Educational Psychology
Windows on Classrooms

Sixth Edition

Paul Eggen

University of North Florida

Don Kauchak

University of Utah

PEARSON

Merrill
Prentice Hall

Upper Saddle River, New Jersey
Columbus, Ohio

Library of Congress Cataloging in Publication Data
Eggen, Pau l D.
    Educational psychology: windows on classrooms / Paul Eggen, Don Kauchak—6th ed.
      p. cm.
    Includes bibliographical references (p.) and indexes.
    ISBN 0-13-110840-9 (paper)
      1. Educational psychology—Study and teaching (Higher)—United States. 2. Learning,
Psychology of—Case studies. I. Kauchak, Donald P. II. Title.

LB1051.E463 2004   370.15—dc21
2003041244

⊗

*This book is dedicated to Clifton Eggen and
Martin Kauchak. They gave us their best.*

⊗

Vice President and Executive Publisher: Jeffery W. Johnston
Assistant Vice President and Publisher: Kevin M. Davis
Editorial Assistant: Autumn Crisp
Development Editor: Julie Peters
Production Editor: Sheryl Glicker Langner
Design Coordinator: Diane C. Lorenzo
Photo Coordinator: Valerie Schultz
Cover Designer: Bryan Huber
Cover image: Getty One
Production Manager: Laura Messerly
Director of Marketing: Ann Castel Davis
Marketing Manager: Amy June
Marketing Coordinator: Tyra Poole

This book was set in Garamond by Carlisle Communications, Ltd. It was printed and bound by
Courier Kendallville, Inc. The cover was printed by Phoenix Color Corp.

Photo Credits: Photo credits are on page 650

Pearson Education Ltd.   Pearson Education Australia Pty. Limited
Pearson Education Singapore Pte. Ltd.   Pearson Education North Asia Ltd.
Pearson Education Canada, Ltd.   Pearson Educación de Mexico, S.A. de C.V
Pearson Education—Japan   Pearson Education Malaysia Pte. Ltd.

10 9 8 7 6 5 4 3 2 1
ISBN: 0-13-110840-9

Preface

The literature of educational psychology continues to rapidly evolve, and we have written the sixth edition of *Educational Psychology: Windows on Classrooms* to remain on the cutting edge of theory and research in the field. At the same time, we have expanded on the theme that has made this book successful: to be the most applied text on the market. Our goals are to provide accurate, clear, and precise descriptions of research and theory combined with the suggestions that make these theories applicable in classroom practice. The subtitle "Windows on Classrooms" refers to our presentation of authentic classroom activities that are designed to provide you, our readers, with a realistic look at classrooms today and what they might become tomorrow.

To this end, this new edition has a deeper focus and commitment to being:

- Case-based *throughout* each chapter
- Exceptionally applied
- Filled with practice for the PRAXIS™

The edition is also expanded to include a new chapter that provides a detailed examination of the construction of understanding, a second chapter that presents a classroom model of student motivation, and a third chapter that focuses on the processes and issues involved in standardized testing.

The following pages illustrate the features and new additions to this text.

A BOOK THAT *TRULY INTEGRATES* *CASES* THROUGHOUT CHAPTERS

To capture the real world of learning and teaching, we capitalize on the use of case studies. All chapters begin with an extended case study. These cases are detailed and rich and are integrated and elaborated throughout the chapters to make theory concrete and applicable. The process of situating theory in the context of real-world practice is consistent with the most recent learning and motivation research. In this regard, the book is a model for effective instruction and provides our readers with repeated opportunities to construct meaningful understandings of the book's contents.

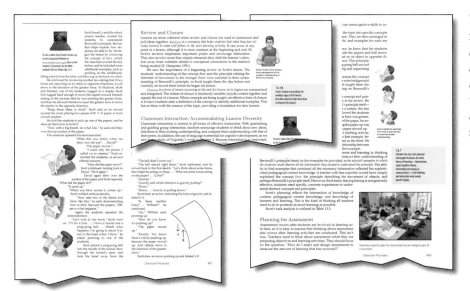

Elaborated Cases. The book does not merely reference the opening case, but it actually integrates and enriches the case as the chapter develops. Illustrations and captions are provided on pages throughout the chapter to call students' attention to the key points in the case study.

Videos to Accompany Cases. Twelve of the chapter cases have a video counterpart. These video segments are included on two videotapes, "Looking Through Classroom Windows 1 and 2", in order of their appearance in the book. Viewing video cases and discussing and analyzing them can deepen understanding of concepts presented in the chapter. See the table on page 26 listing the topic, grade level, and content focus of each video case.

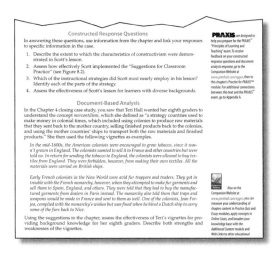

End-of-Chapter Case Analysis. Chapter-ending cases, called "Windows on Classrooms," provide additional practice in understanding chapter concepts through analysis of the classroom-based case. Moreover, constructed-response questions and document-based analysis questions give students opportunities to practice analyzing cases for the PRAXIS™ "Principles of Learning and Teaching" Exam—and for professional practice.

A BOOK THAT IS EXCEPTIONALLY APPLIED

As might be expected from a case-based text, a central goal of *Educational Psychology: Windows on Classrooms* is to help its readers be able to use educational psychology as teachers. The text examines every theory and concept through its application in classrooms, and a number of features help students connect content to classrooms.

Classroom Connections at the Elementary, Middle School, and High School Levels. This box in each chapter offers strategies for applying the content to specific learning and teaching situations. Each strategy is illustrated with an example, derived largely from the authors' experiences in schools, for elementary classrooms, middle and junior high classrooms, and high school classrooms in all content areas.

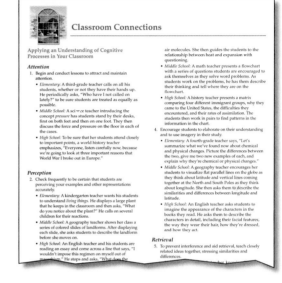

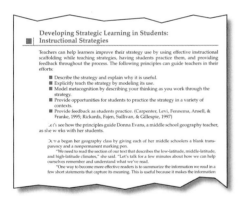

Instructional Strategies. New *Instructional Strategies* sections lay out very concrete guidelines for applying key chapter content. These sections, which are situated in case studies that run through the text, explicitly show teachers' efforts to apply the guidelines. This helps readers bridge the gap between theories and classroom practice.

Web Clips. Brief video clips on the Companion Website offer a front-row seat to real classrooms of students and teachers. Authentic examples of chapter content are identified in the margins of each chapter so that students can link directly to a clip illustrating an educational psychology concept and understand what that concept looks like in an authentic setting. See the *Classrooms on the Web* module on the Website.

Margin Questions. Readers are placed in active learning roles by reading margin questions encouraging them to: a) explain a specific aspect of the content on the basis of theory and/or research, b) relate the immediate topic to one studied in an earlier chapter, or c) relate a topic to a real-life experience.

A BOOK THAT HELPS STUDENTS PRACTICE FOR THE PRAXIS™

PRAXIS™ has moved to a greater emphasis on case-based questions, so the entire text will help students with the PRAXIS™ by helping them become more familiar and comfortable with cases. In addition, a number of features aimed at getting students ready for the PRAXIS™ "Principles of Learning and Teaching" Exam have been added to the text and its accompanying website.

Constructed Response Questions & Document-Based Analysis. New Constructed Response and Document-Based Analysis questions following each end-of-chapter case provides students with experiences in responding to items similar to those they will find on the PRAXIS™ exam.

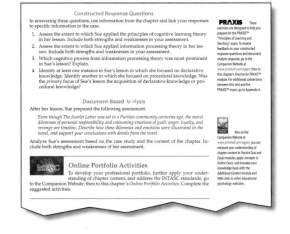

Feedback on the Companion Website. The "Practice for PRAXIS™" module on the Companion Website provides feedback for the Constructed Response and Document-Based Analysis questions.

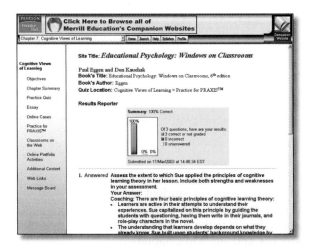

Appendix Linking Book Content to PRAXIS™ content. A new Appendix ties the content in the book to the PRAXIS™ "Principles of Learning and Teaching" Exam.

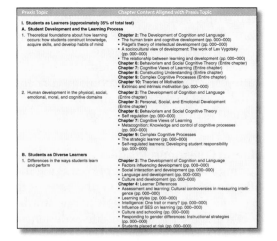

KEY CONTENT
IN THIS EDITION

New Chapter on Motivation

This edition's coverage of motivation has been expanded to two chapters. Included are the latest theoretical advances in areas such as goal theory, self-determination theory, expectancy x value theory, attribution theory, and self-worth theory, as well as deeper looks at behaviorist and humanistic views of motivation. See Chapters 10 and 11.

New Chapter on the Construction of Understanding

Constructivist, and particularly social constructivist, views of learning are increasingly emphasized as a framework for guiding instruction, and this edition includes an entire chapter devoted to these theories and their implications for teaching. See Chapter 8.

New Chapter on Assessment Through Standardized Testing

Testing and accountability are increasingly emphasized in today's schools, and a new chapter has been added to help teachers prepare for these real-world aspects of teaching. See Chapter 15.

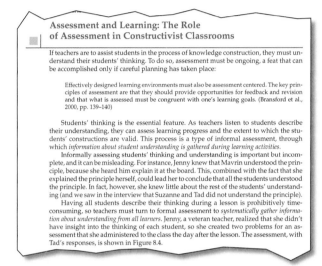

Assessment and Learning: The Role of Assessment in Constructivist Classrooms

If teachers are to assist students in the process of knowledge construction, they must understand their students' thinking. To do so, assessment must be ongoing, a feat that can be accomplished only if careful planning has taken place:

> Effectively designed learning environments must also be assessment centered. The key principles of assessment are that they should provide opportunities for feedback and revision and that what is assessed must be congruent with one's learning goals. (Bransford et al., 2000, pp. 139–140)

Students' thinking is the essential feature. As teachers listen to students describe their understanding, they can assess learning progress and the extent to which the students' constructions are valid. This process is a type of informal assessment, through which *information about student understanding is gathered during learning activities.*

Informally assessing students' thinking and understanding is important but incomplete, and it can be misleading. For instance, Jenny knew that Mavrin understood the principle, because she heard him explain it at the board. This, combined with the fact that she explained the principle herself, could lead her to conclude that all the students understood the principle. In fact, however, she knew little about the rest of the students' understanding (and we saw in the interview that Suzanne and Tad did not understand the principle).

Having all students describe their thinking during a lesson is prohibitively time-consuming, so teachers must turn to formal assessment to *systematically gather information about understanding from all learners.* Jenny, a veteran teacher, realized that she didn't have insight into the thinking of each student, so she created two problems for an assessment that she administered to the class the day after the lesson. The assessment, with Tad's responses, is shown in Figure 8.4.

New Assessment Feature

Assessment research indicates that classroom environments that promote as much learning as possible are assessment centered. To be consistent with this research, each chapter of the text has a section titled *Assessment and Learning* that is devoted to a discussion of assessment related to chapter topics. These sections include suggestions for developing assessments that increase learning and explore issues involved in the assessment process.

Technology and Learning: Using Technology to Increase Learner Motivation

Technology is changing education, and nowhere is this impact more strongly felt than in motivation (Barron, Hogarty, Kromrey, & Lenkway, 1999). Research has identified positive effects of technology on motivation in at least four areas:

- *Self-esteem and self-efficacy.* Students using technology experienced increased self-esteem, and beliefs about their capabilities improved (O'Connor & Brie, 1994). In addition, teachers who became proficient with technology increased in perceived self-efficacy (Kellenberger, 1996).
- *Attendance.* An 8-year study of one technology-implementation project found that student absenteeism dropped by nearly 50% after the project was put into place (Dwyer, 1994).
- *Attitudes.* Students participating in a technology-enriched program reported more positive attitudes toward school and more enjoyment of out-of-class activities (McKinnon, 1997).
- *Involvement.* Students in technology-supported programs were more willing to participate in school learning activities (Yang, 1991–1992).

Improved Technology Feature

Technology and its implications for student learning are explored and utilized, first in a regular chapter feature, "Technology and Learning," that looks closely at the way technology can be and *is* used in K–12 classrooms, and again in Chapters 2, 3, and 7 as we ask you to use the CD-ROM experiments and exercises on the "Simulations in Educational Psychology CD-ROM" that accompanies this text. Completing these activities will increase students' understanding of educational psychology concepts.

Increased Coverage of Action Research.

Teacher professionalism is increasing as teachers learn to conduct action research projects in their own classrooms. To reflect this emphasis, a detailed section on the conduct and application of action research is included in Chapter 1.

Focus on Learner Diversity

Teachers are encountering increasingly diverse student populations. To reflect this trend, learner diversity is a theme for this text. Each chapter contains a section on diversity, with its own set of *Classroom Connections*, and Chapter 4 is devoted to this topic.

Supplementary Materials

To further aid your learning and development as a teacher, several supplements have been provided for you and your instructor's use. The entire package—text, video cases, and supplements—is thoroughly integrated. We have written our own supplements, making every effort to ensure that all the components complement each other.

For Students

Expanded Companion Website

The Companion Website for this edition has been considerably expanded with some unique modules. The modules include:

Chapter Outline and Summary	Practice for PRAXIS™
Self-Assessment (Practice Quiz and Essay)	Portfolio Activities and INTASC
Classrooms on the Web/Video Clips	Additional Content and Web Links
Cases	Message Board

Readers continue to have access to an interactive study guide, in *Self-Assessments* with *Practice Quiz* and *Essay*, to help prepare for tests and quizzes. Brief video clips (integrated in the textbook) appear in *Classrooms on the Web* to illustrate key educational psychology concepts. *Cases* provide additional opportunities to practice analyzing genuine classroom scenarios. Feedback for the constructed-response questions and document analysis sections following end-of-chapter cases are provided in a new *Practice for PRAXIS™* module. *Portfolio Activities* are activities designed to support IN-TASC principles that, once completed, will contribute meaningfully to a teaching portfolio.

An *Additional Content* module provides readers with more detailed coverage of topics that go beyond the scope of the content presented in the text. Annotated *Web Links* related to chapter content encourage further investigation on the Internet. *Message Board* is a forum for discussing theories, educational practice, and other topics with educational psychology students and instructors. Go to *www.prenhall.com/eggen*

Simulations in Educational Psychology CD-ROM

All copies of the Sixth Edition will come with custom computer software—the only problem-solving simulations available in educational psychology. The cross-platform CD-ROM packaged with the text contains simulations that help students experience and explore (1) Piaget's developmental stages, (2) misconceptions and the role of prior knowledge in learning, (3) schemas and the construction of meaning, (4) Kohlberg's stages of moral development, and (5) a new assessment simulation, giving students opportunities to practice assessing authentic student schoolwork.

Student Study Guide and Reader

Organized by chapter, this guide includes chapter outlines, chapter overviews, chapter objectives, and application exercises. These exercises put you in an active role as you apply concepts to authentic classroom situations. Feedback is provided for the application exercises.

Each chapter also includes a Self-Help Quiz, using the same format as the items in the *Test Bank* that accompanies the text, answers to the Self-Help Quiz, and suggested responses to the margin questions in the chapters. These items will help you to master course content.

This revised guide also includes an extensive look at learning and teaching in reading, writing, math, and science; this is the former "Learning in the Content Areas" full-length chapter in the previous edition of the textbook.

ASCD/Merrill Website

A joint website between Merrill and ASCD at *www.educator learningcenter.com* offers students and faculty many resources, including instructional strategies, lesson plans, video segments, case studies, listservs, and hundreds of articles from the journal *Educational Leadership.* The site now includes a link to Research Navigator, allowing students to search hundreds of academic journals. A four-month subscription is available to anyone who purchases a Merrill Education textbook.

For Instructors

Online Course Management Systems

Blackboard and CourseCompass are perfect course management solutions that combine quality Merrill/Prentice Hall content with state-of-the-art Blackboard technology. These products allow you to teach this material in an easy-to-use customizable format and add updates instantaneously.

The Video Package

The extensive video package that accompanies this textbook has been expanded for ease of use. Two new videotapes are available. They contain video versions of many of the cases that introduce and conclude each chapter in the text. Students may read cases in their text and see the same familiar teachers and learners on video. The two videotapes, with 6 lessons on each, are organized so that the lessons on the tapes are presented in the same order as they appear in the chapters. *Looking Through Classroom Windows 1* includes lessons that focus on teacher knowledge, cognitive development, information processing, and constructing understanding—all concepts that reflect the content in Chapters 1–8 case studies. *Looking Through Classroom Windows 2* includes lessons on problem solving, complex cognitive processes, motivation in the classroom, essential teaching skills, and assessment.

All other videotapes that have accompanied previous editions are still being offered, including *Concepts in Classrooms* (10 episodes that illustrate several of the most important topics in educational psychology), *Insights into Learning* (cases that "get into learners' heads" and examine student thinking), *A Private Universe* (examining student misconceptions in science), *Double-Column Addition: A Teacher Uses Piaget's Theory* (depicting a constructivist approach to teaching mathematics), *Windows on Classrooms* (cases that focus on the effectiveness of teachers' instruction as they work with their students), and *Educational Psychology Video Package 1 and 2* (video cases that provide an array of classroom experiences).

Instructor's Manual and Media Guide

These two guides have been combined for this edition to facilitate instruction. This manual includes chapter outlines, overviews, and objectives; listings of available acetate/ PowerPoint transparencies and transparency masters; and presentation outlines and case study analyses for each chapter. In addition, it contains directions for using the *CD-ROM for Instructors,* directions for using the *Simulations CD* (for students), information for using the text's Companion Website, and descriptions of the 10 videos that accompany the text, along with questions for discussion and analysis of the videos, including feedback.

Transparencies

A revised transparency package containing over 100 transparencies with larger type makes transparencies easier to read. Full-color and black and white acetate transparencies help organize the information you want students to master. PowerPoint versions of the transparencies are also available on the CD-ROM for Instructors.

Test Bank

Available in print and electronic formats (for both Windows and Mac users) are approximately 1500 test items. Test items fall into two categories: lower-level items in the form of multiple-choice and true-false questions, and higher-level items that require students to apply what they know to mini-cases and essay questions.

CD-ROM for Instructors

A flexible and user-friendly CD-ROM is available for instructors. Features of the printed supplements—the *Study Guide,* the *Instructor's Manual and Media Guide,* and the *Test Bank*—can be accessed on the CD-ROM and printed.

All of the components in this text and the supplements are designed to be consistent with what we know about learning and motivation. We believe they reflect a realistic view of learning and teaching today and as we move into the new millennium. We wish you the best of luck in your study. We hope that you find it both exciting and meaningful.

Acknowledgments

Every book reflects the work of a team that includes the authors, the staff of editors, and the reviewers. We appreciate the input we've received from professors and students who have used previous editions of the book, and gratefully acknowledge the contributions of the reviewers who offered us constructive feedback to guide us in this new edition: Jerrell Cassady, Ball State University; Steve Hoover, St. Cloud State University; Stephen Lehman, University of Nebraska-Lincoln; and Johnmarshall Reeve, University of Iowa. In addition, we acknowledge with our thanks, the reviewers of our previous editions. They are: Kay S. Bull, Oklahoma State University; Thomas G. Fetsco, Northern Arizona University; Newell T. Gill, Florida Atlantic University; Dov Liberman, University of Houston; Hermine H. Marshall, San Francisco State University; Luanna H. Meyer, Massey University–New Zealand; Nancy Perry, University of British Columbia; Jay Samuels, University of Minnesota; Gregory Schraw, University of Nebraska–Lincoln; Dale H. Schunk, Purdue University; Rozanne Sparks, Pittsburg State University; Karen M. Zabrucky, Georgia State University; Patricia Barbetta, Florida International University; David Bergin, University of Toledo; Scott W. Brown, University of Connecticut; Barbara Collamer, Western Washington University; Betty M. Davenport, Campbell University; Charles W. Good, West Chester University; Tes Mehring, Emporia State University; Evan Powell, University of Georgia; Robert J. Stevens, Pennsylvania State University; and Julianne C. Turner, Notre Dame University.

In addition to the reviewers who guided our revisions, our team of editors gave us support in many ways. Kevin Davis, our Publisher, continues to guide us with his intelligence, insight, and finger on the pulse of the field. Julie Peters, our development editor, helped us make the book more accessible to our readers. A very special thanks to Sheryl Langner for her conscientiousness and diligence in producing the book. She has been with us for four editions; in each she has been supportive and flexible, and the professionalism and commitment to excellence that she consistently demonstrates are appreciated more than we can say. Sheryl, stay with us; we need you.

Our appreciation goes to all these fine people who have taken our words and given them shape. We hope that all our efforts will result in increased learning for students and more rewarding teaching for instructors.

Finally, we would sincerely appreciate any comments or questions about anything that appears in the book or any of its supplements. Please feel free to contact either of us at any time. Our e-mail addresses are: peggen@ufl.edu and kauchak@ed.utah.edu.

Good luck.

Paul Eggen
Don Kauchak

Brief Contents

Contents

Part 1: The Learner

Chapter 3
Personal, Social, and Emotional Development   78

Chapter 4
Learner Differences   116

Chapter 5
Learners with Exceptionalities   158

Part 2 Learning

Chapter 6
Behaviorism and Social Cognitive
Theory   194

Chapter 7
Cognitive Views
of Learning   234

Part 3: Classroom Processes

Chapter 10

Theories of Motivation 348

Chapter 14
Assessing Classroom Learning   492

Chapter 15
Assessment Through Standardized Testing   540

Appendix

Note: Every effort has been made to provide accurate and current Internet information in this book. However, the Internet and information posted on it are constantly changing and it is inevitable that some of the Internet addresses listed in this textbook will change.

Educator Learning Center:
An Invaluable Online Resource

Merrill Education and the Association for Supervision and Curriculum Development (ASCD) invite you to take advantage of a new online resource, one that provides access to the top research and proven strategies associated with ASCD and Merrill—the Educator Learning Center. At **www.EducatorLearningCenter.com** you will find resources that will enhance your students' understanding of course topics and of current educational issues, in addition to being invaluable for further research.

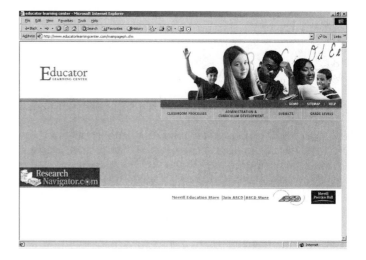

How the Educator Learning Center will help your students become better teachers

With the combined resources of Merrill Education and ASCD, you and your students will find a wealth of tools and materials to better prepare them for the classroom.

Research

- More than 600 articles from the ASCD journal *Educational Leadership* discuss everyday issues faced by practicing teachers.
- A direct link on the site to Research Navigator™ gives students access to many of the leading education journals, as well as extensive content detailing the research process.
- Excerpts from Merrill Education texts give your students insights on important topics of instructional methods, diverse populations, assessment, classroom management, technology, and refining classroom practice.

Classroom Practice

- Hundreds of lesson plans and teaching strategies are categorized by content area and age range.
- Case studies and classroom video footage provide virtual field experience for student reflection.
- Computer simulations and other electronic tools keep your students abreast of today's classrooms and current technologies.

Look into the value of Educator Learning Center yourself

Preview the value of this educational environment by visiting **www.EducatorLearningCenter.com** and clicking on "Demo." For a free 4-month subscription to the Educator Learning Center in conjunction with this text, simply contact your Merrill/Prentice Hall sales representative.

Special Features

Instructional Strategies

Concrete guidelines for applying key chapter content.

Assessment and Learning

Discussions about how assessment is related to learning

Technology and Learning

Discussions about how technology can facilitate learning.

Chapter Outline

Teaching
in the
Real World

1

"Good morning, Keith." Jan Davis, a sixth-grade math teacher, greeted Keith Jackson, a first-year teacher and colleague at Lake Park Middle School. "You look deep in thought."

"I was just thinking about my last-period class. Sometimes I'm not sure what I'm doing. The students are fine when we stick to mechanics, . . . but they hate word problems so much. They always try to take the easiest way out . . . memorize a formula, and if the next problem is even the teeniest bit different from the first, they can't do it.

"I thought I was going to be so great when I got here. I have a really good math background, and I love math. I just knew the kids would love it too, but I'm not so sure anymore. . . . And there are a few who sit in the back of the room like they're almost dead. No one prepared me for this.

"As if that weren't enough, there's Kelly. She disrupts everything I do. I've tried everything. I've ignored her talking, given her referrals, tried to 'catch her being good.' Nothing has worked. She's not really a bad kid. . . . I even took her aside and asked her straight out why she was giving me such a hard time. . . . Actually, I think she's a bit better lately."

"You're in the process of becoming a real teacher," Jan smiled. "You're looking at problems for which there are no easy answers. Very little in teaching is cut-and-dried . . . but then, that's also part of the fun of it.

"Like working with Kelly. You said it seemed to help when you took her aside. I don't think she has another adult she can talk to, and she may simply need someone to be interested in her. . . . And there's no question that kids' personal needs influence their learning.

"About the quiet ones in the back of the room. Let me tell you what works for me. First, I move them up to the front, and I tell them, 'I want you to learn, and I want you up close where I can work with you.' Then I make it a point to call on all of them as equally as possible. One of my university instructors kept talking about a number of research studies indicating the value of calling on all the kids, so I practice it in my classes. Once they get used to it, they really like it. It's one of the most important things I do."

"How about the math part?" Keith asked. "I've tried explaining the stuff until I'm blue in the face."

"As it happens, I'm taking another course to upgrade my certificate, and I've learned a lot. It deals with exactly the stuff you're struggling with, like problem solving. . . . We read these research articles for class that talk about putting the student in the center of the learning process, and then we apply the ideas with our own students.

"Here's an example. We've been reviewing decimals, so at the beginning of class, I put a shopping bag on my desk and said, 'You all like soft drinks, but do you know which is the best buy?' Then I took out a 12-ounce can, a 16-ounce bottle, a liter bottle, a 6-pack, and a 12-pack.

"'Which is the best buy?' I challenged them. We had a lively discussion, and most agreed that bigger is better, but some were skeptical.

"Then I put price tags on each of the containers and broke the students into pairs. Some of them struggled for a while trying to figure out whether they should find the price per can or price per ounce and what to do about liters, but I helped them along. We created a common format for a table, the groups computed their answers, and we compared them as a whole-class activity. They really need to see how math relates to their day-to-day lives.

"It wasn't always smooth, but I learned from it. Sometimes I jumped in too soon when they could have figured it out for themselves, and at other times I let them stumble around too long, and they wasted time. But overall they learned a lot—a lot more than they would have if I had simply stood up and lectured to them."

"I hate to admit this," Keith said almost sheepishly, "but some of my courses at the university suggested just what you did. It was fun, but I didn't think it was *real* teaching."

"Maybe you couldn't relate to it at the time," Jan returned. "You didn't have a class with *live* students who 'didn't get it.'

"My compliments to you," she continued. "The fact that you're thinking about it means you really care about what you're doing. That's what we need in teaching. If you hadn't brought it up, we probably wouldn't have had this talk."

W elcome! You're beginning what we hope will be an interesting and fascinating study; interesting, because this is a book about learning, teaching, and the things that influence them, and fascinating, because even though we focus on school-age children, you'll probably see yourself in many of the experiences described. In some cases, you might even discover that ideas you've held about people, learning, and teaching aren't valid.

As you examine the ways people learn, how they develop intellectually, emotionally, and socially, what makes each person an individual, and why they are motivated by some experiences but not others, you'll be studying the content of educational psychology. You'll also see how you, as a teacher, can apply this content in your work with students.

That's what this book is about. As you study it, remember that the focus in educational psychology is on learning and teaching and factors that influence them.

After you've completed your study of this chapter, you should be able to

- Identify the different types of knowledge required in learning to teach
- Explain the strengths and limitations of descriptive, correlational, and experimental research
- Describe how action research can be conducted in classrooms
- Describe the relationship between research and theory and how both guide classroom practice
- Explain how skilled teachers use educational psychology to improve professional decision making

Educational Psychology: Teaching in the Real World

This is a book about learning, what influences it, and how we as teachers can contribute to it. Our ability to increase student learning strongly depends on our professional knowledge, knowledge that occurs in a variety of forms (Borko & Putnam, 1996). Our goal in studying educational psychology is to develop that knowledge, so we're equipped to make the most effective professional decisions possible.

To begin, complete the following Learning and Teaching Inventory, designed to provide a brief introduction to the different kinds of knowledge needed to understand students, ourselves, and the way learning occurs. Mark each item true or false.

Learning and Teaching Inventory

1. The thinking of children in elementary schools tends to be limited to the concrete and tangible, whereas the thinking of middle and high school students tends to be abstract.
2. Students generally understand how much they know about a topic.
3. Experts in the area of intelligence view knowledge of facts (such as the answer to "On what continent is Brazil?") as one indicator of intelligence.
4. Effective teaching is essentially a process of presenting information to students in succinct and organized ways.
5. Preservice teachers who major in a content area, such as math, are much more successful than nonmajors in providing clear examples of the ideas they teach.
6. Students doing individual work at their seats may react negatively when a teacher comes by and offers help.
7. To increase students' motivation to learn, teachers should praise as much as possible.
8. Teachers who are the most successful at creating and maintaining orderly classrooms are those who can quickly stop disruptions when they occur.
9. Preservice teachers generally believe they will be more effective than teachers who are already in the field.
10. Teachers primarily learn by teaching; in general, experience is all that is necessary in learning to teach.
11. Testing detracts from learning, because students who are tested frequently develop negative attitudes and usually learn less than those who are tested less often.

Let's see how you did. The answer and an explanation for each item are outlined in the following paragraphs. As you read the explanations, remember that they describe students or other people *in general,* and exceptions will exist.

1. *The thinking of children in elementary schools tends to be limited to the concrete and tangible, whereas the thinking of middle and high school students tends to be abstract.*

False: Research indicates that middle school, high school, and even university students can think effectively in the abstract only when they are studying areas in which they have considerable experience and expertise (Lawson & Snitgren, 1982; Pulos & Linn, 1981; Thornton & Fuller, 1981). When we examine development of students' thinking in Chapter 2, you'll understand why and how your understanding of this idea can improve your teaching.

Concepts learned in educational psychology help teachers understand the complex events occurring in classrooms.

2. *Students generally understand how much they know about a topic.*

False: Contrary to what we might think, learners in general, and young children in particular, often are unable to assess what they know (Hacker, Bol, Horgan, & Rakow, 2000; Schommer, 1994). Students' awareness of how they learn and what they already know strongly influences understanding, and cognitive learning theory helps us understand why. (We discuss cognitive learning theory in Chapters 7–9.)

3. *Experts in the area of intelligence view knowledge of facts (such as the answer to "On what continent is Brazil?") as one indicator of intelligence.*

True: The Wechsler Intelligence Scale for Children—Third Edition (WISC-III, Wechsler, 1991), the most popular intelligence test in use today, has several items very similar to the example. Is this an effective way to measure intelligence? Theories of intelligence, which are analyzed in Chapter 4, examine this and other issues related to learner ability.

4. *Effective teaching is essentially a process of presenting information to students in succinct and organized ways.*

False: As we better understand learning, we find that simply explaining information to students often isn't effective in promoting understanding (Bransford, Brown, & Cocking, 2000; Greeno, Collins, & Resnick, 1996; Mayer, 2002). Learners construct their own understanding based on what they already know, and their emotions, beliefs, and expectations all influence the process (Bruning, Schraw, & Ronning, 1999; Bransford et al., 2000; Mayer, 1998b, 1999). Educational psychology helps us understand each of these factors and what we can do to promote learning. (We examine the processes involved in constructing understanding in Chapter 8.)

5. *Preservice teachers who major in a content area, such as math, are much more successful than nonmajors in providing clear examples of the ideas they teach.*

False: One of the most pervasive myths in teaching is that knowledge of subject matter is all that is necessary to teach effectively. In one study of teacher candidates, math majors were no more capable than nonmajors in effectively illustrating and representing math concepts in ways that learners could understand (National Center for Research on Teacher Learning, 1993). Knowledge of content is essential, but understanding how to make that content meaningful to students requires an additional kind of knowledge—knowledge that educational psychology helps us acquire. (We discuss in detail ways of making knowledge accessible to learners in Chapters 2, 6–9, and 13.)

1.1
Many of you probably agreed with item 4's assertion that teaching is a process of transmitting knowledge to learners. Why do many preservice and beginning teachers believe this?

1.2
What is the most likely reason that math majors were no more successful than nonmajors in effectively illustrating math topics?

6. *Students doing individual work at their seats may react negatively when a teacher comes by and offers help.*

    True: Being perceived as intelligent and capable is very important to students, particularly as they get older, and researchers have found that children as young as 6 rated students who were offered unsolicited help lower in ability than others offered no help (Graham & Barker, 1990). Further, when offered unsolicited help, learners themselves often perceive the offer as an indication that the teacher believes they have low ability (W. Meyer, 1982). Theories and research focusing on motivation, which are examined in Chapters 10 and 11, help us understand why learners react this way.

7. *To increase students' motivation to learn, teachers should praise as much as possible.*

    False: Although appropriate use of praise is important, overuse detracts from its credibility. This is particularly true for older students, who discount praise they perceive as unwarranted or invalid. They also interpret praise given for easy tasks as indicating that the teacher thinks they have low ability (Emmer, 1988; Good, 1987a). Your study of motivation in Chapters 10 and 11 will help you understand this and other factors influencing students' desire to learn.

8. *Teachers who are the most successful at creating and maintaining orderly classrooms are those who can quickly stop disruptions when they occur.*

    False: Research indicates that classroom management, one of the greatest concerns of preservice and beginning teachers (Borko & Putnam, 1996), is most effective when teachers prevent management problems from occurring in the first place, instead of responding to problems when they occur (Emmer, Evertson, & Worsham, 2003; Evertson, Emmer, & Worsham, 2003; Kounin, 1970). (Classroom management is discussed in detail in Chapter 12.)

9. *Preservice teachers generally believe they will be more effective than teachers who are already in the field.*

    True: Preservice teachers (like yourself) are often optimistic and idealistic. They believe they'll be very effective with young people, and they generally believe they'll be better than teachers now in the field (Borko & Putnam, 1996). They're also sometimes "shocked" when they begin work and face the challenge of teaching completely on their own for the first time (Borko & Putnam, 1996; Veenman, 1984). Keith's comments in the opening case study illustrate the experience of many beginning teachers: "I thought I was going to be so great when I got here. I have a really good math background, and I love math. I just knew the students would love it too. I'm not so sure anymore. . . . No one prepared me for this." The more knowledge you have about teaching, learning, and learners, the better prepared you'll be to cope with the realities of your first job. Keith's conversation with Jan helped him acquire some of that knowledge. Their discussion focused on topics you'll study throughout this text.

10. *Teachers primarily learn by teaching; in general, experience is all that is necessary in learning to teach.*

    False: Experience is essential in learning to teach, but it isn't sufficient by itself. In many cases, experience can result in repeating the same actions and procedures year after year, regardless of their effectiveness (Putnam, Heaton, Prawat, & Remillard, 1992). Knowledge of learners and learning, combined with experience, however, can lead to high levels of teaching expertise (Cochran & Jones, 1998).

11. *Testing detracts from learning, because students who are tested frequently develop negative attitudes and usually learn less than those who are tested less often.*

> False: In comprehensive reviews of the literature on assessment, experts concluded that frequent, thorough assessment is one of the most powerful and positive influences on learning (P. Black & William, 1998; Brookhart, 1997). (We discuss assessment and its role in learning in Chapters 14 and 15.)

The items you've just examined give a brief sampling of the different kinds of knowledge teachers need to help students learn as much as possible. Helping you acquire this knowledge is our goal in writing this book. Let's examine it in more detail.

Knowledge and Learning to Teach

About the middle of the 20th century, educational psychology experienced a major shift as theorists moved away from viewing learning as the acquisition of specific, observable behaviors and toward seeing it as an internal, mental, and often thoughtful, process (Mayer, 1998b). This shift, commonly described as the "cognitive revolution," has resulted in a much greater emphasis on teachers' knowledge and thinking in the process of learning to teach.

Studies of expertise in a variety of fields confirm the importance of knowledge in the development of expert performance (Bruning et al., 1999), and this is true for teaching as well.

> The accumulation of richly structured and accessible bodies of knowledge allows individuals to engage in expert thinking and action. In studies of teaching, this understanding of expertise has led researchers to devote increased attention to teachers' knowledge and its organization. (Borko & Putnam, 1996, p. 674)

Research indicates that at least four different kinds of knowledge are essential for expert teaching:

- Knowledge of content
- Pedagogical content knowledge
- General pedagogical knowledge
- Knowledge of learners and learning (Peterson, 1988; Shulman, 1987)

Knowledge of Content

We can't teach what we don't understand. This statement appears self-evident, and indeed it has been well documented by research examining the relationships between what teachers know and how they teach (Shulman, 1986; S. Wilson, Shulman, & Richert, 1987). To effectively teach about the American Revolutionary War, for example, a social studies teacher must know not only basic facts about the war but also how the war relates to other aspects of history, such as the French and Indian War, the colonies' relationship with England before the Revolution, and the characteristics of the colonies. The same is true for any topic in any content area.

Pedagogical Content Knowledge

Pedagogical content knowledge is *an understanding of how to make a specific subject comprehensible to others* (Shulman, 1986). Whereas content knowledge is an understanding of a particular topic (e.g., the factors leading to the American Revolution), pedagogical content knowledge is the ability to represent that topic so that it makes sense to students.

To see a video clip of a teacher displaying content knowledge, go to the Companion Website at *www.prenhall.com/eggen*, then to the this chapter's *Classrooms on the Web* module. Click on *Video Clip 1.1.*

Pedagogical content knowledge helps teachers represent difficult-to-learn concepts in meaningful ways.

Paradoxically, researchers have found that sometimes teachers with high levels of content knowledge have trouble representing topics for novice learners (Nathan, Koedinger & Alibali, 2001). Because of their deep understanding, they have trouble "putting themselves in learners' shoes." The importance of developing both the inclination and the ability to represent topics so they're understandable is impossible to overstate.

Teachers who possess pedagogical content knowledge also recognize when topics are hard to understand and illustrate these difficult-to-teach ideas with concrete experiences that make them meaningful. As an illustration, think for a moment about how you might explain the abstract process of multiplying fractions to a fifth-grade student, then do the following activity.

Fold a sheet of plain $8\frac{1}{2} \times 11$ paper into thirds, and draw shading lines across the center one-third of the paper, as shown:

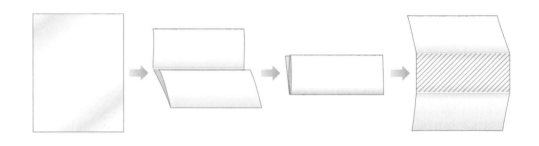

Refold your paper so that the shaded third is exposed:

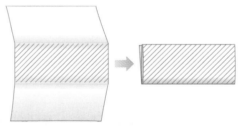

Now fold the paper in half, and in half again, so that one-fourth of the shaded one-third is visible. On that portion, draw lines across the original lines. Then unfold the paper, as shown:

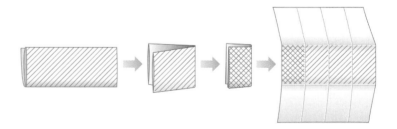

You've just given a concrete example of the process of multiplying fractions. In this case, you demonstrated that $\frac{1}{4} \times \frac{1}{3} = \frac{1}{12}$ (the cross-hatched portion of the paper).

The "subject" was multiplying fractions, and the representation was your folded piece of paper.

Concrete representations of topics like multiplying fractions are important because they make abstract ideas meaningful, which not only helps students learn the idea in the first place but also allows them to apply their understanding in a variety of real-world settings (Mayer & Wittrock, 1996). Intuitively, it doesn't make sense that multiplying two numbers results in a smaller number; so, many students mechanically perform the operation with little understanding. This is why a teacher's ability to create effective representations is so essential. Without the examples, students grasp what they can and memorize as much as possible. Little understanding develops.

Greater pedagogical content knowledge would certainly help Keith understand why his students are "fine when we stick to mechanics" but "hate word problems so much." It is likely that he has relied primarily on explanation ("I've tried explaining the stuff until I'm blue in the face") to help his students understand the problems. This doesn't work very well (Bransford et al., 2000). In contrast, Jan used real-world examples—the containers of soft drinks—to illustrate her abstract topic, demonstrating her more advanced pedagogical content knowledge.

Representations of content exist in a variety of forms, such as:

- *Examples.* A fifth-grade math teacher, DeVonne Lampkin, uses pieces of chocolate to illustrate equivalent fractions (opening case study, Chapter 14). An eighth-grade physical science teacher, Karen Johnson, compresses cotton in a drink cup to illustrate the concept *density* (opening case study, Chapter 2).
- *Demonstrations.* First-grade teacher Jenny Newhall uses water to demonstrate that air takes up space and exerts pressure (closing case study, Chapter 2). A ninth-grade earth science teacher, David Shelton, demonstrates that planets revolve around the sun in the same direction and in the same plane by swinging socks tied to strings (opening case study, Chapter 7).
- *Case studies.* Case studies are used throughout this text to illustrate content. Along with *vignettes,* or short case studies, they are effective ways to illustrate difficult-to-represent or complex topics. For instance, an English teacher illustrated the concept *internal conflict* with this brief vignette: "Andrea didn't know what to do. She was looking forward to the class trip, but if she went, she wouldn't be able to take the scholarship qualifying test." In addition, analysis of video cases, such as the ones that accompany this text, has been used to help teachers think about connections between teaching and student learning (Siegel, 2002).
- *Metaphors.* A world history teacher uses her students' loyalty to their school, their ways of talking, and their weekend activities as a metaphor for the concept *nationalism.* Kathy Brewster, another history teacher, uses her class's "crusade" for extracurricular activities as a metaphor for the actual Crusades (opening case study, Chapter 10).
- *Simulations.* An American government teacher creates a mock trial to simulate the workings of our country's judicial system, and a history teacher has students role-play delegates in a simulated Continental Congress to help his students understand forces that helped shape our emerging country.
- *Models.* A science teacher uses a model of an atom to help students visualize the organization of the nucleus and electrons. The model in Figure 7.2 (on page 239) helps us think about the ways we take in and store information in memory.

1.3
Which form of representation best describes what Jan Davis did in her lesson on decimals and "best buys"? Explain.

From the preceding examples, we can see why item 5 on the Learning and Teaching Inventory is false. Majoring in math does not ensure that a teacher will be able to create examples like the one involving the multiplication of fractions, and majoring in history does not ensure that a social studies teacher will think of using the students' school

To see a video clip of teachers displaying pedagogical content knowledge, go to the Companion Website at *www.prenhall.com/eggen*, then to this chapter's *Classrooms on the Web* module. Click on *Video Clip 1.2.*

1.4

Identify the statement made by Keith Jackson that best indicates his lack of pedagogical content knowledge in trying to teach problem solving to his students. Explain why the statement shows he lacks this knowledge.

activities as a metaphor for the Crusades. The ability to do so requires both a clear understanding of content and pedagogical content knowledge. If either is lacking, teachers commonly paraphrase information in learners' textbooks or provide abstract explanations that aren't meaningful to their students. Your study of educational psychology will help you develop pedagogical content knowledge by increasing your understanding of the ways students learn and the kinds of examples and representations that make topics meaningful for them.

General Pedagogical Knowledge

Knowledge of content and pedagogical content knowledge are domain specific; that is, they depend on knowledge of a particular content area, such as multiplying fractions, the concept *density*, the Crusades, or our judicial system. In comparison, **general pedagogical knowledge** involves *an understanding of general principles of instruction and classroom management that transcends individual topics or subject matter areas* (Borko & Putnam, 1996).

Instructional Strategies

Regardless of the content area or topic, teachers must understand and know how to apply different ways of promoting learning, including strategies and techniques to involve students in learning activities, check their understanding, and keep lessons running smoothly. Jan was applying an important instructional strategy when asking questions designed to engage all of her students (McDougall & Granby, 1996). She was teaching math, but the ability to involve all students is equally important for teaching about the Crusades, about density, or about any other topic. Similarly, teachers must be able to communicate clearly, provide feedback, and perform a variety of other skills to maximize learning for all students. We examine these aspects of general pedagogical knowledge in detail in Chapter 13.

Classroom Management

Teachers must also know how to create classroom environments that are orderly and focused on learning (Emmer et al., 2003; Evertson et al., 2003). To succeed at keeping 20 to 35 or more students actively engaged and working together in learning activities, teachers must know how to plan, implement, and monitor rules and procedures; organize groups; and manage student behavior. The complexities of these processes helps us see why item 8 in the Learning and Teaching Inventory is false. It is virtually impossible to maintain an orderly, learning-focused classroom if we wait for misbehavior to occur. Classroom environments must be designed to prevent, rather than stop, disruptions. Chapter 12 is devoted to a discussion of this topic.

Knowledge of Learners and Learning

Knowledge of learners and learning is essential, "arguably the most important knowledge a teacher can have" (Borko & Putnam, 1996, p. 675). Let's see how this knowledge can influence the way we teach.

Knowledge of Learners

Items 1, 2, 6, and 7 in the Learning and Teaching Inventory all involve knowledge of learners, and each has important implications for the way we teach. For instance, we learned from item 1 that students need abstract ideas illustrated with examples. This means that—even for older students—the more concretely we're able to represent our topics, the more meaningful they'll become. Chapter 2, which focuses on cognitive development, describes how understanding learners increases our pedagogical content knowledge and helps us provide meaningful representations, such as in the example of multiplying fractions.

Item 2 suggests that learners often aren't good judges of either how much they know or the ways they learn. Chapter 7, which discusses the development of metacognition, helps us understand how to guide our students to become more knowledgeable about themselves and more strategic in their approach to learning (Bruning et al., 1999).

Items 6 and 7 have implications for the ways we interact with our students. Intuitively, it seems that offering help and providing as much praise as possible would be positive and effective. However, both research and theories of motivation, which we examine in Chapters 10 and 11, help us understand why this isn't always the case.

Knowledge of Learning

As we better understand the ways people learn, we can understand why item 4 on the Learning and Teaching Inventory is false. For example, evidence overwhelmingly indicates that people don't behave like tape recorders; they don't simply record in memory what they hear or read. Rather, they interpret information in an effort to make sense of it (Bransford et al., 2000; Mayer, 2002). In the process, meaning can be distorted, sometimes profoundly. For instance, look at the following statements, actually made by students:

> "The phases of the moon are caused by clouds blocking out the unseen parts."
> "Coats keep us warm by generating heat, like a fire."
> "*Trousers* is an uncommon noun, because it is singular at the top and plural at the bottom."
> "A triangle which has an angle of 135 degrees is called an obscene triangle."

Obviously, students didn't acquire these ideas from teachers' explanations. Rather, the students interpreted what they heard, experienced, or read, related it to what they already knew, and attempted to make sense of both.

These examples help us see why "wisdom can't be told" (Bransford, 1993, p. 6) and why "explaining the stuff until . . . blue in the face" often isn't enough. Effective teaching is much more complex than simply explaining, and expert teachers have a thorough understanding of the way learning occurs and what they can do to promote it. (We examine learning in detail in Chapters 6–9.)

We now can also understand why item 10 is false. Experience is essential in learning to teach, and no one would argue that it isn't necessary. However, we can already see that teachers won't acquire all the knowledge needed to be effective from experience alone. This is the reason you're studying educational psychology. The knowledge you acquire from it, combined with your experience, will start you on your way to becoming an expert teacher.

1.5
A life science teacher holds up a sheet of bubble wrap and then places a second sheet of bubble wrap on top of the first to help her students visualize the way that cells are organized into tissue. What kind of knowledge does the teacher's demonstration best indicate? Explain.

The INTASC Standards: States Respond to the Need for Professional Knowledge

In response to a growing recognition of the importance of professional knowledge in teaching, a number of states collaborated to create the *Interstate New Teacher Assessment and Support Consortium (INTASC)*, an organization whose goal is to increase the professionalism of beginning teachers. INTASC has set rigorous standards in each of the areas of teacher knowledge discussed in the previous sections. The standards describe what teachers should know and be able to do and are organized around the 10 principles outlined in Table 1.1. The portfolio activities at the end of each chapter in this text are aligned with the standards from INTASC.

To learn more about INTASC, go to the Companion Website at www.prenhall.com/eggen, then to this chapter's *Web Links* module.

Table 1.1 The INTASC principles

Principle	Description
1. Knowledge of subject	The teacher understands the central concepts, tools of inquiry, and structures of the discipline(s) he or she teaches and can create learning experiences that make these aspects of subject matter meaningful for students.
2. Learning and human development	The teacher understands how children learn and develop, and can provide learning opportunities that support their intellectual, social and personal development.
3. Adapting instruction	The teacher understands how students differ in their approaches to learning and creates instructional opportunities that are adapted to diverse learners.
4. Strategies	The teacher understands and uses a variety of instructional strategies to encourage students' development of critical thinking, problem solving, and performance skills.
5. Motivation and management	The teacher uses an understanding of individual and group motivation and behavior to create a learning environment that encourages positive social interaction, active engagement in learning, and self-motivation.
6. Communication skills	The teacher uses knowledge of effective verbal, nonverbal, and media communication techniques to foster active inquiry, collaboration, and supportive interaction in the classroom.
7. Planning	The teacher plans instruction based upon knowledge of subject matter, students, the community, and curriculum goals.
8. Assessment	The teacher understands and uses formal and informal assessment strategies to evaluate and ensure the continuous intellectual, social and physical development of the learner.
9. Commitment	The teacher is a reflective practitioner who continually evaluates the effects of his/her choices and actions on others (students, parents, and other professionals in the learning community) and who actively seeks out opportunities to grow professionally.
10. Partnership	The teacher fosters relationships with school colleagues, parents, and agencies in the larger community to support students' learning and well-being.

Source: Principles from *Model Standards for Beginning Teacher Licensing and Development: A Resource for State Dialogues*, by Interstate New Teacher Assessment and Support Consortium, 1993, Washington, DC: Council of Chief State School Officers. Reprinted with permission.

The Role of Research in Acquiring Knowledge

In the last section, we considered the different kinds of knowledge teachers need to help their students learn. Where did this knowledge originate, how does it accumulate, and how can we acquire it?

One answer is experience, sometimes called "the wisdom of practice" (Berliner, 1988; Leinhardt & Greeno, 1986). Effective teacher education programs help people like you acquire the beginnings of "the wisdom of practice" by integrating clinical experiences in schools with conceptual and theoretical knowledge.

A second source of teacher knowledge is **research,** *the process of systematically gathering information for the purpose of answering one or more questions.* Jan referred to research in her conversation with Keith when she mentioned the changes she's made in her classroom based on "studies indicating the value of calling on all the kids" and "articles for class that talk about putting the student in the center of the learning process." Jan is a veteran with considerable experience, but she continues to grow professionally by staying up-to-date on current research.

Research is the process all professions use to develop a body of knowledge (Gall, Gall, & Borg, 2003). For example, research examining students' writing indicates that students who practice writing with computers compose better quality essays than those who don't, but only if they have well-developed word processing skills (Jerry & Ballator, 1999; Roblyer, 2003). Educators are trying to understand why this occurs and how technology might benefit those learning to write. Without systematically gathering information, we wouldn't be able to answer these questions.

Research provides information that teachers can use in their instructional decision making.

Research exists in many forms. In this chapter, we consider four of the most common:

- Descriptive research
- Correlational research
- Experimental research
- Action research

Jan used research as a source of professional knowledge.

Descriptive Research

Descriptive research, as the term implies, *uses interviews, observations, and surveys to describe opinions, attitudes, or events.* For example, researchers interviewed students to understand their perceptions of caring teachers:

Nichole:	It's more an attitude, ... Like Ms. G. She's like . . . she never says it, but you know, she's just there and she just wants to teach, but she doesn't want to explain the whole deal.
Interviewer:	How do you know that?
Nichole:	I could feel it. The way she acts and the way she does things. She's been here seven years and all the kids I've talked to that have had her before say, "Oooh! You have Ms. G.!" Just like that.
Interviewer:	But a teacher who really cares, how do they act?
Nichole:	Like Mr. P. He really cares about his students. He's helping me a lot and he tells me, "I'm not angry with you, I just care about you." He's real caring and he does teach me when he cares. (Kramer & Colvin, 1991, p. 13)

Interviews can provide valuable insights into both students' and teachers' thoughts.

Observations have also been used in descriptive research. Perhaps the most significant is the work done by Jean Piaget (1952, 1959), a pioneer in the study of cognitive development, one of the cornerstones of educational psychology. Piaget studied the way learners' thinking develops by making detailed observations of his own children. Because of his observations, and a great deal of research conducted by others, we realize, for example, that 10-year-olds don't simply know more than 5-year-olds—they think in ways that are qualitatively different. In the accompanying

8-26

© 1996 Bil Keane, Inc.
Dist. by Cowles Synd., Inc.

"This time try not to miss my bat."

Family Circus cartoon, Dolly's thinks it's her daddy's fault that she missed the previous pitch. A 10-year-old would realize this isn't the case. We understand these differences in children's thinking because of Piaget's, and other researchers', systematic descriptive research. (We examine Piaget's work in detail in Chapter 2.)

Surveys are a third important source of descriptive information. For instance, parents are periodically surveyed to determine their attitudes toward public schools. When asked to name schools' biggest problems, parents have consistently cited lack of student discipline and financial support (L. Rose & Gallup, 2001).

In another descriptive study, researchers administered the popular Myers-Briggs personality test to 4,483 university students who were considering majoring in education and then later checked the students' records to see who graduated and what majors they selected (Sears, Kennedy, & Kaye, 1997). The researchers found that elementary education majors tended to fit a profile described as "warm, sociable, responsible, and caring about people" (p. 201), whereas secondary majors tended to be "oriented to the theoretical, disposed to investigate possibilities and relationships, and drawn to complexity, innovation, and change" (p. 201). The knowledge generated by this research may have implications for both people considering teaching as a career and teacher educators.

Evaluating Descriptive Studies

A great deal of research exists, and teachers need to become proficient at evaluating different studies, not only for their validity but also for their applicability to specific teaching situations. In the case study, Jan noted to Keith that a university instructor referred to "a number of research studies." This information is significant: Several studies reporting similar results provide information that is more likely to be valid than a single, or even a few, studies.

Jan and Keith discuss research.

For descriptive studies, two additional aspects are important. First, the subjects and instruments used should be well described (McMillan, 2000). For instance, the study conducted by Sears et al. (1997) identified the number and characteristics of the population studied (4,483 undergraduate university students considering an education major) as well as the instrument used (the Myers-Briggs personality test). This information allows the reader to judge how applicable the findings are to other similar (and dissimilar) populations.

Second, while they may be tempted to do so, readers must be careful not to predict future behavior based on descriptive studies (McMillan, 2000).

For example, predicting that secondary teachers would respond more positively to innovation and change than would elementary teachers, based on the Sears et al. (1997) study, would not be valid. Nor would it be valid to predict, from the study reported by Kramer and Colvin (1991), that students taught by teachers like Mr. P. would be more motivated or would achieve higher than students taught by teachers like Ms. G. Additional research would be needed to make such predictions.

Finding relationships between variables leads us to correlational research.

Correlational Research

Consider the following questions:

Does a relationship exist between

■ Students' grade point averages and their scores on the Scholastic Aptitude Test (SAT I)?

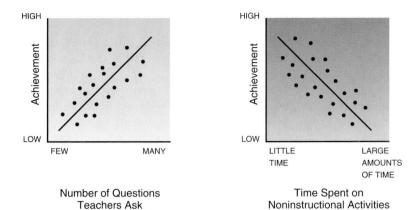

Figure 1.1 Examples of positive (left) and negative (right) correlations

- Students' heights and high school grade point averages?
- Students' absences and their grades in school?

A **correlation** *is a relationship, either positive or negative, between two or more variables.* In our examples, the variables are *grade point averages* and *SAT scores, height* and *high school grade point averages,* and *absences* and *grades.* In the first case, the variables are positively correlated: In general, the higher students' grade point averages, the higher their SAT I scores. No correlation exists in the second: Height and high school grade point averages are not related. In the third case, the variables are negatively correlated: The more school students miss, the lower their grades will be.

Much of what we know about learning and teaching is based on **correlational research,** *the process of looking for relationships between two or more variables.* A great deal of this research attempts to find relationships between teachers' actions and student achievement. For example, researchers have found positive correlations between the number of questions teachers ask and their students' achievement (Shuell, 1996). They have also found negative correlations between achievement and the time teachers spend in noninstructional activities, such as taking roll, passing out papers, and explaining procedures (Brophy & Good, 1986). These relationships are diagrammed in Figure 1.1.

Correlations are represented quantitatively, and they can range from a perfect positive correlation of 1 to a perfect negative correlation of −1. As a very basic example, speed and distance have a correlation of 1. For each increase in the speed we travel, there is a corresponding increase in the distance we cover in the same amount of time. Most correlations are less than a perfect 1 or −1. For instance, the correlation between the number of questions teachers ask and student achievement is about .5, and the correlation between time spent in noninstructional activities and achievement is about −.4 (Good & Brophy, 1986; Shuell, 1996).

Correlational research is valuable because it allows us to make predictions about one variable if we have information about the other (B. Johnson & Christensen, 2000; McMillan, 2000). For instance, because a positive correlation exists between teacher questioning and student achievement, we can predict that students will learn more in classrooms where teachers ask many questions than those where teachers primarily lecture.

Evaluating Correlational Research

As with descriptive research, correlational studies have limitations. Most important, correlational studies describe relationships between variables, but they do not suggest that one variable *causes* the other (Gall et al., 2003; McMillan, 2000). Consider the relationship between grade point average and SAT scores. Obviously, a high grade point average doesn't *cause* a high SAT score. Other factors, such as time spent studying, effective study strategies, and general intelligence are likely to be causes of both. The same kind of reasoning applies to our negative correlation example. Being absent, per se, doesn't cause low grades. Instead, missing opportunities to learn topics, not completing homework assignments, and losing chances to positively interact with peers are some of the likely causes.

1.6

We said that no relationship exists between students' heights and their high school grade point averages. What is the numerical value of this correlation?

1.7

From 1980 to 1994 the number of Asian American students in the United States increased 100%, Hispanic students increased 46%, African American students increased 25%, and Caucasian students increased 10% (U.S. Bureau of the Census, 1996). Are these findings descriptive or correlational research results? Explain.

Experimental Research

Whereas correlational research looks for relationships in existing situations (such as the existing relationship between grade point averages and SAT scores), **experimental research** *systematically manipulates variables in attempts to determine cause and effect.* Experimental studies commonly build upon correlational research. For example, let's look again at the relationship between teachers' questioning and student achievement. In an extension of earlier correlational studies, researchers randomly assigned teachers to a treatment and a control group. **Random assignment** means that *an individual has an equal likelihood of being assigned to either group,* and it is used to ensure that the two groups are comparable. Teachers in the treatment group were trained to provide prompts and cues when students initially failed to answer a question; the researchers attempted to consciously manipulate the variable, *frequency of teachers' prompts,* through training. Teachers in the control group were given no training; they taught as they normally did. Reading scores of the students in both groups were compared at the end of the year. Researchers found that students taught by teachers in the treatment group scored significantly higher on an achievement test than did students taught by teachers in the control group (L. Anderson, Evertson, & Brophy, 1979). In this case, researchers concluded that the ability to provide prompting questions and cues *results in,* or *causes,* increases in achievement.

Evaluating Experimental Research

As with both descriptive and correlational studies, experimental studies should be read with a critical eye. Factors to consider include

- Comparability of experimental and control groups
- Maximum control of extraneous variables
- Sample size
- Clearly described manipulation of the independent variable

For instance, let's consider the Anderson et al. (1979) study again. It would be possible to conclude that prompting caused higher reading achievement only if the treatment and the control groups were similar. If, for example, the students who received prompts had higher ability than students in the control group, conclusions about the effectiveness of the prompts would be invalid. Similarly, if the teachers who were trained to provide prompts had higher initial levels of expertise than teachers in the control group, conclusions about prompting would also be invalid.

Using random assignment and an adequate sample size can also help ensure that experimental and control groups are comparable. For instance, if 20 teachers each have been randomly assigned to experimental and control groups, concluding that teacher expertise has been controlled is more valid than it would be if only 5 teachers existed in each group.

Finally, experimental research must clearly describe the treatment that was provided to the experimental group. The questioning study gave explicit detail about how the teachers in the experimental group were trained to provide cues and prompts. This clear description not only allows the reader to evaluate the research but also allows other researchers to replicate it, which is another way to increase validity.

Action Research

Earlier in the chapter, we saw that the "cognitive revolution" has resulted in a much greater emphasis on teachers' knowledge and learning. Understanding and critically examining others' research is one way to increase teacher knowledge. Another is for teachers to conduct research in their own classrooms. **Action research** is *a form of ap-*

1.8
Teachers who are high in personal teaching efficacy—the belief that they have an important positive effect on students—have higher achieving students than teachers who are low in personal teaching efficacy (Bruning et al., 1999). Is this finding based on descriptive, correlational, or experimental research? Explain your response.

plied research designed to answer a specific school-or classroom-related question (Gall et al., 2003; Wiersma, 2000). It can be conducted by teachers, school administrators, or other education professionals and can include descriptive, correlational, or experimental methods. When they conduct action research projects (and share the results with others), teachers learn about research and begin to understand how self-assessment and reflection can link theory and practice (Sagor, 2000; Schon, 1983). The primary intent in action research is to improve practice within a specific classroom or school (McMillan, 2000). It also increases the professionalism of teachers by recognizing their ability to contribute to the growing body of knowledge about learning and teaching (Bransford et al., 2000).

Action research provides opportunities for teachers to research learning in their classrooms and share their findings with other teachers.

Conducting Action Research in Classrooms: Instructional Strategies

Teachers should follow four essential steps as they attempt to plan and conduct action research studies (Johnson & Christensen, 2000):

- ■ Identify and diagnose a problem that is important to you.
- ■ Systematically plan and conduct a research study.
- ■ Implement the findings to solve or improve a local problem.
- ■ Use the results of the study to generate additional research.

Let's see how eighth-grade English teacher Tyra Forcine attempts to implement these steps in her classroom.

Tyra was sitting in the teachers' lounge after school with a group of colleagues who were discussing problems they were having with homework. "It's frustrating. I can't get my kids to do it," Kim Brown lamented. "A third of them blow it off on some days."

"I solved that problem. . . . I simply don't assign homework," Bill McClendon responded. "I give them a seatwork assignment, we do it after the lesson, and that's it. . . . I'm tired of fighting the homework battle."

"I've heard teachers say that homework doesn't help that much in terms of learning, anyway," Selena Cross added.

"That doesn't make sense to me," Tyra countered, shaking her head. "It has to help. The more kids work on something, the better they have to get at it."

"Well, I'm not sure," Selena shrugged.

The conversation bothered Tyra. She consistently gave her students homework and checked to see that it was done, but because of the conversation, she decided to take a more systematic look at its effects. She started digging around. She tried to find information on several Internet sites and in some of her old college textbooks. Surprisingly, she couldn't find a satisfactory answer, so she decided to do her own research.

A week later, at the start of the third grading period, Tyra began her study. She collected homework every day and gave the students 2 points for having done it fully, 1 point for partial completion, and 0 points for minimal effort or not turning it in. As part of her daily routine, she discussed some of the most troublesome items on the homework. On Fridays she quizzed students on the content discussed Monday through Thursday, and she also gave a midterm test and a final exam. She then tried to see if a relationship existed between students' homework averages and their performance on the quizzes and tests.

At the end of the grading period, Tyra summarized the results. Each student had a homework score, a quiz average, and an average on the two tests.

She called the district office to ask for help in summarizing the information, and together they found a correlation of .55 between homework scores and quiz averages, and a correlation of .44 between homework and test averages.

"I don't get that," Tyra said to Kim and Bill in another teachers' lounge conversation. "I can see why the correlation between the homework and tests might be lower than the one between homework and quizzes, but why aren't both correlations higher?"

"Well . . . ," Kim responded. "You're only giving the kids a 2, 1, or 0 on the homework—you're not actually grading it. So I suspect that some of the kids are simply doing it to finish it, and they aren't really thinking carefully about the work."

"On the other hand," Bill acknowledged, "homework and quizzes and tests are indeed correlated, so maybe I'd better rethink my stand on no homework. . . . Maybe I'll change what I do next grading period."

"Good points," Tyra responded. "I'm going to keep on giving homework, but I think I need to change what I'm doing too. . . . It's going to be a ton of work, but I'm going to do two things: I'm going to repeat my study next grading period to see if I get similar results, and then, starting in the fall, I'm going to redesign my homework so it's easier to grade. I'll grade every assignment, and we'll see if the correlations go up."

"Great idea," Kim nodded." If the kids see how important it is for their learning, maybe they'll take their homework more seriously, and some of the not-doing-it problem will also get better. . . . I'm going to look at that in the fall."

1.9

Suppose that Tyra and her colleagues concluded that doing homework caused an increase in student achievement. Would this be a valid conclusion? Explain why or why not.

Let's take a closer look at Tyra's efforts to conduct action research. First, in her conversation with the other teachers, she did identify a problem that was important to her: To what extent does homework contribute to student performance on quizzes and tests? Addressing problems that are personally meaningful makes action research motivating to teachers (Mills, 2002; Quiocho & Ulanoff, 2002).

Second, she systematically designed and conducted her study, and its efficiency was an important feature. Unfortunately, school systems rarely provide extra time and resources for action research (Bransford et al., 2000), so being able to conduct projects that don't take inordinate amounts of teacher time is important.

Third, Tyra and her colleagues were able to implement the results of her project immediately. Bill, for example, planned to give homework during the next grading period.

Finally, like most research, her project prompted further studies. Tyra planned another study to see if scoring the homework more carefully would increase the correlations between homework and quizzes and tests, and Kim planned to investigate whether more careful scoring would lead to students more conscientiously doing their homework. (We discuss existing research examining the effectiveness of homework in Chapter 7.)

Theories help teachers understand the complex world of classrooms and the connections between teacher actions and student learning.

Perhaps Tyra and her colleagues will reap an additional benefit of conducting action research. As mentioned earlier, engaging in research increases teachers' feelings of professionalism; contributing to a body of knowledge that guides practice helps teachers grow both individually and professionally. And the results of well-designed studies can often be presented at professional conferences and published in professional journals. This allows the knowledge gained to be made public and integrated with other research, two important characteristics in the development of a professional body of knowledge (J. Hiebert, Gallimore, & Stigler, 2002).

Research and the Development of Theory

As research accumulates, results are summarized and patterns emerge. After making a great many observations, for instance, researchers have concluded that the thinking of young children tends to be dominated by their perceptions. For example, when first graders see an inverted cup of water with a card beneath it, as we see in the accompanying picture, they commonly explain that the card doesn't fall because the water somehow holds it against the cup. They focus on the most perceptually obvious aspect of the object—the water—and ignore atmospheric pressure, the actual reason the card stays on the cup.

The statement "The thinking of young children tends to be dominated by perception" is considered a *principle* because it summarizes results consistently supported by large numbers of research studies. Some additional examples of research-based principles include the following:

- Behaviors rewarded some of the time, but not all of the time, persist longer than behaviors rewarded every time they occur.
- People tend to imitate behaviors they observe in others.
- People strive for a state of order, balance, and predictability in the world.

As additional research is conducted, related principles are formed, which in turn generate further studies. As knowledge accumulates, theories are gradually constructed. A **theory** is *a set of related principles derived from observations that, in turn, are used to explain additional observations.* In the everyday world, the term *theory* is used more loosely. For instance, one person will make a point in a conversation, and a second will respond, "I have a theory on that." In this case, the person is merely offering an explanation for the point. In science, *theory* has a more precise, restricted definition.

Theories help organize research findings and can provide valuable guidance for teachers (Gall et al., 2003). Let's look at a brief example. One research-based principle is that reinforced behaviors increase in frequency, and as mentioned earlier, a related principle indicates that intermittently reinforced behaviors persist longer than those that are continuously reinforced (Baldwin & Baldwin, 1998; B. Skinner, 1957). Further, too much reinforcement can actually decrease its effectiveness. A classroom application of these principles occurs in learning activities. If students are praised for their attempts to answer questions (reinforced), they are likely to increase their efforts, but they will persist longer if they are praised for some, but not all, of their attempts (intermittently reinforced). If they are praised excessively, they may actually reduce their efforts.

These related principles are part of the theory of behaviorism, which studies the effects of experiences on behavior. Our illustration, of course, is only a tiny portion of the complete theory. (We examine behaviorism in depth in Chapter 6.) The key feature of any theory is that a comprehensive body of information integrates a number of research-based principles.

Theories are useful in at least two ways. First, they allow us to *explain* behaviors and events. For instance, look at the accompanying cartoon. Piaget's theory of cognitive development, which includes the principle mentioned earlier ("The thinking of young children tends to be dominated by perception"), helps us explain why the child in the cartoon thinks the way he does. Using Piaget's theory, we can explain this behavior by saying that the boy can see only the water and the faucet, and because his thinking is dominated by his perception—what he can see—he concludes that all the water is in the faucet. Similarly, using the theory of behaviorism, we can explain why casino patrons persist in playing slot machines, though coins seldom fall into the trays, by saying that they are being intermittently reinforced.

FAMILY CIRCUS

"How do they fit so much water in that little spigot?"

1.10
Describe how, in our opening case study, Keith used reinforcement theory (behaviors that are reinforced will increase in frequency) to explain and predict Kelly's behavior.

A second value of theories is that they allow us to *predict* behavior and events. For instance, attribution theory—a theory of motivation—allows us to predict that students who believe they are the ones who control how good their grades will be try harder than those who believe their grades are due primarily to luck or the whim of the teacher.

In all three instances, theories—cognitive development theory, behaviorism, and attribution theory—help us understand learning and teaching by allowing us to explain and predict people's actions.

Research and Teacher Decision Making

We've just seen how research and theory provide us with knowledge that we can use to guide our teaching. They don't answer all our questions, however. Just as medical research doesn't tell us exactly how many times a week people can safely eat fatty foods or how much exercise is necessary to maintain a healthy lifestyle, educational research and theory don't spell out every aspect of best classroom practice. For example, Jan cited research indicating that students in classes should be called on as equally as possible, but the research doesn't specify who to call on at a particular moment or how to treat a shy and withdrawn student compared to an outgoing and assertive one. Research and theory help us understand patterns of student learning and effective teaching, but specific decisions are left to teachers.

Jan made informed decisions based on research.

Throughout this text, we'll make statements such as "A teacher's careful judgment is required," "The specific decision will be left up to you," and "You must decide." Teaching includes a great deal of uncertainty and ambiguity. Careful professional judgment and personal decision making are essential for effective teaching.

Unfortunately, teacher decision making can sometimes be complicated by research results that appear contradictory. For example, one such dilemma relates to wait-time, the practice of pausing after a question to give students time to think:

> From Rowe's (1974) research on wait-time, for example, we learn the principle that longer wait-times produce higher levels of cognitive processing. Yet Kounin's (1970) research on classroom management warns the teacher against slowing the pace of the classroom too severely lest the frequency of discipline problems increase. How can the principle of longer wait-times and that of quicker pacing both be correct? (Shulman, 1986, p. 13)

Should we wait longer to give students time to think through a question fully, or will long pauses result in lessons that drag? Research doesn't provide a precise answer, so we must use our professional judgment and decide how long to wait and when to move the lesson along more quickly.

As another example of the need for teacher decision making, consider the following situation:

> April Sumner taught remedial English to a first-period class of inner-city high school students. Students were required to pass the class to graduate from high school, but motivation and attendance were problems.
>
> She liked the class, and because it was small, she knew all her students well. This closeness was rewarding, but the students were also frustrating; they didn't bother to bring any materials to class. Daily reminders didn't seem to help, nor did threats of failure, because many students were repeating the class for the second or third time.
>
> April talked with other teachers. Some said, "Let them sit"; others responded, "Lend them your own" but warned of logistical nightmares and economic disaster when the pencils disappeared and she ran out of paper.

April was hired to teach English, but first she had to solve the materials problem. What would you do? Providing students with pencils reinforces their coming to class unprepared. However, if the teacher doesn't provide them, students can't participate, and research and theory both confirm the importance of active student involvement in learning (Blumenfeld, 1992; Bransford et al., 2000).

It would certainly be easier if we could simply call up a research result, apply it as a rule, and get consistent, predictable results. However, neither the world, nor teaching and learning, work this way. So, to succeed, teachers must cope with uncertainty and try to make informed decisions.

How should research be used in making decisions? Some experts suggest that teachers need to think *critically, practically,* and *artistically* about the research results (Gage & Berliner, 1989). When we do this, we do more than simply apply research—we personalize research results by selecting, modifying, and adapting the suggested applications to best meet the needs of our students. Let's look at these processes.

Critical Decision Making: The Role of Classroom Context

When using research results critically, teachers analyze their own situations and compare them with the settings that produced the results. For instance, in one study, researchers found that first graders called on in a predictable order—such as up and down rows—achieved higher in reading than students called on randomly (Ogden, Brophy, & Evertson, 1977). Does this imply that we should stop the intuitively sensible practice of calling on students at random? Certainly not, for at least three reasons. First, examining the results critically, we find that the study was conducted with first graders in small reading groups, a context very different from most whole-group instruction.

Second, the study was correlational, so concluding that the predictable order *caused* higher achievement is invalid. For example, students' opportunities to participate equally may have been the actual cause (Tierney, Readence, & Dishner, 1990).

Third, the results with first graders haven't been replicated in other settings, whereas additional research has consistently found that equally involving all students increases learning (Brophy & Good, 1986; Kerman, 1979; McDougall & Granby, 1996), and teachers have more effective methods than predictable turns for ensuring equal participation.

The context in which decisions are made also helps us resolve the dilemma with wait-time cited earlier. For example, if a question is thought provoking, the lesson is moving smoothly, and the student "on the spot" is comfortable, we should probably wait. However, if the question calls for a fact, the lesson is dragging, other students are fidgety, or the target student appears uncomfortable, we should reduce the wait-time. The context in which the question is asked helps us decide. Research assists in the process but does not substitute for sound teacher judgment.

We all periodically react with frustration because research seems inconsistent and uncertain, such as in the study with first graders and predictable turns. This is reality, however, and it isn't unique to learning and teaching, or education in general. For instance, a number of studies caution against eating too many eggs, because of their high cholesterol content; others suggest that our bodies manufacture most of the cholesterol in our systems and that diet affects cholesterol level less than previously believed.

All this suggests that individual research studies should be examined critically and interpreted with caution. They provide us with knowledge that we can use to make decisions, but the decisions are left up to us.

Practical Decision Making: The Need for Efficiency

Practicality is a second factor in making informed decisions. To be useful, research must be applied efficiently, with minimal disruption to the class or extra work for the teacher. Classrooms are complex and busy places; researchers estimate that elementary teachers have more than 500 exchanges with individual students in a day (Doyle, 1986). Many, if not most, of these exchanges require a split-second teacher decision. To be practical, research results must be applied efficiently.

For example, research suggesting that all students be called on equally is practical. Although the practice requires teachers to be skilled in questioning, the curriculum, classroom routines, and general patterns of instruction don't have to be radically altered. On the other hand, research also suggests that students taught in a one-to-one, personalized mode of instruction learn best (Bloom, 1984; Slavin, Madden, Karweit, Dolan, & Wasik, 1992), but unfortunately this often isn't feasible.

1.11
Identify at least four decisions that Keith made in his attempts to deal with Kelly. What theory of learning did he use to make the decisions? Explain how they were practical.

April's materials dilemma illustrates the importance of practical decisions and the role of research and theory in making them. As we said earlier, research indicates that students need to be involved in learning activities, so April can't let her students sit passively. She also can't repeatedly give students materials, because—according to her understanding of behaviorism—doing so reinforces their irresponsibility (and she could spend a lot of money distributing pencils to students who consider the whole process a game).

At least two practical solutions to the problem exist. One teacher kept a box of short pencil stubs in his desk (Shulman, 1986). When a student forgot a pencil, the teacher gave the student the shortest stub he could find and required the student to complete the work with it and return it after class. Another teacher required a personal article, such as an earring, bracelet, or belt, as collateral, which she exchanged for the pencil at the end of class (Shulman, 1986). These were simple, practical solutions that worked. In both instances, students started bringing their materials to class.

Artistic Decision Making: Creativity in Teaching

The artistic element, the third dimension of informed decision making, asks teachers to apply the results of research in original and creative ways. Let's look at an example.

After three separate efforts to teach the principle of exposition, development, and recapitulation in music—each of which failed—the teacher was at wit's end. Having repeatedly reminded her students that composers like Wagner depended on the listeners' remembering earlier themes so as to recognize their later elaboration, she was determined to make her students understand musical form, no matter what it took.

The class had little trouble with simple variations and could easily identify themes that were repeated in a related key, but when it came to the development sections, the students' attention focused on the new detail to such an extent that they no longer "heard" the basic motif. For a week or two, the young teacher fretted over the problem. She discarded one idea after another as either too complicated or impractical. Older teachers advised her to go on with something else, suggesting that she was overly ambitious, and that such discrimination was impossible without formal music training. Still, the teacher searched for a solution.

One afternoon during the lunch hour, she noticed a group of students clustered in a corner of the yard. Several girls were swaying their bodies in a rhythmic cadence. Curious, she drew closer and found that the students were listening to a new rock hit. A boy in the center of the group held a tape recorder in his hand. A few moments later, as the teacher continued on her noon duty rounds, a sudden inspiration took hold.

The following day, when her music appreciation class arrived, she asked how many students had tape recorders. A dozen or so students immediately said, "I do." The teacher looked at her students pensively. "I have an idea," she said with sudden animation. "Maybe machines have better memories than people. What would you think," she said, "about trying an experiment? We could play Beethoven's 'Eroica' again, and one of you can record the theme of the second movement when it's first introduced. Then, later, when Beethoven gets into the development section, someone else can record that segment. Finally, when he comes to the recapitulation—the restatement—we'll have a third person record again. Of course," she added, "technically, it won't be a real recapitulation because we'll select passages in the same key. If," she finished triumphantly, "we can synchronize the timing, and start all three recorders at exactly the same instant, we'll play the three recordings together and see if they fit. What do you think?"

Her students looked at her in surprise. Suddenly, however, delight appeared on their faces.

"Neat," one boy exclaimed.

"We'll have to get three recorders with the same speed," another exclaimed. "I'll bring a timer."

Creative teachers design activities that motivate students to learn.

And so it was arranged. They had difficulty starting the recorders simultaneously; there were slight variations in their pitch; and the tempo of the recorded passages was a bit uneven; but the sounds blended sufficiently for the students to recognize their commonality. (L. Rubin, *Artistry in Teaching,* 1985, McGraw-Hill, Inc., pp. 32–33 reproduced with permission of McGraw-Hill)

This teacher capitalized on the principles suggesting that actively involving students and relating abstract ideas to their personal lives increase learning. Through artistic decision making, she applied these ideas to create meaningful lessons. Of course, such creativity doesn't simply happen. It is the result of knowledge—*knowledge of content, pedagogical content knowledge, general pedagogical knowledge,* and *knowledge of learners and learning*—and it is informed by research.

1.12
Describe specifically how the music teacher demonstrated pedagogical content knowledge as well as knowledge of learners and learning in her lesson.

Assessment and Learning: Gathering Information for Decision Making

Decision making is an essential part of expert teaching, just as it is an essential part of other professions, such as medicine, law, or architecture. Throughout this book, we consistently emphasize that decisions be based on information, not personal preference, ideology, or uninformed belief. Research and theory are essential sources of information.

Assessment provides another primary source for decision making. **Assessment** is *the process of systematically gathering information for the purposes of making decisions about learning and teaching.* Action research, which we examined earlier, is one example of assessment-driven decision making: Tyra, Bill, and Kim used the results of Tyra's homework project as a basis for making decisions about their homework policies.

Assessment most commonly focuses on gathering information about student learning progress and making instructional decisions based on that information. It includes observations of students' written work, students' responses to homework, answers to questions in class, and students' answers on teacher-made and standardized tests. It also includes performance assessments, such as watching first graders print or observing students as they create documents in a word processing class.

Effective assessment allows teachers to examine students' thinking. Let's look at a brief example.

DeVonne Lampkin's fifth-grade students were studying fractions. In a homework assignment on reducing fractions to lowest terms, one student, Kevin, correctly reduced ⁵⁄₂₅ to ⅕, apparently reasoning as follows: "Five goes into 5 once, and 5 goes into 25 five times, so the fraction is ⅕.

When he reduced ¹²⁄₃₀, however, Kevin got ½.

As DeVonne discussed the homework with her students, she directed, "Kevin, please explain how you got ½ when you reduced ¹²⁄₃₀ to lowest terms."

Kevin responded, "Twelve goes into 12 once, and 12 goes into 30 twice."

"What is 12 times 2?" DeVonne probed.

"Twenty-four. . . . There was some left over."

Kevin's explanation indicates that he has an incomplete understanding of *fractions-in-lowest-terms* as well as the procedure for reducing fractions. Without examining his thinking, the teacher cannot provide the corrective feedback needed to improve his understanding. Simply scoring homework and other assessments does not reveal what is going on in learners' minds. For instance, if DeVonne had simply marked Kevin's answer wrong when he reduced ¹²⁄₃₀ to ½, she would have learned nothing about his thinking. Asking him to explain his answer was essential because it provided her with information she needed to provide the corrective feedback that would further his learning progress.

Assessment is integral to the learning-teaching process (Bransford et al., 2000), as the example with Kevin's thinking about fractions illustrates. Because it is so important, we have made it a major theme of this text. Each chapter contains an "Assessment and Learning" section that describes how assessment is related to chapter content and how it can be used to promote learning.

Reflection and Decision Making

Keith's reflection increases his teaching effectiveness.

1.13

Identify a specific example in which Jan Davis demonstrated reflection in her teaching.

Teaching involves making an enormous number of decisions, most of which can't be reduced to simple rules. How do teachers know if their decisions are valid and wise? This is a tough question, because they receive little feedback about the effectiveness of their work. They are observed by administrators a few times a year at most and receive only vague, sketchy, and uncertain feedback from students and parents. In addition, they get virtually no feedback from their colleagues, unless the school has a peer coaching or mentoring program (Darling-Hammond, 1996, 1997). To improve, teachers must be able to assess their own classroom performance.

The ability to conduct this self-assessment can be developed, but it requires that teachers develop a disposition for critically examining what they're doing. This is the essence of a simple, yet powerful notion called **reflective teaching,** *the process of conducting a critical self-examination of one's teaching* (Cruickshank, 1987; Schon, 1983). Reflective teachers plan lessons thoughtfully and take the time to analyze and critique them afterward. Very simply, they continually think about what they're doing and ask themselves how they might improve.

Your study of educational psychology supports reflection by providing a foundation of research, theory, and assessment that you can use in critiquing your own teaching. In the opening case study, for instance, Keith's knowledge that students should be actively involved in the learning process and that problem solving is important helped him reflect on his effectiveness. Had he been less well informed, he wouldn't have reacted as strongly when some of his students memorized formulas to "try to take the easiest way out" and had difficulty with problems that were "even the teeniest bit different from the first." He also recognized that the problem solving Jan suggested could improve both student motivation and understanding. His uneasiness about his students' progress and his openness to new ideas indicated a tendency to be reflective, and his knowledge base made the process more effective.

Teachers can acquire the tendency to reflect by continually asking themselves questions, such as those in Figure 1.2, as they teach. More important than the questions themselves is the inclination to ask them. If teachers keep questioning, they can avoid the trap of teaching in a certain way because they've always taught that way. Openness to change and the desire for improvement are two of the most important characteristics of professional growth, and careful reflection can have positive effects on the decisions teachers make.

Reflective teachers analyze their teaching to ensure that learning activities meet the needs of all students.

Figure 1.2 Questions for reflective teaching

- Did I have a clear goal for the lesson? What was the specific goal?
- Was the goal important? How do I know?
- Was my learning activity consistent with the goal?
- What examples or representations would have made the lesson clearer for students?
- What could I have done to make the lesson more interesting for students?
- How do I know whether students understand what I taught? What would be a better way of finding out?
- Overall, what will I do differently to improve the lesson the next time I teach it?

The Use of Case Studies in Educational Psychology

The different kinds of knowledge teachers need to become experts has important implications both for you, who are learning to teach, and for us, who write textbooks designed to help you in this process. Our knowledge of learners and learning reminds us that students of all ages need concrete and real-world representations of the topics they are studying if those topics are to be meaningful.

The use of case studies, such as the one at the beginning of this chapter, is one of the most effective ways to provide concrete illustrations of learning and teaching in the real world of classrooms—classrooms like those in which you will work when you finish your teacher preparation program (Putnam & Borko, 2000). Long popular in other professional fields, such as law and medicine, cases are now being increasingly used in education (Sudzina, 1999).

Because of the value of case studies in illustrating the complex processes involved in teaching and learning, we both introduce and end each chapter in this book with a case study. The introductory case and the chapter closing case serve two different purposes. The beginning case provides a real-world introduction to the content and illustrates the topics presented in the chapter. As topics are discussed, we frequently refer back to the case, in some instances taking dialogue directly from it, to make concepts more meaningful. We also present short vignettes throughout each chapter to further link content to real-world examples.

The closing cases, found in the *Windows on Classrooms* feature, have a different purpose. To encourage critical thinking, decision making, and reflection, we ask you to analyze each case and assess the extent to which the teacher effectively applied the chapter content in his or her classroom. In some cases the teacher's work was quite effective; in others it may not have been. The cases present the richness and complexity of actual classroom problems and provide opportunities to apply chapter content using multiple perspectives (Siegel, 2002).

Video Cases

Video cases can be particularly effective in representing the complexity of classroom learning and teaching. A video can show subtleties of the learning-teaching process that would be difficult to express in writing (Putnam & Borko, 2000). For this reason, 12 of the cases that either introduce or close the chapters also appear on video. You thus have the opportunity to see each episode in an authentic, unrehearsed classroom setting and also read the written transcript of the same lesson. Table 1.2 lists the cases from the text that also appear on video.

The Praxis™ Exam

Increasingly, teachers are being asked to pass competency tests that measure their readiness for working with learners. The most frequently used test is the *Praxis Series*

Table 1.2 Chapter opening or closing cases studies on videotape

Topic	Grade	Content Focus	Chapter and Location
Planting a garden	K	Teacher knowledge	1—Closing case
Symmetry	7th		
Charles's law of gases	10th		
Causes of the Vietnam War	11th		
Properties of air	1st	Cognitive development	2—Closing case
The Scarlet Letter	12th	Information processing	7—Closing case
Constructing understanding of beam balances	4th	Constructing understanding	8—Opening case
Designing and conducting experiments	7th	Constructing understanding	8—Closing case
Finding the area of irregular polygons	5th	Problem solving	9—Opening case
Using graphs to represent information	2nd	Complex cognitive processes	9—Closing case
The characteristics of arthropods	5th	Motivation in the classroom	11—Opening case
Writing effective paragraphs	5th	Motivation in the classroom	11—Closing case
Bernoulli's principle	7th	Essential teaching skills	13—Opening case
The influence of geography on economy	9th	Essential teaching skills	13—Closing case
The properties of fractions	5th	Assessing learning	14—Opening case

New state accountability systems require teachers to demonstrate their understanding of different forms of professional knowledge on tests.

(*praxis* means putting theory into practice), which is required in 35 states (Educational Testing Service, 1999).

An important part of the Praxis Series is the Principles of Learning and Teaching (PLT) tests, three tests specifically designed for teachers seeking licensure in grades K–6, 5–9, and 7–12, respectively. The PLT tests are closely aligned with the INTASC standards discussed earlier in the chapter, and this book addresses most of the topics covered on the tests. These topics are outlined in Appendix A.

The PLT tests have two parts (Educational Testing Service, 2001). One consists of multiple-choice questions similar to those in the test bank that accompanies this text. The second contains case studies (which are called "case histories") that you will be asked to read and analyze in much the same way as you will analyze the chapter-ending case studies in this book. We have designed our end-of-chapter cases to be parallel in format to the PLT format. For instance, in the PLT tests you will read a case study and then respond to "constructed response questions" (Educational Testing Service, 2001); you'll do the same for the cases in this text. In addition, in both the PLTs and this text, you will analyze student or teacher-prepared documents, such as student work, excerpts from student records, teachers' lesson plans, assignments, or assessments. The questions for this "document-based analysis" are found in this text after the constructed response questions at the end of each chapter.

Scoring the Praxis™

The constructed response and document-based analysis questions on the Praxis™ PLTs are scored using a **rubric,** *a scoring scale that describes criteria for grading* (Stiggins, 2001; Goodrich, 1996–1997). (A detailed discussion and examples of rubrics are presented in Chapter 14, beginning on page 507.)

The Praxis™ rubric uses the following 0–2 scale:

Score of 2: The response contains appropriate answers to all parts of the question, demonstrating an understanding both of the details in the case study and of the principles of learning and teaching as outlined in the content categories covered by the test.
Score of 1: The response contains appropriate answers to only part of the question.
Score of 0: The response contains no appropriate responses to any parts of the question. (Educational Testing Service, 2001, p. 82)

An answer is judged as "appropriate" by determining the extent to which it contains information similar to information in a model response constructed by a panel of experts (Educational Testing Service, 2001).

Keys to Success on the Praxis™

What strategies should you employ as you use the exercises in this text to prepare for the Praxis™? Experts offer the following four suggestions (Educational Testing Service, 2001):

- *Answer all parts of the question.* For instance, if the question asks you to identify four characteristics of constructivist learning theory that were demonstrated in the case, be sure that your response includes all four. (We discuss constructivist learning theory in Chapter 8.)
- *Demonstrate an understanding of the theory or pedagogical concepts related to the question.* For instance, if the case involves an application of information processing, you will want to include concepts such as *attention, perception, working memory,* and *metacognition* in your response. (These information processing concepts are discussed in detail in Chapter 7.)
- *Demonstrate a thorough understanding of the case.* In your answers be sure to discuss the case in general as well as specific details within the case that relate to the question.
- *Support your answer with details.* By specifically referring to the case and identifying the theoretical or pedagogical concepts illustrated, you will provide documentation for your answer.

After you answer the constructed response and document-based analysis questions at the end of a chapter, you can receive feedback by going to the chapter's Praxis Practice module on the website at www.prenhall.com/eggen. The feedback includes model responses (score of 2) that incorporate the experts' suggestions.

We hope this introduction has provided a framework for the rest of your study of this book. Its organization and goals are outlined in Table 1.3.

To begin preparing constructed responses and document-based analyses, read the case studies in the Windows on Classrooms feature and answer the questions that follow.

The *Principles of Learning and Teaching Study Guide,* published by the Educational Testing Service, provides additional help in preparing for the Praxis™ exams. For purchase information, go to the Companion Website at *www.prenhall.com/eggen,* then to this chapter's *Additional Content* module.

Table 1.3 Organization of this book

Part and Chapter		Goal
Chapter 1:	Teaching in the Real World	To understand teacher knowledge and the role of research in teacher decision making
Part I:	The Learner	
Chapter 2:	The Development of Cognition and Language	To understand how learners' intellectual capacities and language abilities develop over time
Chapter 3:	Personal, Social, and Emotional Development	To understand how learners' personal characteristics, moral reasoning, and socialization develop over time
Chapter 4:	Learner Differences	To understand how intelligence, culture, socioeconomic status, and gender affect learning
Chapter 5:	Learners with Exceptionalities	To understand how learner exceptionalities affect learning
Part II:	Learning	
Chapter 6:	Behaviorism and Social Cognitive Theory	To understand learning from behaviorist and social cognitive perspectives
Chapter 7:	Cognitive Views of Learning	To understand learning from cognitive perspectives
Chapter 8:	Constructing Understanding	To understand the processes involved in constructing understanding
Chapter 9:	Complex Cognitive Processes	To understand concept learning, problem solving, and the development of strategic learners
Part III:	Classroom Processes	
Chapter 10:	Theories of Motivation	To understand motivation from behaviorist, humanistic, and cognitive perspectives
Chapter 11:	Motivation in the Classroom	To understand how theories of motivation can be used in classrooms
Chapter 12:	Creating Productive Learning Environments: Classroom Management	To understand how to create orderly classrooms focused on learning
Chapter 13:	Creating Productive Learning Environments: Principles of Instruction	To understand how to plan, implement, and assess learning activities
Chapter 14:	Assessing Classroom Learning	To understand processes for assessing student learning
Chapter 15:	Standardized Testing	To understand how standardized tests can be used to increase student learning

Windows on Classrooms

The following episodes illustrate four teachers at different classroom levels working with their students. In the first, Rebecca Atkins, a kindergarten teacher, talks with her children about planting a garden. Richard Nelms, a middle school teacher, illustrates the concept of *symmetry* for his seventh-grade life science students in the second episode. In the third, Didi Johnson, a chemistry teacher, presents Charles's law to her 10th graders. Finally, in the fourth episode, Bob Duchaine, an American history teacher, is discussing the Vietnam War with his 11th graders.

As you read the episodes, think about the different types of professional knowledge that each teacher demonstrated and the kinds of instructional decisions that each made.

Now let's look at Rebecca's work with her kindergarten children.

Rebecca had the children seated on the floor in a semicircle in front of her. She sat on a small chair in front of them and then began, "We had a story on gardening, remember? Who remembers the name of the story? . . . Shereta?"

"Together," Shereta softly responded.

"Yes, 'Together'," Rebecca repeated. "What happened in 'Together'? . . . Andrea?"

"They had a garden," Andrea answered.

"They planted a garden together, didn't they?" Rebecca smiled. "The boy's father helped them plant the garden."

She continued by referring the children to previous science lessons where they had talked about plants and soil and asked them about helping their parents plant a garden.

"I helped them put the seeds in the ground and put the dirt on top of it," Robert offered.

"What kinds of vegetables did you plant? . . . Kim?"

"I planted lots of vegetables . . . tomatoes, carrots."

"Shereta?"

"I planted lettuce in my own garden."

"Travis?"

"I planted okra."

"Raphael?"

"I planted beans."

She then continued, "Tell about the story 'Together.' What did they have to do to take care of the garden? . . . Carlita?"

"Water it."

"Bengemar?"

"Pull the weeds from it."

"Pull the weeds from it," Rebecca repeated enthusiastically. "What would happen if we left those weeds in there? . . . Latangela?"

"It would hurt the soil."

"What's another word for *soil*?"

"Dirt," several of the children said in unison.

"How many of you like to play in the dirt?"

Most of the children raised their hands.

"So, planting a garden would be fun because you get to play in the dirt," Rebecca said enthusiastically.

"I like to play in the mud," Travis added.

"You like to play in the mud," Rebecca repeated with a laugh.

Next, let's turn to Richard's lesson on animal symmetry with his seventh graders.

Richard began his discussion of *symmetry* by using a sponge as an example of an asymmetrical object; he demonstrated radial symmetry using a starfish; and he then turned to bilateral symmetry.

"We have one more type of symmetry," he said. "Jason, come up here. . . . Stand up here."

Jason came to the front of the room and stood on a stool.

"Would you say," Richard began, "that Jason is asymmetrical—that there is not uniformity in his shape?"

The students shook their heads.

He had Jason extend his arms out from his sides and then asked, "Would you consider this *radial*, because he has extensions that go out in all directions? . . . Jarrett?"

"No."

"Why not? Explain that for us."

"There's nothing there," Jarrett said, pointing to Jason's sides.

"There's nothing coming from here, is there?" Richard nodded.

"So, we move into the third type of symmetry," he went on, as Jason continued to stand with his arms extended. "Does anyone know what that is called? . . . Rachel?"

"A type of symmetry," Rachel responded uncertainly.

"Yes, it's a type of symmetry," Richard smiled. "It's called *bilateral*. . . . Bilateral means that the form or shape of the organism is divided into two halves, and the two halves are consistent. . . . If I took a tree saw and started at the top," he said, pointing at Jason's head as the class laughed, "the two halves would be essentially the same. . . . or, if I blocked off one half of Jason, and two hours later saw the other half, do you think I would know who it is? . . . Why is that?" he asked in response to the students nodding and responding yes.

"Because both halves look the same," he reinforced.

"Now, tomorrow," he continued, "we're going to see how symmetry influences the ways organisms function in their environments."

Now, let's turn to Didi Johnson's chemistry lesson.

Didi wanted her students to understand Charles's law of gases, the law stating that an increase in the temperature of a gas causes an increase in its volume when the pressure on the gas remains the same.

To illustrate that heat causes gases to expand, Didi prepared a demonstration in which she placed three identical balloons filled with the same amount of air into three beakers of water. The first was put into a beaker of hot water, the second into a beaker of water at room temperature, and the third into a beaker of ice water, as shown.

"This water is about 100 degrees, which is the boiling point of water, since we're using Celsius," Didi explained as she placed the first balloon in the beaker. "This is room temperature, and this has had ice in it, so it is down around zero Celsius," she continued as she put the other two balloons into the beakers.

She placed another beaker on the top of each balloon to push it down into the water and then conducted a brief review of the behavior of gases.

"Now, today," she said as she began writing on the board, "we're going to discuss Charles's law, but before we put it on the board and discuss it, we're going to see what happened to the balloons. . . . Look up here. . . . How is the size of the balloon related to the temperature of the water we placed it in?"

"The balloon in the hot water looks bigger," Chris responded.

"Can you see any difference in these two?" Didi continued, pointing to the other two balloons.

"The one in the cold water looks smaller than the one in the room temperature water," Chris added.

"You're not going to see as much difference here," Didi explained, "because the difference between freezing and room temperature isn't as great as the difference between room temperature and boiling.

"But from what we see, if you increase temperature, what happens to the volume of the gas?"

"It increases," several students answered.

Didi wrote *Increase in temperature increases volume* on the board. She went on to emphasize that the amount of air in the balloons was the same and that they had essentially kept the pressure constant.

"So who can state Charles's law based on what we've seen here?"

"Increased temperature will increase volume if you have constant pressure and mass," Jeremy offered.

Didi briefly reviewed Charles's law, wrote an equation for it on the board, and proceeded to have her students solve a series of problems using the law.

Finally, let's look at Bob Duchaine as he discusses the Vietnam War.

Bob began his discussion by saying, "To understand the Vietnam War, we need to go back to the beginning. Vietnam had been set up as a French colony in the 1880s, but by the mid-1900s the military situation had gotten so bad for the French that they only controlled the little city of Dien Bien Phu."

Bob explained that the French surrendered in the summer of 1954 and peace talks followed. The talks resulted in Vietnam being split and provisions for free elections.

"These elections were never held," Bob continued. "Ngo Dinh Diem, in 1956, said there will be no free elections: 'I am in charge of the South. You can have elections in the north if you want, but there will be no elections in the south.'"

Bob continued by introducing the domino theory, which suggested that countries such as South Vietnam, Cambodia, Laos, Thailand, Burma, and even India would fall into communist hands much as dominos tip over and knock each other down. The way to prevent the loss of the countries, he explained, was to confront North Vietnam.

"And that's what we're going to be talking about throughout this unit," he said. "The war that we took over from the French to stop the fall of the dominos soon was eating up American lives at the rate of 12 to 15 thousand a year. . . . This situation went from a little simple plan . . . to stop the dominos from falling, to a loss of over 53,000 American lives that we know of.

"We'll pick up with this topic day after tomorrow. . . . Tomorrow you have a fun day in the library."

 These exercises are designed to help you prepare for the PRAXIS™ "Principles of Learning and Teaching" exam. To receive feedback on your constructed response questions and document analysis response, go to the Companion Website at *www.prenhall.com/eggen*, then to this chapter's *Practice for PRAXIS*™ module. For additional connections between this text and the PRAXIS™ exam, go to Appendix A.

Constructed Response Questions

In answering these questions, use information from the chapter and link your responses to specific information in the case.

1. What type or types of knowledge did Rebecca Atkins primarily demonstrate?
2. What type or types of knowledge did Richard Nelms demonstrate in his lesson? Identify at least two decisions that Richard made in an attempt to help his lesson progress smoothly.
3. What type or types of knowledge did Didi Johnson primarily demonstrate? Identify at least two decisions that Didi made in an attempt to help her lesson progress smoothly.
4. What type or types of knowledge did Bob Duchaine primarily demonstrate?

Document-Based Analysis

Three days after the presentation in his lesson, Bob Duchaine gave the following items on a brief quiz.

1. In what decade was Vietnam established as a colony?
2. What country was defeated in the battle of Dien Bien Phu?
3. What year was the battle of Dien Bien Phu fought?

4. Describe the domino theory, including at least two countries, other than Vietnam, that were identified.
5. Who was the leader of South Vietnam that refused to hold the free elections provided for in the peace talks after Dien Bien Phu?

Analyze the effectiveness of Bob's quiz based on the descriptions of effective assessment in the chapter.

 Also on the Companion Website at *www.prenhall.com/eggen*, you can measure your understanding of chapter content in *Practice Quiz* and *Essay* modules, apply concepts in *Online Cases,* and broaden your knowledge base with the *Additional Content* module and *Web Links* to other educational psychology websites.

 ## Online Portfolio Activities

To develop your professional portfolio, further apply your understanding of chapter content, and address the INTASC standards, go the Companion Website, then to this chapter's *Online Portfolio Activities.* Complete the suggested activities.

Important Concepts

action research *(p. 16)*
assessment *(p. 23)*
correlation *(p. 15)*
correlational research *(p. 15)*
descriptive research *(p. 13)*
experimental research *(p. 16)*
general pedagogical knowledge *(p. 10)*

pedagogical content knowledge *(p. 7)*
random assignment *(p. 16)*
reflective teaching *(p. 24)*
research *(p. 13)*
rubric *(p. 27)*
theory *(p. 19)*

Chapter Outline

The
Development
of Cognition
and Language

2

Karen Johnson, an eighth-grade science teacher, walked into the teachers' workroom with a clear plastic drinking cup filled with cotton balls.

"What are you up to?" asked Ken, one of her colleagues. "Drinking cotton these days?"

"I just had the greatest class," Karen exclaimed. "You know how I told you the other day that my third-period students didn't understand density? They would memorize the formula and solve problems but didn't really get it. I also found out they were confused about basic concepts such as mass, weight, size, volume—everything. To them, mass and weight were the same. If something was bigger, they figured it had to be heavier. It had to have more mass and also be more dense. It was a disaster."

"The kids in that group are a little slow, aren't they?" Ken responded.

"That's not really the problem," Karen said, shaking her head. "Their backgrounds are weak, and they've never really done anything other than memorize some definitions and formulas. So what do you expect? I kept thinking they could do better, so I decided to try something a little different, even if it seemed sort of elementary. See," she went on, compressing the cotton in the cup. "Now the cotton is more dense.... And now it's less dense," she pointed out, releasing the cotton.

"Then yesterday I made some different-sized blocks out of the same wood. We speculated about their densities, and some of the kids believed the density of the big block was greater. But then we weighed the blocks, measured their volumes, and computed their densities. As we discussed the results, they gradually began to understand that size is only one factor influencing density.

"This morning," she said with increasing animation, "I had them put water and vegetable oil in little bottles with equal volumes on our balances. When the balance tipped down on the water side, they saw that the mass of the water was greater, so water is more dense. I had asked them to predict which was more dense before we did the activity, and most of them said oil. We talked about that, and they concluded the reason they predicted oil is the fact that it's thicker.

"Here's the good part," she continued, "Calvin—he hates science—remembered that oil floats on water, so it made sense to him that oil is less dense. He actually got excited about what we were doing.

"So we formed a principle: Less dense materials float on more dense materials. Then, even better, Donelle wanted to know what would happen if the materials mixed together, you know, like water and alcohol. You could almost see the wheels turning. So we discussed that and thought about more examples where that might be the case. We even got into population density and how a door screen with the wires close together compared with one with the wires farther apart, and how that related to what we were studying. It was exciting. I really felt as if I was teaching and the students were really into learning for a change, instead of poking each other. A day like that now and then keeps you going."

As you began your study of teaching and learning, one of the first principles you probably heard was, "You must begin where the learner is." If we expect to teach as effectively as possible, we obviously need to understand our learners. One part of this understanding is human development—how students think, feel, and act at different ages and with different kinds of experiences. In this book, we examine three important aspects of this process: personal development, which includes an understanding of who we are and looks at our emotional and moral growth; social development, which examines our changing abilities to relate to each other; and cognitive development, which *describes changes in the ways we think and process information.* We study cognitive development in this chapter and then turn to personal and social development in Chapter 3.

After you've completed your study of this chapter, you should be able to

- Explain how cognitive development is influenced by learning, experience, and maturation.
- Describe basic concepts in Piaget's theory of cognitive development.
- Explain the role of social interaction, language, and culture in Vygotsky's theory of cognitive development.
- Explain how language development contributes to other aspects of development.

In the opening case study, Karen described a problem typical for many teachers: She found that her students had only a superficial understanding of an important concept. Their reactions were also typical. In their efforts to cope with their uncertainty, they memorized a formula, plugged in numbers, and got answers that had little meaning for them.

Why are some concepts, such as *density,* so hard for students to understand? It would be easy to blame "slowness" for their lack of progress, as Ken suggested. You'll learn later in the text, however, about some of the dangers in making such a judgment about student ability. In many instances, students are capable of achieving much more than they demonstrate. Other, more useful explanations are needed.

Development: A Definition

2.1

A first grader tries to shoot basketballs like her brother but has neither the strength nor the skill. She practices, receives tips from her brother, gets bigger and stronger, and by the fourth grade is making baskets consistently. Identify the experiential, the learning, and the maturational aspects of development in this example.

Mike began playing the trumpet as a sixth grader in his middle school band. Evenings were filled with odd sounds coming from his bedroom, and even Chews, his devoted dog, retreated to the relative sanctuary of the living room. As an eighth grader, however, practicing his part in the piece that he and two friends were playing for a concert, he produced very different sounds. Now, after listening to his son play his last concert as a high school senior, Mike's dad was convinced that Mike could play in a professional orchestra.

Three factors influenced Mike's success. First, he practiced and acquired a great deal of experience, and in the process, he also learned much about playing the trumpet. He also simply became stronger and more physically capable as a high schooler than he was earlier; he matured. We use this example to introduce the concept of **development**, *the orderly, durable changes in learners resulting from a combination of experience, learning, and maturation* (Figure 2.1). For all of us, development begins at birth and continues until we die.

In Mike's case, his musical ability developed. Athletes develop their physical skills; all of us try to develop our social skills. In this chapter, we focus on the ways that learners' thinking, reasoning, and intellectual abilities develop. As you study, keep the following questions in mind: "How is the thinking of young children different from the thinking of older learners and adults?" and "How does the thinking of all people change as they learn and acquire experience?" Theories of development help us answer these questions.

Figure 2.1 Factors influencing human intellectual development

Principles of Development

Although development is complex, some general principles exist that apply to all children and all forms of development.

- *Learning contributes to development.* Learning refers to increased understanding or improved abilities, and development occurs when the understanding or abilities are incorporated into the context of a complex activity (Bredo, 1997). For instance, you will learn specific questioning skills in your teacher-training program, and when you're able to use them appropriately in a variety of lessons, your teaching will have developed.
- *Experience enhances development.* Children whose parents have read and talked to them at home have advantages in school, for example. Children exposed to music, physical activities, and social experiences become more capable in these areas than those having less experience.
- *Social interaction is essential for development.* Social interaction allows students to share and compare knowledge, beliefs, and perspectives with one another.
- *Development strongly depends on language.* Language provides a medium for thought and a vehicle for sharing ideas and social experiences.

- *Development is continuous and relatively orderly.* As people mature, learn, and gather experiences, their development continuously advances. They don't suddenly "jump" from one set of abilities to another (Berk, 2001).
- *Individuals develop at different rates.* One middle school girl, for example, will be a young woman, towering head and shoulders over her slower developing classmates. In another case, two fourth graders will vary significantly in their ability to benefit from a learning activity.
- *Development is influenced by* **maturation,** *genetically controlled, age-related changes in individuals.* A 10-year-old will run faster than she did when she was 5, for example, and a first grader won't be able to solve problems a seventh grader can solve. In extreme cases, such as malnutrition or severe sensory deprivation, the environment can retard maturation. In most cases, genes and the environment interact to produce normal growth.

With these principles in mind, we now focus on cognitive development. We begin by considering research on the role of the brain in it, a topic that is receiving considerable attention in education.

Concrete learning experiences contribute to development by encouraging learners to apply and adjust existing schemes.

The Human Brain and Cognitive Development

Should young children be taught a second language at the same time they are learning their first? Is there a critical period during early childhood when artistic and musical abilities are best nurtured and developed? Some educators believe the answers to these questions can be found in research on the brain.

Educators and researchers have turned to neuroscientific or brain research as one mechanism for understanding cognitive development, and discussions of the brain have appeared in respected academic journals. The entire December 1998 issue of *Educational Psychology Review,* for example, is devoted to the topic. Some educators hope to create direct links between research on the physiological development of the brain and educational practice (Wolfe & Brandt, 1998). Areas of the brain and their functions are illustrated in Figure 2.2.

Research on Brain Development

Educators trying to create links between brain development and educational practice point to three major findings from the neuroscience research (Bruer, 1997, 1998, 1999). These findings suggest that

- Rapid brain growth occurs during early stages of development.
- Rapid brain growth results in critical periods of development for processes such as language and perception.
- Enriched environments can result in increased brain growth and development.

Let's consider these findings in more detail.

Early Brain Development. The human brain has between 100 and 200 billion neurons (nerve cells), and the connections between them, called *synapses,* determine the

Figure 2.2   Brain physiology and functions

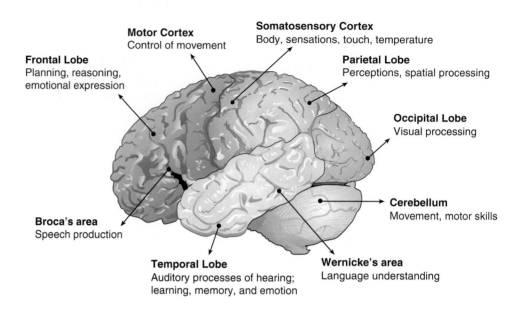

direction and extent of cognitive growth. The addition of synapses probably represents the creation of most forms of memory (Bransford et al., 2000). Scientists have found that synapses form most rapidly around age 4, resulting in synaptic density levels 50% higher than those of adults. In addition, 4-year-olds utilize blood sugar in their brains at twice the rate of adults, indicating increased brain activity (Bruer, 1999). These high levels of neural activity suggest that this time might be optimal for cognitive development, and this finding is a major reason educators are interested in brain development.

Critical Periods.   **Critical periods** are *time spans that are optimal for the development of certain capacities in the brain* (Berk, 2001). If adequate environmental stimulation occurs, development proceeds naturally; if not, it is retarded.

Evidence for critical periods comes from both human and animal research. For example, the brains of young kittens deprived of light for 3 or 4 days degenerate, and longer periods of stimulus deprivation can result in permanent brain damage (Berk, 2001). Research also indicates that after early childhood, it is extremely difficult to learn to speak a foreign language without an accent. At the extreme, the critical period concept suggests "use it or lose it."

Optimal Environments.   Some educators believe that enriched environments during critical periods may enhance cognitive development. Support for this conclusion comes from research with rats indicating that animals reared in complex environments have 25% more synapses per neuron in the visual areas of their brains than rats raised in isolation (Bruer, 1998). In addition, animals raised in these surroundings have more capillaries per nerve cell, suggesting that optimal environments result in increased brain capacity (Bransford et al., 2000). However, although stimulus deprivation can adversely affect brain development, extra stimulation does not necessarily increase it (J. Byrnes & Fox, 1998). Evidence does not exist to suggest that more is better.

2.2
To which of the three influences on development—experience, learning, or maturation—is the concept of critical period most closely related? Explain.

Putting Brain Research Into Perspective

It is tempting to use neuroscience research to infer educational applications. For instance, brain research might prompt some educators to capitalize on critical periods of brain growth by providing enriched environments, in hopes of enhancing cognitive development. However, much of the research on brain development has been done with laboratory animals, and experts are cautious about applications with humans (Bruer, 1998; J. Byrnes & Fox, 1998). Although critical periods probably do occur in humans, our brains retain an enormous ability to benefit from environmental stimulation throughout our lives (Bransford et al., 2000). In addition, evidence for critical periods in the development of traditional academic subjects, such as reading or math, doesn't exist (Geary, 1998). Finally, brain research isn't well developed and doesn't provide educators with specific suggestions about when and how to capitalize on surges in brain growth.

Obviously, we should try to provide the best possible environments for growth and development, but the reasons for doing so can be better found in cognitive research on learning and development. One expert in this area concluded, "Neuroscience has only the broadest outline of principles to offer education at this time. And in a lot of cases, the principles suggest strategies that educators already know" (D'Arcangelo, 2000, p. 71). Bruer (1997) summarizes this position:

> Educational applications of brain science may come eventually, but as of now neuroscience has little to offer teachers in terms of informing classroom practice. There is, however, a science of mind, cognitive science, that can serve as a basic science for the development of an applied science of learning and instruction. Practical, well-founded examples of putting cognitive science into practice already exist in numerous schools and classrooms. Teachers would be better off looking at these examples than at speculative applications of neuroscience. (p. 4)

The cognitive science that Bruer refers to is detailed throughout this text.

We turn now to Piaget's efforts to describe human cognitive development.

Piaget's Theory of Intellectual Development

Jean Piaget (1896–1990) was an unlikely influence on American education. His initial work was in biology, and his writing had to be translated from French into English. He wasn't even originally interested in education, instead being fascinated by *genetic epistemology*, the study of the growth of knowledge in people. He formed the beginnings of his theory by observing his own three children. His research method—intensively observing small numbers of subjects—was very different from the behaviorist tradition so dominant in the United States at the time, and as a result, his work wasn't initially accepted. However, as additional research confirmed his findings, Piaget's work became increasingly influential and has since had a great impact on views of development and learning and on education in the United States. Let's look at his theory now.

The Drive for Equilibrium

Think about some of your everyday experiences. Are you bothered when something doesn't make sense? Do you want the world to be predictable? Are you more comfortable in classes where the instructor specifies the requirements and outlines the grading practices? Do most of your days follow a pattern, or are they just a series of random experiences?

According to Piaget (1952, 1959), people have an innate need to understand how the world works and to find order, structure, and predictability in their existence. He calls this need the drive for **equilibrium**, *a state of cognitive balance between individuals' understanding of the world and their experiences.*

The concept of equilibrium and the need to achieve it are the foundations of Piaget's theory (Piaget, 1952, 1959). When we are able to understand new experiences, we remain at equilibrium; when we aren't, disequilbrium occurs and we change our thinking. Disequilibrium is a major energizing force in development.

Organization and Adaptation: The Development of Schemes

To achieve and maintain equilibrium, people employ two related processes, *organization* and *adaptation*.

Achieving Equilibrium: The Process of Organization

People have a myriad of experiences—sometimes bewildering experiences—in the everyday world. To achieve equilibrium, they organize these experiences into *mental patterns, operations, and systems,* which Piaget called **schemes.** *The process of forming and using schemes in an effort to understand how the world works* is called **organization.**

2.3
Identify at least two schemes you should have formed by now in your study of this chapter.

Schemes are the building blocks of thinking and, as such, vary with age. Infants develop psychomotor schemes such as reaching for and holding objects; school-age children develop more abstract schemes such as classification or proportional reasoning. When you learned to operate a car, you developed a "driving" scheme, which helped you start the car, maneuver in traffic, understand traffic signals and laws, and make routine decisions about your speed.

Piaget used the concept of schemes to refer to a narrow range of abstract operations, such as infants' object permanence scheme (the idea that an object still exists even when we can't see it) or young children's conservation-of-volume scheme (the idea that the amount of liquid doesn't change if it is poured into a different-shaped container) (Piaget, 1952). However, teachers and some researchers (e.g., Wadsworth, 1996) find it useful to extend Piaget's idea to include content-related schemes, such as the "driving" scheme just mentioned or an "adding-fractions-with-unlike-denominators" scheme, when designing instruction to meet the developmental needs of their students. We use this expanded view in our description of Piaget's work.

The formation of schemes abounds in school. For example, young learners come to understand that number is something that can be applied to objects ranging from toys to people, and that the number of objects doesn't change with their spacing or arrangement. Older learners use a classification scheme in science when they decide if crabs or snakes are vertebrates, and language arts students use writing schemes to compose coherent paragraphs. From a content perspective, all the concepts, principles, rules, and procedures that students learn in school are organized into schemes that allow them to make sense of the world.

Maintaining Equilibrium: The Process of Adaptation

As we acquire experiences, our existing schemes often become inadequate, and we are forced to adapt to function effectively. **Adaptation** is *the process of adjusting schemes and experiences to each other to maintain equilibrium.* For example, if you learn to drive a car with an automatic transmission and then later buy a car with a stick shift, you must adapt your "driving" scheme accordingly.

Adaptation consists of two reciprocal processes: accommodation and assimilation (J. Byrnes, 2001). **Accommodation** is *a form of adaptation in which an existing scheme is modified and a new one is created in response to experience.* As you learn to drive with the stick shift, you modify your original "driving" scheme and create a "driving-with-a-stick-shift" scheme. Accommodation functions with its counterpart process, **assimilation,** which is *a form of adaptation in which an experience in the environment is incorporated into an existing scheme.* For instance, once you've learned to drive a car with a stick shift, you likely will also be able to drive a pickup truck with a stick shift. You will have assimilated the experience with the pickup truck into your "driving-with-a-stick-shift" scheme. The relationship between assimilation and accommodation is illustrated in Figure 2.3.

Maintaining equilibrium requires both assimilation and accommodation. If new experiences are only assimilated into existing schemes, the schemes don't change and development doesn't occur. As an extreme example, "flat-earthers," people who cling to the belief that Earth is flat, manage to assimilate experiences with geography into that scheme. On the other hand, if existing schemes can't be made to work, a person faces con-

Figure 2.3 Maintaining equilibrium through the process of adaptation

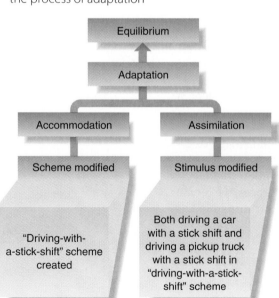

stant disequilibrium. Culture shock—the uneasy feeling people have when they visit a new country and must quickly adjust to different customs, food, and language—is an example. The amount of accommodation required can be overwhelming.

When considering how organization and adaptation lead to cognitive development, an important principle must be kept in mind: *All growth depends on existing schemes;* a scheme is never formed in isolation. For example, a math student's ability to add fractions with unlike denominators develops from an understanding of adding fractions with like denominators, which is based on an understanding of fractions themselves, which begins with an understanding of numbers and numerals (Figure 2.4). This principle is one of the most important contributions of Piaget's developmental theory. It suggests that teachers should select and present topics that build on learners' current understanding and disrupt equilibrium enough to be motivating but not overwhelming. If new information is presented at the same level as existing understanding, it is simply assimilated and development doesn't occur. On the other hand, if it is too different from present understanding, learners cannot link it to what they already know and will maintain equilibrium by discarding the experience instead of accommodating their present schemes.

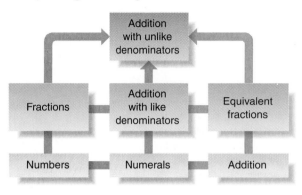

Figure 2.4 Illustration of growth in math depending on existing schemes

2.4
Four-year-old Anna believes that short-haired people are male, and those with long hair, female. When she meets Kevin, who has long hair, she believes he is female, but she changes her mind after talking to him. Later, she meets another long-haired man, Damon, and believes he is male. Describe where assimilation and where accommodation occurred for Anna. Also, explain how these experiences led to development.

Factors Influencing Development

We saw earlier that development results from the combination of learning, experience, and maturation, and we have already discussed maturation. Here we consider Piaget's emphasis on the role of experience in development. Piaget tended to subsume the role of learning under a more general description of experience. In addition, he separated experience with the physical world from social experience in describing their influence on development (Piaget, 1970).

Experience with the Physical World

Let's consider our "driving" scheme again. If we originally learned to drive vehicles with automatic transmissions, for example, and never had experiences with those having stick shifts, our overall ability to drive would be less developed. The same principle applies for development in general. Let's look at a classroom example.

> Carol Mendoza was working with her fifth-grade students on map-reading skills in social studies. She wanted them to understand how the scale on a map represents real distances.
>
> She began by saying, "Look at the map of Ohio in front of you. How far is it from Cleveland to Columbus? . . . Antonio?"
>
> "I . . . I don't know . . . About 4 inches."
>
> Carol could tell from the silence and embarrassed giggles in response to Antonio's answer that most of her students knew little about the scale on their map and how it worked.
>
> "Okay everyone, let's try something," she said after thinking for a moment. "Each of you take out a sheet of paper and a ruler. We're going to make a map of our classroom."
>
> She then had the students work in pairs to measure the room and its contents and draw pictures of what they found. When the students finished, she reconvened the class and led a discussion about the concept of *scale*. The class then made a composite drawing of the classroom using a scale that all agreed on.
>
> The next day Carol returned to the map of Ohio and related the map to their activities of the day before. As the students compared the map they had constructed to the map of Ohio, she could see that they were beginning to understand what "scale" meant.

According to Piaget, concrete, real-world experience exerts a major influence on development. The concrete experience of constructing a "scale" for their classroom gave Carol's students a true understanding of the social studies concept. Carol could have merely written the definition of *scale* on the board and had students memorize it, which would have taken less time and effort, but doing so would have provided little experience and less understanding. We have all memorized definitions that we didn't understand and then promptly forgotten them. They resulted in virtually no development.

The hands-on activities often seen in schools today are applications of Piaget's emphasis on direct experience. For example, using sticks and blocks helps children understand abstract math concepts and operations (Ball, 1992; Hartnett & Gelman, 1998). In our opening case study, Karen gave her eighth graders direct experiences with the concept *density* with activities using cotton balls, water and oil, and other examples. Now, because her students better understand the concept *density*, they're equipped to incorporate that understanding into explanations about weather fronts, hot-air balloons, why people float more easily in the ocean than in lakes, and many others. Their ability to understand and adapt to the outside world has expanded; development has occurred.

Social Experience

Piaget also emphasized the role of **social experience,** *the process of interacting—usually verbally—with others,* in development (Becker & Varelas, 2001; DeVries, 1997). Social experience allows learners to test their schemes against those of others. When schemes are comparable, people remain at equilibrium; when they aren't, equilibrium is disrupted, learners are motivated to adapt their schemes, and development occurs.

The recognition that social interaction is essential for development has strongly influenced education and child-rearing practice. For example, parents organize play groups for their young children, cooperative learning is emphasized in schools, and students are encouraged to conduct experiments and solve problems in groups. The effectiveness of these activities illustrates the value of social interaction.

Stages of Development

Perhaps the most widely known elements of Piaget's theory are his descriptions of stages of development. Piaget's stages describe general patterns of thinking for children at different ages and with different amounts of experience. Progress from one stage to another represents *qualitative* changes in children's thinking, that is, changes in the *kind* of thinking rather than the *amount* (Siegler, 1991). For example, kindergartners' thinking depends largely on their perceptions, a conceptual "what you see is what you get." Fourth graders, in comparison, can go beyond mere perception to think logically if they have experience with concrete materials. More advanced students can think logically about abstract ideas. These are qualitative differences in thinking.

As you study the characteristics of each stage, keep three ideas in mind:

- Children develop steadily and gradually, and experiences in one stage form the foundation for movement to the next (Berk, 2001).
- Although approximate chronological ages are attached to the stages, the rate at which individual children pass through them differs widely, depending on maturation, experience, and culture (Papalia & Wendkos-

Social interaction encourages learners to examine their own schemas and compare them to those of others.

Table 2.1 Piaget's stages and characteristics

Stage	Characteristics	Example
Sensorimotor (0–2)	Goal-directed behavior	Makes jack-in-the-box pop up
	Object permanence (represents objects in memory)	Searches for object behind parent's back
Preoperational (2–7)	Rapid increase in language ability with overgeneralized language	"We goed to the store."
	Symbolic thought	Points out car window and says, "Truck!"
	Dominated by perception	Concludes that all the water in a sink came out of the faucet (the second cartoon in Chapter 1)
Concrete Operational (7–11)	Operates logically with concrete materials	Concludes that two objects on a "balanced" balance have the same mass even though one is larger than the other
	Classifies and serial orders	Orders containers according to decreasing volume
Formal Operational (11–Adult)	Solves abstract and hypothetical problems	Considers outcome of WWII if the Battle of Britain had been lost
	Thinks combinatorially	Systematically determines how many different sandwiches can be made from three different kinds of meat, cheese, and bread

Olds, 1996). In groups of students with the same chronological age, developmental levels may differ significantly (Weinert & Helmke, 1998).

■ Although rates vary, all people pass through each stage before progressing into a later one. No one skips any stage. This means that older children and even adults will process information in ways that are characteristic of young children if they lack experience in an area.

Piaget's stages of development are summarized in Table 2.1 and described in the sections that follow.

Sensorimotor Stage (0 to 2 Years)

In the **sensorimotor stage**, *children use their senses and motor capacities to make sense of the world.* The schemes they develop are based on their physical interactions with their environments, such as using eye-hand coordination to grab objects and bring them to their mouths.

Early in the sensorimotor stage, children do not mentally represent objects; for these children, objects are "out of sight, out of mind." Later in the stage, however, they acquire **object permanence**, *the ability to represent objects in memory.* Children in this stage also develop the ability to imitate, an important skill that allows them to learn by observing others.

Preoperational Stage (2 to 7 Years)

In the **preoperational stage**, *perception dominates children's thinking.* The name of this stage comes from the idea of "operation," or mental activity. A child who can classify different animals as dogs, cats, and bears, for example, is performing a mental operation.

Many dramatic changes occur in children as they pass through the preoperational stage. For example, children make enormous progress in language development, reflecting growth in the ability to use symbols (P. Miller, 1993). They also learn huge numbers of concepts. For example, a child will point excitedly and say, "Truck," "Horse," and "Tree," delighting in exercising these newly formed ideas. These concepts are concrete, however; the truck, horse, and tree are present or associated with the current situation. Children in this stage have limited notions of abstract ideas such as *fairness, democracy,* and *energy.*

2.6
A small child has not acquired object permanence. His mother takes a stuffed toy the child can see and puts it behind her back. What is the child likely to do? What will the child do after object permanence is acquired?

Table 2.2 Characteristics of preoperational thinking

Characteristic	Description	Example
Egocentrism	The inability to interpret an event from someone else's point of view	In the cartoon on page 14, Dolly believes it is her daddy's fault she missed the ball.
Centration (Centering)	The tendency to focus on the most perceptually obvious aspect of an object or event to the exclusion of all others	When we see a gasoline price of 1.45^9 or a clothing item marked $69.95, we tend to center on the $1.45 and the $69, making the items seem less expensive than they really are.
Transformation	The ability to mentally trace the process of changing from one state to another	A person is able to *mentally represent* the process of changing clay from a ball to a pancake shape.
Reversibility	The ability to mentally trace a line of reasoning back to its beginning	A person can *mentally trace* the pancake-shaped clay back to the shape of a ball.
Systematic reasoning	The process of using logical thought to reach a conclusion	A person concludes that it is likely to rain because it is humid and cloudy and it usually rains when it is humid and cloudy.

2.7
Which factor affecting development—experience with the physical world, social experience, or maturation—is probably most important for reducing egocentrism? Why?

The powerful effect of perceptual dominance is also seen in five other aspects of preoperational thinking: **egocentrism, centration,** and *the lack of* **transformation,** *re-*versibility, and **systematic reasoning.** These characteristics are defined in Table 2.2.

Let's see how these factors work together to influence the thinking of children on cognitive tasks that Piaget made famous. In one task, 5-year-olds are shown two rows of nickels such as the following:

When asked if the number of coins in each row is the same, the children say it is. However, when one row is lengthened right in front of the children, like this,

they typically conclude that the bottom row has more coins.

Let's analyze their thinking. First, they *center* on the differences in length of the two rows, which is more perceptually obvious than the more abstract idea of number. Second, because they tend not to *transform,* they don't mentally represent the process of lengthening the bottom row, even though they directly observe it: They see it as a different row, rather than as the earlier one lengthened. Third, they don't *reverse:* They are not able to mentally trace the process of lengthening the row back to its original state. Also, because they tend not to reason systematically, they easily conclude that the bottom row is longer.

A nonconserver is influenced by appearances, believing that the flat pieces of clay have different amounts than the balls of clay even though they were initially the same.

This leads to another widely publicized feature of Piaget's work, his concept of conservation.

Conservation.

> As he's taking an order, the waiter at the pizza place asks, "Do you want that pizza cut into four or eight pieces?"
>
> The customer replies, "You'd better make it four; I couldn't eat eight all by myself!"

This joke illustrates Piaget's concept of **conservation,** *the idea that the "amount" of some substance stays the same regardless of its shape or the number of pieces into which it is divided.* The thinking of children can be demonstrated with a number of conservation tasks. One was illustrated in the example with the coins. A task involving conservation of mass is as follows:

A child is given two balls of clay, as shown.

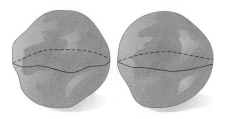

The child is asked which ball has more clay, and she responds that the balls have the same amount. (If she says they have different amounts, she is asked to remove clay from one ball and put it on the other until she says they're equal.) The experimenter then rolls out one of the balls, as shown here:

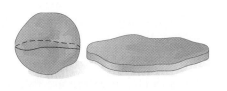

The child is asked if the balls now have the same amount of clay.

To see a video clip of a 6- and a 12-year-old wrestling with conservation of mass, go to the Companion Website at *www.prenhall.com/eggen*, then to this chapter's *Classrooms on the Web* module. Click on *Video Clip 2.1.*

To see a video clip of two students at different developmental levels considering the conservation task with liquids, go to the Companion Website at *www.prenhall.com/eggen*, then to this chapter's *Classrooms on the Web* module. Click on *Video Clip 2.2.*

2.8
Use the concepts *centration*, *transformation*, and *reversibility* to explain why preoperational children don't "conserve" in the clay task.

Preoperational children typically conclude that the amounts are now different because they haven't mentally "conserved" the amount of clay. If the amounts are different, some clay must have magically appeared or disappeared, given that no clay was actually added or removed. Because they display the thinking characteristics described in Table 2.2, preoperational thinkers aren't bothered by this inconsistency.

The same experiment can be done with liquids with the same results; that is, preoperational thinkers conclude that the amounts of liquid are different when poured from identical containers into those with different shapes, even though the amounts remain the same.

Preoperational children don't think about the world in the same way adults do. Their thinking is dominated by perception, their mental representations are limited to concrete objects, and they have difficulty mentally representing change. They've made huge strides from the sensorimotor stage, however; they have a much greater ability to use symbols and words to think about their world.

Concrete Operational Stage (7 to 11 Years)

The **concrete operational stage,** which *is characterized by the ability to think logically about concrete objects,* marks another important advance in children's thinking (Flavell, Miller, & Miller, 1993). For instance, when facing the situation with the coins, concrete operational thinkers conclude that the number in the two rows remains the same. They reason as follows (although they may not be able to precisely verbalize their thinking):

> The number of coins was initially the same.
> No coin was added or taken away.
> Therefore, the number must still be the same.

This represents systematic reasoning and logical thought. It would be reflected by a statement such as "You just made the row longer" or "You just spread the coins apart."

As another case, consider the following:

An experimenter has three sticks. He presents 1 and 2 to you, as shown:

1   2

Now he removes Stick 2 and shows you 1 and 3, as follows:

1   3

2.9
Look again at the cartoon on page 19 in Chapter 1. How would a concrete operational thinker explain the water coming out of the faucet? Describe the thinker's logic.

He then asks, "What do you know about the relationship between Sticks 2 and 3?"

A preoperational thinker cannot deal with this problem. A concrete operational thinker concludes that 2 is longer than 3, reasoning that, because 2 is longer than 1 and 1 is longer than 3, 2 must be longer than 3. This is another example of systematic reasoning and logical thought.

Seriation and Classification.   Seriation and classification are two logical operations that develop during the concrete operational stage (Piaget, 1977), and both are essential for understanding number concepts (Siegler, 1991). **Seriation** is *the ability to* *order objects according to increasing or decreasing length, weight, or volume.* Piaget's research indicates that this ability gradually evolves until it is finally acquired at about age 7 or 8.

Classification is *the process of grouping objects on the basis of a common characteristic.* Before age 5, children can form simple groups. For example, they can separate a pile of cardboard circles into one group of white and another group of black circles. When a black square is added, however, they typically include it with the black circles, instead of forming subclasses of black circles and black squares. By age 7, they can form subclasses, but they still have problems with more complex classification systems. For example, when shown 10 black and 3 white cardboard circles, they conclude that the circles are all cardboard, with 10 black and 3 white. When asked if there are more cardboard or more black circles, however, 6-year-olds typically say there are more black, suggesting that they center on the colors, ignoring the larger class of cardboard circles and the subclass of black cardboard circles.

Formal Operational Stage (Age 11 to Adult)

Although concrete thinkers are capable of logic, their thinking is tied to the real and tangible. Formal thinkers, in contrast, can think logically about the hypothetical and even the impossible. During the **formal operational stage,** *the learner can examine abstract problems systematically and generalize about the results.* These abilities open a range of possibilities for thinking about the world that were unavailable to learners at the earlier stages.

Characteristics of Formal Thought.   Formal thinking has three characteristics (Flavell, 1993):

- Thinking abstractly
- Thinking systematically
- Thinking hypothetically

Differences between concrete and formal operational thinkers on these dimensions are illustrated in Figure 2.5.

Formal operational learners can think logically about abstract and hypothetical ideas.

As shown in Figure 2.5, the formal operational learner can consider the abstract and hypothetical, as in the question about laws. This ability makes the study of courses such as algebra, in which letters and symbols stand for numbers, meaningful on a different level. To the concrete operational child, $x + 2x = 9$ is meaningful only if it is represented concretely, such as:

> *Dave ate a certain number of cookies. His sister ate twice as many. Together they ate 9. How many did each one eat?*

Formal operational learners, in contrast, can think about the equation as a general idea, just as they would in describing the problem with the sticks by saying, "If A is greater than B, and if B is greater than C, then A is greater than C." In doing so, formal thinkers are operating abstractly, an ability that allows them to use the solution for a variety of problems.

Formal thinkers also think systematically and recognize the need to isolate and control variables in forming conclusions. For example, a girl hears her father say, "I've got to stop drinking so much coffee. I've been sleeping terribly the last few nights." She responds, "But Dad, maybe that's not it. You've also been bringing work home every night, and you didn't do that before." She recognizes that her father's sleeplessness may be caused by extra work, rather than by the coffee, and that they can't tell until they isolate each variable.

Formal operational learners can also think hypothetically. For instance, considering what might have happened if the British had won the Revolutionary War requires

Figure 2.5 A comparison of concrete and formal operational thinking

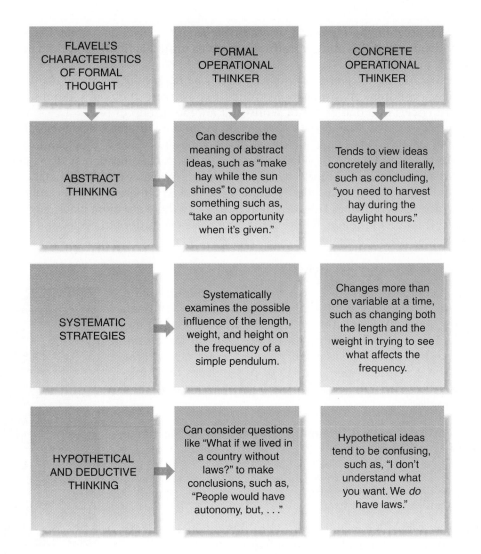

FLAVELL'S CHARACTERISTICS OF FORMAL THOUGHT	FORMAL OPERATIONAL THINKER	CONCRETE OPERATIONAL THINKER
ABSTRACT THINKING	Can describe the meaning of abstract ideas, such as "make hay while the sun shines" to conclude something such as, "take an opportunity when it's given."	Tends to view ideas concretely and literally, such as concluding, "you need to harvest hay during the daylight hours."
SYSTEMATIC STRATEGIES	Systematically examines the possible influence of the length, weight, and height on the frequency of a simple pendulum.	Changes more than one variable at a time, such as changing both the length and the weight in trying to see what affects the frequency.
HYPOTHETICAL AND DEDUCTIVE THINKING	Can consider questions like "What if we lived in a country without laws?" to make conclusions, such as, "People would have autonomy, but, . . ."	Hypothetical ideas tend to be confusing, such as, "I don't understand what you want. We *do* have laws."

hypothetical thinking for American history students. Biology students are asked to consider the results of crossing different combinations of dominant and recessive genes, and art students must imagine multiple perspectives and light sources when they create drawings. Middle and high school classrooms are filled with content requiring formal operational thought.

The difficulty Karen Johnson's students had in understanding the concept *density* further illustrates the need for formal thinking. When students cannot think abstractly and solve abstract problems, they revert to memorizing what they can or, in frustration, give up altogether.

Stages of Development: Research on Student Thinking

We've just seen that much of the middle, junior high, and particularly the high school curriculum is geared toward formal operational thinking, and a strict application of Piaget's work suggests that this is appropriate. Such an application can create a dilemma, however, because research indicates that the thinking of most middle, junior high, and high school students is still concrete operational (Karplus, Karplus, Formisano, & Paulsen, 1979; Lawson & Snitgren, 1982; Thornton & Fuller, 1981). Additional research indicates that almost half of college students aren't

Karen's concrete examples provided the experience needed to advance formal thinking.

able to consistently reason formally, especially in areas outside their majors (De Lisi & Straudt, 1980; Wigfield, Eccles, & Pintrich, 1996). Similar patterns have been found in adults.

> You are likely to find that even well-educated adults have difficulty with abstract thinking! . . . Why is it that so many college students, and adults in general, are not fully formal operational? The reason is that people are most likely to think abstractly in situations in which they have had extensive experience. (Berk, 2000, p. 256)

If older students lack concrete experiences in a particular area, they may even be preoperational in their thinking. As an example, consider the following problem. Eighth graders observed a balance with blocks on it, as shown in Figure 2.6, and were then asked to judge the accuracy of the following propositions:

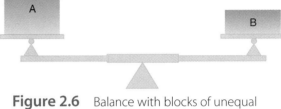

The volume of A is greater than the volume of B.
The mass of A is greater than the mass of B.
The density of A is greater than the density of B.

Figure 2.6   Balance with blocks of unequal volume

The reasoning involved can be described as follows:

We can see that the volume of A is greater than the volume of B.
The balance is level, so the masses are equal.
Given that the masses are equal but the volume of A is greater, the density of A is less than the density of B.

The problem occurs in the present and is tangible; thus, it requires concrete operational thinking. The eighth graders, typically 13 or 14 years old, were chronologically at the formal operational stage, so they should have been able to solve the problem with ease. Researchers found, however, that more than three fourths of the students concluded that both the mass and density of A were greater than the mass and density of B. The students were still dominated by perceptions, concluding that because A is larger, it must have more mass and also be more dense (Eggen & McDonald, 1987). Their reasoning was preoperational!

These findings have important implications for teachers, particularly those in middle schools, junior highs, and high schools (and even universities). Many students come to these learning settings without the concrete experiences needed to think at the level of abstraction often required. Wise teachers realize this and provide concrete experiences for them, as Karen Johnson did with her eighth graders. Otherwise, students will revert to whatever it takes for them to survive—in most cases, memorization without understanding.

2.10
What preoperational characteristic explains why the students would conclude that the bigger block had more mass, even though the balance was balanced? Explain the students' thinking.

Assessment and Learning: Assessing Students' Cognitive Development

We study Piaget's work because it helps us understand our students' thinking. The research you saw in the last section suggests that the thinking of many students isn't at the stage that Piaget's theory predicts it should be. Understanding how students react to the learning tasks we give them allows teachers to better match these tasks to their developmental needs.

Unfortunately, most of the assessment tasks that Piaget used in his research involved one-to-one interviews with children, making it difficult to use these methods with an elementary class of 25 to 30 students and virtually impossible for a middle school or high school teacher who works with 150 or more students a day.

What other options do teachers have for gathering information about the developmental levels of their students? One option is paper-and-pencil measures. The following sections describe some examples:

Assessing Aspects of Formal Operational Thinking

Problems such as the following can be used to assess the extent to which students' thinking is formal operational.

> *A person making sandwiches has turkey, ham, and beef as choices for meat; American and Swiss as choices for cheese; and whole wheat and rye as bread choices. How many different kinds of sandwiches can the person make?*

In using paper-and-pencil measures like this, asking students to show their thinking is essential, because the logic behind the solution is as important as the answer itself.

Formal operational students will attack this problem systematically, perhaps by listing the combinations as follows:

> Turkey, American, whole wheat
> Turkey, American, rye
> Turkey, Swiss, whole wheat
> Turkey, Swiss, rye

Then, seeing that 4 different combinations can be made with turkey and that there are 3 kinds of meat, students can conclude that 12 combinations are possible in all.

Concrete operational students will be more haphazard in their approach, perhaps creating a list like the following:

> Ham, American, rye
> Turkey, American, whole wheat
> Beef, Swiss, whole wheat
> And so on . . .

A second type of assessment problem asks students to describe the meaning of proverbs like "Still water runs deep" and "Make hay while the sun shines." Formal thinkers will describe the proverbs in abstract terms, such as "A quiet person often understands the complexities of existence" and "Take advantage of an opportunity when it presents itself." Concrete thinkers will give more literal interpretations, such as "When water is still, it means that it is very deep" and "A farmer should gather his crops before it gets dark."

Other measures assess the extent to which students can think logically with combinations (Renner et al., 1976).

Assessing Aspects of Concrete Operational Thinking

Similar measures can be used to assess progress toward concrete operational thought. For example, one item measuring conservation of volume first presents students with pictures of two cows that have an equal number of bales of hay to eat (Berk, 2003).

Students are asked, "Does each of these two cows have the same amount of hay to eat?" Students are then shown pictures in which one of the cow's bales are spread out and the other cow's bales remain the same. Students are asked, "Now does each cow have the same amount of hay to eat, or does one cow have more?" Again, asking students to explain the logic of their answers is essential.

Another problem that measures the extent to which students' thinking is concrete operational focuses on seriation.

There are three students named Joanne, Kevin, and Deitra. Deitra is taller than Kevin, and Kevin is taller than Joanne. Which of the following statements is most accurate?

a. *Deitra and Joanne are the same height.*
b. *Deitra is taller than Joanne.*
c. *Joanne is taller than Deitra.*
d. *We don't have enough information to know about their heights.*

Explain your choice.

To see a video clip of students struggling with the pendulum problem, go to the Companion Website at *www.prenhall.com/eggen*, then to this chapter's *Classrooms on the Web* module. Click on *Video Clip 2.3*.

Teachers can also assess students' thinking informally by listening to students talk to one another as they work on problems in the classroom. For example, a middle school science teacher asked his students to design an experiment that would tell them what factors influence the frequency (how many times it swings in a specified time period) of a simple pendulum, such as a paper clip suspended by a string. By listening to their interaction as they worked in groups, he found that they didn't understand the need to control variables to solve the problem. His observations led him to conclude that the students needed additional concrete experiences to advance their development.

We want to offer a word of caution, however, in using assessment exercises like the ones described above to plan instruction. Research indicates that students' thinking strongly depends on background knowledge and experience, perhaps as much as or more than on general developmental levels, such as concrete operations or formal operations (Serpell, 2000; Siegler & Ellis, 1996). For example, students given experiences with exercises such as the "sandwich problem" quickly learn to attack them systematically. However, if they lack adequate background experiences, the thinking of older students will be concrete operational or even preoperational as the research examining the thinking of eighth graders that we described in the last section indicated. This suggests that teachers at all levels should provide students with as many experiences as necessary to help them acquire the background knowledge needed for developmentally advanced thinking.

Technology and Learning: Using Technology to Develop Formal Thinking

If much of the content of middle, junior high, and high school classrooms requires formal thought, yet most students at these ages remain concrete operational, what can be done to bridge the gap? Using concrete demonstrations, as Karen did in attempting to help her students understand the concept *density*, is one solution. Laboratory activities are another. If properly

Computer simulations allow learners to test hypotheses, control variables, and develop their formal thinking abilities.

designed, they provide concrete experiences while simultaneously requiring students to think logically, systematically, and hypothetically, all characteristics of formal thinking (Lawson, 1995).

Hands-on labs are often expensive, time-consuming, difficult to implement, and sometimes even dangerous, discouraging many teachers from using them. Technology provides a viable alternative.

Laboratory Simulations

Researchers have created laboratory simulations that allow students to design experiments using computer technology (Roblyer, 2003). Research on these simulations indicates they can be effective in helping learners develop formal thinking (B. Fisher, 1997; Weller, 1997). Students unable to control variables before their involvement in a simulation were able to do so after, indicating that the simulation provided the experience needed to make the transition to systematic reasoning. Technology-based simulations have also increased students' interest and confidence in science, as well as their ability to interpret data (Lundeberg et al., 1999). To experience a simulation, you might want to try the following exercise.

Using Technology in Your Study of Educational Psychology

Examining Cognitive Development

Simulations can provide students with experiences in designing, implementing, and evaluating experiments like those in a real laboratory. Using the CD-ROM that accompanies this book, you can perform one of your own experiments. This simulation will give you some direct experience in using the CD to examine your own thinking as well as the thinking of students who have completed the experiment in an actual lab setting. To complete the activity, do the following:

- Open the CD, and click on *Pendulum Experiment*.
- Complete the activities, and then answer the following questions.

1. With respect to the pendulum experiment, was your thinking concrete operational or formal operational? What, specifically, did you do in conducting the experiment that indicated your thinking was either concrete or formal operational?

2. Suppose your thinking in this experiment was concrete operational. (It may or may not have been, and if it was, it isn't a negative reflection on your ability.) What is the most likely reason your thinking was concrete operational?

3. Now, let's examine the thinking of students who conducted this same experiment in an actual lab setting. Read the case study at the end of Chapter 8. (You may also watch a video of this same case study. Your instructor can make the video available to you if he or she chooses to do so.) Based on what you read in the written case study or saw in the video case study, decide if the thinking of the students was concrete operational or formal operational. What, specifically, did the students do that indicated concrete or formal operational thought?

Technology-based simulations won't work automatically, however, and careful thought and planning are needed to implement them effectively. The following guidelines can increase their effectiveness:

- Ensure that learners have adequate background knowledge before beginning the simulation. If background knowledge is lacking, provide examples and other representations of the content to develop it.
- To check for understanding, review the procedures involved in the simulation before students complete the activity.
- Make the logic behind operations visible by carefully recapping the experience in a whole-class discussion after the students have completed it.
- Require students to apply the ideas they learn in the simulations to other, real-world problems.

If carefully planned and implemented, technology simulations can provide valuable educational experiences for students.

2.11
Identify at least one advantage and one disadvantage of using a computer simulation, rather than a lab experiment, to examine the effects of heat on different objects.

Applying Piaget's Work in Classrooms: Instructional Strategies

Piaget's theory suggests that teachers should keep the developmental needs of students in mind as they design and implement instruction. The following principles can guide teachers in their efforts:

- Provide concrete experiences that represent abstract concepts and principles.
- Help students link the concrete representations to the abstract idea.
- Use social interaction to help students verbalize their developing understanding.
- Design learning experiences as developmental bridges to more advanced stages of development.

Let's see how the principles guide Kristen Michler, a second-grade teacher, as she works with her students.

Concrete experiences provide opportunities for students to learn abstract concepts by modifying existing schemas.

Kristen Michler was teaching her students about place value. She grouped her students in pairs and gave each pair several craft sticks with 10 beans glued on each and a number of separate beans, as shown here.

"What do we have here?" she began. "Jason?"

"Sticks . . . with beans on them."

"And other beans," Tenesha added.

"And how many beans on each stick? . . . Go ahead and count them."

"Ten," Trang said after a few seconds.

"Yes, good Trang," Kristen smiled. "We have several groups of 10 beans on the sticks, and we also have some beans just sitting by themselves."

"Now . . . everyone hold up one of your sticks," Kristen directed and then turned to the board and wrote *10*. "You have one group of 10 beans, and we write it as the 10 you see here."

"Now, show us this with your beans," she said as she wrote 2 on the board.

She watched, offering brief suggestions to some of the children who were uncertain, to be sure that all the students picked up two beans from their desks and held them in their hands.

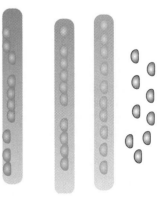

"Good," she said when she saw that all the students had picked up two beans.

"Now, tell me what I have here," she continued as she held up two sticks and three additional beans. "Chin?"

"Two sticks . . . and three others," Chin responded hesitantly.

"Yes," Kristen smiled, "and how many beans on each stick?"

"Ten," Andrea answered.

"Good. . . . So, now I want you to work with your partner for a minute and write the number that these represent," Kristen said, again referring to the two sticks and three separate beans.

She watched as the students talked and wrote numbers on their papers.

"Okay, what did you come up with? . . . Tiffany?"

"Ten and ten and three."

"Okay, what's this?" Kristen asked, holding up one stick.

"Ten," several students said.

"And this?" she continued with the other stick.

"Another 10."

"Good, so how do we write this?"

Seeing uncertainty on the students' faces, Kristen wrote *20* on the board. "See this 2," she pointed. "This represents two groups of 10."

She then wrote *23* on the board and asked, "What is this 3?"

"The three other beans," Clay volunteered.

"Very good thinking, Clay," Kristen smiled. "That's exactly right.

"Okay, now, I'm going to give you a challenge. I want you to work with your partners and show me this with your sticks and beans." She wrote *32* on the board.

She watched as the students worked together to demonstrate the number with their beans and sticks and offered brief suggestions to those that were uncertain.

"Good," she smiled when everyone had finished. "Let's try one more." She wrote *22* on the board.

Again she watched as the students demonstrated the numeral with their beans and sticks.

"Now, let's see what we have," she continued. "Everyone show me this 2," she said, pointing at the 2 in the tens place in 22.

She watched as the students held up two sticks.

"And what is this 2? . . . Bryan?"

". . . Two . . . tens."

"Good," Kristen smiled, nodding. "Now show me this 2." She pointed to the 2 in the units place.

Again she watched as the students held up two beans.

"And what is this 2?"

". . . Two . . . by itself," Brenda volunteered.

"Okay, excellent thinking, everyone."

Kristen had the students practice several more examples, some in which the students demonstrated a number that she had written on the board and others in which they wrote a number that she had demonstrated with the materials.

Let's take a closer look at Kristen's attempts to apply principles based on Piaget's work. First, she used her beans and sticks to represent an abstract idea—the concept of place value. For instance, the idea that the 2 in the tens place represents two groups of 10 but the 2 in the units place represents two individual items is very abstract, particularly for young children. The concrete materials helped Kristen's students understand this difference because they could actually *see* the two groups of 10 as well as the two single items by themselves.

Kristen's lesson shows the value of concrete experiences in math, but they are also important in other content areas. Working with such experiences helps students form mental images of abstract ideas, which lays the foundation for more advanced thinking and development (Chao, Stigler, & Woodward, 2000; Fujimura, 2001). Examples of concrete experiences with other topics are shown in Table 2.3.

Second, Kristen emphasized the link between the concrete materials (the beans and sticks) and the abstraction (the numbers written on the board). For example, she said, "Everyone show me this 2" (pointing at the 2 in the tens place in 22) and "Now show me this 2" (pointing to the 2 in the units place in 22). These conceptual links are essential for understanding. In fact, teachers sometimes mistakenly believe that if their students are

2.12

Think again about Karen Johnson's work with her students. Describe a series of questions that she would need to ask to help her students link the abstract formula for density (density = mass/volume) to her demonstration with the cotton.

Table 2.3 The use of concrete examples in teaching

Topic	Example
Geography: Longitude and latitude	A teacher draws longitude and latitude lines around a beach ball to illustrate that latitude lines are parallel and longitude lines intersect.
Elementary Science: Air takes up space	A first-grade teacher places an inverted cup into a fishbowl of water. To demonstrate that air keeps the water out of the cup, she tips it slightly to let some bubbles escape.
Chemistry: Charles's law (when pressure is constant, an increase in temperature causes an increase in the volume of a gas)	A teacher places one balloon into ice water; a second, equally inflated balloon, into room-temperature water; and a third into hot water. She asks the students to compare the final volumes of each.
History: Mercantilism	A teacher writes short case studies to illustrate England and France trading raw materials from their colonies for manufactured products, forbidding the colonies from trading with others, and requiring English and French ships for transport.

using manipulatives, then learning is automatically taking place. This often is not the case (Ball, 1992). Unless connections are specifically made between concrete materials and the abstractions they represent, students are left uncertain and may even view use of the concrete materials and the discussion of the concepts and symbols as two different lessons.

Third, Kristen used social interaction to help students assimilate ideas into their existing schemes and accommodate schemes when necessary. For instance, when Bryan and Brenda described the difference between the 2 in the tens place and the 2 in the units place, students who didn't understand the difference had to accommodate an existing scheme. The more practice students get in putting their understanding into words, the more opportunities for assimilation and accommodation that occur, and the further development advances. Kristen promoted the social interaction with her questioning, which helped guide the students' thinking as they practiced. She also used group work to further encourage interaction.

Finally, Kristen designed her lesson to be slightly beyond her students' present level of development. We saw that the students were initially uncertain about both representing numbers with the sticks and beans and writing numbers represented by the materials. Using the concrete materials and interacting socially, however, gradually brought the students to understanding. Such understanding can provide a developmental bridge to further advances in thinking, such as what the 4 in 436 means and what it means to "borrow" or "regroup" in a problem such as 45 − 27.

Putting Piaget's Theory into Perspective

As with all theories, Piaget's work has been criticized. In an effort to put his work into perspective, we look at both criticisms and strengths of his theory in this section.

The following are some common criticisms of Piaget's work:

- Piaget underestimated the abilities of young children. Abstract directions and requirements cause children to fail at tasks they can do under simpler, more realistic conditions (Z. Chen & Siegler, 2000; Siegler, 1996). When 3-year-olds are given a simplified conservation-of-number task, for example, such as working with three instead of six or seven items, they're successful (Berk, 2003).

- Piaget overestimated the abilities of older learners; thus, teaching approaches that rely on his findings can cause a problem for both learners and teachers. For example, middle and junior high teachers often assume that their students can think logically in the abstract, but often they cannot. Learners needing, but lacking, concrete experiences then usually revert to memorizing information that they quickly forget.
- Piaget's descriptions of broad developmental stages that affect all types of tasks aren't valid (Siegler, 1991). For example, the progression to concrete operational thinking begins with conservation of mass, proceeds through a range of abilities, and ends with conservation of volume.
- Children's logical abilities depend more strongly on experience and knowledge in a specific area than Piaget suggested (Serpell, 2000; Siegler & Ellis, 1996). For example, if given adequate experiences, students can solve proportional reasoning problems, but without these experiences, they cannot.
- Piaget's work fails to adequately consider the influence of culture on development (Berk, 2001). Cultures determine the kinds of experiences children have, the values they develop, the language they use, and the ways they interact with adults and each other (Rogoff & Chavajay, 1995). (We examine the role of culture in development in our discussion of Lev Vygotsky's work in the next section of the chapter.)

Despite these shortcomings, Piaget's work has been enormously influential. For instance, he has strongly contributed to a major change in the way learning is viewed. Educators now see it as an active process in which learners construct their own understanding of how the world works, instead of seeing it as a process in which students passively receive information or apply rules with little understanding.

Piaget's work has also influenced the curriculum. Lessons are now organized with concrete experiences presented first, followed by more abstract and detailed ideas (Ackerman, 1998). This is how Kristen organized her lesson, and this approach is supported by the National Council of Teachers of Mathematics (2000), a leading professional organization. Similarly, "hands-on" experiences are emphasized in science (American Association for the Advancement of Science, 1993), and language arts curricula encourage the use of children's own experiences in developing reading and writing abilities, instead of requiring memorized words and definitions (Tompkins, 1997). Developmentally based social studies curricula sequence topics from the concrete to the abstract, beginning with a study of children's homes and families and then progressing to their neighborhoods, cities, states, and finally to a study of their culture and those of other nations (Brophy, 1990).

In summary, some of the specifics of Piaget's theory are now criticized, but his emphasis on experience and his idea that learners actively create their own understanding are unquestioned. He continues to have an enormous influence on teaching in this country.

Classroom Connections

Applying an Understanding of Piaget's Views of Development in Your Classroom

1. Provide concrete and personalized examples, particularly when abstract concepts are first introduced.
   - *Elementary:* A kindergarten teacher begins her unit on animals by taking her students to the zoo. She plans for most of the time to be spent in the petting zoo.

- *Middle School:* An English teacher encourages students to role-play different characters in a novel they are reading. The class then discusses the feelings and emotions of the characters.

- *High School:* An American government teacher involves his students in a simulated trial to help them understand the American court system. After the activity, he has participants discuss the process from their different perspectives.

2. Use students' interactions to assess their present levels of development and expose them to the thought processes of more advanced students.

- *Elementary:* After completing a demonstration on light refraction, a fifth-grade science teacher asks students to describe their understanding of what they saw. She encourages other students to ask questions of those offering the explanations.
- *Middle School:* A science teacher gives his students a pretest at the beginning of the year on tasks that require control of variables and proportional thinking. He uses this information to group students for cooperative learning projects, placing students with different levels of development in the same group. He models thinking aloud at the chalkboard and encourages students to do the same in their groups.
- *High School:* A geometry teacher asks students to explain their reasoning as they demonstrate proofs at the chalkboard. She asks probing questions that require the students to clarify their explanations, and she encourages other students to do the same.

3. Provide your students with developmentally appropriate practice in reasoning.

- *Elementary:* A kindergarten teacher gives pairs of children a variety of geometric shapes. He asks the students to group the shapes and then has different pairs explain their grouping while he organizes the shapes on a flannel board according to their explanations. He asks other students if the groupings make sense and if the shapes could be grouped differently. He repeats the process as the students offer other suggestions.
- *Middle School:* An algebra teacher has her students factor this polynomial expression: $m^2 + 2m + 1$. She then asks, "If no 2 appeared in the middle term, would the polynomial still be factorable?"
- *High School:* A history class concludes that people often emigrate for economic reasons. The teacher asks, "Consider a family named Fishwiera, who are upper-class Lebanese. What is the likelihood of them immigrating to the United States?" The class uses this and other hypothetical cases to test the generalizations it has formed.

A Sociocultural View of Development: The Work of Lev Vygotsky

Piaget (1952) viewed developing children as busy and self-motivated individuals who, on their own, explore, form ideas, and test these ideas with their experiences. Lev Vygotsky (1896–1934), a Russian psychologist, provided an alternative view that emphasizes social and cultural influences on the child's developing mind.

As a boy, Vygotsky was instructed by private tutors who used Socratic dialogue, a question-and-answer process that challenges current ideas, to promote higher levels of understanding (Kozulin, 1990). These sessions, combined with his study of literature and experience as a teacher, convinced him of the importance of two factors in human development: social interaction and language (Vygotsky, 1978, 1986). This perspective, a **sociocultural theory of development,** *emphasizes the crucial influence that social interactions and language, embedded within a cultural context, have on cognitive development.*

Let's look at some examples.

Suzanne was reading *The Little Engine That Could* to her 4-year-old daughter, Perri, who sat on her lap. "I think I can, I think I can," she read enthusiastically from the story.

"Why do you think the little engine kept saying, 'I think I can, I think I can'?" she asked Perri as they talked about the events in the story.

". . . We need to try . . . and . . . try and try," Perri finally said after some hesitation and prompting from Suzanne.

Sometime later, Perri was in school, working on a project with two of her classmates.

"I don't get this," her friend Dana complained. "It's too hard."

"No, we can do this if we hang in," Perri countered. "We need to try a little harder."

Monique was struggling with the process of solving word problems in algebra.

"Look at this problem," Mrs. Castillo directed.

Social interaction provides opportunities for students to articulate their own ideas while comparing their developing understanding with that of others.

You have some nickels and dimes in your pocket. You have 9 coins in all, and you have twice as many nickels as dimes. How many of each coin do you have?

"We don't know how many of each you have, so we'll let *n* be the number of dimes. So we have *n* dimes. . . . How many nickels will we have?"

"Twice as many," Monique responded.

"Yes, good," Mrs. Castillo smiled. "How might we write that?"

". . . Like, 2*n*."

"Very good thinking. . . . And how many all together?"

"Nine."

"So, 2*n* plus *n* equals nine."

Monique then found that $3n = 9$, so she had 3 dimes and 6 nickels.

After considerable additional practice, Monique was working on the following problem:

A company's inventory of oil reserves has been lost because of a computer glitch. By manipulating several of the company's inventory programs, a worker learns that the company has 1,000 D (a D is one thousand barrels) in Houston and that it has three times as much 30-weight oil as 10–30-weight oil. The worker has also been able to determine that the ratio of 30 to 10–30 is 2 to 3 in New Orleans and that the company has 900 D in New Orleans.

"I can write this as $3x + x = 1000$, and $2x + 3x = 900$," Monique said to herself after carefully thinking about the problem. She struggled briefly but solved the problem, finding that the company has 750 D of 30 and 250 D of 10–30 in Houston, and 360 D of 30 and 540 D of 10–30 in New Orleans.

Limok and his father looked out and saw a fresh blanket of snow on the ground.

"Ahh, beautiful," his father observed enthusiastically. "Iblik, the best kind of snow for hunting, especially when it's sunny."

"What is *iblik*?" Limok wondered.

"It is the soft, new snow; . . . no crystals," his father responded, picking up a handful and demonstrating how it slid easily through his fingers.

"The seals like it," the father continued. "They come out and sun themselves in it. Then, we only need the spear. Our hunting will be good today."

Sometime later, as Limok and his friend Osool hiked across the ice, Limok saw a fresh blanket of snow covering the landscape.

"Let's go back and get our spears," Limok said eagerly. "The seals will be out and easy to find today."

The relationships between social interaction, language, and culture are outlined in Figure 2.7 and discussed in the sections that follow.

Figure 2.7 Learning and development in a cultural context

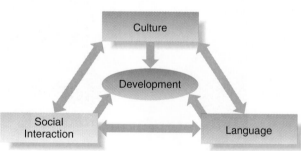

Social Interaction and Development

In contrast with Piaget, who saw social interaction primarily as a mechanism for promoting assimilation and accommodation in individuals, Vygotsky viewed learning and development as arising directly from social interactions. To see how, let's look again at the interactions in our three examples. First, learning took place directly within the context of a social situation in each. Perri learned about perseverance as her mother read and talked to her; Monique learned how to use algebra to solve real-world problems under Mrs. Castillo's guidance; and Limok learned about the conditions conducive to hunting as he interacted with his father. According to Vygotsky's perspective, these individuals' thinking (cognition) developed as a direct result of interactions with other people.

Second, the interactions were between the children and a "more knowledgeable other," an adult in these cases.

Third, through these interactions, the children developed an understanding that they wouldn't have been able to acquire on their own. Whereas Piaget proposed that children explore the world individually, Vygotsky suggested that children need not, and should not, reinvent the knowledge of a culture on their own. This knowledge has been built up over thousands of years and should be *appropriated* (internalized) through social interaction (Leont'ev, 1981).

Both adults—particularly parents, other caregivers, and teachers—and peers play an important role in the process of appropriation. Adults explain, give directions, provide feedback, and guide communication (Rogoff & Chavajay, 1995). Children use conversation to collaborate when solving problems, both in play and in classrooms. This interaction allows the exchange of information and provides feedback about the validity of existing ideas.

Fourth, Perri, Monique, and Limok didn't passively listen to the adults; they were active participants in the interactions. The concept of *activity* is an essential element of sociocultural theory. Vygotsky believed that children learn by doing, by becoming involved in meaningful activities with more knowledgeable people. Activity provides a framework in which dialogue can occur. Through dialogue driven by activity, ideas are exchanged and development occurs.

Language and Development

The role of language is central to Vygotsky's theory, and it plays at least three different roles in development. First, through social interaction, language gives learners access to knowledge others already have. Second, language provides learners with cognitive tools that allow them to think about the world and solve problems. For example, when Limok learned *iblik,* he didn't just learn the word and how to pronounce it; he also learned that it is snow that is soft, fresh, crystal free, and something that increases the likelihood of a successful hunt. Encouraging children to talk about their experiences promotes both learning and development (Pine & Messer, 2000).

2.13
Some educators believe that non-native English-speaking students should be immersed in "English only" programs as soon as possible. On the basis of the information in this section, explain how effective those programs are likely to be.

Third, language serves an individual function; it gives us a means for regulating and reflecting on our own thinking (J. Byrnes, 2001). We all talk to ourselves. For example, we grumble when we're frustrated or angry: "Now where did I put those x%#* keys?" We talk ourselves through uncertain situations: "Oh no, a flat tire. Now what? The jack is in the trunk. Yeah. I'd better loosen the wheel nuts before I jack up the car."

Children also talk to themselves. Walk into a preschool or kindergarten during free play and you'll hear muttering that appears to have no specific audience. If you listen more closely, you'll hear the children talking to themselves as they attempt tasks: "Hmm, which button goes where? . . . I better start at the bottom and put the first button down there." Vygotsky believed this free-floating external speech is the precursor of internalized, private speech.

Private speech is *self-talk that guides thinking and action.* Piaget (1926) observed it in young children and termed it "egocentric speech," reflecting his belief that it was a by-product of the preoperational child's inability to consider the perspectives of others. Vygotsky interpreted private speech differently. He believed that these seemingly targetless mumblings indicated the beginnings of self-regulation. Private speech, first muttered aloud and then internalized, forms the foundation for complex cognitive skills such as sustaining attention ("I had better pay attention now. This is important."), memorizing new information ("If I repeat the number, I'll be able to remember it."), and problem solving ("Let's see, what kind of answer is the problem asking for?"). We saw private speech illustrated when Monique said to herself, "I can write this as $3x + x = 1000$, and $2x + 3x = 900$," as she attempted to solve the algebra problems.

2.14
You have assigned your second graders a series of word problems in math. As they work, you hear audible muttering about the problems. What might you infer from this muttering? Would you expect similar muttering if you were teaching sixth graders?

Research supports Vygotsky's view of private speech. Children use it more frequently when tasks are difficult, as Monique did, or when they are confused about how to proceed (Berk, 2001). In addition, children who use private speech during problem-solving tasks are more attentive and show more improvement than their less talkative peers (Behrend, Rosengren, & Perlmutter, 1992). Also, as Vygotsky predicted, private speech becomes internalized with age, changing from overt mumblings to whispers and lip movements.

Culture and Development

Culture is the third essential concept in Vygotsky's view of development, and it provides the context in which development occurs (Glassman, 2001). The language of a culture becomes a cognitive "tool kit" that children use to conduct their interactions and make sense of the world.

The role of culture was illustrated most concretely in the example with Limok and his father. As they interacted, they used the term *iblik,* which represents a concept unique to Limok's culture. It provided a mechanism for both communication and thinking.

2.15

In mainstream American culture, the concept of *snow* is relatively simple. In contrast, the Inuit people have a great many terms for the concept. What idea (discussed in this section) does this difference illustrate?

The Relationship Between Learning and Development

In the list of principles at the beginning of the chapter, we said that "learning contributes to development." Let's see how learning and development are related in the context of Vygotsky's work.

According to Vygotsky, learning occurs when people acquire specific understanding or develop distinct abilities, and development progresses when understanding or skills are incorporated into a larger, more complex context (Bredo, 1997). Each of the children in our examples, because of their experience with adults, learned something specific: Perri learned the value of perseverance, Monique learned how to solve word problems in algebra, and Limok learned about the conditions for good hunting. Then, later, each of the children incorporated what they had learned into a different and more complex context. Perri, for example, in her interaction with Dana—who wanted to give up—exhorted her to continue making an effort; Perri's behavior indicated an advanced level of development. Monique and Limok had similar experiences. Monique was able to solve a more complex algebra problem on her own, and Limok recognized the conditions for good hunting when he and Osool were merely hiking across the ice.

These descriptions illustrate that learning is necessary for development, development is stimulated by learning, and learning and development both occur in the context of a social situation mediated by language (Bredo, 1997).

■ | Vygotsky's Work: Instructional Strategies

Let's turn now to applications of Vygotsky's work to teaching and learning. The following instructional principles can help guide these applications:

- ■ Embed learning activities in a context that is culturally authentic.
- ■ Create learning activities that involve students in social interactions.
- ■ Encourage students to use language to describe their developing understandings.
- ■ Create learning activities that are in learners' zones of proximal development (this concept is discussed later in the chapter).
- ■ Provide instructional assistance to promote learning and development.

Let's see how the principles guide Jeff Malone, a seventh-grade teacher, as he works with his students.

Jeff began his math class by passing out two newspaper ads for the same CD player. Techworld advertised, "The lowest prices in town"; Complete Computers offered a coupon that allowed customers to "take an additional 15% off our already low prices." After allowing students time to read the two ads, Jeff asked, "So, where would you buy your CD player? Which store has the best buy? . . . Antonia?"

"I think it's Techworld because they say they have the lowest prices in town. And their price is lower than Complete Computers by $5."

"Hmm. Do you all agree? . . . Maria, what do you think?"

"I disagree, because Complete Computers says you can take an additional 15% off their price, so they would be the cheapest."

"How can we find out?" Jeff asked, scanning the room.

After additional discussion, the students decided they needed to find the price with the 15% discount.

To check understanding, Jeff first reviewed decimals and percentages. He organized his students into groups of three and gave each group three problems to solve.

As he moved around the room, he saw that one group—Sandra, Javier, and Stewart— were having trouble. Sandra zipped through the problems; Javier knew that a fraction was needed to find decimals and percentages, but he struggled to compute the decimal; and Stewart didn't know how to begin approaching the problem, so he sat staring at a blank paper.

"Let's talk about how we compute percentages in problems like this," Jeff said, kneeling in front of the group. "Sandra, explain how you did the first problem, and we'll follow along. Then I'll ask someone else to do the next one."

Sandra began, "Okay, the problem asks what percentage of the video games are on sale. Now, I thought, how can I make a fraction? . . . Then I made a decimal out of it and then a percent. . . . Yeah, that's what I did, . . . so here's what I do first."

As she described her thinking, Javier and Stewart listened to what she was saying.

"Okay, let's try this one," Jeff then said. " 'Joseph raised gerbils to sell to the pet store. He had 12 gerbils and sold 9 to the pet store. What percentage did he sell?'

"The first thing," Jeff continued, "I need to find out is what fraction he sold. Now, why do I need to find a fraction? . . . Javier?"

"To . . . then . . . if . . . once we get a fraction, we can make a decimal and then a percent."

"Good," Jeff smiled. "What fraction did he sell? . . . Stewart?"

" . . . 9 . . . 12ths."

"Excellent, Stewart. Now, Javier, how might we make a decimal out of the fraction?"

" . . . Divide the 12 into the 9," Javier responded hesitantly.

"Good," Jeff smiled, and as he watched, he saw that Javier quickly got .75. Stewart also began hesitantly, and then began to grasp the idea.

After all the groups had finished the review problems, Jeff called the class back together and had some of the other students offer explanations. When they struggled to put their explanations into words, Jeff asked questions that guided both their thinking and their descriptions.

He then returned to the CD player problem and asked them to apply their knowledge of percentages to it.

Let's take a closer look at Jeff's attempts to apply principles based on Vygotsky's work. First, he began the lesson with a problem that was real for the students. CDs and CD players are a part of our culture, and shopping is an activity familiar to middle school students. Jeff's problem was culturally authentic.

Second, the students were actively involved in the interactions as they explained their thinking, and third, they used language to describe their understanding. For instance, when Jeff asked Javier why they needed a fraction, and provided encouragement, Javier said, "To . . . then . . . if . . . once we get a fraction, we can make a decimal and then a percent." Javier initially struggled to put his understanding into words, but with additional practice, he will articulate his understanding more easily, and his development will advance.

Fourth, the learning activity was within the students' zones of proximal development. Let's see what that means.

Zone of Proximal Development

When children are able to benefit from the experience of interacting with a more knowledgeable person, they are in the **zone of proximal development,** *a range of tasks that an individual cannot yet do alone but can accomplish when assisted by a more skilled partner.* The zone represents a learning situation in which knowledgeable partners, working with students, can promote development (J. Byrnes, 2001). Learners have a zone of proximal development for each task they are expected to master, and they must be in the zone to benefit from assistance.

To illustrate this idea, let's look again at Jeff's work with Sandra, Javier, and Stewart, each of whom was at a different developmental level. With respect to the percentage problems Jeff initially presented, Sandra was beyond the zone; she was able to accomplish the tasks without assistance. Javier was within the zone; he was able to solve the problems with Jeff's help. Stewart was below the zone, so Jeff had to adapt his instruction to find the zone for Stewart. For instance, Stewart didn't initially know that the problem could be solved by first making a fraction, then a decimal, and finally a percentage. He was able to find the fraction of the gerbils that had be sold to the pet store, however. By asking Stewart to identify the fraction, Jeff adapted his instruction to find the zone for this task and, as a result, promoted Stewart's development. Had he not adapted, Stewart wouldn't have benefitted from the interaction.

On the surface, Jeff's instruction seems quite simple, but it was, in fact, very sophisticated. By observing the students and listening to their responses to his questions, Jeff assessed their current understanding, a process called *dynamic assessment* (Spector, 1992). Then, he adapted the learning activities to the developmental level of each student. For instance, he asked Sandra to explain the problem, which required an advanced level of development. He also guided Javier's efforts to solve the problem, and he simplified the task for Stewart to ensure that it was in the zone for him.

In addition, Jeff designed the tasks to create **shared understanding,** *an understanding that occurs when the teacher and students have a common view of the learning task.* Shared understanding is essential, because learners obviously cannot benefit from support if they don't understand the task. Jeff helped ensure shared understanding by putting his percentage problems into a context that was real for the students' culture and by developing the problems with dialogue instead of a lecture.

Finally, in attempting to apply Vygotsky's work in his teaching, Jeff provided the instructional assistance necessary to promote learning and development. This assistance is a concept called *scaffolding.* Let's look at it.

Scaffolding: Interactive Instructional Support

A toddler was learning to walk. As she took her first tentative steps, her father walked behind her, holding both hands above her head as she awkwardly lurched forward. As she gained confidence, the father held only one hand, walking to the side, keeping an eye out for toys and other objects that could trip her. After awhile, he let go but continued at his daughter's side to catch her if she fell. When the child became tired or the terrain got bumpy, Dad grabbed her hand to make sure she didn't fall and skin a knee. Eventually, his daughter both walked and ran on her own. (Adapted from Cazden, 1988)

Teachers provide individualized scaffolding for students through their numerous personal interactions during the day.

Parents frequently provide scaffolding for their children as they learn new skills. In an educational setting, **scaffolding** is *assistance that allows students to complete tasks they cannot complete independently* (D. Wood, Bruner, & Ross, 1976). Jeff provided scaffolding for Javier and Stewart by asking questions that helped them understand the percentage problems. (Sandra's zone for percentage problems was beyond the requirements of the task, so Jeff helped enhance her development by asking her to verbally model her thinking, a task appropriate for her zone.)

In providing support for Javier and Stewart, Jeff adjusted his questioning to keep the task within the learners' zones of proximal development and helped them move through their zones. When they needed more help, he stepped in; when less was required, he stepped back to allow them to progress on their own. Effective scaffolding is responsive to learners' needs; it adjusts instructional requirements to learners' capabilities and levels of performance (Rosenshine & Meister, 1992). The relationship between the students' zones of proximal development and the scaffolding Jeff provided is illustrated in Figure 2.8.

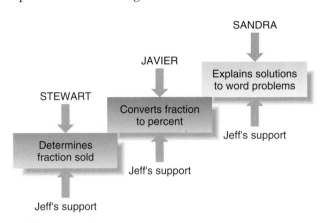

Figure 2.8 Scaffolding tasks in three zones of proximal development

Just as the toddler's development in walking was enhanced by her father's support, learners' development is enhanced by the support of teachers. Without this support, development is impaired. It is important to note, however, that effective scaffolding is only enough support to allow learners to progress *on their own*. Remember that the father provided the support, but the toddler did the walking. Doing tasks for learners delays development.

Different types of instructional scaffolding are outlined in Table 2.4.

Piaget's and Vygotsky's Views of Knowledge Construction

As might be expected, Piaget's and Vygotsky's descriptions of development are similar in some respects and different in others (Fowler, 1994; see Table 2.5). For instance, both views attach importance to language and social interaction, but they differ in their descriptions of the role that each plays in development. Piaget more strongly emphasized individual learners' creations of new knowledge, whereas Vygotsky focused on learners appropriating the knowledge of a culture using language as a tool (Fowler, 1994; Rogoff, 1990). Regardless of differences, however, both views of development recommend that teachers move beyond lecturing and telling as teaching methods and

2.17
Explain how the father accomplished the three instructional tasks—assessing, adapting, providing support—as he helped his toddler daughter progress through the zone of proximal development.

2.18
The distinction between scaffolding and simply explaining is subtle but important. What is the key characteristic of scaffolding that makes it different from simple explaining?

Table 2.4 Types of instructional scaffolding

Type of Scaffolding	Example
Modeling	An art teacher demonstrates drawing with two-point perspective before asking students to try a new drawing on their own.
Think aloud	A physics teacher verbalizes her thinking as she solves momentum problems at the chalkboard.
Questions	After modeling and thinking aloud, the same physics teacher "walks" students through several problems, asking them questions at critical junctures.
Adapting instructional materials	An elementary physical education teacher lowers the basket while teaching shooting techniques and then raises it as students become proficient.
Prompts and cues	Preschoolers are taught that "the bunny goes around the hole and then jumps into it" as they learn to tie their shoelaces.

Table 2.5 A comparison of Piaget's and Vygotsky's views of knowledge construction

	Piaget	Vygotsky
Basic question	How is new knowledge created in all cultures?	How are the tools of knowledge transmitted in a specific culture?
Role of language	Aids in developing symbolic thought. Does not qualitatively raise the level of intellectual functioning. (The level of functioning is raised by action.)	Is an essential mechanism for thinking, cultural transmission, and self-regulation. Qualitatively raises the level of intellectual functioning.
Social interaction	Provides a way to test and validate schemes.	Provides an avenue for acquiring language and the cultural exchange of ideas.
View of learners	Active in manipulating objects and ideas.	Active in social contexts and interactions.
Instructional implications	Design experiences to disrupt equilibrium.	Provide scaffolding. Guide interaction.

toward "structuring reflective discussions of the meanings and implications of content and providing opportunities for students to use the content as they engage in inquiry, problem solving, or decision making" (Good & Brophy, 2000, pp. 416–417).

This view of teaching is grounded in the powerful and widely accepted idea that learners, instead of passively receiving understanding from others, actively construct understanding for themselves. Piaget believed that learners construct understanding essentially on their own, whereas Vygotsky believed that it is first socially constructed and then internalized by individuals. However, both positions suggest that teachers provide experiences, guide discussions, and assume a supportive role in assisting students' attempts at developing understanding. We examine the process of knowledge construction in detail in Chapter 8.

Classroom Connections

Applying Vygotsky's Theory of Development in Your Classroom

1. Use meaningful activity and authentic tasks as organizing themes for your instruction.
   - *Elementary:* A fourth-grade teacher teaches graphing by having the students graph class attendance. Information is recorded for both boys and girls, figures are kept for several weeks, and patterns are discussed.
   - *Middle School:* A science teacher structures a unit on weather around a daily recording of the weather conditions at her school. Each day, students observe the temperature, cloud cover, and precipitation; record the data on a calendar; graph the data; and compare the actual weather to that forecasted in the newspaper.
   - *High School:* An American government teacher tries to help his students understand political polls and the election process. Prior to a national election, he has students poll their parents and students around the

school. Students then have a class election and compare their findings with national results.

2. Use scaffolding to help students progress through their zones of proximal development.
   - *Elementary:* When her students are first learning to print, a kindergarten teacher initially gives them dotted outlines of letters and paper with half lines for gauging letter size. As students become more skilled, she removes these aids.
   - *Middle School:* A science teacher helps her students learn to prepare lab reports by doing an experiment with the whole class and writing the report as a class activity. Later, she instead provides an outline with the essential categories in it. Finally, she simply reminds them to follow the proper format.
   - *High School:* An art teacher begins a unit on perspective by sharing his own work, showing slides, and displaying works from other students. As students work on their own projects, he provides individual

feedback and also shares the projects with the class, asking students to discuss how perspective contributed to each drawing.

3. Structure classroom tasks to encourage student interaction.
   - *Elementary:* After fifth-grade students complete a writing assignment, their teacher has them share their assignments with each other. To assist them in the process, she provides them with focusing questions that students use to discuss their work. Students then rewrite their papers before handing them in to the teacher.
   - *Middle School:* An English teacher uses cooperative learning groups to discuss the literature the class is studying. The teacher asks each group to respond to a list of prepared questions that asks individuals in the groups to take a position on issues raised in the stories. After students discuss the questions in groups, they share their perspectives with the whole class.
   - *High School:* Students in a high school biology class work in groups to prepare for exams. Before each test, the teacher provides an outline of the content covered, and each group is responsible for creating one question on each major topic. The teacher then uses a quiz show format to review for the test, asking students who created a specific question to explain the answer when a mistake is made.

Language Development

A miracle occurs in the time from birth to 5 years of age. Born with a limited ability to communicate, the young child enters school with an impressive command of the language spoken at home. Experts estimate that 6-year-olds know between 8,000 and 14,000 words, and by the sixth grade children's vocabulary expands to 80,000 words (Owens, 1996). As importantly, school-age children can use these words in complex forms of communication.

How does this language ability develop, and how does it contribute to the development of thinking? The answers to these questions are the topics of this section.

Understanding language development is important for at least three reasons:

- As shown in the discussions of Piaget's and Vygotsky's work, language is a catalyst for development. As children interact with peers and adults, they construct increasingly complex ideas about the world.
- Language development facilitates learning in general (Berk, 2001), and it is closely tied to learning to read and write (M. Adams, 1990). As students' language develops, their ability to learn abstract concepts also develops.
- The development of language provides a tool for social and personal development, as we'll see in Chapter 3.

Theories of Language Acquisition

Psychologists who study the growth and development of human language differ in their views of how it is acquired. We discuss four of their theories in this section: behaviorist, social cognitive, nativist, and sociocultural.

Behaviorism

A 2-year-old picks up a ball and says, "Baa."
Mom smiles broadly and says, "Good boy! Ball."
The little boy repeats, "Baa."
Mom responds, "Very good."

Behaviorism explains language development by suggesting that children are reinforced for demonstrating sounds and words (Moerk, 1992; B. Skinner, 1953, 1957). For example, Mom's "Good boy! Ball" and "Very good" reinforced the child's efforts and, over time, language develops. (We examine behaviorism in Chapter 6.)

Language development is facilitated by concrete experiences and opportunities to practice language.

Social Cognitive Theory

"Give Daddy some cookie."

"Cookie, Dad."

"Good. Giselle gives Daddy some cookie."

2.19

Children who grow up in bilingual families typically learn to speak both languages. Which approach—behaviorism or social cognitive theory—better explains this phenomenon? Why?

Social cognitive theory emphasizes the role of modeling, the child's imitation of adult speech, adult reinforcement, and corrective feedback (Bandura, 1986, 1989). In the example, the father modeled an expression, Giselle attempted to imitate it, and he praised her for her efforts. (We examine social cognitive theory also in Chapter 6.)

Both behaviorism and social cognitive theory make intuitive sense. Children probably do learn certain aspects of language by observing and listening to others, trying it out themselves, and being reinforced (Owens, 1996). Scientists who study the development of languages in different cultures, however, believe something else is occurring.

Nativist Theory

A parent listened one morning at breakfast while her 6- and her 3-year-old were discussing the relative dangers of forgetting to feed the goldfish versus overfeeding the goldfish:

six-year-old:	It's worse to forget to feed them.
three-year-old:	No, it's badder to feed them too much.
six-year-old:	You don't say badder, you say worser.
three-year-old:	But it's baddest to give them too much food.
six-year-old:	No it's not. It's worsest to forget to feed them. (Bee, 1989, p. 276)

Virtually all humans learn to speak, and despite diversity, all languages share basic structures, such as a subject–verb sequence at the beginning of sentences, called *language universals* (Pinker, 1994). In addition, children pass through basically the same age-related stages when learning these diverse languages.

Nativist theory *asserts that all humans are genetically "wired" to learn language and that exposure to language triggers this development.* Noam Chomsky (1972, 1976), the father of nativist theory, hypothesized that an innate, genetically driven language acquisition device predisposes children to learn language. According to Chomsky, the **language acquisition device (LAD)** is *a genetic set of language-processing skills that enables children to understand and use the rules governing speech.* When children are exposed to language, the LAD analyzes speech patterns for the rules of grammar—such as the subject after a verb when asking a question—that govern a language. The existence of an LAD would explain why children are so good at producing sentences they have never heard before. For example, our young fish caretakers said "badder," "baddest," "worser," and "worsest." Both behaviorists and social cognitive theorists have trouble explaining these original constructions (Lightfoot, 1999).

2.20

Which of the three theories of language acquisition best explains why virtually all children reach school able to speak a language? Which theory best explains why some children have better language backgrounds than others?

Chomsky's position also has its critics, however (Tomasello, 1995). For instance, it cannot explain why some home environments are better than others for promoting language development and why people acquire certain dialects.

Most developmental psychologists believe that language is learned through a combination of factors that include both an inborn disposition, as Chomsky proposed, and environmental factors that shape the specific form of the language (D. Walker, Greenwood, Hart, & Carta, 1994). In addition, increased emphasis is being placed on the child as an active participant in language learning (Genishi, 1992). This sociocultural view emphasizes the importance of experience and interaction with others in a child's language development. Let's look at it.

Sociocultural Theory

As you saw earlier, language is central to Vygotsky's theory of cognitive development. It provides a vehicle for social interaction, the transmission of culture, and the internal regulation of thinking. Vygotsky's theory also provides insights into the process of language development itself.

As we also saw, activity is central to Vygotsky's theory of development, and language is no exception. Children learn language by practicing it in their day-to-day interactions with adults and peers. Language development appears effortless because it is embedded in everyday activities involving the process of communication.

In helping young children develop language, adults adjust their speech to operate within the children's zones of proximal development (Bruner, 1985). Baby talk and *motherese* use simple words, short sentences, and voice inflections to simplify and highlight important aspects of a message (Baringa, 1997). These alterations provide a form of linguistic scaffolding that facilitates communication and language development.

Children use language to express needs and desires. Parents adapt language to fit the capabilities of the child and then raise the ante by using bigger words and more complex sentences as the child's language skills develop. Teachers and other adults promote language development through interactions that encourage children's use of language and feedback that helps correct, refine, and extend language (Arnold, Lonigan, Whitehurst, & Epstein, 1994).

Stages of Language Acquisition

Children pass through a series of stages as they learn to talk. In the process, they make errors, and their speech is an imperfect version of adult language. Most important, however, are the huge strides they make. Understanding this progress helps teachers promote language growth through their interactions with learners.

Early Language: Building the Foundation

Learning to speak actually begins in the cradle when adults say "Ooh" and "Aah" and "Such a smart baby!" to encourage the infant's gurgling and cooing. These interactions lay the foundation for future language development by teaching the child that language is a process human beings use to communicate.

The first words, spoken between ages 1 and 2, are **holophrases**, *one- and two-word utterances that carry as much meaning for the child as complete sentences.* For example:

"Momma car."	That's Momma's car.
"Banana."	I want a banana.
"No go!"	Don't leave me alone with this scary baby-sitter!

During this stage, the child also learns to use intonation to convey meaning. For example, the same word said differently has a very different message for the parent:

"Cookie."	That's a cookie.
"Cookie!"	I want a cookie.

This intonation is significant: It indicates that the child is beginning to use language as a functional tool.

Two patterns creep into speech at this stage and stay with the child through the other stages. **Overgeneralization** *occurs when a child uses a word to refer to a broader class of objects than is appropriate* (Naigles & Gelman, 1995), such as using the word *car* to also refer to buses, trucks, and trains. **Undergeneralization**, which is harder to detect, *occurs when a child uses a word too narrowly,* such as using *kitty* for a specific cat but not for cats in general. Both overgeneralization and undergeneralization are normal aspects of language development and in most instances are corrected through ordinary listening and talking. A parent or other adult may intervene, saying something like, "No, that's a truck. See, it has more wheels and a big box on it."

Language development closely parallels the development of schemes in children. Overgeneralization occurs when children inappropriately assimilate new information into an existing scheme; undergeneralization occurs when they overaccommodate. Concrete experiences and interactions with adults and peers help young children fine-tune their language.

2.21
Sometimes a child will call all men "Daddy." What is this speech pattern an example of? How could it be remedied?

Fine-Tuning Language

During the "twos," children expand and fine-tune their initial speech (Berk, 2001, 2003). The present tense is elaborated to include verb forms such as

Present progressive:	I eating.
Past regular:	He looked.
Past irregular:	Jimmy went.
Third person irregular:	She does it.

One problem that surfaces in this stage is overgeneralization of grammatical rules, as in the examples "badder," "worsest," and "He goed home." Piaget's work helps explain these utterances. "He goed home" uses an existing scheme (add *-ed* to make past tense), which allows the child to remain at equilibrium, whereas "He went home" requires accommodation—modification of the existing scheme and creation of a new scheme.

Increasing Language Complexity

At about age 3, a child learns to use sentences more strategically. Subjects and verbs are reversed to form questions, and positive statements are modified to form negative statements (O'Grady, 1997). For instance, the child can say not only "He hit him" but also "He didn't hit him" and "Did he hit him?" The idea that the form of language is determined by its function begins to develop more fully in this stage.

The introduction of more complex sentence forms happens at around age 6 and parallels other aspects of cognitive development. For instance, "Jackie paid the bill" and "She had asked him out" become "Jackie paid the bill because she had asked him out." The ability to form and use more complex sentences reflects the child's developing understanding of cause-and-effect relationships.

The typical child brings to school a healthy and confident grasp of the powers of language and how it can be used to communicate with others and think about the world. The importance of this language foundation for reading and writing instruction, as well as learning in general, is difficult to overstate (Berk, 2001, 2003; Tompkins, 1997).

Language Diversity

As we've just seen, language plays a central role in cognitive development and is a powerful tool for acquiring new knowledge. Increasingly, however, our students bring different languages to school, and their facility with English varies greatly (Fashola, Slavin, Calderon, & Duran, 1997; P. Walton, Kuhlman, & Cortez, 1998). Let's look at this diversity and its implications for teaching.

English Dialects: Research Findings

Anyone who has traveled in the United States can confirm that our country has many regional and ethnic dialects. A **dialect** is *a variation of standard English that is distinct in vocabulary, grammar, or pronunciation.* Everyone in the United States speaks a dialect; people merely react to those different from their own (Wolfram, 1991). Some dialects are accepted more than others, however, and language is at the heart of what Delpit (1995) calls "codes of power," the cultural and linguistic conventions that control access to opportunity in our society. What does research say about these dialects?

Research indicates that when students use nonstandard English, teachers have lower expectations for student performance (Bowie & Bond, 1994) and make lower assessments of the students and their work (Hollie, 2001; J. Taylor, 1983). Teachers often confuse nonstandard English with mistakes during oral reading (Washington & Miller-Jones, 1989), and some critics argue that dialects, such as Black English, are substandard.

Linguists, however, argue that these variations are just as rich and semantically complex as standard English (Labov, 1972; Rickford, 1997).

A controversy over *ebonics*—a term created by combining *ebony* and *phonics* and used to describe an African American dialect—erupted in California when the Oakland school board wanted to use ebonics as an interim scaffold to help children learn standard English (McMillen, 1997). Proponents claimed that ebonics would help African American students form a bridge between home and school cultures and better understand instruction. Critics contended that the move was political, would isolate African American children, and would "dumb-down" the curriculum.

Dialects in the Classroom: Implications for Teachers.   Teachers who respond effectively to the cultural diversity in their classrooms accept and value learner differences, and these responses are particularly important when working with students having nonstandard dialects (Hollie, 2001). Dialects are integral to the culture of students' neighborhoods, and requiring that they be eliminated communicates that differences are neither accepted nor valued.

However, standard English allows access to certain educational and economic opportunities, which is the primary reason for teaching it. Students realize this when they interview for a first job or when they plan for post–high school education. So, what should teachers do when a student says, "I ain't got no pencil," or brings some other nonstandard dialect into the classroom? Opinions vary from "rejection and correction" to complete acceptance. The approach most consistent with culturally responsive teaching is to first accept the dialect and then build on it. For example, when the student says, "I ain't got no pencil," the teacher (or adult) might say, "Oh, you don't have a pencil. What should you do, then?" Although results won't be apparent immediately, the long-range benefits—both for language development and attitudes toward school—are worthwhile.

Language differences don't have to form barriers between home and school. **Bidialecticism,** *the ability to switch back and forth between a dialect and standard English,* allows access to both (Gollnick & Chinn, 1998). For example, one teacher explicitly taught differences between standard and Black English, analyzing the strengths of each and specifying respective places for their use. The teacher read a series of poems by Langston Hughes and focused on how Hughes used Black English to create vivid images. The class discussed contrasts with standard English and ways in which differences between the two dialects could be used to accomplish different communication goals (Shields & Shaver, 1990).

English as a Second Language

In an urban fourth-grade class composed of 11 Asian and 17 Black children, Sokhom, age 10, has recently been promoted to the on-grade-level reading group and is doing well. Instead of being "pulled out" of her regular classroom for special instruction in English, she now spends her whole day in the mainstream classroom. At home, she pulls out a well-worn English–Khmer dictionary that she says her father bought at great expense in the refugee camp in the Philippines. She recounts that when she first came to the United States and was in second grade, she used to look up English words there and ask her father or her brother to read the Cambodian word to her; then she would know what the English word was. Today, in addition to her intense motivation to know English ("I like to talk in English. I like to read in English, and I like to write in English."), Sokhom wants to learn to read and write in Khmer and, in fact, has taught herself a little via English.

In another urban public school across the city, Maria, a fifth-grader who has been in a two-way maintenance bilingual education program since pre-kindergarten, has both Spanish and English reading every morning for 1¼ hours each, with Ms. Torres and Mrs. Dittmar, respectively. Today, Mrs. Dittmar is reviewing the vocabulary for the story the students are reading about Charles Drew, a Black American doctor. She explains that "influenza" is what Charles's little sister died of. Maria comments that "you say it [influenza] in Spanish the same way you write it [in English]."

2.22
How would behaviorism explain the development of dialects? How would social cognitive theory explain them?

2.23
State one advantage and one disadvantage of rejecting and correcting nonstandard English. State an advantage and a disadvantage of complete acceptance.

In the same Puerto Rican community, in a new bilingual middle school a few blocks away, Elizabeth, a graduate of the two-way maintenance bilingual program mentioned above, hears a Career Day speaker from the community tell her that of two people applying for a job, one bilingual and one not, the bilingual has an advantage. Yet Elizabeth's daily program of classes provides little opportunity for her to continue to develop literacy in Spanish; the bilingual program at this school is primarily transitional. (Hornberger, 1989, pp. 271–272)

As a result of immigration (more than 7 million people a decade during the 1970s and 1980s and nearly as many in the 1990s), a great many students with limited backgrounds in English are entering American classrooms. Between 1985 and 1991, the number of non-English-speaking and limited-English students—from a wide range of places such as Southeast Asia, the Middle East, and Mexico—increased by more than 50%. Further, between 1991 and 1993, the language minority population in the United States increased 12.6% while the total population increased only 1.02% (Weaver & Padron, 1997).

The diversity is staggering. Currently, more than 3.2 million students who are English language learners (ELLs) attend American schools (U.S. Department of Education, 1998); the 1.4 million who reside in California comprise nearly 40% of the student population (Office of Bilingual Education and Minority Language Affairs, 1999; Stoddart, 1999). Nationwide, the number of students whose primary language is not English is expected to triple during the next 30 years. The most common language groups for ELL students are Spanish (73%), Vietnamese (4%), Hmong (1.8%), Cantonese (1.7%), and Cambodian (1.6%).

This language diversity is a challenge for teachers because most of our instruction is verbal. How should schools respond to this linguistic challenge? Bilingual programs offer one solution.

Types of Bilingual Programs

True bilingual programs offer instruction to non-native English speakers in both English and their primary language. They attempt to maintain and enhance the native language while building on it to teach English. The term *bilingual,* however, has been expanded to refer to a range of programs for ELLs (Echevarria & Graves, 1998; Peregoy & Boyle, 2001). We look at three of them:

- Maintenance bilingual programs
- Transitional bilingual programs
- English as a second language (ESL) programs

2.24
Using Piaget's concepts of equilibrium, assimilation, and accommodation, describe the process of second-language learning in maintenance programs.

2.25
Identify at least one similarity and one difference between maintenance and transitional bilingual programs. From an economic perspective, with the current trend toward a global economy, which approach would be preferable? Explain.

Maintenance Bilingual Programs. Maintenance bilingual programs *maintain and build on students' native language by teaching in both the native language and English* (Peregoy & Boyle, 2001). Also called "two-way" bilingual programs because of the interaction between the two languages (Ovando, 1997), maintenance programs are found primarily at the elementary level, with the goal of developing students who can truly speak two languages. Maria, the fifth grader in the preceding example, had a Spanish as well as an English-speaking teacher to help her develop proficiency in both languages. Maintenance programs have the advantage of retaining and building on students' heritage, language, and culture, but they are difficult to implement because they require groups of students with the same native language and bilingual teachers or teacher teams that have a member who speaks the heritage language.

Transitional Bilingual Programs. Transitional bilingual programs *attempt to use the native language as an instructional aid until English becomes proficient.* Transitional programs begin with the first language and gradually develop the English skills of learners. The transition period is often too short, critics contend, leaving students inadequately prepared for learning in English (Gersten & Woodward, 1995). In addition, loss of the first language and lack of emphasis on the home culture can result in communication gaps between children who no longer speak the first language and parents who don't speak English.

English as a Second Language Programs. Although, technically, all bilingual programs fit this category because mastery of English is a goal, **English as a second language (ESL) programs** *focus explicitly on the mastery of English.* Unlike the other programs, they emphasize learning English outside the regular classroom. Sokhom, the Cambodian student in our example, was initially in a pull-out ESL program until she could function in an English-only environment. Pulling students out of the regular classroom, however, can disrupt the continuity of their instruction as well as their emotional and cognitive equilibrium. ESL programs are common when classes contain students who speak a variety of languages, making maintenance or transitional programs difficult to implement, or when content acquisition is a primary focus, as in high school classrooms.

When working with students from ESL programs, teachers should be careful not to overestimate their students' English proficiency. After about 2 years in a language-rich environment, students develop **basic interpersonal communication skills,** *a level that allows students to interact conversationally with their peers* (Cummins, 1991). Students may need an additional 5 to 7 years to develop **cognitive academic language proficiency,** *a level that allows students to handle demanding learning tasks with abstract concepts in the curriculum.*

2.26
Describe an ESL program based on behaviorist principles. Describe one based on social cognitive theory.

Evaluating Bilingual Programs

Bilingual programs have become increasingly controversial over the years, in some cases being replaced by **immersion,** *approaches that involve hearing and speaking English exclusively in classrooms* (such as English as a second language programs). Critics contend that these programs are

- Divisive, encouraging groups of non-native English speakers to remain separate from mainstream American culture.
- Ineffective, slowing the process of acquiring English for ELL students.
- Inefficient, requiring expenditures for the training of bilingual teachers and materials that could better be spent on quality monolingual programs.

Proponents counter that bilingual programs make sense because they provide a smooth and humane transition to English by building on a student's first language. In addition, they argue that being able to speak two languages has both practical and learning benefits (Garcia, 1993).

Critics' views are prevailing in several states. In a 1998 referendum, California voters passed Proposition 227, a ballot initiative that sharply reduced bilingual education, replacing it with English-only immersion programs for ESL students. A similar measure passed in Arizona in 2000, and other states, such as Utah and Colorado, have considered similar initiatives (Schnaiberg, 1999; Zehr, 2000a, 2000b).

What does research say about the relative benefits of bilingual versus immersion programs? The results are mixed. First, contrary to an argument that newcomers to the United States are learning English more slowly than in previous generations, the opposite appears to be true (Waggoner, 1995). Second, in comparing bilingual to immersion programs, some researchers have found that students in bilingual programs achieve higher in math and reading and have more positive attitudes toward school and themselves (Arias & Casanova, 1993; Diaz, 1983). Further, research indicates that knowledge and skills acquired in a native language—literacy in particular—are "transferable" to the second language (Krashen, 1996).

Effective bilingual programs teach English while building on and enriching student's native language.

These findings make sense. Programs that use a student's native language not only build on an existing foundation but also say to the student, "To do well in school, you don't have to forget the culture of your home and neighborhood."

Research that seems to contradict these results also exists (K. Hayes & Salazar, 2001). For instance, one California school district reported that average standardized test scores for students in the early grades—those most affected by the move from bilingual to immersion programs—improved from the 35th to the 45th percentile in just one year, and additional research found similar positive results across the state (Barone, 2000).

2.27
Use the concept of zone of proximal development to explain the difference between successful and unsuccessful bilingual programs.

Teaching ELL Students: Instructional Strategies

It is likely that you will teach students whose first language is not English. Fortunately, you can use a number of strategies to help ELL students learn both English and academic content. Here are some guiding principles:

- Become familiar with the language backgrounds and capabilities of students.
- Use concrete experiences as reference points for language development.
- Provide opportunities for ELL students to practice language.

Let's see how the principles guide Felicia Marquez, a second-grade teacher, as she works with her students.

Felicia had a group of 8 non-native English speakers in her second-grade class of 24 students. During the first 2 weeks of school, Felicia had made it a point to talk to each of her students and find out as much about them as she could. She also called the students' parents to learn about the home environment. Throughout the year, she paid particular attention to the progress of her students who were learning English along with the rest of their academics.

She was now reading a story to her class from a book liberally illustrated with pictures depicting the events in the story. As she read, she help up the pictures and had the students identify the object or event being illustrated. One picture showed a cave in the woods that the boy and girl in the story decided to explore.

Effective programs for ELL students provide opportunities to learn vocabulary and practice language.

After finishing the story, she began a discussion.

"Tell us something you remember about the story. . . . Carmela?"

". . . A boy and a girl," Carmela responded hesitantly.

"Yes, good, Carmela," Felicia smiled. "The story is about a boy and a girl." She pointed to a picture of the boy and girl.

"Tell us something about the boy and girl. . . . Segundo?"

". . . Lost . . . cave," Segundo offered.

"Yes," Felicia nodded encouragingly. "The boy and girl were exploring a cave and they got lost." She pointed again to the pictures in the book. "Have any of you ever been in a cave?"

After several students shared their experiences with caves, Felicia showed the class more pictures of caves. The class discussed the caves and compared them to the cave in the story.

Felicia then asked, "What do you think *exploring* means? . . . Anyone?"

Let's take a closer look at Felicia's efforts to apply the principles for teaching ELL students. First, Felicia made it a point to learn as much as she could about all of her students and particularly those who were not native English speakers.

Research indicates that a surprising number of teachers are unaware of their students' home languages. For example, one study examining teachers' work with Asian students indicated that teachers recognized only 27% of those who were non-native English speakers (Schmidt, 1992). Teachers can't adjust their teaching to meet the needs of ELL students if they aren't aware that these students exist. Talking with counselors, administrators, other teachers, the students themselves, and parents can help teachers understand their learners' backgrounds. Then teachers can communicate through actions and words that they respect and value this diversity.

Second, Felicia used concrete experiences to facilitate language development. ELL students must concentrate on learning two things at the same time—the subject matter and a new language—so concrete experiences can be particularly useful. For example, Felicia constantly referred back to pictures in the book, which provided concrete frames of references for the story and the new vocabulary students were learning. She also provided additional examples of concepts, such as *caves,* and linked the concepts to information in the stories. Finally, she encouraged students to share their own personal experiences with the concepts. Research shows that linking new information to existing knowledge, while effective for all students, can be especially effective for ELL students (Bulgren et al., 2000).

Third, Felicia provided students with opportunities to practice language. In large part, language is a skill, and students learn English by using it in their day-to-day lives. Students in general, and ELL students in particular, need to spend as much time as possible literally "practicing the language" (Boyd & Rubin, 2001; Fitzgerald, 1995). Too much teacher-centered instruction, in which the teacher does most of the talking while students listen passively, should be avoided (Hernandez, 1997; Peregoy & Boyle, 2001). Instead, students should be provided with concrete experiences and opportunities to talk, write, and read about them. Open-ended questions that allow students to respond without the pressure of giving specific answers are valuable tools for eliciting student responses (Echevarria & Graves, 1998).

Other strategies proven effective with ELL students include

- Modifying speech by slowing down and simplifying vocabulary.
- Supplementing words with gestures, pictures, and other forms of visual representation.
- Using small-group activities to increase interaction.
- Relating new vocabulary to native terms.
- Encouraging writing and reading through creative and interactive tasks. (Ovando, 1997; Verna, Wintergerst & DeCapua, 2001)

These strategies not only help ELL learners but also enrich instruction for all students.

Classroom Connections

Capitalizing on Language Diversity in Your Classroom

1. Begin language development and concept learning activities with concrete experiences.
   - *Elementary:* A fifth-grade teacher, in a unit on fractions, has the students fold pieces of paper into halves, thirds, fourths, and eighths. She then has them shade different sections of the folded papers, describe what they've done, and compare the sections.
   - *Middle School:* A science teacher begins a unit on bones and muscles by having the students feel their own legs, arms, ribs, and heads. As they do this, she identifies the bones on a skeleton in the front of the classroom.
   - *High School:* An English teacher stops whenever an unfamiliar word is used in a reading passage or discussion and asks for an example of it. He keeps a list of these words on a bulletin board and encourages students to use them in class and in their writing.

2. Use instructional strategies that accommodate diversity.
   - *Elementary:* A second-grade teacher enlists older students to come into her classroom to tutor her students in reading. When possible, the tutors speak the same native language as her second graders and provide assistance in both English and the native tongue.
   - *Middle School:* Whenever his students use variations of standard English, a language arts teacher asks the students to explain what the words and phrases mean and tell where they originated. He describes the explanations as interesting and paraphrases them in standard English.
   - *High School:* A physical education teacher uses the "buddy system" to help students with limited English skills participate in class. She asks bilingual students with well-developed English skills to pair with less-proficient students to explain rules and concepts during instruction and games.

3. Provide students with opportunities to actively use language.
   - *Elementary:* A first-grade teacher places students of differing language abilities into groups to work on their assignments. She structures this group work so that students must explain their answers to one another, and she encourages stronger students to help the others.
   - *Middle School:* A social studies teacher has students prepare oral reports in groups. After students practice their reports in the groups, each person presents a part of a report to the whole class. The teacher then meets with each student to provide specific feedback about strengths and areas needing work.
   - *High School:* A sophomore English teacher uses small groups to work on writing projects. When writing assignments are first given, students use the groups to brainstorm ideas. Once first drafts are written, students give one another verbal and written feedback and make revisions. The groups meet one more time to give final approval before the assignments are handed in.

Summary

Development: A Definition

Development, the orderly, durable changes that occur over a lifetime, results from the interaction of the environment and heredity. Although development proceeds in a relatively orderly fashion, individuals can vary considerably in the ways and rates at which they develop. Brain research attempts to forge links between descriptions of how the brain physically grows and operates and cognitive development.

Piaget's Theory of Intellectual Development

Piaget suggested that development is an orderly process that occurs in stages. The quality of experiences in the physical and social world, together with the drive for equilibrium, combine to influence development. Intellectually, developing children organize their experiences into schemes that help them understand the world. Compatible experiences are assimilated into existing schemes; incongruent experiences require an accommodation of these schemes to reestablish equilibrium.

As children develop, they progress through stages characterized by unique ways of understanding the world. During the sensorimotor stage, young children develop eye-hand coordination schemes and object permanence. The preoperational stage includes the growth of symbolic thought, as evidenced by increased use of language. During the concrete operational stage, children can perform basic operations such as classification and serial ordering on concrete objects. In the final stage, formal operations, students develop the ability to think abstractly, reason hypothetically, and think about thinking. Computer-based simulations can provide learners with valuable experiences in controlling variables and systematically analyzing data.

Piaget's work has influenced curriculum and instruction, as evidenced by the emphasis on manipulatives, language experience, hands-on activities, and discovery-oriented instruction.

A Sociocultural View of Development: The Work of Lev Vygotsky

Lev Vygotsky offered an alternate view of development. His theory focuses heavily on language and social interaction, and the role they play in helping learners acquire an understanding of the culture in which they live. Language is a tool people use for cultural transmission, communication, and reflection on their own thinking.

Vygotsky's work has begun to exert influence in classrooms. Teachers are encouraged to engage students in meaningful learning tasks that involve language and social interaction. Learners who can benefit from assistance are in what Vygotsky called the zone of proximal development. Learners within this zone can profit from instructional scaffolding in the form of modeling, questions, prompts, and cues.

Piaget and Vygotsky both agreed that active learners and social interaction are important for development, but they differed in their reasons why. Piaget focused on manipulation of objects and ideas, together with the validation of schemes; Vygotsky emphasized participation in verbal cultural exchange.

Language Development

All views of cognitive development are closely linked to language and its development. Behaviorism, social cognitive theory, and nativist theory explain language development differently; each contributes unique perspectives on this process. Children progress from one- and two-word utterances to elaborate language that involves complex sentence structures by the time they reach school.

Language diversity poses new challenges for teachers. Schools respond to this challenge with bilingual and ESL programs that use differing strategies to teach English.

Windows on Classrooms

At the beginning of the chapter, you saw how Karen Johnson used her understanding of student development to help her students learn about density. In studying the chapter, you've seen how concrete and personalized examples and high levels of interaction facilitate learning and development. In addition, you've seen how an understanding of students' developmental needs can affect the effectiveness of instruction.

Let's look now at another teacher who is working with a group of first-grade students. Read the case study, and answer the questions that follow.

Jenny Newhall gathered her first graders around her on the rug in front of a small table to begin her science lesson. After they were settled, she announced, "Today, we are going to be scientists. Scientists use their senses to find out about the world."

She first reviewed the five senses by asking students for examples. Then she asked, "How do you know if something is real? . . . Jessica?"

When Jessica failed to respond, Jenny continued by holding up a spoon and asking, "Jessica, is this real?"

Jessica nodded, and Jenny continued, "How do you know?"

" . . . "

"What is it?"

". . . A tablespoon."

"How do you know it's a spoon?" Jenny prompted.

After some thought, students agreed they could touch it, see it, and even taste it. Jenny then asked, "Is air real? . . . Anthony?"

Anthony offered, "Yes, because you can breathe it."

Jenny probed further, "Can we see it?"

Her students thought for a moment and shook their heads no.

"Let's think about air for a while," Jenny said as she turned to a large fishbowl filled with water.

"What do you see?" she asked, pointing to the fishbowl.

"A bowl with water in it," one student volunteered.

"What is this?" Jenny continued, holding up an empty water glass.

After spending a few minutes asking students to use their sense of sight to describe various features of the glass, Jenny said, "I'm going to put this glass upside down in the water. What's going to happen? What do you think? . . . Michelle?"

". . . Water will go in the glass."

"No, it'll stay dry," Samantha countered.

To address this difference of opinion, Jenny surveyed the room: "Raise your hand if you think it will get water in it. . . . Okay, . . . raise your hand if you think it'll remain dry. . . . How many aren't sure? . . . Well, let's see if we can find out.

"First, we have to be sure it's dry. Terry, because you're not sure, I want you to help me by feeling the inside of the glass. How does it feel? Is it dry?"

"Yeah," replied Terry after putting his hand into the glass.

Then Jenny asked the students to watch carefully as she pushed the inverted glass under the water, as shown in the following drawing:

"Is the glass all the way under?" she asked, with her hand under the water.

The class agreed that it was.

Terry then offered, "There's water inside it. I can see the water inside."

"Then what will it feel like when I pull it out?" Jenny asked.

"Wet," Terry responded.

Jenny pulled the glass carefully out of the water and asked Terry to check the inside.

"How does it feel?"

"Wet."

Jenny was momentarily taken aback. For the demonstration to work and for students to begin to understand that air takes up space, the inside of the glass had to be dry. After a pause, she said, "Samantha, come up here and tell us what you feel."

Samantha touched the glass. "It's wet on the outside but dry on the inside."

"It's wet!" Terry asserted.

With a look of concern, Jenny said, "Uh, oh! We have two differing opinions. We've got to find out how to solve this problem."

She continued, "Let's dry this glass off and start again. Only this time, we're going to put a paper towel in the glass." She wadded up a paper towel and pushed it to the bottom of the glass. "Now if water goes in the glass, what is the paper towel going to look like?"

The class agreed it would be wet and soggy.

She held up the glass for the class to see. "Okay, it's dry. The paper towel is up in there. We're going to put it in the water again and see what happens."

The class watched carefully as Jenny put the glass into the water again and, after a few moments, pulled it back out.

"Okay, Marisse, come up here and check the paper towel and tell us whether it's wet or dry."

Marisse felt the towel, thought for a moment, and said, "Dry."

"Why did it stay dry? Raise your hand if you can tell us why it stayed dry. What do you think, Jessica?"

"'Cause it's inside and the water is outside?"

"But why didn't the water go into the glass? What kept the water out? . . . Anthony?"

"A water seal."

"A water seal. Hmm, . . . There's all that water on the outside. How come it didn't go inside? How can the towel stay dry?"

A quiet voice volunteered, "Because there's air in there."

"Air! Is that what kept the water out?" Jenny asked with enthusiasm.

"Well, earlier Samantha said that when she was swimming in a pool and put a glass under the water, it stayed dry, but when she tipped it, it got wet inside. Now what do you think will happen if I put the glass under the water and tip it? . . . Devon?"

"It'll get wet."

Jenny removed the paper towel and returned the glass to the fishbowl.

"Let's see. Now watch very carefully. What is happening?" Jenny asked as she slowly tipped the inverted glass, allowing some of the bubbles to escape. "Andrea?"

"There were bubbles."

"Andrea, what were those bubbles made of?"

"They're air bubbles."

"Now look at the glass. What do you see?" Jenny asked, pointing to the half-empty glass upside down in the water. "In the bottom half is water. What's in the top half?"

"It's dry."

"What's up in there?"

"Air."

"Air is up there. Well, how can I get that air out?"

"Tip it over some more," several students responded. When Jenny did that, additional bubbles floated to the surface.

"Samantha, how does that work? When I tip the glass over, what's pushing the air out?"

". . . The water," Samantha offered hesitantly.

"So, when I tip it this way (tipping it until more bubbles came out), what's pushing the air out?"

"Water," several students answered in unison.

Jenny then changed the direction of the lesson by saying, "Now I have something else for you." She showed the students a glass full of water. "What do you think will happen if I tip this glass over?"

Jenny continued by covering the glass with a card and asking what would happen now if she tipped the glass. This time there were disagreements, some suggesting that the water would spill, but others believing that the water would stay in the glass.

Jenny then held the card on the glass, tipped the glass over, and let go of the card. When the students saw that the water didn't spill, Jenny asked for explanations. One of the students suggested that the water acted like "super glue" to keep the card on the glass. Another suggested that air kept the card next to the glass.

After discussing each possibility, Jenny divided the class for some small-group work. In groups of four or five, the students used tubs of water, glasses, cards, and paper towels to experiment on their own. After each student had a chance to try the activities, Jenny again called the children together, and they reviewed and summarized what they had found.

Constructed Response Questions

In answering these questions, use information from the chapter and link your responses to specific information in the case.

1. At what level of cognitive development were Jenny's students likely to be? Was her instruction effective for that level? Explain.

2. Why was the medium of water important for Jenny's lesson? How does this relate to Piaget's levels of development?

3. When Samantha and Terry disagreed about the condition of the inside of the glass, how did Jenny respond? What other alternatives might she have pursued? What are the advantages and disadvantages of these alternatives?

4. Were Jenny's students in the zone of proximal development for the lesson she was teaching? What forms of scaffolding did Jenny provide? How effective was the scaffolding?

PRAXIS These exercises are designed to help you prepare for the PRAXIS™ "Principles of Learning and Teaching" exam. To receive feedback on your constructed response questions and document analysis response, go to the Companion Website at *www.prenhall.com/eggen*, then to this chapter's *Practice for PRAXIS™* module. For additional connections between this text and the PRAXIS™ exam, go to Appendix A.

Document-Based Analysis

A student is given a series of conservation tasks. When two equal pieces of clay are shown to the child, he agrees they are equal, but when one is flattened, he replies, "It's not the same because that one is flattened out like a pancake."

Two equal beakers of liquid are shown to the child, and he concludes that the amounts are equal. When one is poured into a larger beaker, he is asked again whether they are equal. He replies that the one has more "because it's taller."

When two rows of coins are shown to the same child, he agrees that the rows contain the same number of coins. When one row is spread out, he is asked again whether they still contain the same number of coins. He replies that one is "bigger."

The boy's responses indicate thinking at which of Piaget's stages of development. Explain, based on the characteristics of thinking at that stage.

Online Portfolio Activities

To develop your professional portfolio, further apply your understanding of chapter content, and address the INTASC standards, go the Companion Website, then to this chapter's *Online Portfolio Activities*. Complete the suggested activities.

Also on the Companion Website at *www.prenhall.com/eggen*, you can measure your understanding of chapter content in *Practice Quiz* and *Essay* modules, apply concepts in *Online Cases*, and broaden your knowledge base with the *Additional Content* module and *Web Links* to other educational psychology websites.

Important Concepts

accommodation *(p. 38)*
adaptation *(p. 38)*
assimilation *(p. 38)*
basic interpersonal communication skills *(p. 69)*
bidialecticism *(p. 67)*
centration *(p. 42)*
classification *(p. 45)*
cognitive academic language proficiency *(p. 69)*
cognitive development *(p. 33)*
concrete operational stage *(p. 44)*
conservation *(p. 43)*
critical periods *(p. 36)*
development *(p. 34)*
dialect *(p. 66)*
egocentrism *(p. 42)*
English as a second language (ESL) programs *(p. 69)*
equilibrium *(p. 37)*
formal operational stage *(p. 45)*
holophrases *(p. 65)*
immersion *(p. 69)*

language acquisition device (LAD) *(p. 64)*
maintenance bilingual programs *(p. 68)*
maturation *(p. 35)*
nativist theory *(p. 64)*
object permanence *(p. 41)*
organization *(p. 38)*
overgeneralization *(p. 65)*
preoperational stage *(p. 41)*
private speech *(p. 57)*
reversibility *(p. 42)*
scaffolding *(p. 61)*
schemes *(p. 38)*
sensorimotor stage *(p. 41)*
seriation *(p. 44)*
shared understanding *(p. 60)*
social experience *(p. 40)*
sociocultural theory of development *(p. 55)*
systematic reasoning *(p. 42)*
transformation *(p. 42)*
transitional bilingual programs *(p. 68)*
undergeneralization *(p. 65)*
zone of proximal development *(p. 59)*

Chapter Outline

Personal,
Social, and
Emotional
Development

3

"Ahh," Anne Dillard, an eighth-grade English teacher, sighed wearily as she slumped into a chair in the faculty lounge.

"Tough day?" her friend Beth asked.

"Yes. . . . It's Sean again," Anne nodded, straightening up. "I just can't seem to get through to him. He won't do his work, and he has a bad attitude about school in general. I talked with his mother, and she said he's been a handful since birth. He can't get along with the other students, and when I try to talk with him about it, he always says they're picking on him for no reason. I don't know what's going to become of him. The funny thing is, I get the feeling that he knows he's out of line, but he just can't seem to change."

"I know what you mean," Beth responded. "I had him for English last year. He was a tough one . . . very distant. He lost his dad in a messy divorce; his mother got custody of him, and his father just split. Every once in a while, he'd open up to me, but then the wall would go up again. . . . And his younger brother seems so different. He's eager and cooperative, and he seems to get along with everyone. . . . Same home, same situation."

"Sean's a bright boy, too," Anne continued, "but he seems to prefer avoiding work to doing it. I just know that I can help him . . . if I can just figure out how."

In Chapter 2, you studied theories that describe cognitive development, and as a result, you know that younger students think in ways that are qualitatively different from those of older learners and adults. We now want to examine the personal, social, and moral development of our students.

Those who argue that schools should focus solely on academic subjects may ask, Why should teachers understand these areas? The answer is simple: They influence both students' motivation and learning in school and how successfully students cope with life, during and after the formal school years. The better teachers understand these areas of development, the better equipped they are to promote learning and help students grow into happy adults and capable citizens. The need for this understanding grows ever greater as modern life becomes more complex and our students are faced with challenges in the form of alcohol and other drugs, sex, and potential violence.

After you've completed your study of this chapter, you should be able to

- Identify factors that influence personal development
- Describe factors influencing social development
- Explain the implications of Erikson's theory for teaching
- Explain the relationships between self-concept and academic achievement, and what teachers can do to influence each
- Identify different stages of moral reasoning and how they apply to classroom practice

Personal Development

Think about the people you know. Some are very comfortable with themselves, new situations, and people in general, whereas others tend to be shy and uneasy. We all know people who are trusting and see the best in everything, and we also see individuals who are wary and negative.

How did they get that way? What causes differences in people's personalities? What factors have influenced our own development, causing us to interact with others and our environments in the ways we do? We try to answer these questions in this chapter.

Personal development is *the growth of enduring personality traits that influence the way individuals interact with their physical and social environments.* The primary causes of this development are heredity and the environmental influences of parents, other adults, and peers. These factors are outlined in Figure 3.1 and discussed in the sections that follow.

Figure 3.1 Influences
on personal development

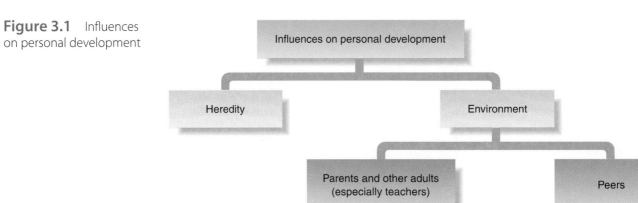

Heredity

People differ in temperament, virtually from birth. They vary in traits such as irritability, adventurousness, happiness, and confidence, and these differences persist over time (Berk, 2001; Caspi & Silva, 1995). Siblings raised in the same environments typically develop very different personalities—perhaps being "a handful since birth," like Sean, or "eager and cooperative," like his brother. These examples illustrate the influence of heredity on personal development.

Parents and Other Adults

Parents also exert a major influence on children's personal development (Grolnick, Kourowski, & Gurland, 1999). This intuitively sensible and widely accepted factor isn't surprising, given the amount of time children, and especially young children, spend with their parents.

Research indicates that certain parenting styles promote more healthy personal development than others (Baumrind, 1991), and the effects of parenting style can last into the college years, influencing students' grades, motivation, and relationships with teachers (Strage & Brandt, 1999).

Interaction with teachers and other adults provides opportunities for students' personal self-development.

Researchers have found two important differences among parents in the ways they relate to their children: their expectations and their responsiveness. Some set high expectations and insist that these expectations are met; others expect little of their children and rarely try to influence them. Responsive parents accept their children and interact with them frequently; unresponsive parents tend to be rejecting or negative. If parents are unresponsive, children view high expectations as unfair, and they often rebel. Using expectations and responsiveness as a framework, researchers have identified four parenting styles and the patterns of personal development associated with them. They are summarized in Table 3.1.

As we see from Table 3.1, an authoritative parenting style—one that combines high expectations and responsiveness—is most effective for promoting healthy personal development. Children need challenge, structure, and support in their lives, and authoritative parents provide them.

Table 3.1 Parenting styles and patterns of personal development

Interaction Style	Parental Characteristics	Child Characteristics
Authoritative	Are firm but caring. Explain reasons for rules, and are consistent. Have high expectations.	High self-esteem. Confident and secure. Willing to take risks, and are successful in school.
Authoritarian	Stress conformity. Are detached, don't explain rules, and do not encourage verbal give-and-take.	Withdrawn. Worry more about pleasing parent than solving problems. Defiant, and lack social skills.
Permissive	Give children total freedom. Have limited expectations, and make few demands on children.	Immature, and lack self-control. Impulsive. Unmotivated.
Uninvolved	Have little interest in their child's life. Hold few expectations.	Lack self-control and long-term goals. Easily frustrated and disobedient.

Each of the other parenting styles can result in developmental problems. Authoritarian parents are rigid and seem unable to communicate caring to their children; permissive parents are emotionally responsive but fail to set and maintain high expectations; uninvolved parents are laissez-faire, providing neither structure nor emotional support.

Healthy parent-child relationships promote personal development by helping children acquire a sense of autonomy, competence, and belonging (Grolnick et al., 1999; Wentzel, 1999a). Such relationships also support the development of personal responsibility—the ability to control one's own actions based on developing values and goals.

Other adults—most commonly teachers—also contribute to students' personal development. The interaction styles of effective teachers are similar to those of effective parents, and the description of authoritative parenting strongly parallels recommended classroom management practices for teachers (W. Doyle, 1986). As you'll see in Chapter 12, effective teachers are clear about classroom rules and procedures, take the time to explain why they are necessary, and involve students in forming them. They have high expectations for their students, but they're simultaneously supportive. When a disruption occurs, they quickly intervene, eliminate the problem, and return just as quickly to learning activities. Like authoritative parents, they are firm but caring, they establish rules and limits, and they expect students to develop and use self-control.

Research indicates that this kind of teacher support leads to increased student motivation, enhanced self-concept, and the development of self-regulation (Branson, 2000; Brophy, 1998; Wentzel, 1999a). Although they spend less time with children than do parents, teachers strongly influence learners' personal development.

3.1
Identify two characteristics of authoritarian parenting that could result in children failing to develop social skills. Identify one characteristic of permissive parenting that could lead to children being unable to set long-term goals.

Peers

Peers influence personal development in two ways: by offering—or not offering—friendship and by communicating attitudes and values.

Friendships are important because they give young people opportunities to practice their developing social skills (Coolahan, Fantuzzi, Mendez, & McDermott, 2000). We all want to be liked and valued by others. Students who are socially accepted and supported by peers are more motivated, achieve higher, have healthier self-concepts, and are generally more satisfied with life than those receiving less support (Wentzel, 1999a). At the other extreme, rejection by peers can lead to loneliness and isolation, poor academic work, and dropping out of school.

Peers continually communicate their attitudes and values to one another, most commonly in day-to-day interactions. Many of these interactions occur in organized clubs or teams, whereas others happen in informal cliques and neighborhood groups (Trawick-Smith, 1997; Wigfield, Eccles, & Pintrich, 1996). Unfortunately, peer influences are sometimes negative, such as when participants in gangs or other school subcultures reject academic achievement. In examining adolescent friendships, researchers have found

3.2
The influence of peers on academic success can be interpreted in different ways. One is selection; for example, low achievers seek out other low achievers. Offer one other interpretation based on the information in this section.

that a student's choice of friends predicts grades, disruptive behaviors, and teachers' ratings of involvement in school. When students select academically oriented friends, their grades improve; when they choose disruptive friends, their grades decline and behavior problems increase (Berndt & Keefe, 1995).

In some instances, ethnicity plays a role in the attitudes communicated by peers (Steinberg, Brown, & Dornbusch, 1996). Sometimes the attitudes are positive, as in the following example:

> One clear reason for Asian students' success is that Asian students are far more likely to have friends who place a great deal of emphasis on academic achievement. Asian-American students are, in general, significantly more likely to say that their friends believe that it is important to do well in school, and significantly less likely than other students to say that their friends place a premium on having an active social life. Not surprisingly, Asian students are the most likely to say that they work hard in school to keep up with their friends. (Steinberg et al., 1996, p. 44)

Unfortunately, the opposite is also true. In some minority groups, academic success is viewed as "selling out" or "becoming white." Media messages sometimes portray successful minority youth as being hip, tough, or cool, but not academically oriented. To combat these messages, minority youth need role models who can demonstrate that being a member of a minority group and being academically successful are compatible (Berndt, 1999).

In this section, we've seen that healthy social relationships are important for personal development. Let's look at social development more closely.

Social Development

Fifth graders Octavio, Mindy, Sarah, and Bill were studying American westward expansion in social studies. They'd been working as a group for 2 weeks and were preparing a report to be delivered to the class. There was some disagreement about who should present the topics.

"So what should we do?" Mindy asked, looking at the others. "Octavio, Sarah, and Bill all want to report on the Pony Express."

"I thought of it first," Octavio argued.

"But everyone knows I like horses," Sarah countered.

"Why don't we compromise?" Mindy asked. "Octavio, didn't you say that you were kind of interested in railroads because your grandfather worked on them? Couldn't you talk to him and get some information for the report? And Sarah, I know you like horses. Couldn't you report on horses and the Plains Indians? . . . And Bill, what about you?"

"I don't care . . . whatever," Bill replied, folding his arms and peering insolently at the group.

Classrooms are social places that require cooperation among students and teachers. **Social development** describes *the advances people make in their ability to interact and get along with others.* Understanding social development helps us guide our students in their attempts to improve their social skills. Social development affects both learning and satisfaction with learning experiences (Coolahan et al., 2000). And as we saw in the last section, the ability to make and keep friends contributes to students' sense of belonging and their overall attitudes toward school.

In the following sections, we examine perspective taking and social problem solving, two important dimensions of social development.

Perspective taking and problem solving are important components in learners' social development.

Perspective Taking

Perspective taking is *the ability to understand the thoughts and feelings of others.* When Mindy suggested that Octavio and Sarah switch assignments because of their interest in different topics, for example, she demonstrated perspective taking.

Research indicates that perspective taking develops slowly and is related to Piaget's stages of cognitive development (Berk, 2001). To measure children's perspective-taking abilities, researchers show children scenarios similar to the one just presented and ask them to explain different people's thinking. Children up to about age 8 typically don't understand Bill's angry response or why Octavio might be happy reporting on railroads. As they develop, their ability to see the world from other people's perspectives grows.

Effective perspective takers handle difficult social situations well, display empathy and compassion (Eisenberg & Fabes, 1998), and are well liked by their peers (Berk, 2001). Those less effective tend to be mistrusting and interpret the intentions of others as hostile, which can lead to arguing, fighting, and other antisocial acts. They also tend to feel no guilt or remorse when they hurt other people's feelings (Dodge & Price, 1994).

To see a video clip of a high school English teacher integrating perspective taking into instruction, go to the Companion Website at *www.prenhall.com/eggen,* then to this chapter's *Classrooms on the Web* module. Click on *Video Clip 3.1.*

3.3
Using Piaget's theory as a basis, explain why young children encounter difficulties with perspective taking. What factor influencing development helps them improve their perspective-taking abilities?

Social Problem Solving

Social problem solving, *the ability to resolve conflicts in ways that are beneficial to all involved,* is closely related to perspective taking. Mindy displayed social problem-solving skills when she suggested a compromise that would satisfy everyone.

Research suggests that social problem solving is similar to problem solving in general (we examine problem solving in Chapter 9) and involves processes that can be described as four sequential steps (Berk, 2001):

1. Observing and interpreting social cues ("Bill seems upset, probably because he isn't getting his first choice.")
2. Identifying social goals ("If we are going to finish this project, everyone must contribute.")
3. Generating strategies ("Can we find different topics that will satisfy everyone?")
4. Implementing and evaluating the strategies ("This will work if everyone agrees to shift their topic slightly.")

Social problem solving is a powerful tool. Students who are good at it have more friends, fight less, and work more efficiently in groups than those who are less skilled (Crick & Dodge, 1994).

Research indicates that, like perspective taking, social problem solving develops gradually (Berk, 2001). Young children, for example, are not adept at reading social cues, and they tend to create simplistic solutions that satisfy themselves but not others. Older children realize that persuasion and compromise can benefit everyone, and they're better at adapting when initial efforts aren't successful.

3.4
Which step of social problem solving is most closely related to perspective taking? Explain. What can teachers do to develop this ability in students?

Violence and Aggression in Schools

Unfortunately, school violence and aggression are increasing, and some experts link this trend to problems with personal and social development (Crick & Dodge, 1996; D. Johnson & Johnson, 1999). The widely publicized Columbine tragedy, in which two students killed a teacher and 12 of their peers, wounded 23 others, and then killed themselves, together with other shooting incidents in schools around the nation dramatically underscore this problem.

National statistics are also disconcerting. For instance, during the 1996–97 school year, 10% of public schools reported at least one serious violent crime, such as murder, rape, assault with a weapon, or robbery. During the same period, almost half of public schools (47%) reported lesser crimes such as vandalism and fighting (Kaufman et al., 1999). Also, during the 1995 school year, 12% of elementary and secondary teachers were threatened by students, 4% were physically attacked, and 9% of teenagers avoided at least one place at school because of concerns for their personal safety (Kaufman et al., 1999). In a survey of South Carolina middle school students, 1 in 4 reported being bullied several times in a 3-month period, and 1 in 10 said the bullying occurred once a week or more (Institute for Families in Society, 1997). Other experts estimate the incidence of bullying is higher and note that it can be physical, verbal, or relational, where students convince their peers to reject or exclude classmates (Kerr, 2000). Schools, which should be safe havens for learning and development, often mirror society with respect to violence and aggression.

Proactive aggression, *aggression that involves overt hostile acts toward someone else,* is the most troublesome pattern. Proactively aggressive students have difficulty maintaining friendships and are at increased risk for engaging in delinquent activities. The development of aggressive tendencies causes problems both in school and in life after the school years (Poulin & Boivin, 1999; Vitaro, Gendreau, Tremblay, & Oligny, 1998).

The causes of aggressive behavior, like development in general, are complex. Genetics plays a role, and beginning in the preschool years boys are more physically aggressive than girls (McDevitt & Ormrod, 2002). Experts estimate that boys bully more than girls by a ratio of 3 to 1, although this ratio may be due to a greater tendency to report physical than verbal bullying (Ma, 2001). In addition, adolescent males are 10 times more likely to be involved in antisocial behavior and violent crime (U.S. Department of Justice, 1999).

Aggression can also be learned, with modeling and reinforcement playing major roles (McDevitt & Ormrod, 2002). For example, bullies typically come from homes where parents are authoritarian, hostile, and rejecting. The parents often have poor problem-solving skills and also advocate fighting as the solution to conflicts (Ma, 2001). In addition, aggression may be linked to deficits in perspective taking, empathy, moral development, and emotional self-regulation (Eisenberg & Fabes, 1998; McDevitt & Ormrod, 2002).

Attempts to prevent aggression and violence in schools focus on peer mediation and programs designed to develop social problem-solving skills. Peer mediation programs attempt to teach students conflict resolution abilities. In one of the best known programs, designed by David and Roger Johnson (1995, 1999), a mediator guides peers through five steps to resolve a conflict:

1. Jointly define the conflict. Get both parties to agree on a definition of the problem, and separate the problem from the personal characteristics of the people.
2. Exchange positions and perspectives. Discuss the problem from each party's perspective.
3. Reverse perspectives. Encourage each student to understand the problem from the other's point of view.
4. Invent solutions beneficial to both parties. Construct alternatives that allow both parties to win.
5. Reach an agreement that satisfies both parties. Encourage students to develop an agreement that is acceptable to both.

The students involved in the conflict not only resolve their own problems but also, in the process, learn how to mediate others' disputes. According to the program developers, schools in which students were trained in conflict resolution and peer mediation had fewer management problems, both within classrooms and on school grounds (Johnson & Johnson, 1999). In addition, students continued to use these conflict resolution strategies both at school and at home.

Programs designed to teach social problem-solving skills focus on substituting peaceful alternatives for force (Goodman, Gravitt, & Kaslow, 1995). With young children, puppet skits may be used to present social dilemmas, which the children discuss and try to solve. Older children often are asked to read and respond to scenarios like the one involving Octavio, Mindy, Sarah, and Bill. Research indicates that students in these programs improve in both their social problem-solving abilities and in their classroom behavior (Gettinger, Doll, & Salmon, 1994).

These strategies attack the problem of violence and aggression at the individual level. Equally important is a school climate that discourages violence and aggression and openly communicates that they won't be tolerated (Ma, 2001). Parental involvement is important, and students need to know that teachers and administrators are committed to safe schools (Kerr, 2000).

Assessment and Learning: Assessing Students' Social Development

As we've seen, social growth is a crucial dimension of a student's overall development (Coolahan et al., 2000; Ladd & Coleman, 1993; Webb & Palincsar, 1996). Being able to assess learners' social development is important if teachers are to help students develop in this domain.

A number of commercially prepared instruments for assessing social development exist (Goodwin & Goodwin, 1993). Most are designed to be administered individually, however, which limits their usefulness to teachers, who have classes of 25 to 30 or more students. Informal observations during day-to-day school activities are often more efficient and effective. They don't require a great deal of additional teacher energy, and they allow teachers to observe students in realistic settings.

Opportunities to assess students' social skills abound. For example, teachers can observe the extent to which students interact effectively with others when they enter and leave the classroom, work in small groups, engage in whole-class discussions, and seek and provide help during seat work.

In addition, teachers can observe students

- Before and after school as they interact with peers on the school grounds
- During recess and other unstructured recreation times
- At lunch and in the cafeteria
- During extracurricular activities, such as club meetings and sports games

These out-of-classroom observations are valuable because they show behavior in different contexts. Students who are shy and withdrawn in classroom activities sometimes blossom in nonacademic settings.

What should teachers look for as they assess students' social development? We have emphasized perspective taking and social problem solving in this chapter. These and other important dimensions are outlined in Table 3.2.

Reliability—the consistency of measurements over time and in different situations—is always an issue in informal measures such as these. Teachers who have concerns about

Table 3.2 Dimensions of social development

Dimension	Indicators
Peer relationships	• Number of friends • Quality of friendships • Balance and harmony in peer interactions
Perspective taking	• Recognizing that people have different perspectives on issues • Accepting different points of view
Social problem solving	• Identifying factors that impede group progress • Offering alternative plans of action • Accepting suggestions of others
Functioning in learning group	• Suggesting different group roles • Accepting group roles offered by others • Contributing ideas effectively • Providing productive feedback to others in group

a child's social development should observe the child in as many different settings as possible before making firm conclusions. If the observations consistently indicate that social skills are lacking or the child has social adjustment problems, a school counselor or school psychologist should be consulted.

■ Promoting Social Development: Instructional Strategies

As with other aspects of learning, social skills can be improved with understanding, practice, and feedback. Schools and teachers can make important contributions to social development through the social skills they model and in the ways they organize and maintain their classroom environments. The following principles can guide teachers in their efforts:

- ■ Use modeling and explicit instruction to teach the kinds of social skills that you would like to see in your students.
- ■ Establish rules governing acceptable classroom behavior.
- ■ Help students understand the rules by providing examples and guiding discussions.
- ■ Have students practice social skills, and give them feedback.

Let's see how the principles guide Teresa Manteras, a first-year teacher, as she works with her sixth-grade students.

"You look a little down, Teresa," said Carla Ambergi, a colleague and teaching veteran of five years. Teresa had slumped into an overstuffed chair in the teachers' lounge. "Everything okay?"

"A little discouraged," Teresa sighed. "I learned about all those cooperative learning activities in my university classes, but when I try them out with my kids, it seems like all they want to do is fight and snip at each other. Maybe I should just lecture. At least then I don't have to continually wrestle with them. I know that's not the solution, but I just don't know how to get where I want to go from here."

"Hang in there," Carla smiled. "They're just not used to working in groups, and they haven't yet learned how to cooperate with each other. Like everything else in life, the more they practice the better they get at it."

"Yes, I know that—but I don't even know where to start. As I turn to help one group, two other groups start arguing."

"Would you like me to come in and observe during my planning period? Maybe I can offer a few suggestions."

"That would be great!" Teresa replied with a big sense of relief.

Carla went in the next day, and after her visit, she and Teresa sat down together. "First," Carla smiled, "I think you do an excellent job of modeling social skills. You consider where the kids are coming from, you treat disagreements as an opportunity to solve problems, and you are consistently courteous and supportive with them. . . . However, your modeling often goes right over their heads. They don't notice what you're doing. So, the first thing I would suggest is that you make your own behaviors explicit. Simply tell the kids what you're modeling, and periodically point out examples in your own behavior, or in the behavior of one of the kids, that illustrate the kinds of social skills you're trying to develop. It will take some time, but it will make a contribution."

"Excellent point," Teresa nodded. "I hadn't quite thought about it that way before."

Carla then helped Teresa develop several rules that specifically addressed student behavior in groups:

1. Listen politely until other people are finished before speaking.
2. Treat other people's ideas with courtesy and respect.
3. Paraphrase other people's ideas in your own words before disagreeing.
4. Encourage everyone in the group to participate.

Teachers can promote learners' social development by acting as a role model and creating classroom environments in which students can practice social skills.

Armed with these new rules and encouragement from Carla, Teresa returned to her classroom the next day. Before breaking the class into groups for project work, she told the students that she was going to model social skills for them and that she wanted them to model social skills for one another. After giving several examples, she presented the new rules and explained why they were necessary. For each rule, Teresa asked volunteers to role-play an example in front of the others. She guided a discussion of each example to ensure that all students understood what it was intended to illustrate.

The students then began their group work. Teresa carefully monitored the groups and intervened when they had difficulties. Once, several groups had the same problem, so she reconvened the class, discussed the problem, and asked students to practice the new skill in their groups. The students were far from perfect, but they were improving.

Let's take a closer look at Teresa's attempts to promote social development. First, Teresa used modeling and explicit instruction to teach the students the social skills she wanted them to develop. Social skills don't magically occur. Just as learning to write, for example, involves understanding grammar and punctuation together with a great deal of practice in writing, developing social skills involves both understanding and practice in interactions with others (Webb & Palincsar, 1996).

Second, Teresa began with a set of rules intended to guide the students as they worked together. This is important because, just as rules exist to help people understand grammar, rules are necessary to guide students during social interaction. She presented only four rules, in part because they supplemented her general classroom rules but also because too many rules increase the likelihood that students will forget one or more of them.

Third, Teresa provided concrete examples of the rules by having students role-play social situations, and then, through discussion, she helped students understand what the role playing illustrated. Her modeling provided additional examples of desirable social skills and behaviors.

Finally, Teresa provided opportunities for the students to practice their social skills during group work, and she gave them feedback during the activities.

Students won't become socially skilled in just one or two activities, but with time, practice, and explicit instruction, such as Teresa provided, they will become more skilled at working with each other in groups (Webb & Palincsar, 1996).

Technology and Learning: Using the Internet to Promote Social Development

As we saw in the last section, teachers can, through their modeling and by explicitly teaching social skills, strongly contribute to students' social development. Another, often overlooked mechanism for promoting social skills is the Internet. It is changing both the way we live and the way we communicate, and teachers can capitalize on it to further promote students' social development.

Researchers have identified both advantages and disadvantages of Internet communication (Fabos & Young, 1999; Jehng, 1997; Johnson & Johnson, 1996). Internet technologies can connect students all over the world, allowing them direct access to diverse personal perspectives—something much more difficult to obtain through other means. Exposure to these perspectives can promote social growth, as can personal relationships that may form through online dialogue. One such relationship developed during an e-mail exchange between a young person in war-torn Kosovo and an American teenager (National Public Radio, 1999). Their correspondence, some of which was broadcast in a National Public Radio segment in 1999, captured a power and emotion that the students may have found impossible to communicate in any other way, including face to face. Both of the young people said that their lives had been changed by the relationship.

Internet interactions also can be more equitable than face-to-face interactions, because factors such as attractiveness, prestige, and material possessions don't come into play (unless people share this information). In addition, communicating on the Internet gives students time to form and present more complete thoughts, interconnect ideas, and think and reflect.

To see a transcript of one of the "Letters from Kosovo," go to the Companion Website at *www.prenhall.com/eggen*, then to this chapter's *Additional Content* module.

Disadvantages also exist, however. For instance, unlike face-to-face conversation, Internet communication uses only the written word, which doesn't allow students to read nonverbal social cues, such as facial expressions and eye contact, or hear vocal signals like emphasis and intonation. Communications research suggests that a large part (some estimates are as high as 90%) of a message's credibility is communicated through nonverbal channels (Mehrabian & Ferris, 1967), so learning to read nonverbal behavior is an important part of social development. Further, spending a great deal of time in front of computers reduces the time students spend in face-to-face social experiences, a situation some experts believe impairs social development (Kuh & Vesper, 1999).

Because Internet communication uses only one channel, writers may be out of touch with their audiences, feeling a sense of anonymity. This can be helpful when it encourages students to disagree or express opinions but can also lead to insensitivity and treating others like objects rather than people.

Finally, some experts warn that although a great many claims have been offered about the positive effects of Internet communication on the development of writing and workplace skills, in addition to social development, well-designed research documenting these claims is still sparse (Fabos & Young, 1999).

3.5

Flaming is the practice of name calling and using epithets on the Internet. Explain why a person would be more likely to behave inappropriately on the Internet than in person.

Classroom Connections

Applying an Understanding of Personal and Social Development in Your Classroom

Personal Development

1. Discuss peer relationships and personal responsibility with students.

    - *Elementary:* At the end of each day, a third-grade teacher calls her students to a "meeting" at which they discuss classroom problems that arose that day, the ways in which classmates should treat one another, and other issues related to personal responsibility.

    - *Middle School:* An eighth-grade homeroom teacher spends time each week discussing topics such as friendship, the need to be personally responsible, and the effort everyone should make to influence friends in positive ways.

    - *High School:* A health teacher encourages his students to think about the influence of peers when they discuss topics such as drugs, diet, and dating. He tries to help them understand how peers can have both a positive and negative influence on their personal development.

Social Development

2. Encourage students to consider the perspectives of others.

    - *Elementary:* A fourth-grade teacher has her students analyze different characters' motives and feelings when they discuss a story they've read. She asks:

How does the character feel? Why does the character feel that way? How would you feel if you were that person?

    - *Middle School:* A middle school science teacher stays after school to provide opportunities for students to ask questions about their work in his class. The conversations often drift to interpersonal problems the students are having with parents or friends. The teacher listens patiently but also encourages students to think about the motives and feelings of the other people involved.

    - *High School:* A history teacher encourages her students to consider point of view when they read reports of historical events. For example, when studying the Civil War, she reminds her students that both sides thought they were morally right, and she asks questions such as these: Why was states' rights such a controversial topic? How did the opponents interpret the Emancipation Proclamation?

3. Involve students in social problem solving.

    - *Elementary:* A third-grade teacher periodically has groups of four students check math homework. He passes out two answer sheets to each group and asks the students to decide how to proceed. When the students don't accept equal responsibilities, or conflicts arise, he encourages the students to work out the problems themselves and intervenes only if they've been unable to resolve the problems.

- *Middle School:* An eighth-grade English teacher sometimes purposefully leaves decisions about individual assignments up to the groups in cooperative learning activities. When disagreements occur, she offers only enough assistance to get the group back on track. If the problem is widespread, she calls a whole-class meeting to discuss the problem.

- *High School:* When students argue about space, the music they listen to, and access to materials and supplies, an art teacher requires the students to discuss the problem and suggest solutions acceptable to everyone.

Integrating Personal, Emotional, and Social Development: Erikson's Theory

Erik Erikson (1902–1994) was interested in personal and emotional development and how they are influenced by the social environment. Because he integrated personal, emotional, and social factors in his theory of development, it is often described as a *psychosocial* theory (Erikson, 1968).

Erikson believed that people, in general, have the same basic needs. Personal development occurs in response to these needs and depends on the quality of the care and support provided by the social environment, particularly caregivers. Development proceeds in stages, each characterized by **crisis,** *a psychosocial challenge that presents opportunities for development.* Although no crisis is permanently resolved, a positive resolution of one psychosocial challenge increases the likelihood of a positive resolution at the next stage.

Erikson's Stages of Psychosocial Development

Erikson believed that movement through his developmental stages reflects changes in an individual's motivation. For instance, he believed that infants are instinctively motivated to establish a sense of trust in the world, and acquiring this trust means that the psychosocial challenge has been met. Failure to meet the challenge—resolve the crisis—leaves the individual with a general uneasiness about people and the larger social context. Each stage represents a unique psychosocial challenge.

Erikson's stages are outlined as follows:

- *Trust Versus Mistrust (Birth to 1 Year).* Trust develops when infants receive consistently loving care from caregivers, most commonly parents. Infants who are left to cry or who receive unpredictable care can develop basic mistrust that leads to fear and suspicion of other people and the world in general (Isabella & Belsky, 1991).
- *Autonomy Versus Shame and Doubt (Ages 1 to 3).* Autonomy develops when children are supported in their efforts to perform tasks, such as tying their shoes, on their own. Overly restrictive parents or ones who punish children for failures such as minor spills or bedwetting can lead children to doubt their own abilities or feel ashamed of their bodies.
- *Initiative Versus Guilt (Ages 3 to 6).* Initiative develops when adults encourage and reward children's efforts to explore and take on new challenges. Parents who criticize or punish initiative cause children to feel guilty about their self-initiated activities.
- *Industry Versus Inferiority (Ages 6 to 12).* Industry develops when learners acquire a sense of competence through successes on challenging tasks. A pattern of failure can lead to feelings of inferiority.
- *Identity Versus Confusion (Ages 12 to 18).* Identity develops when adolescents are allowed to test their attempts at increasing independence within clearly

3.6
How successfully has Sean, from the introductory case study, resolved the trust-mistrust crisis? Support your answer with evidence taken directly from the case study.

3.7
You are teaching a ninth-grade student whom you can't " get going." He will do what is required of him and no more. He does a good job on his required work, however, and seems to be quite happy. Use Erikson's theory to explain his behavior.

established limits. Authoritarian parenting, which is overly restrictive, or permissive parenting, which fails to set limits, both can result in confusion and an uncertain identity.

- *Intimacy Versus Isolation (Young Adulthood).* Intimacy develops when individuals with a clear sense of identity are able to give themselves over to another. People who fail to meet the psychosocial challenge remain emotionally isolated, unable to give and receive love freely.
- *Generativity Versus Stagnation (Middle Adulthood).* Generative adults are committed to guiding the next generation (Erikson, 1980). They work for positive social outcomes, such as a clean environment, a safe and drug-free world, and adherence to the principles of freedom and dignity for all people. An unhealthy resolution of the psychosocial challenge leads to apathy, pseudo-intimacy, or self-absorption.
- *Integrity Versus Despair (Old Age).* Integrity occurs when people believe they've lived their lives as well as possible and accept the inevitability of death with few regrets. Conversely, remorse over things done or left undone, and the feeling that time is running out, leads to despair.

Putting Erikson's Work Into Perspective

Erikson's work was popular and influential in the 1960s and 1970s, but since then developmental theorists have taken issue with it on at least three grounds. First, some researchers argue that Erikson failed to adequately address the important role that culture plays in personal, emotional, and social development. For instance, some cultures discourage autonomy and initiative in young children, perhaps as a way of protecting them from dangers in their environments (X. Chen, Rubin, & Sun, 1992; Harwood, Miller, & Irizarry, 1995).

Second, Erikson based his theory on his work with men, and his description of intimacy as following the development of identity has been criticized. For many women, establishing a sense of intimacy may occur with, or even precede, a focus on identity (Josselson, 1988).

Third, research indicates that most people don't achieve a sense of identity as early as Erikson suggested; it more often occurs after, rather than during, the high school years (Durkin, 1995; Marcia, 1980, 1988; Waterman, 1985). (We discuss identity development later in the chapter.)

Erikson's work is intuitively sensible, however, and it helps us explain much of the behavior we see in others (e.g., Sean, the student with the "bad attitude" in the opening case study). We've all met people we admire because of their positive outlook, openness, and commitment to making the world a better place. We've also encountered those who believe that others are trying to take advantage of them or are somehow inherently evil. We see good minds sliding into lethargy because of a lack of initiative or even substance abuse. We are frustrated by people's apathy and lack of a zest for living. Erikson's work helps us understand these problems.

His work also reminds us that teachers are essential in creating the social environment that contributes to students' personal and emotional growth, and it offers sensible suggestions for working with students during the early childhood, elementary, and adolescent years. Let's look at some of these suggestions.

Supporting Psychosocial Development

Erikson asserted that psychosocial development depends on the quality of the care and support provided by the social environment. The encouragement of teachers is essential in this process as children move from early childhood to adolescence.

Early Childhood

As children enter preschool and kindergarten, they are moving forward, taking on more tasks, and searching eagerly for more experiences. "Let me help!" and "I want to try that" are signs of this initiative. The children are also interacting more with their peers, and their play is becoming more complex and interdependent. As children go through these changes, teachers can do much to help them develop into happy and healthy individuals.

Early childhood and elementary classrooms should provide opportunities for students to develop personal independence and initiative.

> Mrs. Hernandez is watching her kindergarten students work on an art activity.
>
> "Good, Felipe. I see you've used a lot of colors to draw your bird. That's a very pretty bird," she says kindly as she circulates around the room.
>
> "Nice, Taeko. Those are really bright colors. They make me feel happy.
>
> "Look what Raymond did. He cut out his picture when he was done. That's a nice job of cutting."

Felipe and Taeko made their own decisions about coloring, and Raymond decided on his own to cut out the picture when he was finished. The kind of encouragement and reinforcement that Mrs. Hernandez gave strongly supports a child's developing initiative. In contrast, criticism or overly restrictive directions detract from the feeling of independence and, in extreme cases, lead to guilt and dependency. Simple, self-chosen tasks, such as those undertaken by Mrs. Hernandez's students, form the concrete challenges that children use to express their growing initiative. For healthy psychosocial development, a child's activity and performance on a task aren't as important as an adult's response to them. Adult affirmation—such as support and encouragement from teachers—is essential.

The Elementary Years

> "I believe that Atlanta will have a warmer climate than Bogota," Enrique, one of Tim Duncan's fifth graders, commented during a geography lesson.
>
> "That's an interesting idea," Tim responded. "Why do you think so, considering Bogota is much nearer the equator than Atlanta?"
>
> "Bogota is high up . . . and Atlanta isn't in any mountains. It isn't always just being farther south that makes it warm."
>
> "That's very insightful," Tim nodded with a smile. "That's the kind of thinking we want to be doing in here. . . . Excellent, Enrique."

During the elementary years, students are attempting to acquire a sense of belief in their competence. Teachers support these efforts when they provide a challenging menu of learning experiences and help learners succeed in them. This isn't easy, of course. Activities that are so challenging that students frequently fail can leave them with a sense of inferiority and a lack of confidence about their capabilities. On the other hand, success on trivial tasks does little to make students feel competent and develop their sense of industry. Tim's expertise as a teacher helped him find the right mix in his geography lesson.

In a longitudinal study of development, researchers found that of intelligence, family background, and industry, a healthy *sense of industry* was the most significant factor influencing later personal adjustment, economic success, and interpersonal relationships (Vaillant & Vaillant, 1990). This finding is powerful and quite encouraging; if teachers can help students respond to challenges and develop a sense of industry, students can overcome many obstacles later in life.

Conversations with caring adults provide opportunities for adolescents to think about and refine their developing personal identities.

Adolescence

Adolescence is a unique time in which students experience physical, emotional, and intellectual changes. They go through growth spurts, and their coordination doesn't keep up with their bodies. The magnitude of physical change in early adolescence is surpassed only during infancy. Adolescents are frequently confused about how to respond to new sexual feelings. They are concerned with what others think of them and are preoccupied with their looks. They are caught in the awkward position of wanting to assert their independence, yet longing for the stability of structure and discipline. They want to rebel, but they want something solid to rebel against.

These changes and struggles don't necessarily doom teenagers to a period of distress and uncertainty, however. Most negotiate adolescence successfully and maintain positive relationships with their parents and other adults. Contemporary theorists suggest that this is a time of *exploration* for students, because it reflects day-to-day experimentation with different roles and people (Berk, 2001; Grotevant, 1998).

Understanding emotionally developing adolescents helps a teacher better respond to their sometimes capricious behavior. Fads and bizarre clothing and hairstyles, for example, reflect teenagers' urges to identify with groups while simultaneously searching for their individuality. If their behaviors don't interfere with learning or the rights and comfort of others, they shouldn't be major issues. A teacher

Talking honestly with students can promote social development.

can help by taking the time to simply talk with students openly and honestly about their concerns. This is the best advice we can give teachers struggling to reach adolescents.

You may remember that Sean's teachers, Anne and Beth, both tried to get Sean to "open up" to them. Perhaps more significant, however, is the sensitivity the teachers demonstrated in their efforts to reach him. Students, particularly at the middle and junior high levels, need firm, caring teachers, teachers who empathize with them while providing the security of clear limits for acceptable behavior. They don't need a teacher who is a buddy. They need a solid adult who can guide their intellectual and emotional growth (Emmer et al., 2003).

Classroom Connections

Applying Erikson's Work in Your Classroom

1. Know the emotional needs of young people, and use that knowledge as an umbrella under which you conduct your interactions with them.

   • *Elementary:* A kindergarten student responsible for watering the classroom plants knocks one over on the floor. The teacher says evenly, "It looks like we have a problem. What needs to be done?" She pauses and continues, "Sweep up the dirt, and wipe up the water with some paper towels." When the student is done, the teacher gives her a hug and comments, "Everyone makes mistakes. The important thing is what we do about them."

   • *Middle School:* A math teacher designs her instruction so that all students can achieve success and develop a growing sense of industry. Assignments are designed so that each student can do them. Sometimes this requires shortening the assignment or breaking it into smaller parts. Students also have the opportunity to redo assignments if they made an honest effort the first time. The teacher often comments, "Math is for everyone—if you try!"

- *High School:* A biology teacher pays little attention to the attire and slang of his students as long as offensive language isn't used, the rights of others are recognized, and learning occurs.

2. Help students understand that effort leads to success and competence.
- *Elementary:* A second-grade teacher carefully covers each topic and provides precise directions before making seat-work assignments. She conducts "monitored practice" with the first few items to be sure all students get started correctly. When students encounter difficulties, she meets with them separately or in small groups so they don't fall behind.
- *Middle School:* A sixth-grade teacher develops a grading system based partially on improvement so that each student can succeed by improving his or her performance. He meets with students periodically during each grading period to help them monitor their learning progress.

- *High School:* An art teacher uses portfolios and individual conferences to help her students set goals and see their growth over the year. During conferences, she emphasizes individual growth and tries to help students understand how their effort and accomplishments are linked.

3. Be a role model for students, both professionally and personally.
- *Elementary:* A fourth-grade teacher arranges his classroom procedures so that everyone—including himself—is given responsibilities, including homework. He discusses the work that he takes home at night, stressing its importance for teaching and learning.
- *Middle School:* A life science teacher who is working on a master's degree at night shares her experiences with her students, telling them about the new ideas she's learning as well as about the time and effort she's expending in her classes. She wants her students to appreciate the joy of learning as well as understand that all meaningful learning takes work.
- *High School:* A tenth-grade English teacher stresses that discourtesy and mistreatment of others are "mortal sins" in his class. When he presents his classroom rules, he pledges his own courtesy and his commitment to preserving each student's dignity.

The Development of Identity and Self-Concept

One child announced at the dinner table that she was an honest person. When asked how she knew she was honest, she replied, "Because my teacher asked me to help her grade papers!" (W. Purkey & Novak, 1984, p. 27)

"I'll never forget my seventh-grade teacher. At that time I was overweight and wore braces on my teeth. Our teacher asked us to turn in a paper of different types of sentences. To demonstrate an exaggeration, I wrote, 'I am the most beautiful girl in the world.' The teacher wrote back: 'This is an exaggeration?' He'll never know how good he made me feel." (W. Purkey & Novak, 1984, p. 28)

As children develop, they grow not only in size, knowledge, and skills but also in their awareness and views of themselves as learners and people. These views usually are positive when students enter school, but they often become less positive over time (Stipek, 2002). This is especially true for students who experience learning problems (Heward, 1996).

The Development of Identity

As students move through school and beyond, they begin to establish a sense of **identity**, *a definition of who they are, what their existence means, and what they want to accomplish in life.* Social experiences, including informal cliques, organized clubs and teams, and neighborhoods and communities, all contribute to students' developing identities (Trawick-Smith, 2000; Wigfield et al., 1996). In addition, for children who belong to cultural minority groups, ethnic identity is an essential part of this identity development (M. Jones, 1999). (We discuss the development of ethnic identity later in the chapter.)

During the process of identity development, adolescents often identify with a particular peer group, rigidly adhering to a style of dress or way of wearing their hair. The oversized shirts and baggy shorts that junior high teachers commonly see their students wear are displays of these "temporary identities." In time they're replaced with a more individual sense of self and an awareness of lifelong goals.

Patterns in Identity Development

Four seniors were talking about what they planned to do after high school:

> "I'm not sure what I want to do," Sandy commented. "I've thought about veterinary medicine, and also about teaching. I've been working at the vet clinic, and I really like it, but I'm not sure about doing it forever. I guess I should take some kind of interest inventory or something. I don't know."
>
> "I wish I could do that," Ramon replied. "But I'm off to the university full-time in the fall. I'm going to be a lawyer. At least that's what my parents think. It's not a bad job, and lawyers make good money."
>
> "How can you just do that, Ramon?" Nancy wondered aloud. "You don't really want to be a lawyer; you've said that before. Me, I'm not willing to decide yet. I'm only 18. I'm good in biology. I've thought about trying premed, and I'm going to take some more courses in biology-oriented stuff, but I'm not sure I'm ready for that many years of school. I'm going to think hard about it for a while. How about you, Taylor?"
>
> "I'm going into nursing," Taylor answered. "I've been working part-time at the hospital, and it feels really good. I thought I wanted to be a doctor at one time, but I don't think I can handle all the pressures. I've talked with the counselors, and I think I can do the chem and other science courses. I guess we'll see."

The process of identity formation isn't smooth and uniform; it takes different paths, like a railroad train. Sometimes it's sitting on a holding spur beside the main track; at other times it's chugging full speed ahead.

As mentioned earlier, Erikson believed that identity formation takes place some time between the ages of 12 and 18. To study the development of identity, researchers have interviewed adolescents and asked them about their occupational, religious, and political choices (Marcia, 1980). They have found that young people's commitments can be classified as falling within one of four states, outlined in Table 3.3 (Marcia, 1987).

The descriptions in Table 3.3 show how the development of identity can take both positive and negative turns. Identity moratorium is a healthy state and may lead individuals to identity achievement. On the other hand, identity diffusion and identity foreclosure are less healthy states in which adolescents fail to wrestle with choices that will

Table 3.3 States in identity development

State	Description and Example
Identity diffusion	Occurs when individuals fail to make clear choices. Confusion is common. Choices may be difficult, or individuals aren't developmentally ready to make choices. This state is illustrated by Sandy's comments in the vignette.
Identity foreclosure	Occurs when individuals prematurely adopt ready-made positions of others, such as parents. This is an undesirable position, because decisions are based on the identities of others. Ramon's comments suggest this state.
Identity moratorium	Occurs when individuals pause and remain in a holding pattern. Long-range commitment is delayed. Nancy appears to be in this state.
Identity achievement	Occurs after individuals experience a period of crises and decision making. Identity achievement reflects a commitment to a goal or direction. Taylor's comments indicate that he has made this commitment.

Source: Marcia, 1987.

have important consequences for them throughout life. Identity foreclosure happens when adolescents adopt the goals and values of others—usually their parents—without thoroughly examining the implications of those choices for their future lives. Identity diffusion occurs when adolescents fail to seriously consider who they are or what they want to become. This can result in teenagers becoming apathetic, withdrawn, or openly rebellious (Berger & Thompson, 1995; Kroger, 1995).

Research has shown that—in contrast with the predictions of Erikson's theory—identity achievement more often occurs after, than during, high school (Waterman, 1985). This delay was especially true for college students, who had more time to consider what they wanted to do with their lives. These results suggest that the uncertainty of adolescence is related more to increasing independence than to career or gender identity resolution. Conflict with parents, teachers, and other adults peaks in early adolescence and then declines, as teenagers accept responsibility and adults learn how to deal with the new relationships (Offer, Ostrov, & Howard, 1989). These developmental challenges of early adolescence help explain why teaching junior high or middle school students can be particularly challenging.

3.8
Research indicates that identity formation occurs later for American youth (after high school) than for youth in other countries. Why do you think this is so?

The Development of Self-Concept

Self-concept is *a cognitive appraisal of one's own physical, social, and academic competence* (Marsh, 1989; Pintrich & Schunk, 2002). We would describe a girl who believes that she is a good athlete, for example, as having a positive physical self-concept, or a boy who believes he is good at getting along with people as having a positive social self-concept. People who believe they are intellectually competent are said to have high academic self-concepts.

Self-Concept and Self-Esteem

The terms *self-concept* and *self-esteem* are often used interchangeably but in fact are quite distinct. In contrast with self-concept, which is cognitive, **self-esteem**, or **self-worth**, is *an emotional reaction to or an evaluation of the self* (Pintrich & Schunk, 2002). People who have high self-esteem believe that they are inherently worthy people.

Young children tend to have both high self-esteem and positive—sometimes unrealistically positive—self-concepts, probably because they lack social comparisons and receive much support from parents (Berk, 2001; Flavell et al., 1993; Stipek, 2002). Self-esteem tends to drop during the elementary school years, and self-concepts become more realistic as interactions with others give students a more accurate measure of their performance compared to their peers (Hay, Ashman, van Kraayenoord, & Stewart, 1999). As students move into adolescence, self-concept and a developing sense of identity interact, with each influencing the other and both influencing self-esteem.

3.9
Is competition a generally healthy or unhealthy component of the school curriculum? Explain, using information from this section.

Self-Concept and Achievement

The relationship between overall self-concept and achievement is positive but weak (Walberg, 1984). In attempting to understand why, researchers have found that social and physical self-concepts are virtually unrelated to academic achievement (Byrne & Gavin, 1996). This makes sense; we've all known socially withdrawn students who are happy as academic isolates as well as popular students content to earn average grades in school.

3.10
What parts of the total school experience most influence the development of social and physical self-concepts? What does this suggest about the importance of a total school program?

Academic Self-Concept

Academic self-concept is important to teachers because it strongly interacts with school performance. As we saw earlier, children commonly enter school expecting to learn and

Children form their academic self-concepts on the basis of the concrete experiences and feedback they receive in school.

do well (Stipek, 2002), but as they progress, actual accomplishments lead them to alter this expectation. When learning experiences are positive, self-concept is enhanced; when they're negative, it suffers.

An even stronger relationship exists between specific subject matter self-concepts and achievement in those areas (Yeung et al., 2000). For example, people with positive self-concepts in math perform better on math tests (and vice versa). Researchers have also found that concepts of competence in different subjects, such as math and English, become more distinct over time, and students become better able to differentiate between their performances in different areas (Marsh, 1992). Unfortunately, we've all heard people make statements such as "I'm okay in English, but I'm no good in math." Some evidence suggests that comments like these may not reflect actual competence; instead, people for whom societal expectations are low underestimate their abilities (American Association of University Women, 1992).

The relationships between the components of self-concept and achievement are illustrated in Figure 3.2.

Promoting Psychosocial and Self-Concept Development: Instructional Strategies

Teachers play an important role in promoting all forms of learner development, and they are likely to be the most significant influences on students' developing academic self-concepts. They design the learning activities and assessments and provide the feedback that students use to appraise their academic competence. The following principles can guide teachers in their efforts to promote psychosocial and self-concept development:

3.11
What, specifically, is the primary source of information students use to develop their academic self-concepts? Describe what you as a teacher can do to help low achievers form positive self-concepts.

■ Communicate caring and genuine interest in all students.
■ Maintain an authoritative interaction style.
■ Reward autonomy and initiative in your students.
■ Establish appropriately high expectations for all learners.
■ Create learning activities in which students can succeed on tasks they view as challenging.
■ Design grading systems that emphasize increasing competence and avoid competition.

Figure 3.2 The relationships among the dimensions of self-concept and achievement

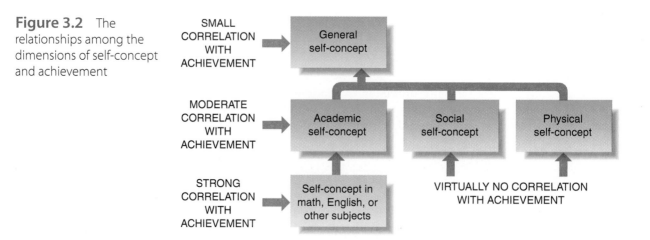

Let's see how the principles guide John Adler, an eighth-grade English teacher, as he works with his students.

"Here are your papers," John said on Friday as he handed back a set of quizzes that had been given the day before. "I'm very proud of you. You're all improving so much, particularly on your writing. Your grammar, spelling, and punctuation are all improving, and you're also becoming more expressive. . . . I realize that I expect a lot from you, but you've always risen to the task.

"Be sure to put your scores in your logs. . . . And be sure to look at your improvement points on your papers and to add them to your logs as well."

"Who improved the most, Mr. Adler?" Jeremy asked.

"We don't care who improved the most," John replied, gently admonishing Jeremy. "Remember, as I've been saying, we're all in this together. I help you as much as I can, you take responsibility for your learning, and each one of us tries to improve as much as possible. . . . That's why I put your scores on the last page of the quizzes. They're your business and no one else's. You should be concerned with improving and increasing your understanding, not with whether you're doing better than the person next to you."

John then went over some of the quiz items that had given the students trouble. He gave some additional examples and closed the discussion by saying, "I know that these were challenging, but if you look back to the beginning of the year, you can see that you're getting better and better on them. That's what this is all about—improving.

"Now, I want to take some time to have a classroom meeting," he said, changing the direction of the discussion. "One of you came to me after school last Friday and expressed some concern about the way some kids are treating each other. . . . Now, she didn't tattle or name any names. She simply expressed a concern, and I'm proud of her. I really like it when someone takes the initiative to make our classroom environment better.

"And I agree with her concern. . . . For instance, I saw one of you get tripped when you walked down the aisle, and another had water splashed on him at the water fountain. . . . I'm also seeing more litter on the floor.

"Frankly, I'm disappointed in some of you. We want an orderly classroom in which we all can to learn, and we're here to help one another. . . . So, I want to hear some ideas. What are we going to do about it?"

Many of the students offered comments, with suggestions ranging from kicking perpetrators out of class to talking to them, to adding some more rules. The students agreed that John had been attempting to enforce the rules fairly but that he had perhaps been a little too lenient in some cases. He acknowledged that possibility, saying that because he felt so strongly about students accepting responsibility, he perhaps went too far.

At the meeting's end, the students agreed to redouble their efforts to be responsible, and John agreed to enforce the rules equally and consistently.

Let's look more closely at John's attempts to promote personal and self-concept development. First, John's efforts to establish an orderly, learning-focused classroom environment demonstrated caring and genuine interest in his students. Like most people, students respond positively to such attitudes:

> When asked about their favorite teachers, students unsurprisingly mention such qualities as caring about them as individuals and seeking to help them succeed as students. . . . However, students also say that they want teachers to articulate and enforce clear standards of behavior. They view this not just as part of the teacher's job but as evidence that the teacher cares about them." (Brophy, 1998, p. 23)

Second, by being caring but firm about standards for behavior, and by soliciting the students' input into classroom rules and procedures, John displayed the authoritative interaction style discussed earlier in the chapter. Authoritative management, with its opportunity for practicing independence within limits, is particularly valuable in eighth-grade classrooms where students are beginning the process of establishing a sense of identity.

Third, John realized that no psychosocial challenge is ever permanently resolved; so, although his students were eighth graders, he rewarded progress associated with earlier stages, such as autonomy and initiative. This was the reason he praised one of his students for taking the initiative to raise the issue of student behavior.

Fourth, John helped promote a sense of industry and positive academic self-concept in his students in several ways. His comments, "I'm very proud of you," "You're all improving so much," and "I realize that I expect a lot from you, but you've always risen to the task," communicated his high expectations and his emphasis on increasing competence.

John also focused on learning and de-emphasized competition when he said, "We don't care who improved the most" and "Each one of us tries to improve as much as possible," in response to Jeremy's question. Finally, by awarding points for improvement, he used his grading system to further emphasize increasing competence.

Research supports John's approach to developing his students' academic self-concepts. Another approach attempts to improve self-concept directly, using strategies such as having minority students study multicultural learning materials, establishing residential summer camps, and implementing support groups and sensitivity training. However, in comparing this approach to John's—improving self-concept through increased academic success—studies consistently support the latter (Beane, 1991; Skaalvik & Valas, 1999). Learners are active, thinking people; without evidence of accomplishment, they're unlikely to conclude that they're competent (Hay et al., 1999; Marsh, Kong, & Hau, 2001).

Helping students positively resolve the psychosocial challenges described by Erikson's theory and develop positive identities and self-concepts isn't easy, and efforts such as John's won't work with all students or even with any student all the time. However, with time and continued effort, teachers make an important difference in students' psychosocial, identity, and self-concept development.

Ethnic Pride: Promoting Positive Self-Esteem and Ethnic Identity

Maria Robles squeezed her mother's hand tightly as they entered the busy doors of her new school. Her mother could tell she was nervous as she anxiously eyed the bigger boys and girls walking down the hallway.

As they stopped in front of the doorway marked *Kindergarten, Room 3*, Mrs. Avilla, a woman with a smiling face, came out to greet them.

"Hola. ¿Cómo te llamas, niña?" (Hello. What is your name, little one?)

Maria was still uneasy, but as she looked at her mother's face, she felt relieved.

"Dile tu nombre" (Tell her your name), her mother prompted, squeezing her hand and smiling.

". . . Maria," she offered hesitantly.

Her mother added quickly, "Maria Robles. Yo soy su madre." (I am her mother.)

Mrs. Avilla looked on her list, found Maria's name, and checked it off. Then she invited them, in Spanish, to come into the room and meet the other boys and girls. Music could be heard in the background. Maria recognized some of her friends who were playing with toys in one corner of the room.

"Maria, ven aquí y juega con nosotros." (Maria, come here and play with us.)

Maria hesitated for a moment and looked up at her mother to see whether it was all right. When her mother smiled and nodded, Maria ran over to join her friends.

Self-Esteem and Ethnicity

We all wonder about our self-worth. Will others like us? Are we worthy of their love? Are we perceived by others as smart? beautiful? handsome? As we saw at the beginning of this chapter, our interactions with others help shape our beliefs, and schools provide an active social environment in which to develop both self-concept and self-esteem.

Especially for minority youth, culture also figures significantly in the development of self-esteem. Researchers have found that the self-esteem of people from minority groups often includes both a personal and a collective component (Wright & Taylor, 1995).

Collective self-esteem refers to *individuals' perceptions of the relative worth of the groups to which they belong*. Families, peers, and the ethnic groups that individuals identify with contribute to their sense of self-worth. When these groups are valued and per-

Teachers can help students develop ethnic pride and positive self-esteem by actively acknowledging and valuing the ethnic and cultural strengths different students bring to school.

ceived as having status, personal identities and self-esteem are enhanced. The opposite is also true.

Children as young as Maria Robles know they are part of an ethnic minority, and research dating back to the 1930s indicates that minority children such as African Americans (Clark & Clark, 1939), Mexican Americans (Weiland & Coughlin, 1979), and Chinese Americans (Aboud & Skerry, 1984) evaluate their ethnic reference groups as being inherently less worthy than the White majority. These findings suggest that simply being part of a minority group can make students feel less confident and less good about themselves; this is a disturbing problem for teachers who are working to promote healthy self-esteem in all students.

What can teachers do to combat this problem? We can make every effort to communicate to students that their ethnic heritage and language are both recognized and valued. In a test of this idea, researchers taught elementary native Canadian children in either their native (heritage) language or in a second language, such as French (Wright & Taylor, 1995). Children educated in their heritage language showed a substantial increase in their personal self-esteem, whereas children educated in the nonheritage second language did not. The researchers concluded that "early heritage language education can have a positive impact on the personal and collective self-esteem of minority language students" (p. 251).

Students who hear their home language used in the classroom learn that the language and the culture in which it is embedded are valued. Like Maria Robles, many students come to school wondering if they will be welcome and questioning whether the knowledge they bring with them will be valued (Jackson, 1999); this anxiousness has an additional dimension for those who speak a minority language. The way a teacher reacts to these students influences their sense of self-worth.

Ethnic Pride and Identity Formation

Membership in an ethnic group also affects identity formation in several ways (Jones, 1999). Sometimes the messages teenagers receive about their ethnic identities are mixed or even negative. An African American journalist reported, "If you were black, you didn't quite measure up. . . . You didn't see any black people doing certain things. . . . Well, it must mean that white people are better than we are" (Monroe, Goldman, & Smith, 1988, pp. 88–89).

3.12
What kinds of information do children from ethnic minorities use in forming these lower evaluations? How does this process compare with the process that occurs in forming personal self-esteem and self-concept?

Similar problems with ethnic identity formation have been documented with Mexican American (Matute-Bianchi, 1986) and Asian American teenagers (Wong-Fillmore, 1992).

On a more positive note, research indicates that students who are encouraged and helped to explore their ethnic identities and who have adopted values from both the dominant culture and their own tend to have a clearer sense of their identity (Nieto, 1999). They also achieve higher, like school more, have higher self-esteem, and have a more positive view of their ability to cope with their environments (Hood, 1999; L. Jackson, 1999).

The research reveals consistent patterns. Minority students need to know that their cultures are valued and that the languages they bring to school are assets rather than obstacles or liabilities (B. Wilson, 1998). Teachers play a crucial role in making every student feel wanted and welcomed by the overt and implicit messages they send through their teaching.

3.13
Explain how positive ethnic role models can assist in identity-resolution tasks, such as independence, career decision making, sexual adjustment, and peer group relations.

Classroom Connections

Developing Positive Self-Concepts in Your Classroom

1. Make students feel wanted and valued in your class. Provide learning experiences that promote success.

   - *Elementary:* A fourth-grade teacher starts the school year by having students write autobiographical sketches and bring in pictures of themselves taken when they were preschoolers. They list their strengths, interests, and hobbies, and describe what they want to be when they grow up.

   - *Middle School:* A homeroom teacher for entering middle schoolers tries to make his classroom a place where students feel safe and secure. He begins the school year with classroom meetings where students get to know one another and form homeroom rules. As the year progresses, he uses these meetings to discuss issues and problems important to students.

   - *High School:* A ninth-grade English teacher begins each school year by announcing that everyone is important in her classes and that she expects everyone to learn. She structures her classrooms around success, minimizing competition. She also stays in her room after school and invites students who are having problems to come by for help.

Capitalizing on Diversity in Your Classroom

2. Build on students' cultures and ethnic backgrounds to develop positive self-esteem.

   - *Elementary:* A first-grade teacher learns that three distinct native languages are spoken in the different homes of his students. With the help of other teachers and parent volunteers, he constructs a chart of common nouns and phrases (e.g., *chair, table, mother, hello*) in the different languages. He uses the chart to explain to his students differences in the languages and to establish commonalities between them.

   - *Middle School:* A social studies teacher in an ethnically diverse school encourages her students to research the countries from which their ancestors came. Students display the information they discover on a poster and bring in things from home, such as clothes and food, to illustrate the cultures of the ancestral countries.

   - *High School:* A tenth-grade English teacher makes a special effort to present literature written by authors from various minority groups. When the class reads the selections, he provides biographical information to help students understand who the authors are and how their experiences as youths shaped their writing.

3. Use ethnic role models as a foundation for the development of students' personal identities.

   - *Elementary:* A third-grade teacher in an inner-city school encourages parents and family members of students to volunteer in the classroom. As the teacher gets to know the volunteers, she encourages them to talk about their jobs and occupations with students.

   - *Middle School:* A language arts teacher in a career exploration unit makes a special effort to invite members of minority groups who have different occupations and professions. He encourages them to talk openly about the challenges and satisfactions they encountered in pursuing their careers.

   - *High School:* A history teacher makes a special effort to educate students about the contributions of women and members of ethnic minorities to American society. As contemporary newspapers and magazines report the accomplishments of individuals who are ethnic minorities, she brings in the articles to share with her students.

Development of Morality, Social Responsibility, and Self-Control

"Listen, everyone. . . . I need to go to the office for a moment," Amanda Kellinger said as her students were completing a seat-work assignment. "You all have work to do, so work quietly until I get back."

The quiet shuffling of pencils and papers could be heard for a few moments, and then Gary whispered, "Psst, what math problems are we supposed to do?"

"Shh! No talking," Talitha said, pointing to the rules posted on the bulletin board.

"But he needs to know so he can do his work," Krystal put in. "It's the evens on page 79."

"Who cares?" Dwain growled. "She's not here. She won't catch us."

What do students think about classroom rules? What influences their interpretations of rules, and how do they learn to follow and modify them? Perhaps more importantly, how do they think about the laws and conventions that govern our society? In the following sections, we continue our discussion of student development, examining changes in children's thinking about issues of right, wrong, fairness, and justice.

Increased Interest in Moral Education and Development

In recent years, interest in moral education and how it should be used to promote moral development has increased markedly (Wynne, 1997). In the popular media, *Newsweek* and *Time* have devoted cover articles to the topic, and in 1999 *U.S. News* addressed the issue of cheating, claiming on its cover, "A new epidemic of fraud is sweeping through our schools."

Disturbing trends also exist in the behavior patterns of our young people. For example, alcohol and drug abuse remain persistent problems among youth (Kuther & Higgins-D'Alessandra, 1997). Out-of-wedlock births to White adolescent females are at historical highs, as are homicide and suicide rates for White adolescent males (U.S. Department of Health and Human Services, 1998).

More recently, the corporate scandals in 2002 that led to the collapse of Enron and WorldCom, and questionable accounting practices in other companies, sent shock waves through the financial community and American society in general. Rampant greed and a sense that anything people could get away with was legitimate seemed to be the "moral" principle of the day. The American public is increasingly looking to moral education for solutions to problems such as these.

The need for moral education has also been voiced within the teaching profession (Goodlad, Soder, & Sirotnik, 1990; Tirri, 2001). Some argue that teaching is an inherently moral activity, with value decisions around every instructional corner (Hansen, 2001). This view separates the morality of teaching practices (e.g., who gets called on, who receives extra help) from the teaching of morality (e.g., how should we treat each other, why we have classroom rules) (Buzzelli & Johnston, 1997). On a broader level, some argue that value conflicts and the decisions that follow are an integral part of applying knowledge within any profession (Stern, 1997).

Moral issues are also embedded in the curriculum. Social studies are not a mere chronology of events; they are the study of humans' responses to situation-specific moral dilemmas, such as war and peace and justice and equality (Sunai & Haas, 1993). Ethical issues are also commonly found in literature designed for young people. For instance, in *Charlotte's Web* Charlotte was faced with the dilemma of saving Wilbur the pig at the loss of her own life. Old Yeller's master had to decide between losing his dog or allowing the potential health menace of rabies. Teachers commonly choose books such as *The Yearling* and *A Tale of Two Cities* not only because they are good literature but also because they introduce moral problems with no clear answers.

Moral education is an essential and integral part of learner development. To become socially and emotionally healthy, learners must acquire the moral compass that values provide and the thinking capacities to apply these values in intelligent ways. Further, research indicates that the moral atmosphere of a school (e.g., democratic and prosocial versus authoritarian) can influence motivation and the value students place on school (Binfet, Schonert-Reicht, & McDougal, 1997; Grolnick et al., 1999). Moral development theory can help us understand these issues.

Piaget's Description of Moral Development

Although most people think of Piaget primarily in the context of cognitive development, he examined the development of ethics and morals as well (1932/1965). He studied cognitive and moral development in much the same way; he presented children with problems and tasks, listened to their reactions, and asked questions to gain insight into their thinking.

Piaget (1932/1965) found that children's responses to moral problems could be divided into two broad stages of development on the basis of a principle he labeled **internalization,** which refers to *the personal source of control for children's thoughts and actions.* In the first stage, **external morality,** *children view rules as fixed and permanent and externally enforced by authority figures.* When Talitha said, "Shh! No talking," and pointed to the rules, she was demonstrating thinking at this stage. It didn't matter that Gary was only asking about the assignment—rules are rules. Dwain, who responded, "Who cares? She's not here. She won't catch us," showed the same kind of thinking—he was focusing on the fact that no authority figure was there to enforce the rule. External morality typically lasts to about age 10. Piaget believed that parents and teachers who stress unquestioning adherence to adult authority retard moral development and encourage students to remain at this level (DeVries & Zan, 1995).

In the second stage, **autonomous morality,** *children develop rational ideas of fairness and see justice as a reciprocal process of treating others as they would want to be treated.* Children at this stage begin to rely on themselves instead of others to regulate moral behavior. Krystal's comment, "But he needs to know so he can do his work," is characteristic of thinking at this stage; she viewed Gary's whispering as an honest request for assistance, rather than a rule infraction.

3.14
Use Piaget's concept of egocentrism (See Chapter 2) to explain the difference between external and autonomous morality. Describe what you as a teacher can do to help students progress from one stage to the next.

Kohlberg's Theory of Moral Development

Steve, a high school senior, was working at a night job to help support his mother, a single parent of three. Steve was a conscientious student who worked hard in his classes, but he didn't have enough time to study.

History wasn't Steve's favorite course, and because of his night work, he had a marginal D average. If he failed the final exam, he would fail the course and wouldn't graduate. He arranged to be off work the night before the exam so that he could study extra hard, but early in the evening his boss called, desperate to have Steve come in and replace another employee who called in sick at the last moment. His boss pressured him heavily, so Steve went to work reluctantly at 8:00 P.M. and came home exhausted at 2:00 A.M. He tried to study but fell asleep on the couch, with his book in his lap. His mother woke him for school at 6:30 A.M.

Steve went to his history class, looked at the test, and went blank. Everything seemed like a jumble. Clarice, one of the best students in the class, happened to have her answer sheet positioned so that he could clearly see every answer by barely moving his eyes.

From what you've read here, would Steve be justified in cheating on the test? You've just experienced a **moral dilemma,** *an ambiguous situation that requires a person to make a moral decision and justify that decision in terms of right and wrong.* Steve was caught in a position that had no clear course of action; any decision had both pos-

Cheating is a persistent problem in classrooms. How students think about this problem and how teachers should respond to it depend on students' levels of moral development.

itive and negative consequences. Students' responses to moral dilemmas provide insight into their moral development (Rest, Thoma, Narvaez, & Bebeau, 1997).

Influenced by the work of Piaget and John Dewey, Lawrence Kohlberg (1929–1987), a Harvard educator and psychologist, used dilemmas to study moral reasoning. While working with teenagers, he found that moral reasoning was developmental, and on the basis of research conducted in cities and villages in Great Britain, Malaysia, Mexico, Taiwan, and Turkey, Kohlberg concluded that the development of moral reasoning is similar across cultures. Using responses to hypothetical moral dilemmas such as the one you just read, Kohlberg (1963, 1969, 1981, 1984) developed a theory of moral development that extended Piaget's earlier work. Like Piaget, he concluded that morality develops in stages, and all people pass through all the stages in the same order but at different rates.

Kohlberg originally described moral development as existing in three levels consisting of two stages each. These levels represent the perspectives people take as they wrestle with moral dilemmas or problems. The levels and stages are outlined in Table 3.4. As you read the descriptions of these stages, remember that the specific response to a moral dilemma isn't the critical issue; the level and stage of moral development are determined by the *reasons* a person gives for making the decision.

To see a video clip of students at different developmental levels wrestling with a moral dilemma, go to the Companion Website at *www.prenhall.com/eggen,* then to this chapter's *Classrooms on the Web* module. Click on *Video Clip 3.2.*

Level I: Preconventional Ethics

The preconventional level is an egocentric orientation focusing on moral consequences for the self. As you might predict, because of their egocentrism, young children reason at this level. Level I consists of two stages: punishment-obedience and market exchange. Some research indicates that 15% to 20% of the U.S. teenage population still reason at this level (Turiel, 1973).

Stage 1: Punishment-Obedience.   In the **punishment-obedience stage,** *people make moral decisions based on their chances of getting caught and being punished.* They determine right or wrong by the consequences of an action. For example, if a child was caught and

Table 3.4 Kohlberg's stages of moral reasoning

Level I Preconventional Ethics	The ethics of egocentrism. Typical of children up to about age 10. Called preconventional because children typically don't fully understand rules set down by others.
Stage 1: Punishment-Obedience	Consequences of acts determine whether they're good or bad. Individuals make moral decisions without considering the needs or feelings of others.
Stage 2: Market Exchange	The ethics of "What's in it for me?" Obeying rules and exchanging favors are judged in terms of the benefit to the individual.
Level II Conventional Ethics	The ethics of others. Typical of 10- to 20-year-olds. The name comes from conformity to the rules and conventions of society.
Stage 3: Interpersonal Harmony	Ethical decisions are based on concern for or the opinions of others. What pleases, helps, or is approved of by others characterizes this stage.
Stage 4: Law and Order	The ethics of laws, rules, and societal order. Rules and laws are inflexible and are obeyed for their own sake.
Level III Postconventional Ethics	The ethics of principle. Rarely reached before age 20 and only by a small portion of the population. The focus is on the principles underlying society's rules.
Stage 5: Social Contract	Rules and laws represent agreements among people about behavior that benefits society. Rules can be changed when they no longer meet society's needs.
Stage 6: Universal Principles	Rarely encountered in life. Ethics are determined by abstract and general principles that transcend societal rules.

punished, the act was morally wrong; if not, the act was right. People who do not take an unguarded purse because they fear getting caught are operating at this stage. The same principle applies in a classroom. A person who argues that Steve is justified in cheating because he can easily see every answer on Clarice's paper, and he probably won't get caught, is reasoning at Stage 1.

Stage 2: Market Exchange. Students reasoning at Stage 2 begin to include others in their moral decision making, but they continue to focus on the consequences of an action for themselves. In the **market exchange stage,** *people feel that an act is morally justified if it results in an act of reciprocity on someone else's part.* Positions such as "An eye for an eye and a tooth for a tooth" and "Don't bite the hand that feeds you" reflect morality at this stage, and "You do something for me and I'll do something for you" is a key characteristic. A naive hedonism is used to judge the rightness or wrongness of an action.

A person reasoning at Stage 2 might argue that Steve should go ahead and cheat because if he doesn't, he'll have to repeat the course and quit his job. From this perspective, "The right thing to do is what makes me the happiest." This reasoning again focuses on the self. A familiar example of Stage 2 ethics is political patronage, the tendency of successful office seekers to give their supporters "cushy" jobs regardless of qualifications.

3.15
What teacher behaviors contribute to students continuing to reason at the preconventional level? What can teachers do to help students move to higher levels?

Level II: Conventional Ethics

As egocentrism declines and development progresses, students become better able to see the world from others' points of view. Moral reasoning no longer depends on the consequences for the individual but instead becomes linked to the perspectives of, and concerns for, others. Values such as loyalty, others' approval, family expectations, obeying the law, and social order become prominent. Stages 3 and 4 reflect this orientation, and a few older elementary school students, some middle school and junior high students, and many high school students exhibit conventional morality (McDevitt & Ormrod, 2002). Much of the adult population reasons at this level.

Stage 3: Interpersonal Harmony. Individuals reasoning at Stage 3 do not manipulate people to reach their goals, as they might at Stage 2. Rather, in the **interpersonal harmony stage,** *people make decisions based on conventions, loyalty, and living up to the expectations of others.* In Stage 3, sometimes called the "nice girl/good boy" stage, a person is oriented toward maintaining the affection and approval of friends and relatives by being a "good" person. For example, a teenager on a date meets a curfew because she doesn't want to worry her parents.

A person reasoning at Stage 3 might offer at least two different perspectives on Steve's dilemma. One could argue that he needs to work to help his family and therefore is justified in cheating. A contrasting view, still at Stage 3, would suggest that he should not cheat because people would think badly of him if they found out.

Those reasoning at Stage 3 run the danger of being caught up in the majority opinion. For example, some people accept that cheating on income taxes is okay because "everybody cheats." We might call Stage 3 the "ethics of adolescence" because of the influence peers have on young people's thinking at this age.

Teachers' interactions with students provide opportunities to promote learner moral development.

Stage 4: Law and Order.   A person reasoning at Stage 4 would argue that Steve should not cheat because "It's against the rules to cheat." In the **law and order stage,** *people follow laws and rules for their own sake.* They don't make moral decisions to please particular people, as in Stage 3; rather, they believe that laws and rules exist to guide behavior and that they should be followed uniformly.

Concern for the orderliness of society is also characteristic of this stage; for example, a person might argue that Steve should not cheat because "What would our country be like if everybody cheated under those same conditions?" Concern for others is still the focus, but rules and order are key criteria. People reasoning at Stage 4 don't care whether the rest of the world cheats on their income taxes; they pay theirs because the law says they should.

3.16
Heavy traffic is moving on an interstate highway at a speed limit of 65. A sign appears that says "Speed Limit 55." The flow of traffic continues as before. How might a driver at Stage 3 and a driver at Stage 4 react? Explain each driver's reasoning.

Level III: Postconventional Ethics

A person reasoning at Level III has transcended both the individual and societal levels and makes moral decisions based on principles. People operating at this level, also called *principled morality,* follow rules but also see that at times rules need to be changed or ignored. Only a small portion of the population attains this level, and most don't reach it until their middle to late 20s.

Some of the great figures in history have sacrificed their lives in the name of principle. Sir Thomas More, who knew that he was, in effect, ending his own life by refusing to acknowledge King Henry VIII as the head of the Church of England, nevertheless stood on a principle. Mohandas K. Gandhi chose jail rather than adhere to England's laws as he applied the principle of nonviolent noncooperation; his work, as well, ultimately led to his death.

Stage 5: Social Contract.   In the **social contract stage,** *people make moral decisions based on socially agreed-upon rules.* A person reasoning at Stage 5 believes that a society of rational people needs such rules in order to function. The laws are not accepted blindly or for their own sake; rather, laws are based on the principle of utility, or "the greatest good for the greatest number," and are followed because people believe in principles such as liberty and the dignity of the individual.

Stage 5 is the official ethic of the United States. The constitutional Bill of Rights is an example of a cultural social contract; for example, Americans agree in principle that people have the right to free speech (the First Amendment to the Constitution), and the legal profession is conceptually committed to interpreting the laws in this light. In addition, the American legal system has provisions for changing or amending laws when new values or conditions warrant it. A person reasoning at Stage 5 would say that Steve's cheating is wrong because teachers and learners agree in principle that grades should reflect achievement. Cheating violates the agreement.

3.17
Describe the reasoning of a person at Stage 5 in responding to the problem of people cheating on their income taxes.

Stage 6: Universal Principles.   At the **universal principles stage,** *the individual's moral reasoning is based on abstract and general principles that are independent of society's laws and rules.* People at this stage define rightness in terms of internalized universal standards that go beyond concrete laws. "The Golden Rule" is a commonly cited example. Because very few people operate at this stage, and questions have been raised about the existence of "universal" principles, Kohlberg de-emphasized this stage in his later writings (Kohlberg, 1984).

Putting Kohlberg's Theory Into Perspective

As with most theories, Kohlberg's has both proponents and critics. Next we examine research that has investigated the theory and look at some of the most common criticisms of his work.

Research on Kohlberg's Theory. Kohlberg's work has been widely researched, and this research has led to the following conclusions (Berk, 2001; McDevitt & Ormrod, 2002):

- Every person's moral reasoning passes through the same stages in the same order.
- People pass through the stages at different rates.
- Development is gradual and continuous, rather than sudden and discrete.
- Once a stage is attained, a person tends to reason at that stage rather than regressing to a lower stage.
- Intervention usually advances a person only to the next higher stage of moral reasoning.

These results are generally consistent with what Kohlberg's theory would predict. Despite this research support, however, there have been questions and criticisms of his work.

Criticisms of Kohlberg's Theory. Kohlberg's work has been criticized on several grounds. First, people's thinking, while tending to be at a certain stage, will show evidence of reasoning at other stages. Also, although Stages 1–4 appear in most cultural groups, postconventional reasoning isn't seen in all cultures, suggesting that Kohlberg's theory is biased in favor of Western thinking (Snary, 1995; Vine, 1986). In describing Stage 5, for example, we used the phrase "principles such as liberty and the dignity of the individual." The "dignity of the individual" certainly reflects Western values. Other cultures, such as the Amish and Native Americans, de-emphasize individuality, placing greater value on cooperation. A person from a more group-oriented culture might respond to the cheating dilemma by saying, "He shouldn't have been placed in a situation like that. Other people should be helping him." Teachers should be sensitive to interpretations of morality that people from different cultures bring with them.

Also, people's moral reasoning depends on context (Rest, Narvaez, Bebeau, & Thoma, 1999). For example, people are much more likely to believe that breaking a traffic law isn't immoral if it causes no one harm. They may consider driving faster than the speed limit on an interstate to be okay but object to passing a parked school bus whose stop sign is out.

Researchers have also found that young children's thinking about morality is more advanced than Kohlberg predicted. For instance, 6-year-olds commonly believe, without being told by authority figures, that behaviors that are harmful or unfair to others are inherently wrong (Laupa & Turiel, 1995; Tisak, 1993). In addition, children as young as 3 can differentiate between **social conventions**, *the rules and expectations of a particular group or society,* and true moral issues. For instance, it's rude to interrupt while someone else is talking, but it isn't morally wrong. (It is, in fact, perfectly acceptable in some societies. [Au, 1992].) Kohlberg's work doesn't differentiate between social conventions and true moral issues until the higher stages of moral reasoning (L. Walker & Pitts, 1998).

Although Kohlberg attempted to make his stages content free, research indicates that thinking about moral dilemmas, like problem solving in general, is influenced by domain-specific knowledge (Bebeau, Rest, & Narvaez, 1999; Bech, 1996). For example, a medical doctor asked to deliberate about an educational dilemma or a teacher asked to resolve a medical issue may be hampered by their lack of knowledge of the factors involved.

Kohlberg's data-gathering methods—interviews in which study participants describe their thinking—have also been questioned, with researchers arguing that self-reported explanations of thought processes have severe limitations. One author noted: "Using interview data assumes that participants can verbally explain the workings of their minds. In recent years, this assumption has been questioned, more and more" (Rest et al., 1999, p. 295).

Finally, Kohlberg's work has been criticized for focusing on moral *reasoning* instead of moral *behavior*. People may reason at one stage and behave at another. However, in support of a moral reasoning–moral behavior connection, Kohlberg (1975) found that only 15% of students reasoning at the postconventional level cheated when given the opportunity to do so, but 55% of conventional thinkers and 70% of preconventional thinkers cheated. In addition, adolescents reasoning at the lower stages are likely to be less honest and to engage in more antisocial behavior, such as delinquency and drug use

---

3.18

All but one of the conclusions here are similar to Piaget's descriptions of cognitive development. Which one is different? Explain how it's different.

(Gregg, Gibbs, & Basinger, 1994). In contrast, reasoning at the higher stages is associated with altruistic behaviors, such as defending free speech, victims of injustice, and the rights of minorities (Berk, 2001; Kuther & Higgins-D'Alessandra, 1997). Moral reasoning and moral behavior are correlated.

Gender Differences: The Morality of Caring.   Some critics of Kohlberg's work also argue that it fails to adequately consider ways in which women and girls think about morality. Early research examining Kohlberg's theory identified differences in the ways men and women responded to moral dilemmas (Gilligan, 1982; Gilligan & Attanucci, 1988). Men were more likely to base their judgments on abstract concepts, such as justice, rules, individual rights, and obligations. Women, in contrast, were more likely to base their moral decisions on personal relationships, interpersonal connections, and attention to human needs.

These differences might suggest a lower stage of moral development for women (Holstein, 1976). Gilligan (1982) argued that the findings, instead, indicate an "ethic of care" in women that is not inferior; rather, Kohlberg's descriptions don't adequately represent the complexity of female thinking. Caring appears to be more central to females' sense of identity. In addition, when asked to identify moral dilemmas, females are more likely to choose real-world interpersonal problems than distant and abstract issues (Skoe & Dressner, 1994).

Gilligan (1977, 1982) suggests that a morality of caring proceeds through three stages. In the first stage, children are concerned primarily with their own needs. In the second, they show concern for others who are unable to care for themselves, such as infants and the elderly. In the third and final stage, they recognize the interdependent nature of personal relationships and extend compassion to all of humanity. To encourage this development, Gilligan recommends an engaging curriculum with opportunities for students to think and talk about moral issues involving caring (Goldberg, 2000).

More recent research on gender differences is mixed, with some studies finding differences and others not (Leon, Lynn, McLean, & Perri, 1997). Like cross-cultural studies, Gilligan's research reminds us of the complexity of the issues involved in moral development.

Finally, Kohlberg focused exclusively on the cognition of moral development—how people reason about moral issues. There is more to moral development, however, as we will see now.

3.19
According to Gilligan, how might a girl respond to the problem of the student not knowing his assignment (see the vignette on p. 101)? How might her response be different from that of a boy?

Emotional Factors in Moral Development

"Are you okay?" her mother asked as Melissa walked in the house after school.

"I feel really bad, Mom," Melissa answered softly. "We were working in a group, and Jessica said something sort of odd, and I said, 'That's dumb. Where did that come from?' . . . She didn't say anything for the rest of our group time. She doesn't get really good grades, and I know saying something about her being dumb really hurt her feelings. I didn't intend to do it. It just sort of fell out."

"I know you didn't intend to hurt her feelings, Sweetheart. Did you tell her you were sorry?"

"No, when I realized it, I just sat there like a lump. I know how I'd feel if someone made me feel dumb."

"Tell you what," her mom suggested. "Tomorrow, you go directly to her, tell her you're very sorry, and that it won't happen again."

"Thanks, Mom. I'll do it as soon as I see her. . . . I feel a lot better."

This vignette is about morality, but it doesn't involve moral reasoning; instead, it deals with emotions. For instance, Melissa felt both **shame,** *the painful emotion aroused when people recognize that they have failed to act or think in ways they believe are good,* and **guilt,** *the uncomfortable feeling people get when they know they've caused distress for someone else.* Hurting someone's feelings isn't good, and Melissa knew that she caused distress for Jessica. Although it's unpleasant, experiencing shame and guilt indicates that moral

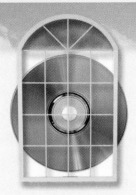

Using Technology in Your Study of Educational Psychology

Assessing Moral Thinking

You've studied Kohlberg's theory of moral development, and now, using the CD-ROM that accompanies this book, you can personally experience dilemmas similar to those that Kohlberg used to study and measure moral development. To complete the activity, do the following:

- Open the CD, and click on *Assessing Moral Development*.
- Complete the activities, and then answer the following questions.

1. Explain how each of the following could potentially influence responses to the different moral dilemmas.
   - The gender of the person involved
   - The focus of the dilemma (i.e., whether it involved a teacher and schooling or a life-saving drug)
   - Whether the decision was positive or negative

2. What do your responses to these questions tell you about assessing moral development?

3. In reacting to the moral dilemmas, did you always respond at the same stage? What does this tell you about assessing moral development?

4. What advantages and disadvantages are there in open-ended versus multiple-choice responses to moral dilemmas? Which would be most effective in assessing an individual's level of moral development? A group's?

---

development is advancing and future behaviors will improve. Most children feel shame and guilt by the middle elementary grades (Damon, 1988).

When Melissa said, "I know how I'd feel if someone made me feel dumb," she was also describing feelings of **empathy,** *the ability to experience the same emotion someone else is feeling.* By being concerned about Jessica's well-being, she showed *sympathy* for Jessica's feelings too. Melissa believed she hurt Jessica's feelings; however, empathy promotes moral and prosocial behavior even in the absence of wrongdoing (Damon, 1988; Eisenberg, 1982). When empathy and sympathy are combined, as they were with Melissa, moral and prosocial behaviors are even more likely (Turiel, 1998).

Empathy develops throughout the school years. In the primary grades, children's empathy tends to be directed primarily toward their friends, classmates, and family, but by late elementary school their empathy extends to more distant groups, such as those who have lost their homes in fires, or victims of accidents (Eisenberg, Carlo, Murphy, & Van Court, 1995).

As teachers, we have many opportunities to promote empathy and prosocial behaviors, such as cooperating, sharing, and comforting classmates who have been hurt. Apologizing to Jessica is another example of a prosocial act.

As we have seen from this discussion, moral development is complex, with both cognitive and emotional components. Kohlberg's work doesn't give a complete picture, but combined with other information about personal, social, and emotional development, it provides insights into the ways people think and feel about moral issues and situations. It also reminds us that moral reasoning and development aren't simply handed down from others. Rather, they result from an individual's own constructed beliefs. (We examine the processes involved in constructing understanding in Chapter 8.) This leads us to some issues involved in moral education.

3.20
To which of Kohlberg's stages are empathy and prosocial behaviors most closely related? Explain.

The Moral Education Versus Character Education Debate

Over the years, debate over the proper place of values and moral education in the curriculum has continued. At present, educational leaders generally agree that moral education is needed, but they disagree about the form it should take. This disagreement has become polarized, with character education at one extreme and moral education at the other (Bebeau et al., 1999; Wynne, 1997).

Character education *emphasizes the transmission of moral values, such as honesty and citizenship, and the translation of these values into character traits or behaviors* (Milson & Mehlig, 2001). This socialization approach to values emphasizes the internalization of societal values such as honesty and truthfulness through modeling and rewards and punishment. Instruction in character education emphasizes the study of values, practicing these values both in school and out, and rewarding displays of these values (Benninga & Wynne, 1998; Lickona, 1998).

Moral education, by contrast, *emphasizes the development of students' moral reasoning rather than the transmission of specified values.* Moral education uses moral dilemmas and classroom discussions to teach moral problem-solving skills and to bring about changes in the way learners think about moral issues.

These positions also differ in their views of learners' and teachers' roles. Character educators view learners as unsocialized at best, potentially evil at worst, and in need of moral guidance. The teacher is to serve as an advocate, explaining and modeling appropriate values and reinforcing learners for displaying desirable behaviors. Moral educators view learners as undeveloped, needing cognitive stimulation to construct better and more comprehensive moral perspectives (Bebeau et al., 1999). A teacher using a moral education approach acts as a problem poser and facilitator, helping students grapple with complex moral problems. These differences are summarized in Table 3.5.

Critics of character education argue that it emphasizes indoctrination instead of education, it ignores the issue of transfer to new situations, and its theoretical underpinnings focus on behavior instead of learner thinking (Kohn, 1997, 1998). Critics of moral education assert that it has a relativistic view of morals that offers no right or wrong answers, and they further criticize the use of hypothetical and decontextualized dilemmas that are removed from real classroom life (Wynne, 1997).

Perhaps the greatest strength of the character education perspective is its willingness to identify and promote core values. For instance, honesty, caring, and respect for others should undergird the way we structure our classrooms, interact with students, and expect them to treat one another. On the other hand, emphasizing student thinking and decision making is important as well, and this is the focus of the moral education perspective.

Table 3.5 A comparison of character and moral education

	Character Education	Moral Education
Goals	Transmission of moral values	Development of moral reasoning capacities
	Translation of values into behavior	Decision making about moral issues
Instruction	Reading about and analyzing values	Moral dilemmas serve as the focus for problem solving
	Practicing and rewarding good values	Discussions provide opportunities to share moral perspectives and analyze others
Role of Teacher	Lecturer/advocate Role model	Problem poser Facilitator
View of Learner	Unsocialized citizen of the community needing moral direction and guidance	Undeveloped Uses information to construct increasingly complex moral structures

Promoting Moral Development: Instructional Strategies

Teachers can be important influences on their students' moral development, both in the kinds of classroom environments they create and in the ways they interact with their students and guide students' interactions with one another. As teachers work to promote their students' moral development, the following principles can help guide their efforts:

- Model ethical thinking, behavior, and empathy in your interactions with students.
- Use classroom management as a vehicle for promoting moral development.
- Encourage students to respect the perspectives of others.
- Use moral dilemmas as concrete reference points for discussions of moral issues.
- Encourage students to articulate and justify their moral positions in discussions.

Let's see how the principles guide Rod Leist, a fifth-grade teacher, as he works with his students.

Discussing moral dilemmas provides students opportunities to analyze and evaluate their own moral views.

Rod began language arts by saying, "We've been reading an interesting story, and now I'd like to focus on a particular part of it. Let's talk a bit about Chris, the boy in the story who found the wallet. Chris was essentially broke, so would it be wrong for him to keep it, and the money in it? . . . Okay, I see a lot of heads nodding. . . . Why? . . . Jolene?"

"Because it didn't belong to him."

"Ray?"

"Why not keep it? It wasn't his fault—"

"That's terrible," Helena interrupted. "How would you like it if you lost your wallet?"

"Helena," Rod admonished, "remember we agreed that in discussions we would let everyone finish their point before we speak. We have a right to disagree with any point, but we're also responsible for our own behavior—in this case, listening to a different point of view and waiting until the person is finished."

"I'm sorry for breaking in. . . . Please finish your point, Ray," Rod added.

"I was saying it wasn't his fault that the person lost it. He didn't do anything. . . . The person shouldn't have dropped it in the first place, and he was broke."

"Okay, Helena, go ahead," Rod said.

". . . How would you feel if you lost something and somebody else kept it? Pretty bad, I think. . . . That's why I think you should give it back."

"That's an interesting point, Helena. It's good for us to try to put ourselves in someone else's shoes," Rod commented. "Of course we would all feel badly if we lost something and it wasn't returned.

"Go ahead, . . . Juan?"

"I agree. It was a lot of money, and Chris's parents would probably make him give it back anyway."

"And what if the person who lost the money really needed it?" Kristina added.

They continued the discussion for another 15 minutes, then Rod said, "These are all good points. . . . Okay, here's what we're going to do. I want each of you to write a short paragraph telling whether you would keep the wallet. If you say yes, explain why you feel it would be right or fair to keep it, and if you say no, explain why you feel it would be wrong to keep it. . . . Then, we'll discuss your reasons some more tomorrow."

Let's take at a closer look at Rod's attempts to promote moral development. To begin, Rod applied our first principle by modeling ethical thinking, behavior, and empathy in his interactions with his students. His simple and brief apology for interrupting the discussion communicated that he obeyed the same rules he expected his students to follow. Also, in saying, "That's an interesting point, Helena. It's good

3.21
Rod's approach included aspects of both character education and moral education. Identify an example from the case study of each.

for us to try to put ourselves in someone else's shoes. Of course we would all feel badly if we lost something and it wasn't returned," he reinforced Helena for being empathic and modeled his own empathy and prosocial behavior.

Efforts to be fair, responsible, and democratic in dealings with students speak volumes about teachers' values and views of morality. Interestingly, research indicates that teachers who reason at the higher stages of Kohlberg's system are more democratic and promote moral development to a greater extent than those reasoning at lower levels (Strom, 1989).

Rod's management system and his response to Helena show his application of our second and third principles. When he stopped Helena to remind her of the class agreement about interrupting and disagreeing with others, he was implementing a feature of his management system to help his students understand fairness, open-mindedness, cooperation, and tolerance for differing opinions. Acquiring this understanding is an important part of self-regulation, which can be developed only if students understand rules, understand why they are important, and agree to follow them (Brantlinger, Morton, & Washburn, 1999).

This kind of learning environment promotes *autonomous morality,* and research supports this approach (Berk, 2001; Boyes & Allen, 1993). In contrast, in an environment where punishment or the threat of punishment is emphasized—a form of *external morality*—students will obey rules but will not improve their self-regulation.

Applying the fourth principle, Rod used the story of the lost wallet as a concrete example that served as a focus for the discussion. And finally, during the discussion and in the writing exercise that followed it, Rod encouraged students to articulate and justify their moral positions on the issue.

Research supports an interactive approach to dealing with topics involving morality. Moral development can be enhanced through classroom discussions that encourage students to examine their own moral thinking and compare it to others' (Kuther & Higgins-D'Alessandra, 1997; Thoma & Rest, 1996). Peer interaction encourages active listening and analysis of different and more complex ways of reasoning about moral issues (Kruger, 1992). And being exposed to more sophisticated thinking can disrupt a person's equilibrium and promote development (Pyryt & Mendaglio, 2001).

Facilitating moral development is complex, however (Narvaez, 1998; Thoma & Rest, 1996). If learners are exposed to moral reasoning too far beyond their present levels, they have trouble connecting the positions to their existing background knowledge, and development doesn't occur. The ideal is one stage beyond learners' present reasoning. Thinking reflecting *interpersonal harmony,* for example, would be effective for students presently reasoning at the stage of *market exchange.* This finding underscores the relationship between cognitive and moral reasoning (Pyryt & Mendaglio, 2001).

The study of moral development also reminds us that much of what teachers do is grounded in moral decisions. When teachers emphasize student responsibility, make rules that prevent them from ridiculing each other, emphasize industry, and advocate honesty, they are teaching about morality. Laws that apply to schools also promote these values. For example, Public Law 94–142, which requires that students with learning exceptionalities be placed in the least restrictive environment possible, is based on an ethical issue: It is not fair to deny a student with an exceptionality access to the mainstream learning environment. (We examine PL 94–142 in detail in Chapter 5.)

Arguments that schools shouldn't teach morals are naive. Values are involved every time a teacher emphasizes one topic over another, and morals reflect the values of individuals as well as cultural groups. A more realistic approach is to become as knowledgeable as possible about the central role that values play in education and how teachers as well as schools can promote moral development. This increases teacher professionalism by providing the background that helps them make informed decisions.

3.22
Explain why teachers reasoning at higher levels would likely be more democratic and involve students more in classroom discussions than teachers reasoning at lower levels.

3.23
Using Piaget's theory, predict the stage of cognitive development a learner must reach to reason at the conventional level. What stage of cognitive development would be required for postconventional reasoning?

3.24
Write a specific statement describing how you would respond to parents who strongly express the opinion that the teaching of morals belongs in the home and that teachers should not deal with the subject.

Classroom Connections

Promoting Moral Development in Your Classroom

1. Openly discuss ethical dilemmas when they arise.
   - *Elementary:* The day before a new student with an exceptionality joins the class, a second-grade teacher invites students to discuss how they would feel if they were new, how new students should be treated, and how they should treat one another in general.
   - *Middle School:* A seventh-grade math teacher has a classroom rule that students may not laugh, snicker, or make remarks of any kind when a classmate is trying to answer a question. In introducing the rule, she has the students discuss the reasons for it and the importance of the rule from other students' perspectives.
   - *High School:* A high school teacher's students view cheating as a game, seeing what they can get away with. The teacher addresses the issue by saying, "Because you feel this way about cheating, I'm going to decide who gets what grade without a test. I'll grade you on how smart I think you are." This

provocative statement precipitates a classroom discussion on fairness and cheating.

2. Model moral and ethical behavior for your students.
   - *Elementary:* In November, fifth-grade students jokingly ask if the teacher votes. The teacher uses this as an opportunity to discuss the importance of voting and each person's responsibilities in a democracy such as ours.
   - *Middle School:* A science teacher makes a commitment to students to have all their tests and quizzes graded by the following day. One day he is asked if he has the tests ready. "Of course," he responds. "I made an agreement at the beginning of the year, and people can't go back on their agreements."
   - *High School:* A group of tenth-grade business education students finishes a field trip sooner than expected. "If we just hang around a little longer, we don't have to go back to school," someone comments. "Yes, but that would be a lie, wouldn't it?" the teacher counters. "We said we'd be back as soon as we finished, and we need to keep our word."

Summary

Personal Development

Personal development is influenced by heredity, parents and other adults, and peers. Parents can positively influence development by providing a structured environment that is both demanding and responsive to children's individual needs. Peers affect development by providing opportunities for social skill development and by influencing the formation of values and attitudes.

Social Development

Social development influences children's ability to make and interact with friends and their ability to learn cooperatively in school. Perspective taking allows students to consider problems and issues from others' points of view. Social problem solving includes the ability to read social cues, generate strategies, and implement and evaluate these strategies.

Integrating Personal, Emotional, and Social Development: Erikson's Theory

Erikson's psychosocial theory, an effort to integrate personal and social development, is based on the assumption that development of self is a response to needs. Development occurs in stages, each marked by a psychosocial challenge called a crisis. As people develop, the challenges change.

According to Erikson, positive resolution of the crisis in each stage results in an inclination to be trusting, autonomous, willing to take initiative, and industrious, from the period of birth through approximately the elementary school years. Continued resolution of crises leaves people with a firm identity, the ability to achieve intimacy, desire for generativity, and finally, a sense of integrity as life's end nears. As teachers work with students, they should keep these developmental challenges in mind and structure their classrooms and interactions with students to facilitate growth in these areas.

The Development of Identity and Self-Concept

The development of identity, in contrast with Erikson's predictions, usually occurs during high school and beyond. Students may take on temporary identities, which are reflected in rigid conformity to styles of dress and other fads. Identity moratorium and identity achievement are healthy states; identity diffusion and identity moratorium are less healthy.

Self-concept, developed largely through personal experiences, describes people's cognitive assessments of their physical, social, and academic competence. Academic self-concept, particularly in specific content areas, is correlated with achievement, but achievement and physical and social self-concepts are essentially unrelated.

Attempts to improve students' self-concepts by direct intervention have been largely unsuccessful. In contrast, attempts to improve self-concept as an outcome of increased success and achievement have been quite successful. This suggests that when teachers direct their efforts toward improving students' effort and achievement, self-concept will improve as well.

Development of Morality, Social Responsibility, and Self-Control

Piaget is identified with cognitive development, but he studied moral development as well. He suggested that individuals progress from the stage of external morality, where rules are enforced by authority figures, to the stage of autonomous morality, where individuals see morality as rational and reciprocal.

Lawrence Kohlberg's theory of moral development was influenced by Piaget's work. Kohlberg presented people with moral dilemmas—problems requiring moral decisions—and, on the basis of their responses to the dilemmas, developed a classification system for describing moral reasoning. At the preconventional level, people make egocentric moral decisions; at the conventional level, moral reasoning focuses on the consequences for others; and at the postconventional level, moral reasoning is based on principle. Kohlberg suggested that these stages of moral development were cross-cultural and that moral development influences moral behavior.

The experience of the unpleasant emotions shame and guilt and the development of empathy mark advances in the emotional component of moral development.

Character education advocates emphasize the study, practice, and reinforcement of moral values. In contrast, moral education proponents emphasize the development of moral reasoning and students' thinking about moral issues.

Teachers can promote moral development in their classrooms by emphasizing personal responsibility and the functional nature of rules designed to protect the rights of others. Students should be encouraged to think about topics such as honesty, respect for others, and basic principles of human conduct. As teachers interact with students, they should recognize the powerful influence they have in influencing the moral development of their students.

Windows on Classrooms

As you've studied this chapter, you've seen how developmental factors influence ways students feel about themselves and the ways they learn. You've seen how environments that combine structure with opportunities for autonomy and decision making and teachers who are sensitive to their students promote personal, social, and emotional development.

Let's look now at a teacher working with a group of middle school students. Read the case study, and answer the questions that follow. As you read, compare the teacher's approach to the suggestions you've studied in the chapter.

"Gee, this is frustrating," Helen Sharman, a seventh-grade teacher, mumbled as she was scoring a set of quizzes in the teachers' workroom after school.

"What's up?" her friend Natasha asked.

"Look," Helen directed, pointing to item 6 on the quiz. A student had edited a sentence like so:

Their's were the first items to be loaded.

"These students just won't think," Helen continued. "Three quarters of them put an apostrophe between the *r* and the *s* in *theirs*. The quiz was on using apostrophes in possessives. I warned them I was going to put some questions on the quiz that would make them think and that some of them would have trouble if they weren't on their toes. I should have saved my breath. . . . Not only that, but I had given them practice problems that were just like those on the quiz. We had one almost exactly like item 6, and they still missed it. . . . And I explained it so carefully," she mumbled, shaking her head.

Helen returned to scoring her papers.

A little later, Natasha asked, "Getting any better?"

"No," Helen said firmly. "Maybe worse."

"What are you going to do?"

"What's really discouraging is that some of the students won't even try. Look at this one. Half of the quiz is blank. This isn't the first time Kim has done this either. When I confronted him about it last time, he said, 'But I'm no good at English.' I replied, 'But you're doing fine in science and math.' He thought about that for a while and said, 'But that's different.' I wish I knew how to motivate him. You should see him on the basketball floor—poetry in motion—but when he gets in here, nothing."

"That can be discouraging. I've got a few like that myself," Natasha replied empathically.

"What's worse, I'm almost sure some of the kids cheated. I left the room to go to the office, and when I returned, several of them were talking and had guilt written all over their faces."

"Why do you suppose they did it?" Natasha returned.

"I'm not sure—part of it might be grade pressure. I grade on the curve, and they complain like crazy, but how else am I going to motivate them? Some just don't see any problem with cheating. If they don't get caught, fine. I really am discouraged."

"Well," Natasha shrugged, "hang in there."

The next morning, Helen returned the quizzes.

"We need to review the rules again," she commented as she finished. "You did so poorly on the quiz, and I explained everything so carefully. You must not have studied very hard."

"Let's take another look," she went on. "What's the rule for singular possessives?"

"Apostrophe *s*," Felice volunteered.

"That's right, Felice. Good. Now, how about plurals?"

"*S* apostrophe," Scott answered.

"All right. But what if the plural form of the noun doesn't end in *s*? . . . Russell?"

"Then it's like singular. . . . It's apostrophe *s*."

"Good. And how about pronouns?"

"You don't do anything," Connie put in.

"Yes, that's all correct," Helen nodded. "Why didn't you do that on the quiz?"

". . ."

"Okay, look at number 3 on the quiz."

It appeared as follows:

The books belonging to the lady were lost.

"It should be written like this," Helen explained, and she wrote *The lady's books were lost* on the chalkboard.

"Ms. Sharman," Nathan called from the back of the room. "Why is it apostrophe *s*?"

"Nathan," Helen said evenly. "Remember my first rule?"

"Yes, Ma'am," Nathan said quietly.

"Good. If you want to ask a question, what else can you do other than shout it out?"

"Raise my hand."

"Good. Now, to answer your question, it's singular. So that's why it's apostrophe *s*.

"Now look at number 6." Helen waited a few seconds and then continued, "You were supposed to correctly punctuate it. But it's correct already because *theirs* is already possessive. Now that one was a little tricky, but you know I'm going to put a few on each quiz to make you think. You'd have gotten it if you were on your toes."

Helen identified a few more items that were commonly missed and then handed out a review sheet.

"Now, these are just like the quiz," she said. " Practice hard on them, and we'll have another quiz on Thursday. Let's all do better. Please don't let me down again.

"And one more thing. I believe there was some cheating on this test. If I catch anyone cheating on Thursday, I'll tear up your quiz and give you a failing grade. Now go to work."

The students worked on the practice exercises as Helen walked among them, offering periodic suggestions.

Constructed Response Questions

In answering these questions, use information from the chapter and link your responses to specific information in the case.

1. How might Erikson explain Kim's behavior in Helen's class?
2. Using findings from the research on self-concept, explain Kim's behavior.
3. Using concepts from Kohlberg's theory, analyze Helen's cheating problem. From Kohlberg's perspective, how well did she handle this problem?
4. If you think Helen's teaching could have been improved on the basis of the information in Chapter 3, what suggestions would you make? Again, be specific.

Document-Based Analysis

Two students are presented with the moral dilemma involving Steve, the high school senior given an opportunity to cheat (see page 102). When asked if cheating would be justified, Student A replies, "No, because he'll get caught and kicked out." Student B replies, "No, because there are classroom and school rules against cheating."

At which of Kohlberg's stages of moral development is Student A? Provide evidence to document your answer. At which stage of development is Student B? Provide evidence to document your answer.

 PRAXIS These exercises are designed to help you prepare for the PRAXIS™ "Principles of Learning and Teaching" exam. To receive feedback on your constructed response questions and document analysis response, go to the Companion Website at *www.prenhall.com/eggen*, then to this chapter's *Practice for PRAXIS™* module. For additional connections between this text and the PRAXIS™ exam, go to Appendix A.

 **Online Portfolio Activities**

To develop your professional portfolio, further apply your understanding of chapter content, and address the INTASC standards, go the Companion Website, then to this chapter's *Online Portfolio Activities*. Complete the suggested activities.

 Also on the Companion Website at *www.prenhall.com/eggen*, you can measure your understanding of chapter content in *Practice Quiz* and *Essay* modules, apply concepts in *Online Cases*, and broaden your knowledge base with the *Additional Content* module and *Web Links* to other educational psychology websites.

Important Concepts

autonomous morality *(p. 102)*
character education *(p. 109)*
collective self-esteem *(p. 98)*
crisis *(p. 89)*
empathy *(p. 108)*
external morality *(p. 102)*
guilt *(p. 107)*
identity *(p. 93)*
internalization *(p. 102)*
interpersonal harmony stage *(p. 104)*
law and order stage *(p. 105)*
market exchange stage *(p. 104)*
moral dilemma *(p. 102)*
moral education *(p. 109)*

personal development *(p. 79)*
perspective taking *(p. 83)*
proactive aggression *(p. 84)*
punishment-obedience stage *(p. 103)*
self-concept *(p. 95)*
self-esteem *(p. 95)*
self-worth *(p. 95)*
shame *(p. 107)*
social conventions *(p. 106)*
social contract stage *(p. 105)*
social development *(p. 82)*
social problem solving *(p. 83)*
universal principles stage *(p. 105)*

Chapter Outline

Learner Differences

4

Tim Wilkinson was a fifth-grade teacher in a large urban elementary school. He had 29 students: 16 girls and 13 boys. His class included 10 African Americans, 3 students of Hispanic descent, and 2 Asian Americans. Most of his students came from low-income families.

Tim smiled as he watched his students bent over their desks busy with seat work. Walking among his students, he glanced at Selena's work. As usual, it was nearly perfect. Everything was easy for her, and she seemed to be a happy, well-adjusted child.

He grinned as he walked by Helen's desk. She was his "special project," and she had begun to blossom in response to his attention and effort. The quality of her work had improved dramatically since the beginning of the year.

As he stepped past Juan, Tim's glow turned to concern. Juan had been quiet from the first day of school, and he was easily offended by perceived slights from his classmates. Because his parents were migrant workers, the family moved constantly, and he had repeated the first grade. Now his parents were separated, and his mother had settled in this area so that the children could stay in the same school.

Juan had to struggle to keep up with the rest of the class. Spanish was his first language, and Tim wasn't sure how much of his directions and instruction Juan understood. What seemed certain, however, was that Juan was falling further and further behind, and Tim didn't know what to do. Not knowing where else to turn, he consulted Jeanne Morton, the school psychologist.

After talking with Tim and meeting with Juan, Jeanne contacted Juan's mother and suggested several tests. One was an individually administered intelligence test. On the basis of the tests, Jeanne eliminated aptitude as a potential source of Juan's problem. "Juan is definitely capable of doing better work," she commented to Tim. They agreed to meet again to consider other alternatives.

Imagine that you are entering your classroom for the first time. A sea of faces appears before you. In some ways, your students seem very much alike; they are nearly the same age, they have similar interests, and they study common subjects. A closer look, however, reveals many differences. You have both boys and girls in your classes, and their ethnic and cultural backgrounds differ. From your study of Chapters 2 and 3, you know that students develop at different rates. Learning is nearly effortless for some; others struggle with even basic ideas. A few have affluent parents; others' parents barely eke out a living. Unfortunately, combinations of these factors put some students at risk of not being able to fully benefit from the educational system.

Suddenly, the sea of faces turns into 30 individuals! In this chapter, we examine differences among learners and their implications for our teaching.

After you've completed your study of this chapter, you should be able to

- Explain how different views of intelligence influence teaching
- Define socioeconomic status and explain how it may affect school performance
- Explain the role culture plays in learning
- Describe the influence of gender on different aspects of school success
- Describe ways that schools and classrooms can be adapted to meet the needs of students placed at risk

In a perfect world, learning would come easily to all students, and teaching would be a continuous pleasure. Teachers know, however, that students vary in ability and in other important ways, as did Selena and Juan in our opening case study. Figure 4.1 illustrates some of the sources of individuality.

Intelligence

All of us, including teachers, have an intuitive notion of intelligence; it's how "sharp" people are, or how much they know, how quickly and easily they learn, and how perceptive and sensitive they are. We react to people, and teachers respond to students, based on these intuitions. But how accurate are they? We examine this and other questions about intelligence in the next section.

Intelligence: What Does It Mean?

Experts define **intelligence** as having three dimensions: *(a) the ability to acquire knowledge, (b) the capacity to think and reason in the abstract, and (c) the ability to solve novel problems* (Snyderman & Rothman, 1987; Sternberg, 1986). Some learning theorists equate a student's ability to acquire knowledge—also called *aptitude*—with the time and quality of instruction the student needs to master a subject (Bloom, 1981; Carrol, 1963). In this view, learners with high aptitude need less time and instruction than those whose aptitude is lower. By noticing that Juan was falling further and further behind, Tim was intuitively reacting to this dimension.

Figure 4.1 Sources of learner individuality

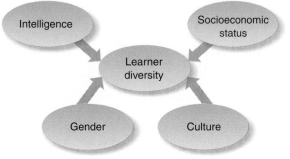

From another perspective, intelligence is simply defined as the attributes that intelligence tests measure. Items like the following are commonly found on these tests, and people's intelligence is inferred from their test performance.

1. Cave:Hole::Bag: _____ (Cave is to hole as bag is to _____?)
   a. paper   b. container   c. box   d. brown
2. Sharon had x amount of money, and this could buy 8 apples. How much money would it take to buy 4 apples?
   a. 8x   b. 2x   c. x/2   d. x^2
3. Inspect the following list of numbers for 5 seconds:
   9 7 4 6 2 1 8 3 9
   Now cover them and name the digits in order from memory.

When we examine these items, it becomes clear that experience is an important factor in test performance (Halpern & LaMay, 2000; Perkins, 1995). Practice with vocabulary and analogies, for example, would improve the score on the first item. The second requires background in math, and even the third, a seemingly simple memory task, can be improved with training (A. Brown, Bransford, Ferrara, & Campione, 1983).

The finding that experience affects intelligence test performance corroborates Piaget's work. In Chapter 2, we saw that experience is an important factor in cognitive development, and children who have the advantage of rich experiences consistently perform better than their less-experienced peers. Clearly, intelligence tests measure more than innate ability.

4.1
How does experience influence a person's aptitude, or "ability to acquire knowledge"? Explain your answer with a specific example.

Intelligence: One Trait or Many?

Because scores on different measures of intelligence, such as verbal ability and abstract reasoning, were highly correlated (a learner scored similarly high or low for all measures), early researchers believed intelligence to be a single trait. For example, Charles Spearman (1927) described it as "g," or general intelligence. Since then theorists have expanded the concept and proposed more specific kinds of intelligence, such as verbal, mathematical, spatial, and perceptual (Jensen, 1987). Several contemporary theories have elaborated on the idea that intelligence is composed of several abilities (Woodcock, 1995). Next we look at two of these theories: Gardner's theory of multiple intelligences and Sternberg's triarchic theory of intelligence.

4.2
If intelligence is a single trait, how might you expect students to perform in different domains or content areas? Does your own performance in different content areas support this single trait view?

Gardner's Theory of Multiple Intelligences

Howard Gardner (1983, 1999b) analyzed people's performance in different domains and concluded that intelligence is not unitary but instead composed of eight relatively independent dimensions. Three observations inspired Gardner's argument (Krechevsky & Seidel, 1998):

1. Research on people with brain damage suggests that neural functioning is specific to a single domain, such as speech or athletic ability.

Spatial intelligence includes the ability to perceive and re-create physical relations in the world.

Bodily-kinesthetic intelligence allows dancers and athletes to use their bodies in effective and creative ways.

2. Most individuals perform unevenly on the variety of skills found in modern society. For example, many people display average ability in verbal or logical dimensions but excel in other areas, such as spatial ability (artists and architects) and interpersonal skills (effective counselors and salespeople).

3. Prodigies, savants, and some others exhibit exceptional talent in specific, isolated domains.

Gardner originally proposed seven intelligences but later added another, called "naturalist intelligence," which he has described as the ability to recognize patterns in nature; identify and classify plants, animals, and minerals; and apply this information in activities such as farming or landscaping. He is also considering a ninth dimension, called *existential intelligence,* which is evident in a person's ability to think about life's fundamental questions, such as "Who are we?" and "Where do we come from?" (Gardner, 1999c). Table 4.1 outlines the eight dimensions currently in his theory.

The concept of multiple intelligences makes intuitive sense. We all know people who don't seem particularly "sharp" analytically but who excel in getting along with others, for example. This ability serves them well, and in some instances, they're more successful than their "brighter" counterparts. Others are extraordinary athletes or accomplished musicians. Gardner would describe these people as high in interpersonal, bodily-kinesthetic, and musical intelligence, respectively.

Gardner's Theory: Applications and Criticisms.   Gardner (1999a) has recommended that teachers adapt instruction to address the different intelligences. Content should be represented in ways that capitalize on as many of the intelligences as possible, and efforts should also focus on helping students understand their strengths and weaknesses in each of the dimensions (Shearer, 2002). Table 4.2 outlines some possibilities. Gardner has warned, however, that not all ideas or subjects can be adapted for each intelligence: "There is no point in assuming that every topic can be effectively approached in [multiple] ways, and it is a waste of effort and time to attempt to do this" (Gardner, 1995b, p. 206).

Gardner's theory also has its critics. Some researchers caution that the theory and its applications have not been validated by research (Berk, 2003; Kail, 1998). Others disagree with the assertion that abilities in specific domains, such as naturalist or musical intelligence, truly qualify as separate forms of intelligence (Bracken, McCallum, & Shaughnessy, 1999).

4.3
On which of Gardner's eight intelligences does the typical school curriculum focus most strongly? On which report card— an elementary or a secondary— are more of the intelligences evaluated? Why is this the case?

Table 4.1 Gardner's theory of multiple intelligences

Dimension	Example
Linguistic Intelligence Sensitivity to the meaning and order of words and the varied uses of language	Poet, journalist
Logical-Mathematical Intelligence The ability to handle long chains of reasoning and to recognize patterns and order in the world	Scientist, mathematician
Musical Intelligence Sensitivity to pitch, melody, and tone	Composer, violinist
Spatial Intelligence The ability to perceive the visual world accurately and to re-create, transform, or modify aspects of the world on the basis of one's perceptions	Sculptor, navigator
Bodily-Kinesthetic Intelligence A fine-tuned ability to use the body and to handle objects	Dancer, athlete
Interpersonal Intelligence The ability to notice and make distinctions among others	Therapist, salesperson
Intrapersonal Intelligence Access to one's own "feeling life"	Self-aware individual
Naturalist Intelligence The ability to recognize similarities and differences in the physical world	Naturalist, biologist, anthropologist

Sources: Adapted from Gardner and Hatch (1989) and Chekley (1997).

Table 4.2 Instructional applications of Gardner's multiple intelligences

Dimension	Application
Linguistic	How can I get students to talk or write about the idea?
Logical-Mathematical	How can I bring in number, logic, and classification to encourage students to quantify or clarify the idea?
Spatial	What can I do to help students visualize, draw, or conceptualize the idea spatially?
Musical	How can I help students use environmental sounds, or set ideas into rhythm or melody?
Bodily-Kinesthetic	What can I do to help students involve the whole body or to use hands-on experience?
Interpersonal	How can peer, cross-age, or cooperative learning be used to help students develop their interactive skills?
Intrapersonal	How can I get students to think about their capacities and feelings to make them more aware of themselves as persons and learners?
Naturalist	How can I provide experiences that require students to classify different types of objects and analyze their classification schemes?

One of the strongest criticisms argues that Gardner's theory fails to account for the role a centralized working memory system plays in intelligent behavior (D. Lohman, 2001). Cognitive research suggests that the ability to maintain, organize, and coordinate information in working memory is essential to problem solving and other reasoning abilities. (We examine working memory in detail in Chapter 7.) For example, when students encounter word problems in math, they have to keep the specifics of the problems in mind as they search their memories for similar problems, select strategies, and then use specific values to solve the problems. This cognitive juggling act occurs in all types of intelligent behavior. Gardner's theory, because it views intelligence as consisting of separate dimensions, ignores the fact that all knowledge is processed in working memory (Lohman, 2001).

Sternberg's Triarchic Theory of Intelligence

Robert Sternberg (Sternberg, 1990; Sternberg & Grigorenko, 2000), another multitrait theorist, sees the ability to function effectively in the real world as an important indicator of intelligence, which he views as consisting of three cognitive parts: (a) processing components—skills used in problem solving, (b) contextual components—links between intelligence and the environment, and (c) experiential components—mechanisms for modifying intelligence through experience. These components and their features are illustrated in Figure 4.2 and discussed in the sections that follow.

Processing Components. The most basic parts of Sternberg's model are the processing components that learners use to think about and solve problems: a metacomponent, a knowledge acquisition component, and a performance component. Sternberg describes them as analogous to manager, trainee, and laborer in a company (Sternberg, 1988). For example, a student faced with the problem of writing a term paper uses the metacomponent (manager) to decide on a topic, plan the paper, and monitor progress as it's written. The knowledge acquisition component (trainee) gathers facts and combines them into related ideas, and the performance component (laboror) does the actual writing. The three work together to produce a final product.

4.4
Illustrate how the three processing components interact, using an example such as buying a car.

Contextual Components: Intelligence and the Environment. Contextual components explain how intelligent behavior involves adaptation. In reaching goals, intelligent people adapt to, change, or select out of the environment when necessary. For example, in an attempt to succeed in a college course, a student adjusts her study strategies in response to a professor's testing procedures (adapts). She can't clearly hear his presentations, so she moves to the front of the class (changes the environment). Despite these efforts, she isn't succeeding, so she drops the class (selects out of the environment). In each case, the student is aware of the effect the environment is having on her learning. Contextual components help us apply our intelligence to the solution of everyday, real-world problems.

4.5
Consider Sternberg's strategies for dealing with the environment— adapting to it, changing it, and selecting out of it. Which do schools emphasize the most? Which should they emphasize most? least?

Figure 4.2 Sternberg's triarchic model of intelligence

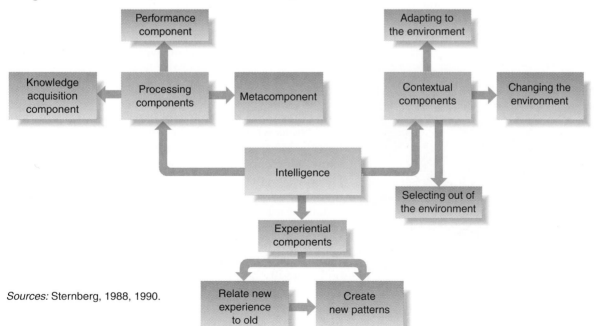

Sources: Sternberg, 1988, 1990.

Experiential Components: Adapting to Unique Experiences. The third arm of Sternberg's (1988, 1990) triarchic model of intelligence involves experience. In Sternberg's view, intelligent behavior includes (a) the ability to effectively deal with novel experiences and (b) the ability to solve familiar problems efficiently and automatically. An intelligent person relates new experiences to old and quickly identifies relationships. The following example shows these experiental components at work:

> A beginning reader encounters the word *she*. The teacher says, "Shheee."
> Then the reader encounters the word *show*. The teacher says, "This word sounds like 'Shho.'"
> Next, the student sees the word *ship*. He tries pronouncing it himself: "Shhip." He now has a rule to decode future words. When *s* and *h* are together, they go "shh."

According to Sternberg, an intelligent child readily recognizes patterns and soon can use rules automatically. The ability to see patterns in information increases with age and makes older children more efficient problem solvers. It is a cornerstone of increased intellectual functioning (Sternberg, 1998a, 1998b).

Improving Intelligence. Because the ability to deal with novel experiences is an indicator of intelligent behavior, Sternberg believes that practice in relating new to existing ideas should improve intelligence (Sternberg, 1998a). For example, if the ability to solve analogies is an indicator of intelligence (and measurable on tests), then practice with analogies would improve intelligence test performance.

In more recent work, Sternberg has extended the idea of improving intelligence by emphasizing three different kinds of thinking: *analytic,* which involves comparing, contrasting, critiquing, judging, and evaluating; *creative,* which includes inventing, discovering, imagining, and supposing; and *practical,* which involves implementing, applying, using, and seeking relevance in ideas (Sternberg, 1998a, 1998b; Sternberg, Torff, & Grigorenko, 1998a, 1998b). Practicing these different ways of thinking, Sternberg argues, allows students to process information in different ways and capitalize on individual strengths (Sternberg et al., 1998a, 1998b; Sternberg, Grigorenko, & Jarvin, 2001). Applications of these different ways of thinking are illustrated in Table 4.3 (Sternberg, 1998a, 1998b).

4.6
Identify at least two ways in which Sternberg's and Piaget's (see Chapter 2) theories are similar. Identify an important implication that these similarities have for schools.

4.7
Identify at least one similarity and one difference between Sternberg's analytic, creative, and practical intelligence and Gardner's multiple intelligences.

Intelligence: Nature Versus Nurture

No aspect of intelligence has been more hotly debated than the issue of heredity versus environment. The extreme **nature view** *asserts that intelligence is solely determined by genetics;* the **nurture view** *emphasizes the influence of the environment.* Differences between these positions are very controversial when race or ethnicity are considered. For example, research indicates that some cultural minority groups, especially African American and Hispanic, collectively score lower on intelligence tests than American White children (McLoyd, 1998).

People who support the nurture view explain this finding by arguing that minority children have fewer stimulating experiences while they are developing. People adhering to the nature view argue that heredity is the more important factor (Jensen, 1998). (A third explanation is that the intelligence tests themselves are faulty and may not truly measure intelligence, a topic we explore shortly.)

Most experts take a position somewhere in the middle, believing that a person's intelligence is influenced by both heredity and the environment (Petrill & Wilkerson, 2000; Shepard, 2001). This view holds that a person's genes provide the potential for intelligence, and stimulating environments make the most of the raw material.

Intelligence can be enhanced by learning activities that emphasize abstract reasoning and problem solving.

Table 4.3 Applying analytic, creative, and practical thinking in different content areas

Content Area	Analytic	Creative	Practical
Math	Express the number 44 in base 2.	Write a test question that measures understanding of the Pythagorean theorem.	How might geometry be useful in the construction area?
Language Arts	Why is *Romeo and Juliet* considered a tragedy?	Write an alternative ending to *Romeo and Juliet* to make it a comedy.	Write a TV ad for the school's production of *Romeo and Juliet*.
Social Studies	In what ways were the Korean War and the Vietnam War similar and different?	In hindsight, what could the United States have done differently in these two wars?	What lessons can we take away from these two wars?
Art	Compare and contrast the artistic styles of Van Gogh and Monet.	What would the Statue of Liberty look like if it were created by Picasso?	Create a poster for the student art show using the style of one of the artists studied.

Unfortunately, most learning environments do not provide enough stimulation to allow people to reach their full potential. For example, researchers tracked children born to low-income parents but adopted as infants into high-income families. The children exposed to enriched environments in high-income households scored an average of 14 points higher on intelligence tests than did siblings who remained in low-income households (Schiff, Duyme, Dumaret, & Tomkiewicz, 1982). School experiences also produce consistent gains in intelligence test (IQ) scores (Ceci & Williams, 1997).

Intelligence also changes over time. One review found IQ changes of 28 points from early childhood to adolescence; one seventh of the students had changes of more than 40 points (McCall, Appelbaum, & Hogarty, 1973). Although some testing error is likely, in many cases intelligence itself was probably altered because of changes in an individual's environment and others' expectations (Perkins, 1995).

Efforts to improve intelligence have also been fruitful. Attempts to directly teach the cognitive skills tapped by intelligence tests have been successful with preschool and elementary students (Sprigle & Schoefer, 1985), adults (Whimbey, 1980), and students with learning disabilities (A. Brown & Campione, 1986). A longitudinal study of disadvantaged, inner-city children also indicated that early stimulation can have lasting effects on intelligence (Garber, 1988).

4.8
Describe specifically the kinds of experiences children—and particularly disadvantaged children—need to increase their scores on intelligence tests.

Assessment and Learning: Cultural Controversies in Measuring Intelligence

As we just saw, experts disagree about the relative contributions of genetics and the environment on intelligence. The question of whether or not existing tests accurately measure intelligence for some cultural minorities is also controversial. For example, African American and Hispanic American students collectively score about 15 points lower on intelligence tests than other segments of the population (Valencia & Suzuki, 2001). Critics point to the tests themselves, contending that, because of their design, they often fail to accurately measure the intelligence of these students. This problem can have serious consequences: African American and Hispanic students are proportionally overrepresented in special education classes and underrepresented in programs for the gifted and talented (Hardman, Drew, & Egan, 2001).

Cultural bias *occurs when one or more items on a test penalize students of a particular ethnic or cultural background.* For example, a student may miss a word problem, not because he can't do the math, but because the scenario described is strange and unfamiliar to members of his cultural group. A number of factors—such as language, opportunities to learn the knowledge and skills measured by the test, and motivation—can influence intelligence test performance (Linn & Gronlund, 2000). For example, language is likely a factor for many Hispanic students, for whom English is a second language, whereas opportunities to learn knowledge and skills may affect African American learners, many of whom attend sub par, segregated schools (Valencia & Suzuki, 2001).

In response to these problems, test designers have attempted to construct culture-fair tests that eliminate or minimize culturally influenced factors (Linn & Gronlund, 2000). Typical strategies to accomplish these goals include

- Using test materials that are primarily nonverbal and include diagrams or pictures familiar to the cultural groups being tested
- Including motivating materials and methods to encourage optimal test performance
- Providing liberal time limits to de-emphasize speed as a factor

The most widely used intelligence tests developed to address cultural bias issues are the Kaufman Assessment Battery for Children (K-ABC) and the Universal Nonverbal Intelligence Test (UNIT) (Valencia & Suzuki, 2001). Several items from the UNIT illustrate how these tests attempt to bypass or minimize language. In one, the examinee uses paper and pencil to navigate increasingly complex mazes. Another measures analogic reasoning with pictures instead of written words. For example, when shown pictures of a canoe and an airplane, and then pictures of an airplane propellor, an airplane wing, a parachute, and an airplane wheel, the examinee is asked to identify the one analogous to a canoe paddle. Ethnic group differences on the UNIT are considerably smaller than differences seen on more traditional, language-based tests, but cultural group differences still persist (McCallum, 1999; Valencia & Suzuki, 2001).

How should teachers respond when examining and using intelligence test scores? We offer two suggestions. First, remember that intelligence test scores are only one measure of academic performance. Quizzes, tests, written work, and responses in class must all be considered to get a complete picture of student potential. Second, don't allow students' scores to unduly influence your expectations.

For example:

Cal, a 10th grader, had been doing well on his essays in English, getting a mix of B's and A's. He recently took the PSAT (Preliminary Scholastic Aptitude Test, commonly given to 10th graders), and his scores were near the median for all students taking the test. Since that time, Cal has been getting mostly C's on his essays, in spite of increasing his effort and talking to Mrs. Vines, his teacher, about what he can do to improve.

It is highly unlikely that the quality of Cal's writing suddenly declined. It is much more likely that because his PSAT score suggested he was an "average" student, Mrs. Vines began to think of him as "average" and scored his essays in ways that corroborated her expectations.

Teachers (perhaps Mrs. Vines) may not realize that they hold lowered expectations for some of their students and may even react badly to such a suggestion. No one wants to be accused of discriminatory practices, and a teacher may be especially defensive if the students being discussed are members of cultural minorities.

The following are some ways teachers can maintain appropriate expectations for all students:

- Treat all of your students as equally as possible. Be aware of both your verbal and nonverbal behavior.
- Use high-quality examples and other representations of content to compensate for differences in background knowledge.
- Assess your students thoroughly and often, and use assessment primarily as a learning tool.
- Keep assessment results confidential, and encourage your students to do the same.
- Provide detailed feedback on all assessments so students can use them as learning opportunities.

(We discuss assessment in every chapter, and we examine assessment practices in detail in Chapters 14 and 15.)

Ability Grouping

Although other adaptations exist (we discuss them in Chapter 5), the most common way schools respond to differences in learner ability is by **ability grouping,** *the process of placing students of similar abilities together and attempting to match instruction to the needs of different groups* (Lou, Abrami, & Spence, 2000). Because ability grouping is so common, yet controversial and politically charged, we examine it in this section.

Ability grouping in elementary schools typically exists in three forms, described and illustrated in Table 4.4. Most elementary teachers endorse ability grouping, particularly in reading and math.

The research on ability grouping reminds teachers of the need for positive expectations for all students.

In middle, junior high, and high schools, ability grouping goes further, with high-ability students studying advanced and college preparatory courses and lower ability students receiving vocational or work-related instruction (Kulik & Kulik, 1982). In some cases, students are grouped only in certain content areas, such as English or math; in other cases, ability grouping occurs across all content areas. The latter practice, called **tracking,** *places students in different classes or curricula on the basis of ability.* Some form of tracking exists in most middle, junior high, and high schools.

Ability Grouping: Research Results

Why is ability grouping so pervasive? Advocates argue that it enhances instruction by allowing teachers to adjust the instructional pace, methods, and materials to better meet students' needs. Because instruction is similar for a particular group, ability grouping is also easier for the teacher.

Critics counter these arguments and cite several problems with all forms of ability grouping:

Table 4.4 Types of ability grouping in elementary schools

Type	Description	Example
Between-class grouping	Divides students at a certain grade into levels, such as high, average, and low	A school with 75 third graders divides them into one class of high achievers, one of average achievers, and one of low achievers.
Within-class grouping	Divides students in a class into subgroups based on reading or math scores	A fourth-grade teacher has three reading groups based on reading ability.
Joplin plan	Regroups across grade levels	Teachers from different grade levels place students in the same reading class.

- Within-class grouping creates logistical problems, because different lessons and assignments are required, and monitoring students in different tasks is difficult (Good & Brophy, 2000; Oakes, 1992).
- Improper placements occur, and placement tends to become permanent. Students from cultural minorities are underrepresented in high-ability classes (Davenport et al., 1998; Mickelson & Heath, 1999; Oakes, 1992).
- Members of low groups are stigmatized, and their self-esteem and motivation declines (Hallinan, 1984).
- Homogeneously grouped low-ability students achieve less than heterogeneously grouped students of similar ability (Good & Brophy, 2000).

4.9

Explain how being placed in a low-ability group might adversely affect students' self-esteem and motivation.

The negative effects of grouping are related, in part, to the quality of instruction. Studies have found that presentations to low groups are more fragmented and vague than those to high groups; they focus more on memorizing than on understanding, problem solving, and "active learning." Students in low-ability classes are often taught by teachers who lack enthusiasm and stress conformity instead of autonomy and the development of self-regulation (Good & Brophy, 2000; S. Ross, Smith, Loks, & McNelie, 1994).

These differences affect students. Self-esteem and motivation to learn decrease, and absentee rates increase. One study found that absenteeism increased from 8% to 26% after one junior high adopted tracking (Slavin & Karweit, 1982), and most of the truants were students in low-level classes. Tracking can also result in racial or cultural segregation of students, negatively influencing social development and the ability to form friendships across cultural groups (Oakes, 1992).

Ability Grouping: Implications for Teachers

Suggestions for dealing with the problems of ability grouping vary. At one extreme, critics argue that its effects are so pernicious that the practice should be abolished completely:

> We suggest . . . that there is a fundamental conflict between the practice of ability grouping and public schools' avowed goal of providing equal opportunity to all students. More equitable alternatives must be sought, even if they involve major changes in classroom organization. (Grant & Rothenberg, 1986, p. 47)

A more moderate position suggests that grouping may be appropriate in some areas, such as reading and math, where learning is more hierarchical and sequential (Good & Brophy, 2000), but that every effort should be made to de-emphasize groups in other content areas. Researchers have found that use of the **Joplin plan**, which *uses homogeneous grouping in reading, combined with heterogeneous grouping in other areas*, can have positive effects on reading achievement without negative side effects (Slavin, 1987). At the junior and senior high levels, between-class grouping should be limited to the basic academic areas, with heterogeneous grouping in others.

When grouping is necessary, specific measures to reduce its negative effects should be taken. Summaries of some suggestions are presented in Figure 4.3. These suggestions are demanding; teachers must constantly monitor both the cognitive and affective progress of their students and make careful decisions about group placements. The need

Figure 4.3
Suggestions for reducing the negative effects of ability grouping

- Keep group composition flexible, and reassign students to other groups when their rate of learning warrants it.
- Make every effort to ensure that the quality of instruction is as high for low-ability students as it is for high-ability students.
- Treat student characteristics as dynamic rather than static; teach low-ability students appropriate learning strategies and behaviors.
- Avoid assigning negative labels to lower groups.
- Constantly be aware of the possible negative consequences of ability grouping.

to maintain high expectations and instructional flexibility in this process cannot be overemphasized (Bixby, 1997).

In addition, certain instructional adaptations may allow teachers to avoid tracking altogether and to reverse the negative effects of previous tracking (Nyberg, McMillin, O'Neill-Rood, & Florence, 1997; Tomlinson, Callahan, & Moon, 1998). Research suggests that teachers' attitudes about tracking, as well as their knowledge of alternate instructional strategies, can have powerful effects on their classroom practice (Tomlinson & Callahan, 2001). When teaching students whose backgrounds vary, effective teachers adapt their instruction by

- Giving students who need it more time to complete assignments
- Providing peer tutors for students requiring extra help
- Using small-group work to provide opportunities for students to help each other
- Breaking large assignments into smaller ones and providing additional scaffolding for those who need it
- Providing options on some assignments, such as giving students the choice of presenting a report orally or in writing

Effective teachers need to adapt instruction to meet the needs of all students, but this need is especially acute at the upper and lower extremes of the ability continuum (Tomlinson, 1995; Tomlinson et al., 1998).

Classroom Connections

Applying an Understanding of Ability Differences in Your Classroom

1. Use intelligence test scores cautiously when making educational decisions. Remember that they are only one indicator of ability.

   - *Elementary:* A first-grade teacher working in an inner-city school consults with the school psychologist in interpreting intelligence test scores. She reminds herself of the effect that language and experience can have on test performance.
   - *Middle School:* When making placement decisions, a middle school team relies on past classroom performance and grades, in addition to standardized test scores.
   - *High School:* In deciding whether to place a student in a special education class, a team of teachers and the guidance counselor consider grades, work samples, and teacher observations, in addition to intelligence test scores.

2. Use instructional strategies that maximize student interest and different abilities.

   - *Elementary:* In a unit on the Revolutionary War, a fifth-grade teacher assesses all students on basic information but bases 25% of the unit grade on special projects, such as researching the music and art of the times, people's lifestyles, or the way they made their money.

   - *Middle School:* An eighth-grade English teacher makes both required and optional assignments. Seventy percent of the assignments are required for everyone; the other 30% provide students with choices, and students negotiate with the teacher on the specific assignments.
   - *High School:* A math teacher allows students two opportunities to pass his quizzes. When they need extra help, he uses peer tutoring and special small-group work as additional aids.

Using Grouping Appropriately in Classrooms

3. View group composition as flexible, and reassign students to other groups when warranted by their learning progress. When using ability groups, make every effort to ensure that the quality of instruction is the same for each ability level. Use heterogeneous grouping whenever possible.

   - *Elementary:* A fourth-grade teacher uses ability groups for reading but whole-class instruction when she does units on other language arts topics such as poetry and American folktales.
   - *Middle School:* A sixth-grade team at a middle school analyzes several types of information, including grades and standardized test scores, when forming classes. The team members meet frequently to compare notes on student progress and to make

decisions about reassigning students to different classes. They contact both students and their parents if learning problems surface.

- *High School:* A history teacher has a colleague observe and monitor his questioning strategies during a series of lessons. He asks the colleague to record his questions and to whom they're addressed to ensure that each ability group receives the same amount of active teaching and an appropriate mix of high- and low-level questions.

Learning Styles

One thing Nate Crowder remembered from his teacher preparation experience was that variety is important in promoting learning and motivation. In social studies, he tended to conduct mostly large-group discussions because many of the students seemed to respond well. Others, however, appeared disinterested, and their attention often wandered.

In an effort to involve all his students, he decided to try some small-group work focusing on problem solving. This approach would work nicely in a unit on cities and the problems they face.

He organized the groups and assigned each a problem. As he watched the group members interact, he was struck by the fact that some of the quietest students in whole-class discussions were leaders in the small groups.

"Great!" he thought. But at the same time, he saw that some of his typically active students were sitting back, uninvolved.

4.10
What are the most likely causes of differences in learning style? Are the causes similar or different from the causes of differences in intelligence? Explain.

Historically, psychologists have used intelligence tests to measure mental abilities and concepts such as *introvert* and *extrovert* to describe different personality types. Researchers who think about the interface between the two areas study **learning styles,** *students' personal approaches to learning, problem solving, and processing information* (Snow, Corno, & Jackson, 1996). Some researchers distinguish between the concepts *learning style* and *cognitive style* (Beaty, 1995), whereas others do not (Snow et al., 1996).

One of the most common descriptions of learning style distinguishes between deep and surface approaches to processing information in learning situations (Snow et al., 1996). Students who use deep-processing approaches view the information they're studying, or the problem they're attempting to solve, as a means to understanding the content; they attempt to link the information to a larger conceptual framework. Those who use a surface approach view the information itself as the content to be learned without attempting to link it to bigger ideas. For instance, as you studied the concept of *centration* in Chapter 2, did you note that it is part of Piaget's theory and relate it to other concepts, such as egocentricity, conservation, and preoperational thinking? Did you also relate it to the fact that adults—and not just young children—often center? If so, you were using a deep-processing approach. On the other hand, if you memorized the definition and identified one or two examples of centering, you were using a surface approach.

As you might expect, deep-processing approaches result in higher achievement if tests focus on understanding, but surface approaches can be successful if tests tend to emphasize fact learning and memorization. Students who use deep-processing approaches also tend to focus on mastering a task (have *learning goals*), engage in a learning activity for its own sake (have *intrinsic motivation*), and regulate their own learning. Those who use surface approaches tend to compare their work to others' (have *performance goals*) and engage in an activity as a means to an end (have *extrinsic motivation*) (Pintrich & Schrauben, 1992; Snow et al., 1996). (We examine types of goals and motivation in detail in Chapter 10.)

For some additional information on learning styles, go to the Companion Website at *www.prenhall.com/eggen*, then to this chapter's *Additional Content* module.

Learning Preferences: Research Results

The term *learning style* is widely used in education, and many inservice workshops for teachers have been designed around it. However, rather than focusing on learning style as we just described it, these workshops typically focus on students' *preferences* for different learning environments. Participants consider room lighting, whether or not music is playing, and where and with whom students want to sit, for instance, and are encouraged to match classroom environments to students' preferences.

Research on the effectiveness of this matching is mixed. Some claim the match results in increased achievement and improved attitudes (Carbo, 1997; Dunn & Griggs, 1995). However, the validity of the tests used to measure learning styles (preferences) has been questioned (Snider, 1990; Stahl, 1999), and additional research has found that attempts to match learning environments to learning preferences have resulted in no increases and, in some cases, even decreases in learning (Curry, 1990; Knight, Halpen, & Halpen, 1992; Snow, 1992; Stahl, 1999).

Learning Styles: Implications for Teachers

Unquestionably, students come to us with different preferences and different ways of attacking learning tasks. The key question is, "What should we as teachers do in response to these differences?" and perhaps more realistically, "What *can* we do about these differences?"

We believe the concept of *learning style* has at least three implications for teachers. First, a consideration of learning style reminds us of the need to vary instruction (Shuell, 1996). Alternatives to teacher-centered lecturing, such as problem-based learning, small-group discussions, and cooperative learning provide flexibility in meeting individual differences.

Second, considering learning style reminds us to help students gain an understanding of the ways they learn most effectively. (*Metacognition*, the concept that describes learners' awareness of and control over their thinking and learning, is examined in depth in Chapter 7.) We also saw earlier that Sternberg (1998a) identified learner self-awareness as one component of intelligent behavior.

Third, considering learning style reminds us that our students are different and increases our sensitivity to those differences. With increased sensitivity, we are more likely to respond to our students as individuals. The classroom becomes a model of tolerance for individual differences, and classroom climate improves.

A sensible compromise in thinking about learning styles is offered by Snider (1990):

> People are different, and it is good practice to recognize and accommodate individual differences. It is also good practice to present information in a variety of ways through more than one modality, but it is not wise to categorize learners and prescribe methods solely on the basis of tests with questionable technical qualities. . . . The idea of learning style is appealing, but a critical examination of this approach should cause educators to be skeptical. (p. 153)

Socioeconomic Status

One of the most powerful factors related to school performance is **socioeconomic status (SES),** *the combination of income, occupation, and level of education that describes a family or individual* (see Figure 4.4). A family's SES provides a sense of their standing in a community: how much flexibility they have in where they live or what they buy, how much influence they have on political decision making, and the educational opportunities their children have. SES consistently predicts intelligence and achievement test scores, grades, truancy, and dropout and suspension rates (Macionis, 2000; McLoyd, 1998). For example, dropout rates for students from the poorest families in the United States exceed 50%, and when compared with students whose families are in the highest income quartile, students in the lowest quartile are 2½ times

Parents promote both cognitive and language development by discussing ideas and experiences with their children.

Figure 4.4 Sources of learner individuality: Socioeconomic status

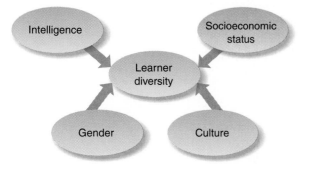

less likely to enroll in college and 8 times less likely to graduate (Levine & Nediffer, 1996; B. Young & Smith, 1999). The influence of SES on learning is summarized in the following statement: "The relationship between test scores and SES is one of the most widely replicated findings in the social sciences" (Konstantopoulos, 1997, p. 5).

Why is SES important to teachers? Consider the following statistics:

- Between 1979 and 1997, the number of children under age 6 living in poverty increased from 3.5 million to 5.2 million.
- The poverty rate for children in 1999 was 19%—approximately the same as 15 years ago—but varied considerably for different populations in the United States. For African Americans and Hispanics, it was 35%, for example, but for Whites, 14%.
- The proportion of children living in single-parent homes has more than doubled since 1970, averaging 25% for all families, with higher rates for African American (60%) and Hispanic families (29%).
- Children under age 6 living with a single mother were 5 times more likely to be poor than those living with both parents (56% compared to 11%).
- The poverty rate for parents with less than a high school education was 62.5%. (Forum on Child and Family Statistics, 1999; Hodgkinson, 2001; National Center for Children in Poverty, 1999; B. Young & Smith, 1999)

Influence of SES on Learning

How does SES influence learning? Researchers have identified three areas in which it plays a role: (a) basic needs and experiences, (b) parental involvement, and (c) attitudes and values. Let's look at them.

Basic Needs and Experiences

As one might expect, SES affects a family's ability to meet basic needs. Some families lack adequate medical care, and some children come to school without proper nourishment (L. Miller, 1995). Homelessness is also a problem; experts estimate that families now account for almost 40% of all the homeless, and the number of homeless children is higher than at any time since the Great Depression (Homes for Homeless, 1999).

Economic problems can lead to family and marital conflicts, which result in less stable and nurturant homes (McLoyd, 1998). Children of poverty may come to school without the personal sense of safety and security that equips them to tackle school-related tasks and problems.

Children of poverty also move more than their peers. Researchers examining student mobility in one urban school system found that only 38% of sixth graders attended the same school throughout their elementary years, and the average elementary school in the system had a 50% turnover rate every 3 years (Kerbow, 1996). These frequent moves are a source of stress for students and a problem for teachers attempting to create coherent instructional programs and develop caring relationships with students (T. Fisher & Mathews, 1999; Nakagawa, 1999).

SES also influences children's background experiences (McLoyd, 1998; Trawick-Smith, 1997). High-SES parents are more likely to provide their children with educational activities outside school, such as visits to art and science museums, concerts, and travel. They also have more learning materials in the home (e.g., computers, encyclopedias, and news magazines) and provide more formal training outside of school (e.g., music and dance lessons). These activities complement classroom learning by providing an experiential base for school activities (Peng & Lee, 1992). Some researchers refer to these experiences as "cultural capital" that forms a foundation for the concepts young children bring to school (Ballantine, 1989). In studying Piaget's work in Chapter 2, we saw that experience is essential for intellectual development. Bloom (1981) estimated that 80% of potential intelligence is developed by age 8; this high percentage underscores the importance of early, family-based experiences.

Parental Involvement

SES also influences parents involvement in children's education and parent-child interaction patterns, which in turn influence learning. (Hess & McDevitt, 1984). High-SES parents tend to be more involved in their children's extracurricular activities, which provides a focal point for parent-child interactions (Peng & Lee, 1992). One mother commented, "When she sees me at her games, when she sees me going to open house, when I attend her Interscholastic League contests, she knows I am interested in her activities. Plus, we have more to talk about" (M. Young & Scribner, 1997, p. 12).

In general, high-SES parents talk to their children more and differently than do low-SES parents. They explain the causes of events and provide reasons for rules, their language is more elaborate, their directions are clearer, and they are more likely to encourage problem solving. Research shows that the way parents teach and interact with their children influences how their children learn at school. When home instruction is understandable and broken into small steps, children are more likely to pay attention in school, expecting the same (Stright, Neitzel, Sears, & Hoke-Sinex, 2001). In addition, high-SES parents are more likely to ask "*wh*" questions (*who, what, when, where,* and *why*), which promote language development and prepare children for the kinds of verbal interaction found in schools. Sometimes called "the curriculum of the home," these rich interaction patterns, together with the background experiences already described, provide a foundation for reading and vocabulary development.

Attitudes and Values

The impact of SES is also transmitted through parental attitudes and values. For example, many high-SES parents value and emphasize autonomy, individual responsibility, and self-control; many low-SES parents place greater emphasis on conformity and obedience (Macionis, 2000).

Values are also communicated by example. For instance, adults who have books, newspapers, and magazines around the home and who read themselves communicate that reading and learning are important. As a result, their children are more likely to read, and students who read at home show higher reading achievement than those who don't (Hiebert & Rafael, 1996). Research also suggests that low-income children have less access to print media than do middle-income children (Neuman & Celano, 2001).

In general, high-SES parents have high expectations for their children and encourage them to graduate from high school and attend college (Trusty & Pirtle, 1998). They also play the "schooling game," steering their sons and daughters into advanced high school courses, for example (D. Baker & Stevenson, 1986), and they aren't hesitant to contact schools for information about their children's learning progress (Marks, 1995). Low-SES parents, in contrast, tend to have lower aspirations, allow their children to "drift" into classes, and rely on the decisions of others (Marks, 1995). Students can get lost in the shuffle, ending up in inappropriate or less challenging classes and tracks.

SES: Some Cautions and Implications for Teachers

It's important to point out that the research findings we've reported are *generalizations*, which means many exceptions to the patterns exist. Obviously, for example, many low-SES parents read to their children, talk to them, encourage their involvement in extracurricular activities, and attend school events. They take their children to museums and zoos and have high expectations for their learning. None of these factors is restricted to high-SES parents. In fact, both of your authors come from low-SES families. Conversely, belonging to a high-SES family does not guarantee a child enriching experiences and caring, involved parents.

4.11
Look ahead to Chapter 10's description of Maslow's hierarchy of needs. Read about the hierarchy and then explain, on the basis of Maslow's work, why children of poverty might be less equipped for learning.

4.12
Of the three components of SES—occupation, income, and level of education—researchers have found the last to be most influential in school performance. Explain why this is the case.

Remembering that many low-income families provide both a rich learning environment and a strong system of parental support can help teachers maintain high expectations for students from low-income families. Teachers can tap into and use this parental support to promote learning for these children.

Work with minority populations documents the untapped potential of family and home resources (Halle, Kurtz-Costes, & Mahoney, 1997). Researchers found "funds of knowledge," informal networks of information that low-SES, minority families can access. For example, fathers who work in construction have knowledge and skills about different ways that math can be applied in the real world (Moll, 1992). Teachers can use these funds of knowledge to make connections with students' homes and help students use and develop pride in the family and community resources available to them.

Teachers can also support learning for all students by providing safe and structured learning environments, using high-quality examples and representations, relating content to students' lives, and promoting high levels of interaction in learning activities. These strategies are effective for all students; for those from low-SES backgrounds, they're essential.

Culture

Think about the clothes you wear, the music you like, the foods you eat, the activities you share with your friends, and the things you do for recreation. These and other factors, such as religion, family structure, and values, are all part of your culture.

Culture refers to *the attitudes, values, customs, and behavior patterns that characterize a social group* (Banks, 1997). Its enormous impact on even the most basic aspects of our lives is illustrated by its influence on something as basic as our eating habits:

> Culture not only helps to determine what foods we eat, but it also influences when we eat (for example, one, three, or five meals and at what time of the day); with whom we eat (that is, only with the same sex, with children or with the extended family); how we eat (for example, at a table or on the floor; with chopsticks, silverware, or the fingers); and the ritual of eating (for example, in which hand the fork is held, asking for or being offered seconds, and belching to show appreciation of a good meal). These eating patterns are habits of the culture. (Gollnick & Chinn, 1986, pp. 6–7)

4.13
Think back to your study of development in Chapter 2. Which theorist—Piaget or Vygotsky—placed more emphasis on culture? Explain.

Like SES, culture influences school success through the attitudes, values, and ways of viewing the world that are held and transmitted by it (see Figure 4.5).

Figure 4.5 Sources of learner individuality: Culture

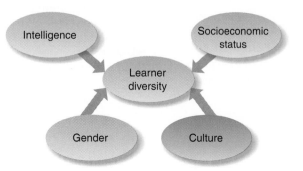

Ethnicity

An important part of culture is a person's ethnic background. **Ethnicity** refers to *a person's ancestry; the way individuals identify themselves with the nation from which they or their ancestors came* (deMarrais & LeCompte, 1999). Members of an ethnic group have a common history, language (although sometimes not actively used), customs and traditions, and value system.

More than 7 million people immigrated to the United States during the 1970s, and another 7 million came during the 1980s. The results of this and later immigration, as well as differences in birth rate for various groups, can be seen in a comparison of 1980, 1990, and 2000 U.S. population figures (see Table 4.5). In the 20-year period, the non-Hispanic White populations showed the greatest decrease, and the Hispanic population showed the greatest increase.

Experts estimate that by the year 2020 the proportion of White students in the school population will decrease by 11%, whereas dramatic increases in the proportions of African American (between 15% and 20%), Hispanic (between 47% and 61%) and Asian/Pacific Islander/American Indian/Alaskan Native (between 67% and 73%) students will be seen

Table 4.5 U.S. Census ethnicity comparisons

Population Group	Percent of Total		
	1980	1990	2000
Non-Hispanic White	79.8	75.6	69.1
Black	11.5	11.7	12.1
Hispanic	6.4	9.0	12.5
Asian	1.6	2.8	3.7
American Indian	0.6	0.7	0.7
Some other race	0.1	0.1	0.2
Two or more races	NA	NA	1.6

Source: Kent, M., Pollard, K., Haaga, J., & Mather, M., 2001.

(B. Young & Smith, 1999). By the year 2020, more than two thirds of the school population will be African American, Asian, Hispanic, or Native American (U.S. Department of Education, 2000a). Each of these groups brings a distinct set of values and traditions that influences student learning.

Culture and Schooling

A second-grade class in Albuquerque, New Mexico, was reading *The Boxcar Children* and was about to start a new chapter. The teacher said, "Look at the illustration at the beginning of the chapter and tell me what you think is going to happen." A few students raised their hands. The teacher called on a boy in the back row.

He said, "I think the boy is going to meet his grandfather."

The teacher asked, "Based on what you know, how does the boy feel about meeting his grandfather?"

Trying to involve the whole class, the teacher called on another student—one of four Native Americans in the group—even though she had not raised her hand. When she didn't answer, the teacher tried rephrasing the question, but again the student sat in silence.

Feeling exasperated, the teacher wondered if there was something in the way the lesson was being conducted that made it difficult for the student to respond. She sensed that the student she had called on understood the story and was enjoying it. Why, then, wouldn't she answer what appeared to be a simple question?

The teacher recalled that this was not the first time this had happened, and that, in fact, the other Native American students in the class rarely answered questions in class discussions. She wanted to involve them, wanted them to participate in class, but could not think of ways to get them to talk. (Villegas, 1991, p. 3)

Why do students respond differently to instruction, and how does culture influence these differences? In the sections that follow, we examine these questions, focusing on the relationships between culture and

- Attitudes and values
- Adult-child interactions
- Classroom organization
- School communication

The Cultural Base of Attitudes and Values

Our students come to us with a long learning history. In their homes, they've learned to talk, dress, care for themselves, and function as family members. On their streets and playgrounds, they've learned to interact with their peers, make friends, and solve interpersonal problems. Through these experiences, they have developed attitudes and values that can either complement or detract from school learning. Research helps us understand how.

Minority role models help minority youth understand how they can succeed without losing their ethnic or cultural heritage.

4.14

Is the concept *accommodation without assimilation* consistent or inconsistent with the idea of America as a "melting pot"? Explain.

Ogbu (1992, 1999b) divides minority cultures in the United States into two broad categories. *Voluntary minorities,* such as recent Chinese, Vietnamese, and Indian immigrants, came to the United States seeking a better life, whereas some *involuntary minorities,* such as African Americans, were brought here against their will, and others, such as Native Americans, Hawaiians, and early Hispanics in the Southwest, were conquered.

Ogbu suggests that these two types of minority groups approach assimilation and integration into American culture (and schooling) in different ways. As a group, voluntary minorities see school as an opportunity for quick assimilation and integration into the economic and social mainstream, and they strongly value schooling and hard work. Involuntary minorities, because of a long history of separatism and low status, defend themselves through **cultural inversion,** *"the tendency for involuntary minorities to regard certain forms of behavior, events, symbols, and meanings as inappropriate for them because these are characteristic of white Americans"* (Ogbu, 1992, p. 8, italics added). To adopt these values and ways of behaving is to reject their own culture.

Attitudes about language and school success are examples of this cultural inversion. Students from involuntary minorities are hesitant to drop the use of nonstandard English dialects in favor of "school English" because it would alienate their peers and distance their families (Ogbu, 1999a). These students may interpret school success as rejecting their native values; to become a good student is to adopt White cultural values and "become White." Students who study and become actively involved in school risk losing the friendship and respect of their peers. Ogbu believes that in many schools students in these groups either don't support school learning or directly oppose it; they form what he calls "resistance cultures" (Ogbu & Simons, 1998). Low grades, management and motivation problems, truancy, and high dropout rates are symptoms of this conflict.

Ogbu encourages teachers to help minority students adapt to the dominant culture (including schools) without losing their cultural identity, a process he calls "accommodation without assimilation." Other terms for this process include "alternation"—the ability to comfortably function in both cultures (Hamm & Coleman, 1997) and "code switching"—talking differently in different contexts (DeMeulenaere, 2001). The challenge for teachers is to help students learn about the "culture of schooling," the norms, procedures, and expectations necessary for success in school, while honoring the value and integrity of students' home cultures.

Minority role models are especially powerful in helping minority youth understand how they can succeed without losing their ethnic or cultural heritage. One student commented:

> It all started in the second grade. One faithful (sic) Career day at Jensen Scholastic Academy in my teacher Mrs. F.'s room an M.D. came to speak to the class about his career as a doctor. Reluctantly I can't remember his name but from that day forward I knew I was destined to be a doctor. From that point on I began to take my work seriously, because I knew to become a doctor grades were very important. Throughout my elementary career I received honors. In the seventh grade I really became fascinated with science, which I owe all to my teacher Mr. H. He made learning fun and interesting. I started to read science books even when it wasn't necessary, or I found myself watching the different specials on Channel 11 about operations they showed doctors performing. When I entered Kenwood Academy I decided to take Honors Biology which was very helpful. I wanted to be in a medical program at U.I.C. but I received a B second semester so I did not get chosen. That incident did not discourage me one bit. Through high school I continued my science classes. (Smokowski, 1997, p. 13)

Minority role models provide learners with evidence that they can not only succeed but can do so without sacrificing their cultural identity.

Cultural Differences in Adult-Child Interactions

Children from different cultures also learn to interact with adults in different ways; sometimes the style of interaction complements communication in schools, and sometimes it doesn't. This phenomenon can be illustrated by one of your authors' personal experiences:

> I was a Chicago-raised person living in the South for the first time. I soon developed a warm relationship with a family having three children, ages 3, 7, and 10. I reacted when the children would always call me "Dr. Kauchak" and my fiancee "Miss Lake," rather than "Don" and "Kathy," as we preferred. We thought these addresses were formal, but quaint. The parents also referred to us in this way, so we didn't press the issue. As we worked in schools, we noticed that middle-class children said, "Yes, ma'am," and, "No, ma'am," when talking with teachers. We came to realize that these formal (to us) ways of addressing adults were expected by both middle-class families and the teachers who came from these families. To encourage these children to call us by our first names would have been inappropriate in social situations and in conflict with accepted behavior in the schools.

Although the experience described reflects a minor (and positive) cultural difference, others can result in misunderstanding or even conflict. One principal's experience working with Pacific Island students (Winitsky, 1994) is an example. The principal had been invited to a community awards ceremony at a local church to honor students from her school. She gladly accepted, arrived a few minutes early, and was ushered to a seat of honor on the stage. After an uncomfortable (to her) wait of over an hour, the ceremony began, and the students proudly filed to the stage to receive their awards. Each was acknowledged, given an award, and applauded. The children returned to their seats in the audience, and the principal had an eye-opening experience:

> Well, the kids were fine for a while, but as you might imagine, they got bored fast and started to fidget. Fidgeting and whispering turned into poking, prodding, and open chatting. I became a little anxious at the disruption, but none of the other adults appeared to even notice, so I ignored it, too. Pretty soon several of the children were up and out of their seats, strolling about the back and sides of the auditorium. All adult faces continued looking serenely up at the speaker on the stage. Then the kids started playing tag, running circles around the seating area and yelling gleefully. No adult response—I was amazed, and struggled to resist the urge to quiet the children. Then some of the kids got up onto the stage, running around the speaker, flicking the lights on and off, and opening and closing the curtain! Still nothing from the Islander parents! It was not my place, and I shouldn't have done it, but I was so beyond my comfort zone that with eye contact and a pantomimed shush, I got the kids to settle down.
>
> I suddenly realized then that when these children . . . come to school late, it doesn't mean that they or their parents don't care about learning . . . that's just how all the adults in their world operate. When they squirm under desks and run around the classroom, they aren't trying to be disrespectful or defiant, they're just doing what they do everywhere else. (Winitzky, 1994, pp. 147–148)

Students bring with them ways of acting and interacting with adults that may differ from the traditional teacher-as-authority-figure role (Trawick-Smith, 2000). The experience with Pacific Island culture gave the principal insights into the ways (and reasons) her students often acted as they did. (We discuss the difficult question of what to do about these differences later in the chapter.)

4.15

Fostering *accommodation without assimilation* requires considerable teacher judgment and tact. Explain specifically how you would deal with the Pacific Island children's concept of time and their spirited behavior in your classroom.

Classroom Organization: Working with and Against Students' Cultures

In most classrooms, emphasis is placed on individual initiative and responsibility, which are often reinforced by grades and competition. Competition demands successes and failures, and the success of one student is often tied to the failure of another (Cushner, McClelland, & Safford, 1992).

Contrast this orientation with the cultural learning styles of the Hmong, a mountain tribe from Laos that immigrated to the United States after the Vietnam War. The Hmong culture emphasizes cooperation, and Hmong students constantly monitor the learning progress of their peers, offering help and assistance. Individual achievement is de-emphasized in favor of group success. One teacher working with the Hmong described her classroom in this way:

> When Mee Hang has difficulty with an alphabetization lesson, Pang Lor explains, in Hmong, how to proceed. Chia Ying listens in to Pang's explanation and nods her head. Pang goes back to work on her own paper, keeping an eye on Mee Hang. When she sees Mee looking confused, Pang leaves her seat and leans over Mee's shoulder. She writes the first letter of each word on the line, indicating to Mee that these letters are in alphabetical order and that Mee should fill in the rest of each word. This gives Mee the help she needs and she is able to finish on her own. Mee, in turn, writes the first letter of each word on the line for Chia Ying, passing on Pang Lor's explanation.
>
> Classroom achievement is never personal but always considered to be the result of co-operative effort. Not only is there no competition in the classroom, there is constant denial of individual ability. When individuals are praised by the teacher, they generally shake their heads and appear hesitant to be singled out as being more able than their peers. (Hvitfeldt, 1986, p. 70)

Consider how well these students would learn if instruction were competitive and teacher centered, with few opportunities for student help and collaboration.

Native Americans and students from other cultures, including Mexican American, Southeast Asian, and Pacific Island students, experience similar difficulties in competitive classrooms (Greenfield, 1994; Triandis, 1995). Their cultures teach them that cooperation is important; they view competition as silly, if not distasteful. When they come to school and are asked to compete, they experience cultural conflict. Raising hands and jousting for the right to give the correct answer isn't congruent with the ways they interact at home. If they're forced to choose between two cultures, they may conclude that schools are not for them. (We examine competitive classroom structures and their impact on motivation in Chapters 10 and 11.)

School-Culture Matches and Mismatches

Some cultural patterns strongly support schooling. In a cross-cultural study comparing Chinese, Japanese, and American child-raising practices, researchers found significant differences in parental support for schooling (Stevenson, Lee, & Stigler, 1986). More than 95% of native Chinese and Japanese fifth graders had desks and quiet study areas at home; only 63% of the American sample did. Also, 57% of the Chinese and Japanese parents supplemented their fifth graders' schoolwork with additional math workbooks, as compared with only 28% of the American parents. In addition, 51% of the Chinese parents and 29% of the Japanese parents supplemented their children's science curriculum with additional work, compared with only 1% of the American parents.

Additional research has examined the phenomenal successes of Vietnamese and Laotian refugee children in American classrooms. In spite of being in the United States less than 4 years, these students earned better than B averages in school, and scores on standardized achievement tests corroborated the grades. This occurred in spite of vast language differences and very different cultures (Caplan, Choy, & Whitmore, 1992).

Gender also interacts with culture to influence school success. In a study of immigrant children, researchers found that girls outperformed boys on a number of academic dimensions (Campo-Flores, 2002). Although boys in the study faced more peer pressure to adopt various aspects of American youth culture such as dress, slang, and even disdain for education, the immigrant girls took a more active and responsible role in helping their parents adapt to American life. This increased responsibility, plus demands to act as translators for parents, thrust the girls into active and positive cultural roles.

In attempting to explain the encouraging patterns of school acculturation and progress among the diverse cultures, the researchers looked to the families. They found heavy emphasis on the importance of hard work, autonomy, perseverance, and pride. These values were reinforced with a nightly ritual of family homework in which both parents and older siblings helped younger members of the family. Indo-Chinese high schoolers spent an average of 3 hours a day on homework; junior high and elementary students spent an average of 2½ hours and 2 hours, respectively. This compares with the 1½ hours a day American junior and senior high students typically spend on homework (Caplan et al., 1992).

In other cases, cultural mismatches between home and school occur (Owens, 1996). A study of differences in language patterns between White and African American students illustrates this possibility (Heath, 1989). For example, when teachers would say, "Let's put the scissors away now," White students, accustomed to this indirect way of speaking, interpreted it as a command; African American students did not. Failure to obey was then viewed as either a management or motivation problem, a result of the mismatch between home and school cultures.

Similar disparities caused problems during instruction. From their home experiences, White children were accustomed to using language to explore abstract relationships and were used to questions requiring specific answers, such as "Where did the puppy go?" and "What's this story about?" African American children were accustomed to questions that were more "open-ended, story-starter" types that didn't have single answers. They "were not viewed as information-givers in their interactions with adults, nor were they considered appropriate conversation partners and thus they did not learn to act as such" (Heath, 1982, p. 119). When these children went to school, they were unprepared for the verbal give-and-take of fast-paced, convergent questioning.

Made aware of these differences, teachers incorporated more open-ended questions in their lessons, and worded commands more directly (e.g., "Put your scissors away now"). They also helped the African American students become more comfortable with answering factual questions. In this way, bridges were built between the students' natural learning styles and the schools.

Culture and Learning: Deficit or Difference?

Efforts have been made to synthesize the information relating culture and school success into theories to further explain the relationship between learning and culture.

Cultural deficit theories *suggest that the linguistic, social, or cultural backgrounds of minority children prevent them from doing well academically* (Villegas, 1991). These theories have at least three weaknesses. First, they don't account for the many successes of different cultural groups. Second, because of their negative orientation, they result in lowered expectations for students from minority groups. Third, they can't explain why some minority students fall even further behind in school as time passes. If deficit theories are valid, the gap should be greatest when students first enter school and should gradually narrow over time (Villegas, 1991). It doesn't.

Cultural difference theories *emphasize the strengths of different cultures and look for ways that instructional practice can recognize and build on those strengths* (Villegas, 1991). Proponents of these theories begin with the premise that different cultural groups have unique ways of learning and that no single way of teaching is most effective for all. They then attempt to understand each cultural group and to adapt instruction to best meet the group's learning needs. Evidence supports their premise, and we discuss implications for teaching students from cultural minorities in the next section.

> **4.16**
> Using Ogbu's concept of *cultural inversion,* explain why some minorities might fall further and further behind the longer they remain in school.

Culturally Responsive Teaching: Instructional Strategies

Culturally responsive teaching *acknowledges cultural differences in classrooms and creates teaching strategies that respond to this diversity* (Gay, 1997). The following principles can guide teachers in their efforts:

- Demonstrate caring for all students by giving them your time and showing personal interest in them.
- Involve all students in learning activities as equally as possible.

Culturally responsive teachers build on the strengths that different students bring to school.

- Use a variety of teaching methods to accommodate different cultural learning styles.
- Communicate that you value the contributions that all cultures can bring to school and society.
- Provide opportunities for students with different backgrounds to interact and work together.

Let's see how the principles guide Gary Nolan, a fifth-grade teacher, as he works with his students.

Gary's class was very diverse. Of his 28 students, six were African American, eight were Hispanic, four were of Asian descent, two were from Morocco, and three recently immigrated from Russia.

"It's time for the rest of the class to come in," Gary said to Hajam, Sergie, and Javier, all three of whom were non-native English speakers. Gary spent a half hour with them every morning working on both their English language skills and their assignments to be sure that they didn't fall behind the other students.

"You're coming along really well," he smiled at them as he got up. "I'll see you here tomorrow morning. . . . Study hard now.

"Good morning, Tu. . . . New hat, Damon? . . . Nice haircut, Shah. . . . How's your new baby sister, Jack?" Gary greeted the students as they came in the door.

The students quickly moved to their desks and put their materials away.

"Who's up today?" he asked.

"Me," Anna said, raising her hand.

"Go ahead, Anna."

Anna got up, moved to the front of the room, and took out two large posters showing the islands of Mallorca and Menorca. "I was born in Mexico, but my father is from Mallorca, and my mother is from Menorca," Anna explained.

"Show everyone on our map," Gary interjected, and as Anna moved toward a large map on the classroom wall, he added, "Don't forget your tags."

Every Tuesday and Thursday morning, Gary had one of the students make a presentation about his or her background. The students brought items that illustrated their cultural heritage, such as foods, pieces of clothing, art objects, stories or poems, or other artifacts, and they placed a push pin with their name on it on the world map in the classroom. Gary repeatedly commented about how lucky students were to have classmates from so many different parts of the world, and he routinely emphasize how much they learned from each other. "Remember when Shah told us about Omar Khayyam?" Gary once asked. "He solved some math problems that people in Europe didn't solve until hundreds of years later. If Shah weren't in our class, we probably would never have learned that. . . . Aren't we lucky?"

Gary also kept a vocabulary chart on the wall with common words and phrases ("Hello," "Good-bye," "How are you?") in Spanish, Vietnamese, Arabic, Russian, and English. And he displayed a large calendar that identified important holidays in different cultures. Students from those cultures made special presentations on the holidays, and all the students' parents were invited to attend. At first, parental attendance was quite low, but lately it had been growing.

When Anna finished her presentation, Gary said, "Okay, everyone, get ready for math." During the lesson, he called on all the students to give everyone an equal chance to participate.

He then broke the students into groups of four for math seat work. Each group member attempted the problem and then compared his or her answer with a partner's. If they couldn't agree, they turned to the other pair in the group. Gary organized the groups so that students of different ethnic backgrounds were in each. He carefully monitored the students to be sure that everyone was attempting the problems and that the students treated each other with courtesy and respect.

Much of culturally responsive teaching deals with feelings, attitudes, and values. All students want to feel that their teachers care about them, that they are welcome and wanted in school, and that they are integral members of their classes. This is particularly important for students from cultural minorities, who sometimes feel alienated from school. Genuine caring is at the core of culturally responsive teaching.

With that thought in mind, let's take a closer look at Gary's attempts to be culturally responsive. First, nothing communicates Gary's caring better than his willingness to spend his personal time to give students extra help. By devoting a half hour every day to work with Hajam, Sergie, and Javier, Gary directly communicated his commitment to them and indirectly communicated commitment to the rest of the class. He also communicated caring for his students by greeting them each morning and making a personal comment to each individual whenever possible. Subtle, but important, gestures such as these let students know they are welcome and important to the class.

Second, Gary also communicated that each student was an important member of the class by involving all of them in his learning activities as equally as possible. Every time he called on a student, he signaled that he expected the student to answer. Nothing better communicates to students that they are valued.

Some teachers believe that students don't *want* to answer. However, if students (including those from cultural minorities) believe they will be *able* to answer, they will want to be called on (Eggen, 2002). Teachers should emphasize that learning is the goal of every discussion and wrong answers are an integral and important part of the learning progress (Eggen & Kauchak, 2002). (We examine strategies for involving all students in learning activities in Chapter 13.)

Third, by combining whole-class and small-group instruction, Gary attempted to accommodate possible differences in cultural learning styles by varying his teaching methods. For example, he apparently had learned that Hajam, Sergie, and Javier were more comfortable in small groups. These adaptations can increase learning for all students (Holliday, 2002; Slavin, 1995).

Teachers can accommodate learning style differences in other ways. For instance, a teacher learned that her Asian American students were overwhelmed by the hustle and bustle of American schools, so she made an extra effort to keep her classroom orderly and quiet (Park, 1997). In another case, knowing that Asian Americans are sometimes reluctant to speak in class, a teacher encouraged participation by asking more open-ended questions, giving students extra more time to respond, and gently encouraging them to speak a bit louder (Shields & Shaver, 1990).

A great deal of variation exists within all cultural groups, however, and teachers should be cautious about overgeneralizing (Dilworth & Brown, 2001). Concluding that a student is likely to be shy and reluctant to respond simply because he is Asian is no more valid than concluding that all White students are aggressive and outgoing. The patterns described in this section are designed merely to sensitize teachers to possible group differences.

Fourth, Gary communicated how much he valued the contributions that all the cultures made to students' learning and to society in general. He demonstrated his feelings in both actions and words—with the students' twice-a-week presentations; the map with tags for ancestral countries; his specific emphasis on the contributions of Omar Khayyam, who was little known to most of the students; and comments like "If Shah weren't in our class, we probably would never have learned that." Wise teachers learn about their students' cultures and use this information to promote their personal pride and motivation (Xu, 2002). This practice not only increases student achievement but also makes parents more positive about school, which in turn enhances student motivation (Shumow & Harris, 1998).

Finally, Gary realized that nothing breaks down barriers between students more quickly than working together cooperatively. So, his group work, in addition to being a different teaching strategy, provided another function: It gave students of different backgrounds the chance to get to know one another.

To see a video clip of a teacher describing how she accommodates one student's culture in her teaching, go to the Companion Website at *www.prenhall.com/eggen*, then to this chapter's *Classrooms on the Web* module. Click on *Video Clip 4.1*.

4.17
Identify at least three advantages, to all students, of learning about different students' cultural backgrounds.

Classroom Connections

Using SES and Culture as Tools to Understand Your Students

1. Make an attempt to learn about the cultures of the students you are teaching.

   - *Elementary:* A third-grade teacher asks her students about their after-school activities and their holiday customs. She designs classroom "festivals" that focus on different cultures and invites parents and other caregivers to help celebrate and contribute to enriching them.

   - *Middle School:* On the first day of class, a seventh-grade English teacher has students write essays about themselves. He has them include a description of their favorite activities and foods, the kind of music they like, and any information they want to include about parents, caregivers, or other close relatives. He asks them to include anything about school that worries them or that they don't like. He writes an essay of his own and shares it with his students.

   - *High School:* A geometry teacher learns something personal about each of her students and refers to this

information in one-on-one conversations. She also conducts help sessions after school. Though focused on academics, the conversations in these sessions often turn to students' lives and the problems they encounter in school.

2. Make students aware of the values and accomplishments of people from ethnic and cultural minorities.

   - *Elementary:* A second-grade teacher emphasizes values, such as courtesy and respect, that are common to all cultures. He has students discuss the ways these values are displayed in different societies.

   - *Middle School:* An art teacher decorates the room with pictures of Native American art and discusses its quality and contributions to art in general.

   - *High School:* An inner-city American history teacher displays pictures of prominent African Americans and discusses the contributions they have made to the American way of life. She notes that many history books underrepresent the contributions of women and members of minority groups.

Gender

What Marti Banes saw on her first day of her advanced-placement chemistry class was both surprising and disturbing. Of the 26 students watching her, only 5 were girls, and they sat quietly in class, responding only when she asked them direct questions. One reason that she had gone into teaching was to share her interest in science with girls, but this situation gave her little chance to do so.

The fact that some of our students are boys and others are girls is so obvious that we may not even think about it. When we're reminded, we notice that boys and girls often act and think differently. These differences are natural—even desirable—but problems can occur if societal or school influences limit the academic performance of either girls or boys. In this section, we examine gender-related student differences and their implications for our teaching (Figure 4.6).

Males and females *are* different. In general, females score higher on tests of verbal ability; boys score higher on tests of visual imagery (Halpern & LaMay, 2000). Girls tend to be more extroverted, anxious, and trusting; less assertive; and have slightly lower self-esteem than males of the same age and background (Feingold, 1995; Halpern & LaMay, 2000). Differences also exist in boys' and girls developmental rates: Girls develop faster, and they acquire verbal and motor skills at an earlier age. In play, girls gravitate toward activities with a social component, such as playing "house" and dress-up. Boys gravitate toward activities with a visual-spatial component, such as block building and playing with cars or dinosaurs. Both boys and girls prefer to play with members of the same sex. These differences, together

Figure 4.6 Sources of learner individuality: Gender

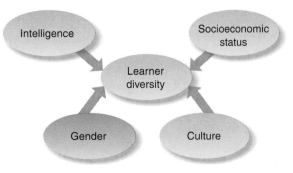

with societal expectations, result in **gender role identity differences,** *beliefs about appropriate characteristics and behaviors of the two sexes.*

Why do these gender differences exist? Like the question about sources of differences in intelligence, this question is controversial. Evidence suggests, however, that gender differences, like differences in intelligence, result from an interaction between genetics and environment. Genes control physical differences such as size and growth rate and probably also influence differences in temperament, aggressiveness, and early verbal and exploratory behaviors (Berk, 2003). With respect to nurture, girls and boys are treated differently by parents, peers, and teachers, and this treatment also influences how they view gender roles over time and what they ultimately become (Biklen & Pollard, 2001; Todt-Stockman, Gaa, Swank, 2001).

What should teachers do about these differences? Again, the suggestions are controversial, with some people believing that most differences between boys and girls are natural and little intervention is necessary, and others arguing that every attempt should be made to minimize gender differences.

Research sheds light on the issue, and some suggests that schools are not meeting girls' needs:

- In the early grades, girls score as high or higher than boys on almost every standardized measure of achievement and psychological well-being. By the time they graduate from high school or college, they have fallen behind boys.
- In high school, girls score lower on the SAT and ACT, important tests for college admission. The greatest gender gaps are in science and math.
- Women score lower on all sections of the Graduate Record Exam, the Medical College Admissions Test, and admission tests for law, dental, and optometry schools. (Sadker, Sadker, & Long, 1997)

Other research suggests that schools also fail to meet the learning needs of boys:

- Boys outnumber girls in remedial English and math classes, are held back in grade more often, and are two to three times more likely to be placed in special education classes.
- Boys consistently receive lower grades than girls and score lower than girls on both direct and indirect measures of writing ability.
- The proportion of both bachelor's and master's degrees earned favors women by a ratio of 53 to 47. (Willingham & Cole, 1997)

4.18
Explain gender differences from both "nature" and "nurture" perspectives. Then explain these differences from an interactionist position.

Differences in the Behavior of Boys and Girls

Boys actively participate in learning activities to a greater extent than girls. They are more likely to ask questions and make comments about ideas being discussed in class, and teachers call on them more often (Sadker, Sadker, & Klein, 1991), probably because boys are more verbally aggressive (Altermatt, Jovanovic, & Perry, 1998).

These gender-related classroom differences are particularly pronounced in science and math classrooms. In one study, researchers found that 79% of a teacher's science demonstrations were carried out by boys. At the third-grade level, 51% of boys reported experiences with microscopes compared to 37% of girls. In an 11th-grade sample, 49% of boys, but only 17% of girls, reported hands-on experiences with electrical equipment (Sadker et al., 1991). These experiences are important because they influence girls' attitudes toward science and their perceptions of their ability to do science (Jovanovic & King, 1998).

Differences in participation become greater as students move through school, with an especially significant decrease in girls' participation during the middle school years. In the seventh grade, girls initiated 41% of the student-teacher interactions, but by eighth grade, this number had decreased to 30% (Sadker et al., 1991). This decrease appears during the time girls are wrestling with gender-role identities. In spite of increased sensitivity to girls' needs, our society still commonly views female roles as submissive and conforming, and middle school girls often feel uncomfortable asserting themselves in classes.

4.19
Explain girls' participation in math and science, using Erikson's stage of *identity versus confusion* (see Chapter 3) as the basis for your explanation.

Boys also display behaviors that detract from learning. They cut class more often than girls, hold more part-time jobs out of school, read less for pleasure, do less homework, and are less likely to take college preparatory classes. In college they party more and watch more TV than girls (Riordan, 1996). These problems have become prominent enough to receive national attention. For example, in the fall of 2002, the television news magazine *60 Minutes* did a feature examining boys' lack of achievement compared to girls in most areas other than those emphasizing math and science.

Although the areas of concern are different, evidence suggests that schools aren't effectively serving the needs of either boys or girls.

Gender Stereotypes and Perceptions

Increased national attention has focused on the problem of gender stereotyping (Riordan, 1996). For example, in 1993 Mattel attempted to market a new "Teen Talk Barbie" which—when you pressed her tummy—said, "I like shopping," "I like boys," and "Math class is tough." The marketing attempt was significant because it immediately caused a storm of protest (the doll was quickly pulled from the market), indicating heightened sensitivity to gender issues, and also because it illustrated the pervasiveness of male and female stereotypes.

Perceptions of Male and Female Domains

Both society and parents communicate—sometimes directly and sometimes unconsciously—different expectations for their sons and daughters. For example, researchers found that mothers' gender-stereotyped attitudes toward girls' ability in math adversely influenced their daughters' achievement in math and reinforced their beliefs that math is a male domain (J. Campbell & Beaudry, 1998). One woman recalled:

> It was OK, even feminine, not to be good in math. It was even cute. And so I locked myself out of a very important part of what it is to be a human being, and that is to know all of oneself. I just locked that part out because I didn't think that was an appropriate thing for me to do. . . . [But] it was not OK for the men to not do well in math. It was *not* OK for them to not take calculus. It was not manly. (Weissglass, 1998, p. 160)

The perception that certain areas, such as math, science, and computer science, are male domains has a powerful effect on career choices. For instance, although achievement differences between boys and girls at the K–12 level are small and declining (Willingham & Cole, 1997), girls are less than half as likely as boys to pursue careers in engineering and physical and computer sciences (American Association of University Women, 1998). The percentages of women who are doctors (20%), lawyers (21%), engineers (8%), and professors in science-related fields (36%) continue to remain low (U.S. Bureau of the Census, 2000). And the problem of gender stereotypic views of math- and science-related careers seems to be especially acute for minority females (O'Brien, Kopola, & Martinez-Pons, 1999). These trends are troubling because the perception of these fields as male domains limits career options for females as well as the pool for future scientists and mathematicians (J. Campbell & Beaudry, 1998).

Single-Gender Classrooms and Schools

One response to perceptions about domains has been the creation of single-gender classes and schools (Mael, 1998). One study found girls more likely to ask and answer questions in a girls-only middle school math class than in coeducational classes (Streitmatter, 1997). Girls

Science activities that actively involve female students in designing and carrying out science experiments help combat gender stereotypes that the sciences are a male domain.

also preferred this environment, saying that it enhanced their ability to learn math and their views of themselves as mathematicians.

Research on single-gender schools has found similar positive effects for both girls and boys. Studies suggest that single gender schools provide a stronger academic climate and reduce distractions (Datnow, Hubbard, & Conchas, 2001). Girls who attend single-gender schools are more apt to adopt leadership roles, take more math and science courses, have higher self-esteem, and have an increased perception of being in control of their own learning. Advocates of all-boy schools claim that they promote male character development and are especially effective with boys from low-income and minority families (Datnow, Hubbard, & Conchas, 1999).

Although research shows generally positive effects of single-gender schooling for both general achievement and achievement in stereotyped fields, like math and science, it raises other issues (Datnow et al., 2001; Mael, 1998). For example, these environments tend to reinforce stereotypical attitudes toward the opposite sex, and they don't prepare students for the real world in which men and women work together (Datnow et al., 1999). More research is needed to examine the long-term effects of these experiments and the impact they have on the intellectual, social, and personal development of both boys and girls.

Responding to Gender Differences: Instructional Strategies

Teachers can do a great deal to make students aware of gender bias and gender stereotyping. The following principles can guide teachers in their efforts:

- Communicate openly with students about gender issues and concerns.
- Eliminate gender bias in instructional activities.
- Present students with nonstereotypical role models.

Let's see how the principles guide Marti Banes, the teacher in the vignette at the beginning of the "Gender" section, as she works with her students.

Marti decided to take steps to deal with the gender issue in her chemistry class. First, she promoted an open discussion. "I almost didn't major in chemistry," she began. "Some of my girl friends scoffed, and others were nearly appalled. 'You'll be in there with a bunch of geeks,' some of them said. 'Girls don't major in chemistry. You'll be in there with 45 guys and two girls,' others added. They all thought science and math were only for guys."

"It *is* for guys," Amy shrugged. "Look at us."

"It isn't our fault," Shane responded, a bit defensively. "The guys didn't try to keep you out of the class."

Several other students made lively comments.

"Listen everyone. I'm not blaming either you guys, or the girls. . . . It's a problem for all of us, and I'm not saying that because I'm a woman. I'd be just as concerned if I were a man, because we're losing a lot of talented people who could be majoring in science. . . . It's a societal problem."

As the discussion continued, she encouraged both the boys and the girls to keep their career options open. "There's no rule that says that girls can't be computer scientists or boys can't be nurses," she emphasized. "In fact, there's an enormous shortage of both." She had similar discussions in her other classes.

During learning activities, she made a special effort to be sure that the girls and the boys participated as equally as possible, and she told the students why she was doing so. In lab activities, she organized groups to include equal numbers of boys and girls in each and monitored the groups closely to be sure that the girls took an active role in designing and conducting the experiments.

For Career Week, Marti invited a female chemistry professor from a nearby university to come into her classes to talk about career opportunities for women in chemistry, and she invited a male nurse from one of the local hospitals to talk about his experiences in a female-dominated profession.

Marti also talked with other science teachers and counselors about gender stereotyping, and they worked on a plan to encourage both boys and girls to consider career options in nonstereotypical fields.

Teachers can play an important role in helping eliminate gender stereotyping in education (Brantlinger et al., 1999; S. Turner, Bernt, & Pecora, 2002). As with many aspects of individual differences, the first step is awareness. Marti attempted to implement our first principle by openly discussing the issue with her classes. The discussions increased both the boys' and the girls' awareness of the fact that people have a stereotyped notion that chemistry is for boys. And the discussions with her colleagues helped increase their sensitivity to gender issues in the school.

Second, knowing that teachers sometimes unconsciously treat boys and girls differently, Marti made a special effort to ensure equal treatment of both, and again she openly communicated why she was making the effort. She called on the girls in equal proportion to the boys, and she monitored the lab activities to be sure that the girls didn't slide into passive roles. She expected the same academic behaviors from both the girls and the boys.

Notice the term "academic behaviors." No one suggests that boys and girls are the same in every way, and they shouldn't be expected to behave in the same ways. Academically, however, boys and girls should be given the same opportunities and encouragement, just as students from different cultures and socioeconomic backgrounds should be.

Third, Marti invited a female chemistry professor and a male nurse into her classes to discuss careers in those fields. Seeing that both men and women can succeed and be happy in nonstereotypical fields can broaden the horizon for girls and boys thinking about career choices.

Classroom Connections

Eliminating Gender Bias in Your Classroom

1. Actively attack gender bias in your teaching.
   - *Elementary:* A first-grade teacher consciously deemphasizes sex roles and differences in his classroom. He has boys and girls share equally in chores, and he eliminates gender-related activities, such as competitions between boys and girls and forming lines by gender.
   - *Middle School:* A middle school language arts teacher selects stories and clippings from newspapers and

magazines that portray men and women in nontraditional roles. She matter-of-factly talks about nontraditional careers during class discussions about becoming an adult.
   - *High School:* At the beginning of the school year, a social studies teacher explains how gender bias hurts both sexes, and he forbids sexist comments in his classes. As classes study historical topics, he emphasizes the contributions of women, and he points out the changes in views of gender over time.

Students Placed at Risk

I was told that "the class was all right, but some children were pretty hopeless." I was also told that the children were used to working through their arithmetic book and were tested at the end of each week. After receiving the first test papers in long division, most of which were disastrous, I did not know what to do. Nothing in my training had prepared me for a class where some children failed because they did not understand the meaning of zero, some because they had not learned how to carry over numbers from one stage to another; others seemed to have very little understanding of division and would try to divide the smaller number by the larger one, while some children seemed confused and unable to make any sense of the set number work.

I subsequently divided the papers into small groups according to the main errors they revealed, and spent my next lunch breaks working with the children on their own specific difficulties. I soon realized that some of the "hopeless" children were pretty bright, but for different reasons had lost confidence in their ability to cope with their schoolwork. However, I found out that when each child was helped to understand the specific problem in arithmetic that had been holding him back, his progress was not only remarkable, but also quite out of proportion to the effort I invested. (Butler-Por, 1987, p. 3)

Failing students can be found in any school, anywhere. Although there are many reasons for school failure, some students share specific background factors and educational problems that decrease their chances for success in school. Do you remember Juan, the young boy in our opening case study? A member of a cultural minority with a low-SES background, Juan had missed a great deal of school, and he was retained in the first grade. His tendency to be easily offended suggests low self-esteem. These characteristics and others (Table 4.6) are common to **students placed at risk,** *learners in danger of failing to complete their education with the skills necessary to survive in a modern technological society* (Slavin, Karweit, & Madden, 1989).

The term *students placed at risk* became widely used after the National Commission on Excellence in Education (1983) proclaimed the United States a "nation at risk." The report emphasized the importance of education in our modern world, and since that time, increased attention has been given to problems and issues relating to students placed at risk. It is a virtual certainty that you will have some of these students in your classes.

Students placed at risk have learning problems and adjustment difficulties, and they often fail, even though they can succeed (Butler-Por, 1987). These students used to be called *underachievers,* but the term *at risk* more clearly reflects the long-term consequences of school failure. Families whose primary breadwinners lack high school diplomas earn 30% less than those with a high school education; over the course of a lifetime, a male high school dropout will earn a quarter of a million dollars less than a high school graduate (Mishel & Frankel, 1991). Many jobs requiring few specialized skills no longer exist, and others are becoming rare in a world driven by technology.

The presence of "male" as a background factor in Table 4.6 needs clarification. Although research indicates that males are more likely to experience difficulties in school and drop out, females who fail to graduate or graduate with inadequate skills are more likely to live in poverty than male dropouts (American Association of University Women, 1992). In addition, many girls drop out because they are pregnant and are left with the burden of single parenting on an inadequate income. Being at risk is a problem facing both male and female students.

4.20
Why are students placed at risk increasingly seen as both educational and economic problems? Will this trend increase or decrease? Why?

Table 4.6 Characteristics of students placed at risk

Background Factors	
Low SES	Minority
Inner city	Non-native English speaker
Male	Divorced families
Transient	

Educational Problems	
High dropout rate	High rates of drug use
Low grades	Management problems
Retention in grade	Low self-esteem
Low achievement	High criminal activity rates
Low involvement in extracurricular activities	Low test scores
Low motivation	Dissatisfaction with and lack of interest in school
Poor attendance	High suspension rates

Resilient children come from homes and classrooms that are supportive but demanding and where caring adults provide nurturant challenge.

Resilience

Research on students placed at risk has increasingly focused on the concept of **resilience,** *a learner characteristic that raises the likelihood of success in school and in other aspects of life, despite environmental adversities* (Wang, Haertel, & Walberg, 1995). This research studies young people who have survived and even prospered despite obstacles such as poverty, poor health care, and fragmented support services. Resilient children have well-developed self-systems, including high self-esteem, optimism, and feelings that they are in control of their destinies (Jew, Green, Millard, & Posillico, 1999). They set personal goals, possess good interpersonal skills, and have positive expectations for success (Benard, 1994; Wang et al., 1995). These strengths pay off in higher achievement, motivation, and satisfaction with school (Waxman & Huang, 1996).

How do these skills develop? Resilient children come from nurturant environments, and one characteristic is striking. In most cases, these children have one or more adults who have taken a special interest in them and hold them to high moral and academic standards—they essentially refuse to let the young person fail (Jew et al., 1999; Stull, 1998). These adults are often parents, but they could also be older siblings or other adults who take a young person "under their wing."

Schools also make an important contribution. Let's look at them more closely.

Schools That Promote Resilience

4.21
Identify two of Gardner's intelligences that are particularly important for resilient children.

Research has identified at least four school practices that promote resilience (Wang et al., 1995). They include the following:

- *High and uncompromising academic standards.* Mastery of content is emphasized, and passive attendance and mere completion of assignments are unacceptable (Corbett, Wilson, & Williams, 1999; Jesse & Pokorny, 2001).
- *Strong personal bonds between teachers and students.* Teachers become the adults that refuse to let students fail, students feel connected to the schools (Parish, Parish, & Batt, 2001), mutual respect between students and teachers is emphasized, and personal responsibility and cooperation are stressed (Battistich, 2001; Kim, Solomon, & Roberts, 1995).
- *Order and high structure.* The school and classes are orderly and highly structured. Reasons for rules are emphasized, and rules and procedures are consistently enforced (Glidden, 1999).
- *Participation in after-school activities.* Activities such as clubs and athletics give students additional chances to interact with caring adults and receive reinforcement for achievement (Davidson, Dell, & Walker, 2001).

Effective schools are both demanding and supportive; in many instances, they serve as homes away from home (Haynes & Comer, 1995). The emphasis placed on school-sponsored activities reduces alienation, increases academic engagement and achievement, and improves students' self-concepts (Davidson, et al., 2001; Jordan, 2001). They also give teachers the chance to know students in contexts outside the classroom. Interestingly, these same characteristics seem to apply to schools in other countries; a study done with similar students in Israel arrived at the same conclusions (Gaziel, 1997).

Teachers Who Promote Resilience

To begin this section, let's look again at Tim Wilkinson's work with his students.

"Good morning, Juan," Tim smiled as Juan walked into the room at 8:15 A.M.

"Hi, Mr. Wilkinson," Juan responded in his accented English. "I worked very hard on the assignment last night, but I still don't get it."

"We'll get it," Tim smiled again as he got up and moved over to the student desk next to Juan's. "You've been coming in every morning for the last 2 weeks, and you've improved so much I can hardly tell you—so keep that in mind. And if you hang in, you know you always get it. . . . Now, let's take a look."

Tim went over each of the problems on the homework with Juan, first by having Juan read the problems aloud and explain what he thought each problem meant. Then he guided Juan through the solution. Whenever Juan's frustration got the better of him, Tim stopped for a minute or two, sent Juan out to get a drink, and they started again.

"See, I told you that you could do this," Tim often said after Juan had completed a problem. "You just have to work hard and believe it."

Tim's personal interest promotes resilience in Juan.

Schools are no more effective than the teachers who work in them (Waxman, Huang, Anderson, & Weinstein, 1997). You know that teachers who promote resilience form strong personal bonds with students and that they "become the adults that refuse to let students fail." You just saw this demonstrated with Tim and Juan. Admittedly, spending time every morning with a student is very demanding, but this kind of commitment is the essence of promoting resilience.

What else do we know about teachers who promote resilience? Research indicates that they talk frequently with students, learn about their families, and share their own lives. They maintain high expectations, use interactive teaching strategies, and emphasize success and mastery of content. They motivate students through personal contacts, instructional support, and attempts to link school to students' lives (Kramer-Schlosser, 1992).

Let's see what students say about these teachers:

Well it's like you're family, you know. Like regular days like at home, we argue sometimes, and then it's like we're all brothers and sisters and the teachers are like our guardians or something.

And the teachers really get on you until they try to make you think of what's in the future and all that. It's good. I mean it makes you think, you know, if every school was like that I don't think there would be a lot of people that would drop out. (Greenleaf, 1995, p. 2)

[This teacher is] always ready to help you. When I first came to this school, I didn't like her, 'til I realized that the only thing she was trying to do was help me.
> Student, Accelerated Academics Academy
> Flint, Michigan

The teachers stay on you . . . they'll keep staying on you until you get your goals.
> Student, Project ACCEL
> Newark, New Jersey

[The teachers] believe you can do the work, and you don't want to let them down.
> Student, Up With Literacy Program
> Long Beach, California
> (Dynarski & Gleason, 1999, p. 13)

Teachers less effective in promoting resilience are more authoritarian and less accessible. They distance themselves from students and place primary responsibility for learning on them. They view instructional support as "babying students" or "holding students' hands." Lecture is a common teaching strategy, and motivation is the students' responsibility. Students perceive these teachers as adversaries, to be avoided if possible, tolerated if not (Kramer-Schlosser, 1992). They also resent the teachers' lack of commitment:

There's this teacher [over at the regular school] . . . you can put anything down and he'll give you a check mark for it. He doesn't check it. He just gives you a mark and says, 'OK, you did your work.' How you gonna learn from that? You ain't gonna learn nothing.
> Student, JFY Academy
> Boston, Massachusetts
> (Dynarski & Gleason, 1999, p. 13)

As with culturally responsive teaching, much of promoting resilience lies in teachers' attitudes and commitment to student success. Effective teachers care about the students as people and will accept nothing less than consistent effort and quality work

To see a video clip of a caring teacher with high expectations, go to the Companion Website at *www.prenhall.com/eggen*, then to this chapter's *Classrooms on the Web* module. Click on *Video Clip 4.2.*

4.22
Refer again to Maslow's hierarchy of needs, outlined in Chapter 10. Using this hierarchy, explain why caring teachers are so important for students placed at risk.

(Freese, 1999; Gschwend & Dembo, 2001). Caring teachers are important for all students; for students placed at risk, they're essential.

Teaching Students Placed at Risk: Instructional Strategies

We have just seen that teachers who promote resilience in students placed at risk are caring and committed. But, in addition to providing this human element, what else can teachers do? In a review of the research in this area, Brophy (1986) concluded, "Research has turned up very little evidence suggesting the need for qualitatively different forms of instruction for students who differ in aptitude, achievement level, socioeconomic status, ethnicity or learning style" (p. 122).

In short, teachers of students placed at risk don't need to teach in fundamentally different ways; they need to provide the structure and support that will ensure student success while at the same time teaching students strategies that allow them to take control of their own learning. The following principles can guide teachers in their efforts:

- Create and maintain an orderly learning environment with predictable routines.
- Combine high expectations with frequent feedback about learning progress.
- Use teaching strategies that actively involve all students and promote high levels of success.
- Use high-quality examples that provide the background knowledge students need to learn new content.
- Stress student self-regulation and the acquisition of learning strategies.

Let's see how the principles guide Diane Smith, a fourth-grade teacher, as she works with her students.

Diane's objective for language arts, scheduled from 12:35 to 1:45 today, was to teach her students to write with comparative and superlative forms of adjectives.

The students filed into the room from their lunch break, immediately went to their desks, and began working on a set of exercises directing them to identify all the adjectives and the nouns they modified in a paragraph displayed on the overhead.

At 12:35, all students were seated and busy. As they worked, Diane surveyed the room and, on a small notepad, identified students who had pencils of different lengths and students whose hair colors varied.

The students finished at 12:45, and Diane began, "Let's see how we did."

She went over the passage with the students, asking them to explain how they knew a word was an adjective and also how they knew what noun it modified. When students had difficulty, she explained the correct answer carefully.

At 12:55 they finished, and Diane announced, "Okay, very good, everyone. Put your pencils down for now, and look up here."

In a few seconds, all the students had their pencils down and were waiting.

"Calesha and Daniel, hold your pencils up so everyone can see. What do you notice? . . . Naitia?"

" . . . Calesha's is red, and Daniel's is blue."

"Okay. What else?" Diane smiled, " . . . Sheila?"

"You write with them."

"Kevin?"

"Calesha's is longer."

"Does everyone see that? Hold them up again."

Calesha and Daniel held their pencils up again, and Diane went to the board and wrote:

Calesha has a long pencil.
Calesha has a longer pencil than Daniel does.

"Now, let's look at Matt and Leroy. What do you notice about their hair? . . . Judy?" Diane asked as she walked down the aisle.

"Leroy's is black, and Matt's is brown," Randy responded.

"Okay. Good, Randy. So who's is darker?"

"LEROY!" several in the class blurted out, as Diane smiled at their eagerness.

"Good!" Diane again went to the board and wrote three more sentences, so the information appeared as follows:

Calesha has a long pencil.   Leroy has black hair.
Calesha has a longer pencil than Daniel does.   Matt has brown hair.
                                     Leroy has darker hair than Matt does.

"Now, how do the adjectives in the sentences compare? . . . Heather?" Diane asked, pointing to *long* and *longer* in the first two sentences.

". . . The ones . . . at the bottom have an -*er* on the end of them," Heather responded hesitantly.

"Yes, good," Diane nodded.

"So, what are we doing in each of the sentences? . . . Jason?" Diane continued.

"We're comparing two things."

"Excellent thinking, Jason," Diane smiled and waved.

She then repeated the process with the superlative form of adjectives by having the students compare three pencils and three different hair colors, and leading them to conclude that superlative adjectives have an -*est* on the end of them.

"So, how do we write adjectives if we compare two things? . . . Todd?"

"We put an -*er* on the end of them."

"And suppose we have three or more things. Then what? . . . Sara?"

"We put an -*est* on them."

"Very good, everyone. In describing nouns, if we're comparing two, we use the comparative form of the adjective, which has an -*er* on the end, and if we have three or more, we have an -*est* on the end of the adjective.

"Now, I have a little challenge for you." Diane reached back and took a softball, a tennis ball, and a golf ball from her desk. "Write two sentences that tell about the sizes of the balls."

The students began writing their sentences, and as they worked, Diane walked up and down the rows, periodically making brief comments.

"Now let's look at some sentences," Diane began after a few minutes. "Someone volunteer, and I'll write it on the chalkboard. . . . Okay, Rashad?"

"The tennis ball is bigger than the golf ball."

"Very good, Rashad. And why did you write *bigger* with an -*er* in your sentence?"

"We're comparing the size of two balls."

"And another one? . . . Bharat?"

"The softball is the biggest one."

She asked Bharat to explain his sentence, and then said "That's excellent. . . . Now, I want you to write a paragraph with at least two sentences that use the comparative form of adjectives and at least two other sentences that use the superlative form of the adjectives. Underline the adjectives in each case."

"And what do we always do after we write something?"

"We read it to be sure it makes sense!" several of the students said simultaneously.

"Very good," Diane smiled knowingly. "We're a team, aren't we?"

The students began writing their paragraphs. As they worked, Diane circulated among them, periodically stopping for a few seconds to comment on a student's work and to offer brief suggestions.

After the students finished, they shared their paragraphs with a partner, who made comments, and the students then revised the paragraphs based on the feedback.

Let's take a closer look at Diane's attempts to structure her lesson in a way that is appropriate for students placed at risk.

First, her classroom was orderly, and she had predictable and well-established routines. For instance, when the students came in from their break, they immediately went to work on the exercises on the overhead without being told to do so. Students placed at risk sometimes come from chaotic home environments, so they have a greater need for order and structure than do students whose home lives are more stable. Teachers meet this need by creating orderly, predictable, productive classroom environments. (We discuss specific strategies for creating orderly learning environments in Chapter 12.)

Second, Diane communicated high expectations for her students in two ways. By calling on individual students (Naitia, Sheila, and Kevin at the beginning of the lesson and several others as the lesson developed), she communicated that she expected all students to pay attention and answer. She also required the students to explain their answers.

Establishing and maintaining high expectations is a simple idea, but it's hard to put into practice. Research indicates that students placed at risk often encounter low standards, and in spite of being encouraged to challenge students, teachers fail to do so (Haycock, 2001). Teacher effort and patience are essential. Diane's students initially had a great deal of difficulty in explaining their answers. Most students have trouble putting their understanding into words when they're first asked to do so; for students placed at risk, it's an even greater challenge. Many teachers simply give up, concluding, "They can't do it." They can't because they haven't had enough practice. It isn't easy, but it can be done.

Also, Diane went over each of the beginning-of-class exercises to provide feedback to any students who were uncertain about the concepts, and the explanations the students provided gave additional feedback. She also gave the students feedback about their sentences at the end of the lesson before she had them work on their paragraphs on their own.

Diane attempted to apply the third principle with questioning that involved all the students in the lesson and kept them engaged throughout. Open-ended questions such as "What do you notice?" and "How do the adjectives in the sentences compare?" virtually assured the students of being able answer successfully.

Interactive teaching methods are effective for all students and essential for students placed at risk (Gladney & Greene, 1997; Hudley, 1998; Wang et al., 1995). In a comparison of more and less effective urban elementary teachers, researchers found that less effective teachers interacted with students only 47% of the time versus 70% of the time for their more effective counterparts (Waxman, Huang, Anderson, & Weinstein, 1997). Cooperative learning strategies, such as Diane having the students make comments about each other's paragraphs, can also be effective for involving and motivating these students (Holliday, 2002).

Fourth, Diane developed her lesson with real-world examples. In our discussion of teachers who promote resilience, we saw that they attempt to link school to students' lives, and Diane did so simply and cleverly by using the students' pencils and hair color to illustrate comparative and superlative adjectives.

Finally, Diane emphasized self-regulation when she asked, "And what do we always do after we write something?" The fact that the students so quickly said, "We read it to be sure it makes sense!" indicates that she placed a great deal of emphasis on this practice.

The challenge for teachers who work with students placed at risk is how to help them be successful while still presenting a challenging intellectual menu. It isn't easy. It requires a caring environment, a great deal of effort from teachers, and administrative support. However, seeing students who were previously unsuccessful and apathetic succeed and meet challenges is enormously rewarding.

To see a video clip of a teacher using questioning strategies with a classroom of diverse learners, go to the Companion Website at *www.prenhall.com/eggen*, then to this chapter's *Classrooms on the Web* module. Click on *Video Clip 4.3.*

4.23
Earlier we found that students placed at risk often have poorer motivation than their more advantaged peers. How do structure and support, active teaching, and frequent feedback address this problem?

Classroom Connections

Using Effective Teaching Practices for Students Placed at Risk in Your Classroom

1. Communicate positive expectations to both students and their parents.
   - *Elementary:* A fourth-grade teacher spends the first 2 weeks of school teaching her students her classroom procedures. She makes short assignments, carefully

monitors students to be certain the assignments are turned in, and immediately calls parents if an assignment is missing.
   - *Middle School:* A math teacher takes extra time explaining his course procedures to his basic math classes. He explains how homework and quizzes contribute to learning and the overall grade. He emphasizes the importance of attendance and effort

and expects all to pass his course. He makes himself available before and after school for help sessions.

- *High School:* An English teacher sends home a description of her class expectations at the beginning of the school year. She makes this letter upbeat and positive and carefully explains student work requirements and grading practices. She enlists the aid of students to translate the letter for parents whose first language is not English and asks parents to sign the letter, indicating they have read it. She also invites questions and comments from parents or other caregivers.

2. Use teaching strategies that elicit high levels of student involvement and success.

- *Elementary:* A fifth-grade teacher arranges the seating in his classroom so that minority and nonminority students are mixed. He combines small-group and whole-class instruction, and when he uses group work, he arranges the groups so they include high and low achievers, minorities and nonminorities, and boys and girls.

- *Middle School:* An earth science teacher gives students a short quiz of one or two questions every day. It is discussed at the beginning of the following day, and students calculate their own averages each day during the grading period. The teacher closely monitors these scores and spends time before school to work with students who are falling behind.

- *High School:* An English teacher builds her teaching around questioning and examples. She comments, "My goal is to call on each student in the class at least twice during the course of a lesson. I also use a lot of repetition and reinforcement as we cover the examples."

Technology and Learning: Equity Issues

Technology has been viewed as the great equalizer, believed to minimize learning gaps between the rich and poor, minority and nonminority, and male and female students. Unfortunately, this view is being disproven, as research suggests a growing "digital divide" among these groups (National Telecommunications and Information Administration, 1999).

The Digital Divides

The first digital divide involves ethnicity. For instance, as shown in Table 4.7, in 1997 54% of White elementary students reported using computers at home, whereas only 21% of African American and 19% of Hispanics reported using them. Disparities were even greater at the high school level.

The second digital divide occurs between high-income and low-income groups. As shown in Table 4.8, students from families with household incomes at about the poverty level reported far less computer use at home and significantly less at school than did students

Teachers can help ensure equal access to technology through strategically assigning central roles to girls and students who are minorities.

Table 4.7 Ethnicity and computer use in 1997

Ethnicity	School Use of Computer		Home Use of Computer	
	Grades 1–8	Grades 9–12	Grades 1–8	Grades 9–12
White	84%	72%	54%	61%
African American	72%	73%	21%	21%
Hispanic	68%	63%	19%	22%

Source: U.S. Department of Commerce, 1998.

Table 4.8 Household income and computer use in 1997

Household Income	School Use of Computer		Home Use of Computer	
	Grades 1–8	Grades 9–12	Grades 1–8	Grades 9–12
$15,000–$20,000	75%	67%	16%	21%
$35,000–$40,000	80%	70%	44%	46%
$75,000 or more	86%	72%	80%	81%

Source: U.S. Department of Commerce, 1998.

whose families earned $75,000 or more. Students from high-income homes clearly have much greater access to computers (Hunter, 2002). In addition, as access increases, student motivation and achievement and improvements in the ways teachers use computers also increase (Cassady, Cassady, Budenz-Anders, Austin, & Pavlechko, 2001). If students are expected to become technologically savvy, they must have access to computers.

Access to high-quality equipment and to the Internet is also a problem for low-income groups (U.S. Department of Commerce, 1999). Schools serving high percentages of students from cultural minorities, and schools located in communities with high poverty rates, tend to have older, lower quality computers without CD-ROM capability or high-speed processors (Bracey, 1999). In 1996 schools with the most economically disadvantaged students (71% or more) had 17 students per Internet-linked computer versus 10 students per computer for schools with fewer than 11% disadvantaged students (U.S. Department of Education, 1998).

Also, in 1998 only 12% of the students at the lower end of the income scale used the Internet at home compared to 59% at the upper end (U.S. Department of Commerce, 1999).

A third digital divide separates males and females. In 1996 boys were three times more likely to enroll in computer clubs and summer computer science classes, and only 15% of users in cyberspace were female (Hale, 1998). At the Massachusetts Institute of Technology, one of the premier science and technology universities in the country, one third of all 1996 graduates were women, but only 15% of computer science graduates were women. In contrast, more than half of all biology majors were women (Hale, 1998). In 1995 women earned only 28% of the bachelor's degrees in computer or information science and 9% of the bachelor's degrees in engineering and related technologies (American Association of University Women, 2000).

At the high school level, in 1996 only 17% of students taking the College Board Advanced Placement Test in computer science were women (American Association of University Women, 1998).

Implications for Teachers

Unquestionably, technology will become increasingly important in our society, and computers can be a powerful learning tool for students. But what can teachers do to ensure that access to technology is more nearly equal?

On a positive note, research suggests that teachers, through modeling, the ways they talk about technology, and the ways they integrate technology into their instruction, have an important influence on students' attitudes toward technology (S. Turner et al., 2002). Other strategies include the following:

■ *Broadening school access to computers* (Holloway, 2000). Giving students class time to finish computer assignments and working with administrators to make computer labs available before and after school can help students who don't have computers at home, as can informing students of places in the community (e.g., public libraries) where they can use computers. Some schools are experimenting with lending students laptop computers, much as band students are loaned musical instruments.

- ■ *Providing positive role models.* Teachers, especially women, can become effective role models by describing how they use technology in their everyday lives. Teachers can invite women and members of minority groups from different professions, such as architecture and construction, to describe how they use technology in their work.
- ■ *Stressing equity in group assignments.* When students work on computers in groups, teachers should openly discuss the need for students to share responsibilities. Research suggests that students working at computers often assign low-status jobs to girls (Volman & van Eck, 2002). Teachers can combat this tendency by assigning students specific roles and monitoring group work.

With awareness and effort, teachers can do much to ensure that all students benefit from the potential of technology.

Summary

Students differ in intelligence, socioeconomic status (SES), culture, and gender, each of which influences learning. Certain combinations of these factors place students at risk of not being able to take full advantage of their educational experience.

Intelligence

Intelligence is the ability to think and reason abstractly, to solve problems, and to acquire new knowledge. Some theories suggest that intelligence is a single entity; others describe intelligence as existing in several forms.

Experts disagree about the contributions of heredity and environment to the development of intelligence. Nature advocates argue that intelligence is genetically determined; nurture proponents contend that it is influenced primarily by a child's cumulative experiences. Most experts believe that intelligence is determined by a combination of the two.

The most common response to differences in ability has been to group students according to those differences. Within- and between-class ability grouping is common in elementary schools; tracking is prevalent in middle and secondary schools. Ability grouping can lower performance and stigmatize students in low-ability classes.

Socioeconomic Status

Socioeconomic status (SES) includes parents' income, occupation, and level of education. SES can strongly influence student attitudes, values, background experiences, and school success.

Culture

Culture helps determine the attitudes, values, customs, and behavior patterns a child brings to school. The match between a child's culture and the school has a powerful influence on school success. Culturally responsive teaching creates links between a student's culture and classroom instruction.

Gender

Gender differences in aptitude or intelligence are minor, and gender-related achievement differences are caused primarily by different treatment of boys and girls. Teachers can minimize achievement differences by treating boys and girls equally and by actively combating gender stereotypes in their teaching.

Students Placed at Risk

Students placed at risk are those in danger of leaving school without the skills needed to function effectively in our modern world. Effective schools for students placed at risk stress high expectations, an academic focus, continuous monitoring of progress, and strong parent involvement. Effective teachers hold high expectations for academic success, use a variety of interactive instructional and motivational strategies, and demonstrate caring through sincere interest in students' lives. Effective instruction for students placed at risk provides greater structure and support, more active teaching, greater student engagement, challenge, and more feedback with higher success rates.

Windows on Classrooms

Throughout this chapter, we've seen how intelligence, SES, culture, and gender can influence learning and how certain combinations of these factors can place students at risk. Teachers can respond to these differences by caring about students as people, being sensitive to differences, capitalizing on students' backgrounds, and maintaining high expectations with appropriate structure.

Let's look now at another teacher working with students having some of these characteristics. Read the case study, and answer the questions that follow.

Teri Hall was an eighth-grade American history teacher in an inner-city middle school. Most of her students were from low-income families.

Today her class was studying the colonization of North America. Teri took roll as the students came into the room, and she finished entering the information into the computer on her desk just as the bell rang.

"What were we discussing yesterday?" Teri began immediately after the bell stopped ringing. "Ditan?"

". . . The beginning of the American colonies."

"Good. . . . Go up to the map, point out where we live, and show us the first British, French, and Spanish colonies. . . . Kaldya?"

Kaldya walked to the front of the room and pointed to four different locations on a large map of North America.

Teri reviewed for a few more minutes and then displayed the following on the overhead:

In the mid-1600s, the American colonists were encouraged to grow tobacco, since it wasn't grown in England. The colonists wanted to sell it to France and other countries but were told no. In return for sending the tobacco to England, the colonists were allowed to buy textiles from England. They were forbidden, however, from making their own textiles. All the materials were carried on British ships.

Early French colonists in the New World were avid fur trappers and traders. They got in trouble with the French monarchy, however, when they attempted to make fur garments and sell them to Spain, England, and others. They were told that they had to buy the manufactured garments from dealers in Paris instead. The monarchy also told them that traps and weapons would be made in France and sent to them as well. One of the colonists, Jean Forjea, complied with the monarchy's wishes but was fined when he hired a Dutch ship to carry some of the furs back to Nice.

"Now let's take a look," she began. "Take a few seconds to read the paragraphs you see on the screen. Then, with your partner, write down as many observations as you can about the subjects of the two paragraphs. Look particularly for what they have in common. You have 5 minutes."

Teri did a considerable amount of group work in her class. She sometimes had the students work in pairs, and at other times in groups of four. The students were seated together, so they could move into and out of the groups quickly. The students initially protested the assignments, because they weren't sitting near their friends, but Teri emphasized that *learning* and getting to know and respect people different from themselves were important goals for the class. Teri persisted, and the groups became quite effective.

Teri watched as the students worked, and at the end of the 5-minute period, she said, "Okay, you've done a good job. . . . Turn back up here, and let's think about this."

The class quickly turned their attention to the front of the room, and Teri said, "Serena, what did you and David come up with?"

". . . Both of the paragraphs deal with a colony."

"Okay, Eric, how about you and Kyo?"

". . . The colonies both produced something their countries, England and France, wanted—like tobacco or furs."

"Excellent observation, you two," Teri smiled. "Go on Gustavo. How about you and Pam?"

". . . They sent the stuff to their country," Gustavo responded after looking at his notes.

"And they couldn't send it anywhere else!" Tito added, warming up to the idea.

"That's very good, all of you. Where do you suppose Tito got that idea? . . . Connie?"

"It says it right in the paragraphs," Connie responded.

"Excellent, everyone! Connie, good use of information to support your ideas."

Teri continued to guide the students as they analyzed the paragraphs. She led the class to conclude that, in each instance, the colonies sent raw materials to the mother country, bought back finished products, and were required to use the mother country's ships to transport all materials.

She then told them that this policy, called *mercantilism*, was a strategy the countries used to make money from their colonies. "Mercantilism helps us understand why Europe was so interested in imperialism and colonization," she went on. "It doesn't explain everything, but it was a big factor.

"Let's look at another paragraph. Does this one illustrate mercantilism? Be ready to explain why or why not when you've made your decision." She displayed the following on the screen:

Canada is a member of the British commonwealth. Canada is a large grain producer and exporter and derives considerable income from selling this grain to Great Britain, France, Russia, and other countries. This trade has also enhanced the shipping business for Greece, Norway, and Liberia, who carry most of the products. Canada, however, doesn't rely on grain alone. It is now a major producer of clothing, high tech equipment, and heavy industrial equipment.

The class discussed the paragraph and, providing evidence from the text, concluded that it did not illustrate mercantilism.

Constructed Response Questions

In answering these questions, use information from the chapter and link your responses to specific information in the case.

1. What strategies did Teri use to eliminate gender bias in her classroom? What else might she have done?

2. One of the principles of effective teaching for students placed at risk recommends the use of high-quality examples that supplement students' background knowledge. How well did Teri apply this principle?

3. Success and challenge are essential for effective instruction for students placed at risk. Evaluate Teri's attempts to provide these components.

4. What strategies did Teri use to actively involve her students?

Document-Based Analysis

A first-grade teacher prepared the following lesson plan for the concept *mammal*.

PRAXIS These exercises are designed to help you prepare for the PRAXIS™ "Principles of Learning and Teaching" exam. To receive feedback on your constructed response questions and document analysis response, go to the Companion Website at *www.prenhall.com/eggen*, then to this chapter's *Practice for PRAXIS™* module. For additional connections between this text and the PRAXIS™ exam, go to Appendix A.

Unit: Warm-Blooded Animals

Objective: First graders will understand mammals, so when given a series of pictures of different animals, they will identify all the mammals.

Rationale: Mammals are the most advanced members of the animal kingdom, and humans are mammals. Understanding mammals will contribute to children's understanding of themselves as well as different ways that animals adapt to ensure their survival.

Content: Mammals are warm-blooded animals that have hair and nurse their young. Most mammals are born live, but some, such as the duck-billed platypus, are egg-layers. Mammals have four-chambered hearts and seven neck vertebrae. Some examples are cows, horses, people, wolves, seals, whales, kangaroos, and tigers.

Procedures:
1. Ask students to give some examples of different kinds of animals. Explain that they are going to learn about a special kind of animal. Emphasize that all can learn this content. Stress the need to pay attention.
2. Show students a guinea pig, and have them touch and feel it.
3. Have them describe what they saw and felt. Accept all answers. Write responses on board. Prompt for "feels warm" and "has hair."
4. Show them a picture of a cow with a calf. Ask how the calf eats. Prompt them to conclude that the calf nurses from its mother.
5. Add "nurses" to "warm-blooded" and "has hair" as characteristics of mammals on the board.
6. Show a picture of a dog. Ask how many of them have a dog. Ask them to describe the picture. Link to essential characteristics of mammals. Prompt if necessary, and positively reinforce for naming correct characteristics.
7. Show them a picture of an eagle sitting on a nest of eggs.
8. Ask students to identify the similarities and differences between the eagle and the guinea pig, cow, calf, and dog.
9. Show them a picture of a mother whale and baby whale. Prompt them to conclude that some mammals live in water.
10. Call for a definition of mammals based on the characteristics they've described. Write it on the board.
11. Ask for additional examples, and help students determine if they are mammals.

Materials: Pet guinea pig; pictures of a cow with calf, a dog, and a nesting eagle

Assessment: Show students a series of pictures of animals. Have them circle those that are mammals.

Assess the effectiveness of the lesson plan for students placed at risk. Identify both strengths and weaknesses. Offer at least two suggestions that would make the lesson more effective for at-risk students.

Also on the Companion Website at *www.prenhall.com/eggen*, you can measure your understanding of chapter content in *Practice Quiz* and *Essay* modules, apply concepts in *Online Cases,* and broaden your knowledge base with the *Additional Content* module and *Web Links* to other educational psychology websites.

Online Portfolio Activities

To develop your professional portfolio, further apply your understanding of chapter content, and address the INTASC standards, go to the Companion Website, then to this chapter's *Online Portfolio Activities.* Complete the suggested activities.

Important Concepts

ability grouping *(p. 125)*
cultural bias *(p. 123)*
cultural deficit theories *(p. 137)*
cultural difference theories *(p. 137)*
cultural inversion *(p. 134)*
culturally responsive teaching *(p. 137)*
culture *(p. 132)*
ethnicity *(p. 132)*
gender role identity differences *(p. 141)*

intelligence *(p. 118)*
Joplin plan *(p. 126)*
learning styles *(p. 128)*
nature view of intelligence *(p. 122)*
nurture view of intelligence *(p. 122)*
resilience *(p. 146)*
socioeconomic status (SES) *(p. 129)*
students placed at risk *(p. 145)*
tracking *(p. 125)*

Chapter Outline

Learners with Exceptionalities

5

Sabrina Curtis, a beginning first-grade teacher in a large inner-city school district, had survived the hectic first weeks of school. She was beginning to feel comfortable as she worked her way into the routines of teaching. At the same time, something bothered her.

"It's kind of frustrating," she admitted, sandwich in hand as she shared her half-hour lunch break with Clarisse, a "veteran" of 3 years who had become her friend and confidant. "I'm teaching the students, but some just don't seem to get it."

"Maybe you're being too hard on yourself," Clarisse responded. "Students *are* different. Remember some of the stuff you studied in college? One thing the professors emphasized was that we should be trying our best to treat students as individuals."

"Well, yes, . . . I understand that, but that seems almost too pat. I still have this feeling. For instance, there's Rodney. You've seen him on the playground. He's a cute boy, but his engine is stuck on fast," she said with a sigh. "I can barely get him to sit in his seat, much less work.

"When he sits down to do an assignment, he's all over his desk, squirming and wiggling. The smallest distraction sets him off. He can usually do the work when he sticks to it, but it's a chal-

lenge. I've spoken with his mother, and he's the same way at home. I wonder if he has some type of learning disability.

"Then there's Amelia; she's so sweet, but she simply doesn't get it. I've tried everything under the sun with her. I explain it, and the next time, it's as if it's all brand new again. I feel sorry for her, because I know she gets frustrated when she can't keep up with the other kids. She seems to lack basic learning strategies, like paying attention and keeping track of her assignments. When I work with her one-on-one, it seems to help, but I wish I had more time to spend with her. She's falling further and further behind."

"Maybe it's not your fault. You're supposed to be bright and energetic and do your best, but you're going to burn yourself out if you keep this up," Clarisse cautioned. "Check with the Teacher Assistance Team. Maybe these students need some extra help."

As you saw in Chapter 4, students differ in several important ways, and effective teachers consider these differences when they work with their students. In some cases, special help and resources are needed for students to reach their full potential. In these cases, the students are said to have **exceptionalities,** a category that includes *learning problems, gifts and talents, or both.*

Special education refers to *instruction designed to meet the unique needs of students with exceptionalities.* In the past, special education often meant separate classrooms. Today, students with exceptionalities are included in regular classrooms to the greatest extent possible, and teachers in these classrooms play an ever-increasing role in their education. This chapter is designed to help you prepare for that role.

After you've completed your study of this chapter, you should be able to

- Describe the laws and regulations that influence teachers' work with students with exceptionalities
- Explain how specific exceptionalities—mental retardation, learning disabilities, behavior disorders, communication disorders, and visual and hearing impairments—affect learning
- Describe several methods of identifying and teaching students who are gifted and talented
- Explain the role of classroom teachers in working with students with exceptionalities
- Explain how instructional strategies can be adapted to meet the needs of students with exceptionalities

Issues like those Sabrina and Clarisse discussed are not uncommon. Although we can't be certain from the brief descriptions, Rodney and Amelia may have problems that prevent them from taking full advantage of their educational opportunities. As teachers, we all work with students who, despite our best efforts, fail to learn as their classmates do.

Changes in the Way Teachers Help Students with Exceptionalities

In the past, students with disabilities were separated from their nondisabled peers and placed in special classrooms or schools. Instruction in these situations was often inferior, however, achievement was no better than in regular education classrooms, and students didn't learn the social and life skills needed to live in the real world (D. Bradley & Switlick, 1997). A series of federal laws redefined the way teachers assist these students.

Individuals with Disabilities Education Act (IDEA)

In 1975 the U.S. Congress passed Public Law 94-142, which made available a free and public education for all students with disabilities in the United States. This law, renamed the Individuals with Disabilities Education Act (IDEA), requires that educators working with students having exceptionalities do the following:

- Provide a free and appropriate public education (FAPE).
- Educate children in the least restrictive environment (LRE).
- Protect against discrimination in testing.
- Involve parents in developing each child's educational program.
- Develop an individualized education program (IEP) of study for each student.

IDEA has affected every school in the United States and has changed the roles of regular and special educators. Let's look at its major provisions.

A Free and Appropriate Public Education (FAPE)

IDEA asserts that every student can learn and is entitled to a free and appropriate public education. IDEA provisions related to FAPE are based on the 14th Amendment to the U.S. Constitution, which guarantees equal protection of all citizens under the law. The U.S. Supreme Court in 1982 defined an *appropriate education* as one specially and individually designed to provide educational benefits to a particular student (Hardman et al., 2002).

Least Restrictive Environment: The Evolution Toward Inclusion

Educators grappling with the challenges of providing a free and appropriate public education for all students realized that segregated classes and services were not meeting the needs of students with exceptionalities. One of the first alternatives considered was **mainstreaming,** *the practice of moving students with exceptionalities from segregated settings into regular classrooms, often for selected activities only.* Popular in the 1970s, it began the move away from segregated services and allowed students with exceptionalities and other students to interact. However, students with exceptionalities were often placed into classrooms without the necessary support (Hardman et al., 2002).

As educators grappled with these problems, they developed the concept of the **least restrictive environment (LRE),** *one that places students in as typical an educational setting as possible while still meeting their special needs.* Broader than the concept of *mainstreaming,* the LRE can consist of a continuum of services, ranging from full-time placement in the regular education classroom to placement in a separate facility. Full-time place-

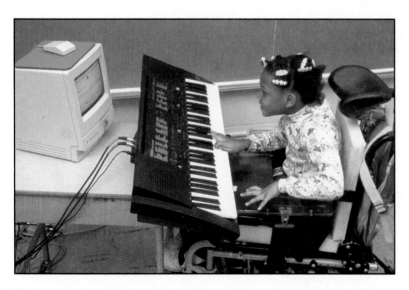

The least restrictive environment provides students with opportunities to develop to their fullest potential.

ment in the regular classroom occurs only if parents and educators decide it best meets the child's needs.

The LRE provision means that you will have learners with exceptionalities in your classroom, and you will be asked to work with special educators to design and implement programs for these students. The LRE means that students with exceptionalities should participate as much as possible in the regular school agenda, ranging from academics to extracurricular activities. The form of these programs varies with the nature of the problem and the capabilities of the students. Figure 5.1 presents a continuum, or cascade, of services for implementing the LRE, starting with the least confining at the top and moving to the most confining at the bottom. Special educators use the word *cascade* to emphasize the connectedness of levels; if students don't succeed at one level, they are moved to the next.

The concept of **adaptive fit,** *the degree to which a student is able to meet the requirements of a particular school setting and the extent to which the school accommodates the student's needs in that setting* (Hardman et al., 2002), is central to the LRE. Adaptive fit requires an individualized approach to working with a student with an exceptionality; it can be determined only after an analysis of the student's needs. As educators grappled with mainstreaming, LRE, and adaptive fit, they gradually developed the concept of inclusion.

Inclusion is *a comprehensive approach to educating students with exceptionalities that advocates a total, systematic, and coordinated web of services.* Inclusion has three components:

1. Include students with special needs in a regular school campus.
2. Place students with special needs in age- and grade-appropriate classrooms.
3. Provide special education support within the regular classroom.

Collaborative Consultation: Help for the Classroom Teacher. Initially, inclusion was viewed as additive; students with exceptionalities received additional services to help them function in regular school settings (Turnbull, Turnbull, Shank, Smith, & Leal, 2002). Gradually, the concept of *coordination* replaced addition; today, collaboration between special and regular educators to ensure that experiences for students with exceptionalities are integrated is strongly emphasized.

Figure 5.1 Educational service options for implementing the LRE

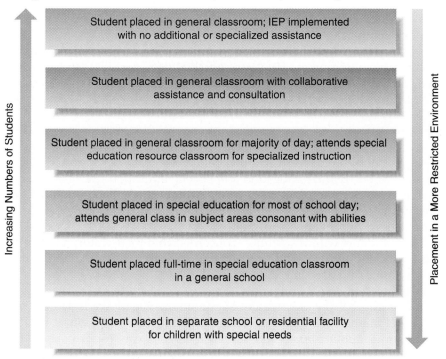

Source: U.S. Department of Education, 2002.

Inclusion creates a web of services to integrate students with exceptionalities into the educational system.

Collaboration is essential if inclusion is to be effective (Hardman et al., 2002). In working with the regular education teacher, the special educator

- Assists in collecting assessment information
- Maintains students' records
- Develops special curriculum materials
- Coordinates the efforts of team members in implementing individualized education programs
- Works with parents
- Assists in adapting instruction

Helping the regular education teacher adapt instruction is perhaps most important. (We discuss adaptations later in the chapter.)

When properly designed and implemented, team teaching can be particularly effective in a collaborative environment. It allows efficient use of special education resources, reduces the stigma of pull-out programs, and creates productive learning environments for all students (Pugach & Wesson, 1995).

Putting Inclusion Into Perspective. The practice of inclusion, while increasing, is controversial, with criticisms coming from regular classroom teachers, parents, and special educators themselves (M. Byrnes, 2002; Turnbull et al., 2002).

Where inclusion works, regular education and special education teachers collaborate extensively (Larrivee, Semmel, & Gerber, 1997). Without this collaboration, full inclusion isn't effective, and regular classroom teachers are resentful of being expected to individualize instruction without adequate support.

Some parents of students with disabilities, concerned that their children might be lost in the shuffle of school life, question the effectiveness of inclusion in providing needed services and often favor special classrooms.

In the special education community, advocates of inclusion contend that placement in a regular classroom is the only way to eliminate the negative effects of segregation (Stainback & Stainback, 1992). Opponents counter that inclusion is not for everyone and that some students are better served in special classes for parts of the day (Holloway, 2001).

Protection Against Discrimination in Testing

In the past, students with disabilities were often placed in special education programs based on inadequate or invalid assessment information. IDEA requires that any testing used in the placement process be conducted in a student's native language by qualified personnel and that no single instrument, such as an intelligence test, be used as the basis for placement. Recently, increased emphasis has been placed on a student's classroom performance and general adaptive behavior (Heward, 2003).

Due Process and Parents' Rights

Due process *guarantees parents' right to be involved in identifying and placing their children in special programs, to access school records, and to obtain an independent evaluation if they're not satisfied with the one conducted by the school.* Legal safeguards are also in place if parents don't speak English; they have the right to an interpreter, and their rights must be read to them in their native language.

Teachers and other professionals meet with parents to design an IEP that meets a student's individual learning needs.

Individualized Education Program

To ensure that inclusion works and learners with exceptionalities don't get lost in the regular classroom, an individualized education program is prepared if a student is found eligible for special education. An **individualized education program (IEP)** is *an individually prescribed instructional plan devised by special education and general education teachers, resource professionals, and parents (and sometimes the student).* It specifies the following:

- An assessment of the student's current level of performance
- Long- and short-term objectives
- Services or strategies to be used
- Schedules for implementing the plan
- Criteria to be used in evaluating the plan's success

A sample IEP is illustrated in Figure 5.2. It has three important features. First, the initials of all participants indicate that its development was a cooperative effort. Second, the information in Columns 3, 4, 5, and 6 and in Section 7 is specific enough to guide the classroom teacher and special education personnel as they implement the program. Third, the mother's signature indicates that a parent was involved in developing the program and agrees with its provisions.

The IEP performs four functions. First, it provides support for the classroom teacher, who may be uncertain about working with students with special needs. Second, it creates a link between the regular classroom and the resource team. Third, it helps parents monitor their child's educational progress. Fourth, and most important, it provides a program to meet the individual needs of the student.

IEPs sometimes provide for work in settings outside the regular classroom, such as a resource room; at other times, they focus exclusively on adaptations in the regular classroom. They are most effective when the two are coordinated, such as when a classroom teacher working on word problems in math asks the resource teacher to focus on the same type of problems (Choate, 1997).

Amendments to the Individuals with Disabilities Education Act

Since 1975 Congress has amended IDEA several times in attempts to ensure that all children with disabilities are protected and provided with a free and appropriate public education (Huefner, 1999; Lewis & Doorlag, 1999). For example, amendments in 1986 extended the rights and protections of IDEA to children aged 3 through 5 and held states

5.1
You suspect that a Hispanic student in your class, who speaks understandable English, has a learning disability in math. Because he speaks understandable English, can he be given a diagnostic test written in English? Explain.

5.2
Explain specifically how an IEP addresses the previously discussed concepts of due process, parental involvement, and least restrictive environment.

Figure 5.2 Individualized education program (IEP)

INDIVIDUAL EDUCATION PROGRAM

Date _____3-1-00_____

(1) Student

Name: Joe S.
School: Adams
Grade: 5
Current Placement: Regular Class/Resource Room

Date of Birth: 10-1-88   **Age:** 11-5

(2) Committee

		Initial
Mrs. Wrens	Principal	D.a.W.
Mrs. Snow	Regular Teacher	AS
Mr. LaJoie	Counselor	JLJ
Mr. Thomas	Resource Teacher	M.T.
Mr. Ryan	School Psychologist	H.R.R.
Mrs. S.	Parent	J.S.
Joe S.	Student	Joe L.

EP from _3-15-00_ to _3-15-01_

(3) Present Level of Educational Functioning	(4) Annual Goal Statements	(5) Instructional Objectives	(6) Objective Criteria and Evaluation
MATH Strengths 1. Can successfully compute addition and subtraction problems to two places with regrouping and zeros. 2. Knows 100 basic multiplication facts. Weaknesses 1. Frequently makes computational errors on problems with which he has had experience. 2. Does not complete seatwork. Key Math total score of 2.1 Grade Equivalent.	Joe will apply knowledge of regrouping in addition and renaming in subtraction to four-digit numbers.	1. When presented with 20 addition problems of 3-digit numbers requiring two renamings, the student will compute answers at a rate of one problem per minute and an accuracy of 90%. 2. When presented with 20 subtraction problems of 3-digit numbers requiring two renamings, the student will compute answers at the rate of one problem per minute with 90% accuracy. 3. When presented with 20 addition problems of 4-digit numbers requiring three renamings, the student will compute answers at a rate of one problem per minute and an accuracy of 90%. 4. When presented with 20 subtraction problems of 4-digit numbers requiring three renamings, the student will compute answers at a rate of one problem per minute with 90% accuracy.	Teacher-made tests (weekly) Teacher-made tests (weekly) Teacher-made tests (weekly)

(7) Educational Services to be provided

Services Required	Date initiated	Duration of Service	Individual Responsible for the Service
Regular reading-adapted	3-15-00	3-15-01	Reading Improvement Specialist and Special Education Teacher
Resource room	3-15-00	3-15-01	Special Education Teacher
Counselor consultant	3-15-00	3-15-01	Counselor
Monitoring diet and general health	3-15-00	3-15-01	School Health Nurse

Extent of time in the regular education program: 60% increasing to 80%
Justification of the educational placement:

It is felt that the structure of the resource room can best meet the goals stated for Joe; especially when coordinated with the regular classroom.

It is also felt that Joe could profit enormously from talking with a counselor. He needs someone with whom to talk and with whom he can share his feelings.

(8) I have had the opportunity to participate in the development of the Individual Education Program.

I agree with Individual Education Program   (✓)
I disagree with the Individual Education Program (   )

Parent's Signature _____Mrs S._____

Source: Adapted from *Developing and Implementing Individualized Education Programs* (3rd ed., pp. 308, 316) by B. B. Strickland and A. P. Turnbull, 1990, Upper Saddle River, NJ: Merrill/Prentice Hall.

accountable for locating young children who need special education. That state service is sometimes called *Child Find*.

Amendments in 1997, known as IDEA 97, attempted to clarify and extend the quality of services to students with disabilities. Some of the most important changes were in the following areas:

- *Nondiscriminatory assessment.* The amendment reaffirms the importance of assessment that does not penalize students for their native language, race, or culture.
- *Due process.* If school officials or the parents of a student with disabilities are not satisfied with the existing educational program, an impartial due process hearing can be requested.
- *IEP.* A copy of the IEP must be provided to parents, and they may bring to IEP meetings a person with knowledge or special expertise regarding their child.
- *Confidentiality.* Districts must keep confidential records of each child, protect the confidentiality of these records, and share them with parents on request.

One of the most controversial aspects of IDEA 97 has been in the area of disciplinary suspensions (Sach, 1999). The law establishes procedural safeguards for students while maintaining the right of districts to suspend students, if necessary, to ensure the safety of other students.

Students with Learning Problems

Educators often create labels to address student differences (Hardman et al., 2002). *Disorder, disability,* and *handicap* are common terms used to describe physical or behavioral differences. **Disorder,** the broadest of the three, refers to *a general malfunction of mental, physical, or psychological processes.* A **disability** is *a functional limitation or an inability to perform a specific act,* such as hear or walk. A **handicap** is *a limitation that an individual experiences in a particular environment,* such as being unable to enter a building in a wheelchair. Some disabilities, but not all, lead to handicaps. For example, a student with a visual disability may be able to wear glasses or sit in the front of the classroom; if these measures allow the student to function effectively, the disability isn't a handicap.

When applied as an educational label, *handicapped* has a narrow focus and a negative connotation. The word *handicapped,* which literally means "cap in hand," originates from a time when people with disabilities were forced to beg in the streets merely to survive. *Exceptional* is a much more comprehensive term. It may be used to describe any individual whose physical, mental, or behavioral performance deviates substantially from the norm, higher or lower. A person with exceptional characteristics is not necessarily an individual with a handicap.

About 5 million students with exceptionalities are enrolled in special programs, two thirds of them for relatively minor problems (Heward, 2003). Approximately 8.5 percent of students in a typical school receive special education services, and the kinds of disabilities they have range from mild learning problems to physical impairments such as deafness and blindness (U.S. Department of Education, 2000). Federal legislation has created categories to identify specific learning problems, and educators use these categories in developing programs to meet the needs of students in each category.

The Labeling Controversy

The use of categories and the labeling that results are controversial (King-Sears, 1997). Advocates argue that categories provide a common language for professionals and encourage specialized instruction that meets the specific needs of all students (Heward, 2003). Opponents claim that categories are arbitrary, many differences exist within them, and categorizing encourages educators to treat students as labels instead of people. Despite the controversy, these labels and categories are widely used, so you

Figure 5.3 The population of students with disabilities

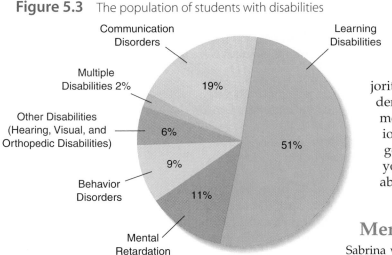

Communication Disorders

Learning Disabilities

Multiple Disabilities 2%

Other Disabilities (Hearing, Visual, and Orthopedic Disabilities)

19%

6%

51%

9%

11%

Behavior Disorders

Mental Retardation

Source: U.S. Department of Education, 2002.

need to be familiar with the terms and how they apply to the students you will be working with.

Figure 5.3 presents the percentage of students in each of the categories commonly used in education. The figure shows that a large majority (more than 70%) of the total population of students with disabilities fall into three categories—mental retardation, learning disabilities, and behavior disorders. The various disabilities in these categories are the ones you will most likely encounter in your classroom. We discuss several categories of disability in the following sections.

Mental Retardation

Sabrina watched her children as they worked on a reading assignment. Most of the class was working quietly, with occasional whispers and giggles. Amelia, in contrast, was out of her seat for the third time, supposedly sharpening her pencil. Sabrina had reminded her once to sit down and this time went over to see what the problem was.

"I can't do this! I don't get it!" Amelia responded in frustration when Sabrina asked her why she hadn't started her work.

After helping her calm down, Sabrina worked with Amelia for a few moments, but she could tell by Amelia's responses and her facial expression that she truly didn't "get" the assignment. Sabrina made a note to herself to talk to a special educator about Amelia.

All first-grade teachers have had experiences similar to Sabrina's. Amelia learns more slowly than others and becomes frustrated when she can't keep up with her peers. Unfortunately, this problem often isn't identified until students are several years into school. Many of these students have mild mental retardation. (You may also encounter the terms *educationally* or *intellectually handicapped,* which some educators prefer.)

The American Association on Mental Retardation (AAMR) defines **mental retardation,** in part, as follows:

> Mental retardation is a disability characterized by significant limitations both in intellectual functioning and in adaptive behavior as expressed in conceptual, social, and practical adaptive skills. This disability originates before the age of 18. A complete and accurate understanding of mental retardation involves realizing that mental retardation refers to a particular state of functioning that begins in childhood, has many dimensions, and is affected positively by individualized supports. (AAMR Ad Hoc Committee on Terminology and Classification, 2002)

The AAMR definition emphasizes two characteristics (Turnbull et al., 2002): limitations in intellectual functioning and limitations in adaptive skills, such as communication, self-care, and social skills. Functioning in both areas can improve when students with mental retardation receive supportive services designed to meet their needs.

Students with mental retardation are likely to display some or all of the following characteristics:

- Lack of general knowledge about the world
- Difficulty with abstract ideas
- Poor reading and language skills
- Poorly developed learning and memory strategies
- Difficulty transferring ideas to new situations
- Underdeveloped motor skills
- Immature interpersonal skills. (Beirne-Smith, Ittenbach, & Patton, 2002)

Some of these characteristics affect learning directly; the effects of others, such as immature interpersonal skills, are less direct but still important.

Before the 1960s, definitions of mental retardation were based primarily on below-average scores on intelligence tests, but this approach had several problems: (a) Tests are imprecise, so misdiagnoses sometimes resulted; (b) disproportionate numbers of minorities and non-English-speaking students were identified as mentally retarded and placed in inappropriate educational settings (Hallahan & Kauffman, 2003; Hardman et al., 2002); and (c) educators found that individuals with the same IQ scores varied widely in their ability to cope with the real world (Heward, 2003). Because of these problems, adaptive functioning became a more important concept in defining mental retardation. It is in this area that teachers' input is essential.

5.3
In Chapter 4, intelligence was defined as "the ability to acquire knowledge, the capacity to think and reason in the abstract, and the ability to solve novel problems." To which of these is adaptive behavior most closely related? Least related?

Levels of Mental Retardation

Educators describe mental retardation as having four levels that relate to the amount of support needed (Turnbull et al., 2002):

- *Intermittent:* Support on an as-needed basis
- *Limited:* Support consistently needed over time
- *Extensive:* Regular (e.g., daily) support required
- *Pervasive:* High-intensity, potentially life-sustaining support required

This classification system replaces the earlier one based on IQ scores alone. That system categorized people as having either mild (50 to 70 IQ), moderate (35 to 50 IQ), or severe and profound (IQ below 35) mental retardation. The transition from the older, IQ-anchored system to the new one is not complete, so you may encounter both in your work.

Programs for Students with Mental Retardation

Programs for students who have intermittent (mild) mental retardation focus on creating support systems to augment existing instruction. These students are often placed in regular education classrooms where teaching is adapted to meet their special needs, and attempts are made to help students fit in socially and academically.

Research indicates that these students often fail to acquire basic learning strategies—such as maintaining attention, organizing new material, and studying for tests—that typically developing students pick up naturally (Choate, 1997; Heward, 2003). Amelia, in our opening case study, is an example of a student who needs additional help to function successfully in school. Sabrina recognized this need and attempted to provide additional support by working with her one-on-one.

Learning Disabilities

Tammy Fuller, a middle school social studies teacher, was surprised when she scored Adam's test. He seemed to be doing so well. He was rarely absent, paid attention, and participated willingly and intelligently. Why was his test score so low? Tammy made a mental note to watch him more closely, because his classroom behavior and his test performance were inconsistent.

In her second unit, Tammy emphasized both independent and cooperative work, so she prepared study guide questions and had students work in groups to study the material. As she moved around the room, she noticed that Adam's sheet was empty; when she asked him about it, he mumbled something about not having time the night before. Because the success of the unit depended on students coming to class prepared, Tammy asked Adam to come in after school to complete his work.

Although students with learning disabilities are found in almost every classroom, these students are often overlooked because learning disabilities are difficult to identify.

He arrived promptly and opened his book to the chapter. When Tammy stopped to check on his progress 10 minutes later, his page was blank; in another 10 minutes, it was still empty.

As she sat down to talk with him, he appeared embarrassed and evasive. When they started to work on the questions together, she discovered that he couldn't read the text.

Some students, like Adam, have average or above average intelligence but, despite their teachers' best efforts, have a difficult time learning. These are students with **learning disabilities** (also called *specific learning disabilities*), *difficulties in acquiring and using reading, writing, reasoning, listening or mathematical abilities* (National Joint Committee on Learning Disabilities, 1994). Problems with reading, writing, and listening are most common, but math-related difficulties are receiving increased attention (Hanich, Jordan, Kaplan, & Dick, 2001). Learning disabilities are believed to be due to central nervous system dysfunction, and they may exist along with, but are not caused by, other disabilities such as sensory impairments or attention problems. Experts stress that the term *learning disability* is broad and encompasses a range of learning problems (Hardman et al., 2002).

5.4
Identify at least one similarity and one difference between learning disabilities and mental retardation.

Students with learning disabilities are the largest group of learners with exceptionalities, approximately 51 percent of the disabled student and 4.5 percent of the total school-age population. The category first became widely used in the early 1960s, and the number of school-aged children diagnosed as having learning disabilities has continually increased (U.S. Department of Education, 2000).

Characteristics of Students with Learning Disabilities

Students with learning disabilities often share a number of problems, outlined in Table 5.1. However, each student is unique, and adaptations should be individualized.

Some of the characteristics in Table 5.1 are typical of general learning problems or immaturity. Unlike developmental lags, however, problems associated with learning disabilities often increase over time. Achievement declines, management problems increase, and self-esteem decreases (Hardman et al., 2002; Heward, 2003). Lowered achievement and reduced self-esteem exacerbate each other and result in major learning problems.

Table 5.1 Characteristics of students with learning disabilities

General Patterns
Attention deficits
Disorganization and tendency toward distraction
Lack of follow-through and completion of assignments
Uneven performance (e.g., capable in one area, extremely weak in others)
Lack of coordination and balance

Academic Performance	
Reading	Lacks reading fluency
	Reverses words (e.g., *saw* for *was*)
	Frequently loses place
Writing	Makes jerky and poorly formed letters
	Has difficulty staying on line
	Is slow in completing work
	Has difficulty in copying from chalkboard
Math	Has difficulty remembering math facts
	Mixes columns (e.g., tens and ones) in computing
	Has trouble with story problems

As with all exceptionalities, identification is the first step, and it must be done early to prevent damaging effects from accumulating. Early identification isn't simple, however—uneven rates of development can easily be mistaken for learning disabilities, and classroom management issues can complicate identification. Students with learning disabilities frequently display inappropriate classroom behavior, and students who misbehave are referred for testing at a much higher rate than those who behave appropriately (Gottlieb & Weinberg, 1999). Students with learning disabilities who comply with rules and complete assignments on time are often passed over for referral. This happened with Adam, in Tammy Fuller's class. These patterns can be gender related: More boys than girls are identified because boys tend to act out more (Heward, 2003). Identification rates also vary from state to state and even within states; in Connecticut, for example, experts found identification rates varying from 7.2 percent to 23.8 percent (Sternberg & Grigorenko, 2001).

The Use of Classroom-Based Information for Identification.   Teachers play a central role in identifying and working with students who have learning disabilities (Mamlin & Harris, 1998). Information taken from teacher-made tests and teachers' direct observations are combined with standardized test scores as sources of information. Often, a discrepancy model is then used to diagnose the problem (Turnbull et al., 2002). The model looks for differences between

1. Intelligence and achievement test performance
2. Intelligence test scores and classroom achievement
3. Subtests on either intelligence or achievement tests

Performance in one area, such as an intelligence test, should predict performance in others; when the two are not comparable, a learning disability may be the cause. Some critics contend that the discrepancy model does not provide specific enough information about the nature of the learning problem and what should be done to correct it (Sternberg & Grigorenko, 2001; Stuebing et al., 2002). Other critics argue that discrepancy models identify a disability only after a problem surfaces, sometimes after several years of failure and frustration (M. Meyer, 2000). Needed, instead, are early screening measures that prevent failure before it occurs.

Earlier, we mentioned the problem of labeling. Critics contend that *learning disability* is a catchall term for students who have learning problems (Spear-Swerling & Sternberg, 1998). Part of this criticism results from the rapid growth of the category—nonexistent in the early 1960s to the largest category of exceptionality at present. Before using the learning disability label, teachers should examine their own instruction to ensure it meets the needs of different students.

Adaptive Instruction.   Students with learning disabilities require modified instruction and teacher support. Because learning disabilities have different causes, strategies need to be tailored to meet each student's needs. One study of college students with learning disabilities illustrates the range of modifications that can increase success (Ruzic, 2001). These students budgeted their time carefully, used other students as resources, and sought feedback from instructors to modify their study strategies. To compensate for reading deficits, they read in quiet environments, read aloud to themselves, and purchased previously highlighted books. In writing, they used a dictionary, frequently substituted an easier word if they had trouble spelling one, and asked other people to proofread their papers. They tape-recorded lectures to compensate for poor note taking and asked for extra time on tests. Students with learning disabilities can survive, and even thrive, if they learn and use effective study strategies.

Attention Deficit/Hyperactivity Disorder

Attention deficit/hyperactivity disorder (ADHD) is *a learning problem characterized by difficulties in maintaining attention because of a limited ability to concentrate.* Hyperactivity and impulsive behaviors are often connected with ADHD. ADHD has long been associated with learning disabilities; in fact, experts estimate as much as a 25 percent overlap between the two conditions (Hardman et al., 2002). ADHD is relatively new as an exceptionality, and it is not listed as a distinct disability category in IDEA. Students with ADHD may qualify for special education under the "other health impairments" disability category in IDEA, however, and others seek educational accommodations and modifications under *Section 504 of the Rehabilitation Act,* which protects individuals with disabilities from being discriminated against because of their disability.

The disorder has received a great deal of media attention, and teachers see many students who seem to fit the ADHD description. High activity levels and inability to focus attention are characteristics of developmental lags, especially in young boys, however, so teachers should be cautious about drawing conclusions on the basis of these characteristics alone.

Characteristics of ADHD include

- Hyperactivity
- Inattention, distractibility, difficulty in concentrating, and failure to finish tasks
- Impulsiveness (e.g., acting before thinking, frequent calling out in class, and difficulty awaiting turns)
- Forgetfulness and inordinate need for supervision

These characteristics suggest that students with ADHD have difficulty controlling the mental functions that monitor and regulate behavior (Barkley, 1998; Davies, Luftig, & Witte, 1999). It's easy to see why students with ADHD have difficulties adjusting to the "sit-down" pace of school life, where many activities are done quietly at a desk (Schlozman & Schlozman, 2000).

ADHD usually appears early (at age 2 or 3 years) and, in at least 50 percent to 70 percent of the cases, persists into adolescence (Purdie, Hattie, & Carroll, 2002). The American Psychiatric Association (2000) estimates that three to four times as many boys as girls are identified, although other experts estimate this ratio higher (Purdie et al., 2002). Treatments range from medication (e.g., the controversial stimulant medication, Ritalin) to reinforcement programs and structured teaching environments (described later in this chapter). Diagnosis and treatment of ADHD are usually done in consultation with medical and psychological experts.

Rodney, in the opening case study, shows several symptoms of ADHD. He's hyperactive, easily distracted, and has difficulties focusing his attention. His teacher is wise in seeking additional help for him. But before she does, she should examine her learning environment to see if it meets Rodney's needs. For example, teachers often find that moving a student like Rodney to a quieter part of the room can eliminate distractions and help him focus on learning tasks. Behavioral interventions using principles of reinforcement and punishment to increase desirable behaviors and reduce problematic ones, such as off-task behaviors, have also been used with some success (Purdie et al., 2002). In addition, experts recommend teaching students how to break assignments into smaller components, requiring them to keep meticulously organized assignment books, and using flash cards and other drills to develop automaticity and confidence (Schlozman & Schlozman, 2000).

Teacher support can help students with exceptionalities adapt to classroom tasks.

5.5
Explain the high ratio of boys to girls with ADHD from a genetic, or nature, position; from an environmental, or nurture, position; and from an interactionist position.

Behavior Disorders

Kyle came in from recess sweaty and disheveled, crossed his arms, and looked at the teacher defiantly. The playground monitor had reported another scuffle. Kyle had a history of these disturbances and was a difficult student. He struggled at his studies but could handle them if provided with enough structure. When he became frustrated, he sometimes acted out, often ignoring the feelings and rights of others.

Ben, who sat next to Kyle, was so quiet that the teacher almost forgot he was there. He never caused problems. In fact, he seldom participated in class. He had few friends and walked around at recess by himself, appearing to consciously avoid other children.

Although their behaviors are very different, Kyle and Ben both display symptoms of a behavior disorder. This term is often used interchangeably with *emotional distur-*

bance, emotional disability, or *emotional handicap,* and you may encounter any of these terms in your work. The term *behavior disorder* is preferred because it focuses on overt behaviors that can be targeted and changed.

Students with **behavior disorders** display *serious and persistent age-inappropriate behaviors that result in social conflict, personal unhappiness, and often school failure.* The terms *serious* and *persistent* are important. Many children occasionally fight with their peers, and all children go through periods when they want to be alone. When these patterns are chronic and interfere with normal development and school performance, however, a behavior disorder may exist.

Students with behavior disorders often have academic problems, some of which are connected with learning disabilities. The combination of these problems results in high absentee rates, low achievement, and a dropout rate of near 50 percent, the highest of any group of students with special needs (U.S. Department of Education, 1999).

Students with behavior disorders often have the following characteristics:

- Impulsiveness and difficulty interacting with others in socially acceptable ways
- Acting out and failure to follow school or classroom rules
- Poor self-concept
- Lack of awareness of the severity of their problems
- Frequent absences from school and deteriorating academic performance (Hardman et al., 2002; Turnbull et al., 2002)

Estimates of the frequency of behavior disorders vary (Hardman et al., 2002). Some suggest that about 1 percent of the total school population and about 9 percent of the special education population have the problem (U.S. Department of Education, 2002), whereas others suggest that the incidence is closer to 6 percent to 10 percent of the total population (Hallahan & Kauffman, 2003). Identification is a problem because the characteristics are elusive, making diagnosis difficult (Turnbull et al., 2002).

Kinds of Behavior Disorders

Behavior disorders can be *externalizing* or *internalizing* (Hallahan & Kauffman, 2003). Students like Kyle fall into the first category, exhibiting characteristics such as hyperactivity, defiance, hostility, and even cruelty. Males are three times more likely to be labeled as having an externalizing behavior disorder than females, and low-SES and minority status also increase students' chances of having this type of disorder. Evidence suggests that some aggressive behaviors are learned from aggressive

Externalizing behavior disorders are characterized by hyperactivity and defiant behaviors, whereas internalizing disorders are characterized by behaviors related to social withdrawal and anxiety.

5.6

Identify at least one similarity and one difference between students with learning disabilities and those with behavior disorders.

5.7

Which behavioral management strategy would likely be least effective in working with Kyle, the student who had been in the scuffle at recess? Explain.

parents and peers (Hallahan & Kauffman, 2003). Externalizing children often don't respond to typical rules and consequences.

Internalizing behavior disorders are characterized by social withdrawal, guilt, depression, and anxiety, problems more directed at the self than others. Like Ben, these children lack self-confidence and are often shy, timid, and depressed—sometimes suicidal. They have few friends and are isolated and withdrawn (Lambros, Ward, Bocian, MacMillan, & Gresham, 1998). Because they don't have the high profile of the acting-out student, many go unnoticed, so a teacher's sensitivity and awareness are crucial in identifying these students.

Teaching Students with Behavior Disorders

Students with behavior disorders require a classroom environment that invites participation and success while providing structure through clearly stated and consistently enforced rules and expectations.

Behavioral management strategies are commonly used to reinforce positive behaviors and eliminate negative ones (Alberto & Troutman, 1999). They include

- *Positive reinforcement:* Rewarding positive behaviors (e.g., praising a student for behaving courteously)
- *Replacement:* Teaching appropriate behaviors that substitute for inappropriate ones (e.g., teaching students to express personal feelings instead of fighting)
- *Ignoring:* Not recognizing disruptive behaviors in an attempt to avoid reinforcing them
- *Time-out:* Isolating a child for brief periods of time
- *Overcorrection:* Requiring restitution beyond the damaging effects of the immediate behavior (e.g., requiring a child to return one of his own cookies in addition to the one he took from another student)

A systematic use of these strategies, called *applied behavioral analysis,* is discussed in detail in Chapter 6.

Teaching self-management skills can also be effective (Heward, 2003). For instance, students might be helped to identify behaviors they want to increase (such as making eye contact with the teacher) or decrease (such as finger snapping or playing with a pencil). Over a period of time, they record the number of times they display the behaviors. They then graph the results, so they have a concrete record of their progress. The teacher also meets with them—frequently at first—to reinforce progress and to set new goals. Self-management strategies have succeeded in increasing desired behaviors, such as paying attention, as well as decreasing undesirable behaviors, such as talking out and leaving one's seat without permission (Alberto & Troutman, 1999).

Teacher Flexibility and Sensitivity.   Students with behavior disorders can be frustrating, and teachers sometimes forget that they have unique needs. An incident with a 4-year-old boy illustrates this point. He had been referred to a school psychologist for aggressive behaviors and acting "out of control." She found him friendly, polite, and cooperative, and the session went smoothly until the child announced he was done. When she tried to get him to continue, he became hysterical and ran out of the room.

> I assumed the testing phase of the evaluation was over and started writing a few notes. . . . A few minutes later, however, the little boy returned . . . and said that he was ready to continue. After another 10 minutes or so . . . the child again said, "I'm done now," to which I replied, "That's fine." The child calmly got out of his chair, walked around the room for a minute, and then sat down to resume testing. This pattern was repeated. . . .
>
>   It was easy to see in a one-to-one testing situation that this child recognized the limits of his concentration and coped with increasing frustration by briefly removing himself. . . . It is equally easy to see, however, how this behavior created problems in the classroom. By wandering around, he would be disrupting the learning of other children. When the teacher tried to make him sit back down, she was increasing his frustration by removing from him the one method he had developed for coping. (Griffith, 1992, p. 34)

But how do teachers manage behavior like this in the regular classroom? The psychologist suggested marking an area in the back of the room where the child could go when he became frustrated. With this safety valve in place, the teacher could return to her teaching and work with the boy on other, long-term coping strategies. By attempting to understand the acting-out child as an individual, the teacher was able to work smoothly with her other students while meeting his needs.

Communication Disorders

Communication disorders are *exceptionalities that interfere with students' abilities to receive and understand information from others and express their own ideas or questions.* They exist in two forms. **Speech disorders** (sometimes called *expressive disorders*) *involve problems in forming and sequencing sounds.* Stuttering and mispronouncing words, such as saying, "I taw it" for "I saw it," are examples. **Language disorders** (also called *receptive disorders*) *include problems with understanding language or using language to express ideas.* Language disorders are often connected to other problems, such as a hearing impairment, learning disability, or mental retardation.

As shown in Table 5.2, there are three kinds of speech disorders. If they are chronic, a therapist is usually required, but sensitive teachers can help students cope with the emotional and social problems that are often associated with them.

Because they affect learning, language disorders are more serious. The vast majority of students learn to communicate quite well by the time they start school, but a small percentage (less than 1 percent) continue to experience problems expressing themselves verbally. Symptoms of a language disorder include

- Seldom speaking, even during play
- Using few words or very short sentences
- Overrelying on gestures to communicate

The causes of language disorders include hearing loss, brain damage, learning disabilities, mental retardation, severe emotional problems, and inadequate developmental experiences in a child's early years.

If teachers suspect a speech or language disorder, they should keep cultural diversity in mind. As you saw in Chapter 4, English is not the primary language for many students. The difficulties these students encounter in learning both content and a second language should not be confused with communication disorders. English language learners will respond to an enriched language environment and teacher patience and understanding. Students with communication disorders require the help of a speech and language specialist.

Helping Students with Communication Disorders

Primary tasks for teachers working with students who have communication disorders include identification, acceptance, and follow-through during classroom instruction. As with other exceptionalities, teachers play an important role in identification because they are in the best position to assess students' communication

Table 5.2 Kinds of speech disorders

Disorder	Description	Example
Articulation disorders	Difficulty in producing certain sounds, including substituting, distorting, and omitting	"Wabbit" for *rabbit* "Thit" for *sit* "Only" for *lonely*
Fluency disorders	Repetition of the first sound of a word (stuttering) and other problems in producing "smooth" speech	"Y, Y, Y, Yes"
Voice disorders	Problems with the larynx or air passageways in the nose or throat	High-pitched or nasal voice

Adaptive instructional materials—such devices and books that use large print or Braille—allow students with visual disabilities to integrate into the regular classroom.

abilities in classroom settings. Modeling and encouraging acceptance are crucial because teasing and social rejection can cause lasting emotional damage. It is not easy being a student who talks differently or who cannot communicate fluently. In interacting with these students, a teacher should be patient and refrain from correcting their speech, which calls attention to the problem. Also, cooperative and small-group activities provide opportunities for students to practice their language skills in informal and less threatening settings.

Visual Disabilities

Approximately 20 percent of children and adults have some type of vision loss (Hardman et al., 2002). Fortunately, most problems can be corrected with glasses, surgery, or therapy. In some situations—approximately 1 child in 1,000—the impairment cannot be corrected. People with this condition have a **visual disability,** *an uncorrectable visual impairment that interferes with learning.*

Nearly two thirds of serious visual disabilities exist at birth, and most children are screened for visual problems when they enter elementary school. Some visual problems appear during the school years as a result of growth spurts, however, and teachers should remain alert to the possibility of an undetected impairment in students. Some symptoms of visual problems are outlined in Figure 5.4.

Research on people with visual disabilities indicates that they differ from their nondisabled peers in some areas of knowledge, ranging from understanding spatial concepts to a general knowledge of the world (Hardman et al., 2002). Word meanings in language development may not be as rich or elaborated because of the students' lack of visual experience with the world. As a result, hands-on experiences are even more important for students with visual disabilities than they are for other learners.

Working with Students Who Have Visual Disabilities

Suggestions for working with students with visual disabilities include seating them near chalkboards and overheads, verbalizing while writing on the board, and ensuring that duplicated handouts are dark and clear (Heward, 2003). Large-print books and magnifying aids can be used to adapt instructional materials. Peer tutors can provide assistance in explaining and clarifying assignments and procedures.

Lowered self-esteem and learned helplessness are two possible side effects of a visual disability. Learned helplessness results from teachers and other students overreact-

5.8
Would Piaget or Vygotsky (see Chapter 2) more strongly favor instructional modifications emphasizing hands-on experiences for students who are visually disabled? Explain how the two theorists would differ in their suggestions for using the materials.

Figure 5.4 Symptoms of potential visual problems

- Holding the head in an awkward position when reading, or holding the book too close or too far away
- Squinting and frequently rubbing the eyes
- Tuning out when information is presented on the chalkboard
- Constantly asking about classroom procedures, especially when information is on the board
- Complaining of headaches, dizziness, or nausea
- Having redness, crusting, or swelling of the eyes
- Losing place on the line or page and confusing letters
- Using poor spacing in writing or having difficulty in staying on the line

Sources: Hallahan and Kauffman, 2003; Hardman et al., 2002.

ing and doing for the student what he or she, with training, can do alone. This can result in an unhealthy dependence on others and can compound self-esteem problems (Hallahan & Kauffman, 2003).

Hearing Disabilities

Hearing disabilities can be divided into two categories. A **partial hearing impairment** is *an impairment that allows a student to use a hearing aid and to hear well enough to be taught through auditory channels.* For the student who is **deaf,** *hearing is impaired enough so that other senses, usually sight, are used to communicate.* Approximately 1.5 percent of students with exceptionalities have a hearing disability (U.S. Department of Education, 2002). Of the students with a hearing loss requiring special education, approximately 40 percent are served in general education classrooms for at least 80 percent of the school day. The percentage of these students in regular classrooms has increased dramatically in recent years and suggests that teachers will increasingly work with them in the future.

Hearing disabilities may result from rubella (German measles) during pregnancy, heredity, complications during birth or pregnancy, meningitis, and other childhood diseases. In almost 40 percent of cases involving hearing loss, the cause is unknown; this makes prevention and remediation more difficult.

Testing by a trained audiologist in a school screening program is the best method of identifying students with hearing problems, but not all schools have these programs, and problems can be overlooked if students miss the screening. When such an omission occurs, the classroom teacher's awareness of the indicators of hearing difficulties is essential. These are outlined in Figure 5.5.

Working with Students Who Have Hearing Disabilities

Lack of proficiency in speech and in language are learning problems that may result from hearing disabilities. These problems affect learning that relies on reading, writing, and listening—major sources of information in the classroom. Teachers should remember that these language deficits have little bearing on intelligence; learners can be successful if given the appropriate help.

Programs for students with hearing disabilities combine regular classroom instruction with additional support. Support programs for students who are deaf include lipreading, sign language, and finger spelling. Total communication, which uses the simultaneous presentation of manual approaches (signing and finger spelling) and speech (through speech reading and residual hearing), is increasing in popularity (Hardman et al., 2002).

Instructional adaptations to help students with hearing disabilities include

- Supplementing auditory presentations with visual information and hands-on experiences
- Speaking clearly and orienting yourself so students can see your face

Figure 5.5 Indicators of hearing impairment

- Favoring one ear by cocking the head toward the speaker or cupping a hand behind the ear
- Misunderstanding or not following directions, and exhibiting nonverbal cues (e.g., frowns or puzzled looks) when directions are given
- Being distracted or seeming disoriented at times
- Asking people to repeat what they have just said
- Poorly articulating words, especially consonants
- Turning the volume up loud when listening to audio recordings, radio, or television
- Showing reluctance to participate in oral activities
- Having frequent earaches or complaining of discomfort or buzzing in the ears

Source: Adapted from Kirk and Gallagher, 1989.

- Minimizing distracting noise
- Frequently checking for understanding

It is also helpful to have nondisabled peers serve as tutors and work in cooperative groups with students who have hearing disabilities. Teaching nondisabled students elements of American Sign Language and finger spelling provides an added dimension to their education.

Assessment and Learning: Assessment Trends in Special Education

Because of the heavy emphasis on category-specific identification and remediation, assessment plays an essential role in special education. It performs two major functions: (a) diagnosis to determine eligibility for services and (b) determination of needs so that appropriate intervention programs can be designed.

In the past, special educators relied heavily on standardized intelligence tests in the assessment process. Because intelligence tests are criticized as too narrow for diagnosing students' needs (Sternberg & Grigorenko, 2001) and because many factors—such as language proficiency, socioeconomic status, and cultural background—can affect performance (Vaughn et al., 2000), experts now urge teachers to avoid making any educational decisions about students with exceptionalities on the basis of intelligence tests alone (Heward, 2003). IDEA in fact requires a school to conduct a *multifactored evaluation* to determine whether a student is eligible for special education.

As part of the evaluations, teachers are increasingly using curriculum-based measurements, which attempt to link assessments more closely to instructional objectives. Teachers also are more closely examining students' adaptive behaviors.

Curriculum-Based Assessment

Curriculum-based assessment *attempts to measure learners' continuous performance in specific areas of the curriculum* (Meltzer & Reid, 1994), such as finding the main idea in reading or using problem-solving strategies in math. In math, for example, technology-based systems can monitor the number of problems done, number correct, and error patterns in students' work. They also provide both teachers and students with weekly progress reports (Vaughn, Bos, & Schumm, 2000). This continual feedback can then be used to teach students to monitor their own learning progress. Teachers report that computerized curriculum-based assessment systems increase students' academic performance and teach students test-taking skills (N. Phillips, Fuchs, & Fuchs, 1995).

Adaptive Behavior

Adaptive behavior refers to *a person's ability to manage the demands and perform the functions of everyday life.* The ability to adapt to changing situations is essential to success and satisfaction, both in school and out (Hardman et al., 2002). Accurate assessment of a student's adaptive behaviors provides teachers with baseline information about the skills a student already possesses and areas that need more attention.

A number of formal instruments are available to assess students' adaptive competence (Heward, 2003). For example, the *American Association on Mental Retardation Adaptive Behavior Scale—Schools* contains 104 items with several questions per item (Lambert, Nihera, & Leland, 1993). This instrument assesses areas such as students' ability to comprehend oral and written directions, express themselves, persist on tasks, and make friends.

Adaptive skills can also be assessed informally (Hardman et al., 2002). Informal assessment focuses on students' abilities to initiate and complete classroom tasks and interact effectively with other students. Teachers play an essential role in providing this information so IEP teams can make well-informed recommendations for instructional services.

Students Who Are Gifted and Talented

What is it like to be gifted or talented in a regular classroom? Here are the thoughts of one 9-year-old:

> Oh what a bore to sit and listen,
> To stuff we already know.
> Do everything we've done and done again,
> But we still must sit and listen.
> Over and over read one more page
> Oh bore, oh bore, oh bore.
> Sometimes I feel if we do one more page
> My head will explode with boreness rage
> I wish I could get up right there and march right out the door.
> (Delisle, 1984, p. 72)

Although we don't typically think of gifted and talented students as having an exceptionality, they are frequently unable to reach their full potential in the regular classroom. **Students who are gifted and talented** are *those at the upper end of the ability continuum who need support beyond regular classroom instruction to realize their full potential.* At one time, the term *gifted* was used to identify these students, but the category has been enlarged to include both students who do well on IQ tests (typically 130 and above) and those who demonstrate above-average talents in such diverse areas as math, creative writing, and music (G. Davis & Rimm, 1998; Subotnik, 1997).

Common characteristics of gifted and talented students include

- Ability to learn more quickly and independently than their peers
- Advanced language, reading, and vocabulary skills
- More highly developed learning and metacognitive strategies
- Higher motivation on challenging tasks and less on easy ones
- High personal standards of achievement

The challenge for classroom teachers is to provide an instructional agenda rich enough to help these children develop.

The history of gifted and talented education in the United States began with a longitudinal study of gifted students by Louis Terman and his colleagues (Terman, Baldwin, & Bronson, 1925; Terman & Oden, 1947, 1959). Using teacher recommendations and IQ scores, he identified 1,500 gifted individuals to be tracked over a lifetime (the study is projected to run until 2010). The researchers found that, in addition to being high academic achievers, these students were better adjusted as children and adults, had more hobbies, read more books, and were healthier than their peers. This study, combined with more current research, has done much to dispel the stereotype of gifted students as maladjusted and narrow "brains" (Moon, Zentall, Grskovic, Hall, & Stormont-Spurgin, 1997).

Current views of gifted and talented students emphasize diverse abilities and needs. The current definition used by the federal government describes them as

> Children and youth with outstanding talent who perform or show the potential for performing at remarkably high levels of accomplishment when compared with others of their age, experience, or environment.
>
> These children and youth exhibit high performance capability in intellectual, creative, and/or artistic areas, possess an unusual leadership capacity, or excel in specific academic fields. They require services or activities not ordinarily provided by the schools.
>
> Outstanding talents are present in children and youth from all cultural groups, across all economic strata, and in all areas of human endeavor. (*National Excellence*, 1993, pp. 54–57)

A recent survey found that many state departments of education have incorporated components of the *National Excellence* definition into their definitions of giftedness and talent (Stephens & Karnes, 2000).

5.9

Identify at least one similarity between the *National Excellence* definition of giftedness and Gardner's (1983, 1995a) description of intelligence found in Chapter 4.

Another popular definition uses three criteria (Renzulli, 1986):

1. Above-average ability
2. High levels of motivation and task commitment
3. High levels of creativity

According to this definition, not only are gifted people "smart," but they also use this ability in focused and creative ways.

More recent work in the area of gifted education has shifted away from the conception of giftedness as a general characteristic and toward talents in specific areas (Feldhusen, 1998a, 1998b). Attempts are made to match instruction to the areas in which talents exist (Treffinger, 1998).

Creativity: What Is It?

Creativity is *the ability to identify or prepare original and varied solutions to problems*. Creativity and intelligence are related but not identical (Sternberg & Grigorenko, 2001; Torrance, 1995); intellectual ability that is at least average is a necessary, but not sufficient, prerequisite for creativity. Like intelligence, creativity is probably influenced by both genetics and the environment.

Research by Sternberg (1997) suggests that creativity uses three kinds of intelligence: synthetic, which helps a creative person to see a problem in a new way; analytic, which allows a person to recognize productive ideas and allocate resources to solve problems; and practical, which helps a creative person use feedback to promote ideas. In all three, the emphasis is on problem solving in real-world settings.

Divergent thinking, the ability to generate a variety of original answers to questions or problems, is an important component of creativity (G. Davis & Rimm, 1998). Divergent thinking has three dimensions:

5.10

A science class is discussing the problem of pollution and the environment. Explain how the creative elements of fluency, flexibility, and originality might be applied to the solution of this problem.

- *Fluency:* The ability to produce many ideas relevant to a problem
- *Flexibility:* The ability to break from an established set to generate new perspectives
- *Originality:* The facility for generating new and different ideas

To illustrate each dimension, let's consider a social studies class discussing the problem of world hunger. Fluency would result in many solutions to the problem, such as growing food in domes in deserts, or altering humans' genetic makeup so that they require less food; flexibility would cast the problem in a new light (e.g., from economic or political rather than traditional perspectives); and originality would produce new and creative solutions to the problem (e.g., superpower cooperation).

Howard Gardner (1993) (see Chapter 4) has defined the creative person as one "who regularly solves problems, fashions products, or defines new questions in a domain in a way that is initially considered novel but that ultimately becomes accepted" (p. 35). Gardner views creativity as a recurring trait, rather than as a one-time event, that typically occurs within, rather than across, domains, such as within art or music but not both.

As with most aspects of learning, creativity requires background knowledge (Shaughnessy, 1998; Sternberg & Lubart, 1995). Knowledge makes a person aware of what has gone before, prevents "reinventing the wheel," and allows a person to concentrate on new ideas instead of existing ones.

Creativity is usually measured by giving students a verbal or pictorial stimulus and asking them to generate as many responses as they can, such as listing as many uses as possible for a brick (e.g., doorstop, bookshelf, paperweight, weapon, building block) or suggesting ways to improve a common object such as a chair (G. Davis & Rimm, 1998).

Many experts believe creativity is an essential component of giftedness.

Pictorial tasks involve turning an ambiguous partial sketch into an interesting picture. Responses are then evaluated for fluency, flexibility, and originality. Current ways of measuring creativity are controversial, with critics charging that existing tests are too narrow and fail to capture its different aspects (Ward, Ward, Landrum, & Patton, 1992).

Identifying Students Who Are Gifted and Talented

Meeting the needs of gifted and talented students requires early identification and service. Failure to do so can result in gifted underachievers with social and emotional problems linked to boredom and lack of motivation (Clinkenbeard, 1992; Dai, Moon, & Feldhusen, 1998; Louis, Subotnik, Breland, & Lewis, 2000). Current identification practices often miss students who are gifted and talented because they rely heavily on standardized test scores and teacher nominations (G. Davis & Rimm, 1998; Gallagher, 1998). Experts recommend more flexible and less culturally dependent methods, such as creativity measures, tests of spatial ability, and peer and parent nominations, in addition to teacher recommendations (G. Davis & Rimm, 1998; Shea, Lubinski, & Benbow, 2001). In addition, it is important to point out that although the majority of states have laws requiring that schools *identify* those who are gifted and talented, in 2002 only 26 states had laws requiring that schools *provide services* to these students (ERIC Clearinghouse, 2002).

Females and students from cultural minorities are typically underrepresented in programs for the gifted, and the reasons include limited definitions of giftedness, lack of culturally and gender sensitive means of assessing potential, and over-reliance on standardized tests (Tomlinson, Callahan, & Lelli, 1997; Van Tassel-Baska, 1998). For example, standardized tests usually require students to respond orally or in writing, in English. Although test makers do produce versions of the tests in other languages, such as Spanish, these tests are not widely available. Thus, ESL students who take the English version may earn scores that don't accurately measure their true potential. Also, students from cultural minorities may not understand the "classroom game" as well as other students, which teachers interpret as lack of potential (Subotnik, 1997). In addition, female students and those from cultural minorities often lack gifted role models, or mentors, who have succeeded in school or in work (Pleiss & Feldhusen, 1995; Tomlinson et al., 1997).

As with all exceptionalities, teachers play an essential role in identifying gifted and talented learners because they work with these students every day and can identify strengths that tests may miss. However, research indicates that teachers often confuse conformity, neatness, and good behavior with being gifted and talented (G. Davis & Rimm, 1998; Hunsaker, Finley, & Frank, 1997).

What should teachers look for? Experts have identified the following indicators (G. Davis & Rimm, 1998):

- Desire to work alone
- Imagination
- Highly developed verbal ability
- Flexibility in thinking
- Persistence on challenging tasks
- Boredom with routines tasks
- Impulsiveness and little interest in details

Working with these students is challenging; their giftedness places unique demands on teachers, and the flexibility of teachers' responses can make school a happy or an unhappy experience for them.

Teaching Gifted and Talented Students: Instructional Strategies

Programs for gifted and talented students are usually based on either **acceleration**, which *keeps the curriculum the same but allows students to move through it more quickly,* or **enrichment**, which *provides advanced and varied content.*

Enrichment activities provide opportunities for gifted students to explore alternative areas of the curriculum.

Educators disagree over which approach best serves students' needs. Critics of enrichment charge that it often involves busywork and point to research suggesting that students benefit from acceleration (Feldhusen, 1998a, 1998b; Schiever & Maker, 1997). Critics of acceleration counter that comparisons are unfair because the outcomes of enrichment, such as creativity and problem solving, are not easily measured on standardized achievement tests. They further argue that the regular curriculum is narrow, and social development can suffer when younger students who want accelerated content must take classes with older students. The question remains unanswered, and the debate is likely to continue.

Gifted and talented students typically are involved in either self-contained classes or pull-out programs that occupy a portion of the school day. Self-contained classes usually include both acceleration and enrichment; pull-out programs usually focus primarily on enrichment. Table 5.3 provides examples of both.

If you have gifted and talented students in your classes, and they're pulled out for part of the day, you'll be expected to provide enrichment activities during the time they're with you. The following principles can guide teachers as they attempt to adapt instruction to meet the needs of these students:

5.11

What are the advantages and disadvantages of acceleration and enrichment for the classroom teacher?

■ Assess frequently to identify areas in which students have already mastered essential content.
■ Provide alternative activities to challenge students' abilities and interests.
■ Utilize technology to provide challenge.

Let's see how the principles guide Jared Taylor, a sixth-grade teacher, as he works with his students.

Jared began the school year by administering a comprehensive series of pretests in basic skills areas. The tests helped him identify students who would need extra help as well as those who had already mastered content he would be teaching. By consulting with the special education teacher and with teachers from the previous year, he learned that he had three students—Darren, Sylvia, and Gabriella—who had been identified as gifted. They met with a teacher of the gifted twice a week in a pull-out program. Jared's task was to provide a motivating menu for them while they were in his class.

To accomplish the task, Jared pretested all of the students before beginning a new unit, and he also closely monitored Darren's, Sylvia's, and Gabriella's homework. When he saw that they had mastered the content, he provided enrichment in three ways.

Table 5.3 Options in enrichment and acceleration programs

Enrichment Options	Acceleration Options
• Independent study and independent projects	• Early admission to kindergarten and first grade
• Learning centers	• Grade skipping
• Field trips	• Subject skipping
• Saturday programs	• Credit by exam
• Summer programs	• College courses in high school
• Mentors and mentorships	• Correspondence courses
• Simulations and games	• Early admission to college
• Small-group investigations	
• Academic competitions	

First, he offered alternative learning activities. For instance, in a unit on plants in science, Jared arranged with the librarian to provide resources for a project on plants, and he met with the students to help them design the goals and scope of the project.

Second, Jared created a series of learning centers that were available to all the students. He designed centers focusing on weather, geometry, music, and art that students could go to when they finished their required work and had free time. Each center had materials to read as well as projects to complete. When Darren, Sylvia, and Gabriella demonstrated that they had mastered the content the other students were studying, he substituted projects from the centers for them.

Third, Jared supplemented his curriculum with technology. He worked with the district's media coordinator to locate a number of software programs and educational websites that provided both enrichment and acceleration. For example, an online tutorial allowed students to experiment with algebra concepts. A social studies software program called Oregon Trail had students participate in a simulated journey west via wagon train.

Jared attempted to apply the principles by first gathering as much information as he could to assess Darren's, Sylvia's, and Gabriella's understanding of the topics he was teaching. When he believed they had mastered a topic, he substituted enrichment activities for the regular topic. Acceleration may have many benefits, but it is extremely difficult to implement in the regular curriculum. Jared's approach was manageable—it didn't require an inordinate amount of extra work—and it also provided enriching experiences for his gifted students.

The Teacher's Role in Inclusive Classrooms

As we have seen, the way students receive special education has changed over time, and today regular education teachers have three important responsibilities in working with students who have exceptionalities. The first is to help identify students who may need additional help, and the second is to modify instruction to best meet individuals' needs. The teacher's third responsibility is to promote acceptance of all students in the classroom.

Identifying Students with Exceptionalities

Current approaches to identification are team-based, and because teachers continually work with students, they are the key members. When teachers identify learning problems that they can't solve by modifying their instructional strategies, other educators are called in and additional data—from standardized test scores, performance measures, and interviews with parents and other teachers—are gathered.

If the data suggest that additional help is needed, a "prereferral team" is formed, usually consisting of a school psychologist, a special educator, and the classroom teacher. The team further evaluates the problem and suggests additional classroom modifications to create a better adaptive fit. Parents are also often asked to support teachers' efforts (Mamlin & Harris, 1998).

Before a student is referred for a special education evaluation, teachers are expected to

Teachers use assessment to gather essential information to identify students with exceptionalities.

document the problem and strategies they've tried to solve it (Hallahan & Kauffman, 2003). They should describe

- The nature of the problem
- How it affects classroom performance
- Dates, places, and times problems have occurred
- Strategies they have tried
- Assessment of the strategies' effectiveness

5.12
Why are tests, quizzes, papers, and other work samples important in the referral process? Are they more or less important than standardized test results? Explain.

The classroom teacher should also check the student's records for any previous evaluations, physical problems, or participation in other special programs (Hallahan & Kauffman, 2003).

Teachers should also communicate with parents before initiating a process. IDEA requires their involvement, they can provide valuable information about the student's educational and medical history, and notifying them is a professional courtesy.

When considering a referral, the teacher should check with school administrators or the school psychologist to learn about the school's policy. A referral initiates the evaluation process. If the evaluation results in a recommendation for special services, an IEP is then prepared.

Teaching Students with Exceptionalities: Instructional Strategies

Almost certainly, some of the students in your classroom will have exceptionalities, and you will be expected to teach them as effectively as possible. The following principles can guide teachers in their efforts:

- Use effective teaching practices that promote learning for all students.
- Provide additional instructional support.
- Design seat-work and homework activities to match the needs of students with exceptionalities.
- Adapt and supplement reading materials to meet the learning needs of students.
- Actively teach learning strategies.
- Implement plans for the social integration and growth of learners with exceptionalities.

To begin examining the principles, let's look back to Chapter 4 and to Diane Smith's lesson on comparative and superlative forms of adjectives. (page 148). In Chapter 4, we emphasized that a caring and supportive environment was important for all students and essential for learners with diverse backgrounds and students placed at risk. In addition to these emotional factors, we saw that Diane created an orderly learning environment with predictable routines, combined high expectations with frequent feedback about learning progress, used high-quality examples and teaching strategies that involved all students and promoted high levels of success, and stressed student self-regulation and the acquisition of learning strategies. Diane's approach utilized the "effective teaching practices that promote learning for all students" that we see in our first principle here.

These practices apply as much to learners with exceptionalities as they do to other students (C. Mercer & Mercer, 1998; Swanson & Hoskyn, 1998):

> Research on regular versus special classroom placement suggests that the achievement progress of special education students depends not so much on what kind of classroom they are assigned to as on the amount and quality of the instruction they receive there. In general, the classroom management and instruction approaches that are effective with special students tend to be the same ones that are effective with other students. (Good & Brophy, 2000, p. 274)

Although the effective instruction practices that work for all students also work with learners having exceptionalities, teachers will need to make the modifications outlined in our principles. Let's look at them.

Instructional Support

Our second principle says, "Provide additional instructional support." To help students overcome a history of failure and frustration and to convince them that renewed effort will work, teachers often have to provide additional instructional support. For instance, while the majority of the class is completing a seat-work assignment, the teacher can work individually with a student, or with a small group. (To see an example, look at Mike Sheppard's work with his students in the closing case study for this chapter.)

Peer tutoring has been used effectively, providing benefit to both the tutor and the person receiving the tutoring (D. Miller, Barbetta, & Heron, 1994), and home-based tutoring programs that involve parents can also be successful. Teachers work with parents and explain specifically what parents can do in working with their youngster (Barbetta & Heron, 1991).

Additional adaptations are outlined in Table 5.4.

Sabrina's individual work with Amelia helped her keep up with the class.

Seat Work and Homework

To help ensure student success, seat-work and homework assignments may need to be adapted (Vaughn et al., 2000). Students with learning problems need to be taught in small steps with careful scaffolding and feedback following every step.

Homework should be an extension of seat work successfully completed in class. Again, parents' assistance can be helpful; they can orally administer a quiz each night on material being studied, for example, and they can confirm with a signature that the homework and quiz have been completed. These adaptations are demanding for the teacher, but the effort brings reward when students begin making progress.

5.13
According to research, most modifications for students with exceptionalities are more of "degree" than of "kind." What does this mean? Explain this statement using homework as a focus.

Table 5.4 Instructional adaptations for students with exceptionalities

Skill Area	Adaptations
Math	• Model correct solutions on the chalkboard. • Use peer tutors to explain problems. • Break long assignments into several shorter ones. • Encourage the use of calculators and other manipulative aids.
Reading	• Use old textbooks and other alternative reading materials at the appropriate level. • Use study guides that identify key concepts. • Preteach difficult concepts before presenting a reading passage. • Encourage group assignments in which students assist each other.
Spelling	• Avoid spelling as a grading criterion. • Focus on spelling words used in science, social studies, and other areas. • Stress mastery of several short spelling lists, rather than one long list. • Encourage students to proofread papers, circling words of which they're uncertain.
Writing	• Increase time allotted for writing assignments. • Allow assignments to be typed, rather than handwritten. • Allow reports to be taped or dictated to others. • Encourage daily writing through the use of short, creative assignments.

Reading Materials

Reading poses particular problems because students needing special help are often unable to read the required materials. Teachers can adapt with some or all of the following in one-on-one sessions with students:

- Set goals at the beginning of assignments.
- Provide advance organizers that summarize passages.
- Introduce key concepts and terms before students read the text.
- Create study guide questions that focus attention on important information.
- Ask students to summarize information in the text. (C. Mercer & Mercer, 1998; Vaughn et al., 2000)

These strategies increase reading comprehension with typically developing learners (Barr, 2001; E. Hiebert & Raphael, 1996), and using them with students with exceptionalities provides an additional level of support.

Learning Strategies

Strategy training is one of the most promising approaches to helping students with learning problems (Swanson & Hoskyn, 1998). A *learning strategy* is a plan for accomplishing a learning goal. For example, in applying a strategy to learn a list of 10 spelling words, a student might say to himself,

> "Okay, . . . 10 words for the quiz on Friday. That shouldn't be too hard. I have 2 days to learn them.
>
> "Let's see. These are all about airports. Which of these do I already know—*airplane, taxi, apron,* and *jet*? No problem. Hmmm, . . . some of these aren't so easy, like *causeway* and *tarmac*. I don't even know what a 'tarmac' is. I'll look it up. . . . Oh, that makes sense. It's the runway. I'd better spend more time on these words. I'll cover them up and try to write them down and then check 'em. Tonight, I can get Mom to give me a quiz, and then I'll know which ones to study extra tomorrow."

To see a video clip of a teacher introducing her students to a learning strategy, go to the Companion Website at *www.prenhall.com/eggen,* then to this chapter's *Classrooms on the Web* module. Click on *Video Clip 5.1.*

5.14
Describe specifically how a teacher might instruct students to more strategically attack the spelling list in the example.

This student was strategic in three ways. First, separating the words he already knew from those he didn't, spending extra time on the difficult ones, and looking up *tarmac* in the dictionary show he had clear goals. Second, he took a deliberate approach to the task, allocating more time to the words he didn't know and skipping the ones he did. Third, he monitored his progress through quizlike exercises.

Students with learning difficulties often approach tasks passively or use the same strategy for all goals (C. Mercer & Mercer, 1998; Swanson, 2001). In studying 10 spelling words, for instance, they may merely read the words, instead of trying to actually spell them, or they may spend as much time on the words they already know as on those they don't know. In contrast with most students, who acquire learning strategies naturally as they progress through school, students with learning problems often have to be explicitly taught them (Gersten & Baker, 2001). Teacher modeling and explanation, together with opportunities for practice and feedback, are essential (De La Paz, Swanson, & Graham, 1998).

Social Integration and Growth

Finally, our sixth principle suggests implementing plans for the social integration and growth of learners with exceptionalities. Students with disabilities are often labeled as different, fall behind in their academic work, misbehave in class, and sometimes lack social skills (Hallahan & Kauffman, 2003). As a result, other students often develop negative attitudes toward them, and the impact of these attitudes on their confidence and self-esteem are among the most difficult obstacles they face (Moon et al., 1997; Pearl et al., 1998). Special efforts are needed to promote the acceptance of students with exceptionalities in regular classrooms. These efforts include developing classmates' understanding and acceptance of them, helping them learn acceptable behaviors, and using strategies to promote social interaction among the students.

Developing Classmates' Understanding and Acceptance. Nondisabled students' negative attitudes are often the result of a lack of understanding. Providing information about disabilities can help change attitudes toward students with exceptionalities (Heward, 2003). Openly discussing disabilities and emphasizing that people with disabilities want to have friends and be liked, want to succeed, and want to be happy—just as everyone else does—can do much to change attitudes. These discussions can reduce stereotypes about learners with exceptionalities and break down the barriers between them and other students. Literature and videos that explore the struggles and triumphs of people with disabilities, and guests that have overcome disabilities, are also valuable sources of information.

Helping Students Learn Acceptable Behaviors Students with exceptionalities can help themselves by learning what constitutes acceptable behavior (Pearl et al., 1998). Counseling and applied behavioral analysis are two strategies that can be used to help students improve their behavior (Elbaum & Vaughn, 2001). (For an example of applied behavioral analysis in a classroom, turn to page 210 in Chapter 6.) Modeling, together with coaching, is also effective.

Modeling and coaching can be particularly helpful for teaching students social skills. Students with disabilities often lack the skills needed to make friends (Choi & Heckenlaible-Gotto, 1998); they may avoid other students or alienate them unknowingly. To teach a student how to initiate play, for example, a teacher might say, "Barnell's over there on the playground. I think I'll say, 'Hi, Barnell! Want to play ball with me?' Now you try it, and I'll watch."

Teachers can also model social problem solving; for instance, a teacher might comment, "Hmm, . . . Mary has a toy that I want to play with. What could I do to make her want to share that toy?" These direct approaches have proved successful in teaching social skills such as empathy, perspective taking, negotiation, and assertiveness (Choi & Heckenlaible-Gotto, 1998; Vaughn et al., 2000).

Strategies for Promoting Interaction and Cooperation. One of the most effective ways to promote acceptance of students with exceptionalities is to call on them—with about the same frequency as you call on other students. This sends a powerful message: It communicates that all students are valued and are expected to participate and succeed. Cooperative learning and peer tutoring are two other strategies that can be used to promote interaction among students. (For a discussion of cooperative learning, turn to page 298 of Chapter 8).

Peer tutoring places students in pairs or groups of three (pairs are most common) and provides them with learning activities, practice, and feedback. For example, after introducing a new concept in math, the teacher assigns students in pairs to work on practice exercises. Students take turns tutoring and being tutored, one doing the sample problems and the other checking the answers and providing feedback. Various combinations have been used: high and low ability, students with and without exceptionalities, and students with exceptionalities tutoring each other. If well organized and carefully monitored, any of these combinations can be successful while also promoting social interaction and improved attitudes toward those with exceptionalities (Elbaum, Vaughn, Hughes, & Moody, 1999; D. Fuchs, Fuchs, Mathes, & Simmons, 1997). For peer tutoring to be most effective, students with exceptionalities must have frequent opportunities to tutor and be tutored.

Simply putting students together and putting one in the role of tutor won't work, however; training students to be interactive and task oriented in their tutoring and feedback dramatically improves the quality of the tutoring (L. Fuchs, Fuchs, Kazdan, & Allen, 1999).

Cross-age tutoring, in which older students with exceptionalities tutor younger ones, can be especially promising (Top & Osgthorpe, 1987). The older students' academic self-concepts increase, which makes sense—providing help for a younger student increases tutors' feelings of competence, which motivation theories describe as a basic need in all people (Ryan & Deci, 2000).

Unquestionably, having learners with exceptionalities in your classroom will increase your workload. On the other hand, helping a student with a disability adapt and even thrive can be one of the most rewarding experiences you will ever have as a teacher.

5.15
Would a student with mental retardation, a learning disability, or a behavior disorder be more likely to have problems with social integration and growth? Explain your thinking.

Technology and Learning: Assistive Technology

Technology offers an impressive variety of tools to help us teach students with exceptionalities. **Assistive technology** refers to *technological adaptations that help students with exceptionalities use computers and other forms of technology.* Some students, such as those who are blind or who have physical impairments, cannot interact with a standard computer unless adaptations are made. Adaptive changes can be made to either input or output devices (Lewis & Doorlag, 1999).

To use computers effectively, students must be able to input their words and ideas. This can be nearly impossible for nonreaders or those with visual or other physical disabilities. One adaptation includes devices that enhance the keyboard by making it larger and easier to see, arranging the letters alphabetically to make them easier to find, or replacing letters with pictures. Keyboards that allow students to type in Braille are also available.

Additional adaptations completely bypass the keyboard. For example, students with limited or no use of their hands can use switches activated by a body movement, such as a head nod, to interact with the computer and input information. Touch screens allow students to go directly to the computer monitor to indicate their responses (Newby, Stepich, Lehman, & Russell, 2000).

Output devices include monitors and printers. Adaptations to the standard computer monitor either bypass visual displays or increase their size. To increase print size, a student may use a large-screen monitor or magnification device. Students who are blind may use a speech synthesizer that translates printed words into sounds or Braille adapters that can convert regular print into Braille.

In addition to alternative input and output devices, many other tools are available for students with exceptionalities. For example, software programs can be used to help students with learning disabilities learn to read and write (MacArthur, Ferretti, Okolo, & Cavalier, 2001). Reading programs help teach students phonetic skills, and other programs simplify word processing demands in writing (Vaughn et al., 2000). These technologies are important because they prevent disabilities from becoming handicaps. Their importance to students with exceptionalities is likely to increase as technology becomes a more integral part of classroom instruction.

Technology can be used to provide students who have exceptionalities with opportunities for practice with frequent and specific feedback.

Classroom Connections

Teaching Students with Exceptionalities in the Regular Classroom

1. Discuss the subject of exceptionalities in an open and positive manner.
   - *Elementary:* A second-grade teacher uses role playing and modeling to illustrate problems such as teasing and taunting others. She emphasizes treating students who look or act differently with the same respect that other students receive.

- *Middle School:* An English teacher uses literature, such as *Summer of the Swans*, by Betsy Byars (1970), as a springboard for talking about individual differences. Students are encouraged to reflect on their own individuality and how important this is to them.

- *High School:* An English teacher leads a discussion of students' favorite foods, activities, movies, and music, and also discusses topics and issues that concern them. He uses the discussions as a springboard for helping create a sense of community in the classroom.

Creative teachers design learning activities that allow students of differing abilities to interact and learn about one another.

2. Adapt instruction to meet the needs of students with exceptionalities.
   - *Elementary:* A third-grade teacher carefully monitors students during seat work. She often gathers students with exceptionalities in a small group to provide additional assistance with assignments.
   - *Middle School:* A sixth-grade math teacher organizes his students in groups of four for seat-work assignments. Each student does a problem and confers with a partner. When two students disagree, they confer with the other pair in their group. The teacher carefully monitors the groups to be sure that all four are participating as equally as possible.
   - *High School:* A science teacher assesses frequently and provides detailed feedback on all assessment items. She spends time in one-on-one conferences with any students having difficulty.

3. Teach students with exceptionalities learning strategies.
   - *Elementary:* A fourth-grade math teacher emphasizes questions such as the following in checking answers to word problems: Does the solution answer the problem? Does it make sense? Are the units correct? He reinforces this process throughout the school year.
   - *Middle School:* A math teacher teaches problem-solving strategies by thinking aloud at the chalkboard while she's working through a problem. She breaks word problems into the following steps:
     1. Read: What is the question?
     2. Reread: What information do I need?
     3. Stop and think: What do I need to do—add, subtract, multiply, or divide?
     4. Compute: Put the correct numbers in and solve.
     5. Label and check: What answer did I get? Does it make sense?

   - *High School:* An English teacher teaches and models step-by-step strategies. A unit on writing one-paragraph essays teaches students to use four steps: (a) Write a topic sentence, (b) write three sentences that support the topic sentence, (c) write a summary sentence, and (d) reread and edit the paragraph. The teacher models the strategy and provides positive and negative examples before asking the students to write their own.

Teaching Students Who Are Gifted and Talented in Your Classroom

4. Provide supplementary activities that challenge students who are gifted and talented.
   - *Elementary:* A fifth-grade teacher allows his gifted and talented students to substitute projects of their choice for homework assignments once they have demonstrated that they have mastered the regular curriculum.
   - *Middle School:* A pre-algebra teacher pretests students at the beginning of each unit. Whenever a student has mastered the concepts and skills, he or she receives an honor pass to work on an alternative activity in the school media center. The activities may be extensions or applications of the concepts taught in the unit, or they may involve learning about mathematical principles or math history not usually taught in the regular curriculum.
   - *High School:* A social studies teacher caps off every unit with a hypothetical problem, such as "What would the United States be like today if Great Britain had won the Revolutionary War?" Students work in groups to address the question, and the teacher gives extra credit to those who want to pursue the topic further in a paper or project.

Summary

Changes in the Way Teachers Help Students with Exceptionalities

In the past, students with exceptionalities were often segregated from the regular classroom. Mainstreaming began the process of integrating them with nondisabled students, and inclusion takes the process further by creating a web of services. Inclusion is most effective when regular education and special education teachers closely collaborate on instructional adaptations for learners with exceptionalities.

Federal laws and regulations require that students with exceptionalities be taught in the least restrictive environment, guarantee the right to parental involvement through due process, protect against discrimination in testing, and provide learners with IEPs.

Students with Learning Problems

Categorizing students with exceptionalities is widespread and controversial. Categories include mental retardation, learning disabilities, behavior disorders, communication disorders, visual disabilities, and hearing disabilities. Students from cultural minorities are disproportionately categorized as having learning problems.

Students Who Are Gifted and Talented

Gifted and talented students display unique abilities in specific domains. Acceleration moves these students through the regular curriculum at a faster rate; enrichment provides alternative instruction to encourage student exploration.

The Teacher's Role in Inclusive Classrooms

Teachers' responsibilities in inclusive classrooms include identifying learners with exceptionalities and adapting instruction for them. In the process of identification, teachers describe and document learning problems and strategies they've tried. Effective instruction for students with disabilities uses characteristics of instruction effective with all students. In addition, teachers provide additional instructional support, modify homework assignments and reading materials, and help students acquire learning strategies.

An additional responsibility is to promote social acceptance for students with disabilities through modeling, practice, and feedback. Attitudes of other students can be improved through instructional approaches that focus on increased understanding and through strategies such as peer tutoring and cooperative learning, which provide students with opportunities to interact in productive ways.

Windows on Classrooms

As you've studied this chapter, you've examined characteristics of students with exceptionalities, and you've learned that all students can learn if instruction is adapted to meet their needs. Efficient use of time, a supportive academic climate, effective classroom management, high success rates, and frequent and informative feedback are important in helping students with exceptionalities achieve their maximum potential.

Let's look at a junior high school math teacher and his efforts to work with students who have exceptionalities. Read the case study, and answer the questions that follow.

Mike Sheppard taught math at Landrom Junior High School. Yesterday he had introduced his seventh-grade pre-algebra class to a procedure for solving word problems. He modeled the solution of several examples, using the procedure, and then assigned five problems for homework.

Mike had 28 students in his second-period class, including five students with exceptionalities: Herchel, Marcus, and Gwenn, who experienced learning problems, and Todd and Horace, who had problems monitoring their own behavior. Herchel, Marcus, and Gwenn each had problems with decoding words, reading comprehension, and writing. Other teachers described Todd as verbally abusive, aggressive, and lacking in self-discipline. He was extremely active and had a difficult time sitting through a class period. Horace was just the opposite: a very shy, withdrawn boy.

At 10:07 today, Herchel, Marcus, and Gwenn were among the first of Mike's students to file into class. As the students entered, they looked in anticipation at the screen in the front of the room. Mike typically displayed one or more problems on the overhead for the students to complete while he took roll and finished other beginning-of-class routines.

Mike watched for Herchel, Marcus, and Gwenn to take their seats, and then he slowly read the displayed problem:

On Saturday the Trebek family drove 17 miles from Henderson to Newton, stopped for 10 minutes to get gas, and then drove 22.5 miles from Newton through Council Rock to Gildford. The trip took 1 hour and 5 minutes, including the stop. On the way back, they took the same route but stopped in Council Rock for lunch. Council Rock is 9.5 miles from Gildford. How much farther will they have to drive to get back to Henderson?

As Mike read, he pointed to each displayed word. "Okay," he smiled after he finished reading. "Do you know what the problem is asking you?"

"Could you read the last part again, Mr. Sheppard?" Gwenn asked.

"Sure," Mike nodded and repeated the part of the problem that described the return trip, again pointing to the words as he read.

"All right, jump on it. Be ready because I'm calling on one of you first today," he again smiled and made sure to make eye contact with each of the students with learning problems.

The students were in their seats, and most were studying the screen as the bell rang at 10:10. Mike quickly took roll and then walked to Todd's desk.

"Let's take a look at your chart," he said. "You've improved a lot, haven't you?"

"Yeah, look," Todd responded, proudly displaying the following chart.

	2/9–2/13	2/16–2/20	2/23–2/27
Talking out	ꝋ ꝋ ꝋ ꝋ ꝋ ꝋ	ꝋ IIII ꝋ	ꝋ II
Swearing	ꝋ ꝋ	ꝋ II	IIII
Hitting/ touching	ꝋ III	ꝋ IIII	III
Out of seat	ꝋ ꝋ ꝋ III	ꝋ ꝋ ꝋ IIII	ꝋ ꝋ ꝋ III
Being friendly	II	IIII	ꝋ II

"That's terrific," Mike whispered to Todd as he leaned over the boy's desk. "You're doing much better. We need some more work on 'out-of-seat,' don't we? I don't like getting after you about it, and I know you don't like it either," he went on. "Stop by at the end of class. I have an idea for you that I think will help. Don't forget to stop. . . . Okay. Get to work on the problem." Mike gave Todd a light thump on the back and returned to the front of the room.

"Okay, everyone. How did you do on the problem?"

Amid a mix of "Okay," "Terrible," "Fine," "Too hard," some nods, and a few nonresponses, Mike began, "Let's review for a minute. . . . What's the first thing we do whenever we have a word problem like this?"

He looked knowingly at Marcus, remembering a pledge he had made to himself to call on one of the five students first today. "Marcus?"

"Read it over at least twice," Marcus replied.

"Good. . . . That's what our problem-solving plan says," Mike continued, pointing to the following chart hanging on the chalkboard:

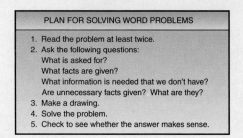

PLAN FOR SOLVING WORD PROBLEMS

1. Read the problem at least twice.
2. Ask the following questions:
   What is asked for?
   What facts are given?
   What information is needed that we don't have?
   Are unnecessary facts given? What are they?
3. Make a drawing.
4. Solve the problem.
5. Check to see whether the answer makes sense.

"Then what do we do? . . . Melissa?"

"See what the problem asks for."

"Very good. What is the problem asking for? . . . Rachel?"

". . . How much farther they'll have to drive?"

"Excellent. Now, think about this. Suppose I solved the problem and decided that they had 39½ miles left to drive. Would that make sense? Why or why not? Everybody think about it for a moment."

Mike hesitated for several seconds and then said, "Okay. What do you think? . . . Herchel?"

". . . I . . . I . . . don't know."

"Oh, yes you do," Mike encouraged. "Let's look. . . . How far from Henderson to Gildford altogether?"

"Thir—," Rico began until Mike put his hand up, stopping him in midword. He then waited a few seconds as Herchel studied a sketch he had made on his paper:

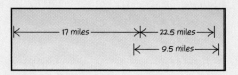

". . . 39½ miles," Herchel said uncertainly. "Oh! . . . The whole trip was only that far, so they couldn't still have that far to go."

"Excellent thinking, Herchel. See, I told you that you knew.

"Now go ahead, Rico. How far do they still have to go?"

"Thirty miles," Rico, one of the higher achievers in the class, responded quickly.

"Good," Mike nodded. "Someone explain carefully how Rico might have gotten that. . . . Go ahead, Brenda."

". . . The total distance is 39½ miles over, and they came back 9½ . . . so, 39½ minus 9½ is 30."

"Good, Brenda. That's a good, clear description."

"Now," Mike continued, "is there any unnecessary information in the problem?"

"Yes!" several students responded at once.

"Okay. Like what? . . . Horace?" Mike asked, lowering his voice slightly and moving toward Horace's desk.

" . . . "

"Look at the problem," Mike encouraged softly.

" . . . "

"How long did the trip take?"

". . . An hour and 5 minutes."

"And again, what does the problem ask us for?" Mike continued, nodding to Horace.

". . . How much farther they had to drive."

"Excellent, so the amount of time they took is irrelevant," Mike smiled, raising his voice and turning back to the front of the room.

Mike guided the class toward identifying other items of unnecessary information in the problem and then asked the students to hold up three fingers if they had solved the problem correctly, two fingers if they had solved it but got an incorrect answer, and one finger if they had gotten no solution.

Seeing about a third of the class holding up three fingers, he thought wryly, "We're going to need some extra work on this material.

"Okay. Not too bad for the first time through," he continued cheerfully. "Let's take a look at your homework."

Mike reviewed each homework problem just as he did the first one, asking students to relate each problem's parts to the steps in the problem-solving plan, drawing a sketch on the chalkboard, and calling on a variety of students to supply specific answers and describe their thinking as they worked their way to the solutions.

With 20 minutes left in the period, he assigned 10 more problems for homework, and the students began working. Once the class was working quietly, Mike gestured to Herchel, Marcus, and Gwenn to join him at a table at the back of the room.

"How'd you do on the homework?" Mike asked. "Do you think you get it?"

"Sort of," Gwenn responded, and the other two nodded.

"Good," Mike smiled. "Now, let's see what we've got. But before we start, Herchel, let's take a look at the drawing you made on our practice problem. . . . Go ahead and get it out."

Herchel got out the sketch:

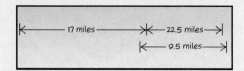

"Take a good look at it," Mike directed. "What looks funny? . . . Gwenn, you and Marcus look too."

"The 9½ miles is longer than the 22½ miles," Gwenn answered.

"Exactly," Mike nodded. "Now remember, this has to make sense. We know that 22½ is longer than 9½ and that 22½ is longer than 17. So, when you make your sketches, be sure they make sense. Now, you all can do this work. So, I want to see good work from each of you," he finished, nodding encouragingly.

"Okay. Go ahead and read the first problem, Gwenn."

"Ramon b . . . b . . . "

"Bought," Mike interjected.

"Bought," Gwenn continued, ". . . bought a CD for $13.95." She finished reading the problem, haltingly, and with Mike's help.

"Okay. What are we trying to find in this problem?"

"How much more the first CD cost than the cassette?" Marcus answered.

"Good. You all understand the problem?"

The three nodded.

"Okay. Let's look at the next one. . . . Go ahead and read it, Marcus."

Mike reviewed each of the problems to be sure the students could read them and comprehend the information. As the group worked, other students periodically came to the table, and Mike momentarily stopped to answer their questions. He also stopped briefly to go over and speak to Connie and Pamela, who were whispering.

When about 5 minutes were left in the period, Mike told the three students, "Run back to your desks now and see whether you can get one or two problems done before the bell rings."

Soon the bell rang, and the students began filing out of the room. Mike caught Todd's eye, Todd stopped, and Mike led him to a small area in the back of the room where a partition had been set up. The area was partially enclosed but facing the front of the class.

"Here's what we'll do," Mike directed. "When you have the urge to get out of your seat, you quietly get up and move back here for a few minutes. Stay as long as you want, but be sure you pay attention to what we're doing. When you think you're ready to move back to your seat, go ahead. All I'm asking is that you move back and forth quietly and not bother the class. . . . What do you think?"

Todd nodded, and Mike put a hand on his shoulder. "You're doing so well on everything else; this will help, I think. You're a good student. You hang in there. . . . Now, get out of here," Mike smiled. "Here's a pass into Mrs. Miller's class."

Constructed Response Questions

In answering these questions, use information from the chapter and link your responses to specific information in the case.

1. How did Mike create a warm academic climate for his students? Cite specific evidence from the case study.

2. How did Mike attempt to ensure success in his teaching?

3. What did Mike do to alter instruction for his students with learning disabilities? How effective were these modifications?

4. What did Mike do to meet the needs of his students with behavior disorders? How effective were these interventions?

Document-Based Analysis

In developing the individualized education program in Figure 5.2, the following procedures were used.

Mrs. Snow, the regular teacher, initiated the process when she noticed that Joe responded infrequently in class and didn't seem to understand her directions. The resource teacher, Mr. Thomas, met with Joe and then referred him to Mr. Ryan, the school psychologist, for testing. In a note to Mr. Ryan, Mrs. Snow suggested that English may not be Joe's first language. After administering an intelligence test to Joe, the school psychologist concluded that he was intelligent enough to stay in the regular class but would need special help. After several unsuccessful attempts to contact Joe's mother, a single parent who worked three jobs, the group decided to meet anyway without her.

Analyze the extent to which the processes used in initiating and completing the IEP were consistent with accepted procedures.

Online Portfolio Activities

To develop your professional portfolio, further apply your understanding of chapter content, and address the INTASC standards, go to the Companion Website, then to this chapter's *Online Portfolio Activities*. Complete the suggested activities.

PRAXIS These exercises are designed to help you prepare for the PRAXIS™ "Principles of Learning and Teaching" exam. To receive feedback on your constructed response questions and document analysis response, go to the Companion Website at *www.prenhall.com/eggen*, then to this chapter's *Practice for PRAXIS*™ module. For additional connections between this text and the PRAXIS™ exam, go to Appendix A.

 Also on the Companion Website at *www.prenhall.com/eggen*, you can measure your understanding of chapter content in *Practice Quiz* and *Essay* modules, apply concepts in *Online Cases*, and broaden your knowledge base with the *Additional Content* module and *Web Links* to other educational psychology websites.

Important Concepts

acceleration *(p. 179)*

adaptive behavior *(p. 176)*

adaptive fit *(p. 161)*

assistive technology *(p. 186)*

attention deficit/hyperactivity disorder (ADHD) *(p. 169)*

behavior disorders *(p. 171)*

communication disorders *(p. 173)*

creativity *(p. 178)*

curriculum-based assessment *(p. 176)*

deaf *(p. 175)*

disorder *(p. 165)*

disability *(p. 165)*

due process *(p. 163)*

enrichment *(p. 179)*

exceptionalities *(p. 159)*

handicap *(p. 165)*

inclusion *(p. 161)*

individualized education program (IEP) *(p. 163)*

language or receptive disorders *(p. 173)*

learning disabilities *(p. 168)*

least restrictive environment (LRE) *(p. 160)*

mainstreaming *(p. 160)*

mental retardation *(p. 166)*

partial hearing impairment *(p. 175)*

special education *(p. 159)*

speech or expressive disorders *(p. 173)*

students who are gifted and talented *(p. 177)*

visual disability *(p. 174)*

Chapter Outline

Behaviorist Views of Learning
Contiguity • Classical Conditioning • Operant Conditioning • Behaviorism in the Classroom: Instructional Strategies • Putting Behaviorism into Perspective

Social Cognitive Theory
Comparing Behaviorism and Social Cognitive Theory • Modeling • Vicarious Learning • Effects of Modeling on Behavior • Technology and Learning: The Impact of Symbolic Modeling on Behavior • Processes Involved in Learning from Models • Effectiveness of Models • Self-Regulation • Social Cognitive Theory in the Classroom: Instructional Strategies • Assessment and Learning: Self-Modeling as an Assessment Tool • Putting Social Cognitive Theory into Perspective

Addressing Diversity: Behaviorism and Social Cognitive Theory
Classical Conditioning: Learning to Like and Dislike School • Motivating Hesitant Learners • Capitalizing on Minority Role Models

Behaviorism and Social Cognitive Theory

6

Tim had been doing fairly well in Algebra II—getting a few C's but mostly B's on the weekly quizzes. In fact, the tenth grader had become fairly confident until the last test, when something inexplicably went wrong. For some reason, he became confused, got solutions mixed up, panicked, and failed the quiz. He was devastated.

On the next quiz, he was so nervous that when he started, the first few answers he circled had wiggly lines around them from his shaking hand. This happened during the following quiz too.

"I'm not sure I can do this," he concluded. "Maybe I should drop algebra."

His hand also started to shake when he took chemistry tests, even though he hadn't done poorly on any of them. Fortunately, he still did fine in his English and world history classes.

One day Mrs. Lovisolo, his Algebra II teacher, had a talk with him. She reminded him that he had only failed one quiz and hadn't been making his usual effort as he studied.

"Thanks, Mrs. Lovisolo," Tim said, on the brink of tears, "but math . . . is so hard for me. I don't know."

"I don't want to hear those words," she said with a supportive smile. "Now I want you to relax. You can do this work. I'm going to keep an eye on you in class, and if you're having trouble, just let me know, and we'll work together after school. Okay?"

"Okay," Tim said, and although he remained unconvinced, he vowed to redouble his efforts.

After class, Tim mentioned his troubles to his friend Susan, who always did so well on the algebra quizzes.

"I think they're tough," she commented, "so I really study for them. How about if we get together?"

Tim reluctantly agreed, and on Thursday, the night before the next quiz, he went to Susan's home to study with her. He saw how she selected problems from the book and solved them completely in writing, rather than just reading over the sample problems and explanations. As she began working on her third problem, he asked her why she was doing another one.

"I try to do as many different kinds as I can, to be sure I don't get fooled on the quiz," she explained. "That way, I'm more confident when I go into it. . . . See, this one is different. . . . The first thing I look for is how it's different. Then I try it.

"I sometimes even make a little chart. I try to do at least three problems of each type we study, and then I check them off as I do them. It's sort of fun—I can see I'm making some progress. If I get all of them right, I treat myself with a dish of ice cream."

"Good idea," Tim nodded. "I usually do a couple and if I'm okay on them, I quit."

Tim set a new goal to do three of each type, selecting the odd problems so that he could check the correct answers in the back of the book. Also, when Mrs. Lovisolo used a term in class that he didn't understand, he wrote it down, together with the definition, and then studied it so that he immediately understood what she meant when she used it in her explanations.

He did much better on the next test. "Whew, what a relief," he said to himself.

He was still a little nervous for the following week's quiz, but his effort had paid off, and he did very well; in fact, his score was the highest for the year.

"Maybe I can do this after all," he concluded with an inward smile.

Learning is at the core of any study of educational psychology, and a primary focus of this text is what teachers can do to promote learning for all students. This chapter is the first of four devoted to theoretical descriptions of that topic.

We begin by examining behaviorism, a view of learning that, in spite of controversy, continues to be widely applied in schools, especially in the area of classroom management (Reynolds, Sinatra, & Jetton, 1996). We then turn to social cognitive theory, which has historical roots in behaviorism but goes well beyond it to examine processes, such as learners' beliefs and expectations, that behaviorists don't consider. In Chapters 7, 8 and 9, we extend this discussion to examine cognitive learning in greater detail.

After you've completed your study of this chapter, you should be able to

- Explain examples of learning through classical conditioning
- Explain student behavior by using concepts such as *reinforcement, punishment, generalization, discrimination, satiation,* and *extinction*
- Identify examples of modeling and vicarious learning in classroom situations
- Explain modeling outcomes, processes, and effectiveness in examples of student learning
- Describe how self-regulation influences student learning

Figure 6.1   Types of learning in behaviorism

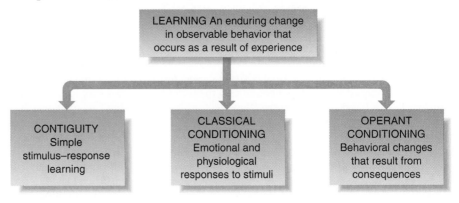

LEARNING An enduring change in observable behavior that occurs as a result of experience

CONTIGUITY
Simple stimulus–response learning

CLASSICAL CONDITIONING
Emotional and physiological responses to stimuli

OPERANT CONDITIONING
Behavioral changes that result from consequences

Behaviorist Views of Learning

Tim's experience in the opening case illustrates the theme of this section. The incident involved **learning**, which, according to behaviorism, is *a relatively enduring change in observable behavior that occurs as a result of experience* (B. Skinner, 1953; Gredler, 2001). Notice that this definition focuses on observable behaviors; behaviorism doesn't consider ideas, insights, goals, or needs that are "in learners' heads."

Our definition also says that the change in behavior is relatively enduring. Temporary changes resulting from illness, injury, or emotional distress are not classified as learning.

Nor are changes in behavior resulting from maturation. For example, a 15-year-old can carry a large bag of groceries that his 6-year-old brother can't even lift. He is bigger and stronger as a result of maturation. Parents say with excitement that their small child has "learned" to walk, but although some experience with crawling is a factor, walking depends more on maturation than on learning.

Let's look again at Tim's situation. He makes wiggly lines around his problems. This behavior is observable, and it was relatively enduring. His making wiggly lines was a result of his experience on the earlier test. It is a "learned" behavior. Other learned behaviors are illustrated in the case study, and we discuss them throughout the chapter.

In the sections that follow, we examine three types of learning according to behaviorism. They are outlined in Figure 6.1.

6.1

Identify two other types of enduring behaviors that wouldn't be called *learning*. Give an example of each.

Contiguity

Someone asks you, "What is 7 times 8?" and you immediately respond, "56." Your response is the result of learning that occurs through **contiguity**, or *the simple pairing of stimuli and responses, so that if they occur together often enough, experiencing one results in the other* (Catania, 1998; Guthrie, 1952). Stimuli are all the sights, sounds, smells, and other input the senses receive from the environment. Responses are the behaviors that result from the association. If you pair 7 × 8 with 56 often enough, you respond "56" when you hear "What is 7 times 8?" Hearing "What is 7 times 8?" is the stimulus, and "56" is the response. Contiguity occurs in classrooms in activities such as drill-and-practice with flash cards. Tim was applying the principle of contiguity when he wrote new terms and definitions and practiced them.

Contiguity is also an essential component of classical conditioning. Let's take a look.

Flash cards and drill-and-practice help students learn through contiguity.

Classical Conditioning

Consider the following examples of learning:

- Tim failed his algebra quiz, and he was devastated and anxious. He was anxious again during his next quiz.
- Suppose you're out on a lake, you fall overboard, nearly drown, and are terrified. The next time you're near a large body of water, you feel a sense of fear similar to the one you experienced in your boating accident.
- Sharon Van Horn greets Damon (and each of her other first graders) in a friendly, courteous manner every day when he comes into her classroom, and her greeting makes him feel good. Later, Damon experiences a comfortable feeling when entering Mrs. Van Horn's room, even when she isn't there.

An understanding of classical conditioning helps teachers see how supportive classroom environments and warm and caring teachers result in positive feelings toward schools and learning.

These examples illustrate **classical conditioning,** *a form of learning in which an individual learns to produce an involuntary emotional or physiological response that is similar to an instinctive or reflexive response.* Both real-world and classroom examples of classical conditioning are quite common (Pintrich & Schunk, 2002). For instance, we react warmly when we smell Thanksgiving turkey and are uneasy when we enter a dentist's office. If we had a bad experience when trying to play baseball, we may be anxious the next time we try to play. Most of us have experienced test anxiety to some degree, and some children become physically ill in anticipation of school. In each of these examples, a response was learned through classical conditioning.

Classical conditioning was originally described by Ivan Pavlov, a Russian physiologist who won a Nobel Prize in 1904 for his work on digestion. As a part of his research, he had his assistants feed dogs meat powder so that their rates of salivation could be measured. As the research progressed, however, the dogs began to salivate at the sight of the assistants, even when they weren't carrying meat powder (Pavlov, 1928). This startling phenomenon caused a turn in Pavlov's work and opened the field of classical conditioning.

To understand how classical conditioning works, one must understand four concepts, as well as the process of *association*. The concepts are as follows (Baldwin & Baldwin, 1998):

- An **unconditioned stimulus (UCS)** is *an object or event that causes an instinctive or reflexive (unlearned) physiological or emotional response.* In Pavlov's experiment, the UCS was the meat powder.
- An **unconditioned response (UCR)** is *the instinctive or reflexive (unlearned) physiological or emotional response caused by the unconditioned stimulus.* The dogs' salivation in the presence of the meat powder was the UCR.
- A **conditioned stimulus (CS)** is *an object or event that becomes associated with the unconditioned stimulus.* The lab assistant was the CS.
- A **conditioned response (CR)** is *a learned physiological or emotional response that is similar to the unconditioned response.* The dogs' salivation in the absence of the meat powder was the CR.

Making an association is the key to learning in classical conditioning. Pavlov's dogs *learned* to salivate at the sight of the lab assistants because they *associated* the lab assistants with the meat powder. Their salivation in response to the meat was unlearned; in response to the lab assistants, it was learned. A learner makes an association when an unconditioned stimulus and a conditioned stimulus have a contiguous relationship—that is, when they occur together.

6.2
Some children become ill in anticipation of school. What concept from classical conditioning is illustrated by the child's ill feeling? Did the child learn to feel ill, or was the ill feeling unlearned? Explain.

Table 6.1 Classical conditioning examples

Example	Stimuli and Responses			
Tim	UCS *Failure*	→	UCR *Devastation and anxiety* (unlearned and involuntary)
	CS *Quizzes*	→	CR *Anxiety* (learned and involuntary)
	Quizzes associated with failure		Anxiety similar to original anxiety
You	UCS *Near drowning*	→	UCR *Terror* (unlearned and involuntary)
	CS *Water*	→	CR *Fear* (learned and involuntary)
	Water associated with nearly drowning		Fear similar to original terror
Damon	UCS *Mrs. Van Horn's manner*	→	UCR *Good feeling* (unlearned and involuntary)
	CS *The classroom*	→	CR *Comfort* (learned and involuntary)
	Classroom associated with Mrs. Van Horn's manner		Comfort similar to original good feeling

Tim learned to be anxious because he associated quizzes with failure.

Now let's return to the three examples of learning that introduced this section. Intuitively, we think of "learning" as involving some knowledge (e.g., knowing the causes of the War of 1812) or skill (e.g., being able to find 42% of 65). Emotions can also be learned, however, and classical conditioning helps explain how. In our examples, Tim learned to be anxious during algebra quizzes, you learned to fear water, and Damon learned to be comfortable when he came into Mrs. Van Horn's classroom. In each case, the conditioned response was *involuntary*; that is, Tim, you, and Damon were not able to control the emotions that were learned (Baldwin & Baldwin, 1998). The mechanisms involved in each example are summarized in Table 6.1.

Classical Conditioning in the Classroom

Because Tim's and Damon's experiences represent a range of cases that can be explained with classical conditioning, they should help sensitize teachers to the importance of the emotional reactions students have toward learning experiences and school in general. Some researchers, in fact, suggest that the emotional reactions learners associate with the topics they study are the most important experiences they take away from schools (Gentile, 1996). For example, the anxiety with which many students respond to math topics impedes their achievement in math. Students are often uneasy about a new school, class, or topic; however, if they are treated with respect and encouragement by their teachers, they will begin to associate school and studying with the teacher's efforts. Eventually, the school will elicit comfortable and safe feelings in students. This is an important goal, and one that can be achieved with classical conditioning.

6.3
We said that the "school will elicit comfortable and safe feelings in students." What concept is illustrated by the *school* and what concept is illustrated by the *safe feelings*? Explain.

Generalization and Discrimination

Let's look once more at our opening case study. In addition to being nervous when he took Algebra II quizzes, Tim started to get nervous when he took chemistry tests, even though he hadn't done poorly on any of them. His fears had generalized to chemistry. **Generalization** *occurs when stimuli similar, but not identical, to a conditioned stimulus elicit the conditioned response.* Tim's chemistry tests were stimuli similar to his algebra quizzes, and they elicited the conditioned response—nervousness—by themselves.

The process can also work in a positive way. Students who associate a classroom with the caring of one teacher may, through generalization, have similar reactions to other classes, club activities, and school-related functions.

The opposite of generalization is **discrimination,** which is *the ability to give different responses to related but not identical stimuli.* For example, Tim was nervous during chemistry tests but not during those in English and history. He discriminated between English and algebra, as well as between history and algebra.

6.4
Think about your boating accident again. Suppose you're fearful when you're near the ocean or a wide river, but you're comfortable in swimming pools. Explain your reactions using the concepts in this section.

Extinction

After working with Susan and changing his study habits, Tim started to feel less nervous. In time, if he continued to succeed, his nervousness would disappear—that is, the conditioned response would become extinct. **Extinction** occurs *when the conditioned stimulus occurs repeatedly in the absence of the unconditioned stimulus and no longer elicits the conditioned response* (Baldwin & Baldwin, 1998). In Tim's case, repeated quiz taking (the conditioned stimulus) without failure (the unconditioned stimulus) would eventually result in him no longer feeling nervous. In a similar way, if you learn how to swim, and you repeatedly go into large bodies of water without an incident similar to your original accident, eventually your fear of water will disappear.

Classroom Connections

Applying Contiguity in Your Classroom

1. Carefully consider the forms of fact learning for which students will be responsible. Provide frequent review and drill to cement the contiguous links between the facts.
   - *Elementary:* An elementary teacher takes a few minutes each morning to review multiplication facts in a drill-and-practice activity.
   - *Middle School:* An eighth-grade history teacher wants students to remember several important dates. She identifies the dates and their significance on a handout and tells students they're responsible for knowing the information. She reviews the material with them periodically before they are tested.
   - *High School:* A chemistry teacher wants his students to know the chemical symbols for common elements. He periodically conducts brief reviews where the students are asked to write the symbol for a list of elements.

Applying Classical Conditioning in Your Classroom

2. Provide a safe and orderly environment so that the classroom will elicit positive emotions.
   - *Elementary:* A first-grade teacher greets each of her students with a smile when they come into the room in the morning. She makes an attempt to periodically ask each of them about their family, a pet, or some other personal part of their lives.

- *Middle School:* A seventh-grade teacher makes a point of establishing and enforcing rules that forbid students to ridicule each other in any way, particularly when they're involved in class discussions or responding to teacher questions. He makes respect for one another a high priority in his classroom.
- *High School:* A geometry teacher attempts to reduce anxiety by specifying precisely what information students are accountable for on tests. She provides sample problems for practice and offers additional help sessions twice a week.

3. When questioning students, put them in safe situations and take steps to ensure a positive outcome.
   - *Elementary:* A fourth-grade inner-city teacher tries to get all his students to participate by asking reluctant responders or low-achieving students open-ended questions such as "What do you notice about the problem?" and "How would you compare the two examples?" He tells students, "These are questions for which any answer is appropriate."
   - *Middle School:* When her seventh graders are unable or unwilling to respond, a seventh-grade math teacher prompts them until they give an acceptable answer. (Effective prompting techniques are discussed in Chapter 13.)
   - *High School:* A world history teacher calls on all students in his class, so that being in his class becomes associated with responding and making an effort.

Applying principles of operant conditioning can help teachers create effective learning environments.

Operant Conditioning

In our discussion of behaviorist views of learning, we progressed from simple stimulus-response pairings, which apply to fact learning (contiguity), to more complex stimulus-response relationships (classical conditioning). We then used these relationships to help explain involuntary emotional and physiological reactions to classroom activities and other events. However, as you may have observed, neither simple contiguity nor classical conditioning can explain the fact that people often initiate behaviors, rather than merely respond to stimuli. In other words, people "operate" on their environments; this idea is the source of the term *operant conditioning.*

This leads us to the work of B. F. Skinner (1904–1990), a behavioral psychologist whose influence was so great that heads of psychology departments in the late 1960s identified him as the most influential psychologist of the 20th century (Myers, 1970). Skinner argued that learners' actions are controlled more by the consequences of a behavior than by the events preceding it. A **consequence** is *an outcome (stimulus) that occurs after the behavior and influences future behaviors.* For example, a teacher's praise after a student answers is a consequence. Being stopped by the highway patrol and fined for speeding is also a consequence. Test results and grades are consequences, as are recognition for outstanding work and reprimands for inappropriate behavior. **Operant conditioning,** then, is *a form of learning in which an observable response changes in frequency or duration as the result of a consequence.*

Operant and classical conditioning are often confused. To help clarify the differences, a comparison of the two is presented in Table 6.2. We see that learning occurs as a result of experience for both, but the type of behavior is different, and the behavior and stimulus occur in the opposite order for the two.

We said in the introduction to the chapter that behaviorism, although controversial, is widely used as a tool for managing student behavior in classrooms (Reynolds et al., 1996). Operant conditioning, in particular, is used in this area. (We consider classroom management in depth in Chapter 12.)

Let's turn now to a detailed discussion of operant conditioning and the different consequences of behavior as they are presented in Figure 6.2.

6.5
A child approaches a dog and is bitten. From that point on, the child is filled with fear and runs away whenever a dog approaches. Describe the classically conditioned aspect as well as the operantly conditioned aspect of this example.

Table 6.2   A comparison of operant and classical conditioning

	Classical Conditioning	Operant Conditioning
Behavior	Involuntary (person does not have control of behavior)	Voluntary (person has control of behavior)
	Emotional	
	Physiological	
Order	Behavior follows stimulus.	Behavior precedes stimulus (consequence).
How learning occurs	Neutral stimuli become associated with unconditioned stimuli.	Consequences of behaviors influence subsequent behaviors.
Example	Learners associate classrooms (initially neutral) with the warmth of teachers, so classrooms elicit positive emotions.	Learners attempt to answer questions and are praised, so their attempts to answer increase.
Key researcher	Pavlov	Skinner

Figure 6.2 Consequences of behavior

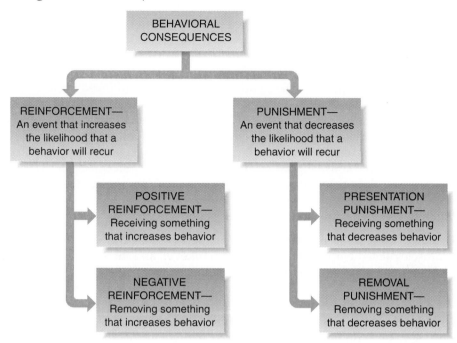

Reinforcement

Imagine that during a class discussion you make a comment, and your instructor responds, "That was a very insightful idea. Good thinking." The likelihood that you'll try to make another comment in the future increases. The instructor's comment is a **reinforcer**, *a consequence that increases the frequency or duration of a behavior.* **Reinforcement,** *the process of applying reinforcers to increase behavior,* exists in two forms: positive and negative.

Positive Reinforcement. Positive reinforcement is *the process of increasing the frequency or duration of a behavior as the result of presenting a reinforcer.* In classrooms we typically think of a positive reinforcer as something desired or valued, such as your instructor's comment. However, any increase in behavior as a result of being presented with a consequence is positive reinforcement, and teachers sometimes unintentionally reinforce behavior with their reprimands. For instance, suppose a student is involved in some mild horseplay, the teacher reprimands him, and his misbehavior actually increases. The reprimand is a positive reinforcer because it was *presented* to the student and the student's behavior *increased.*

Teacher praise in all its forms is perhaps the most common positive reinforcer in classrooms. High test scores, "happy faces" for young children, tokens that can be cashed in for privileges, and stars on the bulletin board can all be positive reinforcers for students.

Teachers also use positive reinforcement when they take advantage of the **Premack principle** (named after David Premack, who originally described it in 1965), *the phenomenon in which a more desired activity serves as a positive reinforcer for a less desired activity.* For example, when a geography teacher says, "As soon as you've finished your summaries, you can start working on your maps," he knows that the promise of map work, a positive reinforcer for his students, will entice them to complete their summaries.

Likewise, attentive looks from students, student questions, high student test scores, and compliments from students or their parents are positive reinforcers for teachers.

Negative Reinforcement. You've just completed a strenuous workout, and your body is "achy," so you decide to take aspirin or ibuprofen to get some relief and help you sleep better. It works, and the next time you work out, you take the pain reliever again. In fact, sometimes you take it before you work out to avoid getting the aches and pains. These examples illustrate the concept of **negative reinforcement,** *the process of removing or avoiding a stimulus to increase behavior* (B. Skinner, 1953). Just as positive reinforcers do not need

To see a video clip of a second grader's reaction to being positively reinforced, go to the Companion Website at *www.prenhall.com/eggen*, then to this chapter's *Classrooms on the Web* module. Click on *Video Clip 6.1.*

6.6
Praise, though well intended, isn't always a positive reinforcer. How do we know when it isn't?

to be desirable, negative reinforcers do not need to be undesirable: Removing any stimulus that increases behavior is negative reinforcement. Think of the term *negative*, in negative reinforcement, as it is used to describe mathematics, not emotions. In our example, the "achy" muscles were the stimuli that were removed (or subtracted) when you took the pain reliever, so your pill-taking behavior increased; you took it more readily the next time. You also avoided the achy muscles on another occasion by taking the pain reliever before you worked out. In both cases, you were negatively reinforced for taking it.

As another example, suppose on Monday you have a student who chronically misbehaves, so in frustration, you finally send her to the dean of students. However, on Tuesday, her misbehavior occurs even sooner than it did Monday, and you send her out again. Your intent was to stop the misbehavior, but in fact, you negatively reinforced her. How do we know? We know she has been reinforced because she misbehaved sooner on Tuesday than she did on Monday; her behavior is increasing. Also, the stimulus—the classroom environment—has been removed (subtracted) by sending her out of the room.

Notice that when negative reinforcement is applied, one of two circumstances exists:

6.7
Judy is off task in your class, and you admonish her. However, in a few moments she's off task again. What concept from operant conditioning does this situation illustrate? Explain.

- Learners are in the situation before they demonstrate the behavior. Your muscles ached before you took the pain reliever, and the student was in the classroom before she was sent to the dean.
- Learners can avoid a consequence (you took the pain reliever to avoid the achy muscles).

Shaping.   Suppose you have a student who is extremely shy and reluctant to interact with his peers. You know that acquiring social skills is an important part of students' overall development, so you encourage him to try to be more outgoing and plan to reinforce him for doing so. It is unlikely, however, that you will see a sudden, dramatic change in his behavior.

In this case, you can *reinforce successive approximations of the desired behavior* through a process called **shaping.** For instance, you watch him carefully and at first reinforce him for any interaction with others, including simple smiles. Later, you reinforce him for greeting other students when they come into the classroom in the morning. Finally, you reinforce him only for more complex interactions with others.

Shaping can also be used in learning activities. When students are initially struggling with difficult ideas, you can reinforce their efforts and partially correct responses. Let's look at two teachers' thinking as an example.

"I start out praising every answer even if it's only partially right," Maria Brugera commented. "I also praise them for trying even if they can't give me an answer. Then as they improve, I praise them only for better, more complete answers, until finally they have to give well thought-out explanations before I'll say anything."

"I don't," Greg Jordan responded. "I like to give a lot of praise, but I think praising every answer takes too much time. I also think if you do too much, you lose your credibility, so I start right off praising them only when they give me a really good answer."

Although Maria was obviously after the correct answer, she considered student effort a beginning step and a partially correct response an even closer approximation of the desired behavior. Through shaping, she hoped to eventually get complete and thoughtful answers from her students.

Reinforcement Schedules.   Maria's and Greg's conversation illustrates an important subtlety in operant conditioning: The timing and spacing of reinforcers can have different effects on learners' behaviors. These effects are illustrated in **reinforcement schedules,** *descriptions of the patterns in the frequency and predictability of reinforcers* (Baldwin & Baldwin, 1998). For instance, even though you may not have played them, you likely understand how slot machines work. You insert a coin, pull the handle (or push a button), and hope for some coins in return. Sometimes a few coins drop into the tray; many times they don't. The coins you receive are reinforcers, which increase the likelihood that you'll continue playing. Because you receive the coins only periodically, you're on an **intermittent reinforcement schedule,** *a pattern in which a behavior is reinforced only periodically.* If you received coins every time you pulled the handle, you would be on a **continuous reinforcement schedule,** *a pattern in which every response is reinforced.* This is the schedule Maria used; she praised all of her students' answers.

Let's look at your experience a bit further. Because the coins you received (your reinforcer) depended on the number of times you pulled the handle, and you were unable to predict when you might get the coins, you were being reinforced on a *variable ratio schedule.* The reinforcement depended on number of responses—a *ratio* of the number of handle pulls to number of coin drops—and the schedule was *variable,* or changing, because you were unable to predict when you would be reinforced. If, somehow, you were able to predict the number of times you needed to pull the handle before receiving coins, your reinforcement would be on a *fixed-ratio schedule.*

Sometimes the pattern of reinforcement relates to time rather than number of responses. Suppose you're in a class that meets Mondays, Wednesdays, and Fridays; you have a quiz each Friday; and your instructor returns the quiz each Monday. You study conscientiously on Tuesday, Wednesday, and Thursday evenings, but you aren't reinforced for studying until the following Monday when you receive your grade. In this case, you are on a *fixed-interval schedule.* Reinforcement occurs at an *interval*—every Monday after the study sessions—and the schedule is *fixed* because you can predict when the reinforcer will be given. If your instructor gave unannounced quizzes, meaning you couldn't predict when they would be given, you'd be on a *variable-interval schedule.*

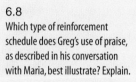

6.8
Which type of reinforcement schedule does Greg's use of praise, as described in his conversation with Maria, best illustrate? Explain.

The relationships among the types of reinforcement schedules are illustrated in Figure 6.3, and additional classroom examples are outlined in Table 6.3.

How do the timing and spacing of reinforcers—the schedules—affect behavior? Each type of schedule has advantages and disadvantages. A continuous schedule yields the fastest rates of initial learning, so it can be effective, for example, when students are acquiring new skills such as solving simultaneous equations in algebra. On the other hand, new behaviors are less likely to persist; that is, learners quickly stop displaying the behaviors when the reinforcers are removed.

Intermittent schedules also have disadvantages. With fixed schedules, behavior increases rapidly just before the reinforcer is given and then decreases rapidly and remains low until just before the next reinforcer is given. For instance, although you chose to conscientiously study for your Friday quiz every Tuesday, Wednesday, and Thursday evening, some students might cram on Thursdays and then not study again until the following Thursday. To avoid this problem, a teacher might give "pop" quizzes, reinforcing on a variable-interval schedule. This strategy, however, can cause high anxiety in

Figure 6.3 Schedules of reinforcement

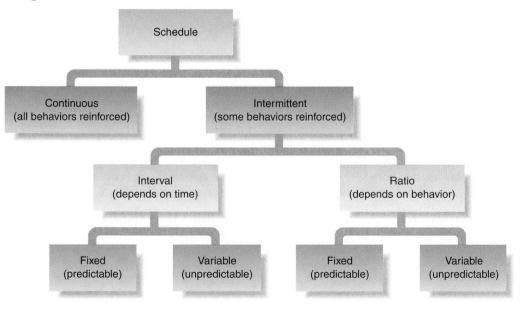

Table 6.3   Reinforcement schedules and examples

Schedule	Example
Continuous	A teacher "walks students through" the steps for solving simultaneous equations. Students are liberally praised at each step as they first learn the solution.
Fixed-ratio	The algebra teacher announces, "As soon as you've done two problems in a row correctly, you may start on your homework assignment so that you'll be able to finish by the end of class."
Variable-ratio	Students volunteer to answer questions by raising their hands and are called on at random.
Fixed-interval	Students are given a quiz every Friday.
Variable-interval	Students are given unannounced quizzes.

6.9
To encourage on-task behaviors, a teacher uses a beeper that periodically makes a noise. If students are on task when the beeper goes off, the class earns points toward a party. What reinforcement schedule is the teacher using? Explain.

6.10
The disappearance of Tim's nervousness would be an example of extinction with classical conditioning. Identify one similarity and one important difference between extinction in classical conditioning and extinction in operant conditioning.

students and detract from their motivation to learn. The best compromise is probably brief, frequent, announced quizzes once a week or even more often (Eggen, 1997; Kika, McLaughlin, & Dixon, 1992).

Extinction.   We noted in the last section that continuous schedules result in behaviors that quickly disappear when the reinforcers are eliminated. When this happens, we say that **extinction**, or *the disappearance of a conditioned response as a result of nonreinforcement*, has occurred. Let's look at an example.

> Renita, a tenth-grader, enjoyed school and liked to respond in her classes. She was attentive and raised her hand, eager to answer most teachers' questions.
> Mr. Frank, her world history teacher, asked a few questions but usually lectured. Renita raised her hand when he did ask a question, but someone would usually blurt out the answer before she could respond.
> Renita rarely raises her hand now and often catches herself daydreaming in world history.

This situation demonstrates how operantly conditioned behaviors can become extinct and, further, how important the way we teach is in promoting student attention and learning. For Renita, being called on reinforced both her attempts to respond and her attention. Because she wasn't called on, she wasn't reinforced, and her behaviors were becoming extinct.

Often, teachers don't interact enough with their students; this is unfortunate because classroom interaction and learning are closely related (Good & Brophy, 2000; McCarthy, 1994). Renita's experience illustrates one aspect of this relationship, and our study of behaviorism helps us understand the mechanisms at work.

Satiation.   Behaviors decrease when they are inadequately reinforced, but they can also decrease when they are reinforced too much. If teachers give too much praise, for instance, they may inadvertently stop students from displaying desired behaviors. They might also overreinforce on purpose, to decrease unwanted behaviors:

> Isabelle Ortega was having a problem with Janice, Tyra, and Kasana passing notes in her seventh-grade English class, so she developed the following plan. She required each girl to write a personal note to the other two and to do so near the end of class while the other students began their homework. The note could not be related to classwork, nor could it be copied, and Isabelle required a full page. She didn't read any of the notes but did inspect them to be certain they were of proper length.
> At the end of the second day, the girls asked whether they could stop writing notes and work on their homework, and at the end of the third day, Isabelle stopped the process. Since that time, she has had no problems with note writing in her class.

Writing notes was reinforcing for Janice, Tyra, and Kasana, so Isabelle applied the concept of **satiation,** which is *using a reinforcer so frequently that it loses its* **potency,** or *ability to* *strengthen behaviors.* In addition, Greg Jordan demonstrated that he was aware of the possibility of inadvertently satiating students when he chose to be judicious in his use of praise.

The example with Isabelle also illustrates the importance of teacher sensitivity and professional judgment. For instance, she made a point of not reading any of the notes, so she didn't embarrass the students or violate their privacy, and she required that the topic be a personal note so that note writing, and not class work, became the aversive behavior. Her actions showed that she cared about her students and also that she expected them to learn. Had these factors not existed, her application of satiation might not have succeeded.

Punishment

Positive and negative reinforcers are consequences that increase behavior. Some consequences, called **punishers,** *weaken behaviors or decrease their frequency. The process of using punishers to decrease behavior* is called **punishment.**

There are two kinds of punishment. As shown earlier in Figure 6.2, **presentation punishment** occurs *when a learner's behavior decreases as a result of being presented with a punisher.* It occurs, for example, when a teacher puts her fingers to her lips, signaling "Shh," and students stop whispering. The students are *presented* with the teacher's signal, and their behavior, whispering, *decreases.*

Removal punishment occurs *when a behavior decreases as a result of removing a stimulus, or as the result of the inability to get positive reinforcement.* For example, suppose students are misbehaving and they are assigned a half hour of detention after school. Under normal conditions, students are free to use their after-school time as they choose. When in detention, this freedom and the opportunity to interact with classmates is taken away. If they're not used excessively, both presentation and removal punishment can be effective management techniques (Skiba & Raison, 1990; A. White & Bailey, 1990).

A common and somewhat controversial application of removal punishment in elementary classrooms is called *time-out.* A misbehaving student is removed from the class and physically isolated in an area away from classmates. The rationale is that removal from the class eliminates the student's chances to get positive reinforcement, so isolation acts as a form of removal punishment.

6.11
Explain how allowing students to talk with one another during detention or even allowing them to finish their homework might defeat the purpose of detention.

Using Punishers: Research Results.   What long-range impact does the use of punishment have on learners? Is it effective? Does it work? Should it ever be used?

Research has identified several problems associated with using punishment:

- *Physical punishment can teach aggression.* Punished individuals often demonstrate similar behaviors at a later time (Bandura, 1986).
- *Punishment causes more vigorous responding.* Students who have learned to defy authority figures, for example, are likely to be even more defiant after receiving punishers (Nilsson & Archer, 1989).
- *Punishment suppresses behavior only temporarily.* Punishment isn't a long-term solution to the problem of misbehavior unless the person administering the punishers is willing to continually use them (Walters & Grusec, 1977).
- *Punishment causes an individual to avoid both the punishers and the person administering them.* A punished individual may learn more sophisticated ways to avoid getting caught, and students avoid teachers who use punishment frequently (Cressey, 1978).
- *Punishment causes negative emotions.* Through classical conditioning, learners begin to associate the classroom with being punished, so classrooms become conditioned stimuli that produce negative emotions (Baldwin & Baldwin, 1998). Learners may generalize their aversion to their assignments, other teachers, and the school as well (Jenson, Sloane, & Young, 1988).

Some critics of behaviorism argue that behavioral techniques in general, and punishers in particular, are undesirable and should never be used (Kohn, 1996a). Others emphasize positive reinforcement as an alternative to punishment. For example, everyone's heard the maxim "Catch 'em being good." Research indicates that systems focusing on positive behaviors are vastly superior to those emphasizing a decrease in inappropriate behaviors (R. Williams, 1987).

Focusing exclusively on positive behaviors isn't a panacea, however. If all punishers are eliminated, some students actually become more disruptive (Pfiffer, Rosen, & O'Leary, 1985; Rosen, O'Leary, Joyce, Conway, & Pfiffer, 1984). It's unrealistic to think that punishment can be totally avoided; it is probably necessary in some cases (Axelrod & Apsche, 1983; Maccoby, 1992). For example, chronic or severely disruptive behavior destroys the learning environment, and if the only alternative is removing disruptive students from the classroom, this action is appropriate. Remember, however, that punishers only suppress undesirable behaviors; students must still be taught how to behave appropriately.

Sensitivity and good judgment are required in using punishers. The most effective solution is a combination of clear classroom rules with consequences that are administered fairly and consistently. We examine these issues in detail in Chapter 12 when we discuss classroom management.

The Influence of Antecedents on Behavior

To this point, we have discussed the influence of consequences—reinforcers and punishers—on behavior. But behavior is also influenced by **antecedents**, *stimuli that precede behaviors*. Antecedents of behaviors that were reinforced in the past increase the likelihood of eliciting the behavior in the future, and antecedents of behaviors that were punished in the past decrease the likelihood of eliciting the behavior (Baldwin & Baldwin, 1998).

In the next sections, we consider three types of antecedents:

- Environmental conditions
- Prompts and cues
- Past reinforcers (that lead to generalization and discrimination)

Environmental Conditions.   When we walk into a dark room, our first inclination is to turn on the lights. The darkness is an environmental antecedent that causes us to turn on the lights, for which we're reinforced because we're now able to see. We've been reinforced for tuning on the lights in the past, so we repeat the behavior. On the other hand, a traffic light turning red is an antecedent that causes us to stop, because running the light increases the likelihood of being punished.

At school, group work in the classroom can be an antecedent that results in student cooperation, which can then be reinforced. Similarly, if students are reinforced for interacting and playing cooperatively on the playground, that environment can become an antecedent that increases the likelihood of positive behaviors. On the other hand, a competitive environment can be an antecedent for aggressive behavior (Bay-Hinitz, Peterson, & Quilitch, 1994).

These examples remind us that the kind of environments we create—both in classrooms and the school in general—can have important effects on our students' behaviors.

Prompts and Cues.   **Prompts** and **cues** are *specific antecedent stimuli intended to produce behaviors teachers want to reinforce*. For example:

Alicia Wendt was working with her fourth graders on adverbs. She wrote this sentence on the chalkboard:

John quickly jerked his head when he heard his name called.

Then she asked, "What is the adverb in the sentence? . . . Wendy?"
Wendy didn't answer.
"Look at the sentence. What did John do?"
". . . He . . . jerked his head."

"How did he jerk it?"
"...Quickly."
"So what is the adverb?"
"...It...is... *quickly.*"
Alicia smiled, "Yes! Well done, Wendy."

Alicia's questions were prompts that helped
Wendy produce the desired response (behavior), which Alicia then reinforced.

Cues come in other forms as well. When a
teacher moves to the front of the class, turns off
the light switch, or walks among the students as
they do seat work, she is cuing them to turn
their attention toward her, become quiet, or remain on task. In each case, the desired behavior
can then be reinforced. Expert teachers use both
verbal and nonverbal cues to develop routines
that result in smoothly running classrooms
(Cazden, 1986; Doyle, 1986).

Generalization and Discrimination. Past reinforcers also serves as antecedents for responses to
similar, but not identical, stimuli. For instance,
look at the shapes in Figure 6.4. If a child is reinforced for identifying number 1 as a square, she is
more likely to also identify 2, 3, and 4 as squares.
They differ in size and orientation, but they all
have the essential characteristics of squares. On
the other hand, if she labels 5 a square and is told
"No, it's a rectangle because two of the sides are
longer," she is less likely to identify 6 as a square.

Teacher questions act as effective cues to elicit responses from a number of
students.

If the child identified 2, 3, and 4 as squares, she generalized. **Generalization** is *giving
the same response to similar, but not identical, stimuli.* If she no longer identified 6 as a
square, she discriminated. **Discrimination** is *giving different responses to similar, but not
identical, stimuli.*

Similarly, after dissecting a shark or frog, biology students recognize the heart in each
case. A shark's heart is two-chambered, whereas a frog's is three-chambered. Nevertheless,
the students learn that they are both hearts despite these differences; they have generalized.
They also learn to discriminate between the animals' hearts and their other body organs.

6.12
A structured classroom—one that
is orderly and in which routines are
predictable—can be an
antecedent. Which kind of
antecedent is it? Explain.

Behaviorism in the Classroom: Instructional Strategies

Although behaviorism isn't commonly used as a basis for guiding instruction, it does
guide teachers in two important tasks: creating productive learning environments and
utilizing applied behavioral analysis. Let's look at them.

6.13
Generalization and discrimination
also occur in classical conditioning.
Identify one similarity and two
differences between
generalization and discrimination
in classical conditioning and
generalization and discrimination
in operant conditioning.

Figure 6.4 Squares and a rectangle

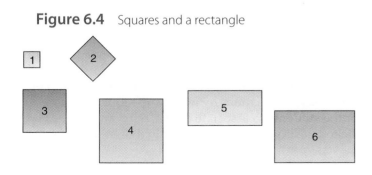

Creating Productive Learning Environments

A **productive learning environment** is *one that is orderly and focuses on learning.* The need for a classroom environment that is safe and orderly is one of the most consistent findings in educational research (Doyle, 1986; Emmer et al., 2003; Evertson et al., 2003). Although behaviorism doesn't provide teachers with all the answers for creating an orderly environment, it can contribute to the process. The following principles can guide teachers in their efforts:

■ Treat students with respect and courtesy so that your classroom and school elicit positive emotions.
■ Create environmental antecedents that produce desired behaviors.
■ Reinforce students' efforts and increasing competence.
■ Establish clear standards for acceptable behavior.
■ Emphasize positive consequences (reinforcers) for meeting behavioral standards, and use punishers only when reinforcers are ineffective.

Let's see how the principles guide Erika Williams, a fourth-grade teacher at Hyde Park Elementary School, as she works with her students.

Erika opened her door just before 8:40 A.M., when students at Hyde Park Elementary were permitted to enter their classrooms. She greeted each of her 26 students individually as they came into the room.

"Good morning, Chin."

"Oh, nice haircut, Calvin."

"How's your new little brother, Tenisha?"

"Feeling better today, Katie?"

"Put your stuff away quickly," she said brightly after all the children were in the room. "We have very important work to do today."

Erika's room was decorated with posters of exotic locations around the world, samples of student projects, pictures of each of the students in the class, and other items. A poster at the front of the room listed important classroom rules:

▥ Bring all materials to class each day.
▥ Treat your classmates with courtesy and respect.
▥ Raise your hand to speak.
▥ Wait for permission before leaving your seat.

The students, who were chattering among themselves, quickly stopped as they saw Erika move to the front of the room to begin the day's math lesson. "You did very good work on the quiz," she commented as she began handing back a quiz the students had taken the day before. "You are getting to where you understand fraction word problems so well that you're hard to stump even with challenging ones. . . . We only have three problems that gave us some trouble, and we're going to understand them by the time we're finished today."

Erika discussed the three problems in detail and then prepared to introduce the new material for the day.

"Before we begin, I want to remind you that everyone was on a white card for both yesterday and the day before," she smiled and motioned toward a wall display that contained index cards she used to track student behavior. "I'm so proud of you. Keep this up and you will all have earned enough points for the class party, which is only a week away."

Let's take a closer look at Erika's attempts to create a productive learning environment. First, she attempted to create a safe emotional climate by implementing concepts from classical conditioning. People respond positively to displays of warmth and, in time, begin to associate their environments with those displays. Erika consciously attempted to capitalize on these associations by warmly greeting her students each morning. Her goal was for the students to associate their classroom with her behavior, so that the classroom elicited positive emotions similar to those they felt when she greeted them.

Second, when she moved to the front of the room, the students quickly stopped their chatter and got ready for the day's work. Her movement was an environmental antecedent that cued the students' behavior. Using antecedents in this way further increases order and saves the teacher energy.

Third, Erika praised the students' increasing competence when she said, "You are getting to where you understand fraction word problems so well that you're hard to stump even with challenging ones." Research indicates that using praise to reinforce students' growing competence can increase their intrinsic motivation to learn (Deci & Ryan, 1991; Deci, Vallerand, Pelletier, & Ryan, 1991). (We examine the use of reinforcers and their impact on student motivation in detail in Chapter 10.)

Finally, Erika created a classroom management system with clear standards for behavior, an emphasis on reinforcement, and the use of punishment only when reinforcers no longer worked.

Let's look at her system in more detail. At the front of Erika's classroom was a large poster that held a packet of six index cards for each student. The cards were color-coded as follows:

To see a video clip of Erika's classroom management system in operation, go to the Companion Website at *www.prenhall.com/eggen*, then to this chapter's *Classrooms on the Web* module. Click on *Video Clip 6.2*.

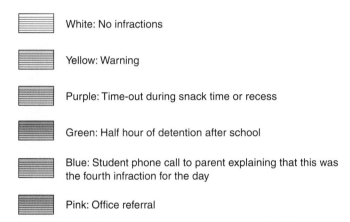

White: No infractions

Yellow: Warning

Purple: Time-out during snack time or recess

Green: Half hour of detention after school

Blue: Student phone call to parent explaining that this was the fourth infraction for the day

Pink: Office referral

Source: D. Lampkin, personal communication, June 6, 2002.

Erika emphasized positive reinforcement with her system. Every student whose white card remained at the front of the stack for the day was reinforced by being given a point. Points were recorded, and every 2 weeks the students could use their points to purchase materials from the "classroom store," which included items ranging from pencils and notebooks to footballs and gym bags. (Erika had solicited some of the items, such as gym bags, from local businesses, and Erika's principal had allowed her to use school funds to purchase pencils and notebooks.) Pencils cost 3 points, notebooks cost 10, and large items cost from 80 to 100.

In addition to being able to purchase items from the store, all students who accumulated 12 points in a month (remaining on a white card for 3 of 5 days each week for 4 weeks) could participate in a class party where the students could bring snacks and play games during the afternoon on the last Friday of the month.

Erika reported that because the incentives for desirable behavior were clear and concrete, she rarely had to revert to punishment. And, when she did, she emphasized removal rather than presentation punishment. For instance, a first infraction sent the student to the front of the room to "turn your card." This meant that the white card was moved to the back of the packet, so the yellow card was exposed, indicating that the student had been warned. A second infraction exposed the purple card and resulted in a 10-minute time-out, and so on. Time-out is a form of removal punishment, as is detention, the punishment for a third infraction.

According to Erika, students rarely committed a third infraction. The students knew a detention meant that their parents or other caregivers would be notified, since they would have to come to the school to pick up their child on the detention day. So, students seldom got past purple cards.

Applied behavioral analysis provides teachers with the tools to help students change their own behavior.

Every student began fresh each day, meaning a white card was at the front of the stack, and the student again had a chance to earn a point for the day.

Although Erika's management system included punishment as a possibility, it strongly emphasized reinforcement. In addition, she used reinforcers to increase motivation and also used concepts from classical conditioning to create a positive emotional climate.

Applied Behavioral Analysis

In addition to helping teachers create productive learning environments, behavioral principles can also help teachers as they work with individuals who are chronically disruptive.

To see how one teacher used behavioral principles, let's look back at the closing case study in Chapter 5 with Mike Sheppard and his seventh-grade pre-algebra class. You may recall that Todd, one of Mike's 28 students, was described by other teachers as verbally abusive, aggressive, and lacking in self-discipline. Mike saw that he was very active and had a difficult time sitting through a class period. After working with Todd to help him learn to control his behavior, Mike saw many positive changes. Four of five target behaviors had improved over a 3-week period:

	2/9–2/13	2/16–2/20	2/23–2/27
Talking out	ЖЖ ЖЖ ЖЖ ЖЖ ЖЖ	ЖЖ IIII ЖЖ	ЖЖ II
Swearing	ЖЖ ЖЖ	ЖЖ II	IIII
Hitting/touching	ЖЖ III	ЖЖ IIII	III
Out of seat	ЖЖ ЖЖ ЖЖ III	ЖЖ ЖЖ ЖЖ IIII	ЖЖ ЖЖ ЖЖ III
Being friendly	II	IIII	ЖЖ II

How was Mike able to accomplish these results? He was *systematically applying behavioral principles in an effort to change specific behaviors in an individual*, a process called **applied behavior analysis** (Baldwin & Baldwin, 1998). (It is also called *behavior modification*, but this term has a negative connotation for some people, so experts prefer the term we use here.) Applied behavior analysis has been used successfully to enable people to increase physical fitness, overcome fears and panic attacks, learn social skills, and stop smoking (Gould & Clum, 1995; Green & Reed, 1996). It is widely used in working with students who have exceptionalities (Werts, Caldwell, & Wolery, 1996), such as Todd, who had a behavior disorder.

Applied behavior analysis is an application of the basic principles of operant conditioning—any behavior that isn't reinforced or is punished will decrease, and behaviors that are reinforced will increase. Applying these principles typically involves the following steps:

- ▪ Identify target behaviors.
- ▪ Establish a baseline for the target behaviors.
- ▪ Choose reinforcers and punishers (if necessary).
- ▪ Measure changes in the target behaviors.
- ▪ Gradually reduce the frequency of reinforcers as behavior improves.

Identify Target Behaviors. The first step is to identify specific behaviors that the teacher wants to change and then measure their frequency. Mike identified five target behaviors: *talking out, swearing, hitting/touching* (other students), being *out-of-seat*, and *being* *friendly.* Some experts might argue that Mike included too many target behaviors and might further suggest that "being friendly" isn't specific enough. As with virtually all teaching-learning applications, these decisions are a matter of professional judgment.

Establish a Baseline. Establishing a baseline for the target behaviors simply means measuring their frequency to establish a reference point for comparison. For instance, during the baseline period (the week of 2/9 to 2/13), Todd talked out in class 20 times, swore 10 times, hit or touched another student 8 times, was out of his seat 18 times, and was friendly to other students only twice. (Ordinarily, the teacher—or an objective third party—makes observations to determine the baseline. For the sake of this discussion, we can assume that Mike, not Todd, created the behavior tally for the first week.) This baseline allowed both Mike and Todd to see what changes would occur in each of the target behaviors.

Choose Reinforcers and Punishers. Before attempting to change behavior, the teacher must identify the particular reinforcers and punishers that are likely to work for an individual student. Ideally, an applied behavior analysis system is based on reinforcers instead of punishers, and this is what Mike used with Todd. In some cases, however, punishers may be necessary, and if they are, they should also be established in advance.

Mike used personal attention and praise as his primary reinforcers, and their effectiveness is indicated by the changes in Todd's behavior. If the undesirable target behaviors had not decreased, Mike would have needed to modify his system by identifying and then trying some additional reinforcers and perhaps some punishers as well.

In addition to attention and praise, another reinforcer increased the effectiveness of Mike's system. Because (after the baseline was established) Mike made Todd responsible for monitoring his own behavior, Todd saw evidence of his improvement; he could see, for example, that the frequency of talking out dropped from 20 to 14 incidents by the end of the second week. This improvement, in itself, was reinforcing.

6.14
We saw no evidence of punishment in Mike's work with Todd. Using behaviorism as a basis, explain why Todd's undesirable behaviors decreased over the course of the 3 weeks.

Measure Changes in Behavior. After establishing a baseline and determining possible reinforcers and punishers, the target behaviors are measured for specified periods to see if changes occur. For example, Todd talked out 6 fewer times in the second week than in the first. Except for "out of seat," improvement occurred for each of the other behaviors during the 3-week period.

The first intervention produced no change in Todd's out-of-seat behavior, so Mike designed an additional intervention. To help Todd satisfy his need for activity yet not disturb the class, Mike prepared a place where Todd could go when the urge to get out of his seat became overwhelming.

Reduce Frequency of Reinforcers. Although the case study does not illustrate it, Mike would have gradually reduced the frequency of his reinforcers as Todd's behavior improved. Initially, a teacher might use a continuous, or nearly continuous, schedule; later, the schedule would become more intermittent. Reducing the frequency of reinforcers helps maintain the desired behaviors and increases the likelihood that they will generalize to other classrooms and to behaviors out of school.

Like all interventions, applied behavior analysis won't work magic, and its application can be labor intensive. In most cases, for example, teachers can't assume that a student will accurately measure the target behaviors, so they have to monitor those behaviors themselves. This makes managing an already-busy classroom even more complex.

Also, personal attention and praise were effective reinforcers for Todd, but if they hadn't been, Mike would have needed others. Finding a reinforcer that is simple to administer and that fits in easily with school procedures can be more difficult than it seems.

These problems notwithstanding, applied behavior analysis gives teachers an additional tool to use when working with students with behavior disorders, especially when conventional methods, such as a basic system of rules and procedures, don't work. Its effectiveness depends on the professional judgment and skill of the teacher.

Putting Behaviorism Into Perspective

Like any theory, behaviorism has both proponents and critics. In this section, we examine some of the arguments on both sides.

Many of the criticisms focus on the following areas:

- The ineffectiveness of behaviorism as a guide for instruction
- The inability of behaviorism to explain higher order functions
- The impact of reinforcers on intrinsic motivation
- Philosophical positions on learning and teaching

Let's look at at each area.

First, instruction based on behaviorism suggests that information should be broken down into specific items, which allows learners to display observable behaviors that can then be reinforced. For instance, most of us have completed exercises such as:

Juanita and (I, me) went to the football game.

If we identified "I" as the correct choice, we were reinforced. If we selected "me," we were given corrective feedback, so we learned to appropriately generalize and discriminate. Much of what we learn is not effectively acquired through reinforcement of specific, decontextualized items of information, however. For example, we learn to write effectively by practicing writing in meaningful contexts, not by responding to exercises like the one just displayed.

Further, behaviorism emphasizes learners' responses to environmental stimuli, such as reinforcers and punishers. Learners, however, commonly demonstrate misconceptions and sometimes "off-the-wall" ideas for which they haven't been reinforced. These ideas are better explained by theories suggesting that students are trying to make sense of their world. (We examine these theories in detail in Chapters 7, 8, and 9.)

Second, behaviorism cannot adequately explain higher order functions, such as language. For instance, Chomsky and Miller (1958) demonstrated that even people with small vocabularies would have to learn sentences at a rate faster then one per second throughout their lifetimes if their learning was based on specific behaviors and reinforcers.

Third, research suggests that offering reinforcers for engaging in intrinsically motivating activities can decrease interest in the tasks (Ryan & Deci, 1996). The use of rewards may detract from intrinsic interest in learning.

Finally, some critics of behaviorism hold the philosophical position that schools should attempt to promote learning for its own sake rather than learning to gain rewards (Anderman & Maehr, 1994). Other critics argue that behaviorism is essentially a means of controlling people, rather than a way to help students learn to control their own behavior (Kohn, 1993).

On the other hand, we all know that our experiences undeniably influence the ways we behave—an idea at the core of behaviorism. For example, virtually all teachers understand that a timely, genuine compliment can increase both learner motivation and the way students feel about themselves. Also, how many of us would continue working if we stopped receiving paychecks, and do we lose interest in our work merely because we get paid for it?

Further, research indicates that reinforcing appropriate classroom behaviors, such as paying attention and treating classmates well, decreases misbehavior (S. Elliot & Busse, 1991), and behaviorist classroom management techniques are often effective when others are not (Maccoby, 1992).

Finally, proponents argue, if reinforcers enhance skills, such as learning a mathematical operation, the ability doesn't disappear merely because praise or some other reinforcer has been removed (J. Cameron & Pierce, 1996; Chance, 1993).

Behaviorism isn't a complete explanation for learning. As with most of what we know about teaching and learning, effective applications of behaviorism require the careful judgment of intelligent teachers.

Classroom Connections

Applying Operant Conditioning in Your Classroom

Reinforcers and Punishers

1. When using behavioral methods, use reinforcement rather than punishment if possible. When punishment is necessary, use removal instead of presentation punishment.
   - *Elementary:* After giving an assignment, a first-grade teacher circulates around the room and gives tickets to students who are working quietly. The tickets may be exchanged for opportunities to play games and work at learning centers.
   - *Middle School:* A seventh-grade teacher gives students "behavior points" at the beginning of the week. If students break a rule, they lose a point. At the end of the week, a specified number of remaining points may be traded for tickets that can be used to purchase special privileges, such as choosing a seat in class.
   - *High School:* A math teacher increases the potency of grades as reinforcers by awarding bonus points for improvement. After an average for each student is determined, she offers them incentive points for scoring higher than their averages.

Generalization and Discrimination

2. Promote generalization and discrimination by encouraging students to make comparisons among examples and other information.
   - *Elementary:* Her teacher praises a third grader who, on her own, notices that frogs and toads are not the same and that frogs climb trees but toads don't.
   - *Middle School:* A life science teacher, in a unit on deciduous and coniferous plants, asks students to compare a pine and an oak tree. He helps them identify the essential differences between the trees by asking specific questions.
   - *High School:* An English teacher gives students examples of similes, metaphors, alliterations, and personifications in poems. She has the students identify the specific characteristics of each.

Reinforcement Schedules

3. Use appropriate schedules of reinforcement.
   - *Elementary:* At the beginning of the school year, a first-grade teacher plans activities that all students can do.

He praises liberally and rewards frequently. As students get used to first-grade work, he requires more effort.
   - *Middle School:* A sixth-grade teacher intermittently provides written compliments for consistent work and effort. She knows that students who do steady, average to above-average work and are not disruptive tend to be taken for granted and are often "lost in the shuffle."
   - *High School:* A geometry teacher gives frequent announced quizzes to prevent the decline in effort that can occur after reinforcement with a fixed-interval schedule.

Shaping

4. Shape desired behaviors.
   - *Elementary:* A second-grade teacher openly praises a student whose behavior is improving. As improvement continues, the teacher requires longer periods of acceptable behavior before he praises the student.
   - *Middle School:* A language arts teacher begins a unit on paragraphing by asking students to write a five-sentence paragraph. As she scores this assignment, she is generous with positive comments, but as time goes on and the students' work improves, she is more critical.
   - *High School*: An Algebra II teacher reinforces students as they make the initial steps in solving sets of equations. As their skills improve, he reduces the amount of reinforcement.

Antecedents

5. Provide cues for appropriate behavior.
   - *Elementary:* Before students line up for lunch, a first-grade teacher reminds them to stand quietly while waiting to be dismissed. When they're standing quietly, she compliments them on their good behavior and lets them go to lunch.
   - *Middle School:* After completing a lesson and assigning seat work, a seventh-grade English teacher circulates around the room, reminding students both verbally and nonverbally to begin working.
   - *High School:* When a chemistry teacher's students are unable to respond correctly, he prompts them with additional questions that help them respond acceptably.

Social Cognitive Theory

"What are you doing?" Jason asked Kelly as he came around the corner and caught her in the act of swinging her arms back and forth.

"I was trying to swing at a ball like the pros do, but I haven't been able to quite do it," Kelly responded with a red face. "I was watching a game on TV last night, and noticed the way those guys swing. It always looks so easy, but they hit it so hard. It just seems like I should be able to do that. It was running through my head, so I just had to try it."

Three-year-old Jimmy crawled up on his dad's lap with a book. "I read too, Dad," he said as his father put down his own book to help Jimmy up on his lap.

You're driving 65 miles an hour on the interstate, and you're passed by a sports car that must be going at least 75. The posted speed limit is 55. A moment later, you see the sports car that passed you pulled over by a highway patrol. You immediately slow down.

What do these incidents have in common, and how would behaviorism explain them? First, they all involve learning by observing the behavior of others; Kelly and Jimmy were attempting to imitate behaviors they observed, and you observed the consequences for the other driver and modified your own behavior as a result.

Second, behaviorism focuses on changes in behavior that have direct causes existing outside the learner. For instance, in our opening case study, taking algebra quizzes directly caused Tim's hand to shake. And if the driver of the sports car drives 55 after being fined, we conclude that being fined directly caused him to drive slower. So, behaviorism has difficulty explaining our examples, since nothing directly happened to the individuals in each case. Kelly, Jimmy, and you changed your behavior based simply on observations of others.

Research that looks at how people learn from observing others was pioneered by Albert Bandura (1925–). From his work emerged **social cognitive theory**, which *examines the processes involved as people learn from observing others and gradually acquire control over their own behavior* (Bandura, 1986, 1997). Social cognitive theory has its historical roots in behaviorism but goes well beyond it. Let's examine the relationships between the two.

Comparing Behaviorism and Social Cognitive Theory

At this point you might be asking yourself, "If behaviorists focus on observable behavior (as opposed to thinking and other processes 'in learners' heads'), and the term *cognitive* implies memory, thinking, and knowing, why is a cognitive learning theory being included in the same chapter with behaviorism?"

Here's why. We said earlier that social cognitive theory has its historical roots in behaviorism. For example, many authors continue to include aspects of social cognitive theory in books focusing on behavioral principles (e.g., Baldwin & Baldwin, 1998), and some people still prefer the terms *observational learning* or *social learning theory* to social cognitive theory. However, *social cognitive theory* is the preferred label by leaders in the field (Bandura, 1986; Bruning, et al., 1999; Pintrich & Schunk, 2002; Schunk, 2000). In addition, the two theories have several similarities:

- They agree that experience is an important cause of learning (as do other cognitive descriptions, such as those found in Piaget's and Vygotsky's work).
- They both include the concepts of reinforcement and punishment in their explanations of behavior.
- They agree that feedback is important in promoting learning.

However, social cognitive theory differs from behaviorism in at least three ways: (a) the way learning is viewed, (b) the way interactions among behavior, the environment, and personal factors are described, and (c) the way reinforcement and punishment are interpreted. Let's look at these differences.

Views of Learning

Whereas behaviorists define learning as a change in observable behavior, social cognitive theorists view **learning** as *a change in mental structures that creates the capacity to demonstrate different behaviors.* This internal process may or may not result in immediate behavioral change. The role of cognitions in this internal process is evident in the preceding examples. Kelly, for example, didn't try to imitate the baseball swing until the next day; her observations of the players on television had to be stored in her memory. Also, her comment, "It just seems like I should be able to do that," suggests a belief or expectation about her ability that influenced her behavior. The concept of expectations also helps explain your behavior when you saw the other car pulled over. You expected to be pulled over if you kept speeding, so you slowed down. Beliefs and expectations are mental processes that behaviorists don't consider.

Interactions Among Behavior, the Environment, and Personal Factors

Behaviorism suggests a "one-way" relationship between the environment and behavior; that is, the environment directly causes behavior. Social cognitive theory's explanation is more complex, suggesting that behavior, the environment, and personal factors, such as beliefs and expectations, all influence one another. For instance, Tim's low score on his algebra quiz (an environmental factor) influenced his belief (a personal factor) about his ability to do algebra. His belief, in turn, influenced his behavior (he adapted his study habits), and his behavior influenced the environment (he went to Susan's home to study). Social cognitive theorists call these mutual influences *reciprocal causation.*

Interpretations of Reinforcement and Punishment

Behaviorists and social cognitive theorists agree that reinforcement and punishment are important concepts, but they interpret the influence of these concepts differently. As we've already said, behaviorists view reinforcers and punishers as direct causes of behavior; for social cognitive theorists, reinforcers and punishers cause *expectations* instead. For example, if you study hard and do well on a test, you expect to do well on a second test by studying in the same way. When you see someone being reinforced or punished for a certain behavior, you expect to be reinforced or punished for a similar behavior. When you saw the sports car pulled over by the highway patrol, for instance, you slowed down because you expected to be pulled over if you continued speeding. Like beliefs, expectations are mental processes.

The fact that people form expectations means they're aware of which behaviors will be reinforced. This is important because, according to social cognitive theory, reinforcement changes behavior only when learners know what behaviors are being reinforced (Bandura, 1986). Tim believed that his changed study habits were the cause of his improved scores, so he maintained those habits. If he had believed that some other strategy was more effective, he would have used that strategy. He wasn't merely responding to reinforcers; he was actively assessing the effectiveness of his strategy.

Because Tim believed that his changed study habits improved his scores, he maintained those habits.

The importance of student cognitions has two implications for teachers. First, teachers should explain what behaviors will be reinforced, so students can adapt their behavior accordingly, and second, they should give feedback so learners know what behaviors have been reinforced. For instance, if a student gets full credit for an essay item on a test but doesn't know why the credit was given, she may not know how to respond correctly the next time.

Nonoccurrence of Expected Consequences

Social cognitive theory also helps explain behavior when expectations aren't met. For example, suppose your instructor gives you a homework assignment, you work hard on it, but she doesn't collect it. The nonoccurrence of the expected reinforcer (credit for the assignment) can act as a punisher; you will probably be less inclined to work hard for the next assignment.

Students are able to learn a wide range of complex behaviors through modeling.

Just as the nonoccurrence of an expected reinforcer can act as a punisher, the nonoccurrence of an expected punisher can act as a reinforcer (Bandura, 1986). A student who breaks a classroom rule, for example, and isn't reprimanded (punished) is more likely to break the rule in the future. Students expect to be punished for breaking rules. When the expected punisher doesn't occur, the fact that it doesn't acts as a reinforcer.

Modeling

Modeling, *the tendency of individuals to imitate behaviors they observe in others,* is a central concept of social cognitive theory. Tim, for example, observed that Susan was successful in her approach to studying for exams. As a result, he imitated her behavior; direct imitation of behavior is one form of modeling. The term *modeling* is sometimes mistakenly used in place of the term *imitation.* For instance, someone might say, "Tim modeled Susan's study habits." This is incorrect. Models "model" behavior and observers "imitate" those behaviors (Pintrich & Schunk, 2002).

The importance of modeling in our everyday lives is difficult to overstate. Modeling helps explain the powerful influence of culture on student learning, which we described in Chapter 4. Parents are urged to use correct grammar and pronunciation in talking to their infants, in hopes of promoting language development. Studies of disadvantaged youth indicate that a lack of effective adult role models is one reason they have difficulty handling the problems they encounter (Ogbu, 1987, 1999b).

In addition to direct modeling (as illustrated by Tim's imitation of Susan's behavior or children imitating their parents), at least two other forms of modeling exist: symbolic and synthesized (Bandura, 1986). They are described and illustrated in Table 6.4. Common to each is the fact that people learn by observing the actions of others.

Cognitive Modeling

An application of modeling that is increasingly emphasized in instruction is called **cognitive modeling,** which involves *modeled demonstrations, together with verbal descriptions of the model's thoughts and actions* (Pintrich & Schunk, 2002). Let's look at an example.

6.15
What form of modeling does the teacher wish to promote by showing her students a videotape of Dr. Martin Luther King Jr.'s famous "I Have a Dream" speech? Explain.

Table 6.4   Different forms of modeling

Type	Description	Example
Direct modeling	Simply attempting to imitate the model's behavior	Tim imitates Susan in studying for exams. A first grader forms letters in the same way a teacher forms them.
Symbolic modeling	Imitating behaviors displayed by characters in books, plays, movies, or television	Teenagers begin to dress like characters on a popular television show oriented toward teens.
Synthesized modeling	Developing behaviors by combining portions of observed acts	A child uses a chair to get up and open the cupboard door after seeing her brother use a chair to get a book from a shelf and seeing her mother open the cupboard door.

"Wait a minute," Jeanna Edwards said as she saw Joanne struggling with the microscope. "Let me show you once more. . . . Now, watch closely as I adjust it. This is important because these slides crack easily. The first thing I think about is getting the slide in place. Otherwise, I might not be able to find what I'm looking for in the microscope. Then I want to be sure I don't crack the slide while I lower the lens, so I watch from the side. Finally, I slowly raise the lens until I have the object in focus. You were trying to focus as you lowered it. It's easier and safer if you try to focus as you raise it. Now go ahead and try it."

Cognitive modeling allows learners to benefit from the thinking of experts. As Jeanna demonstrated how to use the microscope, she also described her thinking, "The first thing I think about is. . . ." When teachers describe their thinking out loud, or when they encourage other students to explain their thinking, they provide learners with specific, concrete examples of how to think about and solve problems. Students have the opportunity to imitate both their behaviors and their thinking.

Vicarious Learning

Although merely observing the actions of other people can affect a learner, people also learn by observing the consequences of other's actions. **Vicarious learning** *occurs when people observe the consequences of another person's behavior and adjust their own behavior accordingly* (Schunk, 2000). For example, in the opening case study, Tim saw how well Susan did on quizzes with her approach to studying, so he was vicariously reinforced through her success. When students hear a teacher say, "I really like the way Jimmy is working so quietly," they are being vicariously reinforced, and when a student receives a verbal reprimand for leaving his seat without permission, other students in the class are vicariously punished. You were vicariously punished by observing the other driver pulled over. You observed the consequences for his speeding and your behavior decreased.

Our expectations contribute to vicarious learning. Tim expected to be reinforced for imitating Susan's behavior, and the other students expect to be reinforced for imitating Jimmy's behavior. As we said earlier, you expected to be punished if you continued speeding, so you slowed down.

Modeling and vicarious learning work together to affect behavior in several ways, which we look at next.

Effects of Modeling on Behavior

Modeling can affect behavior in at least four ways:

- Learning new behaviors
- Facilitating existing behaviors
- Changing inhibitions
- Arousing emotions

Learning New Behaviors

By attempting to imitate behaviors they observe in others, people can acquire abilities they weren't able to display before observing the model. When students watch a teacher demonstrate how to solve an equation in algebra for the first time, make a precise cut with a wood saw, run a smooth bead with a welder, or demonstrate a communication skill, they're trying to capitalize on this important aspect of modeling. Kelly's comment, "I was trying to swing at a ball like the pros do, but I haven't been able to quite do it," indicates that she was attempting to learn a new behavior when she watched the ball players on television.

To see a video clip of a teacher modeling a solution to a problem in chemistry, go to the Companion Website at *www.prenhall.com/eggen*, then to this chapter's *Classrooms on the Web* module. Click on *Video Clip 6.3.*

Facilitating Existing Behaviors

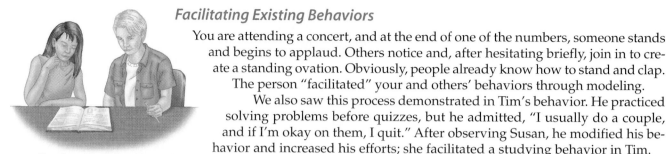

Susan's modeling facilitated improved studying behaviors in Tim.

You are attending a concert, and at the end of one of the numbers, someone stands and begins to applaud. Others notice and, after hesitating briefly, join in to create a standing ovation. Obviously, people already know how to stand and clap. The person "facilitated" your and others' behaviors through modeling.

We also saw this process demonstrated in Tim's behavior. He practiced solving problems before quizzes, but he admitted, "I usually do a couple, and if I'm okay on them, I quit." After observing Susan, he modified his behavior and increased his efforts; she facilitated a studying behavior in Tim.

Changing Inhibitions

An **inhibition** is *a self-imposed restriction on one's behavior,* and modeling can either strengthen or weaken it. Unlike actions that facilitate existing behaviors, modeling that changes inhibitions involves socially unacceptable behaviors, such as breaking classroom rules (Pintrich & Schunk, 2002).

For example, students are less likely to break a classroom rule if one of their peers is reprimanded; their inhibition about breaking the rule has been strengthened. Jacob Kounin (1970), one of the pioneer researchers in the area of classroom management, called this phenomenon the *ripple effect.* On the other hand, if a student speaks without permission and isn't reprimanded, other students are more likely to do the same. The inhibition is weakened. In each situation, expectations play a role. If students see a peer reprimanded or not reprimanded for breaking a rule, they expect the same result for similar behavior.

Arousing Emotions

6.16
Teachers who model persistence in problem-solving tasks have students who persist longer than teachers who don't (Zimmerman & Blotner, 1979). What form of modeling occurs in such situations? Which modeling effect is best illustrated by the students' increased persistence? Explain.

Finally, a person's emotional reaction can be changed by observing a model's display of emotions. For example, observing the uneasiness of a diver on a high board may cause an observer to become more fearful of the board as well. If you see a couple having a heated argument at a party, you may find yourself feeling awkward and embarrassed. Notice here that the emotions modeled aren't necessarily the same ones aroused. You see anger modeled, but your emotions are more likely to be embarrassment or uneasiness.

On the positive side, the emotional arousal effect of modeling is a strong endorsement for teacher enthusiasm. Observing teachers genuinely enjoying themselves as they discuss a topic can help generate similar excitement in students.

From these examples, we see that modeling can result in behavioral, cognitive, and even affective (emotion-related) outcomes. Behavioral outcomes occur when behaviors are learned or facilitated; cognitive outcomes result from observing the consequences of others' actions, such as the example in which a student broke a classroom rule; and affective outcomes are the result of modeling emotions.

Technology and Learning: The Impact of Symbolic Modeling on Behavior

We tend to forget that the computer is not the only technology that affects learning. Television and other forms of video are significant with respect to social cognitive theory because of the impact of symbolic modeling on behavior and the almost universal exposure to television.

Hundreds of studies done over nearly four decades have produced a number of disconcerting findings about television viewing (Berk, 2001). For example, excessive television viewing is associated with adjustment problems, including difficulties with family and peer relations (Liebert, 1986). These effects often are felt by children with lower measured intelligence and those who come from low-income families, who tend to watch more television that their more advantaged peers (Huston, Watkins, & Kunkel, 1989).

Symbolic Modeling and Television Viewing

Literally thousands of studies have consistently confirmed that symbolic modeling influences behavior. This research began with Bandura's classic studies in the 1960s indicating that children who watched aggressive models either on film or depicted as cartoon characters behaved more aggressively in free play than those who saw no models (Bandura, Ross, & Ross, 1963).

Since then, research—carefully controlled for factors such as intelligence, socioeconomic status, school achievement, and child-rearing practices—consistently has indicated that exposure to violence on television increases mean-spirited and hostile behavior in young people (Donnerstein, Slaby, & Eron, 1994). It has been described as "an extensive how-to course in aggression" (Slaby, Roedell, Arezzo, & Hendrix, 1995, p. 163), and it tends to "harden" children to aggression, making them more willing to tolerate it in others (Drabman & Thomas, 1976).

Television can have both positive and negative effects on learners through the role models it provides.

Televised violence also has an emotional arousal effect. Heavy viewers of televised violence tend to see the world as a scary place where aggression is widespread and hostility is an acceptable means of solving problems (Donnerstein et al., 1994).

Finally, research indicates that television tends to reinforce stereotypes. For example, people from cultural minorities are underrepresented, and when they do appear, they tend to be depicted as villains or victims of violence (Graves, 1993). Women tend to be cast as victims and in stereotypically feminine roles, such as wife, mother, teacher, or secretary (Signorielli, 1993). Since this research was done, efforts have been made to counter these stereotypes, but progress is slow and wavering. For example, NBC was strongly criticized in its 1999 programming for underrepresenting African Americans, so much so that it was a frequent topic of jokes on talk shows.

> **6.17**
> What modeling effect is best illustrated when "mean-spirited and hostile behavior in young people" is increased? Explain.

Television and Symbolic Modeling: Guidelines for Teachers and Parents

The message from research on television viewing and behavior is clear and consistent. Excessive exposure to television, and particularly televised violence, is harmful. As teachers, we should work with parents, encouraging and helping them to promote healthy television viewing. Some suggestions for parents follow:

- *Limit television.* Make and stick to clear rules for television viewing, limit what children can watch, and avoid using television as a babysitter.
- *Avoid using TV as a consequence.* Don't use television to reward or punish behavior; it makes it even more attractive.
- *Model healthy viewing.* When possible, watch TV with your children, discuss the content, and express disapproval when it's inappropriate. Watch programs with children that are informative and prosocial.
- *Be an authoritative parent.* Counter the negative effects of television by adopting the authoritative child-rearing practices discussed in Chapter 3: Be firm but caring, provide reasons for rules, behave consistently, and hold high expectations (Slaby et al., 1995).

As teachers, we can also encourage our students to watch informative and prosocial programming, and we should model healthy viewing. Although frequently criticized, television also has the potential to be a positive force for learning and behavior.

Processes Involved in Learning from Models

Modeling can result in learning and facilitating behaviors, changing inhibitions, and arousing emotions, but how does this take place? Learning from models involves four processes: *attention, retention, reproduction,* and *motivation* (Bandura, 1986). They're illustrated in Figure 6.5 and summarized as follows:

- *Attention*: A learner's attention is drawn to the critical aspects of the modeled behavior. For example, Tim paid attention to Susan's study strategies.
- *Retention*: The modeled behaviors are transferred to memory by mentally verbalizing or visually representing them. Tim mentally recorded Susan's behaviors.
- *Reproduction*: Learners reproduce the behaviors that have been stored in memory. Tim imitated Susan's study habits.
- *Motivation*: Learners are motivated by the expectation of reinforcement for reproducing the modeled behaviors. Tim was motivated to imitate Susan's behaviors because he expected to be reinforced for doing so.

Several aspects of these processes are important for teachers. To learn from models, the learner's attention must be drawn to the essential aspects of the modeled behavior (Bandura, 1986). For example, preservice teachers often go into schools and observe veterans in action. If they don't know what they're looking for, the observations don't result in a great deal of learning. As teachers, we need to call attention to the important aspects of the skill we're modeling.

Also, attending to the modeled behaviors and, presumably, recording them in memory don't ensure that learners will be able to reproduce them. Additional scaffolding and feedback are often required. (We examine this issue in detail when we discuss instructional strategies later in the chapter.)

Finally, although motivation appears as a separate component in Figure 6.5, it is integral to each of the others. Motivated learners are more likely than unmotivated learners to attend to a model's behavior, to record the behavior in memory, and to reproduce it. Learners who make a conscious effort to do these things will be more successful than those who remain passive.

Effectiveness of Models

When we refer to the "effectiveness" of a model, we're describing the likelihood that an observer will imitate the model's behavior. An observer is more likely to imitate an

Figure 6.5 Processes involved in learning from models

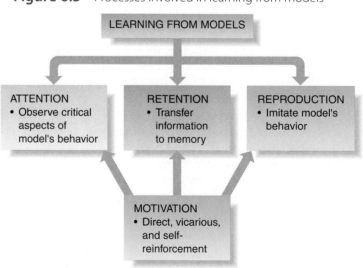

effective than an ineffective model. A model's effectiveness depends primarily on three factors:

- Perceived similarity
- Perceived competence
- Perceived status

When we observe a model's behavior, we are more likely to imitate it if we perceive the model as similar to us (Schunk, 1987). In addition, several models are more effective than a single model, or even a few, because the likelihood of finding a model perceived as similar increases as the number of models increases.

This helps us understand why presenting nontraditional career models and teaching students about the contributions of women and people from minority groups are important. For example, although learners will imitate models of either gender, girls are more likely to believe that engineering is a viable career choice if they observe the work of a female rather than a male engineer. Similarly, a Hispanic student is more likely to believe he can accomplish challenging goals if he sees the accomplishments of a successful Hispanic adult than if the adult is a nonminority.

Perception of a model's competence, the second factor that increases a model's effectiveness, interacts with perceptions of similarity. People are more likely to imitate models perceived as competent than those perceived as less competent, regardless of similarity. Although as classmates Susan and Tim were similar, Tim would have been unlikely to imitate her behaviors if she had not been a successful student.

The third factor, status, is acquired when individuals distinguish themselves from others in their fields. People tend to imitate high-status individuals—such as professional athletes, popular rock stars, and world leaders—more often than others. At the school level, athletes, cheerleaders, and in some cases even gang leaders have high status for many students.

Teachers are also influential models. Despite concerns expressed by educational reformers and teachers themselves, they remain and will continue as high-status models for students.

Status has a spill-over effect; high-status models are often tacitly credited for competence outside their own areas of expertise. This is the reason you see professional basketball players (instead of nutritionists) endorsing breakfast cereal, and actors (instead of engineers) endorsing automobiles and motor oil.

> **6.18**
> One group of students watched teachers successfully solve problems, a second group watched peers do the same, and a third saw no models. Which group successfully solved the most problems, and which solved the fewest? Explain, based on the information in this section.

Self-Regulation

Earlier, we saw that learners' beliefs and expectations can influence both behavior and the environment. This is accomplished through **self-regulation,** *the process of accepting responsibility and control for one's own learning.* Self-regulated learners use their own thoughts and actions to reach academic learning goals; they identify goals and adopt and maintain strategies for reaching these goals.

For example, Tim chose to go to Susan's home to study, and he developed a pattern of changed study strategies, which he monitored himself. Behaviorists are unable to explain why, after going to Susan's house, Tim changed and continued his efforts without reinforcement; he was reinforced only after he made the conscious choice to change, monitor, and sustain his study strategies. To behave as he did, Tim had to be self-regulated; the consequences of his actions existed too far in the future to affect his behavior in the present (Bandura, 1986). If he hadn't been self-regulated, he wouldn't have maintained the behavior until it could be reinforced.

Cognitive Behavior Modification

In recent years, a trend in education has been to increase learners' responsibilities in the learning process (Stipek, 1996; Zimmerman & Schunk, 1989), and a number of programs have been developed to teach self-regulation. These programs commonly combine cognitive self-management strategies with the targeting of specific behaviors (Alberto & Troutman, 1999). One such program is **cognitive behavior modification,** which has been defined as *"the modification of overt behavior through the manipulation of covert thought processes"* (Hallahan & Sapona, 1983, p. 616, italics added). It includes aspects of behaviorism because it assumes that the basic principles of reinforcement are operating, but it differs from behaviorism in that it emphasizes using a person's cognitive operations to achieve a change in behavior (Stipek, 1996).

Cognitive behavior modification requires that students take more responsibility for their own learning by doing the following:

- Setting their own goals
- Monitoring their behavior
- Assessing their behavior
- Administering their own rewards (Ainly, 1993; Meichenbaum, 1977; Pintrich & Schrauben, 1992)

Goal Setting. Goals provide direction for a person's actions and provide ways for measuring progress. Susan set the goal of working at least three of each type of algebra problem, and Tim imitated her behavior by setting goals of his own.

Goals set by students themselves, especially goals that are challenging but realistic, are more effective than those imposed by the teacher (Schunk, 1994; Spaulding, 1992). An important objective for teachers is to help students learn to set effective goals.

6.19

Think about your work in this class. Identify at least two goals that you could use to increase your learning. Now describe a simple form of self-observation you could use to monitor your progress toward the goals.

Self-Observation. Once they have set their goals, self-regulated learners monitor their progress. Susan, for example, said, "I sometimes even make a little chart. I try to do at least three problems of each type we study, and then I check them off as I do them." Self-observation allowed Susan to monitor her progress.

Students can be taught to monitor a variety of behaviors. For example, they can keep a chart and make a check every time they catch themselves "drifting off" during an hour of study, every time they blurt out an answer in class, or—on the positive side—every time they use a desired social skill (Alberto & Troutman, 1999).

Self-observation combined with appropriate goals can change student behavior, sometimes dramatically (Mace, Belfiore, & Shea, 1989). With effort and teacher support, study habits and concentration can be improved and social interactions can be made more positive and productive.

Self-Assessment. Schools historically have been places where a person's performance is judged by someone else. Although teachers can provide valuable feedback in assessing student performance, they don't have to be the sole judges; in addition, students can learn to assess their own work (Stiggins, 1997). For example, students can assess the quality of their solutions to word problems by learning to ask themselves whether their answers make sense and to compare their answers with estimates. Tim was involved in a form of self-assessment when he checked his answers against those given at the back of the book.

Developing self-assessment skills takes time, and students won't automatically be good at it. The best way to help students develop these skills is to be sure their goals are specific and quantitative, as were Susan's and Tim's. Helping students make valid self-assessments based on accurate self-observations is one of the most important instructional tasks teachers face.

Self-Reinforcement. We all feel good when we accomplish a goal, and we often feel guilty when we don't, vowing to do better in the future (Bandura, 1989). As learners become self-regulated, they learn to reinforce or punish themselves for meeting or failing to meet their goals.

Self-reinforcers can be an internal pat on the back, or they can be something more tangible, such as the dish of ice cream Susan treated herself to when she got all of her problems right. A powerful form of self-reinforcement is the feeling of accomplishment that can result from setting and meeting challenging goals. A self-punisher might simply be the denial of the "pat" or the treat.

Self-reinforcement is somewhat controversial. Some researchers argue that it is unnecessary; in other words, goals, self-observation, and self-assessment should be sufficient (S. Hayes et al., 1985). Others argue that self-reinforcement can be a powerful strategy, particularly for low achievers. In one study, low-achieving students were taught to award themselves points, which they could use to buy privileges, when they did well on their assignments. Within a few weeks, the low achievers were achieving as well as their classmates (Stevenson & Fantuzzo, 1986). Bandura (1986) has argued that rewarding oneself for good work can lead to higher performance than goals and self-monitoring alone.

Cognitive behavior modification isn't without problems. For instance, research indicates that learners tend to set very lenient goals (Wall, 1983), and they sometimes cheat when allowed to reinforce themselves (Speidel & Tharp, 1980). Researchers emphasize that learners need guidance in setting goals, and they need to be monitored for cheating. Although effective, cognitive behavior modification strategies are not always easy to implement (Stipek, 1996).

We examine specific strategies for developing learner self-regulation in Chapter 11.

Social Cognitive Theory in the Classroom: Instructional Strategies

Social cognitive theory has a wide range of applications, both in classrooms and in the world at large. As we said earlier, the influence of modeling on people's behaviors, for example, is hard to overstate.

In classrooms, the following principles can help guide teachers at they attempt to capitalize on the characteristics of social cognitive theory:

- Behave in ways you want students to imitate.
- Enforce classroom rules and procedures fairly and consistently.
- Capitalize on modeling effects and processes to promote learning.
- Put students in modeling roles.
- Capitalize on guests as role models when possible.

Let's see how the principles guide Sally Campese, an eighth-grade algebra teacher, as she works with her students.

"Good morning, everyone," Sally greeted the students, as she moved to the front of the classroom. "I have a new little wrinkle that we're going to incorporate into our work. I recently subscribed to a 'word-of-the-day' online service, and I'm going to share the word with you." On the board, she wrote

Recidivism—a tendency to lapse into a previous condition

"We don't want any recidivism with respect to our work habits," she smiled.

"This is an algebra class," Todd noted. "Why are we thinking about words in here?"

"This is first a class about learning," Sally returned. "I want to keep on learning, and I want you all to feel the same way. . . . No recidivism," she smiled again.

"You're gung ho about everything, aren't you, Mrs. Campese?" Jeff grinned.

Teachers act as powerful role models in the classroom, influencing both cognitive and affective outcomes.

Sally gave Jeff a slight smile and then turned to Jamie, who was coming through the door, "I'm sorry, but you're late."

In Sally's classroom, students were warned the first time they were tardy for the week and were given a half hour of detention for a second tardy.

"I know," Jamie nodded wryly, realizing she had been warned.

"Just a reminder before we start. Remember, I've invited a man named Javier Sanchez in to speak on Friday. You remember that I told you Mr. Sanchez is an engineer in one of the big firms in town, and he's going to tell you about engineering and why math is so important for all of us.

"Okay, look up here," Sally said, turning to the day's topic. "We're having a little difficulty with some of these problems, so let's look at a few more examples.

"Try this one," she said, writing on the chalkboard:

$$4a + 6b = 24$$
$$5a - 6b = 3$$

Sally watched as the students tried the problem, and seeing that Gabriel had solved it successfully, said, "Gabriel, go ahead and describe your thinking for us as you solved the problem."

"I saw that there's a $6b$ in the first equation and a negative $6b$ in the second equation. . . . So, I added the two equations together, . . . and that's how I did it."

"Excellent, Gabriel. . . . And what do we get when we add the equations? . . . Hue?"

". . . Nine a plus zero b equals 27."

Sally wrote $9a + 0b = 27$ on the board.

"Okay," she continued. "What is the value of a? . . . Chris?"

". . . Three."

"And how did you get that?"

"Zero b is zero, and then I divided both sides by 9, so I have $1a$ equals 3."

"Good! That's right. Now let's find the value of b. What should we do first? . . . Mitchell?"

Let's take a closer look at Sally's attempts to apply social cognitive theory. First, by initiating the "word-of-the-day" activity, she attempted to model a desire to learn for her students. The fact that her class was an algebra class may have made her efforts even more significant. Her modeling communicated that learning in all its forms is valuable and that being in algebra class didn't mean students could learn only about algebra. Efforts such as Sally's might not make all students enthusiastic learners, but they contribute, as Jeff's comment, "You're gung ho about everything, aren't you, Mrs. Campese?" indicates. We saw earlier in the chapter that teacher enthusiasm can arouse students' emotions, and Sally was attempting to capitalize on this factor.

Second, Sally consistently enforced her classroom rules about lateness. Jamie's tardiness may have been minor, but students would have expected the consequence (the warning). Not following through might have resulted in the nonoccurrence-of-an-expected-punisher acting as a reinforcer, which would have increased the likelihood of Jamie being tardy a second time. Also, if Sally hadn't warned Jamie, the other students' inhibitions about being tardy would have been weakened, increasing the chance that they, too, would come to class late.

Third, Sally capitalized on the processes—*attention, retention, reproduction,* and *motivation*—involved in modeling. She realized that students must first attend to modeled behavior if they're going to retain it in memory, and she also realized that attention and retention don't necessarily make students able to reproduce the desired behavior. So, she guided the students with questions rather than simply explaining the solution. Students are more attentive in question-and-answer sessions than they are during teacher explanations (Good & Brophy, 2000; Lambert & McCombs, 1998), so Sally's students were more likely to retain the modeled solutions in memory. And because they were guided through each step in the reproduction of the solution, the students were more likely to be able to reproduce solutions on their own later.

Fourth, when Sally said, "Gabriel, go ahead and describe your thinking for us as you solved the problem," she was attempting to use Gabriel as a model for the rest of the stu-

6.20
What modeling effect could result from not enforcing the tardiness rule when Jamie came into class late? Explain.

6.21
What concept from your study of Vygotsky's work in Chapter 2 is illustrated by Sally guiding the students with her questioning? Explain.

dents. Because of perceived similarity, peers can be very effective models (Schunk, 2000). Gabriel described her own thinking, so she was also a *cognitive model.*

Finally, by inviting a successful professional engineer to speak to her classes, Sally hoped to expose her students to a guest role model who would be perceived as competent. Javier Sanchez, a Hispanic, would also be effective because of his perceived similarity to students from cultural minorities. Teachers usually cannot routinely invite guests into their classrooms, but having a guest speak even two or three times a year can do much to capitalize on the influence of minority role models.

Assessment and Learning: Self-Modeling as an Assessment Tool

If perceived similarity makes models more effective, then why not take advantage of the individuals most similar to the learners? These individuals are the learners themselves. In **self-modeling,** *behavioral changes result from people observing and reflecting on their own behaviors* (Dowrick, 1983).

In a typical self-modeling episode, an individual is videotaped while performing an activity—perhaps teaching a lesson, completing a gymnastics routine, or even solving a math problem. The videotaped episode then provides specific, concrete information that can be used for assessment and feedback. Self-modeling is particularly informative for behaviors that learners cannot effectively observe and perform at the same time (such as teaching a lesson). Self-modeling has been used to develop social, vocational, motor, cognitive, and teaching skills (Schunk, 2000).

Self-Modeling in Assessment

As an assessment tool, videotaping and self-modeling can be very powerful. For instance, think about viewing a taped episode of yourself teaching a class. Although you would be understandably apprehensive, your interest and motivation would be very high.

The process typically involves four steps:

- Instruction and scaffolded practice
- Videotaped performance
- Self-assessment of performance based on observing the videotape
- Discussion and analysis of self-assessment and performance with an expert

The process begins with instruction and scaffolded practice. For instance, in the example of your videotaped lesson, the desired technique would be explained and modeled for you by your instructor, you would practice on your own or in front of your peers, and then you would be videotaped.

Because videotaping provides an exact copy of performance, self-assessment is an essential part of self-modeling. If you watched yourself teach a lesson, for example, you would probably identify subtle aspects of your instruction that you hadn't been aware of. For instance, self-assessment would provide information about the consistency of your verbal and nonverbal behavior, speech patterns, and mannerisms that you may or may not want to change. It would also provide information about the clarity of your presentation, questions, and responses to students. Many of these processes are essentially automatic, so viewing yourself on videotape would supply information unavailable in any other way.

Motivation and a sense of increasing competence are primary benefits of self-modeling (Schunk, 2000). If you saw yourself successfully teach a lesson, for example, your beliefs about your capabilities would increase, which would further increase your motivation.

Error-filled performances are somewhat problematic, however (Hosford, 1981). Individuals viewing a videotaped episode in which they're performing poorly may become discouraged. In these cases, the support of an expert is essential. He or she can provide encouragement as well as feedback and suggestions for improving the performance. If it does improve, the benefits to motivation can be even greater than those enjoyed after a flawless first performance, because the improvement suggests that capability is increased with effort (Schunk, 1989).

Our illustrations of self-modeling have so far focused on teaching technique, but self-modeling has also been used successfully with basic skills. For instance, low-achieving math students received instruction and practice with fraction skills. Some of the students were then videotaped and shown the tapes in which they successfully solved fraction problems. The self-modeling students scored higher on a subsequent achievement measure than did students who received similar instruction but were not videotaped. Seeing themselves successfully perform on a videotaped episode was essential to the self-models' progress (Schunk & Hanson, 1989).

Putting Social Cognitive Theory into Perspective

Like all descriptions of learning and behavior, social cognitive theory has strengths and weaknesses. For example, we have repeatedly emphasized the importance of modeling as a tool for promoting learning and changes in behavior. And social cognitive theory overcomes some of the limitations of behaviorism by helping us understand the importance of learner cognitions, in the form of beliefs and expectations, on their actions.

However, like any theory, social cognitive theory has limitations:

- It cannot explain why learners attend to and imitate some modeled behaviors but not others.
- It doesn't account for the learning of complex tasks, such as learning to write (beyond mere mechanics).
- It cannot explain the role of context and social interaction in complex learning environments. For example, research indicates that student interaction in small groups facilitates learning (Greeno et al., 1996; Shuell, 1996). The processes involved in these settings extend beyond modeling and imitation.

We identify these limitations as a reminder that every theory of learning is incomplete, able to explain some aspects of learning but not others. This is why it's important for teachers to understand different views of learning together with their strengths and limitations.

Classroom Connections

Applying Social Cognitive Theory in Your Classroom

1. Use cognitive modeling in your instruction. Act as a role model for your students.

   - *Elementary:* A kindergarten teacher uses cognitive modeling in helping her children form letters by saying, "I start with my pencil here and make a straight line down," as she begins to form a *b*.
   - *Middle School:* A seventh-grade teacher has a large poster at the front of his room that says, "I will always

treat you with courtesy and respect, you will treat me with courtesy and respect, and you will treat each other with courtesy and respect."

   - *High School:* A physics teacher solving acceleration problems involving friction writes $F = ma$ on the chalkboard and says, "I know I want to find the net force on the object. So, then I think about what the problem tells me. . . . Someone, go ahead and tell us one thing we know about the problem."

2. As students are learning to reproduce skills, provide group practice by walking them through examples before having them practice on their own.

- *Elementary:* A fifth-grade class is adding fractions with unlike denominators. The teacher displays the problem ¼ + ⅔ = ? and then begins, "What do we need to do first? . . . Karen?" She continues until the class works through the problem and then does a second example the same way.
- *Middle School:* After showing students how to find exact locations using longitude and latitude, a seventh-grade geography teacher says to his students, "We want to find the city closest to 85° west and 37° north. . . . First, what do these numbers tell us? . . . Leslie?" He continues to guide the students through the example until they locate Chicago as the closest city.
- *High School:* After demonstrating several proofs, a geometry teacher wants her students to prove that angle 1 is greater than angle 2 in the accompanying drawing. She begins by asking, "What are we given in the problem?" After the students identify the given information, she asks, "What can we conclude about segments *BE* and *BD*?" She continues until they have completed the proof as a group.

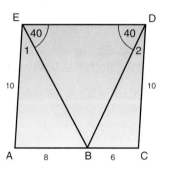

3. Use vicarious reinforcement to increase the effectiveness of modeling.
- *Elementary:* As students in one reading group move back to their desks, a first-grade teacher comments loudly enough for the class to hear, "I like the way this group is returning to their desks. Karen, Vicki, Ali, and David each get a star because they have gone so quickly and quietly."
- *Middle School:* An eighth-grade English teacher displays several examples of well-written paragraphs

on the overhead. He comments, "These are each well written. They have excellent paragraph structure, and each shows some imagination."
- *High School:* An art teacher hands back students' pottery projects. She displays several well-done pieces and comments, "Look at these, everyone. These are excellent. Let's see why. . . ."

(The English and art teachers accomplished three things. First, the students whose paragraphs or pottery were displayed were directly reinforced, but they weren't put on the spot because the teachers didn't identify them. Second, the rest of the students in the classes were vicariously reinforced. Third, the teachers gave the classes feedback and provided models for future imitation.)

4. Promote self-regulation in your students.
- *Elementary:* A third-grade teacher helps his students design a checklist with which they can assess their own behavior. The first behavior they monitor is leaving their seats without permission. Initially, the teacher reminds them to make a check when they are out of their seats, and later he discretely monitors the students to see if they've given themselves a check. The students record a plus sign on the list for each day that has no checks.
- *Middle School:* A pre-algebra teacher helps her students create a rating scale to assess their progress on homework. For each assignment, they circle a 3 on the scale if they complete the assignment and believe they understand it, a 2 if they complete it but are uncertain about their understanding, and a 1 if they do not complete it.
- *High School:* An English teacher helps his students set individual goals by asking each to write a study plan. He returns to the plan at the end of the unit and has each student assess his or her progress.

Addressing Diversity: Behaviorism and Social Cognitive Theory

As Carlos entered his second-grade classroom early Tuesday morning, he heard salsa music in the background. The walls of his classroom were decorated with colorful prints from Mexico and Central America, and vocabulary cards in both Spanish and English were hung around the room.

"Buenos días, Carlos. How are you today?" Donna Evans, his teacher, asked. "You're here very early."

"Buenos días. . . . I'm fine," Carlos responded, smiling as he went to his desk to take out his homework from the night before.

Donna watched Carlos for a few moments as he worked in the empty room. "What are we working on today, Carlos?"

"I cannot do it! I do not understand," Carlos replied in his halting English, frustration in his voice.

Donna looked over his shoulder at the 12 math problems she had assigned for homework. He had done the first two correctly, but he had forgotten to borrow on the next three and had left the last seven undone.

"Carlos, look," she said, kneeling down so that she was at eye level with him. "You did the first two just fine. Look here. . . . How is this problem different from this one?" she asked, pointing to the two following problems:

$$36 \qquad 45$$
$$-14 \qquad -19$$

". . . The numbers . . . are different."

"Okay," she smiled. "What else?"

". . . This one . . . is bigger," he said, pointing to the 45 and then to the 36.

"How about the 9 and the 5? . . . Which is bigger?"

". . . This," he said, pointing at the 9.

"Good, and how about the 6 and the 4?"

". . . Here," he answered and referred to the 6.

"And where is the bigger one in each case?"

". . . There," Carlos said, pointing to the 6 in the first problem, ". . . and there," pointing to the 9 in the second.

"Very good, Carlos. It is very important to know where the bigger number is," she continued. "Now let's work this one together. Watch what I do."

Donna worked with Carlos to solve the next two problems, carefully discussing her thinking as they went along and comparing problems that required regrouping to those that did not.

"Now try the next three on your own," she said, "and I'll be back in a few minutes to see how you're doing. Remember what Juanita's father said about becoming a scientist when he came and visited our class. You have to study very hard and do your math. I know you can do it, especially because you already did it on the first two. . . . Now go ahead."

Carlos nodded and then bent over his work. A short while later, he was finishing the last of the three problems as the other students entered into the classroom. Donna went to him, checked his work, and commented, "Very good, Carlos. You got two of them right. Now check this one. You have just enough time before we start."

In another elementary school in the same city, Roberto shuffled into class and hid behind the big girl in front of him. If he was lucky, his teacher wouldn't discover that he hadn't done his homework—12 problems! How could he ever do that many? Besides, he wasn't good at math.

Roberto hated school. It seemed so strange and foreign. His teacher would sometimes frown when he spoke because his English wasn't as good as most of the other students'. Sometimes when the teacher talked, he couldn't understand what she was saying.

Even lunch wasn't much fun. If his friend Raul wasn't there, he would eat alone. One time when he sat with some other students, they started laughing at the way he talked, and they asked what he was eating. He had tortillas that day. He couldn't wait to go home.

As we saw in Chapter 4, for students from different cultures schools sometimes seem strange and cold, and classrooms threatening. School tasks are difficult, and failure is common. Behaviorism and social cognitive theory can help teachers understand why schools aren't friendlier places for these students and what can be done about it.

Classical Conditioning: Learning to Like and Dislike School

Earlier in the chapter you saw how both Sharon Van Horn, who was mentioned briefly for greeting her student Damon each morning, and Erika Williams, the teacher with the index-card system, attempted to capitalize on classical conditioning to make their classrooms inviting. Donna Evans did the same thing. Carlos had an instinctively positive emotional reaction to Donna's warmth and caring, and in time her classroom became associated with her manner. We can all create warm and supportive learning environments for our students through the way we interact with them and with the rules and procedures we establish.

Unfortunately, the opposite can also be true, as it was in Roberto's case. School was not associated with positive feelings for him, and he didn't feel wanted, safe, or comfortable.

6.22
Using the concepts *unconditioned stimulus, unconditioned response, conditioned stimulus,* and *conditioned response,* explain how Donna Evans's room made Carlos feel good about being there.

Motivating Hesitant Learners

When students are struggling, how can modeling and appropriate use of reinforcers enhance their efforts? The answer to this question influences both initial learning and life-long views of competence.

Let's look again at Donna's work with Carlos:

- She reinforced him for the problems he had done correctly.
- She provided corrective feedback to help him understand where he had made mistakes.
- She reduced the task to three problems to ensure that the reinforcement schedule would be motivating.
- She used both direct and cognitive modeling to show him the correct procedures for solving the problems.
- She helped Carlos increase his sense of accomplishment by encouraging him and by providing only enough assistance so that he could do the problems on his own.

In her work with Carlos, Donna supported his efforts by applying concepts from both behaviorism and social cognitive theory. This support can increase both learner motivation and achievement.

Roberto's experience was very different. To him, the classroom was a strange and unfriendly place. His teacher didn't greet him, and nothing in the classroom made him feel welcome. When the problems seemed impossible, no one came to help. He had already "learned" that he wasn't "good" at math.

Capitalizing on Minority Role Models

Earlier we saw that Sally Campese brought an engineer named Javier Sanchez into her class to discuss the importance of math. Perhaps more important, Mr. Sanchez's presence provided clear evidence that a person of Hispanic background can succeed in a demanding academic field. Donna Evans did the same thing when she invited Juanita's father into her class. Little sends a more powerful message to Hispanic youth.

In their efforts to provide role models for minority youth, teachers often overlook the opportunity to use symbolic models. Editorial columnists, such as William Raspberry, Walter Williams, and Clarence Page—all African American—are nationally syndicated, and they frequently express opinions about prosocial values, such as the need to accept responsibility for personal behavior and success. Their pictures always appear with their columns, so teachers merely need to watch the newspapers and clip columns that are relevant to their goals. Minimal effort is required, and again, minority youth receive a powerful message.

In Chapter 4, we examined the ways students from different backgrounds and cultures respond to schooling. In this chapter, behaviorism and social cognitive theory help us understand how factors such as caring, reinforcement, modeling, and feedback can be used to help all students learn successfully.

Classroom Connections

Capitalizing on Diversity in Your Classroom

1. Make your classroom a place that welcomes all students.
   - *Elementary:* An elementary teacher invites students to bring in posters and pictures to decorate their room. On Friday afternoons during earned free time, he allows them to bring in and play music.
   - *Middle School:* An inner-city social studies teacher displays pictures of historical minority figures around her room. Throughout the year, she refers to these people and emphasizes that American history is the story of all people.
   - *High School:* An English teacher has his students study poetry written by people of Asian, Middle Eastern, European, African, and Native American descent. He emphasizes that people from all parts of the world have expressed themselves in poetry and that we can learn something from each of them.

2. Provide instructional support to ensure as much success as possible.
   - *Elementary:* A fifth-grade teacher uses student graders to provide immediate feedback on math assignments. Two students are chosen each week and are provided with answers for each day's assignment. After students have completed their work, they have it checked immediately; if their scores are below 80%, they see the teacher for help.
   - *Middle School:* A sixth-grade math teacher carefully discusses each day's homework. Students are given the chance to repeat homework assignments to ensure that they understand the concepts and skills involved.
   - *High School:* An English teacher assigns a research paper at the beginning of the term. She breaks the assignment into parts, such as doing a literature search, making an outline, and writing a first draft. She meets with students each week to check their progress and give them feedback.

Summary

Behaviorist Views of Learning

Contiguity helps explain fact learning through the pairing of stimuli and responses. Classical conditioning occurs when a formerly neutral stimulus becomes associated with a naturally occurring (unconditioned) stimulus to produce a response similar to an instinctive or reflexive response. Classical conditioning helps teachers understand emotional reactions such as test anxiety and how students learn to be comfortable in school environments.

Operant conditioning focuses on voluntary responses that are influenced by consequences. Praise, high test scores, and good grades are consequences that increase behavior and are called *reinforcers*, whereas reprimands are consequences that decrease behavior and are called *punishers*. The schedule of reinforcers influences both the rate of initial learning and the persistence of the behavior.

Applied behavior analysis systematically uses the principles of operant conditioning to change severe or chronic behavior problems. It is used quite commonly with students who have exceptionalities.

Social Cognitive Theory

Social cognitive theory extends behaviorism and focuses on the influence that observing others has on behavior. It considers, in addition to behavior and the environment, learners' beliefs and expectations. Social cognitive theory suggests that reinforcement and punishment affect learners' motivation, rather than directly cause behavior.

Modeling lies at the core of social cognitive theory. Modeling can be direct (from live models), symbolic (from books, movies, and television), or synthesized (combining the acts of different models). It can cause new behaviors, facilitate existing behaviors, change inhibitions, and arouse emotions. In learning from models, observers go through the processes of attention (observation), retention in memory, reproduction of the observed behavior, and motivation to produce the behavior in the future.

Learners become self-regulated when they set learning goals on their own, monitor their progress toward the goals, and assess the effectiveness of their efforts.

Addressing Diversity: Behaviorism and Social Cognitive Theory

When teachers treat all students with courtesy and respect, students associate classroom environments with their teachers' caring manner and, through classical conditioning, learn to respond to school with positive emotions. Teachers can also increase learners' feelings of competence by modeling effort and persistence and reinforcing genuine accomplishments.

Professionals and business people who are members of cultural minorities can serve as role models, sending powerful messages to minority youth about the ability to succeed at school and still maintain a cultural identity. Teachers can use nationally syndicated columnists who are ethnic minorities as symbolic models for promoting personal responsibility and other prosocial values.

Windows on Classrooms

You've seen how contiguity, classical and operant conditioning, modeling, vicarious learning, and self-regulation can be used to explain the behavior of students. Let's look now at a teacher attempting to apply some of these concepts as he works with his middle school students. Read the case study, and answer the questions that follow.

Warren Rose, a seventh-grade math teacher, had his students involved in a unit on decimals and percentages. He began class on Thursday by saying, "All right, let's review what we did yesterday."

Hearing some mumbles, he noted wryly, "I realize that percentages and decimals aren't your favorite topic, and I'm not wild about them either, but we have no choice, so we might as well buckle down and learn them.

"Let me show you a few more examples," he continued, displaying the following problem on the overhead:

You are at the mall, shopping for a jacket. You see one that looks great, originally priced at $84, marked 25% off. You recently got a check for $65 from the fast-food restaurant where you work. Can you afford the jacket?

"Now, . . . the first thing I think about when I see a problem like this one is, 'What does the jacket cost now?' I have to figure out the price, and to do that I will take 25% of the $84. . . . That means I first convert the 25% to a decimal. I know when I see 25% that the decimal is understood

to be just to the right of the 5, so I move it two places to the left. Then I can multiply 0.25 times 84."

Warren demonstrated the process as he spoke, working the problem through to completion. He had his students work several examples at their desks and discussed their solutions.

He then continued, "Okay, for homework, do the odd problems on page 113."

"Do we have to do all six of them?" Robbie asked.

"Why not?" Warren responded.

"Aww, gee, Mr. Rose," Will put in, "they're so hard."

"Yes," Ginny added. "And they take so long."

Several other students chimed in, arguing that six word problems were too many.

"Wait, people, please," Warren held up his hands. "All right. You only have to do 1, 3, 5, 7, and 9."

"Yeah!" the class shouted.

"Yikes, Friday," Helen commented to Jenny as they walked into Warren's room Friday morning. "I, like, blanked out last week. I get so nervous when he makes us go up to the board, and everybody's staring at us. If he calls me up today, I'll die."

Warren discussed the day's homework and then said, "Okay, let's look at this problem."

A bicycle selling for $145 is marked down 15%. What is the new selling price?

"First, let's estimate, so that we can see whether our answer makes sense. About what should the new selling price be? . . . Helen?"

". . . I'm not sure," Helen said.

"Callie, what do you think?"

"I think it would be about $120."

"Good thinking. Describe for everyone how you arrived at that."

"Well, 10% would be $14.50, . . . so 15% would be about another $7. That would be about $21, and $21 off would be a little over $120."

"Good," Warren nodded. "Now, let's go ahead and solve it. What do we do first? . . . David?"

". . . We make the 15% into a decimal."

"Good, David. Now, what next? . . . Leslie?"

"Take the 0.15 times the 145."

"Okay. Do that everybody. . . . What did you get?"

". . . $200.17," Cris volunteered. "Whoops, that can't be right. That's more than the bicycle cost to start with. . . . Wait, $21.75."

"Good," Warren smiled. "That's what we're trying to do. We are all going to make mistakes, but if we catch ourselves, we're making progress. Keep it up. You can do these problems. Now what do we do?" he continued.

"Subtract," Matt volunteered.

"All right, go ahead," Warren directed.

". . . $142.83," Molly answered.

"Now, think about that for a second. What was our estimate?"

"What? . . . Oh, yeah, . . . No, wait, $123.25."

"What did you do the first time?" Warren queried.

". . . Decimal point in the wrong place."

"Okay, good work. Now, let's look at another one."

Warren then had the class work two additional problems, and as he began to assign homework, several of the students chimed in, "How about just four problems tonight, Mr. Rose. We always have so much math to do."

"Okay," Warren shrugged, "numbers 2, 6, 7, and 8 on page 114."

Warren continued monitoring the students until 2 minutes were left in the period. "All right, everyone, the bell will ring in 2 minutes. Get everything cleaned up around your desks, and get ready to go."

PRAXIS These exercises are designed to help you prepare for the PRAXIS™ "Principles of Learning and Teaching" exam. To receive feedback on your constructed response questions and document analysis response, go to the Companion Website at *www.prenhall.com/eggen*, then to this chapter's *Practice for PRAXIS™* module. For additional connections between this text and the PRAXIS™ exam, go to Appendix A.

Constructed Response Questions

In answering these questions, use information from the chapter and link your responses to specific information in the case.

1. Describe where classical conditioning occurred in the case study. Identify the classical classical conditioning concepts in your description.

2. Warren inadvertently allowed himself to be punished in two different places in the case study. Explain where they occurred, and describe their likely impact on learning.

3. Warren's modeling had both positive and negative features. Identify and explain one positive and one negative feature.

4. Warren capitalized on the positive aspects of perceived similarity in the case study. Explain where and how this occurred.

Document-Based Analysis

A seventh-grade teacher has the following list of rules and consequences displayed on the bulletin board at the front of her room:

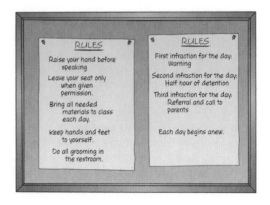

Assess these rules and consequences with respect to using behaviorism as a mechanism for creating a productive learning environment. Identify both their strengths and weaknesses based on the content of the chapter.

 ## Online Portfolio Activities

To develop your professional portfolio, further apply your understanding of chapter content, and address the INTASC standards, go to the Companion Website, then to this chapter's *Online Portfolio Activities*. Complete the suggested activities.

 Also on the Companion Website at *www.prenhall.com/eggen*, you can measure your understanding of chapter content in *Practice Quiz* and *Essay* modules, apply concepts in *Online Cases,* and broaden your knowledge base with the *Additional Content* module and *Web Links* to other educational psychology websites.

Important Concepts

antecedents *(p. 206)*
applied behavior analysis *(p. 210)*
classical conditioning *(p. 197)*
cognitive behavior modification *(p. 221)*
cognitive modeling *(p. 216)*
conditioned response *(p. 197)*
conditioned stimulus *(p. 197)*
consequence *(p. 200)*
contiguity *(p. 196)*
continuous reinforcement schedule *(p. 203)*
cues *(p. 206)*
discrimination *(pp. 199, 207)*
extinction *(pp. 199, 204)*
generalization *(pp. 198, 207)*
inhibition *(p. 218)*
intermittent reinforcement
  schedule *(p. 203)*
learning *(pp. 196, 215)*
modeling *(p. 216)*
negative reinforcement *(p. 201)*
operant conditioning *(p. 200)*

positive reinforcement *(p. 201)*
potency *(p. 204)*
Premack principle *(p. 201)*
presentation punishment *(p. 205)*
productive learning environment *(p. 208)*
prompts *(p. 206)*
punishers *(p. 205)*
punishment *(p. 205)*
reinforcement *(p. 201)*
reinforcement schedules *(p. 202)*
reinforcer *(p. 201)*
removal punishment *(p. 205)*
satiation *(p. 204)*
self-modeling *(p. 225)*
self-regulation *(p. 221)*
shaping *(p. 202)*
social cognitive theory *(p. 214)*
unconditioned response *(p. 197)*
unconditioned stimulus *(p. 197)*
vicarious learning *(p. 217)*

Chapter Outline

Cognitive Views of Learning

7

David Shelton was planning a unit on the solar system for his ninth-grade earth science class. He prepared two color transparencies, one showing the sun throwing globs of gases into space and the other presenting a model of the solar system that illustrated the planets in their orbital planes. He also prepared a large matrix which he taped to the back wall of the room.

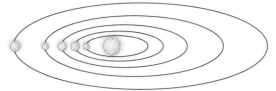

One Theory of How the Solar System Was Formed

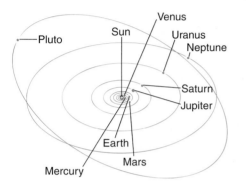

Transparency model of the solar system

David introduced the unit on Monday and assigned groups to gather information for the chart. Books, videos, and computers were available in the classroom.

	Diameter (miles)	Distance from sun (miles)	Length of year (orbit)	Length of day (rotation)	Gravity (compared to Earth's)	Average surface temperature	Characteristics
Mercury							
Venus							
Earth							
Mars							
Jupiter							
Saturn							
Uranus							
Neptune							
Pluto							

On Tuesday he displayed and discussed the transparencies and instructed the class to use the displays as frames of reference for their study. The students spent the rest of the period collecting and putting information into the chart. [The completed chart appears on p. 252.]

On Wednesday David began by saying, "Let's review what we've found so far. Then I'm going to do a little demonstration, and I want you to think about how it relates to what you've been doing." After a brief review of Tuesday's lesson, he tied a pair of athletic socks to a 3-foot piece of string, another pair to a 5-foot string, and whirled the two around his head simultaneously to demonstrate that the planets revolve around the sun on the same plane and in the same direction.

After the class made observations about what they saw, he continued, "Now our jobs get a bit more challenging. Today I want each group to identify a piece of information from the chart that can be explained with information from a different part of the chart, like why Mercury is so hot on one side and so cold on another. While you're doing that I'd also like you to think about how the solar system was formed."

He reminded them to keep the information from the transparencies in mind, and the groups went to work. As they worked, David moved from group to group, answering questions and making brief comments.

"Pluto wasn't part of the solar system to begin with," Juan commented to Randy and Tanya in one group.

"What do you mean?" Randy wondered.

"I was watching 'Nova' with my mom, and the person talking said that scientists think Pluto was an asteroid, or some other body floating around, and the sun kind of grabbed it. . . . See, when Mr. Shelton did that thing with the socks, they stayed sorta level," he continued, moving his hand back and forth to demonstrate a flat plane.

"What's that got to do with it?" Randy asked, still uncertain.

"Well, look," said Juan, pointing to the model on the transparency.

"Gee, I didn't even notice that," Randy shrugged.

"Oh, I get it, now! . . . Pluto isn't level with the rest of them," Tanya jumped in. "I got kinda lost when Mr. Shelton was explaining all that yesterday, but now it makes sense. . . . And look there," she added, pointing to the chart. "See how small Pluto is? It's the littlest, so it would be easy to capture."

"And it's the last one," Randy added, beginning to warm to the task. "I better write some of this stuff down, or I'll never remember it."

David listened as the students talked, and then he suggested, "I think you're doing a super job, but you might be forgetting something. Take another look at the sun transparency, and see how it relates to what you're talking about. . . . Look at how the globs are coming off the sun, and look at the title of the transparency. . . . Try to visualize the globs becoming planets, and the whole idea will be easier to remember."

The students studied the transparency for a moment, and Juan finally said, "Look, all those globs are even, too, you know, level, like the socks. . . . And it says, 'One Theory of How the Solar System Was Formed.' So, that's how the planets were made."

"Now, what was that again about Pluto being the littlest?" Randy wondered. "What's that got to do with anything?"

"If it was really big and floating around out there, the sun's gravity might not be strong enough to grab it," Juan offered.

"But it's easier to grab if it's little," Tanya added.

The groups continued their work for a few more minutes, and then David called the class together to discuss what the information they found suggested about the origins of the solar system. On Thursday they continued to discuss patterns and relationships in the information in the chart.

"For tomorrow's homework," David said near the end of Thursday's period, "I want you to answer the following questions. As always, be sure to use correct grammar, spelling, and punctuation." On an overhead transparency, he displayed these questions:

1. Saturn's diameter is 9 times greater than Earth's, and Uranus's diameter is 4 times greater than Earth's, but the gravity on both planets is less than Earth's. Why?
2. Explain why Mercury's temperature ranges from 300° below zero to 800° above zero.

3. Explain why Venus is our hottest planet.
4. Explain why Mercury has virtually no atmosphere.

"You have about 10 minutes till the bell rings," David announced. "If you start and have any difficulties, I'll help you. I know this is a challenge, but you've done a super job on this unit, and I know you're up to the task."

In this chapter, the second that explores learning, we turn away from an emphasis on changes in observable behaviors and toward a focus on the mental processes people use to make sense of their world, answer questions, and solve problems. The use of these processes is central to cognitive learning theories, which we examine here and in Chapters 8 and 9.

After you have studied this chapter, you should be able to

- Identify the principles on which cognitive learning theories are based
- Describe the components of our information processing system, including memory stores and cognitive processes
- Describe how metacognition influences learning
- Implement ways to promote schema development in your classroom
- Explain the role of assessment in classroom applications of cognitive learning theory

In Chapter 6, we saw that behaviorism is able to explain changes in observable behavior that have direct causes, such as a student stopping talking when a teacher looks at him and puts her finger to her lips. Although it's alive and well, particularly in the area of classroom management, behaviorism is unable to explain changes in behavior that don't have a direct cause, such as a driver slowing down when he sees another car stopped by a highway patrol. This type of behavior is explained by social cognitive theory, which, particularly with the powerful influence that modeling has on people's behaviors, also continues to thrive. It has its own limitations, however. We examine them and alternative perspectives on learning next.

Cognitive Perspectives on Learning

To begin this section, let's visit a group of college friends.

Marcus, an outgoing university student, chats with his friends at a party:

Marcus:	Everyone say "Pots."
His friends:	Pots.
Marcus:	All together now, say "Pots."
His friends:	Pots.
Marcus:	Once more together.
His friends:	Pots.
Marcus:	What do you do at a green light?
His friends:	Stop.

They catch themselves and laugh, realizing what they've said.

This activity, while simple, illustrates important aspects of cognitive explanations for thinking and learning. First, neither behaviorism nor social cognitive theory can explain why people tend to answer "Stop" to the question. The question is the stimulus, and it is clear. No modeling or any consequence for a model has occurred. According to behaviorism, the answer should be "Go." That many people say "Stop" suggests that they base their answer on thoughts or expectations instead of the stimulus itself.

It wasn't only examples such as the one above that made researchers aware that behaviorism and social cognitive theory were not answering their questions. Research conducted during World War II that examined the development of complex skills, the inability of behaviorism to adequately explain how people learn language (Chomsky, 1959), and the development of computers also led to a search for alternative explanations for people's behaviors. The result was the "cognitive revolution," which marked a shift away from behaviorism and toward cognitive theories of learning. The cognitive revolution occurred some time between the mid-1950s and early 1970s (Bruning et al., 1999), and its influence on education has steadily increased since that time (Greeno et al., 1996; Mayer, 1996).

Principles of Cognitive Learning Theory

Cognitive learning theories *explain learning by focusing on changes in mental processes and structures that occur as a result of people's efforts to make sense of the world.* Cognitive learning theories are used to explain tasks as simple as remembering a phone number and as complex as solving ill-defined problems.

Cognitive learning theories are grounded in four basic principles:

- Learners are active in their attempts to understand their experiences.
- The understanding that learners develop depends on what they already know.
- Learners construct, rather than record, understanding.
- Learning is a change in a person's mental structures.

Learners Are Active

Cognitive learning theories are grounded in the belief that learners are active in their attempts to understand how the world works, and as we saw in Chapter 2, this belief is consistent with both Piaget's and Vygotsky's views of learner development. Learners do much more than simply respond to reinforcers and punishers: They search for information that helps them answer questions, they modify their understanding based on new knowledge, and they change their behavior in response to their increased understanding. Cognitive learning theorists view humans as "goal-directed agents who actively seek information" (Bransford et al., 2000, p. 10).

Understanding Depends on What Learners Know

In their attempts to understand how the world works, learners interpret new experiences based on what they already know and believe. For instance, often children continue to believe that the earth is flat even after teachers explain that it is a sphere. Some children then picture a pancake-like flat surface inside or on top of a sphere (Vosniadou & Brewer, 1989). They reason that people aren't able to walk on a ball, and the idea of a flat surface—an idea children know and understand—helps them explain how people are able to stand or walk on the earth's surface. This example also helps us see why explaining, by itself, is often ineffective for changing learners' understanding.

Learners Construct Rather Than Record Understanding

Learners don't behave like tape recorders, recording in their memories—in the form in which it is presented—everything a teacher tells them or what they read. Instead, they use what they already know to construct understandings of what they hear or read that makes sense to them. In their efforts to make the new information understandable, they may dramatically modify it, as did the children who pictured the pancake on the sphere.

Most researchers now accept the idea that learners construct their own understanding (Greeno et al., 1996; Mayer, 1998b, 2002). We examine the process of knowledge construction in detail in Chapter 8.

A Definition of Learning

From a cognitive perspective, **learning** is *a change in a person's mental structures that creates the capacity to demonstrate different behaviors.* Notice the phrase "creates the capacity." From a cognitive perspective, learning can occur without any immediate change in behavior; evidence of the change in mental structures may occur much later.

The "mental structures" that change include schemas, beliefs, goals, expectations, and other components "in the learner's head." In David's lesson, for example, Randy consciously thought about his need to take notes; and Tanya, Randy, and Juan all formed relationships, in their minds, connecting information from the chart, transparencies, and demonstration. Neither behaviorism nor social cognitive theory can adequately explain these students' efforts.

How is information "in the learner's head" acquired, and how is it stored? We attempt to answer these questions in the next section as we examine information processing, one of the first and most thoroughly researched descriptions of how people learn and remember (Hunt & Ellis, 1999; Sternberg, 1999).

7.1
In our study of behaviorism, we didn't discuss any mental processes. Why not?

Figure 7.1   Model of an oxygen atom

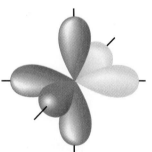

Information Processing

Information processing is *a theory of learning that explains how stimuli enter our memory systems, are selected and organized for storage, and are retrieved from memory* (Mayer, 1998b). The most prominent cognitive learning theory of the 20th century, it has important implications for teaching today (Mayer, 1998b, 1999).

Models: Aids to Understanding

Think back for a moment to courses you've taken during your years of school. You probably studied geography, perhaps chemistry, and now you're taking educational psychology. In geography, you examined the face and makeup of the earth, and in chemistry, you studied the structure of the atom. Because you could directly experience only a small portion of the earth, you used maps and globes. A globe is a miniature representation of the earth, faithful in shape and proportion; it is a model. Likewise, in chemistry you could not directly observe an atom with all its individual parts, so you studied a model, such as the one in Figure 7.1, to help you visualize the tiny particles. In this case, the **model** is *a representation that allows learners to visualize what they can't observe directly.*

We encounter a similar situation when we try to visualize what occurs during information processing. We can't directly observe either the mental stores or the processes involved when we work with information, but we can refer to a model to help us visualize and understand what's happening. The model in Figure 7.2 represents a current view of how cognitive psychologists think the mind processes information (R. Atkinson & Shiffrin, 1968; Leahey & Harris, 1997).

The computer is often used as an analogy for information processing. For example, both computers and humans acquire, store, and retrieve knowledge and make decisions. Computers take symbols as input, apply operators to them, and produce output; humans do, as well (Mayer, 1996). For example, when faced with a math problem, we use symbols in the form of numbers and written language (input), work on the problem (oper-

Models allow students to visualize abstract relationships that are often difficult to understand.

Figure 7.2 An information processing model

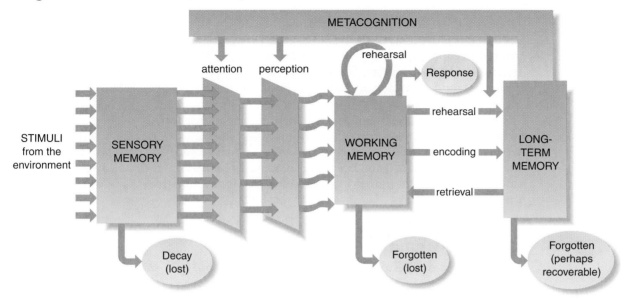

ate on it), and produce a solution (output). A computer's symbols are electronic; ours are written and spoken language and numbers.

The information processing model has three major components:

- Information stores
- Cognitive processes
- Metacognition

Information stores are *repositories that hold information,* analogous to a computer's main memory and hard drive. The information stores in the information processing model are *sensory memory, working memory,* and *long-term memory.*

Cognitive processes are *intellectual actions that transform information and move it from one store to another.* They include *attention, perception, rehearsal, encoding,* and *retrieval.* Cognitive processes are analogous to the programs that process information—the software—in computers.

Metacognition, the third component of the information processing model, is *the awareness of and control over one's own cognitive processes* (E. Hiebert & Raphael, 1996). In David's lesson, Randy said, "I better write some of this stuff down, or I'll never remember it." He was demonstrating an awareness of his ability to remember, and he exercised control over remembering by taking notes; Randy was being metacognitive. (Metacognition is discussed in more detail later in the chapter.)

Some researchers describe the combination of these components as our "cognitive architecture" (Sweller, van Merrienboer, & Paas, 1998). Just as the architecture of a building is the structure in which its activities occur, our information processing system is the framework within which information is acquired, moved, and stored.

Let's look now at the information stores: sensory memory, working memory, and long-term memory. We'll then consider the cognitive processes and metacognitive abilities that move and shape the transfer of information.

Sensory Memory

Hold your finger in front of you, and rapidly wiggle it. You'll see a faint "shadow" that trails behind your finger as it moves. This "shadow" is the image of your finger that has been briefly stored in your visual sensory memory. Likewise, when someone says, "That's an oxymoron," you may briefly retain "Ox see moron" in your auditory sensory memory even though it has no meaning for you.

> Pluto is last. Pluto wasn't part of the first solar system. Pluto is the littlest planet. Pluto isn't in same orbet as the other planats.

7.2
In Figure 7.2, fewer lines connect "attention" and "perception" than connect "sensory memory" and "attention." What is this intended to help us visualize and understand?

Sensory memory is *the information store that briefly holds stimuli from the environment until they can be processed* (Neisser, 1967). The material in sensory memory is "thought to be completely unorganized, basically a perceptual copy of objects and events in the world" (Leahey & Harris, 1997, p. 106). Sensory memory is nearly unlimited in capacity, but if processing doesn't begin almost immediately, the memory trace quickly fades away. Sensory memory is estimated to retain information for about 1 second for vision and 2 to 4 seconds for hearing (Leahey & Harris, 1997; Pashler & Carrier, 1996).

Sensory memory is an essential beginning point for further processing. In trying to read, for example, it would be impossible to get meaning from a sentence if the words at the beginning were lost from your visual sensory memory before you got to the end. The same is true for spoken language. Sensory memory allows you to hold information long enough to attach meaning to it and transfer it to working memory, the next store.

Working Memory

Working memory, historically called *short-term memory*, is *the store that holds information as a person processes it*. Working memory is the conscious part of our information processing system; it is where deliberate thinking takes place (Sweller et al., 1998). We aren't aware of the contents of either sensory memory or long-term memory until they're pulled into working memory.

Limitations of Working Memory

The most striking feature of working memory is its limitations (Bruer, 1993; Sweller et al., 1998). It can hold only about seven items of information at a time (G. Miller, 1956), and it holds the information for a relatively short period (about 10 to 20 seconds for adults), particularly when new information is being received (Greene, 1992). Selecting, organizing, and otherwise processing information take up working memory space also, so often we can handle even fewer than seven items. In fact, we "are probably only able to deal with two or three items of information simultaneously when required to process rather than merely hold information" (Sweller et al., 1998, p. 252).

The limited capacity of working memory has important implications for teaching and learning. Consider the following:

- Writing often improves more rapidly if learners are initially allowed to ignore handwriting quality, grammar, and spelling (De La Paz & Graham, 1997; Graham, Berninger, Weintraub, & Schafer, 1998; McCutchen, 2000).
- Students write better quality essays using word processors if their word processing skills are well developed. If not, handwritten essays are superior (Roblyer, 2003).
- In spite of research about its ineffectiveness and enormous staff development efforts to promote more sophisticated forms of instruction, lecturing persists as the most common teaching strategy (Cuban, 1984).

How does working memory influence these situations? In the first, focusing on handwriting, grammar, and spelling occupies so much working memory space that little is left for the construction of quality products. In

Working memory is the "workbench" where students think about and solve problems.

the second, students lacking word processing skills use too much of their working memory capacity on the mechanics of word processing, leaving too little for composing high-quality essays. And, in the third, sophisticated strategies, such as guided discovery, place a heavy load on teachers' working memories. Monitoring student understanding and behavior, keeping goals in mind, and questioning students must occur simultaneously. For many teachers, this working memory load is too great, so they reduce it by reverting to lecture, a much simpler strategy.

The characteristics of working memory are summarized in Figure 7.3.

7.3
Using the information in this section, explain why Tanya, from the opening case, might have "got kinda lost when Mr. Shelton was explaining all that yesterday." What implications does this have for our teaching?

Cognitive Load Theory: Overcoming the Limitations of Working Memory

When we encounter new information, our learning is influenced by some factors out of our control, such as the amount and complexity of the material. However, as teachers and learners, we can control other factors, such as the way we design instruction and the strategies we use to make information understandable. **Cognitive load theory** *recognizes the limitations of working memory and emphasizes instruction that can accommodate its capacity* (Sweller et al., 1998).

Cognitive load theory emphasizes three factors that can help accommodate the limitations of working memory:

- Chunking
- Automaticity
- Dual processing

Chunking. **Chunking** is *the process of mentally combining separate items into larger, more meaningful units* (G. Miller, 1956). As an illustration, try this simple exercise. Look at the following row of letters for 5 seconds:

A E E E G G I I I I L N N N N R R S S T T

Figure 7.3 Characteristics of working memory

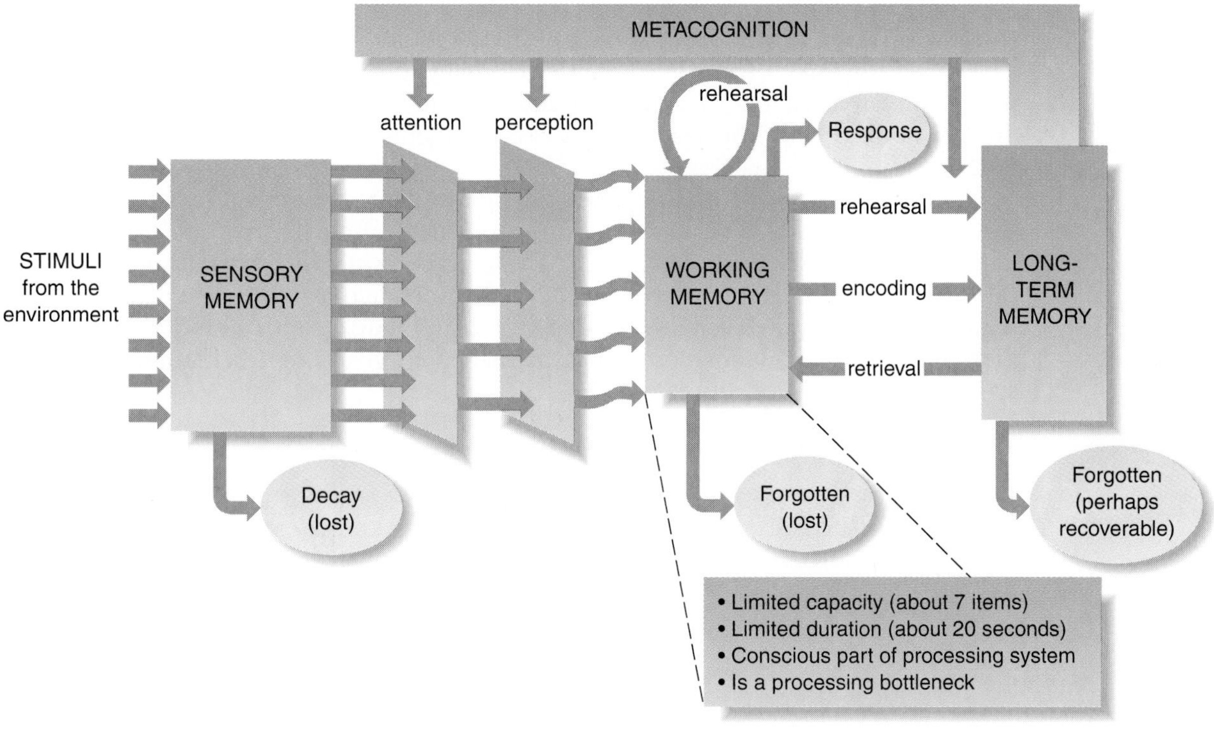

Now cover the row, and try to write down all 21 letters in any order. How did you do? Most people cannot remember the entire list, even though the letters are presented in alphabetical order, all but two are repeated and grouped together, and people are told there are 21 letters in all. The number of items exceeds the capacity of their working memories.

Now look at the same letters presented as follows:

LEARNING IS INTERESTING

7.4
Why would a health club prefer to advertise its telephone number as 2HEALTH rather than 243-2584?

The letters now are simple to remember because they have been "chunked" into three meaningful words (three units) and into a meaningful sentence (one unit).

Table 7.1 presents other examples of chunking. In each case, you can see that remembering the chunk requires less working memory space than the individual items because you can remember the chunked information as a single unit.

Automaticity. A second way of overcoming the limitations of working memory is to make the processes involved in a task automatic. **Automaticity** is *the use of mental operations that can be performed with little awareness or conscious effort* (Healy et al., 1993; Schneider & Shiffrin, 1977). Driving a car is an example of the power and efficiency of automaticity. Once driving becomes automatic, for instance, people can drive, talk, and listen (and sometimes shave or put on makeup) at the same time.

Learning skills to the point of automaticity provides one solution to the three problems involving working memory cited in the last section. If grammar, spelling, and punctuation skills become automatic, students can devote their working memories to composing the written products. Similarly, if word processing skills are automatic, students don't have to devote working memory spaces to them; instead they can concentrate on creating well-organized essays.

The problem involving teaching strategies has important implications for your growth as a teacher. For instance, questioning is at the core of a number of sophisticated teaching strategies, such as guided discovery, but for many teachers, it isn't automatic. This means you must practice essential skills, such as questioning, until they become automatic if you expect to use strategies like guided discovery in your teaching.

Dual Processing. **Dual processing** is *the way two parts, a visual and an auditory component, work together in working memory* (Baddeley, 1992). Whereas each of the parts is limited in capacity, they work independently and additively (Mayer, 1997, 1998a; Sweller et al., 1998). The visual processor supplements the auditory processor and vice versa.

To understand how dual processing helps students remember, let's think back to David's lesson. He used visuals—color transparencies and a matrix—*at the same time* he discussed them with his students. A simultaneous presentation of visual and verbal (auditory) information is important because it provides two routes to representing information in memory (Mayer, 1997). Indeed, research suggests that students will learn more if verbal explanations are supplemented with visual representations (Mayer &

Table 7.1 Saving working memory space through chunking

Information Unchunked	Information Chunked
u, n, r	run
2492520	24 9 25 20
l, v, o, I, o, u, e, y	I love you.
seeletsthiswhyworks	Let's see why this works.

Moreno, 1998). Unfortunately, teachers often use words, alone, to present information, wasting some of working memory's processing capability.

Long-Term Memory

Long-term memory is *our permanent information store.* It's like a library with millions of entries and a network that allows them to be retrieved for reference and use. It differs from working memory in both capacity and duration. Whereas working memory is limited to approximately seven items of information for a matter of seconds, long-term memory's capacity is vast and durable. Some experts suggest that information in it remains for a lifetime (Schunk, 2000).

One of the most widely accepted descriptions of long-term memory differentiates between **declarative knowledge,** *knowledge of facts, definitions, procedures, and rules,* and **procedural knowledge,** *knowledge of how to perform tasks* (J. Anderson, 1990; Hergenhahn & Olson, 2001). For example, a learner who says, "To add fractions, you must first have like denominators," knows the rule for adding fractions but might not be able to actually do the computation. Knowing the rule is a form of declarative knowledge; being able to add the fractions requires procedural knowledge. Declarative knowledge can be determined directly from a person's comments, whereas procedural knowledge is inferred from the person's performance. To develop procedural knowledge, students must practice skills, such as adding fractions or writing essays, and receive feedback about their performance. Talking about or explaining the skills isn't sufficient.

7.5
Look again at David's homework assignment. Did it primarily require declarative knowledge or procedural knowledge? Explain.

Representing Declarative Knowledge in Memory: Schemas

Many researchers believe that declarative knowledge is stored in long-term memory in the form of **schemas** (also called *schemata*), *organized networks of information* (J. Anderson, 1990; E. Hiebert & Raphael, 1996; Voss & Wiley, 1995). Schemas combine simpler forms of information, such as propositions, linear orderings, and images (Gagne, Yekovich, & Yekovich, 1993). For instance, "Pluto is a planet" is a *proposition,* the smallest bit of information that can be judged true or false. *Linear orderings* rank information according to some dimension, such as the planets in their order from the sun, and *images* store physical characteristics as mental pictures, such as a visualization of the globs from David's transparency.

Schemas are individually constructed, dynamic (change in response to new information), and contextual (depend on the situation in which they're learned) (Wigfield, Eccles, & Pintrich, 1996). The illustration in Figure 7.4 of Randy's and Juan's schemas for the solar system helps us see how the two boys organized the information from David's class in different ways. Randy has linked Pluto, the solar system, and Earth to the Sun. His knowledge about the globs, orbital plane, and origins is isolated, however, because they aren't linked to the rest of the information. In comparison, Juan understands how the origins of the solar system, the orbital plane, the location of Earth, and Pluto's size and distance from the Sun are all connected, as indicated by the links between the items in his schema. We discuss the importance of these connecting links shortly.

Schemas as Scripts.   In addition to organizing information, schemas can also guide our actions. For example, when students first go into a college class, they may ask themselves such questions as

- What are the instructor's expectations?
- What are the course requirements?
- How should I prepare for quizzes and other assessments?
- How will I interact with my peers?

Figure 7.4 Schemas illustrating Randy's (on the left) and Juan's understanding

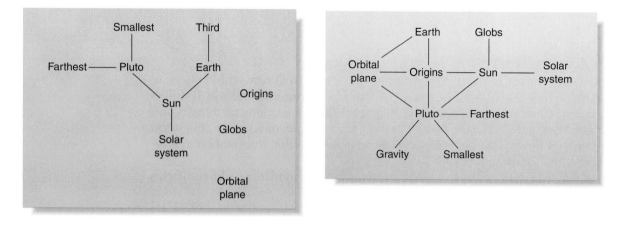

Answers come from their understanding of the proper way to operate in college classes, developed over years of experience. **Scripts**, which are *"schema representations for events"* (Bruning et al., 1999, p. 60 [italics added]), provide plans for action in particular situations like this. For example, you have a script that guides your behavior as you prepare for, attend, and participate in your class. In this regard, scripts contain procedural knowledge, as well as propositions about ways to interact with other students, images of past classes, and linear orderings about what tasks to complete first.

Organizing Knowledge in Memory: Implications for Learning and Teaching. The fact that we organize knowledge in memory in the form of schemas is important for learners and teachers for two reasons. First, schemas help explain why background knowledge and the way it's organized in memory are so important for additional learning (Nuthall, 1999b, 2000). Second, schemas reduce the load on learners' working memory.

To illustrate the first point, let's look at some of the dialogue from David's class:

Juan:	Pluto wasn't part of the solar system to begin with.
Randy:	What do you mean?
Juan:	I was watching 'Nova' with my mom, and the person talking said that scientists think Pluto was an asteroid, or some other body floating around, and the sun kind of grabbed it. . . . See, when Mr. Shelton did that thing with the socks, they stayed sorta level.
Randy:	What's that got to do with it?
Juan:	Well, look. (pointing to the model on the transparency)
Randy:	Gee, I didn't even notice that.

Juan's understanding is clearly much deeper than Randy's, and we can began to understand why by looking again at Figure 7.4. We see that both schemas contain 10 individual items of information, but Randy's has only 6 "links" in it, compared to 12 in Juan's. The difference explains why Juan was able to tie David's demonstration to both a television documentary and information in the unit, whereas Randy initially didn't notice one of the relationships.

How do schemas reduce the load on learners' working memories? We know that working memory capacity is limited. However, "although the number of elements is limited, the size, complexity, and sophistication of elements [are] not" (Sweller et al.,

7.6
Describe how Juan's schema would look if he had simply memorized the information about the planets' names, their order from the sun, and their orbital planes.

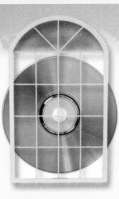

Using Technology in Your Study of Educational Psychology

The Importance of Background Knowledge

You've just read about how schemas influence the way learners perceive and encode new information, and retrieve old information from long-term memory. Using the CD-ROM that accompanies this book, you can experience firsthand how schemas influence learning. To complete the activity, do the following:

- Open the CD, and click on *Bartlett's Ghosts.*
- Complete the activities, and then answer the following questions.

1. What did the relative number of omissions, transformations, and additions tell you about your schema for the information contained in "Bartlett's Ghosts"?

2. From a classroom perspective, which are most problematic: omissions, transformations, or additions? What can teachers do to minimize these different kinds of schematic errors?

3. How would your memory for the information contained in "Bartlett's Ghosts" be influenced by increased knowledge in the following areas?
   - Boats and canoes
   - Native American burial customs
   - Previous exposure to this story

4. What implications do your responses to these questions have for instruction?

1998, p. 256). This is also illustrated in Juan's and Randy's schemas. Because all the items in Juan's schema are connected, it behaves as a chunk (Bransford et al., 2000), so it takes up only one working memory slot. Because Randy's schema is less connected, it takes up four slots: one for the seven interconnected items and one each for "origins," "globs," and "orbital plane." When Randy thought about the origins of our solar system, the load on his working memory was much greater than the load on Juan's, making additional processing more difficult for him.

So that students can benefit from organized schemas, teachers should not only try to help them understand individual ideas but also help them relate the ideas to one another. The more interrelated the ideas, the greater the capacity students have to learn new information.

Representing Procedural Knowledge in Memory: Conditions and Actions

Earlier we said that procedural knowledge involves knowing how to perform tasks. In using procedural knowledge, however, learners must be able to adapt their processing to different conditions. In the example with adding fractions, if the denominators are the same, we merely add the numerators. If they're different, we must find a common denominator and then add the numerators. The conditions for adding fractions with like, compared to unlike, denominators are different, and the ability to add them correctly depends on recognizing these conditions and acting appropriately.

All procedural knowledge depends on declarative knowledge; for example, students must first understand fractions and the rules for adding them before they can adapt to the different conditions. As another example, you will practice both

Learners develop effective procedural knowledge by actively applying concepts and ideas in different contexts.

classroom management and questioning skills as you move through your teacher preparation program, but you must understand the principles of sound management and the characteristics of effective questioning or you won't know how to practice most efficiently. This is why you study theories of learning in this class—they help you understand when and why different instructional strategies are effective.

Developing Procedural Knowledge. Procedural knowledge is developed in three stages: declarative, associative, and automatic (J. Anderson, 1995; Gagne et al., 1993).

In the *declarative stage,* learners acquire declarative knowledge about the procedure; for example, they learn where to place the fingers on a keyboard or the rules for adding fractions. Some researchers call it *planning knowledge,* emphasizing an understanding of the steps to be followed (Star, 2002). Learners are not yet able to perform the action in this stage.

During the *associative stage,* learners can perform the procedure but must think about what they are doing, and their thoughts occupy most of their working memory (J. Anderson, 1990). For example, novice typists who must compose essays focus most of their energies on correctly using the keyboard during this stage and are generally unable to compose high-quality written products.

With additional practice, learners finally move to the *automatic stage,* when they can perform the process with little conscious thought. (Remember our discussion of automaticity earlier in the chapter.) Most of the typists' working memory is focused on other activities, such as what they're composing; little thought is given to the movement of their fingers on the keyboard.

Developing Procedural Knowledge: Implications for Learning and Teaching. The stages involved in developing procedural knowledge have important implications for learning and teaching. First, reaching the automatic stage takes a great deal of time and practice (Bruning et al., 1999), so students must be provided with as many opportunities to practice as possible. Research indicates that complex procedural knowledge, such as the ability to speak and write a foreign language, continues to improve even after thousands of hours of practice (Bruning et al., 1999).

Second, the way procedural knowledge is developed helps us understand why context is so important. For example, when learning to apply grammar and punctuation rules, learners should practice with a variety of written products, including their own writing, rather than with isolated sentences. Having students complete decontextualized exercises, such as commonly occur in worksheets, doesn't provide them with opportunities to identify different conditions and apply the appropriate actions.

As another example, when learning how to solve subtraction problems, students should practice in a variety of realistic settings. Many students identify the current condition based on the section they're studying in their textbook; for example, they use the subtraction operation because they're on the subtraction section of a chapter (Bransford et al., 2000). This suggests that students who are working on problems that require subtraction should also be given problems that require addition, multiplication, and division. In this way, they can learn to identify different conditions and apply the appropriate actions.

As a review, take a moment now to examine Figure 7.5, which summarizes the characteristics of long-term memory.

7.7
You are practicing your questioning skills in a pre-internship classroom experience. Identify some different conditions that could affect the way you use your questioning skills.

Figure 7.5   Characteristics of long-term memory

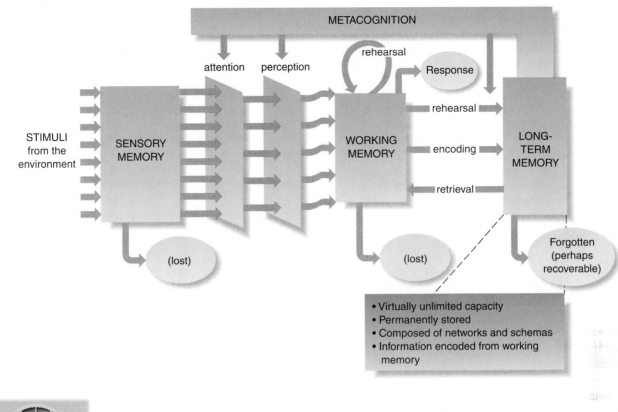

Classroom Connections

Applying an Understanding of Memory Stores in Your Classroom

Sensory Memory

1. To keep students from losing the trace of a sensory memory, give them a chance to attend to one stimulus before presenting a second stimulus.
   - *Elementary:* A second-grade teacher asks one question at a time and gets an answer before asking a second question.
   - *Middle School:* A pre-algebra teacher displays two problems on the overhead and waits until students have copied them before she starts talking.
   - *High School:* In a geography lesson, a teacher puts a map on the overhead and says, "I'll give you a minute to look at the geography of the countries on the map in the front of the room. Then we'll go on."

Working Memory

2. So as not to overload students' working memory, conduct lessons with questioning.
   - *Elementary:* A first-grade teacher gives students directions for seat work by presenting them slowly

and one at a time. He asks different students to repeat the directions before he has them begin.
   - *Middle School:* A teacher in a woodworking class begins by saying, "The hardness and density of wood from the same kind of tree vary, depending on the amount of rainfall the tree has received and how fast it grows." Then, she waits a moment, holds up two pieces of wood, and says, "Look at these wood pieces. What do you notice about the rings on them?"
   - *High School:* An Algebra II teacher "walks" students through the solution to problems by having a different student describe each succeeding step to the solution.

3. Provide frequent practice to develop automaticity, and present information in both verbal and visual forms.
   - *Elementary:* A first-grade teacher has his students practice their writing by composing two sentences each day about an event of the previous evening.
   - *Middle School:* To capitalize on the dual-processing capability of working memory, an eighth-grade history teacher prepares a flowchart of the events that led up to the Revolutionary War. As she questions the students about the topic, she refers to the flowchart for

each important point and encourages students to use the chart to organize their note taking.

- *High School:* As a physics teacher discusses the relationship between force and acceleration, he demonstrates by pulling a cart along the desktop with a constant force so the students can see that the cart accelerates.

Long-Term Memory

4. To develop schemas, encourage students to explore relationships between ideas, and between new ideas and prior understanding.

  - *Elementary:* During story time, a first-grade teacher asks the students to explain how the events in a story contribute to the conclusion.

- *Middle School:* In developing the rules for solving equations by substitution, an algebra teacher asks, "How does this process compare to what we did when we solved equations by addition? What do we do differently? Why?"

- *High School:* To help his students understand cause-effect relationships in their study of ancient Greece, a world history teacher asks questions such as the following: "Why was shipping so important in ancient Greece?" "Why was Troy's location so important, and how does its location relate to the location of some of today's cities, such as New York, Chicago, and San Francisco?" and "Why did Greek city-states exist (instead of larger nation-states)?"

Cognitive Processes

Let's look again at our information processing model, now with a focus on the processes—*attention, perception, rehearsal, encoding,* and *retrieval*—that move information from one store to another. They're highlighted in Figure 7.6 and discussed in the sections that follow.

Attention: The Beginning of Information Processing

Consider the room you're in right now. You are probably unaware of many of the stimuli present—perhaps pictures, furniture, other people moving and talking, the whisper of an air conditioner. Other stimuli, however, attract your **attention,** which is *the process of consciously focusing on a stimulus.* In Figure 7.6 "attention" appears next to "sensory memory," and it is where processing begins. All additional processing depends on the extent to which learners pay attention to appropriate stimuli and ignore distractions.

To see a video clip of teachers' attempts to attract students' attention, go to the Companion Website at *www.prenhall.com/eggen,* then to this chapter's *Classrooms on the Web* module. Click on *Video Clip 7.1.*

Figure 7.6 Cognitive processes in the information processing model

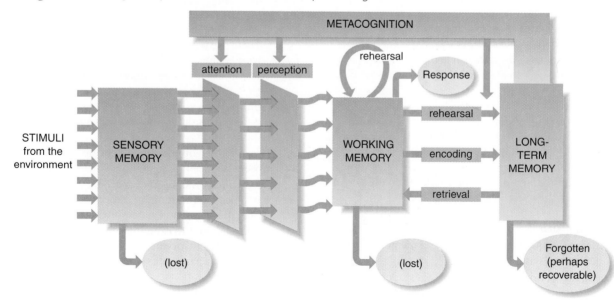

Effective teachers use a variety of visual aids to attract and maintain students' attention.

Attracting and Maintaining Student Attention. Because attention is where learning begins, attracting and maintaining student attention are crucial. Teachers should plan their lessons so students attend to what is being taught and ignore outside noises and other irrelevant stimuli. If a teacher pulls a live, wriggling crab out of a cooler to begin a lesson on crustaceans, for example, even the most disinterested student is likely to pay attention. Similarly, if students are actively involved in learning activities, they're much more attentive than if they're expected to passively listen to lectures (Blumenfeld, 1992). In the lesson in the opening case study, David used several attention getters. His demonstration with the strings and socks was probably most significant, but his transparencies and matrix were effective as well.

Some additional examples of attention getters are outlined and illustrated in Table 7.2. Because of its importance, one deserves increased emphasis: *calling on students by name.* The use of students' names is one of the most powerful attention getters that exists, and effective teachers learn their students' names as quickly as possible and call on individual students instead of directing questions to the class as a whole. When this becomes a pattern, attention and achievement increase (Kauchak & Eggen, 2003; McDougall & Granby, 1996; Shuell, 1996).

7.8
Research indicates that teacher enthusiasm improves student learning and motivation. Explain the positive effects of enthusiasm using information about cognitive processes. Now explain the effects based on social cognitive theory.

Table 7.2 Strategies for attracting attention

Type	Example
Demonstrations	A science teacher pulls a student in a chair across the room to demonstrate the concepts *force* and *work.*
Discrepant events	A world history teacher who usually dresses conservatively comes to class in a sheet, makeshift sandals, and a crown to begin a discussion of ancient Greece.
Charts	A health teacher displays a chart showing the high fat content of some popular foods.
Pictures	An English teacher shows a picture of a bearded Ernest Hemingway as she introduces 20th-century American novels.
Problems	A math teacher says, "We want to go to the rock concert on Saturday night, but we're broke. The tickets are $45, and we need about $20 for gas and something to eat. We make $5.50 an hour in our part-time jobs. How many hours do we have to work to be able to afford the concert?"
Thought-provoking questions	A history teacher begins a discussion of World War II with the question, "Suppose Germany had won the war. How might the world be different now?"
Emphasis	A teacher says, "Pay careful attention now. The next two items are very important."
Student names	In his question and answer sessions, a teacher asks his question, pauses briefly, and then calls on a student by name to answer.

Perception: The Meaning Attached to Stimuli

Look at the picture in the margin. Do you see a young woman, or do you see an old woman? Why do you think you see one versus the other? This classic example illustrates the nature of **perception**, *the process people use to attach meaning to stimuli.* The meaning attached to the picture, for example, may be "old woman" or "young woman." When we asked if you "see" a young or an old woman, technically we were asking, "Do you 'perceive' a young or an old woman?" Neither behaviorism nor social cognitive theory is able to explain why people perceive stimuli differently, and this is one reason we examine cognitive theories of learning.

The importance of accurate perceptions in learning is difficult to overstate. Students' perceptions of what they see or hear are what enter working memory, and if these perceptions aren't accurate, the information that is ultimately stored in long-term memory will also be inaccurate.

To see a video clip of learners who reveal different perceptions during a classroom lesson, go to the Companion Website at *www.prenhall.com/eggen*, then to this chapter's *Classrooms on the Web* module. Click on *Video Clip 7.2.*

7.9
What is the concept we use to describe how background knowledge is organized in memory?

The Influence of Background Knowledge on Perception. Cognitive learning theory stresses the importance of background knowledge, as we saw earlier, and such knowledge has a powerful influence on perception. For instance, Randy didn't "notice" that Pluto's plane differed from that of the other planets because his perception of the information on the transparency and demonstration was affected by his lack of background knowledge.

As another example, science students are studying the formation of calcium deposits from hard water and see the following on the chalkboard:

$$CaCO_3 + CO_2 + H_2O \rightarrow Ca + 2HCO_3$$

For learning to be effective, students must accurately perceive several aspects of this equation, such as these:

- A symbol without a subscript (e.g., Ca, C) signifies one atom of the element in the compound.
- Some elements have two letters in their symbols (Ca); others have only one (H).
- The subscript indicates the number of atoms of the element (such as O_3, O_2, and H_2).

Whether students do indeed perceive these features accurately and go on to understand how calcium deposits form depends on what they already know about chemical equations.

An effective way of checking students' perceptions is to review by asking open-ended questions (Kauchak & Eggen, 2003). For example, after writing the equation on the chalkboard, the science teacher might ask, "Look at the equation. What do you notice about it?" If students can't identify essential information, such as the elements involved, the numbers of each in the compounds, and what the arrow means, the teacher knows that their background knowledge and perceptions are inaccurate or incomplete, and she can then adjust her review to cover these features.

Rehearsal: Retaining Information Through Repetition

You want to dial a phone number, so you look it up and repeat it to yourself a few times until you dial it. You have rehearsed the number to keep it in working memory until you're finished with it. **Rehearsal** is *the process of repeating information over and over, either aloud or mentally, without altering its form.* It is analogous to rehearsing a piece of music. When people do so, they play the music over and over as written; they don't alter it or change its form.

Although rehearsal usually causes information to stay in working memory only until it is used, if rehearsed enough, information can sometimes be transferred to long-term memory, as may have happened with your home or cellular phone number (R. Atkinson & Shiffrin, 1968). Rehearsal is a simple, but inefficient, method of transferring information, however, and not surprisingly, it's one of the first memory strategies that develops in young children (Berk, 2001).

Meaningful Encoding: Making Connections in Long-Term Memory

Encoding is *the process of representing information in long-term memory* (Bruning et al., 1999). When David said to his students, "Try to visualize the globs becoming planets, and the whole idea will be easier to remember," he was attempting to help the students visually encode some of the information they were studying. Learners can also verbally encode information when they form schemas that relate ideas to each other.

When we encode information—try to represent it in our long-term memories—our goal should be to make it as meaningful as possible. **Meaningfulness** *describes the number of connections or links between an idea and other ideas in long-term memory* (Gagne et al., 1993). For example, we saw earlier that Randy formed 6 links in his schema about the solar system, whereas Juan formed 12. Juan's schema was more meaningful because the various components were more interconnected.

The concept of meaningfulness helps us understand why background knowledge and the formation of schemas are so important. The more background information that exists, and the more interrelated the knowledge (the more elaborate the schemas), the more locations a learner has to connect new information and the more likely it is to be meaningfully encoded.

Teachers can help ensure meaningful encoding by promoting three things:

- Organization
- Elaboration
- Activity

They are outlined in Figure 7.7 and discussed in the sections that follow.

Organization.   **Organization** is *the process of clustering related items of content into categories or patterns that illustrate relationships.* Research in reading (Eggen, Kauchak, & Kirk, 1978), memory (Bower, Clark, Lesgold, & Winzenz, 1969), and classroom instruction (Mayer, 1997; Nuthall, 1999b) confirm the value of organization in promoting learning.

Information can be organized in several ways:

- *Charts and matrices*: Useful for organizing large amounts of information into categories. David used a matrix in his lesson to help his students organize their thoughts about the planets. The completed matrix is shown in Table 7.3.
- *Hierarchies:* Effective when new information can be subsumed under existing ideas. We made frequent use of hierarchies in our discussion of behaviorism in

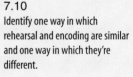

7.10
Identify one way in which rehearsal and encoding are similar and one way in which they're different.

To see a video clip of a teacher using a matrix to organize information, go to the Companion Website at *www.prenhall.com/eggen*, then this chapter's *Classrooms on the Web* module. Click on *Video Clip 7.3.*

Figure 7.7   Making information meaningful

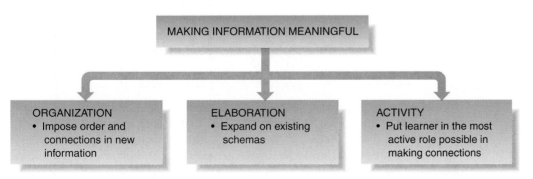

Table 7.3 David's completed planet matrix

	Diameter (miles)	Distance from Sun (millions of miles)	Length of Year (orbit)	Length of Day (rotation)	Gravity (compared to Earth's)	Average Surface Temperature (°F)	Characteristics
Mercury	3,030	35.9	88 E.D.[a]	59 E.D. counterclockwise	.38	300 below to 800 above zero	No atmosphere; no water; many craters
Venus	7,500	67.2	225 E.D.	243 E.D. clockwise	.88	900	Thick cloud cover; high winds; no water
Earth	7,900	98.0	365½ E.D.	24 hours counterclockwise	1	57	Atmos. of 78% nitrogen, 21% oxygen; 70% water on surface
Mars	4,200	141.5	687 E.D.	24½ hours counterclockwise	.38	67 below zero	Thin carbon dioxide atmos.; white caps at poles; red rocky surface
Jupiter	88,700	483.4	12 E.Y.[b]	10 hours counterclockwise	2.34	162 below zero	No water; great red spot; atmos. of hydrogen, helium, ammonia
Saturn	75,000	914.0	30 E.Y.	11 hours counterclockwise	.92	208 below zero	Atmos. of hydrogen, helium; no water; mostly gaseous; prominent rings
Uranus	31,566	1,782.4	84 E.Y.	24 hours counterclockwise	.79	355 below zero	Atmos. of hydrogen, helium; no water
Neptune	30,200	2,792.9	165 E.Y.	17 hours counterclockwise	1.12	266 below zero	Atmos. of hydrogen, helium; no water
Pluto	1,423	3,665.0	248 E.Y.	6½ days counterclockwise	.43	458 below zero	No atmos.; periodically orbits closer to sun than Neptune

[a] Earth days.
[b] Earth years.

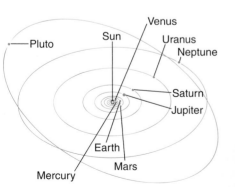

Chapter 6 (such as in Figure 6.2, "Consequences of Behavior").
Figure 7.8 contains an additional example from an English lesson.

- *Models:* Helpful for representing relationships that cannot be observed directly. The model of the solar system on David's transparency and the information processing models in this chapter are examples.
- *Outlines:* Useful for representing the organizational structure in a body of written material. For instance, a detailed outline of this chapter appears on pages 97–98 of your *Student Study Guide.*

Other types of organization include graphs, tables, flowcharts, and maps (Merkley & Jefferies, 2001). Each is intended to represent relationships among the different parts (Mayer, 1997). Learners should be encouraged to use these organizers as personal study strategies to help them in their efforts to make information meaningful.

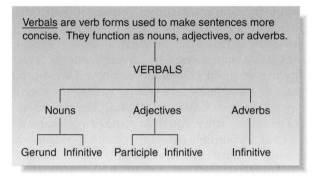

Figure 7.8
Organizational hierarchy in English

Keep in mind that organizing content doesn't guarantee that students will learn effectively. If the organizational structure doesn't make sense to learners, they will (mentally) reorganize it in a way that does, whether or not it is correct; they will memorize snippets of it; or they will reject or ignore it.

Interaction is essential to making the organization of new material meaningful to learners. David, for example, not only organized content by using a demonstration, transparencies, and a matrix, he also guided his students' developing understanding with questioning and discussion. Organization combined with high levels of teacher-student interaction help make relationships meaningful to students.

Dual-Coding Theory: Imagery in Long-Term Memory. We said earlier that some information may be encoded visually whereas other information is encoded verbally. Organizers such as charts, hierarchies, maps, and models can be used to enhance the visual encoding process by capitalizing on **imagery,** *the process of forming mental pictures* (N. Schwartz, Ellsworth, Graham, & Knight, 1998). **Dual-coding theory** *suggests that long-term memory contains two distinct memory systems: one for verbal information and one that stores images* (Paivio, 1986, 1991). For instance, as we study information processing, we can visualize the model (see Figure 7.2). We see that working memory is smaller than sensory and long-term memory, which reminds us that working memory has limited capacity. We also see that the lines emerging from perception are curved, which helps us remember that people perceive information differently. The fact that we can both read about and create an image of the model helps us capitalize on the dual-coding capacity of long-term memory. The model is more meaningfully encoded than it would be if we had to rely on words alone (J. Clark & Paivio, 1991; Willoughby, Porter, Belsito, & Yearsley, 1999). Dual-coding theory again reminds us of the importance of supplementing verbal information with visual representations.

Research suggests that imagery can also make problem solving easier (Kozhevnikov, Hegarty, & Mayer, 1999). Visualizing abstract relationships between problem components helps students differentiate between essential and nonessential information in problems. For example, if students are attempting to find the areas of irregularly shaped polygons, instructing them to visually impose a grid over the figure encourages them to think in area dimensions and also helps them filter out irrelevant information such as the figure's color or physical orientation.

7.11
Dual-coding theory and dual-processing theory (page 242) are closely related, but not identical. Explain how they're different.

Organizational aids help learners construct organized and integrated schemas.

Elaboration. To understand how elaboration can facilitate meaningful encoding, let's look again at David's lesson. He began his Wednesday class by saying, "Let's review what we've found so far. Then I'm going to do a little demonstration, and I want you to think about how it relates to what you've been doing." By having students review their current understanding and expanding on it with his demonstration, David capitalized on **elaboration,** *the process of increasing the meaningfulness of information by forming additional links in existing knowledge or adding new knowledge* (Willoughby, Wood, & Khan, 1994). It occurs in a noisy party, for example, when you miss some of a conversation; you fill in details, trying to make sense of an incomplete message. You do the same when you read or listen to a lecture. You expand on (and sometimes distort) information to make it fit your expectations and current understanding.

Elaboration can enhance meaningfulness in one or both of two ways. For example, when Tanya said, "Oh, I get it! Pluto isn't level with the rest of them," she formed an additional link in her schema without adding any new information. This is one type of elaboration.

David's review capitalized on a second type of elaboration. It reactivated his students' schemas (organized background knowledge), to which the information from Wednesday's lesson could be attached (O'Reilly, Symons, & MacLatchy-Gaudet, 1998). Teacher questioning, such as David's, can be a powerful tool to encourage student elaboration (Seifert, 1993; J. Simpson, Olejnik, Tam, & Suprattathum, 1994).

Teachers can also promote elaboration through three additional strategies:

- *Providing examples:* Specific cases that illustrate ideas
- *Forming analogies:* Comparisons in which similarities are created between otherwise dissimilar ideas (Bulgren et al., 2000; Mayer & Wittrock, 1996)
- *Using mnemonic devices:* Strategies that link items or ideas by forming associations that don't exist naturally in the content (Leahey & Harris, 1997)

7.12
You've taught your students the concept of *adverb*. Ask a question that would be effective for promoting elaboration.

Working with examples—by constructing, finding, or analyzing them—is perhaps the most powerful of the elaboration strategies (Cassady, 1999). Whenever learners can create or identify a new example of an idea, they elaborate on their understanding of that idea. Our extensive use of examples throughout this book demonstrates our belief in this strategy, and we encourage you to focus on the examples to increase your understanding of the topics you're studying. You can do the same with the concepts you teach.

When examples aren't available, using **analogies,** *relationships that are similar in some but not all respects,* can be an effective elaboration strategy (Bulgren et al., 2000). For instance, in an attempt to make information processing more meaningful to you, we presented an analogy between it and a computer. As another example, consider the following analogy from science:

> *Our circulatory system is like a pumping system that carries the blood around our bodies. The veins and arteries are the pipes, and the heart is the pump.*

The veins and arteries are similar, but not identical, to pipes, and the heart is a form of pump. The analogy is an effective form of elaboration because it links new information to something learners already know about—the workings of a pumping system.

Mnemonic devices *link knowledge to be learned to familiar information* (Bruning et al., 1999). Acronyms, such as HOMES (Huron, Ontario, Michigan, Erie, and Superior) and SCUBA (self-contained underwater breathing apparatus) are examples, as are phrases like "Every good boy does fine," for E, G, B, D, and F (the names of the notes in the treble clef), and rhymes such as the spelling aid "*i* before *e* except after *c*." When learners think of the mnemonic, they link it to the items or information it represents. Mnemonics are used to help remember vocabulary, names, rules, lists, and other kinds of factual knowledge; Table 7.4 lists some additional examples.

Activity. You and two friends are studying this book. You read and then attempt to write an answer to each of the margin questions in the chapters. After finishing each answer, you look at the feedback in the *Student Study Guide*. As your friends study, they simply read each margin question and then immediately read the answer.

Table 7.4 Types and examples of mnemonic devices

Mnemonic	Description	Example
Method of loci	Learner combines imagery with specific locations in a familiar environment, such as the chair, sofa, lamp, and end table in a living room.	Student wanting to remember the first seven elements in order visualizes hydrogen at the chair, helium at the sofa, lithium at the lamp, and so on.
Peg-word method	Learner memorizes a series of "pegs"—such as a simple rhyme like "one is bun" and "two is shoe"—on which to-be-remembered information is hung.	A learner wanting to remember to get pickles and carrots at the grocery visualizes a pickle in a bun and carrot stuck in a shoe.
Link method	Learner visually links items to be remembered.	A learner visualizes *homework* stuck in a *notebook* which is bound to her *textbook*, *pencil*, and *pen* with a rubber band to remember to take the (italicized) items to class.
Key-word method	Learner uses imagery and rhyming words to remember unfamiliar words.	A learner remembers that *trigo* (which rhymes with tree) is the Spanish word for "wheat" by visualizing a sheaf of wheat sticking out of a tree.
First-letter method	Learner creates a word from the first letter of items to be remembered.	A student creates the word *Wajmma* to remember the first six presidents in order: Washington, Adams, Jefferson, Madison, Monroe, and Adams.

Your approach is more effective because *you've placed yourself in a more active role than have your friends.* Attempting to answer the question and then checking the feedback is an active process; merely reading the question and then checking the feedback is relatively passive. We've included the questions in the margins to encourage you to interact with the content you're studying, and research indicates that this increase in activity improves learning (Bransford et al., 2000).

As we saw at the beginning of the chapter, active learning is a principle of cognitive learning theories. For example, geometry students who measure shapes such as triangles and rectangles, use their measurements in problem solving, and discuss the logic behind their strategies solve complex problems more effectively than students who are provided with explanations of geometric problems, regardless of how clear the explanations are (Nuthall, 1999b).

"Activity" isn't as simple as it appears on the surface, however. For instance, because hands-on activities are strongly encouraged in science instruction, teachers often assume that learning is taking place if learners are working with materials, such as magnets and other objects. This isn't necessarily the case. If the goal isn't clear, or if students aren't encouraged to describe connections between what they're doing and information they already understand, learning may not be happening. "Hands-on" activities don't guarantee "minds-on" activities (Mayer, 1999).

The same is true with manipulatives in math (Ball, 1992), cooperative learning, and other strategies intended to promote active learner participation. Because students are physically active, or are talking, teachers assume that learning is taking place. This often isn't true.

Activity can also be deceiving at an individual level, as we saw in our example of the study habits of educational psychology students. From a learning perspective, continually asking yourself if you are as active as possible in your study will pay off in increased understanding.

From a teaching perspective, try to use strategies that put students in the most active roles possible. For example:

- Put content in the form of problems to solve and questions to answer, instead of information to be memorized.

7.13
Highlighting is a common study strategy. Some students highlight entire paragraphs of their text, whereas others highlight only sentences and small sections. Which of the two groups is more "active" in their study? Explain.

Active learning encourages students to encode information in meaningful ways.

- Combine explanations with questioning to help students integrate new content with old.
- Ask questions that require students to apply their understanding, rather than simply recall information.
- Require students to provide evidence for conclusions, instead of merely forming the conclusions themselves.
- Develop lessons around examples and applications, instead of definitions.
- Use tests, quizzes, and homework that require application, rather than rote memory.

Each of these strategies requires purposeful, cognitive activity in which students make connections and thoroughly process content.

Levels of Processing: An Alternate View of Meaningful Encoding

Look at the following questions related to David's lesson.

"Which planet is the fourth one from the sun?"
"Why do you suppose Mercury is so hot on one side and so cold on the other?"
"What patterns can you find in the information in the chart?"

Which would produce the most learning?

Levels of processing is *a view of learning suggesting that the more deeply information is processed, the more meaningful it becomes.* Although originally proposed as an alternative to the three-store information processing model you've been studying (Craik & Lockhart, 1972), the levels-of-processing view has been modified to describe different ways that information is encoded in long-term memory (Cermak & Craik, 1979).

For instance, asking students to explain why Mercury is so hot on one side and so cold on the other requires them to understand that Mercury is a small planet, without enough gravity to hold an atmosphere (which helps prevent extreme temperature fluctuations). In addition, students must know that its periods of rotation and revolution are the same, so the same side of the planet always faces the sun, making that side very hot while leaving the opposite side very cold. Being able to answer the question requires students to link all this information in a complex, meaningful schema. This is a deep level of processing.

Finding patterns among the chart information would also take deep processing, whereas merely identifying Mars as the fourth planet is "shallow" processing that requires making few meaningful connections. Teachers should continually ask students to search for relationships in the information they're studying, which will result in deeper, more meaningful processing and better learning and retention.

Forgetting

No discussion of cognitive processes would be complete without considering **forgetting**, *the loss of, or inability to retrieve, information from memory.* Forgetting is both a very real part of people's everyday lives ("Now, where did I put those car keys?") and an important factor in learning.

Let's look again at the information processing model first presented in Figure 7.2. There we see that information lost from both sensory memory and working memory is unrecoverable. On the other hand, information in long-term memory has been encoded. Why can't the learner find it?

Forgetting as Interference. One view of forgetting uses the concept of **interference**, *the loss of information because something learned either before or after detracts from understanding* (M. Anderson & Neely, 1996; Schunk, 1996). For example, students learn that possessives are formed by adding an apostrophe *s* to singular nouns. Then they study plural possessives and contractions and find that the apostrophe is used differently. Students' understanding of plural possessives and contractions can interfere with their understanding of singular possessives and vice versa.

Interference increases when breadth of content coverage is emphasized over in-depth understanding, a common problem in today's schools (R. Dempster & Corkill, 1999). Textbooks that include too many topics create problems for students attempting to relate and differentiate ideas.

Teachers can reduce interference by emphasizing the relationships between topics using review and comparison. After a new topic is introduced, they should compare it with closely related information that students have already studied, identifying easily confused similarities. Doing so elaborates on the original schema, which reduces interference.

Another way to lessen interference is to teach closely related ideas together—for example, adjective and adverb phrases, longitude and latitude, and adding and subtracting fractions with similar and different denominators (Hamilton, 1997). In doing so, teachers should highlight relationships for students, emphasize differences, and identify areas that are easily confused.

Forgetting as Retrieval Failure. A second view of forgetting ties it to individuals' inability to retrieve information from long-term memory.

> This test is a bear. Maybe I should have studied more last night. Oh, well, almost done.
> Now for the fill-in-the-blanks section. First question: Landing site for the Allied invasion of France? I know that. I remember reading it in the text and seeing it in my notes.
> Paris? No, that's inland. We talked about Calais. No, that was a diversion to trick Germany. . . . I know that I know it. . . . Why can't I think of the name?

Unless learners can **retrieve** information—*pull it from long-term memory into working memory for further processing*—it's useless. Many researchers believe that learners don't literally "lose" information when they forget; rather, they can't retrieve it (Ashcraft, 1989). Retrieval failure is like putting information into a file folder and then trying to figure out where you stored the folder; the information is there but can't be found.

As with acquiring procedural knowledge, retrieval strongly depends on context (Burke, MacKay, Worthley, & Wade, 1991). For instance, you know a person at work or school, but you can't remember her name when you see her at a party; her name was encoded in the work or school context, and you're trying to retrieve her name in the context of the party. David accommodated the need for context when he presented his information about Pluto in different ways. He didn't merely say that the first eight planets had one origin and that Pluto had another. Instead, he presented the information in the context of the planets' orbital planes, their direction of revolution, and the origin of the solar system.

Meaningfulness is the key to retrieval. The more detailed and interconnected knowledge is in long-term memory, the easier it is to retrieve (Nuthall, 1999a). By encouraging his students to learn and connect the new information in a variety of ways, David increased the likelihood that it would be meaningful and increased the chance of later retrieval (J. Martin, 1993).

7.14
How can science teachers most effectively put their topics into "context"? How can math teachers contextualize their topics?

Classroom Connections

Applying an Understanding of Cognitive Processes in Your Classroom

Attention

1. Begin and conduct lessons to attract and maintain attention.
   - *Elementary:* A third-grade teacher calls on all his students, whether or not they have their hands up. He periodically asks, "Who have I not called on lately?" to be sure students are treated as equally as possible.
   - *Middle School:* A science teacher introducing the concept *pressure* has students stand by their desks, first on both feet and then on one foot. They then discuss the force and pressure on the floor in each of the cases.
   - *High School:* To be sure that her students attend closely to important points, a world history teacher emphasizes, "Everyone, listen carefully now, because we're going to look at three important reasons that World War I broke out in Europe."

Perception

2. Check frequently to be certain that students are perceiving your examples and other representations accurately.
   - *Elementary:* A kindergarten teacher wants his students to understand *living things.* He displays a large plant that he keeps in the classroom and then asks, "What do you notice about the plant?" He calls on several children for their reactions.
   - *Middle School:* A geography teacher shows her class a series of colored slides of landforms. After displaying each slide, she asks students to describe the landform before she moves on.
   - *High School:* An English teacher and his students are reading an essay and come across a line that says, "I wouldn't impose this regimen on myself out of masochism." He stops and asks, "What does the author mean by 'masochism'?"

Meaningful Encoding

3. Carefully organize the information you present to students, and put them in active roles.
   - *Elementary:* A third-grade teacher illustrates that heat causes expansion by placing a balloon-covered soft drink bottle in a pot of hot water and by presenting a drawing that shows the spacing and motion of the

air molecules. She then guides the students to the relationship between heat and expansion with questioning.
   - *Middle School:* A math teacher presents a flowchart with a series of questions students are encouraged to ask themselves as they solve word problems. As students work on the problems, he has them describe their thinking and tell where they are on the flowchart.
   - *High School:* A history teacher presents a matrix comparing four different immigrant groups, why they came to the United States, the difficulties they encountered, and their rates of assimilation. The students then work in pairs to find patterns in the information in the chart.

4. Encourage students to elaborate on their understanding and to use imagery in their study.
   - *Elementary:* A fourth-grade teacher says, "Let's summarize what we've found now about chemical and physical changes. Picture the differences between the two, give me two new examples of each, and explain why they're chemical or physical changes."
   - *Middle School:* A geography teacher encourages her students to visualize flat parallel lines on the globe as they think about latitude and vertical lines coming together at the North and South Poles as they think about longitude. She then asks them to describe the similarities and differences between longitude and latitude.
   - *High School:* An English teacher asks students to imagine the appearance of the characters in the books they read. He asks them to describe the characters in detail, including their facial features, the way they wear their hair, how they're dressed, and how they act.

Retrieval

5. To prevent interference and aid retrieval, teach closely related ideas together, stressing similarities and differences.
   - *Elementary:* A fifth-grade teacher, knowing that her students confuse *area* and *perimeter,* has them lay squares side by side to illustrate area, and she has them measure the distance around the filled area to illustrate perimeter. She then moves to irregular plane figures and repeats the process.
   - *Middle School:* An English teacher presenting a unit on verbals displays a passage on the overhead that includes both gerunds and participles. He then asks the students to compare the way the words are used in

the passage to demonstrate that gerunds are nouns and participles are adjectives.

- *High School:* A biology teacher begins a unit on arteries and veins by saying, "We've all heard of hardening of the arteries, but we haven't heard of 'hardening of the veins.' Why not? Are we using the term *artery* to mean both, or is there a difference? Why is hardening of the arteries bad for people? I'm going to write these questions down so that we keep them in mind as we study arteries, veins, and capillaries."

Metacognition: Knowledge and Control of Cognitive Processes

Have you ever said to yourself, "I'm going to sit near the front of the class so I won't fall asleep," or "I'm beat today. I'd better drink a cup of coffee before I go to class"? If you have, you were being *metacognitive*. As we saw at the beginning of the chapter, metacognition is *the awareness of and control over one's own cognitive processes.*

Attention is one of those processes. If you knew that you might fall asleep, you demonstrated an awareness of your ability to attend. If you chose to sit in the front of the class or drink coffee, you exercised control over it. You were being meta-attentive, one kind of metacognition.

Students who are aware of the way they study and learn achieve more than those who are less aware (Bruning et. al., 1999). In other words, students who are metacognitive learn more than those who aren't.

Let's look at four reasons why. First, students who are aware of the importance of attention are more likely to create effective learning environments for themselves. The adaptation can be as simple as moving to the front of the class, so as not to miss important information, or turning off a distracting radio while studying.

Second, metacognition enhances accurate perception. Learners who know they might misperceive something can attempt to find corroborating information. By doing so, they demonstrate awareness of and control over perception.

Third, metacognition helps regulate the flow of information through working memory. For example, we all find ourselves in situations where we have to remember a phone number. If we're going to dial the number immediately, we simply rehearse; if we're going to call later, we probably write the number down. Each decision is strategic, influenced by our awareness and control over our memories. This is an example of **metamemory**, which is *knowledge of and control over our memory strategies* (Schraw & Moshman, 1995). Randy, in David's lesson, demonstrated metamemory when he said, "I better write some of this stuff down, or I'll never remember it." He was aware of his memory's limitations, and he exercised control over them by choosing to take notes. The ability to monitor the processing of information in working memory is essential because of its limited capacity (K. Wilson & Swanson, 1999).

Finally, metacognition influences the meaningfulness of encoding. For example, learners who know that encoding is more effective if different items of information are linked, rather than stored in isolation, may consciously look for relationships in the topics they study. This influences their study strategies, and ultimately, how much they learn.

The metacognitive components of the information processing model are illustrated in Figure 7.9.

Randy's metacognition helps him remember important information

The Development of Metacognition

As students mature and develop, their tendency to be metacognitive increases, and they learn to use **strategies**, *plans for accomplishing specific learning goals* (Berk, 2001). For instance, summarizing is an effective strategy for increasing comprehension of a written

7.15
As you're reading a section of this book, you stop and go back to the top of the page and reread one of the sections. Is this an example of metacognition? Explain.

Figure 7.9 Metacognition in the information processing model

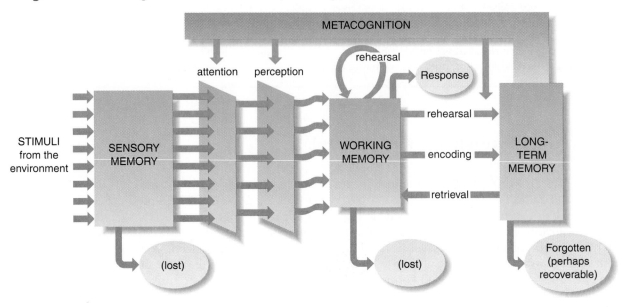

passage, and a mnemonic can be an effective strategy for remembering lists of words such as the names of the Great Lakes. Young learners' metacognitive abilities are limited; they don't realize that they can influence how much they learn. However, as learners develop, they acquire an increasing number of strategies, and their strategies become more selective and efficient (Berk, 2001).

Meta-Attention: The Development of Attention Strategies.   Research indicates that older children are more aware of the importance of attention than their younger counterparts, are better at directing their attention toward important information in a learning task, and are better at ignoring distracting and irrelevant stimuli (Berk, 2001).

Although meta-attention develops naturally, teachers' efforts can enhance it. Let's look at an example.

> Connie Mahera began working with her first graders by saying, "We know how important it is to pay attention." She then modeled attention by focusing on a sample seat work assignment, working carefully, and keeping her eyes on the paper.
>
> Then she had Mrs. Morton, her parent volunteer, talk to the class. She listened intently to Mrs. Morton, maintaining eye contact and keeping her hands and body still. She next modeled inattention in both an interactive and a seat work situation.
>
> She then asked, "Now, am I paying attention?" as she modeled inattention to seat work by gazing out the window and playing with objects on her desk. She demonstrated several more examples, had the students classify them as attention or inattention, and then told the students, "I am going to click the cricket, and if you're paying attention each time I click it, make an X in a box." She then gave each student a sheet of paper with several boxes drawn on it.
>
> The next morning and for several consecutive mornings, Connie demonstrated and had students demonstrate attentive and inattentive behaviors as part of the class routine. As time went on, students' attention improved markedly. (based on Hallahan et al., 1983)

Young children don't realize that they're inattentive, and this awareness needs to be developed. With time and teacher assistance, meta-attention increases and students become more self-regulated.

Metamemory: The Development of Memory Strategies. An 8-year-old described her strategy for remembering a telephone number:

> Say the number is 663-8854. Then what I'd do is say that my number is 663, so I won't have to remember that really. And then I would think now I've got to remember 88. Now I'm eight years old, so I can remember, say my age two times. Then I say how old my brother is, and how old he was last year. And that's how I'd usually remember that phone number. [Interviewer: Is that how you would most often remember a phone number?] Well, usually I write it down. (Kreutzer, Leonard, & Flavell, 1975, p. 11)

This 8-year-old used a sophisticated memory strategy, linking the numbers to information that she already knew.

As with attention, older children and adults are much better than young children at using strategies for remembering information (Short, Schatschneider, & Friebert, 1993). For example, nursery school students given a list of objects to memorize in order didn't use rehearsal as a strategy. Fourth graders, in contrast, both rehearsed aloud and anticipated succeeding items by naming them before they were shown by the experimenter (Flavell, Friedrichs, & Hoyt, 1970). Similar patterns have been found with categorizing and imagery; kindergartners don't use them as strategies, whereas fourth graders can and do (Berk, 2001).

Older learners are also more aware of their memory limitations (Everson & Tobias, 1998; Sternberg, 1998b). For example, when asked to predict how many objects they could remember from a list, nursery school students predicted 7 but were able to remember fewer than 4 (Flavell et al., 1970). Adults given the same task predicted an average of 5.9 and actually remembered 5.5 (Yussen & Levy, 1975).

The example with Connie Mahera and her first graders demonstrated how instruction can help children develop their meta-attention. Instruction can also make students aware of their memory capacities and the importance of matching strategies to the demands of a task. To remember a class assignment, for instance, simply writing it down is enough. For more complex tasks, like understanding a written passage, more sophisticated strategies such as summarizing or outlining are required. Helping students develop this awareness is an important step in their being able to take responsibility for their own learning.

> **7.16**
> What is the most effective way you have of helping students develop their metacognitive abilities? Hint: Think about your study of Chapter 6.

Classroom Connections

Applying an Understanding of Metacognition in Your Classroom

1. Systematically integrate metacognition into your instruction, and model metacognitive strategies.

   - *Elementary:* A fourth-grade teacher plays an attention game with his students. During a lesson, he holds up a card with the sentence "If you're paying attention, raise your hand." He then acknowledges those who are and encourages them to share their strategies for maintaining attention during class.

   - *Middle School:* A social studies teacher tries to teach metamemory by saying, "Suppose you're reading, and the book states that there are three important differences between capitalism and socialism. What should you do?"

   - *High School:* An economics teacher frequently models metacognitive strategies by making statements such as, "Whenever I read something new, I always ask myself, 'How does this relate to what I've been studying?' For example, how is the liberal economic agenda different from the conservative agenda?"

The Impact of Diversity on Information Processing

As a warm-up activity for his world geography class, Mike Havland asked his students to look at a "modern" map of Europe displayed on the overhead.

As Carl looked at the map, he thought it looked familiar. "Yeah," he thought, "there's England, France, Germany, and Russia. Hey, there's Yugoslavia. That's where Goran's grandparents came from."

Next to him, Celeena, who grew up in a military family that had traveled all over Europe, was also looking at the map, but with a look of disbelief. "How old is this map?" she thought. "Look at Yugoslavia. It doesn't exist anymore. It's been torn apart. Hmm, where's Barcelona? . . . Oh yeah. Down there on the coast of Spain. We saw it when we went to the Olympics several years ago."

After a few minutes, Mike began. "Okay, everyone. It's important to have some idea of the geography of Europe, because the geography reflects an important idea that we'll return to again and again." With that, he wrote on the chalkboard:

The history of Europe reflects a tension between nationalism and intercountry cooperation such as the adoption of a common currency, the Euro.

He continued by saying, "As you've already noticed, the face of Europe is continually changing. The Europe of today is very different from what you see on this map, and the changes happened only a few years ago."

As he was talking, he noticed a few nods but more blank looks. Celeena sat knowingly, while Carl thought, "What's he talking about? nationalism? the Euro? What is this?"

Teachers know that background knowledge strongly influences perception and encoding. Students come to class with widely varying experiences, and addressing this diversity is one of the biggest challenges teachers face (Veenman, 1984).

Diversity and Perception

7.17

Which concept is more accurate when comparing students' background knowledge: *different schemas* or *less well-developed schemas?* Explain using information in this section.

As you saw in Mike's lesson, Carl perceived the map of Europe as an accurate representation, but to Celeena it was an antiquated document. What students perceive depends on what they already know, and Celeena had background knowledge Carl didn't possess. As another example, one person seeing a movie on the Vietnam conflict interprets the war as an effort to stop the spread of communism, whereas another perceives it as the imposition of American values on a distant country. The difference depends on what viewers already have learned about the conflict as well as their beliefs and values.

The fact that learners' schemas influence the way they perceive information has been verified in areas as varied as chess, reading, math, and physics (Glover, Ronning, & Bruning, 1990).

Diversity, Encoding, and Retrieval

Just as background knowledge influences learners' perceptions, it also influences how effectively learners encode new information. For example, Celeena's rich geography background made Mike's opening statements meaningful to her. The statements meant little to Carl; he had no information in his memory to which he could link ideas such as "nationalism" and "intercountry cooperation." We've all been in conversations, heard presentations, or read written passages that made no sense to us. In such cases, we may lack the background to which new information can be linked, so meaningful encoding doesn't occur.

The diverse experiential backgrounds of students can be used to enrich the learning experiences of all students.

Instructional Adaptations for Background Diversity

What can teachers do when students aren't able to encode the information presented in a lesson? Research suggests several strategies (M. Brenner et al., 1997; Nuthall, 1999b):

- Begin lessons by asking students what they know about the topic you plan to teach.
- Supplement background experiences with rich examples and representations of the content.
- Use open-ended questions to assess student perceptions of your examples and representations.
- Use the experiences of students in the class to augment the backgrounds of those lacking the experiences.

For instance, Mike could say, "Celeena, you lived in Europe. What do people there say about the conflict in the former Yugoslavia?" Also, because nationalism was an organizing idea for much of what would follow, Mike could ask, "What does *nationalism* mean? Give an example of strong and weak nationalism." If students are unable to respond, he could then change his plans and focus on illustrating and discussing the concept, which would provide the necessary background for later learning. For example, he could use the school as context for his discussion of nationalism by describing school spirit, pride in the school, and the school's traditions as analogies for the feelings of nationalism in European countries. The analogies would make the concept of nationalism meaningful for students, and encoding would improve (Zook, 1991). The ability to adapt lessons in this way is one characteristic of teaching expertise.

Classroom Connections

Capitalizing on Diversity in Your Classroom

1. Assess students' background knowledge and perceptions throughout lessons.
   - *Elementary:* Because he has a number of recent immigrant children in his class, a fourth-grade teacher begins a unit on communities by requesting, "Tell us about the communities that you lived in before coming to this country." He has students whose English skills are more fully developed work as interpreters for other students. He then uses the information as a framework for the study of their community.
   - *Middle School:* To supplement her students' background knowledge, a science teacher introduces the study of refraction by having students put coins in opaque dishes and backing up until they can't see the coins. She then has partners pour water into the dishes until the coins become visible. Finally, she shows a model illustrating how the light rays are bent when they enter and leave the water.
   - *High School:* An art teacher begins a unit on perspective by asking students to sketch a three-dimensional scene. He has students put their names on the back of the sketches and then discusses the sketches during the following class period.

Information Processing in the Classroom: Instructional Strategies

As we saw at the beginning of the chapter, cognitive learning theories assume that learners are active and emphasize the importance of students' background knowledge on new learning. This is as true for information processing as it is for any other cognitive theory.

Well-developed schemas facilitate initial learning and aid later retrieval and use. Teachers can help learners develop coherent and connected schemas in two ways: (a) by using teaching strategies that encourage students to form relationships in the topics they study and (b) by developing procedural knowledge to the point of automaticity. Let's look at them.

Schema Production: Acquiring Integrated Declarative Knowledge

As discussed earlier, schemas reduce the load on working memory because although the number of items it can hold is limited, the size of the items is not (Sweller et al., 1998). In fact, some prominent researchers call the development of schemas a form of chunking (Bransford et al., 2000).

You may recall that schemas organize declarative knowledge, such as the facts about the solar system in David's lesson. Many other classroom lessons focus on schema development to facilitate acquiring declarative knowledge. For instance, students studying 19th-century literature examine relationships among plot, character development, and symbolism in a novel such as *Moby Dick*; geography students study the relationships between landforms, climate, and economy in different regions of the world; and biology students examine differences between parasitic and nonparasitic worms and how these differences are reflected in their body structures.

Promoting Schema Production in Classrooms: An Instructional Strategy

7.18
Think about some of the case studies in other chapters in this text. Identify at least two in which the acquisition of declarative knowledge was the primary goal.

Schema production in classrooms can be developed in three phases that occur in repeated cycles. The cycles are grounded in the following processes:

- *Information acquisition.* The process begins when students acquire knowledge about the topic, either by having the teacher present information or by having students acquire it on their own, as students did in David's lesson. If teachers provide information, the presentations must be kept short to prevent overloading students' working memories.
- *Comprehension monitoring.* After students acquire some knowledge, the teacher asks a series of questions designed to keep them in active roles, check their perceptions, and begin the process of schema development.
- *Integration.* The teacher asks additional questions designed to help students develop complex schemas that promote chunking, reduction of the load on working memory, and encoding into long-term memory.

Let's look at an example of these classroom processes in a 10th-grade American history class. As you read the case study, try to identify the points where the processes occur.

Darren Anderson was discussing the events leading up to the American Revolutionary War. To introduce the topic, she pointed to a time line above the chalkboard and began, "About where are we now in our progress?"

"About there," Adam responded, pointing to the middle of the 1700s on the time line.

"Yes, good," Darren smiled. "That's about where we are. However, I would like for us to understand what happened before that time, so we're going to back up a ways—actually, all the way to the early 1600s. When we're finished today, we'll see that the Revolutionary War didn't just happen; there were events that led up to it that made it almost inevitable. . . . That's the important part of history . . . to see how events that happen at one time affect events at other times, and all the way to today.

"For instance, the conflict between the British and the French in America became so costly for the British that they began policies in the colonies that ultimately led to the Revolution. That's what we want to begin looking at today. What were the events that led to the conflict between the British and French? . . . Here we go."

She then began, "We know that the British established Jamestown in 1607, but we haven't really looked at French expansion into the New World. Let's look again at the map.

"Here we see Jamestown," she said pointing to the map, "but at about the same time, a French explorer named Champlain came down the St. Lawrence River and formed Quebec City, here." She pointed again to the map. "Over the years, at least 35 of the 50 states were discovered or mapped by the French, and several of our big cities, such as Detroit, St. Louis, New Orleans, and Des Moines, were founded by the French." She continued pointing to a series of locations she had marked on the map.

"Now, what do you notice about the location of the two groups?"

After thinking a few seconds, Alfredo offered, "The French had a lot of Canada, . . . and it looks like this country too." He pointed to the north and west on the map.

"It looks like the east was . . . British, and the west was French," Troy added.

"Yes, and remember, this was all happening at about the same time," Darren continued. "Also, the French were more friendly with the American Indians than the British were. The French had what they called a seignorial system, where the settlers were given land if they would serve in the military. So, . . . what does this suggest about the military power of the French?"

"Probably powerful," Josh suggested. "The people got land if they went in the army."

"And the American Indians probably helped, because they were friendly with the French," Tenisha added.

"Now, what else do you notice here?" Darren asked, moving her hand up and down the width of the map.

"Mountains?" Danielle answered uncertainly.

"Yes, exactly," Darren smiled. "Why are they important Danielle? What do mountains do?"

". . . The British were sort of fenced in, and the French could expand and do as they pleased."

"Good. And now the plot thickens. The British needed land and wanted to expand. So they headed west over the mountains and guess who they ran into? . . . Sarah?"

"The French?" Sarah responded.

"And conflict broke out. Now, when the French and British were fighting, why do you suppose the French were initially more successful than the British? . . . What do you think? . . . Dan?"

"Well, . . . they had that seig . . . seignorial system, so they were more eager to fight, because of the land and everything."

"Other thoughts? . . . Bette?"

"I think that the American Indians were part of it. The French got along better with them, so they helped the French."

"Okay, good thinking everyone, now let's think about the British. . . . Let's look at some of their advantages."

Let's take a closer look at Darren's efforts to promote schema production. She first attempted to capture students' *attention* by explaining how events in the past influence the way we live today. Then, unlike David in our opening case study (who had his students acquire much of the background knowledge on their own), she *presented information* about Jamestown, Quebec, and French settlements in the present-day United States. After this brief presentation, she used questioning to involve her students in the *comprehension monitoring* phase. To illustrate, let's review a brief portion of the dialogue.

Darren:	Now, what do you notice about the location of the two groups?
Alfredo:	The French had a lot of Canada, . . . and it looks like this country too. (pointing to the north and west on the map)
Troy:	It looks like the east was . . . British, and the west was French.

Darren's questions were intended to put students in *cognitively active roles*, check their *perceptions*, and begin the process of *schema production*. Satisfied that their perceptions were accurate, she returned to presenting information when she said, "Yes, and remember, this was all happening at about the same time." She continued by briefly describing the French seignorial system and pointing out that the French and American Indians were friendly.

Then she again turned back to the students.

Teacher questions attract attention and encourage learners to integrate information into coherent schemas.

Darren:	So, . . . what does this suggest about the military power of the French?
Josh:	Probably powerful. The people got land if they went in the army.
Tenisha:	And the Native Americans probably helped, because they were friendly with the French.

The two segments appear similar on the surface, but there is an important difference. In the first, Darren was *monitoring comprehension*. The students' responses to the question, "Now, what do you notice about the location of the two groups?" helped her assess their perceptions of what she had presented in the first segment. In the second, she attempted to promote the production of schemas by encouraging students to *integrate* the seignorial system, the relationship between the French and the American Indians, and French military power. Darren's goal for the entire lesson was the development of complex schemas that would provide an understanding of the cause-effect relationships between the French and Indian Wars and the American Revolutionary War.

Teachers often use simple presentations when topics focus on declarative knowledge, and this strategy can be useful when goals include helping students to

7.19
In which phase—*information acquisition, comprehension monitoring,* or *integration*—does schema production actually occur? Explain.

- Acquire information not readily accessible in other ways
- Integrate information from a variety of sources
- Understand different points of view (Bransford et al., 2000; Henson, 1988)

Teacher-facilitated schema production, as we saw in Darren's history lesson, can meet each of these goals and, in addition, has two important advantages over traditional teacher presentations. First, it puts students in active roles. Teacher presentations, by themselves, don't ensure that students will be passive, but research indicates that learners are less likely to be cognitively engaged during extended periods of listening than they are in discussions and question-and-answer activities (Blumenfeld, 1992). Second, through questioning teachers can help students form links between the ideas they're learning, which increases meaningfulness and aids encoding and retrieval.

Meaningful Verbal Learning: The Work of David Ausubel

In her lesson, Darren also applied some of the thinking of David Ausubel (1968, 1977), a pioneer in the emphasis on integrated schemas in meaningful learning. Reacting to what he felt was overemphasis on discovery learning and inquiry at the time, Ausubel contended that the major goal of schooling should be the development of schemas that students could use to acquire additional information.

To promote schema development, Ausubel recommended that teachers begin lessons with an *advance organizer,* an overview or cognitive roadmap, for the content to follow. Darren provided this kind of lesson introduction: "For instance, the conflict between the British and the French in America became so costly for the British that they began policies in the colonies that ultimately led to the Revolution. That's what we want to begin looking at today. What were the events that led to the conflict between the British and French?"

The content to follow should be carefully organized to be meaningful, and the teacher should play an active role in guiding the students' schema production, as Darren did in the comprehension monitoring and integration segments of her lesson.

Although Ausubel's work has received less attention in recent years, his emphasis on learning meaningful declarative knowledge is corroborated by research (Bruning et al., 1999; Merkley & Jefferies, 2001).

Understanding and Automaticity: Acquiring Procedural Knowledge

Much of what students learn in schools is in the form of declarative knowledge, but they also acquire a great deal of procedural knowledge. For example, young children practice math problems using basic operations, chemistry students balance equations and solve a variety of problems, geography students use longitude and latitude to pinpoint locations, and students at all levels write. Each of these tasks involves procedural knowledge.

Earlier we defined procedural knowledge as knowledge of how to perform tasks. To reduce the load on working memory and to ensure that schemas are integrated, procedural knowledge must be developed to the point of automaticity. Such automaticity is most likely to be acquired if students understand the process and are given as many opportunities to practice as possible (Bruning et al., 1999).

Effective teachers play an active role in helping students understand when and how procedural knowledge is used.

Promoting Understanding and Automaticity: An Instructional Strategy

As with the acquisition of declarative knowledge, procedural knowledge is developed in three phases:

- *Introduce and review.* Teachers attempt to attract students' attention and review previous work to check their perceptions and assist them in accessing background knowledge from long-term memory.
- *Develop understanding.* Teachers help learners acquire declarative knowledge about the procedure, connect this knowledge to the skill being learned, and encode this understanding in long-term memory.
- *Provide practice.* Students practice, first under the watchful eye of the teacher (the associative stage) and finally on their own to develop automaticity.

Let's look at an example of these classroom processes in a second-grade math lesson.

Sam Barnett wanted his second graders to understand how to add two-digit numbers. He began by saying, "Today we are going to go a step further with our work in addition so that we'll be able to solve problems like this." He displayed the following on the overhead:

Jana and Patti are friends. They were saving special soda cans to get a free compact disc. They can get the CD if they save 35 cans. Jana had 15 cans and Patti had 12. How many did they have together?

After giving the students a chance to read the problem, Sam continued, "Now, what are we being asked?"

". . . How many cans Jana and Patti have together," Devon answered haltingly.

"Why is that important? . . . Flavia?"

"So they can see how close they are to getting their CD," Flavia responded.

"Sure," Sam smiled. "If they know how many they have, they'll know how close they are. If they don't, they're stuck. That's why it's important."

All of Sam's students had boxes on their desks that contained craft sticks with 10 beans glued on each as well as a number of loose, individual beans. Sam reviewed single-digit

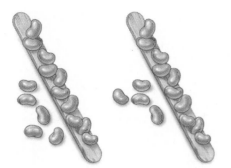

addition by having the students demonstrate their answers to single-digit problems, such as 8 + 7 and 9 + 5, with their sticks and beans.

He then turned back to the problem, had the students demonstrate 15 and 12 with their beans, and wrote the following on the board:

15
+12

"Now, watch what I do here," he continued. "When I add 5 and 2, what do I get? Let me think about that. . . . 5 and 2 are 7. Let's put a 7 on the board," he said as he walked to the board and added a 7.

"Now show me that with your beans." He watched as the students combined 5 beans and 2 beans on their desks.

"Now, we still have to add the tens. What do we get when we add two 10s? . . . Let's see. One 10 and one 10 is two 10s. Now, look where I've put the 2. It is under the tens column because the 2 means two 10s." With that, he wrote the following on the chalkboard:

15
+12
27

"So, how many cans did Jana and Patti have together? . . . Alesha?"

". . . 27?"

"Good, Alesha. They had 27 altogether."

Sam had the students demonstrate with their beans and explain what the 7 and the 2 in 27 meant, and then asked, "Now, we saw that I added the 5 and the 2 before I added the two 10s. Why do you suppose I did that? . . . Anyone?"

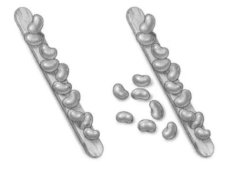

". . . You have to find out how many ones you have to see if we can make a 10," Callie offered.

"That's excellent thinking, Callie. That's exactly right. We'll see why again tomorrow when we have some problems in which we'll have to regroup, but for now let's remember what Callie said.

"So let's look again," he went on. "There's an important difference between this 2," he said, pointing to the 2 in 27, "and this 2," pointing to the 2 in the 12. "What is this difference? . . . Katrina?"

"That 2 . . . is two groups of 10, . . . and that one is just 2 by itself."

"Yes, that's good thinking, Katrina. Good work, everyone. . . . Show me this 2," Sam directed, pointing to the 2 in 27.

The students held up two sticks with the beans glued on them.

"Good, and show me this 2." He pointed to the 2 in the 12, and the students held up two beans.

"Great," Sam nodded. He had the students demonstrate their answers to three additional problems, and then said, "When we've had enough practice with our sticks and beans to be sure that we really, really understand these problems, we'll start practicing with the numbers by themselves. We're going to get so good at these problems that we'll be able to do them without even thinking about it."

He assigned 10 more problems and watched carefully as the students worked at their desks.

Let's take a closer look at Sam's attempts to promote understanding and automaticity and to implement each of the phases in his activity.

Introduce and Review. Information processing begins with *attention*, and Sam used the attention-getting characteristics of a realistic problem to begin his lesson. He then checked students' perceptions by having them describe what the problem asked and reviewed what they had already done to pull background knowledge from long-term memory back into working memory. The value of this process is well established by research (Gersten et al., 1999), and although its importance seems obvious, nearly a fourth of all lessons begin with little or no introduction (Brophy, 1982).

Develop Understanding. As mentioned earlier, an essential part of encoding procedural knowledge involves recognizing different conditions and applying procedures appropriate for those conditions. The second phase is essential for this purpose. Here, students acquire the declarative knowledge that allows them to adapt when applying their procedural knowledge in different conditions. When they fail to connect procedural knowledge to declarative knowledge (organized in schemas), students apply procedures mechanically or use superficial strategies, such as subtracting when they see the words "how many more" in a math problem (Mayer, 1999; Novick, 1998).

Sam's emphasis on developing understanding can be seen in this interaction:

Sam:	So let's look again. There's an important difference between this 2 (pointing to the 2 in 27) and this 2 (pointing to the 2 in the 12). What is this difference? . . . Katrina?
Katrina:	That 2 . . . is two groups of 10, . . . and that one is just 2 by itself.
Sam:	Yes, that's good thinking, Katrina. Good work, everyone. . . . Show me this 2 (pointing to the 2 in 27).

The students held up two sticks with the beans glued on them.

Sam:	Good, and show me this 2 (pointing to the 2 in the 12).

The students then held up two beans.

Sam used questioning and concrete examples throughout this phase, and their importance is difficult to overstate. Questioning puts students in active roles, helps break up an explanation to avoid overloading working memories, and promotes encoding. Concrete examples take advantage of working memories' dual processing capabilities.

Teachers often fail to fully develop understanding as called for in this step. They may emphasize memorization, fail to ask enough questions, or move too quickly to practice (Rittle-Johnson & Alibali, 1999). Or they may involve learners in hands-on activities but then fail to establish the connection between the materials (e.g., sticks and beans) and the abstractions they represent (the numbers on the board) (Ball, 1992).

Practice: The Associative and Automatic Stages. Once students have developed an understanding of the procedure, they can begin practicing with teacher assistance—the *associative stage* of practice. Initially, the teacher uses questioning to provide enough scaffolding to ensure success, but not so much that students' sense of challenge and accomplishment is reduced (Gersten et al., 1999; Rosenshine & Meister, 1992). Sam had his students work a problem, and they discussed it carefully while he assessed their understanding. He continued with this process until he believed that the students were ready to work on their own.

The teacher then attempts to help students gradually make the transition from the associative to the *automatic stage*. During this transition, students move from consciously thinking about the skill to performing it automatically. The teacher reduces scaffolding and shifts responsibility to students. The goal is automaticity, so working memory space can be devoted to high-level applications (Sweller et al., 1998).

Teacher monitoring continues to be important even after students can carry out the procedures automatically. Effective teachers carefully monitor students to assess their developing understanding; less effective teachers are more likely to merely check to see that students are on task (e.g., on the right page and following directions).

Homework. When properly used, homework can help students achieve automaticity (Cooper, Lindsay, Nye, & Greathouse, 1998; Stein & Carnine, 1999). "Properly used" means that teachers assign homework that is an extension of what students have studied and practiced in class (Bransford et al., 2000). Also, although grading homework can be time-consuming, teachers should have some mechanism for giving students credit and providing feedback if students are to take homework seriously and use it as a learning tool.

The effects of homework are especially strong at the junior high and high school levels, and frequency is important (Cooper, Valentine, Nye, & Lindsay, 1999). For example,

7.20
Sam's lesson focused on procedural knowledge. Did his students also acquire any declarative knowledge? Explain.

7.21
What does *scaffolding* mean? Identify one effective way, other than questioning, that teachers can provide scaffolding.

7.22
Using social cognitive theory as a basis, explain why assigning but not collecting and grading homework is ineffective practice.

Table 7.5 Characteristics of effective homework

Characteristic	Rationale
Extension of classwork	The teacher teaches; homework reinforces.
High success rates	Success is motivating. Success leads to automaticity. No one is available to provide help if students encounter problems.
Part of class routines	Becomes a part of student expectations, increases likelihood of students completing assignments.
Graded	Increases accountability and provides feedback.

Source: Based on work by Berliner (1984) and Cooper (1989).

five problems every night are more effective than 25 once a week. Effective homework has four characteristics, which are outlined in Table 7.5.

Researchers attempting to explain why homework is less effective with younger students identified at least two factors (Cooper & Valentine, 2001). First, young children may have poorly developed study and attention skills, which limit the amount of time they productively spend on homework. Second, children who are struggling to learn an idea can encounter even greater problems at home where distractions and lack of help may hamper learning efforts. Elementary teachers who assign homework should monitor students' progress closely to ensure that the homework is contributing to learning.

Teachers should view homework as an integral part of a comprehensive plan to teach students responsibility and self-regulation (Cooper et al., 1998; Corno & Xu, 1998) and should solicit parents' support in this effort (Cooper, Jackson, Nye, & Lindsay, 2001). Homework requires that students take initiative and accept responsibility in several ways; for example, they must remember to take materials home, find a quiet place to work, actually complete the assignment, and attempt to understand the topics. Parents can provide the at-home support that is so important for younger and less motivated students. Teachers can enlist their aid with notes, phone calls, and individual conferences. (We examine strategies for involving parents in Chapter 12.)

Classroom Connections

Helping Students Acquire Declarative and Procedural Knowledge in Your Classroom

Declarative Knowledge

1. Design lessons to maintain students' attention and promote schema production.
   - *Elementary:* A third-grade teacher presents three word problems, each requiring different sets of operations. She has the students compare the problems, decide what operations are required, and explain how they know. She has written the problems without familiar word clues, such as "how many more" and "how many altogether," to prevent students from responding mindlessly.

   - *Middle School:* An American history teacher discussing immigration in the 19th and early 20th centuries compares immigrant groups of the past with today's Cuban population in Miami, Florida, and Mexican immigrants in San Antonio, Texas. He asks the students to summarize the similarities and differences between the two groups with respect to the difficulties they encounter and the rates of assimilation into the American way of life.

   - *High School:* A biology teacher is presenting information related to transport of liquids in and out of cells, identifying and illustrating several of the concepts in the process. After about 3 minutes, she stops presenting information and asks, "Suppose a cell is in a hypotonic solution in one case and a hypertonic solution in another. What's the difference between the two? What would happen to the cell in each case?"

Procedural Knowledge

2. Emphasize understanding and provide practice to develop automaticity.

- *Elementary:* A fourth-grade teacher giving a lesson on possessives displays sentences such as the following and asks, "How are these pairs of sentences different, and what makes them different?"

  The student's books were lost.
  The students' books were lost.

  Who can tell me the boy's story?
  Who can tell me the boys' stories?

  He then has the students write paragraphs that incorporate both singular and plural possessives.

- *Middle School:* In a unit on percentages and decimals, a math teacher comments that the star quarterback for the state university completed 14 of 21 passes in the last game. "What does that mean? Is that good or bad? Was it better than the 12 of 17 passes completed by the opposing quarterback?" she asks. She calculates the percentages with the class and then has the students practice finding percentages in other real-world problems.

- *High School:* A ninth-grade geography teacher helps his students locate the longitude and latitude of their city by "walking them through" the process, using a map and a series of specific questions. He then has them practice finding the longitude and latitude of other cities, as well as finding the major city nearest sets of longitude and latitude locations.

Assessment and Learning: The Role of Assessment in Cognitive Instruction

The principles of cognitive learning theory, together with the characteristics of learners' cognitive architectures—information stores, cognitive processes, and metacognition—have two additional implications for teachers. They are (a) assessment must be an integral part of the teaching-learning process, and (b) instruction must be aligned.

Assessment and Instruction

Assessment provides teachers with insights into how students are processing information. Because background knowledge, beliefs, and expectations vary, learners' perceptions of what they study also vary. The understanding that is encoded can be unique to individuals and cannot be predicted without ongoing assessment. Bransford and colleagues (2000) noted, "Formative assessments—ongoing assessments that make students thinking visible to both teachers and students— . . . permit the teacher to grasp students' preconceptions, understand where the students are in the 'developmental corridor'. . . and design instruction accordingly" (p. 24). Assessment also provides students with feedback that allows them to revise and improve their thinking, which ultimately increases the amount that they learn.

These assessments are not Friday quizzes for which information is memorized the night before, and for which students are ranked compared to their peers. Rather, they combine teacher feedback to students' answers and comments in class discussions, modeled responses for written assignments, and teacher comments on student work and quizzes that measure deep understanding of the topics being studied. Their purpose is to promote knowledge construction, not to grade or rank students according to their performance.

Assessment was an integral part of the teaching-learning process in David's, Darren's, and Sam's lessons. David's homework (the questions about the planets), for example, required an application of sophisticated schemas. In addition, feedback and discussion of the homework would further increase schema production.

Darren was able to assess her students' understanding at various points in her American history lesson by asking questions in both the comprehension-monitoring and integration phases. In each instance, her assessments helped her decide if she could continue the lesson as planned, or if she needed to reteach some parts of the topic.

Assessment was also an integral part of Sam's lesson on two-digit addition. Students' answers to his questions as he worked to develop understanding gave him a measure of their developing schemas to that point, and he carefully monitored their work as they began the practice that ultimately led to automaticity. Both kinds of assessment provided him with the information he needed to make instructional decisions.

The Importance of Alignment

Instructional alignment is *the match between goals, learning activities, and assessments.*

> Without this alignment, it is difficult to know what is being learned. Students may be learning valuable information, but one cannot tell unless there is alignment between what they are learning and the assessment of that learning. Similarly, students may be learning things that others don't value unless curricula and assessments are aligned with the broad learning goals of communities. (Bransford et al., 2000, pp. 151–152)

Alignment helps students understand what is important to learn and helps teachers match instructional strategies and assessments to learning goals. Instruction was aligned in David's, Darren's and Sam's lessons. Each had a clear goal in mind, their learning activities remained focused on the goal, and assessment of the students' learning progress was ongoing.

Maintaining alignment is a challenge. For instance, if a teacher's goal is for students to be able to write effectively, yet learning activities focus on isolated grammar skills, the instruction is out of alignment. It is similarly out of alignment if the goal is for students to apply math concepts, but the learning activities have students practicing computation problems. The question instructional alignment encourages teachers to ask is, "What does my goal (e.g., "apply math concepts") actually mean, and do my learning and assessment activities actually lead to the goal?"

Putting Information Processing Into Perspective

Information processing was the most influential cognitive learning theory in the 20th century (Mayer, 1998b). It has, however, been criticized for failing to adequately consider personal factors in learning, such as students' emotions (Derry, 1992; Mayer, 1996), and the social context in which learning occurs (Greeno et al., 1996). Critics also argue that information processing doesn't adequately emphasize the extent to which learners construct their own understanding, one of the principles of cognitive learning theory stated at the beginning of the chapter (Derry, 1992). (We examine the process of knowledge construction in detail in Chapter 8.)

However, virtually all cognitive descriptions of learning, including those endorsing the principle that learners construct understanding, accept the architecture of information processing, including, for example, a limited-capacity working memory, a long-term memory, cognitive processes that move the information from one store to another, and the regulatory mechanisms of metacognition (Hunt & Ellis, 1999; Mayer, 1998b; Sternberg, 1999; Sweller et al., 1998). These components of our cognitive architectures help us explain learning events that neither behaviorism nor social cognitive theory can explain. Further, they help provide a framework for the process of constructing understanding, which you will see in your study of the next chapter.

Summary

Cognitive Perspectives on Learning

Although elements of cognitive learning theory have a long history, what is commonly termed the "cognitive revolution" occurred at about the middle of the 20th century. Cognitive views of learning evolved, in part, because behaviorism was unable to explain complex phenomena such as language learning and problem solving as well as a number of everyday events, such as why people respond differently to the same stimulus.

Cognitive learning theory assumes that learners are active in their attempts to understand the world, new understanding depends on prior learning, learners construct understanding, and learning is a change in people's mental structures rather than a change in observable behavior.

Information Processing

Information processing is a cognitive view of learning that compares human thinking to the way computers process information. Information stores—sensory memory, working memory, and long-term memory—hold information; cognitive processes, such as attention, perception, rehearsal, encoding, and retrieval, move the information from one store to another.

Information received by sensory memory is moved to working memory through the processes of attention and perception. Working memory, with its limited capacity, can easily be overloaded and become a bottleneck to further processing. The capacity of working memory can, in effect, be increased through chunking, by making aspects of processing automatic, and by capitalizing on its dual-processing capabilities.

Information processing theory assumes that knowledge is encoded in long-term memory in complex interrelationships (schemas) of declarative knowledge (knowledge of facts, concepts, and other ideas) and procedural knowledge (knowledge of how to perform operations, such as how to write an essay). Information processing is governed by metacognition—a person's awareness of and control over the processes that move information from one store to another. As metacognitive knowledge and skills improve, learners develop the capacity for self-regulation.

Information Processing in the Classroom: Instructional Strategies

Teachers apply information processing in their classrooms when they help students acquire declarative and procedural knowledge. Schema production is an effective instructional strategy for helping students acquire integrated declarative knowledge and is accomplished in three cyclical steps that involve acquiring information, checking comprehension, and integrating knowledge. Procedural knowledge can be developed in strategies that include review and presentation to activate background knowledge and develop understanding, which is followed by practice that leads to automaticity.

Assessment is an essential component of the teaching-learning process. It gives teachers information about students' understanding and provides students with feedback about their learning progress.

Windows on Classrooms

In the opening case study, David Shelton planned and conducted his lesson in an effort to make the information meaningful for his students. In the following case, a teacher conducts a lesson with a group of high school students studying the novel *The Scarlet Letter*. Read the case study, and then answer the questions that follow.

Sue Southam, an English teacher at Highland High School, wanted her students to examine timeless issues, such as moral dilemmas involving personal responsibility and emotions like guilt, anger, loyalty, and revenge.

She decided to use Nathaniel Hawthorne's *The Scarlet Letter* as the vehicle to help her reach her goals. The novel, set in Boston in the 1600s, describes a tragic and illicit love affair between the heroine (Hester Prynne) and a minister (Arthur Dimmesdale). The novel's title refers to the letter *A*, meaning "adulterer," which the Puritan community makes Hester wear as punishment for her adultery. The class had been discussing the book for several days; the focus for the current lesson was Reverend Dimmesdale's character.

Sue began by reviewing the novel's plot to date.

She then asked about Hester's illicit lover. When the class identified Dimmesdale as the father of Hester's baby, Sue challenged them by asking, "How do you know the baby is Dimmesdale's? What are the clues in the text in Chapter 3? . . . Nicole?"

"He acted very withdrawn. He doesn't want to look her in the face and doesn't want to be involved in the situation."

"Okay, anything else, any other clues?"

"The baby . . . it points at Reverend Dimmesdale."

"Good observation. That is a good clue."

After several more comments, Sue paused and said, "I'd like to read a passage to you from the text describing Dimmesdale. Listen carefully, and then I'd like you to do something with it."

After reading the paragraph, Sue continued, "In your logs, jot down some of the important characteristics in that description. If you were going to draw a portrait of him, what would he look like? Try to be as specific as possible. Try that now."

Sue gave the students a few minutes to write in their logs and then continued by saying, "Let's see whether we can find out more about the Dimmesdale character through his actions. I'd like you to listen carefully while I read the speech by Reverend Dimmesdale in which he confronts Hester Prynne in front of the congregation and exhorts her to identify her secret lover and partner in sin. Think about both Dimmesdale's and Hester's thoughts while I'm reading."

She read Dimmesdale's speech, and after she finished, she divided the class into "Dimmesdales" and "Hesters" around the room.

Then she said, "Dimmesdales, in your logs I want you to tell me what Dimmesdale is really thinking during this speech. . . . Hesters, I want you to tell me what Hester is thinking while she listens to Dimmesdale's speech. Write in your logs in your own words the private thoughts of your character. Do that right now, and then we'll come back together in a few minutes."

After giving the students a few minutes to write in their logs, she organized them into groups of four, with each group composed of two Hesters and two Dimmesdales. Once students were settled, she said, "In each group, I want you to start off by having Dimmesdale tell what he is thinking during the first line of the speech. Then I'd like a Hester to respond. Then continue with Dimmesdale's next line, and then Hester's reaction. Go ahead and share your thoughts in your groups."

She gave students 5 minutes to share their perspectives, then called the class back together: "Okay, let's hear it. A Dimmesdale first. Just what was he thinking during his speech? . . . Mike?"

"The only thing I could think of was, 'Oh God, help me. I hope she doesn't say anything. If they find out it's me, I'll be ruined.' And then here comes Hester with her powerful speech," Mike concluded, turning to his partner in the group, Nicole.

"I wrote, 'Good man, huh. So why don't you confess then? You know you're guilty. I've admitted my love, but you haven't. Why don't you just come out and say it?'" Nicole added.

"Interesting. . . . What else? How about another Hester? . . . Sarah?"

"I just put, 'No, I'll never tell. I still love you, and I'll keep your secret forever,'" Sarah offered.

Sue paused for a moment, looked around the room, and commented, "Notice how different the two views of Hester are. Nicole paints her as very angry, whereas Sarah views her as still loving him." Sue again paused to look for reactions. Karen raised her hand, and Sue nodded to her.

"I think the reason Hester doesn't say anything is that people won't believe her because he's a minister," Karen suggested. "She's getting her revenge just by being there reminding him of his guilt."

"But if she accuses him, won't people expect him to deny it?" Brad added.

"Maybe he knows she won't accuse him because she still loves him," Julie offered.

"Wait a minute," Jeff interrupted, gesturing with his hands. "I don't think he's such a bad guy. I think he feels guilty about it all, but he just doesn't have the courage to admit it in front of all of those people."

"I think he's really admitting it in his speech but is asking her secretly not to tell," Caroline added. "Maybe he's really talking to Hester and doesn't want the rest of the people to know."

The class continued, with students debating the hidden meaning in the speech and trying to decide whether Reverend Dimmesdale is really a villain or a tragic figure.

"Interesting ideas," Sue said as the end of the class neared. "And who haven't we talked about yet? . . . Sherry?"

". . . Hester Prynne's husband?"

". . . Who's been missing for several years," Sue added.

"Tomorrow, I'd like you to read Chapter 4, in which we meet Hester's husband. That's all for today. Please put the desks back. . . . Thank you."

Constructed Response Questions

In answering these questions, use information from the chapter and link your responses to specific information in the case.

1. Assess the extent to which Sue applied the principles of cognitive learning theory in her lesson. Include both strengths and weaknesses in your assessment.

2. Assess the extent to which Sue applied information processing theory in her lesson. Include both strengths and weaknesses in your assessment.

3. Which cognitive process from information processing theory was most prominent in Sue's lesson? Explain.

4. Identify at least one instance in Sue's lesson in which she focused on declarative knowledge. Identify another in which she focused on procedural knowledge. Was the *primary* focus of Sue's lesson the acquisition of declarative knowledge or procedural knowledge?

PRAXIS These exercises are designed to help you prepare for the PRAXIS™ "Principles of Learning and Teaching" exam. To receive feedback on your constructed response questions and document analysis response, go to the Companion Website at *www.prenhall.com/eggen*, then to this chapter's *Practice for PRAXIS™* module. For additional connections between this text and the PRAXIS™ exam, go to Appendix A.

Document-Based Analysis

After her lesson, Sue prepared the following assessment.

Even though The Scarlet Letter was set in a Puritan community centuries ago, the moral dilemmas of personal responsibility and consuming emotions of guilt, anger, loyalty, and revenge are timeless. Describe how these dilemmas and emotions were illustrated in the novel, and support your conclusions with details from the novel.

Analyze Sue's assessment based on the case study and the content of the chapter. Include both strengths and weaknesses of her assessment.

Also on the Companion Website at *www.prenhall.com/eggen*, you can measure your understanding of chapter content in *Practice Quiz* and *Essay* modules, apply concepts in *Online Cases,* and broaden your knowledge base with the *Additional Content* module and *Web Links* to other educational psychology websites.

Online Portfolio Activities

To develop your professional portfolio, further apply your understanding of chapter content, and address the INTASC standards, go to the Companion Website, then to this chapter's *Online Portfolio Activities.* Complete the suggested activities.

Important Concepts

analogies *(p. 254)*
attention *(p. 248)*
automaticity *(p. 242)*
chunking *(p. 241)*
cognitive learning theories *(p. 237)*
cognitive load theory *(p. 241)*
cognitive processes *(p. 239)*
declarative knowledge *(p. 243)*
dual-coding theory *(p. 253)*
dual processing *(p. 242)*
elaboration *(p. 254)*
encoding *(p. 251)*
forgetting *(p. 256)*
imagery *(p. 253)*
information processing *(p. 238)*
information stores *(p. 239)*
instructional alignment *(p. 272)*
interference *(p. 257)*

learning *(p. 238)*
levels of processing *(p. 256)*
long-term memory *(p. 243)*
meaningfulness *(p. 251)*
metacognition *(p. 239)*
metamemory *(p. 259)*
mnemonic devices *(p. 254)*
model *(p. 238)*
organization *(p. 251)*
perception *(p. 250)*
procedural knowledge *(p. 243)*
rehearsal *(p. 250)*
retrieve *(p. 257)*
schemas *(p. 243)*
scripts *(p. 244)*
sensory memory *(p. 240)*
strategies *(p. 259)*
working memory *(p. 240)*

Constructing
Understanding

8

Jenny Newhall, a fourth-grade teacher, wanted her students to understand the principle behind beam balances—that they balance when the weight times the distance on one side of the fulcrum equals the weight times the distance on the other. She began the lesson by dividing the students into groups of four, giving each group a balance with a numerical scale and presenting the following problem:

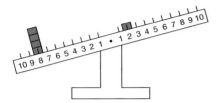

Jenny told the students that they were to figure out how to balance the beam, but *before adding tiles to the actual balances,* they needed to write down possible solutions on paper and convince their groupmates that their solutions would work. The class went to work.

An interviewer from the nearby university was visiting the class that day, and he sat in the back observing the students. Jenny circulated around the room a while and then joined one of the groups—Molly, Suzanne, Tad, and Drexel—as the students were attempting to solve the problem.

Suzanne began by offering, "There are 4 on the 8 and 1 on the 2. I want to put 3 on the 10 so there will be 4 on each side."

Here's the solution she proposed to her group:

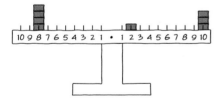

Molly agreed with Suzanne's proposal, but she offered the following reasoning for the same solution: "I think we should put 3 on 10, because 4 on the 8 is 32 on one side. And since we only have 2 on the other side, we need to make them equal. So 3 on 10 would equal 30, and so we'd have 32 on both sides."

The groups continued to discuss their solutions for several minutes, and then Jenny instructed the students to try out their ideas on the actual balances. She reassembled the class and called for a student with a successful solution to come to the board and explain it. A sketch of the beam balance appeared on the chalkboard.

Mavrin volunteered and wrote out his ideas on the sketch:

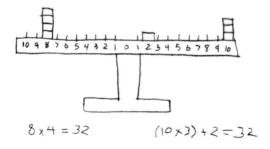

$8 \times 4 = 32$ $\qquad$ $(10 \times 3) + 2 = 32$

Jenny reviewed Mavrin's solution, thinking out loud as she proceeded, "Over on this side he wrote 8 times 4 equals 32, because he had 4 tiles on the 8. Then, when he started out with the 2 over here, he needed something that added up to 30, so he came over here and put 3 on the 10. He has an excellent number sentence up here. . . . Ten times 3 equals 30, plus 2 more equals 32."

Jenny continued by giving the students two additional problems and assigned some homework.

Following the lesson, the interviewer talked with some of the students to assess their thinking and understanding. He focused his interview on Molly, Suzanne, Tad, and Drexel and began by giving them another problem for the beam balance.

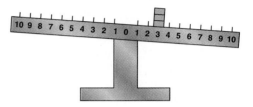

After giving the students some time to consider the problem, the interviewer said, "Suzanne, go ahead and offer a solution."

"What I did was 2 plus 3 equals 5" she responded, pointing to the right side of the beam, "and 2 plus 1 plus 2 equals 5." She pointed to the left side.

Here's her proposed solution:

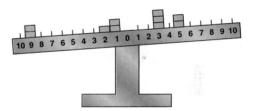

The interviewer then asked, "Molly, what do you think of that solution?"

"It won't work. . . . It doesn't matter how many blocks there are," Molly answered, shaking her head. "It's where they're put."

"Okay, what do you think, Drexel?"

Drexel shook his head no.

"Why don't you think so?"

"Because of Molly's reasoning," Drexel answered, motioning toward Molly. "It doesn't matter how many blocks you have; it's where you put them."

"Tad, how about you? . . . What do you think?"

"Same as them, I guess," Tad responded hesitantly.

The students tried Suzanne's solution, and the beam tipped to the left.

"If you took 1 off the 9, it might work," Suzanne suggested.

"Why do you think that'll work?"

"Because that's the farthest to the end, and sometimes the farthest to the end brings it down more."

"So, if it's farther to the end it brings it down more than if it's not so far to the end?" the interviewer repeated.

The interviewer then gave the students the following additional problem and asked for solutions:

Molly offered, "Put 1 on the 8 and 4 on the 1."

"That's what Molly thinks," the interviewer nodded. "What do you think? Tad?"

"Yeah," Tad answered slowly.

"You do think it'll work. . . . Now give us a nice, clear explanation for why it'll work," the interviewer smiled.

"Okay," Tad began, peering intently at the balance for several seconds. Then he began slowly, "Oh, okay, you put it on a times table. . . . Three times 4 is 12, . . . and 4 times 1 is 4, . . . and 8 times 1 is 8, and 8 plus 4 is 12."

"And so it should work, you think. . . . Suzanne, what do you think?"

". . . I think it'll work."

"You think it'll work . . .," the interviewer repeated. "Okay, who has another solution?"

"One on the 2 and 1 on the 10," Drexel said quickly.

"Okay, I want you to tell us whether or not that'll work, Suzanne."

". . . I think it will."

"Okay, explain why you think it will."

"Because . . . 10 times 1 equals 10," Suzanne began hesitantly, "and 2 times 1 equals 2, and 10 plus 2 equals 12. . . . So it'll be even."

"Okay, Tad what do you think?"

"Um, yeah because it's the same thing as last time. It adds up to 12. Ten times 1 is 10, and 2 times 1 is 2, and 10 and 2 are 12," Tad explained.

The interviewer then tried the solution out on the beam balance and asked, "What do you think, Tad?"

"Perfect," Tad grinned.

"Perfect," the interviewer laughed, finishing the interview.

I n Chapter 7, you saw that "Learners construct, rather than record, understanding" is a basic principle of cognitive learning theory. As with all learning theories, views of knowledge construction vary, and these views interpret the principle in different ways. In this chapter, we examine different interpretations of the knowledge construction process, aspects on which most researchers agree, and the implications they have for learners and teachers.

After you've completed your study of this chapter, you should be able to

- ▪ Identify the essential elements of constructivist views of learning
- ▪ Describe differences between social constructivist and cognitive constructivist perspectives
- ▪ Explain how knowledge construction and learners' cognitive architectures are related
- ▪ Describe classroom applications grounded in knowledge construction frameworks

To begin our study of this chapter, let's look again at the thinking of the students in Jenny's lesson and consider three questions:

- ▪ Suzanne concluded, "There are 4 on the 8 and 1 on the 2. I want to put 3 on the 10 so there will be 4 on each side." Her conclusion was valid, but her thinking wasn't. How did she arrive at this conclusion?
- ▪ Considering that all the group members had similar experiences during the lesson, why were Molly and Drexel able to reason correctly when Suzanne was not?
- ▪ Tad's and Suzanne's understanding of what made the beam balance evolved during the interview. Both students demonstrated little change during the lesson itself. Why?

We try to answer these questions in this chapter.

What Is Constructivism?

Constructivism is a broad term that is used in different ways by philosophers, teachers, educational psychologists, and others (D. Phillips, 2000). Philosophers, for example, debate questions about reality, the validity of understanding, and whether or not misconceptions exist. At one end of the philosophical continuum, a *radical constructivist* perspective suggests that "no individual's viewpoint thus constructed should be viewed as inherently distorted or less correct than another's" (Derry, 1992, p. 415). In other words, because individuals construct forms of understanding that make sense to them, those individual interpretations of the world are as valid as any others. This is an interesting issue for philosophers, but it's a problem for educators. If all understanding is equally good, "we might just as well let students continue to believe whatever they believe" (Moshman, 1997, p. 230).

For teachers, constructivism raises questions about the appropriateness of different goals, approaches to instruction, and assessment. Issues related to teaching include if and when teachers should intervene as students head down "blind alleys," how much information students should memorize, and the most effective ways to assess understanding. We examine these more pragmatic questions in this chapter.

For educational psychologists, **constructivism** is *a view of learning suggesting that learners construct their own understanding of the topics they study rather than having that understanding transmitted to them by some other source* (such as another person or something they read) (Bransford et al., 2000; Bruning et al., 1999).

This definition helps us understand Suzanne's thinking. Suzanne didn't get her solution from Jenny, another teacher, or something she read: She "constructed" the conclusion on her own. Constructivism adds to our understanding of learning, because no other theory—alone—can explain Suzanne's reasoning. It is unlikely that she had been reinforced for this thinking, as a behaviorist explanation would require, and it's equally unlikely that it had been modeled for her, so social cognitive theory can't provide an explanation either. And information processing doesn't directly address the issue of learners' unique constructions and misconceptions. Suzanne's thinking illustrates the principle that learners construct, rather than record, understanding. The principle has enormous implications for teachers, as we'll see later in the chapter.

Constructivism suggests that learners construct their own understanding rather than having it transmitted by some other source.

> **8.1**
> Think about your study of Chapter 7. Where in our information processing systems does the process of constructing understanding occur? In what form does the understanding that's constructed exist, and where is it stored? Explain.

Different Views of Constructivism

We said that views of knowledge construction vary (Bruning et al., 1999; Greeno et al., 1996). The emphasis theorists place on different aspects of the knowledge construction process, and particularly social interaction, is the primary source of this variation. We examine two positions.

Cognitive constructivism, which is based largely on Piaget's work, *focuses on individual, internal constructions of knowledge* (Greeno et al., 1996; Meter & Stevens, 2000; Nuthall, 1999a). Cognitive constructivism stresses individuals' search for meaning as they interact with the environment and test and modify existing schemas (Packer & Goicoechea, 2000). Social interaction is important, but primarily as a catalyst for individual cognitive conflict (Fowler, 1994). When one child suggests an idea that causes disequilibrium in another, for example, the second child resolves the disequilibrium by individually reconstructing his or her understanding.

Social constructivism, which is strongly influenced by Vygotsky's (1978) work, *suggests that knowledge is first constructed in a social context and is then appropriated by individuals* (Bruning et al., 1999; M. Cole, 1991; Nuthall, 1999a). According to social constructivists, the process of sharing individual perspectives—sometimes called *collaborative elaboration* (Meter & Stevens, 2000)—results in learners constructing understanding together that wouldn't be possible alone (Greeno et al., 1996).

To see how these positions differ, let's begin by listening to two children on a playground:

> Devon: (Holding a beetle between his fingers and pointing at a spider) Look at the bugs.
>
> Gino: Yech. . . . Put that thing down. (gesturing to the spider) Besides, that's not a bug. It's a spider.
>
> Devon: What do you mean? A bug is a bug. They look the same.
>
> Gino: Nope. Bugs have six legs. See. (touching the legs of the beetle) He has eight legs. . . . Look. (pointing to the spider)
>
> Devon: So, . . . bugs . . . have . . . six legs, and spiders have eight? Hmm?

Cognitive constructivists would interpret this episode by saying that Devon's equilibrium was disrupted as a result of the discussion, and—individually—he resolved the problem by reconstructing his thinking to accommodate the evidence Gino pointed out. Social constructivists, in contrast, would argue that Devon's understanding was increased as a direct result of the exchange with Gino. They would also assert that the dialogue, itself, played an essential role in helping Devon arrive at a clearer understanding of insects and spiders.

What do these positions have to do with teachers and teaching? A literal interpretation of cognitive constructivism emphasizes learning activities that are experience based and discovery oriented. According to this position, for example, children learn math ideas more effectively if they discover the ideas while manipulating concrete objects such as blocks and sticks, rather than if the ideas are presented by a teacher or other expert (Pressley, Harris, & Marks, 1992).

This interpretation posed a dilemma for educators who first learned of it because it "fundamentally distrusted all attempts to instruct directly" (Resnick & Klopfer, 1989, p. 3). The interpretation suggests that teacher-student interaction is important for learner growth but that teachers need to guard against imposing their thoughts and values on developing learners (DeVries, 1997). Direct instruction should be minimal. So, other than providing materials and a supportive learning environment, what is the teacher's role? This question hasn't been satisfactorily answered (Airasian & Walsh, 1997; Greeno et al., 1996).

A social constructivist interpretation helps resolve the dilemma. From this perspective, Devon's understanding was increased as a direct result of the exchange with Gino, so it "does not suggest that educators get out of the way so children can do their natural work, as Piagetian theory often seemed to imply" (Resnick & Klopfer, 1989, p. 4). Social constructivism highlights teachers' roles and suggests that they consider all the traditional questions of teaching: how to organize and implement learning activities, motivate students, and assess learning. The answers, however, focus on facilitating students' constructions of understanding through social interaction (Greeno et al., 1996; Shuell, 1996). According to social constructivism, creating situations in which learners can exchange ideas and collaborate in solving problems is an important teacher role (R. Anderson et al., 2001; Meter & Stevens, 2000).

Characteristics of Constructivism

Despite their differences, most constructivists agree on four characteristics that influence learning (Bruning et al., 1999; Mayer, 1996). They're outlined in Figure 8.1 and discussed in the sections that follow.

Learners Construct Understanding That Makes Sense to Them

As we first saw in Chapter 7, learners constructing understanding is an accepted principle of all cognitive learning theory. Among theorists, "the view of the learner has changed from that of a recipient of knowledge to that of a constructor of knowledge"

8.2
Would information processing theory support the contention that learners should discover math facts, such as 6 × 9 = 54? Explain, using the characteristics of working memory as a basis for your explanation.

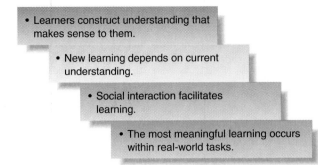

Figure 8.1 Characteristics of constructivism

- Learners construct understanding that makes sense to them.
- New learning depends on current understanding.
- Social interaction facilitates learning.
- The most meaningful learning occurs within real-world tasks.

(Mayer, 1998b, p. 359). Learners are not tape recorders; they don't record and store in their memories an exact copy of what they hear or read. Rather, they interpret stimuli on the basis of what they already know, and they construct understanding that makes sense to them (Nuthall, 2001).

We saw this process in Jenny's students, and cognitive constructivism helps us understand the growth in Suzanne's thinking. She had a clear (to her) schema that guided her thinking. For her, it made sense to think that having an equal number of tiles on each side of the fulcrum would cause the beam to balance. She retained that view, as indicated by her thinking at the beginning of the interview, and it changed only after her observations of the beam balance, the interviewer's questions, and Molly's and Drexel's comments led her to confront it directly. Ideas introduced during the discussion caused cognitive conflict and resulted in reconstruction of her understanding.

Social constructivism helps explain changes in Tad's thinking. His uncertain response, "Same as them, I guess," when the interviewer asked him what he thought about Molly's and Drexel's thinking, suggested that he didn't have a schema that guided his reasoning. He initially depended on the ideas of the others, and his understanding increased as a direct result of the exchange.

8.3
Learners are often very reluctant to modify their existing understanding of the way the world works. Using Piaget's work as a basis, explain this reluctance.

New Learning Depends on Current Understanding

We described the role of current understanding (background knowledge) when we discussed the importance of making information meaningful in Chapter 7. Constructivists go further, emphasizing that new learning is interpreted in the immediate context of current understanding. For instance, learners commonly conclude that summer is warmer than winter (in the Northern Hemisphere) because Earth is closer to the Sun in summer. This makes sense. The closer to a candle or a hot burner we hold our hands, the warmer they feel; therefore, based on this experience, our conclusion that we're closer to the Sun makes more sense than the actual explanation involving the tilt of Earth's axis. An understanding of the seasons is constructed in the context of experience with candles and stove burners.

The influence of background knowledge helps answer our second question: "Considering that all the group members had similar experiences during the lesson, why were Molly and Drexel able to reason correctly when Suzanne was not?" The answer is simple. Molly and Drexel had background knowledge that Suzanne lacked. *Why* they had greater background knowledge is uncertain and could depend on a number of factors, such as more experiences provided by parents, other caregivers or teachers, greater motivation, or higher ability. Examples of differences in background knowledge are common, and constructivism helps us understand why students reason as they do. No other theory is able to provide this understanding.

Social Interaction Facilitates Learning

Social interaction, interpreted from either a cognitive or social constructivist perspective, is widely accepted as important, and Jenny's lesson illustrates its influence on learning. Suzanne, for example, had a clear schema that guided her thinking, and she retained this understanding in spite of hearing correct explanations offered by Molly, Mavrin, and

Jenny during the lesson. But when the interviewer directly challenged her thinking, the interaction helped change her reasoning. Tad's experience was similar. Most of his understanding evolved during the interview when he was more actively involved in the discussion. We discuss the importance of interaction in more detail when we examine the implications of constructivism for teachers.

Meaningful Learning Occurs Within Real-World Tasks

Think about Jenny's lesson again. She used concrete materials to help her students advance their current understanding of beams that balance, and the knowledge they gained could later increase their understanding of teeter totters and force and resistance in many everyday tools that are levers. The lesson used a **real-world task** (often called an *authentic* task), *a learning activity that develops understanding similar to understanding that would be used outside the classroom.* In these tasks, students practice thinking through situations (Needels & Knapp, 1994). *Thinking* is the key: "Authentic activities foster the kinds of thinking and problem-solving skills that are important in out-of-school settings, whether or not the activities themselves mirror what practitioners do" (Putnam & Borko, 2000, pp. 4–5). This means that a history class examining the impact of Harriet Beecher Stowe's *Uncle Tom's Cabin* on the American Civil War, and an English class considering the historical literary significance of *Beowulf*, are also involved in authentic activities if they make students' thinking visible.

Implications of Constructivism for Teaching

Because all learners construct understanding that makes sense to them, individuals' conceptions of the topics they study will vary, sometimes dramatically. What can teachers do to accommodate these differences? We examine this question next.

The Teacher's Role in Constructivist Classrooms

In classrooms where instruction is grounded in constructivism, the focus shifts from teachers to students, because students are the ones constructing understanding. The teacher's role is to get "students to take responsibility for their own learning, to be autonomous thinkers, to develop integrated understandings of concepts, and to pose—and seek to answer—important questions" (Brooks & Brooks, 1993, p. 13). This is certainly a worthwhile ideal. However, it is sometimes misinterpreted to suggest that teachers shouldn't establish clear goals prior to instruction or shouldn't intervene when students struggle or develop misconceptions. Doing so, according to this view, makes the teacher an authority figure, reduces learner autonomy, or bases instruction on behaviorist learning theory. Constructivists discount this interpretation:

Having learning goals clearly specified ahead of time and challenging students to meet them doesn't mean . . . that teachers should always and only engage in "teaching by telling," or that teachers should not take care in dealing with students' mistakes. It is clearly wrong for teachers to simply assert their authority and use humiliating tactics with a student who gives a mistaken answer to "What's the square root of 9?" And it's pedagogically ineffective not to explore why

Teachers play a crucial role in guiding learners' knowledge construction.

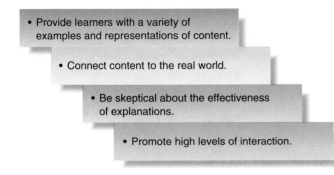

Figure 8.2 Suggestions for classroom practice

- Provide learners with a variety of examples and representations of content.
- Connect content to the real world.
- Be skeptical about the effectiveness of explanations.
- Promote high levels of interaction.

8.4
Which idea in the Howe and Berv excerpt is most important for teachers who base their instruction on constructivist views of learning? Explain.

the student got the answer he did. But it's also wrong not to correct the student's error judiciously but unequivocally. (Howe & Berv, 2000, p. 38)

In constructivist classrooms, teachers still play a central role in guiding students' learning.

Teachers who base their instruction on constructivist views of learning have clear goals, and their instruction is aligned, as is all effective instruction (Bransford et al., 2000). And they judiciously intervene when students struggle (A. Brown & Campione, 1994; Howe & Berv, 2000). They do, however, go beyond what has historically been traditional teaching in several ways. Let's look at them.

Suggestions for Classroom Practice

Knowing that learners construct—instead of record—understanding has important implications for the way we teach. In the following sections, we explore four suggestions for classroom practice. They're also outlined in Figure 8.2.

Provide a Variety of Examples and Representations of Content

We emphasized the importance of prior understanding in both Chapter 7 and in this chapter. So, what can teachers do when students lack sufficient background knowledge?

The answer is simple (but not necessarily easy): *Teachers should supplement existing background knowledge with examples and other representations of content that students can use to construct understanding.* The importance of high-quality examples and other representations of content is impossible to overstate; they are what learners use to construct their understanding (Cassady, 1999; Eggen, 2001). They allow learners to explore ideas from different perspectives; they "criss-cross the conceptual landscape" (Spiro, Feltovich, Jacobson, & Coulson, 1992). Other than "How can I make my goals clear?" perhaps the most basic planning question teachers can ask is "What can I show students or have them do that will illustrate this topic?" In Jenny's lesson, for example, the actual beam balances and the problems she posed were essential if the students were to construct a valid understanding of the principle. The importance of examples and concrete learning activities applies to all topics at all grade levels. Table 8.1 includes some additional illustrations of ways teachers that you've studied in this text have represented their topics.

8.5
We discussed four types of teacher knowledge in Chapter 1: knowledge of content, pedagogical content knowledge, general pedagogical knowledge, and knowledge of learners and learning. Which is best illustrated by a teacher's ability to effectively represent content for learners? Explain.

Technology and Learning: Using Technology to Represent Content. Although high-quality representations are essential, some topics are difficult to illustrate (Mayer, 2001). We can simply drop a paper clip and a ball of clay, for example, to demonstrate that objects of different weights fall at the same rate, but it's virtually impossible to illustrate an object's actual acceleration. Here, technology can be a powerful tool because it allows learners to observe events that can't be seen with the unaided eye. For example, Figure 8.3 illustrates the position of a falling ball at uniform time intervals. We see that the distance between the images increased, indicating that the ball was falling faster and faster. An image like this (perhaps created by time-lapse photography or mapped by a computer) presents an example of acceleration that is virtually impossible to represent in any other way.

Table 8.1 Teachers' representations of content

Teacher and Chapter	Goal	Representations
Jan Davis, Chapter 1	For students to understand decimals	12-ounce soft drink can 16-ounce bottle Liter bottle 6-pack of soft drinks 12-pack of soft drinks 24-can pack
Karen Johnson, Chapter 2	For students to understand *density*	Cotton balls in drink cup Wooden cubes Water and vegetable oil Population density Screen door screen
Jenny Newhall, Chapter 2	For students to understand that air takes up space	Demonstration with drinking glass and paper towel Releasing air bubbles Hands-on experiences
Diane Smith, Chapter 4	For students to understand comparative and superlative adjectives	Three pencils of different lengths combined with sentences written on the board Three hair colors combined with sentences on the board
David Shelton, Chapter 7	For students to understand characteristics of the solar system	Transparencies of a solar system model and of "globs" thrown off by the sun Matrix with characteristics of the planets

Figure 8.3 Illustration of a falling ball

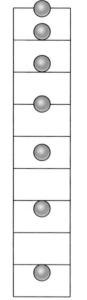

To examine simulations in more depth, you may want to visit several websites where they're discussed in greater detail. Go to the Companion Website at *www.prenhall.com/eggen*, and click on this chapter's *Web Links* module.

As another example, learners can use computer software to simulate a frog dissection, rather than cut up an actual frog. Although the simulation doesn't give students the hands-on experience, it is less expensive because it can be used over and over, it is more flexible because the frog can be "reassembled," and the simulation avoids sacrificing a frog for science.

Animations presented in multimedia formats that combine words and pictures can be effective because they capitalize on the dual-processing capability of working memory. Multimedia animations have helped students understand topics such as the addition and subtraction of signed numbers (Moreno & Mayer, 1998), a car's braking system, the formation of lightning, and the workings of a tire pump (Mayer, 1997, 1998a).

When using technology to support knowledge construction, researchers have found small groups to be an effective supplement, because they give students opportunities to discuss their understanding and build on the ideas of others (Boling & Robinson, 1999; Lou, Abrami, & d'Appollonia, 2001).

Connect Content to the Real World

The more closely connected to the real-world content representations are, the more effective they'll be. Jenny created a real-world problem with the beam balance, and other teachers you've studied in this book did the same. For example, Jan Davis (Chapter 1) used soft drink containers to illustrate how decimals can be used to determine the best buys in supermarkets, Karen Johnson (Chapter 2) used population density and screen door screens to illustrate *density*, and Mike Sheppard (Chapter 5) used a problem with distances from the children's school to teach number operations. Other examples of real-world, or authentic, tasks include social studies students identifying the longitude and latitude of their school, language arts students writing persuasive essays for a school or class newspaper, and science students explaining the need for seatbelts in cars.

Be Skeptical About Explanations

Teaching has historically been viewed as a process of transmitting information to learners, either by teachers or written materials. Although cognitive learning theory, in general, and constructivism, in particular, attempt to dispel this notion, many teachers continue to believe that the most effective way to help learners understand something is to explain it to them (Borko & Putnam, 1996). To promote knowledge construction, teachers need to talk less and listen more to the ideas students are forming (Aulls, 1998).

Teachers shouldn't conclude that learners will not or cannot construct understanding from explanations: "Constructivists assume that all knowledge is constructed from previous knowledge, irrespective of how one is taught . . . even listening to a lecture involves active attempts to construct new knowledge" (Bransford et al., 2000, p. 11). Nor should teachers decide to never explain topics to students. Teachers should combine explanations with hands-on experiences and examples and remember to be skeptical about whether explanations alone have led to learning. You may recall that, in Jenny's lesson, Suzanne and Tad both heard three clear and accurate explanations for the beam balance problem—Molly's, Mavrin's, and Jenny's—yet Suzanne's schema at the beginning of the interview hadn't changed, and Tad hadn't formed a schema for the principle. This brings us to the essential role of social interaction in learning.

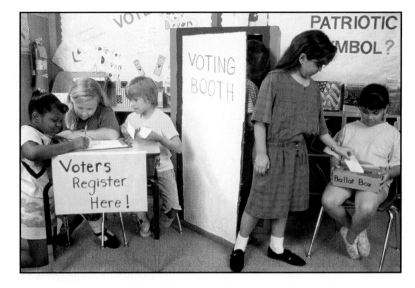

Social interaction embedded within authentic learning tasks provides opportunities for learners to share ideas and analyze and refine their own thinking.

To see a video clip of Molly, Mavrin, and Jenny giving their explanations, go to the Companion Website at *www.prenhall.com/eggen*, then to this chapter's *Classrooms on the Web* module. Click on *Video Clip 8.1.*

Promote High Levels of Interaction

Although essential, effective representations of content won't—by themselves—necessarily produce learning, and we've seen that explaining is often ineffective. This was vividly illustrated in Jenny's lesson. Suzanne's correct solution to Jenny's first problem was a clear example; all the information the students needed to understand the principle was illustrated in it. And, again, explaining didn't work for either Suzanne or Tad. Without the discussion led by the interviewer, Suzanne would have continued to think that the number of tiles on each side of the fulcrum was what made the beam balance, and Tad wouldn't have formed a clear schema. Social interaction is critical to the success of many learning activities.

Social interaction provides learning benefits for the students and instructional benefits for the teacher. They are outlined in Table 8.2 and discussed in the paragraphs that follow.

Learning Benefits for Students. Students benefit from social interaction in at least three ways:

- Sharing ideas
- Appropriating understanding
- Articulating thinking

To see them illustrated, let's look again at the dialogue following the interviewer's first problem.

> **8.6**
> Suzanne focused on the number of tiles and ignored the distance from the fulcrum. What concept from Piaget's theory (in Chapter 2) is illustrated by this kind of thinking? Explain.

Table 8.2 Benefits of social interaction

Description	Example
Benefits to Students	
Sharing ideas	Suzanne, Molly, and Drexel offered ideas, and Suzanne changed her thinking based on the exchange.
Appropriating understanding	By observing Molly's and Drexel's thinking, Tad acquired and internalized an understanding of what made the beam become balanced.
Articulating thinking	The process of putting his thinking into words helped Tad's understanding evolve.
Benefits to Teachers	
Promoting learning	Through questioning, Jenny encouraged students to consider the relationship between length and weight.
Focusing attention	Social interaction guided the attention of Suzanne and Tad as they tried to solve the problem.
Accommodating working memory	Suzanne's and Tad's ideas were encoded as the students articulated them, minimizing the load on working memory.
Assessing learning progress	The interaction in the interview allowed Suzanne's misconception and Tad's lack of understanding to be revealed.

Interviewer:	Suzanne, go ahead and offer a solution.
Suzanne:	What I did was 2 plus 3 equals 5 (pointing to the right side of the beam) and 2 plus 1 plus 2 equals 5 (pointing to the left side).
Interviewer:	Molly, what do you think of that solution?
Molly:	It won't work. . . . It doesn't matter how many blocks there are. It's where they're put.
Interviewer:	Okay, what do you think, Drexel?
Drexel:	(Shakes his head no)
Interviewer:	Why don't you think so?
Drexel:	Because of Molly's reasoning. It doesn't matter how many blocks you have; it's where you put them.
Interviewer:	Tad, how about you? . . . What do you think?
Tad:	(Hesitantly) Same as them, I guess.

The students tried Suzanne's solution, and the beam tipped to the left.

To see a video clip of this interaction, go to the Companion Website at *www.prenhall.com/eggen*, then to this chapter's *Classrooms on the Web* module. Click on *Video Clip 8.2*.

Suzanne:	If you took 1 off the 9, it might work.
Interviewer:	Why do you think that'll work?
Suzanne:	Because that's the farthest to the end, and sometimes the farthest to the end brings it down more.

The opportunity for students to share ideas is perhaps the most powerful outcome of social interaction. Suzanne offered her solution (based on her original schema), Molly and Drexel explained why it wouldn't work, and her understanding of how to balance the beam gradually evolved, as indicated by her suggestion to take one of the tiles off the end.

This socially based process of knowledge construction is sometimes described as occurring from the "outside in" (D. Brenner, 2001). Learners first think collaboratively, building on each others' understanding and negotiating meanings when ideas differ. After understanding is developed in a social environment, individuals can then internalize the knowledge (Meter & Stevens, 2000).

Sharing ideas helps students learn not only *what* to think but also *how* to think and interact productively with others. For example, in one study students were discussing reintroducing wolves into northern forests, and some students spontaneously asked, "Yeah, but what if you were a rancher? Wouldn't you be upset if a wolf came and ate your cattle?" The students demonstrated perspective taking, and other students gradually adopted this way of thinking. Researchers called the spread of reasoning strategies "snowballing" (R. Anderson et al., 2001).

Tad's responses in the interview illustrate the process of *appropriating understanding*—developing new meaning as a direct result of interaction (Leont'ev, 1981). His first comment, "Same as them, I guess," indicated that he didn't have a clear schema for what made the beam balance at the beginning of the interview. He gradually acquired and internalized understanding based on the interaction with Suzanne, Molly, and Drexel.

After appropriating understanding, Tad solidified it by articulating his thinking in an explanation for the interviewer's second problem. The task of putting ideas into words is a cognitively demanding activity (as anyone who has tried to write something can attest) that is especially powerful in promoting learning (Bransford et al., 2000; Mason & Boscolo, 2000). Let's look at some more dialogue.

Molly:	Put 1 on the 8 and 4 on the 1.
Interviewer:	That's what Molly thinks. What do you think? Tad?"
Tad:	(Slowly) Yeah.
Interviewer:	You do think it'll work. . . . Now give us a nice, clear explanation for why it'll work.
Tad:	Okay. (peering intently at the balance for several seconds) Oh, okay, you put it on a times table. . . . Three times 4 is 12, . . . and 4 times 1 is 4, . . . and 8 times 1 is 8, and 8 plus 4 is 12.

To see a video clip of Tad describing his thinking, go to the Companion Website at *www.prenhall.com/eggen*, then to this chapter's *Classrooms on the Web* module. Click on *Video Clip 8.3*.

In the videotape from which the chapter's opening case study was taken, we can almost see "the wheels turning" in Tad's head as he hesitantly describes his understanding.

An understanding of the importance of putting ideas into words also helps answer our third question from early in the chapter: "Tad's and Suzanne's understanding of the principle evolved during the interview. Both demonstrated little change during the lesson itself. Why?" During the whole-class discussion, both students were cognitively passive as Molly, Mavrin, and Jenny provided correct explanations for the problem, whereas they were cognitively active during the interview. They were directly involved in the interaction and needed to respond to Molly's and Drexel's arguments and the interviewer's questions. Putting their developing understanding into words spurred their cognitive activity.

Teachers play a crucial role in ensuring that student interaction results in learning (Webb, Farivar, & Mastergeorge, 2002). For small-group activities, teachers must structure the tasks so that meaning and understanding, versus simply getting the right answer, are emphasized. While the groups work, teachers need to monitor interactions carefully to ensure that ideas are being discussed and explained. Finally, they should

Interactive questioning provides opportunities for teachers to assess students' learning progress.

8.7
In addition to putting students into passive roles, lengthy explanations have at least three other disadvantages. Identify them.

hold students accountable for understanding, not just completing the task, when they conduct or create assessments.

Instructional Benefits for Teachers. Teachers also benefit when students interact with one another or with them. These benefits include

- Promoting learning
- Focusing learners' attention
- Working within students' working memory capacities
- Assessing learning progress

Questioning—a social interaction between teacher and student—plays a major role in instruction grounded in constructivism (Nystrand, Wu, Gamoran, Zeiser, & Long, 2001). Teachers facilitate knowledge construction by asking questions that pose problems, require students to consider existing schemas, and relate specific items of information to each other. Jenny did this in both small-group and whole-group discussions. In addition, the small-group interaction provided opportunities for Jenny's students to ask their own questions, which is particularly powerful in knowledge construction (Nystrand et al., 2001).

We saw the importance of focusing attention in Jenny's lesson and the interview. During the lesson, for example, Suzanne's attention was focused on one aspect of the example—the number of tiles. She didn't direct her attention to the distance from the fulcrum until Molly and Drexel brought it up while discussing her solution during the interview. (Molly said, "It doesn't matter how many blocks there are. It's where they're put.")

In Chapter 7, we saw that working memory limitations are among the most important characteristics of our cognitive architectures. Verbal explanations can quickly overload working memory, which is one reason that they don't work very well. In contrast, students can articulate their understanding only as rapidly as it's being processed; therefore, teachers can accommodate the limitations of students' working memories by encouraging students to put their understanding into words. We saw this illustrated when Tad described his thinking.

Assessment and Learning: The Role of Assessment in Constructivist Classrooms

If teachers are to assist students in the process of knowledge construction, they must understand their students' thinking. To do so, assessment must be ongoing, a feat that can be accomplished only if careful planning has taken place:

> Effectively designed learning environments must also be assessment centered. The key principles of assessment are that they should provide opportunities for feedback and revision and that what is assessed must be congruent with one's learning goals. (Bransford et al., 2000, pp. 139–140)

Students' thinking is the essential feature. As teachers listen to students describe their understanding, they can assess learning progress and the extent to which the students' constructions are valid. This process is a type of informal assessment, through which *information about student understanding is gathered during learning activities.*

Informally assessing students' thinking and understanding is important but incomplete, and it can be misleading. For instance, Jenny knew that Mavrin understood the principle, because she heard him explain it at the board. This, combined with the fact that she explained the principle herself, could lead her to conclude that all the students understood the principle. In fact, however, she knew little about the rest of the students' understanding (and we saw in the interview that Suzanne and Tad did not understand the principle).

Having all students describe their thinking during a lesson is prohibitively time-consuming, so teachers must turn to formal assessment to *systematically gather information about understanding from all learners.* Jenny, a veteran teacher, realized that she didn't have insight into the thinking of each student, so she created two problems for an assessment that she administered to the class the day after the lesson. The assessment, with Tad's responses, is shown in Figure 8.4.

Figure 8.4 Beam balance problems for assessment

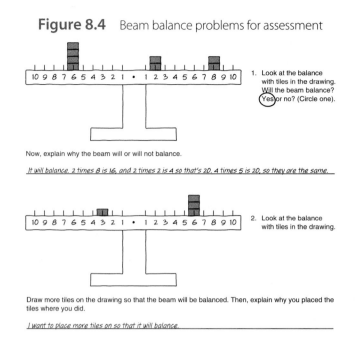

Now, explain why the beam will or will not balance.

It will balance. 2 times 8 is 16, and 2 times 2 is 4 so that's 20. 4 times 5 is 20, so they are the same.

Draw more tiles on the drawing so that the beam will be balanced. Then, explain why you placed the tiles where you did.

I want to place more tiles on so that it will balance.

From the information in Figure 8.4, we can see that Tad's schema for the balanced-beam principle was still "a work in progress." He was able to determine that the beam would balance in the first problem, but he was unable to draw or write a solution to the second problem. His experience was not unique. Jenny's assessment indicated that several of the students in the class were still uncertain about solving problems with beam balances. When well done, formal assessment provides teachers with a look into students' heads, and it gives students feedback and practice with additional problems.

> **8.8**
> Assessments grounded in constructivist views of learning have an essential characteristic. What is this characteristic? Explain.

Classroom Connections

Applying Constructivism in Your Classroom

1. To accommodate differences in background knowledge, provide a variety of representations of the content you want students to understand.

   • *Elementary:* A third-grade teacher doing a unit on chemical and physical change has the students melt ice, crumple paper, dissolve sugar, break toothpicks, and make Kool-Aid to illustrate physical change. She then has them burn paper, pour vinegar into baking soda, and chew soda crackers to illustrate chemical change.

   • *Middle School:* An English teacher working with his students on the concept *internal conflict* presents excerpts such as these:

   Kelly didn't know what to do. She was looking forward to the class trip, but if she went she wouldn't be able to take the scholarship qualifying test.

   Calvin was caught in a dilemma. He saw Jason take Olonzo's calculator but knew that if he told Mrs. Stevens

   what he saw, Jason would realize that it was he who reported the theft.

   • *High School:* While teaching about the Great Depression, a social studies teacher has students read excerpts from *The Grapes of Wrath,* presents a video of people standing in bread lines, shares statistics on the rash of suicides after the stock market crash, and passes out descriptions of Franklin D. Roosevelt's back-to-work programs.

2. Develop learning activities around real-world problems.

   • *Elementary:* In a lesson relating geography and lifestyle, a third-grade teacher has students describe the way they dress for their favorite forms of recreation. She also asks students who have moved from other parts of the country to do the same for their previous locations. She then guides them as they construct an understanding of the effect of geography on lifestyle.

   • *Middle School:* In a unit on percent increase and decrease, a math teacher has students look for examples of marked-down clothes while shopping. He also brings in newspaper ads. The class discusses the examples and calculates the amount saved in each case.

- *High School:* To help her students understand the importance of persuasive writing, an English teacher brings in three examples of "Letters to the Editor." The students discuss the letters, determine which is most effective, and with the teacher's guidance, identify the characteristics of persuasive writing.

3. Promote high levels of interaction, and avoid relying on explanations.

- *Elementary:* A fourth-grade teacher has his students take 8 identical wooden cubes and make one stack of 5 and another stack of 3. He has them discuss the mass, volume, and densities of the two stacks. Then, with questioning, he guides them to conclude that the mass

and volume of the stack of 5 are greater than the mass and volume of the stack of 3 but that the densities of the two stacks are equal.

- *Middle School:* An algebra teacher "walks" students through the solutions to problems by calling on individual students to provide specific information about each step of the solution and explain why a step is necessary. Every time a student has difficulty, the teacher asks additional questions to help students understand the step.

- *High School:* A social studies teacher involved in a lesson comparing the geographies and economies of several countries in the Middle East has students work in groups of three to identify similarities and differences in specific regions. The students develop a chart comparing the different regions, and these charts form the basis for a whole-class discussion.

Constructivism in Classrooms: Instructional Strategies

We have considered the implications of constructivism for classroom practice. We turn now to some specific strategies that, when well done, are grounded in constructivist views of learning. They include

- Guided discovery
- Inquiry
- Classroom discussions
- Cooperative learning

Before we begin, let's see why these strategies have been selected and what they have in common. Earlier in the chapter, we said that learners construct understanding regardless of the teaching method (Bransford et al., 2000). If this is true, and learners construct understanding from a lecture, for example, what makes one strategy a more effective application of constructivism than any other?

We can answer this question by returning to the "Suggestions for Classroom Practice" that we saw earlier in the chapter:

- Provide a variety of examples and other representations of content.
- Connect content to the real world.
- Be skeptical of explanations.
- Promote high levels of interaction.

Our discussion also included an additional suggestion:

- Make assessment an integral part of the teaching-learning process.

These suggestions become the principles that guide teachers as they plan and conduct instruction based on constructivism. Examples and other representations provide background knowledge, and connecting content to the real world capitalizes on the authentic tasks proponents of constructivism endorse. Skepticism about explanations leads to greater use of examples and to an emphasis on social interaction, which in turn makes students' thinking visible and helps learners co-construct understanding. Assessment as an integral part of the teaching-learning process provides teachers with information about the thinking of all the students and makes providing informative feedback possible.

Lecture obviously does not apply these principles. It relies totally on explanation, involves minimal interaction, and doesn't include informal assessment.

The strategies we're recommending here are examples of **learner-centered instruction,** *instruction that pays "careful attention to the knowledge, skills, attitudes, and beliefs that learners bring to the educational setting"* (Bransford et al., 2000, p. 133, italics added).

8.9

Look back at Darren Anderson's (page 264) and Sam Barnett's (page 267) lessons in Chapter 7. Were their lessons learner centered? Explain, using information from this section.

When teachers use learner-centered strategies, they focus as much, or more, on *why* and *how* students arrive at their answers as they do on the answers themselves. Each of the strategies we're including is learner centered and includes the principles that guide teachers as they plan and conduct instruction based on constructivism. (The emphasis on learner-centered instruction has resulted in a number of initiatives, one of the most prominent being the American Psychological Association's *Learner-Centered Psychological Principles* [American Psychological Association Board of Educational Affairs, 1995]).

To see the APA's learner-centered principles, go to the Companion Website at *www.prenhall.com/eggen*, then to this chapter's *Additional Content* module.

Let's look at the specific strategies now.

Guided Discovery

In **guided discovery,** *a teacher identifies a content goal, arranges information so that patterns can be found, and guides students to the goal.* Guided discovery is often contrasted with "pure" or unstructured discovery, such as learners determining, without any help from the teacher, that "light" objects (those less dense than water) float. Unstructured discovery is less effective than guided approaches (Hardiman, Pollatsek, & Weil, 1986; Schauble, 1990) because, without help, students often become lost and frustrated, and this confusion can lead to misconceptions (A. Brown & Campione, 1994). In addition, false starts are common, so time isn't used efficiently. As a result, unstructured discovery is rarely seen in today's classrooms, except in student projects and investigations.

When guided discovery is done well, research supports its effectiveness: "Guided discovery may take more or less time than expository instruction, depending on the task, but tends to result in better long-term retention and transfer than expository instruction" (Mayer, 2002, p. 68). The most likely reason for these outcomes is that teachers spend less time explaining—the primary strategy in expository instruction—and more time asking questions, so students have more opportunities to share thinking and articulate understanding (Bay, Staver, Bryan, & Hale, 1992; Hillocks, 1984).

Let's look at the use of guided discovery in a classroom.

> **8.10**
> We said, "When guided discovery is done well, research supports its effectiveness." What is necessary if instruction is "done well"? Explain.

Judy Nelson was beginning a study of longitude and latitude in social studies with her sixth graders. In preparation, she bought a beach ball, found an old tennis ball, and checked her wall maps and globes.

She began by having students identify where they live on the wall map and then said, "Suppose you were hiking in the wilderness and got lost and injured. You have a cell phone, but you need to describe exactly where you are. How might you do that? You have a map of the area with you, but it's a topographic map showing rivers and mountains." As students discussed the problem, they realized that typical ways of locating themselves—such as cities and street signs—wouldn't work.

She continued, "It looks as if we have a problem. We want to be able to tell rescuers exactly where we are, but we don't have a way of doing it. Let's see if we can figure this out."

She then held up the beach ball and globe and asked her students to compare the two. They identified north, south, east, and west on the beach ball, and she drew a circle around the center of the ball, which they identified as the equator. They did the same with the tennis ball, which she then cut in half, allowing them to see the two hemispheres.

Judy continued by drawing other horizontal lines on the beach ball and saying, "Now, compare the lines with each other."

". . . They're all even," Kathy volunteered.

"Go ahead, Kathy. What do you mean by even?" Judy encouraged.

". . . They don't cross each other," Kathy explained, motioning with her hands.

"Okay," Judy nodded, smiling.

Discovery-oriented lessons provide authentic learning tasks for students.

Judy asked for and got additional comparisons, such as, "The lines all run east and west," and, "They get shorter as they move away from the equator." Judy wrote them on the chalkboard. After the class was done making comparisons, Judy introduced the term *latitude* to refer to the lines they'd been discussing.

She continued by drawing vertical lines of longitude on the beach ball and identified them as shown below:

Discussion then followed:

Judy:	How do these lines compare with the lines of latitude?
Tricia:	. . . They go all around the ball.
Judy:	Good. And what else?
Elliot:	. . . Length, . . . they're all as long, long as each other, same length.
Thomas:	Lengths of what?
Elliot:	The up-and-down lines and the cross ones.
Judy:	What did we call the cross ones?
Elliot:	. . . Latitude.
Jime:	We said that they got shorter. . . . So how can they be the same length?
Tabatha:	I think those are longer (pointing to the longitude lines).
Judy:	How might we check to see about the lengths?
Jime:	. . . Measure them, the lines, like with a tape or string or something.
Judy:	What do you think of Jime's idea?

The students agreed that it seemed to be a good idea, so Judy helped hold pieces of string in place while Jime wrapped them around the ball at different points, and the class compared the lengths.

Chris:	They're the same (holding up two "longitude" strings).
Nicole:	Not these (holding two "latitude" strings).

After comparing the strings, Judy then asked students to work in pairs to summarize what they found. They made several conclusions, which Judy helped them rephrase. Then she wrote the following conclusions on the board:

Longitude lines are farthest apart at the equator; latitude lines are the same distance apart everywhere.

Lines of longitude are the same length; latitude lines get shorter north and south of the equator.

Lines of longitude intersect each other at the poles; lines of latitude and longitude intersect each other all over the globe.

Judy continued, asking, "Now, how does this help us solve our problem of identifying an exact location?" With some guidance, the class concluded that location can be pinpointed by where the lines cross. She noted that this is what they'll focus on the next day. (From Eggen, Paul, & Kauchak, Don, *Strategies for Teachers: Teaching Content and Thinking Skills*, 4/e. Published by Allyn and Bacon, Boston, MA. Copyright © 2001 by Pearson Education. Adapted by permission of the publisher.)

Let's look at Judy's lesson now and examine the extent to which she applied the constructivist principles (the "Suggestions for Classroom Practice"). Four aspects of her lesson are important:

- She began her lesson with a real-world problem, having the students find their exact location if they got lost.

- Because her students lacked background knowledge, she provided it by illustrating longitude and latitude with the beach and tennis balls, the strings, and the globe and maps. The information students needed to understand the concepts was observable in the examples.
- The lesson involved a great deal of social interaction, and the students' thinking was visible throughout. Judy did very little explaining; instead, she guided the students' developing understanding with her questioning.
- Assessment was an integral part of the lesson. As the students' responded, Judy informally assessed their understanding, and she made slight adjustments in the lesson based on the responses. This is an essential part of instruction grounded in constructivist views of learning.

Several of the lessons you've already read about used guided discovery to varying degrees, such as Jenny Newhall's in Chapter 2, and Diane Smith's and Teri Hall's, both in Chapter 4. You may want to refer again to these case studies to further develop your understanding of guided discovery.

Inquiry

Inquiry is *a strategy in which learners gather facts and observations and use them to investigate real-world problems* (Kauchak & Eggen, 2003). The term *inquiry* may seem distant from our everyday living, but in fact, we hear about inquiry problems all the time. For instance, the question of how much exercise is required to provide aerobic benefit is an inquiry problem. The finding that secondhand smoke is harmful is the result of an inquiry investigation. Probes into alleged wrongdoing and attempts to explain catastrophes, such as airline crashes, are inquiry problems. And the conclusion that students learn more in learner-centered than in expository lessons is based on a series of inquiry investigations.

Inquiry typically includes the following steps:

- Identify a question or problem.
- Form hypotheses to answer the question or solve the problem.
- Gather data to test the hypotheses.
- Draw conclusions from the data.
- Generalize on the basis of the conclusions.

Let's look at the use of inquiry in a classroom.

Alfredo Sanchez, a health teacher, was involved in a unit on drugs and drug use. The class had discussed the influence of drugs on the nervous system and the possible overuse of prescription drugs, and the students were now considering over-the-counter medications.

"My dad takes two aspirin every night before he goes to bed," Jacinta offered during the discussion. "Do you think that's bad for him?"

"What kind of aspirin?" Jamie wondered out loud.

"Brand A, I think. . . . Actually, yes, he makes jokes that Brand A is the best."*

"Mr. Sanchez, is Brand A really the best?" Jacinta asked.

"That's an interesting idea," Alfredo nodded. "The company would have us believe that it's the only one that's any good, and more Brand A is sold than any other brand. . . . But do we know if Brand A really is better?"

"My mom takes the cheapest stuff she can find," Luanne shrugged. "We went to the drugstore to get a prescription, and the prescription guy said they're all alike."

"Really interesting!" Alfredo smiled. "Let's see what we can find out about aspirin. . . . Let's think about it for a few minutes. How could we get a handle on whether or not Brand A really is better than another brand, like maybe Brand B? . . . Turn to the person next to you, take 2 minutes, and see if you can come up with some ways of answering that question. We'll brainstorm for a few minutes, and we'll go from there."

---

*The words *Brand A* and *Brand B* have been substituted for the names of the products.

The students talked among themselves for the brief period, Alfredo called them together, and they began to share their ideas.

"We thought we could look at the bottle to see if they have the same stuff in them . . . . If one has more stuff, maybe it's better," Nina offered.

"Good idea," Alfredo nodded. "Who else? . . . Tamara?"

"We could check to see which one dissolved faster, . . . because they talk about how fast they're supposed to work, . . . like if one dissolved faster than another one, it's better."

"Also very good thinking," Alfredo smiled, pleased with the responses.

The class considered additional factors, such as which brand might relieve pain the most quickly and what some experts thought about whether or not different brands varied in quality.

"That's excellent," Alfredo said brightly. "That's really excellent thinking. . . . These are all good hypotheses—our best guesses about how to answer our questions. Let's go to work on them."

Deciding that the class would first focus on the ingredients and the question of which brand dissolved faster, Alfredo organized the students into teams. The next day he brought in four different brands of aspirin, and the teams checked the ingredients. They also dropped samples of each brand into the same amount of water and measured the length of time it took them to dissolve.

The students saw that the ingredients were the same in each brand, and after several trials they found that each dissolved at about the same rate, so they agreed that they would have to reject their ideas about ingredients and dissolving rate.

"It looks like all aspirin are alike," Jacinta commented as the lesson came to a close.

8.11

Identify the places in the lesson where students formed hypotheses, gathered data, drew conclusions from the data, and generalized on the basis of the information.

Alfredo also attempted to apply the constructivist principles. Like Judy, he began with a real-world problem—the question of whether or not one brand of aspirin was better than another. And the fact that the problem evolved from students' questions made it even more meaningful. Students' background knowledge evolved as they formed hypotheses and gathered data. For instance, as part of their investigation, they learned that the ingredients of each brand were the same, and they also learned incidental information about the role and effects of advertising.

A great deal of interaction took place, both in the whole-group discussion and the small-group investigations, and the students' thinking was visible throughout the lesson. As he monitored the students during group work, Alfredo was able to informally assess their understanding, and he provided only enough guidance to ensure that they were making progress.

Discussion

Discussion is another instructional strategy based on constructivist views of learning. **Discussion** is *a strategy designed to stimulate thinking, help learners reconstruct understanding by challenging attitudes and beliefs, and develop interpersonal skills* (Keefer, Zeitz, & Resnick, 2000; Meter & Stevens, 2000). These skills include

- Learning to listen to others
- Developing tolerance for dissenting views
- Learning democratic processes

As with all learning, these skills are developed with practice, and in discussions social interaction is the mechanism that provides that practice. During discussions students are involved in negotiation, co-construction of meaning, and collaborative elaboration, all social constructivist processes (Meter & Stevens, 2000).

We saw earlier that providing examples and other representations of content—to build background knowledge—was one of the principles that each of the strategies attempts to apply. Background knowledge is essential for effective discussions. If it is lacking, they can disintegrate into exchanges of random conjectures, uninformed opinions, and "pooled ignorance." To ensure that background knowledge is adequate, teachers usually teach one or more lessons on the topic before planning a discussion. For example, in Chapter 7 we saw how Darren Anderson provided her students with background knowledge about events leading up to the American Revolutionary War, checked their perceptions of the information she provided, and encouraged schema production by helping them integrate the ideas in the lesson.

Let's look now at how Darren attempts to expand on her earlier lesson to help the students examine their ideas and reconstruct some of them using a discussion as the strategy.

She began, "Today, I'd like us to consider the idea that the British had important advantages over the colonists but wasted them. . . . Think about this idea while I write it on the board."

She wrote

The British advantages during the Revolutionary War should have ensured victory.

"Okay," she went on. "Now that you've had time to think, take a stab at this. . . . Shirley, go ahead."

"I agree," Shirley began. "They had lots of soldiers and guns and equipment. They should have won."

"I agree too," Martha added. "They had more soldiers, and they were . . . real soldiers. And . . . "

"But the soldiers were in the wrong place most of the time," Hank interjected.

"Hold on a second, Hank. That's a good idea, but please give Martha a chance to finish," Darren admonished gently. "Anything else, Martha?"

"Well, . . . I was just going to say that because they were real soldiers, they were better trained."

"Yeah, but the British started the war. You know, we talked about all the taxes, like on tea, and the people in the colonies got mad, because it wasn't fair," Ed added.

"Not really," Joan countered. "I think the colonists started it. They shot first."

"That is an interesting issue," Darren smiled, "but what is the question we're examining here? Ken?"

"If the British should have won the war or not."

"Yes, good, Ken. Let's keep that in mind, everyone. On the other hand, if you want to argue that the issue of who started the war is relevant, please go ahead."

After hesitating briefly, both Ed and Joan shook their heads, indicating that they didn't want to pursue the issue, so Darren continued.

"Now, Hank, what were you saying?"

"Well, even though the British had more soldiers, it didn't always help them."

"Why do you say that, Hank?"

"Well, like we talked about Saratoga. . . . That general . . . Burgoyne, sent a bunch of his soldiers to Philadelphia and wasted them. He was supposed to go to Albany. So, that's what I mean—they didn't seem to be too smart about the way they fought."

"That's an interesting thought, Hank. Jeremy, do you have something to add?"

"Also the British had, . . . those that were paid to fight . . . "

"Mercenaries," Darren added.

"Yeah, mercenaries, they were just being paid to fight, so they didn't fight very hard."

"So, what exactly are you saying?"

"Well, having lots of soldiers isn't necessarily the most important. Like if they didn't really want to fight . . . that would matter. . . . The people in the colonies lived here, so they fought harder, I think."

"Okay! Very good, everyone. Now, return to our question on the board. What other advantages or disadvantages did the British have that influenced the outcome of the war?"

By definition, discussion requires interaction, and interaction was evident throughout Darren's lesson. Also, the students' background knowledge appeared to be adequate, judging from Hank's comment about General Burgoyne wasting the soldiers he sent to Philadelphia and Jeremy's point that mercenaries may have been less motivated than the colonists.

The teacher's role in discussions is to assess both students' thinking and their use of interpersonal skills. When necessary, the teacher provides guidance. Let's look at an example.

Shirley: I agree (that the British should have won.) They had lots of soldiers and guns and equipment. They should have won.

Martha: I agree too. They had more soldiers, and they were . . . real soldiers. And . . .

| Hank: | (Interjecting) But the soldiers were in the wrong place most of the time. |
| Darren: | Hold on a second, Hank. That's a good idea, but please give Martha a chance to finish. |

It's unlikely that Hank intended to be rude. He interrupted Martha without thinking about it, and Darren's reminder helped him realize what he had done. The more practice students have with this type of social negotiation, the better their skills become.

Now, let's see how Darren monitored the students' thinking.

Ed:	Yeah, but the British started the war. You know, we talked about all the taxes, like on tea, and the people in the colonies got mad, because it wasn't fair.
Joan:	Not really. I think the colonists started it. They shot first.
Darren:	That is an interesting issue, but what is the question we're examining here? Ken?
Ken:	If the British should have won the war or not.
Darren:	Yes, good, Ken. Let's keep that in mind, everyone.

During this exchange, Darren intervened only when necessary, and she kept the intervention short. This can be difficult. Many teachers have trouble shifting from an information-giving role to that of facilitator (Dillon, 1987). They tend to dominate discussions and turn them into miniature lectures (Cazden, 1986; Cuban, 1984). Discussions are intended to involve students with the topic and one another, not with the teacher.

Cooperative Learning

As its name implies, cooperative learning relies on social interaction to facilitate knowledge construction. Several of the teachers in cases you've already studied used it as part of their instruction—Jan Davis in Chapter 1, David Shelton and Sue Southam in Chapter 7, and Jenny Newhall in this chapter, for example. It has become one of the most popular instructional strategies in schools today; one survey found that 93% of elementary teachers used some form of cooperative learning in their classrooms. However, many teachers equate cooperative learning with getting students into groups to discuss a topic and tend to ignore research about components that are essential if cooperative learning activities are to promote learning (Antil, Jenkins, Wayne, & Vadasy, 1998).

When implemented effectively, a cooperative learning activity can involve all students in learning, something that is difficult in large groups. In whole-class discussions, opportunities for participation are limited, so those less confident get few chances to present and defend their views. Often, they drift off.

Cooperative learning activities can also be effective for teaching students to collaborate in their thinking (Keefer et al., 2000; Meter & Stevens, 2000). Cooperative learning advocates, grounding their positions in Vygotsky's work, argue that groups of learners co-construct more powerful understandings than individuals can construct alone (Lehman, Kauffman, White, Horn, & Bruning, 1999; O'Donnell & O'Kelly, 1994; Summers, Woodruff, Tomberlin, Williams, & Svinicki, 2001). This co-constructed knowledge can then be appropriated by individuals (D. Brenner, 2001).

Cooperative learning activities encourage knowledge construction through social interaction.

Although a single definition doesn't exist, most researchers agree that **cooperative learning** consists of *students working together in groups small enough (typically two to five) so that everyone can participate in a clearly assigned task* (Cohen, 1994; D. Johnson & Johnson, 1994; Slavin, 1995). They also agree that cooperative learning shares at least four other common features:

- Goals direct the groups' activities.
- Social interaction is emphasized.
- Learners must depend on one another to reach the goals.
- Students are held individually accountable for attainment of learning goals.

The third characteristic, called *positive interdependence* (D. Johnson & Johnson, 1994) or *reciprocal interdependence* (Cohen, 1994), is important because it emphasizes the crucial role that peer cooperation plays in learning. Accountability is also essential because it keeps students focused on the goals and reminds them that learning is the purpose of the activity (Antil et al., 1998; Slavin, 1995).

Introducing Cooperative Learning

Introducing students to cooperative learning requires careful planning and organization. Poorly organized cooperative learning activities often result in less learning that whole-group lessons.

Suggestions for initially planning and organizing cooperative learning activities include the following:

- Seat group members together, so they can move back and forth from group work to whole-class activities with little disruption.
- Have materials ready for easy distribution to each group.
- Introduce students to cooperative learning with short, simple tasks, and make goals and directions very clear.
- Specify the amount of time students have to accomplish the task (and keep it relatively short).
- Monitor the groups while they work.
- Require that students produce a product as a result of the cooperative learning activity (such as written answers to specific questions).

These characteristics were illustrated in Jenny's lesson at the beginning of the chapter. The groups were seated together, the task was clear and specific, she required that students write down their conclusions, and perhaps most importantly, she carefully monitored the progress of the groups.

8.12
Teachers will sometimes give all students in a cooperative group the same grade. Is this likely to be effective practice? Explain, using your understanding of social cognitive theory (Chapter 6) as the basis for your answer.

Cooperative Learning Strategies

Different models of cooperative learning are all grounded in the constructivist principles we outlined earlier, but they are designed to accomplish different goals. We look at four models in the following paragraphs.

Reciprocal Questioning. **Reciprocal questioning** is *a cooperative learning activity in which students work in pairs to ask and answer questions about the content of a lesson or text* (King, 1994). The teacher initially provides question stems as models, and students use the stems to create specific questions about the lesson content. The pairs then take turns asking and answering them. Some examples of question stems based on Darren's lesson are outlined in Table 8.3. Teachers should encourage students to ask questions that connect topics, either in the immediate lesson or to ideas previously discussed.

Scripted Cooperation. **Scripted cooperation** is *a cooperative learning strategy in which a pair of students work together to elaborate each other's thinking* (Dansereau, 1985; O'Donnell & O'Kelly, 1994). The strategy is most effective for high-level tasks, such as solving nonroutine word problems in math, summarizing a reading passage, or editing written

Table 8.3 Reciprocal questioning stems and questions

Questioning Stem	Sample Question
Summarize . . .	Summarize the advantages the British had during the war. Summarize the advantages the colonists had during the war.
Why was . . . important?	Why was the tax on tea in the colonies important?
What does . . . mean?	What does *mercenary* mean?
Why was . . . important?	Why was the fact that some of the British soldiers were mercenaries important?
How does . . . relate to what we've already discussed?	How does the Revolutionary War relate to the French and Indian War, which we've already discussed?

drafts (of a persuasive essay, for instance). In math, for example, one member of a pair offers his or her solution (or partial solution) to a complex word problem. The other member then comments on the solution and offers additional suggestions. The responsibility then returns to the first member, who continues elaborating on the solution.

In reading, both members of the pair might read a passage. The first student then offers a summary, and the second comments on it, identifying errors or information the first member has missed. Then both students try to elaborate on the content, identifying links between it and earlier passages, creating examples that illustrate the information in the passage, and forming analogies. Students then switch roles and continue with the process through the rest of the assignment.

Jigsaw II. Jigsaw II is *a form of cooperative learning in which individual students become experts on subsections of a topic and teach those subsections to others.* Typically done in teams of three to five, Jigsaw II is designed to help students acquire declarative knowledge. A topic could be the relationship between geography and the economy and political systems in Central American countries, for example. One student from each team might focus on the geography, another on the climate, a third on the economies, and a fourth on the political systems. Individuals study their subtopics and then attend "expert meetings," during which students assigned to a particular subtopic, such as the climate, meet, compare notes, and clarify their understanding. "Experts" then teach the other members of their teams. Each member contributes a different piece of the knowledge puzzle, thus the name "Jigsaw." All members are held accountable for the content.

Student Teams Achievement Divisions. Created by Robert Slavin (1995), **Student Teams Achievement Divisions (STAD)** is *a form of cooperative learning that capitalizes on the role of social interaction to help students acquire facts, concepts, and procedural knowledge.* When STAD is used to develop procedural knowledge, it typically follows a teacher presentation and guided practice. Independent practice is then replaced by team study, during which students complete exercises on teacher-prepared worksheets and compare their results with those of their teammates. During team study, students are encouraged to explain their thinking and to focus on the reasons behind the answers, rather than on just getting the exercises right (Farivar & Webb, 1999; Webb, Farivar, & Mastergeorge, 2002). The teacher intervenes only if team members are unable to resolve disagreements about answers. Team study is complete when all teammates understand and can explain the problems or exercises.

Team study is followed by quizzes, which are scored as they would be in any other situation. If individuals score higher on a quiz than their average to that point in the class, they are awarded improvement points, and individual improvement points contribute to team awards. Improvement points contributing to team awards is a mechanism designed to promote positive interdependence.

A number of other cooperative learning strategies exist, and although they differ in format, all incorporate the instructional principles.

Classroom Connections

Applying Instructional Strategies Effectively in Your Classroom

Guided Discovery

1. Provide examples that include all the information students need to understand the topic, and guide student interaction.

   - *Elementary:* A third-grade teacher begins a unit on reptiles by bringing a snake and turtle to class. He also includes colored pictures of lizards, alligators, and sea turtles. He has students describe the live animals and pictures and then guides them to an understanding of the essential characteristics of reptiles.

   - *Middle School:* A seventh-grade English teacher embeds examples of possessive pronouns and singular and plural possessive nouns in the context of a paragraph. She then guides the students' discussion as they develop explanations for why particular sentences (such as "The girls' and boys' accomplishments in the middle school were noteworthy, as were the children's feats in the elementary school") were punctuated the way they were.

   - *High School:* A world history teacher presents students with vignettes such as this one:

     You're part of an archeological team, and at one site you've found some spear points. In spite of their ages, the points are still quite sharp, having been chipped precisely from hard stone. You also see several cattle and sheep skulls and some threads that appear to be the remains of coarsely woven fabric.

     He then guides the students to conclude that the artifacts best represent a New Stone Age society.

Inquiry

2. Guide students as they gather data about real-world problems.

   - *Elementary:* On a large table, a kindergarten teacher sets several tubs of water and a variety of objects, including wooden blocks, plastic spoons, paper clips, marbles, rubber bands, and pieces of tin foil. She asks the children to identify the objects they believe will float and then has them experiment to check their "guesses."

   - *Middle School:* A middle school science teacher asks her students what they think determines how fast a fluid will evaporate. After discussing the question, the students decide to place equal amounts of water in containers with different surface areas, they put equal amounts of water in identical containers at different temperatures, and they compare the evaporation rates of equal amounts of water, vinegar, rubbing alcohol,

and cooking oil. They measure the amount of fluid in each container each day.

   - *High School:* An English teacher asks the students to consider what influences the size of different issues of newspapers throughout the week. They compare the content, amount of advertising, editorials, and topics of different newspapers to search for patterns in each of the variables they've identified.

Discussion

3. Ensure that students have adequate background knowledge, and keep discussions focused on a specific question or issue.

   - *Elementary:* A fourth-grade teacher wants his students to understand how unkind comments can hurt their classmates' feelings. He begins by asking the students for examples of comments that have hurt their feelings, and they then discuss the reasons that the comments may or may not have been appropriate.

   - *Middle School:* A life science teacher is planning a discussion of global warming. Before the discussion, she presents information about the depletion of the Amazon rain forest, U.S. data on carbon dioxide emissions, and data on air emissions from Eastern European countries.

   - *High School:* A history teacher involved in a discussion of the efficacy of the U.S. involvement in Vietnam asks simply, "Considering the historical context, was America's decision to go into Vietnam a wise one?" He then keeps the students focused on America's initial decision to enter the conflict. When they discuss the war's outcome, he refocuses them on the original decision.

Cooperative Learning

4. Provide clear directions for groups, and carefully monitor students as they work.

   - *Elementary:* A second-grade teacher begins the school year by having groups work together on short word problems in math. When students fail to cooperate, she stops the groups and immediately discusses group problems with the class.

   - *Middle School:* A life-science teacher has students create and answer questions about the characteristics, organelles, and environments of one-celled animals. He periodically offers suggestions to the pairs to help them ask more meaningful questions.

   - *High School:* A geometry teacher has pairs use scripted cooperation to solve proofs. When they struggle, she offers hints to help them continue to make progress.

Cooperative Learning: A Tool for Capitalizing on Diversity

Although it's essential for constructing understanding, social interaction doesn't always occur naturally and comfortably; people tend to be wary of others from different cultures and backgrounds. Common in nonschool social settings, this tendency also occurs in schools. Students of particular ethnic groups tend to spend most of their time together, so they don't learn that all of us are much more alike than we are different (Webb, Baxter, & Thompson, 1997).

Teachers can't mandate tolerance, trust, and friendship among students with different backgrounds; they need additional tools, and cooperative learning can be one of them. Research supports this idea. Students working in cooperative groups improve their social skills, accept students with exceptionalities, and develop friendships and positive attitudes with others who differ in achievement, ethnicity, and gender (Slavin, 1995).

One teacher reported the following:

> A special education student in the sixth grade was transferred to our classroom, a fifth/sixth grade. The classroom she was in has several special education students. The first—I'll call her Sara—was having behavior difficulties in her first classroom and was about to be expelled because of her unacceptable behavior with her peers. We offered her the opportunity to try our room with no special education students and with cooperative learning techniques being applied in various subjects along with TAI (cooperative learning) math. Sara was welcomed by her new classmates. We added her to one of the TAI math learning teams, and the students taught her the program's routine. Sara worked very steadily and methodically trying to catch up academically and to fit in socially. She began to take more pride in her dress and grooming habits. I have been working with Sara on her basic facts in preparation for the weekly facts quizzes. Her attitude toward her schoolwork and her self-concept have blossomed within the length of time she has been in our classroom. (Nancy Chrest, Fifth/Sixth Grade Teacher, George C. Weimer Elementary School, St. Albans, WV, cited in Slavin, 1995, p. 42)

The positive effects seen in Sara's situation likely stem from at least four factors:

- Students with different backgrounds working together
- Group members having equal status
- Students learning about each other as individuals
- The teacher emphasizing the value of cooperation among all students (Slavin, 1995)

As learners work together, they do indeed find that they are much more alike than different, and they develop friendships across cultural, gender, and ability lines, which tends to break down peer-group boundaries. Let's see how Maria Sanchez, a third-grade teacher, attempted to accomplish these very goals in her classroom.

As Maria watched her third graders work, she was simultaneously pleased and uneasy. They had improved a great deal in their math and reading, but there was little mixing among her minority and nonminority students—and among other groups as well. She worried about six students from Costa Rica who were struggling with English and four students with exceptionalities who left her class every day for extra help.

To promote a more cohesive atmosphere, Maria decided to try cooperative groups. Over the weekend, she organized the students into groups of four, with equal numbers of high- and low-ability readers in each group. She also mixed the students by ethnicity and gender, and she made sure that no group had more than one student for whom English was a second language or more than one student with an exceptionality.

Teachers need to carefully plan so that diversity complements the knowledge construction process in small groups.

On Monday she organized the groups and explained how they were to work together. To introduce the process, she sat with one group and modeled cooperation and support for the others.

Then she sent the groups to different parts of the room. One student from each group read a paragraph, and a second asked questions of the third and fourth members, using stems that Maria provided. At her signal, they changed roles. As they worked, she moved around the room, encouraged the involvement of all group members, and prevented individuals from dominating the groups.

Her first session was demanding but fairly successful. "Phew," she thought to herself at the end of the day. "This isn't any easier, but it already seems better."

Let's take a closer look at the way Maria planned and implemented her activity. First, because her goal was to develop interpersonal relationships, she carefully organized the groups so that high- and low-ability students, boys and girls, minority and nonminority, and students with and without exceptionalities were represented in the groups as equally as possible. One of the most common mistakes that beginning teachers make is to let students form their own groups.

Second, knowing that effective interaction must be planned and taught, she modeled positive behaviors, such as providing emotional support for other members of the group, listening, asking questions, and staying on task. Teachers can also have role-plays, show videotapes of effective groups, and teach interaction strategies, such as questioning, to help students learn cooperation skills (Fitch & Semb, 1992; King, 1999). These skills are especially valuable for students from minority groups, who are often hesitant about seeking and giving help (Webb & Farivar, 1994).

Third, by using a form of reciprocal questioning, Maria began with a task that required cooperation and communication. By rotating students through these roles, she encouraged participation from all group members and helped prevent higher status or more aggressive students from dominating the activity. Research suggests that teachers need to carefully plan activities so that all members can contribute to the group (Cohen, 1998). Other tasks that can be used to encourage cooperation include presenting and checking math problems, practicing spelling and grammar exercises, and solving open-ended problems (Cohen, 1994; Quin, Johnson, & Johnson, 1995).

Finally, Maria carefully monitored the students while they worked. Initial training is important, but, alone, it won't ensure cooperation. Groups need constant monitoring and support, particularly when cooperative learning is first introduced (Cohen, 1994). The younger the children, the more supervision and support they need. If problems persist or occur in more than one group, teachers can reconvene the class for additional training.

Classroom Connections

Capitalizing on Diversity in Your Classroom

1. Use the composition of cooperative learning groups to capitalize on the strengths of students with diverse backgrounds, and design tasks that require group cooperation.

   - *Elementary:* A second-grade teacher waits until the third week of the school year to form cooperative learning groups. Before that time, she observes her students and gathers information about their interests, talents, and friendships. She then uses the information in making decisions about group membership.

   - *Middle School:* A sixth-grade math teacher uses cooperative learning groups to provide practice and feedback in his class. When he assigns word problems, he asks students to work in pairs to compare and explain their answers. They may ask for help only when they're unable to resolve disagreements.

   - *High School:* An English teacher has students work in groups to provide feedback on one another's writing. Students in each group take turns reading and reacting to another group member's work on the basis of style and clarity. They then make suggestions for revision.

2. Use warm-up, introductory, and team-building exercises to promote interaction within groups.
   - *Elementary:* A kindergarten teacher sometimes interrupts cooperative learning activities when she detects problems, such as students arguing about who gets to perform a certain task. She tells them they must learn to cooperatively solve their problem, and she models cooperation in simulations and think-alouds.
   - *Middle School:* A geography teacher encourages group solidarity by having members interview each other

about such things as their ancestors' countries of origin, favorite foods, hobbies, songs, and vacations. Each interviewer then presents this information to other members of the group.
   - *High School:* An English teacher introduces cooperative learning with an icebreaker called "Truth and Lies." Each person in the group says four things about himself or herself, three of which are true and one of which is a lie. The others try to guess which one is the lie.

Putting Constructivism into Perspective

Constructivism has made an enormous contribution to our understanding of learning and to classroom practices. It is powerful because it helps us understand why background knowledge and interaction are so important for developing deep understanding, and it also helps us understand why monitoring student thinking is essential. Because we know that students construct their own conceptions, we better understand why they don't grasp an idea that's been discussed several times, why they seem to ignore a point that's been emphasized, and why they retain misconceptions that we've attempted to help them eliminate. With this understanding, our frustration can be reduced and our patience increased. Constructivism also helps us understand why explaining, alone, is ineffective, and why worksheets and drill fail to produce much learning.

Constructivism is, however, often misunderstood and misinterpreted:

> A common misconception regarding "constructivist" theories of knowledge . . . is that teachers should never tell students anything directly but, instead, should always allow them to construct knowledge for themselves. This perspective confuses a theory of pedagogy (teaching) with a theory of knowing. (Bransford et al., 2000, p. 11)

8.13
Does the concept "behaviorist teacher" exist? Explain.

This distinction is important. For example, although the terms are commonly used, the concepts "constructivist teacher" and "constructivist instruction" don't exist. As Bransford and colleagues (2000) pointed out, constructivism is a *theory of learning* ("knowing"); it is not a theory of instruction. Theories of learning are useful because they help us "get into kids' heads," as was necessary to understand Suzanne's lack of progress in Jenny's lesson in the opening case study.

The relationship between constructivism and teaching method is a different issue. For example, guided discovery is often described as a "constructivist" approach to instruction. Properly done, it is an effective teaching strategy; improperly done, it is no more effective and no more "constructivist" than any other technique.

As another example, "Social interaction facilitates learning" is sometimes interpreted to mean that a teacher who uses cooperative learning is "constructivist," whereas one who relies on large-group activities is not. In fact, both teachers may be basing their instruction on constructivist views of learning, or neither teacher may be. Large-group instruction, effectively done, may promote construction of understanding, and cooperative learning, improperly done,

By carefully listening to students, teachers can assess the progress of knowledge construction.

may not. Confusing learning and instruction can lead to misconceptions about appropriate method and oversimplified suggestions for classroom practice.

One potential problem when using social interaction in instructional strategies is the assumption that group processes and products equate with individual learning. In other words, if the group accomplishes a task, does that ensure that individual members can also do it? Research suggests not (B. Barron, 2000; Southerland, Kittleson, & Settlage, 2002). Students may be able to do things in groups that they are unable to do alone. This finding underscores the crucial role that assessment plays in instruction grounded in constructivitist views of learning.

Also, as with any theory, constructivism doesn't provide a complete picture of learning and its implications for teaching. For instance, research suggests that many skills must be practiced to automaticity (K. Harris & Graham, 1996; Weinert & Helmke, 1995). This research is better explained by information processing than by constructivism, and in fact, discussions of constructivism tend to ignore learners' cognitive architectures (Eggen, 2001). Students will construct valid understandings of the topics they study, for instance, only to the extent to which they pay attention, correctly perceive the information they're studying, and avoid having their working memories overloaded. Further, students who are metacognitive about their learning are more successful than their peers who are less aware. Attention, perception, working memory, and metacognition are all concepts from information processing theory, and ignoring them leaves important parts of the learning puzzle unattended.

In addition, constructivism fails to address modeling, a concept from social cognitive theory, and one of the most powerful tools teachers have for promoting learning. Ignoring social cognitive theory not only provides an incomplete picture of learning but also robs teachers of an important tool in their repertoires.

Fortunately, many of the controversies that historically have been associated with constructivism seem to have been resolved. For instance, most researchers now reject the idea that misconceptions don't exist and that all students' unique constructions of understanding are equally valid (Derry, 1992; Moshman, 1997; D. Phillips, 1997, 2000).

In addition, the teacher's role in classroom applications of constructivism has been clarified. These applications don't suggest that the teacher has a diminished role in promoting learning; in fact, they provide for an increased and more sophisticated one. Traditional teaching roles, such as establishing clear goals and aligning instruction, are as important for applications of constructivism as they are for applications of any other theory (Airasian & Walsh, 1997; Bransford et al., 2000, A. Brown & Campione, 1994; Howe & Berv, 2000; Osborne, 1996; D. Phillips, 1995, 2000). In addition, instead of merely presenting information (commonly described as a *transmission view* of instruction), teachers must listen to students as they describe their understanding and, when necessary, intervene to help students construct complete and valid schemas. The ability to monitor students' thinking, assist in the knowledge construction process, and intervene soon enough to prevent misconceptions, but not so soon that students' responsibility for learning is diminished, is very sophisticated and demanding instruction.

Summary

What Is Constructivism?

Constructivism is a broad term that is used in different ways by different people. Philosophers examine questions about the nature of reality and the validity of understanding. Teachers consider their roles and different approaches to instruction. Educational psychologists view constructivism as a theory of learning suggesting that learners construct—rather than record—understanding of what they study.

Different Views of Constructivism

Cognitive constructivism, grounded primarily in Piaget's work, emphasizes individual construction of understanding. Social interaction is used to disrupt individual equilibrium, which is reestablished by the individual.

Social constructivism, based on the thinking of Vygotsky, suggests that the process of social interaction results in understanding that didn't exist in any individual. Knowledge initially exists in the social environment, and it is eventually internalized by individuals.

Characteristics of Constructivism

That learners construct, rather than record, understanding is the basic principle of constructivism. In addition, constructivists strongly emphasize the importance of prior knowledge, the role of social interaction, and the value of real-world tasks in the process of constructing understanding.

Implications of Constructivism for Teaching

Constructivism has important implications for teaching, but its interpretation sometimes leads to misconceptions. People sometimes confuse learning theory and instructional theory, tacitly believing that teachers should avoid setting clear goals, guiding instruction, or correcting student misconceptions. Constructivism supports none of these practices.

Instruction based on constructivism emphasizes high-quality examples and representations of content, high levels of student interaction, and content connected to the real world. Teachers who ground their instruction in constructivism realize that lecturing and explaining often fail to promote deep understanding in learners.

Constructivism in Classrooms: Instructional Strategies

Instruction that most effectively applies constructivism in classrooms emphasizes both students' answers and how students arrived at those answers. Effective instruction makes students' thinking open and visible. Guided discovery, inquiry, discussion, and cooperative learning, when well done, can each involve students in knowledge construction and make their thinking visible.

Teachers using guided discovery present students with information and guide them to find patterns in the data. Inquiry begins with a problem, follows with hypotheses that offer tentative solutions to the problem, and ends with data gathering to test the solutions. Discussions involve students in activities in which their interpersonal skills are developed and reconstruction of understanding can occur. Cooperative learning involves students in groups of two to five in tasks that require the efforts of each to succeed.

Putting Constructivism into Perspective

Constructivism helps us understand why learners arrive at some of the seemingly illogical conclusions that they do. However, as with any theory, constructivism doesn't provide a complete picture of learning. Attention, perception, metacognition, and the limitations of working memory all influence learning, as does modeling and judiciously applied reinforcers. These concepts come from information processing, social cognitive theory, and behaviorism. Effective teachers draw from the best of all theories to promote as much learning as possible.

Windows on Classrooms

At the beginning of the chapter, you saw how Jenny Newhall attempted to design and conduct a lesson that would help learners construct an understanding of balanced beams.

In the following case, a science teacher has his students examine the factors that influence the frequency of a simple pendulum. Read the case study, and answer the questions that follow.

Scott Sowell, a middle school science teacher, wondered why his seventh graders continued to have trouble controlling variables. "Funny, we did the plant experiment as a whole class, and they seemed to get it. . . . I explained it so carefully," he thought to himself. He decided to give them some additional practice with controlling variables by working with simple pendulums in small groups.

The next day, Scott began by demonstrating a simple pendulum. He asked the students what factors they thought would influence the frequency of a pendulum, explaining that *frequency* meant the number of swings in a certain time period. After some discussion, they suggested length, weight, and angle of release.

"Okay, your job as a group is to design your own experiment," Scott said. "Think of a way to test how each one of these affects the frequency. Use the equipment at your desk to design and carry out the experiment. Go to it."

One group of four—Marina, Paige, Wensley, and Jonathan—tied a string to a ring stand and measured its length, as shown:

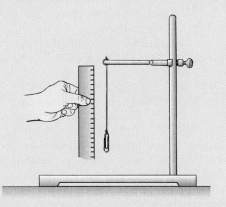

"Forty-nine centimeters," Wensley noted, measuring the length of the string.

"The frequency is the seconds . . . and the what?" Marina asked Scott as he came by the group.

"The frequency is the number of swings in some time period. What time period are you using?" Scott responded.

The group agreed to use 15 seconds and then did their first test with the 49-centimeter length and one paper clip as weight. Marina counted 21 swings.

A few minutes later, Scott again walked by the group, looked at their results, and said, "So you've done one test so far. . . . What are you going to do next? . . . I'm going to come back after your next test and look at it." He then moved to another group.

The group conducted their second test by shortening the string *and* adding a second paper clip.

"Mr. Sowell, we found out that the shorter it is and the heavier it is, the faster it goes," Marina reported to Scott when he returned to the group.

"So tell me how you found out that the length affected it," Scott asked as he knelt down in front of the students.

"We made it long, and then we shortened it, and we made it heavier," Marina explained.

"So in Test 1, the length was 49, and the frequency was 21 swings in 15 seconds, and the weight was one paper clip?" Scott queried. "What did you change between Test 1 and Test 2?"

"The amount of paper clips," Marina explained.

"So you changed the weight? What else did you change?"

"The length," Wensley noted.

"So you changed the weight and the length. . . . Which caused that higher frequency?"

"The length," Paige responded.

"I think weight," Marina countered.

"Weight," Wensley added.

"The weight," Jonathan nodded.

"So, you three think weight," Scott replied, pointing at Marina, Jonathan, and Wensley in turn. "And you think length," he said, nodding to Paige. "Why can't you look at these two sets of data and decide?"

"Well, like the length . . . and the weight changed. None of them stayed the same, so it has to be different," Marina offered.

"What was the first thing you said?"

"They both changed," Wensley and Jonathan said simultaneously.

"Think about that," Scott directed as he moved to another group.

"Everything needs to stay the same except for one thing," Jonathan offered as the group started back to work.

"Okay, I know," Paige suggested. "Keep the two paper clips and put the length back to 49."

"So what are we going to keep the same, and what are we going to change?" Jonathan asked.

"We're testing the weight, so let's keep the length the same," Wensley answered.

Increasing the length back to 49 and keeping the two paper clips on the end of the string, they pulled the paper clip to the side, released the pendulum, and counted the swings.

"21," Marina noted, getting the same result as in their first test.

"You need to come up with a conclusion about length, about weight, and about angle," Scott reminded them as he moved from group to group.

The group had already determined the angle of release—which they referred to as the "height"—by measuring the distance between the top of the table and the bottom of the paper clip, as shown:

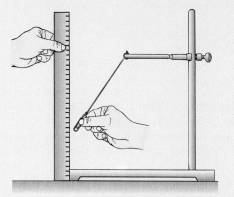

"We're going to keep the same height," Marina suggested.

"And the same length, 49," Wensley added.

The students added a third paper clip and conducted another test.

"So what does that tell you about weight?" Scott asked when he saw the test.

The students talked briefly, concluding that the weight made a difference in spite of the fact that they found the number of swings to be the same in each test. They then turned to testing the angle, or "height."

"It's the same," Paige noted after two tests, seeing that the frequencies were the same when the angles were different.

"It's the same because, remember, the weight changed," Marina responded, concluding that the difference in weight (three paper clips compared to two) accounted for the frequency being the same when the angles were different.

"What did you find out?" Scott asked as he returned to check on their progress.

Marina began, "Okay, Mr. Sowell, we figured out that the shorter it is, the faster the frequency is, . . . and the heavier it is . . . the faster the frequency is."

Scott asked the students to explain their findings about the height.

"In the first one, the height was 56 and the weight was 3, and it came out to 21, and in the second one, the height was higher and the weight was lower, so it was still 21," Marina said, again concluding that the change in weight

explained why the frequency was the same when the angles were different.

"Let's do it out loud before you write it. . . . Talk to me about length," Scott directed.

"The longer the string is, the slower the frequency is," Wensley said.

"The angle?"

"The higher the angle is, the faster the frequency is," Wensley continued.

"What about weight?"

"The heavier it is, the faster it goes," Marina added.

"I want to look at these again. . . . Write those down for me."

The students wrote their conclusions as Scott walked to the front of the room and rang a bell to call the class together.

"When I call your group, I want the speaker for your group to report your findings to the class," he continued to the class as a whole.

One by one, the spokespeople for the groups came to the front of the room to report their findings. In general, the groups concluded that each variable—the length, weight, and angle—affected the frequency.

"Let's take a look at something here," Scott said, placing a ring stand onto his demonstration table. He attached a paper clip to the pendulum, put it in motion, and asked a student to count the swings. He added a second paper clip and again had the students count, to demonstrate that weight doesn't affect the frequency. He had a student state the conclusion and write it on the board. Then he did a second demonstration to show that angle also has no effect on the frequency and again asked a student to make a conclusion.

After the demonstrations, he said, "Now I want someone to give me a conclusion about what we learned about designing experiments and how we use our variables. . . . Who wants to talk about that? . . . Wensley? Tell me what we learned about how to set up an experiment. What did we learn from this?"

"Each time, you do a different part of the experiment, only change one of the variables," Wensley explained.

"Why is that?"

"You're only checking one thing at a time. If you do two, there might be an error in the experiment."

"Okay, . . . if you change more than one thing at one time, why would it be difficult?"

"Because . . . because you got to see the way one thing turns out, because if you change two things . . . two different things . . . you can't tell which one caused the change," Wensley continued.

"Good, okay, for example, if you were testing weight and length, your group had to finally decide that we can't change weight at the same time as we change length, because when we test it . . . "

"You couldn't compare them," Marina responded.

"Right, you couldn't compare them. You couldn't tell which one was causing it, could you? . . . It might go faster, but all of a sudden you'd say, well is it the weight or is it the length?"

Scott then asked if there were any questions, and hearing none, he dismissed the class.

Constructed Response Questions

In answering these questions, use information from the chapter and link your responses to specific information in the case.

1. Describe the extent to which the characteristics of constructivism were demonstrated in Scott's lesson.
2. Assess how effectively Scott implemented the "Suggestions for Classroom Practice" (see Figure 8.2).
3. Which of the instructional strategies did Scott most nearly employ in his lesson? Identify each of the parts of the strategy.
4. Assess the effectiveness of Scott's lesson for learners with diverse backgrounds.

Document-Based Analysis

In the Chapter 4 closing case study, you saw that Teri Hall wanted her eighth graders to understand the concept *mercantilism*, which she defined as "a strategy countries used to make money in colonial times, which included using colonies to produce raw materials that they sent back to the mother country, selling finished products back to the colonies, and using the mother countries' ships to transport both the raw materials and finished products." She then used the following vignettes as examples.

> *In the mid-1600s, the American colonists were encouraged to grow tobacco, since it wasn't grown in England. The colonists wanted to sell it to France and other countries but were told no. In return for sending the tobacco to England, the colonists were allowed to buy textiles from England. They were forbidden, however, from making their own textiles. All the materials were carried on British ships.*

> *Early French colonists in the New World were avid fur trappers and traders. They got in trouble with the French monarchy, however, when they attempted to make fur garments and sell them to Spain, England, and others. They were told that they had to buy the manufactured garments from dealers in Paris instead. The monarchy also told them that traps and weapons would be made in France and sent to them as well. One of the colonists, Jean Forjea, complied with the monarchy's wishes but was fined when he hired a Dutch ship to carry some of the furs back to Nice.*

Using the suggestions in the chapter, assess the effectiveness of Teri's vignettes for providing background knowledge for her eighth graders. Describe both strengths and weaknesses of the vignettes.

 **Online Portfolio Activities**

To develop your professional portfolio, further apply your understanding of chapter content, and address the INTASC standards, go to the Companion Website, then to this chapter's *Online Portfolio Activities*. Complete the suggested activities.

PRAXIS These exercises are designed to help you prepare for the PRAXIS™ "Principles of Learning and Teaching" exam. To receive feedback on your constructed response questions and document analysis response, go to the Companion Website at *www.prenhall.com/eggen*, then to this chapter's *Practice for PRAXIS*™ module. For additional connections between this text and the PRAXIS™ exam, go to Appendix A.

 Also on the Companion Website at *www.prenhall.com/eggen*, you can measure your understanding of chapter content in *Practice Quiz* and *Essay* modules, apply concepts in *Online Cases*, and broaden your knowledge base with the *Additional Content* module and *Web Links* to other educational psychology websites.

Important Concepts

cognitive constructivism *(p. 281)*
constructivism *(p. 281)*
cooperative learning *(p. 299)*
discussion *(p. 296)*
guided discovery *(p. 293)*
inquiry *(p. 295)*
Jigsaw II *(p. 300)*

learner-centered instruction *(p. 292)*
real-world task *(p. 284)*
reciprocal questioning *(p. 299)*
scripted cooperation *(p. 299)*
social constructivism *(p. 281)*
Student Teams Achievement Divisions
  (STAD) *(p. 300)*

Chapter Outline

Complex Cognitive Processes

9

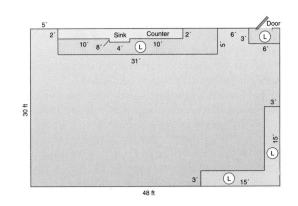

Laura Hunter, a fifth-grade math teacher, was concerned about her students' tendency to memorize procedures for finding answers in math instead of understanding what they were doing or why. After reflecting on the issue, she decided, "I'm going to use a real problem in finding the areas of irregularly shaped figures instead of the ones in the book—something they can relate to."

She decided to have students find the area of the carpeted portion of their classroom. The floor under the computers was covered with linoleum, and the carpeted portion had an irregular shape.

After completing her beginning-of-class routines on Monday, she reviewed *perimeter* and *area* by asking, "Can someone tell us what perimeter is? . . . Sam?"

"It's the length of the line going around the outside."

"Good. And what was the example we used? . . . Like if we were building a playground, it would be the . . . ?"

"Fence," several students said simultaneously.

"Yes, . . . and what would the area be?"

"The inside of the shape," Elise volunteered.

"Right, like how many squares of outdoor carpeting we would need to cover it," Laura responded.

To introduce the problem for the day, she displayed the following on the overhead:

"First, we need to identify the problem," Laura began. "Here it is. We're going to get carpeting for this room, but Mr. Garcia, our principal, doesn't know how much to order. Your job is to figure that out."

Laura broke the students into groups, and each group worked for several minutes to decide how they would represent the problem. As a class, the students discussed what they had found, and Laura then had them measure different parts of the room in their groups. Using the information they gathered, Laura constructed a diagram of the room, gave each group a copy, and told the students that the *L* on the drawing stood for *linoleum*.

"Okay, look back up here at our overhead," Laura instructed the class. "This diagram represents our problem. . . . What's your next job?"

After several seconds, Nephi volunteered, "We didn't measure the area we want. We still have the whole inside of the classroom. We just measured the perimeter."

"Okay, you guys understand what Nephi's saying?" Laura asked.

"Yeah," several students responded.

"Okay," Laura nodded. "That's the part you're going to be working on with your team. . . . You need to select a strategy; decide how you're going to find the area of this part," she directed, pointing to the carpeted area in the diagram. "I only want to know the area of the carpet. . . . Go ahead and get started."

The students reassembled their groups, and as they worked on the problem, different groups identified two basic strategies. One was to find the area of the whole room and subtract the area of the linoleum; the other was to find the area of an interior rectangle and then add the extra areas of carpeting.

"Okay, let's look back up here at our diagram," Laura directed after reassembling the class. "I saw different strategies as I was walking around. Raise your hand and tell me what one of the strategies was. . . . Yashoda?"

"We multiplied the perimeter. And then we subtracted the places where the linoleum was."

"Okay, when you multiplied the perimeter, what did it give you?"

"1,440."

"Okay, that's called the . . . ?"

"Area," several students responded.

"Okay, and what was your next step?"

"Then we subtracted where the linoleum was."

"Okay, raise your hand if your team used that strategy."

Students from some of the groups raised their hands.

"Raise your hand if you tried a different strategy."

Several other students raised their hands.

"Matt, explain what your team did," Laura directed.

"We had two strategies. First, we squared it off, like covering up this," he responded, referring to a carpeted rectangle inside all the areas that had linoleum. "Then we got the area of the middle, and then we were going to add the other pieces . . . to it."

After all the groups reported, Laura put their diagrams on the bulletin board, and then said, "Okay, tell me your answer. How many square feet of carpet did you get?"

"1,173," one of the groups reported.

"Okay," she said, then nodded to another group.

"1,378."

"1,347," a third group reported.

"1,440," a fourth group added.

"1,169," another group offered.

"1,600," the last group put in.

"Well, are you guys comfortable with that?"

Several of the students said no.

"If you were the person purchasing the carpet, would you be comfortable with that?" Laura continued.

Most of the students again shook their head no.

"So, what might we do to try to be more accurate?" Laura asked. "Talk to your team for a minute."

The students talked to their teammates and offered some suggestions, such as measuring the room again, checking once more to see if the strategy made sense, and even asking the janitor about the dimensions of the room.

Chuckling at the last suggestion, Laura said, "That's a strategy that we might call 'Ask an expert,'" and she then had the students get ready for recess, planning to address the problem again the next day.

In this chapter, we extend our study of learning to examine the processes students use to acquire concepts, solve problems, employ learning strategies, and transfer their understanding from one context to another. As we examine these topics, we'll demonstrate how they're grounded in the cognitive learning theories you studied in Chapters 7 and 8.

After you've completed your study of this chapter, you should be able to

- Explain the application of concept learning to classroom activities
- Apply problem-solving strategies to well-defined and ill-defined problems
- Explain how critical thinking can be developed in students
- Describe how study strategies can be used to increase student learning
- Discuss ways of increasing transfer of learning

9.1

Identify at least two concepts that you studied in each of these chapters: 5, 6, 7, and 8.

In our opening case study, we saw that Laura's students struggled to accurately determine the carpeted area of their classroom. Solving the problem depended on the students' procedural knowledge and their ability to accurately measure different parts of the room, devise strategies for finding the carpeted portions, and calculate the areas. Some of the groups' answers varied by more than 400 square feet, a fact that helps us understand why problem solving is one of the "complex cognitive processes" suggested in our chapter title. The students' ability to solve the problem was made more complex because their declarative knowledge about the concepts *area* and *perimeter* was uncertain. We examine these complex processes in the sections that follow, beginning with concept learning.

Effective teachers use concrete examples to help students learn concepts and relate them to the real world.

Concept Learning

Think about some of the topics that you've studied in this book. Among many others, you examined *equilibrium, centration,* and *zone of proximal development* in Chapter 2, *initiative* and *self-esteem* in Chapter 3, and *intelligence* and *socioeconomic status* in Chapter 4. Each is a concept, as was *perimeter* and *area* in Laura's lesson.

Concepts: Categories That Simplify the World

Concepts are *mental structures that categorize sets of objects, events, or ideas,* and they represent a major portion of the school curriculum (Klausmeier, 1992). For example, learners would identify each of the polygons in Figure 9.1 as a triangle, even though the shapes vary in size, configuration, and orientation. "Triangle" is a

Figure 9.1 Triangles

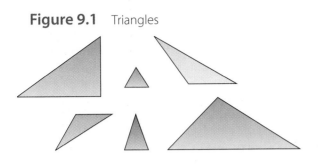

mental structure into which all examples of three-sided, closed plane figures can be placed.

Concepts help us simplify the world. The concept *triangle,* for example, allows people to think and talk about the examples in Figure 9.1 as a group, instead of as specific objects. Having to remember each separately would make learning impossibly complex and unwieldy. Additional examples of concepts in language arts, social studies, math, and science are listed in Table 9.1. This is only a brief list, and you can probably think of many more. Students also study, for example, *major scale* and *tempo* in music, *perspective* and *balance* in art, and *aerobic exercise* and *isotonic exercise* in physical education. In addition, many other concepts occur in the curriculum that don't neatly fit into a particular content area, such as *honesty, bias, love,* and *internal conflict.*

Theories of Concept Learning

Theorists have offered several different explanations of how people form concepts. In this section, we consider three theories that focus on *characteristics, prototypes,* and *exemplars,* respectively.

Some concepts, such as *square, triangle* or *perimeter,* have well-defined **characteristics** (sometimes called *attributes* or *features*), which are *the concept's defining elements* (Medin, Proffitt, & Schwartz, 2000). For instance, "plane," "closed," "equal sides" and "equal angles" are the characteristics of the concept *square.* Learners can identify examples of squares based on a rule stating that squares must have these attributes. Other characteristics—such as size, color, or orientation—aren't essential, so learners don't have to consider them in making their classifications.

Early researchers (e.g., Bruner, Goodenow, & Austin, 1956) suggested that learners acquire concepts by identifying the essential characteristics of a concept and classifying examples accordingly. Concepts are differentiated from one another on the basis of the rules for each (Bourne, 1982), so this is a *rule-driven* theory of concept learning.

Many concepts don't have well-defined characteristics, however, so creating rules to help differentiate them is difficult. For instance, what are the characteristics of the concepts *Democrat* or *Republican?* Despite frequent exposure to the terms in our popular news, most people are unable to define the concepts in even a somewhat precise way. Common concepts, such as *car,* also can have "fuzzy boundaries" (B. Schwartz & Reisberg, 1991). For instance, some people describe sport utility vehicles as cars, but others don't. How about minivans? And railroad "cars" also exist.

Table 9.1 Concepts in different content areas

Language Arts	Social Studies	Science	Math
Adjective	Culture	Acid	Prime number
Verb	Longitude	Conifer	Equivalent fraction
Plot	Federalist	Element	Set
Simile	Democracy	Force	Addition
Infinitive	Immigrant	Inertia	Parabola

A second theory of concept learning suggests that concepts such as *Democrat, Republican,* and even *car* are represented in memory by a **prototype,** *the best representative of a concept, category, or class* (Hampton, 1995; Medin et al., 2000). For example, George W. Bush, Justice Clarence Thomas, and others might be prototypes for the concept *Republican,* and many choices also exist for *Democrat.* Similarly, a common passenger car, like a Ford Taurus or Toyota Camry, might be a prototype for *car.*

Prototypes aren't necessarily physical examples, such as a person or object. Rather, they may be a mental composite, constructed from examples that individuals experience (Reisberg, 1997; B. Ross & Spalding, 1994). For instance, a person who has encountered a number of different dogs might construct a prototype that doesn't look exactly like any particular breed.

A third theory of concept learning holds that learners don't necessarily construct a single prototype from the examples they encounter; rather they store **exemplars,** *the most highly typical examples of a concept* (Medin et al., 2000). For instance, instead of constructing a prototype, the person having experience with dogs may store images of a golden retriever, cocker spaniel, collie, dachshund, and German shepherd in memory as *exemplars.*

Each theory can explain different aspects of concept learning. For instance, concepts such as *square* or *odd number* are likely encoded in terms of characteristics. Others—such as *car*—are probably represented as prototypes, and still others—such as *dog* or *bird*—may be encoded as exemplars.

Examples: The Key to Learning and Teaching Concepts

Why do virtually all people, including small children, understand concepts like *square* and *triangle,* whereas few have a clear understanding of *democracy, justice,* or *bias?* And what can teachers do to help learners understand all concepts, regardless of their difficulty?

When a concept has a small number of concrete characteristics, concept learning is simplified (Tennyson & Cocchiarella, 1986). For example, "plane," "closed," and "three straight lines" are the characteristics of the concept *triangle.* It has only three essential characteristics, and they're observable. We know that the concept is easy to learn because most students in kindergarten can identify triangles. However, concepts like

9.2

Of the concepts *noun* and *culture,* which should be easier to learn? Explain, basing your answer on the information in this section.

Through interactive questioning, teachers help students analyze examples for their essential characteristics.

democracy, justice, and *bias* don't have well-defined characteristics, and people's proto-types and sets of exemplars for them vary markedly. These concepts are much harder to learn than a concept like *triangle,* and consequently they're much harder to teach.

We saw in Chapter 8 that examples and other representations are essential for con-structing understanding. Learners construct concepts, so examples and representations are important to concept learning as well. Regardless of a concept's complexity, the key to teaching a concept is giving students experience with a carefully selected set of ex-amples and nonexamples combined with a definition (Tennyson & Cocchiarella, 1986). An ideal example *contains all the information learners need to construct a valid concept.* If the examples are constructed on the basis of a well-defined rule, such as the rules for *square, adjective,* or *force,* they will illustrate all of the essential characteristics. If not, the exam-ples will help learners construct a valid prototype or set of exemplars.

Analogies can also be used to make new concepts meaningful (Bulgren et al., 2000). For example, comparing the temperature control systems of mammals (new concept) to the temperature control system of a house helps students make connections to experi-ences stored in long-term memory. Graphic organizers that highlight similarities and differences in the two concepts can also be effective instructional aids.

In teaching concepts, teachers may present the definition and then illustrate it with examples, or they may choose to use a guided discovery approach in which they pres-ent a sequence of examples and guide students' construction of the concept.

Concept Mapping: Embedding Concepts in Complex Schemas

Concepts don't exist in isolation. Rather, they're related to each other in complex schemas. **Concept mapping** is *a strategy that helps learners construct visual relationships among concepts* (Mayer, 2002). Concept mapping capitalizes on the effects of organization, imagery, and the dual-processing capabilities of working memory—ideas we discussed in Chapter 7—to make the relationships meaningful (Robinson, Katayama, Dubois, & Devaney, 1998).

Concept mapping benefits both students and teachers (Hall, Hall, & Saling, 1999). Creating concept maps puts students in active roles by encouraging them to visually represent relationships among concepts, and teachers can use the maps to assess stu-dents' understanding of these relationships. For example, the student who created the concept map in Figure 9.2 for closed plane figures didn't include figures with more than four sides or curved shapes other than circles. Seeing that the learner's understanding is incomplete, the teacher can provide examples of other figures with straight lines, such as pentagons and hexagons, as well as other curved figures, such as ellipses.

To see a video clip of a teacher presenting examples of the concept *Haiku poem* to her students, go to the Companion Website at *www.prenhall.com/eggen*, then to this chapter's *Classrooms on the Web* module. Click on *Video Clip 9.1.*

9.3
You're teaching the concept *reptile,* and you've shown common examples, such as a lizard, alligator, snake, and turtle. Identify at least one important additional example and one important nonexample that you should provide.

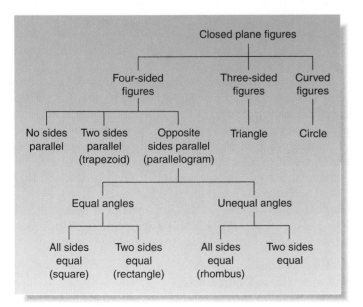

Figure 9.2 Concept map for closed plane figures

Figure 9.3 First
learner's network for the
concept *novel*

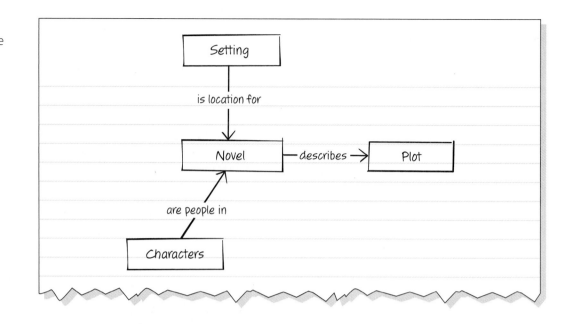

The concepts in Figure 9.2 are organized hierarchically, but not all relationships among concepts are hierarchical, so other types of concept maps may be more appropriate (Wallace, West, Ware, & Dansereau, 1998). Figures 9.3 and 9.4 illustrate two students' understandings of the concept *novel* represented in a **network,** *a concept map illustrating nonhierarchical relationships.*

The first student's concept of *novel* is simplistic; it includes only basic components— *plot, setting,* and *characters.* The second student's concept is more complex and sophisticated; factors that influence the quality of a novel are also included. As with the example of closed plane figures, teachers can use information from networks to assess students' understanding and help them further develop the concept.

The type of concept map students use should be one that best illustrates relationships among the concepts (Wallace et al., 1998). Hierarchies often work best in math and science; in other areas, such as reading or social studies, a network may be more effective.

For an example of a concept map for *operant conditioning,* which you studied in Chapter 6, go to the Companion Website at www.prenhall.com/eggen, then to this chapter's *Additional Content* module.

Concept Learning: Misconceptions and Conceptual Change

9.4

Which of the concepts from Piaget's work (Chapter 2) best help you understand why students' conceptions are so resistant to change? Explain.

In the last section, we saw that concepts become meaningful when they're linked in schemas. Learners construct these schemas, and as with all knowledge construction, learners' background knowledge, expectations, beliefs, and emotions influence their thinking (Dole & Sinatra, 1998). Sometimes their constructions are invalid, however, and once embedded in schemas, they can be very resistant to change (Leander & Brown, 1999; Posner, Strike, Hewson, & Gertzog, 1982; Shuell, 1996).

An example of a concept that students commonly misunderstand is *negative reinforcement.* In this text, we have emphasized that it is a process that *increases* behavior, yet probably because of the emotional reaction to the term *negative,* many of our students continue to view negative reinforcement as a process that *decreases* behavior, inappropriately equating it with punishment. Similar examples can be found in other areas. For instance, science students confuse *reptiles* and *amphibians,* geography students have problems with *longitude* and *latitude,* and language arts learners have difficulty differentiating between figures of speech such as *simile* and *metaphor.*

Teaching for *conceptual change* attempts to address this issue (Dole & Sinatra, 1998; Nissani & Hoefler-Nissani, 1992; Posner et al., 1982). From a conceptual change perspective, at least three conditions are required for students to change their thinking:

- The existing conception must become dissatisfying.
- An alternative conception must be understandable.
- The new conception must be useful in the real world.

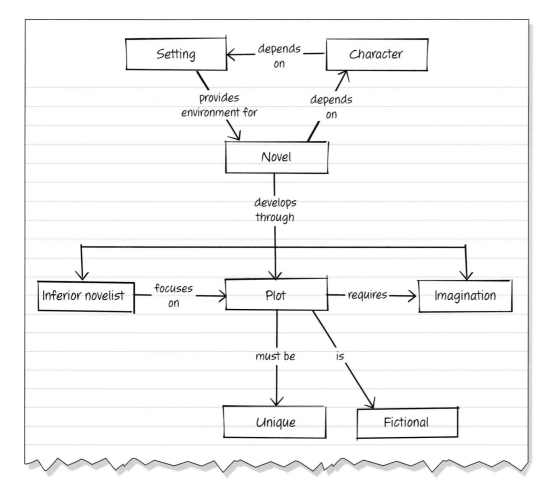

Figure 9.4 Second learner's network for the concept *novel*

As an example, let's think back to Suzanne's thinking about balanced beams in Chapter 8. According to her original conception (schema), an equal number of tiles on each side of the fulcrum was what made the beam balance. The instruction in the lesson didn't result in conceptual change; she retained her original conception in spite of explanations offered by other students and the teacher. What led to conceptual change? First, she modified her schema only after it became dissatisfying: The group tried her solution during the post-lesson interview, and it didn't work (the beam didn't balance). Second, as indicated by her ability to later explain a solution that involved both the number of tiles and the distance, an alternative conception was understandable. And third, the alternative conception was fruitful; it was useful in the lesson, and it could be applied to real-world examples such as teeter totters.

Even with these conditions in place, the process of conceptual change is not easy, as anyone who has attempted to convince someone to change their thinking about a topic will attest. Research suggests that considerable cognitive inertia exists, requiring teachers to take an active role in the conceptual change process (Southerland et al., 2002). Scaffolding, in the form of questions, prompts, and additional examples, often is necessary.

To see a case study in which a teacher attempts to teach for conceptual change, go to the Companion Website at *www.prenhall.com/eggen*, then to this chapter's *Additional Content* module.

Learning and Teaching Concepts: Instructional Strategies

Let's turn now to concept learning in classrooms. To help learners construct valid concepts, teachers should apply instructional strategies grounded in the information in the preceding sections. The following principles can guide teachers in their efforts:

- Provide a wide enough variety of examples to prevent learners from undergeneralizing about the concept.

- Use nonexamples to prevent students from overgeneralizing about the concept.
- Sequence the examples beginning with the most typical and ending with those least familiar.
- Help students with schema construction by linking the concept to related concepts.

Let's see how the principles guide Carol Lopez as she attempts to teach her fifth graders the concept *adjective*.

Carol began by displaying the following vignette on the overhead:

John and Karen, with her brown hair blowing in the wind, drove together in his old car to the football game. They soon met their very best friends, Latoya and Michael, at the large gate near the entrance. The game was incredibly exciting, and because the team's running game was in high gear, the home team won by a bare margin.

"Take a minute and read this little story," Carol began.

She waited briefly and then said, "We've discussed nouns, so let's see what you remember. Identify a noun in the passage. . . . Bharat?"

"*John*," Bharat responded and then quickly added, "and *Karen*."

"Okay," Carol smiled. "Another one, . . . Omar?"

"Mmm . . . *hair*."

Carol continued until the students had named all of the nouns in the vignette, and then she asked, "What do we know about Karen's hair? . . . Jesse?"

"It's brown."

"Good. . . . And what do we know about John's car? . . . Katilya?"

"It's old."

"Excellent, and what kind of game did they attend?"

"A football game," several students said at once.

Carol continued having the students describe what they knew about the nouns, and when they were finished, she said, "All these words that describe nouns are called *adjectives*. . . . Now let's take a little closer look at them. . . . What's different about *exciting* compared to other adjectives like *brown* and *old* and *football* and *best*? . . . Duk?"

"It . . . doesn't come right in front of the noun . . . like the others do?"

"Excellent thinking, Duk. . . . Look at that everyone. . . . Adjectives don't always have to come before the noun. . . . Now, what is important about *running* and *football*? . . . Sharon?"

"*Running* looks like a verb, . . . and *football* looks like a noun."

"Yes they do, . . . but how do we know they're adjectives? . . . Lakesha?"

"They describe nouns, . . . like *football* describes *game*, and . . . *running* does too."

"Bravo, Lakesha. That's also very good thinking."

"Now, we saw that most of the adjectives come right before the noun but that they don't always have to. . . . Let's take a look at the word *the*, like in *the entrance* and *the game*. How do we know that they're not adjectives? . . . Think about that everyone."

After several seconds, Yolanda offered, "They don't tell us anything about the noun. . . . It just says, 'the' entrance. It doesn't describe it."

"Outstanding, Yolanda," Carol smiled.

She then had the students look at the words *very* and *incredibly* and explain why they weren't adjectives. Finally, she had them write a short paragraph that included three or more adjectives, with at least one coming after the noun. "And," Carol required as a challenge for the students, "they all must be different than the ones we studied here."

Carol collected the paragraphs, put three of them on overhead transparencies without names (to avoid having the class know whose paragraphs were being analyzed), and discussed them the next day. During the discussion, she asked the students to explain why the suggested examples were or were not adjectives and whether or not they were used properly.

Let's take a closer look at Carol's lesson as an application of concept learning. First, she provided a variety of examples, and she wrote the passage so that the most obvious examples—*brown* and *old*—were presented first. Second, she emphasized less obvious examples, such as *exciting* and *running*, to prevent the students from undergeneralizing by concluding that all adjectives precede nouns or by excluding words that look like other parts of speech. Third, she had the students identify adverbs, such as *very* and

9.5

Explain why understanding that *running* is an adjective in Carol's lesson represents a complex cognitive process. How would a behaviorist explain this type of learning?

incredibly, as nonexamples so that students would not overgeneralize by including all words that "describe" as adjectives.

Finally, Carol promoted schema production by embedding her examples in a real-world context. In the real world, we encounter adjectives in newspapers, books, and other written materials, so the examples embedded in context were more effective than examples of adjectives presented in isolation, or even in sentences, would have been.

Although the type of examples and the context will vary depending on the concept, the kind of thinking that teachers do in effectively applying concept learning will be similar to Carol's. And even though the concept *adjective* obeys a well-defined rule, concept learning is a complex cognitive process, as we saw in the lesson.

9.6
Cite evidence from the case study that supports the contention that Carol attempted to base her instruction on constructivist views of learning.

Classroom Connections

Applying Concept Learning in Your Classroom

1. Use examples that include all the information learners need to understand the concept, and include nonexamples of the concept.
   - *Elementary:* A fourth-grade teacher presents a crab and shrimp, together with pictures of a spider, beetle, and grasshopper, to illustrate the concept *arthropod.* He also includes a clam, earthworm, and the students themselves as nonexamples.
   - *Middle School:* A geometry teacher presents her students with drawings of similar triangles such as those shown below:

     She has the students measure the sides and angles of the two triangles. They see that the sides of one are twice as long as the sides of the other, and the angles in the two are equal. She includes additional examples of similar triangles and other pairs of triangles that are not similar.
   - *High School:* A physical education teacher is helping his students learn to serve a tennis ball. He videotapes

several people, some with good serves and others less skilled. He shows the class the videotapes and has the students identify the differences in the serves.

2. Link new concepts to related concepts.
   - *Elementary:* A kindergarten teacher wants her class to understand that living things exist in many different forms. She has the children identify themselves, their pets, grass near the school grounds, and plants in their classroom all as living things. They identify "the ability to grow and change" and "the need for food and water" as two characteristics the examples have in common.
   - *Middle School:* An English teacher wants his students to understand similarities and differences between descriptive and persuasive writing. He displays paragraphs illustrating each and has the class identify their similarities and differences.
   - *High School:* A social studies teacher asks her students to compare cultural revolutions to other revolutions they have studied, such as the Industrial Revolution and the American Revolution, pointing out similarities and differences in each case.

Problem Solving

As an introduction to this section, think about the following:

- You want to write a greeting card to a friend who has moved to New York, but you don't know her home address.
- You're planning to paint your living room. To determine how much paint you should buy, you need to know the area of the ceiling and walls.
- You're a teacher, and your seventh graders resist thinking on their own. They expect to find the answer to every question specifically stated in the textbook.

Although they look different, each incident describes a **problem,** which *exists when you're in a state that differs from a desired end state and there is some uncertainty about reaching* *the end state* (Bransford & Stein, 1984). In other words, "a problem occurs when a problem solver has a goal but lacks an obvious way of achieving the goal" (Mayer & Wittrock, 1996, p. 47). In the preceding cases, our goals were finding the address, knowing the area of the ceiling and walls, and having students think on their own. A broad definition of *problem* is beneficial because it recognizes the pervasiveness of problem solving in our everyday lives. Thinking of problems in this way allows people to apply general strategies to solve different kinds of problems (Bruning et al., 1999).

Well-Defined and Ill-Defined Problems

Experts on problem solving find it useful to distinguish between well-defined and ill-defined problems (Eysenck & Keane, 1990; Simon, 1978). A **well-defined problem** *has only one correct solution and a certain method for finding it* (Bruning et al., 1999), whereas an **ill-defined problem** *has more than one acceptable solution, an ambiguous goal, and no generally agreed-upon strategy for reaching a solution* (Dunkle, Schraw, & Bendixon, 1995; Mayer & Wittrock, 1996). Our first two examples are well defined; your friend has only one home address, the area of the ceiling and walls of your living room is specific, and straightforward strategies for finding each exist. Many problems in math, physics, and chemistry are well defined.

In contrast, students' not wanting to think for themselves is an ill-defined problem. The goal state isn't clear—teachers are often not even sure what "thinking" means—and a readily agreed-on strategy for getting students to "think" doesn't exist. The problem can be solved with several strategies, and several "right" answers can be found.

As teachers, we have an ill-defined problem of our own. Research indicates that our students are not very good at solving problems (Bruer, 1993; Mayer, 2002; Mayer & Wittrock, 1996), and our goal is obviously for them to become better at it. In attempting to get a handle on this problem, we can identify at least two subproblems. First, most of learners' experiences in schools focus on well-defined problems, such as the example about wanting to paint our living room, but the majority of the problems we encounter in life are ill defined. For instance, you're encountering an ill-defined problem as you study this book. Your goal is to understand the content and do well in the class, but "understanding" is ambiguous, and many paths to understanding exist. Taking careful notes, studying with classmates, highlighting appropriate parts of the text, and completing the exercises in the Student Study Guide are all possibilities.

Our second subproblem is the fact that problem solving is personal and contextual (Mayer & Wittrock, 1996). A well-defined problem for one person is ill defined for another, and some evidence indicates that solving well-defined and ill-defined problems requires different abilities (N. Hong & Jonassen, 1999). Laura's lesson is an example. Finding the amount of carpeting necessary for the room is well defined for experienced problem solvers; they simply determine the total area of the floor and subtract the areas covered by linoleum. Only one answer exists, and the solution is straightforward. For Laura's students, however, the problem was ill defined. Their understanding of the goal wasn't clear, some of them were uncertain about the difference between area and perimeter—as an interview after the lesson revealed—and they used different strategies to reach the goal. Evidence of their uncertainty is indicated in their answers, which ranged from 1,169 square feet to 1,600 square feet (more than the total area of the room), and no group got 1,186 square feet, the actual amount of carpeting required.

We've seen that our students are not very good at solving problems, and helping them become better problem solvers is one of the biggest challenges teachers face. In an attempt to solve our problem, we offer three strategies:

- Help students understand a problem-solving model that can be applied in a variety of domains.
- Describe for students the characteristics of expert problem solvers that might be used as models for novices.
- Present a specific set of strategies to help students improve their problem-solving abilities.

9.7
You're involved in a relationship with a member of the opposite sex, but the relationship isn't as satisfying as you would hope. Is this a well-defined or an ill-defined problem? Explain.

To see a video clip in which students confuse the concepts *area* and *perimeter*, go to the Companion Website at *www.prenhall.com/eggen*, then to this chapter's *Classrooms on the Web* module. Click on *Video Clip 9.2.*

A Problem-Solving Model

Although some research suggests that problem solving is domain specific (Mayer, 2002), experts believe that within those specific domains (such as geometry, English, or history) general approaches to problem solving can improve students' problem-solving abilities (Bruning et al., 1999). Since the 1950s, computer scientists and cognitive psychologists have worked in this area, and their efforts have led to the general problem-solving model illustrated in Figure 9.5 and discussed in the sections that follow (based on work by Bransford & Stein, 1984).

By breaking down problem solving into specific steps, such as identifying and representing the problem, teachers can help students develop problem-solving strategies to use in many situations.

Identifying the Problem

> Question: There are 26 sheep and 10 goats on a ship. How old is the captain?

Amazingly, in one study, 75% of the second graders who were asked this question answered 36 (cited in Prawat, 1989)! Obviously, they didn't understand the problem.

At first glance, it appears that identifying a problem is straightforward, but in fact, it is one of the most difficult aspects of problem solving. It requires patience and a willingness to avoid committing to a solution too soon (J. Hayes, 1988). Obstacles to effectively identifying problems include the following:

- *Lack of domain-specific knowledge.* As in all areas of learning, background knowledge is essential for problem solving (Mayer, 1998a; Tuovinen & Sweller, 1999).
- *Lack of experience in defining problems.* Most problem solving in schools involves well-defined problems in math in elementary schools and in math, chemistry, and physics in middle and high schools (Bruning et al., 1999).
- *The tendency to rush toward a solution before the problem has been clearly defined.* Novice problem solvers tend to "jump" into a solution before they've clearly identified the problem (Lan, Repman, & Chyung, 1998), as did the second graders who added the sheep and goats to get the age of the captain.
- *The tendency to think convergently.* Beginning problem solvers tend to focus on one approach to solving problems and often persist with this approach even when it isn't working. Learning to think *divergently* results from experiences that require divergent thinking.

9.8
What is the most effective thing a teacher can do to prevent students from rushing toward a solution before they fully understand the problem? Explain.

Representing the Problem

A problem can be represented in at least three ways (Mayer, 2002). The problem can be (a) restated in different words that are more meaningful, (b) related to a previous problem, and (c) represented in visual form (an example is the diagram that Laura's students used). If the problem can't be restated or related to a similar problem, visually representing it can be effective. This puts the problem in a larger context and connects it to learners' existing background knowledge (Lovett & Anderson, 1994; Mevarech, 1999). Research suggests that successful problem solvers use visual representations as scaffolds when encountering particularly difficult problems (Lowrie & Kay, 2001). Many problems are complex enough to overload working memory, and putting problems on paper reduces this load.

Figure 9.5 A general problem-solving model

Selecting a Strategy

After the problem has been identified and represented, a strategy for solving it must be selected.

Algorithms. Let's look at another problem:

A coat costing $90 is marked 25% off. What is the sale price of the coat?

For most of us, this is a well-defined problem. We simply take 25% of 90, subtract the result from $90, and get $67.50 as the sale price. We used an **algorithm**, *a rule prescribing a specific set of steps for solving the problem.* Algorithms vary widely in their complexity. For instance, when we subtract whole numbers with regrouping, add fractions with unlike denominators, and solve algebraic equations, we use simple algorithms. By contrast, computer experts use complex algorithms to solve sophisticated programming problems.

Heuristics. Many problems can't be solved with algorithms, however. They don't exist for ill-defined problems and many that are well defined. In those cases, problem solvers use **heuristics**, *general, widely applicable problem-solving strategies* (Mayer & Wittrock, 1996). *Trial and error* is one example of a heuristic. It's an inefficient strategy, but one that problem solvers often try first when faced with unfamiliar problems and one that provides learners with experience, which is important for acquiring expertise (J. Hayes, 1988; Wagner & Sternberg, 1985).

9.9
Think again about the ill-defined problem of a personal relationship that is not satisfying. Describe a means-ends analysis that might be used to solve the problem.

Means-ends analysis, *a strategy in which the problem solver attempts to break the problem into subgoals and works successively on each,* is another heuristic. It is one of the most effective strategies for solving ill-defined problems. In the case of the seventh graders who don't want to "think," for example, we might operationally define "thinking" as an inclination to search for relationships in the topics they study and to make conclusions based on evidence. With this as our goal, we can then design learning activities that give the students practice in these areas.

Drawing analogies, *a strategy that is used to solve unfamiliar problems by comparing them with problems already solved,* is a third problem-solving heuristic (Mayer, 1992, 2002). It can be difficult to implement, however. Learners often can't find problems in their memories analogous to the one they want to solve, or they may make inappropriate connections between the two problems.

Ultimately, experience and background knowledge are essential for successfully selecting a strategy, and no heuristics can replace them (Pittman & Beth-Halachmy, 1997).

Implementing the Strategy

Clearly defining and representing the problem and selecting an appropriate algorithm or heuristic are keys to successfully implementing a strategy. If these processes have been effective, implementation is routine. If learners cannot implement a strategy, they should rethink the original problem or the strategy they've selected. Laura's students, for example, had an uncertain understanding of *area* and *perimeter,* and they lacked experience in defining problems, which made selecting an effective strategy hard for them. Their difficulties occurred well before they were to implement their strategies.

Evaluating the Results

Evaluating results is the final step in our problem-solving model, and it is often a challenge for students. For example:

> One boy, quite a good student, was working on the problem "If you have six jugs, and you want to put two thirds of a pint of lemonade into each jug, how much lemonade will you need?" His answer was 18 pints. I [Holt] said, "How much in each jug?" "Two thirds of a pint." I said, "Is that more or less than a pint?" "Less." I said, "How many jugs are there?" "Six." I said, "But that doesn't make any sense." He shrugged his shoulders and said, "Well, that's the way the system worked out." (Holt, 1964, p. 18)

Situations like this are common in classrooms. Once students get an answer, they're satisfied, regardless of whether or not it makes sense (Schunk, 1994). This also occurred in Laura's class, where several of her students were satisfied with widely discrepant answers.

Some experts believe that teachers can help students who fail to evaluate their results by emphasizing the thinking involved in problem solving instead of focusing on the answer (Mayer, 2002). Each step should make sense, and teachers should constantly require students to justify their thinking. In addition, requiring estimates beforehand is important. Estimates require understanding, and answers and estimates that are far apart raise questions. The habit of estimating is an important disposition that teachers should encourage.

9.10
Is the tendency of students to accept solutions that don't make sense a well-defined or an ill-defined instructional problem? Explain. Describe specifically what you might do to help the boy with the lemonade problem arrive at a valid solution.

Expert-Novice Differences in Problem-Solving Ability

Having examined a problem-solving model, let's now look at the characteristics of **experts**, *individuals who are "highly skilled or knowledgeable in a given domain"* (Bruer, 1993, p. 12, italics added). Research has identified four important differences between experts and novices in problem-solving ability (Bruning et al., 1999; Glaser & Chi, 1988). They're outlined in Table 9.2 and discussed in the paragraphs that follow.

The pattern we see in Table 9.2 is that experts better overcome the limitations of working memory than do novices. Experts represent problems more effectively because their complex schemas allow them to "chunk" large amounts of information into single units that don't exceed working memory's capacity. Much of their procedural knowledge is automatic, which further reduces the load on working memory and leaves more of its available space to focus on representing the problem and selecting a strategy (Bruer, 1993). In addition, they are metacognitive in their approach to solving unfamiliar problems. They plan carefully, try new strategies when existing ones are unproductive, and carefully monitor results.

How do experts acquire these characteristics? The answer is simple. They possess a great deal of both domain-specific and general knowledge, which are acquired through experience. Because of their experience, they can use heuristics, such as drawing analogies, effectively. Bransford (1993) described the process as follows: "Specific experiences are represented in memory as 'cases' that are indexed and searched so that they can be applied analogically to new problems that occur" (p. 4).

For example, expert teachers possess a wide range of general knowledge, and they have a broad and deep understanding of learning, student characteristics, and the content they teach (Bruning et al., 1999). The same is true for experts in physics, computer science, history, music, and any other area. Unfortunately, no simple path to expertise exists, and some researchers estimate that it takes up to 10,000 hours to develop true expertise in a domain, such as teaching or computer science (Ericsson, 1996).

How can an understanding of expertise help us in our efforts to teach learners to become better problem solvers? Let's take a look.

Table 9.2 Expert-novice differences in problem-solving ability

Area	Experts	Novices
Representing problems	Search for context and relationships in problems.	See problems in isolated pieces.
Problem-solving efficiency	Solve problems rapidly and possess much knowledge that is automatic.	Solve problems slowly, and focus on mechanics.
Planning for problem solving	Plan carefully before attempting solutions to unfamiliar problems.	Plan briefly when attempting solutions to unfamiliar problems; quickly adopt and try solutions.
Monitoring problem solving	Demonstrate well-developed metacognitive abilities; abandon inefficient strategies.	Demonstrate limited metacognition; persevere with unproductive strategies.

Developing Expertise: Role of Deliberate Practice

Research on the development of expertise clearly suggests that it requires a great deal of experience in and knowledge about the area being studied. If students are to develop their problem-solving skills in math, for example, they must solve a great many problems, including those that are ill defined. Drill-and-practice that requires the application of memorized algorithms won't do it.

Recognizing this need, researchers have become interested in the concept of deliberate practice and its role in the acquisition of expertise (Ericsson, 1996; Ericsson, Krampe, & Tesch-Romer, 1993). Deliberate practice has four essential characteristics:

- Learners must be motivated to think about the task and must exert effort.
- Instruction should take learners' background knowledge into account.
- Feedback to learners about errors and how to improve performance must be provided.
- Practice should provide opportunities for learners to repeatedly perform similar (but not identical) tasks.

Deliberate practice can overcome differences in native ability; researchers have found that deliberate, extensive practice provides opportunities for all students to improve their problem-solving abilities. Researchers state emphatically,

> In summary, our review has uncovered essentially no support for the fixed innate characteristics that would correspond to general or specific natural ability (in the development of expertise), and, in fact, has uncovered findings inconsistent with such models. (Ericsson et al., 1993, p. 399)

This doesn't imply that native ability is irrelevant; acquiring expertise will be easier for some than for others. It does mean, however, that if we're willing to work hard enough and long enough, we can acquire expertise and so can our students. In the vast majority of cases, talent doesn't block our road to competence. This is an encouraging finding.

We've now discussed presenting a general problem-solving model and describing the characteristics of expert performance, two of the strategies we identified for improving students' problem-solving abilities. We turn now to the third: teaching specific strategies for improving students' skills.

9.11

Which heuristic is deliberate practice most likely to help students use effectively: trial and error, means-ends analysis, or drawing analogies? Explain.

Helping Learners Become Better Problem Solvers: Instructional Strategies

How can we help our students develop problem-solving expertise? Information processing theory and constructivism, combined with research on problem solving, help us answer this question. To help learners acquire expertise, effective teachers apply this theory and research using the following principles:

- Present problems in real-world contexts.
- Capitalize on social interaction.
- Provide scaffolding for novice problem solvers.
- Teach general problem-solving strategies.

Let's return to Laura Hunter's work with her students to see how she attempted to implement these principles.

> Laura began Tuesday's math lesson by saying, "Yesterday, many of you said you weren't comfortable with the fact that we didn't agree about the amount of carpet we need for our classroom, so we'd better do some more work on it. . . . Let's take a look at our diagram again." She displayed the diagram on the overhead.

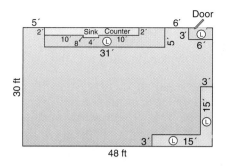

She then went on, "Which step in our problem-solving model are we now in?"

After a brief buzz, the students agreed that they were going back to implementing their strategies. Laura reviewed the two strategies they had used and then asked, "Which one do you want to try first?"

"Let's take the whole thing and subtract the linoleum pieces," Matt volunteered.

Laura asked if that was okay with everyone, and seeing their positive nods, she continued, "It seems that there might be some confusion about area and perimeter, so I want you to look at the diagram and figure out the perimeter first. . . . When you're finished, I'm going to ask you how you got it."

Her review revealed some uncertainty in the students' thinking. When Laura asked Kelly how she found a perimeter of 89 feet, Kelly explained that she added 48, 30, 5 and 6. Damon calculated the perimeter as 150 by adding 48, 15, 15, 6, 31, 5, and 30. Some other students' answers varied, too, suggesting they hadn't added the numbers correctly.

After spending additional time discussing the perimeter and finally agreeing that it was 156 feet, Laura turned back to the subject of area and reviewed it in a similar way, with the class concluding that the total area of the room was 1,440 square feet.

"So, what do we do next?" she continued.

"Subtract those parts," Elise offered, pointing to the parts on the diagram marked *L*.

"How do we know that we must subtract?"

"There isn't any carpet there, . . . and it's part of the whole room," Adam volunteered.

"Okay, let's do it," Laura smiled. "Let's try this first," pointing to the top part of the diagram. "How long is this part? . . . Fred?"

"Thirty-one feet."

"Good, . . . so, how about our width; how wide is this section? Is it 2 feet or 5 feet? . . . Paige?"

"Five feet."

"Why is it 5?"

"The 2 is just that . . . the sink counter. . . . The linoleum goes under the whole 5 feet."

"Good thinking, Paige," Laura smiled. "Okay, everyone calculate the area of that part, figure out the area by the door, and then try the part here," pointing to the linoleum at the lower right.

Most of the students got the first two areas, but many were uncertain about the third.

Laura then went to the chalkboard and wrote the following:

15 × 3 = 45 square feet
12 × 3 = 36 square feet
45 + 36 = 81 square feet

"Now, let's see where this came from," Laura directed. "Look carefully at it, also look at the diagram, and I'm going to ask you to explain these numbers."

Laura waited for a minute and then said, "Someone explain where these numbers came from."

After several seconds, Nephi offered, "The 15 is the length of that part," pointing to the bottom of the diagram. "And the 3 is how wide it is . . . so, the area is 45."

"Forty-five what?" Laura probed.

"Square feet," Nephi added quickly.

"Now, let's be good critical thinkers. . . . Can someone explain the 12 times 3?"

"I've got it!" Anya nearly shouted after several seconds. "It's because you already have that much," waving her hand back and forth.

"Come up and show us."

Anya then went to the overhead and altered the diagram as shown at right:

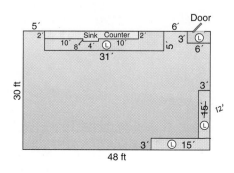

"I was thinking, . . . see, we already have this," she said, pointing to the lower right corner of the drawing. "So, this length is 12, not 15. . . . So, it's 12 times 3."

"What do the rest of you think? . . . Thank you, Anya," Laura smiled.

They agreed that Anya's thinking made sense, and Laura then asked, "Now what do we do?"

"Add up those amounts," Jared suggested.

The class added the areas of the linoleum sections and got a total of 254 square feet.

"So, how much carpet do we need?" Laura said finally. "How are we going to figure that out?"

"Subtract," Sam offered.

"Subtract what?"

"The 254 from . . . 1,440."

"And what is the 1,440?"

"The whole area, the area of the whole room."

The class agreed that Sam's thinking was valid, so Laura continued, "All right, . . . tomorrow we're going to look at the other strategy, where you take the inside area and add the other parts. . . . For your homework, I want you to figure out what the inside length and width are. Be sure you're ready to explain how you got them when we start. You have 15 minutes. Go ahead and get started."

The students began, and as they worked, Laura monitored them carefully and offered suggestions when they had questions or appeared confused.

Let's take a closer look at Laura's Tuesday lesson, its relationship with Monday's lesson, and Laura's attempts to help learners develop problem-solving expertise.

9.12

Identify at least three ways in which Laura's assignment (as opposed to traditional seat work) illustrated deliberate practice.

Present Problems in Real-World Contexts

By building her lessons around the carpeted area of her classroom, Laura presented a real-world problem, which was consistent with our first principle as well as with constructivism. Using real-world experiences significantly improves problem-solving ability (Bransford & Schwartz, 1999). In addition, Laura took the students' background knowledge into account by reviewing *perimeter* and *area* and intervening when she realized that the students had misconceptions about differences between the two concepts.

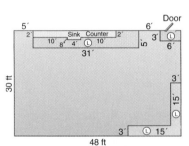

Laura's lesson was built around a real-world problem, allowed time to address misconceptions, included questioning, and focused on student thinking.

Capitalize on Social Interaction

Laura developed both lessons using a great deal of social interaction. The need for social interaction is also supported by constructivism, and problem-solving research indicates that encouraging students to discuss and analyze problems increases their understanding and promotes transfer (B. Barron, 2000; Mevarech, 1999). The benefit of social interaction was particularly evident when Laura asked Kelly to explain how she got 89 feet as an answer for the perimeter. Without the interaction, Kelly's misconception wouldn't have been revealed. Laura also emphasized the students' thinking, rather than correct answers, which is crucial if students are to develop problem-solving expertise (Mayer, 2002). (This doesn't imply that correct answers are not important. Rather, it suggests that the thinking involved in arriving at the correct answer is as important as the answer itself.)

An additional aspect of the interaction in Laura's lessons is significant. In Monday's lesson, much of the students' work was done in small groups, whereas on Tuesday Laura conducted a whole-class lesson. Although the format was different for the two lessons, the interaction was as important in one as in the other. Tuesday's lesson was as grounded in constructivism as was Monday's.

Social interaction in small groups provides opportunities for students to learn new problem-solving strategies from others.

Provide Scaffolding for Novice Problem Solvers

Seeing that students struggled with some parts of the problem-solving process, and particularly with effectively implementing their strategies, Laura provided much more scaffolding in Tuesday's lesson than she did in Monday's.

Questioning was her primary form of scaffolding. She asked a great many questions during Tuesday's lesson; in fact, she developed it almost entirely through questioning. Her questioning also helped ensure that the students' thinking would remain open and visible throughout. This emphasis is an essential characteristic of instruction grounded in constructivist views of learning.

In addition to questioning, three other forms of scaffolding can be helpful: visually representing problems, arranging cognitive apprenticeships, and analyzing worked examples. We saw how she built Tuesday's lesson around the visual representation (diagram) of their problem. Let's look at the other two forms of scaffolding.

Cognitive Apprenticeship. Cognitive apprenticeship is *a form of scaffolding that occurs when a less skilled learner works at the side of an expert* (Collins, Brown, & Holum, 1991; Collins, Brown, & Newman, 1989). The expert can be either the teacher or another student. When Laura used Anya as a model, for instance, and encouraged Anya to describe her own thinking as she explained the results on the board, Laura was employing a form of cognitive apprenticeship. Teachers also capitalize on cognitive apprenticeships when they model, think aloud, coach, and gradually remove support as the apprentice (student) becomes more confident and proficient.

This leads us to the idea of worked examples.

Analyzing Worked Examples. Worked examples are *problems and complete solutions that are presented simultaneously.* An expanding body of research confirms that presenting worked examples, combined with analyzing and discussing them in detail, makes problem solving more meaningful than traditional instruction does. In traditional instruction, teachers typically model solutions to problems that students then try to imitate, often with little understanding (Mayer, 2002; Mwangi & Sweller, 1998). These results have been found with learners ranging from lower elementary to university students, and we saw them illustrated in Laura's lesson (R. Atkinson, Derry, Renkl, & Wortham, 2000).

Laura had written the following on the board:

15 × 3 = 45 square feet

12 × 3 = 36 square feet

45 + 36 = 81 square feet

This worked example, combined with Anya's think-aloud and the discussion that followed, made the problem meaningful for students. Worked examples alone are insufficient, however; without discussion, learners often miss important aspects of the process and are likely to try to memorize the steps in it instead of developing genuine understanding (Chi, Bassok, Lewis, Reimann, & Glaser, 1989).

Worked examples are especially helpful when students are first learning a procedure. As they acquire experience, increased emphasis should be placed on applying the procedure in different contexts (R. Atkinson et al., 2000; Kalyuga, Chandler, Tuovinen, & Sweller, 2001). Research indicates that learners prefer worked examples to traditional instruction (Renkl, Stark, Gruber, & Mandl, 1998). This motivational factor is particularly important as teachers try to provide the extensive deliberate practice necessary to develop expertise.

Teach General Problem-Solving Strategies

Although general strategies in the absence of domain-specific knowledge have limited value, within specific domains, such as mathematics, they can increase problem-solving abilities (Higgins, 1997; Mayer, 1992, 2002). Emphasizing general strategies is effective because it helps students become more metacognitive about their problem solving (Mayer, 2002).

9.13
Explain why general problem-solving strategies would be more effective within a particular domain, such as social studies or science, than across domains.

Identify the problem

↓

Represent the problem

↓

Select a strategy

↓

Carry out the strategy

↓

Evaluate results

Laura used the model as a framework for teaching general problem- solving strategies.

Laura attempted to teach general problem-solving strategies by using the problem-solving model as a framework for her lessons. She emphasized each step in Monday's lesson, and she began Tuesday's lesson by asking, "Which step in our problem-solving model are we now in?"

Laura also modeled the attitudes necessary to promote thinking and the development of expertise. She had an accepting attidude—her students knew that taking risks and making mistakes was acceptable. She also carefully planned the use of strategies—she had the class focus on one strategy on Tuesday, and she planned to consider a second the next day.

Teachers can also help students acquire general problem-solving skills through coaching (Collins et al., 1989; Mayer, 1998a). For example, as students work, the teacher can ask questions, such as the following, to help students become more metacognitive in their efforts:

What (exactly) are you doing? (Can you describe it precisely?)
Why are you doing it? (How does it fit into the solution?)
How does it help you? (What will you do with the outcome when you obtain it?)
(Schoenfeld, 1989, p. 98)

In time and with practice, students become more metacognitive, and their skills improve.

Using Technology to Improve Problem-Solving Ability

We said earlier that practice and experience, which requires motivated learners, is essential for developing expertise and that motivation is higher when students encounter realistic and interesting problems. Technology can be helpful in meeting these requirements (Huffman, 2001). Let's look at an example from middle school math:

Jasper Woodbury sees an ad for a boat docked at Cedar Creek and decides to take a look. His dock is at mile 132.6, and in looking at his navigational map, he guesses it will take him about 2 hours to get to Cedar Creek. On the radio, he hears that the temperature is 91, the sunset will be at 7:52 P.M., and the wind is from the west at 4 mph.

Jasper goes to Larry's to get gas, which is $1.29⁹ with 4¢ off per gallon for cash. Jasper provides a pint of his own oil, which he adds to the tank before Larry puts the fuel in. When Larry looks at the pump, he sees that Jasper has gotten 5.0 gallons for a total of $6.30. Larry gives Jasper change from a 20-dollar bill, which is all the cash Jasper has.

After a minor repair on his boat, costing $8.25, Jasper continues to Cedar Creek, which is at mile 156.6. He makes it all the way on one tank of gas.

Jasper looks at an advertised boat and decides to buy it. The gas tank holds 12 gallons, and the boat burns about 5 gallons per hour at a cruising speed of 7½ mph. Sal, the previous owner, warns him that the running lights don't work, so she always gets home before the sun goes down.

They settle on a price for Sal's boat, and Jasper pays her with his last check.

Jasper looks at his watch and sees that it's 2:35 P.M.

Challenge:
When should Jasper leave for home?
Can he make it without running out of fuel?

The problem you just read is an abbreviated "story summary" of the episode "Journey to Cedar Creek," taken from the problem-solving series called The Adventures of Jasper Woodbury (Cognition and Technology Group at Vanderbilt, 1997). Researchers developed this and other video-based episodes because many of the problems students face in math don't capture the realism and complexity of life-related applications (S. Williams, Bareiss, & Reiser, 1996). The problems in each episode are purposefully left ill defined to give students practice in problem finding and separating relevant from irrelevant information and to give

9.14

Each of the steps in the problem-solving model are important, but one is essential for learners attempting to solve Jasper's problem. Which one? Explain.

Technology can provide learners with complex problems to solve in realistic contexts.

students experiences in using means-ends analysis to identify subgoals, such as finding out how much money Jasper has left. The problems also provide students with deliberate practice. Students must work collaboratively over several class periods, during which they share their thinking and receive feedback from the teacher and their classmates.

The developers, the Cognition and Technology Group at Vanderbilt (1992), claim that middle school students using the Jasper series were more successful and had more positive attitudes toward math than students in traditional programs, and they report teacher comments that corroborate these results. Although these results are intuitively sensible, they haven't been corroborated by researchers who aren't invested in the program. Also, success with the program is likely to require a great deal of skilled scaffolding from teachers.

To examine the complete story summary, together with other problems, solutions, and extensions, go to the Companion Website at *www.prenhall.com/eggen*, then to this chapter's *Web Links* module. The annotated website will appear in the list.

Problem-Based Learning

Think again about Scott Sowell's lesson at the end of Chapter 8, Laura Hunter's lessons in this chapter, and the Jasper Woodbury series you just read about: They all illustrate **problem-based learning**, *a teaching strategy that uses problems as the focus for developing content, skills, and self-direction* (Krajcik, Blumenfeld, Marx, & Soloway, 1994; Richason, 2001). Problem-based learning strategies typically have the following characteristics:

- Lessons begin with a problem, and solving the problem is the focus of the lesson (T. Duffy & Cunningham, 1996; Grabinger, 1996).
- Students are responsible for investigating the problem, designing strategies, and finding solutions (Slavin, Madden, Dolan, & Wasik, 1994). Groups need to be small enough (e.g., four to five students) so that all students can actively participate in the process (M. Lohman & Finkelstein, 2000).
- The teacher guides students' efforts with questioning and other forms of scaffolding (Maxwell, Bellisimo, & Mergendoller, 1999; Stepien & Gallagher, 1993).

As we saw in Scott's and Laura's lessons, the third characteristic is essential. Both needed to judiciously intervene, because their students experienced difficulties in solving the problems. In spite of considerable guidance, Scott's students retained misconceptions about the effect of weight and angle on the frequency of the pendulum until the whole-group discussion, and Laura's students hadn't successfully solved the problem at the end of Monday's lesson. In response to these difficulties, Scott used a direct approach near the end of his lesson, and Laura guided her students more specifically on Tuesday than she did on Monday. Some authorities would argue that both Scott and Laura should have intervened sooner and more specifically, whereas others would suggest that the experience the students gained, in spite of the fact that they struggled, was a worthwhile goal in itself.

In addition, some evidence indicates that content learned in problem-based lessons is retained longer and transfers better than content learned when other strategies are used (T. Duffy & Cunningham, 1996; Sternberg, 1998b), although additional research is needed to confirm these findings (Mergendoller, Bellisimo, & Maxwell, 2000).

If you plan to try problem-based activities in your classes, these guidelines may be valuable:

- *Begin with a clear problem.* Even though the students are responsible for designing and implementing the solution, the initial problem must be clear and precise.
- *Organize the activity carefully.* Be sure groups are small, roles are clear, and materials are readily accessible (M. Lohman & Finkelstein, 2000).
- *Carefully monitor students as they work.* If students are proceeding based on a misconception, you should intervene.

9.15
What concept from "Making Information Meaningful" in Chapter 7 best explains why students might retain content longer in problem-based learning lessons?

Problem-based learning provides opportunities for students to use learning strategies and develop their metacognitive abilities.

(For instance, it would have been unwise of Scott to let his students continue to simultaneously change two variables as they worked on the pendulum problem.)

■ *Conduct a whole-class discussion to summarize the groups' work and provide feedback about the overall process.*

As with virtually any teaching strategy, problem-based learning can be effective, but it won't work automatically. It must be designed and implemented by a skilled teacher who carefully monitors the process.

Classroom Connections

Teaching Problem Solving in Your Classroom

1. Use real-world problems and promote high levels of social interaction.
   - *Elementary:* A fourth-grade teacher emphasizes the first stage of problem solving by having her students practice putting problems into their own words. She asks them to discuss the problem with a partner before beginning to work on it and discusses the problem as a whole group before having them solve it individually or in groups.
   - *Middle School:* A middle school teacher has a "problem of the week" activity. Each student in the class is required to bring in at least one "real-world" problem each week. The teacher selects from among them, and the class works on them in groups. He is careful to ensure that each student has a problem selected during the year.
   - *High School:* An Algebra II teacher requires her students to explain each step as they "walk" through

the solutions to problems. She emphasizes that understanding the reasons is as important as getting the right answers.

2. Provide students with practice and scaffolding as they develop their problem-solving skills.
   - *Elementary:* A third-grade teacher begins a lesson on graphing by asking students how they might determine what people's favorite jelly beans are. He guides them as they identify the problem and how they might represent and solve it.
   - *Middle School:* A seventh-grade pre-algebra teacher uses categories such as "We Know" and "We Need to Know" as scaffolds for analyzing all word problems. Using this framework, the students solve a minimum of two word problems a day.
   - *High School:* A high school teacher in a unit on statistics and probability requires her students to practice making estimates before actually solving problems. They then compare the solutions to the estimates with the goal of making more accurate estimates.

The Strategic Learner

Do you think about the way you study for the courses you're taking? Do you ask yourself if your efforts are as effective as possible? Do you adapt to different conditions, such as skimming if you want only an overview of the content or summarizing if you want a deeper understanding? You should, and in the following discussion you'll see why.

Metacognition: The Foundation of Strategic Learning

In Chapter 7 we saw that **metacognition** is *the awareness of and control over one's own cognitive processes.* Compared to lower achievers high achievers are more aware of the way they study and learn, and they take more steps to improve both. In other words, they're more metacognitive about their learning.

Metacognition is the mechanism used to match a strategy to a goal (C. Weinstein, 1994). You may recall from Chapter 7 that strategies are *plans for accomplishing specific learning goals.* When students take notes, for example, they're using a strategy. Increased understanding is their goal, and taking notes is a plan they're using to reach it. When expert learners use this strategy, they ask questions such as:

- Am I taking enough notes, or am I taking too many?
- Am I writing down important ideas in my notes, or are they filled with trivial details?
- Am I simply reading my notes when I study, or do I attempt to elaborate on them with examples?

These questions demonstrate metacognition, which involves continually asking questions about the effectiveness of our learning strategies.

Although most strategy research has focused on reading (Bruning et al., 1999), other studies have examined strategy use in areas such as problem solving in math and science, writing, and study skills (Rosenshine, 1997). This research indicates that effective strategy users, in addition to being metacognitive about their learning, have two other characteristics: (a) a broad background of knowledge and (b) a repertoire of strategies.

Broad Background Knowledge

We've seen how important background knowledge is for cognitive learning in general, and it is no less important for strategy use (Alao & Guthrie, 1999). Trying to encode information and represent it in memory without a strong knowledge base makes strategy use extremely difficult (Alexander, Graham, & Harris, 1998). In a study in which reciprocal teaching (a strategy used to increase comprehension) was used with science students, researchers found that without sufficient background knowledge students used the strategy only to "predict trivia, to summarize details, and to clarify big words" (C. Anderson & Roth, 1989, p. 300). In contrast, students with extensive background knowledge are able to use deep processing strategies to generate questions, create images, and use analogical thinking (Chinn, 1997).

A Repertoire of Strategies

Just as expert problem solvers draw upon a wealth of experiences, effective strategy users have a variety of strategies from which to choose. For instance, they can take notes, skim, use outlines, generate diagrams and figures, take advantage of bold and italicized print, and capitalize on examples (Hacker, Dunlosky, & Graesser, 1998). They can also use heuristics, such as means-ends analysis, to break ill-defined problems into manageable parts. Without a repertoire of strategies, learners cannot match strategies to different goals.

Becoming a strategic learner takes time and effort. Research indicates that, in spite of being aware of more sophisticated strategies, most students use primitive ones, such as simple rehearsal, regardless of the difficulty of the material. Unfortunately, students rarely receive strategy instruction before high school (E. Wood, Motz, & Willoughby, 1998).

9.16
Which theory of learning—
behaviorism, social cognitive theory, information processing, or *constructivism*—best supports the value of strategy use for increasing learning? Explain.

Study Strategies

Study strategies are *specific plans students use to increase their understanding of written materials and teacher presentations.* In the following sections, we examine basic study skills and a variety of comprehension-monitoring strategies.

Basic Study Skills

Basic study skills are simple, commonly used strategies, such as highlighting and note taking. Again, metacognition is the key to their success; their effectiveness depends on decisions about what is important enough to highlight, include in notes, or use in organizing ideas (Moreland, Dansereau, & Chmielewski, 1997; J. Wiley & Voss, 1999).

Study strategies such as note taking and outlining are effectively learned through teacher modeling, think-alouds, and discussion.

Being metacognitive is not easy, and students often have difficulty identifying important information. For example, some students avoid these decisions by highlighting entire sections, tacitly believing that they're studying when, in fact, they're doing little more than reading and physically marking the text. These students are metacognitively "inert"; they're studying passively instead of actively. Other students are more active, but they miss valuable ideas in a passage because they focus on only the first sentence of paragraphs, items that stand out, such as those in boldface or italics (Mayer, 1984), or those that are intrinsically interesting (Harp & Mayer, 1998).

Note taking is similar to highlighting; its effectiveness depends on the learner's decisions about what is important enough to write down. As with highlighting, some students take notes passively—even though they write furiously—by attempting to write down everything the teacher says, thereby avoiding decisions about what is important or how ideas are interconnected.

Comprehension Monitoring

Comprehension monitoring is *the process of checking to see if you understand the material you're reading or hearing* (Palincsar & Brown, 1984). It is an advanced study strategy that requires well-developed metacognition. Low achievers and others who aren't metacognitive rarely check their understanding, so they're unable to adapt when they don't comprehend what they're reading or hearing (L. Baker & Brown, 1984). Three comprehension-monitoring strategies are summarizing, elaborative questioning, and PQ4R.

Summarizing. **Summarizing** is *the process of preparing a concise description of verbal or written passages.* Learning to summarize takes time and training, but upper elementary students and higher can become skilled with it (Pressley, Johnson, Symons, McGoldrick, & Kurita, 1989). Training usually involves walking students through a passage and helping them identify unimportant information, construct general descriptions for lists of items, and generate topic sentences for paragraphs. Although time-consuming, training results in increased comprehension (T. Anderson & Armbruster, 1984; A. Brown & Palincsar, 1987).

Elaborative Questioning. **Elaborative questioning** is *the process of drawing inferences, identifying examples, and forming relationships in the material being studied.* It is perhaps the most effective of the comprehension-monitoring strategies (Dole, Duffy, Roehler, & Pearson, 1991; E. Wood, Willoughby, McDermott, Motz, Kaspar, & Ducharme, 1999). Three elaborative questions are especially effective:

- What is another example of this idea?
- How is this topic similar to or different from the one in the previous section?
- How does this idea relate to other big ideas I have been learning?

To illustrate these strategies, consider your own study of this chapter. As you were studying the section on problem solving, you could have asked yourself questions, such as

What is another example of a well-defined problem in this class?
What is another example of an ill-defined problem?
What makes the first well defined and the second ill defined?

9.17
Using information processing as a basis, explain why students have the tendency to avoid making the decision about what is important, focusing instead, for example, on the first sentence of paragraphs.

9.18
Which of the three elaborative questions would likely be most valuable for concept learning? Explain.

How are problem-solving and learning strategies similar? How are they
   different?
Could concept learning ever be problem solving? Why or why not?

Elaborative questioning like this creates links between new information and knowledge
in long-term memory, which makes the new information more meaningful and increases
learning.

PQ4R.   *PQ4R* is a complex study strategy that teaches students to use a series of sequential steps to monitor comprehension while reading. The steps are

1. *Preview:* Survey headings to understand how the material is organized.
2. *Question:* Create elaborative questions as you survey the content.
3. *Read:* Read the material, and try to answer the elaborative questions as you're
   reading.
4. *Reflect:* Create and try to answer additional elaborative questions after you've
   finished reading the passage.
5. *Recite:* Summarize what you've read, and include relationships between the
   passage and earlier passages.
6. *Review:* Reread parts of the passage for which you were unable to ask or answer
   your elaborative questions.

PQ4R combines the features of both summarizing and elaborative questioning into a single strategy, and it has had some success in improving learners' use of study strategies
(A. Adams, Carnine, & Gersten, 1982).
    Virtually any strategy will be successful or unsuccessful, depending on how it's
used. Effort is the key. If learners are metacognitive and use a strategy actively, it will
work; if they aren't, it won't.

Developing Strategic Learning in Students:
Instructional Strategies

Teachers can help learners improve their strategy use by using effective instructional
scaffolding while teaching strategies, having students practice them, and providing
feedback throughout the process. The following principles can guide teachers in their
efforts:

- Describe the strategy and explain why it is useful.
- Explicitly teach the strategy by modeling its use.
- Model metacognition by describing your thinking as you work through the
  strategy.
- Provide opportunities for students to practice the strategy in a variety of
  contexts.
- Provide feedback as students practice. (Carpenter, Levi, Fennema, Ansell, &
  Franke, 1995; Rickards, Fajen, Sullivan, & Gillespie, 1997)

Let's see how the principles guide Donna Evans, a middle school geography teacher,
as she works with her students.

Donna began her geography class by giving each of her middle schoolers a blank transparency and a nonpermanent marking pen.
    "We need to read the section of our text that describes the low-latitude, middle-latitude,
and high-latitude climates," she said. "Let's talk for a few minutes about how we can help
ourselves remember and understand what we've read.
    "One way to become more effective readers is to summarize the information we read in a
few short statements that capture its meaning. This is useful because it makes the information

easier to remember—in our situation, it'll help us compare one climate region with another. We can use this skill whenever we're studying a specific topic, such as climates or culture and economics, which we'll study later. You can do the same thing when you study different classes of animals in biology or parts of the court system in your government class.

"Now go ahead and read the passage, and see if you can decide what makes a low-latitude climate a low-latitude climate," she said.

After giving the class a few minutes to read the section, Donna continued, "As I was reading, I kept asking myself what makes the low-latitude climates what they are. . . . Here's how I thought about it. I read the section, and I saw that the low latitudes could be either hot and wet or hot and dry. Close to the equator, the humid tropical climate is hot and wet all year. A little farther away, it has wet summers and dry winters. For the dry tropical climate, high-pressure zones cause deserts, like the Sahara."

Donna displayed a transparency that included the information she had provided and said, "Now, let's all give it a try with the section on the middle-latitude climates. Go ahead and read the section, and try to summarize it the way I did. . . . I want you to write your summaries on your individual transparencies, so we can all see what you've written. As you get better and better with the strategy, we'll quit writing our summaries down, and you'll be able to use it on your own."

The class read the passage, and after they finished, Donna began, "Okay. Who can give me a summary? Someone?. . . . Go ahead, Dana."

Dana displayed her summary on the overhead, and Donna and other class members responded, adding information and comments to what Dana said. Donna then had Omar, Taeko, and Jesse display their summaries, the class practiced again with the section on the high-latitude climates, and Donna had other students display these summaries.

Throughout the school year, Donna continued to have the students practice summarizing a day or two each week.

Let's take a closer look at Donna's efforts to develop strategic learners. First, she described the skill and its use by saying, "One way to become more effective readers is to summarize the information we read in a few short statements that capture its meaning. This is useful because it makes the information easier to remember."

Second, she modeled the skill, including metacognition, when she said, "As I was reading, I kept asking myself what makes the low-latitude climates what they are. . . . Here's how I thought about it."

Then, she had the students practice by reading the passage and preparing a summary. She had students display their summaries on the overhead, so the process of giving and receiving feedback was clear to all. And she continued the process throughout the school year.

Notice also that although Donna focused explicitly on summarizing, she also modeled self-questioning when she said, "I kept asking myself what makes the low-latitude climates what they are." Helping students combine strategies makes strategy instruction even more effective (G. Duffy, 1992).

9.19

Explain one specific way in which Donna's approach was an application of information processing, and also explain one way in which her approach was an application of social cognitive theory.

Critical Thinking

Critical thinking is *a person's ability and inclination to make and assess conclusions based on evidence.* For example, an advertisement says, "Doctors recommend . . . more often," touting a health product. A person thinking critically is wary because the advertisement provides no evidence for its claims. Similarly, a critical thinker listens to another person's argument with skepticism because people often have unconscious biases.

The development of critical thinking is at the core of cognitive approaches to teaching, and as with the development of problem-solving, expertise, and learning strategies, it takes practice (Halpern, 1995). A classroom climate that values different perspectives and high levels of discussion is essential, and as we've said repeatedly, reasons for answers are as important as the answers themselves.

Although critical thinking is related to study skills, the two differ in scope. Study skills focus on learning from teacher presentations and written materials. Critical thinking is broader; it is used to process information from a variety of sources (Beach, 1999; E. Jones, 1995). For example, you might summarize a newspaper editorial to increase your

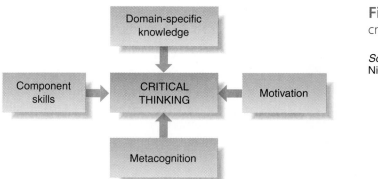

Figure 9.6 Elements of critical thinking

Source: Adapted from Nickerson, 1988.

comprehension of it. When looking for evidence for the author's position or identifying unstated assumptions in what the author says, you're going beyond comprehension; you are thinking critically.

Over the years, many programs have been developed to teach different aspects of thinking outside traditional content courses, but research indicates that the skills taught in these programs rarely transfer to the regular curriculum (Bransford, Goldman, & Vye, 1991). As a result, current critical thinking instruction emphasizes explicitly teaching thinking within the context of the regular curriculum (A. Brown, 1997; Kuhn, 1999).

Current approaches are generally organized around four basic elements (Mayer, 2002; Nickerson, 1988), illustrated in Figure 9.6 and described in the following sections.

Component Skills

Component skills are *the "tools" of thinking;* they are the *cognitive processes learners use to make and assess their conclusions* (Mayer, 2002). With some variation from one source to another (Beyer, 1988; Halpern, 1998), most experts include the skills summarized in Table 9.3.

Research on the teaching of critical thinking supports the idea of focusing on component skills, which are specifically described, modeled, and practiced with feedback (Mayer, 2002; Sternberg, 1998b, 1998c). In addition, integrating critical thinking into the regular school curriculum helps students develop a deeper understanding of the topics they study (Bransford et al., 1991; Van Leuvan, Wang, & Hildebrandt, 1990).

9.20
What is the most likely reason that efforts to teach thinking outside the context of the regular curriculum have been unsuccessful?

Table 9.3 Component skills in thinking

Skill	Subskill
Observing	Recalling Recognizing
Finding patterns and generalizing	Comparing and contrasting Classifying Identifying relevant and irrelevant information
Forming conclusions based on patterns	Inferring Predicting Hypothesizing Applying
Assessing conclusions based on observation	Checking consistency Identifying bias, stereotypes, clichés, and propaganda Identifying unstated assumptions Recognizing overgeneralizations or undergeneralizations Confirming conclusions with facts

Asking students to compare, contrast, analyze, and make predictions encourages them to use and develop higher level cognitive processes.

To illustrate the use of component skills, let's look at some dialogue from Laura's Tuesday lesson.

Laura:	(After the students concluded that the total area of the room was 1,440 square feet) So, what do we do next?
Elise:	(Pointing to the parts on the diagram marked *L*) Subtract those parts.
Laura:	How do we know that we must subtract?
Adam:	There isn't any carpet there, . . . and it's part of the whole room.
Laura:	Okay, let's do it. Let's try this first. (pointing to the top part of the diagram) How long is this part? . . . Fred?
Fred:	Thirty-one feet.
Laura:	Good, . . . so, how about our width; how wide is this section? Is it 2 feet or 5 feet? . . . Paige?
Paige:	Five feet.
Laura:	Why is it 5?
Paige:	The 2 is just that . . . the sink counter. . . . The linoleum goes under the whole 5 feet.

A little later in the lesson, they continued:

Laura:	Now, let's be good critical thinkers. . . . (She presents the worked example.) Can someone explain the 12 times 3?
Anya:	I've got it! It's because you already have that much. (referring to the 15 foot by 3 foot area)
Laura:	Come up and show us.

Anya then went to the overhead and altered the diagram to show that one area was 15 feet by 3 feet and another was 12 feet by 3 feet.

Anya:	I was thinking, . . . see, we already have this. (pointing to the 15 foot by 3 foot area) So, this length is 12, not 15. . . . So, it's 12 times 3.

In the dialogue we see how Laura integrated component critical thinking skills into her instruction. When she asked, "How do we know that we must subtract?" she was asking the students to justify their thinking and confirm a conclusion (that they must subtract) with a fact (there isn't any carpet there, and it's part of the room). She did the same thing when she asked Paige if the width was 2 feet or 5 feet, and Paige also had to recognize that the width of the sink counter was irrelevant to the problem. Identifying relevant and irrelevant information is another component skill. Then, Anya applied her understanding of the problem when she was able to explain the 12 × 3 in the worked example.

Domain-Specific Knowledge

We have repeatedly emphasized the importance of background knowledge for all aspects of cognitive learning, and it is no less important for critical thinking. As in other areas, background knowledge is domain specific; the ability to think critically in history, for example, doesn't ensure that a person will also be able to think critically in chemistry. Nickerson (1988) summarized the importance of domain-specific knowledge to thinking: "To think effectively in any domain one must know something about the domain and, in general, the more one knows the better" (p. 13).

9.21
Which of the component skills could a preoperational learner use? A concrete operational learner? A formal operational learner? Explain.

Metacognition

Metacognition is important for all cognitive processing; it provides direction for our cognitive efforts. In the context of critical thinking, being metacognitive means that learners know when to use the component skills, how they relate to domain-specific knowledge, and why they're used. Effective thinkers not only find patterns and form conclusions based on evidence, for example, but they also are keenly aware of what they're doing and why.

Some researchers argue that metacognition is *the* essence of critical thinking, and the development of metacognition is even more important than the component skills we identified earlier (Kuhn, 1999). Explicitly teaching and talking about thinking as it occurs in the classroom are effective ways to develop these metacognitive abilities (M. Adams, 1989; Butler, 1998).

Motivation

Experts are becoming increasingly aware of the role motivation plays in thinking (Pintrich & Schunk, 2002; Resnick, 1987). Learner motivation determines the attitudes and dispositions students bring to their learning experiences. Examples include

- The inclination to rely on evidence in making conclusions
- The willingness to respect opinions that differ from our own
- A sense of curiosity, inquisitiveness, and a desire to be informed
- A tendency to reflect before acting
- The willingness to "let go" of previous ideas, beliefs, and assumptions (Bransford & Schwartz, 1999; Nickerson, 1988; Tishman, Perkins, & Jay, 1995)

Much of a teacher's effort in developing thinking is directed toward helping learners acquire these attitudes and dispositions. For example, we want our students to ask themselves, "Where is the author coming from?" when they read a political commentary, knowing that political orientation will slant the author's opinion. In school we want learners to be skeptical about the truth of rumors, and in classroom settings we want them to constantly wonder, "What does this relate to?" and, "How do we know?"

Attitudes and dispositions usually can't be taught directly. Students disposed to think critically have teachers who model these attitudes for them and teachers who establish an emotional climate that supports critical thinking.

Classroom Connections

Promoting Strategic Learning in Your Classroom

Study Strategies

1. Teach study strategies across the curriculum.
   - *Elementary:* A second-grade teacher models elaborative questioning and encourages her children to ask themselves, after each lesson of the day, what the lesson was about and what they learned from it.
   - *Middle School:* A sixth-grade teacher introduces note taking as a listening skill and then provides note-taking practice in science and social studies by using skeletal outlines to organize his presentations and

having his students use them as a guide for their note taking.
   - *High School:* A biology teacher closes each lesson by having her students provide summaries of the most important parts of the lesson. She adds material to the summaries that are incomplete.

Critical Thinking

2. Plan and conduct lessons to promote thinking.
   - *Elementary:* A fourth-grade teacher makes an effort to ask questions that promote thinking in his students. He has a list he calls "The Big Five" and looks for

opportunities to ask them whenever he can: (a) What do you see? observe? (b) How are these alike? How are they different? (c) Why? (d) What would happen if . . . ? (e) How do you know?

- *Middle School:* A sixth-grade world history teacher develops the content in her units with charts, graphs, and tables. She begins units by asking her students to make comparisons among items of information in the charts and conclusions based on the comparisons. She requires that they provide evidence for each of the conclusions based on information they see in the charts.

- *High School:* An English teacher works to help his students analyze literature. As they talk about a work, he regularly asks, "How do you know that?" and, "What in the story supports your idea?"

Transfer of Learning

Consider the following situation:

You get into your car, put the key into the ignition, and the seat belt buzzer goes off. You quickly buckle the belt. Or, anticipating the buzzer, you buckle the belt before you insert the key.

Think for a moment. What concept from behaviorism does your behavior—buckling the seat belt—best illustrate? Behaviorists would describe this as an example of *negative reinforcement.* If you identified it as such, you have demonstrated **transfer,** *"the effect of previous learning on new learning or problem solving"* (Mayer, 2002, p. 4, italics added). You have applied your understanding of the concept *negative reinforcement* to the new example of the seat belt. Transfer is crucial in learning because it allows students to apply information—on their own—to new contexts:

Schools are not able to teach students everything they will need to know, but rather must equip students with the ability to transfer—to use what they have learned to solve new problems successfully or to learn quickly in new situations. (Mayer & Wittrock, 1996, p. 49)

Merely recalling information doesn't involve transfer. If, for example, your instructor has previously discussed buckling the seat belt as an example of negative reinforcement and if you later identify it as such, there is no transfer. You merely remembered the information. With respect to problem solving, transfer occurs when students can solve problems they haven't previously encountered, and in the case of learning strategies, transfer occurs, for example, when students use elaborative questioning in areas other than reading.

Transfer can be either positive or negative. Positive transfer occurs when learning in one context facilitates learning in another, whereas negative transfer occurs when learning in one situation hinders performance in another (Mayer & Wittrock, 1996). As a simple example, if students know that a mammal nurses its young and breathes through lungs and then conclude that a whale is a mammal, they are demonstrating positive transfer. If they believe that a fish is an animal that lives in the sea and then conclude that a whale is a fish, they are demonstrating negative transfer.

9.22
One learner transfers understanding of a topic to a new situation, whereas another learner does not. Describe likely differences in the two learners' schemas.

General and Specific Transfer

At one time, educators believed that taking courses such as Latin, Greek, and mathematics were valuable not only for learning Latin, Greek, and math but also to "discipline" the mind. The hope was that these courses would strengthen learners' general thinking ability. Such an occurrence would have demonstrated **general transfer,** *the ability to take knowledge or skills learned in one context and apply them in a broad range of different contexts.* If, for example, becoming an expert chess player would help a person learn math more easily because both require logic, general transfer would occur. **Specific transfer** is *the ability to apply information in a context similar to the context in which it was originally learned.* If having learned that *photos* means "light" in Greek results in a learner better understanding words such as *photography* and *photosynthesis,* specific transfer has occurred.

Unfortunately, as researchers found more than 80 years ago and have since repeatedly confirmed, general transfer rarely or never occurs (Driscoll, 1994; Perkins & Salomon, 1989; E. Thorndike, 1924). Transfer is usually specific. Studying Latin, for example, results in learners' acquiring expertise in Latin and specific transfer to the Latin roots of English words; it does little to improve thinking in general.

Factors Affecting the Transfer of Learning

At least six factors affect students' ability to transfer:

- Similarity between learning situations
- Depth of learners' original understanding
- Quality of learning experiences
- Context for learners' experiences
- Variety of learning contexts and experiences
- Emphasis on metacognition

Similarity Between Learning Situations

As our discussion of general and specific transfer implies, the more closely the two learning situations are related, the more likely transfer is to occur. For instance, if students have seen examples of mammals such as dogs, cats, horses, and deer, they are likely to identify a cow as a mammal because cows are similar to the other examples. They are less likely to transfer the concept to bats because bats aren't as closely related to the original examples.

With respect to problem solving, when first graders are first given this problem,

Angi has two pieces of candy. Kim gives her three more pieces of candy. How many pieces does Angi have now?

they do well on this later one:

Bruce had three pencils. His friend Orlando gave him two more. How many pencils does Bruce have now?

When they're given the problem about Angi and Kim followed by this problem,

Sophie has three cookies. Flavio has four cookies. How many do they have together?

they perform less well (Riley, Greeno, & Heller, 1982). The first two problems are more closely related than the first and third. These results demonstrate that transfer tends to be very specific.

Depth of Original Understanding

Transfer requires a high level of original understanding (Bransford & Schwartz, 1999). This may seem obvious, but research indicates that students often fail to transfer because they don't understand the topic in the first place (A. Lee, 1998; A. Lee & Pennington, 1993).

The more practice and feedback learners are given with the topics they study, the deeper their understanding will be, and the more likely transfer will occur (Bransford et al., 2000; Bransford & Schwartz, 1999; Gick & Holyoak, 1987). When planning curricula, "schools should pick the most important concepts and skills to emphasize so that they can concentrate on the quality of understanding rather than on the quantity of information presented" (Rutherford & Algren, 1990, p. 185).

As constructivist views of learning imply, social interaction also facilitates transfer by enriching original understanding. As students share ideas and identify relationships in the topics they're studying, they gain insights into the ways ideas apply in different settings (Vanderstoep & Seifert, 1994).

If learners' original understanding is shallow or lacking, teachers must try to provide learners with a variety of high-quality examples presented in context, just as they do for students who lack background knowledge (see Chapter 8).

Quality of Learning Experiences

Quality refers to the extent that examples and other content representations *include all the information that students need to understand the topic,* and the words *learning experience* suggest an experience where the reasons for answers are as important as the answers themselves (Rittle-Johnson, & Alibali, 1999).

For some examples of high-quality learning experiences related to concept learning, think back to some of your earlier study. For instance, Karen Johnson's compressed cotton (in the opening case of Chapter 2) was a high-quality example because *students could see the essential characteristic* of the concept *density*—that is, that the amount of cotton (the mass) hadn't changed, but that the space it took up (the volume) decreased. Similarly, Diane Smith's pencils on page 148 of Chapter 4 were high-quality examples because, again, the students *could see* the features (*long, longer, longest*) that she meant to point out. Karen and Diane also chose concrete examples, which are particularly meaningful for learners (Bransford & Schwartz, 1999; Mayer, 2002).

For high-quality experiences related to problem solving, think back to some of Laura's questions. When she asked, "How do we know that we must subtract?" "Why is it (the width of the sink) 5 (versus 2)?" and "Now, let's be good critical thinkers. . . . Can someone explain the 12 times 3?" she was emphasizing the reasons for the answers. This emphasis ensured the quality of the learning experience.

Context for Learners' Experiences

In Chapter 7, we saw that learners encode both the information they're learning and the context in which that information exists (J. Brown, Collins, & Duguid, 1989). This is important because contextualized information is more meaningful than information learned in the abstract.

In general, *context* refers to real-world application. As an example, look back at Carol Lopez's concept learning lesson (on page 318). Instead of using isolated words or sentences, she presented examples of the concept *adjective* in the context of a written passage, which is similar to the way students read information in books, newspapers, and other written materials in the world outside the classroom. Similarly, students' understanding of the law of inertia is more likely to transfer if students learn why we wear seat belts and why cars sometimes "miss" curves. Students would also be likely to transfer learning from Laura's carpeting problem, a real-world problem that was meaningful to them.

Context is a double-edged sword, however. Although contextualized concepts and problems are more meaningful than those presented in the abstract, overly contextualized information can impede transfer because learners' understanding is tied too tightly to the original context (Bransford & Schwartz, 1999).

This raises the issue of situated learning.

Situated Learning. **Situated learning** (or *situated cognition*) is *learning that is social in nature and depends on, and cannot be separated from, the context in which it is learned* (Brown et al., 1989; Greeno, 1998; Putnam & Borko, 2000; Rogoff, 1990). According to this view, a student who learns to solve subtraction and division problems while determining a car's gas mileage on a trip, for example, has a different kind of understanding than one who solves subtraction and division problems in exercises in school.

9.23
The law of inertia says that moving objects continue moving in a straight line unless a force acts on them. Describe a simple "high-quality" example that could be used to illustrate this law.

We saw this illustrated in Laura's lesson. She embedded her lesson in the context of a practical problem that her students could directly relate to. As the interview after the lesson revealed, however, students had difficulty transferring their understanding of the problem to irregularly shaped objects outside the context of their classroom.

Situated learning is somewhat controversial. At the extreme, it suggests that transfer is virtually impossible because all learning is bound to the situation in which it occurs. But evidence for transfer does exist (J. Anderson, Reder, & Simon, 1996). For instance, a person skilled at driving in a large city rarely has trouble driving in a rural area, and people who are skilled readers of textbooks can also read newspapers and magazines with ease.

However, without question, context influences learning and transfer. This leads us to the notion of variety in learning experiences.

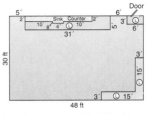

Laura's students needed additional instruction and practice before their understanding transferred to new contexts.

To see a video clip of the students discussing the areas of irregularly shaped figures, go to the Companion Website at *www.prenhall.com/eggen*, then to this chapter's *Classrooms on the Web* module. Click on *Video Clip 9.3*.

Variety of Learning Contexts and Experiences

For knowledge and skills learned in one context to be applied in other contexts, teachers must present concepts and problems in a variety of contexts (Cognition and Technology Group at Vanderbilt, 1997). Variety is perhaps the most important factor affecting the transfer of understanding.

Ensuring variety also means covering a topic in several ways, which is sometimes called providing "multiple knowledge representations" (Brenner et al., 1997; Spiro et al., 1992). As learners construct understanding that prepares them for transfer, each case or example adds connections and perspectives that others miss. Also, the greater the variety, the greater the chance the example will be similar to examples and contexts in learners' existing background knowledge. And as we saw earlier, similarity is one of the factors that influences transfer.

For instance, a lesson on reptiles would have adequate variety if examples of snakes lying in grass and draped over trees, alligators with their noses barely above water and sunning themselves on land, land turtles and sea turtles, and lizards in a variety of habitats are included to help students understand the breadth and depth of the concept in real-world contexts. Inadequate variety results in students' undergeneralizing and forming an incomplete concept.

The same applies to problem solving and strategic learning—the greater the variety of applications, the greater the likelihood that students' understanding will transfer (Sternberg & Frensch, 1993). Informative feedback about correct and incorrect answers and procedures are essential if learning and transfer are to occur (Phye, 2001).

Emphasis on Metacognition

An emphasis on metacognition—encouraging students to monitor, reflect upon, and improve their learning strategies and problem solving— also increases transfer (Renkl et al., 1998; Tobias & Everson, 1998).

Interestingly, some evidence indicates that general transfer may exist for attitudes and dispositions (Prawat, 1989). For example, the inclination to be open-minded, to reserve judgment, to search for facts to support conclusions, and to take personal responsibility for learning is a general disposition. Domain-specific knowledge is

Transfer is facilitated by quality learning experiences in a variety of contexts.

required for understanding the conclusion and the relevant facts, but the disposition is a general orientation. Teachers can encourage transfer of these dispositions through modeling across disciplines and by the day-in and day-out message that learning is a meaningful activity facilitated by metacognition.

Assessment and Learning: The Role of Assessment in Transfer

As we've repeatedly emphasized, assessment is an integral part of effective learning environments (Bransford et al., 2000; Shepard, 2000) because learners construct, rather than record, understanding. Insight into individual learners' thinking is essential if teachers are to help them develop deep and valid understandings of the topics they study. Therefore, as we've also emphasized, assessment must focus as much on the reasons for students' answers as on the answers themselves.

With these thoughts in mind, let's consider the assessment of concept learning, problem solving, and strategic learning. In each case, our understanding of transfer provides some guidance: Specifically, we can use *variety, quality,* and *context* as frameworks for assessing the extent to which transfer has occurred. In the case of concept learning, students' abilities to either identify or produce additional examples of a concept give teachers information about the extent to which the concept has transferred. Carol Lopez's lesson on adjectives is an example. Her assessment had at least four important features:

- Her assessment was an integral part of the teaching-learning process. Having students write a paragraph using adjectives was a natural extension of the learning activity.
- The students were required to produce examples that hadn't been discussed in class, so the assessment promoted variety.
- The examples were embedded in the context of a written passage, so the exercise was a real-world (authentic) task.
- The next day she had the students explain whether or not the examples were used correctly, which helped them link the examples to essential characteristics.

Two of Carol's assessment procedures were particularly noteworthy. First, by requiring students to explain if the examples were correctly used, she emphasized—and gained insight into—students' thinking. Second, by displaying and analyzing the paragraphs, she provided the class with valuable feedback about their work. Feedback not only gives students information about their understanding and performance but also communicates that the purpose of assessment is to improve learning (instead of giving grades).

Effective assessments of problem solving require learners to solve a variety of high-quality problems in authentic contexts. Every problem needn't be taken from the real world, however. As we quoted earlier: "Authentic activities foster the kinds of thinking and problem-solving skills that are important in out-of-school settings, whether or not the activities themselves mirror what practitioners do" (Putnam & Borko, 2000, pp. 4–5). So, in general, assessments that make students' thinking visible are both valid and valuable.

Assessing students' use of learning strategies is a more demanding task. The use of learning strategies can be informally assessed by listening to students describe their thinking during learning activities, but formally assessing it is difficult. Traditional assessments are generally inappropriate, so alternative assessments are required. (We examine this issue in Chapter 14 when we discuss alternative assessment.)

Classroom Connections

Promoting Transfer in Your Classroom

1. Provide examples and applications of the content you teach in a variety of different contexts.
   - *Elementary:* A third-grade teacher selects samples of student writing to teach grammar and punctuation rules. She displays samples on overheads and uses the samples as the basis for her instruction.
   - *Middle School:* A science teacher begins a discussion of light refraction by asking students why they can see better with their glasses on than they can without them. He then illustrates refraction with a variety of demonstrations, such as immersing a pencil in a glass of water and looking at objects through magnifying lenses. The class discusses the demonstrations in detail.
   - *High School:* A geometry teacher illustrates applications of course content with examples from architecture. She also uses photographs from magazines and slides to illustrate how math concepts relate to the real world.

2. Plan examples and representations that provide all the information students need for understanding the topics they study.
   - *Elementary:* A fifth-grade teacher illustrates the concept *volume* by putting 1-cm cubes in a box 4 cm long, 3 cm wide, and 2 cm high. He has the students count the cubes as he puts them in the box, until it is filled with 24 cubes. He uses questioning to help students understand the idea that the box has a volume of 24 cubic centimeters.
   - *Middle School:* A history teacher writes short cases to illustrate concepts, such as *mercantilism*, that are hard to understand from text alone. She guides students' analyses of the cases, helping them identify the essential characteristics of the concepts.
   - *High School:* An English teacher prepares a matrix illustrating the characters, setting, and themes for several of Shakespeare's plays. Students use the information in summarizing and drawing conclusions about Shakespeare's works.

Summary

Concept Learning

Concepts help people make sense of the world by allowing them to categorize experiences in the environment. The theory that learners construct an understanding of concepts based on their common characteristics is a rule-driven theory. Prototype theory suggests that concepts are constructed on the basis of the best representative of its class, and exemplar theory suggests that concepts are represented in memory as lists of highly typical examples.

Concepts with few concrete characteristics are easier to learn than those with many characteristics or characteristics that are abstract. Learners construct understanding of concepts by analyzing a variety of examples in which the characteristics are observable or which are the best prototypes or exemplars available.

Problem Solving

Problems describe situations in which individuals have goals but lack obvious ways of reaching them. Well-defined problems have clear goals and straightforward paths for reaching them; the goals for ill-defined problems are ambiguous and the means of attaining them aren't clear.

Experts in any domain have well-developed schemas that help accommodate the limitations of working memory. They organize knowledge into complex schemas that allow them to represent problems as "chunks" and process problems automatically.

In addition, their vast experiences help them to be metacognitive about their problem-solving efforts. Novices often represent problems in isolated pieces and don't monitor their efforts effectively. Teachers can help students become better problem solvers by helping them understand and acquire the problem-solving strategies of experts.

The Strategic Learner

A strategy is a plan for achieving a specific learning goal. Metacognition is the key to effective strategy use. In addition, strategic learners have broad background knowledge and a repertoire of strategies to choose from in attempting to reach their goals.

Study skills are strategies used to increase comprehension of information in teacher presentations and written text. Comprehensive strategies (like PQ4R) as well as specific strategies (like summarizing and elaborative questioning) are effective for monitoring and improving comprehension.

Critical thinking is the process of making and assessing conclusions based on evidence. Critical thinking requires thorough domain-specific knowledge, the ability to use component skills, well-developed metacognitive ability, and dispositions for open-mindedness. Research indicates that critical thinking is most effectively developed in the context of specific topics.

Transfer of Learning

Transfer occurs when learners are able to apply previously learned information in a new context. Specific transfer involves an application in a situation closely related to the original; general transfer occurs when two learning situations are quite different. Transfer depends on the depth of original understanding, the quality and variety of the representations learners study, and the context in which learning experiences are embedded. Research indicates that transfer tends to be specific, but metacognitive and self-regulatory skills may transfer across domains.

Windows on Classrooms

At the beginning of this chapter, you saw how Laura Hunter planned and conducted her lesson in an effort to promote thinking and problem solving in her students. Let's look now at a teacher with a group of second graders involved in a lesson on graphing. Read the case study, and answer the questions that follow.

Suzanne Brush had her second graders involved in a unit on graphing. She introduced the day's lesson by saying that she was planning a party for the class, but she had a problem: She didn't know the class's favorite flavor of jelly bean.

Several students offered suggestions for solving the problem, and they finally settled on giving each student a variety of jelly beans to taste and having them indicate which was their favorite.

Anticipating that students would want to taste the jelly beans, Suzanne had already prepared a plastic bag with seven different-flavored jelly beans for each student. After students tasted the beans, Suzanne said, "Okay, I need your help. . . . How can we organize our information so that we can look at it as a whole group?. . . . Jacinta?"

"See how many people like the same one, and see how many people like other ones," Jacinta responded.

"Okay. . . . Can you add to that? . . . Josh?"

"You can write their names down and see how many . . . like each flavor," Josh answered uncertainly.

"That was right in line with what Jacinta said," Suzanne smiled and nodded. "Here's what we're going to do. Stacey mentioned earlier that we could graph the information, and we have an empty graph up in the front of the room," she continued, moving to the front of the room and displaying the outline of a graph:

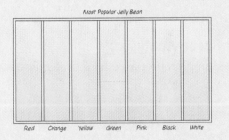

She explained that she had some colored cardboard pieces that matched the colors of the jelly beans and that the names of the colors were written below the columns on the graph. She directed students to come to the front of the room and paste the colored pieces that represented their favorite jelly beans on the graph.

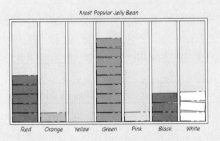

"Now, look up here," she smiled. "We collected and organized the information, so now we want to analyze it. I need you to tell me what we know by looking at the graph. . . . Candice?"

"People like green," Candice answered.

"How many people like green?"

". . . Nine."

"Nine people like green. . . . And how did you find that out? Can you go up there and show us how you read the graph?"

Candice went up to the graph and moved her hand up from the bottom, counting the green squares as she went.

Suzanne continued having the students make observations, and then she changed the direction of the lesson by saying, "Okay, here we go. . . . How many more people liked green than red? . . . Look up at the graph, and set up the problem on your paper."

Suzanne watched as the students looked at the graph and began setting up the problem. She stopped briefly to offer Carlos some help, continued watching the students as they finished, and then said, "I'm looking for a volunteer to share an answer with us. . . . Dominique?"

"Nine plus 5 is 14," Dominique answered.

"Dominique says 9 plus 5 is 14. Let's test it out," Suzanne said, asking Dominique to go up to the graph and show the class how she arrived at her answer.

As Dominique walked to the front of the room, Suzanne said, "We want to know the difference. . . . How many more people liked green than red, and you say 14 people, . . . 14 more people liked green. Does that work?" Suzanne said, pointing at the graph.

Dominique looked at the graph for a moment and then said, "I mean 9 take away 5."

"She got up here and she changed her mind," Suzanne said with a smile to the rest of the class. "Tell them."

"Nine take away 5 is 4," Dominique said.

"Nine take away 5 is 4," Suzanne continued, "so how many more people liked green than red? . . . Carlos?"

"Four," Carlos responded.

"Four, good, four," she smiled at him warmly. "The key was, you had to find the difference between the two numbers."

Suzanne had students offer additional problems, they solved and explained them, and she then continued, "I have one more question, and then we'll switch gears. How many people took part in this voting?"

Suzanne watched as students considered the problem for a few minutes, and then said, "Matt? . . . How many people?"

"Twenty-four."

"Matt said 24. Did anyone get a different answer? So we'll compare. . . . Robert?"

"Twenty-two."

"How did you solve the problem?" she asked Robert.

"Nine plus 5 plus 3 plus 3 plus 1 plus 1 equals 22," he answered quickly.

"Where'd you get all those numbers?"

"There," he said, pointing to the graph.

"He went from the highest to the lowest, and the answer was 22."

Suzanne then broke the children into groups and had them work at centers where they gathered and summarized information in bar graphs. They tallied and graphed the number of students who had birthdays each month, interviewed classmates about their favorite soft drinks, and called pizza delivery places to compare the cost of comparable pizzas.

As time for lunch neared, Suzanne called the groups back together. After the students were settled, she said, "Raise your hand if you can tell me what you learned this morning in math."

"How to bar graph," Jenny responded.

"So, the graph is a way of organizing information, so we can look at it and talk about it. Later we'll look at some additional ways of organizing information," Suzanne said as she ended the lesson.

Constructed Response Questions

In answering these questions, use information from the chapter and link your responses to specific information in the case.

1. How effectively did Suzanne teach problem solving in her lesson? To what extent did she apply the instructional strategies for helping students become better problem solvers?

2. To what extent did Suzanne encourage critical thinking in her lesson? What could she have done to give students more practice in developing critical-thinking abilities?

3. How effective would Suzanne's lesson have been for promoting transfer? What could Suzanne have done to increase the likelihood of transfer in her students?

4. Describe the ways that Suzanne assessed the children's understanding of bar graphs. Describe what she could have done to improve her assessment.

Document-Based Analysis

In Chapter 4, you saw the following lesson plan prepared by a first-grade teacher.

Unit: Warm-Blooded Animals

Objective: First graders will understand mammals, so when given a series of pictures of different animals, they will identify all the mammals.

Rationale: Mammals are the most advanced members of the animal kingdom, and humans are mammals. Understanding mammals will contribute to children's understanding of themselves as well as different ways that animals adapt to ensure their survival.

Content: Mammals are warm-blooded animals that have hair and nurse their young. Most mammals are born live, but some, such as the duck-billed platypus, are egg-layers. Mammals have four-chambered hearts and seven neck vertebrae. Some examples are cows, horses, people, wolves, seals, whales, kangaroos, and tigers.

Procedures:
1. Ask students to give some examples of different kinds of animals. Explain that they are going to learn about a special kind of animal. Emphasize that all can learn this content. Stress the need to pay attention.
2. Show students a guinea pig, and have them touch and feel it.
3. Have them describe what they saw and felt. Accept all answers. Write responses on board. Prompt for "feels warm" and "has hair."
4. Show them a picture of a cow with a calf. Ask how the calf eats. Prompt them to conclude that the calf nurses from its mother.
5. Add "nurses" to "warm-blooded" and "has hair" as characteristics of mammals on the board.

6. Show a picture of a dog. Ask how many of them have a dog. Ask them to describe the picture. Link to essential characteristics of mammals. Prompt if necessary, and positively reinforce for naming correct characteristics.

7. Show them a picture of an eagle sitting on a nest of eggs.

8. Ask students to identify the similarities and differences between the eagle and the guinea pig, cow, calf, and dog.

9. Show them a picture of a mother whale and baby whale. Prompt them to conclude that some mammals live in water.

10. Call for a definition of mammals based on the characteristics they've described. Write it on the board.

11. Ask for additional examples, and help students determine if they are mammals.

Materials: Pet guinea pig; pictures of a cow with calf, a dog, and a nesting eagle

Assessment: Show students a series of pictures of animals. Have them circle those that are mammals.

In Chapter 4, you assessed the lesson plan for students placed at risk. Now assess the effectiveness of this lesson plan for promoting transfer based on the discussion in the chapter. Include both strengths and weaknesses.

Suppose this lesson plan were designed for seventh graders. Again, assess the effectiveness of the plan for the older students. Describe developmental differences between first graders and seventh graders that would influence teachers' thinking in both cases.

Online Portfolio Activities

To develop your professional portfolio, further apply your understanding of chapter content, and address the INTASC standards, go to the Companion Website, then to this chapter's *Online Portfolio Activities*. Complete the suggested activities.

 Also on the Companion Website at *www.prenhall.com/eggen*, you can measure your understanding of chapter content in *Practice Quiz* and *Essay* modules, apply concepts in *Online Cases*, and broaden your knowledge base with the *Additional Content* module and *Web Links* to other educational psychology websites.

Important Concepts

algorithm *(p. 322)*
characteristics *(p. 313)*
cognitive apprenticeship *(p. 327)*
component skills *(p. 335)*
comprehension monitoring *(p. 332)*
concept mapping *(p. 315)*
concepts *(p. 312)*
critical thinking *(p. 334)*
drawing analogies *(p. 322)*
elaborative questioning *(p. 332)*
examplars *(p. 314)*
experts *(p. 323)*
general transfer *(p. 338)*
heuristics *(p. 322)*

ill-defined problem *(p. 320)*
means-ends analysis *(p. 322)*
metacognition *(p. 330)*
network *(p. 316)*
problem *(p. 319)*
problem-based learning *(p. 329)*
prototype *(p. 314)*
situated learning *(p. 340)*
specific transfer *(p. 338)*
study strategies *(p. 331)*
summarizing *(p. 332)*
transfer *(p. 338)*
well-defined problem *(p. 320)*
worked examples *(p. 327)*

Chapter Outline

Theories of
Motivation

10

"We'd better get moving," Susan urged Jim as they approached the door of Kathy Brewster's classroom. "The bell is gonna ring, and you know how Brewster is about this class. She thinks it's *so* important."

"Did you finish your homework?" Jim asked and then stopped himself. "What am I talking about? You've done your homework in every class since I've known you."

"Sure, I don't mind it that much. . . . It bothers me when I don't get something, and sometimes it's even fun. My dad helps me. He says he wants to keep up with the world," Susan laughed.

"In some classes, I just do enough to get a decent grade, but not in here," Jim responded. "I used to hate history, but I sometimes even read ahead a little, because Brewster really makes you think. It's actually interesting the way she's always telling us about the way we are because of something that happened a zillion years ago—I never thought about this stuff in that way before."

"Gee, Mrs. Brewster, that assignment was impossible," Harvey grumbled as he walked in.

"That's good for you," Kathy smiled. "I know it was a tough assignment, but you need to be challenged. It's hard for me, too, when I'm studying and trying to put together new ideas, but if I hang in, I always feel like I can get it."

"Aw, c'mon, Mrs. Brewster. I thought you knew everything."

"I wish. I have to study every night to keep up with you people, and the harder I study, the smarter I get," Kathy said. "And . . . I feel good about myself when I do."

"But you make us work so hard," Harvey continued in feigned complaint.

"Yes, but look how good you're getting at writing," Kathy smiled again, pointing her finger at him. "I think you hit a personal best on your last paper. You're becoming a very good writer."

"Yeah, yeah, I know," Harvey smiled on his way to his desk, "and being good writers will help us in everything we do in life." The rationale was one the students continually heard from Kathy.

"Stop by and see me after class," Kathy quietly said to Jenny as she entered the room. "I'd like to talk to you for a minute."

I n ideal classrooms, students pay attention, ask questions, and want to learn. They do their assignments without complaint and study without being coaxed or cajoled. But teachers don't teach in an ideal world. They often have students who don't seem motivated to work on the classroom tasks set out for them (Hidi & Harackiewicz, 2000; McCombs & Pope, 1994).

Teachers contribute a great deal to students' desires to learn and to take responsibility for their learning. They aren't successful with every student, but with a positive approach to motivation, they can influence many (Stipek, 1996).

In this chapter, we examine theory and research on student motivation. Then, in Chapter 11, we translate these theories and research into a model that teachers can use to improve motivation in their classrooms.

After you've completed your study of this chapter, you should be able to

- Describe differences between extrinsic and intrinsic motivation
- Explain learner motivation on the basis of behavioral, humanistic, and cognitive theories
- Apply rewards in ways that can increase intrinsic motivation
- Utilize strategies that can increase students' intrinsic motivation
- Describe how affective factors in learners influence their motivation

Motivation is *a force that energizes, sustains, and directs behavior toward a goal* (Pintrich & Schunk, 2002), and researchers have found a high correlation between motivation and achievement (McDermott, Mordell, & Stoltzfus, 2001; Wang, Haertel, & Walberg, 1993; R. Weinstein, 1998).

Children's motivation to learn lies at the very core of achieving success in schooling. Given rapid technological advances, an ever-changing knowledge base, and shifting workplace needs, a continuing motivation to learn may well be the hallmark of individual accomplishment across the lifespan. (R. Weinstein, 1998, p. 81)

In general, motivated students

- Have positive attitudes toward school and describe school as satisfying
- Persist on difficult tasks and cause few management problems
- Process information in depth and excel in classroom learning experiences (Stipek, 1996)

Not surprisingly, motivated students are a primary source of job satisfaction for teachers.

Extrinsic and Intrinsic Motivation

Motivation can be described in two broad categories. **Extrinsic motivation** is *the motivation to engage in an activity as a means to an end,* whereas **intrinsic motivation** is *the motivation to be involved in an activity for its own sake* (Pintrich & Schunk, 2002). Extrinsically motivated learners may study hard for a test because they believe studying will lead to high test scores or teacher compliments, for example; intrinsically motivated learners study because they want to understand the content and they view learning as worthwhile in itself. These relationships are illustrated in Figure 10.1.

Kathy's instruction increased Jim's intrinsic motivation.

Although we think of extrinsic and intrinsic motivation as two ends of a continuum (meaning the higher the extrinsic motivation, the lower the intrinsic motivation and vice versa), they are actually on separate continua (Covington, 2000; Pintrich & Schunk, 2002). For example, students might study hard both because a topic is interesting and because they want good grades in a class. Others might study only to receive the good grades. The first group is high in both extrinsic and intrinsic motivation; the second is high in extrinsic motivation but low in intrinsic motivation. Research indicates that intrinsically motivated students achieve higher than those who are only extrinsically motivated (Gottfried, 1985).

Extrinsic and intrinsic motivation are contextual and can change over time. Jim, from our case study, for example, appears to be extrinsically motivated in other classes ("In some classes, I just do enough to get a decent grade") but intrinsically motivated in Kathy's class ("I used to hate history, but . . . Brewster really makes you think. It's actually interesting"). Kathy's class was different enough from others to influence his intrinsic motivation.

Researchers have determined that learners are intrinsically motivated by activities or experiences that

10.1
On the basis of the information in the case study, would you describe Susan as being high in both extrinsic and intrinsic motivation, or high in one and low in another? Explain.

Figure 10.1 Extrinsic and intrinsic motivation

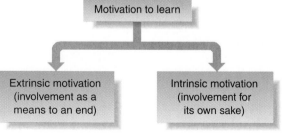

- *Present a challenge.* Goals are moderately difficult, and success isn't guaranteed (Lepper & Hodell, 1989; Ryan & Deci, 2000; R. White, 1959).
- *Give the learner control.* Learners feel as though they have some command or influence over their own learning (Lepper & Hoddell, 1989, N. Perry, 1998; Ryan & Deci, 2000).
- *Evoke curiosity.* Experiences are novel, surprising, or discrepant with learners' existing ideas (Lepper & Hoddell, 1989).
- *Involve fantasy.* Experiences allow learners to make believe (Lepper & Hodell, 1989).

In addition, some researchers suggest that experiences with aesthetic value—those that evoke emotional reactions and particularly those associated with beauty—may be intrinsically motivating as well (Ryan & Deci, 2000).

Jim's comments suggest that Kathy capitalized on aspects of *challenge* as well as *curiosity* in her teaching: "Brewster really makes you think. It's actually interesting the way she's always telling us about the way we are because of something that happened a zillion years ago—I never thought about this stuff in that way before."

Motivation to Learn

Teachers are sometimes given the impression that their instruction should be so interesting and stimulating that students will be intrinsically motivated all the time. This is a worthwhile ideal, but it isn't a realistic expectation for all, or even most, learning activities:

> In short, intrinsic motivation cannot constitute a sufficient and stable motivational basis for schooling in general or a predesigned curriculum in particular. It . . . encourage[s] an orientation toward activity based on immediate satisfaction rather than on values. Contrary to claims made by some psychologists, intrinsically motivated students will not be consistently motivated. Certain aspects of the curriculum will interest them, while others will not; at times they will study, and at times they will not. Thus students who rely exclusively on intrinsic motivation are likely to neglect a large part of their school work. (Nisan, 1992, p. 129)

Experts suggest that *motivation to learn* is a more meaningful concept. **Motivation to learn** is the *"student's tendency to find academic activities meaningful and worthwhile and to try and get the intended learning benefits from them"* (Brophy, 1998, p. 162, italics added). Students with a motivation-to-learn orientation make an effort to understand topics whether or not they find the topics intrinsically interesting or the process of studying them enjoyable. They maintain this effort because they believe that the understanding that results is valuable and worthwhile.

The theories of learning presented in Chapters 6 through 9 can also help us understand motivation, and in fact, some researchers argue that learning and motivation are so interdependent that a person can't fully understand learning without considering motivation (Pintrich, Marx, & Boyle, 1993). In the following sections, we examine behavioral, humanistic, and cognitive theories of motivation. A framework for these theories is outlined in Figure 10.2.

Behavioral Views of Motivation

Behavioral theories view motivation as a change in behavior as a result of experience with the environment (Pintrich & Schunk, 2002). Because, as you learned in Chapter 6, reinforcers increase behavior, they can also increase motivation. Praise, comments on homework, high test scores, and good grades are common classroom reinforcers.

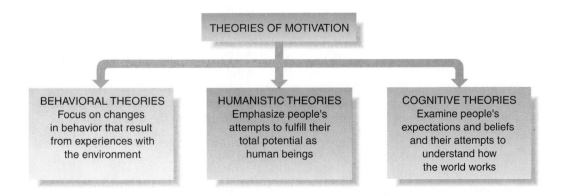

Figure 10.2
Theoretical views of motivation

Effective teachers use reinforcers selectively to increase learning and motivation.

Using Rewards in Classrooms

Although the use of rewards is controversial (Harter & Jackson, 1992; Kohn, 1992, 1996b), it is still common. (Rewards are *intended* reinforcers; we don't know if they actually reinforce behavior until we see if the behavior increases.) Some examples of rewards used in elementary classrooms include

■ Approval, such as teacher praise or being selected as a class monitor
■ Consumable items, such as candy or popcorn
■ Entertainment, such as playing a computer game
■ Success in competition, such as being the first to finish a game or drill

In middle and secondary classrooms, common rewards are

■ High test scores and good grades
■ Teacher comments on papers
■ Teacher compliments delivered quietly and individually
■ Free time to talk to classmates

Criticisms of Behavioral Approaches to Motivation

The use of rewards is criticized on several grounds. Some objections are philosophical—critics argue that schools should cultivate intrinsic motivation and believe that using rewards sends students the wrong message about learning (Anderman & Maehr, 1994). Other critics cite research indicating that the use of rewards decreases interest in intrinsically motivating tasks (Kohn, 1996b; Ryan & Deci, 1996; B. Schwartz, 1990).

A significant weakness of behavioral approaches to motivation is that they provide an incomplete explanation for motivation. Although motivation and learning are closely related, they are not identical. Reinforcers can be extrinsic motivators, but their effects are not automatic—rather, they depend on learners' expectations, beliefs, and other thoughts. If students' reinforcement histories are inconsistent with their present beliefs, they are more likely to act based on their beliefs. For instance, if a student believes he isn't capable of completing a demanding assignment, he will be unlikely to work hard on it despite being reinforced in the past for completing assignments. Behaviorism doesn't consider learner beliefs, so it isn't able to explain why the student won't exert the effort on the assignment.

10.2
When overused, rewards (such as praise) can lose their effectiveness. What concept from behaviorism explains why they become ineffective?

■ ## Using Rewards in Classrooms: Instructional Strategies

Although critics argue that rewards shouldn't be used in classrooms, eliminating them entirely isn't realistic. They provide one tool teachers can use with their students. For instance, they can encourage students to begin tasks that are not intrinsically motivating, and once students are involved, other factors such as interest and challenge can come into play. If they're used with thought and care, rewards can increase both motivation to learn and intrinsic motivation. The following principles can guide teachers in their use of rewards:

■ Use rewards for tasks that are not initially intrinsically interesting (Morgan, 1984).
■ Base rewards on the quality of the work, not mere participation in an activity (Deci & Ryan, 1985, 1987).
■ Use rewards to communicate increasing competence (Rosenfield, Folger, & Adelman, 1980).

Let's see how the principles guide Amanda Shah and Luanne Hawkins, two seventh-grade teachers, as they work with their students.

"Let's go over your homework," Amanda Shah directed as she handed her seventh graders their papers. "Take a look at number 3, where it says, 'A jacket at Coat Mart, originally priced at $65, was marked down to $40. What is the percent decrease in the cost of the jacket?' Explain how you did that one, . . . Omar?"

"I . . . first subtracted the 40 from the 65, so that was $25. . . . Then I took 65 into the 25 and got 0.38, so it was marked down 38%."

"Why did you divide the 25 by 65 instead of by 40?" Amanda probed.

"I needed to compare the marked-down price to the original price," Omar explained. "If I divided by 40, I would be comparing it to the new price, and that doesn't make sense."

"That's excellent thinking, Omar," Amanda smiled. "You showed a good understanding of the difference between percent decrease and percent increase.

"I know that these word problems were hard when we first started them," she continued, "but you're all improving so much that you actually like them now. . . . Let's look at a couple more. . . . Explain how you did number 5, . . . Cassy."

"Get busy on your homework everyone," directed Luanne Hawkins, the teacher in the room next to Amanda's. "Problems just like these will be on your test on Friday, so if you don't understand them now, you'll have trouble with them on the test. . . . If you have difficulties, raise your hand, and I'll come around and help you."

The students busied themselves with their homework, and 15 minutes later Luanne announced, "You're all doing your homework so conscientiously, I'm very proud of you. Not one of you has misbehaved or gone off task this whole time. . . . Since you've been so good, you can talk quietly among yourselves as soon as you're finished."

Let's take a closer look at Amanda's and Luanne's use of rewards. Amanda used her praise to communicate that the students were doing high-quality work when she said, "That's excellent thinking, Omar. You showed a good understanding." When she said, "I know that these word problems were hard when we first started them, but you're all improving so much that you actually like them now," she was using a reward to encourage her students on a task that was not intrinsically interesting. And in the same statement she communicated that their competence was increasing. Using rewards in this way can increase intrinsic motivation, motivation to learn, and students' beliefs about their capabilities (Deci & Ryan, 1991; Deci et al., 1991).

In contrast, when Luanne praised and rewarded her students ("Since you've been so good, you can talk quietly among yourselves"), she was trying to control students' behavior rather than provide information about quality of work or increased competence. Further, she offered the students free time for simply doing the homework, not necessarily doing it thoroughly or accurately. Rewards that control behavior or are given for simple participation in an activity decrease intrinsic motivation (Deci & Ryan, 1991; Eisenberger & Cameron, 1998).

From these examples, we see that the use of rewards is neither uniformly appropriate nor uniformly inappropriate. Further, when judiciously implemented, they can actually enhance intrinsic motivation.

10.3
Identify another practical reason why telling students they can talk as soon as they've finished their homework is not effective.

Humanistic Views of Motivation

In the mid-1950s when the "cognitive revolution" in learning was emerging (see Chapter 7), a movement called *humanistic psychology* also began. **Humanistic psychology** *views motivation as people's attempts to fulfill their total potential as human beings* (Pintrich & Schunk, 2002). This perspective remains popular both in schools and in the workplace.

Development of the Whole Person

In the first half of the 20th century, our understanding of motivation was dominated by two major forces: behaviorism and psychoanalysis. Behaviorism focused on reinforcement in its explanations for motivation. Psychoanalysis, influenced by the famous

For a discussion of Freud and his theories, go to the Companion Website at *www.prenhall. com/eggen*, then to this chapter's *Additional Content* module.

Sigmund Freud (1856–1939), described people as motivated by unconscious drives and directed by an *id, ego,* and *superego.* Humanistic psychology developed as a reaction against this "reductionist" thinking; instead, it emphasizes the total person—physical, emotional, interpersonal, and intellectual—and one's drive for "self-actualization," our inborn need to fulfill our potential (Maslow, 1968, 1970). During the 1950s, this orientation became known as a "third force" alongside behaviorism and psychoanalysis.

Development of the Whole Person: Maslow's Hierarchy of Needs

Abraham Maslow (1968, 1970), one of the fathers of the humanistic movement, developed a hierarchy reflecting the needs of the "whole person" (see Figure 10.3). For instance, we see the *physical person* in survival and safety needs, the *social person* in belonging needs, the *emotional person* in self-esteem needs, and *intellectual, aesthetic,* and *self-actualized persons* in growth needs. Let's look at these needs in more detail.

Deficiency and Growth Needs. Maslow (1968, 1970) described human needs as existing in two groups: *deficiency needs* and *growth needs*. **Deficiency needs** are *needs that, when they are unfulfilled, energize people to meet them;* these needs occupy the bottom of the hierarchy (Figure 10.3). According to Maslow, people won't move to higher needs, such as intellectual achievement, unless the deficiency needs—survival, safety, belonging, and self-esteem—have all been met.

Once deficiency needs are met, an individual can focus on **growth needs**, *needs that expand and increase as people have experiences with them.* In contrast with deficiency needs, growth needs are never "met." For instance, as people develop a greater understanding of literature, their interest in it actually increases rather than decreases. This can explain why some people seem to have an insatiable desire for learning or why an individual never tires of fine art or music.

Maslow believed that all people strive for self-actualization, although less than 1% truly achieve it (Maslow, 1968). Those that do have the following characteristics:

- Clear perceptions of reality
- Autonomy, independence, and self-acceptance
- Problem-centeredness instead of self-centeredness
- Spontaneity in thought and action
- Sympathy to the conditions of other people

10.4
To what does behaviorism "reduce" people? To what does psychoanalysis reduce people?

10.5
On the basis of Maslow's work, would you conclude that people with a high need for aesthetic appreciation have high self-esteem? Have they met their need for intellectual achievement? Explain each answer.

Figure 10.3 Maslow's hierarchy of needs

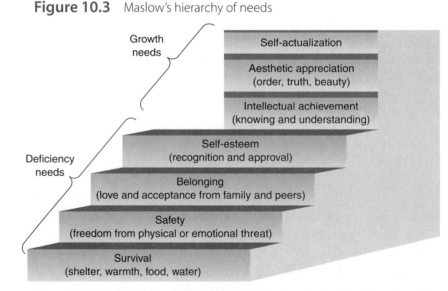

Source: Adapted from *Motivation and Personality* 2nd Edition by Abraham H. Maslow. Copyright 1954 by Harper & Row, Publishers, Inc. Copyright © 1970 by Abraham H. Maslow. Reprinted by permission of HarperCollins Publishers Inc.

They also develop deep bonds with a few people rather than superficial relationships with many, and they have peak experiences marked by feelings of excitement, happiness, and insight. The concept *peak experience* originated with Maslow.

Putting Maslow's Work Into Perspective. Maslow's work, while attractive to many people, has been strongly criticized. One of the most commonly voiced criticisms is the lack of research evidence to support his description of needs (Pintrich & Schunk, 2002). A second is the inconsistency and lack of predictive ability in his hierarchy. For instance, we probably all know of people with serious illnesses or disabling conditions (threats to their physical or emotional well-being) who are able to accomplish significant intellectual achievements and who seek order, truth, and beauty. Maslow's hierarchy would predict that this could not happen.

On the other hand, applications of Maslow's work in schools seem to support its validity. Schools provide free or reduced cost breakfasts and lunches because it makes sense that hungry children won't be motivated to learn. Other practices strive to make students feel safe—both physically and emotionally—in schools because those who feel unsafe are less motivated to learn (Lambert & McCombs, 1998).

Humanistic theories of motivation remind us to treat students as developing human beings.

Also, think about some of your day-to-day experiences. For example, when you shop, you probably first react to the "human" side of salespeople—how friendly and helpful they are. When students talk about their teachers, and this includes university students, their first comments usually center on how "nice" they are, not how intelligent they appear. These ideas remind us that we're all personal and social beings, and our needs in these areas usually precede our intellectual needs. Ignoring the human side of teaching leaves out an essential domain.

The Need for Positive Regard: The Work of Carl Rogers

Carl Rogers, a humanistic psychologist who founded "person-centered" therapy, also emphasized people's attempts to become self-actualized (Rogers, 1963). According to Rogers, the actualizing tendency is oriented toward personal growth, autonomy, and freedom from control by external forces. The tendency is innate, but experiences with others can foster or hinder growth and the development of autonomy (Rogers, 1959). Of those experiences, **unconditional positive regard,** or *the belief that someone is worthy and acceptable regardless of their behavior*, is one of the most essential.

Unconditional positive regard is hard to come by, however. Parents usually feel unconditional positive regard for their small children, valuing them even if they don't accept all their behaviors. But as children get older, parents' regard sometimes becomes *conditional*, or contingent on certain actions, such as acceptable behavior or high grades. Outside of their families, people almost always experience conditional regard, because society does not distinguish between people and their actions. So in schools, high achievers are afforded higher regard than their lower achieving peers, for example, and students who participate and excel in extracurricular activities are regarded more positively than those less successful. According to Rogers (1959, 1963), this conditional regard hinders personal growth. Instead, Rogers recommended treating all students as developing individuals with potential.

10.6
A student is annoying you with her disruptions of your learning activity. Should you be expected to treat her with unconditional positive regard? How do you handle her disruptions? How do you treat her at the start of the next day?

Humanistic Views of Motivation: Instructional Strategies

According to humanistic psychologists, two elements of the teaching-learning process are essential to the development of motivation: a strong student-teacher relationship and a positive classroom climate (Hamachek, 1987). The following principles can guide teachers as they build such relationships and climates:

- Treat students as people first and students second.
- Provide students with unconditional positive regard by separating their behaviors from their intrinsic worth.
- Create safe and orderly classrooms where students believe they can learn and where they are expected to do so.
- Consider teaching-learning experiences from students' points of view.

Let's see how the principles guide Kathy Brewster, the teacher from the opening case study, as she works with her students. We rejoin her after her class.

Kathy's expectations and unconditional positive regard helped Harvey reach his full potential.

To see a video clip of another classroom where students and teacher have a positive relationship, go to the Companion Website at *www.prenhall.com/eggen*, then to this chapter's *Classrooms on the Web* module. Click on *Video Clip 10.1.*

As the students were leaving the room, Jenny stopped at Kathy's desk. "You wanted to see me, Mrs. Brewster? . . . What's up?"

"I've been watching you for a few days, and you don't seem to be yourself. You're somewhere else. . . . Is everything okay?"

"I . . . yes, . . . no, not really," Jenny said, her eyes starting to fill with tears. "My mom and dad are having trouble, and I'm really, really scared. I'm afraid they're going to break up."

"Do you want to talk?"

". . . No, . . . not right now."

Kathy reached over, touched Jenny on the shoulder, and said, "I realize that there isn't anything that I can do directly, but I'm here if you want to talk about it, . . . or anything else . . . anytime."

"Thanks, . . . I'll remember that," Jenny smiled weakly as she turned to go.

As Kathy was working after school, Harvey poked his head into the room.

"Come in," she smiled. "How's the writer?"

"I just came by to say I hope I didn't offend you this morning, complaining so much about all the work."

"Not at all. . . . I haven't given it a second thought.

"I guess you already know how much you've done for me," Harvey continued. "You believed in me when the rest of the world wrote me off. . . . My drug conviction is off my record now, and I haven't used in over a year. I couldn't have made it without you. You made me work and put in all kinds of extra time with me. You pushed me and wouldn't let me give up on myself. I was headed for trouble, and now . . . I'm headed for college."

"We all need a nudge now and then," Kathy smiled. "That's what I'm here for. I appreciate it, but there's no need to thank me. I didn't do it; you did. . . . Now, scoot. I'm thinking up a rough assignment for you tomorrow."

"Mrs. Brewster, you're relentless," Harvey waved as he headed out the door.

A caring student-teacher relationship and a positive classroom climate are clearly evident in Kathy's work with her students. She was concerned about both Jenny and Harvey first as people, not as students. She asked Jenny to stop by because she saw that Jenny was not herself. And early in the year she spent a great deal of time with Harvey, more at a human level than at an academic one. She also treated him with unconditional positive regard; she separated his drug conviction from his intrinsic worth as a person. This, combined with her high expectations, helped motivate him to make changes in his behavior.

In the real world, unfortunately, teachers can't "save" every troubled student; it simply isn't that easy. You can make a difference with many, however, and for those that you do, you will have made an immeasurable difference.

Classroom Connections

Applying Behavioral Views of Motivation Effectively in Your Classroom

1. Reward students for genuine accomplishments and increasing competence, not for mere participation, nor to control behavior.
   - *Elementary:* Positive example—A second-grade teacher does a drill-and-practice activity on math facts each morning. All students who get all the facts correct or improve from the previous day have stars placed by their names on a wall chart. Negative example—A third-grade teacher says, "Every one of you turned in your math homework today, so each of you gets 2 bonus points on your math average."
   - *Middle School:* Positive example—An English teacher underlines well-written passages in her students' essays, comments positively about them, and explains why the sections warrant the comments. Negative example—A seventh-grade life science teacher says, "You worked so well together when we did our group activity, so we won't have any homework over the weekend."
   - *High School:* Positive example—A biology teacher comments to his class about an upcoming test, "Study hard for this test, everyone. The material we've been working on is very important, and your understanding will be a big help as we move on to the next topic." Negative example—Another biology teacher comments to his class about an upcoming test, "Study hard for this test. If you don't study, you might fail, and you could wind up back in this class again next year."

Applying Humanistic Views of Motivation Effectively in Your Classroom

2. Create a safe environment, and try to treat students with unconditional positive regard.
   - *Elementary:* A first-grade teacher encourages and accepts all students' comments and questions. She tells students that mistakes are a part of learning and treats them that way during learning activities.
   - *Middle School:* A seventh-grade teacher demands that all students treat each other with respect. The personal criticisms and sarcasm common in middle schools are strictly forbidden. He carefully models courtesy and respect for students and communicates that he expects respect in return.
   - *High School:* A geometry teacher spends time before and after school helping students with problems and assignments. She also listens attentively when students talk about personal problems and uncertainties.
3. Help meet students' deficiency and growth needs.
   - *Elementary:* A fourth-grade teacher calls on each of his students to be certain they all feel that they're a part of the learning activity. He makes them feel safe by helping them respond correctly when they are initially unable to answer.
   - *Middle School:* A seventh-grade teacher asks two of the more popular girls in her class to introduce a new girl to some of the other students and to take her under their wings until she gets acquainted.
   - *High School:* An American Government teacher brings in a newspaper columnist's political opinion piece, comments that it was interesting to her, and asks students for their opinions on the issue.

Cognitive Theories of Motivation

"C'mon, let's go," Melanie urged her friend Yelena as they were finishing a homework assignment.

"Just a sec," Yelena muttered. "I just can't seem to figure this out. I don't know why I missed this one. I thought I did the whole thing right, and it all made sense, but the answer turned out wrong."

"Let's work on it tonight. Everybody's leaving," Melanie urged.

"Go ahead, I'll catch up to you in a minute. I know that I can figure this out. . . . I just don't get it right now."

From this brief exchange, we see that behaviorism provides us with little insight into Yelena's actions. Although getting the right answer would be reinforcing, it doesn't account for Yelena's efforts to understand why the problem made sense but still came out wrong. Also, behaviorism doesn't consider beliefs or expectations. Yelena's comment, "I know that I can figure this out," indicates that she believed she could resolve the discrepancy and expected to do so. She persisted because of her beliefs and expectations, not because of past reinforcers. Humanistic theory tells us that Yelena's intellectual achievement need is greater than Melanie's, but that explanation doesn't offer any suggestions for what we, as teachers, might do. We study cognitive theories of motivation because they address important aspects of motivated behavior that can't be explained by behaviorism or humanistic views.

Cognitive theories of motivation *focus on learners' beliefs, expectations, and needs for order, predictability, and understanding.* We saw the influence of beliefs and expectations in Yelena's behavior, and the need to understand is at the heart of cognitive motivation theory: "Children are seen as naturally motivated to learn when their experience is inconsistent with their current understanding or when they experience regularities in information that are not yet represented by their schemata" (Greeno et al., 1996, p. 25). For example, why does a young child so eagerly explore the environment? Why does a 4-year-old become engrossed in puzzle "play"? Why was Yelena unable to leave until she solved the problem? Cognitive theorists suggest that each is motivated by the need to understand and make sense of the world.

Piaget described the need for understanding in his concept of *equilibrium* (see Chapter 2), which forms the cornerstone of his theory. When people cannot explain experiences with their existing schemes, they are motivated to modify the schemes, which ultimately results in development.

Cognitive theories of motivation help explain a variety of human behaviors, such as

- Why people are intrigued by brain teasers and other problems with no practical application
- Why people are curious when something occurs unexpectedly
- Why students ask questions about incidental and unrelated aspects of lessons
- Why people persevere on activities and then quit after they've mastered the tasks
- Why people want feedback about their performance, even if it's negative feedback

These behaviors all relate to an innate desire to understand the way the world works. In the following sections, we examine five cognitive theories of motivation:

- Expectancy **x** value theory
- Self-efficacy theory
- Goal theory
- Attribution theory
- Self-determination theory

A note of clarification before we begin: Although some experts (e.g., Graham & Weiner, 1996; Pintrich & Schunk, 2002) distinguish between *cognitive* and *social cognitive* theories of motivation, the line can sometimes be blurred, and we believe, for teachers in K–12 classrooms, that this distinction isn't essential. We discuss both specific cognitive theories and social cognitive approaches under the general framework of cognitive motivation theory. As you study the text that follows, keep expectations, beliefs, and the general need to understand how the world works in mind as the connecting thread that binds the theories together.

Expectancy x Value Theory

Expectancy x value theory *suggests that people are motivated to engage in an activity to the extent that they expect to succeed times the value they place on the success* (Wigfield & Eccles, 1992, 2000). The x is important, because anything "times" zero is zero, so if either the *expectancy* for success or the *value* placed on success is at or near zero, motivation will also be near zero. For example, as a young man, one of your authors toyed with the idea of a career in music. However, his lack of ability was obvious, resulting in low expectation for success. This resulted in low motivation for pursuing a career in music and a fortunate turn to a very rewarding one studying learning, motivation, and human behavior.

Expectancy **x** value theory would explain why many students with a history of low achievement handicap themselves by not trying. Repeated failure results in success expectations that are so low that motivation is also very low.

Let's look at *expectancy for success* in more detail, and then we'll turn to a discussion of factors influencing *task value.*

Expectancy for Success

Expectancy for success answers the question, "Am I able to do this task?" (Eccles, Wigfield, & Schiefele, 1998; Wigfield, 1994; Wigfield & Eccles, 1992). It is influenced by two primary factors: (a) perception of task difficulty and (b) self-schemas. These relationships are outlined in Figure 10.4.

The influence of task difficulty on success expectations is obvious. When people perceive a task as extremely difficult, they are less likely to expect success than when they perceive the task as easier.

The influence of self-schemas is more complex. In Chapter 7, you saw that *schemas* are organized networks of information stored in memory. **Self-schemas** are *organized networks of information about ourselves.* They include our self-concepts and sets of beliefs about the kinds of people we are (Pintrich & Schunk, 2002). One boy, for example, might have a self-schema that includes a cognitive evaluation of his abilities in math (math self-concept) and his belief that he's outgoing, reasonably attractive, but not athletic. This self-schema affects his expectancy for success: Because he has a positive self-concept of ability in math, for example, he will have a higher expectation for success than someone whose self-concept is less positive.

Expectancy for success is important in classrooms. Learners with high success expectations persist longer on tasks, choose more challenging activities, and achieve higher than those whose expectations are lower (Eccles et al., 1998; Wigfield, 1994).

Factors Influencing Task Value

Task value, the second component of expectancy **x** value theory, answers the question, "Why should I do this task?" and is influenced by four factors (Eccles et al., 1998), outlined in Figure 10.5.

Intrinsic Interest.   **Intrinsic interest** is *the characteristics of a topic or activity that induce a person's willing involvement in it* (Schraw & Lehman, 2001). "Because it's interesting" is an intuitively sensible answer to "Why should I do this task?" In our opening case study, Jim *willingly* read ahead in his history book because of his developing interest.

10.8
Trivial tasks tend to lower students' motivation (Lepper & Hodell, 1989). Using expectancy x value theory, explain why this would be the case.

To see a video clip of a teacher attempting to create student interest in a topic, go to the Companion Website at *www.prenhall.com/eggen,* then to this chapter's *Classrooms on the Web* module. Click on *Video Clip 10.2.*

Figure 10.4   Expectancy for success in expectancy x value theory

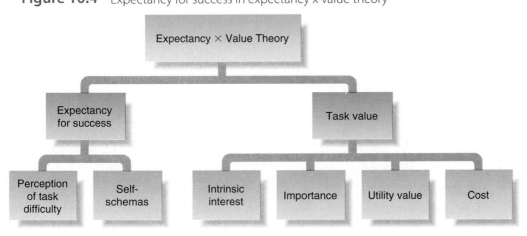

Figure 10.5 Task value in expectancy x value theory

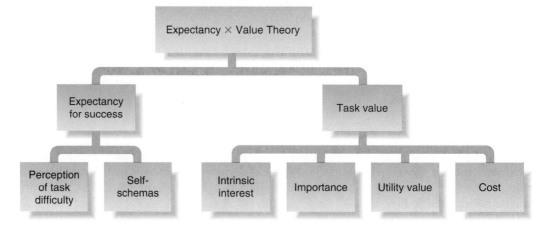

Some topics, such as *death, danger, power, money, romance* and *sex*, seem to be universally interesting (Hidi, 2001). This explains why so many movies and television programs focus on one or more of these topics. For younger students, scary stories, humor, and animals also seem to be generally interesting (Worthy, Moorman, & Turner, 1999).

Although these topics have limited importance in the school curriculum, other, more commonly occurring factors can increase learner interest. They include

- Logical and coherent presentations
- Concrete examples
- Personalized content
- Student involvement

Students' interest is also increased when they're given choices about learning activities and reading materials. And as with most factors in learning and motivation, the more background knowledge students have about a topic, the more interest they have in it (Schraw & Lehman, 2001; Schraw, Flowerday, & Lehman, 2001). We examine strategies for increasing student interest in more detail in Chapter 11.

Importance.   "Because it's important" also helps answer the question "Why should I do this task?" **Importance** is *the extent to which a topic or activity allows a person to confirm or disconfirm important aspects of his or her self-schemas* (Wigfield & Eccles, 1992). If a person believes she is a good athlete, for instance, doing well in an athletic event will be important to her, because it confirms her belief about her athletic ability. Similarly, doing well in math will be important to a student with a positive self-concept of math ability, because doing well is evidence that the self-concept is valid.

Utility Value.

Javier has high motivation to learn in algebra. "I don't always get it completely, so I have to really study, and that can get a little old at times," he comments, "but I know that algebra is required for all the rest of the math courses I'll take, and I want a good math background for college."

For Javier, studying algebra has high **utility value,** *the perception of a topic or activity as useful*

> **10.9**
> Look again at Laura Hunter's lesson at the beginning of Chapter 9. Describe two ways in which she attempted to increase her students' interest in her lesson.

Learning tasks that are interesting, challenging, and that students value increase student motivation.

for meeting future goals, including career goals (Wigfield & Eccles, 1992). He doesn't believe he is particularly good in algebra, and he isn't intrinsically interested in it, but he believes that studying will be valuable to him in the future. At this point, Javier's motivation is primarily extrinsic, but as we saw in the last section, increased understanding leads to increased interest (Schraw & Lehman, 2001; Schraw et al., 2001). As his understanding of math improves, his intrinsic motivation is likely to increase as well. This example helps us see how extrinsic motivation, intrinsic motivation, and motivation to learn interact and support one another.

Cost.   Cost is *the perceived negative aspects of engaging in a task* (Wigfield & Eccles, 1992). The amount of time Javier has to spend studying algebra, for instance, is a cost; time spent studying is time he doesn't have for other, more desirable activities. If the cost is too high, a person may choose to not be involved in the activity. For instance, you may choose to not take a demanding course at this point in your program because you already have a heavy load.

Emotional costs also exist. If a person gets very nervous speaking in front of people, he may choose not to present at a meeting or a conference because the emotional cost is too high. Emotional costs are influenced by **affective memories,** *past emotional experiences related to a topic or activity* (Pintrich & Schunk, 2002). For instance, if the nervous young man went "blank" once when about to make a presentation, the affective memory of this experience would increase the emotional cost and decrease the likelihood of him again involving himself in the activity. As we saw in Chapter 6, affective memories are most likely triggered by classical conditioning (Pintrich & Schunk, 2002).

Self-schemas, including self-concepts, are important in expectancy x value theory. We turn now to a discussion of more specific beliefs about capability, how they're formed, and what impact they have on motivation.

Self-Efficacy: Beliefs About Capability

In your study of social cognitive theory in Chapter 6, you saw that an individual's beliefs can influence both behavior and the present environment. One of the most important is **self-efficacy,** *a belief about one's own capability to organize and complete a course of action required to accomplish a specific type of task* (Bandura, 1986; Schunk, 1994).

Self-efficacy bears some similarity to specific self-concepts, such as self-concept of ability in math, but an important difference exists. As you saw in our discussion of expectancy x value theory (and in Chapter 3), people with positive self-concepts in math, for instance, believe they're *generally* competent in math. Self-efficacy, however, focuses on organizing and completing courses of action, which describes a more specific and situational view of motivation (Bong & Clark, 1999). For example, a student with high self-efficacy for math, when faced with a series of problems involving systems of equations, believes she is capable of solving them. This same student may not believe she is capable of solving these problems using an unfamiliar method, however. Research indicates that self-efficacy doesn't necessarily generalize across areas (P. Smith & Fouad, 1999). The specificity of self-efficacy beliefs is important for teachers because it suggests that students' beliefs about their capabilities can be quite narrow and nontransferable; therefore, teachers must consider students' beliefs in different contexts.

Factors Influencing Self-Efficacy

Four factors influence people's beliefs about their capability of succeeding on specific tasks (Bandura, 1986). They are outlined in Figure 10.6 and discussed in the paragraphs that follow.

Past performance on similar tasks is the most important. A history of success in giving oral reports, for example, increases a person's self-efficacy for giving future reports. Observing the modeling of others, such as those delivering excellent reports, increases self-efficacy by raising expectations and providing information about how a skill should be performed (Bandura, 1986; Kitsantas, Zimmerman & Cleary, 2000).

10.10
Cite a specific example from Kathy Brewster's conversation with Harvey (p. 349) that illustrates emphasis on utility value in his learning. Explain.

10.11
Using the concepts from classical conditioning, explain how a person might have learned to be nervous in anticipation of giving a presentation. Referring again to classical conditioning, explain how the person might overcome this nervousness.

10.12
Explain the relationship between *self-concept* and *self-esteem*. (Hint: Think about your study of these concepts in Chapter 3.)

10.13
Teachers can promote learners' self-efficacy by providing only enough guidance to be sure that they make genuine progress toward a solution on their own. What concept from your study of learner development in Chapter 2 does this sort of guidance describe?

Figure 10.6 Factors influencing self-efficacy

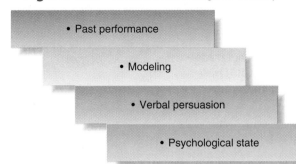

- Past performance
- Modeling
- Verbal persuasion
- Psychological state

Although limited in its effectiveness, verbal persuasion, such as a teacher commenting, "I know you will give a fine report," can also increase self-efficacy. It probably does so indirectly by encouraging students to try challenging tasks; if students succeed, efficacy increases.

Finally, physiological factors, such as fatigue or hunger, can reduce efficacy even though they're unrelated to the task, and emotional states, such as anxiety, can reduce efficacy by filling working memory with thoughts of failure.

The Influence of Self-Efficacy on Learner Behavior

Students who believe they are capable of succeeding—those high in self-efficacy—expect to do so, and this expectation strongly affects their motivation. For instance, compared to low-efficacy students, high-efficacy learners accept more challenging tasks, exert more effort, persist longer, use more effective strategies, and generally perform better (Eccles et al., 1998; Wigfield, 1994; Wigfield & Eccles, 1992). These characteristics are outlined in Table 10.1.

Developmental differences in self-efficacy exist. For instance, young children generally have high efficacy, sometimes unrealistically high—they believe they are capable of accomplishing most of the tasks set out for them (Eccles et al., 1998). As they move through school, they become less confident, which may reflect more realistic beliefs. They also become more aware of, and are more concerned with, their performance compared to that of their peers (A. Elliot & McGregor, 2000). Promoting high self-efficacy in students is an important goal for all teachers.

Goals and Goal Orientation

Goals can also have a powerful influence on motivation. To understand how, let's look at how several students might have thought about a group project in the world history class taught by Kathy Brewster, from the opening case study.

- *Susan:* This should be interesting. I don't know much about the Renaissance, and it began a whole new emphasis on learning all over the world. Mrs. Brewster has given us a lot of responsibility, so we need to come through. We need to make a presentation she'll like.
- *Damien:* I'll get my Dad to help us. He's really up on history. Our presentation will be the best one of the bunch.

Table 10.1 The influence of self-efficacy on behavior and cognition

	High Self-Efficacy Learners	Low Self-Efficacy Learners
Task orientation	Accept challenging tasks	Avoid challenging tasks
Effort	Expend high effort when faced with challenging tasks	Expend low effort when faced with challenging tasks
Persistence	Persist when goals aren't initially reached	Give up when goals aren't initially reached
Beliefs	Believe they will succeed	Focus on feelings of incompetence
	Control stress and anxiety when goals aren't met	Experience anxiety and depression when goals aren't met
	Believe they're in control of their environment	Believe they're not in control of their environment
Strategy use	Discard unproductive strategies	Persist with unproductive strategies
Performance	Perform higher than low-efficacy students of equal ability	Perform lower than high-efficacy students of equal ability

- *Sylvia:* Yikes! Everyone in my group is so smart. What can I do? They'll think I'm the dumbest one.
- *Charlotte:* This should be fun. We can get together to work on this at one of our houses. If we can get the project out of the way fairly quickly, I might have time to get to know Damien better.
- *Antonio:* I don't know anything about this. I'd better do some studying before we start. I don't want the rest of my group to think I'm not pulling my weight.
- *Patrick:* I like group activities. They're usually easy. Somebody is always gung ho and does most of the work.

Each of the six students' thinking reflects a **goal**, *an outcome an individual hopes to achieve* (Locke & Latham, 1990). As the examples illustrate, students have a variety of goals. For instance, Susan's primary goal was to understand the Renaissance, Charlotte wanted to socialize, and Patrick simply wanted to do as little work as possible. Each of these goals influences motivation and learning.

Learning and Performance Goals

Much of the research literature examining goals, motivation, and achievement has focused on differences between learning and performance goals (Pintrich, 2002; Stipek, 2002). For example, consider the following goals:

- To understand each topic covered in this class
- To score in the top third of the class on the next quiz
- To run a road race in less time than my friend Melanie

The first goal is a *learning goal,* whereas the second and third are *performance goals.* A **learning goal** (sometimes called a *mastery goal*) *focuses on mastery of a task, improvement, and increased understanding* (Dweck & Leggett, 1988; Pintrich, 2000). Susan's desire to understand the Renaissance is another example. In comparison, a **performance goal** *focuses on competence or ability and how it compares to the competence or ability of others* (A. Elliot & McGregor, 2000; A. Elliot & Thrash, 2001). Scoring in the top third of the class and running a race in less time than your friend require you to compare your performance to others. Damien wanting to make the best presentation was a *performance-approach goal;* he wanted to look intelligent and competent. Sylvia wanting to avoid looking dumb or incompetent was a *performance-avoidance* goal.

Some researchers use the labels *ego-involved* and *task-involved* (Nicholls, 1984), or *ability-focused* and *task-focused* (Maehr & Midgley, 1991), for performance and learning goals, respectively, but there is enough conceptual overlap that "performance" goal and "learning" goal are appropriate labels (Pintrich & Schunk, 2002).

Learning goals are highly desirable. Research indicates that students who adopt them have high efficacy; they persist in the face of difficulty; attribute success to internal, controllable causes; accept academic challenges; and use effective strategies, such as elaborative questioning and summarizing (Alexander et al., 1998; Bruning et al., 1999). Learning goals lead to sustained interest and effort even after formal instruction has been completed.

The influence of performance goals on motivation is more complex. To begin with, many students adopt both learning and performance goals; they want to both understand the topic and score near the top of their classes, for example (Harackiewicz, Barron, Taurer, Carter, & Elliot, 2000; A. Young, 1997). Also, students who want to demonstrate competence, a *performance-approach* orientation, tend to be confident and have high self-efficacy (Middleton & Midgley, 1997). On the other hand, students with a *performance-avoidance* orientation tend to lack self-confidence and have low self-efficacy (Skaalvik, 1997). For

Learning goals focus students' efforts on understanding and mastering challenging and complex content.

10.14

Consider this goal: "To get an A on my next essay." Rewrite it so it is a learning goal rather than a performance goal.

students with a performance-avoidance orientation, performance goals can strongly detract from motivation (Midgley & Urdan, 2001).

Even though a performance-approach orientation doesn't detract from motivation and achievement for all learners, learning goals have at least two advantages compared to performance goals. The first is control. For instance, when your goal is to understand the topics covered in the class, you are in control of setting, monitoring, and revising the goal. In contrast, if you have the performance goal of scoring in the top third of the class and the topics covered on your next quiz turn out to be very difficult, you may not score in the top third even though you studied carefully—you're out of control. Also, because performance goals are based on performance compared to others, your control over attaining them is further reduced. No matter how hard you study or train, you will not score in the top third of the class or beat your friend in a road race if your classmates and your friend put in a better performance.

The second advantage of learning goals lies in students' responses to mistakes and failure. They are both part of learning, and the way we respond to them is important for motivation. Failure on a learning goal can lead to increased effort or a change in strategies. Failure on a performance goal can lead to anxiety and a performance-avoidance orientation in the future (Midgley, Kaplan, & Middleton, 2001).

Unfortunately, as students progress through school, their performance orientation tends to increase while their learning orientation tends to decrease (A. Elliot & McGregor, 2000). Teachers sometimes unwittingly contribute to this orientation by emphasizing that students need to get good grades if they want to go to college, displaying grades, or discussing differences in students' performances on tests and written work.

Goals and Theories About the Nature of Intelligence

Some researchers (e.g., Dweck, 1999; Dweck & Leggett, 1988) believe that the tendency to adopt learning or performance goals is related to individuals' personal theories about the nature of intelligence. Some people hold an **entity view of intelligence,** which is *the belief that ability is stable and out of an individual's control;* others hold an **incremental view of intelligence,** which is *the belief that ability can be improved with effort.* According to Dweck and her colleagues, people with an entity view are likely to adopt performance goals, whereas those with an incremental view are more apt to adopt learning goals.

Let's see why. Scoring in the top third of the class on a quiz, for example, could be interpreted as an indicator of high ability, and evidence of high ability is important if intelligence is viewed as fixed. On the other hand, if intelligence is viewed as alterable, failure merely indicates that more effort is required, and with that effort, intelligence can be increased.

10.15

How do entity views of intelligence develop? Incremental views? What implications do the development of these views have for teachers?

According to Dweck and Leggett (1988), holding an entity view isn't a problem if individuals' confidence in their intelligence is high; they will seek challenging tasks and persist in the face of difficulty. However, if confidence in their intelligence is low, they're likely to avoid challenge, because failure suggests low ability. In contrast, individuals with an incremental view are more likely to seek challenge and persist even if they aren't confident about their ability, because failure merely indicates that more work is required. And as competence increases, so does intelligence.

An incremental view of intelligence can lead to increased motivation and, with it, higher achievement (McClelland, 1985). This is the view that Kathy Brewster modeled when she said, "the harder I study, the smarter I get."

Social Goals

Let's look again at the students' thinking that introduced the section "Goals and Goal Orientation." Charlotte, for example, thought, "If we can get the project out of the way fairly quickly, I might have time to get to know Damien better." In comparison, Antonio thought, "I don't know anything about this. I'd better do some studying before we start. I don't want the rest of my group to think I'm not pulling my weight." Both goals, although different from each other, are social goals; more specifically, Antonio had a *social responsibility goal.* Other social goals include gaining teacher or peer approval, achieving status among peers, honoring commitments, and assisting and supporting others (Dowson & McInerney, 2001; Wentzel, 1996).

Social goals sometimes enhance and sometimes detract from motivation. Charlotte's social goal of getting to know Damien better, for instance, conflicted with a learning goal—she wanted to "get the project out of the way fairly quickly" to meet the goal. Predictably, low achievers report this orientation much more often than do high achievers (Wentzel, 1991).

On the other hand, a social responsibility goal, such as Antonio's, tends to be associated with higher motivation and achievement (Wentzel, 1996). More significantly, students who simultaneously pursue learning goals and social responsibility goals, such as seeking approval and being responsible, achieve higher than those less oriented toward social responsibility (Wentzel, 1996, 1999b, 2000). Susan's thinking illustrates that of high achievers. She wanted to understand the Renaissance—a learning goal—but at the same time she felt responsible and sought Mrs. Brewster's approval.

Students who adopt both learning and social responsibility goals have higher achievement than those less oriented toward social responsibilty.

Work-Avoidance Goals

Students like Patrick are a source of challenge and frustration for teachers—they simply want to avoid work. Students with *work-avoidance goals* feel successful when tasks are easy or they can accomplish the tasks without exerting much effort (Dowson & McInerney, 2001; Gallini, 2000). They also tend to use ineffective learning strategies, make minimal contributions to group activities, ask for help even when they don't really need it, and complain about challenging activities. Most of the research on students with work-avoidance goals has been done at the middle school level, and more is needed to determine how they originate (Dowson & McInerney, 2001; Gallini, 2000).

The different types of goals and their influence on motivation and achievement are summarized in Table 10.2

Using Goals Effectively

Goal setting has been widely used to increase motivation and performance in the business world (Locke & Latham, 1990), and the importance of goals is being increasingly recognized in education. Goals increase self-efficacy because people set goals they believe they can meet and doing so increases their sense of competence.

Many learners—including university students—study without clear goals in mind, however (Alexander et al., 1998; Rosenshine, 1997). Students copy and reorganize their

Table 10.2 Goals, motivation, and achievement

Type of Goal	Example	Influence on Motivation and Achievement
Learning goals	To understand the influence of the Renaissance on American history	Leads to sustained effort, high self-efficacy, willingness to accept challenges, and high achievement.
Performance-approach goals	To produce one of the best essays on the Renaissance in the class	Can lead to sustained effort and high self-efficacy for confident learners. Can increase achievement.
		Can detract from willingness to accept challenging tasks, which decreases achievement.
Performance-avoidance goals	To avoid the appearance of low ability in front of peers and teachers	Detracts from motivation and achievement, particularly for learners lacking confidence
Social goals	To be perceived as reliable and responsible	Enhances motivation and achievement, particularly when combined with learning goals.
	To make friends and socialize	Can detract from motivation and achievement if social goals compete for time with learning goals.
Work-avoidance goals	To complete an assignment with as little effort as possible	Detracts from effort and self-efficacy. Strongly detracts from achievement.

Figure 10.7 Effective use of goals

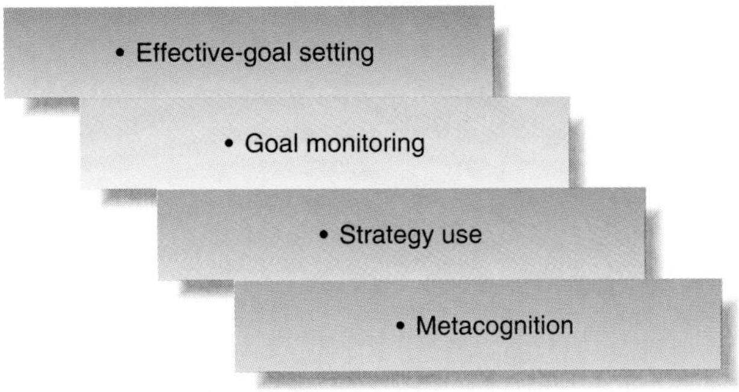

- Effective-goal setting
- Goal monitoring
- Strategy use
- Metacognition

notes, for instance, but don't ask themselves if doing so contributes to their understanding. They tacitly seem to think that spending time equals learning.

Using goals effectively involves four processes. They're outlined in Figure 10.7 and discussed in the paragraphs that follow.

Effective-Goal Setting. What is an effective goal; that is, what kind of goal are we most likely to stick with and eventually attain? To begin answering this question, consider the following goals:

- To learn more in my classes
- To get into better shape
- To lose 20 pounds by the end of this year
- To answer and understand all the margin questions for each chapter of this text

How effective is each one? The first two are general, and as a result, monitoring progress on them and identifying strategies to achieve them is difficult. What, specifically, will you do to learn more, or to get into better shape, for instance? The third goal is too distant. Losing 20 pounds is likely a worthwhile goal, but the end of the year is too far into the future. Goals that are close at hand increase self-efficacy more than distant ones, because meeting them is more easily observed. The fourth goal is effective. It is specific, moderately challenging, and can be attacked immediately. It can also be readily monitored and it lends itself to strategy use.

To summarize, effective goals have three characteristics:

- They are specific (versus broad and general).
- They are immediate or close at hand (versus distant).
- They are moderately challenging.

10.16
Rewrite each of the first three goals on the list to make them more effective.

The appropriate degree of challenge isn't easy to specify, but it's important. Goals that are too easily reached don't increase self-efficacy as much as those more challenging. On the other hand, goals that are too challenging may reduce expectations for success so much that overall motivation is decreased.

In order for goals to work, people must be committed to them (Pintrich & Schunk, 2002). The best way to increase goal commitment in schools is to guide students in setting their own goals, rather than imposing goals on them (Ridley, McCombs, & Taylor, 1994). However, teachers and parents can play a powerful role in influencing the kinds of goals learners set (McNeil & Alibali, 2000). Students must be committed to goals or the motivating influence of using them will be lost.

Goal Monitoring. Once people have committed to a set of goals, monitoring them leads to a sense of accomplishment, promotes self-efficacy, and can be a pleasant emotional experience. For instance, let's look at our fourth goal again. There are 26 questions in the margins of this chapter, so suppose on Monday you set the goal of answering all the questions by the following Sunday. If on Wednesday you've answered the first 13 questions, and you believe you understand them, you feel good about your progress; you've answered half of the questions in less than half the week. You have concrete evidence of your progress, and your self-efficacy increases. In addition, you've taken responsibility for your own learning, which further increases your sense of accomplishment.

Self-monitoring of goals also has more general value (Schunk, 1997; Wolters, 1997). For example, suppose a student named Sheila monitors the amount of time devoted to "studying," and she finds that she is actually spending a considerable amount of time on activities that don't contribute to learning, such as getting up to change the volume of the radio, or reorganizing notes without actually learning from them. This realization can motivate her to shut the radio off and look for relationships among the ideas in her notes. If she believes her changed habits increase her learning, her motivation will be sustained (Schunk, 1997).

Strategy Use. Use of appropriate strategies is the third process required for effective goal use. For example, simply reading the margin questions and then reading the answers is a poor strategy, because you are studying passively. Actually constructing an answer to the question in writing and then checking the feedback is much more effective. Also, waiting until Saturday to start answering the margin questions doesn't work as well as answering four or five each day.

Effective strategy use requires a repertoire of strategies (Bruning et al., 1999). For instance, suppose you've set the goal of writing two summary sentences for each section of the chapter. You obviously must be skilled with summarizing in order to use the strategy.

Metacognition. Finally, the entire process of using goals is grounded in metacognition. For instance, think again about Sheila, the student who realized—when she began monitoring her study time—that she was spending less time "studying" than she had previously thought. She first had to be aware enough of her study habits to begin monitoring her time, and she then had to exercise control over her strategies by shutting off the radio.

The importance of metacognition is hard to overstate. For instance, suppose you're writing definitions of concepts on note cards, but your instructor's tests and quizzes measure application. If you're metacognitive, you'll quickly realize that you're using an ineffective strategy and you'll change your goals, such as deciding to complete the exercises in the Student Study Guide. The change in strategy, resulting from metacognition, is almost certain to increase your understanding.

Teachers can help learners become more metacognitive by modeling their own thinking and by encouraging students to think about the way they study. The message that teachers want to communicate is that learning is conscious, intentional, and requires effort (Alexander et al., 1998).

10.17
Again consider this goal: To understand each topic covered in this class. Is this an effective goal? Explain why or why not.

Attribution Theory

We said earlier in this chapter that students who adopt learning goals attribute success to internal, controllable causes. What does "attribute" mean, and why is it important for motivation? We answer these and other questions in this section.

Let's begin by looking at five students' responses to the results of a test.

"How'd you do, Bob?" Anne asked.

"Terrible," Bob answered sheepishly. "I just can't do this stuff. I'm no good at writing the kind of essays she wants. . . . I'll never get it."

"I didn't do so good either," Anne replied, "but I knew I wouldn't. I just didn't study hard enough. I knew I was going to be in trouble. I won't let that happen again."

"Unbelievable!" Armondo added. "I didn't know what the heck was going on, and I got a B. I don't think she read mine."

"I got a C," Billy shrugged. "Not bad, considering how much I studied. I could have done a lot better, but I couldn't get into it for this test."

"I just went blank," Ashley said with a crestfallen look. "I looked at the test, and all I could think of was, 'I've never seen this stuff before. Where did it come from?'"

We saw earlier that cognitive theories of motivation are grounded in the assumption that people are motivated by a need to understand and make sense of the world. We can explain Bob's, Anne's, and Armondo's reactions on this basis. (We consider Billy's and Ashley's reactions later in the chapter.) They all had innate desires to understand why they got the grades they did, so they created explanations (perceived causes) for their successes and failures. These explanations are called *attributions*. Bob explained his failure by saying that he wasn't good enough (he lacked ability), Anne used lack of effort as her explanation, and Armondo wrote the issue off to luck. In addition to ability, effort, and luck, learners also attribute successes and failures to other factors such as the difficulty of the task, effective or ineffective strategies, lack of help, interest, unfair teacher practices, or clarity of instruction. Ability, effort, luck, and task difficulty are the most frequent perceived causes of success or failure (B. Weiner, 1990).

Attribution theory is *a cognitive theory of motivation that attempts to systematically describe learners' explanations for their successes and failures.* Attributions occur on three dimensions (B. Weiner, 1992, 1994a, 1994b). The first is called *locus* (the location of the cause); it is either within or outside the learner. Ability and effort are within the learner, for example, whereas luck and task difficulty are outside. The second is *stability*, whether or not the cause can change. Effort and luck are unstable because they can change, whereas ability is considered stable in attribution theory. The third is *control*, the extent to which students accept responsibility for their successes or failures, or are in control of the learning situation. Learners control their effort, for example, but they cannot control luck or task difficulty. These relationships are outlined in Table 10.3.

Impact of Attributions on Learners

Attributions influence learners in at least four ways:

- Emotional reactions to success and failure
- Expectations for future success
- Future effort
- Achievement

Let's look at our students again. Anne did poorly, but she attributed it to lack of effort, for which she was responsible (she can control her effort). As a result, guilt was her emotional reaction. She can also expect to be more successful in the future because effort is unstable. Her comment "I won't let that happen again" suggests that she will increase her effort, which is likely to increase her achievement (Weiner, 1994a).

Bob's emotional reaction was shame and embarrassment because he attributed his failure to lack of ability, which he viewed as uncontrollable. He doesn't expect future success ("I'll never get it"), and his effort and achievement are likely to decrease (Weiner, 1994a).

Motivation tends to increase when students attribute failure to lack of effort, as Anne did, because effort can be controlled. Motivation tends to decrease when students attribute failure to uncontrollable causes (such as luck, or ability if it is viewed as stable), as Bob did (Ames, 1992).

Research indicates that people tend to attribute success to internal causes, such as hard work or high ability, and failures to external causes, such as bad luck or the behaviors of others (Marsh, 1990). When students do poorly, for example, they commonly attribute their failure to poor teaching, boring topics, tricky tests, or some other external cause.

Attributions also influence teachers. For instance, if they believe students are succeeding because of their teaching, they're likely to continue making the effort (Shahid, 2001). On the other hand, if they believe learners are doing poorly because of students' lack of background knowledge, poor home lives, or some other cause beyond their control, their teaching efforts decrease.

Learned Helplessness

Let's look at Bob's attributions again. He attributed his failure to lack of ability, which he viewed as an internal, uncontrollable cause. In the extreme, his attribution can lead to **learned helplessness**, *the feeling that no amount of effort can lead to success* (D. Seligman,

10.18
Explain Armondo's emotional reaction, expectation for future success, future effort, and achievement, based on his attributing his success to luck. If he had attributed his failure to a difficult task, how would you explain these characteristics?

Table 10.3 Characteristics of attributions in relation to three dimensions of attributions

Attributions	Locus (location of cause)	Stability (of cause)	Control (of learning situation)
Ability	Inside the learner	Stable (cannot change)	Learner out of control
Effort	Inside the learner	Unstable (can change)	Learner in control
Luck	Outside the learner	Unstable (can change)	Learner out of control
Task difficulty	Outside the learner	Stable (cannot change)	Learner out of control

1975). This perspective leads to overwhelming feelings of shame and self-doubt that result in giving up without trying.

Learned helplessness has both an affective and a cognitive component. Students with learned helplessness have low self-esteem and often suffer from anxiety and depression (Graham & Weiner, 1996). Cognitively, they expect to fail, so they don't take advantage of opportunities to increase understanding and develop skills, which results in low achievement and an even greater expectation for failure (Weiner, 1994a). Students placed at risk who have histories of failure are particularly susceptible to learned helplessness. Fortunately, efforts to intervene with students experiencing learned helplessness have been successful. We turn to this topic now.

Attribution Training

Learners can improve the effectiveness of their attributions through training (Robertson, 2000). In a pioneering study, Dweck (1975) provided students who demonstrated learned helplessness with successful and unsuccessful experiences. When the students were unsuccessful, the experimenter specifically stated that the failure was caused by lack of effort or ineffective strategies. Comparable students were given similar experiences but no training. After 25 sessions, the learners who were counseled about their effort and strategies responded more appropriately to failure by persisting longer and adapting their strategies more effectively. Subsequent research has corroborated Dweck's findings (Forsterling, 1985; M. Seligman, 1995). Strategy instruction was most effective for students who believed that they were already trying hard. This research suggests that teachers can have important influences on the ways students interpret their performance by teaching them learning strategies and encouraging them to attribute success to effort.

Beliefs, Goals, and Attributions: Instructional Strategies

Teachers can apply the cognitive theories of motivation that we've discussed to this point in several ways. The following principles can guide teachers in their efforts:

- Attempt to increase learner self-efficacy by modeling efficacy and providing evidence of accomplishment.
- Encourage internal attributions for successes and controllable attributions for failures.
- Emphasize the utility value of increased skills.
- Promote student interest by modeling your own interest, personalizing content, providing concrete examples, involving students, and offering choices.
- Emphasize learning and social responsibility goals, effective strategies, and metacognition.

Earlier in the chapter, we saw how Kathy Brewster applied humanistic views of motivation in her interactions with Jenny and Harvey. Let's flash back to her teaching and see how the principles we've just listed guide her as she works with her whole class.

Kathy finished her beginning-of-class routines and then pulled down a map in the front of the room. "Let's review for a moment to see where we are. We began our discussion of the Crusades yesterday. How did we start?"

"We imagined that we all left Lincoln High School and that it was taken over by people who believed that extracurricular activities should be eliminated," Carnisha volunteered.

Student beliefs about their own ability as learners can be enhanced by experiences in which challenging tasks are successfully accomplished.

"Good," Kathy smiled. "Then what?"

"We decided we'd talk to them. . . . We'd be on a 'crusade' to change their minds."

"Very good. . . . Now, what were the actual Crusades all about? . . . Selena?"

"The Christians wanted to get the Holy Land back from the Muslims."

"And why? . . . Becky?"

"The holy lands were important for the Christians. I suppose they just wanted them because of that."

"Also, the map shows how much territory the Muslims were getting, and the people in Europe were . . . like afraid the Muslims would take over their land," Cindy added.

"Good thought, Cindy. . . . They certainly were a military threat. In fact, the conflict that occurred in Kosovo is a present-day reminder of the clash between Christians and Muslims. How else might they have been threatening?"

"Maybe . . . economically," Brad suggested. "You're always telling us how economics rules the world."

"Excellent, Brad," Kathy laughed. "Indeed, economics was a factor. In fact, we'll see that the military and economic threats of the Muslims, together with the religious issue, were factors that led to Columbus's voyage to the New World. . . . Think about that. The Muslims in 1000 A.D. have had an influence on us here today.

"Now, for today's assignment," Kathy continued, "you were asked to write a paragraph answering the question, 'Were the Crusades a success or a failure?' You could take either position. The quality of your paragraph depends on how you defended your position, not on the position itself. Remember, the ability to make and defend an argument is a skill that goes way beyond a specific topic like the Crusades.

"So, let's see how we made out. Go ahead. . . . Nikki?"

"I said they were a failure. . . . The Europeans didn't accomplish what they were after—getting the Holy Land back for Christianity," Nikki said. "There were several Crusades, and after only one did they get sort of a foothold, and it only lasted . . . like about 50 years, I think."

"How about you, Joe?"

"I said they were a success because the Europeans learned new military strategies that they later used . . . here, in the Americas. If it hadn't been for the Crusades, they wouldn't have learned the techniques, . . . at least not for a long time. The Crusades even changed our ideas about guerrilla fighting."

"Also good, Joe," Kathy nodded. "This is exactly what we're after. Nikki and Joe took opposite positions in their paragraphs, but they each provided several details in support.

"Let's look at another one. . . . What was your position, Anita?"

"I said they . . . were a success. Western Europe took a lot from their culture . . . in the Middle East. Like, some of the spices we eat today first came to Europe then."

"Now isn't that interesting!" Kathy waved energetically. "See, here's another case where we see ourselves today finding a relationship to people who lived 1,000 or more years ago. That's what history is all about."

"Brewster loves this stuff," David whispered to Kelly, smiling slightly.

"Yeah," she replied. "History has never been my favorite subject, but some of this stuff is actually kind of neat."

"Okay. One more," Kathy continued, "and we'll move on."

The class reviewed another example, and then Kathy told the students to revise their paragraphs based on what they had discussed and turn in a product for peer review the next day.

"Remember, think about what you're doing when you make your revisions," she emphasized. "Read your paragraph after you write it, and ask yourself, 'Do I actually have evidence here or simply an opinion?' . . . The more aware you are when you write, the better your work will be. And remember, we made a commitment to ourselves at the beginning of the year to help each other as much as we could when we give each other feedback on our writing. . . . So, I know that you'll come through.

"One more reminder," Kathy said as the period was nearly over, "group presentations on the Renaissance are on Wednesday and Thursday. You decide what groups will present on each day. For those who chose to write the paper on the Middle Ages, remember we agreed that they're due next Friday."

Let's take a closer look at Kathy's attempts to apply the principles related to beliefs, goals, and attributions. Three of the principles were illustrated in Kathy's interaction with Harvey in the case study at the beginning of the chapter. First, she attempted to increase Harvey's self-efficacy by saying, "Yes, but look how good you're getting at writing. I think you hit a personal best on your last paper." Evidence of accomplishment is the most important factor that influences self-efficacy, and her comment provided some evidence. She also modeled self-efficacy when she said, "It's hard for me, too, when I'm studying and trying to put together new ideas, but if I hang in, I always feel like I can get it."

Evidence of accomplishment increased Harvey's self-efficacy.

Second, her response to Harvey encouraged him to attribute his success to effort and increased ability—both internal causes. Third, Harvey's comment, "Yeah, yeah, I know, and being good writers will help us in everything we do in life," indicates that Kathy also emphasized the utility value of what they were learning.

Kathy attempted to increase her students' interest in the topic in several ways. She modeled her own interest, as indicated by David's comment, "Brewster loves this stuff," and she personalized the topic with the analogy of crusading to prevent the school from eliminating extracurricular activities. Personalizing the topic also created a concrete example of a "crusade," and her students were highly involved throughout the learning activity. The influence of Kathy's attempts to increase interest were reflected in Kelly's response to David when she said, "Yeah, history has never been my favorite subject, but some of this stuff is actually kind of neat."

Kathy also increased interest by giving her students choices. She allowed the students to choose from two assignments (a presentation on the Renaissance or a paper on the Middle Ages), to decide which groups would present on certain days, and to negotiate the due date for the papers ("remember that we agreed that they're due next Friday").

Kathy attempted to apply the last principle by encouraging the students to be strategic and metacognitive about their writing. She said, "Remember, think about what you're doing when you make your revisions. Read your paragraph after you write it, and ask yourself, 'Do I actually have evidence here or simply an opinion?' The more aware you are when you write, the better your work will be."

Her emphasis on goals went even further when she said, "And remember, we made a commitment to ourselves at the beginning of the year to help each other as much as we could when we give each other feedback on our writing. . . . So, I know that you'll come through." Her comment promoted social responsibility, and as we saw in our discussion of goals earlier in the chapter, the combination of social responsibility goals and learning goals increases motivation and achievement more than either alone (Wentzel, 1991).

As we said at the beginning of the chapter, teachers won't be successful with every student, but with a positive approach to motivation, they can influence many. This is what Kathy tried to do as she worked with her students.

Self-Determination Theory

One of the most comprehensive cognitive motivation theories is *self-determination theory* (Deci, 1980; Deci & Ryan, 1985, 1991; Ryan & Deci, 2000). It examines both extrinsic and intrinsic motivation and describes a continuum of increasing self-determination that proceeds through stages of extrinsic motivation and ends in intrinsic motivation. Although the theory is based primarily on cognitive views of motivation, it incorporates aspects of humanistic views as well.

Self-determination is *the process of deciding how to act on one's environments* (Deci, 1980; Ryan & Deci, 2000). According to self-determination theory, having choices and making decisions is intrinsically motivating, and people wouldn't be content if all their needs were satisfied and they could not make decisions about those choices. Self-determination theory assumes that people have three innate psychological needs: competence, control or autonomy, and relatedness (Ryan & Deci, 2000).

The Need for Competence

The need for **competence**, *the ability to function effectively in the environment*, can be described at a variety of levels. At a basic anthropological level, for instance, if an organism can't function effectively in its environment, it isn't likely to survive. In the workplace, competent people succeed and grow in their careers. In schools, competent students are successful learners and high achievers, and they find school rewarding and satisfying. Competence and self-efficacy are sometimes equated (Ryan & Deci, 2000; Pintrich & Schunk, 2002).

The need for competence helps explain the motivating effects of both challenge and curiosity. Meeting challenges provides evidence that competence is increasing, whereas accomplishing trivial tasks provides little information about competence. In addition, meeting challenges is emotionally satisfying (Stipek, 2002). Curiosity addresses similar competence needs. Resolving experiences that are novel and discrepant with existing understanding also indicates increasing competence.

The need for competence is similar to the need for mastery of the environment that was described by R. White (1959) in a paper that is now viewed as a classic. He suggested that people acquire proficiency and skill "because it satisfies an intrinsic need to deal with the environment" (p. 318). The need for competence is also consistent with the need to understand the reasons for our successes and failures that are a part of attribution theory (B. Weiner, 1986), as well as the need for achievement that is basic to historical descriptions of achievement motivation theory (J. Atkinson, 1958).

As with self-efficacy, the most important factor influencing students' perception of competence is evidence and feedback indicating that their understanding and skills are improving. As perception of competence increases, so does self-determination (Deci & Ryan, 1987).

Teachers also influence students' perceptions of competence in other, more subtle ways. They include

- Attributional statements
- Praise and criticism
- Emotional displays
- Offers of help

Attributional Statements.   **Attributional statements,** *comments teachers make about the causes of students' performances,* can influence students' beliefs about their competence. For instance, a teacher is talking to a student who is struggling with a problem. With respect to motivation, which statement is more effective?

> "That's a very good effort. I know that these problems are difficult for you."
> "I believe if you tried a little harder, you'd be able to solve this problem."

According to attribution theory, the second is clearly better. The first attributes failure to lack of ability, and although the teacher may be concerned about the learner's feelings, it undermines beliefs about competence (Stipek, 1996). In contrast, attributing failure to lack of effort communicates that the learner has the ability to complete the task, and with increased effort, competence can be achieved.

Once the learner has succeeded in solving the problem, which statement is more effective?

> "You're getting very good at this."
> "Well done. I see that you've been working hard on this."

In this case, the first is likely to be better. It suggests that the student is becoming competent, whereas the second says little about increasing competence (Nicholls & Miller, 1984; Schunk, 1983).

Praise and Criticism.   Intuitively, using praise appears to be a straightforward motivational strategy—the more praise, the greater the motivation. It isn't that simple, however. Older students may perceive praise as reward for effort, rather than for accomplishment, or they may interpret praise for performance on easy tasks as an indication that the teacher believes they have low ability or are not competent (Graham, 1991; Stipek, 1996).

10.19
Identify a specific example in Kathy's work with her students where she attempted to meet their needs for competence.

To see a video clip of a teacher attempting to provide students with evidence of increasing competence, go to the Companion Website at *www.prenhall.com/eggen*, then to this chapter's *Classrooms on the Web* module. Click on *Video Clip 10.3.*

Giving criticism also appears to be straightforward—we should avoid it because it decreases motivation. However, research indicates that criticism can sometimes have a positive effect on learners' perceptions of competence (Parsons, Kaczala, & Meece, 1982). Learners interpret criticism of subpar performances (not typical for the particular learners) as an indication that the teacher believes they have high ability.

Emotional Displays.　Teachers' emotional reactions to learners' successes and failures can also affect their perceptions of competence. For example, when teachers express annoyance and frustration in response to learner failure, learners are likely to attribute their failure to lack of effort, which further implies that they can achieve competence with increased effort. Students who receive sympathy from teachers are likely to attribute their failure to lack of ability (Graham, 1984). Attributing failure to lack of ability implies that learners don't have the capacity to become competent (Stipek, 1996).

Offers of Help.　Offering students unsolicited help can also be pernicious. For instance, researchers have found that children as young as 6 rated a student offered unsolicited help lower in ability than another offered no help (Graham & Barker, 1990). Further, learners who are offered help may feel negative emotions, such as incompetence, anger, worry, or anxiety (Meyer, 1982).

Research on attributional statements doesn't imply that teachers should avoid praising students, expressing sympathy, offering help, or encouraging effort. Rather, the research should remind us that we must be aware of how our actions will be interpreted by learners. As always, the way we respond to students requires sensitivity and careful judgment.

10.20
You are supervising students doing seat work, and one of them raises his hand and asks for help. Should you provide help? Is the student asking for help more likely to be a high or a low achiever? Explain, using information from this section.

The Need for Control

The need for **control** (or *autonomy*), *the ability to alter the environment when necessary,* is the second innate need described by self-determination theory. As we saw earlier, control is one source of intrinsic motivation (Lepper & Hodell, 1989). Conversely, being out of control detracts from intrinsic motivation and causes stress. For instance, it is widely believed that the stress of assembly line work comes from workers having little control over their environments.

The concept of *need for control* put forth in self-determination theory is similar to historical discussions of the topic, such as *locus of control* (Rotter, 1966) and *personal causation* (deCharms, 1968, 1984). Also, control and competence are strongly related. As learners' competence increases, so do their perceptions of control (Bruning et al., 1999).

What can teachers do to promote perceptions of control in their students? The most obvious answer is to give them choices, as Kathy did by allowing her students to either make a presentation on the Renaissance or write a paper on the Middle Ages. When providing choices isn't possible, perceptions of control can be enhanced in other ways. Some include

- Soliciting student input in creating classroom rules and procedures
- Encouraging students to set and monitor learning goals
- Creating high levels of student participation in learning activities
- Emphasizing effort and strategy attributions while de-emphasizing the role of ability in success
- Using assessments that emphasize learning and provide feedback

Teachers can increase learner autonomy and motivation by allowing students to choose some learning goals and activities.

10.21
In addition to offering the students choices, identify at least two other ways in which Kathy helped increase her students' perceptions of control. Explain.

Soliciting student input into rules and procedures and setting learning goals are intuitively sensible ways to increase perceptions of control. And in our discussion of expectancy x value theory, we saw that student participation was one way to increase student interest. These suggestions, together with effort and strategy attributions, are all grounded in cognitive views of motivation, so here we see a link between these views and self-determination theory. (We examine the relationships between self-determination and assessment shortly.)

The Need for Relatedness

The third innate need described by self-determination theory is the need for **relatedness,** *the feeling of connectedness to others in one's social environment resulting in feelings of worthiness of love and respect.* The need for relatedness is similar to the need for belonging as described in Maslow's hierarchy (Maslow, 1968, 1970) and the need for *affiliation* as described by other early researchers (e.g., Exline, 1962; Terhune, 1968).

Research supports the need for relatedness (Connell & Wellborn, 1990). Teachers who are available to students and who like, understand, and empathize with them have learners who are more emotionally, cognitively, and behaviorally engaged in classroom activities than teachers rated lower in these areas (McCombs, 1998; E. Skinner & Belmont, 1993). Further, students who feel as though they belong and who perceive personal support from their teachers report more interest in their class work and describe it as more important than students whose teachers are more distant (Goodenow, 1993). In addition, students who view their teachers as supportive are more likely to set desirable social goals, such as developing social responsibility (Wentzel, 1996).

10.22
What concept from humanistic views of motivation is seen in the idea of an environment "where each student is valued regardless of academic ability or performance"? Explain.

Collectively, these findings suggest that an accepting and supportive classroom environment, where each student is valued regardless of academic ability or performance, contributes to relatedness and is important for both learning and motivation (Stipek, 1996).

Assessment and Learning: The Role of Assessment in Self-Determination

As we've emphasized throughout this book, assessment is an essential part of the learning-teaching process. This raises an issue, however, because some research indicates that evaluation detracts from self-determination and intrinsic motivation (Deci & Ryan, 1987).

As with most aspects of learning and teaching, this issue isn't simply a matter of do or do not emphasize assessment. It depends on how the process of assessment is handled. For instance, assessments that students view as punitive or controlling detract from intrinsic motivation, whereas assessments that provide information about increasing competence can increase intrinsic motivation (Deci & Ryan, 1987; Eggen, 1997). The following are some suggestions for using assessments effectively:

- Provide clear expectations for students, and align assessments with the expectations (Pintrich & Schunk, 2002).
- Assess frequently and thoroughly (Bangert-Drowns, Kulik, & Kulik, 1991; Dochy & McDowell, 1997).
- Allow students to drop one or more of their lowest test or quiz scores for purposes of grading (Eggen, 1997).
- Provide detailed feedback about responses to assessments, and emphasize the reasons for answers more than the answers themselves (Deci & Ryan, 1987; Pintrich & Schunk, 2002).
- Avoid social comparisons in communicating assessment results (Patrick, Anderman, Ryan, Edelin, & Midgley, 1999; Pintrich & Garcia, 1991; Stipek, 1996).

10.23
Which theory of motivation best explains the need for providing detailed feedback on assessments? Explain.

Our goal in assessment should be to establish a climate that gives students perceptions of control and emphasizes learning and increased competence. Clear expectations and alignment make assessments predictable, which increases perceptions of control. Frequent assessment gives students information about their increasing competence, which also increases self-efficacy. Allowing students to drop one or more scores for purposes of grading emphasizes that learning and increased competence is the primary role of assessment. Detailed feedback that emphasizes reasons for answers further communicates that the role of assessment is to increase learning. Detailed feedback also contributes to students' perceptions of control, because students learn where they need improvement and what strategies they might use to accomplish it. Finally, avoiding social comparisons promotes a learning-focused rather than a performance-focused environment. As a symbolic gesture, some teachers write students' scores on the back page of tests and quizzes and encourage students to avoid sharing their scores with each other. Although students will still probably share their scores, the practice is a tangible symbol that assessments are private and their purpose is to increase learning, not see who is the "smartest."

Developing Students' Self-Determination: Instructional Strategies

Self-determination theory has a number of implications for teachers. Applying the following principles can contribute to motivation to learn and students' self-determination:

- Use assessments that increase intrinsic motivation.
- Reinforce increasing competence instead of compliance or mere participation in an activity.
- Create classroom environments and learning activities that give students as much control as possible.
- Design learning activities that challenge learners' existing understanding and skills.
- When possible, begin learning activities with events that are inconsistent with learners existing understanding and beliefs.
- Treat students with unconditional positive regard, and communicate that you are committed to their learning.

Let's see how the principles guide Elaine Goodman, a fifth-grade teacher, as she works with her students on a unit on fractions. We join her class as she is going over a weekly test, in this case an assessment of her students' progress in adding and subtracting fractions.

"You did very well on the test," Elaine smiled. "But I knew that you would. We've been practicing on problems like these for a week, and your understanding is getting deeper and deeper. And I'm very proud of how courteous those of you who finished so quickly were to the others who took a little longer.

"Now, we want to look at a few of the problems again," she directed, turning the discussion to the test. "Let's look at number 3."

Elaine read the problem:

You were at a party at Jon's [a boy in the class] house, and you ate one slice of the first pizza and two slices of the second pizza. How much did you eat altogether?

"We know that the answer is five twelfths of a pizza, but more important than the answer is understanding how we got it," Elaine began. "So, does someone want to come up to the board and explain how you got five twelfths? . . . Go ahead, Ajma," she said, seeing Ajma's raised hand.

"OK . . . I knew the answer couldn't be 3 over the total number of slices because the size of the slices wasn't the same," Ajma explained at the board. "I needed to add ⅙ of the first pizza and ⅜ of the second pizza, so I found the lowest common multiple for 6 and 8, which is 24. . . . For ⅙ I multiplied the top and bottom by 4, and for ⅜ I multiplied the top and bottom by 3."

Ajma wrote her calculations on the board:

$$\frac{1\,(4)}{6\,(4)} = \frac{4}{24}$$

$$\frac{2\,(3)}{8\,(3)} = \frac{6}{24}$$

"And why did you multiply both the top and bottom?" Elaine probed.

"Well, 4 over 4 is the same as 1, and so is 3 over 3, so I'm really multiplying by 1, and that doesn't change the number," Ajma explained.

"Excellent explanation, Ajma," Elaine smiled. "Go on."

"Then I added the two fractions and got $^{10}\!/_{24}$, and that reduces to $^{5}\!/_{12}$."

Elaine then had students explain other problems on the test, providing guidance when necessary. She completed the discussion by going over the last two problems. On each of her tests, Elaine gave the students the option of doing only one of the last two problems. If they did both problems, they earned bonus points.

When they finished discussing the test, she commented, "You're all getting very good at adding and subtracting fractions, and you're improving on your word problems every day. Keep up the good work." With a grin, she added, "We're going to understand this so well that no one can stump us."

"Now, remember again," she said finally, "If any of you want a little extra help, I'm always here at 8:15 in the morning, so we have 45 minutes before school actually starts to go over anything you need.

"Now, let's think about this," she said, changing the direction of the discussion. "When we multiply numbers, like 6 times 8, we get what?"

"Forty eight!" the students shouted in unison.

"Yes," Elaine smiled, "And 48 is a bigger number than either 6 or 8, isn't it? . . . How about when we divide, like 42 divided by 7?"

"Six. . . . A smaller number," Kiki responded.

"Exactly," Elaine nodded. "But here's the kicker. When we multiply fractions, like $^{2}\!/_{3}$ times $^{1}\!/_{4}$, you know what we get? . . . . Two twelfths, or $^{1}\!/_{6}$. . . . And what do you notice about $^{1}\!/_{6}$ compared to $^{2}\!/_{3}$ or $^{1}\!/_{4}$?"

"It's smaller," several of the students responded simultaneously.

"And when we divide fractions, it's just the opposite. One half divided by $^{1}\!/_{4}$ is—you're not going to believe this—2. . . . Now, how can that be?

"That's going to be our challenge for the next few days. . . . We're going to understand why multiplying fractions gives us a smaller number and dividing fractions gives us a bigger number. What do you think? . . . Are you up to it?"

"Yeah!" the students shouted.

"Of course you are," Elaine smiled. "You've been up to every challenge all year. . . . Let's get started."

Let's take a closer look at Elaine's attempts to develop her students' self-determination. First, her assessment procedures were consistent with the suggestions for using assessments to increase intrinsic motivation. Her expectations were clear, she assessed frequently, and her test was aligned with her goals. Perhaps most importantly, she emphasized understanding more than correct answers and discussed the completed problems carefully, so the students received detailed feedback about their learning progress.

Second, Elaine emphasized students' increasing competence with her praise and statements such as "You're all getting very good at adding and subtracting fractions, and you're improving on your word problems every day" and "We're going to understand this so well that no one can stump us." We saw in our discussion of behavioral approaches to motivation that feedback about increasing competence can increase intrinsic motivation (Deci & Ryan, 1987).

Third, Elaine sought to give students control over their learning. Because she realized that giving students choices is difficult when teaching basic skills such as operations with fractions, she instead gave them choices on the last items of her tests and an opportunity to do the alternate problem as a bonus. She also attempted to increase perceptions of control in her students by using meaningful and personalized examples (such as using students' names in the problems), and she promoted high levels of participation in all her lessons.

Fourth, Elaine introduced the multiplication and division of fractions by showing how they were discrepant compared to multiplying and dividing whole numbers. She then issued a challenge and reminded the students that they had met all her challenges throughout the year. Accepting and meeting challenges increases students' perceptions of competence, self-efficacy, and beliefs about their ability to control their own learning. Each increases intrinsic motivation (Deci, 1975; Harter, 1978; R. White, 1959).

Finally, by reminding the students that they could come in any day before school for extra help, Elaine communicated that she cared about the students and was committed to their learning. This kind of commitment helps meet students' needs for relatedness.

As we said earlier, efforts such as Elaine's won't turn all students into highly motivated learners. Motivation to learn is a goal we should all strive for, however, and in doing so, we can increase motivation for many.

10.24
Identify at least four ways in which Kathy Brewster attempted to promote self-determination in her students.

Classroom Connections

Applying Cognitive Theories of Motivation Effectively in Your Classroom

Expectancy x Value Theory

1. Develop expectations for success and self-efficacy by giving students only as much help as they need to make progress on challenging tasks.

   - *Elementary:* After displaying a problem, a fourth-grade teacher asks students to suggest ways of solving it. Each strategy is thoroughly discussed, and the teacher points out areas in which the students' problem solving is improving.

   - *Middle School:* A seventh-grade English teacher has his students write paragraphs on transparencies. He displays and discusses students' products and makes suggestions for improvement. He continually emphasizes how much the quality of the paragraphs is increasing.

   - *High School:* An art teacher has students keep a portfolio of their art creations. She has them periodically review their products to demonstrate the progress they're making.

2. Promote task value by using concrete examples to increase interest, and emphasize the importance of the topics students study.

   - *Elementary:* A third-grade teacher brings large shrimp and a lobster into his class. His students work in pairs to examine and describe the shrimp. The class discusses their findings, compares them to findings about the lobster, and they arrive at a description of crustaceans.

   - *Middle School:* A seventh-grade math teacher working on percentage problems brings in newspaper advertisements for marked-down products. The class determines the actual reduction in cost, and the teacher then emphasizes the importance of understanding how much people save in promotions.

   - *High School:* An English teacher displays examples of effectively and ineffectively written attempts to make and defend an argument. She uses the examples to emphasize the importance of being able to clearly express oneself in writing.

Goal Theory and Goal Orientation

3. Promote learner responsibility with goal setting and self-monitoring. Emphasize learning goals.

   - *Elementary:* A fifth-grade teacher confers with students as they begin a writing project. He has each write down a schedule for completing the project. He meets with each student periodically to evaluate goals and modify them if necessary.

   - *Middle School:* An eighth-grade history teacher promotes metacognition by saying to her students, "It's very important to think about and be aware of the way you study. If you have your stereo on, ask yourself, 'Am I really learning what I'm studying, or am I distracted by the stereo?'" She emphasizes that learning is the ultimate goal and that being aware of the way they study will increase their understanding.

   - *High School:* An English teacher promotes strategy use with this direction: "Let's read the next section in our books. After we've read it, we're going to stop and make a one-sentence summary of the passage. This is something each of you can do as you read on your own. If you do this, your understanding of what you're reading will dramatically increase."

Attribution Theory

4. Model and encourage students to attribute success to increasing competence and failure to lack of effort or ineffective strategies.
   - *Elementary:* As they initially work on word problems, a second-grade teacher carefully monitors student effort during seat work. When he sees assignments that indicate effort, he makes comments to individual students, such as "Your work is improving all the time" and "Your hard work is paying off, isn't it?"
   - *Middle School:* A sixth-grade English teacher comments, "I wasn't good at grammar for a long time. But I kept trying, and I found that I can do it. I'm good at grammar and writing now. You can get better at it, too, but you have to work at it."
   - *High School:* A chemistry teacher comments, "The way we're attacking balancing equations is working much better, isn't it? You tried to memorize the steps before, and now you're understanding what you're doing. And you're getting better and better at it."

Self-Determination Theory

5. Begin lessons with questions and activities that challenge students' understanding and arouse curiosity.
   - *Elementary:* A fifth-grade teacher drops an ice cube into a cup of clear alcohol (which the students initially think is water), and the ice cube drops to the bottom of the cup. "We know that ice floats on water," she says. "How can we explain what just happened?"
   - *Middle School:* A math teacher has a problem of the week that requires the students to bring in a challenging, everyday problem for the class to solve.
   - *High School:* A biology teacher beginning a unit on body systems says, "Our skull is nearly solid and very hard. But when we're very young, it's quite flexible and there are even gaps or holes in it. Why might this be the case?"

6. To provide evidence about increasing competence, provide clear and prompt feedback on assignments and tests.
   - *Elementary:* A fourth-grade teacher has his students write their answers to word problems on transparencies. The class discusses the different solutions and analyzes how they are similar and different, and the teacher praises solutions that are creative or insightful.
   - *Middle School:* A pre-algebra teacher returns all tests and quizzes the following day and discusses frequently missed problems in detail. She comments that the students skills are continually improving.
   - *High School:* A world history teacher has students identify specific archeological evidence for sites that represent Old Stone Age compared to New Stone Age civilizations. When warranted, he comments that the students' ability to link evidence to conclusions in their reports has improved significantly.

Affective Factors in Motivation

Earlier in the chapter, we presented a vignette in which five students describe their reasons for success or failure on a recent test (p. 367). Three of the students made comments that could be explained by attribution theory, but two of the students did not. Here's what they said:

> "I got a C," Billy shrugged. "Not bad, considering how much I studied. I could have done a lot better, but I couldn't get into it for this test."
>
> "I just went blank," Ashley said with a crestfallen look. "I looked at the test, and all I could think of was, 'I've never seen this stuff before. Where did it come from?'"

The factors behind Billy's and Ashley's comments are the topics of the next two sections.

Self-Worth Theory

Billy made a point of saying that he *did not* study for the test. Self-worth theory helps us explain why he would behave this way.

As we saw in Chapter 3, **self-worth** (or *self-esteem* as it is more commonly called) is *an emotional reaction to or evaluation of the self* (Pintrich & Schunk, 2002).) Research suggests that all people have a basic need to protect their sense of self-worth. This need is represented in a universal search for self-acceptance, which is so great that some consider it to be "the highest human priority" (Covington, 1992). Because our society so strongly values ability and competence, self-worth theorists argue, students will often go to great lengths to protect a sense of their own ability (Covington, 1992; Graham & Weiner, 1996).

Self-worth theory helps us understand Billy's remarks. By emphasizing that he didn't study and saying, "I could have done a lot better," Billy implied that he had the ability to do well. In attributing his low performance to lack of effort, he was attempting to preserve the perception of high ability and, with it, his self-worth.

Research reveals some interesting patterns in student behavior with respect to effort and ability. For instance, some students attempt to hide the fact that they've studied hard for a test, so if they do well, they can, at least in the eyes of their peers, attribute their success to high ability. Other students engage in "self-handicapping" strategies that protect their self-worth (Covington, 1992, 1998; A. Martin, Marsh & Debus, 2001). These include setting unrealistically high goals, so failure can be attributed to task difficulty; procrastinating ("I could have done a lot better, but I didn't start studying until after midnight"); making excuses, such as suggesting that the teacher was poor or the tests were tricky; anxiety ("I understand the stuff, but I get nervous in tests"), or making a point of not trying, as Billy did. In the latter case, students believe that, because they didn't try, a failure doesn't show low ability; in other words, "what they have achieved is 'failure with honor'" (Ames, 1990). These self-handicapping behaviors are most common among low achievers, who often choose to not seek help when it's needed (Middleton & Midgley, 1997).

Perceptions of ability and self-worth change as children develop. For instance, when asked, most kindergarten-aged children claim to be the smartest students in their class. And young children assume that people who try hard are smart, and people who are smart try hard (Stipek, 2002). As students move through school, they develop differential views of ability and effort, have a greater need to be perceived as having high ability, and increasingly view expending effort as an indicator of low ability. Social comparative information, such as grades and all forms of evaluations based on competition, is one of the most significant factors in this process. Children as young as second or third grade begin to judge their ability and competence based on social comparisons (Stipek, 2002).

Although teachers cannot eliminate all social comparisons—most are required to assign grades, for example—they can model effort, emphasize learning instead of performance, and avoid social comparisons as much as possible to help reduce students' emphasis on preserving perceptions of high ability.

10.25
Perceptions of ability exert a stronger influence on self-worth in older than in younger students. Using your understanding of learner development as a basis, explain why this is the case.

Arousal and Anxiety

At one time or another, virtually all of us have been nervous and uncomfortable when anticipating a test or class presentation. Perhaps our heart rates increased, our mouths felt dry, we had "butterflies," or we worried about failing. Ashley undoubtedly had similar sensations when she took her test: "I just went blank. I looked at the test, and all I could think of was, 'I've never seen this stuff before. Where did it come from?'" Like us, Ashley experienced **anxiety,** *a general uneasiness and feeling of tension.* It may also include a sense of foreboding.

The relationship between anxiety, motivation, and achievement is curvilinear; some is good, but too much can be damaging. For example, some anxiety can increase motivation and learning. It makes us work and study hard and develop competence. Relatively high anxiety improves performance on well-practiced tasks where our expertise is high (Covington & Omelich, 1987). Too much anxiety, however, can

Teachers who emphasize learning over performance and use assessment as a tool for learning can reduce the negative effects of test anxiety.

10.26

Using information processing as the basis, explain why relatively high anxiety does not detract from performance on well-practiced tasks.

decrease motivation and achievement. Its main source is fear of failure and, with it, the loss of self-worth (K. Hill & Wigfield, 1984). Low achievers are particularly vulnerable.

Information processing theory helps us understand the debilitating effects of anxiety. First, highly anxious students can have difficulty concentrating, so they don't pay attention as well as they should. Second, because they worry about—and even expect—failure, they often misperceive the information they see and hear. Third, test-anxious students sometimes use superficial learning strategies, such as memorizing definitions of concepts, in their efforts to cope with the topics they study. Instead, they should use productive strategies—such as searching for similarities and differences among topics, summarizing, and self-questioning—which can lead to integrated, meaningful schemas that reduce the load on working memory. Finally, during assessments test-anxious students often waste working memory space on thoughts such as "I'll never get this," leaving less space available for thinking about the task.

Research suggests that the primary problem with highly test-anxious students is that they don't learn the content very well in the first place, which further increases their anxiety when they're required to perform on tests (Wolf, Smith, & Birnbaum, 1997; Zeidner, 1998).

Strategies that promote understanding—such as clear expectations, high-quality examples and student involvement, specific feedback on assessments, modeling effective learning strategies, and providing outside help—can do more than anything else to help students cope with anxiety. When understanding increases, failure decreases. In time, fear of failure and the anxiety it produces will also decrease.

Accommodating Affective Factors in Motivation: Instructional Strategies

Students will always have concerns about self-worth and at times be anxious. However, in addition to using strategies that promote understanding, applying the following principles can help teachers reduce the negative effects of these affective factors:

- Model effort attributions and personal improvement, and de-emphasize competition and ability (Midgley, Arunkumar, & Urdan, 1996).
- Emphasize incremental rather than entity views of intelligence.
- Give students the opportunity to practice exercises similar to those they'll encounter on assessments.
- Assess frequently, announce all assessments, and give students ample time to complete assessment activities.

We saw these principles applied in Kathy's and Elaine's work with their students. For instance, at the beginning of the chapter in response to Harvey, Kathy said, "I have to study every night to keep up with you people, and the harder I study, the smarter I get. And . . . I feel good about myself when I do." Comments like this are intended to link effort to increasing competence and self-worth and model incremental views of ability. Modeling and emphasizing a work ethic, and the impact of effort on success, can help change students' perceptions of the connection between self-worth and ability. Further, emphasizing an incremental view of ability can reduce the risk involved in trying but failing, because failure implies only that more effort or improved strategies are needed to increase competence. As with many aspects of working with students, this type of modeling and emphasis won't work magic, but it can make a significant difference in students' beliefs about ability and self-worth.

Both Kathy and Elaine emphasized deep understanding, which is the most important factor in reducing anxiety. They both gave students opportunities to practice the understanding and skills they expected students to demonstrate on their assessments: Kathy allowed her students to revise their essays, and Elaine gave her students the chance to practice problems similar to those on the test ("We've been practicing on problems like these for a week, and your understanding is getting deeper and deeper"). Elaine's comment, "I'm very proud of how courteous those of you who finished so quickly were to the others who took a little longer," suggests that she also was aware of the importance of providing adequate time in reducing anxiety.

We've now discussed different theories of motivation and related research. In Chapter 11, we synthesize this body of knowledge into a classroom model designed to help teachers increase student motivation at all levels.

Classroom Connections

Accommodating Affective Motivational Factors in Your Classroom.

1. Emphasize that self-worth is an outcome of effort and ability is incremental.

   • *Elementary:* As her students initially work on word problems, a second-grade teacher carefully monitors student effort in seat work. When students' assignments indicate individual effort, she makes comments to those students, such as "You're really understanding what we're doing. Your hard work is paying off, isn't it?"

   • *Middle School:* A life-science teacher comments, "You're really starting to see the connections between these animals' body structures and their ability to adapt to their environments. I'm really feeling good about the progress we're making, and I'll bet you're feeling good about yourselves."

   • *High School:* As students' understanding of balancing equations increases, a chemistry teacher comments,

   "You people are getting smarter all the time. You've really gotten good at this stuff."

2. To reduce anxiety, emphasize focusing attention on the content of tests, provide practice, and give students ample time to finish assessments.

   • *Elementary:* A second-grade teacher monitors his students as they work on an assessment. When he sees their attention wander, he reminds them to concentrate on their work.

   • *Middle School:* An eighth-grade algebra teacher gives her students extensive practice with the types of problems they'll be expected to solve on their tests.

   • *High School:* At the beginning of a unit test, a physics teacher suggests, "Go immediately to the first problem you're sure you know how to solve. Force any thoughts not related to physics out of your heads, and don't let them back in."

Summary

Extrinsic and Intrinsic Motivation

Extrinsic motivation refers to motivation to engage in an activity as a means to an end; intrinsic motivation is motivation to be involved in an activity for its own sake. Learners can be high in both extrinsic and intrinsic motivation, low in both, or high in one and low in the other. The type of motivation learners experience also depends on the context they are in, and their motivations can change over time. Challenge, control, curiosity, fantasy, and aesthetic value all promote intrinsic motivation.

Behavioral Views of Motivation

Behaviorism suggests that motivation results from effective reinforcers. Critics of behavioral approaches to motivation contend that reinforcers detract from intrinsic motivation and cause learners to focus on the reinforcers instead of learning. Reinforcers can be effective, however, if they're based on quality of the work and communicate increasing competence.

Humanistic Views of Motivation

Humanistic views of motivation focus on the learner as a whole person and examine the relationships among physical, emotional, intellectual, and aesthetic needs. A positive classroom climate and caring student-teacher relationship are essential to the development of student motivation.

Maslow's hierarchy, beginning with survival and safety needs, progressing through belonging and esteem needs, and ending with intellectual and aesthetic needs, reflects the "whole person" that is central to humanistic views of motivation.

Carl Rogers also emphasized people's attempts to become self-actualized and suggested that unconditional positive regard is essential in the development of it.

Cognitive Theories of Motivation

Cognitive theories of motivation focus on learners' beliefs, expectations, and needs for order and understanding. Expectancy x value theory suggests that motivation depends on the extent to which people expect to be successful times the value they place on success.

Self-efficacy, or beliefs about the capability of completing specific tasks, influences learners' perseverance and willingness to accept challenges.

Students bring a variety of goals into the classroom, including learning goals, performance goals, and social goals. Goal setting can significantly increase task value. Effective goals are moderately challenging, specific, and near term. Learning-focused goals lead to more sustained motivation and higher achievement than do performance-focused goals. Learners with an incremental view of ability are more likely to set learning-focused goals, whereas learners with an entity view of ability are more likely to set performance-focused goals.

Attribution theory assumes that learners have an innate need to understand their successes and failures. Common explanations, or attributions, include effort, ability, luck, and task difficulty.

Self-determination theory assumes that the need for competence, control, and relatedness are basic in people. Making expectations clear and achievable, using high-quality and personalized examples, involving students, and giving students choices all increase learners' perceptions of control and autonomy.

Affective Factors in Motivation

According to self-worth theory, the ability to achieve is strongly valued in our society, and people's self-worth is strongly linked to their perceptions of their ability. Some learners will procrastinate, blame others, and engage in other self-handicapping behaviors to protect their perceptions of high ability.

Anxiety reduces performance primarily by filling working memory space with thoughts about failure and the negative consequences of that failure. Research indicates that one of the primary problems for test-anxious students is that they don't understand the content very well to start with. With increased understanding, failure decreases, which in turn lessens fear of lowered performance.

We saw throughout the chapter how Kathy Brewster, Amanda Shah, and Elaine Goodman attempted to apply an understanding of theories of motivation in their teaching. They used feedback to communicate increasing competence, promoted self-efficacy, created interest, and tried to develop their students' feelings of competence and control. They also maintained high levels of student involvement in all their lessons.

We turn now to a case study of another teacher presenting a lesson on the Crusades to a different group of students. Read the case study, and then answer the questions that follow. As you read, compare Damon Marcus's approach to Kathy Brewster's.

Damon Marcus watched as his students took their seats, and then announced, "Listen, everyone, I have your tests here from last Friday. Liora, Ivan, Lynn, and Segundo, super job on the test. They were the only A's in the class."

After handing back the tests, Damon moved to the chalkboard and wrote the following:

    A - 4   D - 4
    B - 7   F - 3
    C - 11

"You people down here better get moving," Damon commented, pointing to the D's and F's on the chalkboard. "This wasn't that hard a test. Remember, we have another test in 2 weeks. We need some improvement. C'mon, now. I know you can do better. Let's give the four people with A's a run for their money.

"You can look over your papers, but be sure to turn them in by the end of the class period," Damon continued, as he turned to the day's lesson.

"Now let's get going. We have a lot to cover today. . . . As you'll recall from yesterday, the Crusades were an attempt by the Christian powers of Western Europe to wrest control of the traditional holy lands of Christianity away from the Muslims. Now, when was the First Crusade?" Damon asked, looking over the classroom.

"About 1500, I think," Clifton volunteered.

"No, no," Damon shook his head. "Remember that Columbus sailed in 1492, which was before 1500, so that doesn't make sense. . . . Liora?"

"It was about 1100, I think."

"Excellent, Liora. Now, remember, everyone, you need to know these dates, or otherwise you'll get confused. I know that learning dates and places isn't the most pleasant stuff, but you might as well get used to it because that's what history is about and they'll be on the next test."

While this was going on, Brad whispered to Donna, "Let me look at your test a sec. I got only 1 point on this one, and I don't get it." Donna handed Brad her test, and he carefully read her answer and then read his own again.

"I still don't get it," he whispered and shrugged as he handed back her paper.

"Ask him about it," Donna suggested.

Damon continued, "The First Crusade was in 1095, and it was called the 'People's Crusade.' There were actually seven Crusades in all, starting in 1095 and continuing until enthusiasm for them had ended in 1300."

Damon continued, "The Crusades weren't just religiously motivated. The Muslim world was getting stronger and stronger, and it was posing a threat to Europe. For example, it had control of much of northern Africa, had expanded into southern Spain, and even was moving into other parts of southern Europe. So it was a threat economically and militarily."

Damon continued presenting information about the Crusades, and then, seeing that about 20 minutes were left in the period, he said, "Now, I want you to write a summary of the Crusades that outlines the major people and events and tells why they were important. You should be able to finish by the end of the class period. If you don't, turn your papers in tomorrow at the beginning of the class period. You may use your notes. Go ahead and get started while I come around and collect your tests."

As Damon started to collect the tests, Brad came up to his desk and said, "Mr. Marcus, I don't get this. I only got 1 out of 5 on this one. But Donna got a 4, and the answers say almost the same thing."

"Let me look at Donna's," Damon requested.

Brad went back and got Donna's test. Damon looked at both tests and turned to Brad, "Donna's answer was better organized and clearer than yours."

He continued down the aisles, collecting students' tests. As he went by, he saw that Jeremy had written only a few words on his paper. "Are you having trouble getting started?" Damon asked quietly and sympathetically.

"Yeah, . . . I don't quite know how to get started," Jeremy mumbled.

"I know you have a tough time with written assignments. Let me help you," Damon nodded.

He took a blank piece of paper and started writing as Jeremy watched. He wrote several sentences on the paper and then said, "See how easy that was? That's the kind of thing I want you to do. Go ahead—that's a start. Keep that so you can see what I'm looking for. Go back to your desk, and give it another try."

PRAXIS   These exercises are designed to help you prepare for the PRAXIS™ "Principles of Learning and Teaching" exam. To receive feedback on your constructed response questions and document analysis response, go to the Companion Website at *www.prenhall.com/eggen*, then to this chapter's *Practice for PRAXIS™* module. For additional connections between this text and the PRAXIS™ exam, go to Appendix A.

Constructed Response Questions

In answering these questions, use information from the chapter and link your responses to specific information in the case.

1. Assess Damon's use of praise to communicate increasing competence in his students.

2. With respect to humanistic views of motivation, assess the extent to which Damon helped students meet the deficiency needs and contribute to the growth needs in Maslow's hierarchy.

3. With respect to expectancy x value theory, how effectively did Damon promote intrinsic interest in the topic?

4. Assess Damon's effectiveness in promoting students' feelings of self-efficacy and competence.

5. Assess Damon's effectiveness in accommodating students' needs to preserve feelings of self-worth.

Document-Based Analysis

Damon's students were writing a summary of the Crusades, including people and events and why they were important. As Damon walked by Jeremy, he saw that Jeremy had written only a few words on his paper, and they had the following exchange:

Damon:	(With sympathy) Are you having trouble getting started?
Jeremy:	Yeah, . . . I don't quite know how to get started.
Damon:	I know you have a tough time with written assignments. Let me help you. (Damon took a blank piece of paper and started writing as Jeremy watched.)
Damon:	See how easy that was? That's the kind of thing I want you to do. Go ahead—that's a start. Keep that so you can see what I'm looking for. Go back to your desk, and give it another try.

Assess Damon's interaction with Jeremy based on the content of the chapter.

Companion Website   Also on the Companion Website at *www.prenhall.com/eggen*, you can measure your understanding of chapter content in *Practice Quiz* and *Essay* modules, apply concepts in *Online Cases*, and broaden your knowledge base with the *Additional Content* module and *Web Links* to other educational psychology websites.

Online Portfolio Activities

To develop your professional portfolio, further apply your understanding of chapter content, and address the INTASC standards, go to the Companion Website, then to this chapter's *Online Portfolio Activities*. Complete the suggested activities.

Important Concepts

affective memories *(p. 361)*
anxiety *(p. 379)*
attribution theory *(p. 368)*
attributional statements *(p. 372)*
cognitive theories of motivation *(p. 358)*
competence *(p. 371)*
control *(p. 373)*
cost *(p. 361)*
deficiency needs *(p. 354)*
entity view of intelligence *(p. 364)*
expectancy x value theory *(p. 358)*
extrinsic motivation *(p. 350)*
goal *(p. 363)*
growth needs *(p. 355)*
humanistic psychology *(p. 353)*
importance *(p. 360)*

incremental view of intelligence *(p. 364)*
intrinsic interest *(p. 359)*
intrinsic motivation *(p. 350)*
learned helplessness *(p. 368)*
learning goal *(p. 363)*
motivation *(p. 349)*
motivation to learn *(p. 351)*
performance goal *(p. 363)*
relatedness *(p. 374)*
self-determination *(p. 371)*
self-efficacy *(p. 361)*
self-schemas *(p. 359)*
self-worth *(p. 378)*
unconditional positive regard *(p. 355)*
utility value *(p. 360)*

Chapter Outline

Motivation in the Classroom

11

DeVonne Lampkin, a fifth-grade teacher at Abbott Park Elementary School, wanted her students to understand the essential characteristics of arthropods and to know subcategories of the phylum, such as crustaceans, insects, and arachnids. After briefly reviewing other major animal groups the class had studied, she turned to the day's lesson.

"Today we are going to learn about arthropods, and I want you to figure out their essential characteristics by looking at an example," she began. She reached into a cooler and took out a whole lobster as the students screeched and shouted oohs and aahs.

"Yes, you can touch it," DeVonne said in response to students' queries. She asked Stephanie to carry the lobster around the room so everyone could see it closely.

"You need to observe very carefully," DeVonne encouraged, "because I'll be asking you to tell me what you see in a minute."

After everyone had a chance to touch the lobster, tap its shell, and wiggle its legs, DeVonne walked to the front of the room and asked, "Okay, who can tell me one thing that you noticed?"

"Hard," Tu responded.

"Gross," Saleina added.

"Wet," Kevin put in.

DeVonne listed the students' observations on the board and prompted the students to conclude that the lobster had three body parts and segmented legs. On the list, she highlighted the three essential characteristics of arthropods: hard outer covering (exoskeleton), three-part body, and segmented legs.

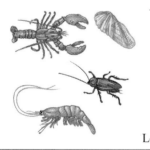

Reaching into her bag again, DeVonne pulled out a cockroach. Amid more squeals, she walked around the class holding it with tweezers.

"Everyone knows what this is, don't you? Now, more importantly, I want to know, . . . can this be an arthropod? . . . Remember our essential characteristics. . . . Look carefully and tell me."

The students decided that it had three body parts and segmented legs but disagreed on whether or not it had an exoskeleton.

"What happens when we step on one?" DeVonne asked.

"It crunches," Anthony answered after thinking for a few seconds.

"So, does it have a hard shell?"

When the class concluded that it did, DeVonne produced a clam from her cooler.

"Is this an arthropod? . . . Look carefully at it and compare it to the characteristics on the board," she instructed.

Some of the students concluded that the clam was an arthropod, because it had a hard shell.

"How many body parts?" DeVonne prompted.

The students realized that it didn't have three, and then A.J. commented, "It doesn't have any legs."

"Good observation," DeVonne smiled.

The class concluded that the clam was not an arthropod.

"Now," DeVonne said sheepishly, "Do you think Mrs. Sapp (the school principal) is an arthropod? . . . Tell us why or why not."

Amid more giggles and laughter, some of the students concluded that she was, whereas others decided that she wasn't. After considerable discussion, Tu observed, "She doesn't have an exoskeleton," and the class nodded in agreement.

DeVonne had the students form pairs or groups of three and then passed out whole shrimp for examination. As she distributed them, she calmed the excited students and asked them to observe the shrimp carefully and decide whether or not they were arthropods.

During the whole-group discussion that followed, DeVonne discovered that some of the students were still uncertain about the idea of an *exoskeleton*, so she directed the students to peel the shrimp and feel the head and hard, outer covering. After seeing the peeled covering, they concluded that the shrimp did, indeed, have an exoskeleton.

Finally, DeVonne introduced the subcategories of arthropods, including insects, arachnids, and crustaceans. She had the students classify addition examples into each subcategory and then closed the lesson.

I n Chapter 10, you studied theories and research that help us understand why certain teacher actions—such as praising students for their increasing competence, creating a positive classroom environment, using concrete and personalized examples, promoting high levels of involvement, and providing detailed feedback about performance on assessments—increase students' motivation to learn. In this chapter, we synthesize these theories and research into a model for promoting student motivation that can be applied in all classrooms and at all grade levels.

After you've completed your study of this chapter, you should be able to

- Describe the difference between a learning-focused environment and a performance-focused environment
- Explain the role of motivation in developing self-regulation
- Explain how teacher personal characteristics promote student motivation
- Describe how classroom climate variables promote student motivation
- Identify instructional factors that promote student motivation

Class Structure: Creating a Learning-Focused Environment

To begin this section, let's review some aspects of DeVonne's lesson.

- She involved everyone by having each student feel the lobster and make observations. She also had the students work in pairs or groups of three to observe the shrimp.
- She personalized the topic by asking the students if Mrs. Sapp, their principal, was an arthropod.
- She promoted a climate of cooperation rather than competition; the students were encouraged to collaborate as they made their observations.
- She praised the students' increasing competence as they made their conclusions about the different examples.

In Chapter 10, we discussed the differences between learning goals, which emphasize increased understanding and mastery of tasks, and performance goals, which focus on demonstrating high ability—particularly ability compared to that of others. Whether a student adopts one type of goal or the other depends on many factors, but one important influence is the classroom environment. **Learning-focused environments** *emphasize learning goals* (Ames & Archer, 1988; Patrick et al., 1999; Stipek, 1996), whereas **performance-focused environments** *concentrate on performance goals*.

DeVonne attempted to create a learning-focused environment in her classroom. If, instead, she had compared the students' observations to one another, or made comments such as "C'mon, we can make better observations than that," she would have promoted a performance-oriented environment. The differences in the two types of environments are summarized in Table 11.1 (Ames & Archer, 1988; Maehr, 1992).

Within this learning-oriented framework, we present a model for promoting student motivation that synthesizes the theory and research you studied in Chapter 10 (Eggen & Kauchak, 2002). It is outlined in Figure 11.1 and has four components:

1. Self-regulated learners: Developing student responsibility
2. Teacher characteristics: Personal qualities that increase student motivation
3. Climate variables: Creating a motivating environment
4. Instructional variables: Developing interest in learning activities

The variables in the model are interdependent; a single variable cannot be effectively applied if the others are lacking. Keep this in mind as you study the following sections.

11.1
A teacher says, "Excellent job on the last test, everyone. More than half the class got an A or a B." On the basis of the information in this section, how appropriate is this comment? Explain.

Table 11.1 Comparisons of learning-focused and performance-focused classrooms

	Learning-Focused	Performance-Focused
Success defined as . . .	Mastery, improvement	High grades, doing better than others
Value placed on . . .	Effort, improvement	High grades, demonstration of high ability
Reasons for satisfaction . . .	Meeting challenges, hard work	Doing better than others, success with minimum effort
Teacher oriented toward . . .	Student learning	Student performance
View of errors . . .	A normal part of learning	A basis for concern and anxiety
Reasons for effort . . .	Increased understanding	High grades, doing better than others
Ability viewed as . . .	Incremental, alterable	An entity, fixed
Reasons for assessment . . .	Measure progress toward preset criteria, provide feedback	Determine grades, compare students to one another

Figure 11.1 A model for promoting student motivation

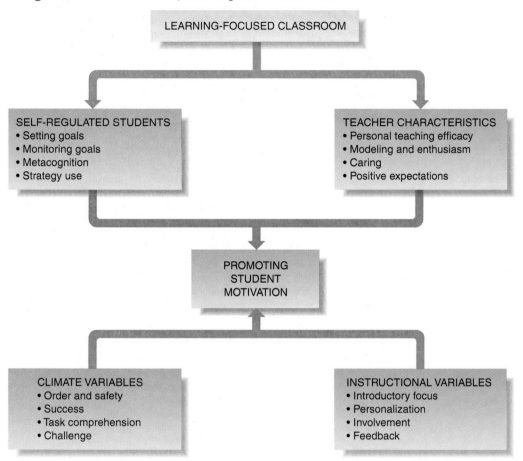

Self-Regulated Learners: Developing Student Responsibility

Lack of student effort and responsibility is a common lament in many teachers' conversations. All teachers want students to be responsible, and most emphasize this goal to students, but many are less successful than they would like to be:

> "My kids are so irresponsible," Kathy Hughes, a seventh-grade teacher grumbled in a conversation at lunch. "They don't bring their books, they forget their notebooks in their lockers, they come without pencils. . . . I can't get them to come to class prepared, let alone get them to read their assignments."
>
> "I know," said Mercedes Blount, one of Kathy's colleagues, smiling wryly. "Some of them are totally spacey, and others just don't seem to give a rip."

What can be done to help students learn to become more responsible or, ideally, *self-regulated*? **Self-regulation,** *the process of accepting responsibility and control for one's own learning,* begins with goals. As we saw in Chapter 10, setting and monitoring goals, metacognition, and use of strategies are all necessary if goals are to be used effectively. We also saw that students must be committed to goals in order for them to work. Although students are more likely to commit to goals they set themselves (Ridley, McCombs, & Taylor, 1994), many aren't inclined to set goals, and even if they are, they don't know what goals to set and how to set them. In the following two sections, we look at ways for teachers to help students along the road to self-regulation.

11.2
Identify the three characteristics of effective goals presented in Chapter 10. Explain the difference between *goal content* and *goal orientation.*

Developing Self-Regulation: Applying Self-Determination Theory

Student self-regulation is a developmental process that, with teacher support, gradually increases. It begins with accepting personal responsibility (Deci & Ryan, 1991; Ryan, Connell, & Deci, 1985), sometimes described in terms of setting *social responsibility goals* (Stipek, 2002; Wentzel, 1993). Setting appropriate goals is easy enough, but getting students to commit to and monitor them is often another story.

Here we can find some suggestions in self-determination theory. Although focusing on intrinsic motivation, the theory acknowledges that initially not all behaviors are intrinsically motivated (Ryan & Deci, 2000; Pintrich & Schunk, 2002). Learners pass through stages of extrinsic motivation as their self-determination increases. At the first stage, called *external regulation* (Deci & Ryan, 1985; Ryan & Deci, 2000), students attempt to meet goals to receive rewards and avoid punishers. As their self-regulation develops, students gradually learn to meet their responsibility and learning goals because, for example, they believe that meeting the goal is important for helping them get better grades. Although this behavior is still extrinsically motivated, it represents increasing self-regulation. As students develop further, they attempt to meet the goals because doing so is consistent with their self-schemas. For instance, if a student monitors goal achievement because she begins to view herself as a responsible person, she has made further progress toward self-determination.

Eventually (and ideally) learners set and monitor goals for their own sake—behavior that is intrinsically motivated and, by definition, self-determined (Pintrich & Schunk, 2002). In the real world, many students never get to this point; however, for those that do, the probability of long-term achievement and success are greatly enhanced. As a teacher, you are invaluable in helping self-determination develop.

11.3

Concepts such as *self-schemas* and *importance* are part of what theory of motivation that was discussed in Chapter 10?

Helping Students Develop Self-Regulation: Instructional Strategies

Because self-regulation is developmental, teachers need to initially scaffold students' efforts and then gradually turn more and more responsibility over to them. The following principles can help guide this process:

- Emphasize the relationship between accepting responsibility and learning.
- Solicit student input in the process of establishing class procedures that include student responsibility.
- Help students understand responsibility by treating it as a concept and link consequences to actions.
- Model responsibility, a learning focus, and metacognition, and guide students as they initially set goals.
- Provide concrete mechanisms to help students monitor and assess goal achievement.

Let's see how the principles guide Sam Cook, a seventh-grade geography teacher, as he works with his students.

Sam began the first day of school by saying, "Welcome to Carver Middle School everyone. I'm looking forward to a very good year this year, and I'm sure you are too."

Teachers can help students develop self-regulation by involving them in setting classroom rules and by emphasizing individual responsibility.

Sam had the students introduce themselves, and then he asked, "Now, why are we here—here in this class and here in school?"

The students sat silently for a few seconds, not quite sure where Sam was headed.

Finally, Dana responded hesitantly, "To learn . . . about . . . geography."

"Exactly!" Sam responded. "That's why we go to school—to learn. It's what school is all about. The more we learn, the smarter we get, and the smarter we get, the better off we are. . . . So, in order to create a classroom that helps us learn as much as possible, we need to work together. I need to try to help you, and you need to help yourselves. For instance, I need to think carefully about what we're trying to accomplish, and I need to bring the examples that I'll use to help you understand our topics. . . . That's my part.

"So, what is your part? . . . What do you need to be thinking about and what do you need to bring to class every day to be sure you learn as much as possible?"

"Pencil," Alyssa offered.

"Sure," Sam responded. "What else?"

"Our book," Darrell added.

"Absolutely," Sam nodded.

With Sam's guidance, the students agreed that they needed to be in their seats when the bell rang and they needed to bring their books, binders with paper, and pencils or pens to class each day. They also agreed that they needed to both do their homework conscientiously and understand it, not simply get it done.

"Now, who is responsible for all this?" Sam asked.

"We are," several students responded simultaneously.

"Yes," Sam responded emphatically, "I am responsible for my part, and you are responsible for your parts.

"Now, let's think about this," Sam continued. "What kinds of things happen when we aren't responsible?"

The students made a few comments, and Sam said, "Let's take a look at a couple examples."

He displayed the following on the overhead:

Josh is very careful to bring all his materials to school. He has a checklist that he uses to mark off each of his items and to be sure that he's done and understands his homework in each class. If he's uncertain about any part of his homework, he always asks the next day.

Josh is doing very well in school. He likes his classes and says they're really interesting and that he's learning a lot. His teachers respect how conscientious he is.

Andy is often in trouble with his teachers because he frequently forgets to bring his book, notebook, or pencil to class. He sometimes forgets his homework in his locker, so he doesn't get credit for the assignment. Andy's homeroom teacher called his mom to discuss his irresponsibility, and now Andy can't watch TV for a week.

Andy is struggling in some of his classes. He says he's bored and doesn't feel like he's learning very much.

"What are some differences you notice between Josh and Andy?" Sam asked after giving the students a minute to read the vignettes.

"Josh brings his stuff and Andy doesn't," Shawnta offered.

"Andy gets in trouble with his teachers," Wesley added.

"Josh is learning a lot more than Andy is," Mayle put in.

"It's his own fault," Ronise said.

"Those are all good comments, and yours is particularly important," Sam responded, nodding to Ronise. "If we don't take responsibility for ourselves, and we don't study, whose fault is it if we don't learn?"

"Our own," several of the students responded.

"Yes," Sam emphasized. "We're all responsible for ourselves."

Sam suggested that perhaps the students should set some goals that would help them take responsibility for their own learning. With his guidance they made suggestions, and he wrote them on the board.

The next day, Sam distributed a monitoring sheet (see Figure 11.2) he had prepared after the discussion. The students suggested that they put the sheet in the front of their notebooks and check off the items the first thing each morning. As the sheets accumulated, the students would have a "responsibility portfolio" that gave them a long-term record of their progress.

Figure 11.2 Monitoring sheet

Week of _____		Name_____			
Responsibility Goals	**Monday**	**Tuesday**	**Wednesday**	**Thursday**	**Friday**
Bring sharpened pencil	✓	✓			
Bring notebook					
Bring textbook					
In seat when bell rings					
Learning Goals	**Monday**	**Tuesday**	**Wednesday**	**Thursday**	**Friday**
Finish homework					
Understand homework					

Sam asked the students how they would determine whether or not they understood their homework. After some discussion, they agreed that they would either explain it to another person or explain their answers in class.

Finally, they agreed that all students who got 15 checks for the responsibility goals and 8 or more checks for the learning goals for the week would have free time for the last half of the period on Fridays, during which they could bring snacks and play games. Those that failed to achieve 18 checks on the responsibility goals would spend "quiet time" alone during that period, and those that received fewer than 8 checks for the learning goals would spend time with Sam working on areas that needed improvement.

Let's take a closer look at Sam's efforts to help his students develop self-regulation. First, Sam began the year by emphasizing that they were all there to learn and that their classroom environment and procedures were designed to help them learn as much as possible. He also emphasized the relationship between accepting responsibility and learning. In this way, he began the process of establishing a learning-focused environment.

Second, Sam solicited students' input into the procedures. Being asked for input contributes to students' feeling of control, a basic human need according to self-determination theory (Ryan & Deci, 2000). It also increases the likelihood that students will commit to the goals they create.

11.4

Using information from this section, describe what would be a "controlling" strategy for promoting self-regulation.

Third, Sam treated *responsibility* as a concept and illustrated it with an example and a nonexample. Students sometimes fail to take responsibility because they don't fully understand the relationship between their behaviors and the consequences of those behaviors. By using examples to illustrate the consequences of behaving responsibly versus irresponsibly, Sam used an *informational* rather than a *controlling* strategy for promoting self-regulation, which contributes to intrinsic motivation (Koestner, Ryan, Bernieri, & Holt, 1984).

Fourth, Sam modeled responsibility, goal setting, and goal monitoring, and the goals Sam's students developed were consistent with goal theory. They were specific, near term—they were monitored a week at a time—and, for Sam's students, moderately challenging.

Finally, Sam prepared a concrete structure (the sheet) to help students monitor their goals, which, in itself, can contribute to intrinsic motivation. As Sam's students accumulate checks on their monitoring sheets, they are likely to feel a sense of self-efficacy, even though the process is as basic as bringing required materials to class. Gradually, they should not only accept responsibility for following these procedures but also learn to make decisions that will increase their own learning.

We see that Sam's students were initially at the level of *external regulation* as described by self-determination theory; they wanted to meet goals to receive rewards and avoid punishers. Students who met the goals would be rewarded with free time, students who didn't meet the learning goals would receive support from the teacher, and students who didn't meet the responsibility goals would spend "quiet time" during the free period. As self-regulation develops, the students should begin setting their own goals because they see that setting and monitoring goals increase learning.

The preceding example focuses on middle school students, but self-regulation can also be a goal for young children. To account for developmental level, however, the process should be adapted. The case study on page 434 of Chapter 12 describes how Martha Oakes teaches her first graders to put away their worksheets. Martha incorporates some of the principles we saw Sam use. For instance, she teaches the procedure as a concept, she models the procedure, and she expects the students to accept responsibility for following it. And Martha asserts that her first graders are capable of making productive contributions in classroom meetings. These are all part of the development of self-regulation.

Classroom Connections

Promoting Self-Regulation in Your Classroom
Promote learner responsibility with goal setting, self-monitoring, and metacognition.

- *Elementary:* A fourth-grade teacher presents a "problem of the week" each Monday in math. The students set the goal of preparing a solution to the problem, which they place in their math portfolios. When they've completed the solution, they place a check on the first page of their portfolio. When they've explained the solution to a parent, sibling, or other adult, they place a second check on the sheet. The class discusses solutions on Fridays.

- *Middle School:* A seventh-grade geography teacher provides a study guide for her students. The students set the goal of answering and understanding all the study guide questions each week. They check off each question when they've answered it and believe they understand it.

- *High School:* Physics students set the goal of creating one real-world application of each of the topics they study. When they believe they have a particularly good application, they offer it to the class for analysis and discussion.

Teacher Characteristics: Personal Qualities That Increase Student Motivation and Learning

That teachers make a difference in student learning is a theme of this text, and it is true for motivation as well. Teachers create learning environments, implement instruction, and establish learning-oriented or performance-oriented classrooms. None of the other components of our motivation model are effective if the teacher characteristics—*personal teaching efficacy, modeling and enthusiasm, caring,* and *positive expectations*—are lacking. These characteristics are highlighted in Figure 11.3.

Personal Teaching Efficacy: Beliefs About Teaching and Learning

In Chapter 10, we saw that self-efficacy is an individual's beliefs about his or her capability to succeed at specific tasks. **Personal teaching efficacy,** *a teacher's belief that he or she is capable of getting all students to learn and succeed regardless of their background knowledge or ability* (Bruning et al., 1999), is an extension of this concept. Teachers who are high in personal teaching efficacy take responsibility for the success or failure of their own instruction (V. Lee, 2000).

Figure 11.3 Teacher characteristics in the model for promoting student motivation

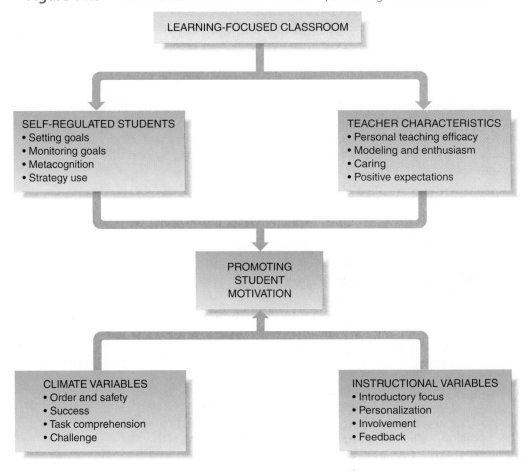

When students aren't learning as much as they can, high efficacy teachers don't blame it on lack of intelligence, poor home environments, uncooperative administrators, or some other external cause. Instead, they redouble their efforts, convinced they can increase student learning. They work students hard and maintain high expectations for them (we discuss expectations later in this section). They create classroom climates in which students feel safe and free to express their thinking without fear of embarrassment or ridicule. They praise students for their increasing competence, avoid the use of rewards to control behavior, persevere with low achievers, and maximize the time available for instruction. Low-efficacy teachers, in contrast, lower their expectations, focus less on students, spend less time on learning activities, "give up" on low achievers, and are more critical when students fail (Kagan, 1992). High-efficacy teachers adopt new curriculum materials and change strategies more readily than do low-efficacy teachers (Poole, Okeafor, & Sloan, 1989). High-efficacy teachers also value and promote student control and autonomy more than low-efficacy teachers (Woolfolk & Hoy, 1990).

Low personal teaching efficacy contributes to negative emotions, stress, and teacher burnout. Not surprisingly, students taught by high-efficacy teachers learn more and are more motivated than those taught by low-efficacy teachers (Tschannen-Moran, Woolfolk-Hoy, & Hoy, 1998).

Many individual students can learn from a high-efficacy teacher, but the entire student body can benefit from a **high-collective-efficacy school,** *a school in which most of the teachers are high in personal teaching efficacy.* Such schools are particularly notable for the effect they have on the achievement levels of students from diverse socioeconomic backgrounds. As you may recall from Chapter 4, the correlation between low socioeconomic status and low achievement test scores and grades has been documented in numerous research studies (Macionis, 2000; McLoyd, 1998). In high-collective-efficacy schools, however, low-SES students have achievement gains nearly as high as those of high-SES students from low-collective-efficacy schools (Lee, 2000). Also, differences in achievement gains among low, middle, and high-SES students in high-collective-efficacy schools are smaller than they are in low-collective-efficacy schools (Lee, 2000). In other words, such schools help reduce achievement differences between groups who typically benefit quite differently from schooling.

What can you do to promote collective efficacy? You can certainly remain positive when colleagues are cynical or pessimistic, and you can remind your fellow teachers of the research that consistently confirms how important teachers are in promoting learning and motivation for all students.

Modeling and Enthusiasm: Communicating Genuine Interest

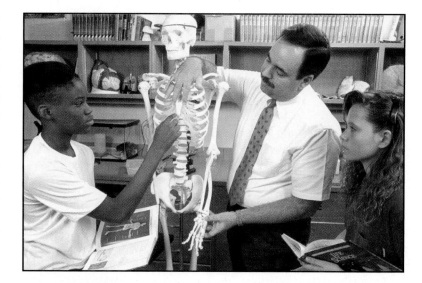

Enthusiastic teachers increase motivation by sharing their interest in the subjects they teach.

Teachers communicate their beliefs about teaching and learning through the behaviors they model. Motivating students is virtually impossible if teachers model distaste or lack of interest in the topics they teach. Statements such as the following are devastating to motivation:

> "I know this stuff is boring, but we have to learn it."
> "I know you hate proofs."
> "This isn't my favorite topic, either."

In contrast, even routine and potentially uninteresting topics are more motivating if teachers model interest in them. For instance, a teacher communicates interest in the influence of geography on our lives with this statement: "New York, Chicago, San Francisco, and Seattle didn't become prominent and important cities for no reason. Their success is related to their geography." Likewise, a teacher models interest in grammar by showing a well-written and an error-filled paragraph and commenting, "Look how much better an impression this one makes on the reader."

Statements such as these capture the essence of enthusiasm because they communicate the teachers' genuine interest in their topics. Unlike pep talks, theatrics, or efforts to entertain students, genuine interest and enthusiasm can induce in students the feeling that the information is valuable and worth learning (Good & Brophy, 2000). In fact, students with enthusiastic teachers have greater autonomy, self-efficacy, and achievement than those with less enthusiastic teachers (R. Perry, 1985; R. Perry, Magnusson, Parsonson, & Dickens, 1986).

Teachers can influence student motivation by modeling other positive learner characteristics as well. A teacher who says, "The harder I study the better I understand what I read—and I keep on getting smarter," is modeling effort attributions and incremental views of intelligence. In doing so, he or she is increasing the likelihood that students will imitate these beliefs in their own thinking. And, other than direct experience, modeling is the most powerful factor affecting learners' self-efficacy (Bruning et al., 1999).

Caring: Meeting the Need for Relatedness

- A first-grade teacher has a student who calls her "Mom."
- A fifth-grade teacher walks out on the playground during recess to chat with his students.
- A high school teacher makes a special effort to make a new student feel welcome.

11.5
Look again at Damon Marcus's lesson in the Chapter 10 closing case. Would you describe Damon as a high-efficacy or a low-efficacy teacher? Explain carefully.

11.6
Which theory of learning—behaviorism, social cognitive theory, information processing, or constructivism—best explains the positive effects of enthusiasm? Explain on the basis of that theory.

Teachers demonstrate caring by their willingness to spend time interacting with their students.

These teachers foster relatedness—a basic human need according to self-determination theory (see Chapter 10). A growing body of research confirms the importance of students feeling connected to the classrooms in which they learn (Freese, 1999; Stipek, 2002). Not only that, but students can be motivated to learn by "safe, trusting, and supportive environments characterized by . . . quality relationships with caring adults that see their unique potential" (McCombs, 1998, p. 399). The teacher caring emphasized in humanistic views of motivation reminds us that we don't teach math, science, or language arts—we teach people. We should focus on the learner as a whole person, including emotional and social needs as well as intellectual ones.

Caring refers to a teacher's *ability to empathize with and invest in the protection and development of young people* (Chaskin & Rauner, 1995). The importance of caring is captured in this comment by a fourth grader: "If a teacher doesn't care about you, it affects your mind. You feel like you're a nobody, and it makes you want to drop out of school" (Noblit, Rogers, & Mc-Cadden, 1995, p. 683).

11.7
Which need in Maslow's hierarchy is most nearly met by teacher caring? Explain.

Wentzel (1997) offers an additional student perspective. She asked middle school students, "How do you know when a teacher does and does not care about you?" The students reported that attentiveness to them as human beings was important, but perhaps more striking was their belief that teachers who care make serious efforts to promote learning and hold students to appropriately high standards. This finding suggests that caring is more than warm, fuzzy interactions with students. In addition to understanding how students feel, caring teachers are committed to their students' growth and competence (Noddings, 1995, 1999; Wentzel, 1997).

A final perspective is offered in a study by E. Skinner and Belmont (1993). When the researchers assessed teacher perceptions of their personal involvement with students, they found that teachers who said they liked and enjoyed their students and who knew about their personal lives had students who felt higher levels of control and autonomy than those whose teachers were less involved with them. Also, students' feelings of control predicted their engagement in classroom activities; those who felt the most control and autonomy were the most engaged.

DeVonne's positive feelings about her students increased their sense of control and autonomy, which also increased their engagement.

Communicating Caring

How do teachers communicate caring to students? Although the ways are individual, research has identified several characteristics, outlined in Table 11.2 (Freese, 1999; Noddings, 1999; Wentzel, 1997). Two common threads appear in the descriptions of the characteristics: giving time and showing respect.

We all have just 24 hours in our days, and choosing to allocate some of that time to an individual student communicates caring better than any other single factor. Helping students who have problems with an assignment or calling a parent after school hours communicates that teachers care about student learning. Spending personal time to ask a question about a baby brother or compliment a new hairstyle communicates caring about a student as a human being.

Showing respect is also essential to communicate caring and promote student motivation. Teachers can show respect in subtle ways, such as the way they look at students

Table 11.2 Characteristics of caring teachers

Category	Description
Showing respect	Teachers are polite, treat students with respect, listen to their comments and questions, are patient when students make mistakes, and respond to legitimate needs for second chances and help.
Valuing individuality	Teachers know students as human beings, noticing and commenting on changes in dress, habits, and behavior.
Giving personal attention	Teachers listen to students and help them with schoolwork and extracurricular activities as well as personal relationships and other nonacademic problems.
Creating safe learning environments	Teachers have fair rules but do not apply them rigidly, and they encourage students to do their best and to freely express their thoughts and ideas without fear of embarrassment or ridicule.

and how long they wait for students to answer questions, but maintaining standards is one of the most important:

> One of the best ways to show respect for students is to hold them to high standards—by not accepting sloppy, thoughtless, or incomplete work, by pressing them to clarify vague comments, by encouraging them not to give up, and by not praising work that does not reflect genuine effort. Ironically, reactions that are often intended to protect students' self-esteem—such as accepting low quality work—convey a lack of interest, patience, or caring. (Stipek, 2002, p. 157)

Respect is a two-way street, however. Teachers should model respect for students, and in turn they have the right to expect students to respect them and one another. "Treat everyone with respect" is a rule that should be enforced. Occasional rudeness can be overlooked, but teachers should clearly communicate that chronic disrespect will not be tolerated.

Teacher Expectations: Increasing Perceptions of Competence

Positive expectations is the last of the four teacher characteristics in our model for promoting student motivation (Figure 11.3).

> Teacher expectations about students' learning can have profound implications for what students actually learn. Expectations affect the content and pace of the curriculum, the organization of instruction, evaluation, instructional interactions with individual students, and many subtle and not-so-subtle behaviors that affect students' own expectations for learning and thus their behavior. (Stipek, 2002, p. 210).

To promote learning and increase student motivation, teachers must strive to make all students feel competent, an innate need according to self-determination theory. Unfortunately, teachers' expectations for students can lead them—often innocently—to say and do things that instead communicate a feeling of incompetence.

Teachers communicate high learner expectations through interactive teaching strategies that actively involve all students.

Sometimes teachers communicate competence or incompetence to the entire class through their demeanor or their general approach to classroom management. For example, compare the following two comments:

"This is a new idea we've been working on, and it will be challenging, but if you work hard I know you can all get it. I want you to start right in while the ideas are still fresh in your mind. I'll be coming around, so if you have any questions just raise your hand."

"This material is hard, but we've got to learn it. I want everyone to start right away, and no fooling around. Jesse, did you hear me? Some of you will probably have trouble with this, and I'll be around as soon as I can to straighten things out. No messing around until I get there."

The first teacher acknowledged that the assignment was difficult, but she expected students to successfully complete it. She communicated confidence in their competence. The second, by saying, "Some of you will probably have trouble with this," implied that the students were not competent and that she didn't expect them to be able to complete the assignment.

More often, however, teachers have expectations that influence their behavior in ways that directly affect individual students and detract from both achievement and motivation. Specifically, they treat students they perceive to be high achievers differently than those they perceive as low achievers (R. Weinstein, 1998). This differential treatment takes four different forms (Good, 1987a, 1987b; Good & Brophy, 2000):

- *Emotional support:* Teachers have more interactions with perceived high achievers; their interactions are more positive and include a greater number of smiles; they make more eye contact, stand closer, orient their bodies more directly toward the students; and they seat students closer to the teacher.
- *Teacher effort and demands:* Teachers give perceived high achievers clearer and more thorough explanations, their instruction is more enthusiastic, they ask more follow-up questions, and they require more complete and accurate student answers.
- *Questioning:* Teachers call on perceived high achievers more often, they allow the students more time to answer and provide more encouragement, and they prompt perceived high achievers more often.
- *Feedback and evaluation:* Teachers praise perceived high achievers more and criticize them less. They offer perceived high achievers more complete and lengthier feedback and more conceptual evaluations.

Differential treatment in turn influences learners' own beliefs and expectations for success. In fact, teachers' expectations for a student—whether high or low—can serve as a **self-fulfilling prophecy,** *a phenomenon in which a person tends to perform in certain ways that result from and confirm beliefs about the person's abilities.* We can explain the phenomenon with expectancy × value theory and self-efficacy theory. As we saw in Chapter 10, expectations for success depend on learners' perceptions of the difficulty of the task and their beliefs about whether or not they will do well on an upcoming test or other future assignment. Communicating positive expectations suggests to students that they will be successful on this test or assignment. Then, when they are successful, their self-efficacy increases, and a positive relationship between motivation and achievement is created. The reverse also occurs. Communicating low expectations can "lead children to confirm predictions about their abilities by exerting less effort and ultimately performing more poorly" (R. Weinstein, 1998, p. 83).

Children of all ages are aware of the different expectations teachers hold for students (Stipek, 2002). In one study, researchers concluded: "After ten seconds of seeing and/or hearing a teacher, even very young students could detect whether the teacher talked about or to an excellent or a weak student and could determine the extent to which that student was loved by the teacher" (Babad, Bernieri, & Rosenthal, 1991, p. 230).

Teacher expectations for learning strongly influence the amount that students actually do learn. Students in schools in which *all* students are expected to learn achieve more than those in schools that have varying expectations (Baker, Terry, Bridger, & Winsor, 1997; Lambert & McCombs, 1998; Wharton-McDonald, Pressley, & Hampston, 1998).

One of our goals in writing this section was to increase teachers' awareness. Expectations are subtle and sometimes unconscious. Teachers may not realize that they hold different expectations for their students. With awareness and effort, teachers will do their best to maintain appropriately high expectations for all students. Their efforts need not be Herculean. When teacher Elaine Lawless began calling on her students as equally as possible, she saw immediate benefits: "Joseph made my day. He said to one of the other kids, 'Put your hand down. Mrs. Lawless calls on all of us. She thinks we're all smart'" (Elaine Lawless, personal communication, February 19, 2002).

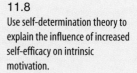

11.8
Use self-determination theory to explain the influence of increased self-efficacy on intrinsic motivation.

Demonstrating Personal Qualities That Increase Motivation: Instructional Strategies

Teachers can demonstrate the personal qualities that promote student motivation in a number of ways. The following principles can guide them in their efforts:

- Strive to believe in yourself and your capability to get all students to learn.
- Model responsibility, effort, and interest in the topics you're teaching.
- Demonstrate commitment to your students' learning by spending personal time with them.
- Maintain appropriately high expectations for all students.

Let's see how the principles guide DeVonne Lampkin as she continues to work with her fifth graders.

"Wow, you're here early," Karla Utley, another teacher in the school, said to DeVonne at 7:45 one morning. "You don't have to be here until 8:30."

"I've got some kids coming in," DeVonne returned. "I did a writing lesson yesterday, and we evaluated some of their paragraphs as a whole class. Several of the kids, like Tu and Saleina, did really well . . . but some of the others are a ways behind. And I saw the same thing when I looked at the rest of the papers after school. Some of the kids don't quite get it. So Justin, Picey, and Roseanne are coming in before school this morning, and we're going to practice some more. They aren't my highest achievers, but I know I can get more out of them than I am right now. They're good kids; they're just a little behind. . . . Particularly Roseanne. She's only been in the States for a year, and she didn't speak a word of English when she came. She's made tons of progress, but it's tough."

At 8:00 DeVonne was waiting as Justin, Picey, and Roseanne came in the door. She smiled at them and said, "We're going to practice a little more on our writing. I know that you can all be good writers. It's the same thing for me. I have practiced and practiced and practiced, and now I'm good at it. You can do the same thing. . . . Let's look at your paragraphs again."

She displayed Justin's paragraph on the overhead again (his was one of the papers evaluated in class the day before) and asked, "What did we suggest that you might do to improve this?"

"He needs to stay on either the boy or the house," Roseanne offered.

"Yes," DeVonne nodded.

Together, the group looked at each of the students' original paragraphs and made specific suggestions for improvement.

DeVonne demonstrated caring by spending out-of-class time with her students.

DeVonne then said, "Okay, now each of you rewrite your paragraphs based on our suggestions. When we're finished, we'll look at them again."

The three students rewrote their paragraphs, and the four of them again discussed what they had done.

"Much improvement," DeVonne said encouragingly once they had finished. "If we keep at it, we're going to get there. . . . I'll see you again tomorrow at eight."

Let's take a closer look at DeVonne's efforts to demonstrate personal qualities that increase student motivation. First, her comments to Karla, "I know I can get more out of them than I am right now," and "They're good kids," indicate that she believes in herself and her capability to get all of her students to learn; that is, she has high personal teaching efficacy. Her comments also provide insight into her expectations. She expects *all* students to learn, not just high achievers like Tu, Saleina, and some of the others.

In the process of working with the small group, DeVonne also modeled responsibility and effort: "I have practiced and practiced and practiced, and now I'm good at it. You can do the same thing. . . . Let's look at your paragraphs again."

Perhaps most significantly, DeVonne demonstrated a high level of caring by arriving in school 45 minutes early to devote her time to helping students who needed extra support. She kept the study session upbeat and encouraging and displayed the respect for the students that is so essential for promoting motivation.

We said at the beginning of the chapter that the elements of our motivation model (Figure 11.3) are interdependent, and we see this interdependence in DeVonne's work with her students. For example, they tried to meet her expectations because they believed she cared about them and their learning, and she modeled her own interest in what they were doing. If students don't believe teachers are committed to their learning, having high expectations can actually be counterproductive because students may perceive them as threatening or unfair. Similarly, it is virtually impossible to hold students to high standards if teachers don't model interest in the topics they're teaching. One characteristic, or even two, aren't enough. Teachers must display all the personal characteristics to impact students' motivation to learn.

Classroom Connections

Demonstrating the Personal Characteristics in the Model for Promoting Student Motivation in Your Classroom

1. Show students you care by showing respect and giving them your personal time.
   - *Elementary:* A first-grade teacher greets each of her students every day as they come into the classroom. She makes it a point to talk to each of the students about something personal several times a week.
   - *Middle School:* A geography teacher calls parents as soon as he sees a student having even minor academic or personal problems. He solicits their help in monitoring the students and offers his assistance in solving problems.
   - *High School:* An Algebra II teacher conducts help sessions after school three nights a week. Students are invited to attend to get help with homework or discuss any other personal concerns about the class or school.

2. Model interest in the topics you're teaching.
   - *Elementary:* During quiet reading time, a fourth-grade teacher comments on a book she's interested in and reads while the students are reading.
   - *Middle School:* A life science teacher brings in clippings from the local newspaper that relate to science and asks students to do the same. He discusses them at the beginning of class and pins them on a bulletin board for students to read.
   - *High School:* A world history teacher frequently describes connections between classroom topics and their impact on today's world.

3. Maintain appropriately high expectations for all students.
   - *Elementary:* A second-grade teacher makes a conscious attempt to call on all her students as equally as possible and to expect as much as she can from each.
   - *Middle School:* When his students complain about word problems, a seventh-grade pre-algebra teacher

reminds them of how important word problems are and tells them that the only way to become good at solving the problems is to continue to practice. Each day in class, he guides a detailed discussion of at least two complex word problems.

- *High School:* When her American history students turn in sloppily written essays, the teacher displays a well-written model on the overhead and then requires a second, higher quality product. She continues this process throughout the year.

Climate Variables: Creating a Motivating Environment

As students spend time in classrooms, they get feelings about whether or not the classroom is a desirable place to learn. *The feelings evoked by the classroom environment* create the **classroom climate.** *In a healthy climate, teacher and classroom characteristics promote students' feelings of safety and security, together with a sense of success, challenge, and understanding* (see Figure 11.4). In other words, students are treated as competent people. They understand the requirements of learning tasks, perceive them as challenging, and believe they will succeed if they make reasonable effort (Brophy, 1987b; Clifford, 1990). Let's look at these climate variables.

Order and Safety: Classrooms as Secure Places to Learn

To illustrate a healthy classroom climate, let's look back at DeVonne's classroom. Her students obviously felt completely safe: They willingly participated in her learning activities, and they seemed unconcerned about how their questions and answers would be received. Such feelings are an ideal to strive for in all classrooms.

Figure 11.4 Climate variables in the model for promoting student motivation

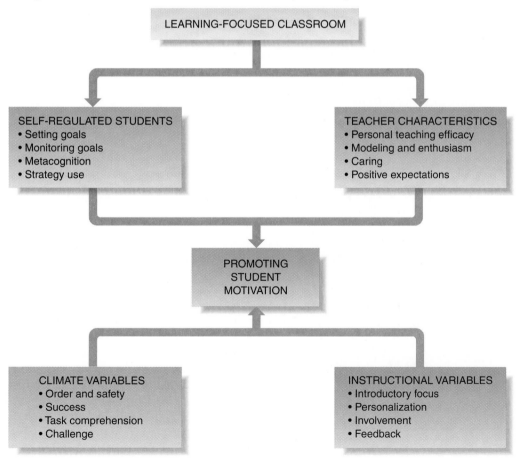

To see the Learner-Centered Psychological Principles, go to the Companion Website at *www.prenhall.com/eggen*, then to this chapter's *Additional Content* module.

11.9
Use behaviorism to explain why students criticized for offering personal or creative thoughts would be unlikely to repeat the behavior. Using social cognitive theory, explain how criticizing a student would impact the rest of the class.

The need for safety can be explained with both humanistic and cognitive theories of motivation. For instance, safety is a basic deficiency need (preceded only by survival) in Maslow's hierarchy. Researchers who corroborate Maslow's theory describe effective schools as safe places where trust, order, cooperation, and high morale predominate (Rutter, Maughn, Mortimore, Ouston, & Smith, 1979). Also, the research-based *Learner-Centered Psychological Principles* (Alexander & Murphy, 1998; American Psychological Association Board of Educational Affairs, 1995) specifically address the need for emotional safety.

Teachers set the tone for this essential variable by modeling respect and courtesy. Students who are criticized for venturing personal or creative thoughts about a topic will not feel safe—and will be unlikely to take the risk a second time.

The need for order can be explained in at least two ways. First, an orderly environment is predictable, so it helps meet students' needs for equilibrium. Second, in Chapter 10 we saw that competence was defined as the ability to function effectively in one's environment. Students are able to function more effectively when the environment is orderly and predictable than when it is chaotic and uncertain. So, order contributes to students' perceptions of competence (Connell & Wellborn, 1990), which is basic, according to self-determination theory.

Success: Developing Learner Self-Efficacy

Once a safe and orderly environment is established, student success becomes the most important climate variable. The need for success is fundamental according to expectancy x value theory.

Unfortunately, not all students are successful, but teachers can increase the likelihood of success for most students in several ways. In addition to making students feel competent to increase their self-efficacy, as discussed earlier, strategies include

- Beginning lessons with open-ended questions that assess learners' current understanding
- Using a variety of high-quality examples and representations that provide background knowledge and promote understanding
- Developing lessons with questioning and prompting students when they have difficulty answering
- Providing scaffolded practice before putting students on their own
- Conducting ongoing assessments and providing detailed feedback about learning progress

Success, like most aspects of teaching and learning, isn't as simple as it appears, however. Let's look at this idea further.

Teachers promote self-efficacy through challenging activities that students can complete successfully.

Challenge: Increasing Perceptions of Competence and Self-Determination

A long line of theory and research confirms the need not only for success but also for challenge. As you saw in Chapter 10, challenge is one of the characteristics of intrinsically motivating activities. It makes students want to participate. Moreover, learners are more likely to value success on a task if they perceive the task as challenging (J. Atkinson, 1964; Brehm & Self, 1989; Clifford, 1990), an idea that is consistent with expectancy x value theory.

The reason learners value success on challenging tasks can also be explained with self-determination theory. Succeeding on challenging tasks increases perceptions of competence to a greater extent than succeeding on trivial tasks. Perceptions of increasing competence are satisfying in themselves because they lead to people's feelings that they're able to function effectively in their environments, which in turn contribute to feelings of control (autonomy) (Baron, 1998; Kloosterman, 1997; Schunk, 1994; Wasserstein, 1995). Feelings of competence and control lead to increased effort and persistence. This helps us understand why, for example, children persevere in learning to ride a bicycle, even though they fall repeatedly, and why they lose interest in a skill after it's mastered.

Teachers capitalize on the motivating features of challenge by encouraging students to identify relationships in the topics they study and the implications these relationships have for new learning. Limiting discussions to isolated, and often meaningless, facts has the opposite effect. When students complain about the difficulty of their tasks, effective teachers don't decrease the challenge—they provide scaffolding to ensure that students are able to meet it.

Task Comprehension: Increasing Perceptions of Control and Value

Consider the following teacher statements:

> "Today's lesson is nothing new if you've been here."
> "Get your nose in the book; otherwise, I'll give you a writing assignment."
> "This test is to see who the really smart ones are." (Brophy, 1987a, p. 204)

These are statements actually made by teachers! Now, consider these statements:

> "We're going to be getting a lot of practice with our writing throughout this year. We want to be good writers because being able to express ourselves in writing will help us in everything we do in life outside of school."
> "The geography of an area influences virtually all aspects of our lives, the way we make money, how we spend our leisure time, and even the way we dress. This is why we study it, and we'll look for these relationships in each of our upcoming units."

If the teachers who made the first three statements had thought about their impact on students' motivation, it's unlikely that they would have made the statements. The second set, in contrast, enhances **task comprehension,** *the understanding that results when learners are told what they are supposed to be learning and why they are learning it* (Blumenfeld, 1992; Good & Brophy, 2000).

Task comprehension contributes to a motivating classroom environment in several ways. First, clearly understanding what they're learning and why they're learning it increases students' feelings of control, which, according to self-determination theory, is essential for intrinsic motivation. Second, motivation depends on students believing that what they're learning is worthwhile (Good & Brophy, 2000). Understanding why they're studying a topic contributes to students' perceptions of the topic's utility value, *the perception of a topic or activity as useful for meeting future goals, including career goals* (see Chapter 10). According to expectancy x value theory, utility value contributes to perceptions of task value. Third, task comprehension leads to greater self-regulation. Understanding what they're learning and why helps learners identify appropriate goals, select effective strategies, and maintain their effort in the face of difficulty.

As with teacher characteristics, climate variables are interdependent. A challenging assignment can be motivating, for example, if students feel safe. If they're worried about the consequences of making mistakes or offering conjectures, the motivating effects of challenge are lost. Similarly, if students don't understand the point in an activity or expectations aren't clear, neither success nor challenge will increase motivation. All the climate variables depend on the extent to which teachers care about students and hold them to high standards.

11.10

Explain specifically how *challenge* differs from *teacher expectations*.

11.11

Task comprehension also contributes to a concept from Piaget's theory (Chapter 2). Name the concept, and explain task comprehension's contribution.

Classroom Connections

Applying the Climate Variables in the Model for Promoting Student Motivation in Your Classroom

1. Create a safe and orderly learning environment.
   - *Elementary:* A second-grade teacher establishes and practices daily routines until they're predictable and automatic for students.
   - *Middle School:* An eighth-grade American history teacher leads a discussion examining the kind of environment the students want to work in. They conclude that all comments, "digs," and discourteous remarks should be strictly forbidden. The teacher enforces the agreement with complete consistency.
   - *High School:* An English teacher constantly reminds her students that all relevant comments about a topic are welcome, and she models acceptance of all ideas. She requires all students to listen courteously when a classmate is talking.

2. Help students succeed on challenging tasks.
   - *Elementary:* A fifth-grade teacher comments, "We're really getting good at percentages. Now I have a problem that is going to make us all think. It will be tough, but I know that we'll be able to do it." After students attempt the solution, he guides a detailed discussion of the problem and ways to solve it.
   - *Middle School:* A sixth-grade English teacher always has the class practice three or four homework exercises as a whole group and discusses them before students begin to work independently.
   - *High School:* As she returns their homework, a physics teacher gives her students worked solutions to the most frequently missed problems. She has the students put the homework and the worked examples in their portfolios to study for the biweekly quizzes.

3. Carefully describe objectives and rationales for your assignments.
   - *Elementary:* A third-grade teacher says, as he gives students their daily math homework, "We know that understanding math is really, really important, so that's why we practice word problems every day."
   - *Middle School:* A seventh-grade English teacher carefully describes her assignments and due dates and writes them on the board. Each time, she explains why the assignment is important.
   - *High School:* A biology teacher displays the following on an overhead: *We don't just study flatworms because we're interested in flatworms. As we look at how they've adapted to their environments, we'll get additional insights into ourselves.* He then says, "We'll repeatedly look at this idea to remind ourselves why we study each organism."

Instructional Variables: Developing Interest in Learning Activities

Teacher and climate variables form a general framework for motivation. Within this context, the teacher can do much in specific learning activities to enhance learner motivation.

From an instructional perspective, a motivated student can be viewed as "someone who is actively engaged in the learning process" (Stipek, 1996, p. 85). But how do we promote and maintain active engagement? In Chapter 10, we saw that the ability to arouse curiosity is one characteristic of intrinsically motivating activities, so curiosity increases interest (Lepper & Hodell, 1989). Also, students' interest increases when they are involved in learning activities and their teachers use personalized and concrete examples that apply in the real world (Bruning et al., 1999); it also increases as their background knowledge develops (Schraw et al., 2001; Schraw & Lehman, 2001). Interest is important because it, like engagement, has been linked to learner attention, comprehension, and achievement (Krapp, Hidi, & Renninger, 1992; McDaniel, Waddill, Finstad, & Bourg, 2000; Mayer, 1998a).

To increase interest, our goal is to initially capture students' attention and then maintain their involvement in the learning activity. These factors are illustrated in Figure 11.5.

Figure 11.5 Instructional variables in the model for promoting student motivation

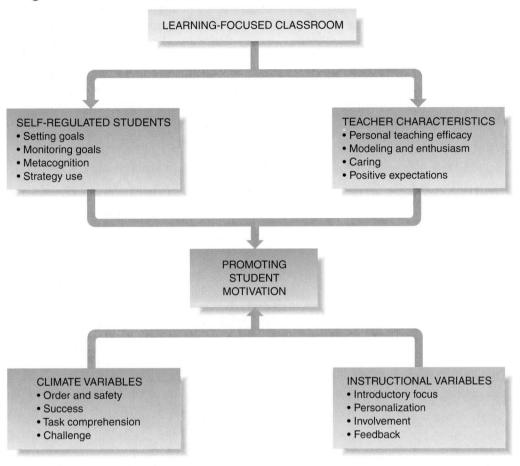

LEARNING-FOCUSED CLASSROOM

SELF-REGULATED STUDENTS
- Setting goals
- Monitoring goals
- Metacognition
- Strategy use

TEACHER CHARACTERISTICS
- Personal teaching efficacy
- Modeling and enthusiasm
- Caring
- Positive expectations

PROMOTING
STUDENT
MOTIVATION

CLIMATE VARIABLES
- Order and safety
- Success
- Task comprehension
- Challenge

INSTRUCTIONAL VARIABLES
- Introductory focus
- Personalization
- Involvement
- Feedback

Introductory Focus: Attracting Students' Attention

To begin this section, think about the way DeVonne began her lesson on arthropods: She brought out a whole lobster for the students to see and touch. The squeals and oohs and aahs indicated that she had clearly attracted their attention. Let's look at a couple more examples.

As an introduction to the topic of cities and their locations, Marissa Allen, a social studies teacher, hands out a map of a fictitious island. On it are physical features such as lakes, rivers, mountains, and bays. Information about altitude, rainfall, and average seasonal temperature is also included. Marissa begins, "Our class has just been sent to this island to settle it. We have this information about its climate and physical features. Where should we make our first settlement?"

Darrell Keen, a science teacher, passes a baseball and a golf ball around the room and has the students hold them. After the students confirm that the baseball feels heavier, he climbs up onto his desk and holds the two balls in front of him. As he prepares to drop them, he says, "I'm going to drop these balls at the same time. What do you predict will happen?"

By beginning their lessons in these ways, the teachers were attempting to increase interest by creating **introductory focus**, *direction for a lesson that is established by using an attention-getting technique or tool that also provides a framework for the lesson.* Introductory focus often capitalizes on the effects of curiosity and novelty, which we already know are characteristics of intrinsically motivating activities.

Effective teachers use introductory focus to draw students into their lessons.

To see a video clip in which teachers attempt to attract students' attention and provide frameworks for their lessons, go to the Companion Website at *www.prenhall.com/eggen*, then to this chapter's *Classrooms on the Web* module. Click on *Video Clip 11.1*.

Teachers can increase curiosity with unique problems, such Marissa's fictitious island problem; by asking paradoxical questions ("If Rome was such a powerful and advanced civilization, why did it fall apart?"); by using demonstrations with seemingly contradictory results (the two balls that Darrell planned to drop will hit the floor at the same time); or with eye-catching examples, such as DeVonne's lobster.

Unfortunately, few teachers plan their lesson introductions; in one study, only 5% of teachers made an explicit effort to draw students into the lesson (L. Anderson, Brubaker, Alleman-Brooks, & Duffy, 1984). Providing for effective introductory focus need not be difficult, however. All that is required is some conscious effort to connect the content of the lesson to students' backgrounds and interest. Additional examples are provided in Table 11.3.

Once learners are attracted to the lesson and a conceptual framework is provided, the lesson has to maintain their attention. Personalization, involvement, and feedback can help meet this goal.

Table 11.3 Tools and techniques for providing introductory focus

Tool/Technique	Example
Problems and questions	• A literature teacher shows a picture of Ernest Hemingway and says, "Here we see 'Papa' in all his splendor. He seemed to have everything—fame, adventure, romance. Yet he took his own life. Why would this happen?" • A science teacher asks the students to explain why two pieces of paper come together at the bottom (rather than move apart) when students blow between them. • An educational psychology instructor introducing social cognitive theory displays the following vignette: *You're driving 75 mph on the interstate—with a posted speed limit of 65—when another car blazes past you. A minute later, you see the car stopped by the highway patrol. You immediately slow down. How would behaviorism explain you slowing down?*
Inductive sequences	• An English teacher displays the following: *I had a ton of homework last night! I was upset because I had a date with the most gorgeous girl in the world! I guess it was okay, because she had on the ugliest outfit ever!* The students find a pattern in the examples and develop the concept *hyperbole*. • An educational psychology instructor begins a discussion of development with these questions: Are you bothered when something doesn't make sense? Do you want the world to be predictable? Are you more comfortable in classes when the instructor specifies the requirements, schedules the classes, and outlines the grading practices? Does your life in general follow patterns more than random experiences? The class looks at the pattern and arrives at the concept of *equilibrium*.
Concrete examples	• An elementary teacher begins a unit on amphibians by bringing in a live frog. • A geography teacher draws lines on a beach ball to demonstrate that longitude lines intersect at the poles and latitude lines are parallel to each other. • An educational psychology instructor introduces the concept *negative reinforcement* by describing his inclination to take a pain killer to reduce his discomfort after a demanding workout.
Objectives and rationales	• A math teacher begins, "Today we want to learn about unit pricing. This will help us decide which product is a better buy. It will help us all save money and be better consumers." • A world history teacher says, "Today we're going to look at the concept of *mercantilism*. It will help us understand why, throughout history, Europe came to the New World and went into South Asia and Africa." • An educational psychology instructor says, "We know that learners construct, rather than record, understanding. Today we want to see what that principle suggests about the way we should teach most effectively."

Personalization: Links to Students' Lives

Katrina Cardoza, a sixth-grade world history teacher at Matthew Gilbert Middle School, began a discussion of factors leading to World War I by displaying the following vignettes:

The students at Matthew Gilbert are very loyal to their school. "They don't talk the way we do," they comment when students from other schools are mentioned. The students at Matthew Gilbert also say things like, "We go to the same church, and we like to hang out together on the weekends.

"We're Gilbertites. We don't want to be anybody else, and we don't want anyone telling us what to do."

Students at Mandarin Middle School have similar thoughts. "I don't like the way they talk at Gilbert," some of them have been overheard saying. "They want to hang around with each other after school, and we want to go to the mall. I don't want anybody from there to tell us what to do.

"We're Mandariners, and we want to stay that way."

Katrina used questioning to help the students arrive at the notion that both sets of students were loyal to their school, their language, and their school culture. She then used this information as an analogy to help the students understand the concept *nationalism*.

Chris Emery, a science teacher, began an unit on genetics by saying, "Reanne, what color are your eyes?"

"Blue," Reanne responded.

"And how about yours, Eddie?"

"Green."

"Interesting," Chris smiled. "When we're done with this unit, we'll be able to figure out why Reanne's are blue and Eddie's are green, and a whole bunch of other things related to the way we are."

Katrina and Chris both attempted to increase their students' interest through **personalization** (Bruning et al., 1999; Cordova & Lepper, 1996; Mayer, 1998a), *the process of using intellectually and/or emotionally relevant examples to illustrate a topic.* A concept such as *nationalism* is distant from middle schoolers lives, so it isn't likely to be intrinsically interesting. On the other hand, students often feel a strong sense of loyalty to their school, so Katrina capitalized on this feeling to create an analogy between the school and the way people in Europe felt about their countries prior to World War I. Effective social studies teachers frequently use personalization to help students see how events that happened long ago or far away relate to their own lives (Hallden, 1998).

As with creating introductory focus, personalizing content need not require a great deal of extra work. For instance, once Katrina had prepared her vignettes, they could be used over and over. And Chris's introduction required no extra work, only some thought about the way he would introduce his topic.

Personalization is valuable for several reasons. First, it is intuitively sensible and widely applicable. A survey of experienced teachers described personalization as one of the most important ways to promote student interest in learning activities (Zahorik, 1996), and additional research supports Zahorik's findings (Schraw & Lehman, 2001). Second, students feel a sense of control when they study topics in which they're interested (E. Skinner, 1995; E. Skinner, Wellborn, & Connell, 1990). Third, as we saw with Katrina's examples, personalized content is meaningful because it encourages students to connect new information to structures already present in long-term memory (Moreno & Mayer, 2000). As you saw in Chapter 7, meaningfulness increases learning (Schunk, 2000). Finally, as you saw in our discussion of expectancy **x** value theory in Chapter 10, personalization is an effective way to increase learners' intrinsic interest in a topic.

11.12
In addition to being effective for introductory focus, concrete examples provide an essential learning function. Explain this function. (Hint: Think about constructing understanding.)

11.13
Describe how DeVonne used personalization in her lesson on arthropods.

Personalization creates links between students' lives and the content they are learning.

Table 11.4 Teachers' attempts to personalize topics

Teacher and Chapter	Attempt at Personalization
Karen Johnson (Chapter 2)	Used the population density of students' state and the density of window screens to illustrate the concept *density.*
Diane Smith (Chapter 4)	Used differences in the lengths of students' pencils and differences in students' hair color to illustrate comparative and superlative adjectives.
Mike Sheppard (Chapter 5)	Used distances from the students' hometown to neighboring towns as the basis for word problems in math.
Laura Hunter (Chapter 8)	Used finding the area of the classroom as a basis for developing skills in finding the areas of irregularly shaped figures.
Suzanne Brush (Chapter 9)	Used students' favorite flavor of jelly beans, their modes of transportation to school, and the cost of pizzas at local restaurants as a basis for a lesson on bar graphing.
Kathy Brewster (Chapter 10)	Used the class's "crusade" to prevent extracurricular activities from being eliminated at the school as an analogy for the Crusades in history.

Several of the teachers that you've already studied in this book have capitalized on the motivational effects of personalization. The teachers and the way they attempted to personalize their topics are outlined in Table 11.4.

Involvement: Increasing Intrinsic Motivation

<table>
<tr><td>

11.14

Is the concept of *involvement* the same as the concept of *activity* presented in Chapter 7? Explain.

</td></tr>
</table>

Introductory focus and personalization pull students into lessons, but unless the topic is intriguing or timely, neither is likely to sustain interest. The key to maintaining motivation is increasing **involvement,** *the extent to which students are actively participating in a learning activity.*

Think about your experience at lunch or a party. When you're talking and actively listening, you pay more attention to the conversation than you do when you're on its fringes. The same applies in classrooms. Deliberate teacher efforts to promote involvement result in increased interest and learning (Blumenfeld, 1992).

When students are actively involved in a learning activity, their innate need for control can be satisfied (Bruning et al., 1999). Also, as we saw in Chapter 7, being in an active role is essential for meaningful learning. As students learn more, their perceptions of competence increase, and this also increases perceptions of control. Some educational leaders suggest that putting students in active roles is one way to personalize instruction (Schraw & Lehman, 2001).

Let's look at two specific strategies for increasing student involvement: open-ended questioning and hands-on activities.

Using Open-Ended Questioning to Promote Involvement

Questioning is the most generally applicable tool teachers have for maintaining involvement. Students' attention is at a peak when they're being asked questions but drops during teacher monologues (Lemke, 1982). Although we discuss questioning in detail in Chapter 13, we introduce *open-ended questioning* here because it is particularly effective in improving involvement and motivation (Kauchak & Eggen, 2003). **Open-ended questions** are *questions for which a variety of answers are acceptable.*

One type of open-ended question is a request for observations. For instance, recall what DeVonne asked after the students examined the lobster:

Open-ended questions increase involvement and motivation.

DeVonne:	Okay, who can tell me one thing that you noticed?
Tu:	Hard.

Saleina: Gross.
Kevin: Wet.

Virtually any answer to her question would have been acceptable. As another example, a teacher giving a lesson on Shakespeare's *Julius Caesar* might ask the following:

"What has happened so far in the play?"
"What are some of the major events?"
"What is one thing you remember about the play?"

Like DeVonne's question, these questions ask for simple observations.

A second type of open-ended question asks for comparisons. For instance, a teacher giving a lesson on amphibians and reptiles might ask these questions:

"How is a frog similar to a lizard?"
"How are the frog and a toad similar to or different from each other?"

In the lesson on *Julius Caesar,* the teacher might ask these:

"How are Brutus and Marc Antony similar? How are they different?"
"How does the setting for Act I compare with that for Act II?"

Because many answers are acceptable, open-ended questions are safe and virtually ensure success—two of the climate variables we discussed earlier. By combining safety and success, a teacher can encourage even the most reluctant student to respond without risk or fear of embarrassment. Also, because they can be asked and answered quickly, open-ended questions can help solve the problem of involving 30 or more members of a class during a single lesson. Without the use of at least some open-ended questions, calling on reluctant responders often enough to increase their interest can be difficult.

To see a video clip of a teacher using open-ended questions to promote involvement, go to the Companion Website at *www.prenhall.com/eggen*, then to this chapter's *Classrooms on the Web* module. Click on *Video Clip 11.2.*

11.15
Open-ended questions also serve a valuable function related to information processing. What is that function? (Hint: Think about the information processing model.)

Using Hands-On Activities to Promote Involvement

Hands-on activities are another effective way of promoting involvement and student interest (Zahorik, 1996). When students are working with manipulatives in math, concrete materials in science, maps and globes in geography, or computers in language arts, their level of interest increases significantly. The level of involvement in DeVonne's lesson, for example, was at its highest when her groups worked with the shrimp. In addition, hands-on activities add variety to learning activities, and variety has been found to create learner interest (Zahorik, 1996).

Additional strategies for promoting involvement and interest are described in Table 11.5. Improvement drills add an element of gamelike novelty to otherwise routine activities, and personal improvement increases self-efficacy. Having students use

Table 11.5   Strategies for promoting involvement

Technique	Example
Improvement drills	Students are given a list of 10 multiplication facts on a sheet. Students are scored on speed and accuracy, and points are given for individual improvement.
Games	The class is divided equally according to ability, and the two groups respond in a game format to teacher questions.
Individual work spaces	Students are given their own chalkboards on which they solve math problems and identify examples of concepts. They hold the chalkboards up when they've solved the problem or when they think an example illustrates a concept. They also write or draw their own examples on the chalkboards.
Student group work	Student pairs observe a science demonstration and write down as many observations of it as they can.

chalkboards in individual work spaces is similar to having them solve problems on paper at their desks, but the chalkboards allow sharing and discussion, and students often will use them to attempt problems they wouldn't try on paper.

Group work, in which students work together toward common learning goals, can also promote motivation by increasing involvement (Baron, 1998; West, 1997). Group work provides opportunities for students to interact and compare their ideas with others. All the teachers in the cognitive learning chapters—David Shelton and Sue Southam in Chapter 7, Jenny Newhall and Scott Sowell in Chapter 8, and Laura Hunter and Suzanne Brush in Chapter 9—used group work to promote student involvement and interest. We also saw that DeVonne used group work when she had the students work with the shrimp.

Feedback: Meeting the Need to Understand

That students need feedback is a basic principle of learning best explained by constructivism. Because learners construct their own understanding, they require feedback to determine the extent to which their constructions are valid.

The importance of feedback for motivation is supported by cognitive theories of motivation. For instance, as learning increases, perceptions of competence and control also increase, and feedback indicating that competence is increasing contributes to self-efficacy. In addition, feedback helps us meet our innate desire—put forth in attribution theory—to understand why we perform the way we do.

Feedback also contributes to self-regulation. Feedback gives learners information about progress toward goals, and when they're met, self-efficacy increases. If they're not met, students can then increase their effort or change strategies.

Research confirms these theoretical explanations, indicating that feedback has powerful motivational value when it is specifically *intended to improve learning* (Clifford, 1990). Feedback that involves social comparisons or has a performance orientation rather than a learning orientation can detract from motivation (Crooks, 1988; Maehr, 1992; Schunk, 1994). Performance-oriented feedback has a particularly detrimental effect on less able students, and it detracts from intrinsic motivation for both low and high achievers.

11.16
Provide an example of "learning-oriented" and another example of "performance-oriented" feedback. Explain the difference between the two.

Applying the Climate and Instructional Variables in Your Classroom: Instructional Strategies

Throughout the chapter, we've emphasized that the variables in our model for promoting student motivation are interdependent. This is particularly the case with climate and instructional variables. The following principles can help teachers capitalize on this interdependence as they attempt to apply the model in their classrooms:

- Establish rules and procedures that create and maintain a safe, orderly learning environment.
- Clearly describe expectations and the reasons for studying particular topics.
- Attempt to link topics to students' personal lives.
- Establish and maintain high levels of student involvement in learning activities.
- Provide specific and detailed feedback on student work.

Let's see how the principles guide David Crawford, a world history teacher at Baker County High School, as he works with his students.

As the bell rang at the start of the period, David surveyed the class and saw that everyone was in their seats and had their notebooks on their desks. He then began, "Okay, everyone, think about some of the technology that we have in today's world—some of the common things that we all take for granted. Go ahead, . . . Brenda."

"Computers."

"Sure, that's an important one. . . . What else?"

"Cell phones," Mayte offered.

"Cars," Erin added.

"Electricity," Darrell put in.

"All good examples," David nodded. "Now, we tend to think of technology as something that has existed only recently, but in fact it's been there throughout history, and we can tell a great deal about a people or a civilization by looking at the technology and artifacts from that civilization. . . . What do we mean by *artifact*? . . . Anyone?"

"It's like a relic or something left behind," Danae offered.

"Exactly. Good, Danae. . . . Now, today we're going to examine some artifacts to see what they might tell us about the people who left them behind. Being able to make these kinds of conclusions will give us the thinking tools to better understand each of the civilizations we study as we look at the history of the world."

David reached into a box and pulled out two animal skulls, a piece of coarsely woven fabric, and two stone spear points that were ground to fine edges. He placed the items on the right side of a table at the front of the room. On the left side he put two other stone spear points that were also sharp but chipped, several pieces of charcoal, three small animal bones, and a fragment from an animal skin.

11.17
To what part of the information processing model in Chapter 7 do questions like "What do we mean by *artifact*?" and "What do archeologists do?" most closely relate? Explain.

"We'll call this Civilization A, and this one Civilization B," David said, pointing first to the materials on the left and then to those on the right.

The class observed the artifacts and with David's guidance concluded that the two skulls were from a cow and a sheep and the bones were leg and rib bones from a smaller animal like an antelope.

"Now," David said animatedly, "you're going to be sophisticated archeologists. . . . What do archeologists do?"

"Study ancient people based on their artifacts," Jamie volunteered.

"Good, . . . so here we go. You are archeological teams, and you've found these two sites," he said, pointing at the objects on the two sides of the table. "I want you to work with your partners and write down as many conclusions as you can about the people from each site, or any comparisons between the two, such as which one you believe was more advanced. In each case, you must provide evidence for the conclusion that you've made. . . . Think hard and carefully about this, and see what you can come up with. . . . I know you're up to it. . . . I'll give you 10 minutes. . . . Come up and look more closely at the objects if you want to."

The students began, and David moved around the room as they worked. He read the conclusions the students were writing and periodically asked "How do you know that?" or "What does that tell you?"

"Everybody ready?" David asked at the end of the 10 minutes.

"No," several students said.

"Okay, a couple more minutes."

A few minutes later, David said, "Okay, everyone look this way. . . . What did you come up with?"

"We think those are newer," Lori said, pointing at the chipped spear points.

"No way," Rodney interjected.

"Rod," David said sternly, "remember that we can disagree all we want, but we extend the courtesy of letting other people finish, and we always listen to what they have to say."

"Sorry."

"Go ahead, Lori."

"The points are sharp, and they're sort of like art."

"Okay, Rod, go ahead," David said after Lori had finished.

"Those look like they're ground," Rodney responded, indicating the spear points with the fine edges. "And grinding takes a newer technology than chipping."

The class continued discussing the artifacts. From the cow and sheep skulls and the coarse cloth, the students concluded that Civilization B had domesticated animals and the ability to weave. And they decided that the antelope bones and animal skin showed that Civilization A probably consisted of hunter-gatherers who did not yet weave cloth.

When they had completed the discussion, David said, "Okay, for tonight, I want you to read the discussion of the Old, Middle, and New Stone Ages on pages 35–44 of your books and decide what ages these artifacts probably belonged to. . . . You did a great job today. You made some excellent conclusions and provided good evidence for most of them. . . . Turn in your papers; the period is nearly over."

Let's take a closer look at David's attempts to apply the principles in his teaching. First, his classroom was a very orderly and safe environment. For instance, all the students were at their desks with their notebooks out when the bell rang, indicating that this was a routine. Research indicates that well-established routines are an essential part of an orderly learning environment (Emmer et al., 2003; Evertson et al., 2003). In addition, a rule apparently existed in David's class requiring students to treat each other with courtesy and open-mindedness, as indicated by his comment to Rodney, "Rod, remember that we can disagree all we want, but we extend the courtesy of letting other people finish, and we always listen to what they have to say." This kind of atmosphere helps students feel safe enough to offer conclusions without fear of embarrassment.

Second, David attempted to capitalize on *introductory focus* by beginning the lesson with examples of present-day technology and saying, "Being able to make these kinds of conclusions will give us the thinking tools to better understand each of the civilizations we study as we look at the history of the world." By helping the students understand why archeologists study artifacts and why they were going to do the activity that followed, David also promoted *task comprehension.*

Third, he attempted to personalize the activity by beginning the lesson with a look at today's technology and by putting the students in the role of archeologists.

Fourth, he challenged the students to make conclusions based on what they saw and to support their conclusions with evidence. As you saw in Chapter 9, the ability to make conclusions based on evidence is the essence of critical thinking. As students see evidence of their increasing ability to think critically, their perceptions of competence increase, which contributes to self-determination and intrinsic motivation.

Finally, David's students were highly involved in the lesson, and success was enhanced because the task—making conclusions—was open-ended. Any conclusion that the students could support was acceptable.

This brings us to the topic of assessment, feedback, and motivation.

Assessment and Learning: Using Feedback to Increase Interest and Self-Efficacy

To examine the role of assessment and its influence on learning and motivation, let's return to David's work with his students.

Assessment with feedback is an essential component of classroom motivation.

The next day David began the period by saying, "One of our goals for yesterday and throughout the year is to be able to provide evidence for the conclusions we make. . . . You generally did a good job on this, but we need a little more practice in some cases. . . . I'm going to display the conclusions and evidence that some of you offered. . . . Now remember the spirit we're doing this in. It's strictly for the sake of learning and improvement. It's not intended to criticize any of you. Keep that in mind.

"I've typed what you wrote on transparencies, so you all can remain anonymous. . . . Let's take a look at what three different groups wrote," David said as he displayed the following:

Conclusion:	The people had cloth.
Evidence:	There is cloth in Civilization B.
Conclusion:	The people in Civilization B made their own clothes, but those in A wore animal skins.
Evidence:	There is a piece of an animal skin in A and a piece of cloth in B.
Conclusion:	The people in Civilization B were more likely to survive.
Evidence:	They had cows and sheep, so they didn't have to find wild animals. The cloth piece suggests that they wove cloth, so they didn't have to use animal skins.

"What comments can you make about the three sets of conclusions?"

"The first one isn't even really a conclusion," Shantae offered. "You can see the cloth, so it really doesn't say anything."

"Good observation, Shantae. . . . Yes, a conclusion is a statement based on a fact; it isn't the fact itself."

The class then discussed the second and third examples and agreed that the conclusions were based on solid evidence.

"This is the kind of thing we're looking for," David commented. "I know that you're all capable of this kind of thinking, so let's see it in your next writing sample."

He then brought out a can of soup and asked students to make some conclusions about the civilization that might have produced such an artifact and to give evidence that supported each conclusion.

The class, beginning to understand the process, made several comments, and David wrote the students' conclusions and evidence on the board.

Detailed feedback that results from assessment is critical to learning and motivation. Some of David's students had little experience in making and defending conclusions. Collecting and reading their papers was a form of assessment, and without the assessment combined with feedback, they were unlikely to understand the difference between good and poor conclusions. Likewise, language arts students won't construct an understanding of what makes a good essay without having their work assessed and being provided feedback on that work. And math students won't learn to problem solve if their efforts aren't assessed and they don't receive feedback on their progress.

As we said earlier, feedback (resulting from assessment) is motivating because it gives learners evidence that they are becoming more competent. As they use feedback to improve the quality of their work, and they see that the quality actually is increasing, their self-efficacy and self-determination both increase. None of this is possible without ongoing assessment and feedback based on that assessment.

As we close this section, we want to make a final comment about instruction that can increase learner motivation, and this comment relates to teacher effort and preparation time. Without question, it took both effort and time for David to find, buy, borrow, or make the proper instructional materials—the animal skulls, the chipped and ground spear points, the fragment of animal skin, and the coarse cloth. However, in the future, now that the materials are assembled, he can use them over and over with virtually no preparation time. It takes time to gather high-quality examples to represent the topics you teach, but the benefits to both learning and motivation make the effort more than worth it.

> **11.18**
> What theory of motivation in Chapter 10 strongly supports the need for feedback in increasing learning motivation? Explain.

Classroom Connections

Applying the Instructional Variables in the Model for Promoting Student Motivation in Your Classroom

1. Plan lesson introductions to attract students' attention and provide an umbrella for the lesson.
   - *Elementary:* A fourth-grade teacher introduces a lesson on measuring by bringing in a cake recipe and ingredients that have to be modified if everyone in the class is going to get a piece of cake. During the lesson, the class modifies the recipe. The teacher bakes the cake overnight and brings it to class the next day.

   - *Middle School:* A physical science teacher begins many of her lessons with a simple demonstration, such as dropping an ice cube into a container of water and another into a container of alcohol to show that ice floats on water but sinks in alcohol. The demonstration then serves as the focal point of the lesson.

- *High School:* An English teacher introduces *A Raisin in the Sun* this way: "Think about a Muslim family in Detroit. What do you think they talk about? What is important to them? How do you think they felt after the events of September 11, 2001? Keep those questions in mind as we read *A Raisin in the Sun*. It will provide us with insights into how another minority group, African Americans, thought and felt at another time in America."

2. Personalize content whenever possible.
   - *Elementary:* A fourth-grade teacher begins a lesson comparing animals with exoskeletons and those with endoskeletons by having the students squeeze their legs and their arms. He then passes out a number of crayfish and has the students compare the crayfish to themselves.
   - *Middle School:* A seventh-grade teacher begins a lesson on percentages by bringing in an advertisement for computer games and products from a local newspaper. The ad says "10% to 25% off marked prices." After working with the class to compute percentages on several examples, she returns to the ad and asks students to compute their savings on various items.
   - *High School:* A history teacher begins a unit on World War II by having students interview someone who served in the military at the time. The class uses the results of the interviews to remind themselves of the "human" dimension of the war.

3. Involve all students in learning activities.
   - *Elementary:* Each day a second-grade teacher passes out a sheet with 20 math facts on it. The students quickly write the answers and then score the sheets. Students who improve their scores from the previous day or get all 20 facts correct receive a bonus point on their math averages.
   - *Middle School:* A seventh-grade pre-algebra teacher has students work in pairs to complete seat-work assignments. They are required to work each problem individually, check with each other, and ask for help if they can't agree on the solution.
   - *High School:* An English teacher randomly calls on all students as equally as possible, whether or not they raise their hands. At the beginning of the year, he explains that this is his practice, that his intent is to encourage participation, and that students will soon get over any uneasiness about being "put on the spot." Whenever students cannot answer, he prompts them so they'll be able to give an acceptable answer.

4. Provide prompt and informative feedback about learning progress.
   - *Elementary:* A fourth-grade teacher discusses the most frequently missed items on each of her quizzes, asking students to explain why the correct answers are correct and considering the questions from different perspectives whenever possible.
   - *Middle School:* A seventh-grade teacher writes on a student paper, "You have some very good ideas. Now you need to rework your essay so that it is grammatically correct. Look carefully at the notes I've made on your paper."
   - *High School:* A world history teacher displays an "ideal answer" on the overhead for each of the items on his homework assignments and essay items on his tests. Students compare their answers to the ideal and take notes with suggestions for improving their responses.

Technology and Learning: Using Technology to Increase Learner Motivation

Technology is changing education, and nowhere is this impact more strongly felt than in motivation (Barron, Hogarty, Kromrey, & Lenkway, 1999). Research has identified positive effects of technology on motivation in at least four areas:

- *Self-esteem and self-efficacy.* Students using technology experienced increased self-esteem, and beliefs about their capabilities improved (O'Connor & Brie, 1994). In addition, teachers who became proficient with technology increased in perceived self-efficacy (Kellenberger, 1996).
- *Attendance.* An 8-year study of one technology-implementation project found that student absenteeism dropped by nearly 50% after the project was put into place (Dwyer, 1994).
- *Attitudes.* Students participating in a technology-enriched program reported more positive attitudes toward school and more enjoyment of out-of-class activities (McKinnon, 1997).
- *Involvement.* Students in technology-supported programs were more willing to participate in school learning activities (Yang, 1991–1992).

The following comment provides a student perspective:

Interviewer: What do you think are the major advantages of using a computer to help you learn geometry?

Paul: If it's fun, it makes you want to learn something! It's fun! (Schofield, Eurich-Fulcer, & Britt, 1994, p. 602)

The Motivating Effects of Technology: Theoretical Explanations

The motivating characteristics of technology can be explained using self-efficacy, expectancy **x** value theory, and self-determination theory. First, technology may be unique in its ability to increase self-efficacy (Schunk & Ertmer, 1999). The expertise that students develop as they learn to compose on a keyboard, modify and manage files, use spreadsheets and databases, use the Internet, and communicate with others by e-mail gives them a sense of personal satisfaction. As their skills improve, students turn to more sophisticated activities, such as making technologically enhanced presentations, developing and improving their own websites, and creating their own simulations. Expertise with these activities is also personally satisfying and can significantly increase self-efficacy.

Second, expectancy **x** value theory tells us that intrinsic interest increases learners' perceptions of task value, and technology can significantly increase interest in activities that may not otherwise attract students. For instance, practice is necessary to develop basic skills to automaticity, which is necessary for freeing working memory space to work on higher level tasks, such as problem solving (Bruning et al., 1999). Technology can help provide the variety and novelty necessary to maintain students' interest as they practice.

From a self-determination perspective, technology can keep learning activities challenging by adapting the difficulty level of problems, decreasing the time available as expertise develops, and providing immediate and customized feedback. And challenge increases self-determination by increasing perceptions of competence and control as learners meet the challenges.

Because technology allows students to set the pace of the activity and choose the kind and amount of help they receive, they achieve more control over their learning than is often possible in whole-group or even small-group activities. Also, computer assistance is private and personal, so students experience less embarrassment and are more likely to seek help:

Interviewer: How was getting help from the computer different from getting help from Mr. Adams?

Kim: Well, some people, like when you have a teacher, man, you don't ask the teacher. You feel really embarrassed, you know. Sometimes I do. Like if you don't understand something. The computer—it's just a computer. It helps you and you wouldn't mind. (Schofield et al., 1994, p. 599)

Finally, authentic problems presented in realistic contexts (e.g., students are asked if Jasper can make it home without running out of fuel; see Chapter 8) are motivating (R. Davis, 1994). They capitalize on the intrinsically motivating effects of challenge and novelty, and solving real-world problems increases self-efficacy. Researchers investigating the effects of computer-based problem solving observed the following:

By the time the bell to start class rings, three fourths of the students in class today have problems on the screen and are working on them. The others (have all logged in and) appear to be waiting

Used properly, technology can be a tool for increasing learner motivation.

for their problems to appear. . . . I'm struck by the fact that the students have started their work without a word from the substitute teacher who is in charge of class today. (Schofield et al., 1994, p. 593)

Technology and Motivation: Cautions and Guidelines for Teachers

Using technology to increase motivation isn't as simple as it appears on the surface. If technology is to be used effectively, teachers must be very clear about the goals they expect to accomplish with it (Harrington-Lueker, 1997). Vague notions of "surfing the Net" or simply giving students access to computers aren't adequate. Students may—at least initially—enjoy the novelty, but spending time in front of computers doesn't necessarily produce learning.

Although computers and other forms of technology may increase interest, researchers caution that the quality of software varies greatly (R. Davis, 1994), and merely being busy isn't an accurate indicator of student learning. Researchers have found that student engagement with computers can vary from superficial contacts with content to more productive and intense, goal-oriented interactions (Bangert-Drowns & Pyke, 1999).

With the research on technology and motivation in mind, the following are some guidelines for teachers:

- *Establish clear learning goals.* Students should use computers and other forms of technology for clear learning purposes, such as developing automaticity with basic skills or practicing solving complex problems.
- *Assess software before students work with it.* The quality of instructional software varies greatly. It should be thoroughly examined to be sure that it is consistent with learning goals and compatible with learners' background knowledge.
- *Emphasize both process and product goals.* Encourage students to reflect on their experiences in working with technology, both with respect to how technology works and also how it can be used as a learning tool. Ask students to explain why they are using a certain procedure, what they're trying to accomplish, and how they know that they're making progress.
- *Vary the uses of technology.* Technology can be used to enhance learning in a number of ways. It can be used for practice with feedback, problem solving, word processing, and locating information on the Internet. Provide students with opportunities to learn about technology and these different uses.

To examine a website that teachers can use to review software, go to the Companion Website at *www.prenhall.com/eggen*, then to this chapter's *Web Links* module.

The kinds of software teachers choose and the way they present and monitor computer tasks can have important influences on learning. If study time isn't spent on activities related to clear, meaningful goals, or if software isn't matched to students' backgrounds, using technology may actually detract from learning (Bangert-Drowns & Pyke, 1999).

Motivation and Diversity

When we examine the research on the school success of students from ethnic minority groups, we see a pattern. On most measures—achievement test scores, retention in grade, and dropout rates—many minority students in the United States perform less well than nonminorities (Macionis, 2000; Mullis, Dossey, Foertsh, Jones, & Gentile, 1991). Although some differences can be linked to socioeconomic status, disparities remain. Many minority students leave school unprepared for today's demanding world.

Teachers can create powerful links to school through their caring and supportive interactions with students.

Educators have turned to motivational research in an attempt to address these problems, but the picture remains cloudy. For example, researchers have attempted to explain the lower-than-expected achievement of African American students by hypothesizing deficits in need for achievement, perceptions of autonomy, and self-efficacy. However, in a comprehensive review of this literature, Graham (1994) concluded that deficits don't exist in these areas and that African American students "maintain a belief in personal control, have high expectance, and enjoy positive self-regard" (p. 55). Researchers have also found that African American and Latina mothers are enthusiastic about education and hold high expectations for their children's future (Stevenson, Chen, & Uttal, 1990).

The picture is further complicated by the fact that motivation varies among communities, families, and peers within specific minority groups. For example, researchers have found that motivational issues in inner-city African American communities differ from those in suburban or rural ones (Graham, 1994; Slaughter-Defoe, Nakagawa, Takanashi, & Johnson, 1990), and some families approach the task of motivating their children differently than do others (Steinberg, Dornbusch, & Brown, 1992). Similar differences exist in Asian and Latino families. Peer groups sometimes complement school achievement and other times detract from it (Goodenow, 1992b; Steinberg et al., 1992).

Motivation Problems: Student Perspectives

We want to emphasize again that many students from minority groups are highly motivated and highly successful. This obviously isn't a problem. When problems exist, however, researchers have attempted to find reasons. From students' perspectives, the following problems often exist:

- Lack of connection between classroom content and students' lives
- Alienation from school
- Disengagement and lack of involvement in classes
- Distant and inflexible teachers

Students report feeling alienated from school, like outsiders at a party. This feeling results from factors such as cultural discontinuities, language barriers, and academic problems (Ogbu, 1992; Wong-Fillmore, 1992). In one study, researchers asked about connections between school and students' personal happiness:

Interviewer:	What do you really like about school? What makes you happy?
Diane:	Nothing really. I just come because I have to. Because I don't want to grow up being stupid.
Interviewer:	There's nothing you look forward to?
Diane:	Ummm . . . (defiantly stares; challenges.) Getting an education?
Interviewer:	Do you think there's a way to get an education without coming to school?
Diane:	(shakes her head no)
Interviewer:	It has to be this way?
Diane:	(softly; no eye contact) Yeah. (Kramer & Colvin, 1991, p. 6)

Another student, who was discussing his decision to leave school at age 16, described his alienation in this way:

Student:	I wouldn't go to nobody.
Interviewer:	Not even a counselor?
Student:	No.
Interviewer:	That seems funny. Don't you work in the office?
Student:	Yeah, but I don't talk to them [student emphasis]. (Kramer-Schlosser, 1992, p. 132)

Disengagement is another problem. Teachers report that students don't come to class or that when they do they are reluctant to participate.

They'll try to sit at the edges or the back of the classroom and they actually try to become less visible to me, or they'll act up so they get sent out of the classroom and there's less time, less chance I'll call on them or hold them accountable. . . . Usually they don't join the class. (Kramer & Colvin, 1991, p. 12)

Adding to these problems are student perceptions that teachers just don't care. One student described her teachers this way:

Nichole:	People here don't have many people to talk to. I don't. The teachers . . . some of them don't care about their students. They say, "They [administrators] want me to teach and I'm going to do it no matter what." I don't like that. I like them to say, "I'm here to teach and help you because I care." That's what I like. But a lot of them are just saying, "I'm here to teach so I'm gonna teach." I don't think that's right.
Interviewer:	Do they actually say that?
Nichole:	It's more an attitude, and they do say it. Like Ms. G. She's like . . . she never says it, but you know, she's just there and she just wants to teach, but she doesn't want to explain the whole deal.
Interviewer:	How do you know that?
Nichole:	I could feel it. The way she acts and the way she does things. She's been here seven years and all the kids I've talked to that have had her before say, "Oooh! You have Ms. G.!" Just like that.
Interviewer:	But a teacher who really cares, how do they act?
Nichole:	Like Mr. P. He really cares about his students. He's helping me a lot and he tells me, "I'm not angry with you, I just care about you." He's real caring and he does teach me when he cares. (Kramer & Colvin, 1991, p. 13)

The pattern we see is a lack of connection to both school and classes. Students attend school, sit in classes, but don't feel a part of them. They question whether anyone cares about them, and from their perspective, the classes have little meaning for their daily lives.

Motivation Problems: Possible Solutions

Research offers some possible solutions to the problem of student alienation and disengagement. Students must feel that they belong and can contribute to the classroom community. They need to value the classes they take and find them meaningful.

Teachers are critical to the success of this process. Those who are effective at motivating students from minority groups and students placed at risk have the following characteristics:

- They are enthusiastic, supportive, and have high expectations for student achievement.
- They create learner-centered classrooms with high levels of student involvement.
- They make a special effort to connect classroom content to students' lives. (Kramer & Colvin, 1991; Kramer-Schlosser, 1992)

Teachers need to make all students feel welcome and to demonstrate that they sincerely care. They also need to communicate that they hold positive expectations and that they'll work with learners who agree to try. One teacher, identified as effective in working with at-risk students of all cultural backgrounds, described his efforts in this way:

I believe that marginal students who begin the year poorly and improved did so because they knew I would do all I could to help them to be a success in school. I told them I would explain, and explain, and explain until they understood. They were worth every moment it would take. No one ever has to fail. (Kramer-Schlosser, 1992, p. 137)

Having teachers who are caring, enthusiastic, and hold high expectations—important for all students—is essential for minority learners and students placed at risk. Order and safety, challenge, success, and feedback also make classrooms accessible and inviting for students on the margins. Paying careful attention to these variables will enable teachers to increase motivation for all students.

Summary

Class Structure: Creating a Learning-Focused Environment

Learning-focused environments focus on learning goals, those that emphasize increased understanding and mastery of tasks. Performance-focused environments emphasize performance goals, those that focus on demonstrating high ability, and particularly ability compared to others. Learning-focused environments increase student motivation, whereas performance-focused environments can detract from motivation for all but the highest achievers.

Self-Regulated Learners: Developing Student Responsibility

Self-regulation is students' ability and inclination to accept responsibility for and control their learning. It includes setting and monitoring goals, metacognition, and the use of learning strategies.

Self-regulation is developmental, and learners may initially set and monitor goals to receive rewards and avoid punishers. As their self-determination increases, they gradually demonstrate self-regulated behaviors because of utility value or because doing so is consistent with their self-schemas. Ideally, learners will eventually set and monitor goals for their own sake, which is intrinsically motivated behavior.

Teacher Characteristics: Personal Qualities That Increase Student Motivation

Personal teaching efficacy, modeling, caring, and having high expectations are personal characteristics that can increase student motivation. Teachers who are high in personal teaching efficacy believe they are able to help students learn, regardless of student background knowledge or other factors.

Modeling courtesy and respect is essential for motivation, and demonstrating genuine interest in the topics they teach is the essence of teacher enthusiasm.

Teachers demonstrate that they care about their students by being willing to spend personal time with them and demonstrating respect for each individual. One of the most effective ways to demonstrate respect is to hold students to high standards. Holding students to high standards also communicates that teachers expect all students to be successful.

Climate Variables: Creating a Motivating Environment

Motivating environments are safe, secure, and orderly places that focus on learning. In addition, students are successful on tasks they perceive as challenging. As they meet challenges, they get evidence that their competence is increasing and feel an increased sense of control, both factors that increase intrinsic motivation.

In motivating environments, students understand what they're expected to learn and why they're expected to do so. Understanding what they're learning and why further increases perceptions of control and contributes to task value.

Instructional Variables: Developing Interest in Learning Activities

Teachers attempt to increase motivation by beginning lessons with examples, activities, or questions that attract students' attention and provide frameworks for the information that follows.

Attention and interest are maintained when teachers are able to make content personally relevant to students and keep them highly involved in learning activities.

Feedback about learning progress is essential for both learning and motivation. When feedback indicates that competence is increasing, self-efficacy and self-determination both improve, and intrinsic motivation increases.

Technology and Learning: Using Technology to Increase Student Motivation

Research indicates that technology can heighten learner motivation by increasing self-efficacy and self-esteem, improving student attendance, promoting more positive attitudes toward school and more enjoyment of out-of-class activities, and increasing student involvement in learning activities. Technology may be unique in its ability to increase learners' sense of efficacy.

Motivation and Diversity

Research indicates that many students from minority groups perceive a lack of connection between classroom content and their lives and alienation from school. They tend to be uninvolved in classes and believe that their teachers are distant and inflexible.

Teachers who work successfully with minority students are enthusiastic, supportive, and have high expectations for student achievement; they create learner-centered classrooms with high levels of student involvement; and they make a special effort to connect classroom content to students' lives.

Windows on Classrooms

We saw at the beginning of the chapter how DeVonne Lampkin taught the concept arthropod. Let's turn now to a language arts lesson on the construction of paragraphs that she taught later that same day. Read the case study and answer the questions that follow.

DeVonne Lampkin was working with her fifth-grade students on their writing skills. She planned to have them practice writing paragraphs and conduct self-assessments using criteria given in a 3-point rubric. She completed her after-lunch routines, including handing each student a blank transparency and pen, and then began, "Today, we're going to practice some more on composing good paragraphs. . . . Now, we know the characteristics of a good paragraph, but let's review for a moment. . . . What do we look for in a well-composed paragraph?"

"Topic sentence," several of the students said immediately.

"Okay, what else?"

"Sentences that go with the topic," others added.

"Yes, 'go with the topic' means that the sentences support your topic sentence. You need to have at least four supporting sentences."

DeVonne reminded the students that they also needed to use correct grammar and spelling, and she then displayed the following paragraphs:

> *Computers come in all shapes and sizes. One of the first computers, named UNIVA, filled a room. Today, some large computers are as big as refrigerators. Others are as small as books. A few are even tiny enough to fit in a person's pocket.*

> *Ann's family bought a new color television. It had a 54-inch screen. There were controls for color and brightness. Ann likes police stories. There were also controls for sound and tone.*

After some discussion, the class concluded that the first example met the criteria for an acceptable paragraph, but the second one did not, because the topic sentence didn't have four supporting sentences and the information "Ann likes police stories" didn't pertain to the topic.

"Now, I want you to help me out with one," DeVonne continued. "I'm going to write a topic sentence, and I want you to give me some sentences that will support my topic sentence."

She wrote the following on a transparency:

Basketball is a sport played by both girls and boys.

"Who can give me another sentence?" she continued.

The students offered additional sentences until DeVonne had written a complete paragraph:

Basketball is a sport played by both girls and boys. There are 5 players allowed on the court. The NBA is the men's league. The WNBA is the name of the womens league. Therefore, basketball is for everyone.

She again reminded the students of the criteria for a good paragraph and said, "Now, what you're going to do is write a paragraph on any topic. You're going to write it on the transparencies I gave you at the beginning of class, and then the class is going to grade your paper." DeVonne smiled when she heard several calls of "Woo, woo" from the students.

The students went to work, with DeVonne reminding them several times that they could pick any topic.

When she saw that they had all finished, DeVonne said, "Okay, now we're going to grade the paragraphs." She then reviewed the criteria from the 3-point rubric: A score of 3 meant that all criteria for a good paragraph were met; a score of 2 meant that the paragraph had a topic sentence, the paragraph had fewer than four supporting sentences, some information did not pertain to the topic, and a few grammatical errors were present; and a score of 1 meant that a considerable amount of information did not pertain to the topic and many grammatical errors were present.

"Okay, who wants to go first?" DeVonne asked.

"Me!" several of the students shouted.

"I should have known that," DeVonne smiled. "Okay, Tu, come on up."

Tu displayed his paragraph and read it aloud:

Quidditch is a wizard sport that is famous in the wizard world. There is 7 people allowed on each team. On the field there are 4 balls. The Quaffle is a red soccerball. The two bludgers try to knock players of their brooms. Finally, the Golden Snitch is very small and when caught the team gets 150 points. And that team mostly always win. Therefore, Quidditch is very exciting.

The class discussed his paragraph, agreed that it deserved a 3, and then several students called out, "I want to go next! I want to go next!"

DeVonne asked Justin to display his paragraph:

There was a boy named Josh. He lives in a house with the roof falling in and the windows were broke. He had holes in the wall and the ceiling leaked when it rained. But then again it always rained and thunder over his house. No one goes to his gate because he was so weird. They say he is a vampire.

She then had the students raise their hands to vote on the score for the paragraph. About half gave it a 2, and the remainder gave it a 1.

"Samantha, why did you give it a 2?" DeVonne asked, beginning the discussion of the paragraph.

"He didn't stay on his topic. . . . He needs to stay on either the boy or the house," Samantha noted.

"Haajar? . . . You gave him a 1. . . . Go ahead."

"There was a boy named Josh, and then he started talking about the house. And then the weather and then the boy again," Haajar responded.

"Yes, that's similar to what Samantha said," DeVonne nodded.

A few more students offered comments, and the class agreed that Justin's paragraph deserved a 1.5. Justin took his seat.

"Me, me! I want to do mine!" several students exclaimed with their hands raised.

DeVonne called on Saleina to display her paragraph:

Insects have to have certain things to
be insects. They have to have only
six legs. They have to have an
exo skeleton. They have to have
3 body parts. They are the head
the abdomen, and the thorax.
Therefore, any bug can not be
an insect.

★ 3 ★

"So, why do you feel it should be a 3? . . . Matthew?" DeVonne asked after surveying the class.

"She stayed on the topic, and she gave good details," Matthew answered.

"I am so impressed with you guys," DeVonne said. "Your work is excellent.

"Okay, one more," DeVonne continued. "Joshua."

"No! No!" the students protested.

"Okay, one more after Joshua," DeVonne smiled.

The class assessed Joshua's paragraph and one more, written by Allie.

"Are we going to get to do ours tomorrow?" several of the students asked at the end of the lesson.

Constructed Response Questions

In answering these questions, use information from the chapter and link your responses to specific information in the case.

1. Feelings of safety are essential for student motivation. Assess the extent to which DeVonne's students felt safe in her classroom.

2. Assess DeVonne's application of the instructional variables in her classroom.

3. In spite of the fact that they were having their paragraphs publicly evaluated, DeVonne's students were very enthusiastic about displaying their work. Offer an explanation for their enthusiasm.

4. DeVonne's students' backgrounds are very diverse. Assess her classroom environment for learners with diverse backgrounds.

Document-Based Analysis

Look again at Justin's paragraph below. It was rated a 1.5 by his peers.

> There was a boy named Josh. He lives in a house with the roof falling in and the windows were broke. He had holes in the wall and the ceiling leaked when it rained. But then again it always rained and thunder over his house. Noone every goes to his gate because he was so weird. They say he is a vampire.

Based on the information in the chapter, assess how effectively DeVonne handled the class's evaluation of Justin's work.

Online Portfolio Activities

To develop your professional portfolio, further apply your understanding of chapter content, and address the INTASC standards, go to the Companion Website, then to this chapter's *Online Portfolio Activities*. Complete the suggested activities.

Important Concepts

caring *(p. 396)*
classroom climate *(p. 401)*
high-collective-efficacy school *(p. 394)*
introductory focus *(p. 405)*
involvement *(p. 408)*
learning-focused environments *(p. 388)*
open-ended questions *(p. 408)*

performance-focused environments *(p. 388)*
personal teaching efficacy *(p. 393)*
personalization *(p. 407)*
self-fulfilling prophecy *(p. 398)*
self-regulation *(p. 389)*
task comprehension *(p. 403)*

Chapter Outline

Creating Productive Learning Environments

Classroom Management

12

Judy Harris's ninth-grade geography class was involved in a cultural unit on the Middle East.

As Ginger entered the room, she saw a large map projected high on the screen at the front of the room. She quickly slid into her seat just as the bell stopped ringing. Most students had already begun studying the map and the accompanying directions on the chalkboard: *Identify the longitude and latitude of Cairo and Damascus.*

Judy took roll and handed back a set of papers as students busied themselves with the task. She also collected homework by having the students pass their papers to the front of each row then to the left, so that the papers arrived at the desk directly in front of Judy's.

She waited a moment for students to finish, then pulled down another large map in the front of the classroom.

"We've been studying the Middle East, and you just identified Damascus here in Syria," she began, pointing at the map. "Now, think for a moment and make a prediction about the climate in Damascus. . . . Bernice?"

Judy walked down one of the rows.

"Damascus is about 34 North latitude, I think," Bernice replied.

As soon as Judy walked past him, Darren reached across the aisle and tapped Kendra on the shoulder with his pencil. The 32 students were squeezed into a room designed for 24, so the aisles were narrow. Darren watched Judy's back from the corner of his eye.

"Stop it, Darren," Kendra muttered, swiping at him with her hand.

Judy turned, came back up the aisle, placed her hand on Darren's shoulder, and continued, "Good, Bernice. It's very close to 34."

Standing next to Darren, she asked, "What would that indicate about its temperature at this time of the year? . . . Darren?" She looked directly at Darren.

"I'm not sure."

"Warmer or colder than here?"

"Warmer, I think."

"Okay. Good prediction, Darren. And why might that be the case? . . . Jim?"

"Move up here," Judy said quietly to Rachel, who had been whispering and passing notes to Deborah across the aisle. Judy nodded to a desk at the front of the room as she waited for Jim to answer.

"What did I do?" Rachel protested.

Judy leaned over Rachel's desk and pointed to a rule displayed on a poster and said, "When we talked about our rules at the beginning of the year, we agreed that it was important to listen when other people are talking."

> Listen when someone else is talking.
> Raise your hand for permission to speak.
> Leave your desk only when given permission.
> Bring all needed materials to class each day.
> Treat your classmates with courtesy and respect.

"Quickly, now." She motioned to the desk.

"Damascus is south of us and also in a desert," Jim responded.

"I wasn't doing anything," Rachel protested.

"We don't learn as much when people aren't paying attention, and I'm uncomfortable when my class isn't learning. Please move quickly now," Judy said evenly, looking Rachel in the eye.

"Good analysis, Jim. Now let's look at Cairo," she continued as she watched Rachel move to the new desk.

From the 1960s until the present, national Gallup polls have identified classroom management as one of the most challenging problems teachers face. In 2002, 76% of those polled said discipline was a very or somewhat serious problem in U.S. schools (L. Rose & Gallup, 2002). It's the primary concern of beginning teachers (L. Rose & Gallup, 1999), and disruptive students are an important source of stress for all teachers (Abel & Sewell, 1999). Nearly half of the teachers who leave the profession during the first 3 years do so because of problems with managing students (Curwin, 1992), and management is a primary reason teachers leave urban classrooms (L. Weiner, 2002).

Because of highly publicized incidents of school violence, classroom management has also been a major concern of policy makers, parents, and the public at large (Elam & Rose, 1995). Although incidents of school violence arouse fear and concern, they are rare; in contrast, teachers deal daily with class disruptions and rule infractions. Our goal in writing this chapter is to help teachers master the day-to-day job of establishing and maintaining orderly, learning-focused classrooms.

After you've completed your study of this chapter, you should be able to

- Explain how instruction and classroom management contribute to productive learning environments
- Describe how cognitive approaches to classroom management develop learner responsibility
- Explain how effective planning can prevent management problems
- Identify differences between cognitive and behavioral approaches to management
- Describe how effective intervention techniques can eliminate management problems

Classroom Management: A Definition

Advice to beginning teachers about classroom management was once based on either untested theories or testimonials like "Don't smile until Christmas" (Good & Brophy, 2000). Fortunately, this situation has changed, and a large body of research has emerged to guide teachers as they tackle the task of establishing and maintaining productive and orderly classrooms.

Some of the earliest research on classroom management was done by Jacob Kounin (1970), who concluded that the key to orderly classrooms is the teacher's ability to prevent problems from occurring in the first place, rather than handling misbehavior once it happens. Kounin's findings have been consistently corroborated over the years (Freiberg, 1999a).

Kounin's research was important because it helped teachers understand the difference between **classroom management,** *teachers' strategies that create and maintain an orderly learning environment,* and **discipline,** *teachers' responses to student misbehavior.* Expert teachers place primary emphasis on management, which dramatically reduces their required efforts in the area of discipline.

Commonly overlooked in discussions of classroom management is the role of effective instruction. It is virtually impossible to maintain an orderly classroom in the absence of good teaching, and vice versa (Doyle, 1986). (We examine basic principles of good teaching in Chapter 13). To emphasize this important relationship, we focus on the concept of **productive learning environment,** *a classroom or school environment that is orderly and focuses on learning.* In it students feel safe, both physically and emotionally, and the day-to-day routines—as well as the values, expectations, learning experiences, and rules and procedures—are designed to help students learn as much as possible (Tishman et al., 1995).

The relationship between classroom management and learning is well documented. A comprehensive review of research concluded, "Effective classroom management has been shown to increase student engagement, decrease disruptive behaviors, and enhance use of instructional time, all of which result in improved student achievement" (Wang et al., 1993, p. 262). Additional research has identified safe and orderly classrooms as essential components of an effective school (Barth, 2002; S. Purkey & Smith, 1983).

Effective management also increases learner motivation (Radd, 1998). As you saw in Chapter 11, order and safety are essential for motivation, and students feel a greater sense of autonomy and control in orderly environments (McLaughlin, 1994).

12.1
Identify at least one way in which orderly classrooms contribute to learning and at least one way in which they contribute to motivation. Explain your reasoning.

Classroom Management and the Complexities of the Classroom

Why is classroom management so challenging for teachers? Let's look at two teachers wrestling with management issues.

Ken, an elementary teacher in a third/fourth grade split classroom, shared this incident in his teaching journal:

> *March 3: My class is sitting in a circle. I look up and notice one of the girls, Sylvia, is crying. Joey, she claims, has called her a fat jerk. The rest of the students all look at me to watch my response. I consider the alternatives: send Joey to hallway and talk to him in a few minutes; have Joey sit next to me; ask Joey to apologize; direct Sylvia to get a thick skin; ask Sylvia, "How can you solve this problem?"; send Joey to principal; have Joey write an apology letter; ask Joey, "Why did you do this?"; ignore the situation completely; keep Sylvia and Joey in for recess for dialogue; put Joey's name on board; yell at Joey; send Sylvia and Joey in hallway to work out problem; tell them to return to their seats and write in journals about problem.*
>
> *It took me about 10 seconds to run through these alternatives, and after each one I thought of reasons why it wasn't a good idea. By the time I look up at Sylvia after this brief introspection, she had stopped crying and was chattering away with a friend about something else. On the surface, the problem had gone away. (Winograd, 1998, p. 296)*

Kerry, a middle school English teacher, knew that her students would have difficulty settling down the first day after a four day holiday, . . . and she was right. They chatted excitedly about their weekends and showed one another items they had brought from home, as she urged them to quiet down. Finally, she got them settled and began the day's lesson, but it was a struggle to keep their attention.

The struggle continued throughout the day. . . . By afternoon she was nearly frazzled; the students were winning. Seventh period finally arrived, and the end of the day was within sight. Announcements from the office were supposed to begin the period, but they often came late, so teachers never knew quite when to begin class. Kerry waited, while the students chattered. Finally the announcements were completed and she gave the students a quiz on a movie they had seen. They were quiet during the quiz, but the noise level went up as soon as they were finished. The team leader, whose class was also noisy, walked by and commented, "It's so noisy in here today, I'm going crazy myself!" When the buzzer finally sounded, indicating day's end, Kerry had "had it"; rather than hold them after class as she had threatened earlier, she let them go, just to get rid of them.

It was, in Kerry's words, a day that nearly drove her "crazy." (Bullough, 1989, p. 73)

These vignettes both illustrate the sometimes bewildering world of classroom management. Researchers studying management tasks in classrooms have identified several characteristics of classroom events that make them complex and demanding (Doyle, 1986). They found that classroom events are

- Multidimensional and simultaneous: Large numbers of events and tasks occur at the same time.
- Immediate: Classroom events occur rapidly.
- Unpredictable: Classroom events often take unexpected turns.
- Public: Observers' perceptions of teachers' actions can have unintended consequences.

Let's look at each characteristic.

Classrooms Events Are Multidimensional and Simultaneous. Imagine teaching in a classroom right now. At one level, you are expected to maintain order, attract and keep students' attention, and keep them involved in a learning activity. You might also have to deal with a minor disruption without losing the flow of the lesson, acknowledge a student who requests a bathroom break, and respond to the intercom. At other times you work with a small group while monitoring the rest of the class doing seat work. You keep track of students who are being pulled out of class for varying reasons. These events may be multidimensional, and they often occur simultaneously.

Classrooms Events Are Immediate. Things happen quickly in classrooms, and teachers make somewhere between 800 and 1500 decisions every day (P. Jackson, 1968; Murray, 1986). Beyond the sheer numbers, the fact that many of the decisions need to be made

12.2
Using your understanding of information processing as a basis, explain why the multidimensional and simultaneous nature of classroom events makes classrooms more demanding for beginning than for veteran teachers.

right now adds to the demands on the teacher. Sylvia is crying; Ken needs to do something immediately. The intercom hums; should Kerry start or wait? One of your students pokes another one; do you intervene, or do you ignore it? The students seem confused; what should you do? The need to make nearly split second decisions can be almost overwhelming, particularly for beginning teachers.

Classroom Events Are Unpredictable.

> Diana Miller, a first-grade teacher, wanted to involve her students in a lesson based on a story they had read about shoes, so she brought a shoe into class. Pulling it out of a bag, she began, "What can you tell me about this shoe?"
> "It's red," Mike responded.
> The shoe was black; there was no sign of red anywhere!

12.3
How does the concept of *predictability* relate to Piaget's concept of *equilibrium?* What implications does predictability have for classroom management?

Every teacher plans, and the most effective teachers try to anticipate as many contingencies as possible. Diana had planned carefully, even bringing a real shoe to class. It is impossible to plan for a response like Mike's, however, just as it was impossible for Ken and Kerry to plan for all the events that occurred in their classes. Students and classroom events are often unpredictable, and expert teachers get used to expecting the unexpected. The unpredictable nature of classrooms increases their complexity and challenge.

Classroom Events Are Public.   When we teach, we teach in front of people. In a sense, we are on a stage. Teachers' triumphs and mistakes occur in the public arena for all to see. And mistakes are inevitable. One of your authors, in his first year of teaching, had the following experience:

> I was having a rough time quieting my class as they worked on an assignment. After several futile attempts, I said loudly, "All right, this is it! I don't want to hear one more peep out of this class!"
>
> There was momentary silence, but then from behind the cover of a held-up textbook came a squeaky "Peep." The class watched and waited to see what was going to happen. Finally, I smiled and said, "Very funny. Now let's get down to work." This seemed to break the ice, and the students finally settled down.

Your author learned an important lesson about public pronouncements, which may have unintended—and widespread—consequences. For example, if Ken chose to ignore Joey calling Syvia a fat jerk, it might have communicated to the class that verbally abusing one another was acceptable. On the other hand, what if Ken admonished Joey and later found out that Sylvia was mistaken about what he said? The admonishment might have given the message that a simple accusation was enough to get someone into trouble. These undesirable consequences could have affected the entire class. The public nature of teaching adds to its complexity.

Cognitive Approaches to Management: Developing Learner Responsibility

How should teachers respond to the complexity and demands of teaching? What should be your overriding goal in designing a management system? Cognitive psychology provides some answers.

Cognitive approaches to management emphasize creation of orderly classrooms through the development of learner understanding. The goal in a cognitive approach to management is for students to understand the need for a productive learning environment and accept responsibility for their part in creating one. When a cognitive

Classroom management is made more complex by the multidimensional, simultaneous, immediate, unpredictable, and public aspects of classroom events.

approach is effectively implemented, students obey rules because they view themselves as responsible persons and because it makes sense to do so (as opposed to obeying rules merely because they exist). Teachers promote this orientation by teaching responsibility and placing major emphasis on the reasons for rules and procedures. The link between rules, procedures, order, and learning is clearly understood by all.

Cognitive approaches to management are grounded in both information processing and constructivism. With respect to information processing, management contributes to metacognition and self-regulation by being "one vehicle for the enhancement of student self-understanding, self-evaluation, and the internalization of self-control" (McCaslin & Good, 1992, p. 8). With respect to constructivism, learners construct their own understanding of rules and procedures, just as they construct understanding of any topic. They also construct understanding of what responsibility means, why rules and procedures are necessary, and their role in contributing to productive learning environments. This understanding evolves from discussions of the reasons for rules and procedures and from analyzing examples of appropriate and inappropriate behavior.

Cognitive approaches to management are both sensible and practical. Learners are more likely to obey rules when they understand the reasons for them, one of which is to protect their rights and the rights of others. This responsibility orientation can also contribute to ethical thinking and character development (DeVries & Zan, 1995; Kohn, 1996a). For instance, in time Joey may choose to not call a classmate a fat jerk, because he understands that it hurts feelings, and hurting classmates' feelings is unacceptable. As he becomes more responsible, the complexity of the learning environment and the demands on his teacher are reduced. And he has made an important advance in his personal development. Such gains don't happen overnight. With time and consistency, however, a cognitive approach to management will make a teacher's job easier and contribute to students' development as people.

12.4
A student accepts the responsibility for obeying a rule, reasoning that it is necessary to protect her and her peers' rights. At which of Kohlberg's stages of moral development is the student reasoning? (See Chapter 3.) Explain.

Planning for Effective Classroom Management

In some classrooms, management is nearly invisible. The atmosphere is calm but not rigid, movement and interaction are comfortable, and students work quietly. Teachers give few directions that focus on behavior, they reprimand students infrequently, and the reprimands rarely intrude on learning. Are these ideal situations? Of course. Are they impossible to achieve? No.

Obviously, some classes are tougher to manage than others, and in a few cases it may be difficult to reach the ideals just described. In most instances, however, teachers can create an orderly classroom. Doing so requires careful planning, and beginning teachers often underestimate the amount of time and energy it takes (Bullough, 1989; C. Weinstein, Woolfolk, Dittmeier, & Shankar, 1994).

The cornerstone of effective management is a clearly understood and consistently monitored set of rules and procedures that prevents management problems before they occur (Emmer et al., 2003; Evertson et al., 2003). Prevention is essential; experts estimate that it is 80% of an effective management system (Freiberg, 1999b). Before planning rules and procedures, teachers must consider both the characteristics of their students and the physical environment of their classrooms. The relationship among these factors is illustrated in Figure 12.1.

Figure 12.1 Planning for orderly classrooms

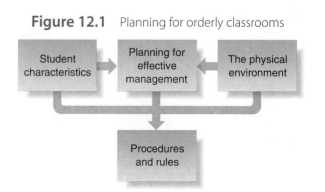

Student Characteristics

Sam Cramer had completed his first semester's clinical work in a high school, and it had been a terrific experience. Except for occasional rough spots, his lessons had gone well. Students were interested and responsive. Management was not a problem.

Table 12.1 Learner characteristics affecting classroom management

Stage	Student Characteristics
Stage 1: Kindergarten through grade 2	• Are compliant, eager to please teachers • Have short attention span, tire easily • Are restless, wander around room • Require close supervision • Break rules because they forget • Need rules and procedures to be explicitly taught, practiced, and reinforced
Stage 2: Grades 3 through 6	• Are increasingly independent, but still like attention and affection from teachers • Respond well to concrete incentives (e.g., stickers, free time), as well as praise and recognition • Understand need for rules and accept consequences; enjoy participating in rule-making process • Know how far they can push • Need rules to be reviewed and consistently and impartially enforced
Stage 3: Grades 7 through 9	• Attempt to test independence; are sometimes rebellious and capricious • Need firm foundation of stability; explicit boundaries and predictable outcomes are critical • Need rules clearly stated and administered
Stage 4: Grades 10 and above	• Behave more stably than in previous stage • Communicate effectively adult to adult • Respond to clear rationales for rules

Source: Learning From Teaching: A Developmental Perspective, by J. Brophy and C. Evertson, 1976, Boston: Allyn & Bacon. Copyright 1976 by Allyn & Bacon. Adapted with permission.

For his second semester, Sam moved to a middle school. It seemed like a different planet. Students were bubbling with excess energy. Giggling, whispering, and note passing were constant distractions. His first lesson was a disaster. The kids wouldn't let him teach!

From your study of Chapters 2 and 3, you know that students think, act, and feel differently at different stages of development. As Sam learned the hard way, students at different grade levels vary in the ways they interpret and respond to rules and procedures, and teachers must anticipate these differences as they plan (Charles, 1999). Descriptions of developmental differences that influence management are outlined in Table 12.1.

Keep in mind that these are general characteristics and individual students vary. As a pattern, however, we see increasing independence and self-regulation as learners develop. Their affection for teachers decreases, and they become more likely to question authority. This trend peaks in early adolescence, making classroom management at this age challenging (Freiberg, 1999a). During the high school years, students begin to behave like young adults and respond well to being treated as such. Students of all ages, however, need the emotional security of knowing that their teachers are genuinely interested in them and sincerely care about their learning.

The Physical Environment

"I can't see the board."

"Fred tripped me."

"What? I can't hear."

Classrooms need to be designed to address issues of visibility, accessibility, and distractibility.

Few classrooms are ideal. Classes are too large, storage space is limited, and maps or overhead projector screens cover the chalkboard. Arranging desks and furnishings is often a compromise between what teachers would like and what is possible. Nevertheless, in their planning teachers should consider the following factors to make the most of the physical environment:

- *Visibility.* The room must be arranged so that all students can see the chalkboard, overhead projector, or other displays.
- *Accessibility.* The room should be designed so that access to high-traffic areas, such as the pencil sharpener and places students put papers, are kept clear and separated from each other.
- *Distractibility.* Desks should be arranged so that potential distractions, such as movement visible through doors and windows, are minimized.

No single arrangement works for all situations. One study found that behavior improved when learners were seated in rows (N. Bennett & Blundel, 1983), but another found that a semicircle was most effective for discussions (Rosenfield, Lambert, & Black, 1985). Teachers should think about their room arrangement when they plan, changing it with their goals and experimenting to see what works best for them.

12.5
Beginning teachers' writing on the board is often too small for students—particularly those at the back of the room—to see, yet the teachers seem to be unaware of this possibility. Using cognitive views of learning (Chapter 7) as a basis, explain why beginning teachers may have this tendency.

Rules and Procedures: Cornerstones of an Effective Management System

Having considered your students' characteristics and your physical environment, you are ready to plan procedures and rules for your classroom. **Procedures** are *the steps for the routines students follow in their daily learning activities,* such as how they turn in papers, sharpen pencils, and make transitions from one activity to another.

As an example, consider the things Judy's students did, in the opening case study. When she asked students to turn in their homework, they passed the papers forward, adding to each stack without being told to do so, and they passed the piles so they ended up near Judy's desk. It was a well-practiced procedure that saved instructional time and involved little teacher effort.

Expert teachers plan and teach procedures until they become routines that students follow automatically. These routines provide a sense of regularity and equilibrium for both students and teachers (Borko & Putnam, 1996). For example, teaching students what they are expected to do after completing assignments and how late or missing homework will be handled are essential procedures for all classrooms. They may seem minor, but they affect the efficiency of the classroom and communicate that learning is the primary purpose of school.

Rules are *descriptions of standards for acceptable classroom behavior,* such as "Listen when someone else is talking." Research confirms the value of rules in creating productive learning environments: "Evidence exists indicating that clear, reasonable rules, fairly and consistently enforced, not only can reduce behavior problems that interfere with learning but also can promote a feeling of pride and responsibility in the school community" (S. Purkey & Smith, 1983, p. 445). Perhaps surprisingly, students also see the articulation and enforcement of rules that set clear standards of behavior "as evidence that the teacher cares about them" (Brophy, 1998, p. 23).

12.6
We said that clearly stated rules and procedures provide behavioral guidelines for students. Explicitly stating these relates to what concept from your study of development in Chapter 2?

Creating and Teaching Rules: Instructional Strategies

A cognitive approach to management requires that learners understand the reasons behind rules so that they can accept responsibility for their own behavior. The following principles can guide teachers in their efforts to promote this understanding:

- State rules positively.
- Minimize the number of rules.

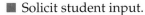

- Solicit student input.
- Emphasize rationales for rules.
- Teach rules as concepts.
- Monitor rules throughout the school year.

To see a video clip of a teacher helping her students understand the reasons behind rules, go to the Companion Website at *www.prenhall.com/eggen*, then to this chapter's *Classrooms on the Web* module. Click on *Video Clip 12.1*.

Let's see how the principles guide the following teachers as they work with their students.

About 20 minutes were left in the period, so English teacher Deanna McDonald told her eighth graders it was time for the class meeting, as she did during all of her classes on Fridays.

"I want to review our rules for a few minutes today," she began. "We've been doing a very good job in here, but when we begin our study of *To Kill a Mockingbird* next week we'll be involved in a lot of discussion. I'd like to talk about what we should be doing to learn as much as possible from our discussions. . . . Go ahead and offer some ideas."

". . . Well, we should listen," Jonique offered after pausing for several seconds.

"Sure, that makes sense. . . . What else, anyone?"

"How about not interrupt. . . . Wait until they finish?" James added after several more seconds.

"That also makes sense. . . . So, suppose we say, 'Listen attentively until a person is finished.' How does that sound?"

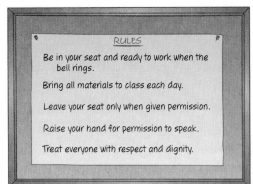

RULES

Be in your seat and ready to work when the bell rings.

Bring all materials to class each day.

Leave your seat only when given permission.

Raise your hand for permission to speak.

Treat everyone with respect and dignity.

Most of the students nodded affirmatively, so Deanna wrote *Listen attentively until a person is finished* on the chalkboard.

"That adds one more rule to our original five," Deanna went on, referring to the class rules posted on the bulletin board.

"And," she continued, "Listening attentively is a part of treating everyone with respect and dignity, so we're actually refining our last rule.

"Now why is this rule so important? . . . Barry?"

"Well . . . it's rude if we don't listen to each other or if we interrupt when someone is talking."

"Of course," Deanna smiled. "What's the very most important reason?"

Hearing no response after a few seconds, she went on, "Why are we here? . . . What's the purpose of school?"

"To learn stuff," Antonio volunteered.

"Absolutely, that's what school's all about. We're here to learn. You learn, I learn, we all learn, and we learn less if we don't listen.

"Plus," she added, "it's important to me that you all participate. Each of you has important ideas to bring to the discussions, and I want you all to have a chance to share those ideas.

"And ultimately, what happens when you leave here?"

"We're responsible for ourselves," Yolanda responded knowingly. "You keep reminding us that no one can really make us do anything. . . . We're the ones in control of what we do."

"That's right, Yolanda," Deanna smiled and nodded with emphasis. "And that, together with being here to learn, is really what we're all about. Out in the world, it's up to us. That's why I'm not going to hold a stick over your head. I want you to listen and be polite because you believe it's important for learning and treating each other well, not because I'll punish you if you aren't.

"But," she continued, "what should you do if you really disagree with something someone says? . . . Kyle?"

"Raise our hand and then tell them?" Kyle answered with a question in his voice.

"Exactly, Kyle. Disagreeing is perfectly okay. One of the reasons we have discussions is to share different perspectives. But we have to listen to the other person before we can disagree.

"Keep this idea in mind, and we'll practice it when we start on *To Kill a Mockingbird* on Monday. . . . I'll remind you if you happen to slip a little."

Let's take a closer look at Deanna's attempts to create effective rules. The first two instructional principles are illustrated in the rules themselves: The rules were stated positively and small in number (there were six rules after the class added one). Rules stated positively specify desired behavior; stated negatively they identify only what students are not to do. To behave responsibly, students must be aware of the rules, and the more they have to remember, the more difficult this is. One of the most common reasons students break rules is that they simply forget them!

Table 12.2 contains additional examples of rules at the elementary, middle, and secondary levels. These are merely examples, and you must decide what rules will work best for you.

The third principle was illustrated when Deanna said, "I'd like to talk about what we should be doing to learn as much as possible from our discussions. . . . Go ahead and offer some ideas." This request solicited the students' input into their sixth rule. Being asked for input promotes students' feelings of ownership and autonomy, it increases the likelihood that they will obey the rules, and it promotes moral development by treating students as moral thinkers (DeVries & Zan, 1995; Kohn, 1996a).

Applying the fourth, and perhaps most important, principle, Deanna strongly emphasized that each of the rules was designed to promote learning—she provided the rationale for the rules. Students are more likely to accept a rule, even when they disagree with it, if they understand why the rule is important. Rationales also contribute to students' feelings that the world is a sensible place and rules exist for reasons. As a result, students' feelings of control and their sense of equilibrium are enhanced.

We see that Deanna used a classroom meeting as a forum for discussing rules and soliciting student input, a process also endorsed by classroom management experts (Glasser, 1985; Nelson, Lott, & Glenn, 1997). These meetings can be used to first establish and then monitor and improve classroom rules. They help create a sense of ownership in students, and they contribute to the development of responsibility and self-regulation.

Does involving students in forming classroom rules work? One middle school teacher reported the following:

> I began with my first-period class. We started slowly, with my asking them about what it would take for the class to work for them. I then told them what it would take for the class to work for me. I was amazed at the overlap. They wanted to know up front what I expected in terms of tests, quantity and quality of work, late assignments, talking in class, and amount and how often they would have homework, where they could sit, grading, and whether classroom participation counted. We talked about the best classes and the

Classroom rules and procedures establish standards for behaviors that allow learning to take place.

To see another middle school teacher's description of soliciting students' input into the rule-making process, go to the Companion Website at *www.prenhall.com/eggen*, then to this chapter's *Additional Content* module.

Table 12.2 Examples of teachers' rules

First-Grade Teacher	Seventh-Grade Teacher	Tenth-Grade Teacher
• We raise our hands before speaking. • We leave our seats only when given permission by the teacher. • We stand politely in line at all times. • We keep our hands to ourselves. • We listen when someone else is talking.	• Be in your seat and quiet when the bell rings. • Follow directions the first time they're given. • Bring covered textbooks, notebook, pen, pencils, and planner to class every day. • Raise your hand for permission to speak or to leave your seat. • Keep hands, feet, and objects to yourself. • Leave class only when dismissed by the teacher. • Do all grooming outside of class.	• Be in your seat before the bell rings. • Stay in your seat at all times. • Bring all materials daily. This includes your book, notebook, pen/pencil, and paper. • Give your full attention to others in discussions, and wait your turn to speak. • Leave when I dismiss you, not when the bell rings.

worst classes. We talked about respect and the need to respect ideas and each other, to listen to and be willing to be an active participant without [verbally] running over other people in the class or being run over. . . . Well, this was five months ago and I was amazed at the level of cooperation. I am well ahead of last year in the curriculum; we have class meetings once a week to see how things are going and adjust as needed. We created a classroom constitution and had a constitutional convention when we felt it needed to be changed. I didn't believe it would make a difference; the students really surprised me with their level of maturity and responsibility and I surprised myself with my own willingness to change. This has been a great year and I am sorry to see it end. (Freiberg, 1999c, p. 169)

Although involving students in classroom management does not solve all management problems, it is an important first step in gaining students' cooperation.

Teaching Rules

The fifth instructional principle, "Teach rules as concepts," reminds us of the importance of students understanding our rules. How can we teach rules as concepts? Let's see how Martha Oakes, a first-grade teacher, attempted to get her students to understand how to put away worksheets.

To see a video clip of an elementary teacher reviewing her rules, go to the Companion Website at *www.prenhall.com/eggen*, then to this chapter's *Classrooms on the Web* module. Click on *Video Clip 12.2*.

> I put each of their names, as well as my own, on a cubby hole on the wall of my room. To demonstrate the process, I did a very short worksheet myself and literally walked it over and put it in my storage spot, talking aloud as I went: "I'm finished with my worksheet. . . . What do I do now? . . . I need to put it in my cubby hole. If I don't put it there, my teacher can't check it, so it's very important. . . . Now, I start on the next assignment."
>
> Then I gave my students the worksheet, directing them to take it to their cubbies, quietly and individually, as soon as they were finished. After they had done that, we spent a few minutes discussing the reasons for taking the finished work to the cubbies immediately, not touching or talking to anyone as they move to the cubbies and back to their desks, and starting right back to work. Then I gave them another worksheet, asked them what they were going to do and why, and had them do it. We then spent a few more minutes talking about what might happen if we didn't put papers where they belong. I asked them whether they had ever lost anything and how this was similar.
>
> Now we have a class meeting nearly every day just before we leave for the day. We discuss classroom life and offer suggestions for improving our classroom. Some people might be skeptical about whether or not first graders can handle meetings like this, but they can. This is also one way I help them keep the procedures fresh in their minds.

Martha's approach illustrates concept learning. Her modeling, the verbalizing of her thinking, and the students actually taking their worksheets to their cubby holes provided the concrete examples they needed to construct their understanding of the process, just as they would use examples to construct their understanding of any concept (Brophy, 1999; Cassady, 1999). Being specific and concrete was essential for Martha's students because they were first graders; simply explaining how they were to deposit their papers wouldn't have been developmentally effective.

To understand concepts, learners of all ages need examples. Even Deanna's students, who were eighth graders, needed examples and nonexamples of "Treating everyone with respect and dignity," for instance, to fully understand what the rule meant. The more thoroughly students understand rules and the reasons for them, the more likely they are to obey the rules.

12.7
On the basis of on our discussion of concept teaching in Chapter 9, explain specifically why the way Martha taught her procedures was effective.

Beginning the School Year

The first few days of the school year are crucial to classroom management, because they create lasting impressions. In fact, research consistently confirms that patterns of behavior for the year are established in these first days (Emmer et al., 2003; Evertson et al., 2003). Effective teachers realize this and are ready to go from the first bell of the first day. Let's look at two teachers as they begin the school year.

Vicki Williams was organizing her handouts on the first day of class. Her eighth graders came into the room; some took their seats, while others milled around, talking in small groups. As the bell rang, she looked up and said over the hum of the students, "Everyone take your seats, please," and she turned back to finish organizing her materials.

Donnell Alexander was waiting at the door for her eighth graders with prepared handouts. As students came in, she distributed the handouts and said, "Take your seats quickly, please. You'll find your name on the desk. The bell is going to ring in less than a minute, and everyone needs to be at his or her desk and quiet when it does. Please read the handout while you're waiting." She was standing at the front of the room, surveying the class as the bell rang. When it stopped, Donnell began, "Good morning, everyone."

In these first few minutes, Vicki's and Donnell's students learned some important ideas. From Vicki they learned, "Being in your seat at the beginning of the period isn't important," whereas Donnell's message was, "Be ready to start when the bell rings." Students quickly understand these differences, and unless Vicki changes her pattern, she will soon have problems—not dramatic perhaps, but chronic and low grade that, like nagging sniffles, won't go away. These kinds of problems cause more teacher stress and fatigue than any other.

Guidelines for beginning the first few days of school are summarized in Table 12.3.

During the first few days of the school year, teachers establish both relationships with students as well as expectations for behavior.

Monitoring Rules

Finally, our sixth instructional principle, "Monitor rules throughout the school year," reminds us of the need to work on management throughout the school year. No matter how good a job you do of teaching rules, monitoring and discussing them will be necessary over time (Emmer et al., 2003; Evertson et al., 2003). Effective teachers react to misbehavior immediately, refer students to the rule that was broken, and discuss why the rule is important and the behavior inappropriate. As an example, let's look again at Judy Harris's work with her students.

To see a video clip of a classroom teacher monitoring her students during seat work, go to the Companion Website at *www.prenhall.com/eggen*, then to this chapter's *Classrooms on the Web* module. Click on *Video Clip 12.3*.

Table 12.3 Guidelines for beginning the school year

Guideline	Examples
Establish expectations	• Explain requirements and grading systems, particularly with older students.
	• Emphasize that learning and classroom order are interdependent.
Plan structured instruction	• Plan with extra care during this period.
	• Conduct eye-catching and motivating activities.
	• Use the first few days to assess learners' skills and background knowledge.
	• Use large- rather than small-group instruction.
	• Minimize transitions from one activity to another.
Teach rules and procedures	• Begin teaching rules and procedures the first day.
	• Frequently discuss and practice rules and procedures during the first few days.
	• Intervene and discuss every infraction of rules.
Begin communication with parents	• Send a letter to parents that states positive expectations for the year.
	• Call parents after the first or second day to nip potential problems in the bud.

Listen when someone else is talking.
Raise your hand for permission to speak.
Leave your desk only when given permission.
Bring all needed materials to class each day.
Treat your classmates with courtesy and respect.

Judy monitored her rules throughout the school year.

Judy: (In response to Rachel's whispering and note passing) Move up here.

Rachel: What did I do?

Judy: (Pointing to the rule) When we talked about our rules at the beginning of the year, we agreed that it was important to listen when other people are talking.

This was effective rule monitoring because Judy called Rachel's attention to the rule and reminded her that the class agreed it was important. She treated the rule as a social contract—modeling moral reasoning at Kohlberg's Stage 5 (see Chapter 3). Other students will obey rules simply because they know the teacher monitors them. Understanding, combined with the knowledge that rules are being monitored, prevents many off-task and disruptive behaviors.

We want to note here that although our discussion has focused on rules, the instructional principles also apply to procedures. Providing reasons for procedures allows students to understand not only what to do but also how their actions contribute to a productive learning environment.

12.8

Using your understanding of information processing as a basis, explain why, from a teacher's perspective, well-established rules and procedures are so important.

Classroom Connections

Planning for Effective Classroom Management

1. Carefully plan and communicate your classroom procedures and rules at the beginning of the school year.
   - *Elementary:* A third-grade teacher prepares and shares a handout for his students and their parents that describes homework procedures, how grades are determined, and how work is made up when a student is absent.
   - *Middle School:* A seventh-grade math teacher prepares a short written list of rules before she starts class on the first day. She then asks students to suggest additional rules that will help make the classroom a positive place to learn.
   - *High School:* A tenth-grade English teacher explains at the beginning of the year how writing drafts will be handled and how peer comments will be used to improve essays. He displays the procedure for peer reviews on the overhead and refers to it each time the class completes writing assignments.

2. Consider the developmental level of your students and your physical environment in preparing and teaching rules and procedures.
   - *Elementary:* At the beginning of the school year, a first-grade teacher takes a few minutes each day to review her procedure for entering class in the morning. She continues until the students follow it without directions.
   - *Middle School:* To prevent distractions, a sixth-grade teacher arranges students' desks so that they are facing away from the classroom window, which looks out on the physical education field.
   - *High School:* A geometry teacher has the custodian move his projection screen into the corner of the room so that it doesn't cover the chalkboard, which he uses to have students present proofs to the class.

Making Rules and Procedures Work

3. Be prepared for the first day of class. Explain and have students practice your classroom procedures.
   - *Elementary:* A kindergarten teacher greets the children as they come to the door of her room. She takes each student by the hand and walks to a seat at a table with the student's name on it. Crayons and other materials are waiting, which students use until everyone arrives.
   - *Middle School:* An eighth-grade history teacher is standing at the door as the students file into the room. "Move to your seats quickly please," he says, "and begin reading the paper that's on your desk. We'll begin discussing it as soon as the bell rings."
   - *High School:* A chemistry teacher takes a full class period to describe and explain safe lab procedures. She distributes a handout describing them to each student, models correct procedures, and explains the reasons behind each. She carefully monitors the students as they work in the lab, reminding them about the importance of safety.

Communication with Parents

Learning is a cooperative venture, and teachers, students, and parents are in it together. In a comprehensive review of factors affecting student learning, researchers concluded the following:

> Because of the importance of the home environment to school learning, teachers must also develop strategies to increase parent involvement in their children's academic life. This means teachers should go beyond traditional once-a-year parent/teacher conferences and work with parents to see that learning is valued in the home. Teachers should encourage parents to be involved with their children's academic pursuits on a day-to-day basis, helping them with homework, monitoring television viewing, reading to their young children, and simply expressing the expectation that their children will achieve academic success. (Wang et al., 1993, pp. 278–279)

Home-school partnerships facilitate classroom management as well as promote higher achievement and motivation.

Communication with parents or other primary caregivers is not an appendage to teaching; rather, it is an integral part of all aspects of teaching and learning, including classroom management.

Benefits of Communication

Research indicates that students benefit from home-school cooperation in at least four ways:

- Higher long-term academic achievement
- More positive attitudes and behaviors
- Better attendance rates
- Greater willingness to do homework (C. Cameron & Lee, 1997; López & Scribner, 1999)

These outcomes likely result from parents' increased participation in school activities, their higher expectations for their children's achievement, and teachers' increased understanding of learners' home environments (C. Weinstein & Mignano, 1993). Determining how to respond to a student's disruptive behavior is easier, for example, when his teachers know that his mother or father has lost a job, his parents are going through a divorce, or there's a serious illness in the family.

Parents can also help reinforce classroom management plans. One teacher gave this report:

> I had this boy in my class who was extremely disruptive. He wouldn't work, kept "forgetting" his homework, distracted other children, wandered about the room. You name it; he did it. The three of us—the mother, the boy and I—talked about what we could do, and we decided to try a system of home rewards. We agreed that I would send a note home each day, reporting on the boy's behavior. For every week with at least three good notes, the mother added one Christmas present. In this way, what the child found under the tree on Christmas Day was directly dependent on his behavior. By Christmas, he had become so cooperative, I couldn't believe he was the same child! After Christmas, I observed some backsliding, so we all agreed to reverse the system: The mother took away one present each time a majority of the week's reports were negative. She didn't have to take many away! (Weinstein & Mignano, 1993, p. 226)

> **12.9**
> What concept from behaviorism is illustrated by giving the child a present for three good notes? What concept is illustrated when the child gets good notes to avoid losing his presents? Explain in each case. Identify one advantage and one disadvantage of the system.

Parent-teacher collaboration can have long-term benefits for teachers and students. For example, teachers who encourage parental involvement report more positive feelings about teaching and their school. They also have higher expectations for parents and rate them higher in helpfulness and follow-through (Epstein, 1996).

Parent involvement programs take many forms. Some of the most common are the following:

- Parent education—helps families understand child and adolescent development and how homes can contribute
- Communication—assists parents in understanding school goals and procedures
- Volunteerism—involves parents in supporting school programs
- Learning at home—teaches parents how to help their children with homework
- Community collaboration—involves parents in identifying community resources and making school policy decisions (Epstein, 2001)

Involving Parents: Instructional Strategies

Virtually all schools have formal communication channels, such as open houses (usually occurring within the first 2 weeks of the year when teachers introduce themselves and describe general guidelines and procedures); interim progress reports, which tell parents about their youngsters' achievements at the midpoint of each grading period; parent-teacher conferences; and, of course, report cards. Although these processes are schoolwide and necessary, as an individual teacher you can enhance existing communication processes. The following principles can guide your actions:

- Establish early communication links with parents and caregivers through an initial letter.
- Be proactive in maintaining communication links with the home.
- Emphasize positive accomplishments.

Let's see how the principles guide Joan Williams, a middle school English teacher, as she makes plans for her classroom.

Although Joan survived her first year of teaching, she vowed over the summer to do more to make her second year more productive and enjoyable. After discussing her first year with several veterans, she concluded that a letter sent home during the first week of class would not only explain her expectations but would involve parents in the process.

She prepared a draft of the letter and on the first day of class shared it with her students, walking them through it and explaining the importance of home-school links. She also asked for their suggestions on rules and procedures to incorporate into her letter. She then took her letter home, revised it, and brought a final copy to school the next day (see Figure 12.2). She made sure all the letters were signed and returned and followed up on those that weren't with phone calls.

Every 3 weeks throughout the year, Joan sent assignments and graded homework home for parents and caregivers to read and sign. She encouraged the parents to contact her if they had any questions about the packets.

During the evening, Joan periodically called parents to let them know about their children's progress. She tried to anticipate problems before they became serious; if students missed more than one assignment she called immediately, emphasizing her personal concern as well as the student's past accomplishments. She also made a point of sending home a note or phoning parents to report positive news—when a student went above and beyond requirements, overcame an obstacle, or showed uncommon kindness, for example.

Her second year wasn't perfect, but Joan felt a tangible difference from her first.

Let's take a closer look at Joan's attempts to involve parents. She applied the first principle by sending parents a letter within the first week of school. A letter home begins the communication process and establishes positive expectations at school and at home.

Joan's letter was effective for several other reasons:

- It expressed positive expectations, and it reminded parents that they are essential for their child's learning.

August 22, 2003

Dear Parents,

I am looking forward to a productive and exciting year, and I am writing this letter to encourage your involvement and support. You always have been and still are the most important people in your youngster's education. We cannot do the job without you.

For us to work together most effectively, some guidelines are necessary. With the students' help, we prepared the ones listed here. Please read this information carefully and sign where indicated. If you have any questions, please call me at Southside Middle School (441-5935) or at home (221-8403) in the evenings.

Sincerely,

Joan Williams

AS A PARENT, I WILL TRY MY BEST TO DO THE FOLLOWING:

1. I will ask my youngsters about school every day. (Evening meal is a good time.) I will ask them about what they're studying and try to learn about it.

2. I will provide a quiet time and place each evening for homework. I will set an example by also working at that time or reading while my youngster is working.

3. Instead of asking if their homework is finished, I will ask to see it. I will have them explain some of the information to see if they understand it.

    Parent's Signature _____

STUDENT SURVIVAL GUIDELINES:

1. I will be in class and seated when the bell rings.
2. I will follow directions the first time they are given.
3. I will bring covered textbook, notebook, paper, and two sharpened pencils to class each day.
4. I will raise my hand for permission to speak or leave my seat.
5. I will keep my hands, feet, and objects to myself.

HOMEWORK GUIDELINES:

1. Our motto is I WILL ALWAYS TRY. I WILL NEVER GIVE UP.
2. I will complete all assignments. If an assignment is not finished or ready when called for, I understand that I get no credit for it.
3. If I miss work because of an absence, it is my responsibility to come in before school (8:15–8:45) to make it up.
4. I know that I get one day to make up a test or turn in my work for each day I'm absent.
5. I understand that extra credit work is not given. If I do all the required work, extra credit isn't necessary.

    Student's Signature _____

Figure 12.2   Letter to parents

- It asked the parents to sign a contract committing to the support of their child's education.
- It specified class rules (described as "guidelines"), and it also outlined procedures for homework, absences, and extra credit.
- It asked students to sign a contract committing them to following the guidelines.
- It used correct grammar and punctuation.

Signatures can't ensure that parents and students will honor the contract, but they symbolize a commitment to working with the teacher and increase the likelihood that the parents and students will attempt to honor the commitment (Katz, 1999). Also, because students had input into the content of the letter, they felt ownership of the process and encouraged their parents to work with them in completing their homework.

The last item on the list bears special mention. The need for error-free written communication should go without saying, but teachers sometimes send home communications with spelling, grammar, or punctuation errors. Don't do it. First impressions are important and lasting. The letter creates a perception of your competence, and errors detract from your credibility (Raths, 2001), which will be important later in soliciting parental support.

Joan was also proactive in maintaining home-school communication, an application of our second principle. Early, positive communication helps get the year off to a good start, and continuing communication maintains the momentum. For example, Joan regularly sent packets of students' work home and asked parents to sign and return them. In addition to creating a concrete link between home and school, this practice gives parents an ongoing record of their child's learning.

One of the most powerful and positive ways to maintain communication is to call parents. When teachers allocate some of their personal time, usually in the evening, to call parents, they communicate caring better than any other way. Also, talking to a parent allows teachers to be specific in describing a student's needs and strengths and gives the teacher the opportunity to further solicit parental support. For example, if a student is missing assignments, the teacher can ask for an explanation and can also encourage the parents to more closely monitor their child's study habits.

Decisions about when to call parents about a problem is a matter of professional judgment. The question "To what extent does this issue influence learning?" is an effective guideline. For instance, a middle school student swearing in class is probably best handled by the teacher. On the other hand, if the student's swearing or other behaviors are disrupting the classroom environment, learning will be affected, and a call to parents is appropriate.

The last principle—"emphasize positive accomplishments"—refers to all types of communication with parents. When teachers call parents about a problem, they should try to describe accomplishments and progress too, as Joan did. But they should also initiate communication for the sole purpose of reporting good news, as Joan also did. All parents need reasons feel proud of their children, and the simple act of looking for those reasons can help teachers as well.

As it continues to expand, technology provides other channels for improving communication. For example, as they become more accessible, both voice mail and e-mail can be used to connect with busy parents (C. Cameron & Lee, 1997). In some schools, newsletters and other communications are being offered in electronic, as well as paper, form.

Communication with Parents: Accommodating Learner Diversity

Classrooms with large numbers of students from cultural minorities present unique communication challenges. Research indicates that "characteristics associated with lower parent participation in school activities included being Hispanic, African American, or Asian American; being of lower-socioeconomic status; having a child enrolled

12.10
Think about your study of motivation and needs in Chapter 10. For parents, which of the needs discussed in that chapter is most nearly met by a teacher's early and continuing communication? Explain.

in either special education or the English-as-a-second-language program" (Griffith, 1998, p. 53). In general, diversity tends to make encouraging parental involvement more challenging.

Economic, Cultural, and Language Barriers

What are some obstacles to greater parental involvement? Research identifies economics, culture, and language as barriers that can limit the school involvement of minority and low-SES parents.

Involvement takes time, and economic commitments often come first. For example, half the parents in one study indicated that their jobs prevented them from helping their youngsters with homework (Ellis, Dowdy, Graham, & Jones, 1992). Often parents lack economic resources (e.g., child care, transportation, and telephones) that would allow them to participate in school activities. Parents want to be involved in their children's schooling, but schools need to be flexible and provide help and encouragement.

Differences between home and school cultures can also create barriers (Delgado-Gaitan, 1992; Harry, 1992). Parents may have experienced schools that were very different from the ones their children attend, and some may have had negative school experiences. One researcher described the problem in this way:

> Underneath most parents is a student—someone who went to school, sometimes happily, sometimes unhappily. What often happens when the parent-as-adult returns to school, or has dealings with teachers, is that the parent as child/student returns. Many parents still enter school buildings flooded with old memories, angers, and disappointments. Their stomachs churn and flutter with butterflies, not because of what is happening today with their own children, but because of outdated memories and past behaviors. (Rich, 1987, p. 24)

These parents require a great deal of encouragement and support to become involved (D. Kaplan, Liu, & Kaplan, 2001).

Out of respect for teachers, many Asian and Latino parents hesitate to become involved in matters they believe are best handled by the school (Harry, 1992). This deference to authority implies, "You're the teacher; do what is best," but it can be misinterpreted as apathy by teachers.

Management style can also be a source of cultural conflict. A study of Puerto Rican families found that parents thought U.S. schools were too impersonal—that teachers didn't "worry about" their children enough. One parent explained, "In the U.S., the teachers care about the education of the child, but they don't care about the child himself and his problems" (Harry, 1992, p. 479). These parents wanted teachers to act more like parents, providing more warmth and structure for their children.

Language can be another barrier. Parents of bilingual students may not speak English, which leaves the child responsible for interpreting communications sent home by teachers. Homework poses a special problem because parents cannot interpret assignments or provide help (Delgado-Gaitan, 1992).

Schools compound the problem by using educational jargon when they send letters home. The problem is especially acute in special education, where legal and procedural safeguards can be bewildering. For example, studies indicate that parents often don't understand individualized education programs (IEPs) or even remember that they've signed one (Harry, 1992).

One solution to the language problem is a telephone network (Peña, 2000). Teachers ask bilingual parents to phone other parents, who can then assist in disseminating the message to others.

Involving Minority Parents

Many parents from cultural minorities feel ill-prepared to assist their children with school-related tasks, but when teachers offer parents specific strategies for working with their children, the home-school gap is narrowed (Gorman & Balter, 1997; Porche & Ross, 1999). Let's look at an example.

12.11
Explain "stomachs churn and flutter with butterflies," using classical conditioning as the basis for your explanation.

Nancy Collins, a middle school English teacher, had students who spoke five different native languages in her class. During the first 2 days of school, she prepared a letter to parents, and with the help of her students, she translated it into each of their native languages. The letter began by describing how pleased she was to have students from varying backgrounds in her class, saying that these backgrounds would enrich all her students' educations.

She continued with a short and simple list of procedures and encouraged the parents to support their children's efforts by

1. Asking their children about school and school work each night
2. Providing a quiet place to study for at least 90 minutes a night
3. Limiting television until homework assignments were finished
4. Asking to see samples of their children's work and grades they've received

She told them that the school was having an open house and the class with the highest attendance there would win a contest. She concluded the letter by reemphasizing that she was pleased to have so much diversity in her class. She asked parents to sign the letter and return it to the school.

The day before the open house, Nancy had each of her students compose a handwritten letter to their parents, asking them to attend the open house. Nancy wrote "Hoping to see you there" at the bottom of each note and signed it.

Nancy's letter accomplished at least three things. First, writing the letter in the students' native languages communicated caring. Second, the letter included specific suggestions. Even parents who cannot read a homework assignment can become more involved if they ask their children to share and explain their work with them. The suggestion also lets parents know they are needed. Third, by encouraging parents to attend the school's open house, Nancy increased the likelihood that they'd attend. If they did, and the experience was positive, their involvement would likely increase.

The process of involving all parents begins with awareness (A. Baker, Kessler-Sklar, Piotrkowski, & Parker, 1999). As we more fully realize that parents from cultural minorities and low-SES backgrounds and those whose children have exceptionalities are often reluctant to become involved in school activities, we can redouble our efforts. We can also try to be as clear and specific as possible in our suggestions for parents as they work with their youngsters.

Finally, if parents speak English, phone calls are as effective with them as they are with nonminority parents. Experts suggest calling parents at work, where they are easier to reach, and scheduling conferences on parents' days off or around their work schedules (Lindeman, 2001). Some teachers even conduct home visits (Bullough, 2001). Although they are very demanding and time consuming, nothing communicates a stronger commitment to a young person's education.

Classroom Connections

Communicating Effectively with Parents

1. Establish communication links between school and home during the first few days of school, and maintain them throughout the year.
   - *Elementary:* A kindergarten teacher makes a personal telephone call to the parents of each of her students during the first week of school. She tells the parents how happy she is to have their children in her class, encourages them to contact her at any time, and gives them her home phone number.
   - *Middle School:* A sixth-grade social studies teacher sends home a "class communicator" each month. It briefly describes the topics the students will be

studying and gives suggestions parents might follow in helping their children. Students are required to write personal notes to their parents on the communicator, describing their efforts and progress.

- *High School:* A geometry teacher sends a letter home at the beginning of the school year describing how he assigns homework every night and has a quiz every Friday. He calls parents when more than one homework assignment is missing. When he calls about homework, he says, "I want to catch these things early. Your son/daughter is a capable student, and I want him/her to get off to a good start."

2. Communicate in nontechnical language, and make specific suggestions to parents for working with their children.

- *Elementary:* A third-grade teacher asks all her parents to sign a contract agreeing that they will (a) designate at least 1 hour an evening when the television is shut off and children do homework, (b) ask their children to show them their homework assignments each day, (c) attend the school's open house, and (d) look at, ask their children about, and sign the packet of papers that is sent home every other week.
- *Middle School:* A sixth-grade teacher goes over a letter to parents with his students. He has them explain to him what each part of the letter says and then asks the students to read and explain the letter to their parents.

- *High School:* A ninth-grade basic math teacher makes a special effort at the beginning of the school year to explain to parents of students with exceptionalities how she'll modify her class to meet their children's needs. She strongly encourages parents to monitor homework and assist if they can.

3. Take extra steps to communicate with the parents of minority children.

- *Elementary:* A second-grade teacher in an urban school enlists the aid of several teachers skilled in various languages. When he sends messages home, he asks these teachers' help in translating the notes into parents' native languages.
- *Middle School:* At the beginning of each grading period, a sixth-grade teacher sends a letter home, in each student's native language, describing the topics that will be covered, the tests and the approximate times they will be given, and any special projects that are required for the period.
- *High School:* A tenth-grade science teacher who has many students whose parents speak little or no English holds student-led conferences in which students themselves report on their progress. She participates in each conference and allows students to serve as translators to relay important information to parents. All students gain practice in communication skills and goal setting.

Dealing with Misbehavior: Interventions

Our focus to this point has been on preventing management problems. We emphasized the interdependence of instruction and classroom management, the importance of planning, and the role of carefully taught and monitored rules and procedures. Despite teachers' best efforts, however, management problems occur, and teachers must intervene in cases of disruptive behavior or chronic inattention. In the following sections, we consider

- General guidelines for successful interventions
- Cognitive approaches to intervention
- Behavioral approaches to interventions

Guidelines for Successful Interventions

Intervening when classroom management problems occur is never easy. If it were, management wouldn't remain a chronic problem for teachers. As you work with your students, we recommend a blend of cognitive and behavioral approaches. Cognitive perspectives emphasize understanding and student responsibility; behaviorist approaches use reinforcers and punishers to establish and maintain order. (As you'll see later in the chapter, reinforcers are much more effective than punishers, but punishers may be necessary in some cases.) Both cognitive and behaviorist approaches have their place in the creation of productive learning environments.

Successful management interventions stop the unwanted behavior while maintaining the flow of the lesson.

Regardless of the theoretical orientation, some general guidelines increase the likelihood that your interventions will be successful. Remember, your goal in managing interventions is to maintain or restore order without detracting from learning.

Demonstrate Withitness.   An essential component of successful interventions is known as **withitness,** *a teacher's awareness of what is going on in all parts of the classroom at all times and the communication of this awareness verbally and nonverbally* (Kounin, 1970). Expert teachers describe withitness as "having eyes in the back of your head." Here are a positive and a negative example of the concept:

> Ron Ziers was explaining the procedure for finding percentages to his seventh graders. While Ron illustrated the procedure, Kareem, in the second desk from the front of the room, was periodically poking Katilyna, who sat across from him. She retaliated by kicking him in the leg. Bill, sitting behind Katilyna, poked her in the arm with his pencil. Ron didn't respond to the students' actions. After a second poke, Katilyna swung her arm back and caught Bill on the shoulder. "Katilyna!" Ron said sternly. "We keep our hands to ourselves! . . . Now, where were we?"
>
> Karl Wickes, a seventh-grade life science teacher in the same school, had the same group of students. He put a transparency displaying a flowering plant on the overhead. As the class discussed the information, he noticed Barry whispering something to Julie, and he saw Kareem poke Katilyna, who kicked him and loudly whispered, "Stop it." As Karl asked, "What is the part of the plant that produces fruit?" he moved to Kareem's desk, leaned over, and said quietly but firmly, "We keep our hands and materials to ourselves in here." He then moved to the front of the room, watched Kareem out of the corner of his eye, and said, "Barry, what other plant part do you see in the diagram?"

Notice the ways in which Karl, but not Ron, demonstrated to his students that he had withitness:

- *Identifying the misbehavior immediately.* Karl responded quickly to Kareem. Ron did nothing until the misbehavior had spread to other students.
- *Correctly identifying the original cause of the incident.* Karl realized that Kareem was the instigator. Ron reprimanded only Katilyna, leaving the students with a sense that the teacher didn't know what was going on.
- *Responding to the most serious infraction first.* Kareem's poking was more disruptive than Barry's whispering, so Karl first responded to Kareem and then simply called on Barry, which drew him back into the activity, making further intervention unnecessary.

Withitness involves more than dealing with misbehavior after it happens. Teachers who are withit also watch for evidence of inattention or confusion; they walk over to, or call on, inattentive students to bring them back into lessons; and they respond to quizzical looks with questions such as "I see uncertain looks on some of your faces. Do you want me to rephrase that question?" Effective teachers are sensitive to students and make adjustments to ensure that they are as attentive and successful as possible.

Preserve Student Dignity.   Preserving a student's dignity is a basic principle of any intervention. As we saw in Chapters 10 and 11, safety is essential for motivation, and your emotional tone when you interact with students influences both the likelihood of their compliance and their attitudes toward you and the class. Loud public reprimands, public criticism, and sarcasm reduce students' sense of safety, create resentment, and detract from a productive learning environment. When students break rules, simply reminding them, telling them why the rule is important, as Judy Harris did in her encounter with Rachel, and requiring compliance is as far as an incident should go.

Be Consistent.   "Be consistent" in management is recommended so often that it has become a cliché. The need for consistency is obvious, but achieving complete consistency in the real world of teaching is difficult, if not impossible. In fact, experts recommend that our interventions be individualized and contextualized, appropriate for the specific student and situation (Doyle, 1986).

12.12
Using your study of information processing in Chapter 7 as a basis, offer a likely reason for Ron's lack of withitness.

12.13
Kounin (1970) describes *overlapping* as a teacher's ability to attend to two incidents at the same time without focusing exclusively on either one. Identify an example of overlapping in the vignette with Karl Wickes and his students.

12.14
Identify the concept from Piaget's work in Chapter 2 that is most closely relates to the need for consistency, and explain how they are related.

For example, most classrooms have a rule about speaking only when recognized by the teacher. Suppose you are monitoring seat work when a student innocently asks a work-related question of another student and then quickly turns back to work. Do you intervene, reminding her that talking is not allowed during seat work? Failing to do so is technically inconsistent, but you don't intervene, and you shouldn't. A student who repeatedly turns around and whispers, though, becomes a disruption, warranting an intervention.

Follow Through.   Following through means doing what you've said you'll do. Without follow-through, a management system breaks down because students learn that teachers aren't fully committed to maintaining an orderly learning environment. This confuses them, leaving them with a sense of uncertainty about their classroom. Once again, the first few days of the school year are very important for establishing rules and communicating your management approach. If you follow through consistently when incidents arise during this period, management becomes much easier during the rest of the year.

Keep Interventions Brief.   Keep all interventions as brief as possible. Researchers have documented a negative relationship between time spent on discipline and student achievement; extended interventions break the flow of the lesson and detract from instructional time (Doyle, 1986).

Judy maintained the flow of her lesson by keeping interventions brief.

In the opening case study, Judy Harris applied this principle in her work with her ninth graders. She simply touched Darren on the shoulder and further communicated her withitness and resolve by moving near him and calling on him, and she spoke quietly to Rachel when directing her to move. Also, none of the interventions disrupted the flow of her lesson.

Avoid Arguments.   Finally, whenever possible, avoid arguing with students. Teachers never "win" arguments. They can exert their authority, but resentment is often the outcome, and the encounter may expand into a major incident. Judy handled this problem skillfully in her encounter with Rachel. She simply referred to the rule, restated her request, and ensured that it was followed. For comparison, consider an alternative scenario:

12.15
What concept, discussed earlier in the chapter, relates to the idea of extended interventions breaking the flow of the lesson?

"I wasn't doing anything."
"You were whispering, and the rule says listen when someone else is talking."
"It doesn't say no whispering."
"You know what the rule means. We've been over it again and again."
"Well, it's not fair. You don't make other students move when they whisper."
"You weren't listening when someone else was talking, so move."

The student, of course, knew what the rule meant and was simply playing a game with the teacher, who allowed herself to be drawn into an argument. Judy didn't, and the incident was disarmed almost immediately.

Having considered these general guidelines, we turn now to cognitive intervention strategies.

Cognitive Interventions

Understanding is at the core of cognitive approaches to management because learner understanding is essential in interpreting rules and teachers' interventions. For example, in the last section, you saw that achieving complete consistency in interventions is virtually impossible. A cognitive approach assumes that students can accommodate minor inconsistencies because they understand the reasons for rules and can interpret differences in situations.

In this section, we examine five factors that influence the way learners understand and respond to our interventions:

- Verbal-nonverbal congruence
- I-messages
- Active listening

■ Problem ownership
■ Logical consequences

Verbal-Nonverbal Congruence

If students are to understand classroom rules and develop responsibility for their actions, teachers' communications must make sense. To make sense, verbal and nonverbal communication must be congruent. Let's examine two examples.

Karen Wilson's 10th graders were working on their next day's English homework as she circulated among them. She was helping Jasmine when Jeff and Mike begin whispering loudly behind her.

"Jeff. Mike. Stop talking, and get started on your homework," she said, glancing over her shoulder.

The two slowed their whispering, and Karen turned back to Jasmine. Soon, though, the boys were whispering as loudly as ever.

"I thought I told you to stop talking," Karen said over her shoulder again, this time with irritation in her voice.

The boys glanced at her and quickly resumed whispering.

Effective interventions require both clear verbal and congruent nonverbal communication.

Isabel Rodriguez was in a similar situation with her ninth-grade algebra class. As she was helping Vicki, Ken and Lance began horsing around at the back of the room.

Isabel quickly excused herself from Vicki, turned, and walked directly to the boys. Looking Lance in the eye, she said pleasantly but firmly, "Lance, we have plenty to do before lunch, and noise disrupts others' work. Begin your homework now." Then, looking directly at Ken, she continued, "Ken, you, too. Quickly now. We have only so much time, and we don't want to waste it." She waited until they were working quietly and then returned to Vicki.

The teachers had similar intents, but their impact on the students was very different. Karen's communication was confusing; her words said one thing, but her body language said another, leaving students unable to make sense of her intent and how they were supposed to function in her classroom. When messages are inconsistent, people attribute more credibility to **nonverbal communication**, *unspoken messages communicated through tone of voice and body language* (Mehrabian & Ferris, 1967).

In contrast, Isabel's communication was clear and consistent. She responded immediately, faced her students directly, emphasized the relationship between order and learning, and made sure her students were on-task before she went back to Vicki. Isabel's verbal and nonverbal behaviors were consistent, so her message made sense. If we expect students to take responsibility for their own behavior, our messages must be consistent and understandable.

Essential elements of nonverbal communication are outlined in Table 12.4.

I-Messages

Successful interventions should focus on the behavior in question and help students understand the effects of their actions on others, including the teacher. To illustrate, let's look again at Judy's encounter with Rachel.

Judy:	(Quietly, in response to Rachel's whispering and note passing) Move up here.
Rachel:	What did I do?
Judy:	When we talked about our rules at the beginning of the year, we agreed that it was important to listen when other people are talking.
Rachel:	I wasn't doing anything.
Judy:	We don't learn as much when people aren't paying attention, and I'm uncomfortable when my class isn't learning. Please move quickly now.

Table 12.4   Characteristics of nonverbal communication

Nonverbal Behavior	Example
Proximity	A teacher moves close to an inattentive student. In another case, a teacher moves to a student and touches her on the shoulder.
Eye contact	A teacher looks an off-task student directly in the eye when issuing a directive.
Body orientation	A teacher directs himself squarely to the learner, rather than over the shoulder or sideways.
Facial expression	A teacher frowns slightly at a disruption, brightens her face at a humorous incident, and smiles approvingly at a student's effort to help a classmate.
Gestures	A teacher puts her palm out (Stop!) to a student who interjects as another student is talking.
Vocal variation	A teacher varies the tone, pitch, and loudness of his voice for emphasis and displays energy and enthusiasm.

In this intervention, Judy sent an **I-message,** *a communication that addresses a behavior, describes the effects on the sender, and identifies feelings generated in the sender.*

The way teachers talk during interventions has both short- and long-term consequences for learners (Gordon, 1974, 1981). In using an I-message, Judy addressed Rachel's behavior rather than her character or personality. When teachers say, "You're driving me up the wall," they're implying weaknesses in students' characters. Focusing on the incident communicates that a student is valued but the behavior is unacceptable. Judy also described the behavior's effect on the sender—herself—and the feelings it generated: "We don't learn as much when people aren't paying attention, and I'm uncomfortable when my class isn't learning." The intent of an I-message is to promote understanding, as it always is in cognitive interventions. Judy wanted Rachel to understand the effects of her actions on others—a step toward responsible behavior and self-regulation.

12.16
Suppose one of your students is talking without permission. Describe an I-message that would be appropriate as a response.

Active Listening

Clear communication is also important in cognitive interventions, and teachers improve communication by being good listeners (Gordon, 1974). When students believe that teachers are listening rather than evaluating what they say, their trust increases and they talk more openly. For example:

Gayle went to Maria Cortez after class and said, "Mrs. Cortez, I don't think I should have gotten a zero on that last assignment."

Maria sat down, focused her attention on Gayle, and said evenly, "You don't think the grade was fair?"

"No," Gayle said, squirming slightly.

"Tell me why."

"I was absent the day you assigned it, and I didn't know that it was due today."

"I understand how you feel, Gayle," Maria responded, leaning forward. "I would feel badly, too, if I got a zero on an assignment. But our procedures say that assignments are due 2 days after you return from an absence, and when you're absent, you're responsible for

Cognitive approaches to management emphasize learner understanding.

finding out what those assignments are. I even reminded you that the assignment was due yesterday. What could you do to prevent this problem in the future?"

"... I guess ... write assignments down in my notebook."

"That's a good idea. Try that. I'm sure it will help."

Maria sat down, gave Gayle her *full attention, and responded to both the intellectual and emotional content of the message.* These are the characteristics of **active listening** (Sokolove, Garrett, Sadker, & Sadker, 1990). Notice also that Maria didn't acquiesce to Gayle's implication of unfairness. Her response was consistent with her procedures, it was predictable, and it further contributed to Gayle's understanding.

Problem Ownership

Before deciding on an intervention, the teacher must determine if it is the teacher's or the student's problem (Gordon, 1981). If it is the student's problem, the teacher guides the student toward a solution; if the problem is the teacher's, then he or she must make some changes to improve the environment.

For example, Gayle's zero was a student problem, and Maria offered her a solution in their discussion. She addressed the immediate problem and also helped Gayle recognize her personal responsibility.

On the other hand, if students are disruptive at the beginning of class, it is likely a teacher problem. Teachers need to create a set of predictable routines that immediately involve students in a learning activity, as Judy did by having students identify the longitude and latitude of Cairo and Damascus. If students are inattentive during learning activities, the teacher may need to alter instruction—for instance, by moving away from lecture and toward more interactive questioning.

Logical Consequences

Logical consequences are *consequences that are conceptually related to the misbehavior; they help learners see a link between their actions and the consequences that should sensibly follow.* For example:

> Allen, a rambunctious sixth grader, was running down the hall toward the lunchroom. As he rounded the corner, he bumped into Alyssia, causing her to drop her books.
>
> "Oops," he replied, continuing his race to the lunchroom.
>
> "Hold it, Allen," said Doug Ramsay, who was monitoring the hall. "Go back and help her pick up her books and apologize."
>
> "Aww."
>
> "Go on," Doug said firmly.
>
> Allen walked back to Alyssia, helped her pick up her books, mumbled an apology, and then returned. As he approached, Doug again stopped him.
>
> "Now, why did I make you do that?" Doug asked.
>
> "Cuz we're not supposed to run."
>
> "Sure," Doug said pleasantly, "but more important, if people are running in the halls, somebody might get hurt, and we don't want that to happen.... Remember that you're responsible for your actions. Think about not wanting to hurt yourself or anybody else, and the next time you'll walk whether a teacher is here or not.... Now, go on to lunch."

12.17

A teacher sees a seventh-grader spit on the door to the classroom. According to the information in this section, which is the more appropriate response: putting the student in after-school detention (which is part of the school's management policy) or having the student wash the door? Explain.

In this incident, Doug helped Allen understand that having to pick up Alyssia's books was a logical consequence of Allen's behavior (running in the hall) and the problems it caused (bumping into Alyssia and causing her to drop her books). Applying logical consequences is a "cognitive" intervention because the goal is learner understanding. Children who understand the effects of their actions on others become more altruistic and are more likely to take actions to make up for their misbehavior (Berk, 2001).

Behavioral Interventions

Ideally, our interventions should help students understand why their behavior is a problem and take personal responsibility. Sometimes, however, learners seem either unable or unwilling to accept responsibility for their behavior, and time or safety concerns require more direct approaches to management. In situations such as these, behavioral interventions can be effective (Reynolds et al., 1996). Experts recommend using behavioral interventions as short-term solutions to specific problems (Freiberg, 1999a); the development of responsibility and self-regulation should still remain our long-term goal.

Let's see how one teacher uses behaviorism in her classroom management.

Behavioral approaches to management stress positive reinforcement for desired behaviors.

Cindy Daines's first graders were sometimes frustrating. Although she tried alerting the groups and having the whole class make transitions at the same time, every transition took several minutes.

To improve the situation, she made some "tickets" from construction paper, bought an assortment of small prizes, and displayed the items in a fishbowl on her desk the next day. She then explained, "We're going to play a little game to see how quiet we can be when we change lessons. . . . Whenever we change, such as from language arts to math, I'm going to give you 2 minutes, and then I'm going to ring this bell." She rang the bell to demonstrate. "Students who have their books out and are waiting quietly when I ring the bell will get one of these tickets. On Friday afternoon, you can turn these in for prizes you see in this fishbowl. The more tickets you have, the better the prize will be."

During the next few days, Cindy moved around the room, handing out tickets and making comments such as "I really like the way Merry is ready to work," "Ted already has his books out and is quiet," and "Thank you for moving to math so quickly."

She knew her strategy was working when she heard "Shh" and "Be quiet!" from the students, so she moved from awarding prizes to allowing the students to "buy" free time with their tickets. Soon she was giving students Friday afternoon parties as group rewards when the class had accumulated enough tickets. She gradually was able to space out the group rewards as the students' self-regulation developed.

Cindy's system used concepts from both behaviorism and social cognitive theory. Her tickets, free time, and Friday afternoon parties were all intended as positive reinforcers for making quick and quiet transitions. In addition, her positive comments ("I really like the way Merry is ready to work," "Ted already has his books out and is quiet") were intended as vicarious reinforcers for the rest of the children. Research indicates that a behavioral system such as Cindy's can be effective in initiating and teaching new behaviors (McCaslin & Good, 1992).

Classroom management systems that emphasize reinforcement are preferable to those that use punishment (Alberto & Troutman, 1999). As you saw in Chapter 6, however, focusing exclusively on positive behaviors doesn't always work; if all punishers are eliminated, some students actually become more disruptive (Pfiffer et al., 1985; Rosen et al., 1984). Although reinforcement is preferable to punishment, it may be necessary in some cases (Axelrod & Apsche, 1983; Maccoby, 1992). Guidelines for using punishers are outlined in Figure 12.3.

12.18
Management systems that focus on desirable behaviors are considered preferable to those that use punishment, yet many teachers largely ignore positive behaviors and focus on undesirable ones. Offer at least two reasons for teachers' tendency to behave this way.

Figure 12.3 Guidelines for using punishers

- Use punishers as infrequently as possible to avoid negative emotional reactions.
- Apply punishers immediately and directly to the behavior.
- Apply punishers only severe enough to eliminate the behavior.
- Avoid using seat work as a punisher.
- Apply punishers logically, systematically, and dispassionately—never angrily.
- Explain and model appropriate alternative behaviors.

Approaches to management have been developed that systematically use reinforcers and punishers in attempts to promote desirable behaviors in students. Assertive discipline is the best known of these systems.

Assertive Discipline: A Structured Approach to Consequences

Assertive discipline is *a classroom management system that emphasizes carefully stated rules and specifically described reinforcers and punishers* (Canter & Canter, 1992). Teachers using an assertive discipline system specify rules, such as "We raise our hands before speaking," "Be in your seat and quiet when the bell rings," and "Stay in your seat at all times" (from Table 12.2). The rules must be clear and specific and must clearly outline standards for behavior. The teacher then describes reinforcers that are given for following the rules and punishers that are administered for breaking them. Sample sets of reinforcers and punishers are illustrated in Table 12.5.

Assertive discipline is controversial. Critics charge that it is punitive, pits teachers against students, and stresses obedience and conformity at the expense of learning and self-control (Brophy, 1999; McLaughlin, 1994). They further argue that research suggests teachers who use assertive discipline are perceived as less supportive and less caring by students (Parker, 1994). Supporters disagree, contending that its emphasis on stated rules and positive reinforcement is proactive, provides a structured environment for both teachers and students, and is effective (Canter, 1988).

Despite controversies, the program has been widely used. A great many school districts in the country have had at least some exposure to assertive discipline. In response to critics, its designers have placed more emphasis on cooperation and developing rapport with students (Canter, 1996). Still, teachers who use the system are advised to supplement it with a more comprehensive approach that emphasizes prevention and effective instruction (Freiberg, 1999a).

Designing and Maintaining a Behavioral Management System

Designing a management system based on behaviorism typically involves the following steps:

- Prepare a list of specific rules, such as "Speak only when recognized by the teacher."
- Specify reinforcers for obeying each rule and punishers for breaking the rules (e.g., the consequences in Table 12.5).

Table 12.5   Sample consequences for following or breaking rules

Consequences for Breaking Rules	
First infraction	Name on list
Second infraction	Check by name
Third infraction	Second check by name
Fourth infraction	Half-hour detention
Fifth infraction	Call to parents

Consequences for Following Rules
A check is removed for each day that no infractions occur. If only a name remains, and no infractions occur, the name is removed.
All students without names on the list are given 45 minutes of free time Friday afternoon to do as they choose. The only restrictions are that they must stay in the classroom, and they must not disrupt the students who didn't earn the free time.

- Display the rules and procedures, and explain the consequences to the students.
- Consistently apply consequences.

A behavioral system doesn't preclude providing rationales or creating the rules with learner input, of course. The primary focus, however, is on the clear specification of behavioral guidelines and application of consequences, in contrast with a cognitive approach, which emphasizes learner understanding and responsibility. (For an example of a behavioral management system, reread the Chapter 6 section "Creating Productive Learning Environments" beginning on page 208).

In designing a comprehensive management system, teachers usually combine elements of both cognitive and behavioral approaches. Behavioral systems have the advantage of being immediately applicable; they're effective for initiating desired behaviors, particularly with young students; and they're useful for reducing chronic misbehavior. Cognitive systems take longer to produce results, but they are more likely to develop learner responsibility.

Despite the most thorough planning and effective implementation, the need for periodic teacher intervention is inevitable. Keeping both cognitive and behavioral approaches to management in mind, let's consider a series of intervention options.

An Intervention Continuum

Disruptions vary widely, from an isolated incident (such as a student briefly whispering to a neighbor during quiet time) to chronic infractions (such as someone repeatedly poking or kicking other students). Because infractions vary, teachers' reactions should also vary. To maximize instructional time, interventions should be as unobtrusive as possible. A continuum of interventions is shown in Figure 12.4 and described in the following sections.

Praising Desired Behavior

A principle of behaviorism is that reinforced behaviors increase. Because promoting desirable behaviors is an important goal, praising desired behavior is a sensible first intervention. Praise occurs less often than might be expected, so efforts to "catch 'em being good" are worthwhile, especially as a method of prevention. Elementary teachers can praise openly and freely, and middle and secondary teachers can make comments such as "I'm extremely pleased with your work this week—keep it up." Making an effort to acknowledge desired behavior and good work significantly contributes to productive learning environments.

Ignoring Inappropriate Behavior

Behaviorism also suggests that unreinforced behaviors become extinct, so one way of reducing undesirable behaviors is to simply ignore them, eliminating any reinforcers teachers might be inadvertently providing (Alberto & Troutman, 1999). This is appropriate, for example, when two students whisper to each other, but soon stop. A combination of praising desired behaviors and ignoring misbehavior can be very effective with minor disruptions (Pfiffer et al., 1985; Rosen et al., 1984).

Figure 12.4 An intervention continuum

Minor infractions				Serious infractions
Praising desired behavior	Ignoring inappropriate behavior	Using indirect cues	Using desists	Applying consequences

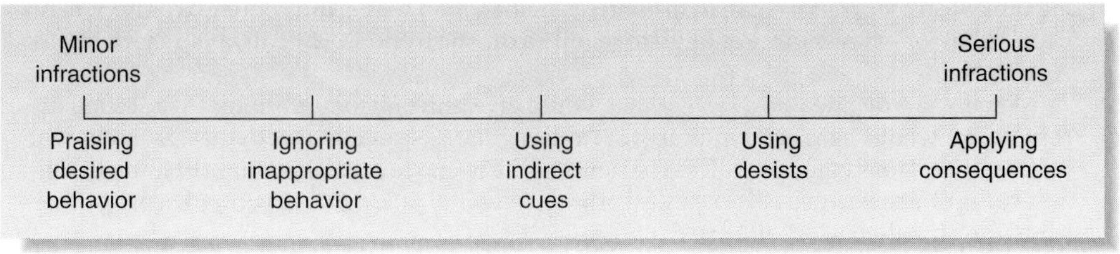

Using Indirect Cues

Effective teachers use indirect cues—such as proximity, methods of redirecting attention, and vicarious reinforcers—when students are displaying behaviors that can't be ignored but can be stopped or diverted without addressing them directly (Jones & Jones, 2001). For example, Judy, in our opening case, moved near Darren and called on him after she heard Kendra mutter. Her proximity stopped his misbehavior, and calling on him and looking directly at him redirected his attention to the lesson.

Vicarious reinforcement can also be effective. Teachers, especially in the lower grades, can use other students as models and vicariously reinforce the rest of the students for imitating their behaviors with statements such as "I really like the way Row 1 is working quietly."

Using Desists

A **desist** is *a verbal or nonverbal communication a teacher makes to a student to stop a behavior* (Kounin, 1970). "Glenys, we leave our seats only when, given permission," "Glenys!", a finger to the lips, or a stern facial expression are all desists. Desists are the most common teacher reactions to misbehavior.

Clarity and tone are important to the effectiveness of desists. For example, "Randy, what is the rule about touching other students?" or "Randy, how do you think that makes Willy feel?" are more desirable than "Randy, stop that," because they link the behavior to a rule or to the behavior's effects. Students react to these subtle differences, preferring rule and consequence reminders to teacher commands (Nucci, 1987).

The tone of desists should be firm but not angry. Research indicates that kindergarten students handled with rough desists actually became more disruptive, and older students are uncomfortable in classes where harsh desists are used (Kounin, 1970). In contrast, gentle reprimands, the suggestion of alternative behaviors, and questioning that maintained student involvement in learning activities reduced time off-task in elementary classrooms by 20 minutes a day (Borg & Ascione, 1982).

Clear communication (including congruence between verbal and nonverbal behavior), an awareness of what is happening in the classroom (withitness), and implementation of effective instruction are essential in effectively using desists. However, even when these important elements are used, simple desists alone sometimes aren't enough.

Applying Consequences

Careful planning and effective instruction will eliminate much misbehavior before it starts. Some minor incidents can be ignored, and simple desists will stop others. When these strategies don't work, however, teachers can apply consequences that are related to the problem.

Logical consequences are preferable because they treat misbehaviors as problems and create a conceptual link between behaviors and consequences. Because classrooms are complex and busy, it isn't always possible to solve problems with logical consequences, however. In these instances, behavioral consequences—consequences solely intended to change a behavior—offer an acceptable alternative:

> Jason was an intelligent and active fifth grader. He loved to talk and seemed to know just how far he could go before Mrs. Aguilar became exasperated with him. He understood the rules and the reasons for them, but his interest in talking seemed to take precedence. Ignoring him wasn't working. A call to his parents helped for a while, but soon he was back to his usual behavior—never quite enough to require a drastic response, but always a thorn in Mrs. Aguilar's side.
>
> Finally, she decided on a system that would give him only one warning. At a second disruption, he would be placed in time-out from regular instructional activities. She met with Jason and explained the new rules. The next day, he began to misbehave almost immediately.
>
> "Jason," she warned, "you can't work while you're talking, and you're keeping others from finishing their work. Please get busy."
>
> He stopped, but 5 minutes later, he was at it again.

12.19
On the basis of your study of social cognitive theory in Chapter 6, explain why rough desists might result in students becoming more disruptive. What other explanations might there be?

"Jason," Mrs. Aguilar said quietly as she moved back to his desk, "I've warned you. Now please go back to the time-out area."

A week later, Jason was working quietly and comfortably with the rest of the class.

Behavior like Jason's is quite common, particularly in elementary and middle schools. This type of behavior certainly causes teacher stress more often than does highly publicized threats of violence and bodily harm. The behavior is disruptive, so it can't be ignored; praise for good work helps to a certain extent, but students get much of their reinforcement from friends; desists work briefly, but teachers tire of constant monitoring. Mrs. Aguilar had little choice but to apply behavioral consequences with Jason.

Consistency is the key to promoting change in students like Jason. Jason understood what he was doing, and he was capable of controlling himself. When he could, with certainty, predict the consequences of his behavior, he quit. He knew that his second infraction would result in a time-out, and when it did, he quickly changed his behavior. There was no argument, little time was used, and the class wasn't disrupted.

12.20
Suppose Mrs. Aguilar has just begun implementing her system with Jason, and she sees him briefly talk to a buddy. Should she ignore the behavior or apply a consequence? Provide a rationale for your response.

Assessment and Learning: The Role of Assessment in Classroom Management

Assessment involves gathering data to be used in making decisions. It usually focuses on learning progress, but it can also provide valuable information about the classroom environment for both teachers and students.

Assessment provides teachers with information about the effectiveness of their management systems, areas that need improvement, and the progress they're making toward their management goals. It also provides information about the progress individual students are making toward self-regulation.

Because classrooms are busy and complex, assessment of a management system can be a challenge. Teachers immersed in the hectic bustle of the classroom may be unable to get an accurate picture of how well their management systems are working. This is where a mentor or colleague can provide valuable information. Let's see how this can occur.

Vicky, a first year teacher, slumped into a chair in the teacher's lounge and let out a soft groan.

"What the matter? You look pooped," Angela, her neighbor and third-year veteran, remarked. "Not getting enough sleep?"

"It's not sleep. It's my kids. Sometimes I think they're winning. I'm struggling to keep the lid on. They're wearing me out."

As they talked, it became apparent that Vicky didn't know where to start in approaching her problem with classroom management.

"If you would like, I'll come into your class while my kids are at P.E. tomorrow," Angela offered.

"That would be great!" Vicky responded with relief.

Angela came in the next day, took notes about the beginnings and endings of Vicky's lesson, made a seating chart of the class, noted what students did when their assignments were complete, and described the amount of time it took the students to settle down after a transition.

When she talked with Angela about her observations that afternoon, Vicky realized that her management problems were primarily related to students bothering other students during transitions. Angela also noted that students who sat next to each were frequently visiting, during lessons and particularly during seat work. Armed with this information, Angela and Vicky worked out a plan to create more specific procedures that students would routinely follow at the beginning of class, during transitions, and after they completed assignments. Vicki also rearranged her seating chart.

Earlier in the chapter we saw that well-established procedures are essential for preventing management problems. Because of lack of experience and the multidimensional nature of her classroom, Vicki was unable to assess her problems on her own; it took Angela's observations to identify the fact that she didn't have clear procedures that the students automatically followed.

Accurate information helps teachers make good management decisions. Teachers can gather accurate information about management problems by identifying whether problems occur at certain times or in certain locations (Alberto & Troutman, 1999). The first approach provides teachers with insights into how their actions and classroom events contribute to problems. The second can help teachers identify areas of the class (e.g., pencil sharpener, equipment storage spaces) as well as clusters of students associated with problems.

Assessment can also provide students with valuable information, which can then be used to develop behavioral contracts or self-management systems. Students are often unaware of their own behaviors or the consequences of those behaviors on others. By asking students to focus on specific behaviors, such as being out of seat or off-task, teachers can help students develop self-regulation. The process begins with assessment.

Student self-monitoring has been found effective in changing a wide range of unproductive behaviors (C. Cole, 1992). For example, if a teacher is trying to decrease call-outs and increase a student's hand-raising, the teacher would first meet with the student, discuss the problem, and ask the student to monitor his or her behavior. Together, they would set a goal for improvement. Goal setting is valuable because it gives the student a tangible target and also teaches the importance of goals in learning (Jones & Jones, 2001).

Assessment then provides both the teacher and student with tangible evidence that progress is being made toward the goal. A simple chart in which the student tallies instances of the problem behavior(s) throughout the day can be effective. (An example of a self-management system in which behaviors are tallied appears on page 189 in the closing case study for Chapter 5). The process of self-assessment alone may reduce unwanted behavior. If it doesn't, the teacher can then apply the needed intervention from the continuum described earlier.

Classroom Connections

Using Interventions Successfully in Your Classroom

1. Use problem-solving strategies and logical consequences to help students develop responsibility. Hold discussions regarding fairness or equity after class and in private.

   - *Elementary:* During weekly classroom chores, two first graders begin a tug-of-war over a cleaning rag and knock over a potted plant. The teacher talks to the students, they agree to clean up the mess, and they write a note to their parents explaining that they will be working in the classroom before school the next week to pay for a new pot.

   - *Middle School:* A social studies teacher tries to help her students learn from her interventions. When she uses indirect cues, she points to the appropriate rule on the bulletin board. In cases of uncertainty, she quickly talks to them in private, reminding them of the rule and the reason for it.

   - *High School:* After having been asked to stop whispering for the second time in 10 minutes, a ninth grader protests that he was asking about the assigned seat work. The teacher reminds him of the two incidents, points out that his behavior is disruptive, and applies a consequence without further discussion. The teacher sits down with him after class, explains why rules exist, and reminds him that he is expected to accept responsibility for his behavior.

2. Use positive reinforcers to initiate and teach desirable behaviors.

   - *Elementary:* A first-grade teacher, knowing that the times after recess and lunch are difficult for many students, institutes a system in which the class has 1 minute after a timer rings to settle down and get out their materials. When the class meets the requirement, they earn points toward free time.

   - *Middle School:* To encourage students to clean up quickly after labs, a science teacher offers them

5 minutes of free time to talk in their seats if the lab is cleaned up in time. Students who don't clean up in time are required to finish in silence.

- *High School:* A ninth-grade basic math teacher is encountering problems getting his students to work quietly in small groups. He discusses the problem with the class and then closely monitors the groups for the next few days, circulating and offering praise and reinforcement when groups are working smoothly.

3. Follow through consistently in cases of disruptive behavior.
   - *Elementary:* A second-grade teacher finds that transitions to and from recess, lunch, and the bathroom are noisy and disruptive. She talks with the class about the problem and initiates a "no talking" rule during these transitions. She carefully enforces the rule, which significantly reduces the noise problem.
   - *Middle School:* A teacher separates two seventh graders who disrupt lessons with their talking, telling them the new seat assignments are theirs until further notice. The next day, they sit in their old seats as the bell is about to ring. "Do you know why I moved you two yesterday?" the teacher says immediately. After a momentary pause, both students nod. "Then move quickly now, and be certain you're in your new seats tomorrow. You can come and talk with me when you believe you're ready to accept responsibility for your talking."
   - *High School:* An eleventh-grade history teacher reminds students about being seated when the bell rings. As it rings the next day, two girls remain standing and talking. The teacher turns to them and says, "I'm sorry, but you must not have understood me yesterday. To be counted on time, you need to be in your seats when the bell rings. Please go to the office and get a late admit pass. If you want to talk with me about this, come in after class." He immediately begins his lesson.

Serious Management Problems: Violence and Aggression

Class is disrupted by a scuffle. You look up to see that Ron has left his seat and gone to Phil's desk, where he is punching and shouting at Phil. Phil is not so much fighting back as trying to protect himself. You don't know how this started, but you do know that Phil gets along well with other students and that Ron often starts fights and arguments without provocation. (Brophy & Rohrkemper, 1987, p. 60)

This morning several students excitedly tell you that on the way to school they saw Tom beating up Sam and taking his lunch money. Tom is the class bully and has done things like this many times. (Brophy & Rohrkemper, 1987, p. 53)

What would you do in these situations? What would be your immediate reaction? How would you follow through? What long-term strategies would you use to try to prevent these problems from recurring? These questions were asked of teachers identified by their principals as effective in dealing with serious management problems (Brophy & McCaslin, 1992). In the following sections, we consider their responses, together with other research examining violence and aggression in schools.

Problems of violence and aggression require both immediate actions and long-term solutions.

Immediate Actions

Immediate actions involve three steps: (a) Stop the incident (if possible), (b) protect the victim, and (c) get help. For instance, in the case of the classroom scuffle, a loud noise—such as shouting, clapping, or slamming a chair against the floor—will often surprise the students enough so they'll stop. At that point, you can begin to talk to them, check to see if the victim is all right, and then take the students to the main office, where you can get help. If your interventions don't stop the fight, you should immediately rush an uninvolved student to the main office for help. Unless you're sure that you can separate the students without danger to yourself, or them, attempting to do so is unwise.

Serious management problems require both short- and long-term strategies.

12.21
Where on the intervention continuum would immediate actions be? Why would other interventions be skipped?

You are legally required to intervene in the case of a fight. If you ignore a fight, even on the playground, parents can sue for negligence on the grounds that you failed to protect a student from injury. However, the law doesn't say that you're required to physically break up the fight; immediately reporting it to administrators is an acceptable form of intervention.

Long-Term Solutions

Long-term, students must be helped to understand that aggression will not be permitted and that they're accountable for their behavior (Brophy, 1996; Limber, Flerx, Nation, & Melton, 1998). In the incident with the lunch money, for example, Tom must understand that his behavior will be reported; it's unacceptable and won't be tolerated.

12.22
Using Piaget's work as a basis, explain why aggressive youth might misperceive others' intentions.

As a preventive strategy, teachers must help students learn how to control their tempers, cope with frustration, and negotiate, rather than fight. One approach uses problem-solving simulations to help aggressive youth understand the motives and intentions of other people. Research indicates that these youngsters often respond aggressively because they misperceive others' intentions as being hostile. Following problem-solving sessions, aggressive students were less hostile in their interpretation of ambiguous situations and were rated as less aggressive by their teachers (Hudley, 1992).

Teaching students broadly applicable personal and social competencies such as self-control, perspective taking, and constructive assertiveness can also reduce aggressive behaviors and can improve social adjustment (Greenberg, 1996; Weissberg & Greenberg, 1998). For example, one effective program taught students to express anger verbally instead of physically and to solve conflicts through communication and negotiation rather than fighting (J. Lee, Pulvino, & Perrone, 1998). One form of communication and negotiation is learning to make and defend a position—to argue effectively. Students taught to make effective arguments, and who learn that arguing and verbal aggression are very different, become less combative when encountering others with whom they disagree (Burstyn & Stevens, 1999). Learning to argue also has incidental benefits: Those skilled in this area are seen by their peers as intelligent and credible.

To decrease aggressive incidents, experts also recommend the involvement of parents and other school personnel (Brophy, 1996; Moles, 1992). A large majority of surveyed parents (88%) said they wanted to be notified immediately if school problems occur (L. Harris, Kagay, & Ross, 1987). In addition, school counselors, school psychologists, social workers, and principals have all been trained to deal with these problems and can provide advice and assistance. Experienced teachers can also provide a wealth of information about how they've handled similar problems. No teacher should face persistent or serious problems of violence or aggression alone.

In conclusion, we want to put violence and aggression into perspective. Although they are possibilities—and you should understand options for dealing with them—the majority of your management problems will involve issues of cooperation and motivation. Many problems can be prevented, others can be dealt with quickly, and some require individual attention. We have all heard about students carrying guns to school and incidents of assault on teachers. Statistically, however, considering the huge numbers of students that pass through schools each day, these incidents remain very infrequent.

Summary

Classroom Management: A Definition

Classroom management focuses on creating and maintaining an orderly learning environment, and discipline involves teacher responses to student misbehavior. Research documents the importance of classroom management for learning and motivation. Cognitive approaches to management emphasize learners' understanding and personal responsibility.

Planning for Effective Classroom Management

Well-planned rules and procedures help establish and maintain orderly classrooms. An effective list of rules should be short, clear, and positive. Understanding reasons for rules is essential, and allowing student input promotes understanding, gives the students a sense of control, and contributes to self-regulation.

Procedures organize classroom routines. Rules and procedures must be carefully taught, monitored, and reviewed. Rules and procedures should be treated as concepts; learners should be provided with examples and nonexamples from which they construct understanding of both. The first few days of the school year are essential for establishing long-term routines.

Communication with Parents

Parents play a crucial role in supporting teachers' management systems. Involving parents increases student achievement, improves attitudes, and results in better attendance and greater willingness to do homework. Formal communication channels include open houses, interim progress reports, parent-teacher conferences, and report cards. Effective teachers also communicate expectations immediately and maintain communication with parents throughout the school year.

Economic, cultural, and language barriers can pose special challenges for teacher-parent communication.

Dealing with Misbehavior: Interventions

Effective teachers keep management interventions brief, preserve student dignity, and follow through consistently. Focusing on positive behavior, ignoring misbehavior, and employing simple desists can eliminate minor disruptions. Logical consequences help students see the connection between their behaviors and the effects of their behaviors on others. More lengthy interventions are sometimes necessary when misbehavior persists or occurs frequently.

Serious Management Problems: Violence and Aggression

In cases of violence and aggression, teachers should immediately stop the incident if possible, protect the victim, and get help. Teachers are required by law to intervene in cases of violence.

Long-term solutions involve teaching students social skills such as perspective taking and social problem solving. Involving parents is essential in cases of aggressive behavior in students.

In the opening case study, you saw how instruction and classroom management converged in Judy Harris's classroom. The following case study introduces another ninth-grade geography teacher, Janelle Powers, also working with her students on a lesson about the Middle East. As you read, look for similarities and differences in the two teachers' approaches to instruction and classroom management. Answer the questions that follow.

Janelle Powers taught ninth-grade geography in a large, urban middle school. With 29 students, her classroom was quite crowded.

This morning, in homeroom, Shiana came through the classroom doorway just as the tardy bell rang.

"Take your seat quickly, Shiana," Janelle directed. "You're just about late. All right. Listen up, everyone," she continued. "Ali?"

"Here."

"Gaelen?"

"Here."

"Chu?"

"Here."

Janelle finished taking the roll and then walked around the room, handing back a set of papers.

"You did quite well on the assignment," she commented. "Let's keep up the good work. . . . Howard and Manny, please stop talking while I'm returning the papers. Can't you just sit quietly for 1 minute?"

The boys, who were whispering, turned back to the front of the room.

"Now," Janelle continued after returning to the front of the room, "we've been studying the Middle East, so let's review for a moment. . . . Look at the map and identify the longitude and latitude of Cairo. Take a minute and figure it out right now."

The students began as Janelle went to her file cabinet to get out some transparencies.

"Stop it, Damon," she heard Leila blurt out behind her.

"Leila," Janelle responded sternly, "we don't talk out like that in class."

"He's poking me, Mrs. Powers."

"Are you poking her, Damon?"

". . ."

"Well?"

"Not really."

"You did, too," Leila complained.

"Both of you stop it," Janelle warned. "Another outburst like that, Leila, and your name goes on the chalkboard."

As the last students were finishing the problem, Janelle looked up from the materials on her desk to check an example on the overhead. She heard Howard and Manny talking and chuckling at the back of the room.

"Are you boys finished?"

"Yes," Manny answered.

"Well, be quiet then until everyone is done," Janelle directed and went back to rearranging her materials.

"Quiet, everyone," she again directed, looking up in response to a hum of voices around the room. "Is everyone finished? . . . Good. Pass your papers forward. . . . Remember, put your paper on the top of the stack. . . . Roberto, wait until the papers come from behind you before you pass yours forward."

Janelle collected the papers, put them on her desk, and then began, "We've talked about the geography of the Middle East, and now we want to look at the climate a bit more. It varies somewhat. For example, Syria is extremely hot in the summer but is actually quite cool in the winter. In fact, it snows in some parts.

"Now, what did we find for the latitude of Cairo?"

"Thirty," Miguel volunteered.

"North or south, Miguel? . . . Wait a minute. Howard? . . . Manny? . . . This is the third time this period that I've had to say something to you about your talking, and the period isn't even 20 minutes old yet. Get out your rules and read me the rule about talking without permission. . . . Howard?"

". . ."

"It's supposed to be in the front of your notebook."

". . ."

"Manny?"

"'No speaking without permission of the teacher,'" Manny read from the front page of his notebook.

"Howard, where are your rules?"

"I don't know."

"Move up here," Janelle directed, pointing to an empty desk at the front of the room. "You've been bothering me all week. If you can't learn to be quiet, you will be up here for the rest of the year."

Howard got up and slowly moved to the desk Janelle had pointed out. After Howard was seated, Janelle began again, "Where were we before we were rudely interrupted? . . . Oh yes. What did you get for the latitude of Cairo?"

"Thirty North," Miguel responded.

"Okay, good. . . . Now, Egypt also has a hot climate in the summer—in fact, very hot. The summer temperatures often go over 100 Fahrenheit. Egypt is also mostly desert, so the people have trouble making a living. Their primary source of subsistence is the Nile River, which floods frequently. Most of the agriculture of the country is near the river."

Janelle continued presenting information to the students for the next several minutes.

"Andrew, are you listening to this?" Janelle interjected when she saw Andrew poke Jacinta with a ruler.

"Yes," he responded, turning to the front.

"I get frustrated when I see people not paying attention. When you don't pay attention, you can't learn and that frustrates me because I'm here to help you learn."

Janelle continued with her presentation.

Constructed Response Questions

In answering these questions, use information from the chapter and link your responses to specific information in the case.

1. Analyze Janelle's planning for classroom management.
2. Evaluate the effectiveness of Janelle's management interventions.
3. The chapter stressed the interdependence of management and instruction. Analyze the relationship between management and instruction in Janelle's class. Include both strengths and weaknesses in the relationship.

Document-Based Analysis

Brenda Litchfield, a third-grade teacher in an inner-city elementary school, developed the following list of rules for her class:

1. Raise your hand before speaking. Otherwise work quietly.
2. Listen when someone else is talking.
3. Don't leave your seat unless the teacher gives permission.
4. Keep your hands to yourself.
5. When in line, stand quietly and don't bother people in front or back of you.
6. Follow directions the first time they are given.
7. Bring necessary materials to class.

Analyze Brenda's rules based on the guidelines in this chapter. Include suggestions for making the rules more effective.

Online Portfolio Activities

To develop your professional portfolio, further apply your understanding of chapter content, and address the INTASC standards, go to the Companion Website, then to this chapter's *Online Portfolio Activities*. Complete the suggested activities.

Important Concepts

active listening *(p. 448)*
assertive discipline *(p. 450)*
classroom management *(p. 426)*
cognitive approaches to management
  (p. 428)
desist *(p. 452)*
discipline *(p. 426)*

I-message *(p. 447)*
logical consequences *(p. 448)*
nonverbal communication *(p. 446)*
procedures *(p. 431)*
productive learning environment *(p. 426)*
rules *(p. 431)*
withitness *(p. 444)*

 PRAXIS These exercises are designed to help you prepare for the PRAXIS™ "Principles of Learning and Teaching" exam. To receive feedback on your constructed response questions and document analysis response, go to the Companion Website at *www.prenhall.com/eggen*, then to this chapter's *Practice for PRAXIS™* module. For additional connections between this text and the PRAXIS™ exam, go to Appendix A.

 Also on the Companion Website at *www.prenhall.com/eggen*, you can measure your understanding of chapter content in *Practice Quiz* and *Essay* modules, apply concepts in *Online Cases*, and broaden your knowledge base with the *Additional Content* module and *Web Links* to other educational psychology websites.

Chapter Outline

Teacher Knowledge and Teacher Thinking
Teacher Knowledge • Teacher Thinking

Planning for Instruction
Deciding What Topics Are Important to Study • Preparing Objectives: Deciding What Students Should Know, Value, or Be Able to Do • Preparing and Organizing Learning Activities • Planning for Assessment • Planning in a Standards-Based Environment

Implementing Instruction:
Essential Teaching Skills
Attitudes • Use of Time • Organization • Communication • Focus: Attracting and Maintaining Attention • Feedback • Questioning • Review and Closure • Classroom Interaction: Accommodating Learner Diversity

Assessment and Learning:
Using Assessment as a Learning Tool

Creating Productive Learning Environments

Principles of Instruction

13

To see a video clip of Scott's review, go to the Companion Website at *www.prenhall.com/eggen*, then to this chapter's Classrooms on the Web module. Click on Video Clip 13.1.

Scott Sowell, a middle school science teacher, wanted his students to understand Bernoulli's principle, the law that helps explain how airplanes are able to fly. He began the lesson by reviewing the concept of *force*, which the class had covered the day before, and he included some additional examples, such as pushing on the chalkboard, lifting a book from the table, and blowing on the back of a chair.

He continued by reviewing another law stating that if two forces are operating on an object in opposite directions, it will move in the direction of the greater force. To illustrate, Scott and Damien, one of the students, tugged on a stapler. Scott first tugged hard enough to move the stapler toward himself, stating in the process that he was exerting the greater force, and then he allowed Damien to exert the greater force to move the stapler in the opposite direction.

"Keep those ideas in mind," Scott said as he moved around the room placing two pieces of 8½ × 11 paper in front of each student.

He told the students to pick up one of the papers, and he showed them how to hold it.

"Now with a big breath, do what I do," he said and blew over the top surface of the paper.

The students repeated his demonstration.

"What did you notice when we blew over the top? . . . David?"

"The paper moved."

"I want only the person I called on to answer," Scott reminded the students, as several offered answers.

"How did the paper move?" Scott continued, turning back to David. "Do it again."

David again blew over the surface of the paper, and Scott repeated, "What did the paper do?"

"It came up."

"When you blow across it, comes up," Scott nodded enthusiastically.

"Now take two of the sheets and blow like this," he said, demonstrating how to blow between the papers. "Observe what happens."

Again the students repeated the demonstration.

"Let's look at one more," Scott went on. "I'll do it first. . . . I have a funnel and a ping-pong ball. . . . Watch what happens. I'm going to shoot Tristan in the head when I blow," he joked, pointing to one of the students.

Scott placed a ping-pong ball into the mouth of the funnel, blew through the funnel's stem, and took his hand away from the

mouth. To the students' surprise, the ball simply spun around in the mouth of the funnel.

The students repeated the demonstration, and Scott again went on, "Let's look at these."

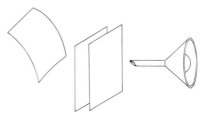

He drew sketches of each of the demonstrations on the board, as shown here, and began guiding an analysis of them.

Referring to the first sketch, Scott asked, "Was I blowing on the top or the bottom? . . . Rachel?"

"The top."

"And what happened there? . . . Heather?"

"The paper rose up."

He then turned to the second sketch and asked, "What did we do to these pieces of paper? . . . Shentae?"

"We blew in between them."

"Yes, we blew in between them," he repeated. "And what happened there . . . Ricky?"

"They came together."

"So we saw this paper rise up," he said, pointing at the first sketch. "We saw these papers come together," he continued, pointing at the second, "and in the third one, what happened?"

"We blew in the funnel," several of the students said simultaneously.

"And what happened? . . . Abe?"

"The ball didn't come out."

"The ball stayed right there," Scott rephrased, and he moved back to the first sketch. "Let's think about some forces that might be acting on these. . . . What are some forces acting on the paper? . . . Colin?"

"Gravity."

"Gravity, and which direction is gravity pulling?"

"Down."

"Down. . . . Gravity is pulling down."

Scott drew an arrow indicating the force of gravity and labeled it *A*.

"Is there another force? . . . William?" he continued.

"Air," William said, pointing up.

"How do you know it's pushing up?

"The paper moved up."

"Exactly. You know there's a force pushing up, because the paper moved up. And objects move in the direction of the greater force."

Scott drew an arrow pointing up and labeled it *B*.

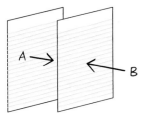

"Now let's move over here," he said, moving to the second sketch and drawing the arrows shown here.

"Where was the force greater here, at A or at B? . . . Talley?"

"B."

"How do you know?"

"The papers moved together."

"Exactly, because if they moved that way, the force that way had to be greater."

"Now let's go here," Scott said and moved over to the sketch of the ball and funnel.

"David. Which force is greater, A or B?"

"B."

"How do you know?"

"The ball stayed in the funnel."

"Now let's look at some trends," Scott continued, moving over to the first sketch. "Which one did we say was greater—A, pulling down, or B, pushing up?"

"B," several students said in unison.

"Which one in number 2—A, pushing out, or B, pushing in?"

"B."

"B. Good. And what about number 3—A or B?"

"B."

"Now I want everyone to look closely. . . . Do you see a relationship between where you blew and which one was stronger? . . . Heather?"

"It seems like wherever you blew, the opposite was stronger."

"So every place you blew, where was the force greater?"

"In the opposite direction."

"So," Scott continued. "This person named Bernoulli, who first discovered this principle, . . . he said that every time you increase the speed of the air, the force goes down. . . . So when I speed up the wind on the top of the paper (holding up the single sheet of paper), the force goes down and this force takes over (motioning to the force underneath the paper).

"Same thing when I blow between two sheets. The force in between goes down, and the outside force takes over."

Scott reviewed the same principle in the example with the ball and funnel and then ended the lesson.

In Chapter 12, we emphasized that productive learning environments are orderly and focused on learning, and we discussed ways of creating and maintain orderly classrooms. We now turn to an examination of the abilities all teachers need to help students learn as much as possible. In doing so, we'll look carefully at Scott's work with his students. In particular, we want to consider his thinking as he planned his lesson, his skills in implementing it, and the way he assessed his students' understanding.

When you're finished with your study of this chapter, you should be able to

- Identify the different types of knowledge expert teachers possess
- Describe the thinking of expert teachers as they plan for instruction
- Identify essential teaching skills that help promote learning for all students at all levels
- Describe the relationships among planning instruction, implementing instruction, and assessing student learning

Teacher knowledge allows teachers to make effective decisions during their planning.

Teacher Knowledge and Teacher Thinking

You're probably taking this course because you are in a teacher preparation program, one for which learning to teach is the goal. A great deal of research has been done on the way people learn to teach, and this research has focused primarily on two factors: teachers' knowledge and the way teachers think about their work (Borko & Putnam, 1996; Calderhead, 1996). We will examine the way Scott planned and conducted his lesson and the way he assessed his students' learning because they were the result of his knowledge and thinking.

Teacher Knowledge

In Chapter 1, we introduced the different kinds of knowledge that expert teachers possess. Each is essential, and they include

- Knowledge of content (Jetton & Alexander, 1997), such as Scott's understanding of the concept *force,* the principle stating that objects move in the direction of the greater force, and Bernoulli's principle itself.
- Pedagogical content knowledge (Shulman, 1986), such as Scott's ability to illustrate Bernoulli's principle with the pieces of paper, ping-pong ball, and funnel.
- General pedagogical knowledge (Borko & Putnam, 1996), such as understanding how to organize orderly classrooms and use questioning skills that involve students and lead to thorough understanding.
- Knowledge of learners and learning (Borko & Putnam, 1996), such as understanding that students need concrete examples when they first encounter a topic and that success on tasks they perceive as challenging increases both motivation and learning.

Scott obviously understood Bernoulli's principle, but more importantly, he demonstrated pedagogical content knowledge in representing the principle with the papers, ball, and funnel. They provided the concrete examples needed to help the students reach the goal of the lesson.

Scott also demonstrated a thorough understanding of learning. A less skilled teacher might have simply explained Bernoulli's principle, but Scott understood that people construct their own understanding of the topics they study and that explaining is often ineffective for guiding this process (Bransford et al., 2000). He also knew that his students would construct their understanding from the examples they experienced, so he carefully developed his lesson around them. At the same time he realized that the examples, alone, weren't enough. To develop a clear understanding of the principle, the students needed to be actively involved in discussing the examples and putting their developing understanding into words (Wink & Putney, 2002). So he guided the discussion with his questioning, and his questioning skills demonstrated his general pedagogical knowledge. *Knowledge of content, pedagogical content knowledge, general pedagogical knowledge,* and *knowledge of learners and learning* each influenced Scott's thinking as he planned and implemented the lesson.

Teacher Thinking

Teacher thinking centers on making decisions intended to promote student learning. These decisions are based on answers to such questions as

- What topics are most important for students to study in the limited school and classroom time available?
- How do I plan lessons to promote as much learning as possible?
- How do I implement instruction to maximize learning?
- How do I select and design assessments to measure the amount of learning that has occurred?
- How do I ensure that instruction and assessments are aligned with the objectives? (L. Anderson & Krathwohl, 2001)

Teacher thinking thus centers on planning for instruction, implementing instruction, and assessing learning (see Figure 13.1). Let's look more closely at each of these areas.

13.1
Could teachers have thorough knowledge of content and inadequate pedagogical content knowledge? Could teachers have pedagogical content knowledge without knowledge of content? Explain in both cases.

13.2
What concept from your study of Vygotsky's work in Chapter 2 is best illustrated by Scott guiding the discussion with his questioning? Explain.

Figure 13.1 Processes involved in teacher thinking about planning, implementation, and assessment

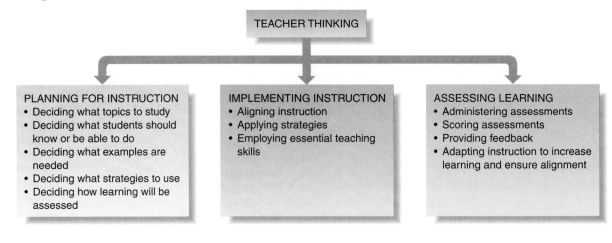

```
                         TEACHER THINKING

PLANNING FOR INSTRUCTION    IMPLEMENTING INSTRUCTION   ASSESSING LEARNING
• Deciding what topics      • Aligning instruction     • Administering assessments
  to study                  • Applying strategies      • Scoring assessments
• Deciding what students    • Employing essential      • Providing feedback
  should know or be able      teaching skills          • Adapting instruction to
  to do                                                  increase learning and
• Deciding what examples                                 ensure alignment
  are needed
• Deciding what strategies
  to use
• Deciding how learning
  will be assessed
```

Planning for Instruction

Planning for instruction includes all the decisions teachers make before working directly with students (Kauchak & Eggen, 2003). Specifically, planning involves making decisions about what topics are most important to study, how the topics will be represented, what teaching strategies will be used, and how learning will be assessed. Assessing learning is ongoing; formal assessments are given after instruction, but many of the decisions about assessment are made during planning.

Deciding What Topics Are Important to Study

"What is important to study?" is one of the most common and long-standing questions that exist in education (L. Anderson & Krathwohl, 2001). Textbooks, curriculum guides, and standards mandated by states or suggested by professional organizations are three common sources that teachers use to help them answer the question. Teachers' personal philosophies, students' interests in the topic, and real-world applications are other sources. Scott, for example, believed that Bernoulli's principle was important for students to learn, because it would help them understand how airplanes are able to fly. This is a real-world application.

Some teachers tacitly avoid making decisions about what is important to study by simply teaching the topics as they appear in their textbooks or curriculum guides (Zahorik, 1991). This can present a problem, however, because more content appears in typical textbooks than can be learned in depth.

Parsimony is essential in setting out educational goals. Schools should pick the most important concepts and skills to emphasize so that they can concentrate on the quality of understanding rather than on the quantity of information presented. (Rutherford & Algren, 1990, p. 185)

You will examine this question in detail in courses that come later in your program.

Clear goals allow teachers to design learning tasks that match students' needs.

Preparing Objectives: Deciding What Students Should Know, Value, or Be Able to Do

Scott decided that Bernoulli's principle was an important topic to study because it had a practical, real-world application. To plan his lesson, however, he needed to make more specific decisions about what his students should know, value, or be able to do. He needed to develop *objectives* for the lesson.

Objectives in the Cognitive Domain

Scott wanted his students to be able to apply Bernoulli's principle to real-world examples. This describes an objective in the **cognitive domain**, *the learning domain that focuses on the cognitive processes involved in learning different forms of knowledge.* Before examining Scott's planning in detail, let's take a brief historical look at objectives in the cognitive domain.

13.3
Do you recall what the term *cognitive* means? Define.

In *Basic Principles of Curriculum and Instruction,* Ralph Tyler (1950) suggested that the most useful form for stating objectives is "to express them in terms which identify both the kind of behavior to be developed in the student and the content or area of life in which this behavior is to operate" (p. 46). Tyler's text became a classic, and other applications of his idea, such as management-by-objectives in the business world, became popular in the 1950s and 1960s. These applications went well beyond Tyler's original conception to include the conditions under which learners would demonstrate the behavior and the criteria for acceptable performance. This specific approach was popularized by Robert Mager (1962) in his highly readable book *Preparing Instructional Objectives.* Mager's work also strongly influenced teaching and remains popular today (Mager, 1998).

A prominent alternative to Mager's approach is one offered by Norman Gronlund (2000). Gronlund has suggested that teachers formulate a general objective, such as *know, understand,* or *apply,* followed by specific learning outcomes that operationally define these terms.

To read more about Gronlund's approach and to see examples of objectives written according to both Mager's and Gronlund's formats, go to the Companion Website at *www.prenhall.com/eggen*, then to this chapter's *Additional Content* module.

Ralph Tyler used *behavior* and *content* in his description of objectives, but more recent thinking about objectives avoids the use of both terms (L. Anderson & Krathwohl, 2001). To reflect the emphasis on cognitive views of learning, and because the term *behavior* was commonly—and mistakenly—equated with behaviorism by many who studied Tyler's original work, educational theorists today recommend stating objectives in terms of students' *cognitive processes* rather than *behaviors.* And because the term *content* isn't precisely defined, they use the term *knowledge:* "We use the term *knowledge* to reflect our belief that disciplines are constantly changing and evolving in terms of the knowledge that shares a consensus of acceptance within the discipline" (L. Anderson & Krathwohl, 2001, p. 13). **Objectives,** then, are *statements that describe the knowledge that students are expected to acquire or construct and a cognitive process that describes what they will be able to do with the knowledge* (L. Anderson & Krathwohl, 2001). For example, "Students will apply Bernoulli's principle to real-world examples" was Scott's objective. Bernoulli's principle is the knowledge, and *apply* is the cognitive process—it specifies what the students will do with that knowledge.

A Taxonomy for Cognitive Objectives

Scott wanted his students to apply Bernoulli's principle to real-world examples, such as why the ping-pong ball stayed in the funnel. Many other objectives involving the same knowledge exist, however. The following are two additional possibilities:

- Students will learn to state Bernoulli's principle in their own words.
- Students will differentiate between relevant and irrelevant information in applications of Bernoulli's principle.

Although all three objectives involve the same knowledge—Bernoulli's principle—the cognitive processes described differ. *Applying* the principle, *paraphrasing* it

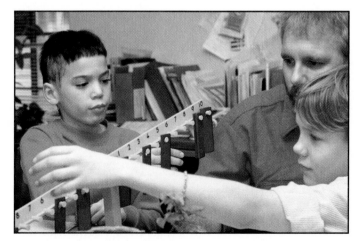

The different levels of the cognitive domain help teachers design learning activities that emphasize problem solving and critical thinking.

13.4
The terms used in Figure 13.2 suggest that the taxonomy is based on which theory of learning—behaviorism, social cognitive theory, information processing, or constructivism? Explain.

13.5
Classify the following objective into one of the cells of the taxonomy and explain your classification: *Students will learn to search for relevant and irrelevant information in applications of all the topics they study.*

(stating it in their own words), and *differentiating* between relevant and irrelevant information are three different cognitive processes.

In response to differences such as these, researchers have developed a system to classify different objectives (L. Anderson & Krathwohl, 2001). A revision of the famous "Bloom's taxonomy" first published in 1956 (Bloom, Englehart, Furst, Hill, & Krathwohl, 1956), the system is a matrix with 24 cells that represent the intersection of four types of knowledge with six cognitive processes. The revision reflects the dramatic increase in understanding of learning and teaching since the middle of the 20th century, when the original taxonomy was created, and it now more nearly reflects the influence of cognitive learning theory on education (L. Anderson & Krathwohl, 2001). The revised taxonomy appears in Figure 13.2.

To understand this matrix, let's analyze the three objectives. Bernoulli's principle is a form of *conceptual knowledge,* or knowledge of "classifications and categories, principles, and generalizations, and theories, models, and structures" (L. Anderson & Krathwohl, 2001, p. 27). The term *apply* appeared in Scott's objective, so his objective would be placed in the cell where *apply* intersects with *conceptual knowledge.* Paraphrasing is a form of understanding, so the second objective would be placed in the cell where *understand* intersects with *conceptual knowledge.* Differentiating is a form of analysis, so the third objective would be in the cell where *analyze* intersects with *conceptual knowledge.*

The taxonomy reminds us that learning is a complex process with many possible outcomes. It also reminds us that we want our students to do much more than "remember" "factual knowledge." Unfortunately, a great deal of schooling focuses as much on this most basic type of objective as it does on the other 23 types combined. Moving to the other forms of knowledge and more advanced cognitive processes is even more important now in the 21st century, as student thinking, decision making, and problem solving are increasingly emphasized.

Objectives in the Affective Domain

Although most of the focus in schools is on cognitive outcomes, teachers have many implicit objectives that don't fit in that domain. For example, science and math teachers want students to like these subjects and appreciate their importance in today's world, but they rarely specify *liking* and *appreciating* as objectives. In these cases, teachers have objectives that fit into the **affective domain,** *the learning domain that focuses on attitudes*

Figure 13.2 A taxonomy for learning, teaching, and assessing

The Knowledge Dimension	The Cognitive Process Dimension					
	1. Remember	2. Understand	3. Apply	4. Analyze	5. Evaluate	6. Create
A. Factual knowledge						
B. Conceptual knowledge						
C. Procedural knowledge						
D. Metacognitive knowledge						

Source: From Lorin W. Anderson & David R. Krathwohl, *A Taxonomy for Learning, Teaching, and Assessing: A Revision of Bloom's Objectives,* © 2001. Published by Allyn and Bacon, Boston, MA. Copyright © 2001 by Pearson Education. Reprinted by permission of the publisher.

Table 13.1 Levels, outcomes, and examples in the affective domain

Level	Outcome	Example
Receiving	Is willing to listen, open-minded	Pays attention in science class
Responding	Demonstrates new behavior, volunteers involvement	Volunteers answers, asks questions
Valuing	Shows commitment, maintains involvement	Reads ahead in text, watches science-oriented programs on television
Organizing	Integrates new value into personal structure	Chooses to take 4 years of science in high school because of interest in science
Characterizing by value	Gains open, firm, and long-range commitment to value	Chooses a branch of science as a career field

Source: Taxonomy of Educational Objectives: Handbook II: Affective Domain by D. Krathwohl, B. Bloom, and B. Masia, 1964, New York: David McKay. Copyright 1964 by David McKay. Adapted by permission.

and values and the development of students' personal and emotional growth.

A classification system for objectives in the affective domain also exists (Krathwohl, Bloom, & Masia, 1964), with a structure parallel to that of the original Bloom's taxonomy in the cognitive domain. The guiding principle behind the affective domain is **internalization,** *the extent to which an attitude or value has been incorporated into a student's total value structure.* The affective domain is outlined in Table 13.1 and illustrated with an example that could be based on Scott's lesson.

Although much of teachers' focus in the affective domain is implicit, they sometimes concentrate on it deliberately. For example, many multicultural lessons have increased awareness of and appreciation for other cultures' values and customs as their objectives. Similarly, learning about disabilities helps students develop more positive attitudes toward people with exceptionalities (Hardman et al., 1999). The affective taxonomy reminds us that attitudes, values, and emotions strongly affect learning and that we should keep these factors in mind when we plan and teach.

> **13.6**
> Suppose Scott said, "One of the things I'm after is for them to get over their fear of science. Otherwise, they'll take only what's required in high school." At what level in the affective taxonomy would this goal be classified?

Objectives in the Psychomotor Domain

A third type of learning involves the **psychomotor domain,** *the learning domain that focuses on the development of students' physical abilities and skills.* It has historically received less emphasis than the cognitive or affective domains, except in physical education, and taxonomies for it weren't developed until the 1970s (Harrow, 1972; E. Simpson, 1972). However, schools are increasing their emphasis on the psychomotor domain as its role in overall development becomes better understood. For instance, kindergarten children practice tying their shoes, and the ability to physically manipulate a pencil is considered in assessing a child's readiness for writing. Science requires using equipment such as microscopes and balances, geometry involves constructions with compasses and rulers, word processing and driver's training require physical skills, and fine motor movements are essential in art and music. These are all objectives in the psychomotor domain.

Growth in the psychomotor domain contributes to healthy self-concepts and increases physical well-being in students.

Table 13.2 Levels, outcomes, and examples in the psychomotor domain

Level	Outcome	Examples
Reflex movements	Involuntary responses	Blinking, knee jerks
Basic fundamental movements	Innate movements, combinations of reflexes	Eating, running, physically tracking an object
Perceptual abilities	Movement following interpretation of stimuli	Walking a balance beam, skipping rope, writing *p* and *q*
Physical abilities	Endurance, strength, flexibility, agility	Pull-ups, toe touching, distance bicycling
Skilled movements	Efficiency in complex movement tasks	Hitting a tennis ball, jazz dancing
Nondiscursive communication	Communication with physical movement, body language	Pleasure, authority, warmth, and other emotions demonstrated with body language

Source: A Taxonomy of the Psychomotor Domain: A Guide for Developing Behavioral Objectives by A. Harrow, 1972, New York: David McKay. Copyright 1972 by David McKay. Adapted by permission.

Table 13.2 presents a description and illustrations of the psychomotor taxonomy using Harrow's (1972) conception as a framework.

The psychomotor domain provides us with a more complete picture of our students as human beings. In addition to helping them grow cognitively and affectively, we want them to develop healthy bodies that they can use throughout their lives.

Preparing and Organizing Learning Activities

Once Scott decided on a topic and specified an objective in the cognitive domain ("Apply Bernoulli's principle to real-world examples"), he then needed to prepare and organize his learning activity. This process involves four steps:

1. Identify the components of the topic—the concepts, principles, and relationships among them that students should understand.
2. Sequence the components of the topic.
3. Prepare examples that students can use to construct their understanding of each component of the topic.
4. Order the examples with the most salient and obvious presented first.

Scott accomplished these steps in a task analysis. Let's look at it.

Task Analysis: A Planning Tool

Task analysis is *the process of breaking content down into component parts and making decisions about sequencing the parts.* A task analysis can take at least three different forms: a behavioral, an information processing, or a subject matter analysis (Alberto & Troutman, 1999; Jonassen, Hannum, & Tessmer, 1989).

In a behavioral analysis, the teacher identifies and sequences the specific behaviors the student must demonstrate to carry out the learning activity (the task). For instance, when learning to do word processing on a computer, the student must learn to turn on the computer; access the desired word processing program; input text; save, move, and delete files, and change formatting. Each of these is necessary before learning more sophisticated skills, such as creating and inserting tables, artwork, and graphics. A task analysis identifies these skills and creates a sequence that makes them meaningful.

In an information processing analysis, the teacher identifies and sequences the specific cognitive processes required for the learning activity. For instance, to solve word problems in math, students must correctly encode the type of problem, retrieve the necessary math facts, apply the appropriate operations, and use metacognitive skills to assess their answers.

In a subject matter analysis, the teacher breaks down the topic into specific concepts and principles and identifies the relationships among them. They are then arranged in a sequence that will make them the most understandable, and examples for each are prepared.

Scott conducted a subject matter analysis. For instance, he knew that his students needed to learn the concept *force* to understand what made the papers and ball move. They also needed to understand that when two forces act on an object in opposite directions, the object moves in the direction of the greater force. This principle helped the students understand why the papers and ping-pong ball moved in the directions they did. This is our first step in preparing and organizing a teaching activity.

Scott then sequenced these topics, the second step. Because the concept *force* and the principle describing the movement of objects were background knowledge for understanding Bernoulli's principle, Scott taught them the day before his lesson and reviewed them before focusing on Bernoulli's principle itself.

Scott then prepared specific, concrete examples of each concept and principle (the third step), and he planned additional examples in his review. He also identified examples that concretely illustrated Bernoulli's principle itself—examples that demonstrated that the faster air moves over a surface, the less force it exerts on the surface. He selected examples that allowed the students to *see* where the air was moving more rapidly and where the force was greater. They could see that the air was moving faster over the top of the paper, for example, because this is where they blew, and the force pushing the paper up was greater than the force of gravity pulling down, because the paper moved up.

Finally, as the last step in preparing and organizing a teaching activity, Scott planned to blow over the single piece of paper as his first example, between the two papers as his second, and the ball and funnel as the third. He ordered his examples in this way because he believed the relationship between the speed of the air and the force was most obvious in the first example.

Scott ordered his examples from most to least obvious to maximize student understanding.

Scott demonstrated sophisticated knowledge of learners and learning in thinking about his planning. He knew that his students would construct their understanding of Bernoulli's principle based on the examples he provided, so he *selected examples in which the students could observe all the information they needed to understand the principle.* His ability to find examples that contained all the necessary information reflected his sophisticated pedagogical content knowledge. A teacher with less expertise would have simply explained the concept *force,* the principle describing the movement of objects, and perhaps Bernoulli's principle itself. However, Scott knew that explaining is not generally effective; students need specific, concrete experiences to understand abstract concepts and principles.

Scott's planning reflects the intersection of knowledge of content, pedagogical content knowledge, and knowledge of learners and learning. This is the kind of thinking all teachers need to do to promote as much learning as possible.

Scott's task analysis is outlined in Table 13.3.

> **13.7**
> Consider the way Scott planned and taught his lesson. On what theory of learning—behaviorism, social cognitive theory, information processing, or constructivism—is his thinking and instruction most nearly based? Explain.

Planning for Assessment

Assessment occurs after students are involved in learning activities, so it is easy to assume that thinking about assessment also occurs after learning activities are conducted. This isn't true. Teachers need to think about assessment while they are preparing objectives and learning activities. They should focus on the question, "How do I select and design assessments to measure the amount of learning that has occurred?"

Teachers need to plan for assessment as an integral part of instruction.

Table 13.3 Scott's task analysis

Task Analysis Step	Example
1. Identify components of the topic.	Scott identified the concept *force*, the principle stating that *objects move in the direction of the greater force* and *Bernoulli's principle* as the components of his topic.
2. Sequence the components.	Scott planned to first teach the concept *force*; second, the principle stating that *objects move in the direction of the greater force*; and third, *Bernoulli's principle*.
3. Prepare examples of each component.	Scott pushed on the board and blew on the object to illustrate *force*. Scott and a student tugged on a stapler to illustrate the principle stating that *objects move in the direction of the greater force*. Scott used the papers, ball, and funnel to illustrate *Bernoulli's principle*.
4. Order the examples that illustrate each component.	Scott used the single piece of paper first, the two pieces of paper second, and the ball and funnel third.

When Scott planned his activity, he prepared a quiz that included three items, as follows:

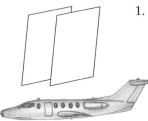

1. Look at the drawing that represents the two pieces of paper that we used in the lesson. Explain what made the papers move together. Make a drawing that shows how the air flowed as you blew between the papers. Label the forces in the drawing as we did during the lesson.
2. Look at the sketch of the airplane. Using the information in the sketch, write one paragraph explaining what makes the airplane fly.
3. Watch the demonstration. Explain why the water came up the straw and sprayed me.

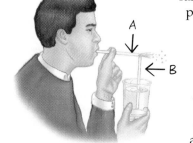

Scott planned a demonstration for item 3. He would blow through Straw A, as in the illustration. As he blew, the water in the cup would come up Straw B and disperse in a fine spray.

Three aspects of Scott's assessment are significant. First, the format for the assessment was the same as the format for his learning activity, and both were outcomes of his thinking as he planned the lesson. He used specific, concrete examples in his lesson, and he also used specific, concrete examples to assess his students' ability to apply the principle to real-world situations.

Second, by thinking about assessment during planning, Scott addressed the question "How do I ensure that instruction and assessments are aligned with the objectives?" Such alignment is essential for promoting as much learning as possible (L. Anderson & Krathwohl, 2001).

Third, Scott's learning environment was, in addition to being knowledge centered and learner centered, assessment centered. This means that assessment was not something added on at the end of his lesson and used primarily to give a grade; it was an integral part of the total teaching-learning process (Bransford et al., 2000).

We look at the importance of assessment in Scott's lesson again near the end of the chapter.

Planning in a Standards-Based Environment

A great deal has been written about Americans and American students lacking knowledge about their history and their world. Research suggests, for example, that 60% of adult Americans don't know the name of the president who ordered the dropping of the atomic bomb, 42% of college seniors can't place the Civil War in the correct half century, and most Americans can't find the Persian Gulf on a map (Bertman, 2000). These examples are in social studies, and even greater concerns have been raised about math, science, and writing knowledge. The result has been a move toward establishing **standards,** *statements that describe what students should know or be able to do at the end of a prescribed period of study.* Some standards are stated specifically, whereas others are quite general. Those stated in general terms are often followed by more specific statements called *benchmarks, expectations, indicators,* and a variety of other names.

Although the standards movement is highly controversial, with critics (e.g., Amrein & Berliner, 2002; Paris, 1998) and proponents (e.g., Bishop, 1998; Hirsh, 2000) lining up on opposite sides, virtually every professional organization in education has prepared lists of standards. Standards exist for core subjects, such as math and English, as well as for subjects such as the arts, foreign language, and physical education (e.g., see Consortium of National Arts Education Associations, 1994; Geography Education Standards Project, 1994; National Association for Sport and Physical Education, 1995; National Council of Teachers of Mathematics, 2000; National Standards in Foreign Language Education Project, 1999). Even support organizations such as the National Parent Teacher Association (2000) have created standards. In addition, the District of Columbia, Puerto Rico, and every state except Iowa have set academic standards for students.

It is virtually certain that your planning decisions will be influenced by standards. What does this mean for you? It means that your school will be held accountable for helping students meet the standards, so you must design learning activities to meet this goal.

Standards are essentially statements of objectives. Considering that standards prescribe objectives, you might think that this would reduce the number of decisions you must make. This usually isn't true, however. Standards vary in their specificity, so you will have to interpret them. In other words, you must answer the question, "Exactly what does this standard mean?" Also, learning activities that help meet the standards are usually not prescribed for teachers.

Finally, teachers must make decisions about aligning learning activities with standards and assessments. In some cases, standards include suggested assessments, which means that you must first interpret the standard in the context of the assessment and then design your learning activity to be aligned with both. If suggested assessments aren't offered, you will have to make decisions about both learning activities and assessments that are aligned with the standard.

Let's look at an example. The following standard for middle school math students was created by the National Council of Teachers of Mathematics (2000):

Number and Operations Standard for Grades 6–8
Instructional programs from prekindergarten through grade 12 should enable all students to compute fluently and make reasonable estimates:

In grades 6–8 all students should:

- work flexibly with fractions, decimals, and percents to solve problems;
- compare and order fractions, decimals, and percents efficiently and find their approximate locations on a number line;
- develop meaning for percents greater than 100 and less than 1. (p. 214)

If you were working with this standard, you would need to decide what "work flexibly with fractions, decimals, and percents to solve problems" means, decide what students must do to meet this objective, and design an assessment. In its standards, the NCTM (2000) suggests the following to assess students' ability to "work flexibly with fractions":

a. If ▓▓▓▓▓▓▓ is ¾, draw the fraction strip for ½, for ⅔, for ⅙, and for ½. Be prepared to justify your answers.

b. ◄———┼——┼———————►
     1   1½

   Using the points you are given on the number line above, locate ½, 2½, and ¼. Be prepared to justify your answer. (p. 214)

13.8
Classify item *a* into one of the cells of the taxonomy in Table 13.1. Classify item *b.* Explain your classifications.

You would need to prepare assessments for the other two objectives in the standard.

As you can see, the thinking involved in planning for standards-based instruction is similar to the thinking involved in any planning. The standard merely begins the decision making process by presenting an objective in a form with varying degrees of specificity. The teacher must make decisions about learning activities and assessments.

Classroom Connections

Applying an Understanding of Expert Planning in Your Classroom

1. Carefully consider the level of your instruction. Make an effort to prepare objectives that require students to do more than remember factual knowledge.
   - *Elementary:* A fourth-grade teacher wants her students to understand the functions of the human skeleton, such as why the skull is solid, the ribs are curved, and the femur is the largest bone in the body. "This is much better than simply having them label the different bones," she thinks.
   - *Middle School:* A seventh-grade geography teacher wants his students to understand how climate is influenced by the interaction of a number of variables. To reach his objective, he gives students a map of a fictitious island, together with longitude, latitude, topography, and wind direction. He then gears his instruction around the conclusions they can make about the climate of the island.
   - *High School:* A biology teacher wants her students to understand the relationships between an organism's body structure and its adaptation to its environment. She has her students identify the characteristics of parasitic and nonparasitic worms and identify differences between the characteristics. The students must then link the differences to the organisms' abilities to adapt to their environments.
2. Be sure that your objectives, learning activities, and assessments are aligned. Prepare assessments during planning, and keep the need for alignment in mind as you plan.
   - *Elementary:* The fourth-grade teacher in her unit on the skeletal system plans an assessment in which the students are asked to consider the following question: "Suppose we humans walked on all fours, as chimpanzees and gorillas do. Describe how our skeletons would be different than they are now."
   - *Middle School:* The geography teacher gives his students another map of a fictitious island with different mountain ranges, wind directions, ocean currents, and latitude and longitude. He then asks them to identify and explain where the largest city on the island would most likely be.
   - *High School:* The biology teacher describes two organisms, one with radial symmetry and the other with bilateral symmetry. She asks her students to identify the one that is most advanced with respect to evolution and to explain their choices.
3. Deliberately plan for objectives in different domains to provide a balanced educational experience.
   - *Elementary:* A third-grade teacher carefully guides his students through basic math skills. He initially focuses on the students being successful. "I want them all to believe that they're capable of being successful math students," he emphasizes.
   - *Middle School:* A physical science teacher plans her initial presentation of inertia around real-world problems, like the use of seat belts in cars, why cars miss curves, and even why a wet dog is able to "shake itself off." She says, "I want students to appreciate science and see that basic science principles apply to 'where they live.'"
   - *High School:* A music teacher plans to begin her unit on different musical forms with songs inspired by the classics but created by prominent rock stars. "Students appreciate the classics once they find out that a lot of rock stars first got their ideas from them," she notes.

Implementing Instruction: Essential Teaching Skills

We've looked at how expert teachers, such as Scott Sowell, think as they plan a lesson. Now we want to turn to a lesson's implementation—that is, the lesson as we observe it.

Imagine sitting in the back of any classroom, regardless of the students' grade level, the content they are learning, or the specific teaching strategy being used. What would we hope to see? We're familiar with the basic skills in reading, writing, and math that all learners need, but there are also **essential teaching skills**, *basic abilities that all teachers, including those in their first year, should have to promote order and learning.* Just as learners must be able to read with comprehension when they study their geography, literature, or science books, teachers must demonstrate the essential teaching skills when promoting understanding and automaticity (an instructional strategy we discussed in Chapter 7), guided discovery and cooperative learning (two of the strategies we discussed in Chapter 8), or problem solving (discussed in Chapter 9). The essential teaching skills support learning for all types of students, content areas, and instructional strategies.

Each of the essential teaching skills is derived from an extensive body of research that emerged in the 1970s and 1980s (Good & Brophy, 2000; Shuell, 1996). (Expert teachers go well beyond these essential skills as they create experiences that maximize learning for their students.) The skills are outlined in Figure 13.3 and discussed in the sections that follow. For the sake of clarity, we describe the essential teaching skills separately, but they are interdependent; none is as effective alone as it is in combination with the others. The interaction and integration of these skills are crucial.

Figure 13.3 Essential teaching skills

Attitudes

Admittedly, "attitudes" are not skills, but positive teacher attitudes are fundamental to effective teaching. As we saw in Chapter 11, teacher characteristics such as *personal teaching efficacy, modeling and enthusiasm, caring,* and *high expectations* promote learner motivation. They are also associated with increased student achievement, which shouldn't be surprising since motivation and learning are so strongly linked (Bruning et al., 1999; Noddings, 1999; Shuell, 1996).

Scott displayed these characteristics in his work with his students. His instruction was energetic and enthusiastic, he demonstrated the respect for students that is an indicator of caring, and his questioning suggested that he expected all of his students to answer. These are the attitudes we hope to see in all teachers.

Use of Time

In addition to having positive attitudes about students' capabilities, effective teachers increase learning by using time efficiently. Time is a valuable resource. Efforts at reform have suggested lengthening the school year, school day, and even the amount of time devoted to certain subjects (Karweit, 1989), but improving learning by increasing time isn't as simple as it appears on the surface. As suggested in Table 13.4, different types of classroom time influence learning in different ways.

Table 13.4 Types of classroom time

Type	Description
Allocated time	The amount of time a teacher or school designates for a content area or topic
Instructional time	The amount left for teaching after routine management and administrative tasks are completed
Engaged time	The amount of time students are actively involved in learning activities
Academic learning time	The amount of time students are actively involved in learning activities *during which they're successful*

13.9

What is the allocated time for the class you're now in? Of this time, how much does your instructor typically devote to instruction? Why is the second question important?

As one moves from allocated time to academic learning time, the correlation with learning becomes stronger (Nystrand & Gamoran, 1989). In classrooms where students are engaged and successful, achievement is high, learners feel a sense of competence and self-efficacy, and interest in the topics is increased (C. Fisher et al., 1980).

Unfortunately, teachers don't always use time effectively. A great deal of class time is spent on noninstructional activities, often more than a third of teachers' allocated time (Karweit, 1989). Further, some teachers seem unaware of the importance of time, viewing it as something to be filled—or even "killed"—rather than a resource that increases learning (Eggen, 1998; D. Wiley & Harnischfeger, 1974). The ideal is to increase instructional, engaged, and academic learning time to make as much use of the allocated time as possible. When each of these types of time is maximized, learning increases (Stallings, 1980).

Organization

How many times have you put something away and later been unable to locate it? Have you ever said, "I've simply got to get organized" or "If he'd just get organized, he could be so effective"? Organization affects our personal lives and our teaching. Teacher organization affects learning because it determines how efficiently time is used (S. Bennett, 1978; Rutter et al., 1979).

Organization is *an essential teaching skill that includes starting on time, preparing materials in advance, establishing routines, and other actions that increase instructional time.* For example, Scott's organization allowed him to devote as much class time as possible to instruction. He began his lesson as soon as the bell rang, he had his materials ready for easy distribution, and he had well-established routines.

13.10

Expert teachers often have their students practice procedures, such as turning in papers, until they are automatic. On what theory of learning is this practice based? Explain.

Routines are extremely important for teachers. Research indicates that experts in every field have as many of their procedures as routinized as possible, which reduces the load on their working memories (Bransford et al., 2000; Bruning et al., 1999). Routines also create a sense of order and equilibrium. We saw in Chapter 2 that people have an innate need for equilibrium and in Chapter 12 that students learn more in orderly environments than in those that are chaotic.

An often overlooked value of routines is the energy they save teachers. Most people don't realize how *physically* demanding teaching is, particularly monitoring hands-on activities or guiding high levels of social interaction. Anything teachers can do to reduce their physical demands, without sacrificing learning, is worthwhile.

Effective organization allows teachers to make the best use of instructional time.

Communication

The link between effective communication, student achievement, and student satisfaction with instruction has been well established (Cruickshank, 1985; Snyder et al., 1991). Also, the way teachers interact with students influences their motivation and attitudes toward school (Pintrich & Schunk, 2002). Four aspects of effective communication are especially important for learning and motivation:

- Precise terminology
- Connected discourse
- Transition signals
- Emphasis

Precise terminology is *language that eliminates vague terms (such as* perhaps, maybe, might, and so on, *and* usually). When teachers use these seemingly innocuous terms in their explanations and responses to students' questions, students are left with a sense of uncertainty about the topics they're studying, and this uncertainty detracts from learning (L. Smith & Cotten, 1980). For example, suppose you asked,

"What do high-efficacy teachers do that promotes learning?" and your instructor responded, "Usually, they use their time somewhat better and so on." Another instructor responded, "They believe they can increase learning, and one of their characteristics is the effective use of time." The first response is muddled and uncertain, whereas the second is clear and precise.

Connected discourse is *instruction that is thematic and leads to a point.* If the point of the lesson isn't clear, if it is sequenced inappropriately, or if incidental information is interjected without indicating how it relates to the topic, classroom discourse becomes "disconnected" or "scrambled." Effective teachers keep their lessons on track, minimizing time on matters unrelated to the topic (Coker, Lorentz, & Coker, 1980; L. Smith & Cotten, 1980).

Transition signals are *verbal statements indicating that one idea is ending and another is beginning.* For example, an American government teacher might signal a transition by saying, "We've been talking about the Senate, which is one house of Congress. Now we'll turn to the House of Representatives." Because not all students are cognitively at the same place, a transition signal alerts them that the lesson is making a conceptual shift—moving to a new topic—and allows them to adjust and prepare for it.

Emphasis, a fourth aspect of effective communication, consists of *verbal and vocal cues and repetition that alert students to important information in a lesson.* Teachers influence what students learn by emphasizing it (Jetton & Alexander, 1997).

For example, Scott raised his voice—a form of vocal emphasis—in saying, "Keep those ideas in mind," as he moved from his review to the lesson itself. When teachers say, "Now remember, everyone, this is very important" or "Listen carefully now," they're using verbal emphasis. Repeating a point—redundancy—is also a form of emphasis. Asking students, "What did we say earlier that these problems had in common?" stresses an important feature in the problems and helps students link new to past information. Redundancy is particularly effective when reviewing abstract rules, principles, and concepts (Brophy & Good, 1986; Shuell, 1996).

Communication and Knowledge of Content: Implications for Teachers

Our discussion of communication has two implications for teachers. First, they should monitor their own speech to ensure that their presentations are as clear and logical as possible. Videotaping lessons and developing lessons with many questions are simple and effective ways to improve clarity. Second, teachers must thoroughly understand the content they teach. If the content is unfamiliar, or if teachers' own grasp of it is uncertain, they should spend extra time studying and preparing. Teachers whose understanding of topics is thorough use clearer language, their discourse is more connected, and they provide better explanations than those whose background is weaker (Carlsen, 1987; Cruickshank, 1985).

Clear understanding is particularly important when teachers guide learners instead of lecturing to them. Guiding learning requires that teachers constantly keep their objectives in mind, keep students involved, and ask appropriate questions at the right times. These are sophisticated abilities that require a deep and thorough understanding of the topics.

Focus: Attracting and Maintaining Attention

We saw in Chapter 11 that introductory focus *attracts students' attention and provides a framework for a lesson.* In addition to attracting attention, it can increase motivation by arousing

Introductory focus attracts students' attention and maintains it during the lesson.

13.11
Does *connected discourse* imply that teachers should avoid interjecting additional material into lessons? Explain.

13.12
What concept is being illustrated when learners link new to past information or create new links in what they already understand? (Hint: Think about your study of Chapter 7.)

Scott's concrete examples provided mental models that helped the students understand an abstract principle.

curiosity. Scott provided introductory focus for his students by beginning his lesson with his demonstrations. They attracted the students' attention, and they provided a context for the rest of the lesson.

Scott's demonstrations also acted as a form of **sensory focus**, or *stimuli*—concrete objects, pictures, models, materials displayed on the overhead, and even information written on the chalkboard—*that are used to maintain students' attention during learning activities.* His demonstrations and drawings gave students something to focus on and provided a mental model to help them conceptualize an abstract principle.

Many of the teachers in the case studies that you've studied in earlier chapters provided sensory focus in their lessons. Examples include:

- Jenny Newhall's demonstration with the cup and water in Chapter 2
- David Shelton's matrix and transparencies in Chapter 7
- Jenny's balances and Suzanne Brush's graph in Chapter 8
- Laura Hunter's classroom diagram in Chapter 9
- Kathy Brewster's map in Chapter 10
- DeVonne Lampkin's examples of paragraphs on the overhead in Chapter 11

Each teacher used sensory focus to help maintain students' attention and remind them of the lesson's topic and direction.

We have strongly emphasized the importance of examples and other representations of content throughout this text, and here we see another function that they provide. If you build lessons around high-quality examples, the examples not only provide the information students need to construct their understanding, but they also provide the sensory focus needed to help maintain attention.

13.13
What makes an example "high quality"? Illustrate your description with an example of your own.

Feedback

The importance of **feedback**—*information learners receive about the accuracy or appropriateness of their verbal responses and work*—in promoting learning is inarguable (Weinert & Helmke, 1995). Feedback allows learners to assess the accuracy of their background knowledge, and it gives them information about the validity of their knowledge constructions. It also helps learners elaborate on their existing understanding. Feedback is also important for motivation (see Chapters 10 and 11) because it provides students with information about their increasing competence (Clifford, 1990) and helps satisfy their intrinsic need to understand how they're progressing.

Effective feedback has four essential characteristics:

- It is immediate or given soon after a learner response.
- It is specific.
- It provides corrective information for the learner.
- It has a positive emotional tone. (Brophy & Good, 1986; Murphy, Weil, & McGreal, 1986)

To illustrate these characteristics, let's look at three examples.

Mr. Dole:	What kind of figure is shown on the overhead, Jo?
Jo:	A square.
Mr. Dole:	Not quite. Help her out, . . . Steve?
Ms. West:	What kind of figure is shown on the overhead, Jo?
Jo:	A square.
Ms. West:	No, it's a rectangle. What is the next figure, . . . Albert?
Ms. Baker:	What kind of figure is shown on the overhead, Jo?
Jo:	A square.
Ms. Baker:	No, remember we said that all sides have the same length in a square. What do you notice about the lengths of the sides in this figure?

In each scenario, the teacher gave immediate feedback. Mr. Dole, however, gave Jo no information about her answer other than it was incorrect; his feedback was not specific and provided no corrective information. Ms. West's feedback was specific, but it gave Jo no corrective information. Ms. Baker, in contrast, provided specific, corrective information in her response.

The examples give us no information about the emotional tone of the teachers' responses. Maintaining a positive emotional tone means avoiding harsh, critical, or sarcastic feedback, which detracts from both learning and student motivation (Pintrich & Schunk, 2002).

We said that effective feedback is immediate or given soon after a learner response. In question and answer sessions, feedback should be immediate. In other cases, such as addressing student responses on test or quiz items, however, delayed feedback often increases understanding more than immediate feedback. In other words, discussing test items the day after the test is given is more effective than discussing them immediately after finishing the test. According to cognitive learning theory, delaying the discussion gives students time to elaborate on their original thinking. Then, receiving feedback helps them confirm or requires them to reconstruct their understanding. In either case, the feedback is more meaningful than immediate feedback would be. It is also best not to withhold feedback for too long—say until a week after the test, when students may be less able to recall the reasons behind their answers. So "delayed" feedback, too, should occur relatively soon after a learner response.

13.14
On the basis of your study of motivation in Chapters 10 and 11, explain why a positive emotional tone in delivering feedback is important.

Praise

Praise is probably the most common and adaptable form of teacher feedback. Research reveals some interesting patterns in its use:

- Praise is used less often than most teachers believe—less than five times per class.
- Praise for good behavior is quite rare, occurring once every 2 or more hours in the elementary grades and even less as students get older.
- Praise tends to depend as much on the type of student—high achieving, well behaved, and attentive—as on the quality of the student's response.
- Teachers praise students based on the answers they expect to receive as much as on those they actually hear. (Brophy, 1981; Good & Brophy, 2000)

Praising students effectively seems simple, but in fact, it is quite complex and requires sound teacher judgment. Developmental differences are important. Young children tend to accept praise at face value even when overdone. Also, young children bask in praise given openly in front of a class, whereas adolescents may react better if it's given quietly and individually (Stipek, 2002). Students who are highly anxious and those from low-SES backgrounds tend to react more positively to praise than students who are confident and those from higher SES backgrounds (Brophy, 1981; Good & Brophy, 2000).

In contrast with young children, older students quickly discount praise they perceive as insincere or unwarranted. Older students may also interpret praise given for easy tasks as indicating that the teacher thinks they have low ability (Emmer, 1988; Good, 1987b). Experts suggest that praise should be delivered to older students in a simple and direct way, using a natural voice. And it should reflect genuine accomplishment (Good & Brophy, 2000).

13.15
Praise that reflects genuine accomplishment helps meet an important intrinsic need in students. What is that need? (Hint: Think about your study of intrinsic motivation in Chapter 10.)

Finally, although research indicates that specific praise is more effective than general praise, if every desired answer is praised specifically, it sounds stilted and artificial and disrupts the flow of a lesson. You must judge the appropriate mix of specific and general praise.

Experts suggest that praise for student answers that are correct but tentative should be specific and provide additional or affirming information, whereas praise for answers delivered with confidence should be simple and general (Rosenshine, 1987).

Written Feedback

Much of the feedback students receive is verbal, but teachers can also provide valuable feedback through their notes and comments on student work. Because writing detailed comments is time-consuming, written feedback is often brief and sketchy, so it gives students little useful information (Bloom & Bourdon, 1980).

One solution to this problem is to provide model responses to written assignments. For instance, to help students evaluate their answers to essay items, teachers can write ideal answers, display them on an overhead, and encourage students to compare their answers with the model. The model, combined with discussion and time available for individual help after school, provides informative feedback that is manageable for the teacher.

Questioning

As instruction becomes more learner centered in response to the cognitive revolution in general and constructivist views of learning in particular, teachers are increasingly being asked to guide learning rather than simply deliver information. Questioning is the most important tool teachers have for meeting this goal (Wang et al., 1993).

A teacher skilled in questioning can assess student background knowledge, cause learners to rethink their ideas, help them form relationships, involve shy or reticent students, recapture students' wandering attention, promote success, and enhance self-worth. Questioning can also be a tool to maintain the pace and momentum of a lesson, important factors in maintaining student engagement (Good & Brophy, 2000; Kounin, 1970).

Skilled questioning is very sophisticated, but with practice, effort and experience, teachers can and do become expert at it (Kerman, 1979; Rowe, 1986). To avoid overloading their own working memories, teachers need to practice questioning strategies to the point of automaticity, which leaves working memory space available to monitor students' thinking and assess learning progress.

Effective questioning

- Is frequent
- Is equitably distributed
- Uses prompting
- Allows adequate wait-time

We consider these characteristics in the following sections.

Questioning Frequency

In his lesson in the opening case study, Scott asked a large number of questions. In fact, he developed his entire lesson with questioning. **Questioning frequency** refers to *the number of times a teacher asks questions during a given period of instructional time.* In general, the more questions teachers ask, the more effective they are (Morine-Dershimer, 1987). Questioning increases student involvement, which increases achievement (Lambert & McCombs, 1998), and increasing involvement also increases a learner's sense of control and autonomy, which are essential for intrinsic motivation (Ryan & Deci, 2000; see Chapter 10).

Questioning allows teachers to guide student learning while also gauging learning progress.

Equitable Distribution

To begin this section, let's look again at some dialogue from Scott's lesson.

Scott: (Referring the students to the sketch of the single piece of paper) Was I blowing on the top or the bottom? . . . Rachel?

Rachel: The top.

Scott:	And what happened there? . . . Heather?
Heather:	The paper rose up.
Scott:	(Referring to the drawing of the two pieces of paper) What did we do to these pieces of paper? . . . Shentae?
Shentae:	We blew in between them.
Scott:	And what happened there? . . . Ricky?
Ricky:	They came together.

In directing each of his questions to a different student and calling on each student by name, Scott demonstrated a concept called **equitable distribution,** *a questioning strategy in which all students in a class are called on as equally as possible* (Kerman, 1979). A majority of teacher questions are not directed to individuals (McGreal, 1985), so the highest achieving and most assertive students answer most of them, and less assertive and lower achieving students fall into a pattern of not responding. Good and Brophy (2000) summarized the relationship between these patterns and teacher expertise as follows:

> A few reticent students who rarely participate in discussions may still get excellent grades, but most students benefit from opportunities to practice oral communication skills, and distributing response opportunities helps keep them attentive and accountable. Also, teachers who restrict their questions primarily to a small group of active (and usually high-achieving) students are likely to communicate undesirable expectations . . . and generally to be less aware and less effective. (p. 395)

Calling on individual students as equally as possible, as Scott did, prevents a vocal minority from dominating question-and-answer sessions. Equitable distribution communicates that the teacher *expects* all students to be involved and participating. When this becomes a pattern, achievement and motivation improve for both high and low achievers, and classroom management problems decrease (Good & Brophy, 2000; McDougall & Granby, 1996; Shuell, 1996).

This pattern is particularly important in teaching students with diverse backgrounds. By calling on all his students, Scott communicated, "I don't care if you're African American, Latino, Asian, White, boy, or girl. I don't care if you're gifted or have a learning disability. I expect you to participate, and I expect you to learn." Nothing better communicates that the teacher and all the students are "in this together."

Equitable distribution is a simple idea but difficult to implement. It requires careful monitoring of students and a great deal of teacher energy. However, its effects can be very powerful for both learning and motivation, and we strongly encourage you to persevere and pursue it rigorously.

Prompting

In attempting equitable distribution, an important question arises. What do you do when the student you call on doesn't answer or answers incorrectly? The answer is **prompting,** *a technique in which a teacher asks questions or makes statements that elicit a student response after the student has failed to answer a previous question or has given an incorrect or incomplete answer.* The value of prompting has been well documented by research (Brophy & Good, 1986; Shuell, 1996).

To illustrate, let's look again at some dialogue from Scott's lesson.

Scott:	What did you notice when we blew over the top? . . . David?
David:	The paper moved.
Scott:	How did the paper move? Do it again.

David again blew over the surface of the paper.

Scott:	What did the paper do?
David:	It came up.

13.16
Equitable distribution most directly applies to which two of the variables in our model for promoting student motivation in Chapter 11? Explain.

To see a video clip of Scott prompting one of his students, go to the Companion Website at *www.prenhall.com/eggen*, then to this chapter's *Classrooms on the Web* module. Click on *Video Clip 13.2.*

As another example, suppose Ken Duran, a language arts teacher, has the following displayed on an overhead:

The girl was very athletic.

He begins a class discussion:

Ken:	Identify an adjective in the sentence, . . . Chandra.
Chandra:	. . .
Ken:	What do we know about the girl?
Chandra:	She was athletic.

13.17

Most teachers, instead of prompting, turn the question to another student, and the student initially asked the question becomes even more reluctant to respond in the future. What concept from behaviorism explains the increasing reluctance?

By providing a focus, Ken elicited an acceptable response from Chandra, keeping her engaged in the activity. She hadn't quite arrived at the answer Ken wanted, but the question kept the process in her zone of proximal development, so she was making learning progress.

Had Chandra still been unable to respond, Ken could have reverted to an open-ended question, such as "What do you notice about the sentence?" or "What can you tell us about the sentence?" which would have virtually ensured an *acceptable* response. Successful prompting doesn't have to result in *the correct answer*; it does need to keep the student successfully engaged.

Prompting isn't always appropriate. For instance, if a teacher asks a simple question that calls for remembering factual knowledge, such as "What is 7 times 8?" or "What is the first amendment to the Constitution?" and the student is unable to answer, prompting has little usefulness; students either know the fact or they don't. Prompting is more effective for conceptual, procedural, and metacognitive knowledge, and cognitive processes beyond remembering (L. Anderson & Krathwohl, 2001).

Wait-Time

After asking a question, teachers should wait a few seconds—alerting all students that they could be called on—before calling on an individual student; they should then wait a few more seconds to give the student time to think (Good & Brophy, 2000). This *period of silence, both before and after calling on a student,* is called **wait-time,** and in most classrooms, it is too short—typically, less than 1 second (Rowe, 1986).

A more precise label for wait-time might be "think-time" because waiting simply gives the student time to think. Increasing wait-time—ideally to about 3 to 5 seconds—has at least three benefits (Rowe, 1974, 1986):

- Students give longer and better responses.
- Voluntary participation increases, and fewer students fail to respond.
- Equitable distribution improves, and responses of students from cultural minorities increase.

Wait-time must be implemented judiciously, however. For example, if students are practicing basic skills, such as multiplication facts, quick answers are desirable, and wait-times should be short (Rosenshine & Stevens, 1986). Also, if a student appears uneasy, the teacher may choose to intervene earlier. However, students need time to respond to demanding cognitive processes such as *apply, analyze, evaluate,* and *create* (L. Anderson & Krathwohl, 2001). In general, increasing wait-time reduces rather than increases student anxiety because a climate of positive expectations and support is established. All students are expected to participate, they're given time to think about their responses, and they know that the teacher will help them if they're unable to answer.

Cognitive Levels of Questions

The kinds of questions teachers ask also influence learning. Which are better: low-level questions that require that students merely remember or questions that demand higher level cognitive processes? The cognitive levels of teacher questions have been widely researched, but the results are mixed. Both low-level questions (e.g., *remember* on the taxonomy) and high-level questions (e.g., *apply* or *analyze* on the taxonomy) correlate positively with achievement, depending on the teaching situation (Good & Brophy, 2000).

The best cognitive level for a question depends on teachers' goals, and teachers should think about asking sequences of questions instead of single questions in isolation (Good & Brophy, 2000). For example, if a teacher wants students to understand the factors leading to the American Revolutionary War, she might begin with a series of lower level questions asking students to remember specific events. She might then go on to higher level questions asking students to identify cause-and-effect relationships among those events. We saw this type of sequence illustrated in Scott's lesson. After completing the demonstrations, Scott first asked the students to remember how the papers and the ball behaved. He followed this sequence with questions asking students to identify the relationship between the speed of the air and the forces it exerted on the objects.

Teachers' first concerns should be what they are trying to accomplish—their goals—not the level of questions they choose to ask. When goals are clear, appropriate questions follow.

Review and Closure

Lessons are more coherent when review and closure are used to summarize and pull ideas together. **Review** is *a summary that helps students link what they have already learned to what will follow in the next learning activity.* It can occur at any point in a lesson, although it is most common at the beginning and end. Effective reviews emphasize important points and encourage elaboration. They also involve more than simple rehearsal; they shift the learner's attention away from verbatim details to conceptual connections in the material being studied (E. Dempster, 1991).

Scott's review of the concept *force* was essential for the students' understanding of Bernoulli's principle.

We saw the importance of a beginning review in Scott's lesson. The students' understanding of the concept *force* and the principle relating the direction of movement to the stronger force were essential to their understanding of Bernoulli's principle, so Scott taught them the day before and carefully reviewed them before he began his lesson.

Closure is *a form of review occurring at the end of a lesson*; in it, topics are summarized and integrated. The notion of closure is intuitively sensible; it pulls content together and signals the end of a lesson. When concepts are being taught, an effective form of closure is to have students state a definition of the concept or identify additional examples. This leaves them with the essence of the topic, providing a foundation for later lessons.

13.18
Scott's closure was perhaps the weakest aspect of his lesson. Describe what he might have done to improve his closure.

Classroom Interaction: Accommodating Learner Diversity

Classroom interaction is central to all forms of effective instruction. With questioning and guiding group interaction, teachers encourage students to think about new ideas, link them to their existing understanding, and compare their understanding with that of their peers. In addition, the use of language is essential for cognitive development, as we saw in our study of Vygotsky's work in Chapter 2. Because interaction is so important, teachers need to understand the interaction patterns of different learners.

Research indicates that interaction patterns vary among different cultural groups. For instance, native Hawaiian children may prefer a collaborative and conversational learning environment that includes students interrupting each other and more than one student talking at a time (Au, 1992). In contrast, Navajo children tend to be less verbally interactive in groups and more independent in their interaction patterns (Tharp & Gallimore, 1988). Additional research indicates that some African American children are more successful at demonstrating their comprehension of a story when they are invited to retell it than when they are required to answer specific questions (Heath, 1989).

To see a video clip of Scott's closure, go to the Companion Website at *www.prenhall.com/eggen*, then to this chapter's *Classrooms on the Web* module. Click on *Video Clip 13.3*.

Effective teachers adapt their questioning strategies to the interaction styles of their students.

These results raise questions. Should teachers allow some students to interrupt each other or to avoid being involved in learning activities if they appear reluctant to participate? Or should teachers require all students to conform to classroom rules and procedures? As with most aspects of teaching and learning, the answer is somewhere in between, and it depends on teacher sensitivity and sound professional judgment. Let's take a look.

Interacting with Diverse Learners: Implications for Teachers

A complex set of factors—involving learner motivation, classroom management, and instructional technique—can influence the success of teacher interactions with learners of different cultural backgrounds. The following general suggestions, however, can help teachers interact successfully with students of all backgrounds:

- Communicate respect for and attraction to different cultures.
- Communicate with all students on a personal level.
- Carefully implement *equitable distribution* when interacting with students.
- Adapt interaction patterns to the characteristics of individuals.
- Socialize students into productive patterns of interaction.

These suggestions certainly require sensitivity and awareness, but they can be readily implemented. First, teachers can communicate respect for and interest in various aspects of different cultures. As an example, consider Mr. Callio, a teacher of a combined first- and second-grade class composed of Hispanic, African American, and White students:

> Mr. Callio holds high expectations for his students and demands strict accountability for the work assigned to them. . . . Mr. Callio's classroom is alive with pictures from different parts of the world, showing the different ethnic, racial, and cultural groups represented in his students. . . . He argues that Spanish is an important language to know and encourages his monolingual English speakers to try to learn it. One of the top students in the class, an African-American male, regularly tries to piece together Spanish sentences. (Knapp, 1995, p. 39)

Second, all students respond to genuine demonstrations of caring and interest in students as human beings. Teachers who believe that all students—regardless of cultural, ethnic, or socioeconomic background—fundamentally want to learn and are capable of doing so are more successful than teachers who don't share those beliefs (V. Lee, 2000).

Third, a careful implementation of equitable distribution will increase the likelihood of successful interactions. Nothing better communicates that you expect all students to achieve and that you're holding them accountable for learning than calling on students with the same frequency, prompting them in the same ways, giving similar feedback, and giving the same quality of help when it is needed. Making equitable distribution the prevailing pattern in your classroom can do more than anything else to communicate that you believe all students can learn and you expect them to do so.

Fourth, within the context of equitable distribution, adaptations can be made. For instance, researchers examining the practices of Anglo and Navajo teachers noticed some significant differences (Winterton, 1977). Anglo teachers interpreted pauses in a Navajo student's response as a sign of a completed answer. Not realizing that long pauses (by Anglo standards) and silences were a regular part of Navajo conversation, they intervened. Interrupted in this way, Navajo students felt uncomfortable and became less willing to participate. Adjusting wait-times produced expected results: In one study of Pueblo Indian children, students whose teachers utilized a longer wait-time participated twice as frequently as those whose teachers used a shorter wait-time (Winterton, 1977).

In addition to increasing wait-time, other simple adaptations can be made. Research indicates that African American students are sometimes uncomfortable with fast-paced convergent questioning (questioning that calls for specific answers). When teachers adapted by asking more open-ended questions, these students were both more motivated and more successful (Heath, 1982). Varying learning activities is another relatively easy adaptation. For instance, group work accommodates the interaction patterns of some students, whereas whole-class discussions accommodate others. Neither exclusively done is as effective as a combination of the two.

The need to adapt is another reason for getting to know students on a personal level (Washington & Miller-Jones, 1989). For example, suppose you interact with a student in a nonacademic setting and learn that he sometimes takes longer to respond than you might expect. As a result, you can increase your wait-time for him in a question-and-answer session.

Finally, teachers should make an effort to socialize students into the interaction patterns that are likely to produce the most learning (Brophy, 1998). For instance, your authors observed a high school class of 21 students, 12 of which were non-Hispanic White, 2 were Hispanic, 2 were Asian, and 5 were African American. At first glance, the most striking feature of the class was the fact that all five African American students were sitting at the back of the room with a physical gap between them and the rest of the class. When we discussed this with the teacher, he commented that they wanted to sit in the back and were very reluctant to move. This is an instance where an imposed seating chart, based on alphabetical order, or some other non-ethnic basis, would be advisable. Although the students may have professed preference for the back, the sense of separation from the rest of the class was apparent, and socializing the students into a more desirable arrangement was important.

Socializing students in this way helps them to accomplish *accommodation without assimilation*, Ogbu's (1987) concept introduced in Chapter 4. The following describes the school's role in this process:

> All of us, regardless of class or cultural background, have to acquire literacies that go beyond our home-based ways of making sense and using language. . . . The key challenge for schools is to introduce and enculturate students into these school-based discourses without denigrating their culturally specific values and ways of using language. (Michaels & O'Connor, 1990, p. 18)

Assessment and Learning: Using Assessment as a Learning Tool

We are now at the third point of the planning-implementing-assessing process. We saw earlier in the chapter that Scott created his assessments as he planned. We look now at the results of his assessment.

Effective teachers use a variety of assessments to gather information about whether learning goals have been achieved.

Let's look at the first item of Scott's three-item quiz again:

1. Look at the drawing that represents the two pieces of paper that we used in the lesson. Explain what made the papers move together. Make a drawing that shows how the air flowed as you blew between the papers. Label the forces in the drawing as we did during the lesson.

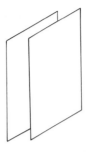

The following are two students' sketches of the flow of air between the papers:

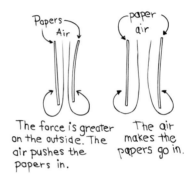

The students' responses illustrate two important needs for teachers to keep in mind as they design and review assessments: To serve as a tool for learning, assessments must (a) provide information about students' thinking and (b) be an integral part of the teaching-learning process.

Scott's assessment was successful in gathering information about what his students were thinking. The responses pictured here show that the two students correctly concluded that the force (pressure) on the outside of the papers pushing in was greater than the force (pressure) on the inside of the papers pushing out. This doesn't provide a great deal of evidence about understanding, however, because this fact was emphasized in the lesson. The students' drawings of the air flow together with their explanations are much more revealing. Rather than correctly concluding that the papers moved together because moving air over a surface exerts less pressure on the surface than does still air, and the still air on the outside of the papers push them together—as demonstrated in the sketch below—the students concluded that the moving air curled around the bottoms of the papers and pushed the papers together. If Scott had not constructed a quiz item that asked for both an explanation and a drawing, he may not have learned what he did about his students' misconceptions.

13.19
What concept from your study of Piaget's work in Chapter 2 is illustrated by the fact that the students concluded that the moving air curled around the bottoms of the papers and pushed them together?

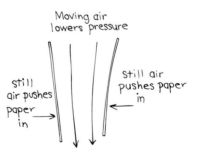

The illustrated results from Scott's assessment also provide concrete evidence of the need for assessment being an integral part of the teaching-learning process, and we can look at the students' responses in two ways. On the one hand, it might be frustrating to find that the students retained an important misconception even after careful instruction. On the other, their responses can be viewed as an opportunity for increased learning. For instance, a detailed discussion of their responses together with examples (demonstrating that air exerts pressure in all directions and that all objects, including air particles, move in a straight line unless a force acts on them) would greatly expand the students' understanding of some basic principles in science. In fact, teaching these principles after the assessment would probably be more effective than trying to teach them before the assessment, because the students' responses to the assessment itself would provide context for the further learning.

Classroom Connections

Demonstrating Essential Teaching Skills in Your Classroom

Attitudes

1. Display the attitudes that increase student motivation and achievement.
   - *Elementary:* A third-grade teacher communicates her personal efficacy and caring by calling a student's parents and soliciting their help as soon as the student fails to turn in an assignment or receives an unsatisfactory grade on a quiz or test.
   - *Middle School:* A seventh-grade teacher commits himself to being a role model by displaying the statement *I will always behave in the way I expect you to behave in this class* on the bulletin board. He uses the statement as a guiding principle in his class.
   - *High School:* A geometry teacher, knowing that her students initially have problems with proofs, conducts help sessions twice a week after school. "I would much rather help them than lower my expectations," she comments.

Organization and Communication

2. Carefully plan and organize materials to maximize instructional time. Communicate clearly.
   - *Elementary:* A first-grade teacher has several boxes filled with frequently used science materials, such as soft drink bottles, balloons, matches, baking soda, vinegar, funnels, and a hot plate. The night before a science demonstration, he spends a few minutes selecting his materials from the boxes and sets them on a shelf near his desk so that he'll have everything ready at the beginning of the lesson.

   - *Middle School:* A eighth-grade American history teacher asks a member of her team to visit her class and check to see how many minutes she spends before actually beginning instruction. She also asks her colleague to check to see if she clearly emphasizes the important points in the lesson, sequences the presentation logically, and communicates changes in topics.
   - *High School:* An English teacher videotapes a lesson he conducts with his students and then studies the tape to check his language and nonverbal communication.

Focus and Feedback

3. Use problems, demonstrations, and displays to provide introductory and sensory focus during lessons. Provide feedback throughout all learning experiences.
   - *Elementary:* A fourth-grade teacher beginning a study of different groups of animals brings a live lobster, a spider, and a grasshopper to class and builds a lesson on arthropods around these animals. After making a list of an arthropod's characteristics on the board, she asks the students if a clam is an arthropod. When some say it is, she provides feedback by referring them to the list and asking them to identify each in the clam. After a short discussion, they conclude that the clam is not an arthropod.
   - *Middle School:* A science teacher dealing with the concept of *kindling temperature* soaks a cloth in a water-alcohol mix, ignites it, and asks, "Why isn't the cloth burning?" He provides feedback during the class discussion by asking guiding questions to help students develop their understanding.
   - *High School:* A physical education teacher shows students a videotape of Justine Henin, a professional

tennis player, executing a nearly perfect backhand. She then videotapes the students as they practice backhands, and they attempt to modify their swings to more nearly imitate Henin's.

Questioning and Review

4. Begin and end each class with a short review. Guide the review with questioning.
   - *Elementary:* A fifth-grade teacher whose class is studying different types of boundaries says, "We've looked at three kinds of boundaries between the states so far today. What are the three, and where do they occur?"
   - *Middle School:* An English teacher begins, "We studied pronoun-antecedent agreement yesterday. Give me an example that illustrates this idea, and explain why your example is correct."
   - *High School:* An art teacher says, "Today we've found that many artists use color to create different moods. Let's summarize some of the features that we've learned about. Go ahead, offer one, someone."

Summary

Teacher Knowledge and Teacher Thinking

Expert teachers have a deep understanding of the topics they teach (knowledge of content), are able to represent the topics in ways that are understandable to learners (pedagogical content knowledge), are able to organize and maintain productive learning environments (general pedagogical knowledge), and understand learning and the characteristics of the students they teach (knowledge of learners and learning).

The different forms of knowledge guide expert teachers' thinking as they make decisions about planning and implementing instruction and assessing learning.

Planning for Instruction

Planning for instruction involves thinking about what is most important for students to learn, objectives students should meet, learning activities that will help students meet the objectives, and ways of assessing learning.

Teachers focus primarily on objectives in the cognitive domain, but the affective domain, which involves attitudes and values, and the psychomotor domain, which involves physical abilities, are also important.

Educators today find themselves in a standards-based environment. Professional organizations, states, and local districts have provided statements of standards, which are descriptions of objectives with varying degrees of specificity. Planning instruction in a standards-based environment is similar to planning instruction in any other environment.

Implementing Instruction: Essential Teaching Skills

Several teaching skills are essential for promoting student learning and contributing to productive learning environments. Effective teachers are high in efficacy; they believe they are responsible for student learning and can increase it. They are caring and enthusiastic, are good role models, and have high expectations for their students.

Effective teachers are well organized, know what's going on in their classrooms, use their time well, and communicate clearly. They represent content in attention-getting ways, provide clear and informative feedback to students, and review important ideas.

Effective teachers use effective questioning strategies. They ask many questions, prompt students who don't answer successfully, employ equitable distribution, and give students time to think about their answers.

Assessment and Learning:
Using Assessment as a Learning Tool

As has been emphasized by prominent researchers, productive learning environments must be assessment centered. Carefully prepared assessments that are aligned with objectives and learning activities can greatly contribute to student learning.

Detailed discussion of assessments after they're given is one of the most important features of the assessment process.

Windows on Classrooms

At the beginning of this chapter, you saw how Scott Sowell planned his lesson, demonstrated the essential teaching skills, and assessed his students' learning. Let's look now at a teacher working with a class of ninth-grade geography students. As you read the case study, consider the extent to which the teacher applied the information you've studied in this chapter in her lesson. Read the case study, and answer the questions that follow.

Judy Holmquist, a ninth-grade geography teacher at Lakeside Junior High School, was involved in a unit on climate regions of the United States. To begin the unit, she had divided the class into groups and had each group gather information about the geography, economy, ethnic groups, and future issues in Florida, California, New York, and Alaska. She then put the students' information into a matrix (shown on the following page).

In today's lesson, Judy wanted the students to understand how the geography of each region influenced its economy.

As the bell signaling the beginning of the class period stopped ringing, Judy referred the students to the matrix, which she had hung at the front of the classroom. She reminded them they would be looking for similarities and differences in the information about the states, organized the students into pairs, and began by saying, "I want you to get with your partner and write down three differences and three similarities you can find by looking at the geography portion of the chart."

The groups began their work, and Judy moved around the classroom, answering questions and making brief suggestions.

A few minutes later, she called the students back together. "You look like you're doing a good job. . . . Okay, I think we're ready.

"Give me a piece of information, Jackie, from the geography column," Judy began, pointing to the chart.

"Mmm, they all have mountains except for Florida."

"Okay, they all have mountains except for Florida," Judy repeated and wrote the information under "Similarities" on the chalkboard.

"Something else. . . . Jeff?"

"They all touch the oceans in places."

"Okay, what else? Give us something else. Go ahead, Todd."

"They're all in four corners."

"Okay, we have four corners."

"What else? . . . Missy?"

"New York and Florida both have coastal plains."

"New York and Florida both have coastal plains," she again repeated, writing the information on the chalkboard.

"Okay, you two in the back. I can hear you. Scott, give us something."

"They all have cold weather in December."

"Okay. . . . Tim?"

"All the summer temperatures are above 50% . . . er 50 degrees," Tim answered to some laughter from the rest of the class.

"How about some differences?" Judy encouraged. "Okay, Chris?"

"The temperature ranges a lot."

"All right. . . . John?"

"Different climate zones."

"Alaska gets below zero. It's the only one that gets below zero," Kiki offered.

"It's the only one that gets below zero in winter. Is that what you said?" Judy asked to confirm Kiki's response, and Kiki nodded.

"Now, let's have a little bit more. I know you've got some more. I see it written on your papers."

"Carnisha, do you have anything to add?"

"All except Alaska have less than 4 inches of moisture in the winter," Carnisha offered.

Section 1 (FLORIDA)

Geography			Economy	Ethnic Groups	Future Issues
	Geography		**Economy**	**Ethnic Groups**	**Future Issues**
	Coastal plain		Citrus industry	Native Americans	Population explosion
F	Florida uplands		Tourism	Spanish	Immigration problems
L	Hurricane season		Fishing	Cubans	Pollution
O	Warm ocean currents		Forestry	Haitians	Tax revisions
R	Temp.	Moisture	Cattle	African American	Money for education
I	Dec. 69	1.8			
D	March 72	2.4			
A	June 81	9.3			
	Sept 82	7.6			

Section 2 (CALIFORNIA)

	Geography		Economy	Ethnic Groups	Future Issues
C	Coastal ranges		Citrus industry	Spanish	Earthquakes
A	Cascades		Wine/vineyards	Mexican	Deforestation
L	Sierra Nevadas		Fishing	Asian	Population explosion
I	Central Valley		Lumber	African American	Pollution
F	Desert		Television/Hollywood		Immigration problems
O	Temp.	Moisture	Tourism		
R	Dec. 54	2.5	Computers		
N	March 57	2.8			
I	June 66	T			
A	Sept. 69	.3			

Section 3 (NEW YORK)

	Geography		Economy	Ethnic Groups	Future Issues
N	Atlantic Coastal Plain		Vegetables	Dutch	Industrial decline
E	New England uplands		Fishing	Native Americans	Decaying urban areas
W	Appalachian Plateau		Apples	Italians	Waste disposal
	Adirondack Mts.		Forestry	French	Crime
Y	Temp.	Moisture	Light manufacturing	Polish	Homelessness
O	Dec. 37	3.9	Entertainment/TV	Puerto Rican	Crowded schools
R	March 42	4.1		African American	
K	June 72	3.7		English	
	Sept. 68	3.9		Irish	
				Russian	

Section 4 (ALASKA)

	Geography		Economy	Ethnic Groups	Future Issues
	Rocky Mountains		Mining	Eskimo (Inuit)	Unemployment
	Brooks Range		Fishing	Native Americans	Cost of living
A	Panhandle area		Trapping	Russian	Oil spills
L	Plateaus between mountains		Lumbering/forestry		Pollution
A	Islands/treeless		Oil/pipeline		
S	Warm ocean currents		Tourism		
K	Temp.	Moisture			
A	Dec −7	.9			
	March 11	.4			
	June 60	1.4			
	Sept. 46	1.0			

"Okay, have we exhausted your lists? Anyone else have anything more to add?"

Judy waited a couple seconds and then said, "Okay, now I want you to look at the economy, and I want you to write down three similarities and three differences you can find by looking at the economy column. You have 3 minutes."

As students again returned to their groups, Judy monitored them as she had earlier.

After they finished, she again called for and received a number of similarities and differences based on the information in the economy column.

She then shifted the direction of the lesson, saying, "Okay, great. . . . Now, let's see if we can link geography and economics. For example, why do they all have fishing?" she asked, waving her hand across the class as she walked toward the back of the room. "John?"

"They're all near the coast."

"Hmm, why do they all have forestry? . . . Okay, Jeremy?"

"They all have lots of trees," he answered to smiles from the rest of the class.

"Now, if they have lots of trees, what does this tell you about their climate?"

"It's warm enough for them to grow."

"But along with being warm enough, it has . . . ?"

"Fertile soil."

"And?"

"Moisture."

"Now, let's look again at our chart. We have fruit in California and Florida. Why do they have the citrus industry there?"

"Jackie, good," she said, seeing Jackie's raised hand. "Never mind."

"Oh, you know," Judy encouraged.

"No."

"Why can we grow oranges down here in Florida?"

"It's the climate."

"All right, because of the climate. Jackie says it's because of the climate. What kind of climate allows the citrus industry? . . . Tim?"

". . . Humid subtropical."

"Okay, humid subtropical. Humid subtropical means that we have what? . . . Go ahead."

"Long humid summers, short mild winters," he replied.

"Now let's look at tourism. Why does each area have tourism?" Judy continued. "Okay, Lance?"

"Because they're all spread out. They're each at four corners, and they have different seasons that they're popular in."

Seeing that the period was nearing a close, Judy said, "Okay, let's deal with one issue. I want you to summarize. . . . Listen up. I want to know what effect climate has on the economy of those regions."

She gave the class 1 minute to work again in their pairs, announcing that she expected to hear from as many people as possible.

"Let's see what you've got for an answer," she said after the minute had passed. "Braden, you had one. . . . I want to know what effect geography has on the economy," she said, pointing at Braden.

"If you have mountains in the area, you can't have farmland," he responded.

"Okay, what else? . . . Becky?"

"The climate affects like what's grown and like what's done inside the section."

"Okay, great. Climate affects what's grown, and what was the last part of that?"

"Like what's done," Becky repeated as the bell rang.

"Okay, great."

"Class dismissed," Judy announced and waved as students began gathering their materials to move to their next class period.

Constructed Response Questions

In answering these questions, use information from the chapter and link your responses to specific information in the case.

1. Describe the types of teacher knowledge Judy displayed in the lesson. Provide evidence from the case study to support your conclusions.

2. Describe Judy's thinking as she planned the lesson. Identify at least three decisions that she made as she planned.

3. Analyze Judy's instructional alignment. Offer any suggestions that you might have that would have increased the alignment of the lesson.

4. Analyze Judy's application of the essential teaching skills in her lesson. Which did she demonstrate most effectively? Which did she demonstrate least effectively?

Document-Based Analysis

Judy prepared the following items on a short quiz following her lesson.

1. In which of the four states was the citrus industry most prominent?
2. In which state was mining the most important part of the economy?

PRAXIS These exercises are designed to help you prepare for the PRAXIS™ "Principles of Learning and Teaching" exam. To receive feedback on your constructed response questions and document analysis response, go to the Companion Website at *www.prenhall.com/eggen*, then to this chapter's *Practice for PRAXIS™* module. For additional connections between this text and the PRAXIS™ exam, go to Appendix A.

Also on the Companion Website at *www.prenhall.com/eggen*, you can measure your understanding of chapter content in *Practice Quiz* and *Essay* modules, apply concepts in *Online Cases,* and broaden your knowledge base with the *Additional Content* module and *Web Links* to other educational psychology websites.

3. Explain why the lumber industry is important in both California and Alaska but not in Florida and New York.
4. Explain why fishing is an important part of the economy in all four states.

Analyze each of the four items with respect to its alignment with Judy's goal.

Online Portfolio Activities

To develop your professional portfolio, further apply your understanding of chapter content and address the INTASC standards, go to the Companion Website, then to this chapter's *Online Portfolio Activities.* Complete the suggested activities.

Important Concepts

affective domain *(p. 467)*
closure *(p. 481)*
cognitive domain *(p. 465)*
connected discourse *(p. 475)*
emphasis *(p. 475)*
equitable distribution *(p. 479)*
essential teaching skills *(p. 473)*
feedback *(p. 476)*
internalization *(p. 467)*
objectives *(p. 465)*
organization *(p. 474)*

precise terminology *(p. 474)*
prompting *(p. 479)*
psychomotor domain *(p. 467)*
questioning frequency *(p. 478)*
review *(p. 481)*
sensory focus *(p. 476)*
standards *(p. 471)*
task analysis *(p. 468)*
transition signals *(p. 475)*
wait-time *(p. 480)*

Chapter Outline

Assessing Classroom Learning

14

DeVonne Lampkin, a teacher at Abbott Park Elementary School (the teacher in the case studies in Chapter 11), was beginning a unit on fractions. She knew that her students had been introduced to fractions in the fourth grade, but she wasn't sure how much they remembered or how much they understood about them. She began her unit by administering a pretest. When she scored the pretest, she found that all of her students could do the following problem:

Draw a figure that will illustrate each of the fractions.

¾   3/8   1/3

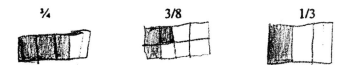

Most could also do this one:

You need 3 pieces of ribbon for a project. The pieces should measure 2 5/16, 4 2/16, and 1 3/16 inches. How much ribbon do you need in all?

$$7 \frac{10}{16}$$

So they seemed to understand the basic concept of *fraction,* and most understood adding fractions with like denominators. But they had difficulties with the following problems, suggesting they were unable to add fractions when the denominators were not alike.

Latoya made a punch recipe for a party.

Punch Recipe
¾ gallon ginger ale   ½ gallon grapefruit juice
1 2/3 gallon orange juice   2/3 gallon pineapple juice

a. **Will the punch she made fit into one 3-gallon punch bowl? Explain why or why not.**

No because when added correctly it is more.

b. **How much punch, if any, is left over?**

None

On Saturday, Justin rode his bicycle 12 ½ miles. On Sunday, he rode 8 3/5 miles.

a. **How many miles did he ride altogether?**

21

b. **How many more miles did Justin ride on Saturday than on Sunday?**

4 miles more.

As a result, DeVonne designed her first lesson to focus on equivalent fractions. She knew that her students needed to understand the concept of *equivalent fractions* to be able to add fractions with unlike denominators.

She began her lesson by passing out chocolate candy bars divided into 12 equal pieces and saying, "We're going to start our unit on fractions, and I think I have a lesson that all of you will like. We're going to learn about fractions using this chocolate candy bar, and when we're all done, you can eat it."

Using the chocolate pieces she introduced the idea of equivalent fractions, illustrating how $\frac{3}{12}$ was the same as $\frac{1}{4}$, $\frac{6}{12}$ was equal to $\frac{1}{2}$, and $\frac{8}{12}$ equaled $\frac{2}{3}$. As students worked on illustrating these problems with their candy bars, DeVonne circulated around the room, asking students to explain their ideas with the pieces in front of them. In the process, she discovered that one student thought that she needed 7 pieces of candy to illustrate the fraction ¾. Through her questioning, DeVonne was able to show the student that she could use 4 pieces to illustrate the fraction.

As the lesson continued, DeVonne went to the board and showed students how to work equivalency problems with numbers. At the end of the lesson, she gave a homework assignment with the following problems:

Write two equivalent fractions for each shaded part.

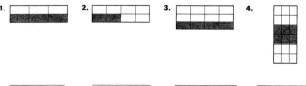

When she scored the homework, she discovered that some students were still having problems with equivalent fractions:

Write two equivalent fractions for each shaded part.

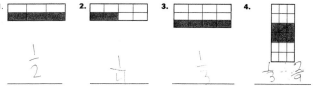

So she designed another hands-on activity to further illustrate the concept.

The next day, she began her new lesson by having the students construct a model fraction city with equivalent-length streets divided into different parts, or fractions:

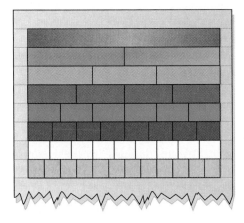

When students were finished making their equivalent strips, she had each student move cars along the different streets to illustrate that ½ = ⅜, ⅓ = ⅜, ¾ = ½, and other equivalent fractions. She then illustrated adding fractions with like denominators, using the cars and strips as concrete frames of reference. When she felt that most students understood equivalent fractions, she again used the same cars and strips to illustrate adding fractions with unlike denominators.

DeVonne then moved to the board and showed how to perform the same operations using numbers and symbols.

Several days later, DeVonne gave a test to see how much her students understood about fractions. Their answers to several items on the test suggested that they seemed to understand equivalent fractions and how to add fractions with unlike denominators:

Write the equivalent fraction.

$$\frac{2}{3} = \frac{8}{12} \qquad \frac{3}{8} = \frac{6}{16} \qquad \frac{4}{5} = \frac{16}{20} \qquad \frac{5}{6} = \frac{50}{60}$$

Write each fraction in simplest terms.

$$\frac{5}{10} = \frac{1}{2} \qquad \frac{8}{12} = \frac{2}{3} \qquad \frac{4}{20} = \frac{1}{5} \qquad \frac{9}{27} = \frac{1}{3}$$

$$\frac{24}{30} = \frac{4}{5} \qquad \frac{16}{18} = \frac{8}{9} \qquad \frac{35}{49} = \frac{5}{7} \qquad \frac{32}{40} = \frac{4}{5}$$

An alien from a far-off planet landed her spacecraft on Earth. She had left her planet with a full tank of super interplanetary fuel. She knew that she'd need at least 3/8 of that fuel to return home from Earth. She used half a tank of fuel to get here. How much fuel did she use all together?

$$\frac{3}{8} + \frac{1}{2} =$$

$$\frac{3}{8} + \frac{4}{8} = \frac{7}{8}$$

Quizzes, tests, and other assessments have a powerful effect on student learning and guide teachers' actions as they help students learn. Despite the importance of classroom assessment, teachers often feel ill-prepared to deal with its complexities (Stiggins, 2001). Experienced teachers express concerns about their ability to write assessment items, to construct valid assessments, and to assign grades. Beginning teachers also express concerns about their ability to assess student progress (Lomax, 1996), ranking this problem fourth after classroom management, motivation, and dealing with individual differences (Veenman, 1984). A study of student teachers found valid assessment practices one of the most challenging aspects of learning to teach (C. Campbell & Evans, 2000).

In this chapter, we address these concerns by examining the effects of assessment on learning and motivation, analyzing teachers' assessment patterns, and describing ways to design effective classroom assessments.

After you've completed your study of this chapter, you should be able to

- Explain basic assessment concepts
- Describe classroom teachers' assessment patterns
- Analyze assessment items for factors that detract from their validity
- Construct alternative assessments in your content area or grade level
- Apply effective assessment procedures in your own classroom

Classroom Assessment

The case study at the beginning of the chapter illustrates the process of assessment, one of the most basic and difficult tasks teachers face in their work. **Classroom assessment** includes *all the processes involved in making decisions about students' learning progress* (Airasian, 2000). It includes observations of students' written work, their answers to questions in class, and performance on teacher-made and standardized tests. It includes performance assessments, such as watching first graders print or observing a word processing class type a letter. It also involves decisions such as reteaching a topic or assigning grades. Combined, these elements make up a teacher's assessment system. In DeVonne's case, her system included monitoring her students' learning progress through homework, quizzes, and tests.

Functions of Classroom Assessment

As we saw in our opening case, classroom assessment provides valuable information that allows teachers to adapt instructional procedures to the learning needs of their students (Kovalik, 2002). In addition to facilitating teacher decision making about learning progress through systematic information gathering, assessment accomplishes two other important goals: (a) increasing learning and (b) increasing motivation.

The relationship between learning and assessment is strong and robust (P. Black & William, 1998a; Shepard, 2001). Students learn more in classes where assessment is an integral part of instruction than in those where it isn't, and brief assessments that provide frequent feedback about learning progress are more effective than long, infrequent ones, like once-a-term tests (Bangert-Drowns et al., 1991; Dochy & McDowell, 1997).

Suggesting a link between testing and motivation is controversial because some critics argue that assessment detracts from motivation. Evidence runs counter to this argument, however (Eggen, 1997; J. Ross, Rolheiser, & Hogaboam-Gray, 2002). Frequent assessment, linked to well-planned goals, encourages learners to pace themselves and keep up with their studies (Tuckman, 1998). Think about your own experiences. In which classes did you learn the most and for which did you study the hardest? Most students exert more effort in classes where they're thoroughly assessed and given frequent feedback. Learners need to understand what they are supposed to learn, why they are learning it, and how they are progressing (Olina & Sullivan, 2002); when assessment provides this information, it increases student motivation (see Chapter 10). Information about progress can exert a powerful influence on the amount and ways students study (Airasian, 2000; Stiggins, 2001).

14.1
How would a behaviorist explain the advantage of frequent, announced quizzes over those given infrequently? (Hint: Think about the concept of reinforcement schedules from Chapter 6.)

Measurement and Evaluation

Two basic processes are involved in assessment: **measurement**, *the process of gathering information about learning,* and **evaluation**, *the process of making decisions on the basis of measurements.* Evaluation essentially entails making a value judgment about a measurement outcome (e.g., does the student's score reflect mastery of an important concept?).

Effective teachers use a range of measurement tools to assess different aspects of student learning. Some use traditional paper-and-pencil formats, and others take advantage of alternative formats to assess critical thinking and problem-solving abilities, as you see in Figure 14.1.

Formal and Informal Measurement

Informal measurement is *the process of gathering incidental information about learning progress during learning activities and discussions with students.* For instance, teachers conduct informal measurement when they listen to students' comments and answers to questions, notice puzzled looks, or see that a student isn't paying attention. In contrast, **formal measurement** is *the process of systematically gathering information about learning progress.* Tests and quizzes are formal measures, as are performance assessments, such as a physical education teacher observing the number of sit-ups a student can do.

14.2
Identify an important similarity and an important difference between formal and informal measurement.

To see a video clip of a teacher using questioning to informally assess her students' background knowledge, go to the Companion Website at *www.prenhall.com/eggen*, then to this chapter's *Classrooms on the Web* module. Click on *Video Clip 14.1*.

Figure 14.1 Traditional and alternative measurement formats

Traditional Measurement Formats	Alternative Measurement Formats
True–false	Specific performance task
Multiple choice	Timed trial
Matching	Exhibition of work
Fill in the blank	Reflective journal entry
Short, open-ended answer	Open-ended oral presentation
Paragraph response to specific question	Oral response to specific question
Paragraph response to open-ended question	Collaborative group project
Essay	Audiovisual presentation
	Debate
	Simulation

Source: From "Plain Talk About Alternative Assessment," by D. Cheek, 1993, *Middle School Journal, 25* (2), pp. 6–10. Copyright 1993 by the Middle School Association. Adapted with permission.

The Need for Systematic Assessment

Informal measurement is essential in helping teachers make the frequent instructional decisions required in every class. In the opening case, DeVonne used questionning and observations of student work to help her understand whether students were understanding equivalent fractions. Teachers also use informal measurement to decide how quickly they can teach a topic, whom they should call on, and when they should stop one activity and move on to the next. Information from informal measurement can provide an alternate, and more complete and accurate, picture of the learning that is occurring in a classroom (Rose, Williams, Gomez, & Gearon, 2002).

Informal measurement has drawbacks, however (Green & Mantz, 2002). Because teachers don't obtain the same information from each student, they don't know about each student's individual progress. Concluding that the whole class understands an idea on the basis of responses from only a few students (who usually have their hands up) is a mistake that teachers often make. Because information is often gathered unsystematically, informal measurement fails to provide a comprehensive picture of ongoing student learning (Green & Mantz, 2002).

Without realizing it, teachers sometimes make decisions as important as assigning grades on the basis of informal measurement. Students who readily respond, have engaging personalities, and are physically attractive are often awarded higher grades than their less fortunate peers (Ritts, Patterson, & Tubbs, 1992). Systematically gathering information about each student's progress is one way to prevent these potential biases.

Systematic measurement is particularly important in the lower elementary grades, where teachers often rely on information from performance assessments, such as handwriting samples and verbal identification of written numerals, to make evaluation decisions. All too often these assessments are subjective, influenced by nonperformance factors. The

Gathering systematic information about each student and keeping current records about students' learning progress help ensure accurate assessment.

question, "Could I defend and document this decision to a parent if necessary?" is a helpful guideline in this process.

Validity: Making Appropriate Evaluation Decisions

Validity is *an indicator of the extent to which an assessment actually measures what it is supposed to measure.* It refers to "an evaluation of the adequacy and appropriateness of the interpretations and uses of assessment results" (Linn & Gronlund, 2000, p. 73). To have validity, the decisions based on a test must be supported by evidence.

Validity describes the link between the information gathered and the decisions made from that information (AERA, APA, NCME, 1999; Shepard, 1993). In classroom practice, the validity of a measurement is the extent to which it is congruent, or aligned, with the teacher's goals. For example, if a classroom test intended for measuring students' understanding of the Civil War contained only factual items on names, dates, and places, the test would be invalid because it failed to measure the connections between and significance of these facts.

Problems concerning validity are at the heart of many controversies in assessment. For example, critics argue that standardized tests are culturally biased and, as a result, are invalid for minority students (Helms, 1992). Other critics assert that questions measuring isolated and decontextualized skills—such as multiple-choice items on standardized tests—give an incomplete and therefore invalid picture of student understanding. This assertion has contributed to the movement toward "alternative" or "authentic" assessment (Herman, Aschbacher, & Winters, 1992; Moss, 1992). We examine alternative assessment in detail later in the chapter.

In classrooms, assessment decisions based on personality, appearance, or other factors unrelated to learning goals are also invalid (Lambating & Allen, 2002). Teachers who give lower scores on essay items because of messy handwriting are using invalid criteria. In these cases, the actions are usually unconscious; without realizing it, teachers often base their assessments on appearance rather than substance.

None of this suggests, however, that teachers are doomed to use invalid assessments. Teachers who continually look for ways to improve their tests, quizzes, and other assessments; analyze trends and patterns in student responses; and conscientiously revise items increase the validity of their assessment system. These actions are a part of the reflective attitude toward teaching that we emphasize throughout this text.

Reliability: Consistency in Measurement

Reliability, an intuitively sensible concept, is *a description of the extent to which measurements are consistent and free from errors of measurement* (Linn & Gronlund, 2000). For instance, if your bathroom scale is reliable, and your weight doesn't change, the readings shouldn't vary from one day to the next. Similarly, if we could repeatedly give a student the same reliable test, the scores would all be the same, assuming no additional learning or forgetting occurred. Unreliable measurements cannot be valid, even if the measurements are congruent with the teacher's goals, because they give inconsistent information.

Ways that teachers can positively influence reliability include the following:

- Use a sufficient number of items or tasks in an instrument, and look for consistency in students' performance from one task to another.
- Ensure that directions are clear so students know what is expected of them.
- Identify specific criteria to evaluate students' performance.
- Administer assessments in similar ways for all students.

Our overriding goal with reliability is to ensure that our assessment techniques accurately and consistently reflect student learning.

14.3
Give an example of a systematic assessment in the class you're in now. What makes it systematic? Give an example of an assessment that is not systematic.

14.4
A teacher gives her students the following writing assignment: "Describe a room in your home. Be sure your grammar and punctuation are correct." When she returns the papers, they have two grades, one for creativity and one for punctuation and grammar. Are both of these grades valid? Explain.

Figure 14.2 The relationships between validity and reliability

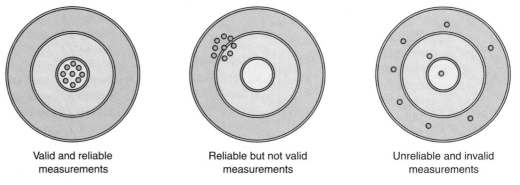

| Valid and reliable measurements | Reliable but not valid measurements | Unreliable and invalid measurements |

Source: Adapted from MEASUREMENT AND ASSESSMENT IN TEACHING 8/E by Linn & Gronlund, © 2000. Reprinted by permission of Pearson Education, Inc., Upper Saddle River, NJ.

Problems with reliability can come from three major sources: the assessment instrument (e.g., a test or quiz) or process, student characteristics, and scoring problems (Sax, 1997). The most glaring challenges to reliability in a test or quiz are ambiguous items and unclear directions. Student characteristics, such as fatigue, anxiety, and lack of motivation, can also pose problems to reliability. Finally, the teacher can also negatively influence reliability through inconsistent scoring procedures, which are common for essay exams as well as computational problems.

One way to think about the relationship between validity and reliability is to visualize a target and a person practicing shooting (Linn & Gronlund, 2000). A valid and reliable shooter consistently clusters shots in the target's bull's-eye. This is analogous to an assessment instrument that accurately and consistently measures the goals of instruction. A reliable but invalid shooter clusters shots, but the cluster is not in the bull's-eye. Assessment instruments that give teachers consistent scores but don't measure the goals of instruction are reliable but not valid. Finally, a shooter that scatters shots randomly over the target is analogous to an assessment instrument that is neither valid nor reliable. These relationships are illustrated in Figure 14.2.

The problem of scoring consistency can be illustrated with essay tests, which are often unreliable. Studies indicate that different instructors with similar backgrounds, ostensibly using the same criteria, have awarded grades ranging from excellent to failure on the same essay (Gronlund, 1993). When inconsistency in scoring occurs, lack of reliability makes the process invalid.

Information from informal measurement is often unreliable because not all students respond to the same question. Uncertainty on one student's face doesn't necessarily mean the other students are confused; likewise, a quick, confident answer from one student doesn't mean the entire class understands the topic. The solution is to use systematic measures, which gather information from all students and are more likely to be reliable.

14.5
Research indicates that increasing the length of a test increases reliability, but studies of child development indicate that attention spans of young children are limited. Explain how teachers can reconcile these findings.

Traditional Assessment Strategies

Teachers have historically assessed learning through teacher-made quizzes and tests, and these forms of assessment are likely to play a central role in classrooms of the future. If well designed and constructed, quizzes and tests can provide valid assessments of many aspects of student learning (Linn & Gronlund, 2000). In the following sections, we examine teachers' assessment patterns and discuss ways of constructing measurement items to make them as reliable and valid as possible.

Teachers' Assessment Patterns

The way in which teachers assess student learning is important because teachers' assessment patterns influence not only immediate learning but also students' cognitive and metacognitive processes (Newmann, 1997; Shepard, 2001). In short, how we assess influences how learners study and think about the content they're learning. Superficial assessment practices that focus on memorization of isolated facts send different messages to students than integrative ones that require critical thinking and problem solving.

Let's look at one teacher's assessment practices.

Laura Torrez's second graders were working on subtracting one-digit from two-digit numbers with regrouping. She put a series of problems on the chalkboard, and as she circulated, her students busily solved them.

"Check this one again, Kelly," Laura said, seeing that Kelly had written

$$\begin{array}{r} 24 \\ -9 \\ \hline 25 \end{array}$$

on her paper.

"I think I'll take a grade on this one," Laura said to herself. She collected the papers after the students finished, scored them, and wrote 9 in her grade book for Kelly because she missed one of the 10 problems from the chalkboard.

Laura's on-the-spot decision to use an in-class learning activity for grading purposes is typical of elementary teachers, particularly at the primary level. They use informal measures more frequently than teachers at the higher levels; they rely on commercially prepared items, such as those that come with a textbook series; and they emphasize affective goals (Guskey, 2002; McMillan, Workman, & Myran, 1999). These patterns are summarized in Table 14.1.

Middle and high school teachers' assessment practices differ from those of elementary teachers in several ways (Guskey, 2002). They depend more on traditional tests and quizzes than on performance measures, and they more commonly prepare their own items instead of relying on published tests. Figure 14.3 summarizes characteristics of these teacher-made items (Bol, Stephenson, O'Connell, & Nunnery, 1998; Stiggins & Conklin, 1992).

Several factors help explain the patterns in Figure 14.3. First, teachers' jobs are complex and demanding, and they respond to this complexity by simplifying their work. Reusing an item is simpler than revising it, for example. Essay items are easy to write but difficult and time-consuming to score; multiple-choice items are just the opposite. The simplest alternatives are the completion and matching formats, which are most popular with teachers. Further, knowledge and recall items, which have only one right answer, are easy to construct, score, and defend.

Table 14.1 Elementary teachers' assessment patterns

Characteristic	Description
Performance measures	Primary teachers rely heavily on actual samples of student work (e.g., the ability to form letters or write numerals) to evaluate student learning (Marso & Pigge, 1992).
Informal measurements	Measurement is often informal, as was the case in Laura's class. She comments, "I take a grade a few times a week. I don't really have a regular schedule that I follow for grading." Further, teachers sometimes give social and background characteristics greater emphasis than ability (McMillan et al., 1999).
Commercially prepared tests	When they do test, elementary teachers depend heavily on commercially prepared and published tests. Teachers in the primary grades rarely prepare their own formal tests, instead using informal assessments or using exercises from texts or teachers' editions (McMillan et al., 1999).
Emphasis on affective goals	Primary teachers emphasize affective goals, such as "Gets along well with others." In one analysis of kindergarten progress reports sent home to parents, more than a third of the categories were devoted to intrapersonal or interpersonal factors (Freeman & Hatch, 1989).

Figure 14.3 Characteristics of teacher-made tests

1. Teachers commonly use test items containing many technical errors.

2. Teachers rarely use techniques such as item analysis and tables of specifications to improve the quality of their items. Once items are constructed, teachers tend to reuse them without revision.

3. Even though teachers state that higher order objectives are important, more than three fourths of all items are written at the knowledge/recall level, and most of those above the knowledge level are in math and science. In other areas, 90% to 100% of the items are written at the knowledge level.

4. About 1% of all teacher-made test items use the essay format. This figure is higher in English classes.

5. The short-answer format is used most frequently, such as:

   Which two countries border on Mexico? _____

   _____

   Why does a cactus have needles, whereas an oak tree has broad leaves?_____

   _____

6. Matching items are common; for example:

   _____ A quadrilateral with one pair of opposite equal sides
   _____ A three-sided plane figure with two sides equal in length
   _____ A quadrilateral with opposite sides equal in length

   a. Parallelogram
   b. Pentagon
   c. Rhombus
   d. Scalene triangle
   e. Square
   f. Isosceles triangle

All teachers, elementary and secondary, lack confidence in their ability to write good test items and use assessment to improve learning (Marso & Pigge, 1992; Plake & Impara, 1997). Because of inadequate training, teachers frequently have difficulty writing clear and precise test items at a level above knowledge and recall (Kahn, 2000). These findings indicate a need for better quality assessments, particularly items that are unambiguous and require more of students than the simple recall of facts and information.

Valid Test Items

Like an entire test, a test item can be valid or invalid. Conceptually, item validity is simple; an item is valid if students who understand the content answer it correctly and if those who don't understand it get the item wrong. For instance, if you have a multiple-choice item with *a* as the answer, but most of the class chooses *c*, the results may indicate a general misconception or a difficult idea, and the item would be valid. If, however, students who knew the information got the item wrong, the item may have been misleading. Sometimes students who *don't* understand the content get an item correct because clues to the answer are included in the item. Learners as young as fifth and sixth graders can use item clues to identify correct choices (Sudweeks, Baird, & Petersen, 1990). Any time a question is misleading or gives away the answer, it is invalid and needs to be fixed.

Teachers confess they have trouble writing effective items but believe many of these problems could be eliminated through increased teacher knowledge and understanding (Carter, 1986). Indeed, the information in this chapter can help you write better, more valid items that will provide you with accurate information about what your students really know.

The easiest and most effective way to evaluate an item is to discuss it with the class. In the case of a frequently missed item, for example, if missing it indicates a general misconception, the topic can be retaught. This is the primary purpose of assessment—to determine the extent to which students understand important ideas. If the item is misleading or gives clues, it can be rewritten. In either case, discussing the students' responses to the item provides important information to the teacher.

Before we turn to a discussion of strategies for constructing specific item types, we need to describe how assessment items are classified. Multiple-choice, true-false, and matching formats are called *selected-response formats,* because they require learners to choose the correct answer from a list of alternatives; completion and essay formats are called *supply formats* because they require learners to produce their own answers (Stiggins, 2001). Items can also be classified as *objective,* which are those on which equally competent learners get the same scores (e.g., multiple-choice items), or *subjective,* where the scores are influenced by the judgment of the person doing the scoring (e.g., essay questions; Linn & Gronlund, 2000).

14.6
Suppose that most of the students in your class chose *d* on a multiple-choice item when the correct answer was *b.* You learn that many of the students misinterpreted what you were asking for in the item. Is the item valid? Is it reliable? What should you do?

Constructing Valid Test Items: Instructional Strategies

Although different item types require specific strategies, there are several general strategies for increasing validity in all formats:

- ■ Write items with a specific learning goal in mind.
- ■ Match item types to learning goals. Different item types are designed to assess different learning goals.
- ■ Continually keep validity in mind as you construct, administer, and revise assessment items.

With these principles in mind, let's examine specific strategies for constructing different item types.

Multiple-Choice Items

The multiple-choice format can be one of the most effective for preparing valid and reliable items at different levels of thinking; most standardized tests use this format, and multiple-choice items are widely used by teachers (Kahn, 2000). Gronlund (1993) has suggested that teachers try writing multiple-choice items first and then switch to another format only if the objectives or content require it. **Multiple-choice format** is *a measurement format that consists of a question or statement, called a stem, and a series of answer choices. The individual responding to the items chooses the correct or best answer.* The *incorrect alternatives* are called **distracters** because they are *designed to distract students who don't understand the content being measured in the item.*

Items may be written so that only one choice is correct, or they may be in a "best-answer" form, in which more than one choice are partially correct but one is clearly better than the others. The best-answer form is more demanding, promotes higher level thinking, and measures more complex achievement. Guidelines for preparing multiple-choice items are summarized in Figure 14.4.

The Stem.   The stem should pose one question or problem for students to consider. With this guideline in mind, analyze the items in Figure 14.5.

The first item in Figure 14.5 is essentially a series of true-false statements linked only by the fact that they fall under the same stem. The second item is misleading, because choice *b* includes both correct and incorrect information. Veins *are* part of the circulatory system, but they carry blood back to the heart rather than away from it. The third item presents a single, clearly stated problem, with the distracters providing possible alternatives.

Distracters.   Although carefully written stems are important, good distracters are also essential for effective multiple-choice items. Distracters should address students' likely

Figure 14.4 Guidelines for preparing multiple-choice items

1. Present one clear problem in the stem of the item.
2. Make all distracters plausible and attractive to the uninformed.
3. Vary the position of the correct choice randomly. Be careful to avoid overusing choice *c*.
4. Avoid similar wording in the stem and the correct choice.
5. Avoid phrasing the correct choice in more technical terms than distracters.
6. Keep the correct answer and the distracters similar in length. A longer or shorter answer should usually be used as an incorrect choice.
7. Avoid using absolute terms (e.g., *always, never*) in the incorrect choices.
8. Keep the stem and distracters grammatically consistent.
9. Avoid using two distracters with the same meaning.
10. Emphasize *negative wording* by underlining if it is used.
11. Use "none of the above" with care, and avoid "all of the above" as a choice.

Source: How to Construct Achievement Tests, 4th ed., by N. Gronlund, 1988, Upper Saddle River, NJ: Prentice Hall. Copyright 1988 by Prentice Hall. Adapted by permission.

Figure 14.5 Multiple-choice items of differing quality

14.7
What is the simplest and most effective way to correct item 2 in Figure 14.5?

1. The circulatory system is the system that
   *a. transports blood throughout the body
   b. includes the lungs
   c. protects the vital organs of the body
   d. turns the food we eat into energy
2. Which of the following is a part and function of the circulatory system?
   *a. The blood vessels that carry food and oxygen to the body cells
   b. The blood veins that carry blood away from the heart
   c. The lungs that pump blood to all parts of the body
   d. The muscles that help move a person from one place to another
3. Which of the following describes the function of the circulatory system?
   *a. It moves blood from your heart to other parts of your body.
   b. It turns the sandwich you eat into energy you need to keep you going throughout the day.
   c. It removes solid and liquid waste materials from your body.
   d. It protects your heart, brain, and other body parts from being injured.

misconceptions so that these mistaken views can be identified and corrected. One way to generate effective distracters is to first include the stem on a test as a short answer or fill-in-the-blank item. As students respond, you can use incorrect answers as distracters for future tests (Stiggins, 2001).

Many problems with faulty multiple-choice items involve clues in distracters that allow students to answer the question correctly without knowing the content. Figure 14.6 contains six items with faulty distracters. See if you can identify features in them that are inconsistent with the guidelines.

In item 1 in Figure 14.6, forms of the term *circulate* appear in both the stem and the correct answer. In item 2, the correct choice is written in more technical terms than the distracters. Teachers fall into this trap when they take the correct choice directly from the text and then make up the distracters. Their informal language appears in the distracters, whereas text language appears in the correct answer.

Figure 14.6 Constructing distracters for multiple-choice items

1. Which of the following is a function of the circulatory system?
   a. to support the vital organs of the body
   *b. to circulate the blood throughout the body
   c. to transfer nerve impulses from the brain to the muscles
   d. to provide for the movement of the body's large muscles

2. Of the following, the definition of *population density* is
   a. the number of people who live in your city or town
   b. the number of people who voted in the last presidential election
   *c. the number of people per square mile in a country
   d. the number of people in cities compared to small towns

3. Of the following, the most significant cause of World War II was
   a. American aid to Great Britain
   b. Italy's conquering of Ethiopia
   c. Japan's war on China
   *d. the devastation of the German economy as a result of the Treaty of Versailles

4. Which of the following is the best description of an insect?
   a. It always has one pair of antennae on its head.
   *b. It has three body parts.
   c. None lives in water.
   d. It breathes through lungs.

5. The one of the following that is not a reptile is a
   a. alligator
   b. lizard
   *c. frog
   d. turtle

6. Which of the following illustrates a verb form used as a participle?
   a. Running is good exercise.
   *b. I saw a jumping frog contest on TV yesterday.
   c. Thinking is hard for many of us.
   d. All of the above.

In item 3, the correct choice is significantly longer than the incorrect choices; a similar clue is given when the correct choice is shorter than distracters. If one choice is significantly longer or shorter than others, it should be a distracter.

In item 4, choices *a* and *c* are stated in absolute terms, which alerts testwise students. Absolute terms, such as *all, always, none,* and *never,* are usually associated with incorrect answers. If used, they should be in the correct answer, such as "All algae contain chlorophyll."

The stem in item 5 is stated in negative terms without this fact being emphasized (the word *not* should be underlined). Also, choice *a* is grammatically inconsistent with the stem. One solution to the problem is to end the stem with *a(n),* so grammatical consistency is preserved.

In item 6, choices *a* and *c* are automatically eliminated because both are gerunds and only one answer can be correct. Also, item 6 uses "all of the above" as a choice; it can't be correct if *a* and *c* are eliminated. That makes *b* the only possible choice. A student could get the item right and have no idea what a participle is.

As you can see, preparing valid multiple-choice items requires both thought and care. With effort and practice, however, you can become skilled at it, and when you do, you have a powerful learning and assessment tool.

> **14.8**
> Rewrite each of the six items in Figure 14.6 so they are consistent with the guidelines.

Assessing Higher Level Learning.   Although most of the examples presented to this point measure lower level, memory outcomes, the multiple-choice format can also be

Figure 14.7
Interpretive exercise used with the multiple-choice format

Look at the drawings above. They represent two identical soft drink bottles covered with identical balloons sitting side-by-side on a table. Bottle A was then heated. Which of the following is the most accurate statement?
a. The density of the air in Bottle A is greater than the density of the air in Bottle B.
*b. The density of the air in Bottle A is less than the density of the air in Bottle B.
c. The density of the air in Bottle A is equal to the density of the air in Bottle B.
d. We don't have enough information to compare the density of the air in Bottle A to the density of the air in Bottle B.

effectively used to assess higher order thinking. In an "interpretive exercise," students are presented with material similar to—but not identical to—information presented in class, and the distracters represent different analyses or "interpretations" of it (Gronlund, 1993). This type of item measures students' ability to analyze or think about course content. The material may be a graph, chart, table, map, picture, or case study.

Figure 14.7 contains a multiple-choice item that is meant to assess higher level learning in science. In this case, the teacher's goal was for science students to to apply information about heat, expansion, mass, volume, and density to a familiar but unique situation. This type of exercise promotes transfer, helps develop critical thinking, and can increase learner motivation.

Matching Items

Multiple-choice format can be inefficient if all of the items require the same set of answer choices, as in the following (asterisk indicates correct answer):

1. The statement "Understanding is like a lightbulb coming on in your head" is an example of

   *a. simile
   b. metaphor
   c. hyperbole
   d. personification

2. "That's the most brilliant comment ever made" is a statement of

   a. simile
   b. metaphor
   *c. hyperbole
   d. personification

The problem can be solved by combining items into a single **matching format**, *a measurement format that requires learners to classify a series of examples using the same alternatives.* The following is an example:

Match the following statements with the figures of speech by writing the letter of the appropriate figure of speech in the blank next to each statement. Each figure of speech may be used *once, more than once,* or *not at all.*

_____ 1. Understanding is like a lightbulb coming on in your head.

_____ 2. That's the most brilliant comment ever made.

_____ 3. His oratory was a belch from the bowels of his soul.

_____ 4. Appropriate attitudes are always advantageous.

_____ 5. Her eyes are limpid pools of longing.

_____ 6. He stood as straight as a rod.

_____ 7. I'll never get this stuff, no matter what I do.

_____ 8. The colors of his shirt described the world in which he lived.

a. alliteration
b. hyperbole
c. metaphor
d. personification
e. simile

Five characteristics of effective matching items are illustrated in the example. First, the content is homogeneous: All the statements are figures of speech, and only figures of speech are given as alternatives. Other topics appropriate for matching items include persons and their achievements, historical events and dates, terms and definitions, authors and their works, and principles and their illustrations (Linn & Gronlund, 2000). Homogeneity is necessary to make all alternatives plausible. Second, the item includes more statements than possible alternatives (to prevent getting the right answer by process of elimination). Third, the alternatives can be used more than once or not at all. Fourth, the entire item fits on a single page. Items with more than 10 statements should be broken into two items, to prevent overloading learners' working memories. Finally, the ground rules of the matching exercise (e.g., options "may be used once, more than once, or not at all") are provided.

14.9
Identify at least two other topics with homogeneous material that could be appropriately measured with the matching format.

True-False Items

The **true-false format** is *a measurement format that includes statements of varying complexity that learners have to judge as being correct or incorrect.* Because they usually measure lower level outcomes, and because students have a 50–50 chance of guessing the correct answer, true-false items should be used sparingly (Linn & Gronlund, 2000). As with the multiple-choice format, guidelines can help teachers improve the items' effectiveness (see Figure 14.8).

The following true-false items illustrate some of the problems described in the guidelines:

Choose One

T　F　1. Mammals are animals with four-chambered hearts that bear live young.

T　F　2. Most protists have only one cell.

T　F　3. Negative wording should never be used when writing multiple-choice items.

T　F　4. All spiders have exoskeletons.

14.10
Recall our discussion of teachers' assessment patterns. Using this as a frame of reference, identify another problem common to the four true-false items.

Item 1 contains two ideas: (a) mammals have four-chambered hearts, and (b) they bear live young. The first is true, but the second is not true in all cases; some mammals, such as the duck-billed platypus, are egg layers. Therefore, the item is false and potentially confusing for students. If both ideas are important, they should be written as separate items. Item 2 contains the qualifying word *most,* which is a clue that the statement is true, and item 3 uses the term *never,* which usually indicates a false statement.

Figure 14.8 Guidelines for preparing true-false items

1. When using the format, write a few more false than true statements. (Teachers tend to write more true than false statements, and students tend to mark answers they're unsure of as "true.")
2. Make each item one clear statement.
3. Avoid clues that may allow students to answer correctly without fully understanding the content.

(As you saw in the previous section, negative wording should be used with caution in multiple-choice items, but to say *never* is false.) In general, true–false items should be free of qualifying terms such as *may, most, usually, possible,* and *often,* and absolutes such as *always, never, all,* and *none.* If qualifiers are used, they're most appropriate in false statements, and absolutes are most effective in true statements. For instance, item 4 uses the absolute *all,* but the statement is true.

Completion Items

1. What is an opinion? _____
2. _____ is the capital of Canada.

Completion format is *a measurement format that includes a question or an incomplete statement that requires the learner to supply appropriate words, numbers, or symbols.* (Items that consist of questions, such as the first example above, are also called *short-answer items.*) As you saw earlier, the completion format is popular with teachers, probably because questions seem easy to construct. This advantage is misleading, however, because completion items have two serious disadvantages.

The first disadvantage is that it is very difficult to phrase a question so that only one possible answer is correct. A number of defensible responses could be given to item 1, for example. Overuse of the completion format puts students in the position of trying to guess the answer the teacher wants, rather than giving the one they think is most correct. The second disadvantage is that unless the item requires solving a problem, completion items usually measure knowledge-level outcomes, as in item 2. Because of these weaknesses, completion formats should be used sparingly (Gronlund, 1993). Table 14.2 presents guidelines for preparing items using this format.

Essay Items: Measuring Complex Outcomes

Essay format is *a measurement format that requires students to make extended written responses to questions or problems.* Essay items are valuable for at least three reasons. First,

14.11
Completion items are classified as *supply formats.* Would you classify them as *objective* or *subjective?* When and why?

14.12
Rewrite completion item 1 so that only one defensible response can be given.

Table 14.2 Guidelines for preparing completion items

Guideline	Rationale
1. Use only one blank, and relate it to the main point of the statement.	Several blanks are confusing, and one answer may depend on another.
2. Use complete sentences followed by a question mark or period.	Complete sentences allow students to more nearly grasp the full meaning of the statement.
3. Keep blanks the same length. Use "a(an)" at the end of the statement or eliminate indefinite articles.	A long blank for a long word or a particular indefinite article commonly provides clues to the answer.
4. For numerical answers, indicate the degree of precision and the units desired.	Degree of precision and units clarify the task for students and prevent them from spending more time than necessary on an item.

they can effectively assess creative and critical thinking and other dimensions of learning not tapped by single-answer, convergent items. Second, teaching students to organize ideas, make and defend an argument, and describe understanding in writing are important goals throughout the curriculum, and essay items are one of the only ways progress toward these goals can be measured (Stiggins, 2001). Third, essay tests can positively influence the way students study and learn. If students know an essay format will be used, they are more likely to look for relationships in what they study and to organize information in a meaningful way (Foos, 1992; Shepard, 2001).

Essay items provide opportunities for teachers to assess writing ability as well as other complex cognitive processes.

Essay items also have disadvantages. Scoring them is time-consuming and sometimes unreliable, and scores on essay items are influenced by writing skill, including grammar, spelling, and handwriting (Airasian, 2000; Haladyna & Ryan, 2001; E. McDaniel, 1994). If writing skill is a desired outcome, the influence is appropriate; if not, it detracts from the validity of the items.

Essay items appear easy to write, but they can be ambiguous, leaving students uncertain about how to respond. The result is that student's ability to interpret the teacher's question is often the outcome measured. Figure 14.9 presents general guidelines for preparing and scoring essay items (Stiggins, 2001). In addition to the suggestions in Figure 14.9, a valuable component in reliably scoring essays is to establish grading criteria in the form of a scoring rubric, described in the next section.

Using Rubrics

A **rubric** is *a scoring scale that describes the criteria for grading* (Goodrich, 1996/97; Stiggins, 2001). Rubrics can be used to assess performances (such as a student speech or presentation) or products (such as an essay or science project). When well constructed, rubrics help students by providing information they can use to guide their thinking as they plan their products or performances. They also provide guidance for the teacher during planning, instruction, and assessment.

Let's see how one teacher uses rubrics to improve her instruction.

Maria Mendoza looked up from the essays her middle school English students had handed in and sighed.

"They just don't get it. How hard is it to write simple paragraphs with a topic sentence, supporting sentences, and a summary? I guess harder than I thought. Oh well. Back to the

Figure 14.9 Guidelines for preparing and scoring essay items

1. Elicit higher order thinking by using such terms as *explain* and *compare*. Have students defend their responses with facts.

2. Write a model answer for each item. This can be used both for scoring and for providing feedback.

3. Require all students to answer all items. Allowing students to select particular items prevents comparisons and detracts from reliability.

4. Prepare criteria for scoring in advance.

5. Score all students' answers to a single item before moving to the next item.

6. Score all responses to a single item in one sitting if possible. This increases reliability.

7. Score answers without knowing the identity of the student. This helps reduce the influence of past performance and expectations.

8. Develop a model answer complete with points, and compare a few students' responses to it, to see if any adjustments are needed in the scoring criteria.

Figure 14.10 Sample rubric for paragraph structure

Criteria	Levels of Achievement		
	1	2	3
Topic Sentence	Not present; reader has no idea of what paragraph is about	Present but does not give the reader a clear idea of what the paragraph is about	Provides a clearly stated overview of the paragraph
Supporting Sentences	Rambling and unrelated to topic sentence	Provide additional information but not all focused on topic sentence	Provide supporting detail relating to the topic sentence
Summarizing Sentence	Nonexistent or unrelated to preceding sentences	Relates to topic sentence but doesn't summarize information in paragraph	Accurately summarizes information in paragraph and is related to topic sentence
Overall Score (9 Possible)			

drawing board. I need to get them to write clear paragraphs before we can work on transitions and the total essay."

As Maria thought about options for making her instruction more effective, she came up with the idea of a scoring rubric.

"If I can just get them to see in concrete terms what I'm after, it'll give them a clearer idea of what to aim for."

After some thought, she developed the rubric in Figure 14.10 and used it the next day to discuss effective and ineffective paragraphs with her class. She also gave students a copy and told them to use it as a guide for their next writing assignment. The following week when they handed their papers in, Maria looked them over anxiously.

"Well, I wouldn't exactly call it a miracle recovery, but these are definitely better than the last batch."

Rubrics were originally created to help teachers with the complex task of grading essays. As we just saw, carefully constructed rubrics can also aid teachers as they plan for instruction and actually teach. Constructing a scoring rubric during planning provides the teacher with specific targets or goals to achieve during instruction. Experts recommend four steps in constructing a rubric (Huba & Freed, 2000):

- Establish criteria based on essential elements that must be present in students' work.
- Decide on number of levels of achievement for each criterion.
- Develop clear descriptors for each level of achievement.
- Determine a rating scale for entire rubric.

In constructing her rubric, Maria first identified three elements essential to an effective paragraph: topic sentence, supporting sentences, and summary sentence (see Figure 14.10). Essential elements should appear in a column along the left side of the rubric matrix (Huba & Freed, 2000). Next, Maria analyzed the most common errors or problems her students encountered in writing their essays and decided on three levels of achievement. She then developed clear descriptors for each level of achievement. Clear descriptors guide students as they write and also provide concrete frames of reference for teachers when they grade. As the final step in rubric construction, Maria determined the weight for the different dimensions to assist her in producing a final grade for the essay. She decided that 9 points would be an A, 7–8 points a B, and 5–6 points would be a C, so a student would be required to be at a level of achievement of 3 on all three criteria to receive an A, for example.

Teachers can also use rubrics to communicate goals during instruction. For example, Maria displayed the rubric she developed and used it to analyze effectively and poorly written paragraphs. The rubric focused students' attention on critical aspects of their writing; the paragraphs provided concrete examples or models.

To see a video clip of a teacher using a rubric to structure her instruction, go to the Companion Website at *www.prenhall.com/eggen*, then to this chapter's *Classrooms on the Web* module. Click on *Video Clip 14.2.*

Rubrics are also helpful during the assessment phase of instruction. They provide a concrete scoring framework to guide teachers and can increase scoring consistency and reliability. For example, one widely used rubric to assess writing skills is the Oregon Six Traits of Writing Rubric (Stiggins, 2001). This rubric focuses on six essential elements of writing quality:

- Ideas (Are ideas presented clearly?)
- Organization (Is the paper clearly organized?)
- Voice (Does the paper reflect the views of the writer?)
- Word Choice (Is vocabulary accurate, clear, and lively?)
- Sentence Fluency (Are sentences clear and varied?)
- Conventions (Are spelling, punctuation, and capitalization correct?)

Within each of these areas, additional descriptors provide specific guidelines to both teachers and students. For example, to receive a top score in organization, an essay should meet the following criteria:

> The organization enhances and showcases the central idea or theme. The order, structure, or presentation of information is compelling and moves the reader through the text.
>
> a. An *inviting introduction* draws the reader in; a *satisfying conclusion* leaves the reader with a sense of closure and resolution.
> b. *Thoughtful transitions* clearly show how ideas connect.
> c. Details seem to fit where they're placed; *sequencing is logical* and *effective.*
> d. *Pacing is well controlled*; the writer knows when to slow down and elaborate, and when to pick up the pace and move on.
> e. The title, if desired, is *original* and captures the central theme of the piece.
> f. Organization *flows so smoothly* the reader hardly thinks about it; the choice of structure matches the *purpose* and *audience.* (Stiggins, 2001, p. 304)

Research on the Oregon Six Traits of Writing Rubric is positive. Developed over 15 years, it provides sufficient clarity and detail to enable different raters to score essays reliably (Stiggins, 2001).

Commercially Prepared Test Items

As we mentioned earlier, many teachers depend on the tests included in textbooks, teachers' guides, and other commercially prepared curriculum materials. Although using these tests obviously saves time, they should be used with caution for at least three reasons (Airasian, 2000):

1. *Goals:* The goals of the curriculum developers may not be the same as your goals. If items don't reflect the goals and instruction in your course, they are invalid.
2. *Quality:* This factor is perhaps most important. Many commercially prepared tests are of low quality.
3. *Level:* Commercially prepared items are commonly written at the knowledge level, measuring memorized information instead of higher order thinking.

The time and labor saved using commercially prepared items are important advantages, however, and teachers can capitalize on these benefits by using the following guidelines:

- Carefully examine your goals before using these items.
- Select those items that are consistent with your goals, and place them in a test file in your computer for easy editing.
- Revise items that need improvement, using feedback from students and analysis of test results.
- Create additional items that help you accurately measure your students' understanding.

14.13
Do the problems—inappropriate goals, quality, and level—of commercially prepared items more commonly affect validity or reliability? Explain.

Remember, only you know what your goals are, and you are the best judge of the extent to which commercially prepared items assess these important goals. Use commercially prepared items selectively and strategically.

Alternative Assessment

Traditional assessments, most commonly in the form of multiple-choice tests, have come under increasing criticism over the last several years (Herman et al., 1992; Reckase, 1997). In response to these criticisms, the use of **alternative assessment**, or *"direct examination of student performance on significant tasks that are relevant to life outside of school"* (Worthen, 1993, p. 445), is growing in importance (Shepard, 2001). A 1999 national survey found that 37 states use some form of alternative assessment in their statewide assessments (Jerald, 2000). Alternative assessments directly measure student performance through "real-life" tasks that ask students to produce rather than reproduce knowledge and develop rather than identify responses (Avery & Palmer, 2001; Wiggins, 1996/97). Examples include

- Writing a persuasive essay
- Designing menus for a week's worth of nutritionally balanced meals
- Identifying and fixing the problems with a lawn mower engine that won't start

In addition to products, such as the essay, teachers using alternative assessments are also interested in students' thinking as they prepare the products, so higher order thinking is strongly emphasized (Paris & Paris, 2001; Putnam & Borko, 2000). Insights into these thought processes provide teachers with opportunities to build on student knowledge and correct student misconceptions (Parke & Lane, 1996/97; Shepard, 2001). For example, a structured interview might be used to gain insights into students' thinking as they design science experiments. These insights can then help teachers modify and improve instruction.

Because of their emphasis on applied, higher level tasks, alternative assessments have the potential to change both instruction and learning (Pomplun, Capps, & Sundbye, 1997). Alternative assessments are also consistent with constructivist views of learning, which recognize that learning is holistic and should be contextualized within authentic tasks (Camp, 1992).

Let's look at two forms of alternative assessments: performance assessments and portfolios.

Performance assessments measure students' ability to demonstrate skills similar to those required in real-world settings.

Performance Assessment

A middle school science teacher noticed that her students had difficulty applying scientific principles to real-world events. In an attempt to improve this ability, she focused on everyday problems, such as why an ice cube floats in one cup of clear liquid but sinks in another, which students had to solve in groups and discuss as a class. On Fridays, she presented another problem. For example, on one Friday she put two clear liquids of the same volume on a balance, and the students had to explain why the balance became unbalanced (a balance measures mass). As they worked, she circulated among them, taking notes that would be used for assessment and feedback.

A health teacher read in a professional journal that the biggest problem people have in applying first aid is not the mechanics per se, but knowing what to do and when. In an attempt to address this problem, the teacher periodically planned "catastrophe" days. Students entering the classroom encountered a catastrophe victim with an unspecified injury. In each case, they had to first diagnose the problem and then apply first-aid interventions. The teacher observed them as they worked and used the information she gathered in subsequent discussions and assessments.

These teachers used performance assessments to gather information about their students' abilities to apply information in realistic settings. A **performance assessment** is *a form of assessment in which students demonstrate their knowledge and skill by carrying out an activity or producing a product* (Airasian, 2000). In using performance assessments, teachers attempt to increase validity by placing students in as lifelike a situation as possible, evaluating their performance against preset criteria (Feuer & Fulton, 1993). The term *performance assessment* originated in content areas such as the performing arts and science, where students were required to perform or demonstrate a skill in a hands-on situation (such as a recital or a laboratory demonstration) rather than recognize correct answers on a teacher-made or standardized test (E. Hiebert & Raphael, 1996).

Parents react positively to performance assessments, judging them to be a valuable source of information about their children's learning progress. They believe that performance assessment provides valuable insights into what students are understanding and that they encourage students to think (Shepard & Bliem, 1995).

14.14
Are essay items performance assessments? Defend your answer, using the information from this section.

Designing Performance Assessments: Instructional Strategies

Experts (e.g., Gronlund, 1993) recommend that teachers follow four principles to design effective performance assessments:

- Specify clearly the type of performance you are trying to assess.
- Decide whether processes or products are the primary focus of your assessment efforts.
- Structure the evaluation setting, balancing realism with pragmatic concerns.
- Design evaluation procedures with clearly identified criteria.

Let's see how these principles guide teachers' actions as they attempt to construct valid performance assessments.

Specifying the Type of Performance

The first step in designing any assessment is to develop a clear idea of what you're trying to measure. A clear description of the skill or process helps students understand what is required and assists the teacher in designing appropriate instruction. An example in the area of speech is outlined in Figure 14.11.

Selecting the Focus of Assessment

Having specified performance outcomes, teachers next decide whether the assessment will focus on processes or products. Processes are often the initial focus, with a shift to products after procedures are mastered (Gronlund, 1993). Examples of both processes and products as components of performance assessments are shown in Table 14.3.

Structuring the Evaluation Setting

A major value of performance assessments lies in their link to realistic tasks; ultimately, teachers want students to apply skills

Figure 14.11 Performance outcomes in speech

Oral Presentation
1. Stands naturally.
2. Maintains eye contact.
3. Uses gestures effectively.
4. Uses clear language.
5. Has adequate volume.
6. Speaks at an appropriate rate.
7. Topics are well organized.
8. Maintains interest of the group.

Source: Gronlund, 1993.

Table 14.3 Processes and products as components of performance

Content Area	Product	Process
Math	Correct answer	Problem-solving steps leading to the correct solution
Music	Performance of a work on an instrument	Correct fingering and breathing that produces the performance
English Composition	Essay, term paper, or composition	Preparation of drafts and thought processes that produce the product
Word Processing	Letter or copy of final draft	Proper stroking and techniques for presenting the paper
Science	Explanation for the outcomes of a demonstration	Thought processes involved in preparing the explanation

learned in the classroom in the real world. Time, expense, and safety may prevent realistic measurement procedures, however, and intermediate steps might be necessary. For example, in driver education, the goal is to produce safe drivers. However, putting students in heavy traffic to assess how well they function behind the wheel is both unrealistic and dangerous. Figure 14.12 contains evaluation options ranging from low to high realism to assess driver education skills.

Simulations provide opportunities for teachers to measure performance with intermediate degrees of realism in cases in which high realism is unfeasible. For instance, a geography teacher wanting to measure students' understanding of the impact of climate and geography on the location of cities might display the information shown in Figure 14.13. Students would be asked to identify the best location for a city on the island and the criteria they used in determining the location. The criteria provide the teacher with additional insights into students' thinking.

14.15

Explain how realism influences validity and reliability. Use the driver education example as a frame of reference.

Designing Evaluation Procedures

The final step in creating performance assessments is to design evaluation procedures. Reliability is a primary concern. Well-defined criteria in the form of scoring rubrics, similar to those used with essay items, increase both reliability and validity (Mabry, 1999; Stiggins, 2001). Clearly written criteria provide models of excellence and performance targets for students (McTighe, 1996/97). Effective criteria have four elements (Herman et al., 1992; Messick, 1994):

1. One or more dimensions that serve as a basis for assessing student performance
2. A description of each dimension
3. A scale of values on which each dimension is rated
4. Definitions of each value on the scale

Let's look now at how these criteria can be used with three different strategies to evaluate learner performance: (a) systematic observation, (b) checklists, and (c) rating scales.

Figure 14.12 Continuum of realism on performance tasks

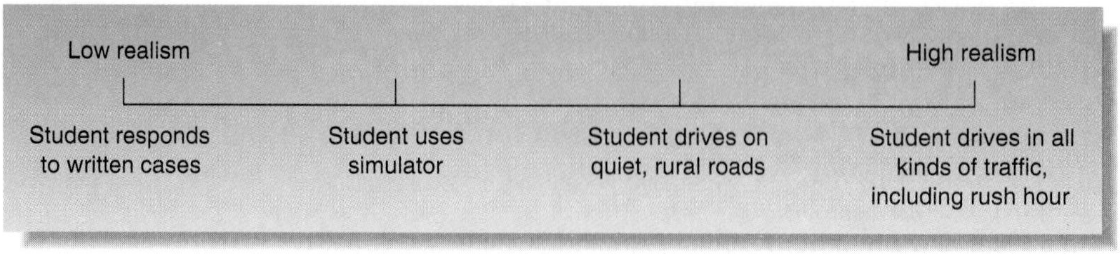

Low realism — High realism

| Student responds to written cases | Student uses simulator | Student drives on quiet, rural roads | Student drives in all kinds of traffic, including rush hour |

Figure 14.13 Simulation in Geography

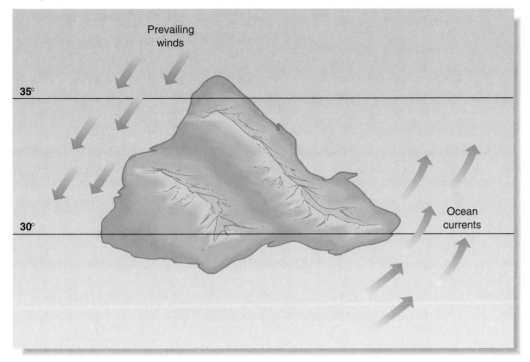

Performance Evaluation Strategies

Teachers observe students in classroom settings all the time. However, these observations typically are not systematic, and records are rarely kept. An attempt to solve these problems is **systematic observation,** *the process of specifying criteria for acceptable performance on an activity and taking notes during observation based on the criteria.* For example, a science teacher attempting to teach her students scientific problem solving might establish the following criteria:

1. States problem or question
2. States hypotheses
3. Identifies independent, dependent, and controlled variables
4. Describes the way data will be gathered
5. Orders and displays data
6. Evaluates hypotheses based on the data

The teacher's observation notes would then refer directly to these criteria, making them consistent for all groups. The notes could be used to give learners feedback and provide information that could be used in future instructional planning.

Checklists extend systematic observation by specifying important aspects of performance and by sharing them with students. **Checklists** are *written descriptions of dimensions that must be present in an acceptable performance of an activity.* When checklists are used, the desired dimensions are typically "checked off" rather than described in notes, as they would be with systematic observation.

Systematic observation incorporating checklists and rating scales allows teachers to assess accurately and to provide valuable information to students about their performance.

Figure 14.14 Checklist for evaluating note taking

Directions: Place a check in the blank for each step performed
_____ 1. Includes essential information
_____ 2. Highlights important facts and ideas
_____ 3. Organizes information to show relationships
_____ 4. Includes questions to clarify information not understood

Checklists might be used to assess students' ability to apply study strategies. For example, an English teacher wanting to assess his students' ability to take notes from a teacher presentation might use a checklist like the one in Figure 14.14. Notes could be added to each dimension, to combine the best of checklists and systematic observation.

Checklists are useful when a criterion can be phrased so that the teacher can answer yes or no to the question "Has this criterion been met?" For instance, with the criterion "Specifies values for controlled variables," it is easy to determine whether a student either did or did not specify the values. In other cases, however, such as "Draws conclusions consistent with the data in the chart," the results aren't cut-and-dried. Conclusions aren't entirely consistent or inconsistent with the data; some conclusions are more thorough or insightful than others. Rating scales address this problem.

Rating scales are *written descriptions of the evaluative dimensions of an acceptable performance of an activity and scales of values on which each dimension is rated.* Rating scales can be constructed in descriptive, graphic, or numerical formats, as shown in Figure 14.15. They allow more precise information to be gathered than is possible with checklists, and the increased detail gives the learner more specific feedback, which gives the teacher and class additional opportunities to evaluate and discuss the performance.

14.16
Create a rating scale that would allow you to assess someone's performance in creating high-quality multiple-choice test items.

Portfolios: Involving Students in Alternative Assessment

Portfolios, another form of alternative assessment, have the additional advantage of involving students in the design, collection, and evaluation of learning products. **Portfolios** are *purposeful collections of student work that are reviewed against preset criteria* (Stiggins, 2001). Because they are cumulative collections of connected works that represent a period of time, they can provide a "motion picture" of learning progress versus the snapshots provided by disconnected tests and quizzes (Ziomek, 1997). The physical portfolio or collection of students' products—such as essays, journal entries, artwork, and videotapes—is not the only assessment; the portfolio assessment also includes students' and the teacher's judgments of learning progress based on these products.

Two features distinguish portfolios from other forms of assessment. First, portfolios collect work samples over time, reflecting developmental changes, and second, portfolios involve students in design, collection, and evaluation. The active involvement of students in portfolios is important for both learning and motivation. One eighth grader had the following comments about a piece she included in her writing portfolio:

Collecting work in portfolios fosters self-regulation because it provides opportunities for students to assess their own learning progress.

In **Ideas and Content** I gave myself a 5. I thought my ideas were clear, and I thought I created a vivid picture of an artist trying to keep his work alive.

Figure 14.15 Three rating scales for evaluating oral presentations

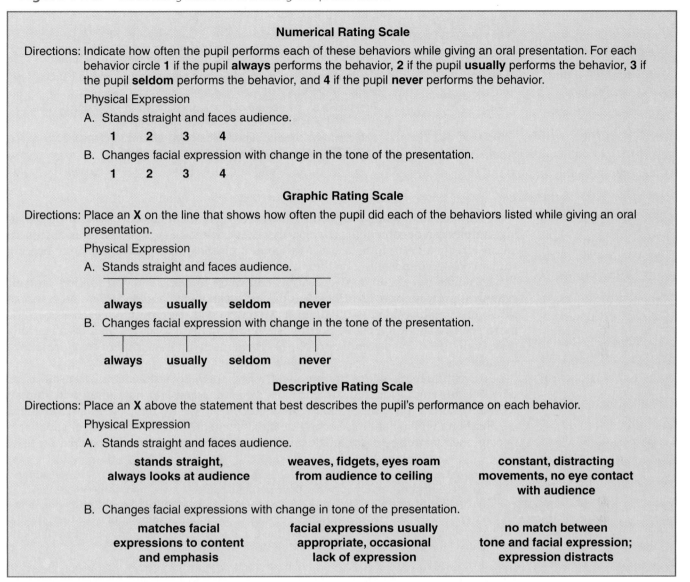

Source: From P. Airasian, *Classroom Assessment*, p. 229. Copyright 1997 by McGraw-Hill Company. Reproduced with permission of the McGraw-Hill Company.

I would also give myself a 5 in **Organization**. My opening does a good job of leading the reader into my paper. . . .

My **Voice** is not as strong as I would have liked it to be. It is hard to take on the voice of another person. I am pretending to be someone else, not myself. I guess I just haven't had enough practice at this. Also, my natural voice tends to be humorous, and clearly, this is the most serious of topics. Anyway, I just did not find quite the voice I wanted, and I gave myself a 4.

My **Sentence Fluency** is pretty strong. You will notice that I vary my sentence beginnings a lot. That's one of my strengths. It's smooth, whether you read it silently or aloud. I think a few sentences are a little short and choppy, though. Some sentence combining would help. So I rated myself a 4 on this trait. (Stiggins, 2001, p. 481)

Involving students in evaluating their own work encourages them to be more reflective and metacognitive about their learning progress.

Table 14.4 Portfolio samples in different content areas

Content Area	Example
Elementary Math	Homework, quizzes, tests, and projects completed over time.
Writing	Drafts of narrative, descriptive, and persuasive essays in various stages of development. Samples of poetry.
Art	Projects over the course of the year collected to show growth in an area like perspective or in a medium like painting.
Science	Lab reports, projects, classroom notes, quizzes, and tests compiled to provide an overview of learning progress.

Portfolios are intended to document and reflect student growth. For example, writing samples can document the changes that occur over a term or course. This documentation can then be used as a basis for communicating with parents and for helping students observe and reflect on their own progress.

Portfolios have been used in teacher education to help candidates reflect on their growth as professionals, identify strengths and weaknesses, and document professional skills during job seeking (Guillaume & Rudney, 1997). Significantly, teachers become more positive about the use of portfolios after using them to assess their own learning (Hootstein, 1999). Examples of portfolio assessments in different content areas are shown in Table 14.4.

At least three questions are involved when portfolio assessments are used. First, who decides what goes into the portfolio? Second, when and how often will student work be placed in portfolios? Finally, on what criteria will students' work be evaluated?

Student involvement in selecting portfolio content gives students the chance to reflect on their learning progress. The following describes one teacher's experience:

> I introduced the idea that their portfolios might present a broader picture—how students have changed or improved, what their particular interests are, and areas where they still have difficulties. This comment led my students to suggest including the following items: an early and a later piece of writing, a rewrite of something, examples of what they like and don't like, a list of books they like and don't, and reading logs that show how their thinking about books has changed. (Case, 1994, p. 46)

The teacher in this vignette also worked with students to jointly establish evaluation criteria. They included (a) how well students explained why they selected particular pieces, (b) the actual pieces, (c) clarity and completeness of the cover letter describing the contents, and (d) neatness and organization. As learners considered what to put in the portfolio, the issue of including only their best work versus pieces demonstrating growth came up. One student commented, "We could all just turn in the papers that got the best grades. But we already got those grades, so what would be the point of making a portfolio?" (Case, 1994, p. 46).

By involving students in these decisions, teachers promote self-regulation by helping them understand how to assess their own growth. Guidelines to make portfolios effective learning tools include the following:

- Embed portfolios into instructional practices. Refer to them frequently as you teach.
- Provide examples of portfolios when introducing them to students.
- Involve students in the selection and evaluation of their work.
- Require students to provide an overview of each portfolio, a rationale for the inclusion of individual works, criteria they used to evaluate, and a summary of progress.
- Provide students with frequent and detailed feedback about their decisions.

14.17
Explain specifically why performance assessments and portfolios are consistent with cognitive views of learning.

Student-led conferences can be an effective way to communicate with parents about portfolio achievements. Researchers found these conferences increased students' sense of responsibility and pride and improved both home-school cooperation and student-parent relationships (Stiggins, 2001). Time constraints and logistics are obstacles to full-scale implementation of student-led conferences, but the educational benefits of increased learner involvement and initiative balance these limitations.

Putting Traditional and Alternative Assessments Into Perspective

The idea of alternative assessments is not new (Worthen, 1993). Oral exams, art exhibits, performances in music, athletics, and business education, proficiency testing in language, and hands-on assessments in vocational areas have been used for years. Increased interest in alternative assessments is likely for at least three reasons.

First, traditional assessments have been increasingly criticized. These criticisms include the following:

- They focus on low-level knowledge and discrete, disconnected content and skills.
- Objective formats, such as multiple-choice, don't measure learners' ability to apply understanding in the real world.
- They measure only outcomes, providing no insight into the processes learners' use to arrive at their conclusions. (Herman et al., 1992; Kahn, 2000; Madaus & O'Dwyer, 1999)

Performance assessments and portfolios respond to these criticisms by attempting to tap higher level thinking and problem-solving skills, emphasizing real-world applications, and focusing on the processes learners use to produce their products (Cizek, 1997; Newman, Secado, & Wehlage, 1995).

Second, critics argue that traditional formats are grounded in behaviorism; they "assume a theory of learning incompatible with current understanding—one that is componential, hierarchical, and unidimensional" (Camp, 1992, p. 243), whereas alternative assessments are more consistent with cognitive views of learning, which stress problem solving and self-regulation (Avery & Palmer, 2001).

Third, designers of alternative assessments hope to increase access to higher education for learners with diverse backgrounds, particularly low-income students (E. Hiebert & Raphael, 1996).

As with many alternatives in education, problems and disadvantages also exist. To begin, little evidence indicates that access to higher education has been improved as the result of the alternative assessment movement (Haertel, 1999; Madaus & O'Dwyer, 1999). In fact, some evidence suggests that alternative assessments may place additional writing demands on minority students, causing them to score as low as, if not lower than, they would have on traditional assessments (Worthen, 1993). Further, insufficient evidence exists to support claims that alternative assessments do a better job than traditional assessments of measuring higher order thinking (Terwilliger, 1997).

Another problem is that implementing alternative assessments can be difficult; without extensive staff development, teachers are unlikely to use them effectively (Avery & Palmer, 2001; E. Hiebert & Raphael, 1996), and the process is very time-consuming, even with support (Ellsworth, 2001; Valencia & Place, 1994). In addition, teachers, faced with the demands of standards-based accountability, often feel tensions between alternative assessments and the more traditional evaluation measures their students will face on tests (Blocher et al., 2002).

Finally, reliability remains an issue. Obtaining acceptable levels of reliability with alternative assessments is possible if care is taken (Nystrand et al., 1992; M. Wilson, Hoskens, & Draney, 2001), but in practice this has been a problem (Haertel, 1999;

Shepard, 2001; Stecher & Herman, 1997). For example, the state of Vermont, in a widely publicized movement, implemented a statewide Portfolio Assessment Program in 1992, but research on the program indicates that scorers assessing the same portfolio often gave very different ratings (Koretz, Stecher, & Diebert, 1993). Additional research on portfolios has identified similar problems (Herman & Winters, 1994).

At the classroom level, allowing students to determine portfolio content also raises the reliability issue. When students choose different items to place in their portfolios, cross-student comparisons are difficult, and reliability in assessing the portfolios suffers. To address this problem, experts suggest supplementing portfolios with traditional measures to obtain the best of both processes (Reckase, 1997).

As with virtually all aspects of learning and teaching, assessment isn't as simple as it appears on the surface; effective measurement and evaluation require sensitive and intelligent teachers. A combination of traditional and alternative assessments—carefully considered and wisely implemented—is likely to be most effective in promoting learning in the classroom (Terwilliger, 1997).

Classroom Connections

Creating Valid and Reliable Assessments in Your Classroom

1. Increase validity through careful planning prior to assessment.
   - *Elementary:* A third-grade teacher compares items on her quizzes, tests, and graded homework to the objectives in the curriculum guide and her unit plan to be sure all the appropriate objectives are covered.
   - *Middle School:* A social studies teacher writes a draft of one test item at the end of each day to be certain the emphasis on his tests is consistent with his instruction. When he puts the whole test together, he uses a table of specifications to ensure that all content areas and difficulty levels are covered.
   - *High School:* After composing a test, a biology teacher rereads the items the next day to eliminate wording that might be confusing or too advanced for her students.

2. Use alternate assessments to increase validity.
   - *Elementary:* A first-grade teacher uses a rating scale to assess his students' oral reading ability. While he listens to each student read, he uses additional notes to help him remember each student's individual strengths and weaknesses.
   - *Middle School:* A math teacher working on decimals and percentages assigns her students the task of

going to three supermarkets and comparing prices on a list of five household items. They are required to determine which store provided the best bargains and what the difference was among the stores on each item.
   - *High School:* A business technology class teacher has students write letters in response to job vacancy notices in the newspaper. The class then critiques the letters in terms of format, grammar, punctuation, and clarity.

3. Use portfolios and performance assessments to develop learner self-regulation.
   - *Elementary:* A fourth-grade language arts teacher uses portfolios as a central organizing theme for his curriculum. Students collect pieces of work over the course of the year and evaluate and share them with other members of the writing teams.
   - *Middle School:* A math teacher asks each student to compile a portfolio of work and present it at parent-teacher conferences. Before the conference, the teacher meets with students and helps them identify individual strengths and weaknesses.
   - *High School:* An auto mechanics teacher makes each student responsible for keeping track of the competencies and skills each has mastered. Each student is given a folder and must document the completion of different shop tasks.

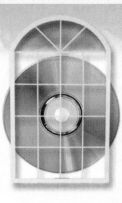

Using Technology in Your Study of Educational Psychology

Assessment in the Balance

You've studied how assessments can promote learning and student self-regulation. Now, using the CD-ROM that accompanies this book, you can personally experience how teachers can use assessment to investigate the thinking of their students. To complete the activity, do the following:

- Open the CD, and click on *Assessment in the Balance*.
- Complete the activities, and then answer the following questions.

1. How can teachers use students' mental models to improve their instruction?

2. How can teachers use student errors to adjust their instruction?

3. How can assessment be used to promote the following goals?
   a. Promote learning.
   b. Develop student self-regulation.
   c. Determine if learning goals have been met.

4. How does alignment influence the quality of assessments?

Effective Assessment Practices: Instructional Strategies

In earlier sections, we examined both traditional and alternative assessment and analyzed how these different forms of assessment influenced learning. Although good items and well-designed alternative measures are essential, there is more to effective assessment. To maximize learning, individual items must be combined into tests; alternative assessments must be carefully planned; students need to be prepared; and assessments must be administered, scored, analyzed, and discussed. In the following sections, we analyze four principles of effective assessment construction:

- Plan systematically using tables of specifications or other organizational guides to ensure a match between learning goals and assessments.
- Prepare students so the assessments you use measure knowledge and skills and not familiarity with test procedures or item types.
- Administer tests and quizzes under optimal conditions to maximize student performance.
- Analyze results to ensure that current and future assessments are accurate and valid.

Let's see how these principles can increase assessment validity and reliability in the classroom.

Planning for Assessment

In planning for assessment, the first task is to increase validity by ensuring assessments are consistent with your goals and instruction. This seems obvious, but because tests are usually prepared some time after instruction is completed, it often doesn't occur. For example, a recent topic given little emphasis in class might have several items related to it, whereas another earlier topic, given much greater emphasis, is covered less thoroughly on the test. A topic may be discussed in class at the applied level, but test items occur at a knowledge level. A goal may call for student performance of some skill, but the assessment consists of multiple-choice questions. Each of these situations reduces the validity of a test.

Tables of Specifications: Increasing Validity Through Planning

One way to ensure that goals and assessments are consistent is to prepare a **table of specifications**, *a matrix that helps teachers generate or organize learning objectives by cognitive level or content area* (C. Campbell & Evans, 2000). For example, a geography teacher based her instruction in a unit on the Middle East on the following list of objectives:

Understands location of cities

1. States location
2. Identifies historical factors in settlement

Understands climate

1. Identifies major climate regions
2. Explains reasons for existing climates

Understands influence of physical features

1. Describes topography
2. Relates physical features to climate
3. Explains impact of physical features on location of cities
4. Analyzes impact of physical features on economy

Understands factors influencing economy

1. Describes economies of countries in the region
2. Identifies characteristics of each economy
3. Explains how economies relate to climate and physical features

Table 14.5 presents a table of specifications for a content-level matrix based on the objectives for the geography unit on the Middle East. The teacher had a mix of items, with greater emphasis on physical features than other items. This emphasis reflects the teacher's objectives, which stressed the influence of physical features on the location of cities, the climate, and the economy of the region. This emphasis also reflects the time and effort spent in class on each area. Ensuring this match between goals, in-

14.18
Two teachers are arguing about the best time to construct a table of specifications—during planning or after a unit has been taught. Describe the advantages and disadvantages of each. Explain.

14.19
A teacher closely follows her curriculum guide, checks off objectives, and writes at least one test item related to each objective as soon as she's finished covering it with her students. Is she being consistent with the concept of tables of specifications by using this procedure? Why or why not?

Table 14.5 Sample table of specifications

Content	Knowledge	Comprehension	Higher Order Thinking and Problem Solving	Total Items in Each Content Area
Cities	4	2	2	8
Climate	4	2	2	8
Economy	2	2	—	4
Physical features	4	9	7	20
Total items	14	15	11	—

struction, and assessment is a primary function of a table of specifications, which helps increase assessment validity.

For alternative assessments, establishing criteria—as discussed in the section on systematic observations, checklists, and rating scales—serves a function similar to that of a table of specifications. The criteria identify performance, determine emphasis, and attempt to ensure congruence between goals and assessments.

Preparing Students for Assessments

DeVonne Lampkin, the fifth-grade teacher in the case study at the beginning of the chapter, was preparing her students for an upcoming test at the end of her unit on fractions. As she made the transition from reading, she stood in front of the room with a transparency in her hand.

"Also, get out your chalkboards and chalk," she reminded students as they got out their math books. She was referring to small individual chalkboards she had made for each of them at the beginning of the year.

"Look up here at our front board," she began, pointing to the chalkboard at the front of the room. "I just want to remind you again that we're having a test tomorrow on finding equivalent fractions and adding fractions with unlike denominators, and we decided that the test will go in your math portfolios. On the test, you will have to add some fractions in which the denominators are the same and others in which the denominators are different. There will also be word problems in which you will need to do the same thing. I'll give the test back Friday, and if we all do well, we won't have any homework over the weekend."

"YEAH!" the students shouted in unison, as DeVonne smiled at their response.

She held up her hand, they quieted down, and she continued. "I have some problems on the test that are going to make you think," she smiled. "But you've all been working hard, and you're getting so smart, you'll be able to do it. You're my team, and I know you'll come through," she said energetically.

"To be sure we're okay," she continued, "I have a few problems that are just like those on the test, so let's see how we do. Write these first two on your chalkboards."

$$\frac{1}{3} + \frac{1}{4} = ? \qquad \frac{2}{7} + \frac{4}{7} = ?$$

DeVonne watched as the students worked on the problems and then held their chalkboards up when they finished. Seeing that three of the students missed the first problem, she carefully reviewed it with the class, comparing it with the second problem.

She then displayed the following three problems:

$$\frac{2}{3} + \frac{1}{6} = ? \qquad \frac{4}{9} + \frac{1}{6} = ? \qquad \frac{2}{9} + \frac{4}{9} = ?$$

Two students missed the second one, so again she reviewed this problem carefully.

"Now, let's try one more," she continued, displaying the following problem on the overhead:

You are at a pizza party with 5 other people, and you order 2 pizzas. The 2 pizzas are the same size, but one is cut into 4 pieces and the other is cut into 8 pieces. You eat 1 piece from each pizza. How much pizza do you eat in all?

Again, DeVonne watched the students work and then reviewed the solution with them when they finished. In the process, she asked questions such as "What information in the problem is particularly important, and how do we know?" "What do we see in the problem that's irrelevant?" and "What should we do first in solving the problem?"

After she displayed two more word problems, she told the students, "The problems on the test are like the ones we practiced in here today." She responded to additional questions from the students and concluded her review by saying, "All right, when we take a test, what do we always do?"

"WE READ THE DIRECTIONS CAREFULLY!" the students shouted in unison.

"Okay, good," DeVonne smiled. "Now, remember, what will you do if you get stuck on a problem?"

"Go on to the next one so we don't run out of time."

"And what will we be sure *not* to do?"

"We won't forget to go back to the one we skipped."

In preparing students for tests, teachers have both long- and short-term goals. Long term, they want students to understand test-taking procedures and strategies and to enter testing situations with a positive attitude and a minimum of anxiety. Short term, they want students to understand the test format and the content being tested. By preparing students, teachers increase the probability that test scores accurately reflect achievement—what students have learned—and thus increase validity.

Teaching Test-Taking Strategies

Teachers can improve students' test-taking strategies by helping them understand the importance of the following strategies:

14.20
Describe at least two specific things DeVonne did to develop test-taking skills in her students.

- Use time efficiently and pace yourself.
- Read directions carefully.
- Identify the important information in questions.
- Understand the demands of different testing formats.
- Find out how questions will be scored.

To be most effective, these strategies should be emphasized throughout the school year, concrete examples should be discussed and linked to the strategies, and students should be given practice with a variety of formats and testing situations. Research indicates that strategy instruction significantly improves test-taking performance, and that young, low-ability, and minority students who have limited test-taking experience benefit the most (S. Walton & Taylor, 1996/97).

Reducing Test Anxiety

"Listen my children and you shall hear. . . . Listen my children and you shall hear. . . . Rats! I knew it this morning in front of Mom."

Like this student, many of us have experienced the negative effects of anxiety in a testing situation. For most of us, the adverse effects of pressure are momentary and minor, with little impairment of performance. For a portion of the school population, however (estimates run as high as 10%), anxiety during testing situations is a serious problem (J. Williams, 1992).

Test anxiety is *a relatively stable, unpleasant reaction to testing situations that lowers performance.* Research suggests that test anxiety consists of two components, affective and cognitive (E. Hong, 1999; Pintrich & Schunk, 2002). Its *affective, or emotional, component* can include physiological symptoms, such as increased pulse rate, dry mouth, and headache, as well as feelings of dread and helplessness and sometimes "going blank." Its *cognitive, or worry, component* involves thoughts, such as worrying about failure (e.g., parents being upset, having to retake the course) and being embarrassed by a low score. During tests, test-anxious students tend to be preoccupied with test difficulty and often cannot focus on the specific items.

Test anxiety is triggered by testing situations that (a) involve pressure to succeed, (b) are perceived as difficult, (c) impose time limits, and (d) contain unfamiliar items or formats (Zohar, 1998). Unannounced or surprise tests, particularly, can trigger adverse amounts of test anxiety.

Frequent assessment within the context of a supportive learning environment can help alleviate test anxiety.

Teachers can do much to minimize test anxiety (Everson, Tobias, Hartman, & Gourgey, 1991), and the most successful of these efforts are usually aimed at the worry component (Pintrich & Schunk, 2002). Suggestions include the following:

- Use criterion-referenced measures to minimize the competitive aspects of tests.
- Avoid social comparisons, such as public displays of test scores and grades.
- Increase the frequency of quizzes and tests.
- Discuss test content and procedures before testing.
- Give clear directions, and ensure that students understand the test format and requirements.
- Teach students test-taking skills.
- Use a variety of measures, including alternative assessments, to measure the range of students' understanding and skills.
- Provide students with ample time to take tests.

Technology can provide a powerful tool to reduce test anxiety. In one study, researchers used computers to provide online practice quizzes and to provide test-takers with flexible time frames to take the test (Cassaday, Budenz-Anders, Pavlenko, & Moch, 2001). Results suggested that test anxiety was alleviated by both measures; the quizzes provided additional confidence for students, and testing flexibility helped relieve time pressures.

Specific Test-Preparation Procedures

Before any test, teachers want to ensure that learners understand test content and procedures and expect to succeed on the exam. In preparing students for her test, DeVonne did three important things:

1. She specified precisely what would be on the test.
2. She gave students a chance to practice similar items under testlike conditions.
3. She established positive expectations in her students and encouraged them to link success and effort.

Clarifying test formats and content establishes structure for students, and this structure reduces test anxiety. Knowing what will be on the test and how items will be formatted leads to higher achievement for all students, particularly those of low ability.

Merely specifying the content often isn't enough, however, particularly with young students, so DeVonne actually gave students practice exercises and presented them in a way that paralleled the way they would appear on her test. In learning math skills, for instance, her students first practiced adding fractions with like denominators, then learned to find equivalent fractions, and finally added fractions with unlike denominators, each in separate lessons. On the test, however, the problems were mixed, and DeVonne gave students a chance to practice integrating these skills before the test. The benefits of this practice are particularly important for young and minority students (S. Walton & Taylor, 1996/97).

Practice with test-like items increases achievement for all students.

Experts urge teachers to differentiate between item teaching and curriculum teaching when they prepare students for tests (W. J. Popham, 2001). In item teaching, teachers organize their instruction around either the actual test items or around a set of look-alike items. The goal is to get students to pass the test. Curriculum teaching, by contrast, focuses on content mastery, with items on a test indicating whether learning has occurred. The distinctions made earlier in Chapters 10 and 11 between learning- and performance-oriented classrooms apply here.

Finally, DeVonne clearly communicated that she expected students to do well on the test. The motivational benefits of establishing positive expectations have been confirmed by decades of research (Pintrich & Schunk, 2002; Stipek, 2002). DeVonne also encouraged attributions of effort and ability for success, and she modeled an

14.21
Using classical conditioning as a basis, explain the emotional component—such as feelings of dread—of test anxiety. Using information processing as a basis, explain how the cognitive component of test anxiety can lower test performance.

14.22
You have an extremely test-anxious student in your class. State specifically what you would do to reduce her anxiety. What should you do if you think her anxiety is a danger to her emotional health?

Monitoring student progress during assessment allows teachers to answer questions and clear up misunderstandings.

incremental view of ability by saying, "But you've all been working hard, and you're getting so smart, you'll be able to do it." You may recall from your study of motivation in Chapters 10 and 11 that encouraging the belief that ability is incremental and can be improved through effort benefits both immediate performance and long-term motivation.

Administering Assessments

When teachers administer tests and quizzes, they want to create conditions that optimize student performance to ensure that assessment results accurately reflect what students know and can do. Let's see how DeVonne does this.

At 10:00 in her classroom the next morning, DeVonne shut a classroom window because delivery trucks were driving back and forth outside. She'd considered rearranging the desks in the room but decided to wait until after the test.

"Okay, everyone," she called. "Let's get ready for our math test." With that, students put their books under their desks.

She waited a moment, saw that everyone's desk was clear, and said, "When you're finished with the test, turn it over, and I'll come and get it. Now look up at the chalkboard. After you're done, work on the assignment listed there until everyone else is finished. Then we'll start reading." As she handed out the tests, she said, "If you get too warm, raise your hand, and I'll turn on the air conditioner. I shut the window because of the noise outside.

"Work carefully," she said after everyone had a copy of the test. "You've all been working hard, and I know you will do well. You have as much time as you need. Now go ahead and get started."

The students quickly began working, and DeVonne stood near the door, watching their efforts.

After several minutes, she noticed Anthony doodling at the top of his paper and periodically glancing around the room. She went over to him, put an arm around his shoulders, and said, "It looks like you're doing fine on these problems," pointing to some near the top of the paper. "Now concentrate a little harder. I'll bet you can do most of the others." She smiled reassuringly and again stood near the door.

DeVonne moved over to Hajar in response to her raised hand. "The lead on my pencil broke, Mrs. Lampkin," she whispered.

"Take this one," DeVonne responded, handing her another. "Come and get yours after the test."

As students finished, DeVonne picked up their papers, and they began the assignment written on the chalkboard.

Let's look at DeVonne's actions in administering the test. First, she arranged the environment to be comfortable, free from distractions, and similar to the way it was when students learned the content. Distractions can depress test performance, particularly in young or low-ability students.

Second, she gave precise directions about how to take the test, how she would collect the papers, and how students should spend their time afterward. These directions helped maintain order and prevented distractions for late-finishing students.

Finally, DeVonne carefully monitored the test during the entire time students worked on it. This not only allowed her to encourage students who became lost or distracted but also discouraged cheating. In the real world, unfortunately, some students will cheat if given the opportunity. However, classroom climate, such as the emphasis on performance versus learning, and the extent to which students feel part of a learning community can strongly influence cheating (Murdock, Hale, & Weber, 2001). In addition, external factors, such as the teacher leaving the room, influence cheating more than whether students are inherently inclined to do so (Blackburn & Miller, 1999; Newstead,

Franklyn-Stokes, & Armstead, 1996). Teacher monitoring during tests also helps students learn to monitor their own test-taking behaviors.

In DeVonne's case, monitoring was more a form of giving support than of being a watchdog. When she saw that Anthony was distracted, she quickly intervened, offered him encouragement, and urged him to increase his concentration. This encouragement is particularly important for underachieving and test-anxious students, who tend to become distracted (J. Elliott & Thurlow, 2000).

14.23
To keep his students informed about the amount of time remaining during a test, a teacher reminds them every 10 minutes. Is this a good idea? How will it affect test anxiety? If at all possible, what should teachers do in scheduling the amount of time students have to take a test?

Analyzing Results

"Do you have our tests finished, Mrs. Lampkin?" the students asked as they got out their math books on Friday morning.

"Of course!" she smiled at them, handing back their papers.

"Overall, you did very well on the test, and I'm very proud of you. I knew all that hard work would pay off."

"There are a few items I want to go over, though," she continued. "We had a little trouble with number 13, and you all made nearly the same mistake, so let's take a look at it."

She waited a moment while the students read the problem and then asked, "Now what are we given in the problem? . . . Saleina?"

"Mr. El had two dozen candy bars.

"Okay. Good. And how many is that? Kevin?"

"Umm . . . two dozen is 24."

"Fine. And what else do we know? . . . Hajar?"

DeVonne continued the discussion and explanation of the problem. She then carefully discussed two other problems that were frequently missed. In the process, she made notes at the top of her test copy, identifying the problems that were difficult. She wrote "Ambiguous" by one problem and underlined some of the wording in it. By another, she wrote, "Teach them how to draw diagrams of the problem." Finally, she put her copy of the test in a file folder, laid it on her desk to be filed, and turned back to the class.

DeVonne's assessment efforts didn't end with administering the test. She scored it and returned it the next day, discussed the results, and provided students with feedback as quickly as possible. This process of providing assessment feedback is important for both achievement and motivation (Bangert-Drowns et al., 1991; Olina & Sullivan, 2002). Feedback allows learners to correct common misconceptions, and knowledge of results promotes student motivation (see Chapter 11). Virtually all teachers provide feedback after a test, and many take up to half a class period to do so (Haertel, 1986). Because student motivation is high, many teachers believe students learn more in these sessions than they do in the original instruction.

In addition, DeVonne made positive comments about the performance of the class on the test. In a study examining this factor, students who were told they did well on a test performed better on a subsequent measure than those who were told they did poorly, even though the two groups did equally well on the first test (Bridgeman, 1974). Research also supports the benefits of individual feedback on tests; students who receive comments such as "Excellent! Keep it up!" and "Good work, keep at it!" do better on subsequent work (Page, 1992). The effects of these short, personalized comments justify the extra work involved.

Finally, DeVonne made notes on her copy of the test before filing it. Her notes reminded her that the wording on one of her problems was misleading, so she could revise the problem before giving it again. This, plus other information taken from the test, will assist her in future planning for both instruction and assessment.

Accommodating Diversity in Classrooms: Reducing Bias in Assessment

When teachers assess their students, they gather data to make decisions about student progress and improve their instruction. Learner diversity, however, often complicates this process. In the following sections, we examine strategies to accommodate this diversity.

To see a video clip of a teacher discussing how she uses assessment results to modify instruction, go to the Companion Website at *www.prenhall.com/eggen*, then to this chapter's *Classrooms on the Web* module. Click on *Video Clip 14.3*.

14.24

Is content bias more a problem with validity or reliability? Explain.

Students from minority groups may lack experience with general testing procedures, different test formats, and test-taking strategies, and they may not understand the purpose of assessments. Also, because most assessments are strongly language based, language may be another obstacle, so the effective testing practices we discussed in the previous section are particularly important for minority students (Heubert & Hausser, 1999; Land, 1997). Teachers can respond to diversity by modifying their assessment procedures in at least three other ways: (a) carefully wording items, (b) making provisions for non-native English speakers, and (c) accommodating diversity in scoring.

Carefully Wording Items

Content bias is always a possibility when assessing students with diverse backgrounds (Hanson, Hayes, Schriver, LeMahieu, & Brown, 1998). For example, learners from minority groups can have difficulties with items that contain information about things uncommon in their culture, such as transportation like cable cars, sports like American football, and musical instruments like the banjo (Cheng, 1987). In addition, holidays like Thanksgiving or U.S. historical figures like Abraham Lincoln, which are well known to most Americans, may be unfamiliar to these students. When these types of terms and events are included in assessment items, teachers are measuring both the intended topic and students' understanding of American vocabulary and culture, and validity suffers.

There is no easy solution to this problem, but teacher awareness and sensitivity are starting points. In addition, encouraging students to ask questions and discussing tests thoroughly after they're given can help uncover unintended bias.

Making Provisions for Non-Native English Speakers

What would you do if your next exam in this class were presented in another language? This prospect gives you some idea of the problems facing non-native English-speaking students during tests. The most effective ways to help these students is to modify the test or the testing procedures. Some suggestions for doing so appear in Table 14.6; of these modifications, simplifying test language and providing extra time for students to use a glossary appear most promising (Abedi, 1999).

Accommodating Diversity in Scoring

Essay exams and alternative assessments can be effective for measuring students' ability to organize information, think analytically, and apply their understanding to real-world problems. However, they also place an extra burden on students who are wrestling with both content and language.

Table 14.6 Modifications to accommodate language diversity

Modifications of the Test	Modifications of the Test Procedures
Simplify test language.	Provide extra time to take the test.
Simplify test directions.	Allow students to use a glossary and dictionary.
Provide visual supports.	Read directions aloud (in the native language is even better).
Assess students in their native languages.	Read the test aloud, and clarify misunderstandings.

Source: Adapted from Butler and Stevens, 1977.

What can teachers do? Valid assessment often requires the use of essays and alternative formats, and teachers cannot ignore students' grammatical errors. One solution is to evaluate essays and performance assessments with two grades: one for content and another for grammar, spelling, and punctuation (Hamp-Lyons, 1992; Scarcella, 1990). In **multiple-trait scoring,** *different dimensions of a product are judged according to different criteria.* For example, a question in science that asks students to propose a solution to the problem of water pollution might be scored using three criteria: (a) the solution to the problem, (b) the understanding of the content, and (c) the way the ideas are developed (Hamp-Lyons, 1992). Breaking the score into three areas allows the teacher to discriminate between understanding of content, problem solving, and ability to use language. These modifications are designed to ensure, as much as possible, that test scores reflect differences in achievement and not cultural bias related to background knowledge, vocabulary, or testing sophistication.

Classroom Connections

Capitalizing on Diversity in Your Classroom

1. Be sure that students and their caregivers understand the importance of assessment in learning.
   - *Elementary:* A third-grade teacher in an inner-city school makes a special effort at the beginning of the school year to explain how homework affects not only learning but grades. She carefully monitors students and notifies parents immediately if work isn't being turned in.
   - *Middle School:* A math teacher in an inner-city magnet school displays his grading system on a wall chart. He carefully explains the system and what it requires of students. He emphasizes that it is designed to promote learning and returns to the chart periodically to remind students of their learning progress.
   - *High School:* A history teacher in a school with high percentages of minority students takes extra time and effort during parent-teacher conferences to explain how she arrives at grades for her students. She saves students' work samples and shares them with the parents during conferences.

2. Adapt testing procedures to meet the needs of all students.
   - *Elementary:* A second-grade teacher adjusts his assessment procedures for his non-native English speakers. He arranges to give these students extra time, and he provides an older student to act as a translator for those whose command of English is still rudimentary.
   - *Middle School:* A social studies teacher encourages her students to ask her about any terms on the test that they don't understand. Unless their understanding of the term is part of what she is measuring, she defines and illustrates the term for students.
   - *High School:* A physics teacher discusses all of the frequently missed items on his tests. He asks students why they responded as they did and what their thinking was. He writes notes during the discussion to revise items that may have been ambiguous or that required knowledge not all students should be expected to know.

Grading and Reporting: The Total Assessment System

To this point, we have discussed the preparation of traditional test items, the design of alternative assessments, and the assessment process itself, which includes preparing students, administering assessments, and analyzing results. Designing a total assessment system requires considering additional issues, such as

- How many tests and quizzes should be given?
- How will authentic assessments be used?

- How is homework counted?
- How is missed work made up?
- How are affective dimensions, such as cooperation and effort, reported in the overall assessment?
- How is performance reported (e.g., letter grade, percentage, descriptive statement)?

These decisions are the teacher's responsibility—a prospect that may seem daunting to beginning teachers, who have little or no experience to fall back on. Merely knowing that the decisions are the teacher's, however, removes some of the uncertainty in the process. We examine these decisions and offer some suggestions in the following sections.

Designing a Grading System

Designing a grading system is an important task that influences both student learning and teacher workload (Guskey, 2002; Haladyna, 1999). A teacher's grading system provides a major communication link between teachers, students, and their parents (Guskey, 2002). When effectively designed and implemented, it can provide feedback to students, create motivational incentives, and help students develop self-regulation. Some guidelines can help in this process:

- Your system should be clear and understandable and consistent with school and district policies.
- Your system should be designed to support learning and instruction by gathering frequent and systematic information from each student.
- Grades should be based on hard data.
- Grading should be fair to all students regardless of gender, class, race, or socioeconomic status.
- You should be able to confidently defend the system to a parent or administrator if necessary. (Linn & Gronlund, 2000; Loyd & Loyd, 1997)

With these guidelines in mind, let's look at elements of an effective system.

Formative and Summative Evaluation

The way a teacher uses quizzes and tests influences learning. Although we often think that the purpose of giving tests and quizzes is to assign grades, a more important function is to provide the teacher and students with feedback about learning progress. In some instances, quizzes and tests are given, scored, and discussed just as any other quiz or test would be, but they are not included in a grading decision. Using assessments in this way is called **formative evaluation** because the *evaluation occurs before or during instruction and is used to provide feedback to students and to monitor their growth.* This feedback is important because it allows students to improve performance, which increases motivation to learn (P. Black & William, 1998b; Brookhart, 1997; Olina & Sullivan, 2002). It also helps students develop metacognitively, by helping them monitor their own learning progress. Formative feedback is also valuable to teachers because it allows them to modify instruction to adapt to student learning problems.

Using tests, quizzes, homework, and alternative assessments to make grading decisions, however, is part of the process called **summative evaluation**, which is *evaluation that occurs after instruction on a given topic and is used for grading purposes.* Although summative evaluations are used as a basis for making decisions about grades, they also provide feedback about learn-

A teacher's grading system can provide one effective way to communicate with students about learning progress.

ing progress, and they should be discussed as thoroughly as any formative evaluation would be. In public schools, most assessments are used for summative evaluations; however, used properly, both formative and summative assessments can be useful in making instructional decisions and motivating students (Stipek, 1996).

Norm-Referenced and Criterion-Referenced Evaluations

Assigning value to students' work is an important part of assessment. This task is as varied as giving "smiley" faces, writing comments on papers, and assigning grades. Norm-referenced and criterion-referenced evaluations are two ways to assign value to student performance. In a **norm-referenced evaluation**, *decisions about an individual student's work are based on comparisons with the work of peers*. In a **criterion-referenced evaluation**, *evaluation decisions are made according to a predetermined standard*.

Norm referencing gets its name from the normal curve (see Figure 15.4 in Chapter 15), and teachers using it might establish a grading curve such as the following:

A   Top 15% of students

B   Next 20% of students

C   Next 30% of students

D   Next 20% of students

F   Last 15% of students

14.25

Think about the effects of formative evaluation on elementary, middle school, and high school students. With which group would formative evaluation be most important? least important? Explain why this would be the case.

By contrast, in a criterion-referenced system, everyone who receives a score of 90 or above on quizzes, tests, or assignments gets an A, for example, everyone above 80% a B, and so on. A more challenging criterion-referenced system uses the following cutoff scores: 94–100, A; 94–88, B; 88–82, C; 82–76, D; below 76, F. A comparison of norm and criterion referencing appears in Table 14.7.

Criterion referencing has two important advantages compared to norm referencing (Stiggins, 2001). First, because it reflects the extent to which goals are met, it more effectively describes content mastery. This allows both students and parents to more accurately understand strengths and weaknesses. Second, criterion referencing de-emphasizes competition, which can discourage students from helping each other, threaten peer relationships, detract from intrinsic motivation, and encourage students to attribute success and failure to innate ability rather than to effort (Ames, 1992; P. Black and William, 1998a; Stipek, 1996). Although criterion referencing alone won't eliminate all these problems, it is preferable to norm referencing.

Although norm referencing is necessary for many standardized tests, it is virtually nonexistent in elementary schools and rarely seen in middle and secondary schools.

14.26

Is the assessment system for the class you're in norm referenced or criterion referenced? What makes it that way?

Table 14.7 A comparison of norm referencing and criterion referencing

	Examples	Characteristics
Norm referencing	Grading on the curve: 15% of students get A's 15% get B's 40% get C's 15% get D's 15% get F's	Compares students' performances to each other Creates a competitive environment
Criterion referencing	94–100 = A 86–93 = B Performance assessments (e.g., recognizes shapes, knows rhyming sounds, knows directions)	Reflects extent to which course goals are being met Reduces student competitiveness

Tests and Quizzes

For teachers in upper elementary, middle, and high schools, tests and quizzes are the cornerstone of a grading system. Some teachers add tests and quizzes together and count them as a certain percentage of the overall grade; others weigh them differently in assigning grades. However it is done, frequent monitoring of progress with feedback to students is important for both achievement and motivation (P. Black & Williams, 1998a; Stipek, 1996). In addition, frequent tests and quizzes provides teachers with valuable information to adapt instruction to learner needs.

Alternative Assessments

If you're using alternative assessments in your classroom, they should be an integral part of your grading system. To do otherwise communicates that they are less important than the traditional measures you're using. If you rate student performance on the basis of well-defined criteria, scoring will have acceptable reliability, and alternative assessments can then be an important part of the total assessment system.

Homework

14.27
Using social cognitive theory, explain why it is important that homework be scored and included in the grading system. What can you do about the possibility that students will copy their homework from others?

Properly designed homework contributes to learning (see Chapter 7). To be most effective, homework should be collected, scored, and included in the grading system (Cooper et al., 1998; Stein & Carnine, 1999). Beyond this point, however, research provides little guidance as to how homework should be managed. Accountability, feedback, and your own workload will all influence this decision. Table 14.8 outlines some options.

As you can see, each option has advantages and disadvantages. The best strategy is one that results in learners making the most consistent and conscientious effort on their homework without costing you an inordinate amount of time.

Assigning Grades: Increasing Learning and Motivation

Having made decisions about tests, quizzes, alternative assessments, and homework, you are now ready to design your total grading system. At this point, you must make two decisions: (a) what to include and (b) the weight to assign each component. Tests,

Table 14.8 Homework assessment options

Option	Advantages	Disadvantages
Grade it yourself	Promotes learning. Allows diagnosis of students. Increases student effort.	Is very demanding for the teacher.
Grade samples	Reduces teacher work, compared with first option.	Doesn't give the teacher a total picture of student performance.
Collect at random intervals	Reduces teacher workload.	Reduces student effort unless homework is frequently collected.
Change papers, students grade	Provides feedback with minimal teacher effort.	Consumes class time. Doesn't give students feedback on their own work.
Students score own papers	Is the same as changing papers. Lets students see their own mistakes.	Is inaccurate for purposes of evaluation. Lets students not do the work and copy in class as it's being discussed.
Students get credit for completing assignment	Gives students feedback on their work when it's discussed in class.	Reduces effort of unmotivated students.
No graded homework, frequent short quizzes	Is effective with older and motivated students.	Reduces effort of unmotivated students.

quizzes, alternative assessments, and homework should all be included. Some teachers build in additional factors, such as effort, class participation, and attitude. This practice, though common in classrooms, is discouraged by assessment experts (R. Linn & Gronlund, 2000; McMillan et al., 1999). Gathering systematic information about affective variables is difficult, and assessing them is highly subjective. In addition, a high grade based on effort suggests to both students and parents that important content was learned, when it may not have been. Factors such as effort, cooperation, preparedness, and class attendance should be reflected in a separate section of the report card.

The practice of inclusion, in which students with exceptionalities spend most or all of the day in general education classrooms, presents special grading challenges for teachers. Research indicates that 60% to 70% of included students receive below-average grades in their general education classes (Munk & Bursuck, 1997/98). The effects of these low grades can be devastating to students who already experience frustrations in attempting to learn and keep up with other students.

To prevent this, teachers often adapt their grading systems by grading on improvement, assigning separate grades for process and for product, and basing a grade on meeting the objectives of an individualized education program (IEP). The dilemma for teachers is how to motivate students while still providing an accurate assessment of learning progress. Experts suggest that districts develop comprehensive grading policies in this area to guide teacher efforts (Munk & Bursuck, 1997/98).

Let's look now at two teachers' systems for assigning grades:

Sun Ngin		**Lea DeLong**	
(Middle school science)		(High school algebra)	
Tests and quizzes	50%	Tests	45%
Homework	20%	Quizzes	45%
Performance assessment	20%	Homework	10%
Projects	10%		

We see that these two grading systems are quite different. Sun Ngin, an eighth-grade physical science teacher, emphasizes both homework and alternative assessments, which include projects and performance assessments. Traditional tests and quizzes count only 50% in his system. Lea DeLong emphasizes tests and quizzes much more heavily; they count 90% in her system. The rationale in each case is simple. Sun indicated that homework was important to student learning, and he believed that unless it was emphasized, students wouldn't do it. He also included projects as an important part of his grades, believing they involve his students in the study of science. He used performance assessments to chart students' progress as they worked on experiments and other hands-on activities. Lea, a secondary Algebra II teacher, thought that students fully understood the need to do their homework in order to succeed on the tests and quizzes, so she de-emphasized this component in her grading system. Instead, she gave a weekly quiz and three tests during a 9-week grading period.

To be effective in promoting learning, your assessment system must be understood by students (Loyd & Loyd, 1997; Thorkildsen, 1996). Even young students can understand the relationship between effort and grades if they are quizzed frequently and if their homework is scored and returned promptly. Conversely, even high school students can have problems understanding a grading system if it is too complex (Evans & Engelberg, 1988).

Parents must also understand your assessment system if they are to become actively involved in their children's learning (Guskey, 2002). Parents view parent-teacher conferences and graded examples of their child's work as most valuable in providing feedback about their children's learning progress, followed closely by report cards (Shepard & Bliem, 1995). Standardized tests, which are given infrequently and often reported in technical language, tend to be rated less favorably by parents. Teachers' clients—both learners and their parents—need to be provided with frequent and clear information about learning progress.

Raw Points or Percentages?

In assigning scores to assignments, quizzes, or tests, teachers have two options. In a percentage system, teachers convert each score to a percentage and then average the percentages as the grading period progresses. In the other system, teachers accumulate raw points and convert them to a percentage only at the end of the period.

To illustrate these options, return to Laura Torrez's work with her second graders, first presented in our discussion of teachers' assessment patterns. Kelly, one of her students, missed 1 of 10 problems on a seat-work assignment. As is typical of many teachers, Laura used a percentage system, and because 9 correct of 10 is 90%, she wrote 90 for Kelly on this assignment. This is a straightforward and simple process.

Suppose now that Laura's students are graded on another assignment; this time, it is 5 items long and Kelly gets 3 of the 5 correct. Her grade on this assignment would be 60. Teachers who use a percentage system typically average the percentages, so Kelly's average at this point would be 75 (the average of 90 and 60). As the example illustrates, this process is flawed. By finding the percentage for each assignment and averaging the two, the assignments are given equal weight. In fact, on the two assignments, Kelly has correctly responded to 12 of 15 problems. If Laura had computed Kelly's percentage based on her raw points to date, Kelly's average would be 80 ($\frac{12}{15} \times 100$), 5 points higher than the average obtained by using a percentage system.

If averaging percentages is flawed, why is it so common? The primary reason is simplicity. In addition to being simpler for teachers to manage, it is easier to communicate to students and parents. Many teachers, particularly those in the elementary and middle schools, have attempted point systems and later returned to percentage systems because of pressure from students, who better understand percentage systems.

Research indicates that computer grade-keeping programs facilitate the use of point systems (Feldman, Kropkf, & Alibrandi, 1996). These researchers also found that the use of a point system in which students are given points for turning in assignments and compiling projects can undermine intrinsic motivation by tacitly communicating that the goal in class is completing tasks and earning points (versus learning). To avoid communicating this message, teachers need to grade on both quality and quantity and continually emphasize the role that instructional tasks play in learning.

As with most aspects of teaching, the choice of a grading system is a matter of professional preference. A percentage system is fair if assignments are similar in length, tests are also similar in length, and tests are given more weight than quizzes and assignments. On the other hand, a point system can work if the teacher simply has the students keep a running total of their points and then communicates the number they must have for an A, a B, and so on at frequent, periodic points in the grading period.

Classroom Connections

Effectively Using Assessment in Your Classroom

1. Use assessments to promote learning in your classroom.
   - *Elementary:* A second-grade teacher continually emphasizes to her students how the work they are doing is designed to promote learning. When she assigns seat work and homework, she talks about the skills they are targeting. When she gives quizzes, she clearly explains what goals are being assessed and why they are important.
   - *Middle School:* A geography teacher attempts to be explicit about what will be covered on assessments by sharing his table of specifications with his students before any test. In addition he explains, "On Thursday's test, you will be asked to explain in an essay question how the physical characteristics of the

northern, middle, and southern colonies affected the economy of each region." The test the next day closely follows this blueprint.

- *High School:* A high school history teacher provides practice for her students under testlike conditions. As she prepares her class for an essay exam, the teacher displays the following question on the overhead: *The southern colonies were primarily agricultural rather than industrial. Using the physical characteristics of the region, explain why this would be the case.* She gives students a few minutes to respond and then discusses the item and appropriate responses to it, reminding students that this is the type of question they will have on the actual test.

2. Use assessment results to provide feedback to students and inform future instructional decisions.

- *Elementary:* A second-grade teacher discusses problems that a significant number of students missed on a math test and then asks the students to rework the problems and hand them back in. If students are still having problems with the content, he reteaches it.

- *Middle School:* After giving a test, a sixth-grade teacher surveys the distribution of student responses. She then revises items that are misleading or that have ineffective distracters. She stores the revisions in the computer for next time.

- *High School:* A freshman English teacher provides extensive individual comments on students' papers. In addition, he identifies problem areas common to the whole class and uses anonymous selections from students' papers to provide concrete feedback.

Technology and Learning: Using Technology to Improve Assessment

The importance of frequent classroom assessment has been a theme throughout this chapter. Frequent assessment requires a great deal of teachers' time and effort, however, and it is here that technology can help.

Because they enable users to store, manipulate, and process large amounts of data quickly, computer technologies are proving to be especially valuable in classroom assessment. Computers can serve three important and time-saving assessment functions (Newby et al., 2000; Roblyer, 2003). These functions are summarized in Table 14.9 and discussed in the paragraphs that follow.

Planning and Constructing Tests

Software test generators have at least three advantages over general word processing programs. First, they produce a standard layout; the teacher doesn't have to worry about spacing or format. Second, they automatically produce various forms of the test—helpful for makeup tests and preventing "wandering eyes." Third, they can be used with commercially prepared test banks, making it easier for teachers to combine the best of the commercially produced items with the items they've constructed. These time- and effort-saving features can make classroom assessment more effective and efficient.

Many test creation programs are commercially available. These include Create-a-Test, Exam Builder, Test Writer, Test-It!, Quick Quiz, and Test Generator. The programs can be used to

- Develop a test file or item bank of multiple-choice, true-false, matching, and short-answer items that can be stored in the system. Within a file, items can be organized by topic, chapter, objective, or difficulty level.
- Select items from the created file bank either randomly, selectively, or by categories to generate multiple versions of a test.
- Modify items and integrate these into the total test.
- Produce student-ready copies and an answer key.

Technology provides teachers with powerful tools to plan, construct, and analyze tests as well as maintain student records.

Table 14.9 Assessment functions performed by computers

Function	Examples
Planning and constructing tests	Preparing objectives
	Writing, editing, and storing items
	Constructing tests
	Printing tests
	Organizing and storing student portfolios
Analyzing test data	Scoring tests
	Summarizing results
	Analyzing items
Maintaining student records	Recording results
	Developing a class summar
	Developing student profiles
	Reporting results to students
	Preparing grade reports

Analyzing Test Data

Technology can also assist in the process of scoring tests and reporting results, saving time for the teacher and providing students with more informative feedback. Software programs are available to machine-score tests (e.g., QuickSCORE), and these programs can perform the following functions:

- Score objective tests and provide descriptive statistics such as test mean, median, mode, range, and standard deviation
- Generate a list of items showing difficulty level, the percentage of students who selected each response, the percentage of students who didn't respond to an item, and the correlation of each item with the total test
- Sort student responses by score, grade/age, or gender (Merrill et al., 1992)

The time and energy saved provide teachers with opportunities to analyze and improve individual items, as well as the entire test, thus improving student learning.

Maintaining Student Records

An effective assessment system frequently gathers information about student performance from a variety of sources. If this information is to be useful to the teacher, it must be stored in an easily accessible and usable form. Computers provide an efficient way to store, analyze, and report student assessments. One teacher commented:

> I keep my grades in an electronic gradebook. By entering my grades into an electronic gradebook as I grade papers, I always know how my students are progressing and exactly where my students stand in relation to each other. It does take a little time to enter the grades, but it makes my job easier during reporting periods. All I have to do is open my disk and record my students' grades on the grade sheet. (Morrison, Lowther, & DeMuelle, 1999, p. 355)

For teachers with some background in technology, general spreadsheet programs can be converted into individualized grade sheets (Forcier, 1999). Commercial software is also available, and most of the programs designed to analyze individual test score data also have the following capabilities:

- Begin a new class file for each class or subject. The files can be organized by name and/or student identification number.
- Average grades, create new grades or change old ones, add extra credit.
- Compute descriptive statistics (such as the mean, median, mode, and standard deviation) for any test or set of scores.
- Weigh numerical or raw scores and translate into letter grades.

- Record the type of activity and the point value for each activity.
- Average grades on a quarterly, semester, and/or yearly basis.

In addition to saving teachers time and energy, these programs are accurate and immediate. If the entered data are correct, teachers can generate grades at the end of a grading period at the touch of a button. In addition, records are readily available at any time, providing students with instant and accurate feedback (Roblyer, 2003). Some programs even have the capacity to print student reports in languages other than English (Forcier, 1999).

Technology and Portfolios

Technology can also be used to organize, store, and display student portfolios (Newby, Stepich, Lehman, & Russell, 2000; Stiggins, 2001). Electronic portfolios address problems of space and accessibility and improve usability because they're stored in a computer. Teachers who have dealt with the logistical problems involved in boxes upon boxes of student portfolios attest to the advantages of electronic storage.

Technology is revolutionizing the teaching-learning process. Nowhere is this impact more important than in the assessment process, and technology's capacity to help assessment contribute more strongly to learning is continually increasing.

Summary

Classroom Assessment

Classroom assessment includes the data teachers gather through tests, quizzes, homework, and classroom observations, as well as the decisions teachers make about student progress. Effective assessment results in increased learning, as well as improved motivation.

Teachers informally measure student understanding during classroom activities and discussions. Formal measurement attempts to systematically gather information for grading and reporting.

Validity involves the appropriateness of interpretations made from measurements. Reliability describes the extent to which measurements are consistently interpreted. Both concepts provide standards for effective assessment.

Traditional Assessment Strategies

Teachers in elementary schools rely on performance measures and commercially prepared items and focus on affective goals more than teachers of older students. Teachers of older students tend to use completion items more than other formats, and their assessments overemphasize memory and low-level outcomes.

Teachers can improve the effectiveness of their assessments by keeping validity and reliability issues in mind when they construct items. Multiple-choice, true-false, matching, completion, and essay items all have strengths and weaknesses that can be addressed through thoughtful item writing.

Alternative Assessment

Alternative assessments, including performance assessments and portfolios, ask students to perform complex tasks similar to those found in the real world. In designing alternative assessments, teachers attempt to place students in realistic settings, asking them to perform high-level tasks involving problem solving in various content areas. Portfolio assessment involves students in the construction of a collection of work samples that documents learning progress. The reliability of alternative assessments can be improved through careful application of predetermined criteria and the use of systematic observation, checklists, and rating scales to evaluate products.

Effective Assessment Practices: Instructional Strategies

Effective assessments are congruent with goals and instruction, and effective teachers communicate what will be covered on assessments, allow students to practice on items similar to those that will appear on tests, teach test-taking skills, and express positive expectations for student performance. Increasing testing frequency, using criterion referencing, providing clear information about tests, and giving students ample time help reduce test anxiety.

Grading and Reporting: The Total Assessment System

Grading and reporting are important functions of an assessment system. Formative evaluation provides feedback about learning, whereas summative evaluation is used for grading purposes. Norm-referenced evaluation compares a learner's performance with that of peers, whereas criterion-referenced evaluation compares students' performance with a standard. Technology can assist teachers in planning, analyzing results, and maintaining student records.

Windows on Classrooms

At the beginning of the chapter, you saw how DeVonne Lampkin used her understanding of assessment to help increase her students' achievement and align her instruction with her students' learning needs. In studying the chapter, you've seen how assessment, in both traditional and alternative forms, can help teachers make strategic decisions about their students' learning progress.

Let's look now at another teacher working with a group of students. Read the case study, and answer the questions that follow. As you read, analyze the teacher's approach in terms of the ideas you've studied in the chapter.

In Ron Hawkins's third-period class on Monday, he began a unit on pronoun cases with one of his Standard English classes. The tardy bell rang at 9:10 as Ron began, "All right, listen, everyone. Today we're going to begin a study of pronoun cases. Everybody turn to page 484 in your text. . . . We see at the top of the page that we're dealing with pronoun cases. This is important in our writing because we want to be able to write and use standard English correctly, and this is one of the places where people often get mixed up. So, when we're finished with our study here, you'll all be able to use pronouns correctly in your writing."

He then wrote the following on the chalkboard:

Pronouns use the nominative case when they're subjects and predicate nominatives. Pronouns use the objective case when they're direct objects, indirect objects, or objects of prepositions.

"Let's review briefly," Ron continued. "Give me a sentence that has both a direct and indirect object in it. . . . Anyone?"

"Mr. Hawkins gives us too much homework," Amato offered jokingly.

Ron wrote the sentence on the chalkboard amid laughter from the students and then continued, smiling, "Okay, Amato. Good sentence, even though it's incorrect. I don't give you enough work. . . . What's the subject in the sentence?"

". . ."

"Go ahead, Amato."

"*Mr. Hawkins*?"

"Yes, good. *Mr. Hawkins* is the subject," Ron replied as he underlined *Mr. Hawkins* in the sentence.

"Now, what's the direct object? . . . Helen?"

"Homework."

"All right, good. And what's the indirect object? . . . Anya?"

"Us."

"Excellent, everybody." Ron continued by reviewing predicate nominatives and objects of prepositions.

"Now let's look at some additional examples up here on the overhead," Ron said, as he displayed the following four sentences:

1. Did you get the card from Esteban and (I, me)?
2. Will Meg and (she, her) run the concession stand?
3. They treat (whoever, whomever) they hire very well.
4. I looked for someone (who, whom) could give me directions to the theater.

"Okay, look at the first one. Which is correct? . . . Omar?"

"Me."

"Good, Omar. How about the second one? . . . Lonnie?"

"Her."

"Not quite, Lonnie. Listen to this. Suppose I turn the sentence around a little and say, 'Meg and her will run the concession stand.' See, that doesn't sound right, does it? 'Meg and she' is a compound subject, and when we have a subject, we use the nominative case. Are you okay on that, Lonnie?"

Lonnie nodded and Ron continued, "Look at the third one, . . . Cheny."

"I don't know . . . whoever, I guess."

"This one is tricky all right," Ron nodded. "When we use whoever and whomever, whoever is the nominative case and whomever is the objective case. In this sentence, whomever is a direct object, so it is the correct form."

After he finished, Ron gave the students another list of sentences in which they were to select the correct form of the pronoun.

On Tuesday, Ron reviewed the exercises the students had completed for homework and gave some additional examples that used who, whom, whoever, and whomever. He then discussed the rules for pronoun-antecedent agreement (pronouns must agree with their antecedents in gender and number). He again had students work examples as he'd done with pronoun cases.

He continued with pronouns and their antecedents on Wednesday and began a discussion of indefinite pronouns as antecedents for personal pronouns—anybody, either, each, one, someone—and had students work examples as done before.

Near the end of class on Thursday, Ron announced, "Tomorrow, we're going to have a test on this material: pronoun cases, pronouns and their antecedents, and indefinite pronouns. You have your notes, so study hard. . . . Are there any questions? . . . Good. I expect you all to do well. I'll see you tomorrow."

On Friday morning as students filed into class and the bell rang, Ron picked up a stack of tests from his desk. The test consisted of 30 sentences, 10 of which dealt with case, 10 with antecedents, and 10 with indefinite pronouns. The final part of the test directed the students to write a paragraph. The following are some sample items from the test:

Part I. For each of the items below, mark A on your answer sheet if the pronoun case is correct in the sentence, and mark B if it is incorrect. If it is incorrect, supply the correct pronoun.

1. Be careful who you tell.
2. Will Rennee and I be in the outfield?
3. My brother and me like water skiing.

Part II. Write the pronoun that correctly completes the sentence.

1. Arlene told us about _____ visit to the dentist to have braces put on.
2. The Wilsons planted a garden in _____ backyard.
3. Cal read the recipe and put _____ in the file.
4. Each of the girls on the team wore _____ school sweater to the game.
5. None of the brass has lost _____ shine yet.
6. Few of the boys on the team have taken _____ physicals yet.

The directions for the final part of the test were as follows:

Part III. Write a short paragraph that contains at least two examples of pronouns in the nominative case and two examples of pronouns in the objective case. (Circle and label these.) Include also at least two examples of pronouns that agree with their antecedents. Remember!! The paragraph must make sense. It cannot be just a series of sentences.

Ron watched as his students worked, and he periodically walked up and down the aisles. Seeing that 15 minutes remained in the period and that some students were only starting on their paragraphs, he announced, "You only have 15 minutes left. Watch your time and work quickly. You need to be finished by the end of the period."

He then continued monitoring students, again reminding them to work quickly when 10 minutes were left and again when 5 minutes were left.

Luis, Simao, Moy, and Rudy were hastily finishing the last few words of their tests as the bell rang. Luis finally turned in his paper as Ron's fourth-period students were filing into the room.

"Here," Ron said. "This pass will get you into Mrs. Washington's class if you're late. . . . How did you do?"

"Okay, I think," Luis said over his shoulder as he scurried out of the room, "except for the last part. It was hard. I couldn't get started."

"I'll look at it," Ron said. "Scoot now."

On Monday, Ron returned the tests, saying, "Here are your papers. You did fine on the sentences, but your paragraphs need a lot of work. Why did you have so much trouble with them, when we had so much practice?"

"It was hard, Mr. Hawkins."

"Not enough time."

"I hate to write."

Ron listened patiently and then said, "Be sure you write your scores in your notebooks. . . . Okay, . . . you have them all written down? . . . Are there any questions?"

"Number 3," Enrique requested.

"Okay, let's look at 3. It says, 'My brother and me like water skiing.' There, the pronoun is part of the subject, so it should be *I* and not *me*.

"Any others?"

A sprinkling of questions came from around the room, and Ron responded, "We don't have time to go over all of them. I'll discuss three more."

He responded to the three students who seemed to be most urgent in waving their hands. He then collected the tests and began a discussion of adjective and adverb clauses.

PRAXIS These exercises are designed to help you prepare for the PRAXIS™ "Principles of Learning and Teaching" exam. To receive feedback on your constructed response questions and document analysis response, go to the Companion Website at *www.prenhall.com/eggen*, then to this chapter's *Practice for PRAXIS™* module. For additional connections between this text and the PRAXIS™ exam, go to Appendix A.

Constructed Response Questions

In answering these questions, use information from the chapter and link your responses to specific information in the case.

1. How well were Ron's curriculum and assessment aligned? Explain specifically. What could he have done to increase curricular alignment?

2. In the section on effective testing practices, we discussed preparing students for tests, administering tests, and analyzing results. How effectively did Ron perform each task? Describe specifically what he might have done to be more effective in these areas.

3. Like most classes, Ron's class was composed of learners with diverse backgrounds. How effective was his teaching and assessment for these students?

4. What were the primary strengths of Ron's teaching and assessment? What were the primary weaknesses? If you think Ron's teaching and assessment could have been improved on the basis of information in this chapter, what suggestions would you make? Be specific.

Also on the Companion Website at *www.prenhall.com/eggen*, you can measure your understanding of chapter content in *Practice Quiz* and *Essay* modules, apply concepts in *Online Cases,* and broaden your knowledge base with the *Additional Content* module and *Web Links* to other educational psychology websites.

Document-Based Analysis

DeVonne Lampkin had the following goal for one of her math lessons: For students to understand equivalent fractions. To measure students' attainment of this goal, she gave the following item:

The Jaguars soccer team won 16 out of the 24 games they played. The Dolphins soccer team won 14 of the 21 games they placed. Is the fraction of the games each team won the same, or is it different? Explain how you know.

On this item, Kevin answered, "The Jaguars won a larger fraction because they won more games."

Analyze DeVonne's item with respect to her goal. What does Kevin's response tell use about his understanding of equivalent fractions? Explain.

Online Portfolio Activities

To develop your professional portfolio, further apply your understanding of chapter content, and address the INTASC standards, go to the Companion Website, then to this chapter's *Online Portfolio Activities.* Complete the suggested activities.

Important Concepts

alternative assessment *(p. 510)*
checklists *(p. 513)*
classroom assessment *(p. 495)*
completion format *(p. 506)*
criterion-referenced evaluation *(p. 529)*
distracters *(p. 501)*
essay format *(p. 506)*
evaluation *(p. 495)*
formal measurement *(p. 495)*
formative evaluation *(p. 528)*
informal measurement *(p. 495)*
matching format *(p. 505)*
measurement *(p. 495)*
multiple-choice format *(p. 501)*

multiple-trait scoring *(p. 527)*
norm-referenced evaluation *(p. 529)*
performance assessment *(p. 511)*
portfolios *(p. 514)*
rating scales *(p. 514)*
reliability *(p. 497)*
rubric *(p. 507)*
summative evaluation *(p. 528)*
systematic observation *(p. 513)*
table of specifications *(p. 520)*
test anxiety *(p. 522)*
true-false format *(p. 505)*
validity *(p. 497)*

Chapter Outline

Standardized Tests

Functions of Standardized Tests • Types of Standardized Tests • Evaluating Standardized Tests: Validity Revisited • The Teacher's Role in Standardized Testing: Instructional Strategies

Understanding and Interpreting Standardized Test Scores

Descriptive Statistics • Interpreting Standardized Test Results

Issues in Standardized Testing

Standards-Based Education and the Accountability Movement • Testing Teachers • Cultural Minorities and High-Stakes Tests • Student Diversity and Test Bias • Eliminating Bias in Standardized Testing: Instructional Strategies • Standardized Testing with Alternative Formats • Issues in Standardized Testing: Implications for Teachers

Assessment Through Standardized Testing

15

"Hello Mrs. Palmer. I'm glad you could come in. It's good to see you again," Mike Chavez, a fourth-grade teacher, said as he offered his hand in greeting.

"Thank you," Doris Palmer responded. "I'm anxious to see how David's doing. His sister always did so well."

"Well, let's take a look," Mike said as he offered Mrs. Palmer a seat next to his desk.

"Here are the results from the Stanford Achievement Test David took earlier this spring," Mike began, referring to a data printout (see Figure 15.1). "There's quite a bit of information here, so let me walk you through it."

After giving Mrs. Palmer a chance to look at the report for a few moments, Mike began by pointing to the reading scores, "Let's take a look at reading first. . . . David is strong there."

"He loves to read. I'm amazed, but he loves going to the library."

"Yes, he always has a book out when he has free time in class. You can see that there are three reading scores—vocabulary, reading comprehension, and total reading. Reading comprehension is especially strong. David's at the 80th percentile locally."

"What does this 5.6 mean?" Mrs. Palmer interjected, pointing to the "Grade Equiv." column. "Should he be in the fifth grade?"

"Not really," Mike smiled. "It simply means that David scored very well on the reading portion of the test. . . . In standardized testing lingo, it means that David's performance on this part of the test was about the same as that of the average fifth grader in the sixth month of school. You should be very pleased, . . . but tests like these don't tell us where kids should be placed.

"You already know he's in our top reading group, and he consistently gets A's in reading," Mike continued. "This test confirms that he's properly placed. . . . I have some other materials from his portfolio that give us some more information."

"So what's the point in the tests if we already know that he's good at reading? They seem to make him nervous."

Figure 15.1   David Palmer's achievement test report

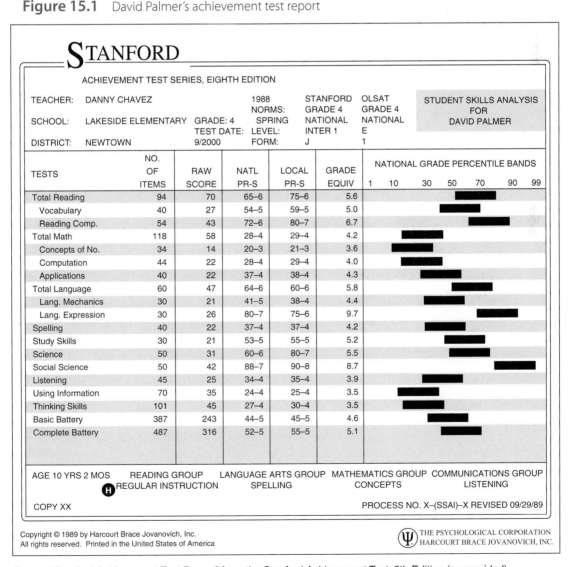

Source: "Stanford Achievement Test Report" from the <u>Stanford Achievement Test: 8th Edition</u> (as provided). Reproduced by permission.

"Good question. We actually use the tests for several reasons. They help us understand how our students are doing compared to other students around the country. They give us an objective, outside measure. And they can help us pinpoint some problem areas in math," Mike continued, pointing at the report. "David isn't quite as strong in math."

"He says he doesn't like math."

Mike smiled. "That's what he says, but I'm not sure that's the whole picture. Look here. Notice how his lowest math score is on concepts of numbers. His percentile rank is 21 locally. . . . And look over here," he noted, pointing to the percentile bands column. "See how this band is lower than most of his others. This could suggest that he has difficulty understanding math concepts."

"You're telling me. Sometimes he comes home and complains about all the problems you have him do. He says he knows the answer but you keep asking him 'why?'"

"That's interesting, Mrs. Palmer, because the test is telling us something that I could see in his work. His work in my class, which I'll show you in a minute, suggests that maybe David tended to rely on memorizing in his earlier math classes. He knew a lot but probably wasn't asked to think that much about what he was learning. Now that he's in fourth grade I'm trying to help him understand *why* he's doing what he's doing. I really believe that it will pay off if he sticks with it . . . and if you and I encourage him to stick with it."

"Well," she responded uncertainly, "if you're sure, we'll hang in there."

"Overall, Mrs. Palmer, I'm very pleased with David's performance," Mike interjected, sensing her uncertainty. "If he can keep his reading scores up and work to get those math scores up some by next year, he will be making excellent progress."

Standardized tests have become a familiar part of the educational landscape. We all took standardized achievement tests as we moved through elementary school, and taking the SAT or ACT has become an accepted rite of passage from high school to college.

Teachers like Mike Chavez play an important role in determining whether or not standardized tests are used effectively. They administer tests, interpret scores for students and their parents, and use test results to inform and improve their teaching. They may even serve on committees involved in making decisions about test selection.

The goal of this chapter is to provide you with information that will help you make sound decisions about using standardized tests in your classroom. After you've completed your study of this chapter, you should be able to

- Describe different uses for standardized tests and explain how they influence educational decisions
- Discuss the different types of standardized tests based on their educational use
- Explain how different types of validity can be used to evaluate standardized tests
- Discuss issues involving standardized testing and explain how they influence classroom teachers
- Explain how student diversity influences measurement validity and discuss strategies that teachers can use to minimize measurement bias

Standardized Tests

A number of questions about students' progress are difficult to answer based on teacher-made instruments alone. For instance: How do the students in my class compare with students across the country? How well is our curriculum preparing students for college or future training? How does a particular student compare to other students of similar ability? **Standardized tests,** *assessment instruments given to large samples of students* (in many cases nationwide) *under uniform conditions and scored according to uniform procedures,* are designed to provide answers to those questions. The scores individuals make on a standardized test are compared to the scores of a **norming group,** *the representative group of individuals whose standardized test scores are compiled for the purpose of constructing national norms.* Individuals in a norming group are similar in age, grade level, and background (Linn & Gronlund, 2000).

Teachers should carefully consider the norming group for a standardized test when interpreting results, because the norming group describes the larger population to which a student is being compared. **National norms** are *scores on standardized tests earned by representative groups of students from around the nation to which an individual's score is compared.* The norming group will include students from urban, suburban, and rural areas; different geographical regions; private and public schools; boys and girls; and different ethnic groups. Based on the student's score on the standardized test, the teacher can determine whether a student is performing above, similar to, or below the general population of students in the nation as a whole.

The influence of standardized testing on education practice can hardly be overstated. The fact that students in other industrialized countries, such as Japan and Germany, score higher than American students on some of these tests has alarmed many in this country (Stedman, 1997). Reform movements that began in the early 1980s and continue today are largely due to concerns about low scores on standardized tests. The results of a morning's testing can often be a powerful factor in decisions about the long-term future of individual students (Gardner, 1992; Hoffman, Assaf, & Paris, 2001).

Standardized testing is also controversial. In a given year, millions of students take state-mandated tests at a cost of more than one billion dollars annually. Many teachers and parents feel that standardized testing is overemphasized, arguing that they adversely affect a balanced school curriculum (Hoffman et al., 2001; Wallace, 2000). In addition, research suggests that beginning teachers are inadequately prepared to deal with new assessment roles thrust upon them by the accountability movement (Lawson & Childs, 2001). To put these concerns in perspective, let's look at some of the ways that standardized tests are used.

15.1

Identify at least two similarities and at least two differences between standardized tests and teacher-made tests.

Functions of Standardized Tests

Standardized tests serve several functions (Ansley, 1997; Stiggins, 2001). They can be used to gather information about learning progress, diagnose individual students' strengths and weaknesses, and make selection and placement decisions, such as deciding which students are eligible for gifted programs. They help schools measure the effectiveness of specific programs, and they are also used to hold schools accountable for student learning.

Student Assessment

The most common function of standardized testing is to provide an external, objective picture of student progress. In our opening case study, for example, David consistently received A's in his reading classes, but this did not tell his parents, teachers, and school administrators how he compared to other children at his grade level. Were his A's due to high achievement or generous grading criteria? Standardized tests provide a yardstick for measuring student achievement across a variety of educational settings, and when combined with teacher-made assessments of student performance, they help provide a complete picture of student progress (Brennan, Kim, Wenz-Gross & Siperstein, 2001).

15.2

Identify at least one advantage and at least one disadvantage of using standardized tests for the purpose of student assessment.

Diagnosis

Standardized tests also help diagnose student strengths and weaknesses (W. J. Popham, 2000). For example, after learning that David scored low on the math section of his achievement test, his teacher might schedule a diagnostic test to gather detailed information about David's strengths and weaknesses in math. These tests are usually administered individually, with the goal of getting specific information about students' achievement in particular aspects of a content area.

Standardized tests provide information about learning progress, diagnose student strengths and weaknesses, and assist in placement decisions.

Selection and Placement

Selecting which students should be placed in specialized or limited-size programs is another use of standardized tests. For instance, students entering a high school may come from "feeder" middle schools, private schools, and schools outside the district. Scores from the math section of a standardized test can help the math faculty place students in classes that will best match their backgrounds and capabilities.

Standardized test results can also be used to make decisions about placement in advanced programs, such as programs for the gifted, and as criteria for university admission. Most of us, for instance, took either the Scholastic Aptitude Test (SAT) or the American College Test (ACT) in high school. Our scores on these standardized tests were important factors in whether or not we were accepted by the college of our choice. Because college students come from different parts of the country, and their backgrounds are diverse, these tests give admission officers a basis for comparison.

15.3
Identify at least one advantage and at least one disadvantage of using standardized tests for selection and placement.

Program Evaluation

Standardized tests can also provide information about instructional programs. For example, an elementary school has moved from a traditional reading program to one that emphasizes writing and children's literature. To assess the effectiveness of this change, the faculty use teacher-made assessments, student work samples, and the perceptions of teachers and parents. However, they still don't know how the students' performance compares with their performance in the previous program or with the performance of peers in other reading programs. Standardized test results can help provide this information.

Accountability

Increasingly, schools and teachers are being held accountable for student learning (Olson, 2000a). Parents, school board members, state officials, and decision makers at the federal level are demanding evidence that tax dollars are being used efficiently. Standardized test scores provide one indicator of this effectiveness.

To see a video clip of one expert's perspective on testing and accountability, go to the Companion Website at *www.prenhall.com/eggen*, then to this chapter's *Classrooms on the Web* module. Click on *Video Clip 15.1*.

The accountability movement has resulted in the creation of a controversial testing program called the National Assessment of Educational Progress, designed to provide information about the quality of education in each of the 50 states (L. Jones, 1996). Critics contend that misuse of standardized test scores can result in narrowing the curriculum and give an inaccurate picture of student learning (Paris, 1998). Proponents claim that standardized tests can provide valuable information about the relative performance of different states, districts, and schools.

Types of Standardized Tests

At least four different kinds of standardized tests are commonly used in educational settings. They include

- Achievement tests
- Diagnostic tests
- Intelligence tests
- Aptitude tests

We examine them in the following sections.

Achievement Tests

Achievement tests, the most widely used type of standardized test, are *designed to measure and communicate how much students have learned in specified content areas.* General-purpose achievement tests measure learning in several content areas—most commonly reading, language, and math but sometimes also one or more areas, such as general knowledge, science, social studies, computer literacy, study skills, or critical thinking. These areas are usually further broken down into more specific skill areas. For example, students taking the Stanford Achievement Test receive not only a Total Language score but also scores that show how they performed on items measuring language mechanics and language expression (see Figure 15.1). Popular achievement tests include the Iowa Test of Basic Skills, the California Achievement Test, the Stanford Achievement Test, the Comprehensive Test of Basic Skills, and the Metropolitan Achievement Test, as well as individual statewide assessments and minimum levels skills tests (Airasian, 2000; Stiggins, 2001).

Standardized achievement tests serve several purposes, including the following:

- Determining the extent to which students have mastered a content area
- Comparing the performance of students with others across the country
- Tracking student progress over time
- Determining if students have the background knowledge to begin instruction in particular areas
- Identifying learning problems

Most standardized achievement tests are batteries of specific tests that are administered over several days. These tests are intended to reflect a curriculum common to most schools, which means they will assess some, but not all, of the goals of a specific school. This is both a strength and a weakness. Because they are designed for a range of schools, they can be used in a variety of locations. On the other hand, this "one size fits all" approach may not accurately measure achievement for a specific curriculum. For example, one study found that only 47% to 71% of the math content measured on commonly used standardized achievement batteries was the same as content covered in popular elementary math textbooks (Berliner, 1984). In a worst-case scenario, this means that students might have had the opportunity to learn less than half the content measured on the test.

15.4
Describe what a teacher might do if a lack of fit is uncovered between a standardized achievement test and the teacher's curriculum.

Schools and teachers should be cautious in selecting and interpreting standardized achievement tests for their students. When selecting a test, it is important to go beyond the name and examine the specific contents described in the testing manual's table of specifications. Comparing the content of the test with your curriculum objectives will help you decide if the test is valid for your use.

Diagnostic Tests

Whereas achievement tests measure students' progress in a variety of curriculum areas, **diagnostic tests** are *designed to provide a detailed description of learners' strengths and weaknesses in specific skill areas.* They are common in the primary grades, where instruction is designed to match the developmental level of the child and to meet needs across several ability levels in math and reading. Diagnostic tests are usually administered individually, and compared to achievement tests, they include a larger number of items, use more subtests, and report scores in more specific areas (Linn & Gronlund, 2000). A diagnostic test in reading, for example, might measure letter recognition, word analysis skills, sight vocabulary, vocabulary in context, and reading comprehension. The Metropolitan Achievement Test, the Detroit Test of Learning Aptitude, the Durrell Analysis of Reading Difficulty, and the Stanford Diagnostic Reading Test are commonly used diagnostic tests.

15.5
Is the issue of "fit" more or less important when using diagnostic tests than when using achievement tests? Explain.

Intelligence Tests

Intelligence tests are *standardized tests designed to measure an individual's ability to acquire knowledge, capacity to think and reason in the abstract, and ability to solve novel problems.* You may recognize these abilities as those included in our definition of *intelligence* in Chapter 4. Attempts to measure intelligence in a valid and reliable way were among the first in the history of standardized testing.

A Short History of Intelligence Tests. Standardized intelligence tests originated in the early 1900s when Alfred Binet was asked by the French minister of public instruction to help develop an instrument to be used in the education of students with mental retardation. He selected a number of school-related skills, such as defining words and making change, and with his partner, Theodore Simon, developed a series of tests based on these skills. They gave the tests to heterogeneous groups of children, eliminating items so difficult that no students passed or so easy that all did. The result was an objective instrument, essentially independent of the influences of social class or the person administering the test, that could be passed by the average child of a given age.

Although intelligence tests were first developed to measure the capabilities of learners with disabilities, they were later broadened to describe the performance of a variety of individuals. Initially, performance was described as a "mental age"; for example, a child succeeding on tasks designed for a typical 8-year-old was said to have a mental age of 8 years.

To overcome problems with older populations—describing a 20-year-old as functioning like a 30-year-old wasn't meaningful, for example—the mental age (M.A.) was divided by the chronological age (C.A.) and multiplied by 100, resulting in the familiar ratio IQ (intelligence quotient). For example, a 6-year-old with a mental age of an 8-year-old would have an IQ of 133 ($\frac{8}{6} = 1.33 \times 100 = 133$).

The importance of Binet and Simon's pioneering work is hard to overstate. For the first time, educators had an objective way of predicting school success; students who performed well on the test usually did well in school and vice versa. The predictions weren't perfect, but they were a vast improvement over people's intuition. The test was translated and brought to the United States by Lewis Terman, a professor at Stanford, and it then became the famous Stanford-Binet. The updated version is one of the two most widely used intelligence tests in schools today.

The Stanford-Binet. The Stanford-Binet is an individually administered assessment of intelligence and cognitive abilities, composed of subtests, much like Binet's original. It comes in a kit that includes all of the testing materials, such as manipulatives and pictures, along with a test manual. Earlier versions heavily emphasized verbal tasks, but the most recent edition is more diverse, targeting five factors—Reasoning, Knowledge, Working Memory, Visual, and Quantitative—which each contain a verbal and nonverbal subtest. Table 15.1 contains descriptions of some sample subtests in the latest revision.

The Stanford-Binet 5th edition (2003) is a technically sound instrument that is second only to the Wechsler scales (described in the next section) in popularity. It has been revised and renormed a number of times over the years, most recently in 2003, using 4,800 schoolchildren, stratified by economic status, geographic region, and community size. The 2000 U.S. Census was used to ensure proportional representation of each of the following subcultures: White, African American, Hispanic, Asian, and Asian/Pacific Islander.

15.6

A 10-year-old has a mental age of an 8-year-old. What is the child's IQ?

15.7

What does the term *renormed* mean? Why is it important that the process of revising and renorming the latest Stanford-Binet involved testing students from minority groups?

Table 15.1 Sample subtests from the revised (5th ed.) Stanford-Binet

Subtest	Example Description
Nonverbal Knowledge	Students are shown picture absurdities (e.g., a man in a bathing suit in the snow) and asked to explain.
Verbal Knowledge	Students are asked to explain the meaning of common vocabulary words.
Nonverbal Working Memory	Students are shown block patterns and asked to describe or reproduce after a brief delay.
Verbal Working Memory	Students are given sentences and asked to provide key words after a brief delay.

Source: Riverside Publishing, 2003.

The Wechsler Scales.   Developed by David Wechsler over a period of 40 years, the Wechsler scales are the most popular intelligence tests in use today (Salvia & Ysseldyke, 1988). The three Wechsler tests, aimed at preschool-primary, elementary, and adult populations, have two main parts: verbal and performance. The Wechsler Intelligence Scale for Children—Third Edition (WISC-III; Wechsler, 1991) is an individually administered intelligence test with 13 subtests, of which 6 are verbal and 7 are performance. (Table 15.2 outlines some sample subtests.) The performance sections

15.8
How do the subtests of the WISC-III compare to the Stanford-Binet? What does this comparison tell you about the test designers' views of intelligence?

Table 15.2 Sample items from the WISC-III

Verbal Section	
Subtest	**Description/Examples**
Information	This subtest taps general knowledge common to American culture: 1. How many wings does a bird have? 2. How many nickels make a dime? 3. What is steam made of? 4. Who wrote "Tom Sawyer"? 5. What is pepper?
Arithmetic	This subtest is a test of basic mathematical knowledge and skills, including counting and addition through division: 1. Sam had three pieces of candy and Joe gave him four more. How many pieces of candy did Sam have altogether? 2. Three women divided eighteen golf balls equally among themselves. How many golf balls did each person receive? 3. If two buttons cost 15¢, what will be the cost of a dozen buttons?
Similarities	This subtest is designed to measure abstract and logical thinking through use of analogies: 1. In what way are a lion and a tiger alike? 2. In what way are a saw and a hammer alike? 3. In what way are an hour and a week alike? 4. In what way are a circle and a triangle alike?

Performance Section	
Subtest	**Description/Examples**
Picture completion	Students are shown a picture with elements missing, which they are required to identify. This subtest measure general knowledge as well as visual comprehension.
Block design	This subtest focuses on a number of abstract figures. Designed to measure visual-motor coordination, it requires students to match patterns displayed by the examiner.

Picture Completion

Block Design

Source: Simulated items similar to those in the *Wechsler Intelligence Scale for Children: Third Edition (WISC-III).* Copyright © 1991 by the Psychological Corporation. Reproduced by permission. All rights reserved. "Wechsler intelligence Scale for Children" and "WISC-III" are registered trademarks of The Psychological Corporation.

Individual intelligence tests such as the Stanford-Binet and WISC-III provide valuable information about individual capabilities.

were added because of dissatisfaction with the strong verbal emphasis of earlier intelligence tests. Like the Stanford-Binet, the Wechsler scales are considered technically sound by testing experts (Anastasi, 1988; R. Kaplan & Saccuzzo, 1993).

The Wechsler's two scales, yielding separate verbal and performance scores, are an asset. For example, a substantially higher score on the performance compared with the verbal scale could indicate a language problem related to poor reading or language-based cultural differences (R. Kaplan & Saccuzzo, 1993). Because performance subtests demand a minimum of verbal ability, these tasks are helpful in studying students who resist school-like tasks, learners with disabilities, and persons with limited education.

Individual Versus Group Intelligence Tests. Individually administered are generally superior to group intelligence tests. Because both the directions and responses are oral, they eliminate errors on answer sheets, and the test administrator can spot signs of fatigue or anxiety. Also, by observing carefully, the test administrator can often determine why students give the responses they do or seek clarification of uncertain answers. These factors are important in interpreting a student's score.

In contrast, group tests are heavily weighted toward verbal skills, and they are more strongly influenced by students' motivation and test-taking experience. Experts emphasize that attentiveness, motivation, and anxiety can all strongly influence intelligence test performance (Snyderman & Rothman, 1987). Because test data are so important in decision making, and individual tests are clearly superior, the use of group tests for individual diagnosis and placement is problematic.

Aptitude Tests

Although *aptitude* and *intelligence* are often used synonymously, aptitude—the ability to acquire knowledge—is only one characteristic of intelligence. **Aptitude tests** are *standardized tests designed to predict the potential for future learning and measure general abilities developed over long periods of time.* Aptitude tests are commonly used in selection and placement decisions, and they correlate highly with achievement tests (Linn & Gronlund, 2000; W. J. Popham, 2000). The concept of *aptitude* is intuitively sensible; for example, people will say, "I just don't have any aptitude for math," implying that their potential for learning math is limited.

The two most common aptitude tests at the high school level are the SAT and ACT, mentioned earlier. They are designed to measure a student's potential for success in college. This potential is heavily influenced by previous experience, however; classroom-related knowledge, particularly in language and mathematics, is essential for success on the tests. But because the tests are objective and reliable, they eliminate teacher bias and the inconsistency of grading practices from different teachers and schools. In this regard, they add valuable information in predicting future success.

The SAT I, a revised version of the original Scholastic Aptitude Test, contains six subsections: three verbal and three math. The verbal subtests include analogies, sentence completion (vocabulary and sentence structure), and critical reasoning; math subtests include standard computation, estimation, and student-produced response questions. Calculators are now allowed during the test.

The ACT Assessment consists of tests in four areas: English, math, reading, and science reasoning. The total test takes about 3 hours, and hand-held calculators are not allowed.

15.9
Group intelligence tests are considered to be particularly inappropriate for younger children. Identify at least two reasons for this.

15.10
Describe how aptitude and intelligence are related.

Evaluating Standardized Tests: Validity Revisited

Wendy Klopman was a little nervous. She had been asked to serve on a districtwide committee to select a new standardized achievement test battery for the elementary grades. Her job was to get feedback from the faculty at her school about two options, the Stanford Achievement Test and the California Achievement Test.

After giving a brief overview of the two tests during a faculty meeting, Wendy opened the floor for questions.

"How much do the two tests cover problem solving?" a fifth-grade teacher asked.

"We're moving our language arts curriculum more in the direction of writing. What about it?" a first-grade teacher wondered.

As the discussion continued, a confused and exasperated colleague asked, "Which one is better? That's really the bottom line. How about a simple answer?"

Wendy couldn't offer a simple answer, not because she was unprepared, but instead because she was asked to make complex and difficult judgements about validity.

In Chapter 14, you saw that validity involves "an evaluation of the adequacy and appropriateness of the interpretations and uses of assessment results" (Linn & Gronlund, 2000, p. 73), and we emphasized the importance of matching assessments and goals. When creating teacher-made tests, teachers must consider the design of the assessments and how the assessments will be used to determine validity. Standardized tests are already constructed, so the teacher must judge only the suitability of a test for a specific purpose.* Validity involves the appropriate use of a test, not the design of the test itself (Messick, 1989; Shepard, 1993).

Experts describe three kinds of validity—*content, predictive,* and *construct*—and each provides a different perspective on the issue of appropriate use.

Content Validity

Content validity refers to *a test's ability to representatively sample the content that is taught and measure the extent to which learners understand it.* Content validity is determined by comparing test content with curriculum objectives, and it is a primary concern when considering standardized achievement tests. The question Wendy was asked about which test was "better" addressed content validity. The "better" test is the one with the closer match between the school's goals and the content of the test (J. Popham, 1998).

15.11
How does a teacher ensure content validity in a teacher-made test? How is the process similar or different from the process for standardized tests?

Predictive Validity

Often educators use standardized tests to predict how students will do in a future course or program of study. **Predictive validity** is *an indicator of a test's ability to gauge future performance.* It is central to the SAT and ACT; these tests are designed to measure a student's potential to do college work. Predictive validity is also the focus of tests that gauge students' readiness for academic tasks in kindergarten and first grade.

Predictive validity is usually quantified by correlating two variables, such as a standardized test score and student grades. A perfect correlation is 1.0; in testing, most are substantially less. For example, a correlation of .42 exists between the SAT and college grades (Shepard, 1993). High school grades are the only predictor that is better (a correlation of .48).

Why isn't the correlation between standardized tests and college performance higher? The primary reason is that the SAT and ACT are designed to predict "general readiness" for college; other factors such as motivation, study habits, and specific content background strongly affect performance.

15.12
Describe a situation in which predictive validity would apply to the use of a standardized achievement test. (Think about the achievement test uses described earlier in the chapter.)

---

*A complete review of more than 1,400 standardized tests of achievement, aptitude, diagnosis, and personality can be found in the *Mental Measurements Yearbook* (Plake, Impara, & Spies, 2003). Originally edited by Oscar Buros, the yearbook provides accurate and critical reviews of all major standardized tests and is an important source of information for selecting and using these tests.

15.13

If a standardized test were a "perfect predictor" of college success, what would the correlation between college performance and the test score be? What would it be if there were no relationship between the score and performance in college?

Construct Validity

Construct validity is *an indicator of the logical connection between a test and what it is designed to measure.* Construct validity is an abstract concept, but it's important in understanding the total concept of validity (Messick, 1989; Shepard, 1993). It answers the question, "Do these items actually assess the ideas the test is designed to measure?"

For instance, many of the items on the SAT do indeed tap the ability to do abstract thinking about words and numbers, tasks that students are likely to face in their college experience. Because of this, the test has construct validity.

The Teacher's Role in Standardized Testing: Instructional Strategies

Teachers play a central role in ensuring that standardized test scores are valid and accurately reflect what students have learned. In addition, teachers play an important role in communicating standardized test results to students and their caregivers and using the results to improve their instruction. The following principles can guide teachers as they perform these essential functions:

- Carefully examine tests to ensure that test content matches learning goals.
- Prepare students so that test performance accurately reflects what they know and can do.
- Administer tests in ways that allow valid comparisons and maximize student performance.
- Communicate results to students and their caregivers to help them make wise educational decisions.

Let's see how these principles operate in the classroom.

Test Selection.   As we just saw, the validity of standardized tests depends on several factors, foremost of which is the match between the test and the purpose for using it. For achievement tests, teachers play a critical role in ensuring a match between test content and classroom instruction. In the past, emphasis was placed on selecting an appropriate test to match teachers' classroom goals. Currently, with the emphasis on district, state, and even nationally mandated tests, emphasis has shifted to teachers' responsibilities for ensuring that students have access to and opportunities to learn the content covered in tests (E. Baker & Niemi, 1996).

A second consideration in test validity is selecting a test that has an appropriate norming group. Teachers should examine norming information provided by test manufacturers to ensure that the norming group matches their students. Mismatches can result in erroneous comparisons and inappropriate conclusions.

Teachers play a crucial role in selecting and administering standardized tests, preparing students, and interpreting results.

Preparing Students.   The teacher's primary role in standardized testing is to prepare students for the tests. Aligning goals and instruction with the standards the tests measure—a demanding and sometimes confusing task—is the first step. Unfortunately, many teachers feel that they don't receive the training necessary to accomplish this task (Hoff, 2001).

In addition, teachers prepare students by teaching general test-taking strategies, such as the following:

- Read and follow all directions.
- Find out how the questions will be scored. For example, is guessing penalized (such as subtracting the number of wrong from the number of right answers), and will points be taken off for spelling, grammar, and neatness in written responses?

- Eliminate options on multiple-choice items and make informed guesses with remaining items (if guessing isn't penalized).
- Pace yourself so that you have enough time to answer all the questions.
- Go back and check your answers if time permits. (Airasian, 2000; Linn & Gronlund, 2000)

Adequately preparing students for standardized tests has become more important as tests are being increasingly used to determine promotion to the next grade and graduation from high school (Hoffman et al., 2001).

In addition to teaching test-taking strategies, teachers can also provide students with practice using items similar to those that will appear on the test. For example, teachers commonly measure spelling by giving weekly quizzes in which students are asked to correctly spell a list of several words. However, when spelling is assessed on most standardized tests, students are given a list of four closely matched words and asked to select the one spelled correctly. To do as well as possible on these items, students need practice with this format.

Administering Tests.   For standardized tests to yield valid results, they must be uniformly administered at different sites and with different populations. Most standardized test makers explain in detail how the test should be administered (Airasian, 2000; McMillan, 1997). Test manuals specify the amount of time for each test and subtest (which should be clearly written on the board for students) and provide scripts for introducing and describing the subtests. If scripts and time frames aren't followed precisely, comparisons with the norming group and other students taking the test can be invalid.

Interpreting Results.   Once test results are returned, teachers are responsible for interpreting them so that they can use them to improve instruction and can share them with students and their caregivers. To determine what areas of instruction may need improvement, teachers may compare beginning- and end-of-year test data to measure growth (Nichols & Singer, 2000). Such pre-post comparisons of specific subtests scores can identify areas of strength as well as those that need improvement. A different strategy is to compare the scores of one year's class with those in earlier years to detect shifts in the curriculum and mismatches between standards and tests.

Teachers are the people primarily responsible for sharing results with students and their caregivers and helping them understand what the scores mean. Standardized test scores should not be reported separate from other information about the student, and teachers should emphasize that test scores are approximate rather than absolute. In addition, teachers should use nontechnical language in discussing the results.

To accurately interpret standardized test results, teachers must understand how these scores are calculated. The next section describes different ways of interpreting and reporting standardized test scores to make them useful to various user groups.

Understanding and Interpreting Standardized Test Scores

The fact that they're given to thousands of students—allowing comparisons with samples across the United States (and in some cases, around the world)—is one of the advantages of standardized tests. But these large samples result in unwieldy data. To process the vast amount of information and to allow users to compare individuals' performances, test publishers use statistical methods to summarize test results.

Descriptive Statistics

As an introduction to the use of statistics in summarizing information, take a look at Table 15.3, which contains scores made by two classes of 31 students on a 50-item test. (As you examine this information, keep in mind that a standardized test would have a

Table 15.3 Scores of two classes on a 50-item test

Class #1	Class #2
50	48
49	47
49	46
48	46
47	45
47	45
46	44 ⎤
46	44
45	44 ⎬ mode
45	44
45	44 ⎦
44 ⎤	43
44 ⎬ mode	43
44	43
44 ⎦	43
43— median	42— median & mean
42— mean	42
41	42
41	42
40	41
40	41
39	41
39	40
38	40
37	39
37	39
36	38
35	38
34	37
34	36
33	35

15.14

Why is the title of this section—"Descriptive Statistics"—an appropriate label? What are the "statistics" in the label "Descriptive Statistics"?

sample much larger than 31 and would probably contain a larger number of items. We are using a class-size example here for the sake of illustration.)

The scores for each class are ranked from highest to lowest, and the mean, median, and mode are labeled. (We discuss the mean, median, and mode in the sections that follow.) As you can see in the table, a simple array of scores can be cumbersome and not very informative, even when the scores are ranked. We need more efficient ways of summarizing the information.

15.15

If the scores in Figure 15.2 reflected ability, which of the two classes would be easier to teach? Why?

Frequency Distributions

A **frequency distribution** is *a distribution of test scores that shows a simple count of the number of people who obtained each score.* It can be represented in several ways, one of which is a graph with the possible scores on the horizontal (*x*) axis and the frequency, or the number of students who got each score, on the vertical (*y*) axis.

The frequency distributions for our two classes are shown in Figure 15.2. This information is still in rough form, but we already begin to see differences between the two

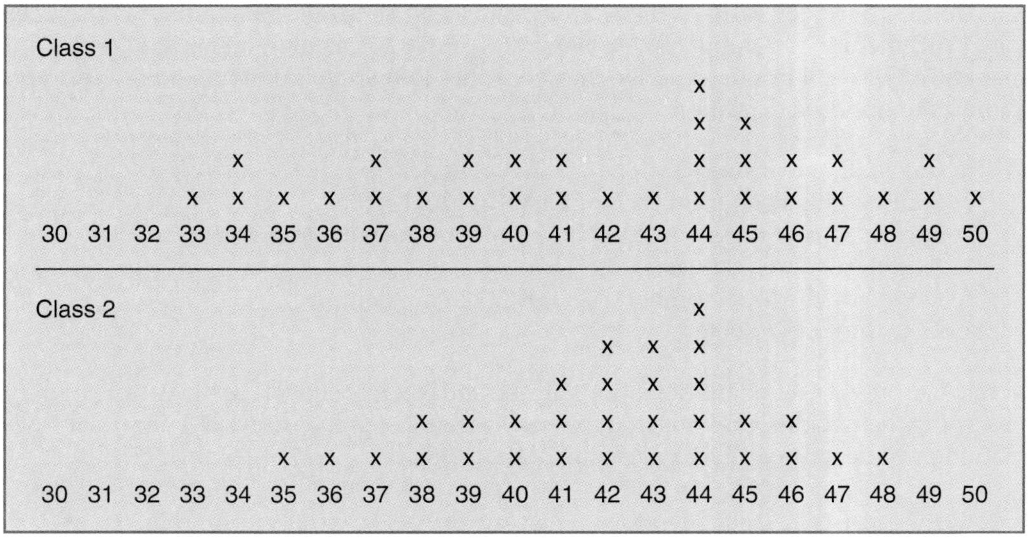

Figure 15.2 Frequency distributions for two classes on a 50-item test

```
Class 1
                                              x
                                              x  x
           x           x        x  x  x       x  x  x  x        x
        x  x  x  x  x  x  x  x  x  x  x  x  x  x  x  x  x  x  x
       30 31 32 33 34 35 36 37 38 39 40 41 42 43 44 45 46 47 48 49 50
       ─────────────────────────────────────────────────────────────
Class 2
                                              x
                                     x  x  x
                                  x  x  x  x
                            x  x  x  x  x  x  x  x  x
                         x  x  x  x  x  x  x  x  x  x  x  x  x  x
       30 31 32 33 34 35 36 37 38 39 40 41 42 43 44 45 46 47 48 49 50
```

classes. For instance, we see a wider range of scores in the first class than in the second and a greater grouping of scores near the middle of the second distribution. Beyond this qualitative description, however, the distributions aren't particularly helpful. We need a better way to quantitatively summarize the information. Measures of central tendency do this.

Measures of Central Tendency

Measures of central tendency—*the mean, median, and mode*—are *quantitative descriptions of how a group performed as a whole.* In a distribution of scores, the **mean** is *the average score,* the **median** is *the middle score* in the distribution, and the **mode** is *the most frequent score.*

To obtain a mean, we simply add the scores and divide by the number of scores. As it turns out, both distributions have a mean of 42 (1,302/31). The class average (mean) of 42 is one indicator of how each group performed as a whole.

The median for the first distribution is 43, because half the scores (15) fall equal to or above 43 and the other half are equal to or below 43. Using the same process, we find that the median for the second distribution is 42.

The median is useful when extremely high or low scores skew the mean and give a false picture of the sample. For example, you commonly hear or read demographic statistics such as "The median income for families of four in this country went from . . . in 1995 to . . . in 2000." The *median* income is reported because a few million-dollar incomes would make the average (mean) income quite high and would give an artificial picture of typical families' standards of living. The median, in contrast, is not affected by these extremes and gives a more realistic picture of the typical American family's economic status. The median provides this type of accuracy when used with test scores.

Looking once more at the two samples, you can see that the most frequent score for each is 44, which is the mode. Small samples, such as those here, often have more than one mode, resulting in "bimodal" or even "trimodal" distributions.

Using our measures of central tendency, you can see that the two groups of test scores are very much alike: They have the same mean, nearly the same median, and the same mode. As you saw from examining the frequency distribution, however, this doesn't give us a complete picture of the two. We also need a measure of their variability, or "spread."

Measures of Variability

To get a more accurate picture of the samples, we need to see how the samples spread out, or vary. One measure of variability is the **range,** *the distance between the top and bottom score in a distribution of scores.* The range in the first class is 17, and in the second it's 13, confirming the spread of scores seen in the frequency distribution. Although easy to compute, the range is overly influenced by one or more extreme scores.

15.16
Sketch a frequency distribution in which the mean, median, and mode differ significantly. What might this type of distribution suggest about the students in that class?

The **standard deviation,** *a statistical measure of the spread of scores,* reduces this problem. With the use of computers, teachers rarely have to calculate a standard deviation manually, but we'll briefly describe the procedure to help you understand the concept. To find the standard deviation

1. Calculate the mean.
2. Subtract the mean from each of the individual scores.
3. Square each of these values. (This eliminates negative numbers.)
4. Add the squared values.
5. Divide by the total number of scores (31 in our samples).
6. Take the square root.

15.17
Try this analogy. Range: Mode :: Standard Deviation:_____. (Range is to Mode as Standard Deviation is to ?)

In our samples, the standard deviations are 4.8 and 3.1, respectively. We saw from merely observing the two distributions that the first was more spread out, and the standard deviation provides a quantitative measure of that spread.

The Normal Distribution

Standardized tests are administered to large (in the thousands) samples of students, and the distribution of scores often approximates a *normal distribution.* To understand this concept, look again at our two distributions of scores and then focus specifically on the second one. If we drew a line over the top of the frequency distribution, it would appear as shown in Figure 15.3.

Now imagine a very large sample of scores, such as we would find from a typical standardized test. The curve would approximate the one shown in Figure 15.4. This is a **normal distribution,** *a distribution of scores in which the mean, median, and mode are equal and the scores distribute themselves symmetrically in a bell-shaped curve.* Many large samples of human characteristics, such as height and weight, tend to distribute themselves this way, as do the large samples of most standardized tests.

15.18
In Figure 15.4, what does the height of the curve at any point represent? What is represented along the horizontal (*x*) axis?

15.19
Reexamine Figure 15.2. Are the scores from the first class more or less like a normal distribution than the scores from the second class? Explain.

The sample of scores in Figure 15.3 has both a mean and median of 42, but a mode of 44, so its measures of central tendency don't quite fit the normal curve. Also, as we see from Figure 15.4, 68% of all the scores fall within one standard deviation from the mean, but in our sample distribution, about 71% of the scores are within one standard deviation above and below the mean. We can see from these illustrations that our samples aren't normal distributions, which is typical of the smaller samples found in most classrooms.

Interpreting Standardized Test Results

Using our two small samples, we have illustrated techniques that statisticians use to summarize standardized test scores. Again, keep in mind that data gathered from standardized tests come from thousands of students instead of the small number in our illustrations. When standardized tests are used, the goal is to compare students from different schools, districts, states, and even countries. To make these comparisons, test makers use raw scores, percentiles, stanines, and grade equivalents. Some of these scores are illustrated in Figure 15.1 on David Palmer's report from the Stanford Achievement Test.

Figure 15.3 Frequency distribution for the second class

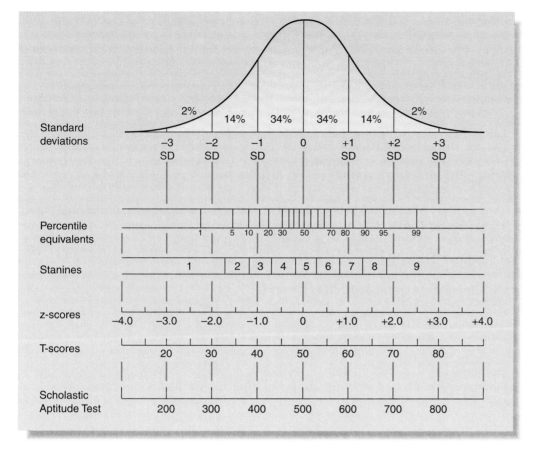

Figure 15.4   Normal distribution

2%	14%	34%	34%	14%	2%

Standard deviations: −3 SD, −2 SD, −1 SD, 0, +1 SD, +2 SD, +3 SD

Percentile equivalents: 1, 5, 10, 20, 30, 50, 70, 80, 90, 95, 99

Stanines: 1, 2, 3, 4, 5, 6, 7, 8, 9

z-scores: −4.0, −3.0, −2.0, −1.0, 0, +1.0, +2.0, +3.0, +4.0

T-scores: 20, 30, 40, 50, 60, 70, 80

Scholastic Aptitude Test: 200, 300, 400, 500, 600, 700, 800

Raw Scores

All standardized tests begin with and are based on raw scores. The **raw score** is simply *the number of items an individual answered correctly on a standardized test or subtest.* For example, we can see in Figure 15.1 that David's raw score for reading comprehension was a 43; David answered 43 out of 54 items correctly. But what does this mean? Was the test easy or hard? How did he do compared to others taking the test? As you can see, this score doesn't tell us much until we compare it to others. Percentiles, stanines, grade equivalents, and standard scores help us do that.

Percentiles

The percentile is one of the most commonly reported scores on standardized tests. The **percentile**, or **percentile rank (PR),** is *a ranking that compares an individual's score with the scores of all the others who have taken the test.* The percentile rank shows the percentage of students in the norming sample that scored at or below a particular raw score. For instance, David's raw score of 43 in reading comprehension placed him in the 72nd percentile nationally and the 80th percentile locally (Figure 15.1). That means his score was as high or higher than 72% of the scores of people who took the test across the nation and 80% of the scores of people who took the test in his district.

Parents and students often confuse percentiles with *percentages.* Percentages reflect the number of correct items compared to the total number possible. Percentile rank, in contrast, tells us how a student did in comparison to other students taking the test.

Teachers need to understand standardized tests so they can interpret them to students and their caregivers.

15.20

A student named Carol is at the 96th percentile rank in number concepts; her friends Marsha and Lenore are at the 86th and 76th, respectively. Is the difference between Carol's and Marsha's scores greater than the difference between Marsha's and Lenore's, or vice versa? Explain.

Percentiles are used because they are simple and straightforward. However, they have a major weakness; they're *rankings*, and the differences between the ranks are not equal (Linn & Gronlund, 2000). For instance, in our first distribution of 31 students, a score of 48 would be in the 90th percentile, 46 would be in the 80th, 44 would be in the 60th, and 43 would be the 50th percentile. In this sample, the difference between scores representing the 90th and 80th percentiles is twice as great (2 points) as the difference between scores representing the 60th and 50th percentiles (1 point). With large samples, this difference can be even more pronounced. Students who score at the extremes in the sample vary more from their counterparts than those who score near the middle of the distribution. This finding is confirmed in Figure 15.4, where we see that the range of scores from the 50th to the 60th percentile is much smaller than the range from the 90th to the 99th percentile.

Percentile bands are *ranges of percentile scores on standardized tests.* (Percentile bands are illustrated for David Palmer's results in the last column of Figure 15.1.) The advantage of a percentile band is that it takes into account the possibility of measurement error (Lyman, 1991). Instead of a single percentile, the band is a range of percentile scores within which an individual's test performance might actually fall. In this respect, percentile bands function somewhat like stanines.

Stanines

The stanine is another score that is commonly used to describe standardized test scores. For example, David's reading comprehension score placed him in stanine 6 nationally and stanine 7 locally (the stanines are given after the dashes in the "Natl PR-S" and "Local PR-S" columns in Figure 15.1). A **stanine (S)**, or *"standard nine,"* is *a description of an individual's standardized test performance that uses a scale ranging from 1 to 9 points.* A stanine refers to a specific percentage of the normal curve's area (see Figure 15.4). Stanine 5 is in the center of the distribution and includes all the scores within one fourth of a standard deviation on either side of the mean. Stanines 4, 3, and 2 are each a band of scores, one half a standard deviation in width, extending below stanine 5. Stanines 6, 7, and 8, also a half standard deviation in width, extend above stanine 5. Stanines 1 and 9 cover the tails of the distribution. A student with a score that falls one standard deviation above the mean will have a stanine score of 7; a student with a score two standard deviations above the mean will have a stanine of 9. Figure 15.4 shows how stanines correspond to other measures we've discussed.

15.21

A student in our first class (illustrated in Table 15.3 and Figure 15.2) scored 47 on the test. In what stanine is this score? In what stanine would a score of 47 be for the second class?

Stanines are widely used because they're simple, and they encourage teachers and parents to interpret scores based on a range instead of fine distinctions that may be artificial. For instance, a score in the 57th percentile may be the result of 1 or 2 extra points on a subtest compared to a score in the 52nd percentile, and the student may have guessed the answer correctly, so the difference between the two wouldn't be meaningful. Both scores would fall in stanine 5, however. Because it describes performance as a range of possible scores, the stanine is probably a more realistic indicator of performance.

On the other hand, reducing the scores to a simple 9-point band sacrifices information. For instance, in our first distribution, with a standard deviation of 4.8, a score of 40 would be in stanine 4, because 40 is slightly more than one-fourth standard deviation below the mean. A score of 44 would be in stanine 6, because it is slightly more than one-fourth standard deviation above the mean. However, a 40 is in the 35th percentile, and a 44 is in the 65th—a considerable difference. It is important to keep the advantages and disadvantages of stanines in mind as you help parents and students interpret standardized test scores.

Grade Equivalents

A third commonly reported score is the **grade equivalent**, *a score that is determined by comparing an individual's score on a standardized test to the scores of students in a particular age group; the first digit represents grade and the second the month of the school year.* For example, David's grade equivalent for total reading is 5.6. This means that he scored as well on the test as the average score for those students taking the test who are in the sixth month of the fifth grade.

As we saw when David's mother asked, "Should David be in the fifth grade?" grade equivalents can be misleading because they oversimplify results and suggest comparisons that aren't necessarily valid. A grade equivalent of 5.6 tells us that David is somewhat advanced in reading. Grade equivalents don't suggest that he should be promoted to fifth grade, nor do they necessarily suggest that he should be reading with fifth graders. Other factors such as social development, motivation, classroom behavior, and performance on teacher-made assessments must be considered in making decisions about students. Because of these limitations and the possibility for misinterpretation, some standardized tests no longer use grade equivalents. Teachers should use caution when using them to communicate with students and parents, and they should never be used in isolation from other measures (Linn & Gronlund, 2000).

15.22
A fourth grader in your class has taken a standardized test, and the summary gives his grade equivalent as 6.7. What does this mean? What implications does this have for your teaching?

Standard Scores

As you saw in our discussion of percentiles, differences in raw scores don't result in comparable differences in the percentile rank. For instance, you saw that it took only 1 raw score point difference—43 compared with 42—to move from the 50th to the 60th percentile, but it took a 2-point difference—48 compared with 46—to move from the 80th to the 90th percentile in our first distribution in Figure 15.2. To deal with this type of discrepancy, standard scores were developed. A **standard score** is *a description of performance on a standardized test that uses standard deviation as the basic unit* (Linn & Gronlund, 2000). Standardized test makers use the mean and standard deviation to report standard scores.

One type of standard score is the **z-score,** which is *the number of standard deviation units from the mean*. A z-score of 2 is two standard deviations above the mean, for example, and a z-score of -1 is one standard deviation below the mean. The **T-score** is *a standard score that defines the mean as 50 and the standard deviation as 10*. A T-score of 70 would be two standard deviations above the mean and would correspond to a z-score of 2. The SAT has a mean defined as 500 and a standard deviation defined as 100. A score of 550 on the verbal part of the SAT means that a student scored one-half deviation above the mean, or at the 68th percentile for this subtest.

Standard scores such as z-scores and T-scores are useful because they make comparisons convenient. Because they are based on equal units of measurement throughout the distribution, inter-group and inter-test comparisons are possible.

15.23
The SAT has a mean of 500 and a standard deviation of 100. You scored 1,050 on the SAT—500 on the math portion and 550 on the verbal section. You scored as well or better than approximately what percentage of the people who took the test in each case?

Standard Error of Measurement

Although standardized tests are technically sophisticated, they contain measurement error; scores represent only an approximation of a student's "true" score. If we gave a student the same test over and over, for example, we would find that the scores would vary. If we averaged those scores, we would have an estimate of the student's "true" score. A **true score** is *the hypothetical average of an individual's scores if repeated testing under ideal conditions were possible.* Although it's impractical to give an individual the same test repeatedly, you can get an estimate of the true score using the **standard error of measurement,** *the range of scores within which an individual's true score is likely to fall.* This range is sometimes termed the *confidence interval, score band,* or *profile band.* For example, suppose Ben has a raw score of 46 and Kim has a raw score of 52 on a test with a standard error of 4. This means that Ben's true score is between 42 and 50, and Kim's is between 48 and 56. At first glance, Kim appears to have scored significantly higher than Ben, but considering the standard error, their scores may be equal, or Ben's true score may even be higher than Kim's. Understanding the concept of standard error is important when we make decisions based on standardized tests. For instance, it would be unwise to place Ben and Kim in different ability groups based solely on the results illustrated here.

15.24
A student in the second class in Figure 15.2 scored 45. If we round the standard deviation to 3 for this sample, what would the student's z-score and T-score be?

Classroom Connections

Using Standardized Tests Effectively in Your Classroom

1. Carefully analyze results to increase instructional alignment.
   - *Elementary:* A fourth-grade team goes over the previous year's test scores to identify areas in the curriculum that need greater attention.
   - *Middle School:* The math teachers in a middle school go over standardized results item by item to identify areas of instructional strength and weakness. Seeing that a large numbers of students missed a particular item, the teachers try to figure out why this occurred.
   - *High School:* English teachers in an urban high school use a scoring rubric to analyze student scores on their essay exams. They share this rubric with their students, pointing out areas where students encountered difficulties in previous years.
2. Communicate test results clearly to both students and their caregivers.

- *Elementary:* Third-grade teachers in an urban elementary school prepare a handout prior to parent-teacher conferences that explains standardized test scores. Included in the handout are numerous examples and answers to frequently asked questions.
- *Middle School:* An interdisciplinary team integrates standardized test scores into a comprehensive packet of assessment materials for students and their caregivers. When they meet with students and these caregivers, they use all the assessment information to identify areas of strength and areas that need improvement.
- *High School:* During an orientation meeting with parents, members of the English Department first give an overview of tests that students will encounter in high school and describe how test scores are reported. During individual meetings with parents, teachers provide specific information about each individual student's scores.

Issues in Standardized Testing

We noted at the beginning of the chapter that standardized testing is controversial. At least three areas of controversy are prominent, as indicated by the amount of publicity they receive both in professional publications and in the popular media:

- Standards-based education and the accountability movement
- Testing teachers
- Cultural minorities and standardized testing

Let's look at them.

High-stakes tests and accountability place new pressures on both teachers and their students.

Standards-Based Education and the Accountability Movement

As we described in Chapter 13, Americans have performed poorly when polled about their world knowledge. Other studies had led to doubts about our science, reading, writing, and math knowledge as well. For example, a nationwide assessment called the National Assessment of Educational Progress (also known as "the Nation's Report Card") indicated that only 38 percent of U.S. eighth graders could figure out a 15 percent tip on a meal, even when given five choices to select from (Stigler & Hiebert, 2000). Social commentators have written much about our inadequacies, and educators have responded by promoting **standards-based education,** *the process of focusing curricula and instruction on predetermined goals.* State content standards in academic subjects have been defined and adopted in every state but Iowa (Olson, 2001).

Standards imply that educational leaders have made decisions about what students at different ages and in particular content areas should know and be able to do. For instance, the following are standards specified by the National Council of Teachers of Mathematics (2000):

In grades 6–8 all students should:

- develop and analyze algorithms for computing with fractions, decimals, and integers and develop fluency in their use;
- develop and use strategies to estimate the results of rational-number computations and judge the reasonableness of the results;
- develop, analyze, and explain methods for solving problems involving proportions, such as scaling and finding equivalent ratios (p. 214)

Accountability is *the process of requiring students to demonstrate that they have met specified standards and holding teachers responsible for students' performance.* Calls for accountability resulted from evidence that students were being promoted from grade to grade without mastering essential content and some students were graduating from high school barely able to read, write, or do basic mathematics.

High-stakes tests are *standardized tests designed to measure the extent to which standards are being met* (Heubert & Hauser, 1999). High-stakes testing, also called *minimum competency testing,* typically has three characteristics: (a) an established standard for acceptable test performance; (b) a requirement that all students of designated grades (such as 5th, 8th, and 10th) take the tests; and (c) the use of test results for decisions about promotion and graduation. When students cannot move to the next grade level or graduate from high school because they fail a test, for example, the "stakes" are very high, thus the term "high-stakes tests."

15.25
Are minimum competency (high-stakes) tests most like aptitude, achievement, or diagnostic tests? Explain.

As you would expect, high-stakes testing is very controversial. Critics argue that teachers spend too much of their class time helping students practice for the tests and that they stifle teacher creativity (Hoffman et al., 2001). They also contend that the cut-off scores are arbitrary, the instruments are too crude to be used in making crucial decisions about individuals, and the tests have a disproportionately adverse impact on minority students, particularly those with limited proficiency in English (Geisinger, 1992; Hafner, 2001).

Pressure to do well on the tests is so great that some teachers and administrators have been driven to cheat; they help students with the tests or even give them answers (Viadero, 2000). In Massachusetts, high-stakes testing became so controversial that the state's largest teacher union, in a highly unusual move, launched a $600,000 television campaign that sharply criticized the Massachusetts Comprehensive Assessment System exam, an exam students in the state had to pass to graduate (Gehring, 2000).

In spite of the criticisms, standards-based education and high-stakes testing are widespread. For example:

- Every state but Iowa has adopted standards in at least some academic subjects.
- Forty-eight states have testing programs designed, in large part, to measure the extent to which students meet the standards.
- Twenty-one states plan to issue overall ratings of their schools based largely on their students' performance on the tests.
- At least 18 states have the authority to close, take over, or overhaul schools that are identified as failing. (Olson, 2000b)

Advocates of minimum competency tests claim the tests help clarify the goals of school systems, send clear messages to students about what they should be learning, and provide the public with hard evidence about school effectiveness (J. Popham, 1993). While conceding that teacher preparation, materials, and the tests themselves need to be improved, they also argue that the tests are the fairest and most effective means of achieving the aim of democratic schooling: a quality education for all students. Further, they assert, educational systems that establish standards and use tests that thoroughly measure the extent to which the standards are met greatly improve achievement for all

15.26

If minimum competency testing were eliminated and decisions about promotion and graduation were left to individual teachers, what advantages and disadvantages would this system have? Could the system work on a national level? Why or why not?

students, including those from disadvantaged backgrounds (Bishop, 1995, 1998). Hirsch (2000) summarized the testing advocates' position: "They [standards and tests that measure achievement of the standards] are the most promising educational development in half a century" (p. 64).

Testing Teachers

Increasingly, teachers are also being asked to pass competency tests that measure their ability to perform basic skills (reading, writing, and mathematics); their background in academic areas, such as chemistry, history, or English; and their understanding of learning and teaching (39 states have this requirement) (Olson, 2000b). The Praxis test series (Educational Testing Service, 1999) contains the most commonly used teacher tests.

The Praxis series (*praxis* means "putting theory into practice") is currently being used in 35 states and consists of three components (Educational Testing Service, 1999):

- *Praxis I: Academic Skills Assessments.* These tests are designed to measure basic or "enabling" skills in reading, writing, and math that all teachers need.
- *Praxis II: Subject Assessments.* These tests are designed to measure teachers' knowledge of the subjects they will teach. In addition to 70 content-specific tests, Praxis II also includes the Principles of Learning and Teaching (PLT) tests and the Professional Knowledge test. (We discussed the PLT tests in Chapter 1, and our closing case studies use the PLTs as a model.)
- *Praxis III: Classroom Performance Assessments.* These tests are designed to use classroom observations and work samples to assess teachers' ability to plan, instruct, manage, and understand professional responsibilities. In addition, Praxis III assesses the teacher's sensitivity to learners' developmental and cultural differences.

Teacher testing has also sparked controversy. Critics argue that teachers' classroom performance depends on factors other than teachers' knowledge (as measured on the tests), the most powerful being teachers' capacities to manage the complexities of classroom life and their ability to work with students (Kohn, 2000; Nagel & Peterson, 2001)). Another issue is that, of teacher candidates who fail the tests, a disproportionate number come from cultural minority groups. Despite the criticisms, the use of these tests—when properly developed and validated—has been upheld in courts (Fischer, Schimmel, & Kelly, 1999; Melnick & Pullin, 2000). The American Federation of Teachers, the second largest professional organization for educators in the United States, now proposes that prospective teachers pass tests that measure understanding of content, such as math and English, and knowledge of teaching principles (Blair, 2000). This proposal signals a change in policy from the past and suggests that teacher testing is not only here to stay but also likely to increase.

Cultural Minorities and High-Stakes Tests

One of the most volatile controversies in high-stakes testing involves critics' claims that the tests are harmful to members of cultural minorities (M. Brennan et al., 2001). This is particularly true for Hispanic and African American students, who on average consistently score lower on standardized tests than do White and Asian students (Bowman, 2000; Viadero & Johnston, 2000). As we mentioned earlier, failing to earn a passing score on high-stakes tests can have serious consequences, such as grade retention or failure to graduate. An example of the controversy occurred in 1999 when the Mexican American Legal Defense and Educational Fund (MALDEF) filed a federal lawsuit seeking to end the practice of requiring students to pass a test to graduate from high school in Texas. MALDEF argued that the Texas Assessment of Academic Skills (TAAS) is unfair to thousands of Hispanic and African American students (Wildavsky, 1999).

The MALDEF lawsuit, although not successful, was just one case in a long line of controversies over race and testing (Heubert & Hauser, 1999; Hoffman et al., 2001). All raise the same question: As standardized tests are increasingly used to measure and improve student performance, will historically lower-scoring African American and Hispanic students be treated fairly? MALDEF's answer to the question is, of course, no, but not all educators, including some in Texas, agree. For example, one school district in Houston made increased scores on the TAAS a high priority and saw dramatic improvement in the performance of students, of whom 86% were Hispanic and 88% economically disadvantaged (Johnston, 2000).

Other educators suggest comprehensive strategies for narrowing the achievement gap between minority and nonminority students, and testing is an integral part of those strategies. Supporters of testing argue that critics tacitly assume that eliminating tests would somehow increase achievement among lower-scoring groups, but it would not, they assert (Viadero & Johnston, 2000).

As least three issues related to high-stakes testing with minority students remain unresolved. One is whether the tests are valid enough to justify using results to make decisions about students' academic lives (Kohn, 2000). A second relates to technical problems involved in testing minorities in general (Land, 1997), and particularly students who speak English as a second language (Abedi, 1999). The question of whether test scores reflect differences in achievement or simply cultural or language differences remains controversial. Third, making decisions about promotion or graduation on the basis of one test score is being increasingly criticized by professional organizations including the American Educational Research Association, the American Psychological Association, and the National Council on Measurement in Education.

Student Diversity and Test Bias

Because of the controversies surrounding standardized testing, increased attention is being focused on efforts to ensure that test results accurately reflect student achievement. An important question to anyone testing students from diverse backgrounds is whether or not the instruments and procedures are fair for all students. Measurement experts have identified at least three types of testing bias that detract from validity (R. Kaplan & Saccuzzo, 1993; Linn & Gronlund, 2000):

- Bias in content
- Bias in testing procedures
- Bias in test use

Bias in Content

Critics contend that the content of standardized tests is geared to White, middle-class American students, and anyone who does not fit this description faces a disadvantage. For example, one item on a standardized intelligence test asks, "From what animal do we get bacon?" First- or second-generation Portuguese children would likely have difficulty with this question because most are unfamiliar with the term *bacon* (Cummins, 1984). They would have little problem, however, if asked "From what animal do we get sausages (*chouricos*)?" since sausage is a staple in Portuguese families.

Bias can also occur in math word problems (Linn & Gronlund, 2000). For example, consider the following percentage problem:

Alex Rodriguez is batting .310 after 100 trips to the plate. In his next three times at bat, he gets a single, double, and home run. What is his batting average now?

Word problems using content that not all children can be expected to know (e.g., how are batting averages computed, and do doubles and home runs count more than singles?) can

Teachers need to continually guard against bias in test content, procedures, and inappropriate uses.

15.27

Does content bias result in more of a problem with validity or reliability? Explain.

unfairly penalize students who don't have the necessary background knowledge. Word problems can also be biased if students miss the problem because of limited reading skills, not because they lack understanding or computational skills in math.

Even the content of pictures used in testing situations can be a source of bias. In one test of English proficiency, students are shown the picture of a smiling boy and asked to describe the picture. The expected response is that he is happy. However, to Vietnamese students, a smiling boy may not be happy; he may be embarrassed, confused, or even angry (Cargill, 1987). Responding with any one of these answers would result in an incorrect response, not from lack of knowledge, but rather from cultural differences.

Bias in Testing Procedures

15.28

Describe at least two things teachers can do to minimize the potential effects of bias in testing procedures.

Bias can also occur in testing procedures. Students from different cultures respond to testing situations differently. They generally become more knowledgeable about testing as they move through the grades and gain experience, but if exposure to testing is limited or if the process isn't compatible with their cultures, performance can be reduced. For example, in one study researchers found that Navajo students were unaware of the consequences of poor test performance, instead treating tests as gamelike events (Deyhle, 1987).

Timed tests are another possible source of bias in testing procedures, particularly for students with limited English proficiency (Scarcella, 1990). Our study of information processing in Chapter 7 helps us understand why. Students with limited knowledge of English require extra time and working memory space to decode the words and comprehend questions. A time limit makes this process more difficult, which can lower test performance. Providing English language learners with more time is one of the most effective ways to ensure that test performance accurately captures what these students know and can do (Hafner, 2001).

Bias in Test Use

15.29

Identify at least three things teachers can do to help students with limited English respond as successfully as possible in testing situations.

Bias can also occur in the use of test results. Experts are concerned about the adverse effects of testing on minority students' progress through public schools and entrance into college (National Commission on Testing and Public Policy, 1990). Evidence suggests that test results are sometimes used in ways that discriminate against minority students and those who do not speak English. For example, a study of 812 students classified as having mental retardation found 300% more Mexican Americans and 50% more African Americans than would be expected from their numbers in the general population. The study population had 40% fewer Anglo Americans than would be expected. Further, people in lower income brackets were overrepresented, whereas people in the upper brackets were underrepresented (J. Mercer, 1973).

Eliminating Bias in Standardized Testing: Instructional Strategies

Teachers can use several instructional strategies to minimize or eliminate test bias and its negative effects. These range from short-term strategies that help students adjust to testing conditions to long-term strategies aimed at modifying test content. All are based on the following testing principles:

- ■ Examine test content before testing, and analyze test results after to help minimize content bias.
- ■ Adapt testing procedures to specific student needs, and teach students to adapt to testing procedures.
- ■ Ensure that standardized test results are only one source of information in individual educational decisions.

Let's see how these principles guide teacher actions in the classroom.

Analyze Test Content

Before administering standardized tests to students, teachers should carefully read over the test to familiarize themselves with test content. What should teachers do if they encounter items or topics that clearly disadvantage a particular group of students? Long term, the thing to do is bring the problem to the attention of the test makers by alerting your school administrator. Short term, the temptation is to address the problem by teaching students the differentially accessible knowledge. This is a difficult professional decision, because clearly teachers should not specifically teach to the content of standardized tests because direct teaching to the test gives students an unfair advantage and jeopardizes the validity of test results.

To assist teachers in this decision, testing experts differentiate between curriculum teaching and item teaching (W. J. Popham, 2001). Curriculum teaching suggests that teachers direct their instruction toward a specific body of content or skills represented by a test and is a valid way to target test-represented content. By contrast, in item teaching, teachers organize their instruction around either actual test items or around a set of look-alike items. Item teaching is indefensible, because it robs both teachers and students of assessment information that can be used to make educational decisions.

In addition to examining test content prior to testing and aligning content with the goals and objectives of the test, teachers can also examine test results for potential content bias. The printouts that detail test performance for a class not only include class means and individual students' scores, they also describe student performance on specific item types. Teachers can use this item-specific information to detect content bias and also to improve their instruction. For example, consider the following tabulation of responses from 28 students on three different multiple-choice items. For each item, B was the correct answer.

1. A	B*	C	D
1	24	1	2
2. A	B*	C	D
4	12	5	7
3. A	B*	C	D
1	4	3	20

Most of the students got item 1 correct, and there was no major problem with alternatives. This indicates that students knew the content and suggests that instruction was aligned with the content of this item. Less than half the class got item 2 correct, and incorrect answers were spread somewhat evenly over the possible choices. This suggests that instruction either wasn't effective or wasn't aligned with the content of the item. For item 3, the majority of students chose the incorrect response D. This pattern suggests either some type of problem with the item or a clear mismatch between instruction and the test item.

This simplified form of item analysis (Linn & Gronlund, 2000) can provide teachers with one analytical tool to identify potential content bias. If a teacher found that significant numbers of students from a particular student group responded in a pattern like that seen for item 3, the teacher should suspect content bias.

Adapt Testing Procedures

A second way to minimize standardized test bias is to adapt testing procedures to the specific needs of students. However, this strategy also poses professional dilemmas for teachers because the validity of standardized test results depends on standard test administration procedures. This problem of adapting test procedures is becoming increasingly important because of the growing use of high-stakes tests, as well as pressures to include diverse populations, such as students with exceptionalities and students with limited English proficiency, in the testing population (Pitoniak & Royer, 2001).

In response to these conflicting pressures, teachers have made accommodations to meet the testing needs of students. The *Standards for Educational and Psychological Testing*, jointly published by the American Educational Research Association, American Psychological Association, and National Council on Measurement in Education (1999), suggest the following accommodation strategies:

- Modifying the presentation format—for example, using Braille or large print booklets for examinees with visual impairments
- Modifying the response format—for example, providing a scribe to mark answers for students who have difficulty writing or typing
- Altering time to provide either extended testing time or frequent breaks
- Modifying the test setting—for example, allowing the test to be individually administered or altering dimensions of the physical setting (such as the lighting)

In testing students with disabilities, the most common adaptations are presenting tests orally, paraphrasing directions or content, and allowing students who have writing problems to dictate their answers (Koretz & Hamilton, 2000). Unfortunately, the legal foundations for these adaptations in specific settings are not clear, and teachers should consult with administrators before adapting standardized test procedures (Pitoniak & Royer, 2001).

Use Alternate Assessment Data Sources

Testing experts are clear on this point: No one test should be used as the sole basis for educational decisions about individual students. At the school level, teachers can help ensure that alternate data sources such as grades, work samples, and classroom observations are used in making educational decisions about individual students. At the policy level, teachers can become vocal advocates for the use of comprehensive assessment data in making these decisions.

Standardized Testing with Alternative Formats

As demands for accountability have increased, traditional multiple-choice formats have also come under fire. Critics contend that

> familiar assessment formats and procedures, . . . give only a single-dimensional indication of what a student can do at the end-point of a learning experience. At best, they allow opportunity only for highly constrained simulations of the actual performances in which we want students to engage, either in the classroom or the world beyond. (Camp, 1992, p. 243)

These critics call for more authentic assessments that measure students' ability to use information in real-life settings.

The use of alternative assessments with large samples of students is a monumental task. Worthen (1993) identified the following areas with unresolved issues that must be addressed if alternative assessments are to be successful on a large scale:

- *Goals and criteria.* Agreement must be reached as to what constitutes a valid measure of predetermined goals. Research indicates that different alternative assessments are often not exchangeable (Madaus & Tan, 1993).
- *Logistics.* Administering and scoring alternative assessments is enormously time-consuming. Further, because alternative assessments are not machine-scored, performances must be judged by at least two people to maintain reliability. This doubles the number of hours required to score an individual response.
- *Validity.* Because alternative assessments are subjective, the assessments are susceptible to questions about their validity.

In spite of these issues, one thing is clear. Asking students to perform tasks similar to those required in the real-world gives educators better information than a score on a

15.30
How can alternative assessment formats increase validity? Explain your answer using the three types of validity discussed earlier.

multiple-choice test. Whether or not questions about logistics and the validity of alternative assessments can be answered remains to be seen.

Issues in Standardized Testing: Implications for Teachers

What do the issues involved in standardized testing have to do with you as a teacher? At least three implications exist. First, although standardized testing is controversial, it is an integral part of schooling and almost certainly will remain so. As you saw earlier in the chapter, you will be expected to interpret standards, align your instruction with them, and prepare students for testing. In addition, you are likely to be held accountable for the students' performance on the tests.

Teachers need to be well informed to make professional decisions about standardized tests.

Second, you will be expected to know more. You will likely be required to take more courses in English, math, science, history, and geography than have been required of teachers in the past. You will also be expected to understand learners and learning and how content can be presented so it's understandable to students. It is very likely that you will be required to pass a test of competence before you're licensed. Standardized testing is a fact of life for teachers as well as students.

Third, and perhaps most important, you must be well informed about the strengths and limitations of standardized tests. Knowing that test bias may exist can help you avoid inappropriately lowering your expectations or stereotyping students based on the results of a single test. Other than students' caregivers, you are the person most important in determining the quality of students' education, and the better informed you are, the more capable you will be of making the best professional decisions possible.

Classroom Connections

Capitalizing on Diversity in Your Classroom

1. Be sensitive to the effects that diversity can have on assessment.

- *Elementary:* Before any of her non-native English-speaking students are referred for special education testing, a first-grade teacher talks with the testing expert and describes the child's background and language patterns.

- *Middle School:* Before administering a statewide eighth-grade math exam, the teacher explains the purpose of the test, explains its format, and provides opportunities for students to practice on different item types that will be on the test. During testing he makes a special effort to speak clearly and write directions and time limits on the board.

- *High School:* A high school English teacher holds special sessions after school to help her students with limited English proficiency prepare for the test. She carefully explains test purposes and formats and provides timed practices to get the students used to the testing procedures they'll encounter.

2. Adapt testing procedures to meet the needs of all students.

- *Elementary:* A third-grade teacher who teaches in an urban school takes extra time before standardized testing to explain the purpose of the tests and to provide opportunities for students to practice. He states positive expectations for all students and carefully monitors them to be sure they understand what is required in responding to the items.

- *Middle School:* Before standardized tests are given each year, a middle school language arts teacher takes time to explain what the tests are for and to teach test-taking strategies. She models the strategies, discusses them with her students, and provides opportunities to practice them under realistic conditions.

- *High School:* A high school math teacher makes a special effort to ensure that the vocabulary on the state standardized test is understood. Before the test, he carefully reviews important concepts the class has learned during the school year.

Summary

Standardized Tests

Standardized tests can be used to assess student academic progress, diagnose strengths and weaknesses, and place students in appropriate instructional programs. These tests can also be used to provide information for program evaluation and improvement.

Achievement tests provide information about what students have learned; diagnostic tests provide in-depth analysis of specific student strengths and weaknesses; intelligence tests are designed to measure students' ability to acquire knowledge, capacity to think and reason in the abstract, and ability to solve novel problems; and aptitude tests are designed to predict potential for future learning.

Validity measures the appropriateness of a test for a specific purpose and includes content, predictive, and construct validity.

Teachers play a central role in standardized testing. They are integral in test selection, student preparation, test administration, and interpreting and communicating results to students and their caregivers.

Understanding and Interpreting Standardized Test Scores

Standardized test scores are interpreted by using descriptive statistics to compare an individual's performance to the performance of a norming group or some criterion. Percentiles, stanines, grade equivalents, and standard scores all allow a student's score to be compared with the scores of comparable students in a norming group.

Issues in Standardized Testing

Accountability, minimum competency testing, and other forms of high-stakes testing point to the increased use of standardized tests for both policy making and individual educational decisions. Advocates argue that standardized tests efficiently assess the educational achievements of large numbers of students. Critics counter that misuse of standardized tests discourages innovation, encourages teaching to low-level skills, and discriminates against students from cultural minorities and those who are non-native English speakers. Bias in standardized testing can occur in the content of tests, in testing procedures, and in test use. Including performance assessments in standardized testing is one possible solution to the problem of low-level outcomes.

Windows on Classrooms

At the beginning of the chapter, we saw how Mike Chavez used standardized testing and interpreted test scores for a parent. Let's look now at another situation in which using standardized tests could help a teacher answer instructional questions. Read the case study, and answer the questions that follow.

Peggy Barret looked up from the stack of algebra tests that she was grading as her colleague, Stan Witzel, walked into the teacher's lounge.

"How's it going?" Stan asked.

"Fine . . . I think. I'm scoring tests from my Algebra I class. That's the one where I'm trying to put more emphasis on problem solving and not so much on the mechanics. I took a class last summer where the professor emphasized problem solving, and I'm giving it a try. Quite a few of the kids are actually getting into the applications now, and they like the problem solving when they do their small-group stuff. The trouble is . . . some of the others are really struggling so, . . . I'm not so sure about it all."

"I wish I had your problems. It sounds like your kids are learning, and at least some of them even like it. What more could a math teacher want?" Stan asked, with a puzzled look on his face.

"Yeah, I know," Peggy replied. "Getting these kids to like any kind of math is a major accomplishment, but still I wonder. . . . It's just that I'm not sure if they're getting all that they should. I don't know whether this class is *really* doing better than last year, . . . or even my other classes this year, for that matter. The tests I give are pretty different in the different classes. I think—or at least I'd like to believe—that the kids are doing better on problem solving, but to be honest about it, I see quite a few of them struggling with the mechanics. I do work on the mechanics, but not as much as in the other classes. . . . I guess what I'm saying is that I'm not sure if I've drawn the line in the right place as far as the emphasis I'm placing on each part of the class."

"Good point," Stan shrugged. "I always wonder when I make changes. Are they missing out on something?"

"As important," Peggy continued, "I wonder how they'll do when they go off to college—if they go to college. Actually, quite a few of them in this class will be going.

"Anyway," she looked over at Stan, "that's what I'm thinking about. . . . Got any good ideas?"

"Good questions, Peggy. I wish I knew, but . . . I guess that's part of teaching."

"Yeah," she said with her voice trailing off, "it seems as if we should be able to get some better information. I can see that some of the kids just don't seem to get it. I would say their background is weak; they seem to be trying. On the other hand, I checked out some of their old standardized test scores, and their math scores weren't that bad. Maybe it's not background. Maybe they just don't belong in my class."

"Say more," Stan encouraged. "Tell me about the kids who are struggling."

"Well, I've got several students who really struggle with word problems. They do fine on computation but fall apart when I ask them to solve word problems. They do fine when they work in small groups—then sometimes they don't even finish the tests I give them . . . like this one."

"Anything that they have in common?" Stan asked.

"Jacinta struggles but tries really hard. Quan is a whiz at computation but struggles when I ask him to think. Carlos actually seems to do fairly well with mechanics but really has problems with word problems. For example, I tried to motivate the class the other day with several word problems involving statistics from our basketball team. Most of the class not only liked them but got them right. Not these three."

"Maybe you ought to talk to Yolanda," Stan suggested. "She's been in this game for awhile and might know about some tests that are available that might help you answer some of your questions."

Constructed Response Questions

In answering these questions, use information from the chapter and link your responses to specific information in the case.

1. What type of standardized test would help Peggy determine the answer to the problem of not knowing "whether this class is *really* doing better than last year, . . . or even my other classes this year"?

2. What type of validity would be the primary concern? Explain.

3. One of Peggy's concerns was the background knowledge of her students: "I would say their background is weak." What type of standardized test might Peggy use to gather data related to this concern?

4. In investigating the problems that her students were having in math, Peggy checked out their overall test scores from past standardized tests. What else might she have done?

Document-Based Analysis

Examine the standardized test report (Figure 15.1) for David Palmer, the student in the opening case study. The following are conclusions based on the results:

1. David answered 62% of the questions on the science subtest correctly.
2. Davis is better at reading than in math.
3. On the basis of his total battery score, David should be placed in fifth grade.
4. David is smarter than his peers in fourth grade.
5. David scored about as well as other fourth graders in math.

Decide which of the conclusions are valid and which are not. Explain why they are or are not in each instance.

Online Portfolio Activities

To develop your professional portfolio, further apply your understanding of chapter content, and address the INTASC standards, go to the Companion Website, then to this chapter's *Online Portfolio Activities.* Complete the suggested activities.

Important Concepts

accountability *(p. 559)*
achievement tests *(p. 544)*
aptitude tests *(p. 548)*
construct validity *(p. 550)*
content validity *(p. 549)*
diagnostic tests *(p. 545)*
frequency distribution *(p. 552)*
grade equivalent *(p. 556)*
high-stakes tests *(p. 559)*
intelligence tests *(p. 545)*
mean *(p. 553)*
measures of central tendency *(p. 553)*
median *(p. 553)*
mode *(p. 553)*
national norms *(p. 543)*

normal distribution *(p. 554)*
norming group *(p. 542)*
percentile (percentile rank, PR) *(p. 555)*
percentile bands *(p. 556)*
predictive validity *(p. 549)*
range *(p. 553)*
raw score *(p. 555)*
standard deviation *(p. 554)*
standard error of measurement *(p. 557)*
standardized tests *(p. 542)*
standard score *(p. 557)*
standards-based education *(p. 558)*
stanine (S) *(p. 556)*
true score *(p. 557)*
T-score *(p. 557)*
z-score *(p. 557)*

Appendix

Using This Text to Practice for the PRAXIS™ Principles of Learning and Teaching Exam

In the United States, approximately thirty-five states use PRAXIS™ exams as part of their teacher licensing requirement. Among the PRAXIS™ tests are three Principles of Learning and Teaching (PLT) tests, one each for teachers seeking licensure for grades K–6, 5–9, and 7–12. *Educational Psychology: Windows on Classrooms* addresses most of the topics covered in the PLT tests.

The Principles of Learning and Teaching exam has two parts (Educational Testing Service, 2001). One consists of multiple-choice questions similar to those in the Eggen and Kauchak test banks, Student Study Guide, and Companion Website interactive Practice Quizzes that accompany this text. The second part is based on cases, which you will be asked to read and analyze, similar to the ones at the beginning and end of each chapter in this text.

There are two types of items in the case-based part of the PRAXIS™ Principles of Learning and Teaching exam: constructed response and document-based. In the first type, you read a case study and are then asked to analyze it, responding to short answer Constructed Response Questions (Educational Testing Service, 2001). In the Document-Based Analysis Questions you evaluate student or teacher-prepared documents, such as student work, excerpts from student records, teachers' lesson plans, assignments, or assessments. We have designed this text to help you succeed on the PRAXIS™ Principles of Learning and Teaching exam by including both types of case-based formats at the end of each chapter and providing feedback to the end-of-chapter questions on the Companion Website at *www.prenhall.com/eggen*.

I. Students as Learners (approximately 35% of total test)

A. Student Development and the Learning Process

1. Theoretical foundations about how learning occurs: how students construct knowledge, acquire skills, and develop habits of mind

Chapter 2: The Development of Cognition and Language
- The human brain and cognitive development (pp. 35–37)
- Piaget's theory of intellectual development (pp. 37–55)
- A sociocultural view of development: The work of Lev Vygotsky (pp. 55–61)
- The relationship between learning and development (p. 58)

Chapter 6: Behaviorism and Social Cognitive Theory (Entire chapter)
Chapter 7: Cognitive Views of Learning (Entire chapter)
Chapter 8: Constructing Understanding (Entire chapter)
Chapter 9: Complex Cognitive Processes (Entire chapter)
Chapter 10: Theories of Motivation
- Extrinsic and intrinsic motivation (pp. 350–351)

2. Human development in the physical, social, emotional, moral, and cognitive domains

Chapter 2: The Development of Cognition and Language (Entire chapter)
Chapter 3: Personal, Social, and Emotional Development (Entire chapter)
Chapter 6: Behaviorism and Social Cognitive Theory
- Self-regulation (pp. 221–223)
Chapter 7: Cognitive Views of Learning
- Metacognition: Knowledge and control of cognitive processes (pp. 259–261)
Chapter 9: Complex Cognitive Processes
- The strategic learner (pp. 330–338)
Chapter 11:
- Self-regulated learners: Developing student responsibility (pp. 389–393)

B. Students as Diverse Learners

1. Differences in the ways students learn and perform

Chapter 2: The Development of Cognition and Language
- Factors influencing development (pp. 39–40)
- Social interaction and development (pp. 56–57)
- Language and development (p. 57)
- Culture and development (p. 58)
Chapter 4: Learner Differences
- Assessment and learning: Cultural controversies in measuring intelligence (pp. 123–125)
- Learning styles (pp. 128–129)
- Intelligence: One trait or many? (pp. 118–122)
- Influence of SES on learning (pp. 130–131)
- Culture and schooling (pp. 133–137)
- Responding to gender differences: Instructional strategies (pp. 143–144)
- Students placed at risk (pp. 144–153)

2. Areas of exceptionality in students' learning

Chapter 2: The Development of Cognition and Language
- Stages of language acquisition (pp. 65–66)
Chapter 5: Learners with Exceptionalities
- Mental retardation (pp. 166–167)
- Learning disabilities (pp. 167–169)
- Attention deficit/hyperactivity disorder (ADHD) (pp. 169–170)
- Behavior disorders (pp. 170–173)
- Communication disorders (pp. 173–174)
- Visual disabilities (pp. 174–175)
- Hearing disabilities (pp. 175–176)
- Students who are gifted and talented (pp. 177–181)

3. Legislation and institutional responsibilities relating to exceptional students

Chapter 5: Learners with Exceptionalities
- Individuals with Disabilities Education Act (pp. 160–163)
- Amendments to the Individuals with Disabilities Act (pp. 163–165)

4. Process of second language acquisition and strategies to support the learning of students for whom English is not a first language

Chapter 2: The Development of Cognition and Language
- Language and development (p. 57)
- Theories of language acquisition (pp. 63–64)
- Stages of language acquisition (pp. 65–66)

B. Students as Diverse Learners—continued

5. Understanding of influences of individual experiences, talents, and prior learning, as well as language, culture, family, and community values on students' learning

Chapter 2: The Development of Cognition and Language
- Language diversity (pp. 66–67)
- English as a second language (pp. 67–68)
- Teaching ELL students: Instructional strategies (pp. 70–72)
- Language diversity (pp. 66–67)

Chapter 3: Personal, Social, and Emotional Development
- Personal development: Peers (pp. 81–82)
- Personal development: Parents and other adults (pp. 80–81)
- Social development (pp. 82–88)
- Promoting psychosocial and self-concept development: Instructional strategies (pp. 86–87)
- Development of morality, social responsibility, and self-control (pp. 101–112)
- Ethnic pride: Promoting self-esteem and ethnic identity (pp. 98–100)

Chapter 4: Learner Differences
- Influence of SES on schooling (pp. 130–131)
- Culture and schooling (pp. 133–137)

Chapter 6: Behaviorism and Social Cognitive Theory
- Addressing diversity: Behaviorism and social cognitive theory (pp. 227–230)

Chapter 7: Cognitive Views of Learning
- The impact of diversity on information processing (pp. 262–263)

6. Approaches for accommodating various learning styles, intelligences, or exceptionalities

Chapter 4: Learner Differences
- Ability grouping (pp. 125–128)
- Learning styles (pp. 128–129)
- Culturally responsive teaching: Instructional strategies (pp. 137–139)
- Responding to gender differences: Instructional strategies (pp. 143–144)
- Teaching students placed at risk: Instructional strategies (pp. 148–150)

Chapter 5: Learners with Exceptionalities
- Identifying students with exceptionalities (pp. 181–182)
- Teaching students with exceptionalities: Instructional strategies (pp.182–185)
- Technology and learning: Assistive technology (p. 186)

Chapter 6: Behaviorism and Social Cognitive Theory
- Addressing: Behaviorism and social cognitive theory (pp. 227–230)
- Capitalizing on minority role models (p. 229)

Chapter 14: Assessing Classroom Learning
- Accommodating diversity in classrooms: Reducing bias in assessment (pp. 526–527)

Chapter 15: Assessment Through Standardized Testing
- Eliminating bias in standardized testing: Instructional strategies (pp. 562–564)

C. Student Motivation and the Learning Environment

1. Theoretical foundations about human motivation behavior

Chapter 3: Personal, Social, and Emotional Development
- Integrating personal, emotional, and social development: Erikson's theory (pp. 89–93)
- Self-concept and achievement (pp. 95–98)

Chapter 6: Behaviorism and Social Cognitive Theory
- Classical conditioning: Learning to like and dislike school (pp. 228–229)

Chapter 10: Theories of Motivation
- Behavioral views of motivation (pp. 351–353)
- Humanistic views of motivation (pp. 353–357)
- Cognitive theories of motivation (pp. 357–378)

2. How knowledge of human motivation and behavior should influence strategies for organizing and supporting individual and group work in the classroom

Chapter 10: Theories of Motivation
- Using rewards in classrooms: Instructional strategies (pp. 352–353)
- Humanistic views of motivation: Instructional strategies (p. 356)

Chapter 11: Motivation in the Classroom
- Class structure: Creating a learning-focused environment (pp. 388–389)
- Self-regulated learners: Developing student responsibility (pp. 389–393)

C. Student Motivation and the Learning Environment—continued

	Chapter 11—continued • Climate variables: Creating a motivating environment (pp. 401–404) • Instructional variables: Developing interest in learning activities (pp. 404–414)
3. Factors and situations that are likely to promote or diminish students' motivation to learn; how to help students become self-motivated	**Chapter 3:** Personal, Social, and Emotional Development • Ethnic pride: Promoting self-esteem and ethnic identity (pp. 98–100) **Chapter 6:** Behaviorism and Social Cognitive Theory • Self-regulation (pp. 221–223) **Chapter 10:** Theories of Motivation • Developing students' self determination: Instructional strategies (pp. 375–377) • Accommodating affective factors in motivation: Instructional strategies (pp. 380–381) **Chapter 11:** Motivation in the Classroom • Self-regulated learners: Developing student responsibility (pp. 389–393) • Teacher expectations: Increasing perceptions of competence (pp. 397–399) • Helping students develop self-regulation: Instructional strategies (pp. 390–393) • Modeling and enthusiasm: Communicating genuine interest (p. 395) • Caring: Meeting the need for relatedness (pp. 395–397) • Climate variables: Creating a motivating environment (pp. 401–404) • Motivation and diversity (pp. 416–419) **Chapter 13:** Creating Productive Learning Environments: Principles of Instruction • Focus: Attracting and maintaining attention (pp. 475–476)
4. Principles of effective classroom management and strategies to promote positive relationships, cooperation and purposeful learning	**Chapter 6:** Behaviorism and Social Cognitive Theory • Motivating hesitant learners (p. 229) **Chapter 11:** Motivation in the Classroom • Class structure: Creating a learning-focused environment (pp. 388–389) • Safety and order: Classrooms as safe place to learn (pp. 401–402) **Chapter 12:** Creating Productive Learning Environments: Classroom Management (Entire chapter)

II. Instruction and Assessment (approximately 35% of total test)

A. Instructional Strategies

1. The major cognitive processes associated with student learning	**Chapter 2:** The Development of Cognition and Language • Applying Piaget's work in the classroom: Instructional strategies (pp. 51–53) • Vygotsky's work: Instructional strategies (pp. 58–61) **Chapter 6:** Behaviorism and Social Cognitive Theory • Social cognitive theory (pp. 214–227) **Chapter 7:** Cognitive Views of Learning (Entire chapter) **Chapter 8:** Constructing Understanding (Entire chapter) **Chapter 9:** Complex Cognitive Processes • Concept learning (pp. 312–319) • Problem solving (pp. 319–330)
2. Major categories, advantages, and appropriate uses of instructional strategies	**Chapter 7:** Cognitive Views of Learning • Schema production: Acquiring integrative declarative knowledge (p. 264) • Understanding and automaticity: Acquiring procedural knowledge (p. 267) **Chapter 8:** Constructing Understanding • Guided discovery (pp. 293–295) • Inquiry (pp. 295–296) • Discussion (pp. 296–298) • Cooperative learning (pp. 298–303)

A. Instructional Strategies—continued

Chapter 13: Creating Productive Learning Environments: Principles of Instruction
• Organization (p. 474)
• Feedback (pp. 476–478)
• Questioning (pp. 478–481)
• Review and closure (p. 481)

3. Methods for enhancing student learning through the use of a variety of resources and materials

Chapter 2: The Development of Cognition and Language
• Technology and learning: Using technology to develop formal thinking (pp. 49–51)
Chapter 3: Personal, Social, and Emotional Development
• Technology and learning: Using the Internet to promote social development (pp. 87–88)
Chapter 4: Learner Differences
• Technology and learning: Equity issues (pp. 151–153)
Chapter 5: Learners with Exceptionalities
• Technology and learning: Assistive technology (p. 186)
Chapter 6: Behaviorism and Social Cognitive Theory
• Technology and learning: The impact of symbolic modeling on behavior (pp. 218–219)
Chapter 9: Complex Cognitive Processes
• Using technology to improve problem solving ability (pp. 328–329)
Chapter 11: Motivation in the Classroom
• Technology and learning: Using technology to increase learner motivation (pp. 414–416)
Chapter 13: Creating Productive Learning Environments: Principles of Instruction
• Focus: Attracting and maintaining attention (pp. 475–476)
Chapter 14: Assessing Classroom Learning
• Technology and learning: Using technology to improve assessment (pp. 533–535)

4. Principles, techniques, and methods associated with major instructional strategies, especially direct instruction and student-centered models

Chapter 3: Personal, Social, and Emotional Development
• Promoting moral development: Instructional strategies (pp. 110–111)
Chapter 7: Cognitive Views of Learning
• Schema production: Acquiring integrative declarative knowledge (p. 264)
• Understanding and automaticity: Acquiring procedural knowledge (p. 267)
Chapter 8: Constructing Understanding
• Guided discovery (pp. 293–295)
• Inquiry (pp. 256–296)
• Discussion (pp. 296–298)
• Cooperative learning (pp. 298–303)
Chapter 9: Complex Cognitive Processes
• Problem-based learning (pp. 329–330)
• Concept mapping: Embedding concepts in complex schemas (pp. 315–316)
• Study strategies (pp. 331–333)

B. Planning Instruction

1. Techniques for planning instruction to meet curriculum goals, including the incorporation of learning theory, subject matter, curriculum development, and student development

Chapter 13: Creating Productive Learning Environments: Principles of Instruction
• Deciding what topics are important to study (p. 464)
• Preparing objectives: Deciding what students should know, value, or be able to do (pp. 464–468)
• Preparing and organizing learning activities (pp. 468–469)
• Planning in a standards-based environment (pp. 470–472)
Chapter 15: Assessment Through Standardized Testing
• Standards-based education and the accountability movement (pp. 558–560)

B. Planning Instruction—continued

2. Techniques for creating effective bridges between curriculum goals and students' experiences

Chapter 6: Behaviorism and Social Cognitive Theory
• Modeling (pp. 216–217)
Chapter 7: Cognitive Views of Learning
• Introduction and review (p. 268)
• Homework (pp. 269–270)
• Attention: The beginning of information processing (pp. 248–249)
• The influence of background knowledge on perception (p. 250)
• Rehearsal: Retaining information through repetition (pp. 250–251)
• Meaningful encoding: Making connections in long-term memory (pp. 251–256)
Chapter 9: Complex Cognitive Processes
• Concept learning (pp. 312–319)
• Problem solving (pp. 319–330)
• Developing strategic learning in students: Instructional strategies (pp. 333–334)

C. Assessment Strategies

1. Types of assessments

Chapter 2: Assessment and learning: Assessing students' cognitive development (pp. 47–49)
Chapter 3: Assessment and learning: Assessing students' social development (pp. 85–86)
Chapter 4: Assessment and learning: Cultural controversies in measuring intelligence (pp. 123–125)
Chapter 5: Assessment and learning: Assessment trends in special education (p. 176)
Chapter 6: Assessment and learning: Self-modeling as an assessment tool (pp. 225–226)
Chapter 7: Assessment and learning: The role of assessment in cognitive instruction (pp. 271–272)
Chapter 8: Assessment and learning: The role of assessment in constructivist classrooms (pp. 290–292)
Chapter 9: Assessment and learning: The role of assessment in transfer (pp. 342–343)
Chapter 10: Assessment and learning: The role of assessment in self-determination (pp. 374–375)
Chapter 11: Assessment and learning: Using feedback to increase interest and self-efficacy (pp. 412–413)
Chapter 12: Assessment and learning: The role of assessment in classroom management (pp. 453–454)
Chapter 13: Assessment and learning: Using assessment as a learning tool (pp. 483–485)
Chapter 14: Assessing Classroom Learning
• Functions of classroom assessment (pp. 495–496)
• Measurement and evaluation (pp. 496–497)
• Performance assessment (p. 511)
• Portfolios: Involving students in alternative assessment (pp. 514–517)
Chapter 15: Assessment Through Standardized Testing
• Functions of standardized tests (pp. 543–544)
• Types of standardized tests (pp. 544–548)

2. Characteristics of assessments

Chapter 14: Assessing Classroom Learning
• Validity: Making appropriate evaluation decisions (pp. 497–498)
• Reliability: Consistency in measurement (pp. 498–499)
• Valid test items (pp. 500–501)
Chapter 15: Assessment Through Standardized Testing
• Evaluating standardized tests: Validity revisited (pp. 548–550)

3. Scoring assessments

Chapter 14: Assessing Classroom Learming
• Using rubrics (pp. 507–509)
• Performance evaluation strategies (pp. 513–514)
• Portfolios: Involving students in alternative assessment (pp. 514–517)
• Analyzing results (pp. 525–526)
Chapter 15: Assessment Through Standardized Testing
• Understanding and interpreting standardized test scores (pp. 551–558)

C. Assessment Strategies—continued

4. Uses of assessments

Chapter 13: Creating Productive Learning Environments: Principles of Instruction
- Planning for assessment (pp. 469–470)

Chapter 14: Assessing Classroom Learning
- Designing a grading system (pp. 528–531)
- Performance assessment (p. 511)
- Portfolios: Involving students in alternative assessment (pp. 514–517)

5. Understanding of measurement theory and assessment-related issues

Chapter 14: Assessing Classroom Learning
- Constructing valid test items: Instructional strategies (pp. 501–510)
- Commercially prepared test items (p. 510)
- Planning for assessments (pp. 520–521)
- Preparing students for assessments (pp. 521–524)
- Administering assessments (pp. 524–525)
- Designing a grading system (pp. 528–531)
- Assigning grades: Increasing learning and motivation (pp. 531–533)

III. Communication Techniques (approximately 15% of total test)

A. Basic, effective verbal and nonverbal communication techniques

Chapter 5: Learners with Exceptionalities
- The labeling controversy (pp. 165–166)

Chapter 8: Constructing Understanding
- Social interaction facilitates learning (pp. 283–284)

Chapter 12: Creating Productive Learning Environments: Classroom Management
- Benefits of communication (pp. 437–438)

Chapter 13: Creating Productive Learning Environments: Principles of Instruction
- Attitudes (p. 473)
- Communication (p. 474–475)

B. Effect of cultural and gender differences on communications in the classroom

Chapter 2: The Development of Cognition and Language
- Language diversity (pp. 66–67)

Chapter 4: Learner Differences
- Culture and schooling (pp. 133–137)
- Gender (pp. 141–144)

Chapter 7: Cognitive Views of Learning
- The impact of diversity on information processing (pp. 262–263)

Chapter 11: Motivation in the Classroom
- Motivation and diversity (pp. 416–419)

Chapter 13: Creating Productive Learning Environments: Principles of Instruction
- Classroom interaction: Accommodating learner diversity (pp. 481–483)

Chapter 14: Assessing Classroom Learning
- Accommodating diversity in classrooms: Reducing bias in assessment (pp. 526–527)

Chapter 15: Assessment Through Standardized Testing
- Student diversity and test bias (pp. 561–562)

C. Types of questions that can stimulate discussion in different ways for particular purposes

Chapter 2: The Development of Cognition and Language
- Social interaction and development (pp. 56–57)
- Language and development (p. 57)

Chapter 3: Personal, Social, and Emotional Development
- Perspective taking (p. 83)
- Social problem solving (p. 83)
- Promoting moral development: Instructional strategies (pp. 110–111)

Chapter 8: Constructing Understanding
- Social interaction facilitates learning (pp. 283–284)

Chapter 13: Creating Productive Learning Environments: Principles of Instruction
- Questioning (pp. 478–481)
- Classroom interaction: Accommodating learner diversity (pp. 481–483)

IV. Profession and Community (approximately 15% of total test)
A. The Reflective Practitioner

1. Types of resources available for professional development and learning

Chapter 1: Educational psychology: Teaching in the Real World
- Knowledge of content (p. 7)
- Pedagogical content knowledge (pp. 7–10)
- General pedagogical knowledge (p. 10)
- Knowledge of learners and learning (p. 10–11)

2. Ability to read and understand articles and books about current views, ideas, and debates regarding best teaching practices

Chapter 1: Educational Psychology: Teaching in the Real World
- Knowledge and learning to teach (pp. 7–11)
- The role of research in acquiring knowledge (pp. 12–20)
- Research and the development of theory (pp. 18–20)

Chapter 13: Creating Productive Learning Environments: Principles of Instruction
- Teacher knowledge and teacher thinking (pp. 462–464)

3. Why personal reflection on teaching practices is critical, and approaches that can be used to do so

Chapter 1: Educational Psychology: Teaching in the Real World
- Conducting action research in classrooms: Instructional strategies (pp. 17–18)
- Research and teacher decision making (pp. 20–24)
- Assessment and learning: Gathering information for decision making (p. 23)
- Reflection and decision making (p. 24)

Chapter 13: Creating Productive Learning Environments: Principles of Instruction
- Teacher knowledge and teacher thinking (pp. 462–464)

B. The Larger Community

1. The role of the school as a resource to the larger community

Chapter 3: Personal, Social, and Emotional Development
- Personal development: Parents and other adults (pp. 80–81)

Chapter 12: Creating Productive Learning Environments: Classroom Management
- Involving parents: Instructional strategies (pp. 438–440)

2. Factors in the students' environment outside of school (family circumstances, community environments, health and economic conditions) that may influence students' life and learning

Chapter 4: Learner Differences
- Influence of SES on learning (pp. 130–131)
- Culture and schooling (pp. 133–137)
- Gender stereotypes and perceptions (pp. 142–143)
- Resilience (pp. 146–151)

Chapter 12: Creating Productive Learning Environments: Classroom Management
- Communication with parents: Accommodating learner diversity (pp. 440–441)

3. Basic strategies for involving parents/guardians and leaders in the community in the educational process

Chapter 6: Behaviorism and Social Cognitive Theory
- Capitalizing on minority role models (p. 229)

Chapter 12: Creating Productive Learning Environments: Classroom Management
- Benefits of communication (pp. 437–438)
- Involving parents: Instructional strategies (pp. 438–440)

4. Major laws related to students' rights and teacher responsibilities

Chapter 5: Learners with Exceptionalities
- Individuals with Disabilities Education Act (pp. 160–163)
- Amendments to the Individuals with Disabilities Education Act (pp. 163–165)

Chapter 15: Assessment Through Standardized Testing
- Standards-based education and the accountability movement (pp. 558–560)
- Cultural minorities and high-stakes tests (pp. 560–561)
- Student diversity and test bias (pp. 561–562)

Glossary

Ability grouping. The process of placing students of similar abilities together and attempting to match instruction to the needs of different groups.

Acceleration. Programs for students who are gifted and talented that keep the curriculum the same but allow students to move through it more quickly.

Accommodation. A form of adaptation in which an existing scheme is modified and a new one is created in response to experience.

Accountability. The process of requiring students to demonstrate that they have met specified standards and holding teachers responsible for students' performance.

Achievement tests. Standardized tests designed to measure and communicate how much students have learned in specified content areas.

Action research. A form of applied research designed to answer a specific school- or classroom-related question.

Active listening. A form of communication in which an individual fully attends to a message and responds to both the intellectual and emotional content of the message.

Adaptation. The process of adjusting schemes and experiences to each other to maintain equilibrium.

Adaptive behavior. A person's ability to manage the demands and perform the functions of everyday life.

Adaptive fit. The degree to which a student is able to meet the requirements of a particular school setting and the extent to which the school accommodates the student's needs in that setting.

Affective domain. The learning domain that focuses on attitudes and values and the development of students' personal and emotional growth.

Affective memories. Past emotional experiences related to a topic or activity, often resulting from classical conditioning.

Algorithm. A rule prescribing a specific set of steps for solving a problem.

Alternative assessment. The direct examination of student performance on tasks similar to those performed in life outside of school.

Analogies. Logical relationships that are similar in some but not all respects.

Antecedents. Stimuli that precede and produce behaviors.

Anxiety. A general uneasiness and feeling of tension, sometimes accompanied by a sense of foreboding.

Applied behavior analysis. The process of systematically applying behavioral principles in an effort to change specific behaviors in an individual.

Aptitude tests. Standardized tests designed to predict the potential for future learning and measure general abilities developed over long periods of time.

Assertive discipline. A classroom management system that emphasizes carefully stated rules and specifically described consequences for obeying and breaking rules (reinforcers and punishers).

Assessment. The process of systematically gathering information for the purposes of making decisions about learning and teaching.

Assimilation. A form of adaptation in which an experience in the environment is incorporated into an existing scheme.

Assistive technology. Technological adaptations that help students with exceptionalities use computers and other forms of technology.

Attention. The process of consciously focusing on a stimulus.

Attention deficit/hyperactivity disorder (ADHD). A learning problem characterized by difficulty in maintaining attention because of limited ability to concentrate.

Attributional statements. Statements made by individuals (usually teachers) about the causes of students' performances.

Attribution theory. A cognitive theory of motivation that attempts to systematically describe learners' explanations for their successes and failures.

Automaticity. The use of mental operations that can be performed with little awareness or conscious effort.

Autonomous morality. A view of right and wrong that involves developing rational ideas of fairness and seeing justice as a reciprocal process of treating others as they would want to be treated.

Basic interpersonal communication skills. A level of language proficiency that allows students to interact conversationally with others.

Behavior disorders. Serious and persistent age-inappropriate behaviors that can result in social conflict, personal unhappiness, and often school failure.

Bidialecticism. The ability to switch back and forth between a dialect and standard English.

Caring. An individual's ability to empathize with and invest in the protection and development of young people.

Centration. The tendency to focus on the most perceptually obvious aspect of an object or event to the exclusion of all others.

Character education. A view of education for ethical development that emphasizes the transmission of moral values, such as honesty and citizenship, and the translation of these values into character traits or behaviors.

Characteristics (sometimes called **attributes** or features). A concept's defining elements.

Checklists. Written descriptions of dimensions that must be present in an acceptable performance of an activity.

Chunking. The process of mentally combining separate items into larger, more meaningful units.

Classical conditioning. A form of learning in which an individual learns to produce an involuntary emotional or physiological response that is similar to an instinctive or reflexive response.

Classification. The process of grouping objects on the basis of a common characteristic.

Classroom assessment. All the processes involved in making decisions about students' learning progress.

Classroom climate. The feelings evoked by the classroom environment. In a healthy climate, teacher and classroom characteristics promote students' feelings of safety and security, together with a sense of success, challenge, and understanding.

Classroom management. Teachers' strategies that create and maintain an orderly learning environment.

Closure. A form of review occurring at the end of a lesson.

Cognitive academic language proficiency. A level of language proficiency that allows students to handle demanding learning tasks with abstract concepts in the curriculum.

Cognitive apprenticeship. A form of scaffolding that occurs when a less skilled learner works at the side of an expert.

Cognitive approaches to management. Approaches to classroom management that emphasize the creation of orderly classrooms through the development of learner understanding.

Cognitive behavior modification. A change in observable behavior that results from changes in thought processes.

Cognitive constructivism. A constructivist view of learning that focuses on individual, internal constructions of knowledge.

Cognitive development. A description of changes in the ways individuals think and process information.

Cognitive domain. The learning domain that focuses on the cognitive processes involved in learning different forms of knowledge.

Cognitive learning theories. Theories that explain learning by focusing on changes in mental processes and structures that occur as a result of people's efforts to make sense of the world.

Cognitive load theory. An information processing theory that recognizes the limitations of working memory and emphasizes instruction that can accommodate its capacity.

Cognitive modeling. Modeling of behavior combined with verbal descriptions of the model's thoughts and actions.

Cognitive processes. Intellectual actions that transform information and move it from one store to another.

Cognitive theories of motivation. Views of motivation that emphasize learners' beliefs, expectations, and needs for order, predictability, and understanding.

Collective self-esteem. Individuals' perceptions of the relative worth of the groups to which they belong.

Communication disorders. Exceptionalities that interfere with students' abilities to receive and understand information from others and express their own ideas or questions.

Competence. The ability to function effectively in the environment.

Completion format. A measurement format that includes a question or an incomplete statement that requires the learner to supply appropriate words, numbers, or symbols.

Component skills. The cognitive processes learners use to make and assess their conclusions during critical thinking activities; the "tools" of thinking.

Comprehension monitoring. The process of checking to see if you understand the material you're reading or hearing.

Concept mapping. A learning strategy that helps learners construct visual relationships among concepts.

Concepts. Mental structures that categorize sets of objects, events, or ideas.

Concrete operational stage. A stage of development in Piaget's theory characterized by the ability to think logically about concrete objects.

Conditioned response (CR). A learned physiological or emotional response that is similar to an unconditioned response.

Conditioned stimulus (CS). An object or event that becomes associated with an unconditioned stimulus.

Connected discourse. Instruction that is thematic and leads to a point.

Consequence. An outcome (stimulus) that occurs after a behavior and influences future behaviors.

Conservation. The idea that the "amount" of some substance stays the same regardless of its shape or the number of pieces into which it is divided.

Construct validity. An indicator of the logical connection between a test and what it is designed to measure.

Constructivism. A view of learning suggesting that learners construct their own understanding of the topics they study rather than having that understanding transmitted to them by some other source.

Content validity. A test's ability to representatively sample the content that is taught and measure the extent to which learners understand it.

Contiguity. The simple pairing of stimuli and responses, so that if they occur together often enough, experiencing one results in the other.

Continuous reinforcement schedule. A pattern in which every response is reinforced.

Control (or **autonomy**). The ability to alter the environment when necessary.

Cooperative learning. An instructional strategy that involves students working together in groups small enough (typically two to five) so that everyone can participate in a clearly assigned task.

Correlation. A positive or negative relationship between two or more variables.

Correlational research. The process of looking for relationships between two or more variables.

Cost. The perceived negative aspects of engaging in a task.

Creativity. The ability to identify or prepare original and varied solutions to problems.

Crisis. A psychosocial challenge, the resolution of which leads to personal and social development.

Criterion-referenced evaluation. The process of making evaluation decisions according to a predetermined standard.

Critical periods. Time spans that are optimal for the development of certain capacities in the brain.

Critical thinking. A person's ability and inclination to make and assess conclusions based on evidence.

Cues (prompts). Specific antecedent stimuli intended to produce behaviors teachers want to reinforce.

Cultural bias. Test bias that occurs when one or more items on a test penalize students of a particular ethnic or cultural background.

Cultural deficit theories. Views suggesting that the linguistic, social, or cultural backgrounds of minority children prevent them from doing well academically.

Cultural difference theories. Positions emphasizing the strengths of different cultures that look for ways that instructional practice can recognize and build on those strengths.

Cultural inversion. The tendency for involuntary minorities to regard certain forms of behavior, events, symbols, and meanings as inappropriate for them because these are characteristic of white Americans. (Definition from Ogbu, 1992, p. 8)

Culturally responsive teaching. Instruction that acknowledges cultural differences in classrooms and creates teaching strategies that respond to this diversity.

Culture. The attitudes, values, customs, and behavior patterns that characterize a social group.

Curriculum-based assessment. Attempts to measure learners' continuous performance in specific areas of the curriculum.

Deaf. Hearing that is impaired enough so that other senses, usually sight, are used to communicate.

Declarative knowledge. Knowledge of facts, definitions, concepts, procedures, and rules.

Deficiency needs. Needs in Maslow's hierarchy that, when unfulfilled, energize people to meet them.

Descriptive research. The use of interviews, observations, and surveys to describe opinions, attitudes, or events.

Desist. A verbal or nonverbal communication a teacher makes to a student to stop a behavior.

Development. The orderly, durable changes in learners resulting from a combination of experience, learning, and maturation.

Diagnostic tests. Standardized tests designed to provide a detailed description of learners' strengths and weaknesses in specific skill areas.

Dialect. A variation of standard English that is distinct in vocabulary, grammar, or pronunciation.

Disability. A functional limitation or an inability to perform a specific act.

Discipline. Teachers' responses to student misbehavior.

Discrimination. The ability to give different responses to related, but not identical, stimuli.

Discussion. An instructional strategy designed to stimulate thinking, help learners reconstruct understanding by challenging attitudes and beliefs, and develop interpersonal skills.

Disorder. A broad label used to describe a general malfunction of mental, physical, or psychological processes.

Distracters. Incorrect choices in multiple-choice test items that are designed to distract students who don't understand the content being measured in the item.

Drawing analogies. A problem-solving strategy that is used to solve unfamiliar problems by comparing them with problems already solved.

Dual-coding theory. An information processing concept that suggests that long-term memory contains two distinct memory systems: one for verbal information and one that stores visual information.

Dual processing. In information processing theory, the way a visual and an auditory component work together in working memory.

Due process. Legal requirements that guarantee parents' right to be involved in identifying and placing their children in special programs, to access school records, and to obtain an independent evaluation if they're not satisfied with the one conducted by the school.

Egocentrism. The inability to interpret an event from someone else's point of view.

Elaboration. The process of increasing the meaningfulness of information by forming additional links in existing knowledge or by adding new knowledge.

Elaborative questioning. A comprehension monitoring strategy that emphasizes drawing inferences, identifying examples, and forming relationships in the material being studied.

Empathy. The ability to experience the same emotion someone else is feeling.

Emphasis. Verbal and vocal cues and repetition that alert students to important information in a lesson.

Encoding. The process of representing information in long-term memory.

English as a second language (ESL) programs. Approaches to learning English that focus explicitly on the mastery of English.

Enrichment. Programs for students who are gifted and talented that provide advanced and varied content.

Entity view of intelligence. The belief that ability is stable and out of an individual's control.

Equilibrium. A state of cognitive balance between individuals' understanding of the world and their experiences.

Equitable distribution. A questioning strategy in which all students in a class are called on as equally as possible.

Essay format. A measurement format that requires students to make extended written responses to questions or problems.

Essential teaching skills. Basic abilities that all teachers, including those in their first year, should have to promote order and learning.

Ethnicity. The way individuals identify themselves with the nation from which they or their ancestors came; a person's ancestry.

Evaluation. The process of making decisions on the basis of measurements.

Exceptionalities. Learning problems, gifts and talents, or both.

Exemplars. The most highly typical examples of a concept.

Expectancy × value theory A cognitive theory of motivation suggesting that people are motivated to engage in an activity to the extent that they expect to succeed times the value they place on the success.

Experimental research. The process of systematically manipulating variables in an attempt to determine cause-and-effect relationships.

Expert. An individual who is highly skilled or knowledgeable in a particular domain.

External morality. A view of right or wrong in which rules are seen as fixed and permanent and externally enforced by authority figures.

Extinction (classical conditioning). The disappearance of a conditioned response as a result of the conditioned stimulus occurring repeatedly in the absence of the unconditioned stimulus.

Extinction (operant conditioning). The disappearance of a response as a result of nonreinforcement.

Extrinsic motivation. The motivation to engage in an activity as a means to an end.

Feedback. Information learners receive about the accuracy or appropriateness of their verbal responses and work.

Forgetting. The loss of, or inability to retrieve, information from memory.

Formal measurement. The process of systematically gathering information about learning progress.

Formal operational stage. A stage of development in Piaget's theory characterized by the ability to think logically, systematically, and hypothetically about combinations of problems.

Formative evaluation. Evaluation of student learning before or during instruction that is used to provide feedback to students and to monitor their growth.

Frequency distribution. A distribution of test scores that shows a simple count of the number of people who obtained each score.

Gender role identity differences. Beliefs about appropriate characteristics and behaviors of the two sexes.

Generalization (classical conditioning). Producing conditioned responses to stimuli that are similar, but not identical, to a conditioned stimulus.

Generalization (operant conditioning). Giving the same response to similar, but not identical, stimuli as a result of reinforcement.

General pedagogical knowledge. An understanding of general principles of instruction and classroom management that transcends individual topics or subject matter areas.

General transfer. The ability to take knowledge or skills learned in one context and apply them in a broad range of different contexts.

Goal. An outcome an individual hopes to achieve.

Grade equivalent. A score that is determined by comparing an individual's score on a standardized test to the scores of students in a particular age group; the first digit represents grade and the second the month of the school year.

Growth needs. Needs in Maslow's hierarchy that expand and increase as people have experiences with them.

Guided discovery. An instructional strategy in which a teacher identifies a content goal, arranges information so that patterns can be found, and guides students to the goal.

Guilt. The uncomfortable feeling people get when they know that they've caused distress for someone else.

Handicap. A limitation that an individual experiences in a particular environment.

Heuristics. General, widely applicable problem-solving strategies.

High-collective-efficacy school. School in which most of the teachers are high in personal teaching efficacy.

High-stakes tests (also called **minimum competency tests**). Standardized tests designed to measure the extent to which standards are being met and to make decisions about issues such as promotion to the next grade level or graduation from high school.

Holophrases. One- and two-word utterances that carry as much meaning for a child as complete sentences.

Humanistic psychology. A view of motivation that emphasizes people's attempts to fulfill their total potential as human beings.

Identity. A definition of the self, what one's existence means, and what one wants to accomplish in life.

Ill-defined problem. A problem that has more than one acceptable solution, an ambiguous goal, and no generally agreed-upon strategy for reaching a solution.

Imagery. The process of forming mental pictures.

I-message. A communication that addresses a behavior, describes the effects of the behavior on the sender, and identifies feelings the behavior generates in the sender.

Immersion. Approaches to learning English that involve hearing and speaking English exclusively in classrooms.

Importance. The extent to which a topic or activity allows a person to confirm or disconfirm important aspects of his or her self-schemas.

Inclusion. A comprehensive approach to educating students with exceptionalities that advocates a total, systematic, and coordinated web of services.

Incremental view of intelligence. The belief that ability can be improved with effort.

Individualized education program (IEP). An individually prescribed instructional plan devised by special education and general education teachers, resource professionals, and parents (and sometimes the student).

Informal measurement. The process of gathering incidental information about learning progress during learning activities and discussions with students.

Information processing. A theory of learning that examines how stimuli enter our memory systems, are selected and organized for storage, and are retrieved.

Information stores. Components of our information processing architecture that hold and process information.

Inhibition. A self-imposed restriction on one's behavior.

Inquiry. An instructional strategy in which learners gather facts and observations and use them to investigate real-world problems.

Instructional alignment. The match between goals, learning activities, and assessments.

Intelligence. The ability to acquire knowledge, the capacity to think and reason in the abstract, and the ability to solve novel problems.

Intelligence tests. Standardized tests designed to measure an individual's ability to acquire knowledge, capacity to think and reason in the abstract, and ability to solve novel problems.

Interference. The loss of information because other information, learned either before or after, detracts from understanding.

Intermittent reinforcement schedule. A pattern in which behavior is reinforced only periodically.

Internalization. The personal source of control for children's thoughts and actions. Also, the extent to which an attitude or value has been incorporated into a student's total value structure.

Interpersonal harmony stage. A stage of moral development characterized by making ethical decisions based on conventions, loyalty, and living up to the expectations of others; sometimes called the "nice girl/good boy" stage.

Intrinsic interest. Characteristics of a topic or activity that induce an individual's willing involvement in its study.

Intrinsic motivation. The motivation to be involved in an activity for its own sake.

Introductory focus. Direction for a lesson that is established by using an attention-getting technique or tool that also provides a framework for the lesson.

Involvement. The extent to which students are actively participating in a learning activity.

Jigsaw II. A form of cooperative learning in which individual students become experts on subsections of a topic and teach those subsections to others.

Joplin plan. An ability grouping plan that uses homogeneous grouping in reading combined with heterogeneous grouping in other areas.

Language acquisition device (LAD). A genetic set of language-processing skills that enables children to understand and use the rules governing speech.

Language disorders. Exceptionalities that involve problems with understanding language and using language to express ideas.

Law and order stage. A stage of moral development characterized by making moral decisions based on following laws and rules for their own sake.

Learned helplessness. The feeling that no amount of effort can lead to success.

Learning (behaviorist). A relatively enduring change in observable behavior that occurs as a result of experience.

Learning (cognitive). A change in a person's mental structures that creates the capacity to demonstrate different behaviors.

Learning disabilities (sometimes called **specific learning disabilities**). Difficulties in acquiring and using reading, writing, reasoning, listening, or mathematical abilities.

Learning-focused environments. Classroom environments that emphasize learning goals such as mastery of tasks, improvement, and increased understanding.

Learning goal (sometimes called a **mastery goal**). A goal that focuses on mastery of a task, improvement, and increased understanding.

Learning styles. Students' personal approaches to learning, problem solving, and processing information.

Least restrictive environment (LRE). A learning environment that places students in as typical an educational setting as possible while still meeting their special needs.

Levels of processing. A view of learning suggesting that the more deeply information is processed, the more meaningful it becomes.

Logical consequences. Consequences that are conceptually related to the misbehavior; they help learners see a link between their actions and the consequences that should sensibly follow.

Long-term memory. The information store in information processing theory that permanently holds information.

Mainstreaming. The practice of moving students with exceptionalities from segregated settings into regular classrooms, often for selected activities only.

Maintenance bilingual programs. Approaches to learning English that maintain and build on students' native language by teaching in both the native language and English.

Market exchange stage. A stage of moral development characterized by feeling that an act is morally justified if it results in an act of reciprocity on someone else's part.

Matching format. A measurement format that requires learners to classify a series of examples using the same alternatives.

Maturation. Genetically controlled, age-related changes in individuals.

Mean. The average score in a distribution of scores.

Meaningfulness. A description of the number of connections or links between an idea and other ideas in long-term memory.

Means-ends analysis. A problem-solving strategy in which the problem solver attempts to break the problem into subgoals and works successively on each.

Measurement. The process of gathering information about learning.

Measures of central tendency. Quantitative descriptions of how a group performed as a whole; the mean, median, and mode.

Median. The middle score in a distribution of scores.

Metacognition. The awareness of and control over one's own cognitive processes. Also, the component in information processing theory that describes a person's awareness of and control over cognitive processes.

Metamemory. Knowledge of and control over memory strategies.

Mnemonic devices. Techniques for promoting meaningfulness that link knowledge to be learned to familiar information.

Mode. The most frequent score in a distribution of scores.

Model. A representation that allows learners to visualize what they can't observe directly.

Modeling. The tendency of individuals to imitate behaviors they observe in others.

Moral dilemma. An ambiguous situation that requires a person to make a moral decision and justify that decision in terms of right and wrong.

Moral education. A view of education for ethical development that emphasizes the development of students' moral reasoning rather than the transmission of specified values.

Motivation. A force that energizes, sustains, and directs behavior toward a goal.

Motivation to learn. A student's tendency to find academic activities meaningful and worthwhile and to try and get the intended learning benefits from them. (Definition from Brophy, 1998, p. 162)

Multiple-choice format. A measurement format that includes a question or statement as a stem, combined with a series of answer choices, the correct or best of which is selected by the individual responding to the item.

Multiple-trait scoring. A scoring practice in which different dimensions of a product are judged according to different criteria.

National norms. Scores on standardized tests earned by representative groups of students from around the nation to which an individual's score is compared.

Nativist theory. A view of language development asserting that all humans are genetically disposed to learn language and that exposure to language triggers this disposition.

Nature view of intelligence. The assertion that intelligence is solely or primarily determined by genetics.

Negative reinforcement. The process of removing or avoiding a stimulus to increase behavior.

Network. A concept map illustrating relationships among concepts that are not hierarchical.

Nonverbal communication. Unspoken messages communicated through tone of voice and body language.

Normal distribution. A distribution of scores in which the mean, median, and mode are equal and the scores distribute themselves symmetrically in a bell-shaped curve.

Norming group. The representative group of individuals whose standardized test scores are compiled for the purpose of constructing national norms.

Norm-referenced evaluation. The process of making evaluation decisions about an individual student's work based on comparisons with the work of peers.

Nurture view of intelligence. The position emphasizing the influence of the environment on intelligence.

Objectives. Statements that describe the knowledge that students are expected to acquire or construct and a cognitive process that describes what they will be able to do with the knowledge.

Object permanence. The developmental ability to represent objects in memory.

Open-ended questions. Questions for which a variety of answers are acceptable.

Operant conditioning. A form of learning in behaviorism whereby an observable response changes in frequency or duration as the result of a consequence.

Organization (essential teaching skill). The essential teaching skill that includes starting on time, preparing materials in advance, establishing routines, and other actions that increase instructional time.

Organization (information processing theory). The process of clustering related items of content into categories or patterns that illustrate relationships.

Organization (Piaget's developmental theory). The developmental process of forming and using mental schemes in an effort to understand how the world works.

Overgeneralization. The process of using a word to refer to a broader class of objects than is appropriate.

Partial hearing impairment. An impairment that allows an individual to use a hearing aid and to hear well enough to be taught through auditory channels.

Pedagogical content knowledge. An understanding of how to make a specific topic comprehensible to others.

Percentile (percentile rank, PR). A ranking of students based on standardized test scores that compares an individual's score with the scores of all the others who have taken the test.

Percentile bands. Ranges of percentile scores on standardized tests.

Perception. The process people use to attach meaning to stimuli.

Performance assessment. A form of assessment in which students demonstrate their knowledge and skill by carrying out an activity or producing a product.

Performance-focused environments. Classroom environments that concentrate on performance goals such as the demonstration of competence, or ability, and how it compares to others.

Performance goal. A goal that focuses on competence or ability and how it compares to the competence or ability of others.

Personal development. The growth of enduring personality traits that influence the way individuals interact with their physical and social environments.

Personalization. The process of using intellectually and/or emotionally relevant examples to illustrate a topic.

Personal teaching efficacy. A teacher's belief that he or she is capable of getting all students to learn and succeed regardless of their background knowledge or ability.

Perspective taking. The ability to understand the thoughts and feelings of others.

Portfolios. Purposeful collections of student work that are reviewed against preset criteria.

Positive reinforcement. The process of increasing the frequency or duration of a behavior as the result of presenting a reinforcer.

Potency. A reinforcer's ability to strengthen behaviors.

Precise terminology. Language that eliminates vague terms (such as *perhaps, might, and so on,* and *usually*).

Predictive validity. An indicator of a test's ability to gauge future performance.

Premack principle. The phenomenon in which a more desired activity serves as a positive reinforcer for a less desired activity.

Preoperational stage. A stage of development in Piaget's theory characterized by perceptual dominance together with vast leaps in conceptual and language development.

Presentation punishment. The decrease in an individual's behavior that occurs as a result of being presented with a punisher.

Private speech. Self-talk that guides thinking and action.

Proactive aggression. Aggression that involves overt hostile acts toward someone else.

Problem. A situation in which an individual is in a state that differs from a desired end state, and the individual is uncertain about reaching the end state.

Problem-based learning. A teaching strategy that uses problems as the focus for developing content, skills, and self-direction.

Procedural knowledge. Knowledge of how to perform tasks.

Procedures. The steps for the routines students follow in their daily learning activities.

Productive learning environment. A classroom or school environment that is orderly and focuses on learning.

Prompting. A questioning technique in which a teacher asks questions or makes statements that elicit a student response after the student has failed to answer a previous question or has given an incorrect or incomplete answer.

Prompts (cues). Specific antecedent stimuli intended to produce behaviors teachers want to reinforce.

Prototype. The best representative of a concept's category.

Psychomotor domain. The learning domain that focuses on the development of students' physical abilities and skills.

Punishers. Consequences that weaken behaviors or decrease their frequency.

Punishment. The process of using punishers to decrease behavior.

Punishment-obedience stage. A stage of moral development characterized by making moral decisions based on the probability of getting caught and being punished.

Questioning frequency. The number of times a teacher asks questions during a given period of instructional time.

Random assignment. Assigning subjects to different groups so that an individual has an equal likelihood of being assigned to any group.

Range. The distance between the top and bottom score in a distribution of scores.

Rating scales. Written descriptions of the evaluative dimensions of an acceptable performance of an activity and scales of values on which each dimension is rated.

Raw score. The number of items an individual answered correctly on a standardized test or subtest.

Real-world task (authentic task). A learning activity that develops understanding similar to understanding that would be used outside the classroom.

Reciprocal questioning. A cooperative learning strategy in which students work in pairs to ask and answer questions about the content of a lesson or text.

Reflective teaching. The process of conducting a critical self-examination of one's teaching.

Rehearsal. The process of repeating information over and over, either aloud or mentally, without altering its form.

Reinforcement. The process of applying reinforcers to increase behavior.

Reinforcement schedules. Descriptions of the patterns in the frequency and predictability of reinforcers.

Reinforcer. A consequence that increases the frequency or duration of a behavior.

Relatedness. The feeling of connectedness to others in one's social environment resulting in feelings of worthiness of love and respect.

Reliability. A description of the extent to which measurements are consistent and free from errors of measurement.

Removal punishment. The decrease in an individual's behavior that occurs as a result of removing a stimulus, or as the result of the inability to get positive reinforcement.

Research. The process of systematically gathering information for the purpose of answering one or more questions.

Resilience. A learner characteristic that raises the likelihood of success in school and in other aspects of life, despite environmental adversities.

Retrieval. The process of pulling information from long-term memory into working memory for further processing.

Reversibility. The ability to mentally trace a line of reasoning back to its beginning.

Review. A summary that helps students link what they have already learned to what will follow in the next learning activity.

Rubric. A scoring scale that describes the criteria for grading.

Rules. Descriptions of standards for acceptable classroom behavior.

Satiation. Providing a reinforcer so frequently that it loses its potency.

Scaffolding. Assistance that allows individuals to complete tasks they cannot complete independently.

Schema (pl. **schemas** or **schemata**). An organized network of information stored in long-term memory.

Schemes. In Piaget's theory of intellectual development, mental patterns, operations, and systems that represent individuals' understanding of the world.

Scripted cooperation. A cooperative learning strategy in which a pair of students work together to elaborate each other's thinking.

Scripts. Schemas that govern behaviors for events.

Self-concept. A cognitive appraisal of one's own physical, social, and academic competence.

Self-determination. The process of deciding how to act on one's environments.

Self-efficacy. A belief about one's own capability to organize and complete a course of action required to accomplish a specific type of task.

Self-esteem (self-worth). An emotional reaction to, or an evaluation of, the self.

Self-fulfilling prophecy. The phenomenon in which a person tends to perform in certain ways that result from and confirm beliefs about the person's abilities.

Self-modeling. Behavioral changes that result from people observing and reflecting on their own actions.

Self-regulation. The process of accepting responsibility and control for one's own learning.

Self-schemas. Organized networks of information about ourselves.

Self-worth. See *self-esteem*.

Sensorimotor stage. The first stage of development in Piaget's theory characterized by children using their senses and motor capacities to make sense of the world.

Sensory focus. Stimuli that are used to maintain students' attention during learning activities.

Sensory memory. The information store in information processing theory that briefly holds stimuli from the environment until they can be processed.

Seriation. The ability to order objects according to increasing or decreasing length, weight, or volume.

Shame. The painful emotion aroused when people recognize that they have failed to act or think in ways they believe are good.

Shaping. The process of reinforcing successive approximations of a desired behavior.

Shared understanding. An understanding that occurs when the teacher and students have a common view of the learning task.

Situated learning (situated cognition). Learning that is social in nature and depends on, and cannot be separated from, the context in which it is learned.

Social cognitive theory. A learning theory that examines the processes involved as people learn from observing others and gradually acquire control over their own behavior.

Social constructivism. A constructivist view of learning that suggests that knowledge is first constructed in a social context and then internalized by individuals.

Social contract stage. A stage of moral development characterized by making moral decisions based on socially agreed upon principles.

Social conventions. The rules and expectations of a particular group or society.

Social development. Advances people make in their ability to interact and get along with others.

Social experience. The process of interacting—usually verbally—with others.

Social problem solving. The ability to resolve conflicts in ways that are beneficial to all involved.

Sociocultural theory of development. Vygotsky's theory of cognitive development characterized by social interaction and language embedded in a cultural context.

Socioeconomic status (SES). The combination of income, occupation, and level of education that describes a family or individual.

Special education. Instruction designed to meet the unique needs of students with exceptionalities.

Specific transfer. The ability to apply information in a context similar to the context in which it was originally learned.

Speech disorders (sometimes called **expressive disorders**). Exceptionalities that involve problems with forming and sequencing sounds.

Standard deviation. A statistical measure of the spread of scores on a standardized test.

Standard error of measurement. The range of scores within which an individual's true score is likely to fall.

Standardized tests. Assessment instruments given to large samples of students under uniform conditions and scored according to uniform procedures.

Standards. Statements that describe what students should know or be able to do at the end of a prescribed period of study.

Standards-based education. The process of focusing curricula and instruction on predetermined goals.

Standard score. A description of performance on a standardized test that uses standard deviation as the basic unit.

Stanine (standard nine, S). A description of an individual's standardized test performance that uses a scale ranging from 1 to 9 points.

Strategies. Plans for accomplishing specific learning goals.

Students placed at risk. Learners who are in danger of failing to complete their education with the skills necessary to survive in a modern technological society.

Students who are gifted and talented. Students at the upper end of the ability continuum who need support beyond regular classroom instruction to realize their full potential.

Student Teams Achievement Divisions (STAD). A form of cooperative learning that capitalizes on the role of social interaction to help students acquire facts, concepts, and procedural knowledge.

Study strategies. Specific plans students use to increase their understanding of written materials and teacher presentations.

Summarizing. The process of preparing a concise description of verbal or written passages.

Summative evaluation. Evaluation of student learning that occurs after instruction on a given topic and is used for grading purposes.

Systematic observation. The process of specifying criteria for acceptable performance on an activity and taking notes during observation based on the criteria.

Systematic reasoning. The process of using logical thought to reach a conclusion.

Table of specifications. A matrix that helps teachers generate or organize learning objectives by cognitive level or content area.

Task analysis. The process of breaking content down into component parts and making decisions about sequencing the parts.

Task comprehension. The understanding that results when learners are told what they are supposed to be learning and why they are learning it; a classroom climate variable in motivating classroom environments.

Test anxiety. A relatively stable, unpleasant reaction to testing situations that lowers performance.

Theory. A set of related principles derived from observations that, in turn, are used to explain additional observations.

Tracking. The process of placing students in different classes or curricula on the basis of ability.

Transfer. The effect of previous learning on new learning or problem solving. (Definition from Mayer, 2002, p. 4)

Transformation. The ability to mentally trace the process of changing from one state to another.

Transitional bilingual programs. Approaches to learning English that attempt to use the native language as an instructional aid until English becomes proficient.

Transition signals. Teachers' verbal statements indicating that one idea is ending and another is beginning.

True-false format. A measurement format that includes statements of varying complexity that learners have to judge as being correct or incorrect.

True score. The hypothetical average of an individual's scores if repeated testing under ideal conditions were possible.

T-score. A standard score that defines the mean as 50 and the standard deviation as 10.

Unconditional positive regard. The belief that someone is worthy and acceptable regardless of the person's behavior.

Unconditioned response (UCR).   An instinctive or reflexive (unlearned) physiological or emotional response caused by an unconditioned stimulus.

Unconditioned stimulus (UCS).   An object or event that causes an instinctive or reflexive (unlearned) physiological or emotional response.

Undergeneralization.   The process of using a word to refer to a narrower class of objects than is appropriate.

Universal principles stage.   A stage of moral development characterized by making moral decisions based on abstract and general principles that are independent of society's laws and rules.

Utility value.   The perception of a topic or activity as useful for meeting future goals, including career goals.

Validity.   An indicator of the extent to which an assessment actually measures what it is supposed to measure.

Vicarious learning.   Learning that occurs when people observe the consequences of another person's behavior and adjust their own behavior accordingly.

Visual disability.   An uncorrectable visual impairment that interferes with learning.

Wait-time.   The period of silence, both before and after calling on a student, during which the student has time to think about and construct an answer.

Well-defined problem.   A problem that has only one correct solution and a certain method for finding it.

Withitness.   A teacher's awareness of what is going on in all parts of the classroom at all times and the communication of this awareness verbally and nonverbally.

Worked examples.   Problems and complete solutions that are presented simultaneously.

Working memory (historically called **short-term memory**). The store in information processing theory that holds and processes information.

Zone of proximal development.   A range of tasks that an individual cannot yet do alone but can accomplish when assisted by a more skilled partner.

Z-score.   A standard score that describes the number of standard deviation units from the mean.

References

AAMR Ad Hoc Committee on Terminology and Classification. (2002). *Mental retardation: Definition, classification, and systems of support* (10th ed.). Washington, DC: American Association on Mental Retardation.

Abedi, J. (1999, spring). CRESST report points to test accommodations for English Language Learning students. *The CRESST Line*, pp. 6–7.

Abel, M., & Sewell, J. (1999). Stress and burnout in rural and urban secondary school teachers. *The Journal of Educational Research, 92*, 287–294.

Aboud, F., & Skerry, S. (1984). The development of ethnic identity: A critical review. *Journal of Cross-Cultural Psychology, 15*, 3–34.

Ackerman, E. (1998). New trends in cognitive development: Theoretical and empirical contributions. *Learning and Instruction, 8*(4), 375–385.

Adams, A., Carnine, D., & Gersten, R. (1982). Instructional strategies for studying content area texts in the intermediate grades. *Reading Research Quarterly, 18*, 27–53.

Adams, M. (1989). Thinking skills curricula. *Educational Psychologist, 24*, 25–77.

Adams, M. (1990). *Beginning to read.* Cambridge, MA: MIT Press.

Aiken, L. (2000). *Psychological testing and assessment* (10th ed.). Boston: Allyn & Bacon.

Ainley, M. (1993). Styles of engagement with learning: A multidimensional assessment of their relationship with strategy use and school achievement. *Journal of Educational Psychology, 85*, 395–405.

Airasian, P. (1997). *Classroom assessment* (3rd ed.). New York: McGraw-Hill.

Airasian, P. (2000). *Classroom assessment* (4th ed.). New York: McGraw-Hill.

Airasian, P., & Walsh, M. (1997). Constructivist cautions. *Phi Delta Kappan, 78*(6), 444–449.

Alao, S., & Guthrie, J. (1999). Predicting conceptual understanding with cognitive and motivational variables. *Journal of Educational Research, 92*(4), 243–254.

Alberto, P., & Troutman, A. (1999). *Applied behavior analysis for teachers* (4th ed.). Upper Saddle River, NJ: Merrill/Prentice Hall.

Alexander, P., Graham, S., & Harris, K. (1998). A perspective on strategy research: Progress and prospects. *Educational Psychology Review, 10*(2), 129–153.

Alexander, P., & Murphy, P. (1998). The research base for APA's learner-centered psychological principles. In N. Lambert & B. McCombs (Eds.), *How students learn: Reforming schools through learner-centered education* (pp. 25–60). Washington, DC: American Psychological Association.

Altermatt, E., Jovanovic, J., & Perry, M. (1998). Bias or responsivity? Sex and achievement-level effects on teachers' classroom questioning practices. *Journal of Educational Psychology, 90*(3), 516–527.

American Association for the Advancement of Science (AAAS). (1993). *Benchmarks for science literacy.* Washington, DC: Author.

American Association of University Women. (1992). *How schools shortchange girls.* Annapolis Junction, MD: Author.

American Association of University Women. (1998). *Gender gaps: Where schools still fail our children.* Annapolis Junction, MD: Author.

American Association of University Women (AAUW) Educational Foundation Commission on Technology, Gender & Teacher Education. (2000). *Tech-survey: Educating girls in the new computer age.* Washington, DC: Author.

American Educational Research Association, American Psychological Association, & National Council on Measurement in Education. (1999). *Standards for educational and psychological testing* (2nd ed.). Washington, DC: American Educational Research Association.

American Psychiatric Association. (1994). *Diagnostic and statistical manual of mental disorders* (4th ed.). Washington DC: Author.

American Psychological Association. (2000). *Diagnostic and statistical manual of mental disorders, text revision: DSMV-IV-TR* (4th ed.). Washington, DC: Author.

American Psychological Association Board of Educational Affairs. (1995). *Learner-centered psychological principles: A framework for school redesign and reform.* Retrieved October 1, 2002, from http://www.apa.org/ed/lcp.html

Ames, C. (1990). Motivation: What teachers need to know. *Teachers College Record, 91*, 409–421.

Ames, C. (1992). Classrooms: Goals, structures, and student motivation. *Journal of Educational Psychology, 84*(3), 261–271.

Ames, C., & Archer, J. (1988). Achievement goals in the classroom: Students' learning strategies and motivation processes. *Journal of Educational Psychology, 80*, 260–267.

Amrein, A., & Berliner, D. (2002). High-stakes testing, uncertainty, and student learning. *Education Policy Analysis Archives, 10*(18). Retrieved October 1, 2002, from http://epaa.asu.edu/epaa/v10n18/

Anastasi, A. (1988). *Psychological testing* (6th ed.). New York: Macmillan.

Anderman, E., & Maehr, M. (1994). Motivation and schooling in the middle grades. *Review of Educational Research, 64*, 287–309.

Anderson, C., & Roth, K. (1989). Teaching for meaningful and self-regulated learning in science. In J. Brophy (Ed.), *Advances in research on teaching* (Vol. 1, pp. 265–309). Greenwich, CT: JAI Press.

Anderson, J. (1990). *Cognitive psychology and its implications* (3rd ed.). New York: Freeman.

Anderson, J. (1995). *Cognitive psychology and its implications* (4th ed.). New York: Freeman.

Anderson, J., Reder, L., & Simon, H. (1996). Situated learning and education. *Educational Researcher, 25*(4), 5–10.

Anderson, L., Brubaker, N., Alleman-Brooks, J., & Duffy, G. (1984). *Making seatwork work* (Research Series No. 142). East Lansing: Michigan State University, Institute for Research on Teaching.

Anderson, L., Evertson, C., & Brophy, J. (1979). An experimental study of effective teaching in first-grade reading groups. *Elementary School Journal, 79,* 193–223.

Anderson, L., & Krathwohl, D. (Eds.).(2001). *A taxonomy for learning, teaching, and assessing: A revision of Bloom's taxonomy of educational objectives.* New York: Addison Wesley Longman.

Anderson, M., & Neely, J. (1996). Interference and inhibition in memory retrieval. In E. Bjork & R. Bjork (Eds.), *Memory* (pp. 237–313). San Diego, CA: Academic Press.

Anderson, R., Nguyen-Jahiel, K., McNurlen, B., Archodidou, A., Kim, S., Reznitskaya, A., Tillmanns, M., & Gilbert, L. (2001). The snowball phenomenon: Spread of ways of talking and ways of thinking across groups of children. *Cognition and Instruction, 19*(1), 1–46.

Anderson, T., & Armbruster, B. (1984). Studying. In D. Pearson (Ed.), *Handbook of reading research* (pp. 657–679). White Plains, NY: Longman.

Ansley, T. (1997). Assessment during the preschool years. In G. Phye (Ed.), *Handbook of classroom assessment* (pp. 265–286). San Diego, CA: Academic Press.

Antil, L., Jenkins, J., Wayne, S., & Vadasy, P. (1998). Cooperative learning: Prevalence, conceptualizations, and the relation between research and practice. *American Educational Research Journal, 35*(3), 419–454.

Arias, M., & Casanova, U. (Eds.). (1993). Bilingual education: Politics, practice, and research. *Ninety-second yearbook of the National Society for the Study of Education, Part 2.* Chicago: University of Chicago Press.

Arnold, D., Lonigan, C., Whitehurst, G., & Epstein, J. (1994). Accelerating language development through picture book reading: Replication and extension to a videotape learning

format. *Journal of Educational Psychology, 86*(2), 235–243.

Ashcraft, M. (1989). *Human memory and cognition.* Glenview, IL: Scott, Foresman.

Atkinson, J. (1958). *Motives in fantasy, action, and society.* Princeton, NJ: Van Nostrand.

Atkinson, J. (1964). *An introduction to motivation.* Princeton, NJ: Van Nostrand.

Atkinson, R., Derry, S., Renkl, A., & Wortham, D. (2000). Learning from examples: Instructional principles from the worked examples research. *Review of Educational Research, 70*(2), 181–214.

Atkinson, R., & Shiffrin, R. (1968). Human memory: A proposed system and its control processes. In K. Spence & J. Spence (Eds.), *The psychology of learning and motivation: Advances in research and theory* (Vol. 2). San Diego, CA: Academic Press.

Au, K. (1992, April). *"There's almost a lesson here": Teacher and students' purposes in constructing the theme of a story.* Paper presented at the annual meeting of the American Educational Research Association, San Francisco.

Aulls, M. (1998). Contributions of classroom discourse to what content students learn during curriculum enactment. *Journal of Educational Psychology, 90*(1), 56–69.

Ausubel, D. (1968). *Educational psychology: A cognitive view.* New York: Holt, Rinehart & Winston.

Ausubel, D. (1977). The facilitation of meaningful verbal learning in the classroom. *Educational Psychologist, 12,* 162–178.

Avery, P., & Palmer, E. (2001, April). *Developing authentic instruction and assessment to promote authentic student performance.* Paper presented at the annual meeting of the American Educational Research Association, Seattle.

Axelrod, S., & Apsche, J. (Eds.). (1983). *The effects of punishment on human behavior.* New York: Academic Press.

Babad, E., Bernieri, F., & Rosenthal, R. (1991). Students as judges of teachers' verbal and nonverbal behavior. *American Educational Research Journal, 28*(1), 211–234.

Baddeley, A. (1992). Working memory. *Science, 255,* 556–559.

Baker, A., Kessler-Sklar, S., Piotrkowski, C., & Parker, F. (1999). Kindergarten and first-grade teachers' reported

knowledge of parents' involvement in their children's education. *Elementary School Journal, 99*(4), 367–380.

Baker, D., & Stevenson, D. (1986). Mothers' strategies for children's school achievement: Managing the transition to high school. *Sociology of Education, 59,* 156–166.

Baker, E. (1989). Mandated tests: Educational reform or quality indicator? In B. Gifford (Ed.), *Test policy and test performance: Education, language, and culture* (pp. 3–23). Boston: Kluwer.

Baker, E., & Niemi, D. (1996). School and program evaluation. In D. Berliner & R. Calfee (Eds.), *Handbook of education psychology* (pp. 926–944). New York: Macmillan.

Baker, J., Terry, T., Bridger, R., & Winsor, A. (1997). Schools as caring communities: A relational approach to school reform. *School Psychology Review, 26,* 586–602.

Baker, L., & Brown, A. (1984). Metacognitive skills of reading. In D. Pearson (Ed.), *Handbook of reading research.* White Plains, NY: Longman.

Baldwin, J., & Baldwin, J. (1998). *Behavior principles in everyday life* (3rd ed.). Upper Saddle River, NJ: Prentice Hall.

Ball, D. (1992, Summer). Magical hopes: Manipulatives and the reform of math education. *American Educator,* pp. 28–33.

Ballantine, J. (1989). *The sociology of education.* Upper Saddle River, NJ: Prentice Hall.

Bandura, A. (1986). *Social foundations of thought and action: A social cognitive theory.* Upper Saddle River, NJ: Prentice Hall.

Bandura, A. (1989). Social cognitive theory. In R. Vasta (Ed.), *Annals of child development* (Vol. 6, pp. 1–60). Greenwich, CT: JAI Press.

Bandura, A. (1997). *Self-efficacy: The exercise of control.* New York: Freeman.

Bandura, A., Ross, D., & Ross, S. (1963). Imitation of film mediated aggressive models. *Journal of Abnormal and Social Psychology, 66,* 3–11.

Bangert-Drowns, R., Kulik, J., & Kulik, C. (1991). Effects of frequent classroom testing. *Journal of Educational Research, 85,* 89–99.

Bangert-Drowns, R., & Pyke, C. (1999, April). *Teacher ratings of student engagement with educational software.*

Paper presented at the annual meeting of the American Educational Research Association, Montreal, Canada.

Banks, J. (1997). Multicultural education: Characteristics and goals. In J. Banks & C. Banks (Eds.), *Multicultural education: Issues and perspectives* (3rd ed., pp. 3–32). Boston: Allyn & Bacon.

Barbetta , P., & Heron, T. (1991). Project Shine: Summer home instruction and evaluation. *Intervention in School and Clinics, 26*, 276–281.

Baringa, M. (1997). New insights into how babies learn language. *Science, 277*, 641.

Barker, G., & Graham, S. (1987). Developmental study of praise and blame as attributional cues. *Journal of Educational Psychology, 79*, 62–66.

Barkley, R. (1998). *Attention-deficit hyperactivity disorder: A handbook for diagnoses and treatment*. New York: Guilford Press.

Baron, J. (1998). Using learner-centered assessment on a large scale. In N. Lambert & B. McCombs (Eds.), *How students learn: Reforming schools through learner-centered education* (pp. 211–240). Washington, DC: American Psychological Association.

Barone, M. (2000). In plain English: Bilingual education flunks out of schools in California. *U.S. News and World Report, 128*(21), 37.

Barr, R. (2001). Research on the teaching of reading. In J. Richardson (Ed.), *Handbook of research on teaching* (4th ed., pp. 390–415). Washington, DC: American Educational Research Association.

Barron, A., Hogarty, K., Kromrey, J., & Lenkway, P. (1999). An examination of the relationships between student conduct and the number of computers per student in Florida schools. *Journal of Research on Computing in Education, 32*, 98–107.

Barron, B. (2000). Problem solving in video-based microworlds: Collaborative and individual outcomes of high-achieving sixth-grade students. *Journal of Educational Psychology, 92*(2), 391–398.

Barth, R. (2002). The culture builder. *Educational Leadership, 59*(8), 6–12.

Battistich, V. (2001, April). Effects of an elementary school intervention on students' "connectedness" to school and social adjustment during middle school. In J. Brown (Ed.), *Resilience education: Theoretical, interactive and empirical applications*. Symposium conducted at the annual meeting of the American Educational Research Association, Seattle.

Baumrind, D. (1991). The influence of parenting style on adolescent competence and substance use. *Journal of Early Adolecence, 11*, 56–95.

Bay, M., Staver, J., Bryan, T., & Hale, J. (1992). Science instruction for the mildly handicapped: Direct instruction versus discovery teaching. *Journal of Research in Science Teaching, 29*, 555–570.

Bay-Hinitz, A., Peterson, R., & Quilitch, H. (1994). Cooperative games: A way to modify aggressive and cooperative behaviors in young children. *Journal of Applied Behavior Analysis, 27*, 435–446.

Beach, K. (1999). Consequential transitions: A sociocultural expedition beyond transfer in education. In A. Iran-Nejad & P. Pearson (Eds.), *Review of research in education* (Vol. 24, pp. 101–140). Washington, DC: American Educational Research Association.

Beane, J. (1991). Sorting out the self-esteem controversy. *Educational Leadership, 49*(1), 25–30.

Beaty, E. (1995). Study contracts and education orientations. In F. Marton, D. Hounsell, & N. Entwistle (Eds.), *The experience of learning* (2nd ed.). Edinburgh: Scottish Academic Press.

Bebeau, M., Rest, J., & Narvaez, D. (1999). Beyond the promise: A perspective on research in moral education. *Educational Researcher, 28*(4), 18–26.

Bech, K. (1996). *The segmentation of moral judgments of adolescent students in Germany: Findings and problems*. Paper presented at the annual meeting of the American Educational Research Association, New York.

Becker, J., & Varelas, M. (2001). Piaget's early theory of the role of language in intellectual development: A comment on DeVries' account of Piaget's social theory. *Educational Researcher, 30*(6), 22–23.

Bee, H. (1989). *The developing child* (5th ed.). New York: Harper & Row.

Behrend, D., Rosengren, K., & Perlmutter, M. (1992). The relation between private speech and parental interactive style. In R. Diaz & L. Berk (Eds.), *Private speech: From social interaction to self-regulation* (pp. 85–100). Hillsdale, NJ: Erlbaum.

Beirne-Smith, M., Ittenbach, R., & Patton, J. (2002). *Mental retardation* (6th ed.). Upper Saddle River, NJ: Merrill/Prentice Hall.

Benard, B. (1994). *Fostering resilience in urban schools*. San Francisco: Far West Laboratory.

Bennett, N., & Blundel, D. (1983). Quantity and quality of work in rows of classroom groups. *Educational Psychology, 3*, 93–105.

Bennett, S. (1978). Recent research on teaching: A dream, a belief, and a model. *British Journal of Educational Psychology, 48*, 27–147.

Benninga, J., & Wynne, E. (1998). Keeping in character: A time-tested solution. *Phi Delta Kappan, 79*(6), 439–448.

Berger, K. S., & Thompson, R. A. (1995). *The developing person through childhood and adolescence*. New York: Worth.

Berk, L. (1996). *Infants, children, and adolescents* (2nd ed.). Boston: Allyn & Bacon.

Berk, L. (2000). *Child development* (5th ed.). Needham Heights, MA: Allyn & Bacon.

Berk, L. (2001). *Development through the lifespan* (2nd ed.). Boston: Allyn & Bacon.

Berk, L. (2003). *Child development* (6th ed.). Needham Heights, MA: Allyn & Bacon.

Berliner, D. (1984). *Making our schools more effective: Proceedings of three state conferences*. San Francisco: Far West Laboratory.

Berliner, D. (1988, February). *The development of expertise in pedagogy*. Paper presented at the annual meeting of the American Association of Colleges for Teacher Education, New Orleans, Louisiana.

Berliner, D., & Biddle, B. (1997). *The manufactured crisis: Myths, frauds, and the attack on America's public schools*. White Plains, NY: Longman.

Berndt, T. (1999). Friends' influence on students' adjustment to school. *Educational Psychologist, 34*, 15–28.

Berndt, T., & Keefe, K. (1995). Friends' influence on adolescents' adjustment to school. *Child Development, 66*, 1312–1329.

Bertman, S. (2000). *Cultural amnesia: America's future and the crisis of memory*. Westport, CT: Praeger.

Beyer, B. (1988). Developing a scope and sequence for thinking skills instruction. *Educational Leadership, 45*(7), 26–30.

Biklen, S., & Pollard, D. (2001). Feminist perspectives on gender in classrooms. In V. Richardson (Ed.), *Handbook of research on learning* (4th ed., pp. 695–722). Washington, DC: American Educational Research Association.

Binfet, J., Schonert-Reicht, K., & McDougal, P. (1997, March). *Adolescents' perceptions of the moral atmosphere of school: Motivational, behavioral, and social correlates.* Paper presented at the annual meeting of the American Educational Research Association, Chicago.

Bishop, J. (1995). The power of external standards. *American Educator, 19,* 10–14, 17–18, 42–43.

Bishop, J. (1998). The effect of curriculum-based external exit systems on student achievement. *Journal of Economic Education, 29,* 171–182.

Bixby, J. (1997, March). *School organization as context for White teachers' talk about race and student achievement.* Paper presented at the annual meeting of the American Educational Research Association, Chicago.

Black, P., & William, D. (1998a). Assessment and classroom learning. *Assessment in Education: Principles, Policy and Practice, 5*(1), 7–75.

Black, P. & Wiliam, D. (1998b). Inside the black box. *Phi Delta Kappan, 80*(2), 139–148.

Black, S. (1998, October). How are you smart? *American School Board Journal,* 26–29.

Blackburn, M., & Miller, R. (1999, April). *Intrinsic motivation for cheating and optimal challenge: Some sources and some consequences.* Paper presented at the annual meeting of the American Educational Research Association, Montreal, Canada.

Blair, J. (2000). AFT urges new tests, expanded training for teachers. *Education Week, 19*(32), 11.

Blanchett, W., & Madsen, J. (2001, April). *An examination of the disconnect between culturally relevant pedagogy and traditional models of evaluation and supervision: Implications for effectively teaching students of color.* Paper presented at the annual meeting of the American Educational Research Association, Seattle.

Blocher, M., Echols, J., Tucker, G., de Montes, L., & Willis, E. (2002, April).

Re-thinking the validity of assessment: A classroom teacher's dilemma. Paper presented at the annual meeting of the American Educational Research Association, New Orleans, LA.

Bloom, B. (1981). *All our children learning.* New York: McGraw-Hill.

Bloom, B. (1984). The search for methods of group instruction as effective as one-to-one tutoring. *Educational Leadership, 41*(8), 4–17.

Bloom, B., & Bourdon, L. (1980). Types and frequencies of teachers' written instructional feedback. *Journal of Educational Research, 74,* 13–15.

Bloom, B., Englehart, M., Furst, E., Hill, W., & Krathwohl, O. (1956). *Taxonomy of educational objectives: The classification of educational goals: Handbook 1. The cognitive domain.* White Plains, NY: Longman.

Blumenfeld, P. (1992). Classroom learning and motivation: Clarifying and expanding goal theory. *Journal of Educational Psychology, 84*(3), 272–281.

Bol, L., Stephenson, P., O'Connell, A., & Nunnery, J. (1998). Influence of experience, grade level, and subject area on teachers' assessment practices. *Journal of Educational Research, 91*(8), 323–330.

Boling, N., & Robinson, D. (1999). Individual study, interactive multimedia, or cooperative learning: Which activity best supplements lecture-based distance education? *Journal of Educational Psychology, 91*(1), 169–174.

Bong, M., & Clark, R. (1999). Comparison between self-concept and self-efficacy in academic motivation research. *Educational Psychologist, 34,* 139–153.

Borg, W., & Ascione, F. (1982). Classroom management in elementary mainstreaming classrooms. *Journal of Educational Psychology, 74,* 85–95.

Borko, H., & Putnam, R. (1996). Learning to teach. In D. Berliner & R. Calfee (Eds.), *Handbook of educational psychology* (pp. 673–708). New York: Macmillan.

Bourne, L. (1982). Typicality effects in logically defined categories. *Memory & Cognition, 10,* 3–9.

Bower, G., Clark, M., Lesgold, A., & Winzenz, D. (1969). Hierarchical retrieval schemes in recall of categorized word lists. *Journal of Verbal Learning and Verbal Behavior, 8,* 323–343.

Bowie, R., & Bond, C. (1994). Influencing future teachers' attitudes toward Black English: Are we making a difference? *Journal of Teacher Education, 45*(2), 112–118.

Bowman, D. (2000). White House proposes goals for improving Hispanic education. *Education Week, 19*(41), 9.

Boyd, M., & Rubin, D. (2001, April). *Elaborated student talk in elementary ESL instruction.* Paper presented at the annual meeting of the American Educational Research Association, Seattle.

Boyes, M., & Allen, S. (1993). Styles of parent-child interaction and moral reasoning in adolescence. *Merrill-Palmer Quarterly, 39,* 551–570.

Bracey, G. (1999). Research: The growing divide. *Phi Delta Kappan, 81*(1), 90.

Bracken, B., McCallum, R., & Shaughnessy, M. (1999). An interview with Bruce A. Bracken and R. Steve McCallum, authors of the Universal Nonverbal Intelligence Test (UNIT). *North American Journal of Psychology, 1,* 277–288.

Braddock, J. (1990). Tracking the middle grades: National patterns of grouping for instruction. *Phi Delta Kappan, 71*(6), 445–449.

Bradley, D. & Switlick, D. (1997). The past and future of special education. In D. Bradley, M. King-Sears, & D. Tessier-Switlick (Eds.), *Teaching students in inclusive settings* (pp. 1–20). Boston: Allyn & Bacon.

Bransford, J. (1993). Who ya gonna call? Thoughts about teaching problem solving. In P. Hallinger, K. Leithwood, & J. Murphy (Eds.), *Cognitive perspectives on educational leadership* (pp. 2–30). New York: Teachers College Press.

Bransford, J., Brown, A., & Cocking, R. (Eds.). (2000). *How people learn: Brain, mind, experience, and school.* Washington, DC: National Academy Press.

Bransford, J., Goldman, S., & Vye, N. (1991). Making a difference in people's abilities to think: Reflections on a decade of work and some hopes for the future. In L. Okagaki & R. Sternberg (Eds.), *Directors of development* (pp. 147–180). Hillsdale, NJ: Erlbaum.

Bransford, J., & Schwartz, D. (1999). Rethinking transfer: A simple proposal with multiple implications. In A. Iran-Nejad & P. Pearson (Eds.),

Review of research in education (Vol. 24, pp. 61–100). Washington, DC: American Educational Research Association.

Bransford, J., & Stein, B. (1984). *The IDEAL problem solver*. New York: Freeman.

Branson, M. (2000). *Self-regulation in early childhood: Nature and nurture*. New York: Guilford Press.

Brantlinger, E., Morton, M., & Washburn, S. (1999). Teachers' moral authority in classrooms: (Re)Structuring social interactions and gendered power. *Elementary School Journal, 99*(5), 490–504.

Bredo, E. (1997). The social construction of learning. In G. Phye (Ed.), *Handbook of academic learning: Construction of knowledge* (pp. 3–45). San Diego, CA: Academic Press.

Brehm, J., & Self, E. (1989). The intensity of motivation. *Annual Review of Psychology, 40,* 109–131.

Brennan, R., Kim, J., Wenz-Gross, M., & Siperstein, G. (2001). The relative equitability of high stakes testing versus teacher-assigned grades: An analysis of the Massachusetts Comprehensive Assessment System. *Harvard Educational Review, 71*(2), 173–212.

Brenner, D. (2001, April). *Translating social constructivism into methodology for documenting learning*. Paper presented at the annual meeting of the American Educational Research Association, Seattle.

Brenner, M., Mayer, R., Moseley, B., Brar, T., Durán, R., Reed, B., & Webb, D. (1997). Learning by understanding: The role of multiple representations in learning algebra. *American Educational Research Journal, 34*(4), 663–689.

Bridgeman, B. (1974). Effects of test score feedback on immediately subsequent test performance. *Journal of Educational Psychology, 66,* 62–66.

Brookhart, S. (1997). A theoretical framework for the role of classroom assessment in motivating student effort and achievement. *Applied Measurement in Education, 10*(2), 161–180.

Brooks, J. (1990). Teachers and students: Constructivists forging connections. *Educational Leadership, 47*(5), 68–71.

Brooks, J., & Brooks, M. (1993). *In search of understanding: The case for constructivist classrooms*. Alexandria,

VA: Association for Supervision and Curriculum Development.

Brophy, J. (1981). On praising effectively. *Elementary School Journal, 81,* 269–278.

Brophy, J. (1982). *Fostering student learning and motivation in the elementary school classroom*. East Lansing: Michigan State University, Institute for Research on Teaching.

Brophy, J. (1986). *Socializing student motivation to learn* (Institute for Research on Teaching Research Series No. 169). East Lansing: Michigan State University.

Brophy, J. (1987a). On motivating students. In D. Berliner & B. Rosenshine (Eds.), *Talks to teachers* (pp. 201–245). New York: Random House.

Brophy, J. (1987b). Syntheses of research on strategies for motivating students to learn. *Educational Leadership, 45*(2), 40–48.

Brophy, J. (1990). Teaching social studies for understanding and higher order applications. *Elementary School Journal, 90,* 351–418.

Brophy, J. (1996). *Teaching problem students*. New York: Guilford Press.

Brophy, J. (1998). *Motivating students to learn*. Boston: McGraw-Hill.

Brophy, J. (1999). Perspectives of classroom management. In J. Freiberg (Ed.), *Beyond behaviorism: Changing the classroom management paradigm* (pp. 43–56). Boston: Allyn & Bacon.

Brophy, J., & Evertson, C. (1976). *Learning from teaching: A developmental perspective*. Boston: Allyn & Bacon.

Brophy, J., & Good, T. (1986). Teacher behavior and student achievement. In M. Wittrock (Ed.), *Handbook of research on teaching* (3rd ed., pp. 328–375). New York: Macmillan.

Brophy, J., & McCaslin, M. (1992). Teachers' reports of how they perceive and cope with problem students. *Elementary School Journal, 93*(1), 3–68.

Brophy, J., & Rohrkemper, M. (1987). *Teachers' strategies for coping with hostile-aggressive students*. East Lansing: Michigan State University, Institute for Research on Teaching.

Brown, A. (1994). The advancement of learning. *Educational Researcher, 23,* 4–12.

Brown, A. (1997). Transforming schools into communities of thinking and learning about serious matters. *American Psychologist, 52,* 399–413.

Brown, A., Bransford, J., Ferrara, R., & Campione, J. (1983). Learning, remembering, and understanding. In J. Flavell & E. Markman (Eds.), *Handbook of child psychology: Vol. 3. Cognitive development* (4th ed., pp. 77–166). New York: Wiley.

Brown, A., & Campione, J. (1986). Psychological theory and the study of learning disabilities. *American Psychologist, 41,* 1059–1068.

Brown, A., & Campione, J. (1994). Guided discovery in a community of learners. In K. McGilly (Ed.), *Classroom lessons: Integrating cognitive theory and classroom practice* (pp. 229–270). Cambridge, MA: MIT Press.

Brown, A., & Palincsar, A. (1987). Reciprocal teaching of comprehension strategies: A natural history of one program for enhancing learning. In J. Borkowski & J. Day (Eds.), *Cognition in special education: Comparative approaches to retardation, learning disabilities, and giftedness*. Norwood, NJ: Ablex.

Brown, J., Collins, A., & Duguid, P. (1989). Situated cognition and the culture of learning. *Educational Researcher, 18,* 32–42.

Brown, R., & McNeill, D. (1966). The "tip-of-the-tongue" phenomenon. *Journal of Verbal Learning and Verbal Behavior, 5,* 325–337.

Bruer, J. (1993). *Schools for thought: A science of learning for the classroom*. Cambridge, MA: MIT Press.

Bruer, J. (1997). Education and the brain: A bridge too far. *Educational Researcher, 26*(8), 4–16.

Bruer, J. (1998). Brain science, brain fiction. *Educational Leadership, 56*(3), 14–18.

Bruer, J. (1999). In search of brain-based education. *Phi Delta Kappan, 89*(9), 649–657.

Bruner, J. (1985). Vygotsky: A historical and conceptual perspective. In J. Wertsch (Ed.), *Culture, communication, and cognition: Vygotskian perspectives* (pp. 21–34). New York: Cambridge University Press.

Bruner, J., Goodenow, J., & Austin, G. (1956). *A study of thinking*. New York: Wiley.

Bruning, R., Schraw, G., & Ronning, R. (1999). *Cognitive psychology and instruction* (3rd ed.). Upper Saddle River, NJ: Prentice Hall.

Bulgren, J., Deshler, D., Schumaker, J., & Lenz, B. K. (2000). The use and effectiveness of analogical instruction in diverse secondary content classrooms. *Journal of Educational Psychology, 92*(3), 426–441.

Bullough, R. (1989). *First-year teacher.* New York: Teachers College Press.

Bullough, R. (2001). *Uncertain lives: Children of promise, teachers of hope.* New York: Teachers College Press.

Burke, D., MacKay, D., Worthley, J., & Wade, E. (1991). On the tip of the tongue: What causes word finding failures in young and older adults? *Journal of Memory and Language, 30,* 542–579.

Burstyn, J., & Stevens, R. (1999, April). *Education in conflict resolution: Creating a whole school approach.* Paper presented at the annual meeting of the American Educational Research Association, Montreal, Canada.

Bushweller, K. (1997, September). Teaching to the test. *American School Board Journal,* pp. 20–25.

Butler, D. (1998). The strategic content learning approach to promoting self-regulated learning: A report of three studies. *Journal of Educational Psychology, 90*(4), 682–697.

Butler-Por, N. (1987). *Underachievers in school: Issues and interventions.* New York: Wiley.

Buzzelli, C., & Johnston, B. (1997, March). *Expressive morality in a collaborative learning activity: The creation of moral meaning.* Paper presented at the annual conference of the American Educational Research Association, Chicago.

Byrne, B., & Gavin, D. (1996). The Shavelson Model revisited: Testing for the structure of academic self-concept across pre, early, and late adolescents. *Journal of Educational Psychology, 88*(2), 215–228.

Byrnes, J. (2001). *Cognitive development and learning* (2nd ed.). Boston: Allyn & Bacon.

Byrnes, J., & Fox, N. (1998). The educational relevance of research in cognitive neuroscience. *Educational Psychology Review, 10,* 297–342.

Byrnes, M. (2002). *Taking sides: Clashing views on controversial issues in special education.* Guilford, CT: McGraw-Hill/Dushkin.

Calderhead, J. (1996). Teachers: Beliefs and knowledge. In D. Berliner & R. Calfee (Eds.), *Handbook of educational psychology* (pp. 709–725). New York: Macmillan.

Cameron, C., & Lee, K. (1997). Bridging the gap between home and school with voice-mail technology. *Journal of Educational Research, 90,* 182–190.

Cameron, J., & Pierce, D. (1996). The debate about rewards and intrinsic motivation: Protests and accusations do not alter the results. *Review of Educational Research, 66,* 39–51.

Camp, R. (1992). Assessment in the context of schools and school change. In H. Marshall (Ed.), *Redefining student learning: Roots of educational change* (pp. 241–263). Norwood, NJ: Ablex.

Campbell, C., & Evans, J. (2000). Investigation of preservice teachers' classroom assessment practices during student teaching. *Journal of Educational Research, 93*(6), 350–353.

Campbell, J., & Beaudry, J. (1998). *Journal of Educational Research, 91*(3), 140–147.

Campos-Flores, A. (2002, July 1). Macho or sweetness? *Newsweek,* p. 51.

Canter, L. (1988). Let the educator beware: A response to Curwin and Mendler. *Educational Leadership, 46*(2), 71–73.

Canter, L. (1996). First, the rapport—then the rules. *Learning, 24*(15), 12–13.

Canter, L., & Canter, M. (1992). *Assertive discipline.* Santa Monica, CA: Lee Canter & Associates.

Caplan, N., Choy, M., & Whitmore, J. (1992). Indochinese refugee families and academic achievement. *Scientific American, 266*(2), 36–42.

Carbo, M. (1997). Reading styles times twenty. *Educational Leadership, 54,* 38–42.

Cargill, C. (1987). Cultural bias in testing ESL. In C. Cargill (Ed.), *A TESOL professional anthology: Culture.* Lincolnwood, IL: National Textbook.

Carlsen, W. (1987, April). *Why do you ask? The effects of science teacher subject-matter knowledge on teacher questioning and classroom discourse.* Paper presented at the annual meeting of the American Educational Research Association, Washington, DC.

Carpenter, T., Levi, L., Fennema, E., Ansell, E., & Franke, M. (1995, April). *Discussing alternative strategies as a context for developing understanding in primary grade mathematics classrooms.* Paper presented at the annual meeting of the American Educational Research Association, San Francisco.

Carr, S., & Punzo, R. (1993). The effects of self-monitoring of academic accuracy and productivity on the performance of students with behavioral disorders. *Behavioral Disorders, 18*(4), 241–250.

Carrol, J. (1963). A model of school learning. *Teachers College Record, 64,* 723–733.

Carter, K. (1986). Test-wiseness for teachers and students. *Educational Measurement: Issues and Practice, 5*(6), 20–23.

Case, S. (1994). Will mandating portfolios undermine their value? *Educational Leadership, 52*(2), 46–47.

Caspi, A., & Silva, P. (1995). Temperamental qualities at age three predict personality traits in young adulthood: Longitudinal evidence from a birth cohort. *Child Development, 66,* 486–498.

Cassady, J. (1999, April). *The effects of examples as elaboration in text on memory and learning.* Paper presented at the annual meeting of the American Educational Research Association, Montreal, Canada.

Cassady, J., Budenz-Anders, J., Pavlechko, G., & Mock, G. (2001, April). *The effects of Internet-based formative and summative assessment on test anxiety, perceptions of threat, and achievement.* Paper presented at the annual meeting of the American Educational Research Association, Seattle.

Cassady, J., Cassady, M., Budenz-Anders, J., Austin, T., & Pavlechko, G. (2002, April). *Integration of computer technology and Internet access in schools and homes of children from low-income backgrounds: Effects on achievement and attitudes.* Paper presented at the annual meeting of the American Educational Research Association, New Orleans, LA.

Catania, A. (1998). *Learning* (4th ed.). Upper Saddle River, NJ: Prentice Hall.

Cazden, C. (1986). Classroom discourse. In M. Wittrock (Ed.), *Handbook of research on teaching* (3rd ed., pp. 432–464). New York: Macmillan.

Cazden, C. (1988). *Classroom discourse.* Portsmouth, NH: Heinemann.

Ceci, S., & Williams, W. (1997). Schooling, intelligence, and income. *American Psychologist, 53,* 185–204.

Cermak, L., & Craik, F. (1979). *Levels of processing in human memory.* Hillsdale, NJ: Erlbaum.

Chance, P. (1993). Sticking up for rewards. *Phi Delta Kappan, 74*, 787–790.

Chao, S., Stigler, J., & Woodward, J. A. (2000). The effects of physical materials on kindergartners' learning of number concepts. *Cognition and Instruction, 18*(3), 285–316.

Charles, C. (1999). *Building classroom discipline* (6th ed). New York: Longman.

Chaskin, R., & Rauner, D. (1995). Youth and caring: An introduction. *Phi Delta Kappan, 76*, 667–674.

Chekley, K. (1997). The first seven . . . and the eighth. *Educational Leadership, 55*, 8–13.

Chen, X., Rubin, K., & Sun, Y. (1992). Social reputation and peer relationships in Chinese and Canadian children: A cross-cultural study. *Child Development, 63*, 1336–1343.

Chen, Z., & Siegler, R. (2000). Intellectual development in childhood. In R. J. Sternberg (Ed.), *Handbook of intelligence* (pp. 92–116). New York: Cambridge University Press.

Cheng, L. R. (1987). *Assessing Asian language performance*. Rockville, MD: Aspen.

Chi, M., Bassok, M., Lewis, M., Reimann, P., & Glaser, R. (1989). Self-explanations: How students study and use examples in learning to solve problems. *Cognitive Science, 5*, 121–152.

Chinn, C. (1997, March). *Learning strategies and the learner's approach to understanding some science concepts.* Paper presented at the annual meeting of the American Educational Research Association, Chicago.

Choate, J. (Ed.). (1997). *Successful inclusive teaching.* Boston: Allyn & Bacon.

Choi, H., & Heckenlaible-Gotto, M. (1998). Classroom-based social skills training: Impact on peer acceptance of first-grade students. *Journal of Educational Research, 91*(4), 209–214.

Chomsky, N. (1959). A review of Skinner's verbal behavior. *Language, 35*, 25–58.

Chomsky, N. (1972). *Language and mind* (2nd ed.). Orlando, FL: Harcourt Brace.

Chomsky, N. (1976). *Reflections on language.* London: Temple Smith.

Chomsky, N., & Miller, G. (1958). Finite-state languages. *Information and Control, 1*, 91–112.

Cizek, G. (1997). Learning, achievement, and assessment: Constructs at a crossroads. In G. Phye (Ed.), *Handbook of classroom assessment* (pp. 1–31). San Diego, CA: Academic Press.

Clark, C., & Peterson, P. (1986). Teachers' thought processes. In M. Wittrock (Ed.), *Handbook of research on teaching* (3rd ed., pp. 255–296). New York: Macmillan.

Clark, J., & Paivio, A. (1991). Dual coding theory and education. *Educational Psychology Review, 3*, 149–210.

Clark, K., & Clark, M. (1939). The development of consciousness of self and the emergence of racial identification in Negro preschool children. *Journal of Social Psychology, 10*, 591–599.

Clifford, M. (1990). Students need challenge, not easy success. *Educational Leadership, 48*(1), 22–26.

Clinkenbeard, P. (1992, April). *Motivation and gifted adolescents: Learning from observing practice.* Paper presented at the annual meeting of the American Educational Research Association, San Francisco.

Cobb, P. (1994). Where is the mind? Constructivist and sociocultural perspectives on mathematical development. *Educational Researcher, 23*, 13–200.

Cochran, K., & Jones, L. (1998). The subject matter knowledge of preservice science teachers. In B. Fraser & K. Tobin (Eds.), *International handbook of science education:* Part II. Dordrecht, The Netherlands: Kluwer.

Cognition and Technology Group at Vanderbilt. (1992). The Jasper Series as an example of anchored instruction: Theory, program description, and assessment data. *Educational Psychologist, 27*, 291–315.

Cognition and Technology Group at Vanderbilt. (1997). *The Jasper Project: Lessons in curriculum, instruction, assessment, and professional development.* Mahwah, NJ: Erlbaum.

Cohen, E. (1991). Strategies for creating a multiability classroom. *Cooperative Learning, 12*(1), 4–7.

Cohen, E. (1994). Restructuring the classroom: Conditions for productive small groups. *Review of Educational Research, 64*, 1–35.

Cohen, E. (1998). Making cooperative learning equitable. *Educational Leadership, 56*(1), 18–21.

Coker, H., Lorentz, C., & Coker, J. (1980, April). *Teacher behavior and student outcomes in the Georgia study.* Paper presented at the annual meeting of the American Educational Research Association, Boston.

Cole, C. (1992). Self–management interventions in the schools. *School Pychology Review, 21*(2), 188–192.

Cole, M. (1991). Conclusion. In L. Resnick, J. Levine, & S. Teasley (Eds.), *Perspectives on socially shared cognition* (pp. 398–417). Washington, DC: American Psychological Association.

Collins, A., Brown, J., & Holum, A. (1991). Cognitive apprenticeship: Making thinking visible. *American Educator, 15*, 38–46.

Collins, A., Brown, J., & Newman, S. (1989). Cognitive apprenticeship: Teaching the crafts of reading, writing, and mathematics. In L. Resnick (Ed.), *Knowing, learning, and instruction: Essays in honor of Robert Glaser* (pp. 453–494). Hillsdale, NJ: Erlbaum.

Connell, J., & Wellborn, J. (1990). Competence, autonomy, and relatedness: A motivational analysis of self-system processes. In M. Gunnar & L. Sroufe (Eds.), *The Minnesota Symposia on Child Psychology* (Vol. 22, pp. 43–77). Hillsdale, NJ: Erlbaum.

Consortium of National Arts Education Associations. (1994). *National standards for arts education: What every young American should know and be able to do in the arts.* Reston, VA: Music Educators National Conference.

Coolahan, K., Fantuzzo, J., Mendez, J., & McDermott, P. (2000). Preschool peer interactions and readiness to learn: Relationship between classroom peer play and learning behaviors and conduct. *Journal of Educational Psychology, 92*(3), 458–465.

Cooper, H. (1989). Synthesis of research on homework. *Educational Leadership, 47*(3), 85–91.

Cooper, H., Jackson, K., Nye, B., & Lindsay, J. (2001). A model of homework's influence on the performance evaluations of elementary school students. *Journal of Experimental Education, 69*(2), 181–199.

Cooper, H., Lindsay, J., Nye, B., & Greathouse, S. (1998). Relationships among attitudes about homework, amount of homework assigned and completed, and student achievement. *Journal of Educational Psychology, 90*(1), 70–83.

Cooper H., & Valentine, J. (2001). Using research to answer practical questions about homework. *Educational Psychologist, 36*(3), 143–153.

Cooper, H., Valentine, J., Nye, B., & Lindsay, J. (1999). Relationships between five after-school activities and academic achievement. *Journal of Educational Psychology, 91*(2), 369–378.

Corbett, D., Wilson, B., & Williams, B. (1999). *FY1998 interim report: The second year of the assumptions, actions, and student performance OERI field-initiated study.* Paper presented at the annual meeting of the American Educational Research Association, Montreal, Canada.

Cordova, D., & Lepper, M. (1996). Intrinsic motivation and the process of learning: Beneficial effects of contextualization, personalization, and choice. *Journal of Educational Psychology, 88*(4), 715–730.

Corno, L., & Xu, J. (1998, April). *Homework and personal responsibility.* Paper presented at the annual meeting of the American Educational Research Association, San Diego, CA.

Covington, M. (1992). *Making the grade: A self-worth perspective on motivation and school reform.* Cambridge, MA: Harvard University Press.

Covington, M. (1998). *The will to learn: A guide for motivating young people.* New York: Cambridge University Press.

Covington, M. (2000). Intrinsic versus extrinsic motivation in schools: A reconciliation. *Current Directions in Psychological Science, 9,* 22–25.

Covington, M., & Omelich, C. (1987). "I knew it cold before the exam": A test of the anxiety blockage hypothesis. *Journal of Educational Psychology, 79,* 393–400.

Craik, F., & Lockhart, R. (1972). Levels of processing: A framework for memory research. *Journal of Verbal Learning and Verbal Behavior, 11,* 671–680.

Cressey, D. (1978). White collar subversives. *The Center Magazine, 11,* 44–49.

Crick, N., & Dodge, K. (1994). A review and reformulation of social information-processing mechanisms in children's social adjustment. *Psychological Bulletin, 115,* 74–101.

Crick, N., & Dodge, K. (1996). Social information-processing mechanisms in reactive and proactive aggression. *Child Development, 67,* 993–1002.

Crooks, T. (1988). The impact of classroom evaluation practices on students. *Review of Educational Research, 58,* 438–481.

Cruickshank, D. (1985). Applying research on teacher clarity. *Journal of Teacher Education, 35*(2), 44–48.

Cruickshank, D. (1987). *Reflective teaching: The preparation of students of teaching.* Reston, VA: Association of Teacher Educators.

Cuban, L. (1984). *How teachers taught: Constancy and change in American classrooms: 1890–1980.* White Plains, NY: Longman.

Cummins, J. (1991). Interdependence of first and second-language proficiency in bilingual children. In E. Bialystol (Ed.), *Language processing in bilingual children* (pp. 70–89). Cambridge, England: Cambridge University Press.

Cummins, J. (1984). *Bilingualism and special education: Issues in assessment and pedagogy.* Clevedon, England: Multilingual Matters.

Cunningham, T. H., & Gram, C. R. (1997, March). *Increasing native English vocabulary recognition through Spanish immersion: Cognate transfer from foreign to first language.* Paper presented at the annual meeting of the American Educational Research Association, Chicago.

Curry, L. (1990). A critique of research on learning styles. *Educational Leadership, 48*(2), 50–52, 54–56.

Curwin, R. (1992). *Rediscovering hope: Our greatest teaching strategy.* Bloomington, IN: National Education Service.

Cushner, K., McClelland, A., & Safford, P. (1992). *Human diversity in education.* New York: McGraw-Hill.

Dai, D., Moon, S., & Feldhusen, J. (1998). Achievement motivation and gifted students: A social cognitive perspective. *Educational Psychologist, 33*(2/3), 45–63.

Damon, W. (1988). *The moral child: Nurturing children's natural moral growth.* New York: Free Press.

Dansereau, D. (1985). Learning strategy research. In J. Segal, S. Chipman, & R. Glaser (Eds.), *Thinking and learning skills* (Vol. 1, pp. 209–239). Hillsdale, NJ: Erlbaum.

D'Arcangelo, M. (2000). How does the brain develop? *Educational Leadership, 58*(3), 68–71.

Darling-Hammond, L. (1996). *What matters most: Teaching for America's future.* Washington, DC: National Commission on Teaching and America's Future.

Darling-Hammond, L. (1997). *The right to learn.* San Francisco: Jossey-Bass.

Datnow, A., Hubbard, L., & Conchas, G. (1999). *How context mediates policy: The implementation of single gender public schooling in California.* Paper presented at the annual meeting of the American Educational Research Association, Montreal, Canada.

Datnow, A., Hubbard, L., & Conchas, G. (2001). How context mediates policy: The implementation of single gender public schooling in California. *Teachers College Record, 103*(2), 184–206.

Davenport, E., Davison, M., Kuang, H., Ding, S., Kim, S., & Kwak, N. (1998). High school mathematics course-taking by gender and ethnicity. *American Educational Research Journal, 35*(3), 497–514.

Davidson, B., Dell, G., & Walker, H. (2001, April). *In-school clubs: Impacting teaching and learning for at-risk students.* Paper presented at the annual meeting of the American Educational Research Association, Seattle.

Davies, S., Luftig, R., & Witte, R. (1999). *Self-management and peer-monitoring within a group contingency to decrease uncontrolled verbalizations of children with attention-deficit/hyperactivity disorder.* Paper presented at the annual meeting of the American Educational Research Association, Montreal, Canada.

Davis, G., & Rimm, S. (1998). *Education of the gifted and talented* (4th ed.). Upper Saddle River, NJ: Prentice Hall.

Davis, R. (1994). The task of improving mathematics classrooms: A reply to Schofield, Eurich-Fulcer, and Britt. *American Educational Research Journal, 31*(3), 608–618.

deCharms, R. (1968). *Personal causation.* San Diego, CA: Academic Press.

deCharms, R. (1984). Motivation enhancement in education settings. In R. Ames & C. Ames (Eds.), *Research on motivation in education*

(Vol. 1, pp. 275–310). New York: Academic Press.

Deci, E. (1975). *Intrinsic motivation*. New York: Plenum Press.

Deci, E. (1980). *The psychology of self-determination*. Lexington, MA: Heath.

Deci, E., & Ryan, R. (1985). *Intrinsic motivation and self-determination in human behavior*. New York: Plenum Press.

Deci, E., & Ryan, R. (1987). The support of autonomy and the control of behavior. *Journal of Personality and Social Psychology, 53*, 1024–1037.

Deci, E., & Ryan, R. (1991). A motivational approach to self: Integration in personality. In R. Dienstbier (Ed.), *Nebraska Symposium on Motivation 1990* (Vol. 38, pp. 237–288). Lincoln: University of Nebraska Press.

Deci, E., Vallerand, R., Pelletier, L., & Ryan, R. (1991). Motivation and education: The self-determination perspective. *Educational Psychologist, 26*, 325–346.

De La Paz, S., & Graham, S. (1997). Effects of dictation and advanced planning instruction on the composing of students with writing and learning problems. *Journal of Educational Psychology, 89*, 203–222.

De La Paz, S., Swanson, P., & Graham, S. (1998). The contribution of executive control to the revising by students with writing and learning difficulties. *Journal of Educational Psychology, 90*(3), 448–460.

Delgado-Gaitan, C. (1992). School matters in the Mexican American home: Socializing children to education. *American Educational Research Journal, 29*(3), 495–516.

De Lisi, R., & Straudt, J. (1980). Individual differences in college students' performance on formal operations tasks. *Journal of Applied Developmental Psychology, 1*, 201–208.

Delisle, J. (1984). *Gifted children speak out*. New York: Walker.

Delpit, L. (1995). *Other people's children: Cultural conflict in the classroom*. New York: The New Press.

deMarrais, K., & LeCompte, M. (1999). *The way schools work* (3rd ed.). New York: Longman.

DeMeulenaere, E. (2001, April). *Constructing reinventions: Black and Latino students negotiating the transofrmation of their academic identities and school performance*. Paper

presented at the annual meeting of the American Educational Research Association, Seattle.

Dempster, F. (1991). Synthesis of research on reviews and tests. *Educational Leadership, 48*(7), 71–76.

Dempster, R., & Corkill, A. (1999). Interference and inhibition in cognition and behavior: Unifying themes for educational psychology. *Educational Psychology Review, 11*(1), 1–88.

Derry, S. (1992). Beyond symbolic processing: Expanding horizons for educational psychology. *Journal of Educational Psychology, 84*, 413–419.

Derry, S., & Lesgold, A. (1996). Toward a situated social practice model for instructional design. In D. Berliner & R. Calfee (Eds.), *Handbook of educational psychology* (pp. 787–806). New York: Macmillan.

DeVries, R. (1997). Piaget's social theory. *Educational Researcher, 26*(2), 4–18.

DeVries, R., & Zan, B. (1995, April). *The sociomoral atmosphere: The first principle of constructivist education*. Paper presented at the annual meeting of the American Educational Research Association, San Francisco.

Deyhle, D. (1987). Learning failure: Tests as gatekeepers and the culturally different child. In H. Trueba (Ed.), *Success or failure?* (pp. 85–108). Cambridge, MA: Newbury House.

Diaz, R. (1983). Thought and two languages: The impact of bilingualism. In Z. Gordon (Ed.), *Review of research in education* (Vol. 10). Washington, DC: American Educational Research Association.

Diaz, R. (1990). Bilingualism and cognitive ability: Theory, research, and controversy. In A. Barona & E. Garcia (Eds.), *Children at risk: Poverty, minority status, and other issues of educational equity* (pp. 91–102). Washington, DC: National Association of School Psychologists.

Dienstbier, R. (Ed.), *Nebraska Symposium on Motivation 1990* (Vol. 38, pp. 237–288). Lincoln: University of Nebraska Press.

Dillon, J. (1987). *Questioning and discussion: A multidisciplinary study*. Norwood, NJ: Ablex.

Dilworth, M., & Brown, C. (2001). Consider the difference: Teaching and learning in culturally rich schools. In V. Richardson (Ed.), *Handbook of research on learning* (4th

ed., pp. 643–667). Washington, DC: American Educational Research Association.

Dochy, F., & McDowell, L. (1997). Introduction: Assessment as a tool for learning. *Studies in Educational Evaluation, 23*(4), 279–298.

Dodge, K., & Price, N. (1994). On the relation between social information processing and socially competent behavior in early school-aged children. *Child Development, 65*, 1385–1397.

Dole, J., Duffy, G., Roehler, L., & Pearson, D. (1991). Moving from the old to the new: Research on reading comprehension instruction. *Review of Educational Research, 61*, 239–264.

Dole, J., & Sinatra, G. (1998). Reconceptualizing change in the cognitive construction of knowledge. *Educational Psychologist, 33*(2/3), 109–128.

Dolgins, J., Myers, M., Flynn, P., & Moore, J. (1993). How do we help the learning disabled? *Instructor, 93*(7), 29–36.

Donnerstein, E., Slaby, R., & Eron, L. (1994). The mass media and youth aggression. In L. Eron, J. Gentry, & P. Schlegel (Eds.), *Reason to hope: A psychosocial perspective on violence and youth* (pp. 219–250). Washington, DC: American Psychological Association.

Dowrick, P. (1983). Self-modeling. In P. Dowrick & S. Biggs (Eds.), *Using video: Psychological and social applications* (pp. 105–124). Chichester, England: Wiley.

Dowson, M., & McInerney, D. (2001). Psychological parameters of students' social and work avoidance goals: A qualitative investigation. *Journal of Educational Psychology, 93*, 35–42.

Doyle, W. (1986). Classroom organization and management. In M. Wittrock (Ed.), *Handbook of research on teaching* (3rd ed., pp. 392–431). New York: Macmillan.

Drabman, R., & Thomas, M. (1976). Does watching violence on television cause apathy? *Pediatrics, 57*, 329–331.

Driscoll, M. (1994). *Psychology of learning for instruction*. Needham Heights, MA: Allyn & Bacon.

Duffy, G. (1992, April). *Learning from the study of practice: Where we must go with strategy instruction*. Paper presented at the annual meeting of the American Educational Research Association, San Francisco.

Duffy, T., & Cunningham, D. (1996). Constructivism: Implications for the design and delivery of instruction. In D. Jonassen (Ed.), *Handbook of research for educational communications and technology* (pp. 170–195). New York: Macmillan.

Dunkle, M., Schraw, G., & Bendixon, L. (1995, April). *Cognitive processes in well-defined and ill-defined problem solving*. Paper presented at the annual meeting of the American Educational Research Association, San Francisco.

Dunn, R., & Griggs, S. (1995). *Multiculturalism and learning style: Teaching and counseling adolescents*. Westport, CT: Praeger.

Durkin, K. (1995). *Developmental social psychology: From infancy to old age*. Cambridge, MA: Blackwell.

Dweck, C. (1975). The role of expectations and attributions in the alleviation of learned helplessness. *Journal of Personality and Social Psychology, 31*, 674–685.

Dweck, C. (1999). *Self-theories: Their role in motivation, personality, and development*. Philadelphia: Taylor & Francis.

Dweck, C., & Bempechat, J. (1983). Children's theories of intelligence: Consequences for learning. In S. Paris, G. Olson, & H. Stevenson (Eds.), *Learning and motivation in the classroom* (pp. 239–255). Hillsdale, NJ: Erlbaum.

Dweck, C., & Leggett, E. (1988). A social-cognitive approach to motivation and personality. *Psychological Review, 95*, 256–273.

Dwyer, D. (1994). Apple Classrooms of Tomorrow: What we've learned. *Educational Leadership, 51*, 4–10.

Dynarski, M., & Gleason, P. (1999, April). *How can we help? What we have learned from evaluations of federal dropout-prevention programs*. Paper presented at the annual meeting of the American Educational Research Association, Montreal, Canada.

Eccles, J., Wigfield, A., & Schiefele, U. (1998). Motivation to succeed. In N. Eisenberg (Ed.), *Handbook of child psychology: Vol. 3. Social, emotional, and personality development* (5th ed., pp. 1017–1095), New York: Wiley.

Echevarria, J., & Graves, A. (1998). *Sheltered content instruction*. Upper Saddle River, NJ: Merrill/Prentice Hall.

Educational Testing Service. (1999). *Principles of Learning and Teaching test bulletin*. Princeton, NJ: Author.

Educational Testing Service. (2001). *Principles of Learning and Teaching study guide*. Princeton, NJ: Author.

Eggen, P. (1997, March). The impact of frequent assessment on achievement, *satisfaction with instruction, and intrinsic motivation of undergraduate university students*. Paper presented at the annual meeting of the American Educational Research Association, Chicago.

Eggen, P. (1998, April). *A comparison of inner-city middle school teachers' classroom practices and their expressed beliefs about learning and effective instruction*. Paper presented at the annual meeting of the American Educational Research Association, San Diego, CA.

Eggen, P. (2001, April). *Constructivism and the architecture of cognition: Implications for instruction*. Paper presented at the annual meeting of the American Educational Research Association, Seattle.

Eggen, P., & Kauchak, D. (2001). *Strategies for teachers: Teaching content and thinking skills* (4th ed.). Needham Heights, MA: Allyn & Bacon.

Eggen, P., & Kauchak, D. (2002, April). *Synthesizing the literature of motivation: Implications for instruction*. Paper presented at the annual meeting of the American Educational Research Association, New Orleans, LA.

Eggen, P., Kauchak, D., & Kirk, S. (1978). Hierarchical cues and the learning of concepts from prose materials. *Journal of Experimental Education, 46*(4), 7–10.

Eggen, P., & McDonald, S. (1987, April). *Student misconceptions of physical science concepts: Implications for science instruction*. Paper presented at the annual meeting of the National Association for Research in Science Teaching, Washington, DC.

Eisenberg, N. (1982). The development of reasoning regarding prosocial behavior. In N. Eisenberg (Ed.), *The development of prosocial behavior*. San Diego, CA: Academic Press.

Eisenberg, N., Carlo, G., Murphy, B., & Van Court, N. (1995). Prosocial development in late adolescence: A longitudinal study. *Child Development, 66*, 1179–1197.

Eisenberg, N., & Fabes, R. A. (1998). Prosocial development. In N.

Eisenberg (Ed.), *Handbook of child psychology: Vol. 3. Social, emotional, and personality development* (5th ed., pp. 701–778). New York: Wiley.

Eisenberg, N., Shell, R., Pasternack, J., Lennon, R., Beller, R., & Mathy, R. (1987). Prosocial development in middle childhood: A longitudinal study. *Developmental Psychology, 23*, 712–718.

Eisenberger, R., & Cameron, J. (1998). Reward, intrinsic interest, and creativity: New findings. *American Psychologist, 53*, 676–679.

Elam, S., & Rose, L. (1995). The 27th annual Phi Delta Kappa/Gallup poll. *Phi Delta Kappan, 77*(1), 41–49.

Elbaum, B., & Vaughn, S. (2001). School-based interventions to enhance the self-concept of students with learning disabilities: A meta-analysis. *Elementary School Journal, 101*(3), 303–330.

Elbaum, B., Vaughn, S., Hughes, M., & Moody, S. (1999). Grouping practices and reading outcomes for students with disabilities. *Exceptional Children, 65*(3), 399–415.

Elliot, A., & McGregor, H. (2000, April). Approach and avoidance goals and autonomous-controlled regulation: Empirical and conceptual relations. In A. Assor (Chair), *Self-determination theory and achievement goal theory: Convergences, divergences, and educational implications*. Symposium conducted at the annual meeting of the American Educational Research Association, New Orleans, LA.

Elliot, A., & Thrash, T. (2001). Achievement goals and the hierarchical model of achievement motivation. *Educational Psychology Review, 13*, 139–156.

Elliot, S., & Busse, R. (1991). Social skills assessment and intervention with children and adolescents. *School Psychology International, 12*, 63–83.

Elliott, D. (1995). *Music matters: A new philosophy of music education*. New York: Oxford University Press.

Elliott, E., & Dweck, C. (1988). Goals: An approach to motivation and achievement. *Journal of Personality and Social Psychology, 54*, 5–12.

Elliott, J., & Thurlow, M. (2000). *Improving test performance of students with disabilities*. Thousand Oaks, CA: Corwin Press.

Ellis, S., Dowdy, B., Graham, P., & Jones, R. (1992, April). *Parental support of *planning skills in the context of homework and family demands.* Paper presented at the annual meeting of the American Educational Research Association, San Francisco.

Ellsworth, J. Z. (2001, April). *Effects of state standards and testing on teacher inquiry and reflective classroom practice: A case study.* Paper presented at the annual meeting of the American Educational Research Association, Seattle.

Emmer, E. (1988). Praise and the instructional process. *Journal of Classroom Interaction, 23,* 32–39.

Emmer, E., Evertson, C., & Worsham, M. (2003). *Classroom management for secondary teachers* (6th ed.). Boston: Allyn & Bacon.

Epstein, J. (1996). Perspectives and previews on research and policy for school, family, and community partnerships. In A. Booth & J. Bunn (Eds.), *Family-school links.* Mahwah, NJ: Erlbaum.

Epstein, J. (2001, April). *School, family, and community partnerships: Preparing educators and improving schools.* Paper presented at the annual meeting of the American Educational Research Association, Seattle.

ERIC Clearinghouse on Disabilities and Gifted Education. (2002). *GT—legal issues.* Retrieved November 20, 2002, from http://ericed.org/faq/gt-legal.html

Ericsson, K. (1996). The acquisition of expert performance. In K. Ericsson (Ed.), *The road to excellence: The acquisition of expert performance in the arts, sciences, sports, and games* (pp. 1–50). Mahwah, NJ: Erlbaum.

Ericsson, K., Krampe, D., & Tesch-Romer, R. (1993). The role of deliberate practice in the acquisition of expert performance. *Psychological Review, 100,* 363–406.

Erikson, E. (1968). *Identity: Youth and crisis.* New York: Norton.

Erikson, E. (1980). *Identity and the life cycle* (2nd ed.). New York: Norton.

Evans, E., & Engelberg, R. (1988). Student perceptions of school grading. *Journal of Research and Development in Education, 21*(2), 45–54.

Everson, H., & Tobias, S. (1998). The ability to estimate knowledge and performance in college: A metacognitive analysis. *Instructional Science, 26*(1–2), 65–79.

Everson, H., Tobias, S., Hartman, H., & Gourgey, A. (1991, April). *Text anxiety in different curricular areas: An exploratory analysis of the role of subject matter.* Paper presented at the annual meeting of the American Educational Research Association, Chicago.

Evertson, C. (1987). Managing classrooms: A framework for teachers. In D. Berliner & B. Rosenshine (Eds.), *Talks to teachers* (pp. 54–74). New York: Random House.

Evertson, C., Emmer, E., & Worsham, M. (2003). *Classroom management for elementary teachers* (6th ed.). Boston: Allyn & Bacon.

Exline, R. (1962). Need affiliation and initial communication behavior in problem solving groups characterized by low interpersonal visibility. *Psychological Reports, 10,* 405–411.

Eysenck, M., & Keane, M. (1990). *Cognitive psychology: A student's handbook.* Hillsdale, NJ: Erlbaum.

Fabos, B., & Young, M. (1999). Telecommunication in the classroom: Rhetoric versus reality. *Review of Educational Research, 69,* 217–259.

Farivar, S., & Webb, N. (1999). Preparing teachers and students for cooperative work: Building communication and helping skills. In C. Brady & N. Davidson (Eds.), *Professional development for cooperative learning.* Albany, NY: SUNY.

Fashola, O., Slavin, R., Calderon, M., & Duran, R. (1997). *Effective programs for Latino students in elementary and middle schools.* Baltimore: Center for Research on the Education of Students Placed at Risk.

Feingold, A. (1995). Gender differences in personality: A meta-analysis. *Psychological Bulletin, 116,* 429–456.

Feldhusen, J. (1998a). Programs and service at the elementary level. In J. VanTassel-Baska (Ed.), *Excellence in educating gifted and talented learners* (3rd ed., pp. 211–223). Denver: Love.

Feldhusen, J. (1998b). Programs and services at the secondary level. In J. VanTassel-Baska (Ed.), *Excellence in educating gifted and talented learners* (3rd ed., pp. 225–240). Denver: Love.

Feldman, A., Kropkf, A., & Alibrandi, M. (1996, April). *Making grades: How high school science teachers determine report card grades.* Paper presented at the annual meeting of the American Educational Research Association, New York.

Feuer, M., & Fulton, K. (1993). The many faces of performance assessment. *Phi Delta Kappan, 74*(6), 478.

Fischer, L., Schimmel, D., & Kelly, C. (1999). *Teachers and the law.* New York: Longman.

Fisher, B. (1997). Computer modeling for thinking about and controlling variables. *School Science Review, 79*(287), 87–90.

Fisher, C., Berliner, D., Filby, N., Marliave, R., Cohen, K., & Dishaw, M. (1980). Teaching behaviors, academic learning time, and student achievement: An overview. In C. Denham & A. Lieberman (Eds.), *Time to learn* (pp. 7–32). Washington, DC: National Institute of Education.

Fisher, T., & Mathews, L. (1999, April). *Examining interventions for highly mobile students and their families.* Paper presented at the annual meeting of the American Educational Research Association, Montreal, Canada.

Fitch, M., & Semb, M. (1992, April). *Peer teacher learning: A comparison of role playing and video evaluation for effects on peer teacher outcomes.* Paper presented at the annual meeting of the American Educational Research Association, San Francisco.

Fitzgerald, J. (1995). English-as-a-second-language learners' cognitive reading processes: A review of research in the United States. *Review of Educational Research, 65*(2), 145–190.

Flavell, J. (1993). *Cognitive development* (3rd ed.). Upper Saddle River, NJ: Prentice Hall.

Flavell, J., Friedrichs, A., & Hoyt, J. (1970). Developmental changes in memorization processes. *Cognitive Psychology, 1,* 324–340.

Flavell, J., Miller, P., & Miller, S. (1993). *Cognitive development* (3rd ed.). Upper Saddle River, NJ: Prentice Hall.

Foos, P. (1992). Test performance as a function of expected form and difficulty. *Journal of Experimental Education, 60*(3), 205–211.

Forcier, R. (1999). *The computer as a productivity tool in education* (2nd ed.). Upper Saddle River, NJ: Merrill/Prentice Hall.

Forsterling, F. (1985). Attributional retraining: A review. *Psychological Bulletin, 98,* 495–512.

Forum on Child and Family Statistics. (1999). *Trends in the well-being of*

America's children and youth. Washington, DC: U.S. Department of Health and Human Services.

Fowler, R. (1994, April). *Piagetian versus Vygotskian perspectives on development and education.* Paper presented at the annual meeting of the American Educational Research Association, New Orleans, LA.

Franklin, W. (1997, March). *African-American youth at promise.* Paper presented at the annual meeting of the American Educational Research Association, Chicago.

Freeman, E., & Hatch, J. (1989). What schools expect young children to know: An analysis of kindergarten report cards. *Elementary School Journal, 89,* 595–605.

Freese, S. (1999, April). *The relationship between teacher caring and student engagement in academic high school classes.* Paper presented at the annual meeting of the American Educational Research Association, Montreal, Canada.

Freiberg, J. (Ed.). (1999a). *Beyond behaviorism: Changing the classroom management paradigm.* Boston: Allyn & Bacon.

Freiberg, J. (1999b). Consistency management and cooperative discipline. In J. Freiberg (Ed.), *Beyond behaviorism: Changing the classroom management paradigm* (pp. 75–97). Boston: Allyn & Bacon.

Freiberg, J. (1999c). Sustaining the paradigm. In J. Freiberg (Ed.), *Beyond behaviorism: Changing the classroom management paradigm* (pp. 164–173). Boston: Allyn & Bacon.

Friedler, Y., Nachmias, R., & Linn, M. (1990). Learning scientific reasoning skills in microcomputer-based laboratories. *Journal of Research in Science Teaching, 27*(2), 173–191.

Friedler, Y., Nachmias, R., & Songer, N. (1989). Teaching scientific reasoning skills: A case study of a microcomputer-based curriculum. *School Science and Mathematics, 89*(1), 58–67.

Fuchs, D., & Fuchs, L. (1994). Inclusive schools movement and the radicalization of special education reform. *Exceptional Children, 60,* 294–309.

Fuchs, D., Fuchs, L., Mathes, P., & Simmons, D. (1997). Peer-assisted learning strategies: Making classrooms more responsive to

diversity. *American Educational Research Journal, 34*(1), 174–206.

Fuchs, L., Fuchs, D., Bentz, J., Phillips, N., & Hamlett, C. (1994). The nature of student interactions during peer tutoring with and without prior training and experience. *American Educational Research Journal, 31*(1), 75–103.

Fuchs, L., Fuchs, D., Kazdan, S., & Allen, S. (1999). Effects of peer-assisted learning strategies in reading with and without training in elaborated help giving. *Elementary School Journal, 99*(3), 201–220.

Fujimura, N. (2001). Facilitating children's proportional reasoning: A model of reasoning processes and effects of intervention on strategy change. *Journal of Educational Psychology, 93*(3), 589–603.

Gabinger, R. (1996). Rich environments for active learning. In D. Jonassen (Ed.), *Handbook of research for educational communications and technology* (pp. 665–692). New York: Macmillan.

Gage, N., & Berliner, D. (1989). Nurturing the critical, practical, and artistic thinking of teachers. *Phi Delta Kappan, 71,* 212–214.

Gagne, E., Yekovich, C., & Yekovich, F. (1993). *The cognitive psychology of school learning* (2nd ed.). New York: HarperCollins.

Gall, M., Gall, J., & Borg, W. (2003). *Educational research: An introduction* (7th ed.). Boston: Allyn & Bacon.

Gallagher, J. (1998). Accountability for gifted students. *Phi Delta Kappan, 79*(10), 739–742.

Gallini, J. (2000, April). *An investigation of self-regulation developments in early adolescence: A comparison between non at-risk and at-risk students.* Paper presented at the annual meeting of the American Educational Research Association, New Orleans, LA.

Gandal, M., & Vranek, J. (2001). Standards: Here today, here tomorrow. *Educational Leadership, 59,* 7–13.

Garber, H. (1988). *Milwaukee Project: Preventing mental retardation in children at risk.* Washington, DC: American Association on Mental Retardation.

Garcia, E. (1993). Language, culture and education. In *Review of research in education* (Vol. 19). Washington, DC: American Educational Research Association.

Gardner, H. (1983). *Frames of mind: The theory of multiple intelligences.* New York: Basic Books.

Gardner, H. (1992). Assessment in context: The alternative to standardized testing. In B. Gifford (Ed.), *Changing assessments: Alternate views of aptitude, achievement, and instruction* (pp. 77–119). Boston: Kluwer.

Gardner, H. (1993). *Creating minds: An anatomy of creativity seen through the lives of Freud, Einstein, Picasso, Stravinsky, Elliot, Graham, and Gandhi.* New York: Basic Books.

Gardner, H. (1995a). "Multiple Intelligences" as a catalyst. *English Journal, 84*(8), 16–26.

Gardner, H. (1995b). Reflections on multiple intelligences: Myths and messages. *Phi Delta Kappan, 77,* 200–209.

Gardner, H. (1999a). *The disciplined mind: What all students should understand.* New York: Simon & Schuster.

Gardner, H. (1999b). The understanding pathway. *Educational Leadership, 57*(3), 12–17.

Gardner, H. (1999c, April). *The well-disciplined mind: What all students should understand.* Paper presented at the annual meeting of the American Educational Research Association, Montreal, Canada.

Gardner, H., & Hatch, T. (1989). Multiple intelligences go to school. *Educational Researcher, 18*(8), 4–10.

Garner, R., Alexander, P., Gillingham, M., Kulikowich, J., & Brown, R. (1991). Interest and learning from text. *American Educational Research Journal, 28,* 643–659.

Gay, B. (1997). Educational equality for students of color. In J. Banks & C. Banks (Eds.), *Multicultural education: issues and perspectives* (3rd ed., pp. 195–228). Boston: Allyn & Bacon.

Gaziel, H. (1997). Impact of school culture on effectiveness of secondary schools with disadvantaged students. *Journal of Educational Research, 90*(5), 310–318.

Geary, D. (1998). What is the function of mind and brain? *Educational Psychology Review, 10,* 377–387.

Gehring, J. (2000). Massachusetts teachers blast state tests in new TV ads. *Education Week, 20*(12), 1, 22.

Geisinger, K. (1992). Testing L.E.P. students for minimum competency and high school graduation. In *Focus on evaluation and measurement* (Vol. 2, pp. 33–68). Washington, DC: U.S. Department of Education.

Gelman, R., Meck, E., & Merkin, S. (1986). Young children's numerical competence. *Cognitive Development, 1,* 1–29.

Genishi, C. (1992, April). *Oral language and communicative competence.* Paper presented at the annual meeting of the American Educational Research Association, San Francisco.

Gentile, J. (1996). Setbacks in the "advancement of learning"? *Educational Researcher, 25,* 37–39.

Geography Education Standards Project. (1994). *Geography for life: National geography standards.* Washington, DC: National Geographic Research and Exploration.

Gersten, R. (1996). The double demands of teaching English language learners. *Educational Leadership, 52*(5), 18–21.

Gersten, R., & Baker, S. (2001). Teaching expressive writing to students with learning disabilities: A meta-analysis. *Elementary School Journal, 101*(3), 251–272.

Gersten, R., Taylor, R., & Graves, A. (1999). Direct instruction and diversity. In R. Stevens (Ed.), *Teaching in American schools* (pp. 81–106). Upper Saddle River, NJ: Merrill/Prentice Hall.

Gersten, R., & Woodward, J. (1995). A longitudinal study of transitional and immersion bilingual education programs in one district. *Elementary School Journal, 95*(3), 223–239.

Gettinger, M., Doll, B. & Salmon, D. (1994). Effects of social problem solving, goal setting, and parent training on children's peer relations. *Journal of Applied Developmental Psychology, 15,* 141–163.

Gick, M., & Holyoak, K. (1987). The cognitive basis of knowledge transfer. In S. Cormier & J. Hagman (Eds.), *Transfer of learning: Contemporary research and applications.* San Diego, CA: Academic Press.

Gilligan, C. (1977). In a different voice: Women's conceptions of the self and of morality. *Harvard Educational Review, 47,* 481–517.

Gilligan, C. (1982). *In a different voice: Psychological theory and women's development.* Cambridge, MA: Harvard University Press.

Gilligan, C., & Attanucci, J. (1988). Two moral orientations: Gender differences and similarities. *Merrill-Palmer Quarterly, 34,* 223–237.

Gladney, L., & Greene, B. (1997, March). *Descriptions of motivation among African American high school students for their favorite and least favorite classes.* Paper presented at the annual meeting of the American Educational Research Association, Chicago.

Glaser, R., & Chi, M. (1988). Overview. In M. Chi, R. Glaser, & M. Farr (Eds.), *The nature of expertise* (pp. xv–xxviii). Hillsdale, NJ: Erlbaum.

Glasser, W. (1985). *Control theory in the classroom.* New York: Perennial Library.

Glassman, M. (2001). Dewey and Vygotsky: Society, experience, and inquiry in educational practice. *Educational Researcher, 30*(4), 3–14.

Glidden, H. (1999). *Breakthrough schools: What are the common characteristics of low income schools that perform as though they are high income schools?* Paper presented at the annual meeting of the American Educational Research Association, Montreal, Canada.

Glover, J., Ronning, R., & Bruning, R. (1990). *Cognitive psychology for teachers.* New York: Macmillan.

Goldberg, M. (2000). An interview with Carol Gilligan: Restoring lost voices. *Phi Delta Kappan, 81*(9), 701–704.

Gollnick, D., & Chinn, P. (1986). *Multicultural education in a pluralistic society* (2nd ed.). Upper Saddle River, NJ: Merrill/Prentice Hall.

Gollnick, D., & Chinn, P. (1994). *Multicultural education in a pluralistic society* (4th ed.). Upper Saddle River, NJ: Merrill/Prentice Hall.

Gollnick, D. M., & Chinn, P. C. (1998). *Multicultural education in a pluralistic society* (5th ed.). Upper Saddle River, NJ: Merrill/Prentice Hall.

Good, T. (1987a). Teacher expectations. In D. Berliner & B. Rosenshine (Eds.), *Talks to teachers* (pp. 159–200). New York: Random House.

Good, T. (1987b). Two decades of research on teacher expectations: Findings and future directions. *Journal of Teacher Education, 37*(4), 32–47.

Good, T., & Brophy, J. (1986). School effects. In M. Wittrock (Ed.), *Handbook of research on teaching* (3rd ed., pp. 570–604). New York: Macmillan.

Good, T., & Brophy, J. (2000). *Looking in classrooms* (8th ed.). New York: Longman.

Goodenow, C. (1992a, April). *School motivation, engagement, and sense of belonging among urban adolescent students.* Paper presented at the annual meeting of the American Educational Research Association, San Francisco.

Goodenow, C. (1992b). Strengthening the links between educational psychology and the study of social contexts. *Educational Psychologist, 27*(2), 177–196.

Goodenow, C. (1993). Classroom belonging among early adolescent students: Relationships to motivation and achievement. *Journal of Early Adolescence, 13,* 21–43.

Goodlad, J., Soder, R., & Sirotnik, K. (Eds.). (1990). *The moral dimension of teaching.* San Francisco: Jossey-Bass.

Goodman, S., Gravitt, G., & Kaslow, N. (1995). Social problem solving: A moderator of the relation between negative life stresses and depression symptoms in children. *Journal of Abnormal Child Psychology, 23,* 473–485.

Goodrich, H. (1996/97). Understanding rubrics. *Educational Leadership, 54*(4), 14–17.

Goodwin, W., & Goodwin, L. (1993). Young children's peer relationships: Forms, features, and functions. In B. Spodek (Ed.), *Handbook of research on the education of young children* (p. 28). New York: Macmillan.

Gordon, T. (1974). *Teacher effectiveness training.* New York: Wyden.

Gordon, T. (1981). Crippling our children with disruption. *Journal of Education, 163,* 228–243.

Gorman, J., & Balter, L. (1997). Culturally sensitive parent education: A critical review of quantitative research. *Review of Educational Research, 67,* 339–369.

Gottfried, A. (1985). Academic intrinsic motivation in elementary and junior high students. *Journal of Educational Psychology, 82,* 525–538.

Gottlieb, J., & Weinberg, S. (1999). Comparison of students referred and not referred for special education. *Elementary School Journal, 99*(3), 187–200.

Gould, R., & Clum, G. (1995). Self-help plus minimal therapist contact in the treatment of panic disorder: A replication and extension. *Behavior Therapy, 26,* 533–546.

Grabinger, R. (1996). Rich environments for active learning. In D. Jonassen

(Ed.), *Handbook of research for educational communications and technology* (pp. 665–692). New York: Macmillan.

Graham, S. (1984). Communicating sympathy and anger to Black and White children: The cognitive (attributional) consequences of affective cues. *Journal of Personality and Social Psychology, 47,* 14–28.

Graham, S. (1991). A review of attribution theory in achievement contexts. *Educational Psychology Review, 3*(1), 5–39.

Graham, S. (1994). Motivation in African Americans. *Review of Educational Research, 64*(1), 55–117.

Graham, S., & Barker, G. (1990). The downside of help: An attributional-developmental analysis of helping behavior as a low ability cue. *Journal of Educational Psychology, 82,* 7–14.

Graham, S., Berninger, V., Weintraub, N., & Schafer, W. (1998). Development of handwriting speed and legibility in grades 1–9. *Journal of Educational Research, 92*(1), 42–49.

Graham, S., & Weiner, B. (1996). Theories and principles of motivation. In D. Berliner & R. Calfee (Eds.), *Handbook of educational psychology* (pp. 63–84). New York: Macmillan.

Grant, L., & Rothenberg, J. (1986). The social enhancement of ability differences: Teacher-student interactions in first- and second-grade reading groups. *Elementary School Journal, 87,* 29–49.

Graves, S. (1993). Television, the portrayal of African Americans and the development of children's attitudes. In G. Berry & J. Asamen (Eds.), *Children and television: Images in a changing sociocultural world* (pp. 179–190). Newbury Park, CA: Sage.

Gredler, M. (2001). *Learning and instruction: Theory into practice* (4th ed.). Upper Saddle River, NJ: Merrill/Prentice Hall.

Green, C., & Reed, D. (1996). Defining, validating, and increasing indices of happiness among people with profound multiple disabilities. *Journal of Applied Behavior Analysis, 29,* 67–78.

Green, S., & Mantz, M. (2002, April). *Classroom assessment practices: Examining impact on student learning.* Paper presented at the annual meeting of the American

Educational Research Association, New Orleans, LA.

Greenberg, M. (1996). *The PATHS project.* Seattle: University of Washington.

Greene, R. (1992). *Human memory: Paradigms and paradoxes.* Mahwah, NJ: Erlbaum.

Greenfield, P. (1994). Independence and interdependence as developmental scripts: Implications for theory, research, and practice. In P. Greenfield & R. Cocking (Eds.), *Cross-cultural roots of minority child development.* Hillsdale, NJ: Erlbaum.

Greenleaf, C. (1995, March). *You feel like you belong: Student perspectives on becoming a community of learners.* Paper presented at the annual meeting of the American Educational Research Association, San Francisco.

Greeno, J. (1998). The situativity of knowing, learning, and research. *American Psychologist, 44,* 134–141.

Greeno, J., Collins, A., & Resnick, L. (1996). Cognition and learning. In D. Berliner & R. Calfee (Eds.), *Handbook of educational psychology* (pp. 15–46). New York: Macmillan.

Gregg, V., Gibbs, J., & Basinger, K. (1994). Patterns of developmental delay in moral judgment by male and female delinquents. *Merrill-Palmer Quarterly, 40,* 538–553.

Griffith, D. (1992, April). Prenatal exposure to cocaine and other drugs: Developmental and educational prognoses. *Phi Delta Kappan, 74,* 30–34.

Grolnick, W., Kurowski, C., & Gurland, S. (1999). Family processes and the development of children's self-regulation. *Educational Psychologist, 34*(1), 3–14.

Gronlund, N. (1993). *How to make achievement tests and assessments.* Needham Heights, MA: Allyn & Bacon.

Gronlund, N. (2000). *How to write and use instructional objectives* (6th ed.). Upper Saddle River, NJ: Merrill/Prentice Hall.

Grotevant, H. D. (1998). Adolescent development in family contexts. In N. Eisenberg (Ed.), *Handbook of child psychology: Vol. 3. Social, emotional, and personality development* (5th ed., pp. 1097–1149). New York: Wiley.

Gschwend, L., & Dembo, M. (2001, April). *How do high-efficacy teachers persist in low-achieving, culturally diverse schools?* Paper presented at the

annual meeting of the American Educational Research Association, Seattle.

Guillaume, A., & Rudney, G. (1997, March). *Stories of struggles and success: Implementing portfolio assessment across the disciplines.* Paper presented at the annual meeting of the National Educational Research Association, Chicago.

Guskey, T. (1994). Making the grade: What benefits students? *Educational Leadership, 52*(2), 14–20.

Guskey, T. (2002, April). *Perspectives on grading and reporting: Differences among teachers, students, and parents.* Paper presented at the annual meeting of the American Educational Research Association, New Orleans, LA.

Guthrie, E. (1952). *The psychology of learning* (Rev. ed.). Gloucester, MA: Smith.

Hacker, D., Bol, L., Horgan, D., & Rakow, E. (2000). Test prediction and performance in a classroom context. *Journal of Education Psychology, 92,* 160–170.

Hacker, D., Dunlosky, J., & Graesser, A. (Eds.). (1998). *Metacognition in educational theory and practice.* Mahwah, NJ: Erlbaum.

Haertel, E. (1986, April). *Choosing and using classroom tests: Teachers' perspectives on assessment.* Paper presented at the annual meeting of the American Educational Research Association, San Francisco.

Haertel, E. (1999). Performance assessment and education reform. *Phi Delta Kappan, 80*(9), 662–666.

Hafner, A. (2001, April). *Evaluating the impact of test accommodations on test scores of LEP students and non-LEP students.* Paper presented at the annual meeting of the American Educational Research Association, Seattle.

Haladyna, T. (1999). *A complete guide to student grading.* Boston: Allyn & Bacon.

Haladyna, T., & Ryan, J. (2001, April). *The influence of rater severity on whether a student passes or fails a performance assessment.* Paper presented at the annual meeting of the American Educational Research Association, Seattle.

Hale, E. (1998, February 14). Cyber gap costs women at work. *Salt Lake City Tribune,* pp. A1, A4.

Hall, R., Hall, M., & Saling, C. (1999). The effects of graphical postorganization strategies on learning from knowledge maps. *Journal of Experimental Education, 67,* 101–112.

Hallahan, D., Hall, R., Ianno, S., Kneedler, R., Lloyd, J., Loper, A., & Reeve, R. (1983). Summary of research findings at the University of Virginia Learning Disabilities Research Institute. *Exceptional Education Quarterly, 4*(1), 95–114.

Hallahan, D., & Kauffman, J. (2003). *Exceptional children* (8th ed.). Needham Heights, MA: Allyn & Bacon.

Hallahan, D., & Sapona, R. (1983). Self-monitoring of attention with learning-disabled children: Past research and current issues. *Journal of Learning Disabilities, 16,* 616–620.

Hallden, O. (1998). Personalization in historical descriptions and explanations. *Learning and Instruction, 8*(2), 131–139.

Halle, T., Kurtz-Costes, B., & Mahoney, J. (1997). Family influences on school achievement in low-income, African American children. *Journal of Educational Psychology, 89*(3), 527–537.

Hallinan, M. (1984). Summary and implications. In P. Peterson, L. Wilkinson, & M. Hallinan (Eds.), *The social context of instruction: Group organization and group processes* (pp. 229–240). San Diego, CA: Academic Press.

Halpern, D. (1995). *Thought and knowledge: An introduction to critical thinking* (3rd ed.). Hillsdale, NJ: Erlbaum.

Halpern, D. (1998). Teaching critical thinking for transfer across domains. *American Psychologist, 53,* 449–455.

Halpern, D., & LaMay, M. (2000). The smarter sex: A critical review of sex differences in intelligence. *Educationl Psychology Review, 12*(2), 229–245.

Hamachek, D. (1987). Humanistic psychology: Theory, postulates, and implications for educational processes. In J. Glover & R. Ronning (Eds.), *Historical foundations of educational psychology* (pp. 159–182). New York: Plenum Press.

Hamilton, R. (1997). Effects of three types of elaboration on learning concepts from text. *Contemporary Education Psychology, 22,* 299–318.

Hamm, J., & Coleman, H. (1997, March). *Adolescent strategies for coping with cultural diversity: Variability and youth outcomes.* Paper presented at the annual meeting of the American Educational Research Association, Chicago.

Hamp-Lyons, L. (1992). Holistic writing assessment for L.E.P. students. In *Focus on evaluation and measurement* (Vol. 2, pp. 317–358). Washington, DC: U.S. Department of Education.

Hampton, J. (1995). Testing the prototype theory of concepts. *Journal of Memory and Language, 32,* 686–708.

Hanich, L., Jordan, N., Kaplan, D., & Dick, J. (2001). Performance across different areas of mathematical cognition in children with learning difficulties. *Journal of Educational Psychology, 93*(3), 615–626.

Hansen, D. (2001). Teaching as a moral activity. In V. Richardson (Ed.), *Handbook of research on learning* (4th ed., pp. 826–857). Washington, DC: American Educational Research Association.

Hanson, M., Hayes, J., Schriver, K., LeMahieu, P., & Brown, P. (1998). *A plain language approach to the revision of test items.* Paper presented at the annual meeting of the American Educational Research Association, San Diego, CA.

Harackiewicz, J., Barron, K., Taurer, J., Carter, S., & Elliot, A. (2000). Short-term and long-term consequences of achievement goals: Predicting interest and performance over time. *Journal of Educational Psychology, 92,* 316–330.

Hardiman, P., Pollatsek, A., & Weil, A. (1986). Learning to understand the balance beam. *Cognition and Instruction, 3,* 1–30.

Hardman, M., Drew, C., & Egan, W. (2002). *Human exceptionality* (7th ed.). Needham Heights, MA: Allyn & Bacon.

Harp, S., & Mayer, R. (1998). How seductive details do their damage: A theory of cognitive interest in science learning. *Journal of Educational Psychology, 90,* 414–434.

Harrington-Lueker, D. (1997). Technology works best when it serves clear educational goals. *Harvard Education Letter, 13,* 1–5.

Harris, K., & Graham, S. (1996). Memo to constructivists: Skills count too. *Educational Leadership, 53,* 26–29.

Harris, L., Kagay, M., & Ross, J. (1987). *The Metropolitan Life Survey of the American Teacher: Strengthening links between home and school.* New York: Louis Harris & Associates.

Harrow, A. (1972). *A taxonomy of the psychomotor domain: A guide for developing behavioral objectives.* New York: McKay.

Harry, B. (1992). An ethnographic study of cross-cultural communication with Puerto Rican American families in the special education system. *American Educational Research Journal, 29*(3), 471–488.

Harter, S. (1978). Effectance motivation reconsidered: Toward a developmental model. *Human Development, 21,* 34–64.

Harter, S. (1998). The development of self-representations. In N. Eisenberg (Ed.), *Handbook of child psychology: Vol. 3. Social, emotional, and personality development* (5th ed., pp. 553–618). New York: Wiley.

Harter, S., & Jackson, B. (1992). Trait versus nontrait conceptualizations of intrinsic/extrinsic motivational orientation. Special issue: Perspectives on intrinsic motivation. *Motivation and Emotion, 16,* 209–230.

Hartnett, P. & Gelman, R. (1998). Early understandings of numbers: Paths or barriers to the construction of new understandings. *Learning and Instruction, 8*(4), 341–374.

Harwood, R., Miller, J., & Irizarry, N. (1995). *Culture and attachment: Perceptions of the child in context.* New York: Guilford Press.

Hay, I., Ashman, A., van Kraayenoord, C., & Stewart, A. (1999). Identification of self-verification in the formation of children's academic self-concept. *Journal of Educational Psychology, 91*(2), 225–229.

Haycock, K. (2001). Closing the achievement gap. *Educational Leadership, 58*(6), 6–11.

Hayes, J. (1988). *The complete problem solver* (2nd ed.). Hillsdale, NJ: Erlbaum.

Hayes, K., & Salazar, J. (2001, April). *Evaluation of the Structured English Immersion Program, final report: Year 1.* Paper presented at the annual meeting of the American Educational Research Association, Seattle.

Hayes, S., Rosenfarb, I., Wulfert, E., Munt, E., Korn, Z., & Zettle, R. (1985). Self-reinforcement effects: An artifact of social standard setting? *Journal of Applied Behavior Analysis, 18,* 201–214.

Haynes, N., & Comer, J. (1995, March). *The School Development Program (SDP): Lessons from the past.* Paper presented at the annual meeting of the American Educational Research Association, San Francisco.

Healy, A., Clawson, D., McNamara, D., Marmie, W., Schneider, V., Rickard, T., Crutcher, R., King, C., Ericsson, K., & Bourne, L. (1993). The long-term retention of knowledge and skills. In D. Medin (Ed.), *The psychology of learning and motivation: Advances in research and theory* (Vol. 30, pp. 135–164). New York: Academic Press.

Heath, S. (1982). Questioning at home and at school: A comparative study. In G. Spindler (Ed.), *Doing the ethnography of schooling.* New York: Holt, Rinehart & Winston.

Heath, S. (1989). Oral and literate traditions among Black Americans living in poverty. *American Psychologist, 44,* 367–373.

Helms, J. (1992). Why is there no study of cultural equivalence in standardized cognitive ability testing? *American Psychologist, 47*(9), 1083–1101.

Henson, K. (1988). *Methods and strategies for teaching in secondary and middle schools.* White Plains, NY: Longman.

Hergenhahn, B., & Olson, M. (2001). An introduction to theories of learning (6th ed.). Upper Saddle River, NJ: Prentice Hall.

Herman, J., Aschbacher, P., & Winters, L. (1992). *A practical guide to alternative assessment.* Alexandria, VA: Association for Supervision and Curriculum Development.

Herman, J., & Winters, L. (1994). Portfolio research: A slim collection. *Educational Leadership, 52,* 48–55.

Hernandez, H. (1997). *Teaching in multilingual classrooms.* Upper Saddle River, NJ: Merrill/Prentice Hall.

Herrnstein, R., & Murray, C. (1994). *The bell curve.* New York: Free Press.

Hess, R., & McDevitt, T. (1984). Some cognitive consequences of maternal intervention techniques: A longitudinal study. *Child Development, 55,* 2017–2020.

Heubert, J., & Hauser, R. (Eds.). (1999). *High stakes testing for tracking, promotion, and graduation.* Washington, DC: National Academy Press.

Heward, W. (1996). *Exceptional children* (5th ed.). Upper Saddle River, NJ: Merrill/Prentice Hall.

Heward, W. (2003). *Exceptional children* (6th ed.). Upper Saddle River, NJ: Merrill/Prentice Hall.

Hidi, S. (2001). Interest, reading, and learning: Theoretical and practical considerations. *Educational Psychology Review, 13,* 191–209.

Hidi, S., & Harackiewicz, J. (2000). Motivating the academically unmotivated: A critical issue for the 21st century. *Review of Educational Research, 70*(2), 151–179.

Hiebert, E., & Raphael, T. (1996). Psychological perspectives on literacy and extensions to educational practice. In D. Berliner & R. Calfee (Eds.), *Handbook of educational psychology* (pp. 550–602). New York: Macmillan.

Hiebert, J., Gallimore, R., & Stigler, J. (2002). A knowledge base for the teaching profession: What would it look like and how can we get one? *Educational Researcher, 31*(5), 3–15.

Higgins, K. (1997). The effect of year-long instruction in mathematical problem-solving on middle-school students' attitudes, beliefs, and abilities. *Journal of Experimental Education, 66,* 5–28.

Hill, K., & Wigfield, A. (1984). Test anxiety: A major educational problem and what can be done about it. *Elementary School Journal, 85,* 105–126.

Hillocks, G. (1984). What works in teaching composition: A meta-analysis of experimental treatment studies. *American Journal of Education, 93,* 133–170.

Hirsch, E. (2000). The tests we need and why we don't quite have them. *Education Week, 19*(21), 40–41.

Hodgkinson, H. (2000/2001). Educational demographics: What teachers should know. *Educational Leadership, 58*(4), 6–11.

Hoff, D. (2001). Missing pieces. *Education Week, 20*(17), 43–52.

Hoffman, J., Assaf, L., & Paris, S. (2001). High-stakes testing in reading: Today in Texas, tomorrow? *Reading Teacher, 54*(5), 482–491.

Holliday, D. (2002, April). *Using cooperative learning to improve the academic achievements of inner-city middle school students.* Paper presented at the annual meeting of the American Educational Research Association, New Orleans, LA.

Hollie, S. (2001, April). *Acknowledging the language of African American students: Instructional strategies.* Paper presented at the annual meeting of the American Educational Research Association, Seattle.

Holloway, J. (2000). The digital divide. *Educational Leadership, 58*(2), 90–91.

Holloway, J. (2001). Inclusion and students with learning disabilities. *Educational Leadership, 58*(6), 86–88.

Holstein, C. (1976). Irreversible, stepwise sequence in the development of moral judgment: A longitudinal study of males and females. *Child Development, 47,* 51–61.

Holt, J. (1964). *How children fail.* New York: Putnam.

Homes for the Homeless. (1999). Information retrieved from http://www.opendoor.com/hfh

Hong, E. (1999, April). *Effects of gender, math ability, trait test anxiety, statistics course anxiety, statistics achievement, and perceived test difficulty on state test anxiety.* Paper presented at the annual meeting of American Educational Research Association, Montreal, Canada.

Hong, N., & Jonassen, D. (1999, April). *Well-structured and ill-structured problem-solving in multimedia simulation.* Paper presented at the annual meeting of the American Educational Research Association, Montreal, Canada.

Hood, D. (1999). *Racial identity attitudes and female African-American students' academic achievement, campus involvement, and academic satisfaction.* Paper presented at the annual meeting of the American Educational Research Association, Montreal, Canada.

Hootstein, E. (1999, April). *Implications of using portfolios with preservice social studies teachers.* Paper presented at the annual meeting of the American Educational Research Association, Montreal, Canada.

Hornberger, N. (1989). Continua of biliteracy. *Review of Educational Research, 59,* 271–296.

Hosford, R. (1981). Self-as-a-model: A cognitive social learning technique. *The Counseling Psychologist, 9,* 45–62.

Howe, K., & Berv, J. (2000). Constructing constructivism, epistemological and pedagogical. In D. Phillips (Ed.), *Constructivism in education: Opinions and second opinions on controversial issues* (pp. 19–40). Chicago: National Society for the Study of Education.

Huba, M., & Freed, J. (2000). *Learner-centered assessment on college campuses.* Boston: Allyn & Bacon.

Hudley, C. (1992, April). *The reduction of peer-directed aggression among highly aggressive African American boys.* Paper presented at the annual meeting of the American Educational Research Association, San Francisco.

Hudley, C. (1998). *Urban minority adolescents' perceptions of classroom climate.* Paper presented at the annual meeting of the American Educational Research Association, San Diego, CA.

Huefner, D. (1999). *Selected changes in IDEA regulations compared to the proposed regulations.* Paper presented at the annual meeting of the American Educational Research Association, Montreal, Canada.

Huffman, D. (2001, April). *Using computers to create constructivist learning environments: The relationship between instruction and achievement in science.* Paper presented at the annual meeting of the American Educational Research Association, Seattle.

Hunsaker, S., Finley, V., & Frank, E. (1997). An analysis of teacher nominations and student performance in gifted programs. *Gifted Child Quarterly, 4*(2), 19–24.

Hunt, R., & Ellis, H. (1999). *Fundamentals of cognitive psychology* (6th ed.). New York: McGraw-Hill.

Hunter, L. (2002). *Internet use in constructivist classrooms.* Doctoral dissertation, University of Utah, Salt Lake City.

Huston, A., Watkins, B., & Kunkel, K. (1989). Public policy and children's television. *American Psychologist, 44,* 424–433.

Hvitfeldt, C. (1986). Traditional culture, perceptual style, and learning: The classroom behavior of Hmong adults. *Adult Education Quarterly, 36(2),* 65–77.

Institute for Families in Society. (1997). *Program to combat bullying in schools.* Columbia: University of South Carolina.

Isabella, R., & Belsky, J. (1991). Interactional synchrony and the origins of infant-mother attachment: A replication study. *Child Development, 62,* 373–384.

Jackson, L. (1999). *"Doing" school: Examining the role of ethnic identity and school engagement in academic performance and goal attainment.* Paper presented at the annual meeting of the American Educational Research Association, Montreal, Canada.

Jackson, P. (1968). *Life in classrooms.* New York: Holt, Rinehart & Winston.

Jacoby, R., & Glauberman, N. (Eds.). (1995). *The bell curve debate: History, documents, opinions.* New York: Random House.

Jehng, J. (1997). The psycho-social processes and cognitive effects of peer-based collaborative interactions with computers. *Journal of Educational Computing Research, 17*(1), 19–46.

Jensen, A. (1987). Individual differences in mental ability. In J. Glover & R. Ronning (Eds.), *Historical foundations of educational psychology.* New York: Plenum Press.

Jensen, A. (1998). *The g factor: The science of mental ability.* Westport, CT: Prager/Greenwood.

Jenson, W., Sloane, H., & Young, K. (1988). *Applied behavior analysis in education.* Upper Saddle River, NJ: Prentice Hall.

Jerald, C. D. (2000). The state of the states. *Quality Counts 2000, Education Week.* Retrieved October 1, 2002, from http://www.edweek.org/sreports/qc00

Jerry, L., & Ballator, N. (1999). *The National Assessment of Educational Progress (NAEP) 1998 writing state reports* (Publication No. NCES 1999463). Washington, DC: National Center for Educational Statistics.

Jesse, D., & Pokorny, N. (2001, April). *Understanding high achieving middle schools for Latino students in poverty.* Paper presented at the annual meeting of the American Educational Research Association, Seattle.

Jetton, T., & Alexander, P. (1997). Instruction importance: What teachers value and what students learn. *Reading Research Quarterly, 32,* 290–308.

Jew, C., Green, K., Millard, J., & Posillico, M. (1999, April). *Resiliency: An examination of related factors in a sample of students from a urban high school and a residential child care facility.* Paper presented at the annual meeting of the American Educational Research Association, Montreal, Canada.

Johnson, B., & Christensen, L. (2000). *Educational research: Quantitative and qualitative approaches.* Boston: Allyn & Bacon.

Johnson, D., & Johnson, R. (1994). *Learning together and alone: Cooperation, competition, and individualization* (4th ed.). Needham Heights, MA: Allyn & Bacon.

Johnson, D., & Johnson, R. (1995). *Teaching students to be peacemakers.* Edina, MN: Interaction Book.

Johnson, D., & Johnson, R. (1996). Cooperation and the use of technology. In D. Jonassen (Ed.), *Handbook of research for educational communications and technology* (pp. 1017–1042). New York: Macmillan.

Johnson, D., & Johnson, R. (1999). The 3 C's of school and classroom management. In R. Freiberg (Ed.), *Beyond behaviorism* (pp. 119–145). Boston: Allyn & Bacon.

Johnston, R. (2000). In a Texas district, test scores for minority students have soared. *Education Week, 19*(30), 14–15.

Jonassen, D., Hannum, W., & Tessmer, M. (1989). *Handbook of task analysis procedures.* New York: Praeger.

Jones, E. (1995, April). *Defining essential critical thinking skills for college students.* Paper presented at the annual meeting of the American Educational Research Association, San Francisco.

Jones, L. (1996). A history of the national assessment of educational progress and some questions about its future. *Educational Researcher, 25*(7), 15–20.

Jones, M. (1999). *Identity as strategy: Rethinking how African American students negotiate desegregated schooling.* Paper presented at the annual meeting of the American Educational Research Association, Montreal, Canada.

Jones, V., & Jones, L. (2001). *Comprehensive classroom management* (6th ed.). Boston: Allyn & Bacon.

Jordan, W. (2001). Black high school students' participation in school-sponsored sports activities: Effects on school engagement and achievement. *Journal of Negro Education, 68*(1), 54–71.

Josselson, R. (1988). The embedded self: I and thou revisited. In D. Lapsley & F. Power (Eds.), *Self, ego, and identity: Integrative approaches* (pp. 91–106). New York: Springer-Verlag.

Jovanovic, J., & King, S. (1998). Boys and girls in the performance-based science classroom: Who's doing the performing? *American Educational Research Journal, 35*(3), 477–496.

Kagan, D. (1992). Implications of research on teacher beliefs. *Educational Psychologist, 27,* 65–90.

Kahn, E. (2000). A case study of assessment in a grade 10 English course. *Journal of Educational Research, 93*(5), 276–286.

Kail, R. (1998). *Children and their development*. Upper Saddle River, NJ: Prentice Hall.

Kalyuga, S., Chandler, P., Tuovinen, J., & Sweller, J. (2001). When problem solving is superior to studying worked examples. *Journal of Educational Psychology, 93*(3), 579–588.

Kaplan, D., Liu, X., & Kaplan, H. (2001). Influence of parents' self-feelings and expectations on children's academic performance. *Journal of Educational Research, 94*(6), 360–365.

Kaplan, R., & Saccuzzo, D. (1993). *Psychological testing* (3rd ed.). Pacific Grove, CA: Brooks/Cole.

Karplus, R., Karplus, E., Formisano, M., & Paulsen, A. (1979). Proportional reasoning and control of variables in seven countries. In J. Lockheed & M. Clements (Eds.), *Cognitive process instruction: Research on teaching thinking skills*. Philadelphia: Franklin Institute Press.

Karweit, N. (1989). Time and learning: A review. In R. Slavin (Ed.), *School and classroom organization*. Hillsdale, NJ: Erlbaum.

Katz, A. (1999, April). *Keepin' it real: Personalizing school experiences for diverse learners to create harmoney intead of conflict*. Paper presented at the annual meeting of the American Educational Research Association, Montreal, Canada.

Kauchak, D., & Eggen, P. (2003). *Learning and teaching: Research-based methods* (4th ed.). Needham Heights, MA: Allyn & Bacon.

Kaufman, P., Chen, X., Choy, S., Chandler, K., Chapman, C., Rand, M., & Ringel, C. (1999). Indicators of school crime and safety, 1998. *Educational Statistics Quarterly, 1*(1), 42–45.

Keefer, M., Zeitz, C., & Resnick, L. (2000). Judging the quality of peer-led student dialogues. *Cognition and Instruction, 18*(1), 53–81.

Kellenberger, D. (1996). Preservice teachers' perceived computer self-efficacy based on achievement and value beliefs within a motivational framework. *Journal of Research on Computing in Education, 29*(2), 124–135.

Kent, M., Pollard, K., Haaga, J., & Mather, M. (2001). *First glimpse from the 2000 U.S. Census*. Retrieved October 1, 2002, from http://www.prb.org/AmeriStatTemplate.cfm

Kerbow, D. (1996). Patterns of urban student mobility and local school reform. *Journal of Education for Students Placed at Risk, 1*(2), 147–169.

Kerman, S. (1979). Teacher expectations and student achievement. *Phi Delta Kappan, 60,* 70–72.

Kerr, M. (2000). Bullying: The hidden threat to a safe school. *Utah Special Educator, 21*(3), 9–10.

Kika, F., McLaughlin, T., & Dixon, J. (1992). Effects of frequent testing of secondary algebra students. *Journal of Educational Research, 85,* 159–162.

Kim, D., Solomon, D., & Roberts, W. (1995, March). *Classroom practices that enhance students' sense of community*. Paper presented at the annual meeting of the American Educational Research Association, San Francisco.

King, A. (1994). Guiding knowledge construction in the classroom: Effects of teaching children how to question and how to explain. *American Educational Research Journal, 31,* 338–368.

King, A. (1999). Teaching effective discourse patterns for small-group learning. In R. Stevens (Ed.), *Teaching in American schools* (pp. 121–139). Upper Saddle River, NJ: Merrill/Prentice Hall.

King-Sears, M. (1997). Disability: Legalities and labels. In D. Bradley, M. King-Sears, & D. Tessier-Switlick (Eds.), *Inclusive settings: From theory to practice* (pp. 21–55). Boston: Allyn & Bacon.

Kitsantas, A., Zimmerman, B., & Cleary, T. (2000). The role of observation and emulation in the development of athletic self-regulation. *Journal of Educational Psychology, 92*(4), 811–817.

Klausmeier, H. (1992). Concept learning and concept thinking. *Educational Psychologist, 27,* 267–286.

Kloosterman, P. (1997, March). *Assessing student motivation in high school mathematics*. Paper presented at the annual meeting of the American Educational Research Association, Chicago.

Knapp, M. (1995). *Teaching for meaning in high-poverty classrooms*. New York: Teachers College Press.

Knight, C., Halpen, G., & Halpen, G. (1992, April). *The effects of learning environment accommodations on the achievement of second graders*. Paper presented at the annual meeting of the American Educational Research Association, San Francisco.

Koestner, R., Ryan, R., Bernieri, F., & Holt, K. (1984). Setting limits on children's behavior: The differential effects of controlling vs. informational styles on intrinsic motivation and creativity. *Journal of Personality, 52,* 233–248.

Kohlberg, L. (1963). The development of children's orientation toward moral order: Sequence in the development of human thought. *Vita Humana, 6,* 11–33.

Kohlberg, L. (1969). Stage and sequence: The cognitive-developmental approach to socialization. In D. Goslin (Ed.), *Handbook of socialization theory and research*. Chicago: Rand McNally.

Kohlberg, L. (1975). The cognitive development approach to moral education. *Phi Delta Kappan, 56,* 670–677.

Kohlberg, L. (1981). *Philosophy of moral development*. New York: Harper & Row.

Kohlberg, L. (1984). *Essays on moral development: Vol. 2. The psychology of moral development*. New York: Harper & Row.

Kohn, A. (1992). *No contest: The case against competition*. Boston: Houghton Mifflin.

Kohn, A. (1993). Why incentive plans cannot work. *Harvard Business Review, 71,* 54–63.

Kohn, A. (1996a). *Beyond discipline: From compliance to community*. Alexandria, VA: Association for Supervision and Curriculum Development.

Kohn, A. (1996b). By all available means: Cameron and Pierce's defense of extrinsic motivators. *Review of Educational Research, 66,* 1–4.

Kohn, A. (1997). How not to teach values. *Phi Delta Kappan, 78*(6), 429–439.

Kohn, A. (1998). Adventures in ethics versus behavior control: A reply to my critics. *Phi Delta Kappan, 79*(6), 455–460.

Kohn, A. (2000). Burnt at the high stakes. *Journal of Teacher Education, 51*(4), 315–327.

Konstantopoulos, S. (1997, March). *Hispanic-White differences in central tendency and proportions of high- and low-scoring individuals*. Paper presented at the annual meeting of the American Educational Research Association, Chicago.

Koretz, D., & Hamilton, L. (2000). Assessment of students with disabilities in Kentucky: Inclusion, student performance, and validity. *Educational Evaluation and Policy Analysis, 22*(3), 255–272.

Koretz, D., Stecher, B., & Diebert, E. (1993). *The reliability of scores from the 1992 Vermont Portfolio Assessment Program* (Tech. Rep. No. 355). Los Angeles: UCLA, Center for the Study of Evaluation.

Korf, R. (1999). Heuristic search. In R. Wilson & F. Keil (Eds.), *The MIT encyclopedia of the cognitive sciences* (pp. 372–373). Cambridge, MA: MIT Press.

Kounin, J. (1970). *Discipline and group management in classrooms.* New York: Holt, Rinehart & Winston.

Kovalik, C. (2002, April). *The value of classroom pretests and posttests to inform instruction.* Paper presented at the annual meeting of the American Educational Research Association, New Orleans, LA.

Kozhevnikov, M., Hegarty, M., & Mayer, R. (1999, April). *Students' use of imagery in solving qualitative problems in kinematics.* Paper presented at the annual meeting of the American Educational Research Association, Montreal, Canada.

Kozulin, A. (1990). *Vygotsky's psychology: A biography of ideas.* Cambridge, MA: Harvard University Press.

Krajcik, J., Blumenfeld, P., Marx, R., & Soloway, E. (1994). A collaborative model for helping middle grade science teachers learn project-based instruction. *Elementary School Journal, 94*(5), 483–497.

Kramer, L., & Colvin, C. (1991, April). *Rules, responsibilities, and respect: The school lives of marginal students.* Paper presented at the annual meeting of the American Educational Research Association, Chicago.

Kramer-Schlosser, L. (1992). Teacher distance and student disengagement: School lives on the margin. *Journal of Teacher Education, 43*(2), 128–140.

Krapp, A., Hidi, S., & Renninger, K. (1992). Interest, learning, and development. In K. Renninger, S. Hidi, & A. Krapp (Eds.), *The role of interest in learning and development* (pp. 3–26). Hillsdale, NJ: Erlbaum.

Krashen, S. (1996). *Under attack: The case against bilingual education.* Culver City, CA: Language Education Associates.

Krathwohl, D., Bloom, B., & Masia, B. (1964). *Taxonomy of educational objectives: The classification of educational goals: Handbook 2. Affective domain.* New York: McKay.

Krechevsky, M., & Seidel, S. (1998). Minds at work: Applying multiple intelligences in the classroom. In R. Sternberg & W. Williams (Eds.), *Intelligence, instruction, and assessment* (pp. 17–42). Mahwah, NJ: Erlbaum.

Kreutzer, M., Leonard, C., & Flavell, J. (1975). An interview study of children's knowledge about memory. *Monographs of the Society for Research in Child Development, 40*(1, Serial No. 15).

Kroger, J. (1993). Ego identity: An overview. In J. Kroger (Ed.), *Discussions on ego identity.* Hillsdale, NJ: Erlbaum.

Kroger, J. (1995). The differentiation of "firm" and "developmental" foreclosure identity statuses: A longitudinal study. *Journal of Adolescent Research, 10,* 317–337.

Kruger, A. (1992). The effect of peer and adult-child transactive discussions on moral reasoning. *Merrill-Palmer Quarterly, 38*(2), 191–211.

Kuh, D., & Vesper, N. (1999, April). *Do computers enhance or detract from student learning?* Paper presented at the annual meeting of the American Educational Research Association, Montreal, Canada.

Kuhn, D. (1999). A developmental model of critical thinking. *Educational Researcher, 28*(2), 16–26, 46.

Kulik, C., & Kulik, J. (1982). Effects of ability grouping on secondary school students: A meta-analysis of evaluation findings. *American Educational Research Journal, 19,* 415–428.

Kuther, T., & Higgins-D'Alessandra, M. (1997, March). *Effects of a just community on moral development and adolescent engagement in risk.* Paper presented at the annual meeting of the American Educational Research Association, Chicago.

Labov, W. (1972). *Language in the inner city: Studies in the "Black" English vernacular.* Philadelphia: University of Pennsylvania Press.

Ladd, G., & Coleman, C. (1993). Young children's peer relationships: Forms, features, and functions. In B. Spodek (Ed.), *Handbook of research on the education of young children* (pp. 57–76). New York: Macmillan.

Lambating, J., & Allen, J. (2002, New Orleans). *How the multiple functions of grades influence their validity and value as measures of academic achievement.* Paper presented at the annual meeting of the American Educational Research Association, New Orleans, LA.

Lambert, N., & McCombs, B. (1998). Introduction: Learner-centered schools and classrooms as a direction for school reform. In N. Lambert & B. McCombs (Eds.), *How students learn: Reforming schools through learner-centered education* (pp. 1–22). Washington, DC: American Psychological Association.

Lambert, N., Nihera, K., & Leland, H. (1993). *AAMR Adaptive Behavior Scale—School: Examiner's manual* (2nd ed.). Austin, TX: Pro-Ed.

Lambros, K., Ward, S., Bocian, K., MacMillan, D., & Gresham, F. (1998). Behavioral profiles of children at risk for emotional and behavioral disorders: Implications for assessment and classification. *Focus on Exceptional Children, 30*(5), 1–16.

Lan, W., Repman, J., & Chyung, S. (1998). Effects of practicing self-monitoring of mathematical problem-solving heuristics on impulsive and reflective college students' heuristics knowledge and problem-solving ability. *Journal of Experimental Education, 67*(1), 32–52.

Land, R. (1997). Moving up to complex assessment systems: Proceedings from the 1996 CRESST Conference. *Evaluation Comment, 7*(1), 1–21.

Larrivee, B., Semmel, M., & Gerber, M. (1997). Case studies of six schools varying in effectiveness for students with learning disabilities. *Elementary School Journal, 98*(1), 27–50.

Laupa, M., & Turiel, E. (1995). Social domain theory. In W. Kurtines & J. Gewirtz (Eds.), *Moral development: An introduction.* Boston: Allyn & Bacon.

Lawson, A. (1995). *Science teaching and the development of thinking.* Belmont, CA: Wadsworth.

Lawson, A., & Childs, R. (2001, April). *Making sense of large-scale assessments: Communicating with teachers.* Paper presented at the annual meeting of the American Educational Research Association, Seattle.

Lawson, A., & Snitgren, D. (1982). Teaching formal reasoning in a college biology course for preservice teachers. *Journal of Research in Science Teaching, 19,* 233–248.

Leahey, T., & Harris, R. (1997). *Learning and cognition* (4th ed.). Upper Saddle River, NJ: Prentice Hall.

Leander, K., & Brown, D. (1999). "You understand, but you don't believe it": Tracing the stabilities and instabilities of interaction in a physics classroom through a multidimensional framework. *Cognition and Instruction, 17*(1), 93–135.

Lee, A. (1998). Transfer as a measure of intellectual functioning. In S. Soraci & W. McIlvane (Eds.), *Perspectives on fundamental processes in intellectual functioning: A survey of research approaches* (Vol. 1, pp. 351–366). Stamford, CT: Ablex.

Lee, A., & Pennington, N. (1993). Learning computer programming: A route to general reasoning skills? In C. Cook, J. Scholtz, & J. Spohrer (Eds.), *Empirical studies of programmers: Fifth workshop* (pp. 113–136). Norwood, NJ: Ablex.

Lee, J., Pulvino, C., & Perrone, P. (1998). *Restoring harmony: A guide for managing conflicts in schools.* Upper Saddle River, NJ: Merrill/Prentice Hall.

Lee, V. (2000). Using hierarchical linear modeling to study social contexts: The case of school effects. *Educational Psychologist, 35,* 125–141.

Lehman, S., Kauffman, D., White, M., Horn, C., & Bruning, R. (1999, April). *Teacher interaction: Motivating at-risk students in Web-based high school courses.* Paper presented at the annual meeting of the American Educational Research Association, Montreal, Canada.

Leinhardt, G., & Greeno, J. (1986). The cognitive skill of teaching. *Journal of Educational Psychology, 78,* 75–95.

Lemke, J. (1982, April). *Classroom communication of science* (Final report to NSF/RISE). Washington, DC: National Science Foundation. (ERIC Document Reproduction Service No. ED222346)

Leon, M., Lynn, T., McLean, P., & Perri, L. (1997, March). *Age and gender trends in adults' normative moral reasoning.* Paper presented at the annual meeting of the American Educational Research Association, Chicago.

Leont'ev, A. (1981). The problem of activity in psychology. In J. Wertsch (Ed.), *The concept of activity in Soviet psychology* (pp. 37–71). Armonk, NY: Sharpe.

Lepper, M., & Hodell, M. (1989). Intrinsic motivation in the classroom. In C. Ames & R. Ames (Eds.), *Research on motivation in education* (Vol. 3, pp. 73–105). San Diego, CA: Academic Press.

Levin, H. (1988, March). *Structuring schools for greater effectiveness with educationally disadvantaged or at-risk students.* Paper presented at the annual meeting of the American Educational Research Association, San Francisco.

Levine, A., & Nediffer, J. (1996). *Beating the odds: How the poor get to college.* San Francisco: Jossey-Bass.

Lewis, R., & Doorlag, D. (1999). *Teaching special students in general education classrooms.* Upper Saddle River, NJ: Merrill/Prentice Hall.

Lickona, T. (1998). A more complex analysis is needed. *Phi Delta Kappan, 79*(6), 449–454.

Liebert, R. (1986). Effects of television on children and adolescents. *Developmental and Behavioral Pediatrics, 7,* 43–48.

Lightfoot, C. (1999). *The development of language: Acquisition, change, and evolution.* Malden, MA: Blackwell.

Limber, S., Flerx, V., Nation, M., & Melton, G. (1998). Bullying among school children in the United States. In M. Watts (Ed.), *Cross-cultural perspectives on youth and violence.* Stamford, CT: JAI Press.

Lindeman, B. (2001). Reaching out to immigrant parents. *Educational Leadership, 58*(6), 62–66.

Linn, R. (2000). Assessments and accountability. *Educational Researcher, 29*(2), 4–16.

Linn, R., & Gronlund, N. (2000). *Measurement and assessment in teaching* (8th ed.). Upper Saddle River, NJ: Merrill/Prentice Hall.

Locke, E., & Latham, G. (1990). *A theory of goal setting and performance.* Upper Saddle River, NJ: Prentice Hall.

Lohman, D. (2001, April). *Fluid intelligence, inductive reasoning, and working memory: Where the theory of multiple intelligences falls short.* Paper presented at the annual meeting of the American Educational Research Association, Seattle.

Lohman, M., & Finkelstein, M. (2000). Designing groups in problem-based learning to promote problem-solving skill and self-directedness. *Instructional Science, 28,* 291–307.

Lomax, R. (1994, April). On *becoming assessment literate. Preservice teachers' beliefs and practices.* Paper presented at the annual meeting of the American Educational Research Association, New Orleans, LA.

Lomax, R. (1996). On becoming assessment literate: An initial look at preservice teachers' beliefs and practices. *Teacher Educator, 31,* 292–303.

López, G., & Scribner, J. (1999, April). *Discourses of involvement: A critical review of parent involvement research.* Paper presented at the annual meeting of the American Educational Research Association, Montreal, Canada.

Lou, Y., Abrami, P., & d'Apollonia, S. (2001). Small group and individual learning with technology: A meta-analysis. *Review of Educational Research, 71*(3), 449–521.

Lou, Y., Abrami, P., & Spence, J. (2000). Effects of within-class grouping on student achievement: An exploratory model. *Journal of Educational Research, 94*(2), 101–112.

Louis, B., Subotnik, R., Breland, P., & Lewis, M. (2000). Establishing criteria for high ability versus selective admission to gifted programs: Implications for policy and practice. *Educational Psychology Review, 12*(3), 295–314.

Lovett, M., & Anderson, J. (1994). Effects of solving related proofs on memory and transfer in geometry problem solving. *Journal of Experimental Psychology, 20*(2), 366–378.

Lowrie, T., & Kay, R. (2001). Relationship between visual and nonvisual solution methods and difficulty in elementary mathematics. *Journal of Educational Research, 94*(4), 248–255.

Loyd, B., & Loyd, D. (1997). Kindergarten through grade 12 standards: A philosophy of grading. In G. Phye (Ed.), *Handbook of classroom assessment* (pp. 481–490). San Diego, CA: Academic Press.

Lundeberg, M., Bergland, M., Klyczek, K., Mogen, K., Johnson, D., & Harmes, N. (1999). *Increasing interest, confidence, and understanding of ethical issues in science through case-based instruction technologies.* Paper presented at the annual meeting of the American Educational Research Association, Montreal, Canada.

Lyman, H. (1991). *Test scores and what they mean* (5th ed.). Upper Saddle River, NJ: Prentice Hall.

Ma, X. (2001). Bullying and being bullied: To what extent are bullies also victims? *American Educational Research Journal, 38*(2), 351–370.

Mabry, L. (1999). Writing to the rubric. *Phi Delta Kappan, 80*(9), 673–679.

MacArthur, C., Ferretti, R., Okolo, C., & Cavalier, A. (2001). Technology applications for students with literacy problems: A critical review. *Elementary School Journal, 101*(3), 273–302.

Maccoby, E. (1992). The role of parents in the socialization of children: An historical overview. *Developmental Psychology, 28,* 1006–1017.

Mace, F., Belfiore, P., & Shea, M. (1989). Operant theory and research on self-regulation. In B. Zimmerman & D. Schunk (Eds.), *Self-regulated learning and academic achievement: Theory, research, and practice.* New York: Springer-Verlag.

Macionis, J. (2000). *Sociology* (6th ed.). Upper Saddle River, NJ: Prentice Hall.

Madaus, G. & O'Dwyer, L. (1999). A short history of performance assessment. *Phi Delta Kappan, 80*(9), 688–695.

Madaus, G., & Tan, A. (1993). The growth of assessment. In G. Cawelti (Ed.), *Challenges and achievements of American education* (pp. 53–79). Alexandria, VA: Association for Supervision and Curriculum Development.

Maehr, M. (1992, April). *Transforming the school culture to enhance motivation.* Paper presented at the annual meeting of the American Educational Research Association, San Francisco.

Maehr, M. & Midgley, C. (1991). Enhancing student motivation: A schoolwide approach. *Education Psychologist, 26,* 399–427.

Mael, F. (1998). Single-sex and coeducational schooling: Relationships to socioemotional and academic development. *Review of Educational Research, 68*(2), 101–129.

Mager, R. (1962). *Preparing instructional objectives.* Palo Alto, CA: Featon.

Mager, R. (1998). *Preparing instructional objectives: A critical tool in the development of effective instruction* (3rd ed.). Atlanta, GA: Center for Effective Performance.

Mamlin, N., & Harris, K. (1998). Elementary teachers' referral to special education in light of inclusion and prereferral: "Every child is here to learn . . . but some of these children are in real trouble." *Journal of Educational Psychology, 90*(3), 385–396.

Mantzicopoulos, P. (1989, April). *Coping with school failure: The relationship of children's coping strategies to academic achievement, self-concept, behavior, and locus of control.* Paper presented at the annual meeting of the American Educational Research Association, San Francisco.

Marcia, J. (1980). Identity in adolescence. In J. Adelson (Ed.), *Handbook of adolescent psychology.* New York: Wiley.

Marcia, J. (1987). The identity status approach to the study of ego identity development. In T. Honess & K. Yardley (Eds.), *Self and identity: Perspectives across the life span.* London: Routledge & Kegan Paul.

Marcia, J. (1988). Common processes underlying ego identity, cognitive/moral development and individuation. In D. Lapsley & F. Power (Eds.), *Self, ego, and identity: Integrative approaches* (pp. 211–225). New York: Springer-Verlag.

Marini, Z., & Case, R. (1994). The development of abstract reasoning about the physical and social world. *Child Development, 65,* 147–159.

Marks, J. (1995). *Human biodiversity: Genes, race, and history.* New York: Aldine de Gruyter.

Marsh, H. (1989). Age and sex effects in multiple dimensions of self-concept: Preadolescence to early adulthood. *Journal of Educational Psychology, 81,* 417–430.

Marsh, H. (1990). Causal ordering of academic self-concept and academic achievement: A multiwave, longitudinal panel analysis. *Journal of Educational Psychology, 82,* 646–656.

Marsh, H. (1992). Content specificity of relations between academic achievement and academic self-concept. *Journal of Educational Psychology, 84*(1), 34–52.

Marsh, H., Kong, C., & Hau, K. (2001). Extension of the internal/external frame of reference model of self-concept formation: Importance of native and non-native languages for Chinese students. *Journal of Educational Psychology, 93*(3), 543–553.

Marso, R., & Pigge, F. (1992, April). *A summary of published research: Classroom teachers' knowledge and skills related to the development and use of teacher-made tests.* Paper presented at the annual meeting of the American Educational Research Association, San Francisco.

Maslow, A. (1968). *Toward a psychology of being* (2nd ed.). New York: Van Nostrand.

Maslow, A. (1970). *Motivation and personality* (2nd ed.). New York: Harper & Row. (Original work published 1954)

Martin, A., Marsh, H., & Debus, R. (2001). Self-handicapping and defensive pessimism: Exploring a model of predictors and outcomes from a self-protection perspective. *Journal of Educational Psychology, 93*(1), 87–102.

Martin, J. (1993). Episodic memory: A neglected phenomenon in the psychology of education. *Educational Psychologist, 28*(2), 169–183.

Mason, L. (1998). Sharing cognition to construct scientific knowledge in school context: The role of oral and written discourse. *Instructional Science 26,* 359–389.

Mason, L., & Boscolo, P. (2000). Writing and conceptual change. What changes? *Instructional Science, 28,* 199–226.

Matute-Bianchi, M. (1986). Ethnic identities and patterns of school success and failure among Mexican-descent and Japanese American students in a California high school: An ethnographic analysis. *American Journal of Education, 95,* 233–255.

Maxwell, N., Bellisimo, Y., & Mergendoller, J. (1999, April). *Matching the strategy to the students: Why we modified the medical school problem-based learning for high school economics.* Paper presented at the annual meeting of the American Educational Research Association, Montreal, Canada.

Mayer, R. (1984). Aids to text comprehension. *Educational Psychologist, 19,* 30–42.

Mayer, R. (1992). *Thinking, problem solving, cognition* (2nd ed.). New York: Freeman.

Mayer, R. (1996). Learners as information processors: Legacies and limitations of educational psychology's second metaphor. *Educational Psychologist, 31*(4), 151–161.

Mayer, R. (1997). Multimedia learning: Are we asking the right questions? *Educational Psychologist, 32*(1), 1–19.

Mayer, R. (1998a). Cognitive, metacognitive, and motivational aspects of problem solving. *Instructional Science, 26,* 49–63.

Mayer, R. (1998b). Cognitive theory for education: What teachers need to know. In N. Lambert & B. McCombs (Eds.), *How students learn: Reforming schools through learner-centered instruction* (pp. 353–378). Washington, DC: American Psychological Association.

Mayer, R. (1999). *The promise of educational psychology: Learning in the content areas.* Upper Saddle River, NJ: Merrill/Prentice Hall.

Mayer, R. (2001). *Multimedia learning.* New York: Cambridge University Press.

Mayer, R. (2002). *The promise of educational psychology: Volume II. Teaching for meaningful learning.* Upper Saddle River, NJ: Prentice Hall.

Mayer, R., & Chandler, P. (2001). When learning is just a click away: Does simple user interaction foster deeper understanding of multimedia messages? *Journal of Education Psychology, 93*(2), 390–397.

Mayer, R., & Moreno, R. (1998). A split-attention effect in multimedia learning: Evidence for dual processing systems in working memory. *Journal of Educational Psychology, 90*(2), 312–320.

Mayer, R., & Wittrock, M. (1996). Problem-solving transfer. In D. Berliner & R. Calfee (Eds.), *Handbook of educational psychology* (pp. 47–62). New York: Macmillan.

McAffee, O., & Leong, D. (2002). *Assessing and guiding young children's development and learning* (3rd ed.). Needham Heights, MA: Allyn & Bacon.

McCall, R., Appelbaum, M., & Hogarty, P. (1973). Developmental changes in mental performance. *Monographs of the Society for Research in Child Development, 38*(3, Serial No. 150).

McCallum, R., (1999). A "baker's dozen" criteria for evaluating fairness in nonverbal testing. *School Psychologist, 53*(2), 41–60.

McCarthy, S. (1994). Authors, text, and talk: The internalization of dialogue from social interaction during writing. *Reading Research Quarterly, 29,* 201–231.

McCaslin, M., & Good, T. (1992). Compliant cognition: The misalliance of management and instructional goals in current school reform. *Educational Researcher, 21*(3), 4–17.

McClelland, D. (1985). *Human motivation.* Glenview, IL: Scott, Foresman.

McCombs, B. (1998). Integrating metacognition, affect, and motivation in improving teacher education. In N. Lambert & B. McCombs (Eds.), *How students learn: Reforming schools through learner-centered education* (pp. 379–408). Washington, DC: American Psychological Association.

McCombs, B., & Pope, B. (1994). *Motivating hard to reach students.* Washington, DC: American Psychological Association.

McCombs, B., & Whisler, J. (1997). *The learner centered classroom and school: Strategies for enhancing student motivation and achievement.* San Francisco: Jossey-Bass.

McCutchen, D. (2000). Knowledge, processing, and working memory: Implications for a theory of writing. *Educational Psychologist, 35*(1), 13–23.

McDaniel, E. (1994). *Understanding educational measurement.* Madison, WI: Brown & Benchmark.

McDaniel, M., Waddill, P., Finstad, K., & Bourg, T. (2000). The effects of text-based interest on attention and recall. *Journal of Educational Psychology, 92*(3), 492–502.

McDermott, P., Mordell, M., & Stoltzfus, J. (2001). The organization of student performance in American schools: Discipline, motivation, verbal learning, and nonverbal learning. *Journal of Educational Psychology, 93*(1), 65–76.

McDevitt, T., & Ormrod, J. (2002). *Child development and education.* Upper Saddle River, NJ: Merrill/Prentice Hall.

McDougall, D., & Granby, C. (1996). How expectation of questioning method affects undergraduates' preparation for class. *Journal of Experimental Education, 65,* 43–54.

McGreal, T. (1985, March). *Characteristics of effective teaching.* Paper presented at the first annual Intensive Training Symposium, Clearwater, Florida.

McKinnon, D. (1997, March). *Longitudinal case study of student attitudes, motivation, and performance.* Paper presented at the annual meeting of the American Education

Research Association, Chicago. (ERIC Document Reproduction Service No. ED408350)

McLaughlin, H. J. (1994). From negation to negotiation: Moving away from the management metaphor. *Action in Teacher Education, 16*(1), 75–84.

McLoyd, V. (1998). Socioeconomic disadvantages and child development. *American Psychologist, 53,* 185–204.

McMillan, J. (1997). *Classroom assessment.* Boston: Allyn & Bacon.

McMillan, J. (2000). *Educational research: Fundamentals for the consumer* (3rd ed.). New York: Longman.

McMillan, J., Workman, D., & Myran, S. (1999). *Elementary teachers' classroom assessment and grading practices.* Paper presented at the annual meeting of the American Educational Research Association, Montreal, Canada.

McMillen, L. (1997, January 17). Linguists find the debate over "ebonics" uninformed. *The Chronicle of Higher Education,* p. A16.

McNeil, N., & Alibali, M. (2000). Learning mathematics from procedural instruction: Externally imposed goals influence what is learned. *Journal of Educational Psychology, 92*(4), 734–744.

McTighe, J. (1996/97). What happens between assessments? *Educational Leadership, 54*(4), 6–12.

Means, B., & Knapp, M. (1991). Introduction: Rethinking teaching for disadvantaged students. In B. Means, C. Chelemer, & M. Knapp (Eds.), *Teaching advanced skills to at-risk students* (pp. 1–27). San Francisco: Jossey-Bass.

Medin, D., Proffitt, J., & Schwartz. H. (2000). Concepts: An overview. In A. Kazdin (Ed.), *Encyclopedia of psychology* (Vol. 2, pp. 242–245). New York: Oxford University Press.

Mehrabian, A., & Ferris, S. (1967). Inference of attitude from nonverbal behavior in two channels. *Journal of Consulting Psychology, 31,* 248–252.

Meichenbaum, D. (1977). *Cognitive behavior modification: An integrative approach.* New York: Plenum Press.

Melnick, S., & Pullin, D. (2000). Can you take dictation? Prescribing teacher quality through testing. *Journal of Teacher Education, 51*(4), 262–275.

Meltzer, L., & Reid, D. (1994). New directions in the assessment of students with special needs. *Journal of Special Education, 28,* 338–355.

Mercer, C., & Mercer, A. (1998). *Teaching students with learning problems* (4th ed.). New York: Macmillan.

Mercer, J. (1973). *Labeling the mentally retarded.* Berkeley: University of California Press.

Mergendoller, J., Bellisimo, Y., & Maxwell, N. (2000). Comparing problem-based learning and traditional instruction in high school economics. *Journal of Educational Psychology, 93*(6), 374–383.

Merkley, D., & Jefferies, D. (2001). Guidelines for implementing a graphic organizer. *Reading Teacher, 54*(4), 350–357.

Merrill, P., Hammons, K., Tolman, M., Christensen, L., Vincent, B., & Reynolds, P. (1992). *Computers in education.* Needham Heights, MA: Allyn & Bacon.

Messick, S. (1989). Validity. In R. Linn (Ed.), *Educational measurement* (3rd ed., pp. 13–103). New York: Macmillan.

Messick, S. (1994). *Standards of validity and the validity of standards in performance assessment* (RM-94-17). Princeton, NJ: Educational Testing Service.

Meter, P., & Stevens, R. (2000). The role of theory in the study of peer collaboration. *Journal of Experimental Education, 69*(1), 113–127.

Mevarech, Z. (1999). Effects of metacognitive training embedded in cooperative settings on mathematical problem solving. *Journal of Educational Research, 92*(4), 195–205.

Meyer, M. (2000). The ability-achievement discrepancy: Does it contribute to an understanding of learning disabilities? *Educational Psychology Review, 12*(3), 315–336.

Meyer, W. (1982). Indirect communications about perceived ability estimates. *Journal of Educational Psychology, 74,* 888–897.

Michaels, S., & O'Connor, M. (1990, Summer). *Literacy as reasoning within multiple discourses: Implications for policy and educational reform.* Paper presented at the Council of Chief State School Officers 1990 Summer Institute.

Mickelson, R., & Heath, D. (1999, April). *The effects of segregation and tracking on African American high school seniors' academic achievement, occupational aspirations, and interracial social networks in Charlotte, North Carolina.* Paper presented at the annual meeting of the American Educational Research Association, Montreal, Canada.

Middleton, M., & Midgley, C. (1997). Avoiding the demonstration of lack of ability: An under explored aspect of goal theory. *Journal of Educational Psychology, 89,* 710–718.

Midgley, C., Arunkumar, R., & Urdan, T. (1996). "If I don't do well tomorrow, there's a reason": Predictors of adolescents' use of academic self-handicapping strategies. *Journal of Educational Psychology, 88*(3), 423–434.

Midgley, C., Kaplan, A., & Middleton, M. (2001). Performance-approach goals: Good for what, for whom, under what circumstances, and at what cost? *Journal of Educational Psychology, 93*(1), 77–86.

Midgley, C., & Urdan, T. (2001). Academic self-handicapping and achievement goals: A further examination. *Contemporary Educational Psychology, 26,* 61–75.

Miller, D., Barbetta, P., & Heron, T. (1994). START tutoring: Designing, training, implementing, adapting, and evaluating tutoring programs for school and home settings. In R. Gardner, D. Sianato, J. Cooper, W. Heward, T. Heron, J. Eshleman, & T. Grossi (Eds.), *Behavior analysis in education: Focus on measurably superior instruction* (pp. 265–282). Pacific Grove, CA: Brooks/Cole.

Miller, G. (1956). Human memory and the storage of information. *IRE Transactions on Information Theory, 2*(3), 129–137.

Miller, L. (1995). *An American imperative: Accelerating minority educational advancement.* New Haven, CT: Yale University Press.

Miller, P. (1993). *Theories of developmental psychology* (3rd ed.). New York: Freeman.

Miller, S., Leinhardt, G., & Zigmond, N. (1988). Influencing engagement through accommodation: An ethnographic study of at-risk students. *American Educational Research Journal, 25,* 465–487.

Mills, G. (2002, April). *Teaching and learning action research.* Paper presented at the annual meeting of the American Educational Research Association, New Orleans, LA.

Milson, A., & Mehlig, L. (2001, April). *The efficacy beliefs of elementary teachers regarding character education.* Paper presented at the annual meeting of the American Educational Research Association, Seattle.

Mischel, W. (1993). *Introduction to personality* (5th ed.). Fort Worth, TX: Harcourt Brace Jovanovich.

Mishel, L., & Frankel, D. (1991). *The state of working America: 1990–1991 edition.* Armonk, NY: M. E. Sharpe.

Moerk, E. (1992). A *first language taught and learned.* Baltimore: Brookes.

Moles, O. (1992, April). *Parental contacts about classroom behavior problems.* Paper presented at the annual meeting of the American Educational Research Association, San Francisco.

Moll, L. (1992). Funds of knowledge for teaching: Using a qualitative approach to connect homes and classrooms. *Theory Into Practice, 3*(1), 132–141.

Monroe, S., Goldman, P., & Smith, U. (1988). *Brothers: Black and poor—a true story of courage and survivors.* New York: Morrow.

Moon, S., Zentall, S., Grskovic, J., Hall, A., & Stormont-Spurgin, M. (1997, March). *Social/emotional characteristics of children with AD/HD and giftedness in school and family contexts.* Paper presented at the annual meeting of the American Educational Research Association, Chicago.

Moreland, J., Dansereau, D., & Chmielewski, T. (1997). Recall of descriptive information: The roles of presentation format, annotation strategy, and individual differences. *Contemporary Educational Psychology, 22,* 521–533.

Moreno, R., & Mayer, R. (1998, April). *Learning from multiple representations in a multimedia environment.* Paper presented at the annual meeting of the American Educational Research Association, San Diego, CA.

Moreno, R., & Mayer, R. (2000). Engaging students in active learning: The case for personalized multimedia messages. *Journal of Educational Psychology, 92*(4), 724–733.

Morgan, M. (1984). Reward-induced decrements and increments in intrinsic motivation. *Review of Educational Research, 54,* 5–30.

Morine-Dershimer, G. (1987). Can we talk? In D. Berliner & B. Rosenshine (Eds.), *Talks to teachers* (pp. 37–53). New York: Random House.

Morrison, G., Lowther, D., & DeMuelle, L. (1999). *Integrating computer technology into the classroom.* Upper Saddle River, NJ: Merrill/Prentice Hall.

Moshman, D. (1997). Pluralist rational constructivism. *Issues in Education: Contributions From Education Psychology, 3,* 229–234.

Moss, P. (1992, April). *Shifting conceptions of validity in educational measurement: Implications for performance assessment.* Paper presented at the annual meeting of the American Educational Research Association, San Francisco.

Mullis, I., Dossey, J., Foertsh, M., Jones, L., & Gentile, C. (1991). *Trends in academic progress.* Washington, DC: U.S. Department of Education, National Center for Education Statistics.

Munk, D., & Bursuck, W. (1997/98). Can grades be helpful and fair? *Educational Leadership, 55*(4), 44–47.

Murdock, T., Hale, N., & Weber, M. (2001). Predictors of cheating among early adolescents: Academic and social motivations. *Contemporary Educational Psychology, 26*(2), 96–115.

Murphy, J., Weil, M., & McGreal, T. (1986). The basic practice model of instruction. *Elementary School Journal, 87,* 83–95.

Murray, F. (1986, May). *Necessity: The developmental component in reasoning.* Paper presented at the sixteenth annual meeting, Jean Piaget Society, Philadelphia.

Mwangi, W., & Sweller, J. (1998). Learning to solve compare word problems: The effect of example format and generating self-explanations. *Cognition and Instruction, 16,* 173–199.

Myers, C. (1970). Journal citations and scientific eminence in contemporary psychology. *American Psychologist, 25,* 1041–1048.

Nagel, G., & Peterson, P. (2001). Why competency tests miss the mark. *Educational Leadership, 58*(8), 46–48.

Naigles, L., & Gelman, S. (1995). Overextensions in comprehension and production revisited: Preferential looking in a study of dog, cat and cow. *Journal of Child Language, 22,* 19–46.

Nakagawa, K. (1999, April). *Portraits of the schools and communities experiencing student mobility.* Paper presented at the annual meeting of the American Educational Research Association, Montreal, Canada.

Narvaez, D. (1998). The influence of moral schemas on the reconstruction of moral narratives in eighth graders and college students. *Journal of Educational Psychology, 90*(1), 13–24.

Nathan, M., Koedinger, K., & Alibali, M. (2001, April). *Expert blind spot: When content knowledge eclipses pedagogical content knowledge.* Paper presented at the annual meeting of the American Educational Research Association, Seattle.

National Association for Sport and Physical Education. (1995). *Moving into the future, national standards for physical education: A guide to content and assessment.* St. Louis, MO: Mosby.

National Center for Children in Poverty. (1999, June). *Young children in poverty: A statistical update.* Columbia University: Joseph Mailmon School of Public Health.

National Center for Research on Teacher Learning. (1993). *Findings on learning to teach.* East Lansing: Michigan State University.

National Commission on Excellence in Education. (1983). *A nation at risk: The imperative for educational reform.* Washington, DC: Government Printing Office.

National Commission on Testing and Public Policy. (1990). *From gatekeeper to gateway.* Chestnut Hill, MA: Boston College Press.

National Council of Teachers of Mathematics. (1989). *Curriculum and evaluation standards for school mathematics.* Reston, VA: Author.

National Council of Teachers of Mathematics. (2000). *Principles and standards for school mathematics.* Reston, VA: Author.

National excellence: A case for developing America's talent. (1993). Washington, DC: U.S. Department of Education, Office of Educational Research and Improvement.

National Joint Committee on Learning Disabilities. (1994). Learning disabilities: Issues on definition. A position paper of the National Joint Committee in Learning Disabilities. In *Collective perspectives on issues affecting learning disability: Position papers and statements.* Austin, TX: Pro-Ed.

National Parent Teacher Association. (2000). *Standards for parent/family involvement programs.* Retrieved October 1, 2002, from http://www.pta.org/programs/INVSTAND

National Public Radio. (1999). E-mails from Kosovo. In *Morning Edition* [Radio series]. Retrieved October 1, 2002, from http://www.npr.org/programs/morning/transcripts

National Standards in Foreign Language Education Project. (1999). *Standards for Foreign Language Learning in the 21st Century.* Lawrence, KS: Author.

National Telecommunications and Information Administration. (1999). *Falling through the Net: Defining the digital divide.* Retrieved October 1, 2002, from http://www.ntia.doc.gov/ntiahome/fttn99/contents.html

Needels, M., & Knapp, M. (1994). Teaching writing to children who are underserved. *Journal of Educational Psychology, 86*(3), 339–349.

Neisser, U. (1967). *Cognitive psychology.* New York: Appleton-Century-Crofts.

Nelson, J., Lott, L., & Glenn, S. (1997). *Positive discipline in the classroom* (2nd ed.). New York: Ballantine Books.

Neuman, S., & Celano, D. (2001). Access to print in low-income and middle-income communities: An ecological study of our neighborhoods. *Reading Research Quarterly, 36*(1), 8–26.

Newby, T., Stepich, D., Lehman, J., & Russell, J. (2000). *Instructional technology for teaching and learning: Designing instruction, integrating computers, and using media.* Upper Saddle River, NJ: Merrill/Prentice Hall.

Newman, F., Secado, W., & Wehlage, G. (1995). *A guide to authentic instruction and assessment: Vision, standards & scoring.* Madison: University of Wisconsin Center for Education Research.

Newmann, F. (1997). Authentic assessment in social studies. Standards and examples. In G. D. Phye (Ed.), *Handbook of classroom assessment: Learning, achievement, and adjustment.* San Diego, CA: Academic Press.

Newstead, J., Franklyn-Stokes, A., & Armstead, P. (1996). Individual differences in student cheating. *Journal of Educational Psychology, 88*(2), 229–241.

Nicholls, J. (1984). Achievement motivation: Conceptions of ability, subjective experience, task choice, and performance. *Psychological Review, 91,* 328–346.

Nicholls, J., & Miller, A. (1984). Conceptions of ability and achievement motivation. In R. Ames & C. Ames (Eds.), *Research on motivation in education: Vol. 1. Student motivation* (pp. 39–73). New York: Academic Press.

Nichols, B., & Singer, K. (2000). Developing data mentors. *Educational Leadership, 57*(5), 34–37.

Nickerson, R. (1988). On improving thinking through instruction. In E. Rothkopf (Ed.), *Review of research in education* (pp. 3–57). Washington, DC: American Educational Research Association.

Nieto, S. (1999). *Identity, personhood, and Puerto Rican students: Challenging paradigms of assimilation and authenticity.* Paper presented at the annual meeting of the American Educational Research Association, Montreal, Canada.

Nilsson, L., & Archer, T. (1989). Aversively motivated behavior: Which are the perspectives? In T. Archer & L. Nilsson (Eds.), *Aversion, avoidance and anxiety.* Hillsdale, NJ: Erlbaum.

Nisan, M. (1992). Beyond intrinsic motivation: Cultivating a "sense of the desirable." In F. Oser, A. Dick, & J. Patry (Eds.), *Effective and responsible teaching: The new synthesis* (pp. 126–138). San Francisco: Jossey-Bass.

Nissani, M., & Hoefler-Nissani, D. (1992). Experimental studies of belief dependence of observations and of resistance to conceptual change. *Cognition and Instruction, 9,* 97–111.

Noblit, G., Rogers, D., & McCadden, B. (1995). In the meantime: The possibilities of caring. *Phi Delta Kappan, 76,* 680–685.

Noddings, N. (1995). Teaching the themes of care. *Phi Delta Kappan, 76,* 675–679.

Noddings, N. (1999, April). *Competence and caring as central to teacher education.* Paper presented at the annual meeting of the American Educational Research Association, Montreal, Canada.

Noddings, N. (2001). The caring teacher. In V. Richardson (Ed.), *Handbook of research on teaching* (4th ed., pp. 99–105). Washington, DC: American Educational Research Association.

Novick, L. (1998, April). *Highly skilled problem solvers use example-based reasoning to support their superior performance.* Paper presented at the annual meeting of the American Educational Research Association, San Diego, CA.

Nucci, L. (1987). Synthesis of research on moral development. *Educational Leadership, 44*(5), 86–92.

Nuthall, G. (1999a). Learning how to learn: The evolution of students' minds through the social processes and culture of the classroom. *International Journal of Educational Research, 31*(3), 141–256.

Nuthall, G. (1999b). The way students learn: Acquiring knowledge from an integrated science and social studies unit. *Elementary School Journal, 99*(4), 303–342.

Nuthall, G. (2000). The anatomy of memory in the classroom: Understanding how students acquire memory processes from classroom activities in science and social studies units. *American Educational Research Journal, 37*(1), 247–304.

Nuthall, G. (2001, April). *Student experience and the learning process: Developing an evidence based theory of classroom learning.* Paper presented at the annual meeting of the American Educational Research Association, Seattle.

Nyberg, K., McMillin, J., O-Neill-Rood, N., & Florence, J. (1997). Ethnic differences in academic retracking: A four-year longitudinal study. *Journal of Educational Research, 91*(1), 33–41.

Nystrand, M., Cohen, A., & Dowling, N. (1992, April). *Reliability of portfolio assessment for measuring verbal outcomes.* Paper presented at the annual meeting of the American Educational Research Association, San Francisco.

Nystrand, M., & Gamoran, A. (1989, March). *Instructional discourse and student engagement.* Paper presented at the annual meeting of the American Educational Research Association, San Francisco.

Nystrand, M., Wu, L., Gamoran, A., Zeiser, S., & Long, D. (2001, April). *Questions in time: Investigating the structure and dynamics of unfolding classroom discourse.* Paper presented at the annual meeting of the American Educational Research Association, Seattle.

Oakes, J. (1992). Can tracking research inform practice? *Educational Researcher, 21*(4), 12–21.

O'Brien, V., Kopola, M., & Martinez-Pons, M. (1999). Mathematics self-efficacy, ethnic identity, gender, and career interests related to mathematics and science. *Journal of Educational Research, 92*(4), 231–235.

O'Connor, J., & Brie, R. (1994). Mathematics and science partnerships: Products, people, performance and multimedia. *Computing Teacher, 22,* 27–30.

O'Donnell, A., & O'Kelly, J. (1994). Learning from peers: Beyond the rhetoric of positive results. *Educational Psychology Review, 6,* 321–349.

Offer, D., Ostrov, E., & Howard, K. (1989). Adolescence: What is normal? *American Journal of Diseases of Children, 14*(3), 731–736.

Office of Bilingual Education and Minority Language Affairs. (1999). *Facts about limited English proficient students.* Washington, DC: U.S. Department of Education. Retrieved from http://www.ed.gov/offices/OBEMLA/rileyfct.html

Ogbu, J. (1987). Variability in minority school performance: A problem in search of an explanation. *Anthropology and Education Quarterly, 18,* 312–334.

Ogbu, J. (1992). Understanding cultural diversity and learning. *Educational Researcher, 21*(8), 5–14.

Ogbu, J. (1999a). Beyond language: Ebonics, proper English, and identity in a Black-American speech community. *American Educational Research Journal, 36*(2), 147–184.

Ogbu, J. (1999b, April). *The significance of minority status.* Paper presented at the annual meeting of the American Educational Research Association, Montreal, Canada.

Ogbu, J., & Simons, H. (1998). Voluntary and involuntary minorities: A cultural-ecological theory of school performance with some implications for education. *Anthropology & Education Quarterly, 29*(2), 155–188.

Ogden, J., Brophy, J., & Evertson, C. (1977, April). *An experimental investigation of organization and management techniques in first-grade reading groups.* Paper presented at the annual meeting of the American Educational Research Association, New York.

O'Grady, W. (1997). *Syntactic development.* Chicago: University of Chicago Press.

Oka, E., Kolar, R., Rau, C., & Stahl, N. (1997, March). *The dynamic nature of collaboration and inclusion.* Paper presented at the annual meeting of the American Educational Research Association, Chicago.

Olina, Z., & Sullivan, H. (2002, April). *Effects of teacher and self-assessment on student performance.* Paper presented at the annual meeting of the American Educational Research Association, New Orleans, LA.

Olson, L. (2000a). Finding and keeping competent teachers. *Education Week, 19*(18), 12–18.

Olson, L. (2000b). Worries of a standards "backlash" grow. *Education Week, 19*(30), 1, 12–13.

Olson, L. (2001). Finding the right mix. *Education Week, 20*(17), 12–20.

O'Reilly, T, Symons, S., & MacLatchy-Gaudet, H. (1998). A comparison of self-explanation and elaborative interrogation. *Contemporary Educational Psychology, 23,* 434–445.

Osborne, J. (1996). Beyond constructivism. *Science Education, 80,* 53–81.

Ovando, C. (1997). Language diversity and education. In J. Banks & C. Banks (Eds.), *Multicultural education: Issues and perspectives* (3rd ed., pp. 272–296). Boston: Allyn & Bacon.

Owens, R. E., Jr. (1996). *Language development* (4th ed.). Boston: Allyn & Bacon.

Packer, M., & Goicoechea, J. (2000). Sociocultural and constructivist theories of learning: Ontology, not just epistemology. *Educational Psychologist, 35*(4), 227–241.

Page, E. (1992). Is the world an orderly place? A review of teacher comments and student achievement. *Journal of Experimental Education, 60*(2), 161–181.

Paivio, A. (1986). *Mental representations: A dual-coding approach.* New York: Oxford University.

Paivio, A. (1991). Dual coding theory: Retrospect and current status. *Canadian Journal of Psychology, 45,* 255–287.

Palincsar, A., & Brown, A. (1984). Reciprocal teaching of comprehension-fostering and comprehension-monitoring activities. *Cognition and Instruction, 2,* 117–175.

Papalia, D., & Wendkos-Olds, S. (1996). *A child's world: Infancy through adolescence* (7th ed.). New York: McGraw-Hill.

Paris, S. (1998). Why learner-centered assessment is better than high-stakes testing. In N. Lambert & B. McCombs (Eds.), *How students learn: Reforming schools through learner-centered education* (pp. 189–209). Washington, DC: American Psychological Association.

Paris, S., & Paris, A. (2001). Classroom applications of research on self-regulated learning. *Educational Psychologist, 36,* 89–101.

Parish, J., Parish, T., & Batt, S. (2001, April). *Academic achievement and school climate—interventions that work.* Paper presented at the annual meeting of the American Educational Research Association, Seattle.

Park, C. (1997, March). *A comparative study of learning style preferences: Asian-American and Anglo students in secondary schools.* Paper presented at the annual meeting of the American Educational Research Association, Chicago.

Parke, C., & Lane, S. (1996/97). Learning from performance assessments in math. *Educational Leadership, 54*(4), 26–29.

Parker, G. (1994). *Gifted students' perceptions of environments in assertive discipline and non-assertive discipline classrooms.* Unpublished dissertation, University of Houston, TX.

Parsons, J., Kaczala, C., & Meece, J. (1982). Socialization of achievement attitudes and beliefs: Classroom influences. *Child Development, 53,* 322–339.

Pashler, H., & Carrier, M. (1996). Structures, processes, and the flow of information. In E. Bjork & R. Bjork (Eds.), *Memory* (pp. 3–29). San Diego, CA: Academic Press.

Patrick, H., Anderman, L., Ryan, A., Edelin, K., & Midgley, C. (1999, April). *Messages teachers send: Communicating goal orientations in the classroom.* Paper presented at the annual meeting of the American Educational Research Association, Montreal, Canada.

Pavlov, I. (1928). *Lectures on conditioned reflexes* (W. Gantt, Trans.). New York: International Universities Press.

Pearl, R., Farmer, T., Van Acker, R., Rodkin, P., Bost, K., Coe, M., & Henley, W. (1998). The social integration of students with mild disabilities in general education classrooms: Peer group membership and peer-assessed social behavior. *Elementary School Journal, 99*(2), 167–185.

Peña, D. (2000). Parent involvement: Influencing factors and implications. *Journal of Educational Research, 94*(1), 42–54.

Peng, S., & Lee, R. (1992, April). *Home variables, parent-child activities, and academic achievement: A study of 1988 eighth graders.* Paper presented at the annual meeting of the American Educational Research Association, San Francisco.

Peregoy, S., & Boyle, O. (2001). *Reading, writing, and learning in ESL* (3rd ed.). New York: Longman.

Perkins, D. (1995). *Outsmarting IQ.* New York: Free Press.

Perkins, D., & Salomon, G. (1989). Are cognitive skills context-bound? *Educational Researcher, 18,* 16–25.

Perry, N. (1998). Young children's self-regulated learning and contexts that support it. *Journal of Educational Psychology, 90*(4), 715–729.

Perry, R. (1985). Instructor expressiveness: Implications for improving teaching. In J. Donald & A. Sullivan (Eds.), *Using research to improve teaching* (pp. 35–49). San Francisco: Jossey-Bass.

Perry, R., Magnusson, J., Parsonson, K., & Dickens, W. (1986). Perceived control in the college classroom: Limitations in instructor expressiveness due to noncontingent feedback and lecture content. *Journal of Educational Psychology, 78,* 96–107.

Peterson, P. (1988). Teachers' and students' cognitional knowledge for classroom teaching and learning. *Educational Research, 17,* 5–14.

Petrill, S., & Wilkerson, B. (2000). Intelligence and achievement: A behavioral genetic perspective. *Educational Psychology Review, 12*(2), 185–199.

Pfiffer, L., Rosen, L., & O'Leary, S. (1985). The efficacy of an all-positive approach to classroom management. *Journal of Applied Behavior Analysis, 18,* 257–261.

Phillips, D. (1995). The good, the bad and the ugly: The many faces of constructivism. *Educational Researcher, 24*(7), 5–12.

Phillips, D. (1997). How, why, what, when, and where: Perspectives on constructivism in psychology and education. *Issues in Education, 3,* 151–194.

Phillips, D. (2000). An opinionated account of the constructivist landscape. In D. Phillips (Ed.), *Constructivism in education: Opinions and second opinions on controversial issues* (pp. 1–16). Chicago: National Society for the Study of Education.

Phillips, N., Fuchs, L., & Fuchs, D. (1995). Effects of classwide curriculum-based measurement and peer tutoring: A collaborative researcher-practitioner interview study. *Journal of Learning Disabilities, 27,* 420–434.

Phye, G. (2001). Problem-solving instruction and problem-solving transfer: The correspondence issue. *Journal of Educational Psychology, 93*(3), 571–578.

Piaget, J. (1926). *The language and thought of the child.* New York: Harcourt, Brace & World.

Piaget, J. (1952). *Origins of intelligence in children.* New York: International Universities Press.

Piaget, J. (1959). *Language and thought of the child* (M. Grabain, Trans.). New York: Humanities Press.

Piaget, J. (1965). The *moral judgment of the child.* New York: Free Press. (Original work published 1932)

Piaget, J. (1970). *The science of education and the psychology of the child.* New York: Orion Press.

Piaget, J. (1977). Problems in equilibration. In M. Appel & L. Goldberg (Eds.), *Topics in cognitive development: Vol. 1. Equilibration: Theory, research, and application* (pp. 3–13). New York: Plenum Press.

Pine, K., & Messer, D. (2000). The effect of explaining another's actions on children's implicit theories of balance. *Cognition and Instruction, 18*(1), 35–51.

Pinker, S. (1994). *The language instinct: How the mind creates language.* New York: William Morrow.

Pintrich, P. (2000). Multiple goals, multiple pathways: The role of goal orientation in learning and achievement. *Journal of Educational Psychology, 92*(3), 544–555.

Pintrich, P., & Garcia, T. (1991). Student goal orientation and self-regulation in the college classroom. In M. Maehr & P. Pintrich (Eds.), *Advances in motivation and achievement* (Vol. 7, pp. 371–402). Greenwich, CT: JAI Press.

Pintrich, P., Marx, R., & Boyle, R. (1993). Beyond cold conceptual change: The role of motivational beliefs and classroom contextual factors in the process of conceptual change. *Review of Educational Research, 63,* 167–199.

Pintrich, P., & Schrauben, B. (1992). Students' motivational beliefs and their cognitive engagement in academic tasks. In D. Schunk & J. Meece (Eds.), *Students' perceptions in the classroom: Causes and consequences* (pp. 149–183). Hillsdale, NJ: Erlbaum.

Pintrich, P., & Schunk, D. (2002). *Motivation in education: Theory,* *research, and applications* (2nd ed.). Upper Saddle River, NJ: Prentice Hall.

Pitoniak, M., & Royer, J. (2001). Testing accommodations for examinees with disabilities: A review of psychometric, legal, and social policy issues. *Review of Educational Research, 71*(1), 53–104.

Pittman, K., & Beth-Halachmy, S. (1997, March). *The role of prior knowledge in analogy use.* Paper presented at the annual meeting of the American Educational Research Association, Chicago.

Plake, B., & Impara, J. (1997). Teacher assessment literacy: What do teachers know about assessment? In G. Phye (Ed.), *Handbook of classroom assessment,* (pp. 54–70). San Diego, CA: Academic Press.

Plake, B., Impara, J., & Spies (Eds.). (2003). *The fifteenth mental measurements yearbook.* Lincoln: University of Nebraska Press.

Pleiss, M., & Feldhusen, J. (1995). Mentors, role models, and heroes in the lives of gifted children. *Educational Psychologist, 30*(3), 159–169.

Pogrow, S. (1990). Challenging at-risk students: Findings from the HOTS Program. *Phi Delta Kappan, 71*(5), 389–397.

Pomplun, M., Capps, L., & Sundbye, N. (1997, March). *Criteria teachers use to score performance items.* Paper presented at the annual meeting of the National Educational Research Association, Chicago.

Poole, M., Okeafor, K., & Sloan, E. (1989, April). *Teachers' interactions, personal efficacy, and change implementation.* Paper presented at the annual meeting of the American Educational Research Association, San Francisco.

Popham, J. (1993). Measurement-driven instruction as a "quick-fix" reform strategy. *Measurement and Evaluation in Counseling and Development, 26,* 31–34.

Popham, J. (1998). *Can instructionally focused low-stakes performance tests foster effective classroom instruction?* Paper presented at the annual meeting of the American Educational Research Association, San Diego, CA.

Popham, W. J. (2000). *Classroom assessment* (3rd ed.). Boston: Allyn & Bacon.

Popham, W. J. (2001). Teaching to the test? *Educational Leadership, 56*(6), 16–20.

Porche, M., & Ross, S. (1999 , April). *Parent involvement in the early elementary grades: An analysis of mothers' practices and teachers' expectations.* Paper presented at the annual meeting of the American Educational Research Association, Montreal, Canada.

Posner, G., Strike, K., Hewson, P., & Gertzog, W. (1982). Accommodation of a scientific conception: Toward a theory of conceptual change. *Science Education, 66,* 211–227.

Poulin, F., & Boivin, M. (1999). Proactive and reactive aggression and boys' friendship quality in mainstream classrooms. *Journal of Emotional and Behavioral Disorders, 7,* 168–177.

Pratton, J., & Hales, L. (1986). The effects of active participation on student learning. *Journal of Educational Research, 79,* 210–215.

Prawat, R. (1989). Promoting access to knowledge, strategy, and disposition in students: A research synthesis. *Review of Educational Research, 59,* 1–41.

Premack, D. (1965). Reinforcement theory. In D. Levine (Ed.), *Nebraska Symposium on Motivation* (Vol. 13, pp. 3–41). Lincoln: University of Nebraska Press.

Pressley, M., Harris, K., & Marks, M. (1992). But good strategy users are constructivists! *Educational Psychology Review, 4,* 3–31.

Pressley, M., Johnson, C., Symons, S., McGoldrick, J., & Kurita, J. (1989). Strategies that improve children's memory and comprehension of text. *Elementary School Journal, 90,* 3–31.

Pugach, M., & Wesson, C. (1995). Teachers' and students' views of team teaching of general education and learning-disabled students in two fifth-grade classes. *Elementary School Journal, 95*(3), 279–295.

Pulos, S., & Linn, M. (1981). Generality of the controlling variable scheme in early adolescence. *Journal of Early Adolescence, 1,* 26–37.

Purdie, N., Hattie, J., & Carroll, A. (2002). A review of the research on interventions for attention deficit hyperactivity disorder: What works best? *Review of Educational Research, 72*(1), 61–100.

Purkey, S., & Smith, M. (1983). Effective schools: A review. *Elementary School Journal, 83,* 427–452.

Purkey, W., & Novak, J. (1984). *Inviting school success* (2nd ed.). Belmont, CA: Wadsworth.

Putnam, R., & Borko, H. (2000). What do new views of knowledge and thinking have to say about research on teacher learning? *Educational Researcher, 29*(1), 4–15.

Putnam, R., Heaton, R., Prawat, R., & Remillard, J. (1992). Teaching mathematics for understanding: Discussing case studies of four fifth-grade teachers. *Elementary School Journal, 93,* 213–228.

Pyryt, M., & Mendaglio, S. (2001, April). *Intelligence and moral development: A meta-analytic review.* Paper presented at the annual meeting of the American Educational Research Association, Seattle.

Quin, Z., Johnson, D., & Johnson, R. (1995). Cooperative versus competitive efforts and problem solving. *Review of Educational Research, 65*(2), 129–143.

Quiocho, A., & Ulanoff, S. (2002, April). *Teacher research in preservice teacher education: Asking burning questions.* Paper presented at the annual meeting of the American Educational Research Association, New Orleans, LA.

Radd, T. (1998). Developing an inviting classroom climate through a comprehensive behavior-management plan. *Journal of Invitational Theory and Practice, 5,* 19–30.

Raths, J. (2001, April). *Indicators of subject matter knowledge in the classroom!* Paper presented at the annual meeting of the American Educational Research Association, Seattle.

Ravetta, M., & Brunn, M. (1995, April). *Language learning, literacy, and cultural background: Second-language acquisition in a mainstreamed classroom.* Paper presented at the annual meeting of the American Educational Research Association, San Francisco.

Reckase, M. (1997, March). *Constructs assessed by portfolios: How do they differ from those assessed by other educational tests?* Paper presented at the annual meeting of the National Educational Research Association, Chicago.

Reis, S. (1992, April). *The curriculum compacting study.* Paper presented at the annual meeting of the American Educational Research Association, San Francisco.

Reis, S., & Purcell, J. (1992). *An analysis of content elimination and strategies used by elementary classroom teachers in the curriculum compacting process.*

Storrs: University of Connecticut, National Research Center on the Gifted and Talented.

Reisberg, D. (1997). *Cognition: Exploring the science of the mind.* New York: Norton.

Renkl, A., Stark, R., Gruber, H., & Mandl, H. (1998). Learning from worked-out examples: The effects of example variability and elicited self-explanations. *Contemporary Educational Psychology, 23,* 90–108.

Renner, J., Stafford, D., Lawson, A., Mckinnon, J., Friot, F., & Kellogg, D. *Research, teaching and learning with the Piaget model.* Norman: University of Oklahoma Press.

Renzulli, J. (1986). The three-ring conception of giftedness: A developmental model for creative productivity. In R. Sternberg & J. Davidson (Eds.), *Conceptions of giftedness.* Cambridge, MA: Harvard University Press.

Resnick, L. (1987). *Education and learning to think.* Washington, DC: National Academy Press.

Resnick, L., & Klopfer, L. (1989). Toward the thinking curriculum: An overview. In L. Resnick & L. Klopfer (Eds.), *Toward the thinking curriculum: Current cognitive research* (pp. 1–18). Alexandria, VA: Association for Supervision and Curriculum Development.

Rest, J., Narvaez, D., Bebeau, M., & Thoma, S. (1999). A neo-Kohlbergian approach: The DIT and schema theory. *Educational Psychology Review, 11,* 291–324.

Rest, J., Thoma, S., Narvaez, D., & Bebeau, M. (1997). Alchemy and beyond: Indexing the defining issues test. *Journal of Educational Psychology, 89*(3), 498–507.

Reynolds, R., Sinatra, G., & Jetton, T. (1996). Views of knowledge acquisition and representation: A continuum from experience-centered to mind-centered. *Educational Psychologist, 31,* 93–194.

Rich, D. (1987). *Teachers and parents: An adult-to-adult approach.* Washington, DC: National Education Association.

Richason, D. (2001, April). *The effects of a problem-based learning pedagogy on student outcomes as they relate to Bloom's taxonomy: A content analysis of student products.* Paper presented at the annual meeting of the American Educational Research Association, Seattle.

Rickards, J., Fajen, B., Sullivan, J., & Gillespie, G. (1997). Signaling, notetaking, and field independence-dependence in text comprehension and recall. *Journal of Educational Psychology, 89*(3), 508–517.

Rickford, J. (1997). Suite for Ebony and phonics. *Discover, 18*(12), 82–87.

Ridley, D., McCombs, B., & Taylor, K. (1994). Walking the talk: Fostering self-regulated learning in the classroom. *Middle School Journal, 26*(2), 52–57.

Riley, M., Greeno, J., & Heller, J. (1982). The development of children's problem-solving ability in arithmetic. In H. Ginsburg (Ed.), *Development of mathematical thinking.* San Diego, CA: Academic Press.

Riordan, C. (1996). *Equality and achievement: An introduction to the sociology of education.* New York: Longman.

Rittle-Johnson, B., & Alibali, M. (1999). Conceptual and procedural knowledge of mathematics: Does one lead to the other? *Journal of Educational Psychology, 91*(1), 175–189.

Ritts, V., Patterson, M., & Tubbs, M. (1992). Expectations, impressions, and judgments of physically attractive students: A review. *Review of Educational Research, 62,* 413–426.

Riverside Publishing. (2003). *Stanford-Binet Intelligence Scales, Fifth Edition.* Retrieved December 21, 2002, from http://www.riverpub.com/products/clinical/sbis5/home.html

Robertson, J. (2000). Is attribution training a worthwhile classroom intervention for K–12 students with learning difficulties? *Educational Psychology Review, 12*(1), 111–134.

Robinson, D., Katayama, A., Dubois, N., & Devaney, T. (1998). Interactive effects of graphic organizers and delayed review on concept application. *Journal of Experimental Education, 67*(1), 17–31.

Roblyer, M. (2003). *Integrating educational technology into teaching* (3rd ed.). Upper Saddle River, NJ: Merrill/Prentice Hall.

Rogers, C. (1959). A theory of therapy, personality, and interpersonal relationships, as developed in the client-centered framework. In S. Koch (Ed.), *Psychology: A study of a science* (Vol. 3, pp. 184–256). New York: McGraw-Hill.

Rogers, C. (1963). Actualizing tendency in relation to "motives" and to consciousness. In M. Jones (Ed.), *Nebraska Symposium on Motivation* (Vol. 11, pp. 1–24). Lincoln: University of Nebraska Press.

Rogoff, B. (1990). *Apprenticeship in thinking: Cognitive development in social context.* New York: Oxford University Press.

Rogoff, B., & Chavajay, P. (1995). What's become of the research on the cultural basis of cognitive development? *American Psychologist, 50,* 859–877.

Rose, K., Williams, K., Gomez, L., & Gearon, J. (2002, April). *Building a case for what our students know and can do: How trustworthy are our judgments?* Paper presented at the annual meeting of the American Educational Research Association, New Orleans, LA.

Rose, L., & Gallup, A. (1999). The 31st annual Phi Delta Kappa/Gallup poll of the public's attitudes toward the public schools. *Phi Delta Kappan, 81,* 41–56.

Rose, L., & Gallup, A. (2001). The 33rd annual Phi Delta Kappa/Gallup poll of the public's attitudes toward the public schools. *Phi Delta Kappan, 83,* 41–58.

Rose, L., & Gallup, A. (2002). The 34th annual Phi Delta Kappa/Gallup poll of the public's attitudes towards public schools. *Phi Delta Kappan, 84,* 41–46, 51–56.

Rosen, L., O'Leary, S., Joyce, S., Conway, G., & Pfiffer, L. (1984). The importance of prudent negative consequences for maintaining the appropriate behavior of hyperactive students. *Journal of Abnormal Child Psychology, 12,* 581–604.

Rosenberg, M. (1989). The effects of daily homework assignments on the acquisition of basic skills by students with learning disabilities. *Journal of Learning Disabilities, 22,* 314–323.

Rosenfeld, D., Folger, R., & Adelman, H. (1980). When rewards reflect competence: A qualification of the overjustification effect. *Journal of Personality and Social Psychology, 39,* 368–376.

Rosenfeld, P., Lambert, S., & Black, R. (1985). Desk arrangement effects on pupil classroom behavior. *Journal of Educational Psychology, 77,* 101–108.

Rosenshine, B. (1987). Explicit teaching. In D. Berliner & B. Rosenshine (Eds.), *Talks to teachers.* New York: Random House.

Rosenshine, B. (1997, March). *The case for explicit, teacher-led, cognitive strategy instruction.* Paper presented at the annual meeting of the American Educational Research Association, Chicago.

Rosenshine, B., & Meister, C. (1992, April). *The use of scaffolds for teaching less structured academic tasks.* Paper presented at the annual meeting of the American Educational Research Association, San Francisco.

Rosenshine, B., & Stevens, R. (1986). Teaching functions. In M. Wittrock (Ed.), *Handbook of research on teaching* (3rd ed., pp. 376–391). New York: Macmillan.

Ross, B., & Spalding, T. (1994). Concepts and categories. In R. Sternberg (Ed.), *Handbook of perception and cognition* (Vol. 12). New York: Academic Press.

Ross, J., Rolheiser, C., & Hogaboam-Gray, A. (2002, April). *Influences on student cognitions about evaluation.* Paper presented at the annual meeting of the American Educational Research Association, New Orleans, LA.

Ross, S., Smith, L., Loks, L., & McNelie, M. (1994). Math and reading instruction in tracked first-grade classes. *Elementary School Journal, 95*(2), 105–118.

Rothman, R. (1991). Schools stress speeding up, not slowing down. *Education Week, 9*(1), 11, 15.

Rotter, J. (1966). Generalized expectancies for internal versus external control of reinforcement. *Psychological Monographs, 80*(1, Whole No. 609).

Rowe, M. (1974). Wait-time and rewards as instructional variables, their influence on language, logic, and fate control: Part one—wait time. *Journal of Research in Science Teaching, 11,* 81–94.

Rowe, M. (1986). Wait-time: Slowing down may be a way of speeding up. *Journal of Teacher Education, 37*(1), 43–50.

Rubin, L. (1985). *Artistry in teaching.* New York: McGraw-Hill.

Rutherford, F., & Algren, A. (1990). *Science for all Americans.* New York: Oxford University Press.

Rutter, M., Maughan, B., Mortimore, P., Ouston, J., & Smith, A. (1979). *Fifteen thousand hours.* Cambridge, MA: Harvard University Press.

Ruzic, R. (2001, April). *Lessons for everyone: How students with reading-related learning disabilities survive and excel in college courses with heavy reading requirements.* Paper presented at the annual meeting of the American Educational Research Association, Seattle.

Ryan, R., Connell, J., & Deci, E. (1985). A motivational analysis of self-determination and self-regulation in education. In C. Ames & R. Ames (Eds.), *Research on motivation in education* (Vol. 2, pp. 13–51). New York: Academic Press.

Ryan, R., & Deci, E. (1996). When paradigms clash: Comments on Cameron and Pierce's claim that rewards do not undermine intrinsic motivation. *Review of Educational Research, 66,* 33–38.

Ryan, R., & Deci, E. (2000). Intrinsic and extrinsic motivations: Classic definitions and new directions. *Contemporary Educational Psychology, 25,* 54–67.

Sach, J. (1999). Department issues IDEA regulations. *Education Week, 18*(27), 1, 40.

Sadker, M., Sadker, D., & Klein, S. (1991). The issue of gender in elementary and secondary education. In G. Grant (Ed.), *Review of research in education* (Vol. 17, pp. 269–334). Washington, DC: American Educational Research Association.

Sadker, M., Sadker, D., & Long, L. (1997). Gender and educational equality. In J. Banks & C. Banks (Eds.), *Multicultural education: Issues and perspectives* (3rd ed., pp. 131–149). Boston: Allyn & Bacon.

Sadoski, M., & Goetz, E. (1998). Concreteness effects and syntactic modification in written composition. *Scientific Studies of Reading, 2,* 341–352.

Sagor, R. (2000). *Guiding school improvement with action research.* Alexandria, VA: Association for Supervision and Curriculum Development.

Salvia, J., & Ysseldyke, J. (1988). *Assessment in special and remedial education* (4th ed.). Boston: Houghton Mifflin.

Samuels, S. (1988). Decoding and automaticity: Helping poor readers become automatic at word recognition. *Reading Teacher, 41*(8), 756–760.

Sax, G. (1997). *Principles of educational and psychological measurement and evaluation.* Belmont, CA: Wadsworth.

Scarcella, R. (1990). *Teaching language-minority students in the multicultural classroom*. Upper Saddle River, NJ: Prentice Hall.

Schauble, L. (1990). Belief revision in children: The role of prior knowledge and strategies for generating evidence. *Journal of Experimental Child Psychology, 49,* 31–57.

Schiever, S., & Maher, C. (1997). Enrichment and acceleration: An overview and new directions. In N. Colangelo & A. Davis (Eds.), *Handbook of gifted education* (2nd ed., pp. 113–125). Boston: Allyn & Bacon.

Schiff, M., Duyme, M., Dumaret, A., & Tomkiewicz, S. (1982). How much could we boost scholastic achievement and IQ scores? A direct answer from a French adoption agency. *Cognition, 12,* 165–192.

Schlozman, S., & Schlozman, V. (2000). Chaos in the classroom: Looking at ADHD. *Educational Leadership, 58*(3), 28–33.

Schmidt, P. (1992). Gap cited in awareness of students' home languages. *Education Week, 11*(32), 11.

Schnaiberg, L. (1999). Arizona looks to its neighbor in crafting plan to take to voters. *Education Week, 18*(38), 9.

Schneider, W., & Shiffrin, R. (1977). Controlled and automatic human information processing: Detection, search, and attention. *Psychological Review, 84,* 1–66.

Schoenfeld, A. (1989). Teaching mathematical thinking and problem solving. In L. Resnick & L. Klopfer (Eds.), *Toward the thinking curriculum: Current cognitive research* (pp. 83–103). Alexandria, VA: Association for Supervision and Curriculum Development.

Schofield, J., Eurich-Fulcer, R., & Britt, C. (1994). Teachers, computer tutors, and teaching: The artificially intelligent tutor as an agent for classroom change. *American Educational Research Journal, 31*(3), 579–607.

Schommer, M. (1994). An emerging conceptualization of epistemological beliefs and their role in learning. In R. Garner & P. Alexander (Eds.), *Beliefs about text and instruction with text.* Hillsdale, NJ: Erlbaum.

Schon, D. (1983). *The reflective practitioner: How professionals think in action.* New York: Basic Books.

Schraw, G., Flowerday, T., & Lehman, S. (2001). Increasing situational interest in the classroom. *Educational Psychology Review, 13*(3), 211–224.

Schraw, G., & Lehman, S. (2001). Situational interest: A review of the literature and directions for future research. *Educational Psychology Review, 13*(1), 23–52.

Schraw, G., & Moshman, D. (1995). Metacognitive theories. *Educational Psychology Review, 7,* 351–371.

Schunk, D. (1983). Ability versus effort attributional feedback: Differential effects on self-efficacy and achievement. *Journal of Educational Psychology, 75,* 848–856.

Schunk, D. (1987). Peer models and children's behavioral change. *Review of Educational Research, 57,* 149–174.

Schunk, D. (1989). Self-efficacy and cognitive skill learning. In C. Ames & R. Ames (Eds.), *Research on motivation in education: Vol. 3. Goals and cognitions* (pp. 13–44). San Diego, CA: Academic Press.

Schunk, D. (1994, April). *Goal and self-evaluative influences during children's mathematical skill acquisition.* Paper presented at the annual meeting of the American Educational Research Association, New Orleans, LA.

Schunk, D. (1996). *Learning theories* (2nd ed.). Upper Saddle River, NJ: Merrill/Prentice Hall.

Schunk, D. (1997, March). *Self-monitoring as a motivator during instruction with elementary school students.* Paper presented at the annual meeting of the American Educational Research Association, Chicago.

Schunk, D. (2000). *Learning theories* (3rd ed.). Upper Saddle River, NJ: Merrill/Prentice Hall.

Schunk, D., & Ertmer, P. (1999). Self-regulatory processes during computer skill acquisition: Goal and self-evaluative influences. *Journal of Educational Psychology, 91*(2), 251–260.

Schunk, D., & Hanson, A. (1989). Self-modeling and children's cognitive skill learning. *Journal of Educational Psychology, 81,* 155–163.

Schwartz, B. (1990). The creation and destruction of value. *American Psychologist, 45,* 7–15.

Schwartz, B., & Reisberg, D. (1991). *Learning and memory.* New York: Norton.

Schwartz, N., Ellsworth, L., Graham, L., & Knight, B. (1998). Accessing prior knowledge to remember text: A comparison of advance organizers and maps. *Contemporary Educational Psychology, 23,* 65–89.

Sears, S., Kennedy, J., & Kaye, G. (1997). Myers-Briggs personality profiles of prospective educators. *The Journal of Education Research, 90,* 195–202.

Seifert, T. (1993). Effects of elaborative interrogation with prose passages. *Journal of Educational Psychology, 85*(4), 642–651.

Seligman, D. (1975). *Helplessness.* San Francisco: Freeman.

Seligman, M. (1995). *The optimistic child.* Boston: Houghton Mifflin.

Serpell, R. (2000). Intelligence and culture. In R. J. Sternberg (Ed.), *Handbook of intelligence* (pp. 549–577). New York: Cambridge University Press.

Shahid, J. (2001, April). *Teacher efficacy: A research synthesis.* Paper presented at the annual meeting of the American Educational Research Association, Seattle.

Shank, R. (1979). Interestingness: Controlling inferences. *Artificial Intelligence, 12,* 273–297.

Shaughnessy, M. (1998). An interview with E. Paul Torrance: About creativity. *Educational Psychology Review, 10*(4).

Shea, D., Lubinski, D., & Benbow, C. (2001). Importance of assessing spatial ability in intellectually talented young adolescents: A 20-year longitudinal study. *Journal of Educational Psychology, 93*(3), 604–614.

Shearer, C. (2002, April). *Using a multiple intelligences assessment to facilitate teacher development.* Paper presented at the annual meeting of the American Educational Research Association, New Orleans, LA.

Shepard, L. (1993). Evaluating test validity. In L. Darling-Hammond (Ed.), *Review of research in education* (Vol. 19, pp. 405–450). Washington, DC: American Educational Research Association.

Shepard, L. (2000). The role of assessment in a learning culture. *Educational Researcher, 29*(7), 4–14.

Shepard, L. (2001). The role of classroom assessment in teaching and learning. In V. Richardson (Ed.), *Handbook of research on learning* (4th ed., pp. 1066–1101). Washington, DC: American Educational Research Association.

Shepard, L., & Bliem, C. (1995). Parents' thinking about standardized tests and performance assessments. *Educational Researcher, 24*(5), 25–32.

Shields, P., & Shaver, D. (1990, April). The *mismatch between the school and home* cultures of academically at-risk students. Paper presented at the annual meeting of the American Educational Research Association, Boston.

Short, E., Schatschneider, C., & Friebert, S. (1993). Relationship between memory and metamemory performance: A comparison of specific and general strategy knowledge. *Journal of Educational Psychology, 85*(3), 412–423.

Shuell, T. (1996). Teaching and learning in a classroom context. In D. Berliner & R. Calfee (Eds.), *Handbook of educational psychology* (pp. 726–764). New York: Macmillan.

Shulman, L. (1986). Those who understand: Knowledge growth in teaching. *Educational Researcher, 15*(2), 4–14.

Shulman, L. (1987). Knowledge and teaching: Foundations of the new reform. *Harvard Educational Review, 57*, 1–22.

Shumow, L., & Harris, W. (1998, April). *Teachers' thinking about home-school relations in low-income urban communities.* Paper presented at the annual meeting of the American Educational Research Association, San Diego, CA.

Siegel, M. (2002, April). *Models of teacher learning: A study of case analyses by preservice teachers.* Paper presented at the annual meeting of the American Educational Research Association, New Orleans, LA.

Siegler, R. (1991). *Children's thinking* (2nd ed.). Upper Saddle River, NJ: Prentice Hall.

Siegler, R. S. (1996). *Emerging minds: The process of change in children's thinking.* New York: Oxford.

Siegler, R., & Ellis, S. (1996). Piaget on childhood. *Psychological Science, 7,* 211–215.

Signorielli, N. (1993). Television, the portrayal of women, and children's attitudes. In G. Berry & J. Asamen (Eds.), *Children and television: Images in a changing sociocultural world* (pp. 229–242). Newbury Park, CA: Sage.

Simon, H. (1978). Information-processing theory of human problem solving. In W. Estes (Ed.), *Handbook of learning and cognitive processes: Vol. 5. Human information processing.* Hillsdale, NJ: Erlbaum.

Simpson, E. (1972). *The classification of educational objectives: Psychomotor domain.* Urbana: University of Illinois Press.

Simpson, J., Olejnik, S., Tam, A., & Suprattathum, S. (1994). Elaborative verbal rehearsals and college students' cognitive performance. *Journal of Educational Psychology, 86*(2), 267–278.

Skaalvik, E. (1997). Self-enhancing and self-defeating ego orientation: Relations with task and avoidance orientation, achievement, self-perceptions and anxiety. *Journal of Educational Psychology, 89,* 71–81.

Skaalvik, E., & Valas, H. (1999). Relations among achievement, self-concept, and motivation in mathematics and language arts: A longitudinal study. *Journal of Experimental Education, 67*(2), 135–149.

Skiba, R., & Raison, J. (1990). Relationship between the use of timeout and academic achievement. *Exceptional Children, 57,* 36–47.

Skinner, B. (1953). *Science and human behavior.* New York: Macmillan.

Skinner, B. (1957). *Verbal behavior.* Upper Saddle River, NJ: Prentice Hall.

Skinner, E. (1995). *Perceived control, motivation, and coping.* Thousand Oaks, CA: Sage.

Skinner, E., & Belmont, M. (1993). Motivation in the classroom: Reciprocal effects of teacher behavior and student engagement across the school year. *Journal of Educational Psychology, 85,* 571–581.

Skinner, E., Wellborn, J., & Connell, J. (1990). What it takes to do well in school and whether I've got it: A process model of perceived control and children's engagement and achievement in school. *Journal of Educational Psychology, 82,* 22–32.

Skoe, E., & Dressner, R. (1994). Ethics of care, justice, identity, and gender: An extension and replication. *Merrill-Palmer Quarterly, 40*(2), 272–289.

Slaby, R., Roedell, W., Arezzo, D., & Hendrix, K. (1995). *Early violence prevention.* Washington, DC: National Association for the Education of Young Children.

Slaughter-Defoe, D., Nakagawa, K., Takanashi, R., & Johnson, D. (1990). Toward cultural/ecological perspectives on schooling and achievement in African and Asian American children. *Child Development,* 363–383.

Slavin, R. (1995). *Cooperative learning: Theory, research, and practice* (2nd ed.).

Needham Heights, MA: Allyn & Bacon.

Slavin, R. (1987). Ability grouping and student achievement in elementary schools: A best-evidence synthesis. *Review of Educational Research, 57,* 293–336.

Slavin, R., & Karweit, N. (1982, April). *School organizational vs. developmental effects on attendance among young adolescents.* Paper presented at the annual meeting of the American Psychological Association, Washington, DC.

Slavin, R., Karweit, N., & Madden, N. (Eds.). (1989). *Effective programs for students at risk.* Needham Heights, MA: Allyn & Bacon.

Slavin, R., Madden, N., Dolan, L., & Wasik, B. (1994). Roots and wings: Inspiring academic excellence. *Educational Leadership, 52,* 10–14.

Slavin, R., Madden, N., Karweit, N., Dolan, L., & Wasik, B. (1992). *Success for all: A relentless approach to prevention and early intervention in elementary schools.* Arlington, VA: Educational Research Service.

Smith, L., & Cotten, M. (1980). Effect of lesson vagueness and discontinuity on student achievement and attitude. *Journal of Educational Psychology, 72,* 670–675.

Smith, P., & Fouad, N. (1999). Subject-matter specificity of self-efficacy, outcome expectancies, interest, and goals: Implications for the social-cognitive model. *Journal of Counseling Psychology, 46,* 461–471.

Smokowski, P. (1997, April). *What personal essays tell us about resiliency and protective factors in adolescence.* Paper presented at the annual meeting of the American Educational Research Association, Chicago.

Snary, J. (1995). In a communitarian voice: The sociological expansion of Kohlbergian theory, research, and practice. In W. Kurtines & J. Gewirtz (Eds.), *Moral development: An introduction.* Boston: Allyn & Bacon.

Snider, V. (1990). What we know about learning styles from research in special education. *Educational Leadership, 48,* 53.

Snow, R. (1992). Aptitude theory: Yesterday, today, and tomorrow. *Educational Psychologist, 27*(1), 5–32.

Snow, R., Corno, L., & Jackson, D., III. (1996). Individual differences in affective and conative functions. In D. Berliner & R. Calfee (Eds.),

Handbook of educational psychology (pp. 243–310). New York: Macmillan.

Snyder, S., Bushur, L., Hoeksema, P., Olson, M., Clark, S., & Snyder, J. (1991, April). *The effect of instructional clarity and concept structure on students' achievement and perception.* Paper presented at the annual meeting of the American Educational Research Association, Chicago.

Snyderman, M., & Rothman, S. (1987). Survey of expert opinion on intelligence and aptitude testing. *American Psychologist, 42,* 137–144.

Sokolove, S., Garrett, S., Sadker, M., & Sadker, D. (1990). Interpersonal communication skills. In J. Cooper (Ed.), *Classroom teaching skills* (pp. 185–228). Lexington, MA: Heath.

Southerland, S., Kittleson, J., & Settlage, J. (2002, April). *The intersection of personal and group knowledge construction: Red fog, cold cans, and seeping vapor or children talking and thinking about condensation in a third grade classroom.* Paper presented at the annual meeting of the National Association for Science Teaching, New Orleans, LA.

Spaulding, C. (1992). *Motivation in the classroom.* New York: McGraw-Hill.

Spearman, C. (1927). *The abilities of man: Their nature and measurement.* New York: Macmillan.

Spear-Swerling, L., & Sternberg, R. (1998). Curing our "epidemic" of learning disabilities. *Phi Delta Kappan, 79*(5), 397–401.

Spector, J. (1992). Predicting progress in beginning reading: Dynamic assessment of phonemic awareness. *Journal of Educational Psychology, 84*(3), 353–363.

Speidel, G., & Tharp, R. (1980). What does self-reinforcement reinforce? An empirical analysis of the contingencies in self-determined reinforcement. *Child Behavior Therapy, 2,* 1–22.

Spiro, R., Feltovich, P., Jacobson, M., & Coulson, R. (1992). Knowledge representation, content specification, and the development of skill in situation-specific knowledge assembly: Some constructivist issues as they relate to cognitive flexibility theory and hypertext. In T. Duffy & D. Jonassen (Eds.), *Constructivism and the technology of instruction: A conversation* (pp. 121–127). Hillsdale, NJ: Erlbaum.

Sprigle, J., & Schoefer, L. (1985). Longitudinal evaluation of the effects of two compensatory preschool programs on fourth- through sixth-grade students. *Developmental Psychology, 21,* 702–708.

Stahl, S. (1999). Why innovations come and go (and mostly go): The case of whole language. *Educational Researcher, 28*(8), 13–22.

Stainback, S., & Stainback, W. (Eds.). (1992). *Curriculum considerations in inclusive classrooms.* Baltimore: Brookes.

Stallings, J. (1980). Allocated academic learning time revisited, or beyond time on task. *Educational Researcher, 9,* 11–16.

Stanovich, K. (1990). Concepts in developmental theory of reading skill: Cognitive resources, automaticity, and modularity. *Developmental Review, 10,* 72–100.

Star, J. (2002, April). *Re-"conceptualizing" procedural knowledge in mathematics.* Paper presented at the annual meeting of the American Educational Research Association, New Orleans, LA.

State Departments of Education. (2000). *Key state education policies of K–12 education: 2000.* Retrieved October 1, 2002, from http://www.ccsso.org/pdfs/KeyState2000.pdf

Stecher, B., & Herman, J. (1997). Using portfolios for large-scale assessment. In G. Phye (Ed.), *Handbook of classroom assessment* (pp. 490-514). San Diego, CA: Academic Press.

Stedman, L. (1997). International achievement differences: An assessment of a new perspective. *Educational Researcher, 26*(3), 4–15.

Stein, M., & Carnine, D. (1999). Designing and delivering effective mathematics instruction. In R. Stevens (Ed.), *Teaching in American schools* (pp. 245–270). Upper Saddle River, NJ: Merrill/Prentice Hall.

Steinberg, L., Brown, B., & Dornbusch, S. (1996). Ethnicity and adolescent achievement. *American Education, 20*(2), 28–35.

Steinberg, L., Dornbusch, S., & Brown, B. (1992). Ethnic differences in adolescent achievement. *American Psychologist, 47*(6), 723–729.

Stephens, K., & Karnes, F. (2000). State definitions for the gifted and talented revisited. *Exceptional Children, 66*(2), 219–238.

Stepien, W., & Gallagher, S. (1993). Problem-based learning: As authentic as it gets. *Educational Leadership, 50*(7), 25–28.

Stern, D. (1997, March). *The role of values conflict in the development of professional attitudes.* Paper presented at the annual meeting of the American Educational Research Association, Chicago.

Sternberg, R. (1986). *Intelligence applied: Understanding and increasing your intellectual skills.* San Diego, CA: Harcourt Brace Jovanovich.

Sternberg, R. (1988). *The triarchic mind.* New York: Viking.

Sternberg, R. (1989). Intelligence, wisdom, and creativity: Their natures and interrelationships. In R. Linn (Ed.), *Intelligence: Measurement, theory, and public policy* (pp. 119–146). Chicago: University of Illinois Press.

Sternberg, R. (1990). *Metaphors of mind: Conceptions of the nature of intelligence.* New York: Cambridge University Press.

Sternberg, R. (1997). A triarchic view of giftedness: Theory and practice. In N. Colangelo & A. Davis (Eds.), *Handbook of gifted education* (2nd ed., pp. 43–53). Boston: Allyn & Bacon.

Sternberg, R. (1998a). Applying the triarchic theory of human intelligence in the classroom. In R. Sternberg & W. Williams (Eds.), *Intelligence, instruction, and assessment* (pp. 1–16). Mahwah, NJ: Erlbaum.

Sternberg, R. (1998b). Metacognition, abilities, and developing expertise: What makes an expert student? *Instructional Science, 26*(1–2), 127–140.

Sternberg, R. (1998c). Principles of teaching for successful intelligence. *Educational Psychologist, 33*(2/3), 65–72.

Sternberg, R. (1999). *Cognitive psychology* (2nd ed.). Fort Worth, TX: Harcourt Brace.

Sternberg, R., & Frensch, P. (1993). Mechanisms of transfer. In D. Detterman & R. Sternberg (Eds.), *Transfer on trial: Intelligence, cognition, and instruction.* Norwood, NJ: Ablex.

Sternberg, R., & Grigorenko, E. (2000). Theme-park psychology: A case study regarding human intelligence and its implications for education. *Educational Psychology Review, 12*(2), 247–268.

Sternberg, R., & Grigorenko, E. (2001). Learning disabilities, schooling, and society. *Phi Delta Kappan, 83*(4), 335–338.

Sternberg, R., Grigorenko, E., & Jarvin, L. (2001). Improving reading instruction: The triarchic model. *Educational Leadership, 59*(6), 48–52.

Sternberg, R., & Lubart, R. (1995). *Defying the crowd.* New York: Free Press.

Sternberg, R., Torff, B., & Grigorenko, E. (1998b). Teaching for successful intelligence raises school achievement. *Phi Delta Kappan, 79*(9), 667–669.

Stevenson, H., Chen, C., & Uttal, D. (1990). Beliefs and achievements: A study of Black, White, and Hispanic children. *Child Development, 61,* 508–523.

Stevenson, H., & Fantuzzo, J. (1986). The generality and social validity of a competency-based self-control training intervention for underachieving students. *Journal of Applied Behavior Analysis, 19,* 269–276.

Stevenson, H., Lee, S., & Stigler, J. (1986). Mathematics achievement of Chinese, Japanese, and American children. *Science, 231,* 693-699.

Stiggins, R. (1997). *Student-centered classroom assessment* (2nd ed.). Upper Saddle River, NJ: Merrill/Prentice Hall.

Stiggins, R. (2001). *Student-centered classroom assessment* (3rd ed.). Upper Saddle River, NJ: Merrill/Prentice Hall.

Stiggins, R., & Conklin, N. (1992). *In teachers' hands.* Albany: State University of New York Press.

Stigler, J., & Hiebert, J. (2000). *The teaching gap.* New York: Free Press.

Stipek, D. (1996). Motivation and instruction. In D. Berliner & R. Calfee (Eds.), *Handbook of educational psychology* (pp. 85–113). New York: Macmillan.

Stipek, D. (2002). *Motivation to learn: Integrating theory and practice* (4th ed.). Boston: Allyn & Bacon.

Stoddart, T.(1999, April). *Language acquisition through science inquiry.* Symposium presented at the annual meeting of the American Educational Research Association, Montreal, Canada.

Strage, A., & Brandt, T. (1999). Authoritative parenting and college students' academic adjustment and success. *Journal of Educational Psychology, 91*(1), 146–156.

Streitmatter, J. (1997). An exploratory study of risk-taking and attitudes in a girls-only middle school math class. *Elementary School Journal, 98*(1), 15–26.

Stright, A., Neitzel, C., Sears, K., & Hoke-Sinex, L. (2001). Instruction begins in the home: Relations between parental instruction and children's self-regulation in the classroom. *Journal of Educational Psychology, 93*(3), 456–466.

Strom, S. (1989). The ethical dimension of teaching. In M. Reynolds (Ed.), *Knowledge base for the beginning teacher* (pp. 267–276). New York: Pergamon Press.

Stuebing, K., Fletcher, J., LeDoux, J., Lyon, G., Shaywitz, S., & Shaywitz, B. (2002). Validity of IQ-discrepancy classifications of reading disabilities: A meta-analysis. *American Educational Research Journal, 39*(2), 469–518.

Stull, J. (1998, April). *Identification and analysis of school characteristics that are effective in fostering educational resilience in students.* Paper presented at the annual meeting of the American Educational Research Association, San Diego, CA.

Subotnik, R. (1997). Teaching gifted students in a multicultural society. In J. Banks & C. Banks (Eds.), *Multicultural education: Issues and perspective* (3rd ed., pp. 361–382). Boston: Allyn & Bacon.

Sudweeks, R., Baird, J., & Petersen, G. (1990, April). *Test-wise responses of third-, fifth-, and sixth-grade students to clued and unclued multiple-choice science items.* Paper presented at the annual meeting of the American Educational Research Association, Boston.

Sudzina, M. (Ed.). (1999). *Case study applications for teacher education.* Needham Heights, MA: Allyn & Bacon.

Summers, J., Woodruff, A., Tomberlin, T., Williams, N., & Svinicki, M. (2001, April). *Cognitive processes of cooperative learning: A qualitative analysis.* Paper presented at the annual meeting of the American Educational Research Association, Seattle.

Sunai, C., & Haas, M. (1993). *Social studies and the elementary/middle school student.* New York: Harcourt Brace Jovanovich.

Surber, J. (2002, April). *Self assessment by college students of exam readiness and exam performance.* Paper presented at

the annual meeting of the American Educational Research Association, New Orleans, LA.

Swanson, H. (2001). Research on interventions for adolescents with learning disabilities: A meta-analysis of outcomes related to higher-order processing. *Elementary School Journal, 101*(3), 331–348.

Swanson, H. & Hoskyn, M. (1998). Experimental intervention research on students with learning disabilities: A meta-analysis of treatment outcomes. *Review of Educational Research, 68*(3), 277–321.

Sweller, J., van Merrienboer, J., & Paas, F. (1998). Cognitive architecture and instructional design. *Educational Psychology Review, 10,* 251–196.

Taylor, J. (1983). Influence of speech variety on teachers' evaluation of reading comprehension. *Journal of Educational Psychology, 75,* 662–667.

Taylor, R. (1987, March). *Knowledge for critical thinking.* Paper presented at the meeting of the Near East South Asia Council for Overseas Schools, Nairobi, Kenya.

Tennyson, R., & Cocchiarella, M. (1986). An empirically based instructional design theory for teaching concepts. *Review of Educational Research, 56,* 40–71.

Terhune, K. (1968). Studies of motives, cooperation, and conflict within laboratory microcosms. In G. Snyder (Ed.), *Studies in international conflict* (Vol. 4, pp. 29–58). Buffalo, NY: SUNY Buffalo Council on International Studies.

Terman, L., Baldwin, B., & Bronson, E. (1925). Mental and physical traits of a thousand gifted children. In L. Terman (Ed.), *Genetic studies of genius* (Vol. 1). Stanford, CA: Stanford University Press.

Terman, L., & Oden, M. (1947). The gifted child grows up. In L. Terman (Ed.), *Genetic studies of genius* (Vol. 4). Stanford, CA: Stanford University Press.

Terman, L., & Oden, M. (1959). The gifted group in mid-life. In L. Terman (Ed.), *Genetic studies of genius* (Vol. 5). Stanford, CA: Stanford University Press.

Terwilliger, J. (1997). Semantics, psychometrics, and assessment reform: A close look at "authentic assessments." *Educational Researcher, 26,* 24–27.

Tharp, R., & Gallimore, R. (1988). *Rousing minds to life: Teaching, learning and schooling in social context.* Cambridge, England: Cambridge University Press.

Thoma, S., & Rest, J. (1996). *The relationship between moral decision-making and patterns of consolidation and transition in moral judgment development.* Paper presented at the annual meeting of the American Educational Research Association, New York.

Thorkildsen, T. (1996, April). *The way tests teach: Children's theories of how much testing is fair in school.* Paper presented at the annual meeting of the National Educational Research Association, New York.

Thorndike, E. (1924). Mental discipline in high school studies. *Journal of Educational Psychology, 15,* 1–2, 83–98

Thorndike, R., Hagen, E., & Sattler, J. (1986). *The Stanford-Binet Intelligence Scale* (4th ed.). Chicago: Riverside.

Thornton, M., & Fuller, R. (1981). How do college students solve proportion problems? *Journal of Research in Science Teaching, 18,* 335–340.

Tierney, R., Readence, J., & Dishner, E. (1990). *Reading strategies and practices: A compendium* (3rd ed.). Boston: Allyn & Bacon.

Tirri, K. (2001, April). *What can we learn from teachers' moral mistakes?* Paper presented at the annual meeting of the American Educational Research Association, Seattle.

Tisak, M. (1993). Preschool children's judgments of moral and personal events involving physical harm and property damage. *Merrill-Palmer Quarterly, 39,* 375–390.

Tishman, S., Perkins, D., & Jay, E. (1995). *The thinking classroom: Learning and teaching in a culture of thinking.* Needham Heights, MA: Allyn & Bacon.

Tobias, S., & Everson, H. (1998, April). *Research on the assessment of metacognitive knowledge monitoring.* Paper presented at the annual meeting of the American Educational Research Association, San Diego, CA.

Todt-Stockman, L., Gaa, J., & Swank, P. (2001, April). *Age and gender differences in the perception of sex-role: Comparing responses from college students and middle-aged college alumni.* Paper presented at the annual meeting of the American Educational Research Association, Seattle.

Tomasello, M. (1995). Language is not an instinct. *Cognitive Development, 10,* 131–156.

Tomlinson, C. (1995). Deciding to differentiate instruction in middle school: One school's journey. *Gifted Child Quarterly, 39*(2), 77–87.

Tomlinson, C., & Callahan, C. (2001, April). *Deciding to teach them all: Middle school teachers learning to teach for academic diversity.* Paper presented at the annual meeting of the American Educational Research Association, Seattle.

Tomlinson, C., Callahan, C., & Lelli, K. (1997). Challenging expectations: Case studies of high-potential, culturally diverse young children. *Gifted Child Quarterly, 41*(2), 5–17.

Tomlinson, C., Callahan, C., & Moon, T. (1998, April). *Teachers learning to create environments responsive to academically diverse classroom populations.* Paper presented at the annual meeting of the American Educational Research Association, San Diego, CA.

Tompkins, G. (1997). *Literacy for the twenty-first century.* Upper Saddle River, NJ: Merrill/Prentice Hall.

Top, B., & Osgthorpe, R. (1987). Reverse-role tutoring: The effects of handicapped students tutoring regular class students. *Elementary School Journal, 87*(4), 413–423.

Torrance, E. (1995). Insights about creativity: Questioned, rejected, ridiculed, ignored. *Educational Psychology Review, 7*(3), 313–322.

Trawick-Smith, J. (1997). *Early childhood development: A multicultural perspective.* Upper Saddle River, NJ: Merrill/Prentice Hall.

Trawick-Smith, J. (2000). *Early childhood development: A multicultural perspective* (2nd ed.). Upper Saddle River, NJ: Merrill/Prentice Hall.

Treffinger, D. (1998). From gifted education to programming for talent development. *Phi Delta Kappan, 79*(10), 752–756.

Triandis, H. (1995). *Individualism and collectivism.* Boulder, CO: Westview Press.

Trusty, J., & Pirtle, T. (1998). Parents' transmission of educational goals to their adolescent children. *Journal of Research and Development in Education, 32*(1), 53–65.

Tschannen-Moran, M., Woolfolk-Hoy, A., & Hoy, W. (1998). Teacher efficacy: Its meaning and measure. *Review of Educational Research, 68*(2), 202–248.

Tuckman, B. (1998). Using tests as an incentive to motivate procrastinators to study. *Journal of Experimental Education, 66*(2), 141–147.

Tulving, E. (1979). Relation between encoding specificity and level of processing. In L. Cermak & F. Craik (Eds.), *Levels of processing and human memory* (pp. 405–428). Hillsdale, NJ: Erlbaum.

Tuovinen, J., & Sweller, J. (1999). A comparison of cognitive load associated with discovery learning and worked examples. *Journal of Educational Psychology, 91*(2), 334–341.

Turiel, E. (1973). Stage transitions in moral development. In R. Travers (Ed.), *Second handbook of research on teaching* (pp. 732–758). Chicago: Rand McNally.

Turiel, E. (1998). The development of morality. In W. Damon (Editor-in-Chief) & N. Eisenberg (Vol. Ed.), *Handbook of child psychology: Vol. 3. Social, emotional, and personality development* (5th ed., pp. 863–932). New York: Wiley.

Turnbull, A., Turnbull, R., Shank, M., Smith, S., &. Leal, D. (2002). *Exceptional lives: Special education in today's schools* (3rd ed.). Upper Saddle River, NJ: Merrill/Prentice Hall.

Turner, J. (1995). The influence of classroom contexts on young children's motivation for literacy. *Reading Research Quarterly, 30,* 410–441.

Turner, S., Bernt, P., & Pecora, N. (2002, April). *Why women choose information technology careers: Educational, social, and familial influences.* Paper presented at the annual meeting of the American Educational Research Association, New Orleans, LA.

Tyler, R. (1950). *Basic principles of curriculum and instruction.* Chicago: University of Chicago Press.

U.S. Bureau of the Census. (1996). *Statistics.* Washington, DC: Author.

U.S. Bureau of the Census. (2000). *Statistical abstract of the United States* (120th edition). Washington, DC: U.S. Government Printing Office.

U.S. Congress. (1978). *Educational Amendment of 1978, P.L. 95–561, IX(A).*

U.S. Department of Commerce. (1998). *Current population survey, 1997.* Washington, DC: Bureau of the Census.

U.S. Department of Commerce. (1999). *Falling through the Net: Defining the digital divide.* Retrieved October 1, 2002, from http://www.ntia.doc.gov/ntiahome/fttn99/contents.html

U.S. Department of Education. (1998). *Advanced telecommunication in U.S.: Public school survey.* Washington, DC: National Center for Educational Statistics.

U.S. Department of Education. (1999). *Digest of education statistics, 1998.* Washington, DC: U.S. Government Printing Office.

U.S. Department of Education. (2000a). *Digest of education statistics, 1999.* Washington, DC: National Center for Educational Statistics.

U.S. Department of Education. (2000b). *Twenty-second annual report to Congress on the implementation of the Individuals With Disabilities Education Act.* Washington, DC: Government Printing Office.

U.S. Department of Education. (2002). *Twenty-fourth annual report to Congress on the implementation of the Individuals With Disabilities Education Act.* Washington, DC: Government Printing Office.

U.S. Department of Health and Human Services [1914–1993]. (1998). *Annual vital statistics report.* Washington, DC: Author.

U.S. Department of Justice. (1999). *Crime in the United States.* Washington, DC: U.S. Government Printing Office.

Vaillant, B., & Vaillant, C. (1990). Natural history of male psychological health, XII: A 45-year study of predictors of successful aging. *American Journal of Psychiatry, 147,* 31–37.

Valencia, R., & Suzuki, L. (2001). *Intelligence testing and minority students.* Thousand Oaks, CA: Sage.

Valencia, S., & Place, N. (1994). Literacy portfolios for teaching, learning, and accountability: The Bellevue Literacy assessment project. In S. Valencia, E. Hiebert, & P. Afflerbach (Eds.), *Authentic reading assessment: Practices and possibilities* (pp. 134-156). Newark, DE: International Reading Association.

Vanderstoep, S., & Seifert, C. (1994). Problem solving, transfer, and thinking. In P. Pintrich, D. Brown, & C. Weinstein (Eds.), *Student motivation, cognition, and learning* (pp. 27–49). Hillsdale, NJ: Erlbaum.

Van Leuvan, P., Wang, M., & Hildebrandt, L. (1990, April). *Students' use of self-instructive processes in the first and second grade.* Paper presented at the annual meeting of the American Educational Research Association, Boston.

Van Meter, P. (2001). Drawing construction as a strategy for learning from text. *Journal of Educational Psychology, 93*(1), 129–140.

Van Tassel-Baska, J. (Ed.). (1998). *Excellence in educating gifted and talented learners* (3rd ed.). Denver: Love.

Vaughn, S., Bos, C., & Schumm, J. (2000). *Teaching exceptional, diverse, and at-risk students in the general education classroom.* Boston: Allyn & Bacon.

Veenman, S. (1984). Perceived problems of beginning teachers. *Review of Educational Research, 54,* 143–178.

Verna, M., Wintergerst, A., & DeCapua, A. (2001, April). *College students benefit by employing second language learning strategies.* Paper presented at the annual meeting of the American Educational Research Association, Seattle.

Viadero, D. (2000). High-stakes tests lead debate at researchers' gathering. *Education Week, 19*(34), 6.

Viadero, D., & Johnston, R. (2000). Lifting minority achievement: Complex answers. *Education Week, 19*(30), 1, 14–16.

Villegas, A. (1991). *Culturally responsive pedagogy for the 1990s and beyond.* Princeton, NJ: Educational Testing Service.

Vine, I. (1986). Moral maturity in socio-cultural perspective: Are Kohlberg's stages universal? In S. Modgil & C. Modgil (Eds.), *Lawrence Kohlberg: Consenses and controversy* (pp. 431–450). Philadelphia: Falmer Press.

Vitaro, F., Gendreau, P., Tremblay, R., & Oligny, P. (1998). Reactive and proactive aggression differentially predict later conduct problems. *Journal of Child Psychology and Psychiatry and Allied Disciplines, 39,* 377–385.

Volman, M., & van Eck, E. (2002, April). *Gender issues in information technology in education.* Paper presented at the annual meeting of the American Educational Research Association, New Orleans, LA.

Vosniadou, S., & Brewer, W. (1989). *The concept of the earth's shape: A study of conceptual change in childhood.* Unpublished manuscript, University of Illinois, Center for the Study of Reading, Champaign, IL.

Voss, J., & Wiley, J. (1995). Acquiring intellectual skills. *Annual Review of Psychology, 46,* 155–181.

Vygotsky, L. (1978). *Mind in society: The development of higher psychological processes* (M. Cole, V. John-Steiner, S. Scribner, & E. Souberman, Eds. & Trans.). Cambridge, MA: Harvard University Press.

Vygotsky, L. (1986). *Thought and language.* Cambridge, MA: MIT Press.

Wadsworth, B. (1996). *Piaget's theory of cognitive and affective development* (5th ed.). White Plains, NY: Longman.

Waggoner, D. (1995, November). Are current home speakers of non-English languages learning English? *Numbers and Needs, 5.*

Wagner, R., & Sternberg, R. (1985). Practical intelligence in real-world pursuits: The role of tacit knowledge. *Journal of Personality and Social Psychology, 52,* 1236–1247.

Walberg, H. (1984). Improving the productivity of America's schools. *Educational Leadership, 41*(8), 19–27.

Walker, D., Greenwood, C., Hart, B., & Carta, J. (1994). Prediction of school outcomes based on early language production and socioeconomic factors. *Child Development, 65,* 606–621.

Walker, L., & Pitts, R. (1998). Naturalistic conceptions of moral maturity. *Developmental Psychology, 34,* 403–419.

Wall, S. (1983). Children's self-determination of standards in reinforcement contingencies: A re-examination. *Journal of School Psychology, 21,* 123–131.

Wallace, D. (2000). Results, results, results? *Education Leadership, 57*(5), 66–67.

Wallace, D., West, S., Ware, A., & Dansereau, D. (1998). The effect of knowledge maps that incorporate gestalt principles on learning. *Journal of Experimental Education, 67*(1), 5–16.

Walsh, D. (1991). Extending the discourse on developmental appropriateness: A developmental perspective. *Early Education and Development, 2*(2), 109–119.

Walters, G., & Grusec, J. (1977). *Punishment.* San Francisco: Freeman.

Walton, P., Kuhlman, N., & Cortez, J. (1998). *Preparing teachers for linguistically and culturally diverse learners: The case for developmental evaluation.* Paper presented at the annual meeting of the American Educational Research Association, San Diego, CA.

Walton, S., & Taylor, K. (1996/97). How did you know the answer was boxcar? *Educational Leadership, 54*(4), 38–40.

Wang, M., Haertel, G., & Walberg, H. (1993). Toward a knowledge base for school learning. *Review of Educational Research, 63*(3), 249–294.

Wang, M., Haertel, G., & Walberg, H. (1995, April). *Educational resilience: An emerging construct.* Paper presented at the annual meeting of the American Educational Research Association, San Francisco.

Ward, T., Ward, S., Landrum, M., & Patton, J. (1992, April). *Examination of a new protocol for the identification of at-risk gifted learners.* Paper presented at the annual meeting of the American Educational Research Association, San Francisco.

Washington, V., & Miller-Jones, D. (1989). Teacher interactions with non-Standard-English speakers during reading instruction. *Contemporary Child Psychology, 14*, 280–312.

Wasserstein, P. (1995). What middle schoolers say about their schoolwork. *Educational Leadership, 53*(1), 41–43.

Waterman, A. (1985). Identity in the context of adolescent psychology. *New Directions for Child Development, 30*, 5–24.

Watson, B., & Konicek, R. (1990). Teaching for conceptual change: Confronting children's experience. *Phi Delta Kappan, 71*, 680–685.

Waxman, H., & Huang, S. (1996). Motivation and learning environment differences in inner-city middle school students. *Journal of Educational Research, 90*(2), 93–102.

Waxman, H., Huang, S., Anderson, L., & Weinstein, T. (1997). Classroom process differences in inner-city elementary schools. *Journal of Educational Research, 91*(1), 49–59.

Weaver, L., & Padron, Y. (1997, March). *Mainstream classroom teachers' observations of ESL teachers' instruction.* Paper presented at the annual meeting of the American Educational Research Association, Chicago.

Webb, N., Baxter, G., & Thompson, L. (1997). Teachers' grouping practices in fifth-grade science classrooms. *Elementary School Journal, 98*(2), 107–111.

Webb, N., & Farivar, S. (1994). Promoting helping behavior in cooperative small groups in middle school mathematics. *American Educational Research Journal, 31*(2), 369–395.

Webb, N., Farivar, S., & Mastergeorge, A. (2002). Productive helping in cooperative groups. *Theory Into Practice, 41*(1).

Webb, N., & Palincsar, A. (1996). Group processes in the classroom. In D. Bertliner & R. Calfee (Eds.), *Handbook of educational psychology* (pp. 841–876). New York: Macmillan.

Wechsler, D. (1991). *The Wechsler Intelligence Scale for Children—Third Edition—WISC-III.* San Antonio, TX: Psychological Corporation.

Weiland, A., & Coughlin, R. (1979). Self-identification and preferences: A comparison of White and Mexican American first and third graders. *Journal of Social Psychology, 10*, 356–365.

Weiner, B. (1986). *An attributional theory of motivation and emotion.* New York: Springer-Verlag.

Weiner, B. (1990). History of motivational research in education. *Journal of Educational Psychology, 82*, 616–622.

Weiner, B. (1992). *Human motivation: Metaphors, theories, and research.* Newbury Park, CA: Sage.

Weiner, B. (1994a). Ability versus effort revisited: The moral determinants of achievement evaluation and achievement as a moral system. *Educational Psychologist, 29*, 163–172.

Weiner, B. (1994b). Integrating social and personal theories of achievement striving. *Review of Educational Research, 64*, 557–573.

Weiner, L. (2002, April). *Why is classroom management so vexing to urban teachers? New Directions in theory and research about classroom management in urban schools.* Paper presented at the annual meeting of the American Educational Research Association, New Orleans, LA.

Weinert, F., & Helmke, A. (1995). Interclassroom differences in instructional quality and interindividual differences in cognitive development. *Educational Psychologist, 30*, 15–20.

Weinert, F., & Helmke, A. (1998). The neglected role of individual differences in theoretical models of cognitive development. *Learning and Instruction, 8*(4), 309–324.

Weinstein, C. (1994). Strategic learning/strategic teaching: Flip sides of a coin. In P. Pintrich,

D. Brown, & C. Weinstein (Eds.), *Student motivation, cognition, and learning* (pp. 257–273). Hillsdale, NJ: Erlbaum.

Weinstein, C. (1999). Reflections on best practices and promising programs: Beyond assertive classroom discipline. In J. Freiberg (Ed.), *Beyond behaviorism: Changing the classroom management paradigm* (pp. 145–163). Boston: Allyn & Bacon.

Weinstein, C., & Mignano, A. (1993). *Elementary classroom management.* New York: McGraw-Hill.

Weinstein, C., Woolfolk, A., Dittmeier, L., & Shankar, U. (1994). Protector or prison guard? Using metaphors and media to explore student teachers' thinking about classroom management. *Action in Teacher Education, 16*(1), 41–54.

Weinstein, R. (1998). Promoting positive expectations in schooling. In N. Lambert & B. McCombs (Eds.), *How students learn: Reforming schools through learner-centered education* (pp. 81–111). Washington, DC: American Psychological Association.

Weissberg, R., & Greenberg, M. (1998). School and community competence-enhancement prevention programs. In W. Damon (Ed.), *Handbook of child psychology* (Vol. 4). New York: Wiley.

Weissglass, S. (1998). *Ripples of hope: Building relationships for educational change.* Santa Barbara, CA: Center for Educational Change in Mathematics & Science, University of California.

Weller, H. (1997, March). *What have we learned from 8 years of research on computer-based science learning? An analysis of 50 research papers.* Paper presented at the annual meeting of the American Educational Research Association, Chicago.

Wentzel, K. (1991). Relations between social competence and academic achievement in early adolescence. *Child Development, 62*, 1066–1078.

Wentzel, K. (1993). Does being good make the grade? Social behavior and academic competence in middle school. *Journal of Educational Psychology, 85*, 357–364.

Wentzel, K. (1996). Social goals and social relationships as motivators of school adjustment. In J. Juvonen & K. Wentzel (Eds.), *Social motivation: Understanding children's school adjustment* (pp. 226–247). Cambridge, England: Cambridge University Press.

Wentzel, K. (1997). Student motivation in middle school: The role of perceived pedagogical caring. *Journal of Educational Psychology, 89,* 411–419.

Wentzel, K. (1999a). Social influences on school adjustment: Commentary. *Educational Psychologist, 34*(1), 59–69.

Wentzel, K. (1999b). Social-motivational processes and interpersonal relationships: Implications for understanding students' academic success. *Journal of Educational Psychology, 91,* 76–97.

Wentzel, K. (2000). What is it that I'm trying to achieve? Classroom goals from a content perspective. *Contemporary Educational Psychology, 25,* 105–115.

Werts, M., Caldwell, N., & Wolery, M. (1996). Peer modeling of response chains: Observational learning by students with disabilities. *Journal of Applied Behavior Analysis, 29,* 53–66.

West, J. (1997, March). *Motivation and access to help: The influence of status on one child's motivation for literacy learning.* Paper presented at the annual meeting of the American Educational Research Association, Chicago.

Wharton-McDonald, R., Pressley, M., & Hampston, J. (1998). Literacy instruction in nine first-grade classrooms: Teacher characteristics and student achievement. *Elementary School Journal, 99,* 101–128.

Whimbey, A. (1980). Students can learn to be better problem solvers. *Educational Leadership, 37,* 560–565.

White, A., & Bailey, J. (1990). Reducing disruptive behaviors of elementary physical education students with sit and watch. *Journal of Applied Behavior Analysis, 23,* 353–359.

White, R. (1959). Motivation reconsidered: The concept of competence. *Psychological Review, 66,* 297–333.

Wiersma, W. (2000). *Research methods in education: An introduction.* Needham Heights, MA: Allyn & Bacon.

Wigfield, A. (1994). Expectancy-value theory of achievement motivation: A developmental perspective. *Educational Psychology Review, 6,* 49–78.

Wigfield, A., & Eccles, J. (1992). The development of achievement task values: A theoretical analysis. *Developmental Review, 12,* 265–310.

Wigfield, A., & Eccles, J. (2000). Expectancy-value theory of achievement motivation. *Contemporary Educational Psychology, 25,* 68–81.

Wigfield, A., Eccles, J., & Pintrich, P. (1996). Development between the ages of 11 and 25. In D. Berliner & R. Calfee (Eds.), *Handbook of educational psychology* (pp. 148–185). New York: Macmillan.

Wiggins, G. (1996/97). Practicing what we preach in designing authentic assessment. *Educational Leadership, 54*(4), 18–25.

Wildavsky, B. (1999, September 27). Achievement testing gets its day in court. *U.S. News and World Report,* pp. 22–23.

Wiley, D., & Harnischfeger, A. (1974). Explosion of a myth: Quantity of schooling and exposure to instruction, major education vehicles. *Education Researcher, 3,* 7–12.

Wiley, J., & Voss, J. (1999). Constructing arguments from multiple sources: Tasks that promote understanding and not just memory for text. *Journal of Educational Psychology, 91*(2), 301–311.

Williams, J. (1992, April). *Effects of test anxiety and self-concept on performance across curricular areas.* Paper presented at the annual meeting of the American Educational Research Association, San Francisco.

Williams, R. (1987). Current issues in classroom behavior management. In J. Glover & R. Ronning (Eds.), *Historical foundations of educational psychology* (pp. 297–325). New York: Plenum Press.

Williams, S., Bareiss, R., & Reiser, B. (1996, April). *ASK Jasper: A multimedia publishing and performance support environment for design.* Paper presented at the annual meeting of the American Educational Research Association, New York.

Willingham, W., & Cole, N. (1997). *Gender and fair assessment.* Mahwah, NJ: Erlbaum.

Willoughby, T., Porter, L., Belsito, L., & Yearsley, T. (1999). Use of elaboration strategies by students in grades two, four, and six. *Elementary School Journal, 99*(3), 221–232.

Willoughby, T., Wood, E., & Khan, M. (1994). Isolating variables that impact on or detract from the effectiveness of elaboration strategies. *Journal of Educational Psychology, 86*(2), 279–289.

Wilson, B. (1998). *African American students' perceptions of their classroom climate and self-esteem.* Paper presented at the annual meeting of the American Educational Research Association, San Diego, CA.

Wilson, K., & Swanson, H. (1999, April). *Individual and age-related differences in working memory and mathematics computation.* Paper presented at the annual conference of the American Educational Research Association, Montreal, Canada.

Wilson, M., Hoskens, M., & Draney, K. (2001, April). *Rater effects: Some issues, some solutions.* Paper presented at the annual meeting of the American Educational Research Association, Seattle.

Wilson, S., Shulman, L., & Richert, A. (1987). 150 different ways of knowing: Representations of knowledge in teaching. In J. Calderhead (Ed.), *Exploring teacher thinking* (pp. 104–124). London: Cassel.

Winitzky, N. (1994). Multicultural and mainstreamed classrooms. In R. Arends (Ed.), *Learning to teach* (3rd ed., pp. 132–170). New York: McGraw-Hill.

Wink, J., & Putney, L. (2002). *A vision of Vygotsky.* Boston: Allyn & Bacon.

Winn, J. (1992, April). *The promises and challenges of scaffolded instruction.* Paper presented at the annual meeting of the American Educational Research Association, San Francisco.

Winograd, K. (1998). Rethinking theory after practice: Education professor as elementary teacher. *Journal of Teacher Education, 49*(4), 296–303.

Winterton, W. A. (1977). The effect of extended wait-time on selected verbal response characteristics of some Pueblo Indian children. *Dissertation Abstracts International, 38,* 620A. (UMI No. 7716130)

Wolf, L., Smith, J., & Birnbaum, M. (1997, March). *Measure-specific assessment of motivation and anxiety.* Paper presented at the annual meeting of the American Educational Research Association, Chicago.

Wolfe, P., & Brandt, R. (1998). What we know. *Educational Leadership, 56*(3), 8–13.

Wolfram, W. (1991). *Dialects and American English.* Upper Saddle River, NJ: Prentice Hall.

Wolters, C. (1997, March). *Self-regulated learning and college students' regulation of motivation.* Paper presented at the annual meeting of the American

Educational Research Association, Chicago.

Wong-Fillmore, L. (1992). When learning a second language means losing the first. *Education, 6*(2), 4–11.

Wood, D., Bruner, J., & Ross, S. (1976). The role of tutoring in problem solving. *British Journal of Psychology, 66,* 181–196.

Wood, E., Motz, M., & Willoughby, T. (1998). Examining students' retrospective memories of strategy development. *Journal of Educational Psychology, 90,* 698–704.

Wood, E., Willoughby, T., McDermott, C., Motz, M., Kaspar, V., & Ducharme, M. (1999). Developmental differences in study behavior. *Journal of Educational Psychology, 91*(3), 527–536.

Woodcock, R. (1995, March). *Conceptualizations of intelligence and their implications for education.* Paper presented at the annual meeting of the American Educational Research Association, San Francisco.

Woolfolk, A., & Hoy, W. (1990). Prospective teachers' sense of efficacy and beliefs about control. *Journal of Educational Psychology, 82,* 81–91.

Worthen, B. (1993). Critical issues that will determine the future of alternative assessment. *Phi Delta Kappan, 74,* 444–454.

Worthy, J., Moorman, M., & Turner, M. (1999). What Johnny likes to read is hard to find in school. *Reading Research Quarterly, 34*(1), 12–27.

Wright, S., & Taylor, D. (1995). Identity and the language of the classroom: Investigating the impact of heritage versus second-language instruction on personal and collective self-esteem. *Journal of Educational Psychology, 87*(2), 241–252.

Wynne, E. (1997, March). *Moral education and character education: A comparison/contrast.* Paper presented at the annual meeting of the American Educational Research Association, Chicago.

Xu, S. (2002, April). *Opportunities and barriers: Teachers learn to integrate diverse students' popular culture into literacy instruction.* Paper presented at the annual meeting of the American Educational Research Association, New Orleans, LA.

Yang, Y. (1991–1992). The effects of media on motivation and content recall: Comparison of computer and print-based instruction. *Journal of Education Technology Systems, 20,* 95–105.

Yazejian, N. (1999, April). *The relationship between school identification and dropping out of school.* Paper presented at the annual meeting of the American Educational Research Association, Montreal, Canada.

Yee, A. (1995). Evolution of the nature-nurture controversy: Response to J. Philipps Rushton. *Educational Psychology Review, 7*(4), 381–394.

Yeung, A., Chui, H., Lau, I., McInerney, D., Russell-Bowie, D., & Suliman, R. (2000). Where is the hierarchy of academic self-concept? *Journal of Educational Psychology, 92*(3), 556–567.

Young, A. (1997). I think, therefore I'm motivated: The relations among cognitive strategy use, motivational orientation and classroom perceptions over time. *Learning and Individual Differences, 9,* 249–283.

Young, B., & Smith, T. (1999). *The condition of education, 1996: Issues in focus: The social context of education.* Washington, DC: U.S. Department of Education. Retrieved October 1, 2002, from http://nces.ed.gov/pubs99/conditio n 99

Young, M., & Scribner, J. (1997, March). *The synergy of parental involvement and student engagement at the secondary level: Relationships of consequence in Mexican-American communities.* Paper presented at the annual meeting of the American Educational Research Association, Chicago.

Yussen, S., & Levy, V. (1975). Developmental changes in predicting one's own span of short-term memory. *Journal of Experimental Child Psychology, 19,* 502–508.

Zahorik, J. (1991). Teaching style and textbooks. *Teaching and Teacher Education, 7,* 185–196.

Zahorik, J. (1996). Elementary and secondary teachers' reports of how they make learning interesting. *The Elementary School Journal, 96*(5), 551–564.

Zehr, M. (2000a). Arizona curtails bilingual education. *Education Week, 20*(11), 1, 21.

Zehr, M. (2000b). Campaigns to curtail bilingual ed. advance in Colorado, Arizona. *Education Week, 19*(39), 19.

Zeidner, M. (1998). *Test anxiety: The state of the art.* New York: Plenum Press.

Zimmerman, B., & Blotner, R. (1979). Effect of model persistence and success on children's problem solving. *Journal of Educational Psychology, 71,* 508–513.

Zimmerman, B., & Schunk, D. (Eds.). (1989). *Self-regulated learning and academic achievement: Theory, research, and practice.* New York: Springer.

Ziomek, R. (1997, March). *The concurrent validity of ACT's Passport Portfolio program: Initial validity results.* Paper presented at the annual meeting of the National Educational Research Association, Chicago.

Zohar, D. (1998). An additive model of test anxiety: Role of exam-specific expectations. *Journal of Educational Psychology, 90*(2), 330–340.

Zook, K. (1991). Effects of analogical processes on learning and misrepresentation. *Educational Psychology Review, 3,* 41–72.

Author Index

Woodruff, A., 298
Woodward, J., 52, 68
Woolfolk, A., 429
Woolfolk-Hoy, A., 394
Workman, D., 499
Worsham, M., 6
Wortham, D., 327
Worthen, B., 510, 517, 564
Worthley, J., 257
Worthy, J., 360
Wright, S., 98, 99
Wu, L., 289-290
Wynne, E., 101, 109

Xu, J., 270
Xu, S., 139

Yang, Y., 414
Yearsley, T., 253
Yekovich, C., 243
Yekovich, F., 243
Yeung, A., 96
Young, A., 363
Young, B., 130, 133
Young, K., 205
Young, M., 87, 88, 131
Ysseldyke, J., 547
Yussen, S., 261

Zahorik, J., 407, 409, 464
Zan, B., 102, 429, 433
Zehr, M., 69
Zeidner, M., 380

Zeiser, S., 289-290
Zeitz, C., 296, 298
Zentall, S., 177
Zimmerman, B., 218, 221, 361
Ziomek, R., 514
Zohar, D., 522
Zook, K., 263

Subject Index

instructional strategies for, 314–319

theories of, 313–314

Concept mapping, 315–316

Conceptual knowledge, 466

Concrete materials, 44–45, 52–53

Concrete operational stage, 41, 44–45, 46, 48–49, 52–53

Concrete representations of topics, 9

Concrete thinking, 4–5. *See also* Cognitive development

Conditioned stimulus/response, 197, 198–199

Conditioning

classical, 197–199, 200, 228–229

operant, 200–213

Conferences

parent-teacher, 438

student-led, 517

Confidentiality of records, 165

Connected discourse, 475

Consequences

applying, 452–453

assertive discipline and, 450

defined, 201

logical, 448, 452–453

nonoccurrence of, 215–216

vicarious learning and, 217

Conservation, 43–44

Consistency, 444–445, 453, 497–498, 509

Constructivism, 279–309

assessment and, 290–291

case studies in, 279–280, 307–308

characteristics of, 282–284, 306

classroom applications of, 291–292, 301, 303–304

cognitive, 281, 282

defined, 281, 305

implications for teaching, 284–290, 306

instructional strategies for, 292–300, 306

perspective on, 304–305, 306

social, 281–282, 326

social interaction and, 281–284, 287–290, 304

technology and, 285–286

as theory of learning, 304

views of, 281–282, 306

Construct validity, 550

Content

intelligence and, 121

knowledge of, 5, 7–10, 12, 463

representations of, 9, 341

Content areas. *See also* Domain-specific knowledge; Mathematics instruction; Reading; Science instruction; Writing

concepts, 313

knowledge of, 5, 7–10, 12, 463

self-esteem and, 96

teaching success and, 5

Content bias, in assessment, 525–526, 561–562, 563, 566

Content validity, 549

Context

problem solving and, 326

procedural knowledge acquisition and, 246

transfer of learning and, 340–341

Contiguity, 196, 199

Continuous reinforcement schedules, 203, 204

Control

defined, 373

as motivator, 368, 373–374

need for, 373–374

technology and, 415

Conventional ethics, 104–105

Convergent thinking, 321

Cooperation

promoting, 185

scripted, 299–300

Cooperative learning, 298–303

classroom application of, 301

defined, 299

diversity and, 135–136, 139, 302–304

instructional strategies in, 298–303

introducing students to, 299

Cooperative learning style, 135–136, 139

Correlation, 15

Correlational research, 14–15

Cost, 361

Creativity, 22–23, 122, 123, 178–179

Crisis, psychosocial theory on, 89

Criterion-referenced evaluation, 529–530

Critical decision making, 21

Critical periods, 36, 37

Critical thinking

case study of, 344–345

instructional strategies for, 334–338

Criticism, 373, 376, 402

Cues, 61, 206–207, 213, 452

Cultural alternation, 134

Cultural bias

intelligence and, 123–124

standardized tests and, 525–526, 561–565, 566

Cultural deficit theories, 137

Cultural difference theories, 137

Cultural diversity, 132–137, 153. *See also* Linguistic diversity; Minority groups

behaviorism and, 227–230, 231

classroom applications and, 100, 140, 565–566

culturally responsive teaching and, 137–139

ethnic pride and, 98–100

high-stakes tests and, 560–561

interaction patterns and, 135, 136–137

learning style and, 135–136, 139

motivation and, 416–419, 420

parent-teacher communication and, 440–443

peer influence and, 82, 134

social cognitive theory and, 227–230, 231

Cultural inversion, 134

Cultural learning styles, 135–136, 139

Culturally responsive teaching, 137–139

Culture

defined, 132

development and, 58

learner differences in, 132–137

resistance, 134

schooling and, 133–137, 153

in sociocultural theory, 58

values and, 133–134

Culture-fair tests, 124

Culture shock, 39

Curiosity motivation, 405–406

Curriculum-based assessment, 176

Deafness, defined, 175

Decision making

artistic, 22–23

assessment and, 23

critical, 21

gathering information for, 23

practical, 21–22

reflective teaching and, 24

research and, 20–24

wait-time and, 20, 21

Declarative knowledge, 243–246, 270–271. *See also* Schemas

Declarative stage, 246

Deep processing approaches, 128

Deficiency needs, 354–355

Deliberate practice, 324

Demonstrations, 9

Descriptive rating scales, 514, 515

Descriptive research, 13–14

Descriptive statistics, 551–554

Desists, 452

Despair, 90

Detention, after-school, 205

Detroit Test of Learning Aptitude, 545

Development, 34, 72. *See also* Child development; Cognitive development; Language development; Moral development; Personal development; Psychosocial development; Social development

Deviation, standard, 554

Diagnostic tests, 543, 545

Dialects, 66–67

"Digital divide," 151–153

Dignity, student, 444

Direct experience, 39–40

Direct modeling, 216

Knowledge. *See also* Background knowledge and experiences; Research
    conceptual, 466
    of content, 5, 7–10, 12, 463
    declarative, 243–246, 270–271
    domain-specific. *See* Domain-specific knowledge
    as indicator of intelligence, 5
    of learners, 10–11
    of learning, 11
    pedagogical, 7–11, 463
    planning, 246
    procedural, 243, 245–246, 267, 271
    role of research in, 12–20
    of teacher, 5, 7–11, 12, 463, 475, 486
    types of, 7–11
Knowledge acquisition component, Sternberg model, 121
Knowledge construction, Piaget and Vygotsky on, 61–62. *See also* Constructivism
Kohlberg's theory of moral development, 102–107, 113
    criticisms of, 106–107
    perspective on, 105–107
    research on, 106
    stages of, 103–105
Kounin, J., 426, 444, 452

Labeling, 165–166, 188
Laboratory simulations. *See* Simulations
Language
    complexity of, 66
    development and, 57, 63–66, 72, 73
    fine-tuning, 66
    knowledge construction and, 62
    in sociocultural theory, 57, 64–65
Language acquisition device (LAD), 64
Language arts, concepts in, 313. *See also* Reading; Writing
Language development, 41, 63–66, 72, 73
    classroom application of, 72
    socioeconomic status and, 131
    stages of, 65–66
    theories of, 63–65
Language disorders, 173–174
Language diversity. *See* Linguistic diversity
Language patterns, cultural differences in, 137
Latinos. *See* Hispanic parents; Hispanic students
Law(s), and exceptionalities, 160, 163, 165
Law and order stage of moral development, 105
LDs (learning disabilities), 167–170
Learned helplessness, 174–175, 368–369
Learner(s)
    knowledge of, 10–11
    self-efficacy of, 362, 402, 412–413, 414

Learner-centered instruction, 139, 298–303
Learner-Centered Psychological Principles (American Psychological Association), 402
Learner-centered strategies, 292–303
    cooperative learning, 139, 298–303
    defined, 292–293
    discussion, 296–298, 301
    guided discovery, 293–295, 301
    inquiry, 295–296, 301
Learner differences
    culture, 132–137
    gender, 136, 140–144, 154
    intelligence, 117–127, 153
    socioeconomic status (SES), 123, 129–132
    students placed at risk, 144–151, 154
Learning. *See also* Transfer of learning
    assessment and, 7, 23, 483–485, 487, 495
    cognitive perspectives on, 236–238, 273
    cooperative. *See* Cooperative learning
    definitions of, 196, 215, 238
    development and, 34, 58
    knowledge of, 11
    motivation to learn, 351
    problem-based, 329–330
    situated, 340–341
    social interaction and, 281–284, 287–290, 304
    technology and, 49–50
    verbal, 266
    vicarious, 217, 452
Learning activities
    information processing model and, 254–256, 258
    motivation and, 409–410, 420
    preparing and organizing, 468–469
Learning and Teaching Inventory, 4–7
Learning disabilities (LDs), 167–170
Learning environments, productive. *See* Productive learning environments
Learning-focused environment, 388–389, 401–404, 419–420
Learning goals, 128, 363–364, 365, 393. *See also* Goal(s); Objective(s)
Learning preferences, 128–129
Learning problems
    behavior disorders, 170–173
    instructional strategies for students with, 184
    learning disabilities, 167–170
    mental retardation, 166–167
Learning strategies, 184. *See also* Strategic learning
Learning styles
    cooperative, 135–136, 139
    cultural, 135–136, 139
    intelligence and, 128–129

Least restrictive environment (LRE), 160–161
Letters, to parents, 438–440
Levels of processing, 256
Linguistic diversity. *See also* Cultural diversity
    classroom applications of, 72
    communication disorders and, 173
    dialects, 66–67
    English as a second language, 67–70
    language patterns, 137
    parent-teacher communication and, 440–443
    self-esteem and, 99
    tests and, 163, 165, 179, 526, 527
Linguistic intelligence, 119
Listening, active, 447–448
Literature, moral dilemmas in, 101
Locus, 368
Logical consequences, 448, 452–453
Logical-mathematical intelligence, 119
Long-term memory, 243–246, 248, 251
    activity, 254–256, 258
    declarative knowledge and, 243–246, 270–271
    elaboration and, 254, 258
    forgetting and, 256–257
    imagery and, 253, 258
    levels of processing and, 256
    metamemory and, 259
    organization and, 251–253
    procedural knowledge and, 243, 245–246, 267, 271
LRE (least restrictive environment), 160–161

Mager's behavioral objectives, 465
Mainstreaming, 160. *See also* Inclusion
Maintenance bilingual programs, 68
Manipulatives, 44–45, 52–53
Market exchange stage of moral development, 104, 111
Maslow, Abraham, 354–355, 374, 382, 402
Massachusetts Comprehensive Assessment System exam, 559
Mastery goal, 363
Matching format, 504–505
Materials. *See* Instructional materials
Mathematics instruction
    adaptive instruction in, 183
    concepts in, 313
    gender differences in, 141, 142
    portfolios in, 516
Matrices, 251
Maturation
    defined, 35
    learning vs., 196
Mean, 553
Meaningfulness, 251, 257
Means-ends analysis, 322
Measurement
    defined, 495

formal, 495–497
informal, 495–497, 499
standard error of, 557
Measures of central tendency, 553
Measures of variability, 553–554
Median, 553
Memory. *See also* Encoding; Long-term
       memory
   affective, 361
   forgetting and, 256–257
   metamemory, 259, 261
   sensory, 239–240, 247
   working, 240–243, 247–248, 259, 321,
       323
Mental retardation, 166–167
Meta-attention, 259, 260
Metacognition, 129
   defined, 239, 330
   goals and, 367
   information processing model and,
       239, 259–261
   strategic learning and, 330–331, 332,
       334, 337
   transfer of learning and, 341–342
Metacomponent, Sternberg model, 121
Metamemory, 259, 261
Metaphors, 9
Metropolitan Achievement Test, 545
Mexican American Legal Defense and
       Education Fund (MALDEF),
       560–561
Minimum competency testing, 559–560
Minority groups. *See also* Cultural
       diversity
   computer use and, 151
   discriminatory testing and, 163, 165,
       179, 526–527
   in gifted and talented programs, 179
   high-stakes tests and, 560–561
   intelligence and, 122, 123, 124
   peer pressure in, 82, 134
   role models and, 134, 221, 229
   voluntary vs. involuntary, 134
Misbehavior, dealing with, 443–453, 457.
       See also Classroom
       management; Discipline;
       Interventions
Misconceptions, 316–317
Mnemonic devices, 254, 255
Mode, 553
Model(s) and modeling, 9, 216–221,
       230–231. *See also* Role models
   behavior, 185
   cognitive, 216–217
   defined, 238
   direct, 216
   effectiveness of, 220–221
   effects on behavior, 217–220
   learning processes in, 220
   motivation and, 220, 224, 225,
       395–401, 402, 419
   in organization, 252

scaffolding and, 61
of social skills, 86–87
symbolic, 216, 218–220
synthesized, 216
television and, 218–219
Model responses, 478
Monitoring. *See also* Metacognition
   comprehension, 264, 266, 332–333
   rules and procedures, 435–436
   self-, 222, 392, 454
Monitoring sheet, 392
Moral development, 101–107, 113
   classroom applications of, 112
   emotional factors in, 107
   gender differences in, 107
   increased interest in, 101
   instructional strategies for
       promoting, 110–111
   Kohlberg on, 102–107, 113
   Piaget on, 102, 113
   promoting, 110–111, 112
   stages of, 103–105
   technology and, 108
Moral dilemmas, 101, 102–103
Moral education, 109, 113
Morality
   autonomous, 102, 111
   external, 102, 111
   principled, 105
Motivation, 349–423
   affective factors in, 378–381, 382
   anxiety and, 379–380, 382
   assessment and, 495, 525, 531
   behaviorism and, 229, 351–353, 357,
       381–382
   case studies of, 349, 353, 356, 369–371,
       375–377, 383–384, 387, 420–422
   classroom applications of, 357,
       377–378, 381, 393, 400–401,
       404, 413–414
   classroom management and, 229
   cognitive theories of. *See* Cognitive
       theories of motivation
   cultural diversity and, 416–419, 420
   defined, 349
   expectations and, 397–399
   expertise and, 324
   extrinsic, 129, 350, 381
   feedback and, 398, 410, 412–413
   goals and, 362–367, 377–378, 382, 390,
       392–393, 416
   humanistic views of, 353–355, 382
   instructional strategies for, 352–353,
       356, 369–371, 380–381, 390–393,
       399–400, 410–412
   interest and, 404–410, 412–413, 420
   intrinsic, 129, 350–351, 381, 408–410
   involvement and, 408–410, 414
   learning-focused environment and,
       388–389, 401–404, 419–420
   modeling and, 220, 224, 225, 395–401,
       402, 419

personalization, 407–408
personal teaching efficacy and,
       393–395, 419
praise and, 6, 372, 376
problems with, 417–419
rewards and, 352–353
self-efficacy and, 361–362, 382, 402,
       412–413, 414
self-regulation and, 389–393, 419
strategic learning and, 337
students' self-efficacy and, 412–413,
       414
teacher caring and, 395–397, 418, 419
teacher understanding of, 12
technology and, 414–416, 420
Motivation to learn, 351
Multifactored evaluation, 176
Multiple-choice format, 502–504
Multiple intelligences (MI), 118–121
Multiple representations of content, 341
Multiple-trait scoring, 527
Multitrait theories of intelligence,
       118–122
   multiple intelligences, 118–121
   triarchic, 121–122
Musical intelligence, 119, 120
Music instruction, 22–23
Myers-Briggs personality test, 14

National Assessment of Educational
       Progress, 544
National Excellence, 177
National norms, 543
Native American students, 133, 134, 136,
       140, 482–483
Nativist theory, 64
Naturalist intelligence, 119, 120
Nature-nurture argument
   gender differences and, 141
   intelligence and, 122–123
Needs
   for affiliation, 374
   for competence, 371–372
   for control, 373–374
   deficiency, 354–355
   growth, 354–355
   hierarchy of, 354–355, 374, 382, 402
   for novelty and challenge, 402–403,
       415
   for relatedness, 374, 395–397
   for safety and order, 401–402, 444
Negative learning transfer, 338
Negative reinforcement (NR), 201–202,
       338
Networks, 316
Non-native English speakers, 67–70
Nonverbal communication, 446, 447
Norm(s), national, 543
Normal distribution, 554, 555
Norming groups, 542, 550
Norm-referenced evaluation, 529–530
Note taking, 330–331, 332

social interaction and, 326
technology and, 328–329
Procedural knowledge, 243, 245–246, 267, 271
Procedures, 431, 436. *See also* Rules
Process goals, 512
Processing, levels of, 256
Product goals, 512
Productive learning environments, 208–210
  attitudes in, 473, 485
  case studies of, 425, 458–459, 461–462, 487–489
  communication in, 474–475, 485, 486
  defined, 426
  feedback in, 476–478, 485–486
  organization in, 474, 485, 486
  questioning in, 478–481, 486
  review and closure in, 481, 486
  time use in, 473–474, 486
Program evaluation, standardized tests for, 544
Progress reports, interim, 438
Prompts and prompting, 61, 206–207, 213, 479–480
Prototypes, 314
Proximal development, zone of, 59–60, 65
Psychoanalysis, 354
Psychomotor domain, 467–468
Psychosocial development, 89–93, 112–113
  in adolescence, 89–90, 92
  in adulthood, 90
  classroom application of, 92–93
  instructional strategies for promoting, 96–98
  perspective on, 90
  stages of, 89–90
  supporting, 90–92
Puerto Rican community, 68, 441
Punishers, 213
  choosing, 211
  defined, 205
  in social cognitive theory, 215
  using, 205–206
Punishment, 205–206, 449–451
Punishment-obedience stage of moral development, 103–104

Question(s) and questioning
  cognitive levels of, 480–481
  elaborative, 332–333
  as essential teaching skill, 478–481, 486
  knowledge construction and, 62
  motivation and, 398, 408–409
  open-ended, 408–409, 480
  reciprocal, 299, 300
  for reflective teaching, 25
  scaffolding and, 61
  wait-time and, 20, 21, 480, 483

Questioning frequency, 478
Quizzes, 530

Random assignment, 16
Range, test, 553
Rating scales, 514, 515
Ratio schedules, 203, 204
Raw point grading, 532
Raw scores, on standardized tests, 555
Reading
  ability grouping and, 126
  adaptive instruction in, 183
  adaptive materials for, 184
  standardized tests on, 545
Real-world tasks, 284, 326
Reasoning, systematic, 42
Receptive disorders, 173–174
Reciprocal causation, 215
Reciprocal questioning, 299, 300
Recordkeeping
  confidentiality and, 165
  technology for, 534–535
Redundancy, 475
Reflective teaching
  defined, 24
  questions for, 25
Regulation. *See* Self-regulation
Rehearsal, 250–251, 258–259
Reinforcement, 201–206
  applied behavioral analysis, 210–211
  classroom management and, 449–450, 452
  language acquisition and, 64
  motivation and, 229, 352–353
  negative, 201–202, 338
  positive, 172, 201
  self-, 222–223
Reinforcement schedules, 202–204, 212, 213
Reinforcers, 213
  choosing, 211
  defined, 201
  reducing frequency of, 211
  in social cognitive theory, 215
Relatedness, need for, 374, 395–397
Reliability, of assessment, 497–499, 509, 518–519, 535
Removal punishment (RP), 205
Replacement, and behavior disorders, 172
Report cards, 438
Representations, 9, 341
Reproduction, and modeling, 220, 224
Research, 12–24
  on ability grouping, 125–126
  action, 16–18
  on brain development, 35–37
  on cognitive development, 46–47
  correlational, 14–15
  decision making and, 20–24
  defined, 13

descriptive, 13–14
development of theory and, 18–20
experimental, 16
knowledge acquisition and, 12–20
on learning preferences, 128–129
on moral development, 106
on punishment, 205
simulations in, 50
Resilience, 146–149
Resistance cultures, 134
Respect, 396–397, 402
Response(s)
  conditioned and unconditioned, 197, 198–199
  defined, 197
  model, 478
Responsibility, developing, 389–393, 419. *See also* Moral development
Responsiveness, parental, 80
Retention, and modeling, 220, 224
Retrieval, information, 256–259, 262
Reversibility, 42
Review, 481, 486
Rewards, 352–353
Rights, of parents, 163
Ripple effect, 218
Rogers, Carl, 355
Role models
  for computer use, 152
  ethnicity and, 134
  exceptionalities and, 185
  gender and, 143, 221
  minority, 134, 221, 229
Routines, 431
  classroom, 149
  in productive learning environments, 474
Rubrics
  defined, 27
  scoring, 507–509
Rules, 431–436
  behaviorist interventions and, 450–451
  defined, 431
  examples of, 433
  Golden, 105
  instructional strategies for, 431–436
  monitoring, 435–436
  moral development and, 105
  teaching, 434

Safety, need for, 401–402, 444
SAT (Scholastic Aptitude Test), 14–15, 16, 544, 548, 549
Satiation, 204–205
Scaffolding, 60–61, 326–327
Schemas, 243–245. *See also* Background knowledge and experiences
  motivation and, 359, 360, 361
  perception and, 262
  production of, 264–266
Schemes, 37–39

Photo Credits

Photo Credits: pp. 2, 78, 92, 122, 284, 360, 464, 482 by David Young-Wolff/PhotoEdit; pp. 5, 104, 289, 402, 496, 507 by Mary Kate Denny/PhotoEdit; pp. 8, 13, 70, 293, 298, 304, 329, 416 by Will Hart/PhotoEdit; pp. 17, 43, 80, 96, 138, 146, 163, 181, 219, 341, 354, 390, 428, 430, 449, 462, 528, 533, 558 by Anthony Magnacca/Merrill; pp. 18, 171 (left), 407, 510 by James L. Shaffer; pp. 22, 24, 60, 142, 160, 187, 246, 256, 369, 513, 524 by Scott Cunningham/Merrill; p. 26 by Ulrike Welsch/PhotoEdit; pp. 32, 51, 110, 125, 178, 197, 253, 266, 312, 363, 435, 437, 474, 478 by Michael Newman/PhotoEdit; pp. 35, 40, 396 by Richard Hutchings/PhotoEdit; p. 45 by Bill Bachman/The Image Works; pp. 49, 287 by Bill Bachman/Photo Researchers; pp. 55, 180, 412, 469, 514, 522, 540, 544 by Tony Freeman/PhotoEdit; pp. 63, 348 by Myrleen Ferguson Cate/PhotoEdit; p. 69 by Anne Vega/Merrill; pp. 82, 186, 249, 379 by Paul Conklin/PhotoEdit; p. 86 by Laima Druskis/PH College; p. 91 by Gail Zucker/Gail Zucker Photography; p. 99 by Bill Aron/PhotoEdit; pp. 102, 240, 314, 447 by Tom Watson/Merrill; p. 116 by Dennis MacDonald/PhotoEdit; pp. 119, 162, 171 (right), 336 by Todd Yarrington/Merrill; pp. 129, 446 by KS Studios/Merrill; p. 134 by Lawrence Migdale/Stock Boston; p. 151 by Arthur Tilley/Getty Images, Inc.–Taxi; p. 158 by Robert Kusel/Getty Images, Inc.–Stone Allstock; pp. 167, 267 by Will & Demi McIntyre/Photo Researchers; p. 174 by Rhoda Sidney/PhotoEdit; p. 194 by Chip Henderson/Getty Images, Inc.–Stone Allstock; p. 196 by Michelle Bridwell/PhotoEdit; p. 200 by Yellow Dog Productions/Getty Images, Inc.–Image Bank; p. 207 by Mark Adams/Getty Images, Inc.–Taxi; p. 210 by Larry Hamill/Merrill; p. 216 by Bonnie Kamin/PhotoEdit; p. 223 by Jim Cummins/Getty Images, Inc.–Taxi; p. 234 by Alan Oddie/PhotoEdit; p. 238 by Lloyd Lemmerman/Merrill; p. 262 by Bob Daemmrich/The Image Works; pp. 278, 424, 561 by Bob Daemmrich/Stock Boston; p. 281 by Jonathan Nourok/PhotoEdit; p. 302 by Laura Dwight/Laura Dwight Photography; p. 310 by Phil Schermeister/Corbis; p. 321 by Steve Skjold/PhotoEdit; p. 326 by Jeff Greenberg/Visuals Unlimited; p. 328 by Randall Hyman; p. 332 by Cleve Bryant/PhotoEdit; p. 352 by Jim Pickerell/Stock Boston; p. 373 by Ellen Senisi/The Image Works; p. 386 by Stephen Frisch/Stock Boston; p. 395 by Bill Bachman/PhotoEdit; p. 397 by F. Pedrick/The Image Works; p. 405 by Jose L. Pelaez/Corbis/Stock Market; p. 415 by James D. Wilson/Getty Images, Inc.–Liaison; p. 433 by Silver Burdett Ginn; p. 443 by Jeff Greenberg/PhotoEdit; p. 455 by Elena Rooraid/PhotoEdit; p. 460 by Gary Conner/PhotoEdit; p. 465 by David Napravnik/Merrill; p. 467 by Robert Finken/Index Stock Imagery; p. 475 by Davis Barber/PhotoEdit; p. 483 by Pearson Learning; p. 492 by Gary Walts/The Image Works; p. 548 by Bob Daemmrich/PictureQuest; p. 550 by Mark Richards/PhotoEdit; p. 555 by Mark Burnett/Stock Boston; p. 565 by Kathy Kirtland/Merrill.